W9-AAI-825

Trouble Logging In?

- Ensure you are using the same email address you used during registration
- If you have forgotten your password, click on the "Forgot Password?" link at your Instructor's Connect Course Web Address
- When logged into Connect, you can update your account information (e.g. email address, password, and security question/answer) by clicking on the *"My Account"* link located at the top-right corner

Home (Assignments)

TIP: If you are unable to begin an assignment, verify the following:

- The assignment is available (start and due dates)
- That you have not exceeded the maximum number of attempts
- That you have not achieved a score of 100%
- If your assignment contains questions that require manual grading, you will not be able to begin your next attempt until your instructor has graded those questions

TIP: Based on the assignment policy settings established by your Instructor, you may encounter the following limitations when working on your assignment(s):

- Ability to Print Assignment
- Timed assignments – once you begin a *"timed assignment,"* the timer will not stop by design

TIP: *"Save & Exit"* vs. *"Submit"* button

- If you are unable to complete your assignment in one sitting, utilize the *"Save & Exit"* button to save your work and complete it at a later time
- Once you have completed your assignment, utilize the *"Submit"* button in order for your assignment to be graded

Library

TIP: The *Library* section of your Connect account provides shortcuts to various resources.

- If you purchased ConnectPlus, you will see an *eBook* link, which can also be accessed from the section information widget of the *Home* tab
- *Recorded Lectures* can be accessed if your instructor is using *Tegrity Campus* to capture lectures. You may al access recorded lectures when taking an assignment by clicking on the projector icon in the navigation bar
- Many McGraw-Hill textbooks offer additional resources such as narrated slides and additional problems, which are accessible through the *Student Resources* link

Reports

TIP: Once you submit your assignment, you can view your available results in the *Reports* tab.

- If you see a dash (-) as your score, your instructor has either delayed or restricted your ability to see the assignment feedback
- Your instructor has the ability to limit the amount of information (e.g. questions, answers, scores) you can view for each submitted assignment

Need More Help?

CONTACT US ONLINE

Visit us at:

www.mcgrawhillconnect.com/support

Browse our support materials including tutorial videos and our searchable Connect knowledge base. If you cannot find an answer to your question, click on "Contact Us" button to send us an email.

GIVE US A CALL

Call us at:

1-800-331-5094

Our live support is available:

Mon-Thurs:	6 am – 9 pm PT
Friday:	6 am – 4 pm PT
Sunday:	4 pm – 9 pm PT

Access Code to accompany

Psychology
Oregon State University
Feist/Rosenberg

CONNECT TO YOUR COURSEWORK ONLINE.
ANYWHERE, ANY TIME.

With McGraw-Hill *Connect*™ *Plus*, engage with your coursework efficiently with learning personalized for you. Get an online eBook and immediate feedback on online assignments, quizzes and practice tests. Even access your instructor's class lecture online. Connect to learning and to what you need for future success!

To register and activate your *Connect Plus* account, simply follow these three easy steps.
1. Go to the **Connect Plus** course URL provided by your instructor.
2. Click on the link to register.
3. When prompted, enter the registration code listed below. Complete the brief registration form that follows online.

This code is unique and not related to any other registration number or ID you may have. The registration code is good for one-time use.

Suggestion: Bookmark your instructor's Connect course URL for fast, easy access.

Questions? Need Help? Visit **www.mhhe.com/support**

REGISTRATION CODE	CDND-JKPN-PJWV-UJBX-68GQ

ONLINE ACCESS CARD FOR CONNECT PLUS

Students: Do Not Throw Away. This is your personalized registration card for online access to assignment material.

 Learning Solutions

The McGraw·Hill Companies

ISBN-13: 978-0-07-755966-3
ISBN-10: 0-07-755966-5

PSYCHOLOGY
Oregon State University

PSYCHOLOGY

Gregory J. Feist
San Jose State University

Erika L. Rosenberg
University of California, Davis

Oregon State University

McGraw Hill **Learning Solutions**

Boston   Burr Ridge, IL   Dubuque, IA   New York   San Francisco   St. Louis
Bangkok   Bogotá   Caracas   Lisbon   London   Madrid
Mexico City   Milan   New Delhi   Seoul   Singapore   Sydney   Taipei   Toronto

Psychology
Oregon State University

This book is a McGraw-Hill Learning Solutions textbook and contains select material from *Psychology* by Gregory J. Feist and Erika L. Rosenberg Copyright © 2010 by The McGraw-Hill Companies, Inc. Reprinted with permission of the publisher. Many custom published texts are modified versions or adaptations of our best-selling textbooks. Some adaptations are printed in black and white to keep prices at a minimum, while others are in color.

1 2 3 4 5 6 7 8 9 0 RJE RJE 13 12 11

ISBN-13: 978-0-07-755965-6
ISBN-10: 0-07-755965-7
Part of
ISBN-13: 978-0-07-756126-0
ISBN-10: 0-07-756126-0

Learning Solutions Manager: Danielle Meier
Production Editor: Patricia Krieger
Printer/Binder: RR Donnelley

To our most precious collaborative work,
Jerry and Evan

about the authors

Gregory J. Feist

Gregory J. Feist is Associate Professor of Psychology in Adult Development at San Jose State University. He has also taught at the College of William & Mary and the University of California at Davis. He received his PhD from the University of California at Berkeley and his undergraduate degree from the University of Massachusetts–Amherst.

Dr. Feist is widely published in the psychology of creativity, the psychology of science, and the development of scientific talent. One of his major goals is establishing the psychology of science as a healthy and independent study of science, along the lines of the history, philosophy, and sociology of science. Toward this end, Dr. Feist has published a book entitled *Psychology of Science and the Origins of the Scientific Mind* (2006, Yale University Press), which was awarded the 2007 William James Book Prize by the Division of General Psychology, American Psychological Association (APA). In addition, he is the founding president of the International Society for the Psychology of Science and Technology and the founding editor in chief of the peer-reviewed *Journal of Psychology of Science & Technology*.

A second major focus for Dr. Feist is the identification and development of scientific talent, as seen in finalists of the Westinghouse and Intel Science Talent Search. His paper (co-authored with Frank Barron) "Predicting creativity from early to late adulthood: Intellect, potential, and personality" won Article of the Year for 2003 in the *Journal of Research in Personality*. His research in creativity has been recognized by an Early Career Award from the Division for Psychology of Aesthetics, Creativity and the Arts (Division 10) of American Psychological Association (APA). Dr. Feist is past president of APA's Division 10 and is currently on the editorial boards of the *Review of General Psychology* and *Psychology of Aesthetics, Creativity and the Arts*. His teaching efforts have been recognized by outstanding teaching awards at both UC Berkeley and UC Davis. Dr. Feist is also coauthor with his father, Jess Feist, of the undergraduate text *Theories of Personality*.

Married to Erika Rosenberg, Dr. Feist is the father of Jerry and Evan.

Erika L. Rosenberg

Erika L. Rosenberg received her PhD in psychology from the University of California, San Francisco, where she studied with Paul Ekman. Dr. Rosenberg served on the faculties at the University of Delaware and the College of William and Mary and currently is a researcher at the Center for Mind and Brain at the University of California at Davis.

Dr. Rosenberg is an emotions researcher, health psychologist, and teacher of meditation. Her research on emotion has examined how feelings are revealed in facial expressions, how social factors influence emotional signals, and how anger affects cardiovascular health. Her research is published in a wide range of psychological journals and books, and she speaks regularly at national and international conferences on the topics of emotions and facial expressions. Her current research interests include collaborative studies that integrate Western psychology with Buddhist practices for improving emotional and cognitive functioning. Dr. Rosenberg is a recognized expert in facial expressions measurement using the Facial Action Coding System (FACS). She consults with scientists, artists, and the media on the use of FACS in a variety of contexts, including innovative applications in computer science, and she teaches workshops worldwide. Dr. Rosenberg is also on the faculty of Nyingma Institute of Tibetan Studies in Berkeley, where she teaches meditation and conducts workshops on working with emotions in daily life and the development of mindfulness and compassion. She has been practicing meditation for 20 years. Dr. Rosenberg and her husband, Greg Feist, have two sons, Jerry and Evan. They live in the San Francisco Bay Area.

brief contents

contents

1 introduction to psychology 2

2 conducting research in psychology 34

3   the **biology** of **behavior**   74

4 sensing and perceiving our world   122

5   human development   168

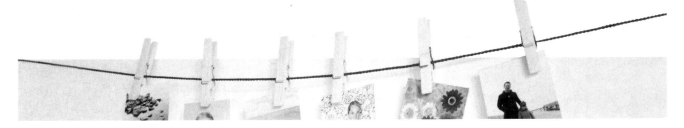

8 learning 292

9 language and thought 332

10 intelligence, problem solving, and creativity 370

11 motivation and emotion   412

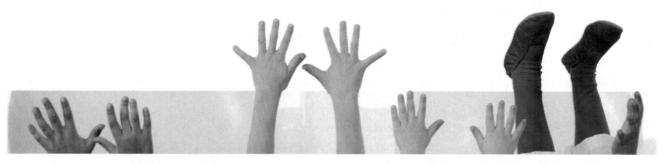

14 social behavior 530

15 psychological disorders   570

16 treatment of psychological disorders   610

foreword by Paul Ekman

Perhaps it was because I had never taken Introductory Psychology that I became a psychologist—or so I used to quip at the start of undergraduate lectures. Fifty years ago the textbooks for introductory courses were a turn-off. Most were dry and segmented. The only reason to read them was to pass introductory psychology in order to get to the higher-level courses you really wanted to take. It was an obstacle you had to jump over. Things have changed!

This textbook—I hesitate to use the word—is fun to read, enlightening, useful, and provocative. I recommend it to anyone—not just undergraduates—who wants a contemporary overview of psychology. In fact, people with no intentions of studying psychology will find this book engaging and interesting, and useful to their life. Wow.

Make no mistake—this is not a how-to book. It is not going to tell you how to get rid of whatever bothers you or find a mate or choose a career or become the most charming person in the world. But it will fascinate you; in each chapter you will learn about the cutting edge of knowledge, how science is done, what it means, and why it is important to understand that most complex of all subjects—why we do what we do and when and how we do it.

My own specialty for forty years has been the study of facial expressions, and in the last decade or so I have reached out to develop a theory about emotion itself and how to lead a better emotional life. So I was surprised to find that when I read Chapter 11, "Motivation and Emotion," I learned something new. This is a comprehensive book; the coverage, even from a specialist's view, is amazing. And in each chapter the reader learns about both the breakthrough discoveries that have fundamentally altered the field of psychology and those scientists responsible for them.

I still find it a bit amazing that I should be ending a foreword to a textbook with the phrase "have fun."

preface

The Interconnected Science of Psychology

As psychologists, we experience that remarkable moment when realization flashes before us. As instructors, we experience that remarkable moment when the glow of recognition lights up students' faces. As students, we experience that remarkable moment when two concepts come together to form the larger picture of psychology. These are the remarkable moments of making connections—when a vast array of topics merge into the interconnected system we call the science of psychology. And making these connections is a goal shared by this text, the field of psychology, instructors, and especially students—who gain valuable experience learning to navigate through the fascinating network of interrelated topics from both the core areas and subfields in the discipline.

The science of psychology as a whole is as exciting as its parts. Just as we see these parts grow in number each day, we see the field grow more integrated as well. As teachers, we continue to explore ways of presenting psychology not as a catalog of unrelated topics, each with its own language, but as an integrated discipline, rich in diversity, but coherent in its methods. We appreciate the need to examine the field in its many parts in order to explore it in depth and to reveal the layers of complexity within each field. We also recognize that we can and should bring these ideas together to connect students to the broader sphere of psychology. The introductory course provides an ideal opportunity to cover psychology with an integrative approach that shows not only the depth and breadth of our field, but also how it all fits together. *Psychology: Making Connections* is designed to make this approach the most effective way of teaching the science of psychology.

> For me, reading *Psychology: Making Connections* was like watching a good movie. It's not just a textbook but a compelling tale of humankind from a psychological perspective. I didn't want the story to end.
>
> KATHERINE LORENZO,
> Macomb Community College

Psychology is an interconnected science.

Making Connections

The overarching theme of this text is *making connections*. Topics in psychology lend themselves to connectivity and integration. For instance, understanding most psychological disorders requires consideration of environments from prenatal to social, and biological factors from genes to molecules, neurons, and brain systems. Also, the most exciting new areas of research bear integrative labels. A prime example is "social cognitive neuroscience," a field that emerged in response to the need to connect different aspects of behavior—such as thinking, feeling, and interacting—with the dynamic brain in order to advance our understanding of behavior.

As educators, we strive to get students thinking from day one about how the elements underlying behavior come together. We aim to engage them in psychology. We have found that the "making connections" theme captivates students as well as instructors. Specifically, our presentation of psychology emphasizes these connective themes:

- Connections between nature and nurture
- Connections between psychologists and scientific discoveries
- Connections between topics across psychology
- Connections among topics within each chapter
- Connections between psychology and students' experience

These themes provide a cohesive, integrative framework for the introductory course. And they inspire students to make active connections themselves.

CONNECTING NATURE AND NURTURE

Psychologists' thinking about the contributions of nature and nurture to our development, thinking, personality, intelligence, desires, relationships, and mental disorders has grown significantly over time. Not so long ago, textbooks set nature against nurture in discussions of behavior and mental life. You would see biological and social theories of personality presented separately, for example, with no attempt made to reconcile the different approaches. Although contemporary texts emphasize that most of human behavior results from the interaction of learned and innate factors, even some interactionist views make overly simplistic divisions.

Teaching psychology today requires a broad view of the dynamic, bi-directional

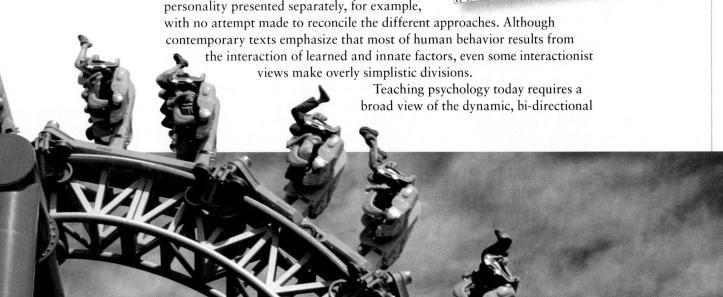

...response (UCR) to stimulus. In this case, ...means "unlearned." (CS) to refer to the ...produced the same ..., the UCS always ...neat powder—the

...eye makes you blink, ...r leg to jerk forth. These ...ific types of environmental ...n in response to food, as fixed

nature & nurture
Through classical conditioning, innate responses—like salivation—can become associated with and changed by almost any experience.

relationship between nature and nurture. *Psychology: Making Connections* embraces the intertwined roles of nature and nurture in behavior and mental life and highlights these connections in every chapter. Here are a few examples:

- *Mirror neurons connect observation and experience.* Imaging technology reveals that certain neuron systems in our brains fire when we pick up objects or manipulate things with our hands. They also fire when we watch someone else perform the same action, in a sense rehearsing our brains for action through observation. This process creates a template for observational learning (Chapter 8, "Learning") and perhaps for empathic connection as well (Chapter 11, "Motivation and Emotion"; Chapter 14, "Social Behavior"). Recent evidence suggests that mirror neuron systems do not appear to work well in children with autism, for whom the social world is mystifying (Chapter 8, "Learning"; Chapter 15, "Psychological Disorders").

> The theme of nature AND nurture is incorporated nicely (which is something that we stress at FSU) and is one that I feel students in both the more liberal arts and hard sciences can relate to.
>
> **JAMES R. SULLIVAN,**
> Florida State University

- *Experience changes the brain.* The mutability of the brain by experience is perhaps the most powerful illustration of the bidirectional effects of nature and nurture. Neuroplasticity may be the buzzword of 21st-century psychology and neuroscience, but the relevant research has been emerging for years. And it has a tremendous impact on all of us, in a very practical way. Learning changes the brain. Developing cognitive and athletic skills can actually cause the brain to grow. We emphasize the ways experience influences the brain in every chapter of the book.

- *Experience affects gene expression.* Genetic influences are not immutable. They are modifiable. Without changing our DNA, experience can directly affect whether certain genes get expressed. What we eat and drink, for example, regulates the genome by turning on some genes and turning off others. Genetically identical animals can grow up fat or thin depending on what their mothers ate while pregnant. We introduce this fascinating concept in Chapter 3 ("The Biology of Behavior") and revisit it in Chapters 5 ("Human Development"), 10 ("Intelligence, Problem Solving, and Creativity"), 13 ("Personality: The Uniqueness of the Individual"), and 15 ("Psychological Disorders").

- *Nature limits the degree to which experience can shape behavior.* There is a genetically determined reaction range for a given trait that sets upper and lower limits on how the trait is expressed. We explore the effect of a reaction range in Chapter 5 ("Human Development"), and in Chapter 10, where we discuss the effects of reaction range on IQ scores.

CONNECTING PSYCHOLOGISTS WITH THEIR SCIENTIFIC DISCOVERIES

Psychology did not come into existence as a fully formed body of knowledge. It emerged from the insight, luck, and hard work of dedicated and creative people. Connecting psychological scientists with their discoveries brings psychology to life for students—it demonstrates that the science of psychology is a dynamic enterprise. This connection is the purpose of the "Breaking New Ground" feature in each chapter. This feature highlights breakthrough discoveries that have fundamentally altered the field of psychology and tells the story of the scientists responsible for them.

To provide students with a full understanding of the thinking in the field, we first lay out the logic behind the assumptions that psychologists held before the pathbreaking research under discussion. We then detail the groundbreaking research, explaining the logic, methods, and results and following up with a discussion—sometimes highlighted by a personal story from the researchers—of how the results forced them and others in the field to change their thinking. These personal accounts humanize the psychology of scientific discovery and make key research more memorable and more meaningful for students. For example, in Chapter 3 ("The Biology of Behavior"), we showcase the discoveries of Elizabeth Gould, Rusty Gage, Peter Erikkson, and others whose work on neurogenesis overturned the accepted dogma of *no new neurons.* In Chapter 11 ("Motivation and Emotion"), we highlight Paul Ekman's discovery of the universality of facial expressions of emotion, which laid to rest the notion that emotions are products of culture alone.

Finally, we explore the implications and changes arising from the paradigm-shifting study. We discuss what the researchers themselves think about the next steps and raise questions that have yet to be answered.

CONNECTING THE MAIN TOPICS IN PSYCHOLOGY

From our own teaching, we see that introductory students struggle with making connections among psychology's various subfields. Not surprisingly, the textbook chapters too often come across to students as isolated topics with

---

breaking new ground
Conditioned Taste Aversion

Remember our story about an aversion to chocolate doughnuts caused by an episode of seasickness after eating a doughnut? This was a case of **conditioned taste aversion,** the learned avoidance of a particular taste when nausea occurs at about the same time as the food. Whether or not the food actually causes the sickness, it is experienced that way in future encounters. In the 1960s, experimental psychologist John Garcia made a remarkable discovery. His groundbreaking research went beyond the limits of conditioning to explain how we learn aversion to tastes.

THE TRADITIONAL LEARNING MODEL

Traditional learning theory would explain conditioned taste aversion as a special case of classical conditioning, in which a neutral or even pleasant taste is linked with the unconditioned causes of nausea. This learned association (say, between a doughnut and nausea) is not much different from the one made by Pavlov's dogs (see Figure 8.11). The catch is that classical conditioning requires repeated pairings of the CS and the UCS to create and maintain a conditioned response. But in the case of the chocolate doughnut, the doughnut (the CS) acquired the ability to induce nausea (CR) after a brief pairing with the motion of the boat (UCS), more than 30 minutes after the doughnut was

---

Breaking New Ground: I thought this was an excellent feature. I think it will help students synthesize the way research works and how it influences their lives. I particularly liked the taste aversion example of this feature in Chapter 8. It perfectly tied in the chapter opening with the chapter content, and I think students will find the explantion very interesting.

ALISHA JANOWSKY, University of Central Florida

little connection to one another, in spite of the fact that the topics of psychology increasingly fold into one another. We understand the limitations imposed by course structure and time, but we also consider integrating the core topics to be a course goal. Therefore we developed a feature we call "Connections" to link topics that are discussed in more than one chapter of the book.

Rather than simply cross-referencing ideas or topics, we provide brief notes and questions in the margin to stimulate interest in how the same topic is treated differently in different areas of psychology. We believe that questions underscoring the breadth of a concept are more likely to tempt curious students to look for coverage in another chapter right then and there. After introducing mirror neurons in Chapter 3 ("The Biology of Behavior"), for example, we refer to them again in four other chapters: "Human Development" (Chapter 5), "Learning" (Chapter 8), "Motivation and Emotion" (Chapter 11), and "Social Behavior" (Chapter 14). We introduce mirror neurons in "The Biology of Behavior" (Chapter 3), simply because it is where the students first learn about the neuron and the brain. In "Learning" (Chapter 8) we have a Connections sidebar with questions referring back to "Human Development" (Chapter 5) and forward to "Social Behavior" (Chapter 14).

> Excellent examples to describe key points!
>
> **DASHA KOUZNETSOVA (student),** CUNY
> Hunter College

connection

Right now you are habituated to dozens of stimuli— including the feel of clothing on your skin. Now you are sensitized to it. How so?
See Chapter 4.

it at all. This
by which o
change in
it) stemm
one, how
orienting
Habi
is it learnin
nor the orient
disappears imme

CONNECTING THE TOPICS WITHIN EACH CHAPTER

Not only do we connect ideas and topics *between* chapters with the "Connections" sidebars, but we also connect all the main ideas and topics *within* each chapter. We do this by ending every chapter with a section called "Making Connections." Integrative discussion reinforces the cumulative nature of science—specifically, how psychological science can arrive at answers to important questions by systematic investigation. For instance, in Chapter 8 ("Learning"), "Making Connections in Learning" looks at why people smoke in terms of the three major models of learning discussed in the chapter (classical

making connections
in learning

Why Do People Smoke?

As you have probably figured out by now, human behavior is complex. So it should be no surprise that any given behavior may be acquired and maintained by means of several types of learning (classical, operant, and/or social), all operating in the context of a human being who has a personality and history. Consider, for example, cigarette smoking (see Figure 8.17). The acquisition of smoking behavior—how people become smokers in the first place—is perhaps best explained by social learning theory (Bandura, 1969, 1986). Think about it: The actual sensory qualities of cigarette smoking on first experience are anything but pleasant—coughing, dizziness, and nausea. But most smokers start smoking as teenagers, and most teens start smoking because they seek some of the rewards that appear to come with smoking: coolness, peer acceptance, looking like an adult. (All of these rewards are secondary reinforcers, which acquire their reinforcing characteristics by means of classical conditioning and operant conditioning.) Kids see that others who smoke get some of these rewards for smoking. Thus they might model smoking behavior in order to obtain these rewards themselves. They might view "being seen

as cool"—a form of peer acceptance—as desirable, and so being seen as cool becomes a reinforcer for the smoking behaviors of others. "Whenever Mom gets stressed, she smokes a cigarette to relax—maybe that will work for me, too" is another example of social learning.

Once someone has become an established smoker, operant conditioning helps maintain smoking behavior. Smoking is bolstered by a number of positive reinforcers: arousal of the sympathetic nervous system (the "rush" of smoking), mild relaxation of the muscles, and, in some cases, increased peer acceptance. Smoking also has a number of negative reinforcers, such as the removal of stress, the removal of social isolation for some smokers, and a reduced appetite. The power of these reinforcers, combined with the physiologically addictive properties of nicotine, make it very difficult to quit smoking. Moreover, the potential punishers of smoking—a substantially increased risk of lung cancer and heart disease—are threats that are so far off in the future for teens that they tend to ignore them. It is for this reason that some psychologists who are concerned with preventing smoking by teens have tried to link smoking with unpleasant images and effects (such as ugliness and social rejection). The hope is that by using both classical and operant conditioning, they can make smoking appear less rewarding. For example, in order to discourage smoking, some public health campaigns show pictures of diseased lungs or smokers who look older than they are. The idea is that by means of classical conditioning people might

and operant conditioning and social learning). In Chapter 2 ("Conducting Research in Psychology"), "Making Connections in Psychological Research" explores studies on environmental enrichment and brain growth and presents experimental, quasi-experimental, correlational, and case-study investigations on how enriched environments shape the brain. Because early brain studies often involved sacrificing animals, this discussion also affords the opportunity to discuss the other major topic of the chapter: ethical issues in psychological research. "Making Connections" integrates the important material covered in the chapter. Reiterating the major ideas in the chapter and showing how they can be applied to a common problem gives students an additional opportunity to learn the material in an integrated way.

> After comparing my text to this one, I find myself preferring this one. I have a strong suspicion that students would prefer this one to our current text.
>
> PAULINA MULTHAUPT,
> Macomb Community College

CONNECTING PSYCHOLOGY WITH STUDENT EXPERIENCE

One of the perennially difficult tasks we face as instructors is to connect course material to students' lives and interests. In *Psychology: Making Connections*, we tie psychology to student experience in two ways. First, we link psychological concepts to tangible, real-world experiences that students will understand. We show, for instance, how texting a friend during lecture necessarily prevents students from attending to what the professor is saying (Chapter 6, "Consciousness").

psychology in the real world

Treating Autism with Applied Behavior Analysis

Autism is a debilitating developmental disorder that usually appears in the first few years of life. It is characterized by drastic deficits in communication and language, social interaction with others, emotional expression and experience, and imaginative play (Kanner, 1943). At one time, autism was considered relatively rare, but with greater awareness and diagnosis, it has become a major mental health concern. Recent estimates suggest that autism affects anywhere from 41 to 45 out of every 10,000 children between the ages of 5 and 8 and that the rate is four times higher in boys than in girls (Fombonne, 2003).

It was long assumed that autism was untreatable. Because most children with autism are unresponsive to social interaction, psychotherapy is largely ineffective. Yet certain behavioral strategies offer the promise of modifying inappropriate social responses. The best-known behavioral treatment for autism is applied behavioral analysis (ABA), developed by Ivar Lovaas at UCLA.

Based on operant conditioning theory, ABA uses reinforcement to increase the frequency of adaptive behaviors in autistic children and, in some cases, punishment to decrease the likelihood of maladaptive behaviors. The intensive program involves ignoring harmful or undesirable behaviors such as hand flapping, twirling, or licking objects, as well as aggressive behaviors. It also involves reinforcing desirable behaviors, such as contact with others, simple

Another way we connect psychology with everyday experience is via "Psychology in the Real World." The purpose of this feature is to show how psychological research can directly affect people's lives. Here are a few examples:

- The prevalence of early hearing loss is increasing in the age of the iPod. (Chapter 4, "Sensing and Perceiving Our World")

- Prolonged stress speeds up the aging process of cells. (Chapter 12, "Stress and Health")

- Personality assessment is used in screening police officers for emotional instability. (Chapter 13, "Personality: The Uniqueness of the Individual")

Connecting psychology to students' lives, we believe, increases the chances that students will be productive individuals who will make positive contributions to the world around them. This is why we teach introductory psychology and why we wrote this book.

ORGANIZATION

Our table of contents follows a fairly typical sequence, primarily because this order of presentation works well in the classroom. It matches most introductory psychology syllabi and also gives instructors the flexibility to cover the material in a different sequence, if desired.

One distinction in our table of contents is the placement of the chapter on memory (Chapter 7) before that on learning (Chapter 8). Learning and memory are intimately linked, which is one reason many universities offer courses in the combined topic of learning and memory. To some extent, it might not matter which chapter comes first. Learning, however, depends on memory processes—as evidenced by the fact that learning is disrupted in people with memory deficits. For this reason, we believe that setting up a basic foundation of memory processes facilitates the understanding of learning.

The second distinction is that we present human development early in the book (Chapter 5), because capacities of thought, feeling, and behavior do not emerge all at once, nor do they remain immutable over the life span. Introducing development early, we have found, instills an appreciation for the dynamic nature of psychological processes. Exposure to developmental principles at the start provides an essential framework for the material in all of the chapters that follow.

> The writing is excellent. The authors have managed to cover the material in a scientifically complete manner without being pedantic or talking down to the students.
>
> **GAYLE BROSNAN-WATTERS,** Slippery Rock University

Coverage

Writing a new text has allowed us to take a fresh look at the content of the course and offer a truly contemporary introduction to psychology. By way of a preview, we highlight some of the topics that we cover in a different way or with a different emphasis.

In our chapter on consciousness (Chapter 6), we consider consciousness as a two-dimensional process with different levels of wakefulness and awareness. We also present meditation as a method for training consciousness rather than as an altered state of consciousness and then discuss neuroscience research on the effects of meditation training on the brain.

In keeping with our theme of making connections between nature and nurture throughout the book, we include a special section on the nature and nurture of various aspects of behavior. For example, in a section on the nature and nurture of learning in Chapter 8, we discuss topics that are not typically covered in a learning chapter, such as imprinting and the role of mirror neurons in imitation.

Intelligence and creativity (Chapter 10) are hallmarks of our species, to which we owe all our cultural, literary, artistic, scientific, and technological

> I am very impressed with the consistency and flow of words and information across the chapters. It is very well written and understandable. I like this text much better than the one we use.
>
> **DIANE FEIBEL,** Raymond Walters College–University of Cincinnati

advances. As such, these topics deserve more coverage in introductory psychology than is typically found in textbooks. In addition to a special section on the nature and nurture of intelligence, therefore, we also examine the effect of gender on intelligence, testing bias, and non-Western views of intelligence, along with the core topics in intelligence. We explore in some depth the nature of savant syndrome and its fascinating "island of giftedness." As part of our discussion of creativity, we look at the nature of genius and how it relates to intelligence, creativity, and the brain and the cognitive and personality factors behind creativity. Later, in the chapter on psychological disorders (Chapter 15), we make a connection to the topic of creativity by reviewing the evidence for an association between creativity and psychological disorders.

In our chapter on motivation and emotion (Chapter 11) we present emotion research in a novel way compared to other texts. Rather than listing and describing various emotion theories and related studies, research on emotion is organized around the emotion process itself. We first look at the appraisal process and associated cognitive theory and research on the generation of an emotion, then move to work on emotional behavior, experience, and physiology, in addition to innovative contributions from affective neuroscience. In this way, we provide a framework for the psychological science of emotion that acknowledges the dynamic flow of affect.

Our coverage of personality (Chapter 13) does more than present the major theoretical perspectives (psychodynamic, humanistic, social-learning, and trait). We also consider the biological and evolutionary underpinnings of personality, the connection between prenatal and infant temperament and adult personality, the evidence for personality in non-human animals, and the evidence for personality stability and change over the lifespan.

On the topic of social behavior (Chapter 14), we offer contemporary findings in the neuroscience of social rejection and empathy along with the classics, including Milgram's work, conformity experiments, and research on the bystander effect. Moreover, we approach social behavior from the point of view that the need to be part of a group is adaptive.

In most chapters, research process figures promote and foster in students a deeper understanding of the science of psychology by focusing on a single study from the text, such as the effect of culture on perception (Chapter 4, "Sensing and Perceiving Our World") and how exercise changes the brain (Chapter 12, "Stress and Health"). Each of these figures emphasizes the four key steps involved in all research: asking a question clearly, designing a clean study that addresses the question, collecting data and interpreting the results, and drawing conclusions about what these results mean to people in general and to other scientists in particular. Moreover, by having the same four-part structure throughout the entire book, these eye-catching graphics reinforce the idea that the scientific method is the foundation of psychological science.

> The research examples were clear and compelling. The layout of the pages was great. The summaries and definitions were well done and will make it easy for students to learn.
>
> **SHIRA GABRIEL,**
> University at Buffalo, State
> University of New York

BIOLOGICAL ACETATES

Introductory Psychology instructors tell us that one of the main goals of their course is to help students master the science underlying psychology. To promote understanding of basic aspects of human biology, we created a dynamic visual presentation of the brain, the nervous system, and the senses. In Chapter 3, "The Biology of Behavior," you will find a series of acetates titled "Touring the Brain and Nervous System," and in Chapter 4, "Sensing and Perceiving Our World," there is another acetate series called "Touring the Senses." Included in these sections are questions designed to focus students' attention on key features of the illustrations, along with answers placed at the end of each series of acetates. Introductory psychology instructors and neuroscientists contributed to the development of these unique transparent images.

QUICK QUIZ STUDY QUESTIONS

Teachers of Introductory Psychology want their students to do well in the course. By applying research in relevant areas of psychology, especially memory, we can make it easier for students to master the key concepts in the course. One way to do this is to break up the content into short chunks, each followed by a brief review section to encourage students to process the material. For this purpose, we have included a few multiple choice "Quick Quiz" questions at the end of each major section of each chapter. These questions provide students with an opportunity to think about what they have read and put it to use.

quick quiz 8.1: Basic Processes and Conditioning Models of Learning

1. Using the definition provided in the text, which is the best example of learning?
   a. A plant moves toward the sun in order to get the best sunlight.
   b. A newborn baby automatically grabs a finger that is placed in its palm.
   c. A cat perks up its ears and looks toward the sound after a bell has rung.
   d. 10-year-old Jerry can snowboard down the mountain after practicing for a week.
2. Because we always use a can opener to open his food, Spalding the cat runs into the kitchen each time he hears someone open the drawer where the can opener is kept. According to the text, Spalding has ———.
   a. remembered what cat food is.
   b. made an association between the drawer opening and being fed.
   c. habituated to noises in the kitchen.
   d. none of the above.
3. A rat presses a lever, resulting in food delivery. The rat then presses the lever more frequently. This is an example of
   a. punishment
   b. higher-order conditioning
   c. reinforcement
   d. extinction
4. In a typical classical conditioning experiment, a neutral stimulus is
   a. repeatedly paired with the UCR
   b. not paired with any other stimulus
   c. repeatedly paired with the CS
   d. repeatedly paired with the UCS

Additionally, the "Quick Quiz" questions are integrated with and representative of the supplemental materials for the text—including the test bank—such that instructors have the choice of including any of them on exams. We achieve this integration by putting all questions into a large common pool of questions and then dispersing them randomly to different sources—the text, the study guide, and the test bank. Students no longer have to worry that questions from their study guide are not representative of test-bank items. Having representative questions in all sources provides incentive and reinforcement for students to answer them as they read the book.

Quick Quiz: Getting a chance to test your knowledge right as you are learning is invaluable to students. It informs them whether they need to reread a section or ask a question in class. All texts should have them!

ALEX SOLDAT, Idaho State University

acknowledgments

Writing this book has been an enormous undertaking of hard work and love. We have felt privileged by the opportunity to delve into the literature of so many areas of psychology in depth, something for which career academics rarely have time. We have also been fortunate to have had the commitment of a vast team of collaborators, to whom we offer our profound gratitude.

We thank the wonderful professionals at McGraw-Hill who have had utter confidence in this project from day one: Mike Sugarman, as executive editor and publisher, has been a man of vision and always said the right things when we needed encouragement and support the most. Editorial Director Beth Mejia, a forceful champion for higher education, has also been a strong advocate for our efforts to make the science of psychology meaningful and relevant to today's students. Judith Kromm, as our developmental editor, has been like a third author in crafting text, interpreting reviews, and helping us learn that strong substance can co-exist with simple and clear writing. Sheryl Adams, as executive director for marketing development, always has her finger on the pulse of the people for whom we wrote the book—instructors and students. As midcareer authors, we sometimes forget how 19- and 20-year-old students think and will respond to the information we are presenting. Sheryl always kept us in line in this regard. Dawn Groundwater, as director of development, was instrumental in keeping the project on task and developing new ideas for how best to package the unique qualities of the book. Jillian Allison, the editorial coordinator at McGraw-Hill, has been a tremendous help in managing the everyday details to keep a project as big as this one running smoothly. We are eternally grateful that, without missing a beat, she provided childcare (her brother Rich) for our sons while we met with McGraw-Hill staff in New York. Our thanks also go to the Editing, Design, and Production team: Production Editor Brett Coker, who guided us through the copyediting and composition stages of production; Creative Director Jeanne Schreiber; Design Manager Preston Thomas; Photo Research Coordinator Alex Ambrose; and Art Manager Robin Mouat, whose talent and creativity are visible throughout this beautiful book. We also must thank freelance editors Sue Ewing, Barbara Conover, and Carolyn Smith, who, along with copyeditor Joan Pendleton, offered invaluable advice in helping to craft the language and clarify text based on reviewer feedback. Finally, we want to acknowledge the wonderful enthusiasm and support that Steve Debow, as President of Humanities, Social Sciences, and World Languages at McGraw-Hill Higher Education, has shown for this project ever since we first presented our ideas.

We also have been honored to have the invaluable input of our friends and colleagues—all experts in their fields—on various topics in the book. In particular we are grateful to Paul Ekman, Elissa Epel, Jess Feist, David Galin,

Mary Gomes, Lee Huntington, Allen Kanner, Alan Kaufman, James Kaufman, Lee Kirkpatrick, Katherine MacLean, Clifford Saron, and Valerie Stone. Our supplements team, whose names and photos appear on p. xxxiv, came together to share their teaching experience and ideas for a superb instructional package, and we owe them our thanks as well for their constructive feedback on the manuscript. Phil Lehman and Tanya Renner deserve special thanks for their editorial reviews. Other colleagues—reviewers, focus group participants, survey respondents, and class testers—are too numerous to acknowledge individually here (see pp. xxxvii–xlii), but their collective interest and encouragement have been inspiring. We have also benefited from having research support from our students, Sarah Greene, Adam Larson, and Jessica Vandeleest.

Additionally, we would like to thank our sons, Jerry and Evan Feist, for enduring the enormous amount of time we spent writing over the past several years. Evan would sometimes come into our office and say "Are you still writing your book?" and we would always have to say "yes, we're still writing." Given that one of us (GF) has also co-authored a book with his father, we wonder if one of the boys may be next. We also thank our parents—Sandra Rosenberg and Jess and Mary Jo Feist—for their love and unending support throughout this entire process.

We are in an unusual situation for ending this acknowledgment section. Often, authors end by thanking their spouses. In this case, spouse also means coauthor. More than one person we have told about this project has said, "Wow! And you're still married!" Not only are we still married, but this project has also deepened our marriage. Projects as big, complex, and difficult as this one test the mettle of any relationship. By affording us the opportunity to work creatively together, this project has strengthened the bond between us. We learned how to play to each other's strengths, balance viewpoints and expertise, and compromise. We were able to work through things late at night, even when one of us did not feel like it. We wonder how other co-authors of introductory psychology textbooks manage to work out the complex problems that arise while writing something this big without such convenience and intimacy as our relationship provides. We are grateful for each other.

Gregory J. Feist and Erika L. Rosenberg

supplements

Psychology: Making Connections is supported by a highly collaborative and integrated program of supplements for instructors teaching and students studying Introductory Psychology. The connections made in the text are stressed and expanded on within the supplements, resulting in a set of tools that will help instructors connect to students and students connect to the material.

McGraw-Hill *Connect Psychology*

McGraw-Hill *Connect Psychology* is a Web-based assignment and assessment platform that gives students the means to better connect with their coursework, with their instructors, and with the important concepts that they will need to know for success now and in the future.

With *Connect Psychology* instructors can deliver assignments, quizzes, and tests online. Nearly all the questions from the text are presented in an auto-gradable format and tied to the text's learning objectives. Instructors can edit existing questions and add new ones; track individual student performance—by question, assignment, or in relation to the class overall—with detailed grade reports; integrate grade reports easily with Learning Management Systems such as WebCT and Blackboard; and much more.

By choosing *Connect Psychology*, instructors are providing their students with a powerful tool for improving academic performance and truly mastering course material. *Connect Psychology* allows students to practice important skills at their own pace and on their own schedule. Importantly, students' assessment results and instructors' feedback are all saved online—so students can continually review their progress and plot their course to success.

Some instructors may also choose *Connect Psychology Plus* for their students. Like *Connect Psychology*, *Connect Psychology Plus* provides students with online assignments and assessments, plus 24/7 online access to an eBook—an online edition of the text—to aid them in successfully completing their work, wherever and whenever they choose.

For Instructors

All of the instructor ancillaries described below can be found on the password-protected instructor's side of the text's Online Learning Center. Contact your local McGraw-Hill sales representative for log-in information. www.mhhe .com/feist1

- **PrepCenter for Introductory Psychology is a comprehensive online media library** that features instructor materials, videos, and images to enhance your lectures and, ultimately, your students' learning experiences. New to PrepCenter are McGraw-Hill's **Dynamic PowerPoints,** which take a concept-based, visual approach to 80 key concepts in Introductory Psychology. Carefully designed and thoroughly reviewed, these PowerPoints can be inserted in chapter outline PowerPoint presentations or used as is. Access PrepCenter through the Instructor's Online Learning Center.

- **Instructors Manual by Alisha Janowsky,** *University of Central Florida,* **and Martha Hubertz,** *Florida Atlantic University:* This manual provides all the tools and resources you need to deliver and enhance your course instruction. The Instructor's Manual includes chapter outlines, key terms, Innovative Instructions suggestions, and video resource lists including suggested YouTube clips relevant to each chapter. Each marginal Nature & Nurture and Connection call-out is reinforced and expanded on in this manual to facilitate teaching psychology as an extensively connected discipline.

- **Test Banks by Marissa Harrison,** *Penn State University–Harrisburg,* **and Lisa Jane Thomassen,** *Indiana University:* Comprising more than 2,400 questions, the test banks are designed to test factual, applied, and conceptual understanding. Test Bank 1 includes primarily factual and applied questions and Test Bank 2 tests conceptual knowledge. The test questions

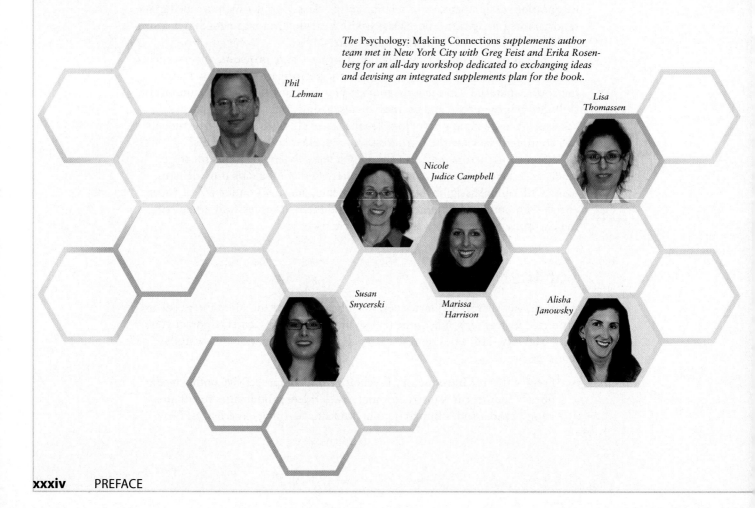

The Psychology: Making Connections *supplements author team met in New York City with Greg Feist and Erika Rosenberg for an all-day workshop dedicated to exchanging ideas and devising an integrated supplements plan for the book.*

Phil Lehman

Lisa Thomassen

Nicole Judice Campbell

Susan Snycerski

Marissa Harrison

Alisha Janowsky

build on the study skills gained through the Student Study Guide and online quizzes and are keyed to major concepts in Introductory Psychology. All items are compatible with **EZTest,** McGraw-Hill's **Computerized Test Bank** program.

- **PowerPoint Presentations by Kim Foreman:** These slides cover the key points of each chapter and include charts and graphs from the text. The PowerPoint presentations serve as an organization and navigation tool and can be used as is or modified to meet your needs.

- **Classroom Performance System Questions by Nicole Judice Campbell, *Oklahoma University:*** These questions, prepared by an instructor experienced in classroom use of "clicker" systems, include a mix of factual and opinion items. Factual questions will let you know what concepts your students are mastering and those with which they are having difficulty; opinion questions present possibilities for class participation and discussion. By switching the system to "anonymous" mode, you can poll opinions and experiences concerning sensitive content.

- **Image Gallery:** The Image Gallery features all the figures from the text. These images are available for download and can be easily embedded in your PowerPoint slides.

For Students

- **Student Study Guide by Susan Snycerski, *San Jose State University:*** This guide takes an active learning approach and includes detailed chapter outlines, vocabulary lists and definitions, practice tests, and reference lists. All materials in this study guide are designed to help students fully grasp the material in the text by shaping study skills.

- **Student Online Learning Center by Phil Lehman, *Virginia Tech:*** This set of student assessment and enrichment activities includes chapter-by-chapter multiple-choice and fill-in-the-blank quizzes. These quizzes build on skills learned through use of the Study Guide.

- **Psych 2.0:** An innovative blend of print and online components, Psych 2.0 combines the best of a study guide with the best of online interactivity. The Psych 2.0 Online Experience Guide, written by Tammy Rahhal of the University of Massachusetts–Amherst and Matthew Schulkind of Amherst College, provides a synopsis, pre-activity TIPS, and post-activity questions for each online activity. The activities themselves offer experiential, observational, and visual learning opportunities for more than 90 key concepts in Introductory Psychology. Accessible as a stand-alone site or an enhanced course cartridge, Psych 2.0 can be easily added to any syllabus or online course. Available at one low price, Psych 2.0 is equally affordable with new or used texts. To view a demonstration of Psych 2.0, please visit http://www.mhhe.com/psych2demo.

CourseSmart

contributors

Manuscript Reviewers

Paula Ahles, Illinois Central College

Peggy L. Akerman, Pensacola Junior College

Jim Allen, SUNY Geneseo

William Altman, Broome Community College

Roxanna Anderson, Palm Beach Community College

Randy Arnau, University of Southern Mississippi

Leslie L. Baylis, University of South Carolina

James L. Becker, Pulaski Technical College

Kenneth Bell, Dodge City Community College

Robert Beneckson, Florida International University

Joy Berrenberg, University of Colorado–Denver

Kathleen Bey, Palm Beach Community College

Stephen Blessing, University of Tampa

Gary Bothe, Pensacola Junior College

Nicole Bragg, Mt. Hood Community College

Nancy Breland, College of New Jersey

Dennis R. Brophy, Northwest College

Gayle Brosnan-Watters, Chandler-Gilbert Community College

Michele Brumley, Idaho State University

Josh Burk, College of William and Mary

David Bush, Utah State University

Gregory D. Busse, American University

Robert Caldwell, Michigan State University

Jarrod N. Calloway, Northwest Mississippi Community College

Michele Camden, Seminole Community College

Nicole Judice Campbell, Oklahoma University

Sandra Carpenter, University of Alabama–Huntsville

Richard Cavasina, California University of Pennsylvania

Wendy C. Chambers, University of Georgia

Stephen Chew, Samford University

Chrisanne Christensen, Southern Arkansas University

Maureen Conard, Sacred Heart University

Shaunna G. Crossen, Penn State University–Schuylkill

Layton Seth Curl, Metropolitan State College of Denver

Dawn Delaney, Madison Area Technical College

Suzanne Delaney, University of Arizona

Penny Devine, Florida Community College–Jacksonville

Dorothy Doolittle, Christopher Newport University

Dale Doty, Monroe Community College

Bonnie Drumwright, California State University, Sacramento

Valerie Farmer-Dugan, Illinois State University

Laura Duvall, Heartland Community College

Steven Dworkin, University of North Carolina–Wilmington

Jane Dycus, Jefferson College

Michael Erickson, University of California, Riverside

Matthew Fanetti, Missouri State University

Debra Farmer, Colorado Northwestern Community College

Valeri Farmer-Dougan, Illinois State University

Diane Feibel, University of Cincinnati–Raymond Walters College

Kevin Filter, Minnesota State University

Tregon Fitch, University of Cincinnati, Clermont College

Shira Gabriel, University at Buffalo, State University of New York

Shannon Gadbois, Brandon University

Jeffrey A. Gibbons, Christopher Newport University

Adam Goodie, University of Georgia

Cameron Gordon, University of North Carolina–Wilmington

Peter Gram, Pensacola Community College

Jeffery Gray, University of Southern Mississippi

Rodney J. Grisham, Indian River State College

Regan Gurung, University of Wisconsin–Green Bay

Lisa Hagan, Metropolitan State College of Denver

Lynn Haller, Morehead State University

Deletha P. Hardin, University of Tampa

Greg Harris, Polk County Community College

Lisa Harrison, California State University, Sacramento

Marissa Harrison, Penn State University–Harrisburg

Diana Hart, Arapahoe Community College

Jason Hart, Christopher Newport University

Lesley Hathorn, Metropolitan State College of Denver

Paul Heintz, Edison Community College

Jeff Henriques, University of Wisconsin–Madison

Paul Herrle, College of Southern Nevada

Debra Hollister, Valencia Community College

Virginia Holloway, University of Florida

Brian Howland, University of Florida–Gainesville

Herman Huber, College of St. Elizabeth

Allen Huffcutt, Bradley University

Harry Hughes, Salt Lake Community College

Margaret Ingate, Rutgers University

Linda M. Jackson, Michigan State University

Alisha Janowsky, Florida Atlantic University–Boca Raton

Lance Jones, Bowling Green State University

Edward P. Kardas, Southern Arkansas University

Don Kates, College of DuPage

Edward Keane, Housatonic Community College

Arthur D. Kemp, University of Central Missouri

Shelia Kennison, Oklahoma State University

Kristin Kilbourn, University of Colorado–Denver

Andrew Kim, Citrus College

G. Jeffrey Klepfer, University of Tampa

Megan L. Knowles, University of Georgia

Ken Koenigshofer, Chaffey College

Gary Krolikowski, SUNY Geneseo

Stephanie Kucera, University of Montana

Karen Kwan, Salt Lake Community College

Josh Landau, York College of Pennsylvania

Elizabeth C. Lanthier, Northern Virginia Community College

Lana Larsen, University of Maryland, University College

Kristin Lazarova, Northeast State Community College

Fred Leavitt, California State University, East Bay

Phil Lehman, Virginia Polytechnic Institute

Tera Letzring, Idaho State University

Katherine Lorenzo, Macomb Community College

Jeffrey M. Love, Penn State University

Greg Loviscky, Penn State–University Park

Lynda Mae, Arizona State University–Tempe

Caitlin Mahy, University of Oregon

Paul Markel, Minot State University

Karen Marsh, University of Minnesota–Duluth

Robert D. Mather, University of Central Oklahoma

Wanda C. McCarthy, University of Cincinnati, Clermont College

Daniel S. McConnell, University of Central Florida

Kathleen C. McCulloch, Idaho State University

Corinne McNamara, Kennesaw State University

Joe Melcher, St. Cloud University

Paul Merritt, Texas A & M University–Corpus Christi

Amori Yee Mikami, University of Virginia

Harold Miller, Brigham Young University–Provo

Mindy Miserendino, Sacred Heart University

Stacie Mitchell, Kirkwood Community College

Paulina Multhaupt, Macomb Community College

David P. Nalbone, Purdue University–Calumet–Hammond

Todd Nelson, California State University, Stanislaus

Daniel M. Niederjohn, Kennesaw State University

Theresa Nowak, Eastern Kentucky University

Geoffrey O'Shea, SUNY College at Oneonta

Lois Pasapane, Palm Beach Community College

Julie Penley, El Paso Community College

Edison Perdomo, Central State University

Brady Phelps, South Dakota State University

Ann Phillips, University of Michigan–Ann Arbor

Lloyd R. Pilkington, Midlands Technical College

Diane Pisacreta, St. Louis Community College

Christy Porter, College of William and Mary

Eileen Price, Midlands Technical College

Elizabeth Purcell, Greenville Technical College

Reginald Rackley, Southern University

Andrea Rashtian, California State University, Northridge

Celia Reaves, Monroe Community College

Tanya Renner, Kapi'olani Community College

Vicki Ritts, St. Louis Community College

Alan Roberts, Indiana University–Bloomington

Larry Rudiger, University of Vermont

Linda Ruehlman, Arizona State University

Joanna Salapska-Gelleri, Florida Gulf Coast University

Juan Salinas, University of Texas at Austin

John Sanders, Garden City Community College

Alan Searleman, St. Lawrence University

Jane P. Sheldon, University of Michigan–Dearborn

Laura Sherrick, Front Range Community College

Cynthia K. Shinabarger Reed, Tarrant County College

Robert Short, Arizona State University

Maria Shpurik, Florida International University

Jessica Shryack, University of Minnesota, Minneapolis

Barry D. Smith, University of Maryland–College Park

Alex Soldat, Idaho State University

Claire St. Peter Pipkin, West Virginia University–Morgantown

Kim Stark-Wroblewski, University of Central Missouri

Genevieve Stevens, Houston Community College

Mark Stewart, American River College

Carla Strassle, York College of Pennsylvania

Joy Stratton, Northern Virginia Community College, Loudoun

Holly Straub, University of South Dakota

Jutta Street, Barton College

James R. Sullivan, Florida State University, Tallahassee

Cyril Svoboda, University of Maryland–University College

Kathleen A. Taylor, Sierra College

Larry Taylor, Parkland University

Pam Terry, Gordon College

Lisa Thomassen, Indiana University

Kandi Turley-Ames, Idaho State University

Barbara VanHorn

Soni Verma, Sierra College

Sheree Watson, University of Southern Mississippi

Eric B. Weiser, Curry College

Brooke Whisenhunt, Missouri State University

Wanda Willard, Monroe Community College

Timothy Williams, Northwest Mississippi Community College

Mark Wolf, Arizona State University

Heather Wolters, Ferris State University/Central Michigan University

Nancy J. Woolf, University of California, Los Angeles

Jennifer Yanowitz, Utica College

Karen Yanowitz, Arkansas State University

Stephen J. Zaccaro, George Mason University

Expert Reviewers

Biology Coverage
C. Robin Timmons, Drew University

Gender Coverage
Sheryl Blahnik, Richland Community College

Chapter 2: Conducting Research in Psychology
William Buskist, Auburn University

Julie Penley, El Paso Community College

Chapter 3: The Biology of Behavior
Charles Evans, LaGrange College

Carlos Grijalva, University of California, Los Angeles

Tanya Renner, Kapi'olani Community College

Chapter 4: Sensing and Perceiving Our World
Gregory Busse, American University

Toby Marx, Union County College

Chapter 5: Human Development
Dan Fawaz, Georgia Perimeter College

Joan Ingram, Northwestern University

Chapter 7: Memory
Barbara Hawley, Davenport University

Steven Mewaldt, Marshall University

Katy Neidhardt, Cuesta College

Chapter 8: Learning
Todd Smith, Lake Superior State University

Deborah Stote, University of Texas at Austin

Chapter 9: Language and Thought
Conor McLennan, Cleveland State University

Patricia Sible, Wayne State University

Chapter 10: Intelligence, Problem-Solving, and Creativity
James Kaufman, California State University, San Bernadino

Robert Sternberg, Tufts University

Chapter 11: Motivation and Emotion
Perrin Cohen, Northeastern University

Lisa Scherer, University of Nebraska–Omaha

Jeff Larsen, Texas Tech University

David Matsumoto, San Francisco State University

Chapter 12: Stress and Health
Nicholas Christenfeld, University of California–San Diego

Raymond Fleming, University of Wisconsin–Milwaukee

Chapter 13: Personality: The Uniqueness of the Individual
Ken Olson, Fort Hays State University

Elizabeth E. Seebach, Saint Mary's University of Minnesota

Chapter 14: Social Behavior
Amy Buddie, Kennesaw State University

Elizabeth Yost Hammer, Xavier University of Louisiana

Jean Twenge, San Diego State University

Chapter 15: Psychological Disorders
Rich Halgin, University of Massachusetts–Amherst

Genevieve Stevens, Houston Community College–Central College

Chapter 16: Treatment of Psychological Disorders
Debra L. Hollister, Valencia Community College

Teleconference Participants

Jason Allaire, North Carolina State University

Gary Bothe, Pensacola Junior College

Dennis R. Brophy, Northwest College

Debra Farmer, Colorado Northwestern Community College

Shannon Gadbois, Brandon University

Diana Hart, Arapahoe Community College

Allen Huffcutt, Bradley University

Herman Huber, College of St. Elizabeth

Linda A. Jackson, Michigan State University

Ken Koenigshofer, Chaffey College

Harold Miller, Brigham Young University–Provo

Brady J. Phelps, South Dakota State University

Andrea Rashtian, California State University, Northridge

Juan Salinas, University of Texas at Austin

Jessica Shryack, University of Minnesota

Carla Strassle, York College of Pennsylvania

Design Reviewers

Charlie Aaron, Northwest Mississippi Community College

Richard Cavasina, California University of Pennsylvania

Dale Doty, Monroe Community College

Sarah Grison, University of Illinois–Urbana–Champaign

Regan Gurung, University of Wisconsin–Green Bay

Ken Koenigshofer, Chaffey College

Jason McCoy, Cape Fear Community College

Julie Morrison, Maricopa Community College

Geoffrey O'Shea, SUNY College at Oneonta

Brady Phelps, South Dakota State University

Celia Reaves, Monroe Community College

Vicki Ritts, St. Louis Community College

Lisa Thomassen, Indiana University

Wanda Willard, Monroe Community College

Jennifer Yanowitz, Utica College

Karen Yanowitz, Arkansas State University

Biological Acetate Reviewers

Scott Bates, Utah State University

Kathleen Bey, Palm Beach Community College

Stephen Chew, Samford University

Tera Letzring, Idaho State University

Robert D. Mather, University of Central Oklahoma

Geoffrey O'Shea, SUNY College at Oneonta

Lawrence J. Ryan, Oregon State University

Scott Safford, Oregon State University

Class Testers

Roxanna Anderson, Palm Beach Community College

James Becker, Pulaski Technical College

William Goggin, University of Southern Mississippi

Beth Lanthier, Northern Virginia Community College

Serge Onyper, St. Lawrence University

Donald Sweeney, College of DuPage

Student Reviewers

Crystal Aya, Hunter College

Julia Calleo, Fashion Institute of Technology

Michelle Carrera, Hunter College

King Moon Chu, Boston University

Stamatina Fileas, SUNY Buffalo

Crystal Godwin, Arkansas State University

Dasha Kouznetsova, Hunter College

Jenna Lynn, Arkansas State University

Tamarah McGaughey, Arkansas State University

Josie Sayegh, University of California–Santa Cruz

Christina K. Ng, SUNY Stony Brook

Bailey Sharp, Arkansas State University

Anna Sorsher, Northeastern University

Christina Szeliga, Hunter College

Introductory Psychology Symposium Attendees

Every year McGraw-Hill conducts several Introductory Psychology Symposia for instructors from across the country. These events offer a forum for instructors to exchange ideas and experiences with colleagues they might not have met otherwise. They also provide an opportunity for editors from McGraw-Hill to gather information about the needs and challenges of instructors of Introductory Psychology. The feedback we have received has been invaluable and has contributed—directly and indirectly—to the development of *Psychology: Making Connections* and its supplements.

Terry Adcock, Parkland College

Mark Alicke, Ohio University

Cheryl Almeida, Johnson & Wales University

Carol Anderson, Bellevue Community College

Grace Austin, Sacramento City College

James Becker, Pulaski Technical College

Bethany Neal-Beliveau, Indiana University-Purdue University Indianapolis

Dan Bellack, Trident Technical College

Kathleen Bey, Palm Beach Community College–Lake Worth

Jennifer Bizon, Texas A&M University

Jeffrey Blum, Los Angeles City College

Susan Boatright, University of Rhode Island

Deb Briihl, Valdosta State University

Tamara Brown, University of Kentucky

Brad Brubaker, Indiana State University

John Cambon, Ozarks Technical Community College

Nicole Judice-Campbell, University of Oklahoma

Lore Carvajal, Triton College

Karen Christoff, University of Mississippi

Diana Ciesko, Valencia Community College–East

Alexis Collier, Ohio State University

Doreen Collins-McHugh, Seminole Community College

Layton Curl, Metropolitan State College of Denver

Chris Curtis, Delta College

David Daniel, James Madison University

Neeru Deep, Northwestern State University of Louisiana

Barbara De Filippo, Lane Community College

Suzanne Delaney, University of Arizona

Bonnie Dennis, Virginia Western Community College

Tom DiLorenzo, University of Delaware

Peggy Dombrowski, Harrisburg Area Community College

Carol Donnelly, Purdue University–West Lafayette

Dorothy Doolittle, Christopher Newport University

Joan Doolittle, Anne Arundel Community College

Dale Doty, Monroe Community College

Katherine Dowdell, Des Moines Area Community College

Shari Dunlavy, Ivy Tech Community College–Fort Wayne

Joelle Elicker, University of Akron

Jay Brophy Ellison, University of Central Florida

Michael Erickson, University of California Riverside

Dan Farwaz, Georgia Perimeter College–Dunwoody

Dave Filak, Joliet Junior College

Tom Fischer, Wayne State University

Ray Fleming, University of Wisconsin–Milwaukee

Donelson R. Forsyth, University of Richmond

Eric Fox, Western Michigan University

Robert Frank, Oakton Community College

Paula Frioli, Truckee Meadows Community College

Dale Fryxell, Chaminade University

Katherine Gibbs, University of California-Davis

Travis Gibbs, Riverside Community College, Moreno Valley Campus

Kendra Gilds, Lane Community College

Daine Grey, Middlesex County College

Sarah Grison, University of Illinois at Urbana–Champaign

Regan Gurung, University of Wisconsin–Green Bay

Mike Hackett, Westchester Community College

Robin Hailstorks, Prince George Community College

Erin Hardin, Texas Tech University

Gregory Eugene Harris, Polk Community College, Winter Haven

Jeffrey Henriques, University of Wisconsin–Madison

Carmon Weaver Hicks, Ivy Tech Community College

Debra Hollister, Valencia Community College

Theresa Holt, Middlesex County College

Natalie W. Hopson, Salisbury University

Vahan Hovsepian, Butte College

Mark Hoyert, Indiana University–Northwest

John Huber, Texas State University San Marcos

Charlie Huffman, James Madison University

Rachel Hull, Texas A&M University

Nita Jackson, Butler Community College

Sean Jennings, Valencia Community College

Linda Jones, Blinn College

Shelia Kennison, Oklahoma State University

Shirin Khosropour, Austin Community College–Pinnacle

Christina Knox, College of the Sequoias

Dana Kuehn, Florida Community College–Deerwood Center

Mark Laumakis, San Diego State University

Natalie Kerr Lawrence, James Madison University

Phil Lehman, Virginia Polytechnic Institute

Tera Letzring, Idaho State University

Dawn Lewis, Prince Georges Community College

Deborah Licht, Pikes Peak Community College

Mark Licht, Florida State University

Paul Livingston, Midlands Technical College

Maria Lopez, Mt. San Jacinto College–San Jacinto Campus

Sonya Lott-Harrison, Community College of Philadelphia

Clem Magner, Milwaukee Area Technical College

Brian Malley, University of Michigan–Ann Arbor

Randall Martinez, Cypress College

Mike Majors, Delgado Community College

Jason McCoy, Cape Fear Community College–Downtown

Robert Melara, City College of New York

Charlene Melrose, Orange Coast College

Steven P. Mewaldt, Marshall University

Joel Morgovsky, Brookdale Community College

Joe Morrissey, Binghamton University

Glenn Musgrove, Broward Community College

Jeff Neubauer, Pima Community College West

John Nezlek, College of William and Mary

Glenda Nichols, Tarrant County College–South

Brian Oppy, Chico State University

Randall Osborne, Texas State University–San Marcos

Donald Orso, Anne Arundel Community College

Jack A. Palmer, University of Louisiana Monroe

Keith Pannel, El Paso Community College

Debra Parish, Tomball College

John Pellew, Greenville Technical College

Jennifer Peluso, Florida Atlantic University

Julie A. Penley, El Paso Community College

David Perkins, University of Louisiana at Lafayette

Claire St. Peter Pipkin, West Virginia University

Deborah S. Podwika, Kankakee Community College

Skip (Susan) Pollock, Mesa Community College

Bryan Porter, Old Dominion University

Alida Quick, Wayne County Community College–Downtown

Christopher Randall, Kennesaw State University

Diane Reddy, University of Wisconsin Milwaukee

Laura Reichel, Front Range Community College

Tanya Renner, Kapi'olani Community College

Tonja Ringgold, Baltimore City Community College

Vicki Ritts, Saint Louis Community College–Meramec

Edna Ross, University of Louisville

Sharleen Sakai, Michigan State University

David Schroeder, University of Arkansas

Michael Schumacher, Columbus State Community College

James Shannon, Citrus College

Wayne Shebilske, Wright State University

Elisabeth Sherwin, University of Arkansas at Little Rock

Harvey Shulman, Ohio State University

Jennifer Siciliani, University of Missouri–St. Louis

Nancy Simpson, Trident Technical College

Jamie Smith, Ohio State University

Lilliette Johnson Smith, Southwest Tennessee Community College

Vivian Smith, Lakeland Community College

Genevieve Stevens, Houston Community College

Mark Stewart, American River College

Pam Stewart, Northern Virginia Community College

Nina Tarner, Sacred Heart University

Rachelle Tennenbaum, Anne Arundel Community College–Arnold

Felicia Friendly Thomas, California State Polytechnic University–Pomona

Lisa Thomassen, Indiana University–Bloomington

Stephen Tracy, Community College of Southern Nevada

Lisa Valentino, Seminole Community College–Sanford

Barbara VanHorn, Indian River Community College

Anre Venter, University of Notre Dame

Ruth Wallace, Butler Community College

Fred Whitford, Montana State University

John W. Wright, Washington State University

Mona Yektaparast, Central Piedmont Community College

Brandy Young, Cypress College

Supplements Reviewers

Leslie L. Baylis, University of South Carolina

James L. Becker, Pulaski Technical College

Stephen Blessing, University of Tampa

Nicole Bragg, Mt. Hood Community College

Chrisanne Christensen, Southern Arkansas University

Shaunna G. Crossen, Penn State University–Schuylkill

Dale V. Doty, Monroe Community College

Allen Huffcutt, Bradley University

Cecile Marczinski, Northern Kentucky University

Geoffrey O'Shea, SUNY College at Oneonta

Julie A. Penley, El Paso Community College

Edison Perdomo, Central State University

Alan Roberts, Indiana University–Bloomington

Tanya Renner, Kapi'olani Community College

McGraw-Hill Connecters

Sheree D'Amico

Anne Fry

Meannine Gauna

Linda Haefer

James Koch

Adam Poston

Mary Ellen Rahn

Pete Vanaria

psychology
making
connections

introduction

to **psychology**

preview
questions

1 *What makes people tick?*

2 *What do psychologists do besides treating mental illness?*

3 *How much of who we are is set by the time we're born, and how much is due to our surroundings?*

Emily Gould, a young editor in New York City, posted her observations about the world and intimate details about her social life in a personal blog. To her, the online community felt safe and friendly. She landed a job as an editor of Gawker.com, a New York-based celebrity gossip blog, which brought her a huge audience and more praise and scrutiny than ever. Emily became obsessed with her blog audience. Her boyfriend complained that she spent less and less time interacting with him and more and more time with her online friends: "Depending on how you looked at it, I either had no life and I barely talked to anyone, or I spoke to thousands of people constantly" (E. Gould, 2008, p. 37).

Among people in their teens and early 20s, blogging and micro-blogging have become common modes of communication. These tools offer quick and cheap ways for people to communicate in real time without disturbing their surroundings (Garrett & Danziger, 2008). Emily wrote about a relationship with a coworker at work that had become almost ▶

▶ entirely electronic. Even when they were sitting side by side, they IM'd nearly all of the time: "Soon it stopped seeming weird to me when one of us would type a joke and the other would type 'Hahahahaha' in lieu of actually laughing" (E. Gould, 2008, p. 36).

Forgoing actual laughter in order to put it in text *is* weird, but it is becoming commonplace. Most 18- and 19-year-olds have used the Internet regularly for at least 6 years of their lives, get online several times per day, and spend an average of 15 hours online per week (Hargittai, 2008). And they spend a lot of time texting their friends (Garrett & Danziger, 2008). So with boundaries between the electronic and real worlds beginning to blur, questions about how humans behave with regard to the electronic realm are important.

Psychologists, people who study human behavior and thought, have begun to study blogging, IM, e-mail, Web sites, and social network sites (SNSs) like MySpace and Facebook (Lewis, Kaufman, & Christakis, in press; Vazire & Gosling, 2004). In real-life interaction, social connections, or *networks,* among people can influence everything from opinion to eating

chapter
outline

patterns to one's likelihood of quitting smoking (Christakis & Fowler, 2007, 2008). Do online SNSs operate in ways that resemble real-world networks? What are the consequences of electronic interaction for our social lives? As we will see in more detail at the end of this chapter, people use practices such as "friending" on SNSs to widen their social circles, which can translate into real-life social benefits (Lange, 2008). IM both enhances and interferes with people's ability to work (Garrett & Danziger, 2008). People often use the Internet as a stepping stone to future meetings in real life (Couch & Liamputtong, 2008). As psychology begins to identify the pros and cons of this overlap between real and virtual worlds, the ways to navigate this realm in a healthy manner become clearer.

You may be wondering just how the study of people's use of technology in all its many forms relates to the study of psychology. The answer is that it involves people thinking, behaving, and interacting, which is what psychology is all about. ■

"On the Internet, nobody knows you're a dog."

What Is Psychology?

Wherever there are people, even online, there is psychology. In one sense, you have been a psychologist for most of your life. Every time you try to explain what someone else is doing—and why—you are thinking psychologically. You do it when you say your friend dominates conversations, because he is self-absorbed. Or when you conclude that your big sister is bossy, because she is older and always gets what she wants. We think and live psychology everyday.

PSYCHOLOGY DEFINED

Many fields of study aim to understand people. Literature helps us understand people through its methods of storytelling, character exploration, setting, and imagery.

History helps us understand people through description and analysis of past events and artifacts. Sociology seeks to understand people in terms of large-scale social forces and with a focus on groups rather than individuals. Psychology is unique in that it is the *science* of understanding individuals—animals as well as people. Formally defined, **psychology** is the scientific study of thought and behavior.

psychology
the scientific study of thought and behavior.

But wait, you might be thinking, "Don't psychologists treat people with mental illness or try to help us figure out how our parents messed us up?" Yes, they do these things too. Some professional psychologists practice or *apply* psychology to diagnose and treat problems of thought and behavior. In fact, psychology is both a clinical practice and a science. The clinical practice side encompasses the services provided in therapists' offices, schools, hospitals, and business. Without fail, when we tell someone that we are psychologists, they immediately think we are clinical psychologists and are analyzing their every move, looking for hidden meaning in everything they do.

You can also find popular psychology in homes, radio talk shows, Internet news sites, and TV news reports. What sets scientific psychology apart from popular psychology—known as *folk psychology*—is the methods used in each. As you will see in Chapter 2, "Conducting Psychological Research," and again in Chapter 16, "Treatment of Psychological Disorders," the methods of scientific and clinical psychologists are quite different from those of lay folk, who sometimes rely on an unreliable body of knowledge known as *common sense*.

In addition to being a clinical practice, psychology is a science. Yet most people you talk to on the street don't think of psychology as a science; rather, they probably think of it only as a clinical practice. Editors of the science magazine *Scientific American*, for instance, commented that "whenever we run articles on social topics, some readers protest that we should stick to 'real science'" ("The Peculiar Institution," 2002, p. 8). Some people are convinced that psychology and other social sciences are not science. They may think that psychology can be considered a therapy or a method of examining thought and behavior, but not a science. Only physics, chemistry, biology, astronomy, genetics, and geology are science in the eyes of some people.

But psychology *is* a science—it is often a social science but increasingly it is also a biological science. To us as psychologists, this is an obvious and not a

Why do people act the way they do? That's what psychologists want to know.

controversial statement. As we will see throughout this book, not only is psychology a science, but it is also considered a core science, along with medicine, earth science, chemistry, physics, and math (Boyack, Klavans, & Börner, 2005).

WHY SHOULD YOU STUDY PSYCHOLOGY?

Reasons for studying psychology vary from person to person. Maybe your advisor suggested it would be a good course to take or maybe you're taking the course because it satisfies a general education requirement. Psychology is considered a part of a good general education because its content is useful to many fields. "Know thyself" is the human dilemma. Studying psychology not only makes you more aware of how people work but also makes you more aware of how *you* work—very practical knowledge to have in many settings. Understanding others' thoughts, feelings, and motives—as well as your own—may help you be a more effective doctor, lawyer, businessperson, or friend. Understanding how children learn, think, reason, and play will help you if you become a parent or a teacher. To learn how one recent college graduate has applied her knowledge of psychology in her life, read the "Psychology in the Real World" box on p. 8.

In a real sense, the study of psychology is as old as the human species. Before people wondered about the stars, rocks, and planets, no doubt they wondered about themselves and others. They did, after all, form relationships, have children, and protect their families. Human babies could not survive without others to care for them. Perhaps that is why people fascinate us. From our first days, we humans are inherently interested in other humans—for survival. Newborns prefer faces to almost any other object. Our very existence is social, and as you will learn, our brains have evolved mechanisms and structures that allow us to understand others in a remarkably complex way (Dunbar, 1996).

As you begin your study of this field, you will learn just how broad the field of psychology is. You may even find a subfield that dovetails with another interest you have already developed.

quick quiz 1.1: What Is Psychology?

1. Psychology is best defined as the study of
   a. mental illness
   b. human behavior
   c. neuroses
   d. human thought and behavior

2. As a field, psychology is
   a. the practice of diagnosing and treating mental illness
   b. a social science
   c. a biological science
   d. all of the above

Answers can be found at the end of the chapter.

psychology in the **real world**

Intro to Psychology in My Everyday Life by Stamatina Fileas (Student at SUNY Buffalo)

It's amazing how taking Introduction to Psychology can take a seemingly normal life and make you more aware of what people do and why. With this realization comes empowerment; awareness opens doors as it opens eyes. To someone who has never taken a psychology class, this may seem ridiculous. You might say, "I do what I do because that is how everyone does it" or "because it works for me." However, the knowledge that comes from this course is a great tool for personal growth and development.

I can think of many ways in which I have encountered things I learned about in my introductory course on a daily basis. There have been so many times when, while reading a chapter, I would look up and tell my roommates about something I had just learned. Then I would overhear them

later telling someone else "Hey did you know . . . ?" It was the ability to take this course from the classroom to real life and the world beyond my desk that made it simpler to grasp and to study.

As a teenager, and even into college, I would babysit to make extra money. Before taking psychology, I would often observe the children and notice how they all had similar patterns of growth, development, and understanding. I would often hear mothers talking about how they could see the changes in their babies daily and were looking forward to the next step in their development. At the time I just assumed that a baby's learning to walk or play peek-a-boo around the same age as its peers was due to coincidence or good parenting. However, when I began learning about growth and development in my psych class, I was shocked to learn that there are characteristics that are visible at specific stages of a child's development. I was amazed when I learned about object permanence, or that until babies reach a certain cognitive level they don't

Subdisciplines of Psychology

cognitive psychology
the study of how people perceive, remember, think, speak, and solve problems.

As a science and a practice, psychology is divided into various areas of investigation. Just as this book consists of chapters on different topics in psychology, the field of psychology is divided into more than 25 distinct, but increasingly interrelated, subdisciplines. Figure 1.1 gives a breakdown of the percentages of doctorates awarded in 2005–2006 in each of the major subdisciplines we discuss.

Cognitive psychology is the study of how we perceive, how we learn and remember, how we aquire and use

FIGURE **1.1**

ADVANCED DEGREES AWARDED IN VARIOUS SUBFIELDS OF PSYCHOLOGY, 2005–2006. Nearly 50 percent of the doctorates were awarded in clinical psychology. (Adapted from 2008 Graduate Study in Psychology.)

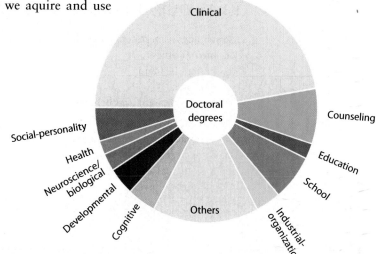

understand that an object they can't see still exists. All of a sudden the fun of peek-a-boo finally made sense!

Another way psychology shed some light on a situation involved my two friends, Jessica and Jennifer. Jessica and Jennifer were twins I had gone to elementary school with. In junior high, Jessica decided to go to a different school than her sister, and she also went to a different high school and college. Though they always tried to be different, it was amazing how similar they actually were. One day we were talking, and they said they didn't believe twins naturally had the inclination to be the same and that, if that were the case, why weren't they like their older brother? They were all born from the same parents, raised in the same home, and had a similar lifestyle. We didn't know. Yet, in my psychology class I found out that biologically, identical twins share the same genes. Many studies have reported that

identical twins separated at birth often have similar interests and futures, as well as similar on IQ test scores. When I emailed Jessica and Jennifer about my discovery they laughed; through the years they had come to realize they had more in common than they wanted to let on and were finally at peace with it.

I must admit, though, that the chapter I paid the most attention to was about mate selection and dating habits. I was so intrigued by how we decide to date someone, how we often choose partners who are as attractive as ourselves, and how the culture we're raised in dictates how and who we date.

Psychology is visible all around us. What you will take away from this course is not just a better appreciation of psychology, but also a better understanding and appreciation of life.

language, and how we solve problems. For example, someone who studies how people visualize objects in their minds is studying cognitive psychology. Those who do research on cognition and learning are often referred to as *experimental psychologists* because they conduct laboratory experiments to address their research questions.

developmental psychology
the study of how thought and behavior change and remain stable across the life span.

Developmental psychology explores how thought and behavior change and show stability across the life span. This perspective allows us to appreciate that organisms—human or otherwise—change and grow; thus, psychological functions likely change as well. Examples of developmental questions in psychology are, How do our reasoning skills or emotional skills change as we age? How does parent–infant bonding affect adult relationships? Does old age bring wisdom?

behavioral neuroscience
the study of the links among brain, mind, and behavior.

Behavioral neuroscience studies the links among brain, mind, and behavior. Neuroscience is a field that cuts across various disciplines and subdisciplines of psychology. One can study brain functions involved in learning, emotion, social behavior, and mental illness, to name just a few areas. A related subdiscipline, **biological psychology,** examines the relationship between bodily systems and chemicals and their relationship to behavior and thought. An example of research in biological psychology that we will look at in Chapter 12 is a study of the effects of stress on hormones and behavior. There is a great deal of overlap between neuroscience and biological psychology. The latter is an older term that

biological psychology
the study of the relationship between bodily systems and chemicals and how they influence behavior and thought.

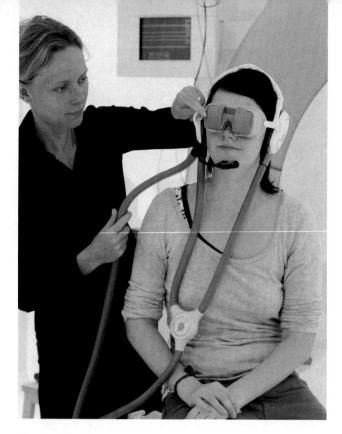

The woman wearing the goggles and headgear is being prepared for a neuroimaging exam in a neuroscience lab.

is being replaced by *behavioral neuroscience* in contemporary psychology. Using painless advanced imaging techniques, behavioral neuroscientists study the structure and functions of the living brain.

Personality psychology considers what makes people unique as well as the consistencies in people's behavior across time and situations. Personality research addresses questions such as whether our personal traits and dispositions change or stay the same from infancy to childhood to adulthood. It also asks whether our consistent tendency to be friendly, anxious, or hostile affects our health, career choice, or interpersonal relationships.

Social psychology considers how the real or imagined presence of others influences thought, feeling, and behavior. Research on prejudice and racism, for example, looks at how a person of one group perceives and treats people in other groups. Social psychologists ask questions like, How does the presence of other people change an individual's thoughts, feeling, or perceptions? Why is someone less likely to help a person in need when there are many people around than when she is alone? Why do otherwise nonaggressive people sometimes behave quite aggressively in certain situations? Why are we attracted to particular kinds of people?

Clinical psychology focuses on the treatment of mental, emotional, and behavioral disorders and ways to promote psychological health. Some clinical psychologists also conduct research and teach. Clinical psychologists work in universities, medical settings, or private practice. As you can see from Figure 1.1, clinical psychology is the single largest subdiscipline in psychology. In the United States, since the late 1940s, the main approach to training in psychology has been the scientist-practitioner model, in which PhDs in clinical psychology should be both therapists and researchers—or at least be trained to be both (Benjamin, 2007). Indeed, psychology is a practice as well as a science.

A related field is *counseling psychology.* Counseling psychologists are more likely than clinical psychologists to work with less severe psychological disorders. They tend to treat and assess relatively healthy people and assist them with career and vocational interests. Counseling training is more likely to occur in schools of education than in psychology departments (Norcross et al., 1998).

Other professionals who provide therapy include clinical psychologists who have obtained a PsyD, which is a professional degree oriented toward nonresearch clinical careers; social workers; marriage and family therapists (who generally have master's degrees); and psychiatrists. Psychiatrists have training in medicine and an MD degree; in addition to offering therapy, they can prescribe drugs.

personality psychology
the study of what makes people unique and the consistencies in people's behavior across time and situations.

social psychology
the study of how living among others influences thought, feeling, and behavior.

clinical psychology
the study of the treatment of mental, emotional, and behavioral disorders and the promotion of psychological health.

connection
Why do crowds make helping a person in distress less likely? Research on the *bystander effect* focuses on this question.
See Chapter 14, p. 557.

health psychology
the study of the role that psychological factors play in regard to physical health and illness.

educational psychology
the study of how students learn, the effectiveness of particular teaching techniques, the social psychology of schools, and the psychology of teaching.

Health psychology examines the role of psychological factors in physical health and illness. Topics in health psychology range from studies of how stress affects people's lives and is linked to illness and immune function to research on the role of social factors in how people interact with the health care system. Some health psychologists work in disease prevention, treatment, and rehabilitation; thus, this area involves clinical practice as well as research.

Educational psychology, connecting cognitive, developmental, and social psychology, examines how students learn, the effectiveness of particular teaching techniques, the dynamics of school populations, and the psychology of teaching. It also attempts to understand special populations of students such as the academically gifted and those with special needs. Educational psychologists are usually academics, theorists, or researchers. *School psychology* is a related field that is generally practiced by counselors in school settings. Approximately 9% of the doctorates in psychology were awarded in educational or school psychology in 2005–2006.

Industrial/organizational (I/O) psychology applies a broad array of psychological concepts and questions to work settings and problems. Such applications can take either a practical focus—such as using personality and social psychology information to select personnel for certain jobs—or a research focus, such as studying whether certain programs improve worker productivity and employment satisfaction. I/O is one of the fastest-growing subdisciplines in psychology, with a nearly 50% increase in the number of PhD programs in this area between 1986 and 2004 (Rogelberg & Gil, 2006).

Two of the smaller and newer disciplines in psychology are sports psychology and forensic psychology. **Sports psychology** examines the psychological factors in sports and exercise (Weinberg & Gould, 1999). It often focuses on improving and increasing athletic performance through techniques such as relaxation and visualization. **Forensic psychology** is a blend of psychology, law, and criminal justice (Adler, 2004). Forensic psychologists make legal evaluations of a person's mental competency to stand trial, the state of mind of a defendant at the time of a crime, the fitness of a parent to have custody of children, or allegations of child abuse. Forensic psychologists also occasionally develop criminal profiles of the type of person who might have committed a particular crime.

As you study the chapters of this text, you may find that one area of psychology especially excites you. Keep in mind, however, that psychology is about how humans think and behave. Thus, all of the topics are useful, many of them are closely intertwined, and there are many reasons for studying psychology, even if you don't become a psychologist. The field of psychology is the outcome of millions of years of humans' interest in their fellow human beings (Feist, 2006). As we will see next, however, the formal history of the field is not quite so old.

nature & nurture
Our feelings can make us more or less susceptible to illness. This connection between nature and nurture is a powerful one.

industrial/ organizational (I/O) psychology
application of psychological concepts and questions to work settings.

sports psychology
the study of psychological factors in sports and exercise.

forensic psychology
field that blends psychology, law, and criminal justice.

quick quiz 1.2: Subdisciplines of Psychology

1. What subdiscipline of psychology examines how thoughts, feelings, and behaviors change over the life span?
   a. developmental psychology
   b. cognitive psychology
   c. personality psychology
   d. educational psychology

2. A psychologist has conducted a series of studies on what part of the brain is most active during a memory task. She is probably
   a. a developmental psychologist
   b. a behavioral neuroscientist
   c. a cognitive psychologist
   d. an industrial/organizational psychologist

3. The main difference between a clinical and counseling psychologist is that counseling psychologists treat
   a. people with more severe psychological disorders
   b. children more than adults
   c. people with less severe psychological disorders
   d. people with learning disabilities only

Answers can be found at the end of the chapter.

The Origins of Psychology

In this section, we look briefly at the origins of the two main forms of psychology: clinical practice and science. The practice of psychology has deeper roots in human history than does the science of psychology. Prehistoric evidence tells us of efforts to heal people's suffering from disturbances of the mind, sometimes in ways we now find alarming. The foundations for psychology as a science date back to the ancient Greeks, and the modern science of psychology originated in the 1870s (Robinson, 1995). First, we consider the practice of psychology.

A BRIEF HISTORY OF THE PRACTICE OF CLINICAL PSYCHOLOGY

Disorders of thought and behavior are no doubt as old as humans—indeed, there is evidence that primates (monkeys and apes) are afflicted with psychological disorders such as depression, anxiety, repetitive and functionless behaviors, and self-injuries (Maestripieri et al., 2006; Novak, 2003; Troisi, 2003). Like any trait shared between species, these behaviors must go back to the ancestors of both species, in this case approximately 6 million years.

Prehistoric Views As far back as the Stone Age (7,000 years ago and maybe even as long as 50,000 years ago), humans tried to cure their fellow humans of various mental problems. Most prehistoric cultures had medicine men or women, known as **shamans,** who would treat the possessed by driving out the demons with elaborate rituals, such as exorcisms, incantations, and prayers. Occasionally, some of these shamans appeared to practice the oldest of all known surgical procedures, trephination.

Trephination involves drilling a small hole in a person's skull, usually less than an inch in diameter (Alt et al., 1997; Weber & Wahl, 2006). Some of these surgeries may have been for medical reasons, such as an attempt to heal a brain injury. Some may also have been performed for psychological reasons, with a goal of

shamans
medicine men or women who treat people with mental problems by driving out their demons with elaborate rituals, such as exorcisms, incantations, and prayers.

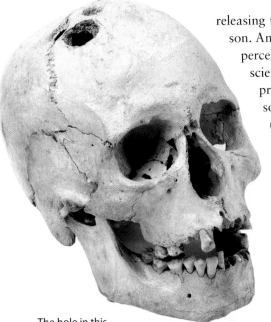

The hole in this skull may have been created by trephination, a prehistoric practice believed to release spirits or demons responsible for psychological disturbances.

releasing the spirits and demons that possessed the afflicted person. Anthropological evidence suggests that a surprisingly large percentage of people survived such surgeries—which today's scientists can confirm by identifying bone growth after the procedure—and the surgeons must have had moderately sophisticated knowledge and understanding of the brain (Alt et al., 1997; Weber & Wahl, 2006).

Ancient Views   The first cultures to focus on natural and physical explanations for disorders were the ancient Egyptians and Greeks. For example, in the second century BCE (Before the Common Era) the ancient Egyptians apparently used narcotics to treat pain (Finger, 1994). The Greek physician Hippocrates (460–377 BCE) was the first to write about a man suffering from a phobia of heights—what we now call acrophobia.

Like the ancient Egyptians and Greeks who came later, the ancient Chinese (2,600 BCE) moved away from supernatural explanations toward natural and physiological explanations of psychological disorders (Tseng, 1973). Specifically, they made connections between a person's bodily organs and their emotions. The heart housed the mind; the liver, the spiritual soul; the lung, the animal soul; the spleen, ideas and intelligence; and the kidneys, will and vitality.

Medieval to Early Modern Views   In Europe during the Middle Ages (400 to 1400 CE [Common Era]), psychological disorders were again attributed to supernatural causes. In the worldview that dominated this era and the Renaissance (1400 to early 1600s), people were possessed by demons, spirits, and the devil—not by physical disorders. These views were taken to an extreme during the Inquisition, when the Catholic Church investigated witchcraft and heresy as part of a broad campaign to eliminate dissent from established Church dogma. Some witchcraft practices were viewed as harmless and even beneficial, but others were branded as the work of the devil. In order to distinguish the good witchcraft from the bad, Church officials held inquisitions and trials (Robinson, 1995). In order to determine whether a person was a witch, they used several different techniques. Sometimes the accused was prodded with a metal pole and spears; if he felt no pain, he was protected by the devil and therefore was a witch. Another common method was the float test. In a *float test* the person's hands and feet were tied, and she was thrown into a lake or river. If she floated, she had to be guilty because only the devil could make someone float; if she sank, she was innocent—but had drowned (Robinson, 1995). The most common punishment for the infrequent survivor of the float test—deemed to be a witch—was being burned at the stake. To be fair, there were numerous writers during the 14th to 16th centuries who argued that witchery was caused not by spirits and supernatural elements but rather by natural ones, such as hallucinations or "melancholia"—what we would now call depression (Robinson, 1995; Veith, 1965).

During the witch hunts of the early modern period of the 16th and 17th centuries, the first facilities for the mentally ill—called **asylums**—were built throughout Europe. The most famous, or infamous, of these was located at St. Mary of Bethlehem in London, England. Although it had served as a hospital for

asylums facilities for treating the mentally ill in Europe during the Middle Ages and into the 19th century.

In the Middle Ages, people who were judged to be witches could be burned at the stake. Some of them may have had psychological disorders that caused them to behave strangely.

the mentally ill and others since the 1300s, Henry VIII designated it as a hospital for the insane in 1547. By then it was really no more than a storage house for the mentally ill and other social castaways. For the most part, people removed mentally ill people from society more than they helped them adjust to society. The conditions were deplorable and chaotic—patients were put in windowless and filthy rooms and were chained and shackled to the walls. The local population, including William Shakespeare, called the place *Bedlam*, a shortened version of "Bethlehem," and that is how the term came to be associated with chaotic and noisy conditions.

moral treatment
19th-century approach to treating the mentally ill with dignity in a caring environment.

In response to these inhumane conditions, reform movements in support of **moral treatment** emerged in Europe and the United States. The main idea was to provide a relaxing place where these patients would be treated with dignity and care. The first major proponent of humane therapies was the Frenchman Philip Pinel in 1783. In the United States the first practitioner of moral treatment was Dorothea Dix. After visiting a prison in 1841 and witnessing the abhorrent and inhumane treatment of the inmates, some of them suffering from psychological disorders, Dix vowed to change these conditions. Over the next 40 years, she personally helped open 30 homes throughout North America (Nolen-Hoeksema, 2007). Moral therapies were among the first forms of treatment that regularly helped people get better.

Modern Views   The last decades of the 1800s also saw the emergence of the first truly modern view of psychological disorders—the idea that they are simply one form of illness and should be treated as all medical conditions are, with appropriate diagnosis and therapy. By the 1880s and 1890s the German psychiatrist Emil Kraepelin collected data on the various kinds of psychological disorders and began systematically classifying and diagnosing them (Shepard, 1995). He popularized the term "dementia praecox" (premature dementia), which he later changed to "schizophrenia," to refer to the major thought disorder known previously as "split mind." He was also the first to distinguish thought disorders (schizophrenia) from the mood disorders of melancholia (depression) and manic depression (bipolar disorder) (Jablensky & Woodbury, 1995). In short, his views were a major influence on diagnostic categories formulated during the 20th century.

Sigmund Freud

Around the turn of the 20th century in Austria, Sigmund Freud developed a form of therapy called psychoanalysis. A clinical approach to understanding and treating psychological disorders, **psychoanalysis** assumes that the unconscious mind is the most powerful force behind thought and behavior and that dreams have meaning and are the most direct route to the unconscious mind (Freud, 1900/1953). It also assumes that our experiences during childhood are a powerful force in the development of our adult personality. Psychoanalysis assumes that people use psychological defenses to protect themselves against threatening impulses, thoughts, feelings, and fantasies. Lastly, it assumes that the unconscious blocking, or repression, of disturbing thoughts and impulses—especially sexual and aggressive impulses—is at the heart of all maladaptive adult behavior.

psychoanalysis a clinically based approach to understanding and treating psychological disorders; assumes that the unconscious mind is the most powerful force behind thought and behavior.

By the middle of the 20th century, three of the major modern developments in clinical psychology had emerged: psychotherapy, drug therapy, and modern criteria for diagnosing mental disorders. For example, one common form of modern therapy—cognitive-behavioral—focuses on changing a person's maladaptive thought and behavior patterns by discussing and rewarding more appropriate ways of thinking and behaving. Although we will consider the modern diagnostic criteria in detail in Chapter 15 and *psychotherapy* (psychological assessment and treatment by a trained therapist) and drug therapy in detail in Chapter 16, it is appropriate to conclude our discussion of the history of psychology as a clinical practice with a brief introduction to the classification system that guides the diagnosis of psychological disorders today.

connection

Deviance, distress, and dysfunction must be present for the diagnosis of psychological disorders. The *DSM* describes specific symptoms of more than 250 different disorders.

See Chapter 15, p. 574.

Psychotherapy techniques, including psychoanalysis, focus on the client's mental state.

When diagnosing psychological disorders, psychologists use the *Diagnostic and Statistical Manual.* Currently in its fourth edition, this standardized reference is referred to as the *Diagnostic and Statistical Manual,* 4th edition, Text Revision—or *DMS-IV-TR* (American Psychiatric Association, 2000). Originally published in 1952, the *DSM* includes diagnoses for more than 250 psychological disorders. The various editions of the *DSM* have incorporated new findings and added new disorders, objectively describing the behaviors and symptoms of each disorder so that psychologists from all perspectives could agree on a single diagnosis for an individual with a given set of symptoms. Occasionally, the authors have even removed behavior patterns (such as homosexuality, which was removed from the list of disorders recognized by the American Psychiatric Association in 1973) that do not meet updated diagnostic criteria.

A BRIEF HISTORY OF SCIENTIFIC PSYCHOLOGY

As with all sciences, scientific psychology can claim philosophy as one of its parent disciplines. By the middle of the 1800s, however, psychology grew away from philosophy to become a science. Let's look briefly at this history.

The Philosophy of Empiricism

Perhaps the most important philosophical question for psychology is the nature of knowledge and how human beings formed knowledge. Does knowledge come from reflection and thinking or from experience? In the 4th century BCE, the Greek philosopher Plato argued for the former and his student Aristotle for the latter. In the 17th century CE, however, the English philosopher John Locke established the view that knowledge and thoughts come from experience, a point of view known as **empiricism.** Specifically, Locke argued that the mind begins as a *tabula rasa*, or blank slate, onto which experience writes the contents of the mind (Locke, 1690/1959).

This view that the mind simply receives what our sensory organs—eyes, ears, nose, skin, and tongue—experience and take in from the outside world is very important in philosophy and much of psychology. Philosophers, in contrast to scientists, do not collect data to test their ideas. Only when researchers started to examine and test human sensations and perception using scientific methods did psychology gain its independence from philosophy. Psychology as a modern empirical science tests predictions about behavior with systematic observations and by gathering data. In the mid- to late 1800s, many German universities were starting scientific laboratories in physics, chemistry, and medicine. In the 1870s they opened the first laboratories in psychology.

The Psychophysics of Human Perception

Because of the profound influence of the empiricists, the first researchers in psychological science developed the field of **psychophysics** to examine the subjective experience of physical sensations. If the mind consists only of what we sense, then understanding the senses will lead to a direct understanding of the mind. German psychophysics researchers in the 1820s focused on the sensations of touch, vision, hearing, and smell. To compare psychophysics and physics, if physicists study the physical properties of light and sound, psychophysicists study human perception of light and sound.

One important principle of psychophysics is that perception of physical properties is not the same as the physical properties themselves. To demonstrate, let's consider the classic question, What weighs more, a pound of feathers or a pound of bricks? You might be thinking "How dumb do they think I am? I've heard that so many times. They weigh the same! A pound is a pound." Maybe . . . for that answer is true only for the objective, physical property of weight. The *perceived* weight of the two—a psychological property—would be very different. Contrary to common sense, when people's estimates of the weights of both items are empirically tested, people think a pound of bricks weighs 2 to 3 times as much as a pound of feathers (Benjamin, 2007). If you don't believe us, try it for yourself. Psychophysics is all about this relationship between the physical and psychological worlds.

In essence, the scientists who first developed psychophysics—Ernst Weber, Gustav Fechner, and Hermann von Helmholtz—were the first experimental

---

empiricism
the view that all knowledge and thoughts come from experience.

psychophysics
the first scientific form of psychology; laboratory studies of the subjective experience of physical sensations.

psychologists. Ernst Weber (1795–1878) did some of the first research in perception and laid the groundwork for what later became known as psychophysics. For instance, he investigated the smallest change in weights or length that people could discern. Building on the work of his mentor, Weber, Gustav Fechner (1801–1889) had a sudden realization in 1850 that one could study the psychological and physical worlds in a new discipline he called psychophysics. Fechner went on to refine some of Weber's principles of perception (Fancher, 1996).

A physician and physicist, Hermann von Helmholtz (1821–1894) not only made important contributions to the study of memory, physiology, and color vision, but also made key contributions to the laws of conservation in physics and to music theory, meteorology, and geometry; he designed a workable telephone years before Alexander Graham Bell (Benjamin, 2007). In addition, he was the first to calculate the speed of a nerve impulse at about 90 feet per second. With the work of these pioneers, psychophysics took the first steps toward establishing psychology as a science.

connections

Helmholtz's work laid the foundation for several areas of psychology, including neuroscience, and sensation and perception.

See Chapter 3, p. 86 and Chapter 4, p. 145.

Wilhelm Wundt

Psychology blossomed into a full-fledged science with the help of Wilhelm Wundt (1832–1920). In 1879 (remember this date!), Wundt set up a psychology laboratory in Leipzig, Germany, now considered the birthplace of experimental psychology. Although others went before Wundt, he is credited with giving psychology its independence from philosophy and physiology (Benjamin, 2007; Fancher, 1996). He did so by applying the scientific methods of physiology to questions of philosophy (Benjamin, 2007). Before Wundt, people evaluated the question of how the mind worked only by way of argument, not by scientific investigation. By establishing a laboratory, Wundt created a place where the best young minds could learn the science of psychology. And come to learn they did. Wundt single-handedly trained more than 180 students in his laboratory. Of these, more than 100 came from countries other than Germany and then returned to their native countries, taking their knowledge of experimental psychology with them.

William James

An American, G. Stanley Hall (1844–1924), was one who went to Germany to learn from Wundt. At Harvard, Hall also studied with William James, who is considered the founder of psychology in the United States. Hall holds the distinction of earning the first PhD (1878) in psychology as James's student. He opened the first psychology laboratory in the United States at Johns Hopkins University in Baltimore, establishing psychology as a science in this country. He also founded the American Psychological Association (APA) and became its first president in 1892. He started the first scientific journal in American psychology, the *American Journal of Psychology*. Finally, he was able to persuade both Sigmund Freud and his famous protégé Carl Jung to make their only journey to the United States and give lectures at Clark University in Massachusetts in 1909.

G. Stanley Hall was also the teacher and mentor of Francis Cecil Sumner (1895–1954). Sumner was the first African American to earn a PhD in psychology (1920). From 1928 until his death in 1954, Sumner chaired the psychology department at Howard University, where he conducted research on equality and justice.

Another of William James's students, Mary Whiton Calkins (1863–1930), became the first female president of APA in 1905. Harvard was an all-male university until 1920, so she and James conducted their coursework in James's home. At one point everyone else in a class quit after they learned a woman would be a classmate. Calkins went on to complete the requirements for the PhD, although Harvard would not grant her the degree simply because she was a woman (Benjamin, 2007). Nevertheless, Calkins had an accomplished academic career. She taught at Wellesley College and conducted much research on dreaming, attention, and self-image (*History of Psychology*, 2002). James acknowledged her work to be among the best students he had ever encountered (Benjamin, 2007).

Structuralism and Functionalism

During its early decades as a science, psychology saw its first major debate. The question was this: Was it more important to study the elements of experience to understand human thought and behavior, or was it more important to study the functions behind human thought and behavior? The first question led to the school of thought known as structuralism, whereas the second led to the school of thought known as functionalism. Edward Titchener (1867–1927), a British-American psychologist trained by Wilhelm Wundt, coined both phrases.

According to **structuralism**, breaking down experience into its elemental parts offers the best way to understand thought and behavior. Structuralists believed that a detailed analysis of experience as it happened provides the most accurate glimpse into the workings of the human mind. Their method was **introspection**, looking into one's own mind for information about the nature of conscious experience. Structuralists divided each experience into its smallest elements. Wundt, the chief proponent of structuralism, wanted to describe human experience in terms of the elements that combined to produce it (Benjamin, 2007). For example, structuralists, like chemists describing elements, would not describe a peach as "a good peach," but rather would describe their experience with the peach as sweet, round, slightly orange, fuzzy, wet, and juicy.

Influenced by Charles Darwin's theory of natural selection, **functionalists** thought it was better to look at why the mind worked the way it did, rather than to describe its parts. The functionalists asked "Why do people think, feel, or perceive, and how did these abilities come to be?" Functionalists used introspection as well. William James, the most famous functionalist, relied on introspection as a primary method of understanding how the mind worked.

James's and Wundt's methods of introspection were impressive attempts to describe the conscious mind. Eventually, however, introspection failed as a method of science because of difficulties in reaching a consensus as to what the experiences were. Moreover, the rise of psychology as the science of *observable* behavior led to the complete rejection of the study of the mind. It also gave way to the rise of behaviorism.

structuralism
19th-century school of psychology that argued that breaking down experience into its elemental parts offers the best way to understand thought and behavior.

introspection
the main method of investigation for structuralists; it involves looking into one's own mind for information about the nature of conscious experience.

functionalism
19th-century school of psychology that argued it was better to look at why the mind works the way it does than to describe its parts.

behaviorism
a school of psychology that proposed that psychology can be a true science only if it examines observable behavior, not ideas, thoughts, feelings, or motives.

Behaviorism   In 1913, a little-known 34-year-old psychologist, John Watson directly challenged the use of introspection. He founded **behaviorism,** which asserts that psychology can be a true science only if it examines observable behavior, not ideas, thoughts, feelings, or motives. In Watson's view, such mental experiences are only hypothetical concepts, as they cannot be directly measured. As long as psychology focused on such internal states, it would forever be a false science, according to Watson.

This dolphin is being trained by means of shaping, a behaviorist technique that rewards animals for small changes in behavior as they learn a desired behavior pattern, such as leaping out of the water on cue.

connection
Watson, Skinner, and behaviorism had tremendous influence on the psychology of learning.
See Chapter 8, p. 301.

Behaviorism is an extreme form of environmentalism, the view that all behavior comes from experience. It is the school of psychology that most clearly expresses John Locke's ideas about our minds being a blank slate.

A decade or so after behaviorism emerged, it became the dominant force in experimental psychology. Its most famous figure, B. F. Skinner (1904–1990), was largely responsible for making behaviorism the major approach in experimental psychology, a position it held for nearly 50 years. Skinner modified Watson's ideas and argued that consequences shape behavior.

Humanistic and Positive Psychology   During the first half of the 20th century, the two major schools of thought in psychology were split along the divide between practice and science. On the therapeutic side were psychoanalysis and Freud, and on the scientific side were behaviorism and Skinner. In the 1940s and 1950s, Abraham Maslow and Carl Rogers presented an alternative to both of these perspectives. They offered a rather straightforward criticism of psychology: Both psychoanalysis and behaviorism ignored people at their best, and neither approach considered what it meant to be psychologically healthy. Maslow and Rogers proposed an alternative called **humanistic psychology,** which promoted personal growth and meaning as a way of reaching one's highest potential.

The humanistic movement waned by the late 1970s, mostly because it had moved away from its research and scientific base. It surfaced again in the late 1990s, however, when Martin Seligman and Mihaly Csikszentmihalyi started the positive psychology movement. **Positive psychology** shares with humanism a belief that psychology should focus on studying, understanding, and promoting healthy and positive psychological functioning. It does so with a better appreciation than humanistic psychology for the importance of studying well-being from a scientific perspective.

humanistic psychology
a theory of psychology that focuses on personal growth and meaning as a way of reaching one's highest potential.

positive psychology
scientific approach to studying, understanding, and promoting healthy and positive psychological functioning.

Gestalt psychology
a theory of psychology that maintains that we perceive things as wholes rather than as a compilation of parts.

connection
Humanistic personality psychologists developed theories of personality based on humans at their best and striving to be better.
See Chapter 13, p. 509.

Cognitivism   After Watson banished thoughts, feelings, and motives as the focal point of the modern science of psychology in the 1910s, research into these topics nearly disappeared from the field for almost 50 years. Two events kept them in the minds of psychologists, however. First, in the 1920s and 1930s, a movement in Germany called Gestalt psychology attracted worldwide attention. Led by Max Wertheimer (1880–1943), **Gestalt psychology** proposed that in perception a unified whole is more than a compilation of parts.

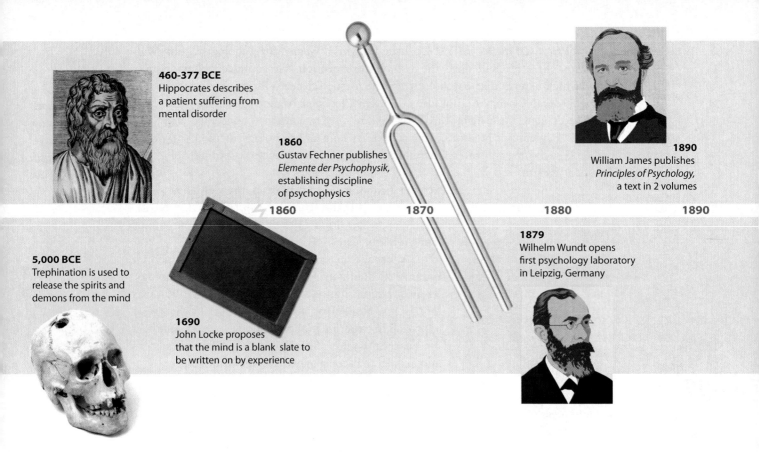

460-377 BCE
Hippocrates describes a patient suffering from mental disorder

1860
Gustav Fechner publishes *Elemente der Psychophysik*, establishing discipline of psychophysics

1890
William James publishes *Principles of Psychology*, a text in 2 volumes

1860   1870   1880   1890

5,000 BCE
Trephination is used to release the spirits and demons from the mind

1690
John Locke proposes that the mind is a blank slate to be written on by experience

1879
Wilhelm Wundt opens first psychology laboratory in Leipzig, Germany

Moreover, our brains actively shape sensory information into perceptions. For example, look at Figure 1.2. You see a triangle within three circles, but no triangle actually exists. The brain, however, organizes your perception of the markings on the page into the shape of a triangle.

Second, mental processes returned to psychology full force in the 1950s and 1960s—just when the influence of behaviorism was at its peak. The new emphasis was really a forgotten focus on the processes that fascinated Fechner, Wundt, and Helmholtz in the 19th century: sensation, perception, and mental processes. The term *mental*, however, had lost its appeal. Instead, a new word for thought and mental processes appeared: *cognition* (Benjamin, 2007; Gardner, 1987).

By the 1960s the field of cognitive science was born, with a focus on the scientific study of thought (Gardner, 1987). In addition to freeing itself from the label *mental*, cognitive science made use of a new modern metaphor—the computer. A fairly recent innovation at the time, the computer seemed to have a lot in common with the human mind. Computers store, retrieve, and process information, just as the brain stores, retrieves, and processes sensations, memories, and ideas. Sensation was the input; perception was the interpretation and processing of the input; and behavior and thoughts were the output. By the 1980s, cognitive science combined many disciplines in addition to psychology—namely, linguistics, philosophy, anthropology, artificial intelligence, and neuroscience (Gardner, 1987).

The British psychologist Frederick Bartlett (1886–1969) wrote a book that promoted a cognitive psychological view in the 1930s. Bartlett stated that memory is not an objective and accurate representation of events but rather a highly personal reconstruction based on one's own beliefs, ideas, and point of view. For

**FIGURE 1.2
A DEMONSTRATION OF GESTALT PSYCHOLOGY.**
You see a triangle even though no triangle actually exists.

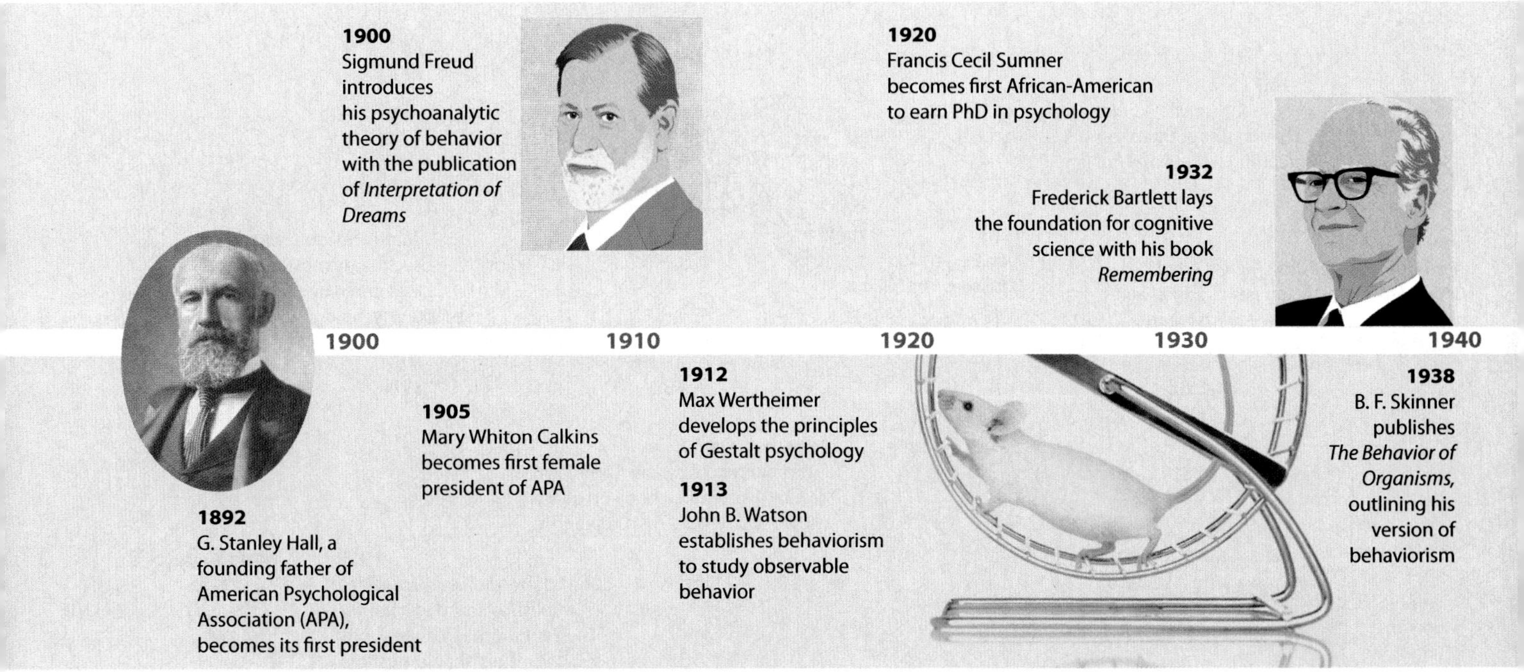

1900
Sigmund Freud introduces his psychoanalytic theory of behavior with the publication of *Interpretation of Dreams*

1920
Francis Cecil Sumner becomes first African-American to earn PhD in psychology

1932
Frederick Bartlett lays the foundation for cognitive science with his book *Remembering*

1900   1910   1920   1930   1940

1912
Max Wertheimer develops the principles of Gestalt psychology

1913
John B. Watson establishes behaviorism to study observable behavior

1905
Mary Whiton Calkins becomes first female president of APA

1892
G. Stanley Hall, a founding father of American Psychological Association (APA), becomes its first president

1938
B. F. Skinner publishes *The Behavior of Organisms*, outlining his version of behaviorism

FIGURE **1.3**
KEY FIGURES AND EVENTS IN THE HISTORY OF PSYCHOLOGY.

example, racial–ethnic stereotypes are frameworks that can alter memory (Graham & Lowery, 2004). If a witness to a crime holds a bias about how likely a crime is to be perpetuated by a person of a certain racial–ethnic background, the witness may misremember the appearance of the accused. This example illustrates that, as Bartlett argued, memory is more a reconstruction of experience in terms of what is most relevant to the witness than an unbiased account of events. Bartlett showed that our cognitive frameworks organize how we experience the world. This view is now well accepted in psychology, though Bartlett's insights were unappreciated in the United States for decades (Benjamin, 2007).

Evolutionary Psychology and Behavioral Neuroscience

By the 1980s, more and more psychologists were becoming receptive to the ideas that who we are, how we got here, and what we do and think are very much a result of brain activity, are influenced by genetic factors, and have a long evolutionary past. Many related fields with older origins came together in the 1980s and 1990s. For example, behavioral neuroscience, behavioral genetics, and evolutionary psychology are each a blend of two or more other disciplines. Evolutionary psychology was jump-started in 1992 when John Tooby and Leda Cosmides (1992) published "The Evolutionary Foundations of Culture" in a seminal book on evolutionary psychology. These developments all began to shift psychology toward a more complex view of the origins of human thought and behavior, enhanced by new brain imaging techniques and the sequencing of the human genome.

Our review of the history of psychological science, summarized in Figure 1.3, has only scratched the surface of how psychologists think about human thought and behavior, about mind, body, and experience. Debates and theories

connection
Our genetic code is not set in stone at birth. Genes are turned on or off by experiences we have, foods we eat, and even foods our mothers ate while pregnant with us.
See Chapter 3, p. 82, and Chapter 5, p. 177.

1953
Abraham Maslow's *Motivation and Personality* outlines the stages of growth leading to personal fulfillment

1950
Karen Horney published *Neurosis and Human Growth* outlining her psychoanalytic social theory as an alternative to Freud's psychosexual theory

1965
Jean Piaget publishes *The Child's Conception of Number*

1998
Martin Seligman starts the positive psychology movement with Mihály Csíkszentmihályi to study and promote psychological well-being

| 1950 | 1960 | 1970 | 1980 | 1990 | 2000 |

1951
Carl Rogers publishes *Client-Centered Therapy,* advocating a new humanistic approach emphasizing personal growth

1974
Eleanor Maccoby and Carol Jacklin publish a seminal book on gender, *The Psychology of Sex Differences.*

1992
John Tooby and Leda Cosmides publish a landmark chapter "The Evolutionary Foundations of Culture" that jumpstarts evolutionary psychology

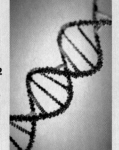

about how and why we think and act the way we do go back thousands of years. Some of the key debates remain unresolved to this day. These systems of thought have profoundly influenced the development of psychology. Let's now consider the major ways of thinking about mind, body, and experience that have shaped modern psychological science.

quick quiz 1.3: The Origins of Psychology

1. What perspective in psychology assumes the unconscious is the most powerful force behind most behavior?
   a. trephination
   b. cognitive psychology
   c. structuralism
   d. psychoanalysis

2. _____ argued that thoughts, feelings, and motives are unimportant in understanding human behavior.
   a. behaviorists
   b. psychoanalysts
   c. functionalists
   d. Gestalt psychologists

3. Positive psychology is a modern form of which school of thought?
   a. structuralism
   b. humanism
   c. functionalism
   d. introspectionism

Answers can be found at the end of the chapter.

Ways of Thinking About Mind, Body, and Experience

The topics covered by psychology sit in the middle of age-old debates and theories about the origins of human thought and behavior. Three major ways of thinking about human experience continue to influence the field today: the nature–nurture debate, the mind–body problem, and evolutionary theory.

THE NATURE–NURTURE DEBATE

For millennia thinkers have argued over what determines our personality and behavior: innate biology or life experience (Pinker, 2004). This conflict is known as the *nature–nurture debate*. The nature-only view is that who we are comes from inborn tendencies and genetically based traits.

Consider this scenario. You are at a restaurant and you see a young family trying to eat a meal. A two-year-old girl is running in circles around a table and won't sit down, despite her parents' best efforts. You mention to the parents that she is quite active. The exhausted mom answers meekly, "Yes, she was born that way!" Other patrons of the restaurant might quietly disapprove of the parent's inability to control the child. Chances are, though, the mom is right. The girl was probably always active, and there may be little they can do to get her to sit down. In fact, a great deal of evidence indicates that our personalities are influenced by genetic factors and remain consistent across the life span (Plomin & Caspi, 1999).

The nurture-only side states that we are all essentially the same at birth, and we are the product of our experiences. As we have already considered, John Locke (1690/1959) popularized the idea that the newborn human mind is a blank slate on which the experiences of life are written. This accumulation of experiences makes us who we are. This view means that anything is possible. You can be anything you want to be. This notion is a very Western, very North American idea. It stands as the cornerstone of democracy, free will, and equality (Pinker, 2002).

Pitting nature against nurture gets us nowhere. It creates a false split, or false dichotomy, that hinders our understanding of the mind and behavior. Almost nothing in psychology can be categorized as either nature or nurture—not learning, not memory, not cognition, not emotion, not even social behavior! These forces work together almost all the time; they are interdependent.

Throughout this book, we will point out many cases in which environmental and genetic forces work together to shape who we are (Rutter, 2002). For example, in the processes of learning and remembering, certain genes in the brain are turned on or off by what happens to us (Kandel, 2006). New connections between brain cells result from these changes in the genes. Consequently, the brains of people and animals reared in richly stimulating environments differ from the brains of people reared in understimulating, neglectful, or abusive environments.

Here's another example: People whose mothers developed an infection during pregnancy are more likely to develop schizophrenia than people whose mothers were healthy during pregnancy (Brown, 2006). Risks of this disorder in offspring increase sevenfold in mothers infected with the flu virus and 10–12-fold in mothers infected with rubella, the virus that causes German measles (Brown, 2006; Brown et al., 2004). Evidence suggests that the crucial event here may be the fact that the mothers are mounting an immune response against an infectious agent during key stages of neural development in pregnancy (Fruntes & Limosin, 2008). A baby of the same genetic makeup who was not exposed to the virus and immune response would be less likely to develop the disorder.

These examples illustrate how what we are born with and what we are exposed to interact to create thought and behavior. For decades many psychologists have shied away from the idea of an interrelationship, clinging to the nature–nurture debate. Old habits do indeed die hard. But to fully appreciate human behavior, we must take a broader view. All creatures are born with genetic instructions, but from the beginning, even before birth, environmental factors alter the ways in which genes are expressed. Rather than pitting nature against nurture, we use the phrase **nature through nurture**: The environment—be it the womb or the world outside—interacts continuously with biology to shape who we are and what we do (Begley, 2007; Ridley, 2003; Pinker, 2004).

nature through nurture
the position that the environment constantly interacts with biology to shape who we are and what we do.

MIND–BODY DUALISM

Since its inception, psychology has been burdened by another big idea of Western thinking—*mind–body dualism*. In the 17th century René Descartes, a French philosopher and mathematician, offered proofs of many important concepts in mathematics (Crump, 2001). But he proposed one idea that crippled the social sciences for years. Descartes stated that the mind and the body are separate entities. This idea is often referred to as *mind–body dualism*. From this perspective, the mind controls the body. The body can occasionally control the mind too, but mainly when we abandon good judgment, such as in the throes of passion. Mostly, in Descartes's view, mind and body are separate.

Dualism, or separation of mind and body, allows for the ideas that a soul survives bodily death, the mind is separate from the brain, humans are superior to animals—and many other philosophies supported by Western thinking. Like nature versus nurture, mind–body dualism represents a false dichotomy—in the sense of being either–or. Mind and body are both useful concepts, but they are exquisitely intertwined. That which we call *mind* results from the functioning of our *brain*, which is indeed part of the body.

Both the nature–nurture and mind–body dichotomies have influenced Western thought and the development of psychology as a field. Notice that we have been talking about *Western* thinking. Indeed, modern psychological science grew from the marriage of Western philosophy and physiology, with Wundt's laboratory in Leipzig as the first child. In contrast, systems of thought from elsewhere in the world—especially Eastern philosophy—have long emphasized the interdependence of body and mind (Begley, 2007; Tulku, 1984). In Eastern thought, body and mind are very much seen as part of one whole. Psychological science is, at last, beginning to arrive at this same conclusion, but it has taken more than a century to get there.

THE EVOLUTION OF BEHAVIOR

One principle that plays an important role in understanding human behavior is evolution. Although we often think we understand the basic theory of evolution, even the basics are more complex than we realize. Here we briefly explain the fundamental processes of evolution.

Evolution means "change." With respect to biological species, **evolution** is the change over time in the frequency with which specific genes occur within a breeding species (Buss, 1999). What does the frequency of gene transmission have to do with behavior? Our genes contain instructions for making all the proteins in our bodies. Proteins, in turn, make up a lot of what we are: cell membranes, hormones, enzymes, and muscle tissue, to name just a few examples. These constituents carry out our intentions, in our brains, in our bodies. Thus, behaviors have genetic bases that are affected by many environmental factors. Human interaction with the world influences which genes are passed on to future generations, and these in turn shape human behavior. These changes take place by *natural selection*.

First described by the 19th-century English naturalist Charles Darwin (1809–1882), **natural selection** is formally defined as a feedback process whereby nature favors one design over another, depending on whether it has an impact on reproduction. This process takes a long time to work, but it ultimately shapes who we are and how species evolve. Charles Darwin's genius and great contribution was not the theory of evolution itself but rather his explanation of *how* evolution works, that is, by natural selection.

Natural selection occurs by chance. Every once in a while, genes change for no apparent reason. Spontaneous changes in genes, called *chance mutations*, can alter the design of a structure or a set of behaviors. Let's suppose, for example, that a chance mutation in a population of green beetles results in a brown beetle. If the brown beetle is less visible to predators, it might have more success in surviving and reproducing, as Figure 1.4 shows. When it reproduces, the brown beetle passes on its "brown" genes to its offspring. The brown offspring have a better survival rate, which means they are more likely to reproduce. Eventually, this physiological trait becomes common among members of the species. The complete change takes many generations, but eventually the entire beetle species will be brown (Tooby & Cosmides, 1992). The key in natural selection is that the behaviors have to increase reproductive success, because reproduction and gene transmission drive the whole process.

The accumulation of chance mutations underlies evolutionary change. Each generation is a product of beneficial modifications from its evolutionary past.

Natural selection creates structures and behaviors that solve adaptive problems. Among the adaptive problems that our early human ancestors faced were avoiding predators, choosing nutritious foods, finding a mate, and communicating effectively with others. **Adaptations** are inherited solutions to ancestral problems that have been naturally selected because they directly contribute in some way to reproductive success (Tooby & Cosmides, 1992). Adaptations evolved to solve problems in past generations—not current ones. In other words, we are living with traits and tendencies that benefited our ancestors. Even though these tendencies might not seem to enhance our fitness in today's world, eons spent in harsher environments have left us predisposed to perform certain social behaviors when a situation calls forth ancient patterns. Consider, for example, our preference for fatty foods. In our evolutionary past, eating fat was a good

---

evolution
the change over time in the frequency with which specific genes occur within a breeding species.

natural selection
a feedback process whereby nature favors one design over another because it has an impact on reproduction.

adaptations
inherited solutions to ancestral problems that have been selected for because they contribute in some way to reproductive success.

strategy. Early humans, as hunter-gatherers, did not know when they would find food. If they found fat, they ate it, because fat could be stored on the body and used later when food might be scarce. For this reason, humans evolved to like fat. Modern society, however, offers easy access to food. Now eating fat is not the best strategy, because we don't need to store it for future use. More food will be available when we need it. So we eat fat, store it up, and carry it around as extra weight. Human cravings have not changed much, even though our environments have.

Evolutionary psychology is the branch of psychology that tries to understand what adaptive problems the human mind may have solved in the distant past and the effect of evolution on behavior today. Rather than just describing what the mind does, evolutionary psychologists are interested in the functions of the human mind (Tooby & Cosmides, 1992). Evolutionary changes in organs and bodily structures—or color, as in our beetle example—are not difficult to understand. But how do human behaviors evolve?

evolutionary psychology
the branch of psychology that studies human behavior by asking what adaptive problems it may have solved for our early ancestors.

Let's consider the emotions as an example of a behavioral adaptation. In Chapter 11, we discuss emotions in detail and explore those feelings that move us powerfully. For now, imagine that you are driving on the highway and the car in the lane next to you has just cut you off. You have to slam on your brakes to keep from smashing into it! You are shaking with fright. The possible car accident is an immediate cause of your fear. But why do you experience this intense bodily reaction called fear in the first place? The answer, from an evolutionary perspective, is that fear was naturally selected to solve an adaptive problem.

What we call fear—including the way it moves our bodies, impels us to act, and makes our hearts race—evolved because it helps us deal quickly and efficiently with danger (Ekman, 2003). Eons ago, a genetic variation occurred in a human that somehow led to a specific way of responding to threatening circumstances—quick action to avoid being killed—and the human was able to avoid harm and reproduce more readily; that is, it had an advantage. Without thinking about it, the ancestor who recognized a beast who could kill her while she was picking berries just wanted to get out of harm's way. Experiencing fear, she was more likely to escape death. This woman survived, reproduced, and passed on a genetic tendency to experience fear to the next generation. Thus, emotions are behavioral adaptations. They are

To understand how Darwin's idea of evolution works, consider a population of beetles:

1 There is variation in traits.
Some beetles are green and some are brown.

2 There is differential reproduction.
Since the environment can't support unlimited population growth, not all individuals get to reproduce to their full potential. In this example, green beetles tend to be eaten by birds and thus do not reproduce, while brown beetles survive to reproduce. There are now fewer green beetles.

3 There is heredity.
The surviving brown beetles have brown baby beetles because this trait has a genetic basis.

Early hunters, like the ones portrayed in this ancient rock painting from the Tadrart Acacus Mountains of Libya, ate fat when it was available and their bodies stored the excess in order to survive when food was scarce. This adaptation has persisted for thousands of years, even though for most people access to food is not a problem.

quick and ready response patterns that tell us whether something is good or bad for our well-being (Ekman, 2003; Lazarus, 1991).

Not all products of evolution are adaptations. Sometimes things evolve because they solved one problem and they just happen to solve another one too. These structures or features that perform a function that did not arise through natural selection are often called *by-products* or, more technically, *exaptations* (Buss, 1999; Gould & Vrba, 1982). An example of a by-product is feathers. Feathers probably evolved for insulation in flightless dinosaurs, but they turned out to be useful for flight in birds, the dinosaurs' descendants. Because feathers did not evolve for that purpose, they are considered by-products ("Exaptations," 2006).

Similarly, humans didn't evolve to speak in fully grammatical sentences or to do scientific research, but once they started doing so, there were legitimate adaptive reasons

nature & nurture
One of the best examples of the intricate interplay between our bodies and the environment (nature and nurture) is evolution by natural selection.

4 There is the end result.

The more advantageous trait, brown coloration, allows the beetle to have more offspring and becomes more common in the population. If this process continues, eventually, all individuals in the population will be brown.

FIGURE **1.4**

HOW NATURAL SELECTION WORKS. Natural selection is one of the basic mechanisms of evolution. This hypothetical example shows how natural selection might change the predominant color of a population of beetles from green to brown.

to continue. Thus, language and science are not adaptations but are by-products of adaptations (Feist, 2006; Pinker, 1994).

Nothing illustrates more vividly than evolution how nature and nurture work together. Depending on how they enable organisms to respond to their environment, certain characteristics of animals predominate or not—like the brown color of the beetle and the fear response in humans. Nature and nurture work together to create our bodies (including our brains) and behavior. They are interdependent—that is, they depend on and interact with each other.

quick quiz 1.4: Ways of Thinking About Mind, Body, and Experience

1. Which phrase most accurately reflects a modern perspective in psychology?
   a. nature over nurture
   b. nature versus nurture
   c. nurture over nature
   d. nature through nurture

2. Charles Darwin's great contribution was the theory of
   a. evolution
   b. how evolution works (natural selection)
   c. psychoanalysis
   d. adaptations

3. Mind–body dualism proposes that
   a. the mind influences the body and the body influences the mind
   b. the mind and body are one
   c. the mind and body are separate
   d. the mind and body are both adaptations

Answers can be found at the end of the chapter.

Connections in Psychology

As we have seen in this chapter, psychology is a very interconnected science. Because humans tend to take things apart to study them in depth, however, psychology can sometimes seem to be a rather segmented field. To show that this is not the case, we will explore connections in psychology throughout the book, focusing particularly on the following ones:

- connections between nature and nurture
- connections between psychologists and scientific discoveries
- connections between topics across psychology
- connections between psychology and your life experience
- connections among topics within each chapter

Connecting nature and nurture is a major theme of the book. We've explained this connection in detail earlier in the chapter. As you read each chapter, we will point out some of the times where this interdependence is pronounced with *Nature & Nurture* notes in the margin.

Connecting psychological scientists with their discoveries brings psychology to life. The purpose behind the stories in the *Breaking New Ground* section in each chapter is to highlight the link between the science

of psychology and the creative work of individuals. The stories explain break-through discoveries that have altered the field of psychology and describe how the scientists responsible for them arrived at their conclusions. There is a psychology behind the science of psychology and there are personal stories for every discovery (Feist, 2006). Seeing the dynamic and often personal side of psychological science leads to a better appreciation of psychology and perhaps to discoveries of your own.

We connect topics covered in different chapters with *Connection* notes in the margins. They link information that you either have or will cover with the material that you are currently learning to help you see how interconnected the various areas of psychology are. For instance, understanding most psychological disorders requires taking into account forces as wide-ranging as prenatal and social environments and as diverse as genes and molecules and social institutions and cultures. *Connection* notes highlight interrelationships among concepts covered in different chapters, such as biology, development, social behavior, and psychological disorders.

The way we connect psychology to your own experience is with examples of real behaviors or events that may be familiar. Each chapter has a section entitled *Psychology in the Real World* to link a core topic in the chapter with your everyday life.

At the end of each chapter, you will find a section titled *Making Connections*. In this section, we explore one topic that connects most of the concepts and ideas in that chapter. For example, in this chapter, we consider how psychologists in different subfields of psychology have begun to study human behaviors as related to electronic social interactions.

making connections
in psychology

Studying Electronic Social Interactions

There are nearly a dozen different ways a person can interact with others electronically—via e-mail, blogs, cell phones, chat rooms, texting, instant messaging, gaming (either solo or multiplayer), videos, photos, bulletin boards, and social network sites (SNSs) (Subrahmanyam & Greenfield, 2008). Humans have taken to electronic forms of interaction like fish to water. As a form of behavior that is evolving at a rapid pace, electronic social interaction holds great interest for psychologists in all of the subfields you read about in this chapter. Let's consider how psychologists from some of these different areas might study electronic communication and its effects on human behavior and thought.

Cognitive Psychology
Cognitive scientists typically are interested in how we learn, remember, think, or reason. They are also interested in attention. The widespread use of cell phones has sparked a number of research questions. The most obvious one concerns how drivers pay attention to driving and carry on a cell phone conversation. Researchers have examined the effect of talking on a hands-free cell phone while driving. They have reported that a person's ability to operate a car while talking on a hands-free cell phone is similar to one's capability while driving drunk (Strayer et al., 2006).

use online dating services tend to be over 30, college-age teens and young adults are increasingly using them as well (Stevens & Morris, 2007; Valkenburg & Peter, 2007). Contrary to what some people originally thought, however, electronic interactions cannot easily be used to hide one's "real personality" and to avoid ever having real face-to-face contact with others. Research on this phenomenon suggests that people use the Internet not simply to interact with others from afar but also to arrange real face-to-face meetings (Couch & Liamputtong, 2008).

Electronic interactions have led to new behaviors and language as the boundaries between public and private have broken down. For instance, being *privately public* means connecting with many other people, while being relatively nonpublic about revealing who you are. Being *publicly private* means you disclose a lot of details of your private life and may or may not limit access to your site (Lange, 2008). Emily Gould, who was profiled at the beginning of the chapter was publicly private—she did not limit access to what she said in her role as editor of Gawker, her site was not password-protected, and she built up a following of thousands of people reading about her most personal and intimate thoughts, feelings, and actions. Another electronic behavior is the concept of "friending." If someone allows you access to their site, they have "friended" you. This in turn raises ancient issues of being "popular," socially excluded, rejected, and accepted. In one tragic case of online rejection, a 13-year-old girl was so distraught over being rejected by a boy online that she committed suicide. The even greater tragedy, however, was that the boy did not exist: A neighbor's mother allegedly made him up to get back at the girl for making disparaging remarks about her daughter.

Emily, by the way, left Gawker.com and reduced her online exposure after some hurtful retribution by readers: "... lately, online, I've found myself doing something unexpected: keeping the personal details of my current life to myself" (Gould, 2008, p. 56).

Personality Psychology

A personality psychologist could ask many questions about electronic interaction and presentations. For example, Are people who interact extensively with other people via Facebook more or less outgoing than those who do not? Whose tube is YouTube anyway (Hargittai, 2008)? Moreover, how much of people's personality is reflected in the style of their Web sites and Facebook pages? This last question has already been researched. Psychologists have studied what kind of personality impressions Web sites create in viewers and whether these impressions of a Web site creator's personality match with their own self-ratings on personality questionnaires. A main finding from research is that when the impressions formed from Web sites are compared to self-reported

Developmental Psychology

Developmental psychologists study how we change over the life span. They might ask questions like these: At what age is a person too young to form electronic social networks? At what age does usage of Internet social networks peak? Will they always be for the younger generation? Will people 60 and older use them? Does gender affect interest and participation in SNSs? How have cell phones and other electronic methods of communicating changed the way teenagers interact with others?

Researchers have already given us answers to some of these questions. For example, some research suggests that older teenage girls and young women are more likely to participate in social networking sites than are boys and young men (Boyd, 2007; Hargittai, 2008). The reason electronic interactions are so popular with adolescents has a lot to do with psychological factors: identity, autonomy, intimacy, and sexuality (Subrahmanyam & Greenfield, 2008). One reason the popularity of electronic interactions declines with age may be that these issues decline in importance as one moves from early adulthood to middle and late adulthood (Erikson, 1982).

Social Psychology

More than just about any other area of psychology, social psychology lends itself to a rich set of research questions regarding electronic interactions. One of the first applications of the Internet for social purposes was online dating services. Such forms of electronic interaction may be a preferred method of contact for people with high social anxiety (Stevens & Morris, 2007). Although most people who

personality data, the Web-based personality evaluations are fairly accurate but the accuracy depends on which personality trait is being rated (Vazire & Gosling, 2004).

There is also the psychologically interesting phenomenon of creating an alternative personality, or avatar, in the gaming world. People sometimes take on personalities that are very different from their own in an online world that allows them to express and say things they would not in direct face-to-face contact. And yet, there is some evidence that it is very difficult to completely shed one's offline personality while in the guise of an online personality (Smith & Kollock, 1999).

Health Psychology

A very innovative and at least partially successful application of electronic media is using the cell phone to access health information and symptoms of various diseases. For example, a program in San Francisco, California, has phone numbers for people to call if they suspect they might have a particular disease, often a sexual disease. The embarrassment of having to ask questions face-to-face is taken away when one can call up or text a phone number to obtain a health diagnosis anonymously.

Clinical Psychology

When do SNSs and other electronic interactions become a problem? Can one become "addicted" to such behavior, and can such interactions become dangerous to those involved? Recall Emily Gould's statement from the opening section of the chapter: "Depending on how you looked at it, I either had no life and I barely talked to anyone, or I spoke to thousands of people constantly."

connection

Can a person actually become addicted to online activities? What does it mean to be addicted to electronic interaction?

See Chapter 15, p. 580.

One of the main criteria for a mental illness is that it interferes with everyday life and functioning. If one is online for 10–12 hours a day, is that healthy? What about the danger involved in meeting someone in person whom you know only from online interaction? Sexual predators use these connections to meet victims. They contact potential victims through chat rooms, instant messages, and e-mail. According to one study, 1 in 5 teens (ages 10–17 years) have been sexually solicited online (Mitchell, Finkelhor, & Wolak, 2001).

We hope this chapter has helped you to appreciate the richness and excitement of psychology as a clinical practice and as a science. One question we also hope you have at this point is, How do psychologists know all of this? How do they do research? In the next chapter, we discuss the techniques by which psychological scientists study mental processes and behavior. Welcome to the fascinating world of psychology.

quick quiz 1.5: Making Connections in Psychology

1. What is the overarching theme of this book?
   a. psychology as fun
   b. making connections
   c. nature through nurture
   d. psychology as a science

2. What area of psychology has reported findings that driving while using a hands-free cell phone is much like driving while being drunk?
   a. behavioral neuroscience
   b. cognitive psychology
   c. developmental psychology
   d. social psychology

3. Researchers have found that
   a. it is difficult to hide one's offline personality when interacting with others online
   b. people form accurate impressions about how open to new experiences a Web site creator might be
   c. personalities can be completely disguised during online interactions
   d. a and b are both correct

Answers can be found at the end of the chapter.

chapter **review**

WHAT IS PSYCHOLOGY?

- Psychology is the scientific study of thought and behavior. We can see psychology all around us—in our own thoughts and feelings, in the behavior of our friends and relatives, and in how we interpret others' behaviors. As a field, it prepares us well not only for life in general, but also for a wide variety of professions in which relating with other people plays a key role.

- As a discipline, psychology is both a practice and a science. Clinical psychologists and counselors treat mental, emotional, and behavioral disorders and promote psychological health. Clinical psychologists also conduct research on psychological disorders and health. They practice psychology. As a science, psychology is the field of study in which researchers examine how the mind works and the rules that govern behavior within and between individuals.

SUBDISCIPLINES OF PSYCHOLOGY

- As a broad field, psychology comprises several subdisciplines, or areas of focused study, including cognitive, developmental, social, personality, health, educational, and industrial/organizational psychology. Neuroscience explores the links among brain, mind, and behavior and thus cuts across other subdisciplines.

THE ORIGINS OF PSYCHOLOGY

- The practice of psychology goes back to prehistoric times. Thousands of years ago humans drilled holes in the skull to treat brain injury and perhaps mental anguish as well. In the Middle Ages, the mentally ill were often treated as if possessed by demons. A few hundred years later, asylums served as storage houses for the severely mentally disabled.

- The late 1800s and early 1900s witnessed the beginning of more humane and more sophisticated treatment of people with psychological disorders. Around the turn of the 20th century, Sigmund Freud developed psychoanalysis to treat people suffering from disorders. By the middle of the 20th century, modern diagnostic criteria for mental disorders, psychotherapy, and drug therapy had emerged.

- The history of psychology as a science is not nearly as old as that of clinical practice, although its origins in philosophy go back to the ancient Greeks. Psychological science emerged from a tradition of empiricism and observations of the world. John Locke's 17th-century view of the mind as a blank slate on which experience writes the contents influences psychology to this day.

- The first psychological scientists did experimental work in perception and laid the groundwork for psychophysics. Only when laboratories started to empirically examine and test human sensations and perception did psychology gain its independence from philosophy and become a science.

- Wilhelm Wundt opened the first laboratory in experimental psychology in Leipzig, Germany, in 1879. Key figures in the birth of scientific psychology in the United States include William James and G. Stanley Hall.

- The biggest development in psychological research in the United States was the birth of behaviorism in the early 20th century. According to behaviorism, all behavior comes from experience. Founded by John Watson, behaviorism reached its pinnacle with B. F. Skinner.

- Behaviorism proved a very useful model for developing methods of studying learning in humans and animals, but it left the unobservable world of the mind unexplained. This all changed with the cognitive revolution of the 1950s and 1960s. Initially, cognitive science used the computer as a model for the way the human mind processes and stores sensations, memories, and ideas.

- Many fields that have older origins came together in the psychology of the 1980s and 1990s: neuroscience, behavioral genetics, and evolutionary psychology.

WAYS OF THINKING ABOUT MIND, BODY, AND EXPERIENCE

- Psychological science in the 21st century has reintegrated biological and environmental explanations of human thought and behavior. The fully modern view squares explanations of behavior with the principles of evolution. It also surpasses old absolutes like the nature–nurture debate and mind–body dualism.

MAKING CONNECTIONS IN PSYCHOLOGY

- The world of electronic interaction provides a context for research in many subdisciplines of psychology. For example, personality psychologists have examined which types of people are more likely to use social networking sites (SNSs); social psychologists have studied whether SNSs operate like real-life social networks; and developmental psychologists have begun to explore how the use of e-mail, SNSs, and texting varies by age and gender.

key terms

adaptations, p. 25
asylums, p. 13
behavioral neuroscience, p. 9
behaviorism, p. 19
biological psychology, p. 9
clinical psychology, p. 10
cognitive psychology, p. 8
developmental psychology, p. 9
educational psychology, p. 11
empiricism, p. 16
evolution, p. 24

evolutionary psychology, p. 26
forensic psychology, p. 11
functionalism, p. 18
Gestalt psychology, p. 19
health psychology, p. 10
humanistic psychology, p. 19
industrial/organizational (I/O) psychology, p. 11
introspection, p. 18
moral treatment, p. 14
natural selection, p. 25

nature through nurture, p. 24
personality psychology, p. 10
positive psychology, p. 19
psychoanalysis, p. 15
psychology, p. 6
psychophysics, p. 16
shamans, p. 12
social psychology, p. 10
sports psychology, p. 11
structuralism, p. 18

quick quiz answers

Quick Quiz 1.1   1. d   2. d   Quick Quiz 1.2   1. a   2. b   3. c   Quick Quiz 1.3   1. d   2. a   3. b
Quick Quiz 1.4   1. d   2. b   3. c   Quick Quiz 1.5   1. b   2. b   3. d

conducting **research** in

psychology

preview **questions**

1 *How is psychology like physics or biology or other sciences?*

2 *How do psychologists study behavior and mental processes?*

3 *Is it safe to participate in psychological research?*

Y ou are at your apartment near campus one summer day when the police knock at your door. After they confirm your identity, they say that you are being arrested on suspicion of armed robbery. They then handcuff your hands behind your back, put you in the police car, and take you down to the police station. There you are booked, finger-printed, and placed in a detention cell. You are then blindfolded and driven to a nearby prison, where you are stripped, sprayed with a delousing agent, and made to stand nude and alone in the cell yard. Finally, you are given a uniform, photographed, and assigned to a prison cell. Yet you have done nothing, and the people who arrested you knew this.

This scenario may seem far-fetched, but it actually happened to 10 male college students in the summer of 1971 in Palo Alto, California. Granted, they had recently agreed to participate in a "psychological study on 'prison life' in return for payment of $15 a day" (Haney, Banks, & Zimbardo, 1973, p. 73). Yet the police officers who arrested them said ▶

▶ nothing about a connection between their arrest and their agreement to participate in such a study.

Philip Zimbardo conducted this study—now known as the Stanford Prison Experiment—to examine whether normal people might behave in extreme ways when thrust into situations that place certain demands on them. In this case, they readily took on roles that made them powerful or powerless (Haney et al., 1973). Zimbardo chose 21 carefully screened male student volunteers and assigned them to be either "guards" or "prisoners" in a simulated prison environment for 2 weeks. All were briefed beforehand about what conditions would be like in the mock prison. All the students signed a form consenting to participate. Six days into the simulation, however, Zimbardo ended the study because the students were playing their roles too well. Prisoners went back and forth between plotting riots and having emotional breakdowns—getting sick and crying, for instance. Guards became

chapter
outline

extremely authoritarian, restricting the prisoners' personal freedom almost completely. They dehumanized the prisoners by referring to each one only by his assigned number—never by name. They put anyone suspected of "disobeying" and being "a bad prisoner" in solitary confinement. The line between fiction and reality, between role and true identity, blurred. In fact, half of the "prisoners" had to be released ahead of schedule because they were experiencing extreme emotional distress as a result of their "incarceration."

The relationship that evolved between "prisoners" and "guards" in the Stanford Prison Experiment closely resembled the relationship between convicts and guards in U.S. prisons. The study has served not only as a springboard for additional research on group behavior, but also as a strong incentive for prison reform. Interest in this study continues even today and takes on new significance in light of more recent cases of abuse of prisoners, such as the mistreatment of Iraqi prisoners by American soldiers following the 2003 U.S. invasion (Zimbardo, 2007). ■

The Nature of Science

Science is about testing intuitive assumptions regarding how the world works, observing the world, and keeping an open mind when our observations surprise us. Fundamentally, science entails collecting information, or data, from the real world and evaluating those data as to whether they support our ideas or not. The Stanford Prison Experiment fulfilled these criteria, and we will refer to this example several times in our discussion of research methods, measures, and ethics.

COMMON SENSE AND LOGIC

Science is more than common sense, logic, and pure observation. Although reason and sharp powers of observation can lead to knowledge, they have limitations. Take common sense—the intuitive ability to understand the world. Often common sense is quite useful. Don't go too close to that cliff. Don't arouse that sleeping bear. Don't eat that rotten food. Sometimes, though, common sense leads us astray. In psychology, our intuitive ideas about people's behavior are often contradictory or flat-out wrong. For example, it is intuitive to most of us that who we are is influenced by our parents, family, friends, and society. But it is equally obvious, especially to parents, that children come into the world as different people, with different temperaments, and people who grow up in essentially the same environments do not have identical personalities. To what extent are we the products of our environment, and how much do we owe to heredity? Common sense cannot answer that question, but science can.

connection

Common sense might suggest that intelligence would be 50% heredity and 50% environment. Is common sense correct?

See Chapter 10, p. 389.

Logic is also a powerful tool in the scientist's arsenal. But it can tell us only how the world *should* work. Sometimes the world is not logical. A classic example of the shortcoming of logic is seen in the work of the ancient Greek philosopher Aristotle. He argued that heavier objects should fall to the ground at a faster rate than lighter objects. Sounds reasonable, right? Unfortunately, it's wrong. For two thousand years, however, the argument was accepted simply because the great philosopher Aristotle wrote it and it made intuitive sense. It took the genius of Galileo to say, "Wait a minute. Is that really true? Is that the way the world works? Let me do some tests to see whether it is true." He did and discovered that Aristotle was wrong (Crump, 2002). The weight of an object does not affect its rate of speed when falling. Science, therefore, must combine logic with research and experimentation.

THE LIMITS OF OBSERVATION

Science also relies on observation, but even observation can lead us astray. Our knowledge of the world comes through our five senses, but our senses can be fairly easily fooled, as any good magician or artist can demonstrate. Even when we are not being intentionally fooled, the way in which the brain organizes and interprets sensory experiences may vary from person to person.

Can you spot the insect in this picture? The walking stick shown here relies on its natural camouflage to make itself appear invisible to deceive predators, demonstrating that observation isn't always a reliable guide to reality.

Another problem with observation is that people tend to generalize from their observations and assume that what they witnessed in one situation applies to all similar situations. Imagine you are visiting another country for the first time. Let's say the first person you have any extended interaction with is rude, and a second briefer interaction goes along the same lines. Granted, you have lots of language difficulties, but nevertheless you might conclude that all people from that country are rude. After all, that has been your experience. But those were only two interactions, and after a couple of days there you might meet other people who are quite nice. The point is that one or two cases do not a generalization make. Scientists must collect numerous observations and conduct several studies on a topic before generalizing their conclusions.

WHAT IS SCIENCE?

Is physics a science? Few would argue that it is not. What about biology? What about psychology? What about astrology? How does one decide? Now that we have looked at some of the components of science and explored their limitations, let's consider the larger question, What *is* science? People often think only of the physical sciences as "science," but science comes in at least three distinct flavors: physical, biological, and social (Feist, 2006). As we saw in Chapter 1, psychology is a social science (see Figure 2.1). The physical sciences are those that study the world of things—the inanimate world of stars, light, waves, atoms, the earth, compounds, and molecules. These sciences include physics, astronomy, chemistry, and geology. The biological sciences study plants and animals in the broadest sense. These sciences include biology, zoology, genetics, and botany. Finally, the social sciences are those that study humans, as individuals, as groups, and collectively. These sciences include anthropology, sociology, economics, and psychology.

Many philosophers and scientists have tackled the question of what science is, but behavioral psychologist B. F. Skinner's answer may be one of the best. He concluded that science is (1) cumulative, (2) a process more than a product, and (3) an attitude (Skinner, 1953). Let's take a closer look at each of these characteristics.

Science Is Cumulative
Are works of contemporary literature more advanced than those of Shakespeare, Tolstoy, or Virginia Woolf? Many literate people would argue that they are not—that these are products of different styles or periods, but that none is superior to the others. Do we know more today about the physical and biological realms than Galileo, Newton, or Darwin did? The answer in this case has to be yes. Scientific knowledge is unique in comparison to knowledge in the humanities, music, art, literature, and philosophy. Science progresses and advances cumulatively. In science, the knowledge base builds on itself and advances in ways that the kind of knowledge the humanities focus on does not.

Science Is a Process More Than a Product
Many students tend to think of science as a set of facts, such as the parts of the body or the structure of a cell. But science is also an active enterprise. It is a way of exploring how the world

FIGURE **2.1**

SIMPLIFIED MAP OF THE SCIENCES: THE STUDY OF THINGS, PLANTS, ANIMALS, AND PEOPLE.

operates, understanding the causes of events, and predicting what might happen under similar conditions in the future more than it is a set of answers. It is a process of gaining knowledge that is ever changing, relatively reliable, but always imperfect. Even the best science is open to modification. Appreciating the way science advances means asking questions, wondering how to test your own ideas, and trying to improve on what is already known.

Science Is an Attitude   Science begins with questioning and rejecting authority—including scientific authority. The first attitude of science, therefore, is to *question authority*. Be skeptical (see Figure 2.2). Don't just take the word of an expert; test ideas yourself. The expert might be right, or not. That advice extends to textbooks—including this one. Wonder. Question. Ask for the evidence. Also be skeptical of your *own* ideas. Our natural inclination is to really like our own ideas, especially if they occur to us in a flash of insight. But as one bumper sticker extols: "Don't believe everything you think." Believing something does not make it true.

As expressed by Carl Sagan (1987), the second attitude of science is *open skepticism*. Be skeptical by default, but ultimately be open to accepting whatever the evidence reveals, however bizarre it may be and however much we may not like or want it to be the case. For example, could placing an electrical stimulator deep in the brain turn off depression like a switch? That sounds like a far-fetched treatment, worthy of skepticism, but it does work for some people (Mayberg et al., 2005). Be skeptical, but let the evidence speak for itself.

The third scientific attitude is *intellectual honesty*. When the central tenet of knowing is not what people think and believe, but rather how nature behaves, then we must accept the data and follow them wherever they take us. If one falsifies results or interprets them in a biased way, then other scientists will not arrive at the same results if they try to confirm them by repeating the study. Every so often we come across a news item about a case in which a scientist faked data in order to get fame or funding. In one well-publicized case in 1989, physicists claimed to have demonstrated the long-sought-after effect of cold fusion, or achieving nuclear fusion (to produce energy) at room temperature, not the extremely high temperatures it normally takes. Unfortunately, so as not to be scooped, the researchers announced that they had achieved cold fusion to the popular press *before* publishing their findings in a scientific journal and, more importantly, before other scientists could re-create their experiment and confirm the results. The fact that scientists must submit their work to the scrutiny of other scientists helps ensure honest and accurate presentation of results.

Don't believe everthing you think

FIGURE **2.2**
SCIENCE IS AN ATTITUDE.

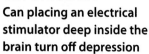
connection
Can placing an electrical stimulator deep inside the brain turn off depression like a switch?
See Chapter 16, p. 623.

Hwang Woo-Suk was a prominent South Korean biomedical researcher who falsely claimed to have cloned human embryonic stem cells. When it was discovered that his data were faked, Hwang lost his university position. Unlike Hwang and a handful of others over many, many years, the vast majority of scientists are intellectually honest and abide by rigorous standards.

All science—whether physics, chemistry, biology, or psychology—shares these general properties of open inquiry that we have discussed. Let's now turn to the specific methods used by scientists in the process of acquiring new and accurate knowledge of the world.

THE SCIENTIFIC METHOD

scientific method
the procedures by which scientists conduct research, consisting of five basic processes: observation, prediction, testing, interpretation, and communication.

Science depends on the use of sound methods to produce trustworthy results that can be confirmed independently by other researchers. The **scientific method** by which scientists conduct research consists of five basic processes: Observe, Predict, Test, Interpret, and Communicate (O-P-T-I-C) (see Figure 2.3). In the *observation* and *prediction* stages of a study, researchers develop expectations about an observed phenomenon. They express their expectations as a **theory**, defined as a set of related assumptions from which testable predictions can be made. Theories organize and explain what we have observed and guide what we will observe (Popper, 1965). Our observations of the world are always either unconsciously or consciously theory-driven, if you understand that theory in this broader sense means little more than "having an expectation." In science, however, a theory is more than a guess. Scientific theories must be tied to real evidence, they must organize observations, and they must generate expectations that can be tested systematically.

theory
a set of related assumptions from which scientists can make testable predictions.

hypothesis
a specific, informed, and testable prediction of the outcome of a particular set of conditions in a research design.

A **hypothesis** is a specific, informed, and testable prediction of what kind of outcome should occur under a particular condition. For example, a study recently appeared that suggests that caffeine increases sex drive in female rats (Guarraci & Benson, 2005). The hypothesis may have stated "Female rats who consume caffeine will seek more couplings with male rats than female rats who do not consume caffeine." This hypothesis specifies a particular form of behavior (coupling with male rats) in a specific group (female rats) under particular conditions (under the influence of caffeine). The more specific a hypothesis is, the more easily each component can be changed to determine what effect it has on the outcome.

To *test* their hypotheses (the third stage of the scientific method), scientists select one of a number of established research methods, along with the appropriate measurement techniques. The methods, which we discuss in detail below, involve choosing a plan for the design of the study, the tools that will create the conditions of the study, and the tools for measuring responses, such as how often each female rat allows a male to mount her. We will examine each of these elements in the section on "Research Methods" below.

In the fourth step of the scientific method, scientists use mathematical techniques to *interpret* the results and determine whether they are significant (not just a matter of chance) and closely fit the prediction or not. Do psychologists' ideas of how people behave hold up, or must they be revised? Let's say that more of the caffeine-consuming female rats coupled with males than did nonconsuming females. Might this enhanced sexual interest hold for all rats or just those few we studied? Statistics, a branch of mathematics that we will discuss shortly, helps answer that question.

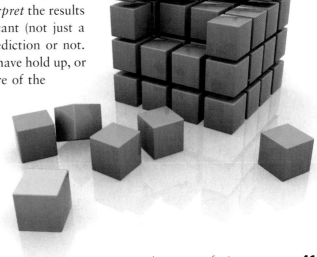

observe
Researchers working with rats observe their behavior.

5 communicate
Publish findings of "Caffeine and mating behavior in female rats" via peer review process.

2 predict
Propose a hypothesis based in theory: Caffeine will make female rats seek more couplings with males.

3 test
Collect data: how often do females on caffeine allow males to mate and how often do females not on caffeine allow males to mate?

4 interpret
Analyze resulting data to confirm or disconfirm the theory-prediction.

FIGURE **2.3**
THE SCIENTIFIC METHOD.
The scientific method consists of an ongoing cycle of observation, prediction, testing, interpretation, and communication (OPTIC). Research begins with observation, but it doesn't end with communication. Publishing results of a study allows other researchers to repeat the procedure and confirm the results.

The fifth stage of the scientific method is to *communicate* the results. Generally, scientists publish their findings in an established, peer-reviewed professional journal. Following a standardized format, the researchers report their hypothesis, describe their research design and the conditions of the study, summarize the results, and share their conclusions. In their reports, researchers also consider the broader implications of their results. What might the effects of caffeine on sexuality in female rats mean for our understanding of caffeine, arousal, and sex in female humans? Publication also serves an important role in making research findings part of the public domain. Such exposure not only indicates that colleagues who reviewed the study found it to be credible, but it also allows other researchers to repeat the research.

replication

the repetition of a study to confirm the results; essential to the scientific process.

Replication is the repetition of a study to confirm the results. The advancement of science hinges on replication of results. No matter how interesting and exciting results are, if they cannot be reliably duplicated, the findings must have been accidental. Whether a result holds or not, new predictions can be generated from the data, leading in turn to new studies. This is how the process of scientific discovery is cumulative. Previous knowledge builds on older knowledge.

WHAT SCIENCE IS NOT: PSEUDOSCIENCE

Do you believe that the planets and stars determine our destiny, that aliens have visited Earth, or that the human mind is capable of moving or altering physical objects? Certainly, astrology, unidentified flying objects (UFOs), and extrasensory perception (ESP) are fascinating topics to ponder. As thinking beings, we try to understand things that science may not explain to our satisfaction. In fact, many of us seem quite willing to believe things that science and skeptics easily dismiss. For example, in a survey of 1,574 U.S. adults in 2002, the National Science Foundation reported (2002) that

- Sixty percent believe some people possess psychic powers or extrasensory perception (ESP).

- Thirty percent believe some reported objects in the sky are really space vehicles from other civilizations.

- From 1991 to 2001 the number of adults who believe in haunted houses, ghosts, communication with the dead, and witches increased by more than 10%; for example, 29% believed in haunted houses in 1991, whereas 42% believed in them in 2001.

- Thirty percent read astrology charts at least occasionally in the newspaper.

- Forty-eight percent believe humans lived at the same time as the dinosaurs.

People often claim there is "scientific evidence" for certain unusual phenomena, but that does not mean the evidence is truly scientific. There is also false science, or *pseudo*science. **Pseudoscience** refers to practices that appear to be and claim to be science, but in fact do not use the scientific method to come to their conclusions. What makes something pseudoscientific comes more from the way it is studied than from the content area. Pseudoscience practitioners (1) make no real advances in knowledge, (2) disregard well-known and established facts that contradict their claims, (3) do not challenge or question their own assumptions, (4) tend to offer vague or incomplete explanations of how

pseudoscience

claims presented as scientific that are not supported by evidence obtained with the scientific method.

they came to their conclusions, and (5) tend to use unsound logic in making their arguments (Derry, 1999; see Figure 2.4).

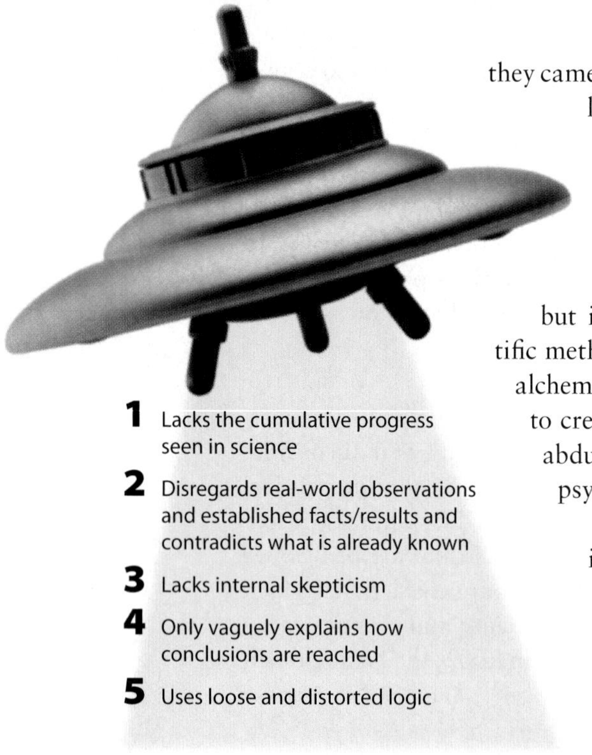

Philosophy, art, music, and religion, for instance, would not be labeled pseudoscience because they do not claim to be science. Pseudoscience may appear to be scientific, but its claims cannot be confirmed with the scientific method. Pseudoscientific claims have been made for alchemy, creation science, intelligent design, attempts to create perpetual motion machines, astrology, alien abduction and extraterrestrial explanations of UFOs, psychokinesis, and some forms of mental telepathy.

Perhaps the most pervasive pseudoscience is astrology, which uses positions of the sun, moon, and planets to explain an individual's personality traits and make predictions about the future. There simply is no credible scientific evidence that the position of the moon, planets, and stars and one's time and place of birth have any influence on personality and its development or one's life course (Shermer, 1997). And yet 30 percent of respondents to the National Science Foundation (2002) survey said they look at the horoscopes in the newspaper at least occasionally.

Overall, some areas of study meet the criteria for pseudoscience—telekinesis, astrology, alien abduction explanations of UFOs, and creation science, to name but a few. But in all fairness, there have been some reliable observations of UFOs and some scientifically sound evidence for telepathy (Rosenthal, 1986; Bem & Horonton, 1994). Reading the scientific literature on these two topics, one has little choice but to conclude that some of these experiences have some validity. Remember, open skepticism is the hallmark of science. If there is scientifically sound evidence for something—even if it is difficult to explain—and it has been replicated, then we have to accept it. The key is to know how to distinguish sound from unsound evidence.

1 Lacks the cumulative progress seen in science

2 Disregards real-world observations and established facts/results and contradicts what is already known

3 Lacks internal skepticism

4 Only vaguely explains how conclusions are reached

5 Uses loose and distorted logic

FIGURE **2.4**
THE CHARACTERISTICS OF PSEUDOSCIENCE.
Skepticism is the best approach to claims that aren't supported by hard scientific evidence.

quick quiz 2.1: The Nature of Science

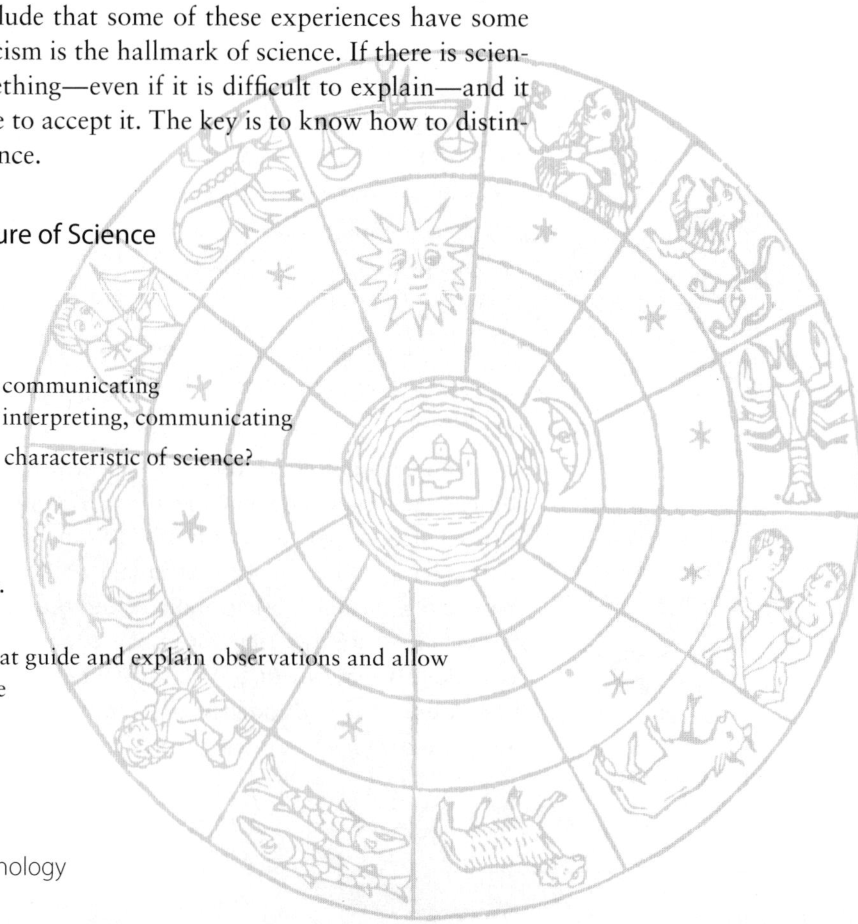

1. The scientific method consists of
   a. observing, predicting, testing
   b. observing, predicting, trying
   c. observing, predicting, testing, communicating
   d. observing, predicting, testing, interpreting, communicating

2. Which of the following is NOT a characteristic of science?
   a. It is cumulative.
   b. It is a set of beliefs.
   c. It is an attitude.
   d. It requires intellectual honesty.

3. Scientific theories are
   a. a set of related assumptions that guide and explain observations and allow testable predictions to be made
   b. educated guesses
   c. hunches
   d. hypotheses

4. What distinguishes science from pseudoscience?
    a. use of statistics
    b. content area studied
    c. open skepticism
    d. the search for truth

Answers can be found at the end of the chapter.

Research Methods in Psychology

Given that science involves testing ideas about how the world works, how do we design studies that test our ideas? This question confronts anyone wanting to answer a psychological question scientifically. Let's turn to the methods and tools psychologists use.

PRINCIPLES OF RESEARCH DESIGN

research design
plans of action for how to conduct a scientific study.

Like other sciences, psychology makes use of several types of **research designs**—or plans for how to conduct a study. The design chosen for a given study depends on the question being asked. Some questions can best be answered by randomly placing people in different groups in a laboratory to see whether a treatment causes a change in behavior. Other questions have to be studied by questionnaires or surveys. Still other questions can best be answered simply by making initial observations and seeing what people do in the real world. And sometimes researchers analyze the results of many studies on the same topic to look for trends.

In this section we examine variations in research designs, along with their advantages and disadvantages. We begin by defining a few key terms common to all research designs in psychology. A general goal of psychological research is to measure change in behavior, thought, or brain activity. A **variable** is anything that changes or "varies" within or between subjects. People differ or vary from one another on age, gender, weight, intelligence, anxiety, and extraversion. These are all examples of variables. Psychologists do research by predicting how and when variables influence each other. For instance, a psychologist who is interested in whether girls develop verbal skills at a different rate than boys focuses on two variables: gender and vocabulary.

variable
a characteristic that changes or "varies," such as age, gender, weight, intelligence, anxiety, and extraversion.

All researchers must pay careful attention to how they obtain participants for the study. The first step in obtaining a sample is for the researchers to decide the makeup of the entire group, or **population**, in which they are interested. In psychology, populations can be all humans, all adolescents, all boys, all girls, all college students, or all students at a particular school. How many in the overall group or population are older than 50 or younger than 20? How many are European American, African American, Asian American, Pacific Islander, or Native American? How many have high school educations, and how many have college educations?

population
the entire group a researcher is interested in; for example, all humans, all adolescents, all boys, all girls, all college students.

Can you think of a problem that would occur if a researcher tried to collect data directly on an entire population? There are many, but the most obvious are

THE FAR SIDE By GARY LARSON

Testing whether fish have feelings

Researchers often work with a small sample of the population they're interested in.

time and money. Most populations are too large to survey or interview directly. So researchers draw on small subsets from each population. These subsets of the population are known as **samples**. A sample of the population of college students, for instance, might consist of students enrolled in one or more universities in a particular geographic area. Research is almost always conducted on samples, not populations. If researchers want to draw valid conclusions or make accurate predictions about the population, it is important that they have samples that accurately represent the population in terms of age, gender, ethnicity, or any other variables that might be of interest. When polls are wrong in predicting who will win an election, it is often because the polled sample did not accurately represent the population.

Another concern for all researchers occurs after participants agree to participate. If the topics are controversial, sensitive, or personal, such as sexual behavior or attitudes toward other ethnic groups, people are likely to respond in ways that may not honestly reflect their true beliefs. In other words, people might tell researchers what they want to hear rather than what they really believe. This tendency toward favorable self-presentation is known as the **social desirability bias**. For example, when asked whether race would play a role in voting for a presidential candidate, most respondents say no. And yet during early presidential primaries of 2008, Barack Obama often received fewer votes from white voters than the pre-election polls would have predicted. This suggests that some voters are falling prey to social desirability when polled about race. They give the socially desirable answer because they don't want to be perceived as being prejudiced.

samples
subsets of the population studied in a research project.

social desirability bias
the tendency toward favorable self-presentation that could lead to inaccurate self-reports.

DESCRIPTIVE STUDIES

Many, if not most, creative ideas for studies start with specific experiences—one person being painfully shy; one person throwing himself on the train tracks to push away someone who had fallen just before the train was about to hit her; or a young woman not being helped as she is stabbed and repeatedly attacked, eventually dying. What is more, the attack occurs in an apartment complex in which 38 other people later confess that they either heard or saw the attack. Only one of the 38 did as much as call the police.

This last case is a real-life story that happened in Queens, New York, in 1964 to a woman named Kitty Genovese. Her case was so shocking that it drove two psychologists—Bibb Latané and John Darley—to begin conducting research on this phenomenon. The area of research known as the "bystander effect" was born.

The point is that single events and single cases often lead to new ideas and new lines of research. When a researcher is interested

connection
What is the "bystander effect" and why, when so many people are around, do individuals not get involved and help others in need?
See Chapter 14, p. 557.

in a particular question or topic that is relatively new to the field, often the wisest first move is to use a descriptive design. In **descriptive designs** the researcher makes no prediction and does not control or manipulate any variables. She simply defines a problem of interest and describes as carefully as possible the variable of interest. The basic question in a descriptive design is, What is variable X?—what is love; what is genius; what is apathy? The psychologist makes careful observations, often in the real world outside the research lab. Descriptive studies usually occur during the exploratory phase of research in which the researcher is looking for meaningful patterns that might lead to some predictions later on; they do not really involve testing hypotheses. Possible relationships or patterns are noted and then used in other designs as the basis for testable predictions (see Figure 2.5). Three of the most common kinds of descriptive methods in psychology are case studies, naturalistic observations, and interviews/surveys.

descriptive designs
study designs in which the researcher defines a problem and variable of interest but makes no prediction and does not control or manipulate anything.

Case Study Psychotherapists have been making use of insights they gain from individual cases for more than 100 years. A **case study** involves observation of one person, often over a long period of time. Much wisdom and knowledge of human behavior can come from careful observations of single individuals over time. Because they are based on a one-on-one relationship lasting over years, case studies offer deep insights that surveys and questionnaires often miss. Sometimes studying the lives of extraordinary individuals, such as van Gogh, Lincoln, Marie Curie, Einstein, or even Hitler can tell us much about creativity, greatness, genius, or evil. An area of psychology called *psychobiography* examines in detail the lives of historically important people and provides an example of the richness and value of case studies and studying individual lives over time (Elms,

case study
a study design in which a psychologist, often a therapist, observes one person over a long period of time.

descriptive studies

What type of questions might be researched?	What is the most suitable method of answering the question?	What is the best use for this kind of study?	What is the main limitation of this kind of study?
Single variable, such as: How do people flirt?	Case study, observation, survey, or interview	To find patterns that might lead to predictions for more complete research project. To start describing observed flirtation behavior	Hypotheses are not tested. Cannot look at cause and effect

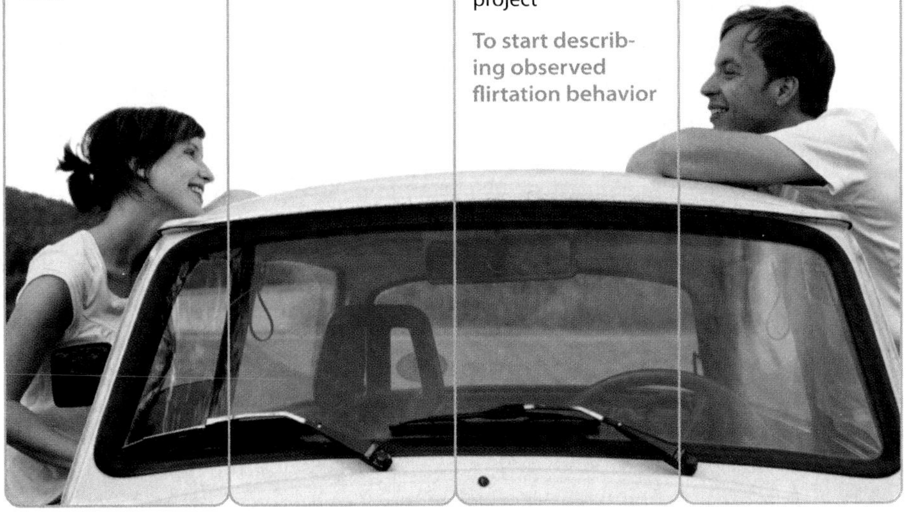

FIGURE **2.5**
CHARACTERISTICS OF DESCRIPTIVE STUDIES.
In descriptive studies, researchers look for patterns that might help them create testable hypotheses.

1993; Runyan, 1982; Schultz, 2005). Like other descriptive research, cases studies do not test hypotheses but can be a rich source for hypotheses. One has to be careful with case studies, however, because not all cases are generalizable to other people. That is why we don't stop with case studies, but use them to develop testable and more general predictions.

Naturalistic Observation   A second kind of descriptive method is **naturalistic observation,** in which the researcher observes and records behavior in the real world. The researcher tries to be as unobtrusive as possible so as not to influence or bias the behavior of interest. Naturalistic observation is more often the design of choice in comparative psychology by researchers who study nonhuman behavior (especially primates) to determine what is and is not unique about our species.

Primatologist Jane Goodall is famous for her observational studies of chimpanzees in the wild.

Developmental psychologists occasionally also conduct naturalistic observations. For example, the developmental psychologist Edward Tronick of Harvard University has made detailed naturalistic observations of infants of the Efe people in Zaire. He has tracked these children from 5 months through 3 years to understand how the communal pattern of child rearing by the Efe influences social development in children (Tronick, Morelli, & Ivey, 1992). Although the traditional Western view is that having a primary caregiver is best for the social and emotional well-being of a child, Tronick's research suggests that the use of multiple, communal caregivers can also foster children's social and emotional well-being.

The advantage of naturalistic observation is that it gives researchers a look at real behavior in the real world, rather than in a controlled setting where people might not behave naturally. Relatively few psychologists use naturalistic observation, however, because conditions cannot be controlled and cause-and-effect relationships between variables cannot be demonstrated.

Interview and Survey   Two related and widely used techniques for gaining information about peoples' thoughts and behaviors are interviews and surveys. They both involve asking people directly or indirectly what they think, feel, or have done. They also both involve specific questions, usually asked precisely the same way to each respondent. Answers can be completely open-ended, allowing the person to answer however she or he wants. More often than not, however, the possible answers are restricted to some kind of rating scale, such as 1 for "completely disagree," 3 for "neither disagree nor agree," and 5 for "completely agree." Historically, interviews were conducted mostly face-to-face, but now both interviews and surveys are more often carried out over the phone or the Internet. Researchers may thus survey thousands of individuals on almost any topic, such as abortion, sex, capital punishment, voting, or gay marriage.

There are numerous pitfalls to collecting data via large-scale interviews and surveys, the two most obvious being the inclusion of people who are not

FIGURE **2.6**

SAMPLING. For practical reasons, research is typically conducted with small samples of the population of interest. If a psychologist wanted to study this population of 22 people, he or she would aim for a sample that represents the makeup of the whole group. Thus, if 27 percent of the population was blue, the researcher would want 27 percent of the sample population to be blue, as shown in the pie chart on the left.

representative of the group at large and biased responses. Think about your own response when you are contacted via phone or e-mail about participating in a scientific survey. Many of us don't want to participate and ignore the request. So how does a researcher know that people who participate are not different from people who don't participate? Maybe those who participate are older or younger, have more education or have less education. In other words, we need to know that the information we collect comes from people who represent the group in which we are interested, which is known as a **representative sample** (see Figure 2.6).

representative sample

a research sample that accurately reflects the population of people one is studying.

The well-known Kinsey surveys of male and female sexual behavior provide good examples of the power and weakness of survey research (Kinsey, Pomeroy, & Martin, 1948; Kinsey et al., 1953). Make no mistake—just publishing such research was shocking to many people and led to an uproar both in the scientific community and in the general public at the time. Kinsey reported, for instance, that up to 50% of the men and only about half as many (26%) of the women interviewed had had extramarital affairs. Another widely cited finding was that approximately 10% of the population could be considered homosexual. The impact of Kinsey's research has been profound. By itself it began the science of studying human sexuality and permanently changed people's views. For example, Kinsey was the first to consider sexual orientation on a continuum from 0 (completely heterosexual) to 6 (completely homosexual) rather than as

Americans were shocked by Alfred Kinsey's initial reports on male and female sexual behavior. Kinsey was the first researcher to survey people about their sexual behavior. For better or worse, his publications changed our attitudes about sex.

an either–or state with only two options. This approach remains a lasting contribution of his studies.

But by today's standards, Kinsey's techniques for interviewing and collecting data were rather primitive. He didn't use representative sampling and oversampled people in Indiana (his home state) and prisons, for example. In addition, he interviewed people face-to-face about their most personal and private details of their sexual behavior, making it more likely they would not be perfectly honest in their responses.

Is there a connection between sugar and children's activity level?

CORRELATIONAL STUDIES

Once an area of study has developed far enough that predictions can be made from descriptive studies, then a researcher might choose to test hypotheses by measuring variables and determining the extent to which one relates to the other. **Correlational designs** measure two or more variables and their relationship to one another. In correlational designs, the basic question is, "Is *X* related to *Y*?" For instance, "Is sugar consumption related to increased activity levels in children?" If so, how strong is the relationship, and is increased sugar consumption associated (correlated) with increased activity levels, as we would predict, or does activity decrease as sugar consumption increases? Or is there no clear relationship?

correlational designs
studies that measure two or more variables and their relationship to one another; not designed to show causation.

Correlational studies are useful when the variables cannot be manipulated. For instance, it would be unethical to raise one group of children one way and another group another way in order to study parenting behavior. But we could use a good questionnaire to find out whether parents' scores are consistently associated with particular behavioral outcomes in children. In fact, many questions in developmental psychology, personality psychology, and even clinical psychology are examined with correlational techniques.

The major limitation of the correlational approach is that it does not establish whether one variable actually causes the other or vice versa. Parental neglect might be associated with antisocial behavior in adolescence, but that does not necessarily mean that neglect causes antisocial behavior. It might, but it might not. Some other variable (e.g., high levels of testosterone, poverty, antisocial friends) could be the cause of the behavior. We must always be mindful that correlation is necessary for causation but not sufficient by itself to establish causation (see Figure 2.7).

correlation coefficient
a statistic that ranges from –1.0 to +1.0 and assesses the strength and direction of association between two variables.

Psychologists often use a statistic called the correlation coefficient to draw conclusions from their correlational study. **Correlation coefficients** tell us whether two variables relate to each other and the direction of the relationship. Correlations range between –1.00 and +1.00, with coefficients near 0.00 telling us there is no relationship between the two variables. This means that knowing about one variable tells you nothing about the other. A classic example of a correlation exists between height and weight. Generally, the taller people are,

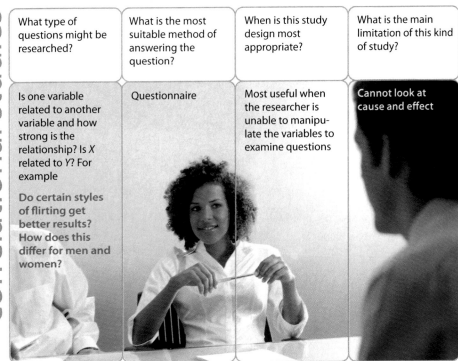

What type of questions might be researched?	What is the most suitable method of answering the question?	When is this study design most appropriate?	What is the main limitation of this kind of study?
Is one variable related to another variable and how strong is the relationship? Is *X* related to *Y*? For example Do certain styles of flirting get better results? How does this differ for men and women?	Questionnaire	Most useful when the researcher is unable to manipulate the variables to examine questions	Cannot look at cause and effect

FIGURE **2.7**
CHARACTERISTCS OF CORRELATIONAL STUDIES.
These studies measure two or more variables and their relationship to one another.

the more they will weigh. As a correlation approaches ±1.00, the strength of the relationship increases.

Correlation coefficients can be positive or negative. If the relationship is positive, then as a group's score on *X* goes up, its score on *Y* also goes up. For instance, let's consider the correlation between students' scores on the midterm and final. By calculating a correlation, we know whether students who do well on the midterm are likely to do well on the final. Data in this example are from 76 students in one of our classes. The correlation was +.57, meaning that students who did well on the midterm in general did well on the final. Likewise, those who did poorly on the midterm tended to do poorly on the final. The correlation, however, was not extremely high (.80 or .90), so there was some inconsistency. Some people performed differently on the two exams. When we plot these scores we see more clearly how individuals did on each exam (see Figure 2.8). Each dot represents one student's scores on each exam. For example, one student scored an 86 on the midterm, but only a 66 on the final.

When interpreting correlations, however, it is important to remember that a correlation does not mean there is a causal relationship between the two variables. *Correlation is necessary but not sufficient for causation.* When one variable causes another, it must be correlated with it. But just because variable *X* is correlated with variable *Y*, it does not mean *X* causes *Y*. In fact, the supposed cause may be an effect, or some third variable may be the cause. What if hairiness and aggression in men were positively correlated? Would that imply that being hairy makes a man more aggressive? No. In fact, both hairiness and aggressiveness are related to a third variable, the male sex hormone testosterone (Simpson, 2001).

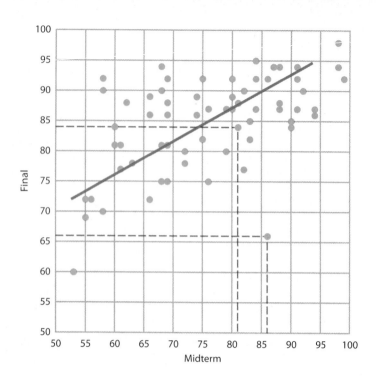

FIGURE **2.8**

EXAMPLE OF SCATTERPLOT OF POSITIVE CORRELATION: STUDENTS' SCORES ON A MIDTERM AND FINAL EXAM. The correlation between scores on the midterm and final is +.57, which means that in general the students who do well on the midterm tend to do well on the final. It also means that students who do poorly on the midterm tend to do poorly on the final. Each circle is a particular student's scores on the midterm and final. For example, one student scored an 81 on the midterm (vertical dashed line) and an 84 on the final (horizontal dashed line). Students above the diagonal line did better on the final than expected. Students below the diagonal line performed worse on the final than expected. For example, one student scored an 86 on the midterm but only a 66 on the final.

EXPERIMENTAL STUDIES

Often people use the word *experiment* loosely to refer to any research study, but in science an experiment is something quite specific. A true **experiment** has two crucial characteristics:

1. Experimental manipulation of a predicted cause—the independent variable—and measurement of the response, or dependent variable.
2. Random assignment of participants to control and experimental groups or conditions—meaning that each participant has an equal chance of being placed in each group.

The **independent variable** in an experiment is an attribute that is manipulated by the experimenter under controlled conditions. The independent variable is the condition that the researcher predicts will cause a particular outcome. The **dependent variable** is the outcome, or response to the experimental manipulation. You can think of the independent variable as the "cause" and the dependent variable as the "effect," although reality is not always so simple. If there is a causal connection between the two, then the responses *depend* on the treatment; hence the name *dependent variable*.

In our sugar-activity example, sugar levels would be the independent variable and activity level the dependent variable. Recall the study of the effect of caffeine on sex drive in rats. Is caffeine the independent or dependent variable? What about sex drive? One of the main shortcomings of the Zimbardo Stanford Prison Experiment was its failure to include obvious dependent variables. That is, the researchers had few ways of measuring how the prisoners and guards behaved as a result of their being assigned to those conditions. They simply observed what happened—and what happened was a lot of conflict and emotional turmoil. In this sense, the prison study was more descriptive than experimental. Figure 2.9 features other examples of independent and dependent variables.

experiment
a research design that includes independent and dependent variables and random assignment of participants to control and experimental groups or conditions.

independent variable
a property that is manipulated by the experimenter under controlled conditions to determine whether it causes the predicted outcome of an experiment.

dependent variable
in an experiment, the outcome or response to the experimental manipulation.

you want to know the effect of X on Y	the IV would be	the DV would be
Number of people present (X) and likelihood of helping someone in distress (Y)	Number of people present	Likelihood of helping
Hours of sleep (X) and performance on a test (Y)	Hours of sleep	Test grade
Relaxation training (X) and blood pressure (Y)	Relaxation training	Blood pressure

FIGURE **2.9**

INDEPENDENT AND DEPENDENT VARIABLES. Remember: the response, or dependent variable (DV), depends on the treatment. It is the treatment, or independent variable (IV), that the researcher manipulates.

random assignment
the method used to assign participants to different research conditions so that all participants have the same chance of being in any specific group.

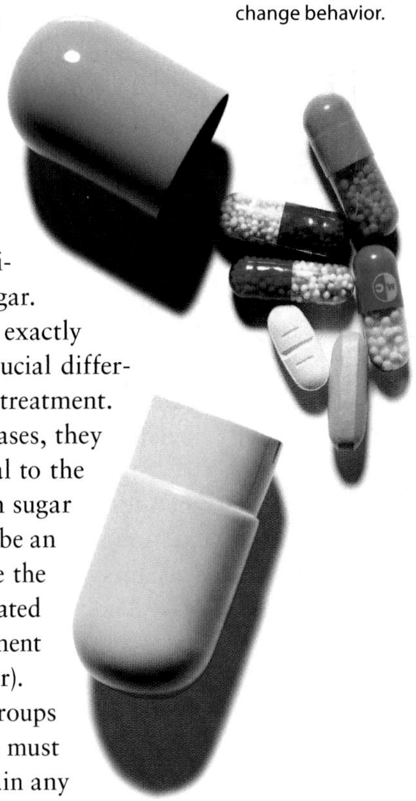

control group
a group of research participants who are treated in exactly the same manner as the experimental group, except that they do not receive the independent variable or treatment.

placebo
a substance or treatment that appears identical to the actual treatment but lacks the active substance.

Random assignment is the method used to assign participants to different research conditions so that each person has the same chance of being in one group as another. Random assignment is achieved either with a random numbers table or some other unbiased technique. Random assignment is critical because it assures that *on average* the groups will be similar with respect to all possible variables, such as gender, intelligence, motivation, and memory when the experiment begins. If the groups are the same on these qualities at the beginning of the study, then any differences between the groups at the end of the experiment are likely to be the result of the independent variable.

Experimenters randomly assign participants to either an experimental group or a control group. The **experimental group** consists of those participants who will receive the treatment or whatever is thought to change behavior. In the sugar consumption and activity study, for example, the experimental group would receive some designated amount of sugar. The **control group** consists of participants who are treated in exactly the same manner as the experimental group, but with the crucial difference that they do not receive the independent variable or treatment. Instead, they often receive no special treatment or, in some cases, they get a **placebo,** a substance or treatment that appears identical to the actual treatment but lacks the active substance. In a study on sugar consumption and activity level, an appropriate placebo might be an artificial sweetener. So the experimental group would receive the actual treatment (sugar), and the control group would be treated exactly the same way but would not receive the actual treatment (instead the control group might receive an artificial sweetener).

Why is it so important for experimental and control groups to be equivalent at the outset of an experimental study? We must minimize the possibility that other characteristics could explain any difference we find after we administer the treatment. If two groups of children are similar at the start and if one group differs from the other

experimental group
a group consisting of those participants who will receive the treatment or whatever is predicted to change behavior.

FIGURE **2.10**
CHARACTERISTICS OF EXPERIMENTAL STUDIES.
With experiments, researchers may find cause and effect based on the independent and dependent variables.

experimental studies

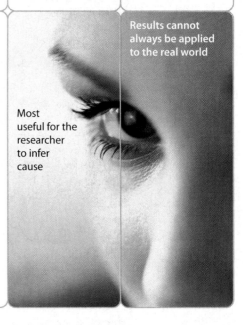

What type of questions might be researched?	What is the most suitable method of answering the question?	What is the best use for this kind of study?	What is the main limitation of this kind of study?
Does the independent variable cause the dependent variable? Does *X* cause *Y*? Do smiles with raised eyebrows versus those without lead to more offers of dates?	Random assignments of participants, controlled experimental conditions in a lab setting	Most useful for the researcher to infer cause	Results cannot always be applied to the real world

on activity level after receiving different amounts of sugar, then we can conclude that the treatment caused the observed effect. That is, different levels of sugar consumption caused the differences in activity level.

In our hypothetical study on sugar and activity, for instance, we would want to include equal numbers of boys and girls in the experimental and control groups and match them with respect to age, ethnicity, and other characteristics, so that we could attribute differences in activity level following treatment to differences in sugar consumption. Suppose we didn't do a good job of randomly assigning participants to our two conditions, and the experimental group ended up with 90% boys and the control group had 90% girls. If, after administering the sugar to the experimental group and the placebo (sugar substitute) to the control group, we found a difference in activity, then we would have two possible explanations: gender and sugar. In this case, gender would be a **confounding variable,** that is, an additional variable whose influence cannot be separated from the independent variable being examined (sugar). As most of the people in the sugar group were also male, we do not know whether male gender or sugar consumption was responsible for the difference in active behavior. These two variables are confounded and cannot be teased apart.

The power of the experimental design is that it allows us to say that the independent variable (or treatment) caused changes in the dependent variable, as long as everything other than the independent variable was held constant (see Figure 2.10). Random assignment guarantees group equivalence on a number of variables and prevents ambiguity over whether effects might be due to other differences in the groups.

In addition to random assignment to control and experimental groups, a true experiment requires experimental control of the independent variable. Researchers must treat the two groups alike and make sure that all environmental

confounding variable
variable whose influence on the dependent variable cannot be separated from the independent variable being examined.

conditions (such as noise level and room size) are equivalent. Again, the goal is to make sure that nothing affects the dependent variable besides the independent variable.

In the experiment on sugar consumption and activity level, for example, the researcher first must randomly assign participants to either the experimental group (in which participants receive some amount of sugar) or the control group (in which participants receive some sugar substitute). The outcome of interest is activity level, and so each group might be videotaped for a short period of time, 30 minutes after eating the sugar or saccharin (the sugar substitute). But what if it turns out that the room in which the experimental group was given the sugar was several degrees warmer than the room where the control group received the sugar substitute, and our results showed that the participants in the warmer room were more active? Could we conclude that sugar led to increased activity level? No, because the heat in that room may have caused the increase in activity level. In this case, room temperature would be the confounding variable. Experimenters must carefully consider all variables that might influence the dependent variable and control them (for example, making sure room temperatures are equal).

How much participants and experimenters know about the experimental conditions to which participants have been assigned can also affect outcome. In **single-blind studies**, participants do not know the experimental condition to which they have been assigned. This is a necessary precaution in all studies to avoid the possibility that participants will behave in a biased way. For example, if participants know they have been assigned to a group that receives a new training technique on memory, then they might try harder to perform well. This would confound the results.

Another possible problem can come from the experimenter knowing who is in which group and unintentionally treating the two groups somewhat differently. This could result in the predicted outcome simply because the experimenter biased the results. In **double-blind studies**, neither the participants nor the researchers (at least the ones administering the treatment) know who has been assigned to which condition. Ideally, then, neither participants nor those collecting the data should know which group is the experimental group and which is the control group. The advantage of double-blind studies is that they prevent experimenter expectancy effects. **Experimenter expectancy effects** occur when the behavior of the participants is influenced by the experimenter's knowledge of who is in which condition (Rosenthal, 1976, 1994). The story of how experimenter expectancy effects were discovered and how they broke new ground is worth telling.

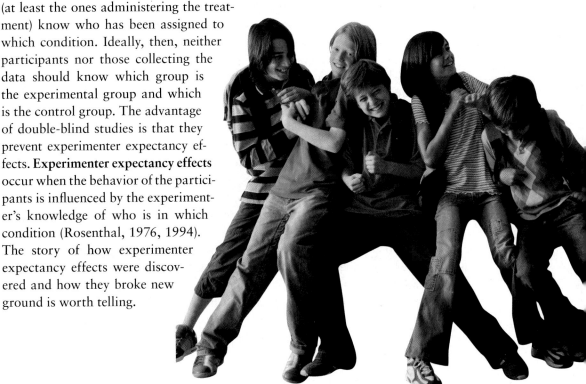

single-blind studies
studies in which participants do not know the experimental condition (group) to which they have been assigned.

experimenter expectancy effects
result that occurs when the behavior of the participants is influenced by the experimenter's knowledge of who is in the control group and who is in the experimental group.

double-blind studies
studies in which neither the participants nor the researchers administering the treatment know who has been assigned to the experimental or control group.

breaking new ground

How the Discovery of Experimenter Effects Changed Psychology

You don't have to be a scientist to understand that it would be wrong and unethical for an experimenter to tell participants how to behave and what to do. Even for the participants to know what group they are in or what the hypotheses of the study are is bad science and biases behavior. But can what the experimenter knows change the behavior of the participants? The answers to these questions might surprise you.

CAN EXPERIMENTERS AFFECT THE OUTCOME OF A STUDY?

Some of the earliest psychology researchers knew that the experimenter's knowledge might slightly change the outcomes of a study. In the 1930s, this effect was given the label *unconscious experimenter bias* (S. Rosenzweig, 1933). But no one thought about studying the impact that experimenters exert on the behavior of the animals or people they are studying until Robert Rosenthal experienced unconscious experimenter bias firsthand.

HOW ROSENTHAL DISCOVERED EXPERIMENTER EFFECTS

Robert Rosenthal

In the mid-1950s, Robert Rosenthal was conducting an experiment to complete his PhD. Rosenthal hypothesized that people who believed they were successful would be more likely to see success in others. To test this idea, he conducted an experiment in which he told one group of participants that they had done well on an intelligence test and another group they had done poorly on an intelligence test. Rosenthal randomly assigned participants to be in one of these conditions (there was also a neutral control condition where participants were not given any feedback after the intelligence test). Then he asked both groups to look at photographs of people doing various tasks and rate how successful they thought the people in the photos were. He reasoned that people told they did well on an intelligence test should see more success in photographs of people doing various tasks than people who were told they did not do well on the test.

Because he had always enjoyed statistics and was a careful researcher, Rosenthal decided to compare the average test scores of the participants assigned to different conditions *before* doing anything to them. The reason is simple: If the treatment causes a difference in behavior for the different groups, the researcher needs to make sure the groups started off behaving the same way before treatment. Otherwise, the researcher does not know if the difference is due to the treatment or to some preexisting condition. To Rosenthal's dismay, the groups were not only different at the outset, but they were also different in exactly the way that favored his hypothesis. The deck was stacked in his favor before he administered the treatment. How did this happen?

Given random assignment, the only difference in the groups at the outset was Rosenthal's knowledge of who was in which group. Somehow by knowing who was in which group he unintentionally created behaviors that favored his hypothesis. He was forced to conclude that even when trying to be "scientific" and "objective," researchers can subtly and unconsciously bias results in their favor.

Afraid that he had ruined his dissertation, Rosenthal asked his professors about this phenomenon, and some casually remarked "Oh yes, we lose a few Ph.D. dissertations now and then because of problems like that!" (Rosenthal, 1994, p. 217). Most psychologists were aware of these kinds of problems, but chalked it up to happenstance rather than seeing an interesting finding to explore and research. Rosenthal combed the literature for research on the topic of unconscious experimenter bias. There was some mention of these bias problems, but no one had ever actually studied the phenomenon (Rosenthal, 1976).

Rosenthal decided to study what he termed *experimenter expectancy effects.* Through several experiments, he confirmed that experimenter expectancies can potentially ruin even the best-designed study. In fact, he discovered that two other surprising factors can unwittingly change the outcome of the study as well. First, if the study involves direct interaction between an experimenter and participants, the experimenter's age, ethnicity, personality, and gender can influence the participants' behavior (Rosenthal, 1976). Second, Rosenthal stumbled upon a more general phenomenon known as self-fulfilling prophecy. A **self-fulfilling prophecy** is a statement that changes events to cause a belief or prediction to become true. If you say "I am going to fail this exam" and do not study, then that belief has become self-fulfilling when you do fail the exam.

self-fulfilling prophecy
a statement that affects events to cause the prediction to become true.

WHAT QUESTIONS REMAIN?

Within 10 years, more than 300 other studies confirmed Rosenthal's results (Rosenthal & Rubin, 1978). Studies showed that experimenter expectancies affect animal participants as well as humans (Rosenthal & Fode, 1963). Rosenthal's demonstration of experimenter expectancy effects and self-fulfilling prophecies also led to the development of double-blind procedures in science. Think about it: If what experimenters know about a study can affect the results, then they'd better be as blind to experimental conditions as the participants are.

Expectancy effects have also been found in classrooms. School principal Lenore Jacobson collaborated with Rosenthal in a study to determine whether teachers create "smart" behavior in classrooms. If a teacher believes that a particular student is "smart" and "special," that teacher may unwittingly treat the student differently, give more detailed feedback, and give the student more challenging material. In turn, these actions could create a higher-performing, "smarter" student. Teacher expectations might become a self-fulfilling prophecy.

That is precisely what Rosenthal and Jacobson (1968, 1992) found in classrooms where 20% of the children were assigned randomly to be "late bloomers"; their teachers were told they would start to show real intellectual gains in the coming year. Sure enough, these late bloomers showed more improvement over the year than any other group of students. Follow-up research one and two years later found that these "late blooming" students had also shown slightly more improvement on intelligence tests than control students. In the 40 years since the original study, dozens of similar studies have confirmed this self-fulfilling prophecy effect in the classroom—although the effect is often not as strong as Rosenthal and Jacobson had reported (Jussim & Harber, 2005).

What other questions does this research raise? Is every researcher and teacher, every research participant and student equally susceptible to expectancy effects? In the workplace, might employer expectations affect employee behavior? What about the relationship between medical doctors and their patients?

META-ANALYSIS

After dozens or more studies have been carried out on the same question, researchers can stand back and analyze the results of the studies as the object of interest. For example, a researcher interested in the effects of media violence on children's aggressive behavior might want to know what all of the research—not just one or two studies—suggests. The method for examining so many research studies is known as **meta-analysis,** and it involves combining the results of all the published and even unpublished results on one question and drawing a conclusion based on the entire set of studies on the topic. To do a meta-analysis, the researcher has to convert the findings of each study to a standardized statistic known as effect size. **Effect size** is a measure of the strength of the relationship between two variables or the magnitude of an experimental effect. The average effect size across all studies tells us what the literature as a whole says on a topic or question. In short, meta-analysis tells us whether all of the research on a topic has or has not led to consistent findings and what the size of the effect is.

meta-analysis
a research and statistical technique for combining all research results on one question and drawing a conclusion.

effect size
a measure of the strength of the relationship between two variables or the magnitude of an experimental effect.

quick quiz 2.2: Research Methods in Psychology

1. Dr. Lovejoy wanted to do research on real-world conditions that lead to aggression in 10-year-old children. She defined aggression as "intent to harm another person" and went to a local elementary school and videotaped a 10-minute recess period. She and her trained coders then coded the behavior of every child and counted the number of times each child acted aggressively. This is an example of what kind of research design?
   a. descriptive
   b. correlational
   c. case study
   d. experimental

2. If Dr. Lovejoy wanted to examine whether certain personality traits make aggression more likely, she would most likely use what kind of research design?
   a. descriptive
   b. correlational
   c. interview
   d. experimental

3. Researchers have consistently found that married men live longer than single men. From this finding, we can conclude that
   a. if a man gets married he adds years to his life
   b. marriage causes men to live longer
   c. being single causes men to die earlier
   d. marriage may or may not cause men to live longer

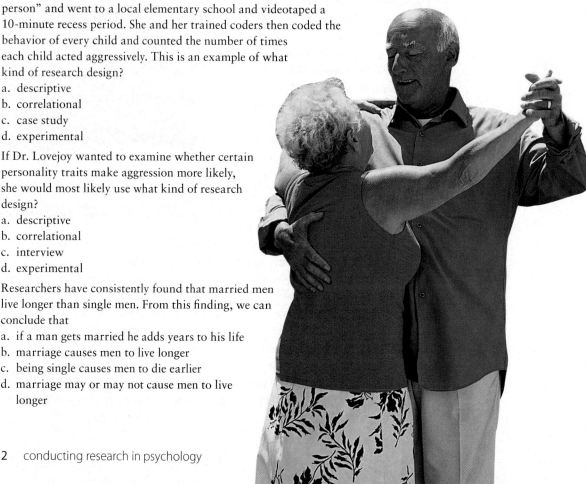

4. In research on whether sugar causes hyperactivity, researchers randomly assign children to receive no sugar, small amounts of sugar, or large amounts of sugar. They then observe and code activity levels. In this case, the sugar level is the
   a. outcome variable
   b. dependent variable
   c. independent variable
   d. control condition

5. In contrast to other kinds of research designs, a true experimental design must have two things:
   a. random assignment of participants to conditions and statistical analysis
   b. random assignment of participants to conditions and manipulation of an independent variable
   c. manipulation of an independent variable and dependent variable
   d. hypothesis testing and observation

Answers can be found at the end of the chapter.

Commonly Used Measures of Psychological Research

When psychologists conduct research, they not only use a variety of research designs to conduct their studies, but they also use a vast array of tools to measure variables relevant to their research questions. The tools and techniques used to assess thought or behavior are called measures. Measures in psychological science tend to fall into three categories: self-report, behavioral, and physiological. To study complex behaviors, researchers may employ multiple measures (see Figure 2.11).

SELF-REPORT MEASURES

self-reports
written or oral accounts of a person's thoughts, feelings, or actions.

Self-reports are people's written or oral accounts of their thoughts, feelings, or actions. Two kinds of self-report measures are commonly used in psychology: interviews and questionnaires. In an interview, a researcher asks a set of questions, and the respondent usually answers in any way he or she feels is appropriate. The answers are often open-ended and not constrained by the researcher. (See the section on "Descriptive Studies" for additional discussion on interviews.)

In a questionnaire, responses are limited to the choices given in the questionnaire. In the Stanford Prison Experiment, the researchers used several questionnaires to keep track of the psychological states of the prisoners and guards. For example, they had participants complete mood questionnaires many times during the study so that they could track any emotional changes they experienced. Participants also completed forms that assessed personality characteristics, such as trustworthiness and orderliness, which might be related to how they acted in a prison environment (Haney et al., 1973).

Self-report questionnaires are easy to use, especially in the context of collecting data from a large number of people at once or in a short period of time.

They are also relatively inexpensive. If designed carefully, they can also provide important information on key psychological variables. A major problem with self-reports, however, is that people are not always the best sources of information about themselves. Why? Sometimes people do not want to reveal what they are thinking or feeling to others for fear of looking bad, the tendency to social desirability that we discussed earlier. Presented with questions about social prejudice, for example, respondents might try to avoid giving answers that would suggest they were prejudiced against a particular group. Another problem with conclusions about human thought and behavior based on self-reports is that we have to assume that people are accurate witnesses to their own experiences. Of course, there is no way to know exactly what a person is thinking without asking that person. It is also true, however, that people do not always have clear insight into how they might behave (Nisbett & Wilson, 1977).

BEHAVIORAL MEASURES

Behavioral measures are based on the systematic observation of people's actions either in their normal environment (that is, naturalistic observation) or in a laboratory setting. For example, a psychologist interested in aggression might bring people into a laboratory, place them in a situation that elicits aggressive behavior, and videotape the responses. Afterward, trained coders would observe the videotapes and, using a prescribed method, code the level of aggressive behavior exhibited by each person. It is important for researchers to train coders to evaluate the video and make sure that the data are being coded in a reliable manner.

behavioral measures measures based on systematic observation of people's actions either in their normal environment or in a laboratory setting.

Behavioral measures are less susceptible to social desirability bias than are self-report measures. They also provide more objective, direct measurements, because they come from a trained outside observer, rather than from the participants themselves. This is a concern for researchers on topics for which people do not always provide accurate information in self-report instruments. In the study of emotion, for example, measuring people's facial expressions from videotape can reveal things about how people are feeling that participants might not want to reveal on questionnaires (Rosenberg & Ekman, 2000). Typically researchers employ behavioral measures because they are interested in natural human behavior.

One drawback of behavioral measures is that people may modify their behavior if they know they are being observed, watched, and/or measured. The major drawback of behavioral measurement, however, is that it is often time-intensive, in terms of the time required to train coders in using the coding schemes, to collect behavioral data, and to prepare the coded data for analysis. As a case in point, one of the most widely used methods for coding facial expressions of emotion requires intensive training,

nature & nurture

Psychology integrates the biological, cognitive, and social contributions to behavior and increasingly uses research methods from other fields (such as medicine and molecular biology) to develop a more comprehensive picture of human behavior.

	Description	Use	Limitations
self-reports	Participants' written or oral accounts of thoughts, actions, feelings.	Interviews and questionaires	Social desirability bias Lack of clear insight into one's own behavior
behavioral measures	Objective observation of actions in either natural or lab settings.	Small scale studies on behavior	Time required to train coders and conduct coding Participants may modify their behavior
physiological measures	Data collection of bodily responses under certain conditions.	Studies to determine the magnitude of physiological change	Specialized training on expensive equipment, on how to collect measurements, and on data interpretation
multiple measures	Several measures combined to acquire data on one aspect of behavior.	Offset limitation of any single measurement Complex behaviors to study	Expensive and time consuming

FIGURE **2.11**
COMMONLY USED MEASURES IN PSYCHOLOGY.

on the order of 100 hours, for people to be able to use it correctly (Ekman, Friesen, & Hager, 2002)! Moreover, it is possible to collect data on only a few participants at once, and therefore behavioral measures are often impractical for large-scale studies.

PHYSIOLOGICAL MEASURES

physiological measures
measures of bodily responses, such as blood pressure or heart rate, used to determine changes in psychological state.

Physiological measures are used to collect data on bodily responses. For years, researchers relied on physiological information to index possible changes in psychological states—for example, to determine the magnitude of a stress reaction. Early research on stress and anxiety focused primarily on electrical changes in involuntary bodily responses, such as heart rate, sweating, and respiration, that are sensitive to changes in psychological states. Some physiologically oriented psychological researchers measure brain activity while people perform certain tasks to determine the rate and location of cognitive processes in the brain.

We will look at specific brain-imaging technologies in Chapter 3. Here we note simply that they have enhanced our understanding of the brain's structure and function tremendously. However, these technologies, and even simple physiological measures, like heart rate, often require specialized training in the use of equipment, collection of measurements, and data interpretation. Further, some of the equipment is expensive and can cost more than $1 million to buy and almost as much each year to maintain. Outside the health care delivery system, only major research universities with medical schools tend to have them. In addition, researchers need years of training and experience in order to use these machines and interpret the data they generate.

connection

What is the best indication of what someone is feeling? Their words? Their facial expressions? Their body language?

See Chapter 11, p. 439.

MULTIPLE MEASUREMENT

Every measure has both strengths and weaknesses. The best way to compensate for the limitations or disadvantages of any particular kind of measurement tool is to use more than one type of measure. **Multiple measurement,** the use of several measures to acquire data on a single aspect of behavior, avoids some of the limitations of individual measures. For example, the researcher who was studying prejudice and wants to avoid social desirability bias might want to include in the study a self-report measure and a behavioral measure, such as observations of how likely an individual is to help a member of a different group. Using the two measures together provides a more accurate portrait of someone's prejudice by building on the strengths of both and offsetting their weaknesses.

multiple measurement the use of several measures to acquire data on one aspect of behavior.

Some studies call for multiple measures, not just because the researchers are trying to offset the limitations of measurement tools, but also because the phenomena under study are complex. One area that requires multiple measures is research on emotions. By their nature, emotions are multifaceted; they create changes in thought, action, bodily systems, and conscious experience. When angry, for example, one individual might contemplate the situation that brought forth the anger, have thoughts of retribution, feel impelled to lunge or attack (but not necessarily act on this impulse), show a facial expression of anger, and experience any number of physiological changes, such as warm skin and a racing heart. Which one of these elements of the emotional response is a definitive measure of anger? We discuss this issue in more detail in Chapter 11 where we examine emotions, but at this point, it is enough to say that emotion is all of these things and no single one of these things. Complex, multifaceted phenomena, such as emotions, can be understood best by measuring the different systems involved.

quick quiz 2.3: Commonly Used Measures of Psychological Research

1. An advantage of self-report questionnaires is that they are easy to administer to large numbers of participants. A disadvantage of questionnaires is that
   a. they cost too much
   b. people do not always accurately report their true thoughts or feelings
   c. scoring responses is subjective
   d. they have low reliability

2. One advantage of behavioral measures compared to self-reported measures is that they
   a. are less prone to social desirability bias
   b. are less time-intensive
   c. are always more valid
   d. cost less

3. A psychologist who is interested in how brain activity relates to behavior will most likely use which kind of measure?
   a. interview
   b. questionnaire
   c. behavioral
   d. physiological

4. Multiple measurement is used to
   a. avoid limitations on any one kind of measurement
   b. capitalize on the strengths of each kind of measurement
   c. understand complex and multifaceted behaviors
   d. all of the above

Answers can be found at the end of the chapter.

Making Sense of Data with Statistics

Once researchers collect data, they must make sense of them. Raw data are difficult to interpret. They are, after all, just a bunch of numbers. It helps to have some way to organize the information and give it meaning. The way scientists do that is with **statistics,** which are the mathematical procedures for collecting, analyzing, interpreting, and presenting numerical data.

Researchers use statistics to describe and simplify what their data look like and to understand how variables relate to one another. They also use effect size to understand the general trends across many published studies on the same question.

To make sense of data researchers use **descriptive statistics** to summarize and organize data. One common way of describing data is to plot the scores in tables or graphs. Graphs provide a visual way of determining what scores occur most frequently. Another way to describe data is by calculating the center, or average, of the scores. There are three different ways to calculate an average, namely, the mean, median, and mode. The **mean** is the arithmetic average of a series of numbers. It is calculated by adding all the numbers together and dividing by the number of scores in the series. An example of a mean is your GPA, which averages the numeric grade points for all of the courses you have taken. The **median** is the score that separates the lower half of scores from the upper half. The **mode** is simply the most frequently occurring score.

Suppose we have a set of scores that vary widely. The mean, median, and mode do not reveal anything about how spread out—or how varied—scores are. For example, one person's 3.0 GPA could come from getting B's in all their courses, while another person's 3.0 could result from getting A's in half their classes and C's in the other half. The second student had much more variable grades than the first. The most common way to represent variability in data is to calculate the **standard deviation,** a statistical measure of how much scores in a sample vary around the mean. A higher standard deviation indicates more variability (or more spread); a lower one indicates less variability or less spread. So in the example above, the student with all B's would have a lower standard deviation than the student with A's and C's.

statistics
collection, analysis, interpretation, and presentation of numerical data.

descriptive statistics
Measures used to describe and summarize research data.

mean
the arithmetic average of a series of numbers.

median
the score that separates the lower half of scores from the upper half.

mode
a statistic that represents the most commonly occurring score or value.

standard deviation
a statistical measure of how much scores in a sample vary around the mean.

Beware of Statistics in Advertising

Learning about research methods plays a crucial role in understanding psychological science, but it offers huge practical advantages as well. You can learn how to look at claims in the news and advertisements with a critical eye. Much of what you learn in this class may be forgotten not long after you leave college. But you are bombarded with advertisements dozens of times each day, something that will continue throughout your life. So let's look briefly at three scenarios that will help you to be a more critical and intelligent consumer of information.

Scenario 1

A billboard advertising a popular hybrid vehicle: *"The car more people would buy again."*

That sounds great! Not only is the car good for the environment (which is one reason to get it), but it also gets great mileage (which will save you money), *and* people like it (they must if they say they would buy it again). Are you sold yet?

Wait a minute. What did the ad actually say? The car more people would buy again. *More* than what? The meaning of this claim depends entirely on what this vehicle is being compared to. The implication is that more people would buy this car again than would buy any other car. But what did they actually compare it to?

> other hybrids?
> all other cars?
> a horse and buggy?

These are things you need to know. Otherwise it is impossible to judge what the statement means, but advertisers regularly leave such information out and hope you will fill in the blank with what helps them most. In this case, they hope and assume you fill in the blank with "all other cars."

Scenario 2

In an ad in the morning paper, Company B reports on research that should really make you want to buy its product. *A recent lab study shows that just a 1/2 oz of their new drug—let's call it "No-Cold"—killed 37,202 germs in a test tube in less than 15 seconds!* (adapted from Huff, 1954).

The implication is that "No-Cold" is a great cold medicine—perhaps better than others—on the basis of these hard scientific data. After all, it killed more than 37,000 germs! Let's take this claim apart. Can you see what is wrong with this statement? Here are a few things to consider:

1. The fact that a substance works well in a test tube does not mean it will work in the human throat or respiratory tract. The test tube is a controlled environment, whereas a host of factors interact in the human body. Temperature, moisture, other bacteria, the human immune system, and phlegm are just a few examples of such factors.

2. The ad doesn't say what kind of germs "No-Cold" killed. Were they the kind that cause colds? In fact, medical researchers still have little idea of the specific viruses

---

Be aware, however, that statistics can be used not only to make sense of data, but also to mislead people. To see how, read "Psychology in the Real World: Beware of Statistics in Advertising."

quick quiz 2.4: Making Sense of Data with Statistics

1. If two sets of scores have the same mean, then
   a. they must have the same variability
   b. they must have similar variabilities
   c. they must have different variabilities
   d. their variabilities could be the same or they could be different

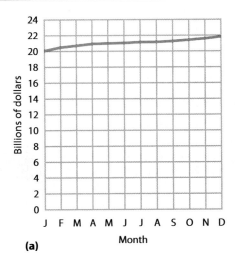
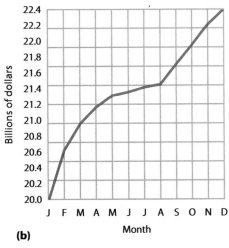

(a)   Month

(b)   Month

FIGURE **2.12**
**BILLIONS OF DOLLARS SPENT
ON EDUCATION.** If you wanted
to persuade someone that education spending is out of control,
which graph woud you use to
make your case?

(germs) that cause colds, though some of them have
been isolated. Were these germs even relevant to colds?
Were they even viruses, for that matter? (The common
cold is caused by a variety of viruses.) Can you identify
any other problems with the ad?

Scenario 3

Graphic displays of data can be misleading. Consider Figures
2.12a and 2.12b, both of which depict the billions of dollars
spent on education over a one-year period. Figure 2.12b
seems to show a much bigger increase in spending on
education than Figure 2.12a. If you look closely, however,
both depict a $2 billion increase in spending over a one-year
period. The information contained in each picture is exactly

the same, but the slopes of the lines differ dramatically. This
difference stems from how the illustrations' vertical axis is
segmented. If you want to imply that the spending increases
in education are insufficient, then you might graph them as
shown in Figure 2.12a. Figure 2.12a has $2 billion increments,
so it shows a gradual increase across the year. Figure 2.12b,
on the other hand, uses $0.2 billion increments. Companies,
journalists, and politicians mislead people all the time by
graphically distorting data.

2. Why is GPA a good example of the statistic "mean"?
    a. because it is calculated by adding scores and dividing by the number of scores
    b. because it is a good measure of how well a student is doing
    c. because it measures the spread or variability of a student's performance
    d. because we can plot it on a graph

3. Scores that are widely spread apart have a
    a. high standard deviation
    b. low standard deviation
    c. high mean
    d. low reliability

Answers can be found at the end of the chapter.

Research Ethics

Some of the most important studies in psychology could not be performed today. One of them is the Stanford Prison Experiment. Recall that this experiment subjected participants to conditions that so altered their behavior that the researchers had to intervene and end the study early. When this study was done, in 1971, there were few ethical limitations on psychological research. Since then, and partly as a consequence of studies like the Stanford Prison Experiment, professional organizations and universities have put in place strict ethical guidelines to protect research participants from physical and psychological harm.

In the Stanford Prison Experiment, college students assigned to the role of either a prison guard or a prisoner acted their parts so well that the distinction between reality and the world created for this study disappeared. The extreme distress experienced by some of the prisoners forced the researchers to end the simulation earlier than planned.

ethics
the rules governing the conduct of a person or group in general or in a specific situation—or more simply, standards of right and wrong.

Ethics are the rules governing the conduct of a person or group in general or in a specific situation, or more simply, standards of right and wrong. What are the ethical boundaries of the treatment of humans and animals in psychological research? In psychology today, nearly every single study conducted with humans and animals must pass through a rigorous review of its methods by a panel of experts. If the proposed study does not meet the standards, it cannot be approved.

Another notable example of research that would violate current ethics guidelines was a classic series of studies by Stanley Milgram in the early 1960s. Milgram's landmark research on obedience is discussed in more detail in Chapter 15, but it is noteworthy here for its pivotal role in the development of ethical guidelines for human psychological research. Like many social psychologists of the mid–20th century, Milgram was both fascinated and horrified by the atrocities of the Holocaust and wondered to what extent psychological factors influenced people's willingness to carry out the orders of the Nazi regime. Milgram predicted that most people are not inherently evil and argued that there might be powerful aspects of social situations that make people obey orders from authority figures. He designed an experiment to test systematically the question of whether decent people could be made to inflict harm on other people.

connection
Can otherwise normal folks be pressured to do cruel things?
See Chapter 14, p. 537.

Briefly, Milgram's studies of obedience involved a simulation in which participants were misled about the true nature of the experiment. Thinking that they were part of an experiment on learning, they administered what they thought were electrical shocks to punish the "learner," who was in another room, for making errors. In spite of protest from the "learner" when increasingly intense shocks occurred, the experimenter pressured the "teachers" to continue administering shocks. Some people withdrew from the study, but most of the participants continued to shock the learner. After the study, Milgram fully explained to his participants that, in fact, the "learner" was never shocked or in pain at all (Milgram, 1974).

Milgram's study provided important data on how easily decent people could be persuaded by the sheer force of a situation to do cruel things. What is more, Milgram conducted many replications and variations of his findings, which helped build knowledge about human social behavior. But was it worth the distress it exerted on the participants? One could ask the same of the Stanford Prison Experiment. The prison study, though dramatic, created much publicity but did not generate a great deal of scientific research. Although the prison experiment led to some reform in U.S. prisons, it is hard to know whether the deception of the participants and the emotional breakdowns some of them experienced was worth it. Do you think it was worthwhile?

ETHICAL RESEARCH WITH HUMANS

The Milgram study is one of the most widely discussed studies in the history of psychology. A number of psychologists were quite upset over the study and protested it on ethical grounds (Baumrind, 1964). The uproar led to the creation of explicit guidelines for the ethical treatment of human subjects. Today all psychological and medical researchers must adhere to the following guidelines:

1. *Informed consent:* Tell participants in general terms what the study is about, what they will do and how long it will take, what the known risks and benefits are, that they have the right to withdraw at any time without penalty, and whom to contact with questions. This information is provided in written form and the participant signs it, signifying consent. If a participant is under the age of 18, informed consent must be granted by a legal guardian. Informed consent is almost always required. It can be omitted only in situations such as completely anonymous surveys.

2. *Respect for persons:* Safeguard the dignity and autonomy of the individual and take extra precautions when dealing with study participants who are less likely to understand that their participation is voluntary, such as children.

3. *Beneficence:* Inform participants of costs and benefits of participation; minimize costs for participants and maximize benefits. For example, many have argued that the Milgram study was worth the distress (cost) it may have caused participants, for the benefit of the knowledge we have gained about how readily decent people can be led astray by powerful social situations. In fact, many of the participants said that they were grateful for this opportunity to gain knowledge abut themselves that they would have not predicted (Milgram, 1974).

4. *Privacy and confidentiality:* Protect the privacy of the participant, generally by keeping all responses confidential.

Confidentiality ensures that participants' identities are never directly connected with the data they provide in a study.

5. *Justice:* Benefits and costs must be distributed equally among participants.

In Milgram's study, participants were led to believe they were taking part in a learning study, when in fact they were taking part in a study on obedience to authority. Is this kind of deception ever justified? The answer (according to the American Psychological Association, APA) is that deception is to be avoided whenever possible but it is permissible if these conditions are met: it can be fully justified by its significant potential scientific, educational, or applied value; it is part of the research design; there is no alternative to deception; and full debriefing occurs afterward. **Debriefing** is the process of informing participants of the exact purposes of the study—including the hypotheses—revealing any and all deceptive practices and explaining why they were necessary to conduct the study and ultimately what the results of the study were. Debriefing is required to minimize any negative effects (e.g., distress) experienced as a result of the deception.

debriefing the explanation of the purposes of a study following data collection.

Deception comes in different shades and degrees. In the Stanford Prison Experiment, all participants were fully informed about the fact that they would be assigned the roles of a prisoner or a guard. In that sense there was no deception. But they were not informed of the details and the extent to which being in this study would be like being in a real prison world. They were not told upfront that if they were assigned to the "prisoner" role, they would be strip-searched. When they were taken from their homes, the "prisoners" were not told this was part of the study. Not informing participants of the research hypotheses may be deceptive, but not telling participants that they might experience physical pain or psychological distress is a much more severe form of deception and is not ethically permissible. Not revealing the hypotheses to participants beforehand not only is permissible but also is necessary to prevent biased and invalid responses.

Today, to ensure adherence to ethical guidelines, **institutional review boards (IRBs)** evaluate proposed research before it is conducted to make sure research involving humans does not cause undue harm or distress. Should Milgram's study have been permitted? Were his procedures ethical by today's standards? To this day, there are people who make strong cases both for and against the Milgram study on ethical grounds, as we have discussed. It is harder to justify what Zimbardo did in the prison experiment.

institutional review boards (IRBs) organizations that evaluate research proposals to make sure research involving humans does not cause undue harm or distress.

ETHICAL RESEARCH WITH ANIMALS

Human participants are generally protected by the ethical guidelines itemized above. But what about animals? They cannot consent, so how do we ethically treat animals in research?

The use of nonhuman species in psychological research is even more controversial than research with humans. There is a long history in psychology of conducting research on animals. Typically, such studies concern topics that are harder to explore in humans. We cannot, for instance, isolate human children from their parents to see what effect an impoverished environment has on brain development. Researchers have done so with animals. Biological psychology and learning are the areas of psychology that most often use animals for research. For instance, to determine what exactly a particular brain structure does, one needs to compare individuals who have healthy structures to

those who do not. With humans this might be done by studying the behavior of individuals with accidental brain injury or disease and comparing it to the behavior of normal humans. Injury and disease, however, never strike two people in precisely the same way, and so it is not possible to reach definite conclusions about the way the brain works by just looking at accidents and illness. Surgically removing the brain structure is another way to determine function, but this approach is obviously unethical with humans. In

Strict laws and ethical standards govern the treatment of animals used in research.

contrast, nonhuman animals, usually laboratory rats, offer the possibility of much more highly controlled studies of selective brain damage. For example, damage could be inflicted on part of a brain structure in one group of rats while another group is left alone. Then the rats' behaviors and abilities could be observed to see if there were any differences between the groups.

Animals cannot consent to research, and if they could, it is unlikely they would agree to any of this. Indeed, it is an ongoing debate as to how much animal research should be permissible at all. Because animal research has led to many treatments for disease (e.g., cancer, heart disease), as well as advances in understanding basic neuroscientific processes (such as the effects of living environment on brain cell growth), it is widely considered to be acceptable. Animal research is acceptable, that is, as long as the general conditions and treatment of the animals is humane.

If informed consent is the key to ethical treatment of human research participants, then humane treatment is the key to the ethical use of animal subjects. The standards for humane treatment of research animals involve complex legal issues. State and federal laws generally require housing the animals in clean, sanitary, and adequately sized structures. In addition, there are separate IRBs to evaluate proposals for animal research. They require researchers to ensure the animals' comfort, health, and humane treatment, which also means keeping discomfort, infection, illness and pain to an absolute minimum at all times. If a study requires euthanizing the animal, it must be done as painlessly as possible.

Despite the existence of legal and ethical safeguards, some animal rights groups argue that any and all animal research should be discontinued, unless it directly benefits the animals. They contend that computer modeling can give us much of the knowledge sought in animal studies and eliminates the need for research with animals. In addition, current brain imaging techniques reduce the need for sacrificing animals to examine their brain structures because they allow researchers to view images of the living human brain (Thompson et al., 2000).

As is true of all ethical issues, complex and legitimate opposing needs must be balanced in research. The need to know, understand, and treat illness must be balanced against the needs of participants and animals to have their well-being and rights protected at all times. Consequently, the debate and discussion about ethical treatment of humans and animals must be ongoing and evolving.

quick quiz 2.5: Research Ethics

1. When conducting research with humans, researchers
   a. never have to obtain informed consent if it interferes with the research
   b. almost always must obtain informed consent
   c. always must obtain informed consent
   d. usually need to obtain informed consent

2. Current guidelines on research ethics state that when studying humans, deception
   a. must be avoided whenever possible
   b. must be part of the research design
   c. must be followed by debriefing
   d. must be fully justified
   e. all of the above

3. Ethical guidelines for research with nonhuman animals state that
   a. informed consent is always required
   b. ethical and humane conditions must exist throughout the entire research process
   c. computer modeling must always be tried before research with animals
   d. deception can be used if fully justified

Answers can be found at the end of the chapter.

making connections
in psychological research

Can Experience Change the Brain?

Can enriching experiences actually improve brain function and/or make the brain grow faster? By looking at different research approaches to this topic and at some of the ethical issues involved, we can see why certain methods are chosen over others and get a sense of the cumulative nature of science.

In the early 1960s a group at the University of California, Berkeley, decided to study the effects of different environments on the brains of rats (Bennett et al., 1964; M. Rosenzweig et al., 1962). In numerous experimental studies, the researchers randomly assigned genetically similar rats to either enriched or impoverished environments for up to 30 days. The enriched environments included many opportunities and apparatus for play and activity, such as running wheels and tubes to climb, as well as food and water. The impoverished environments provided only food and water. As you might have guessed, the independent variable in these experiments was how enriched the environment was; the dependent variables were change in brain size and/or changes in the growth of brain cells. The researchers found that rats raised in enriched environments showed evidence of growth in brain tissue compared to

the animals reared in the impoverished environments. They also replicated their basic finding many times. By doing so, they established that rats raised in the enriched conditions did indeed develop more brain tissue and thicker cortexes. Moreover, because this finding was based on an experimental design with random assignment—the groups of rats were equivalent at the beginning of each experiment—we can conclude that enriching experience actually caused their brains to grow more.

These experiments all involved true experimental designs, in which the animals were randomly assigned to different environmental conditions, all aspects of the study were tightly controlled, and the animals were euthanized afterward to allow for detailed study of brain structure. One of the main reasons we study these phenomena in animals is to learn how these processes work in humans, but ethical limitations prevent human research. Thus, the animals serve as models for how human brain organization and function might be modified by experience in humans.

But do rats serve as good models for how things happen in humans? Although there are many similarities between rat and human brains, there are a multitude of differences in anatomy. This suggests that not everything about brain growth is identical between humans and rats and therefore rat brain organization is not a perfect model for understanding human brain organization.

Another criticism of the animal research on enrichment and brain growth is that what has been labeled as "enrichment" in animal models may indeed represent a more normal mode of activity and that the so-called standard, or more aptly named "impoverished," conditions are not at all like what an animal would experience in the wild and may actually impede normal growth. Ethical guidelines for the treatment of animals have been modified on the basis of the enrichment findings such that nonstimulating conditions are not considered acceptable, though so far only for primates.

Research on humans is necessary to know whether environmental enrichment causes changes in the human brain, but the ways in which we can study such processes in humans are limited. Clearly it would be unethical even to randomly assign babies to live in either enriched or impoverished environments for several years so that we could assess differences in their behavior or brain activity. Which research designs might be appropriate to address these questions with humans?

Probably the most rigorous design that one could

quasi-experimental design
research method similar to an experimental design except that it makes use of naturally occurring groups rather than randomly assigning subjects to groups.

apply in this context is a **quasi-experimental design,** which is much like an experimental design except that it makes use of naturally occurring groups rather than randomly assigning subjects to groups. For example, some humans grow up in more enriched environments than others, benefiting perhaps from specialized training or unique experiences.

Several recent quasi-experimental studies have focused on people who received intensive musical training—something beyond the normal level of experience or enrichment. According to studies of brain images, people who have received intensive musical training, especially those who started music training before age 7, have a thicker corpus callosum (the band of nerve fibers that connects the two halves of the brain) than nonmusicians (Schlaug et al., 1995). This finding means that musicians have more communication between the two sides of the brain than people who have not had such training. Further, brain imaging studies comparing the brains of experienced musicians with those of nonmusicians reveal increased brain growth relative to control subjects in regions associated with music-related skills (Schlaug et al., 1995). Another recent study reported that musicians have a larger cerebellum (an area involved in motor coordination) than nonmusicians (Hutchinson et al., 2003).

Early musical training not only develops a child's appreciation for music, but also correlates with increases in brain size relative to children who don't learn to play an instrument at a young age.

These findings suggest that musical training can change the brain, but because the researchers relied on naturally occurring groups and the groups were not matched, the results are correlational, but *not* causal. That is, we cannot conclude that musical training causes brain growth in particular areas of the brain. Only true experiments, with random assignment, allow us to draw conclusions about cause and effect, so any group differences observed in a quasi-experimental design cannot be attributed to a specific cause. Remember that correlation is not causation, but causation does require correlation.

quick quiz 2.6: Making Connections in Psychological Research

1. What is an enriched environment?
   a. a living situation that provides ample opportunity for play and activity
   b. a living environment that provides optimal nutritional enrichments as well as adequate sleeping space
   c. a living space with room and plenty of water
   d. a living situation with all of the latest toys and games

2. What is the most rigorous study design that can be used to study the effects of enrichment on brain development in humans?
   a. experimental design
   b. case study
   c. correlational design
   d. quasi-experimental design

Answers can be found at the end of the chapter.

chapter **review**

THE NATURE OF SCIENCE

- Science is about empirically testing our ideas and learning whether our understanding of the world is correct.

- The key attitudes of science are skepticism, openness to new ideas based on evidence, and intellectual honesty.

- The scientific method by which research is conducted can be summed up by OPTIC: Observing, Predicting, Testing, Interpreting, and Communicating. Scientists start with observations of the world, make predictions once they see a pattern, devise a study to test predictions, interpret results with the aid of statistics and decide whether the prediction was correct or not, and publish their work to clearly describe findings to others. These new findings lead to new predictions, and the whole process begins anew.

- Pseudoscience lacks cumulative progress, disregards empirical facts, lacks skepticism of its own assumptions, and vaguely describes how it came to its conclusions, which often stem from loose and distorted logic.

RESEARCH METHODS IN PSYCHOLOGY

- Psychologists use three types of research designs to test their ideas: descriptive designs, correlational designs, and experimental designs.

- In descriptive designs, researchers simply observe and describe what they see. They address the question, "What is X?" They don't manipulate anything or have any real predictions to test.

- In correlational designs researchers measure two or more things carefully to see whether or not they are related. They address the question, "Is X related to Y?" These designs use correlational statistics to interpret the results and to make and test hypotheses, but do not allow researchers to draw any conclusions about causality.

- Researchers use correlation coefficients to assess the strength and direction of association between two variables.

- In experimental designs, researchers randomly assign participants to conditions and carefully manipulate the predicted cause (independent variable), then look for differences in outcome (dependent variables). True experiments address the question: "Does X cause Y?"

COMMONLY USED MEASURES OF PSYCHOLOGICAL RESEARCH

- Psychological researchers draw on several types of tools to measure variables relevant to their research questions. These measures fall into three major categories: self-report, behavioral, and physiological.

- Self-reports are people's written or oral accounts of their thoughts, feelings, or actions.

- Behavioral measurements involve systematic observation of people's actions in either their normal life situations (naturalistic observation) or laboratory situations.

- Physiological measures include various types of measures of bodily responses. Each measure has strengths and weaknesses. By employing multiple measures, researchers offset the limitations of any given measure.

MAKING SENSE OF DATA WITH STATISTICS

- Descriptive statistics organize data for interpretation and help researchers evaluate their hypotheses. The mean is the arithmetic average of a set of data. The median is the score that separates the lower half of scores from the upper half.

- Variability is the spread between the lowest and highest values in a set of data. Variability is measured in terms of the standard deviation around the mean.

RESEARCH ETHICS

- Ethics are standards of right and wrong that guide people's behavior.

- Professional ethics have been developed to protect the rights of humans and animals who participate in psychological research. Researchers must obtain informed consent from human participants before a study begins. Animals cannot provide informed consent, but strict ethical guidelines exist to ensure humane living conditions and treatment.

MAKING CONNECTIONS IN PSYCHOLOGICAL RESEARCH

- Research on environmental enrichment and brain growth using experimental designs with animal models and correlational studies with humans illustrates how numerous methodological issues unfold in a given research area.

key **terms**

behavioral measures, p. 60

case study, p. 47

confounding variable, p. 54

control group, p. 53

correlation coefficient, p. 50

correlational designs, p. 50

debriefing, p. 68

dependent variable, p. 52

descriptive designs, p. 47

descriptive statistics, p. 63

double-blind studies, p. 55

effect size, p. 58

ethics, p. 66

experiment, p. 52

experimental group, p. 53

experimenter expectancy effects, p. 55

hypothesis, p. 41

independent variable, p. 52

institutional review boards (IRBs), p. 68

mean, p. 63

median, p. 63

meta-analysis, p. 58

mode, p. 63

multiple measurement, p. 62

naturalistic observation, p. 48

physiological measures, p. 61

placebo, p. 53

population, p. 45

pseudoscience, p. 43

quasi-experimental design, p. 71

random assignment, p. 53

replication, p. 43

representative sample, p. 49

research design, p. 45

samples, p. 46

scientific method, p. 41

self-fulfilling prophecy, p. 57

self-reports, p. 59

single-blind studies, p. 55

social desirability bias, p. 46

standard deviation, p. 63

statistics, p. 63

theory, p. 41

variable, p. 45

quick quiz **answers**

Quick Quiz 2.1: 1. d   2. b   3. a   4. c   **Quick Quiz 2.2:** 1. a   2. b   3. d   4. c   5. b
Quick Quiz 2.3: 1. b   2. a   3. d   4. d   **Quick Quiz 2.4:** 1. d   2. a   3. a
Quick Quiz 2.5: 1. b   2. e   3. b   **Quick Quiz 2.6:** 1. a   2. d

the **biology** of **behavior**

preview
questions

1 *What is the relationship between heredity and behavior?*

2 *How does the nervous system control what we do?*

3 *What does the structure of the brain have to do with psychology?*

4 *How does experience affect the brain?*

5 *What is the endocrine system and why is it important?*

T ake a look at the painting in Figure 3.1. It is pleasing, colorful, and nicely done. It features realistic color, perspective, and shadowing. It seems, perhaps, not extraordinary—except by virtue of its maker. He cannot see at all.

Born blind to an impoverished family in Turkey, Esref Armagan started drawing at a young age; later he began painting with oils and acrylics. Armagan has been actively painting for over 30 years. His work strikes us not only for its beauty but also for how it depicts objects in a way that a sighted person would see them. How can someone who has never seen anything in his life create beautiful paintings that depict realistic images? It seems as if his brain is doing something that his eyes cannot.

You can find a hint of how this is possible at the Tactile Dome, part of the Exploratorium in San Francisco. Once there, you enter a room full of common, recognizable objects ▶

▶ such as a cheese grater, an egg carton, and a sieve. You look at them and feel them. Then you proceed through a pitch-black tunnel. As you find your way through it by touch, you feel the common objects that you saw earlier. When you reach the end, you are prompted to think back and remember your way through the tunnel. Surprisingly, the memory of what you encountered along the path in the dark with your hands is visual! Your brain has taken a tactile experience and unwittingly converted it into a visual memory. How?

chapter
outline

The Tactile Dome and the skills of Esref Armagan both suggest that our experience of the world is not a direct representation of what is out there. The brain can change our experiences—give us visual memories for tactile experiences. The brain is both fixed and flexible in how it acts. While most of us use the rear portion of our brains to process visual information, Esref Armagan uses that area when he paints by the feel of his hands.

In this chapter and the one that follows, we will explore what is known about how the brain works, how it supports behavior, and how it is transformed by experience. Our main task in this chapter is to introduce the biological systems that are most relevant to a basic understanding of psychology. In so doing, we will look at the role of heredity and evolution in shaping the brain and behavior, explore the workings of the nervous system, and learn of the relationship between chemicals called hormones and behavior. ■

Genes and Behavior

We seldom have trouble accepting the idea that heredity is responsible for outward family resemblances, such as the shape of the nose and face, height, and the color of our hair and skin. But when it comes to behavior, many of us are uncomfortable with the idea that heredity might determine what we think and do. Yet heredity very much influences behavior and experience, although it does not operate on thought and behavior in a simple, deterministic way.

Before we can explore how heredity and behavior interact, we must know something about the structures and mechanisms involved in heredity. A **chromosome** is a cellular structure

chromosomes
a coiled-up thread of DNA.

FIGURE **3.1**

***BLUISH VASE* BY ESREF ARMAGAN, A BLIND PAINTER.** Besides being beautiful to look at, Armagan's vivid, realistic paintings and drawings challenge conventional thinking about the brain and its ability to adapt and overcome limitations imposed on it.

that holds our genetic information in threadlike strands of DNA. Humans have 23 pairs of chromosomes in the nucleus of each cell of the body, except red blood cells, which do not have nuclei. **DNA (deoxyribonucleic acid)**, the genetic material that makes up chromosomes, is a large coiled molecule that contains genes. **Genes** are small segments of DNA that contain information for producing proteins. These proteins in turn make up most chemicals and structures in the body (see Figure 3.2). Genes influence specific characteristics, such as height or hair color, by directing the synthesis of proteins. All of the genetic information contained in our DNA makes up our **genome.**

The fact that the individuals in a population are different from one another on a given trait—such as eye color, height, or personality—is a result of genetic differences. More specifically, genes within a population, or entire species, often take different forms. These different forms are known as **alleles** (Clark & Grunstein, 2000; Starr & Taggart, 2004). Individuals inherit one allele from each parent. Sometimes both alleles have the same form, but not always. Each gene in an allele pair can produce different characteristics. Take eye color, for example. The allele inherited from one parent may produce brown eyes, but the allele inherited from the other parent may produce blue eyes. Brown eyes result from a dominant gene. **Dominant genes** show their effect even if there is only one copy of that gene in the pair. So if you have one brown eye allele and one blue eye allele, chances are you will have brown eyes.

DNA (deoxyribonucleic acid)
a large molecule that contains genes.

genes
small segments of DNA that contain information for producing proteins.

genome
all the genetic information in DNA

alleles
different forms of a gene.

dominant genes
genes that show their effect even if there is only one allele for that trait in the pair.

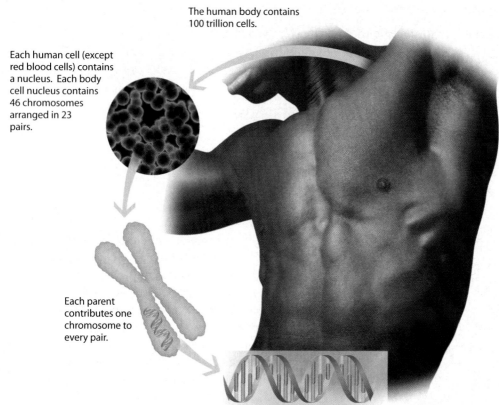

The human body contains 100 trillion cells.

Each human cell (except red blood cells) contains a nucleus. Each body cell nucleus contains 46 chromosomes arranged in 23 pairs.

Each parent contributes one chromosome to every pair.

Each chromosome contains numerous genes, segments of DNA that contain instructions to make proteins—the building blocks of life.

FIGURE **3.2**
DNA, CHROMOSOMES, AND THE HUMAN CELL. Every cell in the human body contains the same genetic material distributed in 23 pairs of chromosomes.

A **recessive gene** shows its effects only when both alleles are the same. Consequently, a person will have blue eyes only if he or she inherits an allele for blue eyes from each parent.

To understand how heredity affects behavior, psychologists turn to the science of **behavioral genetics.** Four principles of behavioral genetics are especially relevant in psychology:

1. The relationship between specific genes and behavior is complex.
2. Most specific behaviors derive from dozens or hundreds of genes—not one or two.
3. By studying twins and adoptees, behavioral geneticists may disentangle the contributions of heredity and environment to behavior.
4. The environment influences how and when genes affect behavior.

Let's consider each of these principles in turn.

THE COMPLEX CONNECTION BETWEEN GENES AND BEHAVIOR

The connection between genes and behavior is complex. To understand how genes influence behavior, we must abandon the notion of simple causation (Rutter, 2006). Genes seldom make behaviors a certainty. For example, no single gene causes anxiety. Anxiety is influenced by both genetic and environmental factors that make it more likely to trouble some people than others.

In a few cases, having a specific gene guarantees an outcome—such as the incurable neuromuscular disease called Huntington's disease—but these outcomes are primarily physical, not behavioral. Typically, a specific gene plays only a small part in creating a given behavior, and genetic influence itself is only part of the story. Environmental events such as smoking during pregnancy, early childhood experiences, stress or trauma, and enriched environments all interact with genes to make specific behaviors more or less likely.

POLYGENIC INFLUENCE ON BEHAVIOR

The second principle of behavioral genetics states that traits tend to be influenced by many genes (Clark & Grunstein, 2000; Hamer & Copeland, 1998). Relatively few human traits result from single genes. And, as stated above, they tend to be physical rather than behavioral characteristics. The hereditary passing on of traits determined by a single gene is known as **monogenic transmission.** Huntington's disease is an example of monogenic transmission.

However, the number of potential outcomes for most traits and behaviors is not small. There is wide variation in intelligence, for example. Numerous genes contribute to intelligence. When many genes interact to create a single characteristic, the process is known as **polygenic transmission.** Other examples of polygenic traits include skin color, personality traits (such as whether a person is likely to be adventurous), height, and weight (Clark & Grunstein, 2000; Ebstein, 2006).

recessive genes
genes that show their effects only when both alleles are the same.

behavioral genetics
the scientific study of the role of heredity in behavior.

connection
Genetics influence about 50% of the differences in performance on intelligence tests, leaving about the same amount to be explained by nongenetic influences.
See Chapter 10, p. 389.

monogenic transmission
the hereditary passing on of traits determined by a single gene.

polygenic transmission
the process by which many genes interact to create a single characteristic.

Actors Maggie and Jake Gyllenhaal inherited their blue eyes from their parents. Blue eyes are a recessive trait, which means that each parent must possess at least one allele for blue eyes.

GENES AND THE ENVIRONMENT

A third principle of behavioral genetics is that teasing apart and identifying genetic and environmental influences on behavior requires special techniques. The extent to which a characteristic is influenced by genetics is known as **heritability**. Researchers use twin studies, adoption studies, twin–adoption studies, and gene-by-environment studies to study heritability.

In order to tease apart the role of genes and environment on behavior experimentally, researchers would have to hold one of these factors constant while varying the other one. That is hard to do because, for obvious ethical reasons, researchers cannot assign people to grow up in the same or different environments. Nor can researchers assign people to be either genetically alike or different. Fortunately, nature does both of these things for us. Researchers take advantage of genetically similar and different people by studying twins, siblings, and unrelated individuals reared together or apart.

heritability
the extent to which a characteristic is influenced by genetics.

Twin Studies   Most of us know or have known at least one set of twins. Maybe it is hard to tell them apart because they look identical, or maybe they're different genders and would never be mistaken for each other. **Fraternal twins** develop from two different eggs fertilized by two different sperm, as are any two siblings born at separate times. Thus, genetically speaking, fraternal twins are no more alike or different than are non-twin brothers and sisters. They may be of the same sex or of different sexes. **Identical twins** develop from a single fertilized egg that splits into two independent cells. As a result, identical twins develop from two embryos with identical genetic information, and they must be of the same sex.

Fraternal and identical twins provide a natural population for research to determine how much of a trait is due to genetics and how much is due to environment. The logic of **twin studies**, studies comparing pairs of fraternal and identical twins, is straightforward. Fraternal twins share half as many genes on average as identical twins (50% compared to 100%). If a trait is genetically influenced, identical twins should be more similar in that trait than fraternal twins will be. If genetics play no role, identical twins will be no more alike than fraternal twins in that specific trait.

fraternal twins
twins that develop from two different eggs fertilized by two different sperm.

identical twins
twins that develop from a single fertilized egg that splits into two independent cells.

twin studies
research into hereditary influence comparing pairs of fraternal and identical twins.

Adoption Studies   Researchers have also studied adopted individuals and compared them to their biological and adoptive parents. Such studies are known as **adoption studies**. Adopted children share none of their genes but most of their environment with their adopted families. Offspring share 50% of their genes with each biological parent and none with their adoptive parents. Yet they share most of their environment with their adoptive parents and none (or little) with their biological parents. If environment is most influential, people will be more similar on a trait to their adoptive parents than to their biological parents. But if genetics is more influential, people will be more similar to their biological parents than to their adoptive parents. If both genetics and environment matter, people will display traits from their biological and adoptive parents. For

adoption studies
research into hereditary influence in which adopted people are compared to their biological and adoptive parents.

example, an adoption study on intelligence would support the power of the environment over genetics if adopted children were more like their adoptive parents than their biological parents in intelligence. In contrast, if adopted children are more similar to their biological parents than adoptive parents in intelligence, we might conclude that genetics are more powerful.

Twin-Adoption Studies

A problem inherent in twin studies is that because identical twins look and act more alike than do fraternal twins, they may also be treated more similarly than regular siblings. Thus, it can be difficult to untangle genetic from environmental effects on any given outcome. In addition, a problem with adoption studies is that they only include people who are 50% genetically similar (biological parents and offspring) and those who are 0% similar (adoptive parents and adoptees)—not those who are genetically identical. The best solution to both of these problems is to study twins, both identical and fraternal, who were raised apart (adopted) and those who were raised together. This is exactly what **twin-adoption studies** do.

The logic of the twin-adoption approach is simple yet powerful. Identical twins are 100% alike genetically, whereas fraternal twins, like all siblings, share only 50% of their genes. Adopted children and their adoptive parents and siblings share no genes. If genes play a strong role in a trait, then the greater the genetic similarity, the greater the similarity on the trait should be. That is, similarity should be strongest in identical twins reared together and next in identical twins reared apart. It should be modest in siblings and biological parent-offspring reared together. Similarity should be weakest in adopted siblings and adoptive parent-offspring. As we will see in later chapters, this pattern holds for intelligence, mental disorders, and even personality, suggesting a moderately strong genetic component to these outcomes.

twin-adoption studies
research into hereditary influence on twins, both identical and fraternal, who were raised apart (adopted) and who were raised together.

Gene-by-Environment Studies

A fourth technique in the study of heritability, **gene-by-environment interaction research**, allows researchers to assess how genetic differences interact with environment to produce certain behavior in some people but not in others (Moffitt, Caspi, & Rutter, 2005). Instead of using twins, family members, and adoptees to vary genetic similarity, gene-by-environment studies directly measure genetic variation in parts of the genome itself and examine how such variation interacts with different kinds of environments to produce different behaviors. Individuals do not differ in whether or not they have a gene, but rather in the form that gene takes. For example, the same gene in different people might vary in

gene-by-environment interaction research
a method of studying heritability by comparing genetic markers that allows researchers to assess how genetic differences interact with environment to produce certain behaviors in some people but not in others.

Twins form a natural population for teasing apart the influences of genetics and environment on development.

the number of particular DNA sequences it has. Some DNA sequences are long in some people and short in others. Differences in the length of DNA sequences represent a *genetic marker*. Researchers first have to locate these genetic markers from blood or saliva samples. Then they assess crucial environmental experiences such as trauma and stress in people with and without the genetic marker. Finally, they determine whether individuals with the genetic marker who were raised in a particular environment are more or less likely to develop some trait, such as extraversion, violence, high intelligence, or schizophrenia. For example, genetic markers interact with a stressful environment to make depression more likely in some people than in others. Researchers report that people who have a short form of a specific DNA sequence linked to depression are more likely to become depressed when under great stress than are individuals who have the long form of the same DNA sequence (Caspi et al., 2003; Kendler et al., 2005).

connection

How do stress and abuse interact with genes to increase vulnerability to depression?
See Chapter 15, p. 586.

EPIGENETICS: HOW THE ENVIRONMENT CHANGES GENE EXPRESSION

A fourth—and in many ways, the most important—principle of behavioral genetics is a relatively new one: Environmental events influence how and when genes are activated or deactivated. Genes can be changed by an individual's behaviors and experiences, and behaviors can be modified by genetic differences. This principle is seen most clearly in **epigenetics** (Rutter, 2006). Epigenetics concerns changes in the way genes get expressed—that is, are activated or deactivated—without changing the sequence of DNA. The food we eat, the drugs we take, and our exposure to certain chemicals in the environment are a few things that can have epigenetic consequences.

nature & nurture
A mother's behavior may influence the expression of genes in her offspring.

epigenetics concerns changes in the way genes are turned on or off without a change in the sequence of DNA.

Experience can turn genes on or off, a field of study known as epigenetics. Studies with rats suggest that parental nurturing may turn off genes that make a child vulnerable to stress.

Because of the need for detailed genetic analysis and for experimentally manipulating genes, epigenetic research tends to be conducted mostly with nonhumans, such as rats. Obese rats possess a specific gene that they pass on to their offspring, who also tend to be obese. However, if obese rats are fed a specific diet (for example, onions, beets, and garlic), they remain obese, but tend to have offspring that are normal weight. It turns out that particular diets can actually affect gene expression by turning on switches that attach to DNA and turn on or off the gene. This result offers a compelling illustration of epigenetics.

An equally compelling example of epigenetics is the effect of parental nurturing on gene expression. Nurturing behavior in rats can produce calmer, less-stressed offspring because genes that are involved in stress reactions are turned off (Weaver, Cervoini, & Champagne, 2004). Rats that lick their offspring (a nurturing behavior) set in motion changes that produce less stressed pups. Licking turns off a gene responsible for producing stress receptors in the growing brains of rat pups. Decreasing these stress receptors makes these pups calmer and less likely to become startled (Watters, 2006).

quick quiz 3.1: Genes and Behavior

1. Genes occur in pairs, or alternate forms of each other, called
   a. chromosomes
   b. alleles
   c. base-pairs
   d. ribosomes

2. Which specific research methodology allows researchers to untangle genetic from environmental effects on behavior?
   a. adoption studies
   b. twin studies
   c. twin–adoption studies
   d. foster care studies

3. Nurturing behavior in rats can produce calmer, less-stressed offspring because genes that are involved in stress reactions are turned off. This is an example of
   a. epigenetics
   b. genetic engineering
   c. recessive genes
   d. dominant genes

Answers can be found at the end of the chapter.

central nervous system (CNS)
the part of the nervous system that comprises the brain and spinal cord.

peripheral nervous system
the part of the nervous system that comprises all the nerve cells in the body outside the central nervous system.

somatic nervous system
nerve cells of the peripheral nervous system that transmit sensory information to the central nervous system (CNS) and those that transmit information from the CNS to the skeletal muscles.

The Nervous System

The human genome contains an estimated 25,000–35,000 genes (Rutter, 2006). At least half of these genes code for proteins in the brain, where they play a central role in seeing, hearing, thinking, memory, learning, movement, and all other behavior. The brain mediates all of our experiences and orchestrates our responses to those experiences.

The nervous system controls all the actions and automatic processes of the body. Ultimately, everything we experience and do results from the activity of nerve cells, which are organized in a net of circuits far more complex than any electrical system you could imagine. Let's look at the organization and basic elements of the nervous system and at how the nervous system transmits information.

ORGANIZATION OF THE NERVOUS SYSTEM

The human nervous system has two main parts and several components, as depicted in Figure 3.3. It is divided into the **central nervous system (CNS),** which includes the brain and spinal cord, and the **peripheral nervous system,** which consists of all the other nerve cells in the body. The peripheral nervous system includes the somatic nervous system and the autonomic nervous system. The **somatic nervous system** transmits sensory information to the brain and spinal cord and from the brain and spinal cord to the skeletal muscles. The **autonomic**

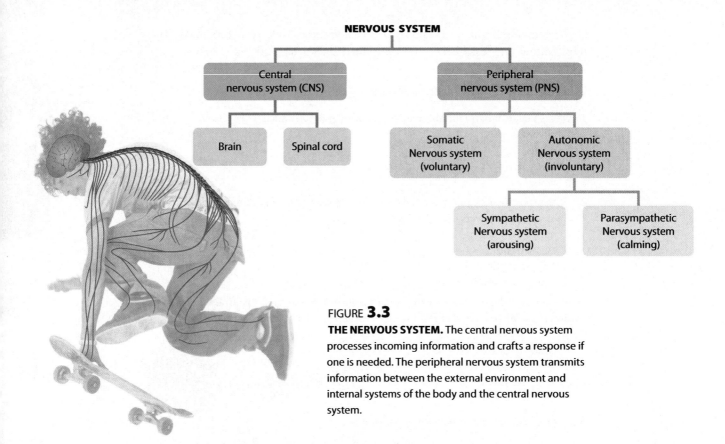

FIGURE **3.3**

THE NERVOUS SYSTEM. The central nervous system processes incoming information and crafts a response if one is needed. The peripheral nervous system transmits information between the external environment and internal systems of the body and the central nervous system.

nervous system (**ANS**) serves the involuntary systems of the body, such as the internal organs and glands.

Autonomic means "self-governing," and to a large extent the structures served by the autonomic nervous system control bodily processes over which we have little conscious control, such as changes in heart rate and blood pressure. The ANS has two main branches: the **sympathetic nervous system** and the **parasympathetic nervous system**. The nerves of these systems control muscles in organs such as the stomach, small intestine, and bladder and in glands such as the sweat glands. The sympathetic branch of the ANS is responsible for what the physiologist Walter Cannon (1939) labeled the *flight-or-fight response;* that is, it activates bodily systems in times of emergency. The main function of the sympathetic nervous system is activating the body, for example, by increasing the heart rate, dilating the pupils of the eyes, or inhibiting digestion. The function of the parasympathetic branch of the ANS is largely one of relaxation, or returning the body to a less active, restful state. All of the systems that are aroused by the sympathetic nervous system are relaxed by the parasympathetic nervous system (see Figure 3.4). Because of its effects on these various bodily systems, the ANS produces many of the physical sensations we experience during emotional arousal, such as a racing heart or sweaty palms.

THE CELLS OF THE NERVOUS SYSTEM: GLIAL CELLS AND NEURONS

Without a nervous system, we would have no sensory experiences—no seeing, hearing, touching, tasting, smelling, or feeling. We would also have no thoughts,

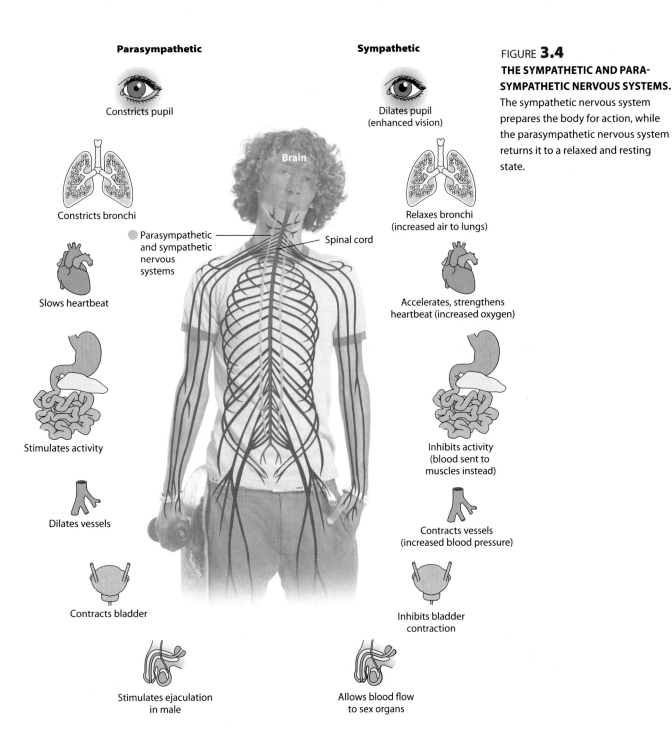

FIGURE **3.4**

THE SYMPATHETIC AND PARA-SYMPATHETIC NERVOUS SYSTEMS. The sympathetic nervous system prepares the body for action, while the parasympathetic nervous system returns it to a relaxed and resting state.

Parasympathetic

Constricts pupil

Constricts bronchi

Slows heartbeat

Stimulates activity

Dilates vessels

Contracts bladder

Stimulates ejaculation in male

Sympathetic

Dilates pupil (enhanced vision)

Relaxes bronchi (increased air to lungs)

Accelerates, strengthens heartbeat (increased oxygen)

Inhibits activity (blood sent to muscles instead)

Contracts vessels (increased blood pressure)

Inhibits bladder contraction

Allows blood flow to sex organs

Brain

Parasympathetic and sympathetic nervous systems

Spinal cord

memories, or emotions. Everything we sense or do is accomplished by means of nerve cells.

The central nervous system is made up of two types of cells: glial cells and neurons. *Glia* is the Greek word for glue. Indeed, **glial cells** serve the primary function of holding the CNS together. Specifically, they provide structural support, promote efficient communication between neurons, and remove cellular debris (Kandel, 2000). We now know that they also play an important role in communication between neurons as well (Allen & Barres, 2005; Pfrieger, 2002).

glial cells

central nervous system cells that provide structural support, promote efficient communication between neurons, and serve as scavengers, removing cellular debris.

Neurons are the cells that process and transmit information throughout the nervous system. Within the brain, neurons receive, integrate, and generate messages. By most estimates, there are more than 10 billion neurons in the human brain. Each neuron has approximately 10,000 connections to other neurons, making for literally trillions and trillions of neural connections in the human brain (Nauta & Feirtag, 1979; Hyman, 2005). Thus, it is understandable that some scientists consider the human brain to be the one of the most complex structures in the known universe. Over the last 125 years, three major principles of neuroscience have emerged concerning the neuron and how it communicates with other neurons (Kandel, 2006):

1. Neurons are the building blocks of the nervous system. All the major structures of the brain are composed of neurons.
2. Information travels within a neuron in the form of an electrical signal by action potentials.
3. Information is transmitted between neurons by means of chemicals called neurotransmitters.

Let's explore each of these principles to better understand the mechanisms of brain function and behavior.

The Structure and Types of Neurons
Whereas most cells in the body have a round shape, neurons are spidery, with long branches and projections. Neurons are so small they cannot be seen with the naked eye, and only a strong microscope can magnify them enough to be viewed and described. In the late 1800s, the Spanish anatomist Santiago Ramón y Cajal deciphered the precise nature and structure of nerve cells, which he named neurons. Cajal was an artist who, while studying anatomy for his drawing, became fascinated by the structure of the body. He then went on to study medicine. His ability to see, imagine, and draw came together in his observations of the neuron. It was Cajal who identified the three major parts of the neuron: cell body, dendrites, and axon. Indeed, Cajal's original sketch of these structures was an amazingly accurate representation.

Sensory and motor neurons working in concert with the brain make this sprinter's elegant strides possible.

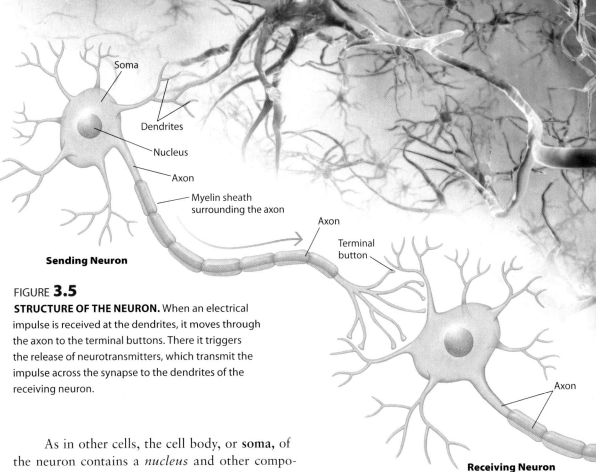

Soma

Dendrites

Nucleus

Axon

Myelin sheath
surrounding the axon

Axon

Terminal
button

Sending Neuron

Axon

Receiving Neuron

FIGURE **3.5**

STRUCTURE OF THE NEURON. When an electrical
impulse is received at the dendrites, it moves through
the axon to the terminal buttons. There it triggers
the release of neurotransmitters, which transmit the
impulse across the synapse to the dendrites of the
receiving neuron.

soma
the cell body of the
neuron.

axon
a long projection
that extends from
a neuron's soma; it
transmits electrical
impulses toward
the adjacent neu-
ron and stimulates
the release of
neurotransmitters.

dendrites
fingerlike projec-
tions from a
neuron's soma that
receive incoming
messages from
other neurons.

terminal buttons
little knobs at
the end of the
axon that contain
tiny sacs of
neurotransmitters.

sensory neurons
nerve cells that
receive incoming
sensory informa-
tion from the sense
organs (eye, ear,
skin, tongue, nose).

As in other cells, the cell body, or **soma,** of
the neuron contains a *nucleus* and other components needed for cell maintenance and function (see
Figure 3.5). Within the nucleus itself are the genes that
direct neural change and growth. Extending from the soma
is a long projection called the **axon,** which transmits electrical
impulses toward the adjacent neuron. On the other side of the soma are
the **dendrites,** fingerlike projections that receive incoming messages from other
neurons.

The axons of some neurons are wrapped in a fatty **myelin sheath.** Just like
rubber around an electrical wire, the myelin sheath insulates the axon so that
the impulse travels more efficiently and strengthens the connection to adjacent
neurons. The process of *myelination* is a gradual one that starts before birth
and continues into early adulthood (Fields, 2008). The junction between the
axon and the adjacent neuron is known as the **synapse.** At the end of the axon,
at each synapse, is a **terminal button** containing tiny sacs of neurotransmitters.
When an electrical impulse reaches the terminal button, it triggers the release of
neurotransmitter molecules into the gap between neurons, known as the *synaptic cleft.* The neurotransmitter carries the signal across the synaptic cleft to the
next neuron.

There are three kinds of neurons: sensory neurons, motor neurons, and
interneurons. **Sensory neurons** receive incoming sensory information from the
sense organs (eyes, ears, skin, tongue, and nose). Any sensation you receive—
anything you see, hear, touch, taste, or smell—activates sensory neurons, which
take the message to the brain for processing. **Motor neurons** take commands
from the brain and carry them to the muscles of the body. Each time you move
any muscle in your body, intentionally or unintentionally, motor neurons are at
work. Recently, researchers have identified motor neurons that are active when
we observe others performing an action as well as when we undertake the same

myelin sheath
the fatty substance
wrapped around
some axons, which
insulates the axon,
making the nerve
impulse travel
more efficiently.

synapse
the junction
between an axon
and the adjacent
neuron, where
information is
transmitted from
one neuron to
another.

motor neurons
nerve cells that
carry commands
for movement
from the brain to
the muscles of the
body.

action. Neurons that behave this way are called **mirror neurons,** and they appear to play an important role in learning (Rizzolatti & Craighero, 2004).

Interneurons communicate only with other neurons. Most interneurons connect neurons in one part of the brain with neurons in another part. Others receive information from sensory neurons and transmit it to motor neurons for action. So if you touched a sharp object, interneurons in the spinal cord would receive pain information from sensory neurons in your fingers and communicate it to motor neurons in the muscles of your arm so that you could pull your hand away. Interneurons are the most common kind of neuron in the brain, outnumbering sensory and motor neurons by at least 10 to 1 (Nauta & Feirtag, 1979).

connections
Mirror neurons support learning by imitation as well as empathy.
See Chapter 5, p. 197, Chapter 8, p. 323, and Chapter 14, p. 560.

mirror neurons
nerve cells that are active when we observe others performing an action as well as when we are performing the same action.

interneurons
neurons that communicate only with other neurons.

Neural Communication: The Action Potential

Neural communication is a two-step process. First, an impulse travels one way from the dendrites along the axon and away from the soma, a process that is both electrical and chemical. Second, the impulse releases chemicals at the tips of the neurons, which are released into the synaptic cleft to transmit the message to another neuron. The first process is known as an action potential, and the second is *neurotransmission,* which we discuss in the next section.

The **action potential** is the positively charged impulse that moves down an axon. This happens by virtue of changes in the neuron itself. The neuron, like all cells in the body, is surrounded by a membrane separating the fluid inside the cell from the fluid outside the cell. This membrane is somewhat permeable, which means that it lets only certain particles move through it. The fluid inside and outside the cell contains electrically charged particles called **ions.** Positively charged sodium and potassium ions and negatively charged chloride ions are the most common. There are also negatively charged proteins in the fluids inside the neuron. Negatively charged ions are called anions (A^-). Channels in the membrane of the neuron allow ions to flow back and forth from between the inside and outside of the cell (these channels are responsible for the membrane permeability). Some of these channels are always open. Others, called *voltage-dependent channels,* open only when an impulse is being transmitted. *Voltage-dependent* means that these channels or passages will open only when certain electrical conditions are met, as we will discuss shortly.

Because of the flow of ions into and out of the neuron, there is a difference in charge inside the cell compared to outside the cell at all times. In the resting state—that is, when no impulse is being transmitted—there is an excess of negatively charged particles inside the axon. The fluid outside the axon has a positive charge. This charge difference between the inside and outside of the neuron is known as a *potential.* When a neuron is in the resting state, the electrical charge difference between the inside and the outside of the axon is –70 millivolts (mV), where the minus sign indicates that the difference in charge is negative. This value is the **resting potential** of the neuronal membrane (see Figure 3.6a).

Neurons do not stay at rest, however. An incoming impulse—which may have been stimulated by events as different as pressure to the skin and the thought of a loved one—can temporarily change the potential. How does this happen? A message received from sense receptors in the skin or from other neurons can change the axonal membrane's permeability, especially to positively charged sodium ions. If an incoming impulse increases the positive charge inside the neuron to a certain threshold, the neuron becomes *depolarized* and fires an action potential. The sodium channels at the top of the axon fly open and

action potential
the impulse of positive charge that runs down an axon.

ions
chemically charged particles that predominate in bodily fluids; found both inside and outside cells.

resting potential
the difference in electrical charge between the inside and outside of the axon when the neuron is at rest.

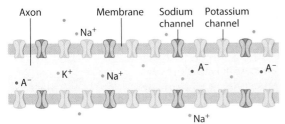

(a) Resting potential: Time 1.
In the resting neuron, the fluid outside the axon contains a higher concentration of positive ions than the inside of the axon, which contains many negatively charged anions (A–).

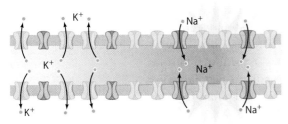

(b) Action potential: Time 2.
An action potential occurs in response to stimulation of the neuron. Sodium channels in the axonal membrane open, and positively charged sodium ions (NA$^+$) pour into the axon, temporarily raising the charge inside the axon up to +40 mV.

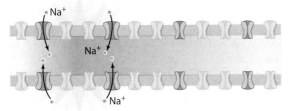

(c) Resting potential restored: Time 3.
As the impulse moves on down the axon, potassium (K$^+$) channels open, allowing more K$^+$ to flood out of the cell, restoring the negative resting potential (–70mV).

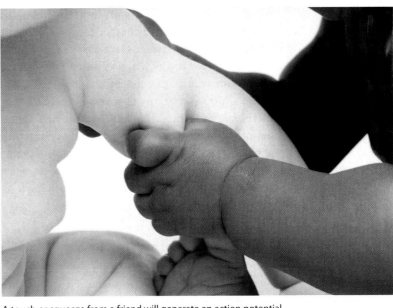

A touch or squeeze from a friend will generate an action potential.

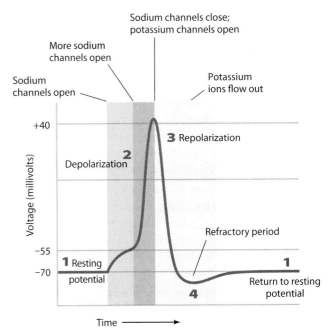

FIGURE **3.6**

Membrane and voltage changes in an action potential. Each change in membrane potential corresponds to specific changes in the axonal membrane.

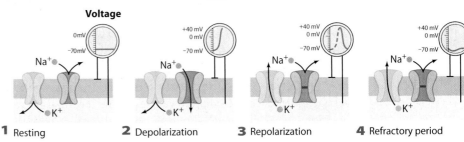

(d) This graph depicts the electrical changes that occur during each stage of an action potential (resting, depolarization, repolarization, refractory period). The top portion shows changes in voltage over time as measured by direct recording from single neurons in animal research. The lower four pictures show the membrane changes that correspond to each stage. The electrical changes of an action potential occur in a few thousandths of a second. During the refractory period, no new action potential can be generated.

positively charged sodium ions pour into the cell. The influx of sodium leads to a brief spike in positive charge, raising the membrane potential from –70 mV to +40 mV. This surge in positive charge is the action potential (see Figure 3.6b).

The creation of an action potential causes the sodium channels to close and potassium voltage-dependent channels to open (see Figure 3.6c). As positively charged potassium ions flow out of the cell, the membrane potential returns to its resting state of –70 mV. While the neuron is returning to its resting state, it temporarily becomes super negatively charged. During this brief period, known as the **refractory period,** the neuron cannot generate another action potential.

We can summarize the electrical changes in the neuron from resting to action potential to refractory period and back to the resting state as follows (see also Figure 3.6d):

1. Resting potential is –70mV.
2. If an incoming impulse causes sufficient depolarization, voltage-dependent sodium channels open and sodium ions flood into the neuron.
3. The influx of positively charged sodium ions quickly raises the membrane potential to +40 mV. This surge in positive charge inside the cell *is* the action potential.
4. When the membrane potential reaches +40 mV, the sodium channels close and potassium channels open. The outward flow of positively charged potassium ions restores the negative charge inside the cell.

This process is repeated all along the axonal membrane, as the impulse moves toward the synapse. As the action potential subsides in one area, it immediately depolarizes the next portion of membrane, causing sodium channels to open there, and continuing or *propagating* the action potential. Like a wave, the action potential travels along the axon, until it reaches the terminal buttons. In myelinated neurons, the action potential travels faster still, as depolarization occurs only at gaps in the myelin sheath and the action potential jumps from gap to gap (see Figure 3.5).

How fast are action potentials anyway? In the 1920s, Edgar Douglas Adrian measured and recorded individual action potentials of sensory neurons and confirmed a speed of about 100 feet per second (Kandel, 2006). Adrian's work also confirmed the existence of thresholds—a point of no return; once the charge inside the neuron exceeds this threshold, the action potential fires and it always fires with the same intensity. This is known as the **all-or-none principle.** In other words, an action potential either fires or it does not; there is no halfway. If the depolarization threshold is not reached, there is no action potential.

Communication Between Neurons: Neurotransmission

The arrival of an action potential at the terminal buttons of a neuron triggers the second phase in neural transmission—the release of neurotransmitters into the synaptic cleft to pass on the impulse to other neurons. Neurotransmitters are packaged in sacs called **synaptic vesicles** in the terminal button. When an action potential reaches the terminal button, the vesicles fuse with the cell membrane of the terminal and release neurotransmitter molecules into the synaptic cleft, where they may be taken up by receptors in the dendrites of adjacent neurons (Schwartz, 2000).

Neurotransmitters bind with receptors in the receiving, or *postsynaptic,* neuron in a lock-and-key type of arrangement (see Figure 3.7). There are different types of neurotransmitters, each of which binds only with a specific receptor. For example, some receptors bind only with the neurotransmitter acetylcholine.

refractory period
the span of time, after an action potential has been generated, when the neuron is returning to its resting state and the neuron cannot generate an action potential.

all-or-none principle
the idea that once the threshold has been crossed, an action potential either fires or it does not; there is no halfway.

synaptic vesicles
tiny sacs in the terminal buttons that contain neurotransmitters.

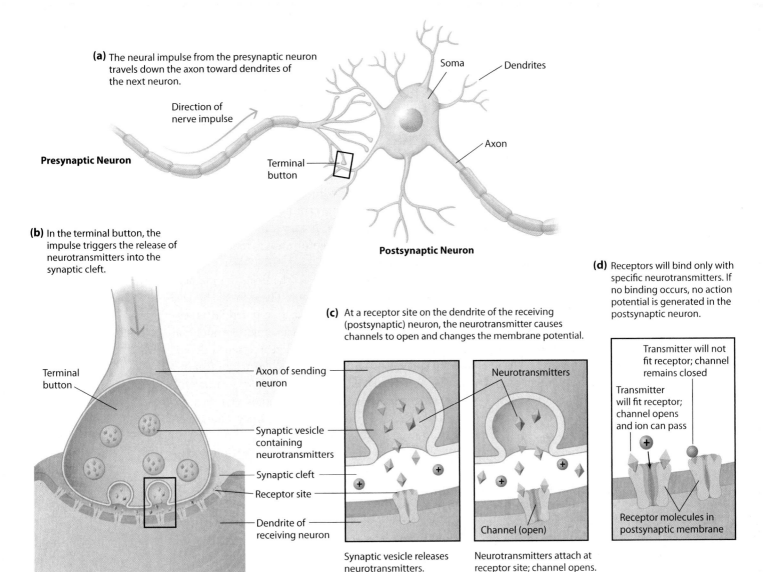

(a) The neural impulse from the presynaptic neuron travels down the axon toward dendrites of the next neuron.

Direction of nerve impulse

Presynaptic Neuron

Soma

Dendrites

Axon

Terminal button

Postsynaptic Neuron

(b) In the terminal button, the impulse triggers the release of neurotransmitters into the synaptic cleft.

Terminal button

Axon of sending neuron

Synaptic vesicle containing neurotransmitters

Synaptic cleft

Receptor site

Dendrite of receiving neuron

(c) At a receptor site on the dendrite of the receiving (postsynaptic) neuron, the neurotransmitter causes channels to open and changes the membrane potential.

Synaptic vesicle releases neurotransmitters.

Neurotransmitters

Channel (open)

Neurotransmitters attach at receptor site; channel opens.

(d) Receptors will bind only with specific neurotransmitters. If no binding occurs, no action potential is generated in the postsynaptic neuron.

Transmitter will not fit receptor; channel remains closed

Transmitter will fit receptor; channel opens and ion can pass

Receptor molecules in postsynaptic membrane

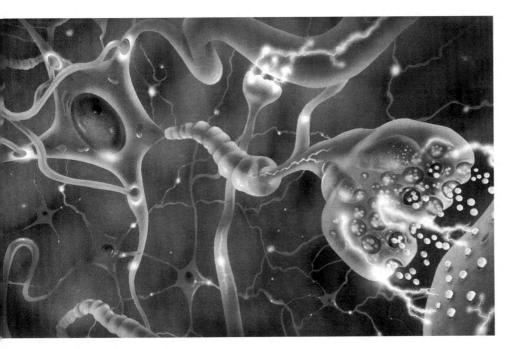

FIGURE **3.7**

HOW SYNAPSES AND NEUROTRANSMITTERS WORK. In (a) two neurons connect, a presynaptic neuron and a postsynaptic neuron. They do not touch, but terminal buttons in the presynaptic neuron form a synaptic cleft with the postsynaptic neuron. In (b) the synaptic cleft has been enlarged to show the synaptic vesicles that carry neurotransmitters. They release neurotransmitters into the cleft where they bind to receptor sites on the postsynaptic neuron. In (c) we see a further enlargement of the neurotransmitters being released into the synaptic cleft and binding to receptor sites in the postsynaptic neuron. To the left is a three-dimensional artistic interpretation of neurons in the brain.

If other neurotransmitters come in contact with acetylcholine receptors, they will not bind to them and no signal will be transmitted.

Not all of the neurotransmitter molecules that are released into the synaptic cleft bind with receptors. Usually, excess neurotransmitter remains in the synaptic cleft and needs to be removed. There are two ways to remove excess neurotransmitter from the synaptic cleft. One involves destruction by enzymes. In this process of **enzymatic degradation,** enzymes specific to that neurotransmitter bind with the neurotransmitter and destroy it. The second method, called **reuptake,** returns excess neurotransmitter to the sending, or *presynaptic*, neuron for storage in vesicles and future use. Another important point is that even the neurotransmitter that binds to the dendrites of the *postsynaptic* neuron does not stay there. Eventually it disengages from the receptor and floats away. This excess neurotransmitter must be removed as well.

After a neurotransmitter has bound to a receptor on the postsynaptic neuron, a series of changes occur in that neuron's cell membrane. These small changes in membrane potential are called **graded potentials.** Unlike action potentials, these are not "all-or-none." Rather, they affect the likelihood that an action potential will occur in the receiving neuron. Some neurotransmitters create graded potentials that decrease the likelihood that a neuron will fire. One such neurotransmitter is GABA (gamma-aminobutyric acid), and so it is called an *inhibitory* neurotransmitter. In contrast, other neurotransmitters create graded potentials that *increase* the likelihood of an action potential, and so they are called *excitatory*. Glutamate is the most common excitatory neurotransmitter in the brain.

Graded potentials increase or decrease the likelihood of an action potential occurring. The excitatory potentials bring the neuron closer to threshold (by making the potential more positive), while the inhibitory potentials bring it further away from threshold (by making the potential more negative). The soma in the postsynaptic neuron *integrates* the graded potentials in the postsynaptic neuron. If the integrated message from these graded potentials depolarizes the axon enough to cross the threshold, then an action potential will occur.

COMMON NEUROTRANSMITTERS

Within the past century, researchers have discovered at least 60 distinct neurotransmitters and learned what most of them do. Of the known neurotransmitters, the ones that have the most relevance for the study of human thought and behavior are acetylcholine, epinephrine, norepinephrine, dopamine, serotonin, GABA, and glutamate (see Figure 3.8). Neurotransmitters are found only in the brain. They are synthesized inside the neuron for the purpose of neurotransmission.

The neurotransmitter **acetylcholine (ACh)** controls muscle movement and plays a role in mental processes such as learning, memory, attention, sleeping, and dreaming. Whether ACh excites muscles or slows them down depends on what kind of receptor receives it. Furthermore, researchers have discovered that the degenerative memory disorder called Alzheimer's disease results at least partly from a decrease in ACh activity and that drugs that enhance ACh aid memory. ACh enhancers are now used to treat memory disorders such as Alzheimer's disease, and they seem to slow the progression of memory loss (Czech & Adessi, 2004; Selkoe, 2002).

Dopamine is released in response to behaviors that feel good or are rewarding to the person or animal. Eating a good meal, doing well on an exam, having an orgasm, or drinking a glass of water when really thirsty—each of these

reuptake
a way of removing excess neurotransmitter from the synapse, in which excess neurotransmitter is returned to the sending, or presynaptic, neuron for storage in vesicles and future use.

dopamine
a neurotransmitter released in response to behaviors that feel good or are rewarding to the person or animal; also involved in voluntary motor control.

enzymatic degradation
a way of removing excess neurotransmitter from the synapse, in which enzymes specific for that neurotransmitter bind with the neurotransmitter and destroy it.

graded potentials
small changes in membrane potential that by themselves are insufficient to trigger an action potential.

acetylcholine (ACh)
a neurotransmitter that controls muscle movement and plays a role in mental processes such as learning, memory, attention, sleeping, and dreaming.

	Major function
Acetylcholine	Slows ANS activity; eating, drinking, neuromuscular junction; involved in learning, memory, sleeping, and dreaming
Dopamine	Plays an important role in arousal, mood (especially positive mood); oversupply correlates with schizophrenia; voluntary muscle control
Epinephrine	Increases ANS activity; flight-or-fight response
Norepinephrine	Affects CNS activity; plays role in increasing alertness, attention
Serotonin	Plays role in mood, sleep, eating, temperature regulation; undersupply correlates with anxiety and depression
GABA	Is the major inhibitory neurotransmitter in the brain; slows CNS function; correlates with anxiety and intoxication
Glutamate	Is the most common excitatory neurotransmitter in the brain; involved in learning and memory; may be involved in schizophrenia.

behaviors stimulates dopamine activity in the brain (Hamer & Copeland, 1998). Because dopamine activity makes us feel good, many drug addictions involve increased dopamine activity. For instance, cocaine blocks the reuptake of dopamine into the presynaptic neuron, leaving it in the synaptic cleft for a longer period of time before it binds to receptors in the postsynaptic neuron (Bradberry, 2007). The result is a feeling of euphoria and pleasure.

Dopamine is also involved in voluntary motor control. One of the more dramatic examples of the effects of dopamine is Parkinson's disease. People who suffer from Parkinson's disease gradually lose the ability to control their muscles and shake—sometimes a little, sometimes a lot. Dopamine-producing neurons die in Parkinson's disease, and eventually the loss of motor control can cause death when muscles involved in swallowing shut down. Most treatments for Parkinson's include drugs that replace or mimic the effects of dopamine.

Epinephrine and **norepinephrine** primarily have energizing and arousing properties. (Epinephrine was formerly called "adrenaline," a term that is still widely used in everyday speech—"Wow! What an adrenaline rush!") Both epinephrine and norepinephrine are produced in the brain and by the adrenal glands that rest on the kidneys. Epinephrine tends not to affect mental states, whereas norepinephrine does increase mental arousal and alertness. When you are alert and paying attention, norepinephrine is involved. Norepinephrine activity also leads to physical arousal—increased heart rate and blood pressure. People who suffer from attention deficit hyperactivity disorder (ADHD) have unusually low norepinephrine levels, and treatment sometimes includes drugs to increase norepinephrine levels (Barr et al., 2002).

Serotonin has some of the most wide-ranging effects on behavior of any of the neurotransmitters. It is involved in dreaming and in controlling emotional states, especially anger, anxiety, and depression. People who are generally anxious and/or depressed often have low levels of serotonin (Caspi et al., 2003; Kendler et al., 2005). Thus, drugs that block the reuptake of serotonin are widely used to treat anxiety and depression.

epinephrine
also known as adrenaline, a neurotransmitter that arouses bodily systems (such as increasing heart rate).

serotonin
a neurotransmitter with wide-ranging effects: involved in dreaming and in controlling emotional states, especially anger, anxiety and depression.

norepinephrine
a neurotransmitter that plays an important role in the sympathetic nervous system, energizing bodily systems and increasing mental arousal and alertness.

People who are consistently angry and/or aggressive (especially males) often have abnormally low levels of serotonin as well. Researchers have shown that when drugs that increase serotonin are given to monkeys who are aggressive, their aggressive tendencies diminish (Suomi, 2005). Likewise, the street drug ecstasy (MDMA), which makes people feel social, affectionate, and euphoric, is known to stimulate extremely high levels of serotonin. Ironically, however, ecstasy ultimately interferes with the brain's ability to produce serotonin, and so depression can be an unpleasant side effect of the drug (de Win et al., 2004).

Gamma-aminobutyric acid, or **GABA,** is a major inhibitory neurotransmitter in the brain. Remember that inhibitory neurotransmitters tell the postsynaptic neurons *not* to fire. It slows CNS activity and is necessary for the regulation and control of neural activity. Without GABA the central nervous system would have no "brakes" and could run out of control. In fact, one theory about epilepsy is that GABA does not function properly in people who suffer from the disorder (Laschet et al., 2007). Many drugs classified as depressants, such as alcohol, increase GABA activity in the brain and lead to relaxing yet ultimately uncoordinated states. Because GABA inhibits much of the CNS activity that keeps us conscious, alert, and able to form memories, large amounts of alcohol consumption can lead to memory lapses, blackouts, loss of consciousness, and even death (White, 2003).

If GABA is the brain's major inhibiting neurotransmitter, then **glutamate** is its major excitatory one. Glutamate is important in learning, memory, neural processing, and brain development. More specifically, glutamate facilitates growth and change in neurons and the migration of neurons to different sites in the brain, all of which are basic processes of early brain development (Nadarajah & Parnavelas, 2002). It also amplifies certain neural signals, making some stimulation more important than others. Glutamate is crucial in early development of the brain because it helps neurons to grow. It also amplifies some neural transmissions so that a person can tell the difference between important and less important information. For example, which is more important? To notice a car skidding out of control in front of you or that your shoes are still the same color they were when you put them on this morning? Glutamate boosts the signals about the car.

connection

Common treatments for depression, which may result in part from a deficiency of the neurotransmitter serotonin, block the reuptake of serotonin at the synapse, making more of it available for binding with post-synaptic neurons.
See Chapter 16, p. 615.

connections

Glutamate does not function properly in people with schizophrenia, and so they become confused. Restoring glutamate function is the focus of new treatments for schizophrenia.
See Chapters 15, p. 594, and 16, p. 616.

GABA (gamma-aminobutyric acid) a major inhibitory neurotransmitter in the brain that tells postsynaptic neurons *not* to fire; it slows CNS activity and is necessary to regulate and control neural activity.

glutamate a major excitatory neurotransmitter in the brain that increases the likelihood that a postsynaptic neuron will fire; important in learning, memory, neural processing, and brain development.

The street drug known as ecstasy stimulates the release of high levels of the neurotransmitter serotonin, which makes people temporarily feel euphoric and affectionate. By interfering with the body's ability to produce serotonin, however, ecstasy eventually may cause depression in some people.

SUMMARY OF THE STEPS IN NEURAL TRANSMISSION

We have considered the complex phenomena of action potentials and neurotransmission and described the neurotransmitters involved in human thought and behavior. Before we discuss the major structures of the brain, let's take time to summarize the process of neural communication.

- The information in neural transmission always travels in one direction in the neuron—from the dendrites to the soma to the axon to the synapses. This process begins with information received from the sense organs or other neurons, which generate a nerve impulse.

- The dendrites are the first part of a neuron to receive a message from other neurons. That message, in the form of an electrical and chemical impulse, is then integrated in the soma. While being integrated in the soma, messages do not yet create an action potential.

- If the excitatory messages pass the threshold intensity, an action potential will occur, sending the nerve impulse down the axon. If the inhibitory messages win out, the likelihood of the postsynaptic neuron firing goes down.

- The nerve impulse, known as the action potential, travels down the axon, jumping from one space in the axon's myelin sheath to the next, because channels are opening and closing in the axon's membrane. Passing in and out of the membrane are ions, mostly sodium and potassium.

- This impulse of opening and closing channels travels like a wave down the length of the axon, where the electrical charge stimulates the release of neurotransmitter molecules in the cell's synapses and terminal buttons.

- The neurotransmitters are released into the space between neurons known as the synaptic cleft. Neurotransmitters released by the presynaptic neuron then connect with receptors in the membrane of the postsynaptic neuron.

- This connection or binding of neurotransmitter to receptor creates electrical changes in the postsynaptic neuron's cell membrane, at its dendrites. Some neurotransmitters tend to be excitatory (for example, glutamate) and increase the likelihood of an action potential. Others tend to be inhibitory (for example, GABA) and decrease the likelihood of an action potential.

- The transmission process is repeated in postsynaptic neurons, which now become presynaptic neurons.

quick quiz 3.2: The Nervous System

1. Which branch of the nervous system is responsible for the fight-or-flight response?
   a. the parasympathetic nervous system
   b. the somatic nervous system
   c. the central nervous system
   d. the sympathetic nervous system

2. The fingerlike projections on neurons that receive input from other neurons are called
   a. dendrites
   b. nuclei
   c. axons
   d. terminal buttons

3. What property of the neuron is most directly responsible for the changes that lead up to an action potential?
   a. sodium ions outside the cell
   b. its permeable membrane
   c. chloride ions inside the cell
   d. the flux of potassium ions

4. What is the most common excitatory neurotransmitter in the brain?
   a. GABA
   b. serotonin
   c. glutamate
   d. acetylcholine

Answers can be found at the end of the chapter.

The Brain

The brain is a collection of neurons and glial cells that controls all the major functions of the body; produces thoughts, emotions, and behavior; and makes us human. This jellylike mass at the top of the spine has been mapped and described in astonishing detail. Here we consider the evolution of the brain, look at key brain regions, and explore what is currently known about their specialized functions. At this point, the picture is still far from complete, and neuroscientists continue to piece it together.

EVOLUTION OF THE HUMAN BRAIN

Evolution provides a fundamental example of how biology and environment interact. As we discussed in Chapter 1, over long periods of time, nature selects traits and behavior that work well in a given environment. Recall the example of the moth population becoming more brown than green, as brown moths blended into their surroundings better and were more likely to survive and reproduce. This natural selection process gradually leads to big changes in living forms and structures—from cells to muscles to brains to new species.

The human brain has been shaped, via natural selection, by the world in which humans have lived. It is worth noting here that brains do not fossilize to allow a present-day analysis, but the skulls that hold them do. By looking at the size and shape of skulls from all animals and over very long time periods, scientists can glean something about how and when human brains evolved. The evolution of the human brain is a fascinating story. Although the details lie well beyond the scope of this book, we can

nature & nurture

The human brain has been shaped, via natural selection, by the world in which we have lived.

consider a general outline of brain evolution (Dunbar, 2001; Jerison, 2000; Klein, 1999).

Flatworms, a species that dates back about 500 million years, were probably the first organisms to have brains. Understand that the flatworm brain consists of scarcely more than a bundle of nerve cells. Within a few million years, the first primitive vertebrates (animals with backbones) appeared. They were jawless fish and they had a bigger mass of nerve cells than flatworms (Jerison, 2000). The first land animals came into existence around 450 million years ago and the first mammals around 200 million years ago. Land animals had more than a bundle of neurons above the spinal cord; they had complex brains with numerous structures. The first primates lived around 55 million years ago—10 million years after the dinosaurs went extinct (Jerison, 2000). Compared to other mammals, birds and reptiles, and fish, primates have relatively large amounts of brain cortex, allowing more complex thinking and problem solving.

The earliest ancestors of humans appeared in Africa about 6 million years ago. One of our closest evolutionary relatives, the Neanderthals (*Homo neanderthalensis*) lived from about 350,000 to 28,000 years ago, when they were replaced by our species (*Homo sapiens*). Neanderthals had brains slightly larger on average than those of modern humans (see Figure 3.9). Nevertheless,

From Neanderthal fossils, scientists have determined that this close ancestor of modern humans had a less complex brain along with many other distinctive anatomical features.

FIGURE **3.9**

EVOLUTION OF THE HUMAN BRAIN OVER THE LAST 4 MILLION YEARS. An early form of prehuman, Australopithecus, had a brain about one-third the size of the modern human (*H. sapiens*) brain. In general, the overall brain size has grown over the course of 4 million years. But note that Neanderthal's brain size was slightly larger than ours. Just as important as overall size for modern human thought and behavior is the relative enlargement of the frontal lobe area. This can be seen in the less sloped forehead of modern humans compared to their earlier ancestors.

Australopithecus
(4 million years ago)

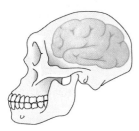

The brain capacity ranges from 450 to 650 cubic centimeters (cc).

Homo erectus
(1.6 million to 100,000 years ago)

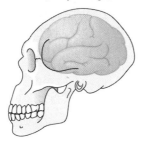

Further development of skull and jaw are evident and brain capacity is 900 cc.

Neanderthal
(350,000 to 28,000 years ago)

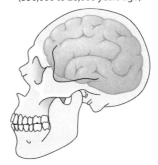

The human skull has now taken shape: the skull case has elongated to hold a complex brain of 1,450 cc.

Homo sapiens
(200,000 years ago to present)

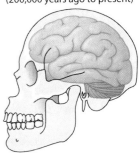

The deeply convoluted brain reflects growth in areas concerned with higher mental processes. (1,300 cc)

these folks did not produce highly complex tools, may have possessed very rudimentary language, and never made symbolic pieces of art, at least none that have been found. In other words, their brains were modern in size but not modern in function. It is possible, therefore, that the human brain took up to 100,000 years to become fully wired and complex, all the while staying the same overall size.

OVERVIEW OF BRAIN REGIONS

In evolutionary terms, then, the human brain is the result of a few hundred million years of natural selection. The three major regions of the brain, in order from earliest to develop to newest, are the hindbrain, the midbrain, and the forebrain (see Figure 3.10). By comparing the relative size of each region in distinct kinds of animals that vary in evolutionary age (see Figure 3.11), we gain an appreciation of how these regions evolved. When we compare brains from these different groups, we see an increase in size of the forebrain in humans and other primates (Jerison, 2000).

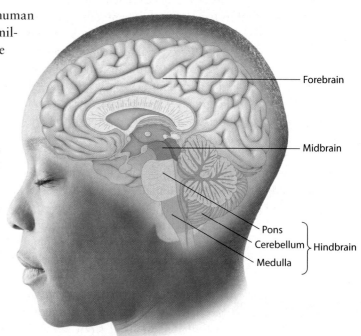

FIGURE **3.10**

THREE MAIN BRAIN STRUCTURES: HINDBRAIN, MIDBRAIN, AND FOREBRAIN. The hindbrain regulates breathing, heart rate, arousal, and other basic survival functions. The midbrain controls eye muscles, processes auditory and visual information, and initiates voluntary movement. The forebrain controls cognitive, sensory, and motor function and regulates temperature, reproductive function, eating, sleeping, and emotions.

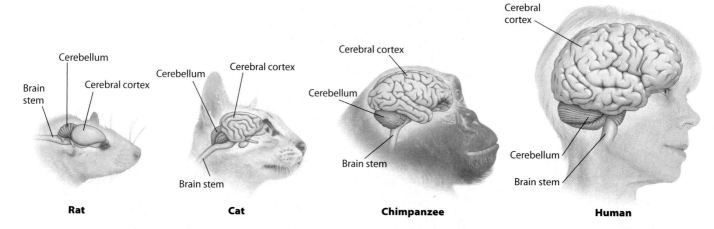

FIGURE **3.11**

BRAIN STRUCTURE OF MAMMALS. Mammals have many of the same brain structures, but of different relative sizes. Notice how much larger the cerebral cortex is in humans than in chimpanzees, cats, and rats. Also notice the increase in brain folds in primates.

pons

a hindbrain structure that serves as a bridge between lower brain regions and higher midbrain and forebrain activity.

cerebellum

a hindbrain structure involved in body movement, balance, coordination, fine-tuning motor skills, and cognitive activities such as learning and language.

Hindbrain The oldest brain region is the hindbrain, the region directly connected to the spinal cord. Hindbrain structures regulate breathing, heart rate, arousal, and other basic functions of survival. There are three main parts of the hindbrain: the medulla, the pons, and the cerebellum.

Extending directly from the spinal cord, the **medulla** regulates breathing, heart rate, and blood pressure. It also is involved in various kinds of reflexes, such as coughing, swallowing, sneezing, and vomiting. **Reflexes** are inborn and involuntary behaviors that are elicited by very specific stimuli (Amaral, 2000). **Pons** means "bridge," and the pons indeed serves as a bridge between lower brain regions and higher midbrain and forebrain activity. For instance, information about body movement and various sensations gets relayed from the cortex via the pons to the cerebellum. The **cerebellum**, or "little brain," contains more neurons than any other single part of the brain. It is responsible for body movement, balance, coordination, and fine motor skills like typing and piano playing. The cerebellum is also important in cognitive activities such as learning and language (Amaral, 2000).

medulla

a hindbrain structure that extends directly from the spinal cord; regulates breathing, heart rate, and blood pressure.

reflexes

inborn and involuntary behaviors—such as coughing, swallowing, sneezing, or vomiting—that are elicited by very specific stimuli.

Midbrain The next brain region to evolve after the hindbrain is the smallest of the three major areas, the midbrain. Different parts of the midbrain control the eye muscles, process auditory and visual information, and initiate voluntary movement of the body. People with Parkinson's disease have problems with midbrain functioning, due to the loss of neurons that use dopamine there, and so they shake uncontrollably. The midbrain, the medulla, and the pons together are sometimes referred to as the *brain stem*.

reticular formation

a network of nerve fibers that runs up through both the hindbrain and the midbrain; it is crucial to waking up and falling asleep.

Running through both the hindbrain and the midbrain is a network of nerves called the **reticular formation.** (Reticular means "netlike.") The reticular formation is crucial to waking up and falling asleep. In other words, it is involved in arousal. Among the first neuroscientists to study the reticular formation were Giuseppe Moruzzi and Horace Magoun. In a classic study, Moruzzi and Magoun electrically stimulated the reticular formation of a sleeping cat, and it immediately awoke. When they *lesioned*, or cut, its connection to higher brain systems, the cat went into a deep coma from which it never recovered. No kind of pinching or loud noises would arouse the cat (Moruzzi & Magoun, 1949).

Forebrain The last major brain region to evolve was the largest part of the human brain, the forebrain. It consists of the cerebrum and numerous other structures, including the thalamus and the limbic system. Collectively, the structures of the forebrain control cognitive, sensory, and motor function and regulate temperature, reproductive functions, eating, sleeping, and the display of emotions. Most forebrain structures are *bilateral*; that is, there are two of them, one on each side of the brain.

thalamus

a forebrain structure that receives information from the senses and relays it to the cerebral cortex for processing.

From the bottom up, the first forebrain structure is the **thalamus,** which receives input from the ears, eyes, skin, or taste buds and relays sensory information to the part of the cerebral cortex most responsible for processing that specific kind of sensory information. For this reason, the thalamus is often called a sensory relay station. In fact, olfaction (the sense of smell) appears to be the only sense that does not have a thalamic relay (Kay & Sherman, 2007).

Swallowing is one of a number of inborn reflexes.

The Limbic System   In the middle of the brain directly around the thalamus lies a set of structures that typically are referred to as the *limbic system* (see Figure 3.12). These are the hypothalamus, the hippocampus, the amygdala, and the cingulate gyrus. Together, the limbic system structures are important in emotion and motivation. However, there is some debate as to whether these structures work together as a system, so some neuroscientists suggest the term limbic system should be abandoned (LeDoux, 2003).

The structure directly below the thalamus is the hypothalamus. In fact, *hypo* simply means "below." The **hypothalamus** is the master regulator of almost all major drives and motives we have, including hunger, thirst, temperature, and sexual behavior. It also controls the pituitary gland, which is responsible for producing and/or controlling the hormones our body produces. Researchers in the 1940s discovered the role the hypothalamus plays in eating: lesioning one part of it produced overeating and obesity in animals, whereas lesioning another part of the hypothalamus led to undereating (Kupfermann, Kandel, & Iversen, 2000). The hypothalamus is also involved in sexual arousal (Karama et al., 2002).

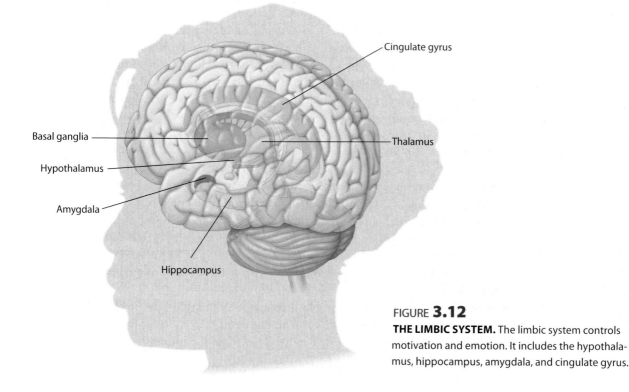

FIGURE **3.12**

THE LIMBIC SYSTEM. The limbic system controls motivation and emotion. It includes the hypothalamus, hippocampus, amygdala, and cingulate gyrus.

Wrapped around the thalamus is the **hippocampus,** which plays a vital role in learning and memory. Sensory information from the sense organs goes to the hippocampus. If these events are important enough, they are processed in the hippocampus and eventually established as lasting memories.

connection

Psychologists learned how essential the hippocampus is in memory and learning through a case study of "H. M.," who had this structure surgically removed on both sides of the brain.
See Chapter 7, p. 257.

As we will see throughout this book, it is well established that learning and memory change the brain. The brain structure most open to change is the hippocampus. It changes with learning and experience. To get a feel for the kind of research that demonstrates this capacity, let's look at recent research conducted with taxi cab drivers in London. Why study taxi drivers in London? They are an ideal group because of the tremendous amount of spatial and geographic knowledge they must have to pass a difficult cab driving test (Maguire, Woollett, & Spiers, 2006). They must know where all the streets are relative to other streets. When neuroscientists examined images of the hippocampus of taxi drivers compared to non–taxi drivers, they found the hippocampus was larger in the taxi drivers. Moreover, the researchers found it was not the stress and frequency of driving that led to this increase in the size of the hippocampus. When they compared bus drivers to taxi drivers, they still found a larger hippocampus in taxi drivers (Maguire et al., 2006). Because bus drivers drive the same route every day, they need to learn much less about the spatial layout of the city than taxi drivers. As this study suggests, learning changes the brain.

The **amygdala** is a small, almond-shaped structure located directly in front of the hippocampus. Anatomically, the amygdala has connections with many other areas of the brain, including the following structures, which appear to be involved in emotion and memory: the hypothalamus, which controls the autonomic nervous system; the hippocampus, which plays a crucial role in memory; the thalamus, which contains neurons that receive information from the sense organs; and the cerebral cortex. By virtue of its prime location, the amygdala plays a key role in determining the emotional significance of stimuli, especially when they evoke fear (Öhman, 2002; Phelps & LeDoux, 2005).

Studies in animals and humans show how important the amygdala is to emotions, especially fear. Electrical stimulation of the amygdala in cats makes them arch their backs in an angry-defensive manner, a response suggesting that anger and aggression involve the amygdala. Moreover, when aggressive monkeys had this region of the brain surgically lesioned, they became tame and nonaggressive. They also became fearless; for instance, rather than fleeing from snakes, they approached them (Klüver & Bucy 1937; Meunier & Bachevalier, 2002). Similarly, in cases of disease, injury, or surgery to the human amygdala, people often lose their aggressive

hippocampus
a limbic structure that wraps itself around the thalamus; plays a vital role in learning and memory.

amygdala
a small, almond-shaped structure located directly in front of the hippocampus; has connections with many important brain regions and is important for processing emotional information, especially that related to fear.

How does this picture make you feel? The structures of the limbic system play a key part in emotion and motivation.

tendencies. They become mild-mannered and nonhostile, yet they also become fearless. Additionally, our ability to recognize certain emotional expressions on other people's faces—especially fear—involves the amygdala (Adolphs et al., 2005; Morris et al. 1996). Without the amygdala, we cannot learn appropriate emotional responses, especially to potentially dangerous situations. The amygdala, along with the hypothalamus and other brain structures, is also activated during sexual arousal (Hamann et al., 2004; Karama et al., 2002).

One of the special functions of the amygdala is to recognize situations for which fear is an appropriate response.

The **cingulate gyrus**, meaning "belt ridge" in Latin, is a beltlike structure in the middle of the brain. Portions of the cingulate gyrus, in particular the front part, play an important role in attention and cognitive control (Botvinick, Cohen, & Carter, 2004). For instance, when people are first trying to figure out a difficult problem and preparing to solve it, parts of the cingulate gyrus are activated (Kounios et al., 2006). In contrast, this area seems to malfunction in people with schizophrenia, who do have major difficulties in focusing their attention (Carter et al., 1997).

cingulate gyrus
a beltlike structure in the middle of the brain that plays an important role in attention and cognitive control.

The **basal ganglia** are a collection of structures surrounding the thalamus that are involved in voluntary motor control. Several movement-related neurological disorders, including Parkinson's disease and Huntington's disease, affect the functioning of neurons in this region. Individuals who have these disorders suffer from jerky, often incontrollable movements. Often considered part of the limbic system, the basal ganglia reside on both sides of the thalamus and above the limbic system. They connect with the cerebral cortex, thalamus, and brain stem (Kopell et al., 2006).

basal ganglia
a collection of structures surrounding the thalamus involved in voluntary motor control.

connection

The amygdala plays a significant role in emotion.

See Chapter 11, p. 446.

The Cerebrum and Cerebral Cortex

The uppermost portion of the brain, the **cerebrum** is folded into convolutions, or folds, and divided into two large hemispheres. When most of us think about the human brain, we typically envision the outer layer, with all of its convolutions. This outer layer is called the **cerebral cortex**. In Latin, *cortex* means "tree bark," which the cerebral cortex resembles. The cortex is only about one-tenth to one-fifth of an inch thick, yet it is in this very thin layer of brain that much of human thought, planning, perception, and consciousness take place. In short, it is the site of all brain activity that makes us most human.

cerebrum
each of the large halves of the brain that are covered with convolutions, or folds.

cerebral cortex
the thin outer layer of the cerebrum, in which much of human thought, planning, perception, and consciousness takes place.

The cerebrum is composed of four large areas called *lobes*, each of which carries out distinct functions. These lobes are bilateral, which means they are located on both the left and right sides of the brain. The four lobes are the frontal, temporal, parietal, and occipital (see Figure 3.13). The *frontal lobes*, in the front of the brain, make up one-third of the area of the cerebral cortex. One important region of the frontal lobe, descending from the top of the head toward the center of the brain, is the *primary motor cortex*. One of the earliest discoveries about the brain's frontal lobes involved the motor cortex. In the 1860s, the German physiologist Eduard Hitzig had noticed while caring for wounded soldiers that touching the surface of a specific side of the brain caused the soldier's body to twitch on the opposite side. From these medical observations, Hitzig and his colleague Gustav Fritsch decided to more systematically test the idea that stimulating distinct parts of the brain would cause the body to move. They found a strip of the frontal cortex in dogs where mild electrical stimulation caused different parts of the body to move. And, indeed, as in the soldiers, stimulating one side of the brain caused the opposite part of the dog's body to move, a feature called *contralaterality*.

contralaterality
the fact that one side of the brain controls movement on the opposite side.

Hitzig and his colleagues also found that as they moved the stimulation along this strip of cortex and stimulated one small region at a time, different parts of the body would move. More importantly, they were the first researchers to discover and study something that few believed: Different parts of the cortex are responsible for different functions—a phenomenon known as *cortical localization*. They were also the first to study localization in a lab (Finger, 1994).

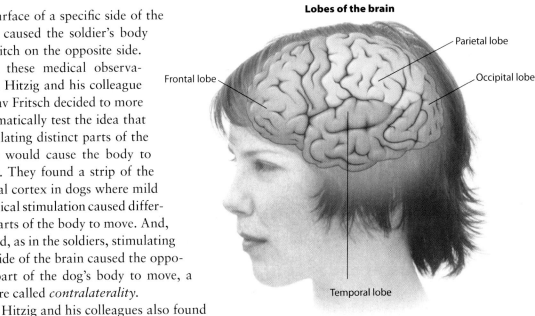

Lobes of the brain

Parietal lobe
Occipital lobe
Frontal lobe
Temporal lobe

FIGURE **3.13**
FOUR LOBES OF THE CEREBRAL CORTEX. Each of the four lobes has a counterpart on the opposite side of the brain. Most important for thinking, planning, and integrating the brain's activity are the frontal lobes. The parietal lobes integrate the sensation and perception of touch. Hearing is the main function of the temporal lobes, and visual information is processed in the occipital lobes.

The frontal lobe carries out many important functions, including attention, holding things in mind while we solve problems, planning, abstract thinking, control of impulses, creativity, and social awareness (Miller & Cummings, 1999). The frontal lobes are more interconnected with other brain regions than any other part of the brain and therefore are able to integrate much brain activity. This integration allows for insight and creative problem solving (Furster, 1999). For example, connections between the frontal lobes and the hippocampus and temporal lobe facilitate tasks involving language and memory, respectively. More than any other part of the brain, the frontal lobes are what make humans human.

It is not a coincidence that the frontal lobes are also the "youngest" part of the brain, evolving to a greater extent in modern humans than in any other species. Similarly, the frontal lobes are the last part of the brain to finish developing in individuals; they do not become mature until we reach our early 20s. One reason why children and teenagers act more impulsively than adults is that their frontal lobes are not fully developed.

Probably the most famous story in neuroscience comes from the first case study of frontal lobe involvement in impulse control and personality (Macmillan, 2000). In September 1848, a 25-year-old railroad foreman, Phineas Gage, was laying railroad ties. While hammering a tamping iron (an iron bar), Gage accidentally ignited gun powder used to lay the track and it exploded. The iron bar shot upward, entered Gage's left cheek, and exited through the top of his skull

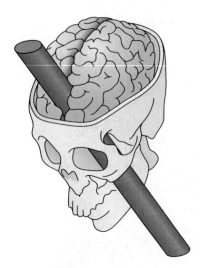

FIGURE **3.14**
PHINEAS GAGE'S ACCIDENT.
Miraculously, Gage survived, but his personality changed dramatically as a result of the injury to his frontal lobe.

after passing through his frontal lobe (see Figure 3.14). The iron bar was traveling so fast that it moved cleanly through Gage's head and landed 25 feet away. Miraculously, not only did Gage survive—but he never even lost consciousness!

Although not severely injured physically (other than the hole in his brain), Gage suffered immediate and obvious changes to his personality. Before the accident, he had been a mild-mannered but clever businessman. After the accident he was stubborn, impulsive, and argumentative, and at times he would say offensive things. Gage's accident was one of the first documented cases of marked personality change following an injury to the frontal lobes.

The *parietal lobes*, which make up the top and rear sections of the brain, play an important role in the sensation and perception of touch. The frontmost portion of the parietal lobes is the *somatosensory cortex*. When different parts of the body are touched, different parts of this strip of cortex are activated. The somatosensory cortex lies directly behind the motor cortex of the frontal lobe. In fact, these two regions are "twins." The areas of the motor and somatosensory cortexes that govern specific parts of the body are parallel to and directly next to each other (see Figure 3.15). For example, the part of the motor cortex involved in moving the lips is directly opposite the region of the sensory cortex where we sense that our lips are being touched.

The *temporal lobes* lie directly below the frontal and parietal lobes and right behind the ears. The temporal lobes have many different functions, but the main one is hearing. The temporal lobes house the *auditory cortex,* where sound information arrives from the thalamus for processing. Here, we "hear" our mother's voice, a symphony, an approaching car, or any other sound. The temporal lobes also house and connect with the hippocampus and amygdala, and so are also involved in memory and emotion.

In the rear of the brain lie the *occipital lobes*. The optic nerve travels from the eye to the thalamus and then to the occipital lobes—specifically, to the *primary visual cortex*. Visual information is processed in the visual cortex; it is here where we "see" and "imagine." Neuroscientists have discovered that different neurons in the visual cortex are activated when we see horizontal lines, diagonal lines, and vertical lines. In other words, individual neurons are specialized for the many different aspects of vision, including shape, color, shadow, light, and orientation (Wurtz & Kandel, 2000).

insula
a small structure inside the cerebrum that plays an important role in the perception of bodily sensations, emotional states, empathy, and addictive behavior.

The **insula** is a small structure that resides deep inside the cerebrum, in the area that separates the temporal lobe from the parietal lobe. The insula is active in the perception of bodily sensations, emotional states, empathy, and addictive behavior (Damasio, 2000; Naqvi et al., 2007). It communicates with structures of the limbic system and higher brain areas involved in decision making. The insula also plays a key role in our awareness of our body as our own (Tsakiris et al., 2007).

Cerebral Hemispheres   The human cerebrum is divided into two equal *hemispheres*. Although they look similar, the hemispheres differ in shape, size, and function. In general terms, the left hemisphere processes information in a more focused and analytic manner, whereas the right hemisphere integrates information in a more holistic, or broader, manner (Beeman & Bowden, 2000). Insights and solutions to ideas are more likely to occur in the right hemisphere.

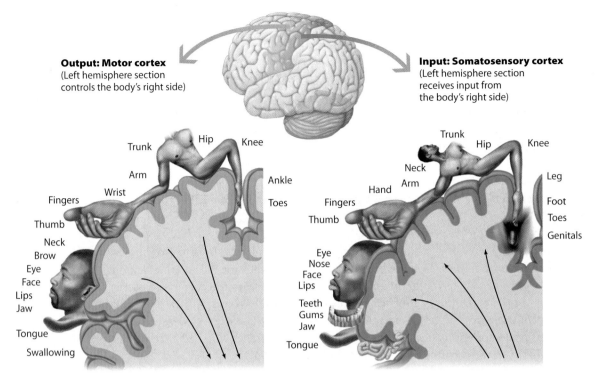

Output: Motor cortex
(Left hemisphere section controls the body's right side)

Input: Somatosensory cortex
(Left hemisphere section receives input from the body's right side)

FIGURE **3.15**

MOTOR AND SOMATOSENSORY CORTEXES OF THE BRAIN. Note that the regions of the motor and somatosensory cortexes are "twins." The face, lips, or toes, for example, activate the same areas of both cortexes. The arrows going down into the lower brain region represent motor neurons and the arrows coming up into the somatosensory cortex correspond to sensory neurons.

corpus callosum
the nerve fibers that connect the two hemispheres of the brain.

The hemispheres do not operate independently, however. The **corpus callosum,** a thick band of nerve fibers connecting the two hemispheres of the brain, provides a channel for extensive communication between hemispheres in both logical and creative tasks.

Perhaps the best-known and biggest functional difference between the cerebral hemispheres is in language. Speech and language comprehension involve two separate regions in the left hemisphere.

The French physician Paul Broca is credited with being the first "neuropsychologist." He deserves this title because his work in the early 1860s demonstrated for the first time that specific parts of the brain controlled particular behaviors (Kandel, 2006). Broca studied a man who had suffered a stroke. This man could understand language, but he could not speak in grammatical sentences. He had a type of **aphasia,** a deficit in the ability to speak or comprehend language. After the man died, Broca performed an autopsy and found that a cyst had damaged the man's left hemisphere. A small region in the left frontal lobe had been damaged, and Broca inferred that this area must be responsible for a person's ability to speak. Broca went on to discover similar damage in eight other aphasia patients (Pinker, 1994). These clinical findings have been confirmed by modern brain imaging techniques: People with aphasia often have damage or lesions in the same region of the left frontal lobe. This region is commonly referred to as **Broca's area,** and this type of aphasia is known as Broca's aphasia. Broca's area is responsible for the ability to produce speech.

aphasia
deficit in the ability to speak or comprehend language.

Broca's area
an area in the left frontal lobe responsible for the ability to produce speech.

Wernicke's area
an area deep in the left temporal lobe responsible for the ability to speak in meaning-ful sentences and to comprehend the meaning of speech.

About 20 years after Broca found the area of the brain now named for him, a German physiologist, Carl Wernicke, discovered that damage to another region of the left hemisphere created a different language problem. This area of the left temporal lobe, now called **Wernicke's area,** is responsible for speech com-prehension. Wernicke's aphasia, in contrast to Broca's aphasia, results in fluent, grammatical streams of speech that lack meaning. For instance, a patient with this disorder who was asked why he was in the hospital responded: "Boy, I'm sweating. I'm awfully nervous, you know, once in awhile I get caught up, I can't mention the tarripoi, a month ago, quite a little, I've done a lot well, I impose a lot, while, on the other hand, you know what I mean, I have to run around, look it over, trebbin and all that sort of stuff" (as quoted in Pinker, 1994, p. 316).

Communication Between the Hemispheres

As we have seen, the two hemispheres of the brain do not operate independently. Information moves between both sides of the brain by way of the corpus callosum. All communication between one side of the brain and the other travels across the corpus callosum.

In the early 1960s a former prisoner of war from World War II developed epileptic seizures as a result of a failed parachute jump. The seizures were so severe that his doctor approached Roger Sperry, a local researcher who had begun to do research on the corpus callosum, for help (Finger, 1994).

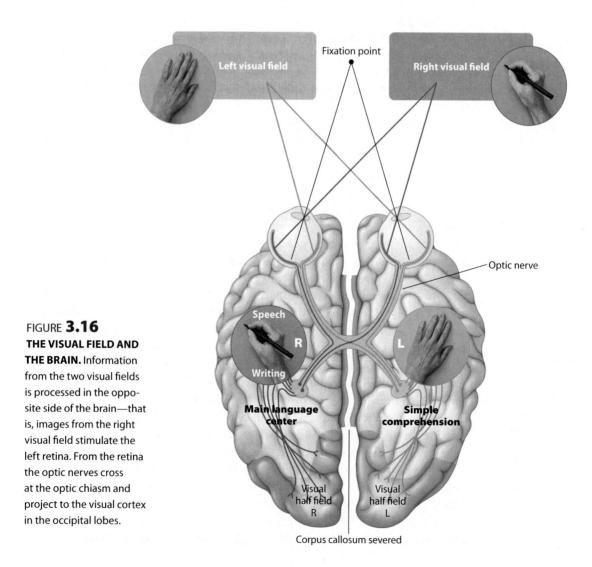

FIGURE **3.16**
THE VISUAL FIELD AND THE BRAIN. Information from the two visual fields is processed in the oppo-site side of the brain—that is, images from the right visual field stimulate the left retina. From the retina the optic nerves cross at the optic chiasm and project to the visual cortex in the occipital lobes.

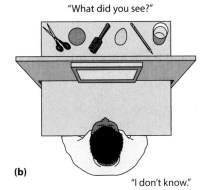

Picture of hairbrush flashed on screen

"What did you see?"

"With your left hand, select the object you saw from those behind the screen."

(a)

(b)

"I don't know."

(c)

FIGURE **3.17**

PERCEPTION AND LANGUAGE IN A SPLIT-BRAIN PATIENT. In (a) a person who has had an operation to cut the corpus callosum is shown an object (hairbrush) to her left visual field. In (b), when asked what she saw, she cannot say, because her language production center (Broca's area) is in her left hemisphere. Because the image is shown to her left visual field, only her right visual cortex perceives it. With a split corpus callosum, there is no way for that information to cross from the right hemisphere to the left. So she is unable to say what she saw. In (c), however, she is able to pick up the object she saw with her *left* hand. Why her left hand? Because it is controlled by her right hemisphere, which did in fact perceive the brush.

Previous medical evidence had suggested that cutting the bundle of nerves between the two hemispheres could stop epileptic seizures. Because the war veteran's seizures had become life threatening, he underwent the surgery under Sperry's guidance and it was very successful. Not only did the man's seizures stop, but there was also no noticeable change in his personality or intelligence. However, Sperry and his colleagues soon discovered a fascinating problem. The man could not name things that were presented to his left visual field, but he could do so with things presented to his right visual field. Why?

Recall that language—both speech and comprehension—resides in the left hemisphere of the human brain. In addition, information from our right visual field (the right portion of the visual scope of each eye) goes to the left occipital cortex, while information from the left visual field (the left portion of the visual scope of each eye) goes to the right occipital cortex (see Figure 3.16 on p. 106). But, because the war veteran had had his corpus callosum cut, the information from the left visual field could not get transferred to the language centers in the left hemisphere. He could, however, consistently pick up with his *left* hand the image he saw! Thus, because the right hemisphere (where the image was projected) controls the left side of the body, he could move his hand to the correct object (see Figure 3.17). This *split-brain research* shows that we can know something even if we cannot name it (Sperry, Gazzaniga, & Bogen, 1969).

BRAIN PLASTICITY AND NEUROGENESIS

When scientists began mapping the brain in the late 19th century, they did so by stimulating various brain regions in animals and observing the behavioral changes that such stimulation caused; they then diagrammed the locations of functions in the cerebral cortex (Kandel, 2006). Such mapping contributed to the notion that brain function was fixed. Certain brain regions had certain functions and that was that. But as far back as the early 20th century, researchers had stimulated different places on the motor cortex in several different monkeys and had found that maps generated from such stimulation varied from monkey to monkey. They were as individual as fingerprints.

A decade or so later, other neuroscientists mapped the motor cortexes of several monkeys many times during a 4-month period. They found that neural areas corresponding to the movement of specific fingers changed to reflect changes in the animal's patterns of movement over that time period (Jenkins et al., 1990). By the 1970s, there was evidence that learning occurs through synaptic change.

These findings were only the tip of the iceberg. Since the 1990s, numerous principles of brain plasticity have emerged (Perry, 2002). First and most generally, **neuroplasticity** is the brain's ability to adopt new functions, reorganize itself, or make new neural connections throughout life, as a function of experience. Second, almost every major structure of the neuron is capable of experience-based change. Third, not all regions of the brain are equally plastic. For example, the part of the brain most involved in learning, the hippocampus, is more plastic than just about any other part of the brain. And fourth, brain plasticity varies with age, being strongest in infancy and early childhood and gradually decreasing with age. Yet, at no time in our lives does the brain lose its ability to grow new neurons. Neuroplasticity occurs in all stages of life, though the different parts of the brain are not equally plastic at all times. The childhood brain is more plastic than the adult brain. The four principles of brain plasticity are summarized in Figure 3.18.

Experience-based change in the nervous system occurs in several ways. Most common are the formation of new neurons, the growth of dendrites in existing neurons, and the formation of new synapses. The process of developing new neurons is known as **neurogenesis.** The growth and formation of new dendrites is called **arborization** (from the Latin *arbor*, or "tree"), because dendrites are like branches on a tree. Probably the best-known example of neuroplasticity, however, is the process known as **synaptogenesis,** the formation of entirely new synapses or connections with other neurons that is the basis of learning.

Although these principles of neuroplasticity are universal—that is, apply to everyone—some of the strongest evidence for them comes out of research on people with different kinds of sensory deficits, such as blindness or deafness. It is in deafness and blindness that we see most clearly how flexible the brain really is. Brain function and localization vary considerably on the basis of the experience of the individual brain.

In most hearing people, the area that is called the *auditory cortex* processes sound. Although it is labeled by its function, anatomically the auditory cortex is actually a section of the temporal lobe. It is called the auditory cortex because the sensory neurons from the inner ear come here. But if those neurons

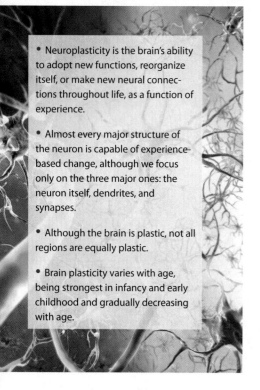

- Neuroplasticity is the brain's ability to adopt new functions, reorganize itself, or make new neural connections throughout life, as a function of experience.

- Almost every major structure of the neuron is capable of experience-based change, although we focus only on the three major ones: the neuron itself, dendrites, and synapses.

- Although the brain is plastic, not all regions are equally plastic.

- Brain plasticity varies with age, being strongest in infancy and early childhood and gradually decreasing with age.

FIGURE **3.18**
FOUR PRINCIPLES OF BRAIN PLASTICITY.

neuroplasticity
the brain's ability to adopt new functions, reorganize itself, or make new neural connections throughout life, as a function of experience.

connection
If a person is not exposed to language much before mid- to late childhood, the ability to speak is limited because the brain loses some of its plasticity as we age.
See Chapter 9, p. 339.

neurogenesis
the development of new neurons.

arborization
the growth and formation of new dendrites.

synaptogenesis
the formation of entirely new synapses or connections with other neurons.

don't pick up any sounds, what does this area of the brain do? Nothing? What a waste of brain tissue that would be.

For centuries scientists and ordinary people have observed that deaf people see better than hearing people and that blind people hear better than sighted people. The neuroscientist Helen Neville always thought there must be truth to these observations. In the process of testing these assumptions, she discovered that—overall—blind people are not better at hearing. They are not more sensitive to softer sounds than sighted people. Similarly, deaf people do not excel at all kinds of vision, nor are they able to see fainter images than do hearing people.

What Neville found, however, was that deaf and blind people are more expert in peripheral sensory experiences. That is, deaf people have better *peripheral* vision than sighted people—they are better at seeing things "out of the corner of their eyes" (Bavelier et al., 2000). They have better motion detection as well, and this also seems to be processed by the auditory cortex. Just as deaf people see better at the periphery, those who are blind don't hear better overall, but their *peripheral* hearing—hearing for things around the edges of a sound field (rather than the center)—is better than that of sighted people. And these peripheral sounds are processed by the visual cortex (Bavelier et al., 2000). According to Neville, "This was some of the first evidence that brain specializations such as auditory cortex are not anatomically determined" (Neville, as quoted in Begley, 2007, p. 84). In short, by virtue of its natural plasticity, the brain compensates for deficits in one sensory modality by reorganizing and rewiring unused regions to take on new functions.

nature & nurture

In blind people, the brain compensates for deficits in vision by reorganizing and rewiring the visual cortex to process sound.

quick quiz 3.3: The Brain

1. This region of the brain was the last to evolve. It is also the biggest part of the brain.
   a. cerebellum
   b. forebrain
   c. hindbrain
   d. pons

2. Which limbic structure plays a crucial role in fear?
   a. hypothalamus
   b. basal ganglia
   c. amygdala
   d. hippocampus

3. Where is the somatosensory cortex?
   a. in the occipital lobes
   b. in the frontal lobes
   c. in the temporal lobes
   d. in the parietal lobes

Answers can be found at the end of the chapter.

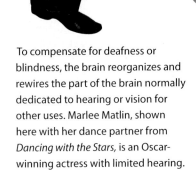

To compensate for deafness or blindness, the brain reorganizes and rewires the part of the brain normally dedicated to hearing or vision for other uses. Marlee Matlin, shown here with her dance partner from *Dancing with the Stars*, is an Oscar-winning actress with limited hearing.

breaking new ground
Neurogenesis in the Adult Brain

Neurons are unique cells in the body. Unlike many other cells, including hair, blood, or skin cells, nerve cells do not grow and die on an hourly basis. Nor do they reproduce. Because of these two facts, discovered by the Spanish physician and Nobel Prize winner Ramón y Cajal more than 100 years ago, the prevailing wisdom was that neurons are incapable of growth, at least after early childhood.

These observations led Cajal to put forth the *neuron doctrine,* which declared that neurons do not regenerate. Until the 1990s, researchers and physicians alike accepted the idea that once a region of the brain was damaged, its function was lost forever. All neural growth and change were understood to be limited to fetal and childhood development, and the adult brain did not change.

EVIDENCE OF NEURON GROWTH

By the early 1960s, an accumulation of evidence began to suggest that adult brains do change. Perhaps the first empirical demonstration of neurogenesis occurred when neuroscientists detected evidence of cell division (evidence of growth) in the brains of adult rats (Bryans, 1959).

In the early 1960s, Joseph Altman published a series of ground-breaking studies with adult rats and cats in scientific journals. Armed with a new cell-labeling technique, Altman found evidence of the growth of new neurons—neurogenesis—in several brain areas that are crucial for learning and memory (Altman & Das, 1966; Gross, 2000). Even though these appeared in prestigious journals, however, Altman's findings were almost completely ignored or discounted. Why? He was working alone and he was a little-known researcher who violated the dogma, or strongly accepted view.

As often happens with ideas that radically challenge basic assumptions and long-held beliefs, neuroscientists and others either trivialized or ignored Altman's findings of adult neurogenesis. What does it take for a movement to change a well-entrenched, century-old idea? Three scientific events took place during the 1980s and 1990s that finally turned the tide of belief. First, a series of studies on birds showed exceptional neuronal growth in many areas of the adult avian brain, including the hippocampus (Nottebohm, 1985). Second, there was increasing evidence for the formation of new synaptic connections in the brains of rats when they were raised in enriched environments, more so than normally occurs with development (Comery et al., 1996). For example, rats that lived in cages with playmates and wheels to run on and toys showed more dendritic growth than those who lived alone in sparse cages (Rosenzweig & Bennett, 1969). Third, in the 1990s, researchers began to find solid evidence for neurogenesis in one particular region of the hippocampus in adult rats, monkeys, and humans. Neurogenesis was no longer something seen only in birds and rats. There was no more denying that neuronal growth occurs in humans.

ENVIRONMENTAL EFFECTS ON NEURON GROWTH

One of the key figures in demonstrating new neural growth in adult primates has been Elizabeth Gould. She and her colleagues have compared rates of neurogenesis and synaptic growth in the brains of primates living in naturalistic settings with those living in lab cages. The naturalistic settings simulated a wild environment, with natural vegetation where the animals could search for food, among other activities. The brains of the animals that lived in these environmentally complex settings showed brain growth in areas important for thinking and feeling. They also had higher rates of neurogenesis and more connections between neurons than the animals reared in cages. In other studies, Gould and her colleagues found that stress and impoverished environments resulted in less neurogenesis in mammals (Mirescu & Gould, 2006; Mirescu et al., 2006).

The person most responsible for demonstrating neurogenesis in humans is Fred "Rusty" Gage (a cousin of the famous Phineas Gage) (Gage, 2002). How? You can guess that researchers cannot train humans and then slice open their brains to see if neural growth occurred. Furthermore, brain imaging techniques that we currently use cannot detect the growth of new cells. One technique, however, lends itself to testing whether new nerve cells grow in the human brain. It involves injecting people with a substance called BrdU, which is incorporated into dividing cells so that they can be identified.

Although it is not legally ethical to inject healthy people with BrdU, Gage and his colleague Peter Erikkson knew that some cancer patients receive this injection as part of their therapy. Because it identifies new cells, it is used to track how aggressively cancerous tumors are growing. After some patients who had been injected with BrdU died, Gage and Erikkson examined their hippocampus tissue. Based on the presence of BrdU, they found new cells in the adult human hippocampus (Begley, 2007; Erikkson et al., 1998). In fact, it was the same part of the hippocampus that earlier had shown the greatest neuronal growth in rats and monkeys.

Because of the onslaught of findings demonstrating neurogenesis in adult animals during the 1990s, the dogma of no new neural growth finally died. Now we know that neurons and their dendrites and synapses change, grow, and die in both young and old animals—including humans—depending on the kind of stimulation they receive from the outside world. To learn about a recently accepted approach to repairing brain damage by stimulating neurogenesis, see "Psychology in the Real World" on pp. 112–113.

quick quiz 3.4: Neurogenesis in the Adult Brain

1. The brain's ability to adopt new functions, reorganize itself, and make new neural connections is known as
   a. neuroplasticity
   b. neurogenesis
   c. the neuron doctrine
   d. localization of function

2. In what region of the human brain is there the most evidence of neurogenesis?
   a. hypothalamus
   b. frontal cortex
   c. amygdala
   d. hippocampus

Answers can be found at the end of the chapter.

Animals reared in naturalistic settings have higher rates of neurogenesis than those reared in cages.

111

Using Progesterone to Treat Brain Injury

For many years, Donald Stein conducted research that fell outside the accepted dogma of neuroscience. His work—focusing on recovery from brain damage—threatened the notion that brain tissue is fixed and irreplaceable. According to Cajal's neuron doctrine—discussed in the text—once brain tissue has been damaged, it cannot be repaired. Two decades ago Stein found—and has continued to amass evidence over the years since then—that the female sex hormone progesterone helps the injured brain repair itself.

In his early research with brain-damaged rats, Stein saw that many (though not all) of the female rats recovered faster than males. He wondered if female sex hormones might be responsible for the difference in recovery times. Further studies helped Stein show that progesterone, a female sex hormone that is released in significant amounts during pregnancy and has a protective effect on the fetus,

may help heal the injured brain. Actually, progesterone is a steroid released by neurons in the brains of both men and women. Stein conducted many experiments in which he damaged rat brain tissue and then manipulated the amount of progesterone given immediately after injury.

At first, no one paid attention to Stein's revolutionary findings. Stein forged ahead with his work anyway, compelled by what the data showed him. His progressive, cumulative finding was that progesterone helps the brain repair itself after injury (Roof et al., 1996; Roof et al., 1994; Stein, Wright, & Kellerman, in press).

Despite continuing to publish his finding in first-rate journals, for many years Stein had difficulty funding his research. Nevertheless, he persisted by working in small labs on shoestring budgets, building his reputation on his mainstream work in memory (Burton, 2007). Finally, people at Emory University—including emergency medicine physician David Wright—showed interest in his work. Wright and Arthur Kellerman suggested conducting a small clinical trial on humans with brain damage. Until then, all efforts

Measuring the Brain

To be able to look into the brain as it is working was a long-time dream of philosophers and scientists. In the last few decades, this has become possible. At least three distinct techniques are now commonly used to measure brain activity in psychological research.

ELECTROENCEPHALOGRAPHY

electroencephalography (EEG) a method for measuring brain activity in which the electrical activity of the brain is recorded from electrodes placed on a person's scalp.

Researchers use **electroencephalography (EEG)** to record the electrical activity of the brain. The procedure involves placing electrodes on a person's scalp. The electrodes, metal disks attached to wires, are usually mounted in a fabric cap that fits snugly over the head. Typically, the person is conducting certain tasks while electrical activity is recorded. EEG is superior to other brain imaging techniques in showing *when* brain activity occurs. It is not very accurate at indicating precisely *where* activity occurs (see Figure 3.19).

The **event-related potential (ERP)** is a special technique that extracts electrical activity from raw EEG data to measure cognitive processes. To examine

event-related potential (ERP) a special technique that extracts electrical activity from raw EEG data to measure cognitive processes.

Bob Woodruff, left, and his wife Lee. Woodruff suffered a traumatic brain injury while reporting on the Iraq war in 2006.

to repair brain damage had been at best ineffective and at worst harmful. Wright, Kellerman, Stein, and colleagues (2007) studied 100 people who came into the emergency room with traumatic brain injury. Patients were randomly assigned either to get treatment as usual or to get a large amount of progesterone. The researchers found that 30 days after injury, those who had received progesterone therapy were more likely to have survived and recovered than those on standard therapy.

Stein's work and the studies of others indicate that progesterone acts via several mechanisms to protect and repair the brain. It can protect or rebuild the *blood-brain barrier* (a membrane that protects the brain from chemicals circulating in the bloodstream), reduce or offset fluid accumulation and swelling of the brain after injury, and limit neuron death (O'Connor, Cernak, & Vink, 2005; Stein et al., in press).

Stein's research and other studies on naturally occurring steroids in the brain have led to more study of the roles of such steroids in brain development and function, as well as in behavior (Mellon, 2007). These substances may play an important role in neuroplasticity (Benarroch, 2007; Plassart-Schiess & Baulieu, 2001). Meanwhile, progesterone therapy shows great promise as a treatment for brain injury, a devastating condition that previously held a very poor prognosis for nearly all those who sustain such injuries.

ERPs, one gathers electrical recordings from an EGG cap on research participants who are performing cognitive or emotional tasks, such as trying to attend to an object on a computer screen, remember a list of words, or view emotionally charged slides. Typically, raw EGG data provide a summary of all the electrical activity in the brain that happens at a particular time. Generally this level of detail is fine for measuring states of wakefulness, for example. But you need more temporal precision if you want to see a brain reaction, say, to a particular stimulus, such as a flashing light or a line. To examine ERPs, researchers use a special averaging process that allows them to filter out all electrical

FIGURE **3.19**
ELECTRO-ENCEPHALOG-RAPHY (EEG). One of the authors (Erika) in an EEG cap for a study on brain activity and facial expression of emotion. The dots on her face allow for video motion capture of facial expression changes.

activity except the activity that is related to the stimulus the person is processing in a controlled experiment.

Because they are based on EEG, ERPs provide excellent temporal resolution (they show brain activity linked with psychological tasks almost immediately in time) but poor spatial resolution. Spatial resolution involves how tiny an area can be pinpointed as being active at a certain time. Two other techniques provide better spatial resolution than EEG: MRI and PET.

MAGNETIC RESONANCE IMAGING (MRI) AND FUNCTIONAL MRI (fMRI)

magnetic resonance imaging (MRI) brain imaging technique that uses magnetic fields to produce detailed images of the structure of the brain and other soft tissues.

MRI stands for **magnetic resonance imaging.** MRI uses magnetic fields to produce very finely detailed images of the structure of the brain and other soft tissues. In MRI, the patient lies on a platform or bed that slides into a tube surrounded by a circular magnet. The magnet, along with radio waves, is used to produce a signal that is then processed by computer. The computer then produces an image with an amazing level of detail (see Figure 3.20). MRI provides static pictures, and it is very useful for looking at structures and abnormalities in structures, such as when someone is injured. MRI does not tell us anything about activity, just structures.

FIGURE **3.20**
BRAIN IMAGING TECHNOLOGY. MRI equipment (right) takes very clear, detailed images of soft tissue, including the brain, but it doesn't record brain activity. Both PET scans and fMRI, in contrast, highlight brain activity.

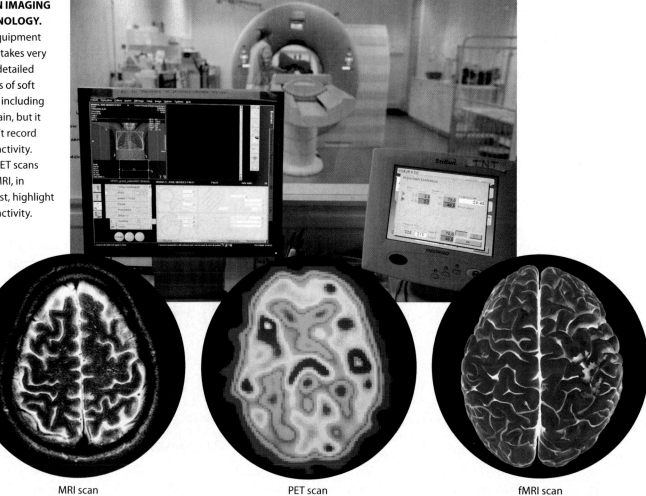

MRI scan   PET scan   fMRI scan

functional magnetic resonance imaging (fMRI)
brain imaging technique that uses magnetic fields to produce detailed images of activity in areas of the brain and other soft tissues.

A variation on MRI, **functional MRI (fMRI)**, does, however, tell us about brain activity. Images from fMRI tell us where activity in the brain is occurring during particular tasks by tracking blood oxygen use in brain tissue, as shown in Figure 3.20. In this way, researchers can see which areas of the brain are using the most oxygen (and presumably are most active) during certain tasks (Casey, Davidson, & Rosen, 2002; Lagopoulos, 2007). When people perform different tasks while they are being scanned, the researchers can distinguish from high-resolution images which areas "light up" or are active during the task. To be sure, they are indirect images of activity based on how the brain uses oxygen rather than a direct "read-out" of nerve impulses.

Although fMRI provides a much better measure of *where* activity occurs than EEG does, it is not without drawbacks. For one thing, it is very expensive. Also, it does not provide very precise measures of *when* activation occurs in response to a particular stimulus or task. It is not entirely clear exactly how directly fMRI images reflect underlying neural activity (Lagopoulos, 2007). Some studies suggest a fairly direct correlation with processing in certain cortical areas (Logothetis et al., 2001). As such, fMRI findings should always be interpreted with care.

POSITRON EMISSION TOMOGRAPHY (PET)

positron emission tomography (PET)
brain imaging technique that measures blood flow to active areas in the brain.

Positron Emission Tomography (PET) measures blood flow to brain areas in the active brain (see Figure 3.20). From these measurements researchers and doctors can determine which brain areas are active during certain situations. PET involves injecting the participant or patient with a harmless radioactive form of oxygen (or glucose). The brain then takes up the oxygen during cell metabolism. Thanks to the radioactive *label* on the oxygen, scanners and computers can be used to create images of the brain regions using that oxygen during a certain task. Although the results are very informative, the use of radioactive substances means PET is not risk-free. fMRI is a much safer way to image metabolism in the brain.

quick quiz 3.5: Measuring the Brain

1. Which brain measurement technique best shows *when* neural activity has occurred?
   a. PET
   b. MRI
   c. EEG
   d. fMRI

2. Which form of brain measurement requires the use of radioactive substances?
   a. PET
   b. MRI
   c. EEG
   d. fMRI

Answers can be found at the end of the chapter.

endocrine system
system of glands that secrete and regulate hormones in the body.

The Endocrine System

hormones
chemicals, secreted by glands, that travel in the bloodstream and carry messages to tissues and organs all over the body.

In the nervous system, neurons communicate information electrochemically by means of membrane changes and neurotransmitters released into synaptic cleft. In the **endocrine system**, glands secrete chemicals called **hormones**, which travel through the bloodstream to tissues and organs all over the body and regulate

FIGURE **3.21**

THE ENDOCRINE SYSTEM. The endocrine system consists of numerous glands found throughout the body. The pancreas, for example, releases insulin, which is important in transporting sugars (glucose) from the bloodstream into the cells. Cells then use the glucose as their energy source. The thyroid gland regulates metabolism.

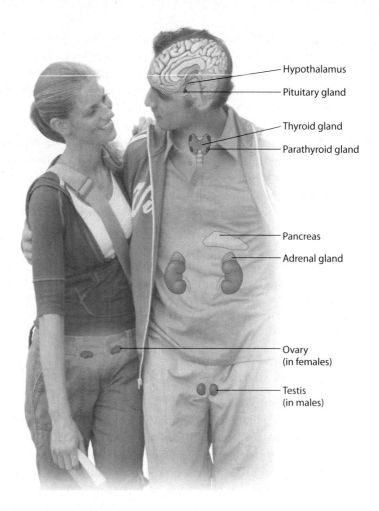

- Hypothalamus
- Pituitary gland
- Thyroid gland
- Parathyroid gland
- Pancreas
- Adrenal gland
- Ovary (in females)
- Testis (in males)

body functions. Hormones also play a crucial role in regulating metabolism, growth, reproduction, mood, and other processes. Figure 3.21 depicts some of the major endocrine glands of the body.

The hypothalamus, shown in Figure 3.21, is a brain structure that controls the pituitary gland. The **pituitary gland** is known as the master gland of the body, because it secretes hormones that control the release of hormones from glands elsewhere in the body.

The *thyroid* gland sits in the neck region and releases hormones that control the rate of metabolism. Metabolism is the process by which the body converts nutritional substances into energy. The *pancreas* releases hormones, including insulin, that play a vital role in regulating the blood sugar levels. The sex glands (ovaries and testes) release sex hormones that lead to development of sex characteristics (such as body hair and breast development), sex drive, and other aspects of sexual maturation.

The **adrenal glands,** which sit atop the kidneys, release hormones in response to stress and emotions. They also help regulate heart rate, blood pressure, and blood sugar. In addition, the adrenal glands produce **catecholamines,** a class of chemicals that includes the neurotransmitters dopamine, norepinephrine, and epinephrine, which control ANS activation. Norepinephrine activates the sympathetic nervous system, increasing heart rate, rate of respiration, and

pituitary gland
the master endocrine gland that controls the release of hormones from glands throughout the body.

adrenal glands
endocrine structures that release hormones important in regulating the stress response and emotions.

catecholamines
chemicals released from the adrenal glands that function as hormones and as neurotransmitters to control ANS activation.

blood pressure in order to support rapid action of the body. The adrenal glands also release stress hormones such as **cortisol,** which is responsible for maintaining the activation of bodily systems during prolonged stress.

The endocrine system works in conjunction with the nervous system and in a dynamic relationship with the brain. An example is its control of the female menstrual cycle. Each month, the hypothalamus sends signals to the pituitary to release hormones that stimulate a woman's ovaries to develop (mature) an egg. As part of the process, the ovary itself releases hormones that prepare the womb to receive a fertilized egg. If the egg is fertilized, the ovaries send hormonal feedback to the hypothalamus, so that it will not stimulate further egg development.

quick quiz 3.6: The Endocrine System

1. How do hormones differ from neurotransmitters?
   a. Hormones are proteins; neurotransmitters are fats.
   b. Hormones carry messages in the bloodstream; neurotransmitters carry messages across synapses.
   c. Hormones have no effect on mood; neurotransmitters do.
   d. all of the above

2. What is the name of the stress hormone released by the adrenal glands?
   a. catecholamine
   b. insulin
   c. thyroxin
   d. cortisol

Answers can be found at the end of the chapter.

making connections
in the biology of behavior

What Esref Armagan's Story Reveals About the Brain

This chapter opened with a profile of the blind artist Esref Armagan. Besides being a fine example of someone creatively overcoming a disability, Armagan's story offers us a way to connect much of the material in this chapter. Let's take a closer look.

When Armagan paints, he uses a Braille stylus (writing instrument) to sketch out his drawing by laying down bumps on paper. With his other hand, he follows the raised bumps to "see" what he has put down (Motluk, 2005). He then transfers this sketch to canvas and applies acrylic paint

with his fingers, one color at a time. Armagan waits for each color to dry before applying another so that they will not blend or smear too much. No one helps him when he paints, and his paintings are entirely his own creations.

Armagan has learned much from talking with other people, such as what the typical colors of certain objects are. He always keeps his paints lined up in the same order so that he can find the right color. His sense of perspective is harder to explain. He portrays perspective with uncanny realism, far beyond what any other blind painter has ever achieved (Kennedy & Juricevic, 2006). He says he learned this from talking with others as well as from feeling his way in the world (*Biography,* n.d.).

Esref Armagan with some of his paintings.

Armagan's skill appears to have at least some inborn basis, given how early he started without receiving any instruction. Before age 6, he would draw in dirt and scratch drawings on the furniture in his home. His parents, wanting to save their furniture, finally gave him drawing materials (Kennedy & Juricevic, 2006; Motluk, 2005)—something not usually offered to blind children. This early, automatic, and almost compulsive behavior suggests that something about how his brain was wired drove young Esref to draw, and genetics likely played a role.

What senses does Armagan use while painting? Like many blind people, Armagan relies mostly on his sense of touch. Interestingly, he needs total silence while working. In many blind people, the so-called "visual" centers of the brain are used to process hearing (Röder, 2006). Maybe Armagan needs silence because he cannot afford to devote the precious resources of his mind's eye to hearing.

How can we explain Armagan's act of painting in the context of the nervous system? As Armagan moves the stylus to create bumps on paper and moves his fingers over those bumps, the sensations from his fingertips stimulate his sensory neurons. These neurons, in turn, stimulate interneurons in different regions of the brain (discussed below),

which eventually stimulate motor neurons to move his hands and fingers in precise ways to execute his painting.

Throughout this entire process, millions of neurons are firing. As Armagan moves his hands and fingers and begins to paint, the neurons send impulses to other neurons. Some of the messages are excitatory; some are inhibitory. If a neuron receives a preponderance of excitatory impulses and the membrane potential changes sufficiently, it will fire in an all-or-none fashion. At this point, the cell membrane opens channels letting potassium out and sodium in. The wave of opening and closing channels moves the impulse down the axon and stimulates the release of neurotransmitters in vesicles that are in the terminal buttons. The neurotransmitters are released into the synaptic cleft where they bind with receptor sites in postsynaptic neurons, get taken back up into the presynaptic neuron, or degrade. The message is then relayed to the next (postsynaptic) neurons.

What neurotransmitters are most likely to be involved in painting? As Armagan sketches and paints, he voluntarily moves his arms, hands, and fingers. Voluntary motor movements of muscles use synapses involving dopamine and acetylcholine. His attention and focus while painting, and his blocking out of auditory stimulation, increase his levels of norepinephrine as well. Additionally, the learning and memory needed for his artistry involve the effects of acetylcholine and glutamate in various parts of the brain.

There is activity throughout his brain, in brain stem structures as well as in the forebrain. As Armagan paints, as is true for anything he does, his breathing, heart rate, body temperature, and even consciousness are regulated by the medulla (see Figure 3.22). Armagan's thalamus transfers and relays most of the sensory information coming into various parts of the brain for different kinds of processing. And there is so much information to process! As he develops new ideas for what he wants to paint, his hippocampus is active in sending those ideas to the frontal lobes for memory or to various cortexes for more permanent storage.

In order to paint, Armagan needs to plan and execute the actions of painting. The frontal lobes play a key role in planning and keeping in mind the tasks needed to paint. His

Touring the Nervous System and the Brain

The Neuron and Synapse ■ The Resting Potential and Action Potential
Structures and Functions in the Human Brain ■ Lobes of the Cerebral Cortex
Visual Information in the Split Brain ■ Central and Peripheral Nervous Systems

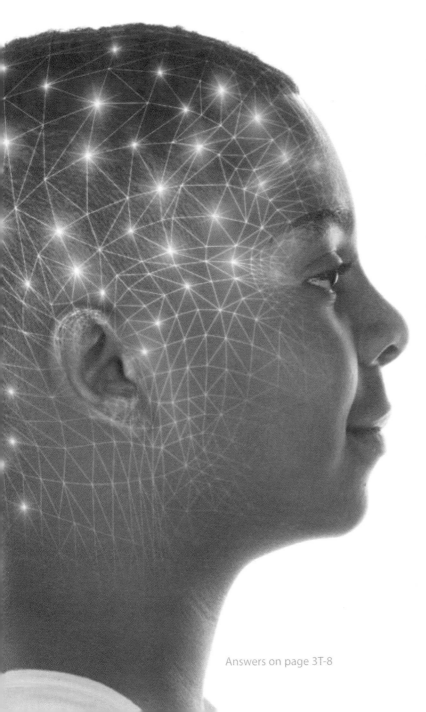

GOALS OF THE TOUR

1   **The Neuron and Synapse.** You will be able to identify parts of the neuron and synapse and describe how they communicate information.

2   **The Resting Potential and Action Potential.** You will be able to describe the membrane changes involved in maintaining the resting potential and in producing the action potential.

3   **Structures and Functions in the Human Brain.** You will be able to identify the brain's key structures and functions.

4   **Lobes of the Cerebral Cortex.** You will be able to identify the location and describe the function of the four lobes of the cerebral cortex.

5   **Visual Information in the Split Brain.** You will be able to describe hemispheric lateralization and communication in the brain.

6   **Central and Peripheral Nervous Systems.** You will be able to identify the parts of the central and peripheral nervous systems and describe the body functions they control.

The Neuron and the Synapse

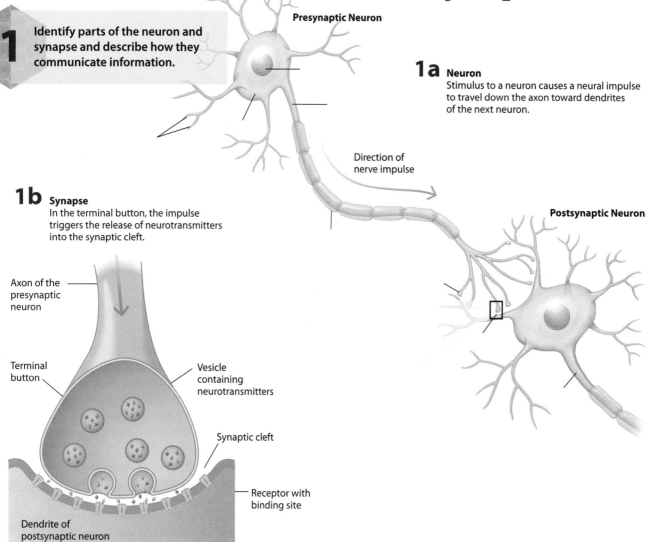

1 Identify parts of the neuron and synapse and describe how they communicate information.

Presynaptic Neuron

1a Neuron
Stimulus to a neuron causes a neural impulse to travel down the axon toward dendrites of the next neuron.

Direction of nerve impulse

Postsynaptic Neuron

1b Synapse
In the terminal button, the impulse triggers the release of neurotransmitters into the synaptic cleft.

Axon of the presynaptic neuron

Terminal button

Vesicle containing neurotransmitters

Synaptic cleft

Receptor with binding site

Dendrite of postsynaptic neuron

The Resting Potential and Action Potential

Direction of
nerve impulse

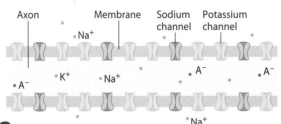

Axon   Membrane   Sodium channel   Potassium channel

Na⁺

K⁺   Na⁺

A⁻   A⁻   A⁻

Na⁺

2a Resting potential

In the resting neuron, the fluid outside the axon contains a higher concentration of positive ions than the inside of the axon, which contains many negatively charged anions (A–).

2a Action Potential

The action potential is an impulse of positive charge that sweeps down the axon.

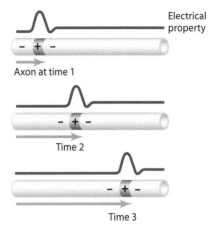

Electrical property

– + –

Axon at time 1

– + –

Time 2

– + –

Time 3

The graph below depicts the electrical changes that occur during each stage of an action potential (**1** resting potential, **2** depolarization, **3** repolarization, and **4** refractory period).

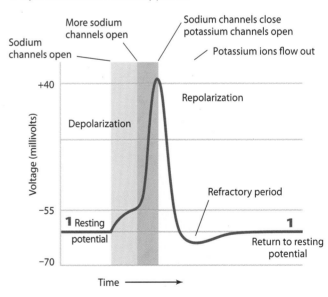

Sodium channels open

More sodium channels open

Sodium channels close potassium channels open

Potassium ions flow out

+40

Depolarization

Repolarization

Voltage (millivolts)

–55

1 Resting potential

1

Refractory period

Return to resting potential

–70

Time

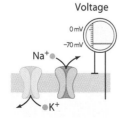

Voltage

0 mV
–70 mV

Na⁺

K⁺

1 Resting potential

Structures and Functions of the Human Brain

3 Identify the brain's key structures and functions.

3a Brain Stem Structures

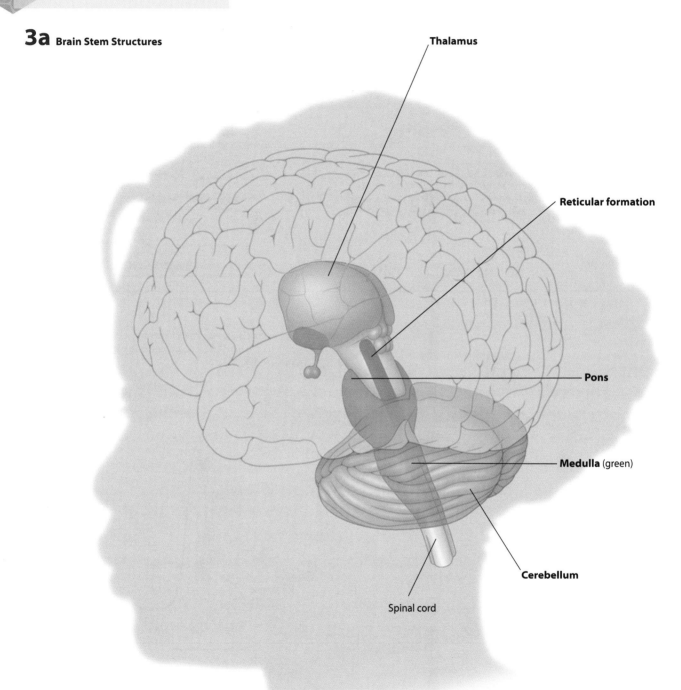

Thalamus

Reticular formation

Pons

Medulla (green)

Cerebellum

Spinal cord

Lobes of the Cerebral Cortex

Identify the location of the lobes of the cerebral cortex and describe their primary function.

4

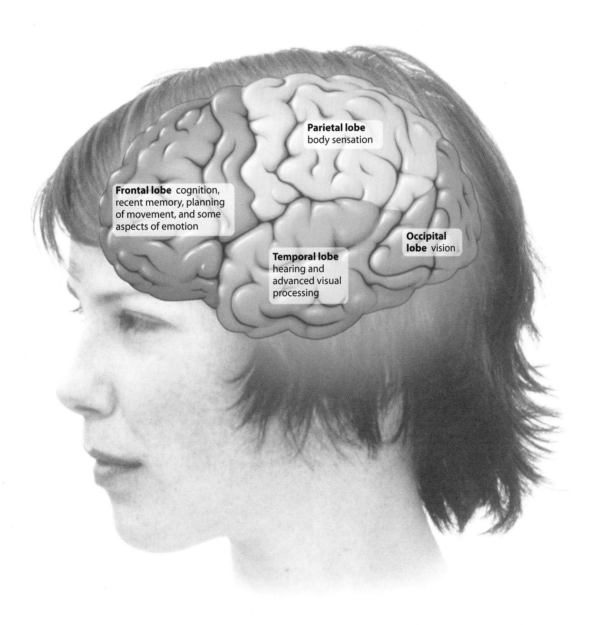

Parietal lobe body sensation

Frontal lobe cognition, recent memory, planning of movement, and some aspects of emotion

Occipital lobe vision

Temporal lobe hearing and advanced visual processing

Visual Information in the Split Brain

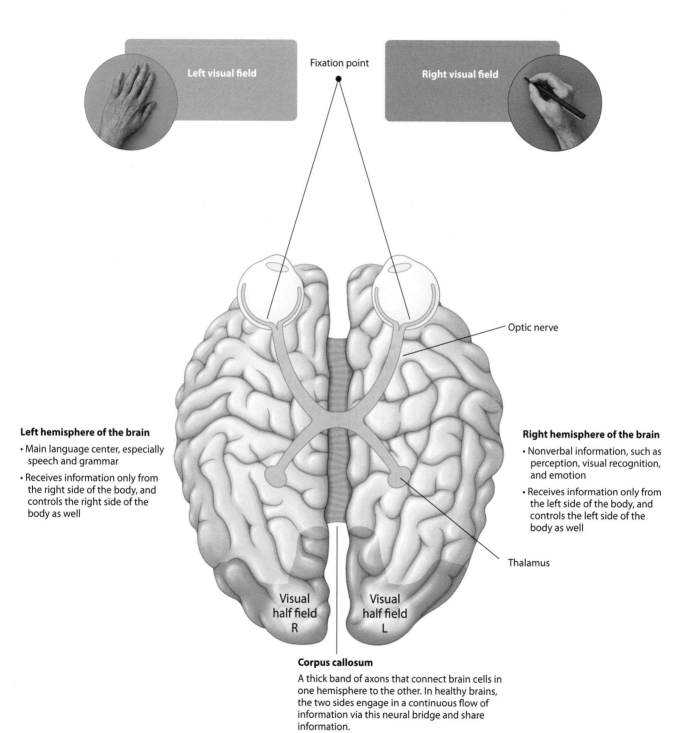

Left visual field

Fixation point

Right visual field

Optic nerve

Left hemisphere of the brain
- Main language center, especially speech and grammar
- Receives information only from the right side of the body, and controls the right side of the body as well

Right hemisphere of the brain
- Nonverbal information, such as perception, visual recognition, and emotion
- Receives information only from the left side of the body, and controls the left side of the body as well

Thalamus

Visual half field R

Visual half field L

Corpus callosum
A thick band of axons that connect brain cells in one hemisphere to the other. In healthy brains, the two sides engage in a continuous flow of information via this neural bridge and share information.

Central and Peripheral Nervous Systems

6a The Central Nervous System

● Central nervous system

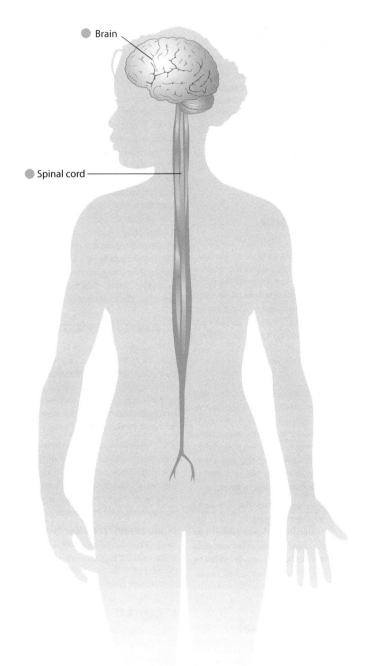

● Brain

● Spinal cord

Identify the parts of the central and peripheral nervous systems and describe the body functions they control.

6

1. THE NEURON AND SYNAPSE

The *neuron* consists of a *soma, dendrites,* and an *axon.* The soma is the structure of the neuron that contains the nucleus, which consists of the genetic material including the chromosomes. The dendrites are branches of the neuron that receive information from other neurons. The axon sends information away from the soma to other neurons or cells.

When a neuron fires, it sends an electrical impulse down the axon, known as the *action potential.* When the impulse arrives at the axon terminal buttons, it causes the release of *neurotransmitter* molecules into the *synapse.* The synapse is the gap junction between two neurons. Neurons communicate with one another by means of chemical signals provided by neurotransmitters that cross the synapse.

The neurotransmitter released by the sending neuron enters the synaptic gap and attaches to a *receptor* on the postsynaptic neuron. The receptor site contains a channel that is typically closed when the receiving neuron is in the resting state (*resting potential*). When the neurotransmitter binds to the receptor site, the receptor channel opens to allow a particular *ion* to enter or leave the neuron. If a neurotransmitter causes channels for a positively charged ion like sodium (Na^+) to open, the postsynaptic neuron will become less negative in charge. The entry of sodium will cause a change in the electrical charge (potential) of the receiving neuron that may make it more likely to generate its own action potential.

2. THE RESTING POTENTIAL AND ACTION POTENTIAL

The neuron maintains electrical properties called an *electrical potential,* which is a difference in the electrical charge inside and outside of the cell. This charge difference is maintained because the membrane of the neuron is *selectively permeable.* This means some molecules can pass through the membrane more freely than others. The membrane is not permeable to large negatively charged protein molecules that are trapped inside the neuron. Inside and outside the neuron are electrically charged particles called *ions* that vary in concentrations. The ions that play an important role in the function of the neuron are sodium (Na^+), potassium (K^+), and chloride (Cl^-). These ions enter or leave the neuron through special channels provided by protein molecules that line the neuron.

The *resting potential* is the electrical property of the neuron when it is not stimulated or not sending a nerve impulse. In a typical neuron this is seen as a -70 mV charge inside relative to the outside of the membrane. During the resting potential, the sodium channels are closed, leaving a higher concentration of sodium ions outside of the neuron membrane. The negative charge of a neuron during the resting state is largely maintained by the negatively charged protein molecules trapped inside the neuron and by the inability of positively charged sodium ions to cross the membrane into the neuron.

If the neuron receives enough excitatory messages to surpass the threshold level, an *action potential* will occur, sending the nerve impulse down the axon. Positively charged sodium ions enter the neuron, and potassium ions move out. The action potential jumps from one space in the axon's myelin sheath to the next, changing membrane qualities at each space. Membrane channels for sodium close to keep sodium ions out of the neuron and potassium channels open to allow potassium to move into the neuron, restoring the resting potential.

3. STRUCTURES AND FUNCTIONS IN THE HUMAN BRAIN

The brain stem structures are embedded within the core of the brain and provide a number of vital functions for survival. These include the medulla, pons, cerebellum, reticular formation, and the thalamus.

The *medulla* is a brain structure just above the spinal cord. It controls a number of life-sustaining reflexes and functions including breathing, coughing, vomiting, and heart rate. The *pons* lies just above the medulla and is particularly involved in sleep and arousal. The *cerebellum* is a large structure at the base of the brain with many folds. It is traditionally known to be involved in motor coordination and balance but also plays a role in attention of visual and auditory stimuli and the timing of movements. The *reticular formation* is an elaborate diffuse network of neurons that runs through the core of the medulla and pons to the base of the thalamus. It plays a role in arousal, attention, sleep patterns, and stereotyped patterns such as posture and locomotion. The *thalamus* is a central structure in the brain that relays auditory, visual, and somatosensory (body senses) information to the cerebral cortex.

The limbic system comprises a number of brain structures involved in motivation, emotion, and memory. The *hypothalamus* is a small structure that is located just below the thalamus. It controls the autonomic nervous system as well as the release of hormones from the pituitary gland. It is involved in a number of functions including eating, drinking, and sexual behavior, and plays an important role in the expression of emotions and stress responses. The *hippocampus* is located in the temporal lobe and plays a role in learning and memory. Adjacent to the hippocampus is the amygdala, which is involved in fear and anxiety. The *cingulate gyrus*, a beltlike structure in the middle of the brain, is involved in attention and cognitive control.

The *cerebral cortex* is the outer layer of the brain and is involved in higher-order functions such as thinking, learning, consciousness, and memory.

4. LOBES OF THE CEREBRAL CORTEX

The *cerebral cortex* is anatomically divided into four lobes: occipital lobe, parietal lobe, temporal lobe, and frontal lobe. The *occipital lobe* is located in the posterior end (back region) of the cortex and is involved in processing *visual information.* The *parietal lobe* makes up the top rear section of the cortex. The parietal lobe is involved in *bodily senses.* The area just in front of the parietal lobe is the *somatosensory cortex.* It is the primary target for the *touch senses* of the body and information for muscle-stretch receptors and joint receptors. The *temporal lobe* is the large portion of each hemisphere near the temples and lies behind the frontal lobe and below the *lateral fissure.* It is the primary region of the cortex that processes *auditory information.* The *frontal lobe* extends from the central sulcus to the anterior limit (forward region) of the brain. The region of the frontal lobe immediately adjacent to the central sulcus is called the *motor cortex* because it controls *fine movements.* The most anterior region is called the *prefrontal cortex;* it is involved in higher brain functions including *cognition* (thought processes), *recent memory,* the *planning of movement,* and some aspects of *emotion.*

5. VISUAL INFORMATION IN THE SPLIT BRAIN

Lateralization refers to the division of labor between the two cerebral hemispheres of the brain. The *left hemisphere* receives sensory information from and controls the movements in the right side of the body. Likewise, images of objects in the right visual field are projected to the left half of the retina of each eye, which in turn sends the information to the visual cortex in the left hemisphere. The left hemisphere also contains the main language area involved in the comprehension and production of language.

The *right hemisphere* receives sensory information from and controls the movements in the left side of the body. Likewise, images of objects in the left visual field are projected to the right half of the retina of each eye, which in turn sends the information to the visual cortex in the right hemisphere. The right hemisphere processes nonverbal information, such as perception, visual recognition, and emotion.

In the healthy brain the two cerebral hemispheres share information with each other across the broad band of axons called the *corpus callosum.* In some instances the corpus callosum is surgically cut, resulting in what is called a *split brain.* In the split brain, information in one cerebral hemisphere is confined to that side of the brain.

6. CENTRAL AND PERIPHERAL NERVOUS SYSTEMS

The nervous system is made up of the *central nervous system* and the *peripheral nervous system.* The central nervous system is comprised of the brain and the spinal cord. The peripheral nervous system consists of all nerve fibers outside of the brain and spinal cord. The peripheral nervous system is made up of two major divisions: the *somatic nervous system* and the *autonomic nervous system.*

The *somatic nervous system* consists of nerve fibers conveying information from the brain and spinal cord to skeletal muscles; this information controls movement and sends information back to the brain via the spinal cord from sensory receptors located in various parts of the body.

The *autonomic nervous system* controls the glands and muscles of the internal organs such as the heart, digestive system, lungs, and salivary glands, and it consists of the sympathetic and the parasympathetic branches. The *sympathetic branch* arouses the body, mobilizes its energy during physical exercise and in stressful situations, and activates the adrenal gland to release epinephrine into the bloodstream. The *parasympathetic branch* calms the body and conserves and replenishes energy.

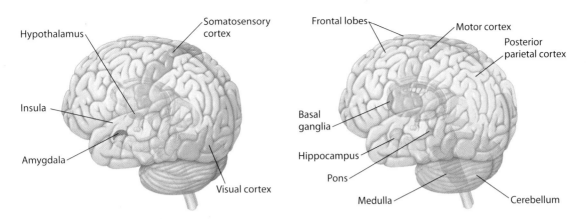

FIGURE **3.22**

SOME OF THE BRAIN REGIONS INVOLVED WHEN ESREF ARMAGAN PAINTS. When he is drawing or painting, Armagan uses many different regions of his brain. Most interestingly, Armagan's visual cortex is active in forming images of what he paints. These images do not stem from his visual system (eyes) but rather from his sense of touch (fingers). When Armagan touches something, his occipital lobes are as active as a sighted person's occipital lobes are when seeing something. In other words, he forms visual images, but they come from touching rather than seeing.

motor cortex controls movement of his legs, arms, hands, and fingers. His basal ganglia help carry out the commands to move the various parts of his body. Perhaps Armagan decides to put his fingers in the paint container to his left. The parietal lobes get involved in orienting his body in space, and the frontal lobes plan the action to reach for the paint pot to his left. When he is ready to move his hand, the signal from these cortical areas travels to the cerebellum to control fine movement, then to the pons, medulla, and finally to the spinal cord to the nerves that control the muscles in his hand and arm. All this occurs in an instant. His brain gets feedback on the position of the hand and makes needed adjustments: a complex interplay among the somatosensory cortex (which receives sensory input from his fingers and arms as he paints), the insula, and the cerebellum.

Armagan is one of the few blind people with the ability to accurately portray depth and perspective in his drawings and paintings. When asked to draw a cube and then rotate it once and then once again, he draws it in perfect perspective, with horizontal and vertical lines converging at imaginary points in the distance (Kennedy & Juricevic, 2006). This ability to render perspective accurately in three dimensions is processed in the parietal lobes near the top and back of his brain. The visual images that Armagan forms from his sense of touch activate the same region of the brain that is active when sighted people see something: the occipital lobe.

When sighted people imagine something, their visual cortex (in the occipital lobe) is active—but in a much weaker way than when they actually look at something. When

Armagan imagines an object, his visual cortex is even less active than that. But when he paints, his occipital cortex becomes so active that it cannot easily be distinguished from a sighted person's visual cortex as he actually sees something (Begley, 2007; Motluk, 2005). Armagan's brain appears to be seeing.

Because Armagan has been blind since birth, his visual cortex has never received any visual input (light). But that part of his brain didn't merely die or stop functioning. In many blind people, the visual cortex takes on hearing functions, enabling them to hear certain types of sounds better than sighted people can (Röder, 2006). Armagan's occipital cortex indeed is very active when he paints, but he is receiving tactile (touch) and not visual input.

Furthermore, in most blind people who read Braille, the visual cortex is active in processing tactile and verbal memory function. But Armagan can't read Braille and his visual cortex is not recruited for any aspect of language. In fact, his memory for language is rather poor. He is a very "visual" person, but his visual images are built from tactile information—just as images are during a walk through the Tactile Dome. There is evidence from neuroscientists who study blind people in general that this plasticity of the occipital lobes is the norm—it usually processes tactile information, verbal information, or both for blind people (Amedi et al., 2005). Armagan's life, abilities, and brain illustrate that the brain is both highly plastic *and* specialized (Begley, 2007). The so-called visual part of his brain found something to do.

chapter **review**

GENES AND BEHAVIOR

- At least four principles of behavioral genetics are important for psychology: (1) The relationship between specific genes and behavior is complex. (2) Most specific behaviors derive from many genes. (3) Behavioral genetics employs studies of twins and adoptees to disentangle the contributions of heredity and environment to behavior. (4) The environment influences how and when genes affect behavior.

- The extent to which a characteristic is influenced by genetics is known as heritability. Researchers use twin studies, adoption studies, twin-adoption studies, and gene-by-environment designs to study heritability.

THE NERVOUS SYSTEM

- There are two kinds of cells in the central nervous system: glial cells and neurons. Glial cells provide structural support, among other important functions.

- Neurons transmit information throughout the nervous system by means of action potentials. Messages are received by the branchlike dendrites and cell bodies of neighboring neurons, which create changes in the membrane of the receiving neuron. If the right conditions are met, that neuron fires in an all-or-none fashion. Action potentials move down the length of the axon as channels in the membrane open and close, allowing ions to move in and out of the axon. The action potential stimulates the release of neurotransmitters from the terminal buttons, into the synaptic cleft.

- Neurotransmitters bind to receptor sites on the dendrites of postsynaptic neurons, allowing an action potential to be generated if the charge threshold is surpassed. Excess neurotransmitter is either taken back into the original neuron or broken down in the synaptic cleft.

THE BRAIN

- The brain is divided into three major regions: the hindbrain, midbrain, and the forebrain.

- The topmost brain structures are the cerebrum and cerebral cortex, which are the seat of abstract reasoning, planning, and higher-order thought.

- The cerebrum comprises four lobes: The frontal lobes are involved in abstract reasoning, self-control, and motor control. The temporal lobes house the auditory cortex; the parietal lobes process tactile and spatial information; and the occipital lobes house the visual cortex.

- The left and right hemispheres of the brain carry out somewhat different functions. The biggest difference between the hemispheres is language, which is usually controlled by the left hemisphere.

- One major shift in our understanding of the brain over the last 15–20 years is how much neurons and brain structures are shaped by experience. New neurons form, new dendrites grow, and new synapses are created across the life span, especially in infancy and early childhood.

MEASURING THE BRAIN

- Various methods offer glimpses into the brain and its functions. Electroencephalography (EEG) measures electrical activity from scalp readings. Magnetic resonance imaging (MRI) measures blood flow changes in the brain without the added risk of the radioactive dyes used in PET scans. The adaptation of MRI to functional MRIs (fMRI) allows researchers to determine which brain areas are active during specific tasks.

THE ENDOCRINE SYSTEM

- In the endocrine system, glands secrete chemicals called hormones, which travel in the bloodstream to tissues and organs all over the body. The pituitary gland, called the master gland of the body, controls the release of hormones from other glands in the body. The adrenal glands secrete hormones involved in sympathetic nervous system responses and stress.

MAKING CONNECTIONS IN THE BIOLOGY OF BEHAVIOR

- The story of Esref Armagan offers a glimpse of the brain in action. For example, as Armagan moves his hands and fingers and begins to paint, the neurons send impulses to other neurons. Activation occurs in many regions of the brain. The cerebellum fine-tunes his movements by attending to whether his body is moving appropriately with the right amount of effort. The visual images that Armagan forms from his sense of touch activate the same region of the brain that is active when seeing people see something: the occipital lobe.

key terms

acetylcholine (ACh), p. 92

action potential, p. 88

adoption studies, p. 80

adrenal glands, p. 116

alleles, p. 78

all-or-none principle, p. 90

amygdala, p. 101

aphasia, p. 105

arborization, p. 108

autonomic nervous system (ANS) , p. 84

axon, p. 87

basal ganglia, p. 102

behavioral genetics, p. 79

Broca's area, p. 105

catecholamines, p. 116

central nervous system (CNS), p. 83

cerebellum, p. 99

cerebral cortex, p. 102

cerebrum, p. 102

chromosomes, p. 77

cingulate gyrus, p. 102

contralaterality, p. 103

corpus callosum, p. 105

cortisol, p. 117

dendrites, p. 87

DNA (deoxyribonucleic acid), p. 78

dominant genes, p. 78

dopamine, p. 92

electroencephalography (EEG), p. 112

endocrine system, p. 115

enzymatic degradation, p. 92

epigenetics, p. 82

epinephrine, p. 93

event-related potential (ERP), p. 112

fraternal twins, p. 80

functional magnetic resonance imaging (fMRI), p. 115

GABA (gamma-aminobutyric acid), p. 94

gene-by-environment interaction research, p. 81

genes, p. 78

genome, p. 78

glial cells, p. 85

glutamate, p. 94

graded potentials, p. 92

heritability, p. 80

hippocampus, p. 101

hormones, p. 115

hypothalamus, p. 100

identical twins, p. 80

insula, p. 104

interneurons, p. 88

ions, p. 88

magnetic resonance imaging (MRI), p. 114

medulla, p. 99

mirror neurons, p. 88

monogenic transmission, p. 79

motor neurons, p. 87

myelin sheath, p. 87

neurogenesis, p. 108

neurons, p. 86

neuroplasticity, p. 108

neurotransmitters, p. 86

norepinephrine, p. 93

parasympathetic nervous system, p. 84

peripheral nervous system, p. 83

pituitary gland, p. 116

polygenic transmission, p. 79

pons, p. 99

positron emission tomography (PET), p. 115

recessive genes, p. 79

reflexes, p. 99

refractory period, p. 90

resting potential, p. 88

reticular formation, p. 99

reuptake, p. 92

sensory neurons, p. 87

serotonin, p. 93

soma, p. 87

somatic nervous system, p. 83

sympathetic nervous system, p. 84

synapse, p. 87

synaptic vesicles, p. 90

synaptogenesis, p. 108

terminal button, p. 87

thalamus, p. 99

twin studies, p. 80

twin-adoption studies, p. 81

Wernicke's area, p. 106

quick quiz **answers**

Quick Quiz 3.1:   1. b   2. c   3. a   Quick Quiz 3.2:   1. d   2. a   3. b   4. c   Quick Quiz 3.3:   1. b   2. c   3. d

Quick Quiz 3.4:   1. a   2. d   Quick Quiz 3.5:   1. c   2. a   Quick Quiz 3.6:   1. b   2. d

sensing and **perceiving**

our world

preview
questions

1 *How does the brain make sense of the world around us?*

2 *What roles do neurons play in vision?*

3 *Why do certain smells bring back powerful memories?*

4 *Why does food taste bad when you have a cold?*

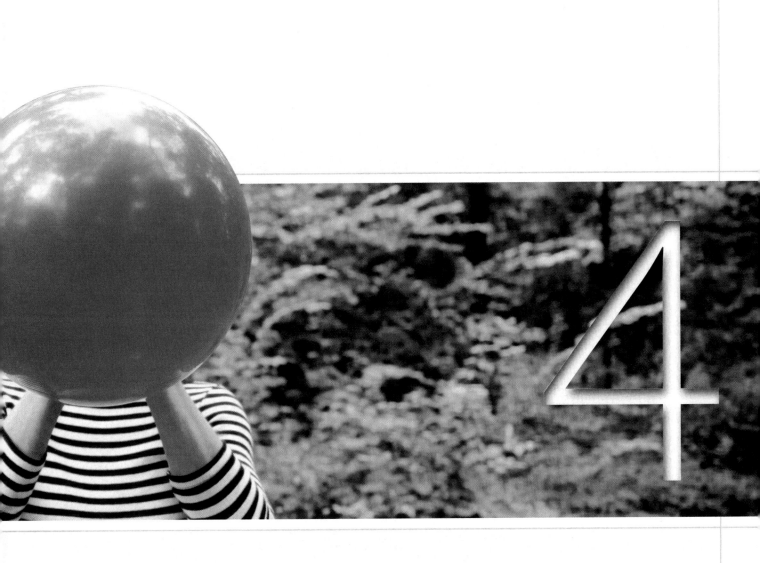

M ike May lost his vision at age 3. Four decades later, he had surgery to repair his eyes, in which doctors replaced the corneas (the clear outer layer of the eye) and other tissues. The surgery gave Mike working eyes. But it takes more than work-ing eyes to see. Mike May could not miraculously "see" right after his surgery. He could barely make out vague shapes, colors, and light. It took him months to learn how to see again. Finally, three years after the surgery, Mike's vision started to approach normal. Many formerly blind people whose vision is restored never fully recover their vision, especially if they have been blind since birth (Kurson, 2007).

The case of Mike May shows how seeing takes place as much in the brain as in the eyes. After the surgery on his eyes, Mike May's brain did not know how to interpret the new ▶

▶ visual information. As discussed in Chapter 3, neurons in the visual cortex often process other kinds of sensory information, such as touch and sound, in people who have no vision. It is possible that after he went blind at age 3, Mike's visual cortex took on different functions. Now his brain had to learn to see again by reorganizing itself and developing new neurons. Seeing requires the right environmental stimulation (in this case, light) and neurons specialized for vision. It requires both sensation and perception, which involve a complex dance of environmental input and biology, of nature and nurture.

Every moment of every day we are bombarded with stimulation—sights, sounds, tastes, smells, and textures. In this chapter we examine the interface between the outside world and our inner experience by looking at how we sense and perceive external stimuli.

chapter **outline**

It is a long journey from light entering the eye to the experience of seeing something, and as Mike May's story suggests, it is by no means a straightforward process. For each of the major sensory systems, we will examine how physical information is transformed into neural signals, how the brain processes that information, and how our knowledge and expectations can shape our sensory experiences. ■

The Long Strange Trip From Sensation to Perception

The better animals can sense what is happening in the world around them, the better they can survive and reproduce. Yet the apparently simple act of knowing that the sound vibrations hitting your ear represent someone calling your name, for example, is a complex process involving the sense organs and the brain. The sense organs transform information from its physical form (whether light or sound waves or chemicals) into a nerve impulse and transmit it to the brain, which organizes that information, interprets it, and then initiates a response. And it all happens in an instant.

This interplay between taking in information from the outside world and interpreting it is what sensation and perception are all about. **Sensation** is the stimulation of our sense organs by the outer world. Our sense organs detect

sensation
a physical process: the stimulation of our sense organs by features of the outer world.

Is there a rainbow at the end of this road? We depend on sensation and perception together to detect, organize, and interpret stimuli in the world around us.

different features of our surroundings: Eyes are sensitive to light waves, ears to sounds, skin to touch and pressure, tongues to tastes, and noses to odors.

Yet sensing does not automatically translate into perceiving. Our brains have to receive the sensory input and then compare it to everything else it already knows, remembers, feels, and thinks. **Perception** is the act of organizing and interpreting sensory experience. It is how our psychological world represents our physical world. If you, for example, had not been taught to read, the words on this page would not be words. They would be shapes. You read and make sense of them because you spent years learning to speak English and then to read it. Your brain transforms the raw sensory experience of black and white marks into meaningful concepts that—we hope—will inspire you to learn and investigate further.

As we mentioned in Chapter 3, the brain organizes and interprets sensory experience to give it meaning. Before the brain can create meaning from sensory information, our sense organs transform physical stimuli from the outer world to a form that the brain can use—action potentials. Let's consider how basic sensory processes transform stimuli into neural information.

perception
a psychological process: the act of organizing and interpreting sensory experience.

BASIC SENSORY PROCESSES

Imagine that you were constantly aware of the sensations that bombard your sense organs, such as the sound of the air conditioner, clock, traffic, and radio; the sight of the chair you're sitting on, the ceiling light, the rug on the floor; the smells in the air; and the feel of your clothing against your skin. If you were constantly sensing all this, you would suffer from sensory overload. Our sensitivity diminishes when an object constantly stimulates our senses, a process we know

FIGURE **4.1**
ABSOLUTE SENSORY THRESHOLDS. These are the smallest amounts of a stimulus that most humans can perceive. (*Source:* Smith, 1998.)

A candle flame seen at 30 miles on a clear night

The tick of a watch under quiet conditions at 20 feet

sensory adaptation
the process by which our sensitivity diminishes when an object constantly stimulates our senses.

as **sensory adaptation.** Sensory adaptation ensures that we notice changes in stimulation more than stimulation itself.

Once we know that a physical stimulus is something to attend to, the sense organs convert it into action potentials. This conversion of physical into neural information is called **transduction.** Transduction happens when cells in the retina change light waves to neural energy, when hair cells in the inner ear change sound waves to neural energy, when chemicals in the air bind to receptors in the nose, when food chemicals stimulate taste buds on the tongue, and when pressure and temperature stimulate nerve cells in the skin.

transduction
the conversion of physical into neural information.

PRINCIPLES OF PERCEPTION

Some of the earliest experiments in psychology were in the field of **psychophysics,** the study of how people psychologically perceive physical stimuli such as light, sound waves, and touch. Some basic principles of perception have emerged from over a century of research in this area. We outline these principles briefly in this section.

psychophysics
the study of how people psychologically perceive physical stimuli such as light, sound waves, and touch.

Absolute Thresholds   What is the smallest object you can see from a distance? What is the softest sound that you can hear? These questions refer to **absolute thresholds,** the lowest intensity level of a stimulus we can detect half of the time. A common way to assess absolute thresholds is for a researcher to present stimuli (light, for example) of different intensities to a research participant. The intensity level that the participant can see 50% of the time is that person's absolute threshold for light. For example, imagine that six light intensities are presented 10 times each. The six intensity values are 150, 160, 170, 180, 190, and 200. Of these values, the participant detects the 180 value 50% of the time. Then 180 is this person's absolute threshold for this light stimulus (Goldstein, 2007).

absolute threshold
the lowest intensity level of a stimulus a person can detect half of the time.

Psychologists have made some general conclusions about thresholds of perception (see Figure 4.1). For example, researchers determined under ideal laboratory conditions that an average person on a very clear night could detect a single

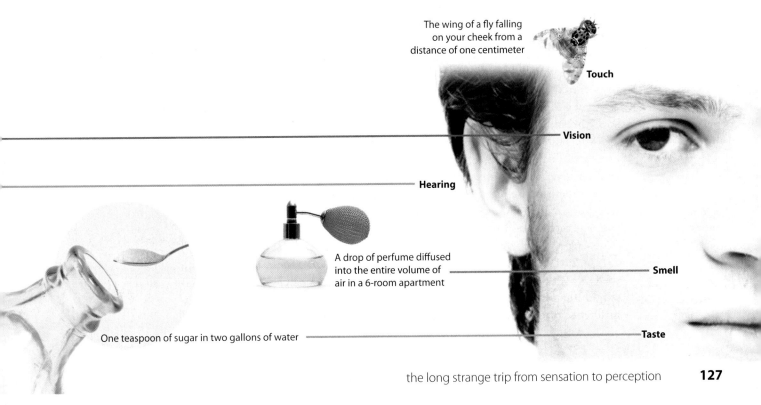

The wing of a fly falling on your cheek from a distance of one centimeter

Touch

Vision

Hearing

A drop of perfume diffused into the entire volume of air in a 6-room apartment

Smell

One teaspoon of sugar in two gallons of water

Taste

candle from 30 miles away or could distinguish 2 gallons of water with only 1 teaspoon of sugar as being different from 2 gallons of pure water (Galanter, 1962).

Signal Detection   There are a few problems, however, with measuring absolute thresholds. First, when a sensory stimulus is near absolute threshold, some people are more likely to say "Yes, I perceive it" and others more likely to say "No, I don't." Put differently, detecting sensations is a matter not only of intensity of the stimulus, but also of the decision-making process of the person in a particular context. **Signal detection theory** takes into account both stimulus intensity and the decision-making processes people use in detecting a stimulus.

Consider the situation in which there are serious consequences if you miss detecting a visual or auditory stimulus. A nurse in emergency medicine, for example, would not want to miss a slight change in a vital sign of a severely injured patient. An air-traffic controller would not want to miss a bleep on his or her screen—it might make the difference between averting a mid-air collision or not. In such situations, people may be more sensitive to sensory input, so much so that they might say they saw or heard something that was not there.

In signal detection research a low-intensity stimulus is presented on some occasions and not presented on other occasions (Green & Swets, 1974; Swets, 1964). Instead of having a 50% detection line, signal detection experiments present only a single low-intensity stimulus. Let's use hearing as an example. A participant has 100 chances to detect a soft tone. During the 100 chances, the tone is either present or not. In signal detection, there are four possible outcomes: a *hit* is correctly detecting a stimulus that is there; a *miss* is failing to detect a stimulus that is there; a *false alarm* is saying that a stimulus exists when it does not; and a *correct rejection* is not reporting a stimulus that is not there. Figure 4.2 summarizes the possible outcomes in signal detection theory. In a signal detection study, the participant's responses create a profile of hits, misses, false alarms, and correct rejections. Using the classic method of absolute threshold, a person's threshold is assumed to be constant (for example, light intensity of 180). But in signal detection, it is assumed that a person's absolute threshold fluctuates, sometimes being more sensitive and other times being less sensitive. Moreover, because the stimulus is often presented in the context of other stimuli (noise for example), signal detection techniques are more like the real world, where many stimuli occur at once and where people's expectations can bias their response.

Difference Thresholds   In addition to the question of absolute threshold, there is a second question: What is the smallest amount of change between two stimuli that a person can detect half of the time? This threshold is known as a **difference threshold**. Difference thresholds are also referred to as *just noticeable*

People whose jobs demand careful attention to sensory stimuli may be more aware of low-intensity signals than the rest of us. They may also be more likely to say they saw or heard something that wasn't there.

signal detection theory
the viewpoint that both stimulus intensity and decision-making processes are involved in the detection of a stimulus.

connection
Attention helps prevent sensory overload by filtering out sensory stimuli that aren't important.
See Chapter 6, p. 221.

difference threshold
the smallest amount of change between two stimuli that a person can detect half of the time.

	"Yes"	"No"
Stimulus Present	Hit	Miss
Stimulus Absent	False alarm	Correct rejection

FIGURE **4.2**
POSSIBLE OUTCOMES IN SIGNAL DETECTION RESEARCH. In signal detection theory, the participant's responses create a profile of hits, misses, false alarms, and correct rejections.

differences (JND) because they involve the smallest difference that is noticeable. Being able to perceive slight differences is essential to a piano tuner, for example, who has to be able to distinguish the slightest change in pitch to tune it.

The laws of just noticeable differences in sensory perception go back to Ernst Weber, who in 1834 discovered that the size of the JND is a constant fraction of the intensity of the stimulus. This is known as **Weber's law.** To put this more concretely: If you are given two weights, and one weighs 100 grams and the other weighs 103 grams, you would probably be able to say "Yes, these two objects are different in weight." But you might not be able to detect the difference between a 100-gram object and a 102-gram object. In this case, 3 grams, or 3%, is the JND. In fact, 3% is the JND for weight perception (Canter & Hirsch, 1955). This means, then, that even if you had much heavier objects, say of 100 and 102 *kilo-grams*, you would not perceive a difference in the weight of these two.

Weber's law
the finding that the size of a just noticeable difference is a constant fraction of the intensity of the stimulus.

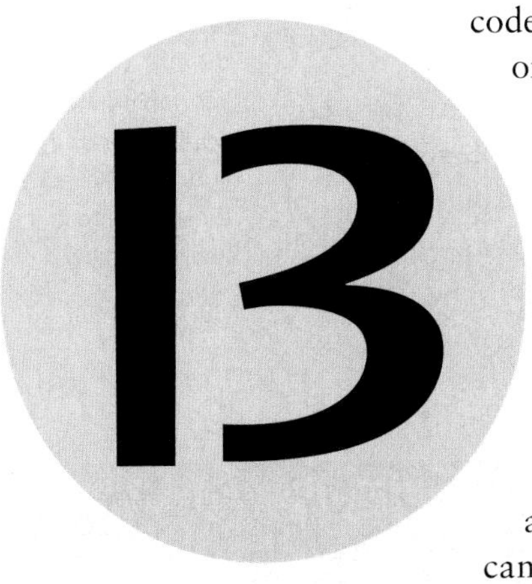

FIGURE **4.3**
A DEMONSTRATION OF PERCEPTUAL SET. People who saw this figure after a series of letters perceived it as a "B." Those who saw it after a series of numbers perceived it as a "13." (Bruner & Minturn, 1955)

Perceptual Set   We have already made clear that perception happens in the brain, after transduction of the stimulus at the sense organ. So our experience of seeing or hearing or tasting is primarily a result of brain processing. Other things going on in the brain at the time of sensory processing can influence perceptual experience. In particular, our frame of mind, which is ultimately coded in the brain, can impact how we perceive things. The effect of frame of mind on perception is known as **perceptual set.** Figure 4.3 reproduces an image from a classic study of perceptual set. Bruner and Minturn (1955) showed two groups of research participants this image. The two groups, however, each saw a different set of items before viewing this image. One group saw a series of numbers; the other saw a series of letters. Of those who saw the numbers first, the vast majority said that this image was the number "13." For those who saw letters first, the vast majority saw the figure as a "B." So, what people had seen prior to the test image created an expectation, or perceptual set, for how they perceived what came next. Many things function as perceptual sets: mood, health, knowledge of how the world works, and cultural upbringing.

perceptual set
the effect of frame of mind on perception; a tendency to perceive stimuli in a certain manner.

quick quiz 4.1: The Long Strange Trip From Sensation to Perception

1. The conversion of physical into neural information is called
   a. transduction
   b. conduction
   c. perception
   d. adaptation

2. Which of the following may act as a perceptual set in constructing our visual experience?
   a. mood
   b. expectation
   c. knowledge of how the world works
   d. all of the above

Answers can be found at the end of the chapter.

Vision

Most mammals rely on smell over all other senses, but humans are visual creatures. We rely so much on our sense of sight that we often ignore other types of information. Why is vision so important? Evolutionarily, being able to see helps us know where we are, what other people might want from us, and whether there is danger nearby. We evolved as hunter-gatherers. In hunting, vision is critical for locating prey and avoiding danger. So is hearing, which is our next-most-relied-upon sense. In gathering food, we use vision to locate the foods we can eat, but we also rely on our sense of smell to know whether a food is safe. But vision is king, and it starts with the eye.

SENSING VISUAL STIMULI

What does the eye do? It bends light, converts light energy to neural energy, and sends that information to the brain for further processing. The eye is the gateway to vision, but very little of what we experience as vision actually happens in the eye. Visual experience happens in the brain, as we learned from Mike May's story. Before we explore the more complicated matter of how the brain sees, let's look briefly at the organ of the eye itself and how it converts light energy to neural energy.

Vision and the Eye   Light enters the eye at the **cornea,** a clear hard covering that protects the lens. It then passes through liquid until it reaches a hole called the **pupil.** Light enters the interior of the eye through the pupil. The colored part of the eye, the **iris,** adjusts the pupil to control the amount of light entering the eye. The light then passes through the **lens,** which bends the light

pupil
the opening in the iris through which light enters the eye.

iris
the muscle that forms the colored part of the eye; it adjusts the pupil to regulate the amount of light that enters the eye.

cornea
the clear hard covering that protects the lens of the eye.

lens
the structure that sits behind the pupil; it bends the light rays that enter the eye to focus images on the retina.

How do 3-D glasses alter the way we perceive a movie?

rays. Muscles around the lens alter its shape, depending on the distance of an object, to allow it to focus light on the retina. The process by which the muscles control the shape of the lens to adjust to viewing objects at different distances is known as **accommodation**.

The **retina** is a thin layer of nerve tissue that lines the back of the eye. The retina consists of several layers of cells. As indicated in Figure 4.4, the light that hits the retina travels through several cell layers before processing begins. The deepest layer of cells, where processing of light energy begins, is the layer of **photoreceptors** (see Figure 4.4). Photoreceptors in the retina convert light energy into neural impulses. Two types of photoreceptors convert light energy into neural energy: rods and cones.

Rods play a key role in night vision, as they are most responsive to dark and light contrast. They work well at low illumination. We have all experienced rods in action. Consider what happens when someone turns out the lights. At first everything is completely dark. Then, with a bit of time, you begin to see

FIGURE **4.4**

THE EYE AND ITS RECEPTOR CELLS. In (a) we see all the main structures of the eye. Notice that the image of the butterfly is projected upside down on the retina in the back of the eye. In (b) we see the layers of cells in the retina, including the photoreceptors (rods and cones). In (c), an enlarged view of the retina shows the layers of the cells involved in processing light. Light hits the retina and is processed first by the photoreceptors (deepest layer), then by the *bipolar cells*, which send it to the ganglion cells.

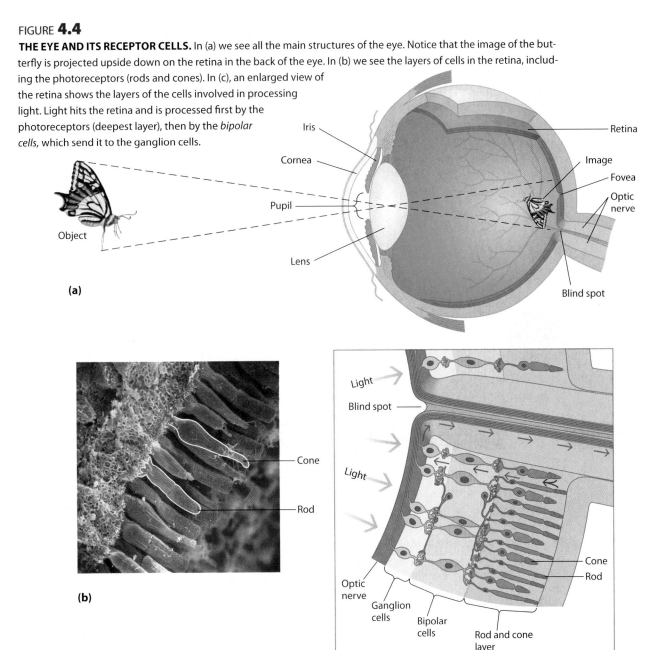

shapes and forms, although you cannot really see colors. The process of adjustment to seeing in the dark, known as **dark adaptation,** reflects the rods at work. This process of adapting to dark can take up to 30 minutes (Rushton, 1961). Rods are very sensitive, however, and sudden exposure to light can quickly cancel out their effectiveness.

dark adaptation
process of adjustment to seeing in the dark.

cones
photoreceptors that are responsible for color vision and are most functional in conditions of bright light.

visual acuity
the ability to see clearly.

     Cones, on the other hand, are responsible for color vision and are most functional in conditions of bright light. They act much more quickly than rods. Upon exposure to light, cones reach maximum effectiveness in about 5 minutes or so, because the chemicals involved in their function replenish quickly (Rushton, 1961). The **fovea,** a spot on the back of the retina, contains the highest concentration of cones in the retina. We see images with the greatest clarity when they are focused on the fovea. So **visual acuity,** or our ability to see clearly, depends on our cones. Those animals with the best acuity have the most cones. Most mammals only have two kinds of cones. Primates—humans included—have three. Birds have four cones (Goldsmith, 2006). Not only do birds see more colors than we, but they also far surpass humans in visual acuity. This gives the saying "to see like a hawk" new meaning.

fovea
spot on the back of the retina that contains the highest concentration of cones in the retina; place of clearest vision.

Vision and the Brain

After transduction at the photoreceptor layer, visual information is processed by different layers of cells in the retina. One of these layers is made up of the *ganglion cells,* the axons of which make up the optic nerve. The **optic nerve** transmits signals from the eye to the brain. The point at which the optic nerve exits the eye is the *blind spot* of the retina because this location has no receptor cells and therefore nothing is seen. Figure 4.5 offers a demonstration of the blind spot.

     When light enters the eye, the lens bends the light in such a way that the image is upside down compared to the orientation of the object in the outside world. Look at Figure 4.4 once again. You will notice that the image of the butterfly is flipped on the retina. The brain reorients the inverted image so that our world is right-side up.

optic nerve
structure composed of the axons of ganglion cells from the retina that carry visual information from the eye to the brain.

FIGURE **4.5**

TEST YOUR BLIND SPOT. Locate the blind spot in your left eye by shutting the right eye and looking at the upper cross with the left eye. Hold the book about 15 inches from the eye and move it slightly closer to and away from the eye until the circle on the left disappears. At this point the circle occupies the blind spot in the left eye. If you then look at the lower cross, the gap in the black line falls on the blind spot and the black line will appear to be continuous. (From Wurtz & Kandel, 2000a, who adapted it from Hurvich, 1981)

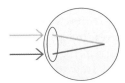

Uncorrected

In **nearsightedness,** the lens focuses the image in front of the retina.

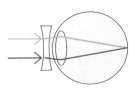

Corrected

In **nearsightedness,** with a minus lens for correction, the image focuses directly on the retina.

Uncorrected

In **farsightedness,** the lens focuses the image past the retina.

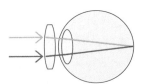

Corrected

In **farsightedness,** with a plus lens for correction, the image focuses directly on the retina.

FIGURE **4.6**

NEARSIGHTEDNESS AND FARSIGHTEDNESS. In nearsightedness, the uncorrected lens of the eye focuses the image short of the retina. In farsightedness, the uncorrected lens focuses the image past the retina. With corrective lenses, the image is accurately projected on the retina.

Another interesting detail about the focusing of the visual image on the retina concerns how well we see. In people with normal vision, the lens projects the image to hit just on the retina. In people who are nearsighted, the image focuses slightly in front of the retina (see Figure 4.6). This means that nearsighted people can see close objects clearly but far objects are fuzzy. In people who are farsighted, the image actually focuses behind the retina. This means they can see far objects clearly but near objects are fuzzy. As people age, the lens becomes less flexible, and it is more likely that the visual image will focus behind the retina. This is an age-related form of farsightedness.

Exactly what happens when visual information arrives in the brain? The optic nerve carries impulses to the thalamus and, ultimately, to the visual cortex of the occipital lobes. This journey is *not* straightforward. As you can see from Figure 4.7, the information from the left visual field is processed in the brain's right hemisphere, and the information from the right visual field is processed in the brain's left hemisphere. How the visual information gets to these hemispheres is a bit complicated. Let's look at this process more closely.

In Figure 4.7, notice that in each eye, each half of the retina (the area at the back) sends out its own axons. So each optic nerve has two strands. One strand from each eye contains axons that travel from the retina to the thalamus and on to the visual cortex of the *same* side of the brain as the eye from which the axons come. The other strand crosses to the *opposite* side of the brain in an area called the **optic chiasm.**

The first stop in the brain for most of the fibers of the optic nerve is the thalamus. If the pathways to the thalamus are cut, visual perception is not possible, beyond some crude ability to detect the presence of a stimulus (Wurtz & Kandel, 2000a). As we discussed in Chapter 3, the thalamus serves as a relay station for most of the major sense inputs to the brain, taking information from

connection

In people whose optic chiasms have been severed (split-brain patients), each eye sees only what is in the opposite visual field.

See Chapter 3, p. 106.

optic chiasm
the point at which strands of the optic nerve from half of each eye cross over to the opposite side of the brain.

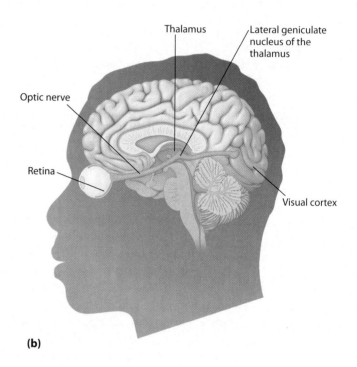

FIGURE **4.7**

THE VISUAL PATHWAYS IN HUMAN VISION. In (a) we see how input from the right visual field is sensed by the left side of the retina of each eye. This input then travels along the optic nerve to the optic chiasm and then to the thalamus (lateral geniculate nucleus). The same happens to input from the left visual field, except it is sensed by the right side of the retina of each eye (blue). From the thalamus, nerve fibers transmit visual information to the visual cortex of the occipital lobes (green). In (b) we see a sideview of the path that visual stimulation takes from the retina via the optic nerve and the thalamus to the visual cortex.

the sense organs and sending it to the relevant area of the cerebral cortex for processing. The thalamus does more than just relay information, however. Real visual processing occurs there. A cluster of the neuron cell bodies in the thalamus form the *lateral geniculate nucleus* (LGN). Visual information creates a point-by-point representation on the tissue of the LGN. What this means is that patterns of neural firing that correspond to the shape projected on a specific region of retina affect a similar layout of cells in the LGN. So the retina and the LGN represent visual information in similar ways (Wurtz & Kandel, 2000a).

Fibers from the LGN in the thalamus then travel to the visual cortex in the occipital lobes. Neurons in the visual cortex analyze the retinal image in terms of its various patterns, contrasts, lines, and edges. Different cortical cells handle different aspects of this analysis. A breakthrough discovery in neuroscience showed just how specific the functions of certain cortical cells can be.

breaking new ground
Functions of Individual Neurons in Vision

For centuries, a common belief was that nerves and the brain worked together as one structure to accomplish specific tasks, such as speech, vision, hearing, and thinking. Toward the end of the 1800s, however, many cases of brain injury demonstrated that injury to different parts of the brain resulted in different speech and behavior disabilities. We saw this in Chapter 3 with Broca's area and speech. These cases provided some of the earliest evidence that different parts of the brain performed different functions.

Until the mid–20th century, however, scholars studying vision focused mostly on the eye. It had long been known, for instance, that rods and cones were the primary photoreceptors and that nerve fibers from each eye crossed at the optic chiasm and projected into the brain. But researchers did not fully understand or appreciate the importance of the brain in vision (Finger, 1994). No one was prepared for the new findings that two neuroscientists, David Hubel and Torsten Wiesel, reported in the 1950s and 1960s.

HOW INDIVIDUAL NEURONS RESPOND TO VISUAL INPUT

Researchers had known for decades that after leaving the retina, optic fibers go to the visual portion of the thalamus (the LGN) and then travel to the visual cortex in the occipital lobes. The work of Hubel and Wiesel—for which they won the Nobel Prize in 1981—showed something astounding. Their work showed us that individual neurons fire only because of very specific visual information. They provided the first evidence that the neurons of the visual cortex are highly specialized for detecting specific features of visual stimuli. They were able to record specialized activity of individual cells in the brain's vision area by implanting electrodes into the visual cortex of cats. As a result, they discovered neurons called **feature detectors** in the visual cortex, which analyze the retinal image and respond to specific aspects of shapes, such as angles and movements (Hubel & Wiesel, 1962, 1979).

feature detectors neurons in the visual cortex that analyze the retinal image and respond to specific aspects of shapes, such as angles and movements.

More specifically, Hubel and Wiesel described three types of neurons in the visual cortex that act as feature detectors. *Simple cells* respond to very specific information, such as a bar of light oriented at a particular angle. Some simple cells respond to only one angle or orientation, other simple cells respond to other angles of orientation, and still others to edges. As seen in Figure 4.8a, a particular simple cell might be receptive only to a diagonal line of a particular orientation. As seen in Figure 4.8b, recordings from this one simple cell show activity only to lines that match its receptive field, which in this case is a diagonal line from about 11 o'clock to 5 o'clock (\ ). The cell begins to fire more often as the stimulus (line) approaches the angle to which the cell is most responsive. As the stimulus passes that orientation on its way back to horizontal, the cell fires less and less often. This is the activity of just one simple cell. Other simple cells are responsive to other orientations, shapes, and sizes of lines.

A simple cell responds only to visual stimuli that stay still or are in the middle of its receptive field. Other cells, called *complex cells,* receive input from many different simple cells and are receptive to particular stimuli in different parts of the receptive field. Unlike simple cells, complex cells are also sensitive to the movement of an image and responds if it appears anywhere in the visual field. In addition, *hypercomplex cells* receive inputs from many complex cells, and so they fire in response to patterns of lines.

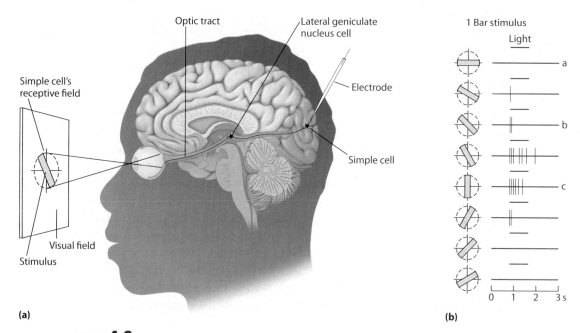

(a)

Simple cell's
receptive field

Optic tract

Lateral geniculate
nucleus cell

1 Bar stimulus

Electrode

Light

a

Simple cell

b

c

Visual field

Stimulus

0 1 2 3 s

(b)

FIGURE **4.8**

NEURAL ACTIVITY OF A SIMPLE CELL THAT IS RECEPTIVE TO ONE PARTICULAR DIAGONAL ORIENTATION. In (a) we see the stimulus on a visual field and how this particular simple cell is receptive to lines tilted from about 11 o'clock to 5 o'clock as if it were a clock face. In (b) each vertical line to the right of the stimulus represents a neural impulse. The cell begins to fire more often as the stimulus (line) approaches the angle to which the cell is the most responsive. As the stimulus passes that orientation on its way back to horizontal, the cell fires less and less frequently. Otherwise, this particular cell does not fire. (Adapted from Wurtz & Kandel, 2000a, p. 534)

To give a concrete example: If some simple cells are responsive to / and others to \, then the hypercomplex cells are sensitive to the entire configuration of \/\/.

If the images and objects are broken up into horizontal and vertical lines, edges, colors, faces, hands, and shapes by the visual cortex, how is it that we ever see whole and integrated images? Reassembling the pieces occurs partly in hypercomplex cells in the visual cortex, but integration mostly happens when the visual cortex sends the images to other parts of the brain, such as the frontal or parietal lobes (Perry & Zeki, 2000; Wurtz & Kandel, 2000b). Thus, the cortex does not passively accept the nerve impulses from the retina and thalamus. The cortex actively transforms the signals by first breaking them down and then putting them back together.

Hubel and Wiesel made an even more monumental discovery when they closed one eye of a newborn cat. In the first weeks in a cat's life, when its brain is growing the most, visual experience is critical for brain structures to develop all the necessary neural connections needed to see well. If a cat is blinded or has its eyes closed for a week or more during this important stage of development, its visual cortex does not develop properly and the animal's vision is forever stunted. If one eye is closed early in life for an extended period of time, the part of the brain receiving messages from the closed eye soon begins to receive and process visual messages from the one good eye. Moreover, it is not merely light that the developing brain needs if vision is to properly develop, but also lines, shapes, and colors—the full visual experience. We see because our brains learn to see.

HOW THESE FINDINGS CHANGED PSYCHOLOGY

The implications of Hubel and Wiesel's findings are quite profound. For instance, we can better understand the case of Mike May, who regained vision as an adult after going blind as a 3-year-old child. If the cortex and other parts of the brain have missed the window of opportunity to fully learn how to reassemble images, as in the case of Mike May, it may be impossible or very difficult to learn it later. After his operation, his brain almost immediately was able to take in color and motion, but not three-dimensional space, depth, faces, and gender (Kurson, 2007). These more complex activities require more than visual training and experience to achieve. His eyes were fine, but his brain had missed the critical period for visual cortical growth and had forgotten how to see.

After Hubel and Wiesel's work, other researchers continued to find other cortical cells that fire in response to certain visual stimuli. Some, for example, respond to faces. If some cells fire when they are stimulated with faces in general, what happens when cells are stimulated with a specific face? Believe it or not, scientists have found evidence of cortical cells in the temporal lobe that respond only to images of certain individuals—for example, images of Bill Clinton, Jennifer Aniston, and Halle Berry (Quiroga et al., 2005). The so-called "Halle Berry neuron" that one individual displayed responds not just to photos of Berry, but also to line drawings of her and to her name printed in white letters against a black background!

nature & nurture

Some neurons fire when they see specific faces; others fire when they see other, specific faces.

This consistency of response by single cells to different types of stimuli—with very different physical features (color photos, lines on paper, and typeface)—associated with Halle Berry shows that individual cells are responsive to abstract categories. Although the temporal lobe is not part of visual processing in most people, the specificity of cell response is very compelling. Does that mean we are born with Halle Berry neurons? No. What it does mean is that based on our exposure and interest in certain things or people, *single cells* can come to represent a category of things, such as all things Halle Berry-ish.

connections
In many areas of development, such as language and learning, there are sensitivity periods when the brain is optimally receptive to environmental stimulation. One researcher found this out when newly hatched goslings (geese) mistook him for their mother.
See Chapter 8, p. 322, and Chapter 9, p. 339.

Do you have a Halle Berry neuron?

quick quiz 4.2: Sensing Visual Stimuli

1. Neurons called _____ in the visual cortex analyze the retinal image and respond to aspects of shapes, such as angles and movements.
   a. subjective contours
   b. shape responsive cells
   c. feature detectors
   d. horizontal cells

2. How did Hubel and Wiesel discover that some cortical neurons responded to seeing lines of a specific orientation?
   a. by using fMRI to study cat brain function during visual tasks
   b. by inserting electrodes into single cells in the visual cortex
   c. through surgical removal of cortical tissue
   d. with EEG

Answers can be found at the end of the chapter.

PERCEIVING VISUAL STIMULI

So far we have followed visual information from light entering the eye to impulses sent to the thalamus and then on the visual cortex, where cells fire in response to very specific features of a visual stimulus. How do we move from detecting edges to perceiving shapes, from noticing lines to identifying objects? A number of processes work together to help us recognize objects in the world. These involve motion, depth, size, grouping, and color perception.

Perceiving Motion   Feature detectors play a role in how we perceive movement and form. We perceive movement when an image moves across the retina. Simple and complex cells respond to either the orientation or direction of moving images. Sometimes these moving images truly reflect movement in the world around us. As we view any scene, several factors contribute to how we perceive movement. One factor is the background against which an object moves, and another factor is the size of the object. When an object moves across a complex background, it appears to move faster than when it moves across a simple background. For example, a deer running across a field with mountains and trees in the background will seem to move faster than one running across a wide open plain, simply because the background objects provide references that help us note the change of position in the deer. The human visual system is quite sensitive to changes in the position of objects, a sensitivity that appears to decline a bit with age (Bennett, Sekuler, & Sekuler, 2007).

Size matters too. Smaller objects appear to move faster than larger objects, when all else is equal. If we see a domestic rabbit and a mule deer run across a wide open plain, the rabbit will appear to be running at a faster speed because of its size. In fact, these two animals run at about the same speed.

We can also be fooled into thinking something is moving when it is not. We refer to this illusion as *apparent motion* because our brains interpret images that move across our retinas as movement. The "moving" lights on a movie theater marquee are a rapid succession of bulbs lighting up in a row. Even though we know the lights are not moving, we still interpret this illusion as movement.

Here's another interesting question. If you press on your eyelid when your eye is open and look straight ahead, you will notice the image shaking around. Yet, you do not perceive this effect as an earthquake. Why? According to research on monkeys, there are neurons that respond only when the image itself moves and not when the eye moves. So when you press on your eye, these neurons that detect image movement, called *real movement neurons,* do not fire. When the image itself moves without eye movement, they do fire (Galletti & Fattori, 2003). This is one way the brain can determine the difference between real and false movement.

depth perception
the ability to see things in three dimensions and to discriminate what is near from what is far.

binocular depth cues
aids to depth perception that rely on input from both eyes.

Depth Perception   We take for granted that we see things in three dimensions and can discriminate what is near from what is far, or what we call **depth perception.** This skill is remarkable, given that the image projected on the retina is two-dimensional. So how does this work? Two major aspects of human visual anatomy and processing allow for depth perception: binocular and monocular depth cues.

Binocular Depth Cues. **Binocular depth cues** rely on input from both eyes. One key binocular cue to depth comes from the fact that the eyes are separated by a few inches, so the images from each eye provide slightly different viewpoints. The difference, or *binocular disparity,* in these retinal images plays a key role in our ability to perceive depth. To see how this works, hold a finger out in front of you. Close one eye, and then close the other eye: You will see how the image shifts slightly to one side, depending on which eye is closed and which eye is opened. The brain integrates these two slightly different two-dimensional images into a single three-dimensional image. Many animals are capable of depth perception, but this quality depends on the location of the eyes in the head.

Another binocular depth cue comes from information provided by the muscles that move the eyeballs around. Put your right finger out in front of you at arm's length. As you move the finger closer to your nose, your eyes come together or move inward. When you move the finger away from you, they move outward. This way that your eyes move inward as an object moves closer to you is known as **convergence.** During convergence of the eyes, the muscles that move the eyeball contract, and the brain makes use of the feedback from these muscles to perceive distance. Convergence is most effective as a depth cue for stimuli that are relatively close to us—that is, within 10 feet (Goldstein, 2007).

Monocular Depth Cues. We derive a great deal of information about depth from the numerous **monocular depth cues** (*monocular* meaning "one eye") that do not require two eyes to be effective. These cues allow people who are blind in one eye to perceive some depth. Our knowledge of many of these cues derives from the seminal work of James Gibson (1950, 1966). Let's discuss some of the most common ones. *Linear perspective* involves parallel lines that converge or come together the farther away they are from the viewer. The more they converge, the greater distance we perceive. See Figure 4.9a for this classic effect in railroad tracks. *Texture gradient* is a monocular depth cue that causes the texture of a surface to appear more tightly packed together and denser as the surface moves to the background. These changes in textural information help us judge depth. Notice in Figure 4.9b that the red poppies are more tightly packed at the top of the picture, which makes us think that those flowers are farther away. Another cue, *atmospheric perspective,* comes from looking across a vast space into the distance in the outdoors. Anyone who has stood at the edge of the Grand Canyon has seen atmospheric perspective at work. We are looking through air and particles in the air (more so when the air is polluted). Objects farther away appear more blurred and bluish as a result (see Figure 4.9c). A final monocular depth cue is called *interposition,* the partial blocking of objects farther away from the viewer by objects closer to the viewer, which happens when objects closer to the viewer often overlap with those farther away. This is a reliable cue to depth. Look at the image in Figure 4.9d of the lemons. The closer lemons hide part of the one behind them.

(a) linear perspective

(b) texture gradient

(c) atmospheric perspective

(d) interposition

FIGURE **4.9**
MONOCULAR CUES TO DEPTH. It isn't necessary to have vision in both eyes to perceive depth using monocular cues.

Perceptual Constancy   We know what familiar objects look like, and we know that when they change position or distance in relation to us, they remain the same. Nevertheless, the images on our retinas change shape and size as objects move through space. The ability of the brain to preserve perception of such objects in spite of the changes in retinal image is known as **perceptual constancy.** We will look at two types of perceptual constancy: those of size and shape.

perceptual constancy
the ability of the brain to preserve perception of objects in spite of changes in retinal image when an object changes in position or distance from the viewer.

Size Constancy. We see things as the same size regardless of the changing size of the image on the retina, because we know what the size of the object is. For example, if you see your friend Jayson, who is about 6 feet tall, walking away from you, the size of his image on your retina shrinks. Yet you do not suddenly think, "Oh no, Jayson is shrinking!" Rather, your knowledge of Jayson's height and your knowledge that people maintain their height even when they move away from you prevent you from interpreting the smaller retinal image as a smaller person. Also, distance cues, such as linear perspective, indicate that the road Jayson is walking on is in the distance and your brain makes use of this information *plus* your knowledge of Jayson's size to keep his size constant in your mind.

A stunning demonstration of distortions in the perception of size is the Ames room. In the photograph below (Figure 4.10a), the child on the right looks enormous compared to the one on the left. It turns out, however, that the room is not rectangular (as we expect it to be) but rather trapezoidal, and the girl on the right is standing much closer to the peephole through which the viewer looks (as depicted in Figure 4.10b). So the distance cues that we tend to rely on are not available, and we perceive the two people as equally far away, which makes the child on the right appear enormous.

(a) (b)

FIGURE **4.10**

THE AMES ROOM. The Ames room was designed to distort perceptions of size (a). When a person looks into the room through a peephole, it appears to be a normal rectangular room and hence the two people seem to be very different sizes: The one on the right is a giant compared to the one on the left. In reality, the two people are the same size. The room is built in such a way that the rear right wall is much closer to the viewer than the left rear wall, masking distance cues on which we tend to rely for size perception (b).

FIGURE **4.11**
SHAPE CONSTANCY. Even though the 2-dimensional retinal image of the door changes in shape from rectangular to trapezoidal when the door is opened, we know the door's shape hasn't changed.

Shape Constancy. People know the shapes of common things just as they know their sizes. The brain uses this knowledge to override changing retinal images that might make the world very confusing indeed. Take a look at Figure 4.11. When we see a door that is closed, it looks like a rectangle (and this is what the 2-D image on our retina looks like). A door that is partially open looks like a trapezoid. Still, we would not think that the door has suddenly changed shape. Again, the brain corrects based on previous knowledge that doors retain their shape when they change position.

Organizing Visual Information: Gestalt Laws of Grouping

How is it that we recognize a set of black marks on a white page as a letter or a shape rather than just a bunch of markings? We know, for example, that the letter "E" is more than just one long vertical line segment plus three shorter horizontal line segments. The Gestalt psychologists recognized that often we perceive wholes as more than merely the sum of their parts. *Gestalt* is a German word that means "form," "pattern," or "shape." German researchers Max Wertheimer, Kurt Koffka, and Wolfgang Köhler studied visual perception in the early 20th century and described a set of principles or laws by which people organize elements of figures or scenes into whole objects. These laws are most easily demonstrated with visual examples, though we can apply them to sounds. For example, when we hear notes strung together in certain patterns, we hear a musical phrase or tune, not just individual notes. Let's examine the major Gestalt laws of visual organization: similarity, continuity, proximity, closure, and figure-ground.

What do you see when you look at Figure 4.12? Most people with normal color vision would report seeing two lines of blue dots alternating with two lines of red dots. You would not say "Oh, 20 dots; some are red and some are blue." Instead, we group the elements that are like one another together into a perceptual unit—the red dots go together and the blue dots go together. This Gestalt tendency to group like objects together is known as **similarity.**

similarity
the Gestalt tendency to group like objects together in visual perception.

FIGURE **4.12**
GESTALT LAWS OF ORGANIZATION: SIMILARITY. People are more likely to see this figure as two rows of blue dots and two rows of red dots than as 20 dots, some red, some blue.

continuity
the Gestalt tendency to see points or lines in such a way that they follow a continuous path.

FIGURE **4.13**

GESTALT LAWS OF ORGANIZATION: CONTINUITY.

connection

The Gestalt law of proximity makes use of the short-term memory technique called "chunking."

See Chapter 7, p. 261.

According to the Gestalt law of **continuity,** we see points or lines in such a way that they follow a continuous path. This sounds rather abstract, so let's look at an example. Consider the first drawing in Figure 4.13. We see a straight line running through a curved line. We do *not* see the first drawing as a result of combining the two pieces from the second drawing.

The Gestalt law of **proximity** says that we tend to group together objects that are near one another. Figure 4.14 shows a series of blue boxes. How would you describe what you see here? Most people say that they see four pairs of boxes, rather than eight boxes, because of the spacing. The first two are closer together than the second and third, and the third and fourth are closer together than the fourth and fifth, and so on.

proximity
the Gestalt tendency to group objects together that are near one another.

FIGURE **4.14**

GESTALT LAWS OF ORGANIZATION: PROXIMITY.

Take a look at Figure 4.15a. Most human observers see these figures as distinct shapes (a circle and two triangles) rather than as lines, curves, and spheres, even though they are incomplete. The **law of closure** occurs when we perceive a whole object in the absence of complete information. The drawing in Figure 4.15b provides another example of how our perceiving brain completes the drawing to see a duck.

FIGURE **4.15**

closure
the Gestalt tendency to see a whole object even when complete information isn't available.

GESTALT LAWS OF ORGANIZATION: CLOSURE. We see the figures (a) as distinct shapes. We see (b) as a duck, not as a bunch of curved line segments.

(a) **(b)**

Another key Gestalt notion concerns how we separate things into *figure* and *ground,* where the figure is the thing that stands in front of a somewhat unformed background. Gestalt psychologists pointed out that we readily separate a figure from its background in order to perceive it. Perhaps the most famous example of figure-ground effects is the face-vase figure, a version of which is shown in Figure 4.16a. Notice that you can view the figure either as a blue vase against a light background or as two facial profiles (with blue space in between them). It is impossible to see both the vase and the faces at the same moment. Dutch painter M. C. Escher regularly used figure-ground effects in his paintings, one of which is also depicted in Figure 4.16b.

(a)

FIGURE **4.16**
FIGURE-GROUND EFFECTS.
In (a), is it a vase or two faces? In
(b), M.C. Escher's *Sky & Water I*, do
you see fish or geese?

(b)

FIGURE **4.17**
**FIGURE AND GROUND EFFECTS IN SCENE
PERCEPTION.** What do you see in this image?
See page 167 to find out what you may have
missed.

Numerous visual illusions stem from
Gestalt figure-ground principles, many
of which have hidden figures as in Figure 4.17. Once you know what to look for
in the picture, the hidden object becomes
figural and you cannot help but see it.
Try it for yourself.

Other visual illusions make use of
the way our brain interprets depth cues
(see Figure 4.18). Which line is longer, the
one on the right or the one on the left? If
you take a ruler to the page you will find
that both line segments are identical in
length, but many people report that the
one on the right looks longer. Why do
we see it that way? This illusion, known
as the Müller-Lyer illusion, results from
our tendency to see the right line as the
inside corner of a room and the left one

FIGURE **4.18**

THE MULLER-LYER ILLUSION.
Which line is longer?

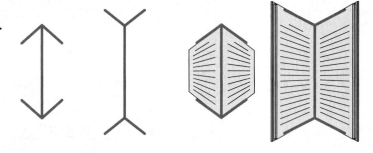

FIGURE **4.19**
**MOON ILLU-
SION.** Distance
cues make the
moon look bigger
at the horizon.

as the outside corner of a room or building, making use of the monocular depth cue of linear perspective.

Another commonly experienced illusion results from monocular depth cues. The *moon illusion* occurs when the moon is closer to the horizon. At that time, it appears to be much larger than when it is in the sky. Of course, the moon is not any larger, so why does this happen? Scientists offer several different explanations for the moon illusion, and although no answer provides one true cause for the illusion, nearly all explanations involve cues to depth perception (Goldstein, 2007). One explanation is that when the moon is near the horizon, we see it against other cues that indicate we are looking off into the distance (such as buildings interposed on the moon, possibly roads that offer cues to linear perspective, and so on). You can see this in Figure 4.19. Another way to look at it is this: When the moon is in the middle of the night sky, there are no cues to distance, no objects with which to compare it, and it is surrounded by a huge sky. Relative to the sky, the moon does not look so big. When the moon is on the horizon, however, we view it against objects whose size we know. Relative to those earthly objects, the moon looks enormous, which it is (Baird, Wagner, & Fuld, 1990).

Visual Perception: Bottom-Up or Top-Down?

Feature detection research suggests that visual perception is a process of building a visual experience from smaller pieces. We put the pieces together, and then we "see" the whole. This perspective is known as **bottom-up processing.** Yet we have also looked at how perceptual set and Gestalt principles can guide how we make visual sense of information. An implied familiar shape, such as that seen in Figure 4.3, overrides our perception of the elements. Processing in which perception of the whole guides perception of smaller elemental features is called **top-down processing.** These two processes would seem to work in opposition, so which is correct? It depends on the nature of the information being processed. Reading, for example, relies on both bottom-up and top-down processing. To recognize a vertical line segment intersected by a shorter line segment as a "t," some building up of elemental features is required. But to make sense of the meaning of a "t" next to an "o" as the word "to," some top-down processing takes over, including your knowledge of English and the meaning of a preposition in a sentence (Johnston & McClelland, 1974; Pelli, Farell, & More, 2003).

bottom-up processing
assembling a perceptual experience.

top-down processing
perception of the whole based on our experience and expectations, which guide our perception of smaller elemental features of a stimulus.

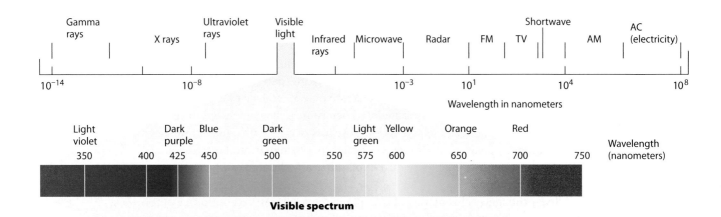

Light violet		Dark purple	Blue		Dark green		Light green	Yellow	Orange	Red
350	400	425	450	500		550	575	600	650	700	750

Wavelength (nanometers)

Visible spectrum

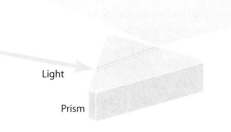

Light

Prism

FIGURE **4.20**

LIGHT WAVES AND THE ELECTROMAGNETIC SPECTRUM. The entire electromagnetic spectrum ranges from gamma waves at the smallest end to AC current at the largest end. Between these two extremes is a very narrow band of wavelengths visible to the human eye. Visible light ranges from about 300 nanometers (violet) to about 750 nanometers (red).

The Perception of Color We tend to think of color as a property of the objects we see. "That rose is red" or "The sky is blue." But color is not a property of objects—it is a property of us. Our perception of color depends on our photoreceptors, our brains, and the physical characteristics of the stimulus we look at. Let's start with the physical stimulus. Color perception is partly determined by wavelength, measured in billionths of a meter or nanometers (nm). The spectrum of color visible to humans ranges from 350 nm, which most of us perceive to be the color blue, to 750 nm, which most of us perceive as red. Light that we perceive as green is at 550 nm. Figure 4.20 shows the spectrum of light visible to humans.

Two Theories of Color Vision. Psychological science has offered two main theories of color perception, each of which explains different aspects of how most humans see color. Let's consider the aspects of perception that each explains.

Young and Helmholtz developed their theory of color vision around the idea that people have three kinds of cones: red, green, and blue. We now know this is anatomically correct, but Young and Helmholtz did not. They inferred it from their experiments on color perception. They reasoned that all color that we experience must result from a mixing of these three colors of light, so they called their theory the **trichromatic color theory.** But mixing light is not like mixing paints. Mix red, green, and blue light together in equal amounts and you get white; with paints, you get a brownish muck. Light color mixing actually occurs inside the eye, in terms of how different kinds of cones respond to different wavelengths of light.

trichromatic color theory
the theory that all color that we experience results from a mixing of three colors of light (red, green, and blue).

The human retina contains three kinds of receptor cones, each sensitive to different wavelengths of light. The red cones fire in response to longer-wavelength light. Green cones respond to medium-wavelength light, and blue cones respond to shorter-wavelength light. Different firing patterns of these various kinds of photoreceptors combine to help create our experience of a wide array of colors. How much each cone is stimulated determines the color we will see. For instance, for most people, the perception of yellow occurs with equal stimulation of red and green cones plus a smidgen of blue cone stimulation. So trichromatic color theory went a long way toward explaining how humans in fact see color. But it has limitations.

Even though trichromatic color explains how photoreceptors process colored light, it cannot explain some aspects of color vision. Take, for example, color afterimages. **Afterimages** are visual images that remain after removal of the stimulus. Figure 4.21 demonstrates a popular color afterimage. Stare at the white spot in the middle of the green and black flag for about 10 seconds and then stare at the black dot in the white rectangle, where you will see, very briefly, a regular red, white, and blue American flag. Trichromatic color theory cannot account for this afterimage, but opponent-process theory can.

Ewald Hering (1878) proposed **opponent-process theory** to explain color vision. He said that cones are linked together in three opposing color pairs: blue/yellow, red/green, and black/white. The members of the color pairs oppose one another, whereby activation of one member of the pair inhibits activity in the other. Opponent-process theory can account for the color afterimage of the American flag. This theory also helps to explain some types of color blindness, as well as why we never experience some colors, such as reddish-green or yellowish-blue.

Current research indicates that both theories account for how human color vision works. The trichromatic theory explains processing at the retina or cone, of which there are three types. Opponent process theory explains more about how cells in the LGN of the thalamus and visual cortex process color information. In these brain areas, some cells are excited by red, for example, and inhibited by green stimuli (Lennie, 2000).

afterimages visual images that remain after removal of or looking away from the stimulus.

opponent-process theory the theory that color vision results from cones linked together in three opposing pairs of colors so that activation of one member of the pair inhibits activity in the other.

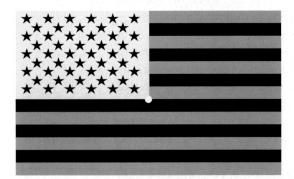
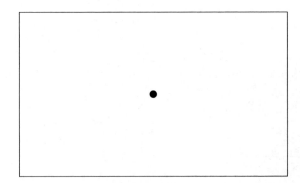

FIGURE **4.21**

COLOR AFTERIMAGE. Stare at the white spot in the middle of the green and black flag for about ten seconds and then stare at the black dot in the white rectangle on the right. You will see, very briefly, a regular red, white, and blue American flag. Trichromatic color theory cannot account for this afterimage, but opponent-process theory can.

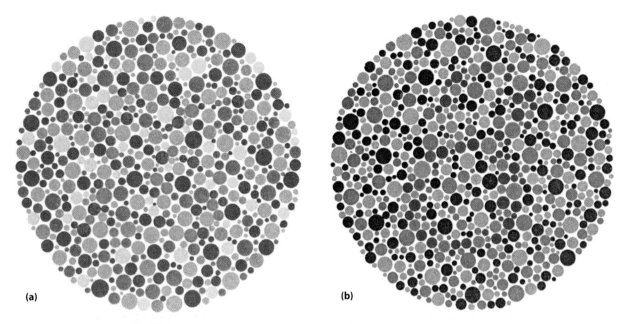

(a) (b)

FIGURE **4.22**

EXAMPLES OF THE ISHIHARA COLOR BLINDNESS TEST. People with normal color vision can see the numbers embedded among the dots of both pictures. People with red-green color blindness can see the "16" in (a) but they cannot see the "8" in (b).

Deficiencies in Color Vision. There are many types of color blindness. Only about 10 people in a million actually fail to see color at all (Goldstein, 2007). More commonly, color blindness refers to a weakness or deficiency in perception of certain colors. Usually this results from an inherited pigment deficiency in the photoreceptors. The most common forms, most often seen in men and boys due to the pattern of inheritance, occurs when certain cones are not as sensitive as they should be. The most common form of color blindness results from a deficiency in red (long-wavelength light) and green (medium-wavelength light) sensitive cones. People with this disorder have trouble distinguishing some shades of green from red, may see green and brown as similar, or might have difficulty distinguishing blue and purple (purple has more red in it, so when a person cannot pick up on the red, purple and blue look alike). Figure 4.22 presents a color blindness test that taps into red–green weaknesses. Yellow–blue deficiencies are less common.

quick quiz 4.3: Perceiving Visual Stimuli

1. What fibers make up the optic nerve?
   a. axons from ganglion cells of the retina
   b. axons from rods
   c. axons from thalamus
   d. occipital neuron axons

2. After leaving the retina, what is the first stop in the brain for processing of visual information?
   a. the occipital cortex
   b. the parietal lobe
   c. the hypothalamus
   d. the thalamus

3. Which of the following is *not* a monocular depth cue?
   a. linear perspective
   b. convergence
   c. texture gradient
   d. interposition

4. The ability of the brain to preserve perception of objects in spite of the changes in retinal image is known as
   a. interrelative consistency
   b. proximity
   c. visual stability
   d. perceptual constancy

Answers can be found at the end of the chapter.

Hearing

We could clearly make the case that for humans seeing is the most important sense. So much of our lives revolves around what we see. The science of vision is much more developed than the science of any other sense. And yet people who are both blind and deaf beg to differ. The deaf and blind American author Helen Keller put it most eloquently when she wrote:

> I am just as deaf as I am blind. The problems of deafness are deep and more complex, if not more important, than those of blindness. Deafness is a much worse misfortune. For it means the loss of the most vital stimulus—the sound of the voice that brings language, sets thoughts astir and keeps us in the intellectual company of man. (Helen Keller, as quoted in Ackerman, 1990, p. 191.)

Just as vision starts when we sense light waves, hearing begins when we sense sound waves. Sound waves must travel through some medium or we cannot hear them. Sound waves can move through fluid or air, but most of the time we hear sound waves that travel through air. Sound waves travel much more slowly than light waves, which is why you hear thunder after you have seen lightning.

Theatres and concert halls are designed to reflect and absorb sound so that wherever you sit, you can hear the performance. For musicians, however, constant exposure to loud music can cause hearing loss.

THE PHYSICS OF SOUND
AND THE PSYCHOLOGY OF HEARING

We perceive different shapes and sizes of sound waves as different sounds. Hearing is affected by three physical properties of the sound wave: its amplitude, frequency, and purity. The height, or *amplitude*, of the sound wave determines what we perceive as loudness. The taller the wave is, the louder the sound. The scale for a sound's loudness is decibels (dB). The scale starts with 0, which is the threshold for normal human hearing. The scale has no upper limit, but sounds above 150–170 dB are seldom registered anywhere. To give you markers for loudness: A whisper is about 30 dB, a regular human conversation is about 55–60 dB, a jackhammer is about 90 dB, a very loud bar or nightclub is around 100–110 dB, a very loud rock concert is about 110–120 dB, and a jet airplane is about 130–140 dB. If you were to ever hear a sound at 160dB, your eardrum would burst. Where might you hear such an incredibly loud noise? Believe it or not, car sound system competitions, such as "dB Drag Racing" regularly achieve sound in the 150–160dB range. The record stands at 171dB. Needless to say, these levels are strictly for competition and no one is in the car during the competition.

The *frequency* of the sound wave, or how many waves occur in a given period of time, we perceive as the sound's pitch. Frequency is measured in units called *hertz (Hz)*, which is how many times the wave cycles per second. The higher the frequency, the higher the pitch. The higher keys on a piano—those further to the right—are of higher pitch than the lower keys, for example. The range for human pitch perception is from about 20 Hz to about 20,000 Hz but most people cannot hear sounds at either extreme. Sounds below 20 Hz are called *subsonic* and above 20,000 are called *ultrasonic*. Most sounds we hear are in the range of 400 to 4,000 Hz. The human voice generally ranges from 200 to 800 Hz, and a piano plays notes ranging from 30 to 4,000 Hz.

The third property of sound waves, *purity*, refers to the complexity of the wave. Some sound waves are pretty simple, made of only one frequency (see Figure 4.23). Most, however, are almost always a mixture of frequencies and how much of a mixture defines its purity. We perceive purity as timbre (pronounced "tamber"). Musicians often refer to timbre as the "color" of sound. Timbre allows us to distinguish a middle C (256 Hz) as being from either a piano or from a violin. They both are 256 Hz and may even be of equal loudness, but we have no trouble telling them apart because they produce waves of different purities.

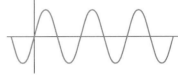

Pure wave

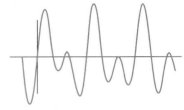

Complex wave

FIGURE **4.23**
PURE AND COMPLEX SOUND WAVES. A pure wave consists of only one wave, whereas a complex wave is a mixture of more than one wave.

THE EAR

The anatomy of the ear is relatively straightforward. First off, as the structures on the sides of our head, our ears have very little to do with hearing itself. These structures, called *pinnae*, collect and funnel sounds into the passage called the *auditory canal*. Once inside this canal, sound vibrations travel to the eardrum, or **tympanic membrane**. The auditory canal and tympanic membrane make up the *outer ear*. The sound waves on the tympanic membrane set into motion the bones of the *middle ear*: the hammer, anvil, and stirrup (see Figure 4.24). These bones do more than just vibrate: They amplify the waves so that they have more

tympanic membrane
the eardrum.

FIGURE **4.24**

ANATOMY OF THE HUMAN EAR. Sound waves hit the outer ear and travel down the auditory canal, where they vibrate the eardrum, which sets in motion the bones of the middle ear (hammer, anvil, and stirrup). The bones vibrate and amplify the waves, where they vibrate the oval window. The vibrations cause fluid in the cochlea to bend the hair cells. Stimulation of the hair cells traduces sound vibrations into electrical impulses. These electrical impulses can generate an action potential in the auditory nerve, which is then sent to the brain's auditory cortex for processing and interpreting.

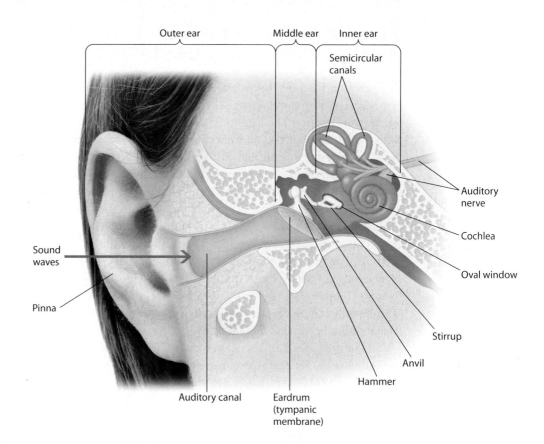

than 20 times the energy they had entering the ear. The hammer hits the anvil and the anvil moves the stirrup. The vibration of the stirrup, in turn, sets into motion a series of important changes in the *inner ear.*

The inner ear includes the cochlea and semicircular canals. The **semi-circular canals** play a key role in maintaining a sense of balance. As the stirrup vibrates, it moves a membrane that covers the inner ear, called the *oval window.* The vibrations on the oval window send movement through the fluid-filled cavity of the cochlea. The **cochlea** is a bony tube, curled like a snail's shell, and filled with fluid. The **basilar membrane** runs through the cochlea. Within the basilar membrane of the cochlea are **hair cells,** which are the sensory receptors for sound just as the photoreceptors are for vision. As the vibrations move through the cochlear fluid, the basilar membrane vibrates, and this makes the hair cells bend. As they bend, the hair cells transduce the sound vibrations into electrical impulses, which may generate an action potential in the **auditory nerve.**

Hair cells vary in size depending on where in the cochlea they are. The smallest hair cells are nearest the oval window, and the largest hair cells are in the coiled-up center part of the cochlea. There is a one-to-one connection between the size of a hair cell and its sensitivity to different frequency of sounds. The smallest cells are sensitive to the highest frequencies (up to 20,000 Hz), and the largest hair cells are sensitive to the lowest frequencies (down to 20 Hz) (see Figure 4.25). The louder the sound, the bigger the vibration in the cochlear fluid, the more stimulation of the hair cells, the faster the rate of action potentials in the auditory nerve, and louder the sound we perceive.

cochlea
a bony tube of the inner ear, which is curled like a snail's shell and filled with fluid.

basilar membrane
a membrane that runs through the cochlea; contains the hair cells.

hair cells
inner ear sensory receptors that transduce sound vibrations into neural impulses.

auditory nerve
the nerve that receives action potentials from the hair cells and transmits auditory information to the brain.

semicircular canals
structure of the inner ear involved in maintaining balance.

Touring the Senses

Parts of the Eye ▪ **Visual Pathways** ▪ **Parts of the Ear** ▪ **The Olfactory Sense**

GOALS OF THE TOUR

1 **Parts of the Eye.** You will be able to identify the structures of the human eye and describe their functions.

2 **Visual Pathways.** You will be able to identify the pathways for visual stimulation and describe the brain's role in visual information processing.

3 **Parts of the Ear.** You will be able to identify the three areas of the ear and describe the key structures of the inner ear.

4 **The Olfactory Sense.** You will be able to describe how the olfactory sense processes a smell.

Answers on page 4T-4

Parts of the Eye and Visual Pathways

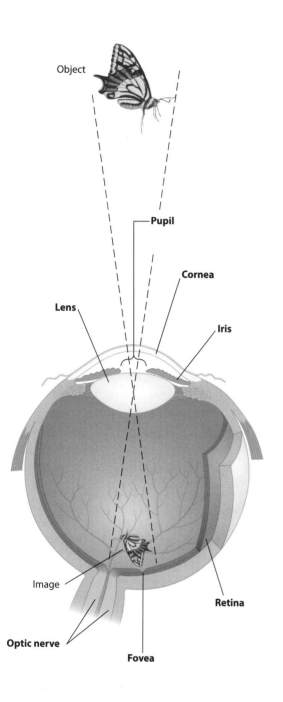

Object

Pupil

Cornea

Lens

Iris

Image

Optic nerve

Retina

Fovea

Left visual field

Right visual field

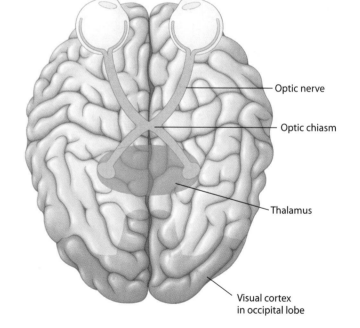

Optic nerve

Optic chiasm

Thalamus

Visual cortex
in occipital lobe

Parts of the Ear and the Olfactory Sense

Identify the three areas of the ear and describe the key structures of the inner ear.

3

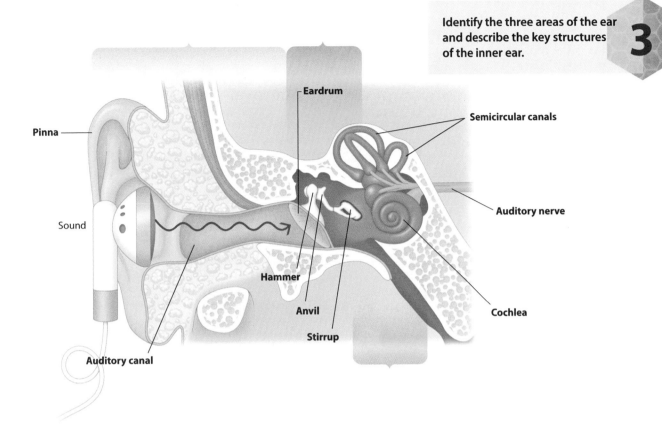

Eardrum

Pinna

Semicircular canals

Sound

Auditory nerve

Hammer

Anvil

Cochlea

Stirrup

Auditory canal

4 Describe how the olfactory sense processes a smell.

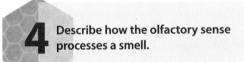

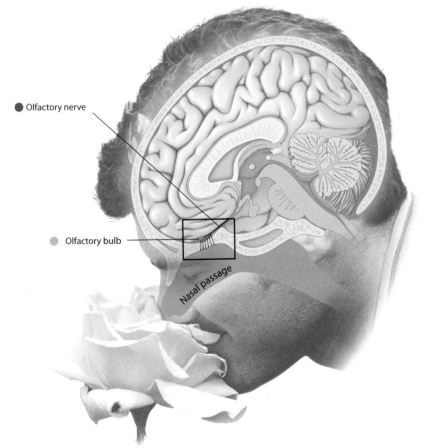

● Olfactory nerve

● Olfactory bulb

Nasal passage

1. PARTS OF THE EYE

The *retina* is made up of a layer of cells in the interior of the eye that contain the *photoreceptors*, the rods and the cones.

The *cornea* is the transparent membrane in the front of the eye that protects the eye and bends light to provide focus.

The *pupil* is the opening that allows light to enter the eye.

The *iris* is the colored muscle that surrounds the pupil and adjusts the amount of light entering into the eye through the pupil. It dilates (opens) or constricts (closes) in response to the intensity (brightness) of the light. It also dilates in response to certain emotions.

The *lens* focuses the image onto the retinal layer on the back surface of the eye. As in a camera, the image projected by the lens onto the retina is reversed.

The *fovea* is the region of the retina that is directly in line with the pupil and contains mostly cones, which are involved in color perception and visual acuity (sharpness).

The *optic nerve* receives inputs from the photoreceptors and sends information to the brain.

2. VISUAL PATHWAYS

Images of objects in the right visual field are projected to the left half of the retina of each eye, which in turn sends the information first to the thalamus for initial processing and then to the visual cortex in the left hemisphere where perception takes place. Likewise, images of objects in the left visual field are projected to the right half of the retina of each eye, which in turn sends the information to the thalamus and then to the visual cortex in the right hemisphere.

3. PARTS OF THE EAR

The *outer ear* is the visible portion of the ear and the auditory canal (ear canal) that funnels sound waves to the eardrum.

The *middle ear* includes the eardrum and three tiny bones (hammer, anvil, and stirrup) that transmit the eardrum's vibrations to a membrane on the cochlea called the oval window.

The *inner ear* includes the snail-shaped tube called the *cochlea*, which translates sound waves into fluid waves, and the semicircular canals, which sense equilibrium.

4. THE OLFACTORY SENSE

Airborne molecules (olfactory chemicals) enter the nasal passage and reach receptor cells located in the olfactory epithelium of the upper nasal passage. The receptors send messages to the brain's olfactory bulb and then onward to the primary smell cortex located in the temporal lobes.

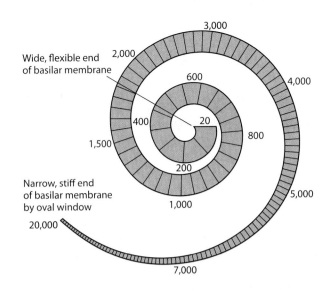

Wide, flexible end of basilar membrane

Narrow, stiff end of basilar membrane by oval window

FIGURE **4.25**

DIFFERENT PARTS OF THE COCHLEA PROCESS DIFFERENT FREQUENCIES OF SOUND. The highest frequencies of sound stimulate the narrowest region of the cochlea. The small hair cells here are sensitive to high-frequency (high-pitch) sounds in the range of 15,000 to 20,000 cycles per second (Hertz). The largest hair cells are in the wide center portion of the cochlea. These hair cells respond to low-frequency (pitch) sounds in the range of 100 to 20 cycles per second range.

If the hair cells in the inner ear become damaged, as can happen when a person is exposed to very loud noises once or moderately loud noises (such as machines) over long periods of time, the person can suffer irreparable hearing loss. For more information about hearing loss, see "Psychology in the Real World."

HEARING IN THE BRAIN

After the sound energy is changed to neural energy in the cochlea, the hair cells synapse with auditory neurons that transmit the sound impulses to the thalamus in the brain. From there, the neural impulses are relayed to various parts of the brain, including the brain stem and the temporal lobes, home of the auditory cortex. Recall that the visual pathways go through the LGN. The auditory pathways go from the cochlea to the *inferior colliculus* in the brain stem and from there to the *medial (middle) geniculate nucleus (MGN) of the thalamus*. It is in the brain that we organize and interpret sounds from the outside world. It is in the brain that hearing takes place. Also the auditory cortex receives inputs from several other cortical regions, including the visual cortex and regions involved in perceiving speech. There are also hemispheric differences in auditory perception: The right auditory cortex is more active in processing nonverbal stimuli, whereas the left auditory cortex is more active in processing speech and language (Zatorre, Evans, & Meyer, 1994).

quick quiz 4.4: Hearing

1. The _____ of a sound wave determines what we perceive as loudness.
   a. frequency
   b. shape
   c. amplitude
   d. width

2. Which structure is responsible for the transduction of sound vibrations into action potentials?
   a. the tympanic membrane
   b. cochlea
   c. stapes
   d. hair cells

Answers can be found at the end of the chapter.

Hearing Loss in the Age of the iPod

Most people take their hearing for granted, but there is a good chance that at some point in your life time you will suffer some degree of hearing loss. It could be minor or it could be major. Studies often divide the causes of hearing loss into categories of age-related and noise exposure, but in fact, these two are related. Being exposed to loud noise levels over long periods of time leads to a loss of hearing after 10 to 15 years.

Noise often leads to age-related hearing loss, especially in the high-frequency range of 5,000–15,000 Hz (Lutman & Spencer, 1991) (see Figure 4.26). For example, in a large-scale study of exposure to noise at work, middle-aged to older men (ages 45 to 70) have their threshold for hearing high-frequency sounds (4,000 Hz and higher) raised by 10 dB compared to men not exposed to such noise at work (Tambs et al., 2006). A 10 dB increase is sound that is 10 times as intense, which we perceive as twice as loud. Factory or machine workers exposed to noise at the 90 dB level for 8 hours a day, 5 days a week suffer permanent hearing loss after 10 years on the job (Bauer et al., 1991; Lutman & Spencer, 1991). Similarly, rock musicians—exposed to noise levels from 95 dB to 107 dB—when tested before and after concerts, showed both temporary and permanent hearing loss (Gunderson, Moline, & Catalono, 1997).

Because of this well-documented loss of high-frequency hearing with age, cell phone users, especially young students, have discovered a way to hear calls during class that their older teachers cannot: Have the ring tone be at a frequency higher than most older people can hear. The best-known high-pitched ringtone is called *mosquito*. Mosquito technology was actually invented by a company to disperse young people in a crowd (because they find it annoying) while leaving the older people unaffected (they cannot hear it). The irony is that some younger people copied the tone and turned

The Bodily Senses

connection
Figure 3.15 shows how the somatosensory cortex maps to specific regions of the body.
See Chapter 3, p. 105.

We feel things on our skin and in our bodily organs. The largest contact surface area any sensory input has with our bodies is the skin, and it is carefully mapped in the somatosensory cortex in the parietal lobe of the brain (Blakeslee & Blakeslee, 2007). Bodily senses also include knowing where our body parts are. In addition, we also sense things inside our bodies—organ pain, levels of heart rate, depth of breathing, to name a few. The senses based in the skin, body, or any membrane surfaces are known as the **bodily senses.** There are at least six distinct bodily or somatic senses: touch, temperature, pain, position/motion, balance, and interoception (perception of bodily sensations). Of these six senses, we will discuss touch and pain.

bodily senses
the senses based in the skin, body, or any membrane surfaces.

it into a ringtone for their cell phone that they can hear, although older people supposedly cannot (Vitello, 2006). However, it doesn't always work as expected. Some 30- and 40-year-olds can, in fact, hear the mosquito ringtone. So watch out: Old folks might be able to hear more than you think. To hear what high-pitched tones of 16,000, 17,000, and 18,000 Hz sound like as well as the mosquito ringtone, try searching the Internet on "mosquito ringtones."

But don't think that hearing loss does not affect younger people. MP3 players, including the iPod, have maximum decibel levels of around 115–120 dB, about the loudness of a rock concert. Researchers at the Centers for Disease Control and Prevention (CDC) reported hearing loss from loud noise in nearly 13 percent of Americans between the ages of 6 and 19 (CDC, 2001). This figure translates to about 5 million young people. Here are some guidelines for listening to an MP3 player without causing long-term damage to your ears (Knox, 2007):

- Limit earphone listening to an hour a day, at a setting no greater than 6 on a 10-notch scale.

- If someone can hear earphone "leakage" from several feet away, it is too loud.

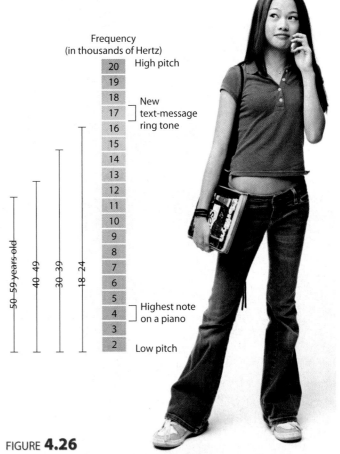

FIGURE **4.26**

HEARING HIGH TONES. Knowing that older adults typically can't hear high-frequency tones, teenagers have downloaded high-pitched ring tones for their cell phones so that they can use them to send and receive text messages during class.

- If someone has ringing in the ears or a feeling of fullness in the ear, or if speech sounds muffled after a listening session, the music was too loud.

TOUCH

Imagine your eyes are closed and someone puts an object in your left hand. You feel it for a minute. You feel its weight, shape, hardness, and temperature. Then the person puts something in your right hand. You conclude, with eyes still shut, that the first was a screwdriver and the second was a pen. How were you able to do this?

The top layers of skin have receptor cells that are sensitive to different tactile qualities—some to shape, some to grooves, some to vibrations and movements. These receptor cells are known as **mechanoreceptors,** and they are like the photoreceptors in the eye or the hair cells in the ear (Goldstein, 2007). There are, in fact, four different kinds of mechanoreceptors, each of which has a unique profile of sensitivity. Some of the mechanoreceptors are slow to change and others

mechanoreceptors receptor cells in the skin that are sensitive to different tactile qualities, such as shape, grooves, or vibrations.

the bodily senses **153**

are fast to change with variations in tactile stimulation. Some are sensitive to fine details, whereas others are not sensitive. For example, slowly drag your fingertip over a quarter. You can feel the bumps and grooves, thanks to fine-detail receptors in your skin. Some mechanoreceptors also sense movement and vibration, such as when someone runs fingers over your forearm. It is important to point out, however, that different areas of skin have different numbers of mechanoreceptors. If someone put a screwdriver and a pen against your feet, for example, you might have trouble telling them apart. You have far fewer mechanoreceptors on the soles of your feet than on your fingertips. This is probably a good thing—it would be overwhelmingly uncomfortable to have extremely sensitive soles.

Like photoreceptors in the eye, mechanoreceptors mark only the beginning of the journey from sensation to perception. The sensory qualities (shape, size, hardness, and temperature) of the screwdriver and pen stimulate different kinds of mechanoreceptors in the skin, but the resulting sensory impulses must travel to the brain to be processed and interpreted. When something touches our fingertips, forearm, or shoulder, a dedicated region of cortex becomes active, and we perceive the sensation of being touched. Tactile sensations from our skin travel via sensory neurons to the spinal cord and up to the brain. The first major structure involved in processing bodily sensations is the thalamus, which relays the impulses to the somatosensory cortex in the parietal lobes.

Repeated sensory and motor tactile experience changes the amount of cortex involved in processing that particular sensation or movement. The general location in the somatosensory cortex stays the same, but areas of the cortex devoted to that experience or function grow (Jenkins et al., 1990). The more one body region is touched or stimulated, the more sensory or motor cortex is used to process information from the mechanoreceptors. For instance, musicians who play stringed instruments such as a violin use the right hand to bow and the left hand to play the notes. Researchers have found that experienced violinists have larger representations, or *brain maps*, of the hand and finger regions of the somatosensory cortex than do nonmusicians (Pantev et al., 2001). Athletes who practice the same movement over and over, whether it is hitting a tennis ball or shooting a basketball, no doubt have similarly well developed sensory and motor cortexes. Once our son Evan finally mastered tying his shoes, we had him do it over and over again, to try to increase the cortical area devoted to those skills.

connection

What are the benefits of touch for premature and low-birth-weight newborns?
See Chapter 5, p. 196.

pain
a complex emotional and sensory experience associated with actual or potential tissue damage.

PAIN

Pain is no fun, but we need it to survive. People born with no pain receptors can be severely injured or killed, because they don't know they have been harmed (Watkins & Maier, 2003). **Pain** is a complex emotional and sensory experience associated with actual or potential tissue damage (Merskey & Bogduk, 1994). It

is usually very unpleasant, but people vary widely in their experiences of pain, what they think is painful, and whether they might even enjoy pain (Schwerdtfeger, 2007). In fact, some people feel no pain during great injury (such as soldiers in battle situations), and others feel pain when no tissue damage is present. The latter situation occurs with *phantom limb pain,* when people who have lost a limb feel pain in the missing arm or leg. Such cases dramatically show how pain is not just a direct result of tissue damage, but an experience in the brain as well. Pain also is enhanced by one's reaction to the injury. Often the emotional reaction to pain creates as much suffering as the actual tissue damage. In fact, physical and emotional pain involve many of the same brain structures (Singer et al., 2004).

Pain Perception How do we sense and perceive pain? It's not merely touch gone too far. In fact, damage to the skin is only one kind of pain. Other forms include organ tissue and nerve damage as well as joint inflammation. Pain from skin damage is called *nociceptive pain.* The skin has pain receptors that are sensitive to heat, cold, chemical irritation, and pressure, all of which are kinds of *nociceptors* (Basbaum & Jessell, 2000). Heat, frostbite, chemical burns, and cutting or hitting your thumb with a hammer all hurt because these events stimulate nociceptors in our skin. The nociceptors send signals to the spinal cord and then to the brain, signaling that damage has occurred. Your brain can then initiate an appropriate response, such as pulling your hand away from the hot burner. You can now see why it is so dangerous not to experience pain!

We now know that the spinal cord may actually play an active rather than passive role in pain perception (Watkins & Maier, 2003). That is, the spinal cord does not simply relay the pain messages from the sensory neurons to the brain; it

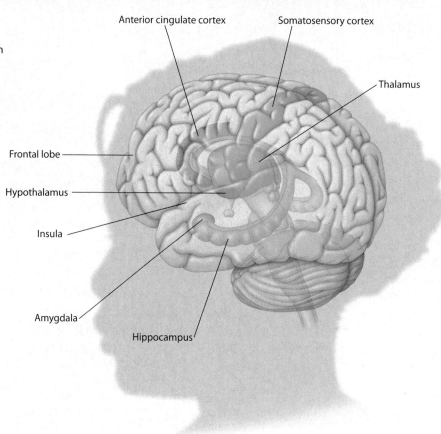

FIGURE **4.27**

THE BRAIN AND PAIN. The structures shown are activated during the perception of physical pain. The anterior cingulate cortex and the insula (located deep within the temporal lobe) are also activated by emotional pain.

Anterior cingulate cortex   Somatosensory cortex

Thalamus

Frontal lobe

Hypothalamus

Insula

Amygdala

Hippocampus

also can enhance those messages. Most surprisingly, it is not neurons in the spinal cord that enhance the pain signals, but rather the glial cells wrapped around the axons (Watkins & Maier, 2003). Once the pain messages get sent and even enhanced by the spinal cord, they move on to the brain.

Many brain structures are involved in the perception of skin damage alone. A partial list of brain structures activated by skin-based pain includes the thalamus, hypothalamus, limbic system, insula, and anterior cingulate cortex (see Figure 4.27; Goldstein, 2007). A recent and somewhat surprising finding is that some of the same brain regions activated when we experience physical pain also are activated during emotional pain—especially when we are rejected by others or see others receive shocks (Eisenberger, Lieberman & Williams, 2003; Singer et al., 2004). The brain regions active in both physical and emotional pain are the anterior cingulate cortex (ACC) and the insula (see Figure 4.27). Even more fascinating, as Singer and colleagues (2004) showed, when we observe a loved one being given a mild shock, only the ACC and the insula become active, not the somatosensory cortex, which is activated when we ourselves are shocked. So when we see someone we love hurt, the aspects of the pain circuit involved with emotion are active, but not the entire circuit.

Explaining Pain   One of the more influential explanations for pain is the one proposed by Ronald Melzack and Patrick Wall (1965, 1988). Their **gate control theory of pain** proposes that the spinal cord regulates the experience of pain by either opening or closing neural channels, called *gates*, involved in pain sensations that get sent to the brain. Smaller neural channels are dedicated to pain sensations, and when they are activated, pain messages get sent to the

gate control theory of pain
idea that the spinal cord regulates the experience of pain by either opening or closing neural channels, called *gates*, that transmit pain sensations to the brain.

brain. Activation of larger neural channels that are involved in the sensation of pain can inhibit the transmission of pain impulses to the brain. This mechanism explains why certain kinds of stimulation—such as acupuncture or even rubbing one's skin—can relieve sensations of pain. The signals from acupuncture may override other, even more intense sensations of pain, such as chronic pain from injury (White, 2006).

What is most interesting about the gate control theory of pain is the idea that inhibitory channels can actually come from the brain as well as the body. Messages sent by the brain itself can close channels in the spinal cord involved in pain sensations. Thoughts, feelings, and beliefs can influence pain sensations, which is one reason why people vary so much in their perception of pain. Different people experiencing the same level of pain may have completely different experiences of their pain. We explore this phenomenon in more detail by examining the role of culture in pain perception in "Making Connections in Sensation and Perception."

Controlling Pain In addition to thoughts and feelings controlling the experience of pain, our bodies have natural painkillers called *endorphins* (for endogenous morphines). When we get hurt, our body responds by releasing these substances (Fields, 2005). Endorphins work by stimulating the release of neurotransmitters that interfere with pain messages in the spinal cord and brain. Endorphin release may explain why people initially experience no pain after a horrible injury from an accident. For example, soldiers and automobile accident victims often report no immediate sensations of pain (Warga, 1987). Only hours afterward or maybe the next day while in a hospital does the pain begin. Endorphins also play a role in acupuncture-based pain relief (Han, 2004).

If thoughts, feelings, and endorphins are not enough to control pain, there are drug treatments. For small aches and pains, many people take aspirin, acetaminophen, ibuprofen, or other similar drugs. These work to control inflammation (Loeser & Melzack, 1999). For more severe pain, doctors may prescribe opioids. Opioids are a class of drug known as *analgesics*, meaning *without pain*. Morphine, heroin, oxycodone, and hydrocodone are all opioids. All but heroin are commonly prescribed for pain relief. They work to deaden or lessen pain by blocking neural activity involved in pain perception. Morphine, for example, is widely used before and after medical procedures and in the care of terminally ill patients. There is a high risk of dependency on opioids, so their use must be carefully monitored.

connection

Why do opioids have a high potential for abuse?

See Chapter 6, p. 245.

quick quiz 4.5: The Bodily Senses

1. The receptor cells for touch that reside in the skin are called
   a. tactile cilia
   b. mechanoreceptors
   c. interoceptors
   d. receptive fields

2. Our bodies have natural painkillers called
   a. analgesics
   b. opioids
   c. endorphins
   d. acetaminophens

Answers can be found at the end of the chapter.

The Chemical Senses: Smell and Taste

Smell and taste are chemical senses, because they respond to contact with molecules from objects we encounter in the world. Smell and taste are very important survival-related senses, for they govern our choices about what we take into our bodies. As such, these senses are very sensitive, are heightened during pregnancy, and can trigger emotional reactions (Profet, 1992; Rolls, 2004).

Unlike receptors for other senses, receptors for chemical molecules are regularly replaced, because they are constantly exposed not only to the chemicals in food but also to dirt and bacteria that can impair function (Goldstein, 2007). Smell and taste receptors are replaced every few weeks. Taste buds are replaced every 1 to 2 weeks.

SMELL (OLFACTION)

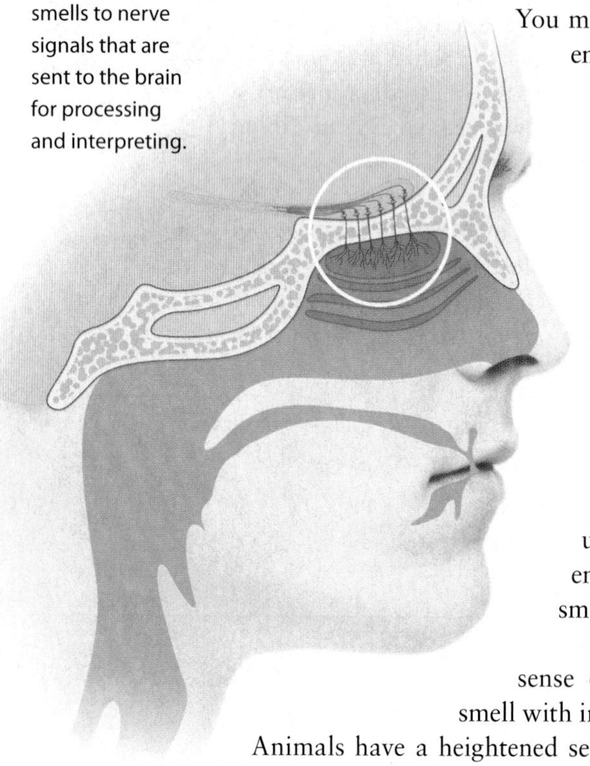

FIGURE **4.28**
OLFACTORY RECEPTORS IN THE NASAL CAVITY. The receptors in the nasal cavity, called cilia, are like the hair cells in the ear. They change chemical stimulation received from smells to nerve signals that are sent to the brain for processing and interpreting.

A small area high in the lining of the nasal cavity contains the **olfactory sensory neurons,** which are the receptors for smell (see Figure 4.28). These neurons contain hairlike projections called *cilia,* which are similar to the hair cells in the inner ear. The cilia convert chemical information in odor molecules into neural impulses.

When chemicals come in contact with the cilia, transduction occurs, and the olfactory message travels to the **olfactory bulb** in the forebrain. The olfactory bulb sends information either directly to the smell-processing areas in the cortex or indirectly to the cortex by way of the thalamus (Buck, 2000). The *primary olfactory cortex* resides in the temporal lobe; the *secondary olfactory cortex* is in the frontal lobe near the eyes.

Some fibers from the olfactory bulb go directly to the amygdala, which sends smell information to the hypothalamus, thalamus, and frontal cortex. You may recall that the amygdala plays a key role in emotional responses and also connects to memory areas like the hippocampus. These connections may explain why smells can instantly evoke an emotional memory (Herz, 2004). The smell of cedar wood, for example, immediately transports one of us (Greg) to his grandmother's attic in Kansas.

Just as there are specific photoreceptors for different primary colors, different odors stimulate different olfactory neurons. In fact, there may be as many as 1,000 different olfactory sensory receptors (Buck, 2000). Greater concentrations of odors will stimulate a greater number of sensory neurons, and this can lead us to perceive the same odor presented at different concentrations as being an entirely different smell.

People differ considerably in their ability to sense odors. Some people lose the ability to sense smell with infection or injury, but usually this is short term. Animals have a heightened sense of smell compared to humans. We rely on dogs to sniff out suspects and bombs for a reason. Grizzly bears can locate dead

olfactory sensory neurons the sensory receptors for smell that reside high up inside the nose.

olfactory bulb a forebrain structure that sends information either directly to the smell processing areas in the cortex or indirectly to the cortex by way of the thalamus.

Humans often employ dogs to locate illegal drugs, explosives, criminals, and missing people by using their keen sense of smell.

animals from miles away and will readily feed on them (*Brown/Grizzly Bear*, n.d.). Sharks can detect one drop of blood in 25 gallons of water (Marks, 2006).

TASTE

A close look at the human tongue reveals all kinds of ridges and bumps. These textured structures, called **papillae**, contain about 10,000 **taste buds**. The cells on the buds that process taste information are called **taste receptor cells**. There are dozens of taste receptor cells in each taste bud. The papillae in the central part of the tongue contain no taste buds and no taste receptor cells, so we do not taste from that region. Human experience of taste results from stimulation of taste buds on the front, sides, and rear of the tongue as shown in Figure 4.29. When chemicals from food or liquid come into contact with the tips of these taste buds, a chain of events unfolds that lead to the experience of taste.

papillae
textured structures on the surface of the tongue that contain thousands of taste buds.

taste buds
structures inside the papillae of the tongue that contain the taste receptor cells.

taste receptor cells
sensory receptors for taste that reside in the taste buds.

Different tastes use different mechanisms to stimulate an impulse in a taste cell. In general, chemicals alter the membranes of taste receptor cells in ways that make them more likely to generate action potentials. Such signals from taste receptor cells in various regions of the tongue then travel down fibers to the brain stem. From the brain stem, taste information travels to the thalamus and frontal lobe. Neurons from the thalamus project taste information to the *taste cortex* in the insula and other regions of the frontal-parietal cortex (Ogawa et al., 2005).

Humans distinguish five basic taste qualities: bitter, sweet, salty, sour, and savory. It used to be thought that receptors for the different tastes resided only in certain regions of the tongue, but we now know that these taste receptor cells are distributed in many regions (Buck, 2000). Although specific receptors exist for each type of taste, the savory experience comes from the combined sensory experience of monosodium glutamate (MSG; a flavor enhancer, traditionally used in many Asian foods) and the perception of savory odors (Kawamura & Kare, 1987; McCabe & Rolls, 2007). The combined influences

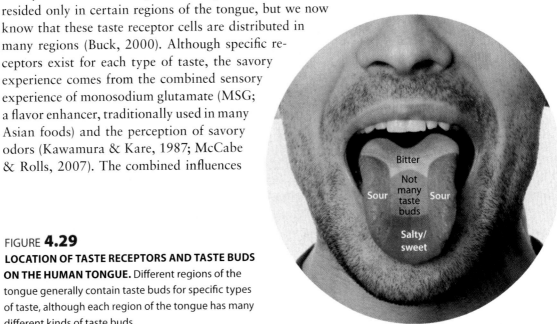

FIGURE **4.29**

LOCATION OF TASTE RECEPTORS AND TASTE BUDS ON THE HUMAN TONGUE. Different regions of the tongue generally contain taste buds for specific types of taste, although each region of the tongue has many different kinds of taste buds.

that produce the savory flavor point to the important roles both taste and smell play in our experiences of flavor in general.

Simply put, the experience of flavor results from the combination of taste plus smell (Goldstein, 2007). Have you ever noticed how dull food tastes when you have a cold? This is because your sense of smell is impaired. Try squeezing your nostrils shut while tasting an apple or any other food. Notice the flavor. Then release your nostrils and take another bite. You will notice more intense "apple-ness" with your nostrils open, because food aromas contribute greatly to the experience of flavor (Lawless et al., 2004). When the nose is shut, olfactory receptors in the passage that connects the oral and nasal cavities do not get stimulated. As a result, less olfactory information is available and taste is impaired. Also, the region of the brain most involved in flavor perception, namely the orbitofrontal cortex (OFC), receives inputs from brain areas involved in olfaction and taste, as well as from areas involved in touch and vision (Rolls, 2000). The OFC is where signals from taste and smell meet. Indeed, this brain area plays a key role in both perception of flavor and satisfaction of appetite, which relies on many senses (Rolls, 2006).

The experience of flavor showcases the brain's ability to combine sensory information to produce a unique sensory experience. In some people, sensory experiences sometimes combine in even more unusual ways. The next section on synesthesia focuses on these cases.

quick quiz 4.6: The Chemical Senses: Smell and Taste

1. The primary olfactory cortex resides in which lobe of the brain?
   a. frontal lobe
   b. temporal lobe
   c. parietal lobe
   d. occipital lobe

2. Humans have taste receptor cells for what flavors?
   a. sweet, sour, bitter, salty, sharp
   b. sweet, sour, salty, sharp, savory
   c. sweet, sour, bitter, salty, savory
   d. sweet, sour, salty, sharp

Answers can be found at the end of the chapter.

Synesthesia

Many of us use expressions such as "he was green with envy" or "her anger was red hot." We use these colors metaphorically, knowing full well he is not really green and her anger is not really red. But what if we literally experienced numbers as colors or touch as tastes? A surprisingly large segment of the population can do just that. They experience what is known as **synesthesia**, which occurs when a person experiences sensations in one sense when a different sense is stimulated (Cytowic, 1989; Ramachandran & Hubbard, 2003). In short, synesthesia occurs when the senses get

synesthesia
an unusual sensory experience in which a person experiences sensations in one sense when a different sense is stimulated.

mixed up and don't stay separate. For example, some people with this condition experience yellow when they hear a tone such as middle C. Others taste shapes. Still others experience numbers as colors, such as 5s as green and 2s as red.

The most common form of synesthesia is this last one, in which people experience numbers or sometimes letters as colors (Ramachandran & Hubbard, 2003). One way that scientists were able to discover that synesthesia was a real perceptual phenomenon and not just a learned association or merely an overly active sense of metaphor was to administer perceptual tests such as the one in Figure 4.30 (5s and 2s). In the figure on the left, there are a few 2s within the 5s. For most of us they are hard to pinpoint and it takes us a while to determine how many there are. But a person who sees 5s as blue and 2s as red, as shown on the right, has no trouble seeing that there are six 2s forming a triangle.

How does synesthesia happen? One explanation is that synesthesia results from a cross-wiring or cross-activation of sensory neurons in various parts of the brain (Hubbard & Ramachandran, 2005; Ramachandran & Hubbard, 2003). Cross-activation occurs when two areas of the brain, normally kept separate, get activated at the same time by the same stimulus. So brain regions involved in color perception get cross-activated with sensations of numbers. As it turns out, one region of the temporal lobe is active in processing both color sensations and numbers and is therefore the most likely area of cross-activation in this form of synesthesia (Hubbard & Ramachandran, 2005; Ramachandran & Hubbard, 2003). Similarly, the orbitofrontal cortex in the frontal lobes has many so-called bimodal neurons (Rolls, 2000). Bimodal neurons respond to more than one sense—such as taste, smell, touch, and vision—and may become cross-activated in synesthesia (Radeau & Colin, 2004). Also, certain hallucinogenic drugs can temporarily create synesthetic experiences, but the brain mechanisms responsible for this kind of synesthesia are not well described (Weil & Rosen, 1998).

FIGURE **4.30**

SYNESTHESIA. People who perceive numbers as colors would have no trouble distinguishing the numbers 5 and 2 in the square on the left. They would see the numbers in color as shown in the example on the right. (From Ramachandran & Hubbell, 2003)

The way a person without synesthesia sees it

The way a person with synesthesia sees it

making connections
in sensation and perception

Differences Across Cultures

Throughout this chapter we have touched on ways in which people differ in sensory perception. For example, some people are more sensitive to bitter tastes than others. Individual differences in perception may result from differences in perceptual set, or frame of mind. Thus, it stands to reason that growing up in a certain environment, with particular beliefs, ways of viewing things, and physical settings might impact how one perceives the world. Culture and place can serve as perceptual sets. Most research on cultural influences on perception has focused on three sense systems: vision, olfaction, and pain.

Cultural Variation in Visual Perception

Differences exist across cultures in response to certain visual images that use monocular cues to depth. Look again at the Müller-Lyer line illusion in Figure 4.18 (p. 144). Recall that linear perspective explains why people see the line on the right as longer than the one on the left, when the lines are in fact equal. The drawing on the right looks like the inner corner of a room, and the one on the left looks like the outer corner of a building. Do people who grow up in a world with no corners view these drawings the same way we do? Researchers have studied the effects of living in a *carpentered world*—an environment with constructed buildings with many right angles—on various people's perceptions of depth. Navajos who have lived at least 10 years in round huts are much less likely to see the lines of Figure 4.18 as differing in length, for they are not accustomed to rooms with edges (Pederson & Wheeler, 1983). A similar effect has been reported in studies of children living in Zambia, in a rural setting with few modern buildings (Stewart, 1973). But Navajos and Zambians who have lived in the presence of corners do experience the Müller-Lyer illusion (Matsumoto & Juang, 2004). Experience modifies perception.

Moreover, Hudson (1960) studied the perception of depth cues in the Bantu people of the Niger-Congo region of Africa. He showed people the picture depicted in Figure 4.31 and others similar to it. He then asked them to explain what was going on in the scene. When people from the United States, Europe, and India viewed such a picture, they said the hunter is going after the gazelle, as the elephant is clearly in the distance. Bantu people, however, said the hunter is attacking the elephant. So the Bantu do not appear to use relative size differences as cues to depth because they don't see the elephant as being in the background. Why? The Bantu people's response may result from not having much experience with two-dimensional drawings like the figure. Interestingly, Bantu who had been educated in European schools say the hunter is going for the gazelle (Matsumoto & Juang, 2004).

As we have just seen, different cultural backgrounds can impact how people make sense of and perceive their world. This is true not just for illusions and depth perception, but also for perceiving and attending to foreground and background.

nature & nurture

People who grow up in cultures without angular buildings do not experience the same visual illusions as those who grew up with angular buildings.

FIGURE **4.31**

PICTURE FOR DEPTH PERCEPTION TASK TESTED ON BANTU. People from Europe, the United States, and India think the hunter is after the gazelle. Bantu tribespeople think he is after the elephant. (Based on Hudson, 1960)

People from Eastern cultures tend to perceive the world more as a whole, with people, objects, and the context being connected and belonging together. Westerners, however, tend to focus most on foreground objects and less on background and the periphery (Nisbett et al., 2001). Figure 4.32 describes research on this question that found cultural influences in how people perceive and recall figural versus background information in visual scenes (Masuda & Nisbett, 2001). These findings are consistent with the more established observation that Eastern people view themselves as embedded in the larger world rather than as independent entities (Markus & Kitayama, 2001). In another example of top-down processing, one's orientation toward life and the world can shape visual perception and memory.

Cultural Variation in Olfactory Experience

Smell is an interesting sense to compare across cultures in part because it is a highly emotional sense. Because smells elicit emotions so readily, cultures often develop strong rules or norms about which smells are okay and which ones aren't. That is, cultures differ widely on the acceptability of odors based on experience, climate, and cuisine. Also, different places vary in their standards for cleanliness and for what is acceptable body odor (Hannigan, 1995). Do people raised so differently with respect to what is typical to smell or what it is okay to smell like show differences in scent detection in controlled experiments?

A highly controlled experiment on scent detection with participants from the United States and Japan suggests remarkable similarity across these two cultures in ability to recognize a wide variety of scents (Kobayashi et al., 2006). There were a few distinct differences, however, that appear to be culturally based. Japanese were much better than Americans at detecting 3 of the 13 smells in final testing. Does that mean the Japanese have superior smell ability? Probably not. Each of these scents (such as condensed milk) is more common in Japan and therefore these results help us to understand that smell recognition is a perceptual process guided by experience with the substances to which we are exposed.

Other aspects of smell may be less susceptible to cultural effects. Consider gender differences in smell perception. Overall, women tend to be more sensitive to smells than men (Brand & Millot, 2001). Scientists at the University of Pennsylvania wanted to know whether such gender differences in smell perception held across cultures and ethnic backgrounds. They tested how well native Japanese and Americans of African, European, and Korean descent could identify odors in a controlled laboratory setting (Doty et al., 1985). Korean Americans performed better than African Americans and White Americans on the odor detection tasks, and both of these groups performed better than the native Japanese. Across all the groups, however, women outperformed men.

nature & nurture
Different cultural backgrounds can impact how people perceive and understand their world.

Cultural differences in pain perception are evident in this photo, taken during the Hindu festival of Thaipusam in Malaysia.

Japanese participant in perception study

1 research question

Do people from an Eastern culture (Japan) focus more on and have better recall for objects in the background and periphery of a scene than people from a Western culture (United States)?

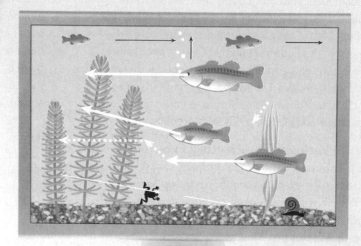

FIGURE **4.32**
HOW CULTURE AFFECTS PERCEPTION OF FOREGROUND–BACKGROUND.
Culture influences the perception of visual information. Japanese people view themselves as more embedded in the larger world and notice backgrounds more than Americans, who feel more independent from their settings. (*Source:* T. Masuda & R. E. Nisbett (2001). Attending holistically versus analytically: Comparing the context sensitivity of Japanese and Americans. *Journal of Personality and Social Psychology 81*, 922–934.)

2 method

For this quasi-experimental study by Masuda and Nisbett (2001), participants came into the laboratory individually and sat down at a computer. They watched a 20-second video of the scene depicted here. The large fish are considered foreground. Plants, small fish, and the other nonmoving animals (rocks and snail) are considered background. Arrows indicate the direction in which the fish and other objects moved during the scene. After viewing the video, participants orally described what they had seen. Trained coders rated the number of statements they made about various aspects of the scene, such as foreground and background fish, the small stationary animals, and the plants.

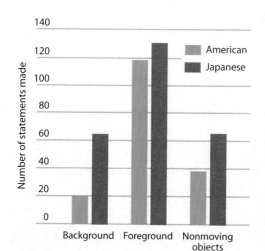

3 results

As predicted, and consistent with cultural values and attitudes, the Japanese commented much more on the background and nonmoving animals (snail and frog) than the Americans did. There was no significant difference in how much people from each culture commented on the large fish in the foreground.

4 conclusion

How we perceive everyday scenes is influenced by our culture. Our brains have been shaped by the assumptions and values of our society. In this case, people in Eastern cultures, such as Japan, tend to focus on background, foreground, and nonmoving objects, whereas those in Western cultures, such as the United States, tend to focus more on the foreground and moving objects only. This research is consistent with the more established observation that Eastern people view themselves as rooted in the larger world rather than as independent individuals.

So the gender differences observed in previous research held for a diverse set of cultural and ethnic backgrounds. Perhaps this is a case where evolutionary pressures override the more subtle effects of ethnic culture or subculture. Women may have more highly developed olfactory perception because they are the ones who bear children. Remember, both olfaction and taste play gatekeeper roles for keeping harmful things out of the body. The sense of smell is greatly enhanced during early pregnancy, which might be because it helps keep the mother from ingesting toxins that might harm the developing baby (Profet, 1992).

Cultural Variation in Pain

Given the large role that subjective factors play in pain perception, many researchers have looked at cultural and ethnic differences in pain. As we have discussed, there are big differences among people in pain tolerance, and we can even experience pain in the absence of any real tissue damage—remember phantom limb pain? As the photograph on page 163 shows, there are clear cultural differences in tolerance for pain!

In one of the most painful of human experiences, childbirth, we see widely differing perceptions of how painful it is. For example, the Yap who live in the South Pacific consider childbirth to be simply a part of everyday life. Yap women routinely work in the fields right up until childbirth and are often back at work the next day. What is even more interesting is that Yap fathers experience the pain of childbirth, and they are the ones who stay in bed to recover after the birth of the child (Kroeber, 1948).

quick quiz 4.7: Making Connections in Sensation and Perception

1. People who grow up in environments with few or no right angles and corners are less likely to be fooled by the _____ illusion.
   a. Ponzo
   b. moon
   c. Müller-Lyer
   d. apparent motion

2. Cultural differences in various kinds of sensory perception, which may stem from differences of belief and physical environments, point to the role of _____ in perceptual experience.
   a. top-down processing
   b. bottom-up processing
   c. elementalism
   d. perceptual constancy

Answers can be found at the end of the chapter.

chapter **review**

THE LONG STRANGE TRIP FROM SENSATION TO PERCEPTION

- Sensation is the stimulation of our sense organs by the external world. Perception is the process by which the brain organizes and interprets sensory experience.

- Stimulation of the sense organs involves taking in sensory energy from the outside world, whether it be sound waves, light waves, chemicals, or pressure. Our sensory system transforms the physical energy into neural energy in a process known as transduction. The brain then organizes the transformed information, interprets it, and initiates a response.

- Absolute thresholds are the lowest level of a stimulus that humans sense. Difference thresholds are the smallest amount of change in stimulus that a person detects. According to Weber's law, the smallest detectable change is a constant proportion of the intensity of the original stimulus.

- The effect of our frame of mind affects our perception of objects and is known as our perceptual set.

VISION

- The eye bends light, converts light energy to electrical energy, and sends that information to the brain for further processing.

- Vision happens in the brain, in the lateral geniculate nucleus (LGN) of the thalamus, and in the visual cortex in the occipital lobes.

- Hubel and Wiesel demonstrated that single cells in the visual cortex act as feature detectors—of which there are three kinds for vision: simple cells, complex cells, and hypercomplex cells. Integration of this feature information occurs in the parietal and temporal cortexes.

- Depth perception is the ability to figure out how far or near objects are. One cue for depth perception is binocular disparity, the fact that our two eyes provide slightly different viewpoints that our brains integrate into a single 3-D image. Monocular depth cues include linear perspective, texture gradient, atmospheric perspective, and interposition.

- The brain organizes visual sensations with Gestalt laws of similarity, continuity, proximity, and closure.

- Separating figures from backgrounds helps us organize visual sensations, but also makes us vulnerable to illusions.

- The retina contains two types of photoreceptor cells called rods and cones. Cones are sensitive to red, green, and blue light waves, whereas rods are sensitive to light and are responsible for dark adaptation.

- The trichromatic theory of color vision states that we perceive the full range of colors as different combinations of three colors. The opponent process theory says that cones are linked together in three opposing color pairs: blue/yellow, red/green, and black/white.

HEARING

- Humans respond to three different properties of sound waves: We perceive amplitude as loudness, frequency as pitch, and purity as timbre.

- The receptor hair cells in the cochlea are sensitive to different frequencies of sound waves and convert the mechanical energy of sound into neural energy for processing in the auditory cortex.

THE BODILY SENSES

- The bodily senses include sensations of touch, temperature, pain, balance, position/motion, and interoception.

- The brain regions most involved in touch are the thalamus and the somatosensory cortex in the parietal lobes. Pain sensations are processed mainly by the insula and the anterior cingulate cortex in the frontal lobes.

THE CHEMICAL SENSES: SMELL AND TASTE

- Smell receptors in the nose contain olfactory sensory neurons, which convert chemical information into neural information. The olfactory message goes to the olfactory bulb and then to the primary olfactory cortex in the temporal lobe.

- Information about taste is processed in the taste buds of the tongue. Humans distinguish five basic taste qualities: bitter, sweet, salty, sour, and savory.

SYNESTHESIA

- Synesthesia occurs when one sensory system is activated by stimulation of a different sensory system, and the neurons are cross-activated in the brain.

- In the most common form of synesthesia, people experience letters or numbers as colors.

MAKING CONNECTIONS
IN SENSATION AND PERCEPTION

- Variations in experience across cultures influence the way people see, smell, and feel pain. Ethnic and cultural differences aside, women are more sensitive to smells than are men.

key **terms**

quick quiz **answers**

Quick Quiz 4.1: 1. a 2. d   Quick Quiz 4.2: 1. c 2. b   Quick Quiz 4.3: 1. a 2. d 3. b 4. d

Quick Quiz 4.4: 1. c 2. d   Quick Quiz 4.5: 1. b 2. c

Quick Quiz 4.6: 1. b 2. c   Quick Quiz 4.7: 1. c 2. a   Solution to Figure 4.17 on page 143:

human
development

A t age 35, Elyse and Paula were identical strangers. Each knew she had been adopted. What each did not know was that she had a twin. The two women grew up thinking they were, like most people, born alone. Imagine the shock and disbelief of finding out in middle adulthood that there is someone else just like you—your identical twin! In Paula's words, "It's as if a slab of cement has landed on my chest, preventing me from inhaling. . . . If I was a cartoon character, there would be stars and question marks circling my skull" (Schein & Bernstein, 2007, p. 31).

As with other pairs of identical twins reared apart, the lives of Elyse and Paula had taken remarkably similar paths. Both studied film and were writers. Not only that, but their interest in film also led them both to claim a German director, Wim Wenders, as their favorite filmmaker and a relatively unknown film of his, *Wings of Desire,* as their favorite movie. Both had experienced episodes of depression. They learned from their adoption agency and ▶

▶ later from their biological uncle that their birth mother had suffered from schizophrenia and depression. A single mother at the time of their birth, she was in the throes of depression and could not care for herself, much less two children. She gave them up for adoption.

The life paths of Elyse and Paula support both the nature and nurture assumptions of development. On the nature side, they both struggle with depression. They share many identical mannerisms and ways of thinking. Their physical appearance and life paths, however, are different enough to also lend support to the assumption that nurture helps mold individuals. For example, they look alike but are not identical. They did look more similar in early childhood, but their features diverged in adulthood.

Because Paula and Elyse are twins who were raised in different families, their story offers a rare view of the

chapter
outline

way heredity and environment shape individuals and make each of us unique. It reflects the process of growth and change across the life span, which is the focus of this chapter. From conception until death, each part of the body, including the brain, as well as each aspect of behavior, keeps developing throughout life, changing us from helpless infants to children who can talk, write, and do math, to adults who can tell when someone might be deceiving us. Humans age and pass through certain developmental milestones in a predictable sequence. Yet, as Paula and Elyse discovered, many of our personal characteristics are relatively stable from birth through adulthood. The study of **human development** is about both change and continuity in the individual across the life span. This process begins before birth, in the prenatal environment of the mother's womb. And so we open the discussion of development at the time of conception. ■

human development
the study of change and continuity in the individual across the life span.

The Developing Fetus

From conception until birth, we grow from a single cell to a fully formed, but still developing, human. The brain is the first major organ to form. The heart develops about a week later. (It is strange to think we have a brain before we have a heart!) A little more than eight months later, when we are born, the brain has more than 100,000,000,000 (100 billion) cells.

We pass more biological milestones before birth than we will in the rest of our lives. Development in the womb is incredibly fast and complex and includes not only physical growth, but psychological development as well.

STAGES OF PRENATAL DEVELOPMENT

germinal stage
the first prenatal stage of development, which begins at conception and lasts two weeks.

Life before birth is commonly divided into three distinct stages: the germinal, embryonic, and fetal stages. The **germinal stage** begins at conception and lasts for two weeks. At conception, the fertilized egg is a single-celled **zygote.** This single

zygote
the single cell that results when a sperm fertilizes an egg.

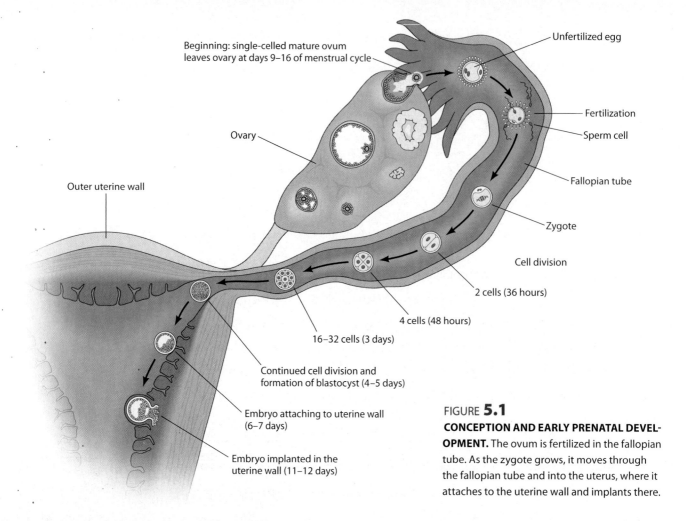

Beginning: single-celled mature ovum leaves ovary at days 9–16 of menstrual cycle

Unfertilized egg

Ovary

Fertilization

Sperm cell

Outer uterine wall

Fallopian tube

Zygote

Cell division

2 cells (36 hours)

4 cells (48 hours)

16–32 cells (3 days)

Continued cell division and formation of blastocyst (4–5 days)

Embryo attaching to uterine wall (6–7 days)

Embryo implanted in the uterine wall (11–12 days)

FIGURE **5.1**

CONCEPTION AND EARLY PRENATAL DEVELOPMENT. The ovum is fertilized in the fallopian tube. As the zygote grows, it moves through the fallopian tube and into the uterus, where it attaches to the uterine wall and implants there.

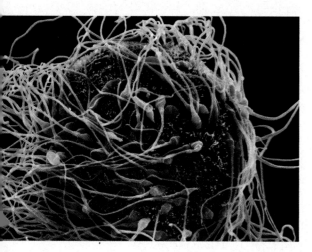

Life begins with the fertilization of an egg. In this highly magnified image, many sperm surround a single egg. Only one sperm will succeed in penetrating the egg.

cell starts dividing rapidly around 36 hours after conception. By day 7, the multicelled organism—now called a *blastocyst*—travels down the mother's fallopian tube and attaches to the uterine wall (see Figure 5.1). This process is far from risk-free: between 30% and 50% of the blastocysts do not implant properly and the pregnancy ends without the woman having known she was pregnant (Gupta et al., 2007).

If implantation was successful, the second stage of prenatal development begins two weeks later. At this point, the growing bundle of cells is officially an **embryo**. The **embryonic stage** is marked by the formation of the major organs: the nervous system, heart, eyes, ears, arms, legs, teeth, palate and external genitalia. Embryonic development continues until about 8 weeks after conception.

In Figure 5.2, we see the timetable for prenatal development. Each bar in Figure 5.2 shows when major structures develop and how long it takes. Notice that the central nervous system (brain and spinal cord) takes the longest amount of time to develop. You can also see that major abnormalities occur only in the early stages of development, when exposure to environmental hazards such as drugs or illness can cause serious defects.

embryo
the term for the developing organism from 2 weeks until about 8 weeks after conception.

embryonic stage
the second prenatal stage, from 2 weeks to 8 weeks after conception, when all of the major organs form.

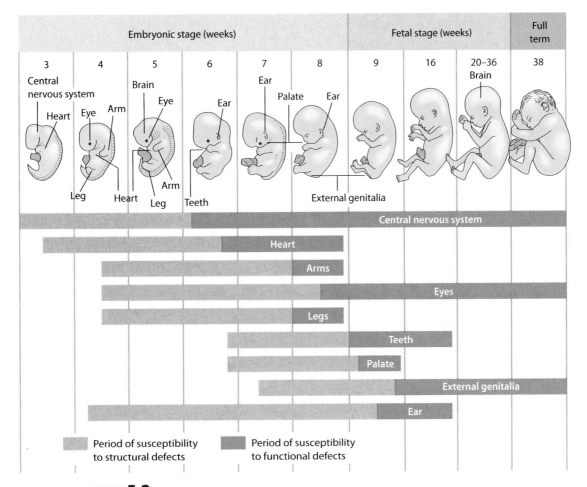

Embryonic stage (weeks)						Fetal stage (weeks)			Full term
3	4	5	6	7	8	9	16	20–36	38

Period of susceptibility to structural defects

Period of susceptibility to functional defects

FIGURE **5.2**

PRENATAL DEVELOPMENT TIMELINE. Each bar shows when major structures develop and how long it takes for development to be completed. Note that the central nervous system begins developing in the third week after conception and continues to nearly the entire time we are in the womb. The blue section of each bar indicates when major abnormalities can occur if growth goes awry. After that crucial period, minor abnormalities can still occur.

fetal stage
the third prenatal stage, which begins with the formation of bone cells 8 weeks after conception and ends at birth.

The key event that distinguishes the embryonic stage from the third stage, the **fetal stage,** is the formation of bone cells at 8 weeks after conception. By this time, all of the major organs have already begun to form. Between 8 and 12 weeks into development, the heartbeat can be detected with a stethoscope. During the fetal stage the organs continue to grow and mature while the fetus rapidly increases in size. Let's look at the important developments of this stage.

BRAIN AND SENSORY DEVELOPMENT BEFORE BIRTH

The first major organ to develop, the brain is still growing rapidly at birth (see Figure 5.3). By the time an infant is born, its head has grown to 25% of its adult weight, whereas its body is only 5% of its adult weight (see Figure 5.4). During the fetal stage, the rate of new neural growth can be approximately 3 million neurons per minute at its peak (Purves & Lichtman, 1985). From months 3 through 5 of pregnancy, neurons move from one part of the brain to their more permanent home in a process known as **neural migration** (Nadarajah & Parnavelas, 2002).

neural migration
the movement of neurons from one part of the fetal brain to their more permanent destination; occurs during months 3–5 of the fetal stage.

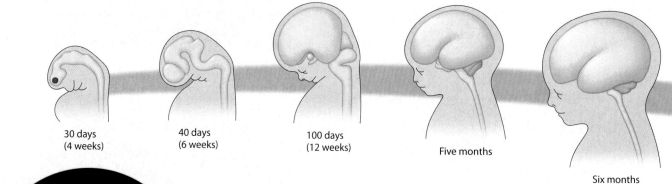

30 days
(4 weeks)

40 days
(6 weeks)

100 days
(12 weeks)

Five months

Six months

FIGURE **5.3**

PRENATAL BRAIN DEVELOPMENT. The size and complexity of the brain increase dramatically in the weeks and months following conception. At birth, the baby's brain weighs about 25% what an adult brain weighs. For comparison, a newborn weighs only about 5 % as much as an adult. The photograph shows the brain at 44 days after conception. Note the well-developed blood vessels which provide blood and oxygen to the rapidly developing brain.

Factors that interfere with normal neural migration, such as prenatal exposure to certain toxins or viruses, can increase the risk of psychological disorders (Kandel, 2006).

Soon after the nervous system has started to form, the embryo begins to move. By 4 to 6 months after conception, the fetus's movements are noticeable (DiPietro et al., 1996). Mothers can feel the fetus moving as early as 16 weeks into pregnancy, although it may feel a little like abdominal gas or "butterflies." Generally, male fetuses are more active than females, suggesting their greater activity levels after birth may be inborn (DiPietro et al., 1996).

The major sensory systems develop at different times and at different rates. The fetus begins to respond to sound around 26 weeks (6 months) after conception (Kisilevsky, Muir, & Low, 1992). A few weeks later, fetuses find their mother's voice soothing, and they prefer the sound of their mother's voice to other voices (DeCasper & Fifer, 1980; DeCasper & Spence, 1986). How can researchers possibly know what a fetus *prefers*? The researchers monitor the fetus's heart rate. Research has shown that a slowed heart rate indicates attention, interest,

Kanye West or Mozart? Can a fetus hear the difference?

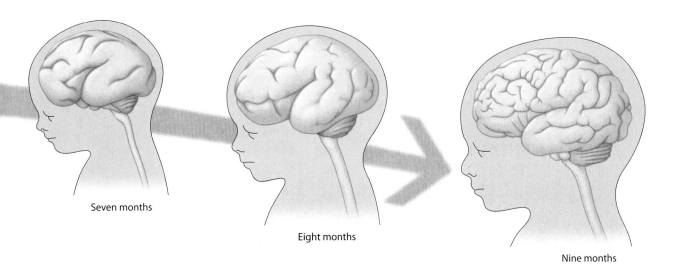

Seven months

Eight months

Nine months

or orienting response, whereas an increased heart rate indicates fear or distress (Groome et al., 2000).

Taste and odor-related chemicals from the mother's diet are present in amniotic fluid (Manella, Johnson, & Beauchamp, 1995). Fetuses are sensitive to odors in the amniotic fluid before birth, and they remember these smells. When pregnant moms consumed anise-flavored foods during the last stages of pregnancy, their newborns liked the smell of anise more than babies whose moms did not consume the anise flavor (Schaal, Marlier, & Soussignan, 2000).

What about prenatal taste? Studies suggest that our taste preferences may start in the womb (Hopson, 1998; Mennella & Beauchamp, 1996). By 13 to 15 weeks after conception, the taste buds of a fetus look very much like an adult's (Bradley, 1972). Researchers do not know whether the fetus uses the taste buds, but babies born prematurely—who would otherwise still be developing in the womb—prefer sweet flavors to other flavors, suggesting that this taste preference exists in the womb (Mennella & Beauchamp, 1996).

The least-well-developed sense in the fetus is vision (Hopson, 1998). Fetuses do not open their eyes. Also, as discussed in Chapters 3 and 4, vision perception occurs in the brain. The brain needs visual stimulation

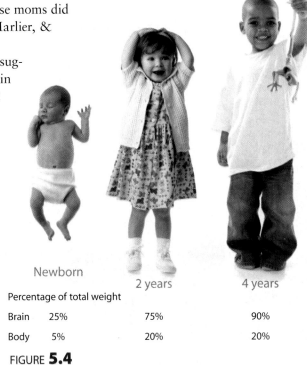

Newborn

2 years

4 years

Percentage of total weight

Brain	25%	75%	90%
Body	5%	20%	20%

FIGURE **5.4**

NEWBORN AND CHILD BRAIN AND BODY AS PERCENTAGE OF ADULT WEIGHT. The size and complexity of the brain increase dramatically in the weeks and months following conception.

to develop the sense of sight (Ptito & Desgent, 2006). Because it is not receiving visual stimulation, the fetus's brain is not developing the appropriate neural connections in the visual cortex to respond to visual imagery. Thus, at birth, infants are near-sighted and cannot see things clearly unless they are close to their face. Infants cannot see as well as adults until they are at least 6 months old, whereas their hearing is almost adultlike soon after birth.

ENVIRONMENTAL INFLUENCES ON FETAL DEVELOPMENT

prenatal programming
the process by which events in the womb alter the development of physical and psychological health.

teratogens
substances that can disrupt normal prenatal development and cause lifelong deficits.

To a fetus, the mother's womb is its only "environment." What a pregnant mother eats, drinks, smokes, feels, and experiences plays an important role in fetal development. **Prenatal programming** refers to the process by which events in the womb alter the development of physical and psychological health (Coe & Lubach, 2008). For instance, chemical substances the mother takes in or is exposed to may shape the development of the brain and other bodily systems in the fetus during the time when they are developing rapidly (Coe & Lubach, 2008). Common factors involved in prenatal programming are maternal nutrition and substances that can cause permanent damage, known as teratogens.

nature & nurture

Chemical substances that a pregnant woman takes in or is exposed to shape the development of the fetus's brain and other bodily systems.

Maternal Nutrition Doctors know that what a pregnant woman eats and drinks is important for the health of the fetus and even for the infant and child for years after birth. For instance, they prescribe folic acid and other vitamins to women who are pregnant or trying to become pregnant because they reduce the rates of abnormalities in the nervous system, which starts developing only 19 days after conception (Ryan-Harshman & Aldoori, 2008).

If the mother does not eat well or eat enough, the risk of various types of problems increases for the unborn child. For example, both schizophrenia and antisocial personality disorder are more likely to occur if the mother is malnourished during pregnancy (Neugebauer, Hoek, & Susser, 1999; Wahlbeck et al., 2001). Iron deficiency in the mother's diet and maternal stress predispose the infant to anemia, or low red blood cell count. This condition affects how well the body functions. In addition, iron deficiencies in children can lead to cognitive impairment, motor deficiencies, and poor emotional functioning (Lozoff et al., 2006).

As it turns out, the body may have a built-in toxin detector. It's called pregnancy sickness, commonly referred to as "morning sickness." Pregnant women often develop aversions to certain foods, and some women get nauseated and even vomit regularly during pregnancy (Profet, 1992). Pregnancy sickness is worst during the first three months of pregnancy, when the fetus's major organs develop and the embryo is most vulnerable to teratogens. Pregnancy sickness occurs most commonly with exposure to foods susceptible to molds (aged cheeses, mushrooms) and to bitter substances (such as coffee), possibly because these foods can cause birth defects (Keeler, 1983).

Maternal nutrition is also one of the most important examples of epigenetics, the study of how the environment affects gene expression (see Chapter 3). Diet is an environmental event. Certain kinds of maternal diet can lead to obesity not only in the person or animal eating a particular diet but also in her offspring. In one study of this phenomenon, researchers took two genetically identical strands of female laboratory mice and randomly assigned them to receive two different kinds of diet while pregnant (Dolinoy & Jirtle, 2008). One group received a diet rich in substances that turn on a gene that causes weight gain. The other group received a diet rich in nutritional supplements (folic acid and B12) that protect against such weight gain. Results showed that the offspring of the pregnant mice that received the diet that turned on the weight gain gene became obese. The diet of the mother while pregnant, not the diet of the animal after birth, led to obesity. Equally noteworthy: The diets of pregnant mice that are rich in vitamin B12 and folic acid protect against obesity in offspring (Dolinoy & Jirtle, 2008; Waterland & Jirtle, 2003).

Teratogens Substances and chemicals that come from the external environment also have an impact on fetal and infant development. Because all major body parts are forming and growing during the embryonic and fetal stages, the fetus is quite susceptible to birth defects during these stages. Known teratogens include viruses, such as those that cause rubella (measles) and the flu; alcohol; nicotine; prescription drugs, such as the antidepressants Prozac and Zoloft; and radiation. Timing determines how detrimental the effects of any given teratogen will be. In general, the earlier in pregnancy the woman is exposed, the more serious the effects. Refer again to Figure 5.2: The blue portion of the bars shows that the time period when major abnormalities can occur is always in the first stages of an organ or structure's development. Viruses, for example, may have a major impact early in pregnancy and relatively little effect toward the end of pregnancy. More specifically, if a pregnant woman develops an infection, such as the flu, especially during months 4–6 of pregnancy, the risk of schizophrenia increases for the child later in life (Brown, 2006; Koenig, 2006).

Maternal substance use can also cause serious prenatal and postnatal problems. Pregnant women who drink alcohol take chances with their developing baby, as there is no known safe level of alcohol consumption during pregnancy (Centers for Disease Control and Prevention, 2007, May 31). The most serious effect of prenatal alcohol exposure is **fetal alcohol spectrum disorder (FASD)**, which causes damage to the central nervous system; low birth weight; physical abnormalities in the face, head, heart, and joints; mental retardation; and behavioral problems (Moore et al., 2007; Sen & Swaminathan, 2007; Uylings, 2006). Brain damage from fetal alcohol exposure may explain many of the problems of FASD (Medina & Krahe, 2008). The effect of fetal alcohol exposure is described as a spectrum of disorders because the types and degrees of deficits can vary tremendously among individuals. FASD affects about 1% of live births in the United States and is a leading cause of mental retardation in this country (Burd et al., 2007; May & Gossage, 2001). FASD has been reported in babies of women who drink excessively as well as in infants whose mothers have only occasionally had drinks during pregnancy, although binge drinking and heavy drinking appear to increase the severity of FASD (May et al., 2008).

connection

Catching the flu while pregnant changes the way neurons grow in the developing fetus and increases vulnerability to schizophrenia later in life.

See Chapter 15, p. 592.

fetal alcohol spectrum disorder
a consequence of prenatal alcohol exposure that causes multiple problems, notably brain damage and mental retardation.

Nicotine exposure from maternal smoking interferes with the oxygen supply to the fetus. It can lead to premature and low-birth-weight babies as well as increased risk for stillbirth (delivery of a dead fetus) (Centers for Disease Control, 2007, August 8; Zigler, Finn-Stevenson, & Hall, 2002).

Prescription drugs also pose risks for the developing fetus. It is not uncommon for women to take prescription drugs during pregnancy, however, especially if they were taking them before they learned they were pregnant. Some studies on animals and humans indicate that the antidepressants Zoloft and Prozac can cause respiratory problems, increased risk of premature birth, and short-lasting effects on motor development, but others suggest there are few risks to the developing fetus (Maschi et al., 2008; Moses-Kolko et al., 2005). The safest course of action, then, would be to avoid these drugs prior to pregnancy.

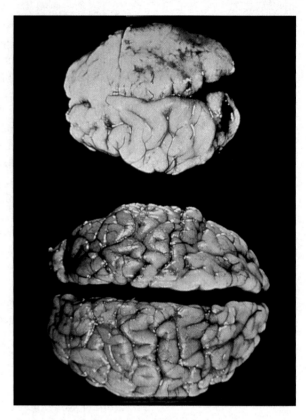

Compared with the brain of a typical child (bottom), the brain of a child with FASD (top) is clearly underdeveloped. Brain abnormalities caused by maternal alcohol use before giving birth result in mental retardation and behavior problems.

quick quiz 5.1: The Developing Fetus

1. Life before birth is commonly divided into three distinct stages: the _____, embryonic, and fetal stages.
   a. gestational
   b. seminal
   c. germinal
   d. cellular

2. How can researchers tell which sounds a fetus prefers to hear?
   a. by measuring the position of the fetus in the womb
   b. by measuring changes in fetal heart rate in response to sounds
   c. by taking a reading of fetal respiration
   d. It is not possible to measure fetal preferences.

3. Teratogens are
   a. substances that can cause birth defects
   b. genes that turn on or off with exposure to viruses
   c. inborn fetal taste preferences
   d. factors that influence the generation of fetal brain tissue

Answers can be found at the end of the chapter.

The Developing Infant and Child

Compared to other primates and to almost all other animals, humans are utterly helpless at birth. Yet because it's still developing, the newborn human brain is more responsive than that of other animals to its surroundings. This distinction allows nurture to shape human nature more than is the case for most animals.

In the first months after birth, development continues at a rapid pace. Not only does the brain keep growing, along with the rest of the body, but infants also begin to gain control of their movements, to learn about their new worlds, and to interact socially with their caregivers. Next we turn to the topic of infancy and childhood. As developmentalists typically do, we consider three domains of development: physical, social and emotional, and cognitive. Physical development includes brain development, growth, motor control, and sensory system development.

PHYSICAL DEVELOPMENT IN INFANCY AND CHILDHOOD

Adults take for granted the ability to act at will. Yet we are really born helpless, unable to act on the world. Motor and sensory systems develop substantially in newborns. In this section, we explore how physical growth, motor skills, and sensory development work along with the developing brain to shape early human experience.

Early Motor Development When we speak of motor development, we are referring to changes in physical movement and body control. Figure 5.5 outlines the major milestones of motor development during the first 15 months. Like any list of milestones we might present in this chapter, the sequence is predictable, but the exact age at which children reach each milestone varies. For example, our son Jerry did not crawl until he was 9 months old, but he walked at 10 months. Our son Evan, on the other hand, crawled at 7½ months and then started walking at about 12 months.

Early in infancy, babies start to show intentional movements. First, they look at their mother with their unfocused gaze, and then they turn their heads to look at her. By about 2 months of age, babies lying on their tummies can lift their

nature & nurture
Because it is not well formed at birth, the newborn human brain is especially responsive to the specific world around it, allowing nurture to shape human nature.

FIGURE **5.5**

MAJOR MOTOR DEVELOPMENT MILESTONES IN INFANCY AND TODDLERHOOD. Some children reach these milestones earlier than others, but most achieve them within the range indicated by the purple bars.

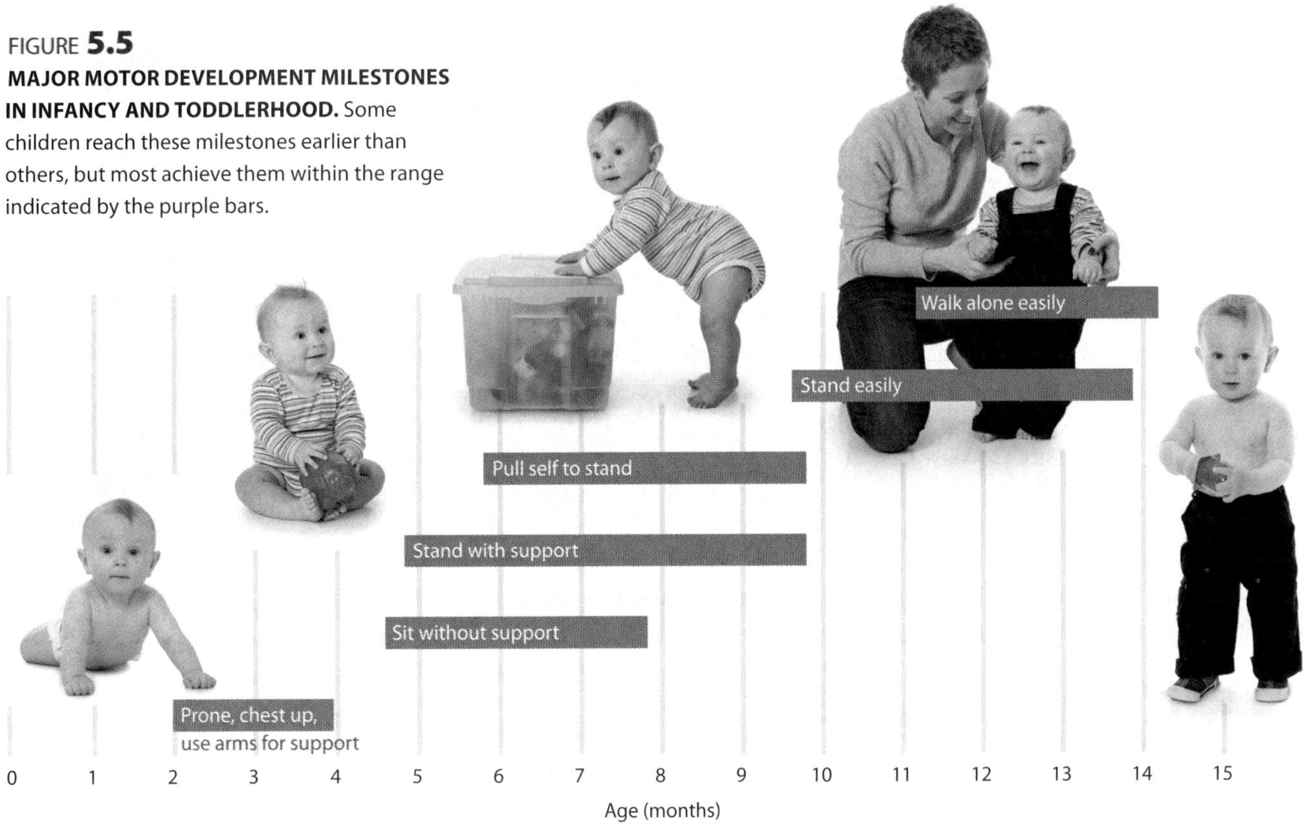

Walk alone easily

Stand easily

Pull self to stand

Stand with support

Sit without support

Prone, chest up, use arms for support

Age (months)
0 1 2 3 4 5 6 7 8 9 10 11 12 13 14 15

heads. At 4 months, they can hold objects. By 6 months, many babies can sit by themselves, without any help. Many babies begin moving themselves around by 7 months, be it by crawling or by scooting on their bellies. About the same time, babies can pull themselves up and hold on to furniture. At about 8 to 9 months, babies walk from sofa to coffee table by holding on to the furniture. Standing and independent walking come soon after. Many babies take their first steps before their first birthday, though it may be some time before they settle into walking alone. Most babies walk without help by 17 months of age (Patterson, 2008).

Other motor responses are more specific. If you give a newborn baby your finger, she will grasp it. Tight. If you stroke her cheek, she will turn her head, open-mouthed in expectation of a breast, a reflex called *rooting*. Grasping and rooting are among several reflexes present at birth—involuntary responses to very specific stimuli. But what about willful action? Within a few months, babies can make voluntary responses. A 3-month-old who is fascinated by a stuffed ring dangling in front of him will suddenly, though not very smoothly, grab for it.

It takes a while before young children can turn knobs and pick up tiny objects. These *fine motor skills* involve the coordination of the actions of many smaller muscles, along with information from the eyes, in the service of some task. Fine motor skill development shows up, for example, in children's drawing skills. Two-year-olds typically show very crude crayon scribbles, but by age 3 or 4 children can make crude drawings of people, and by age 5 most kids can print letters, dress alone, and use silverware (Gardner, 1980; Patterson, 2007). In fact, training in fine motor skills actually aids kindergarteners' attention, especially in girls, showing just how joined cognition and action can be (Stewart, Rule, & Giordano, 2007).

connection

How do we know that the brain "learns" to see?

See Chapter 4, p. 132.

Early Sensory Development

As noted earlier, the five major senses develop at different rates. Hearing is almost fully developed at birth, but a newborn's vision is only about 20-600, meaning infants see an object that is 20 feet away as indistinctly as an adult with normal vision would see an object 600 feet away (see Figure 5.6). Visual sharpness, or acuity, continues to improve during infancy, and by 6 months of age, vision is 20-100. By age 3 or 4, a child's vision is similar to an adult's (Banks & Salapatek, 1983). Newborns are best able to see black and white edges and patterns (Fantz, 1963). Color vision approximates that of adults by 4 months of age (Kellman & Arterberry, 2006).

Experience is crucial in the development of vision, as it is in all aspects of human development. In regard to vision, the occipital cortex of the brain has to be stimulated by visual input in order to develop the proper synaptic connections needed to process visual information. It is for this reason that young infants respond chiefly to visual stimuli within 8 to 12 inches of their face. For full development of the visual sense, these early months are a **critical period,** one of several in human development, when

critical period
specific period in development when individuals are most receptive to a particular kind of input from the environment (such as visual stimulation and language).

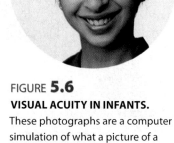

FIGURE **5.6**
VISUAL ACUITY IN INFANTS.
These photographs are a computer simulation of what a picture of a human face looks like to a 1-month-old, 2-month-old, 3-month-old, and 1-year old.

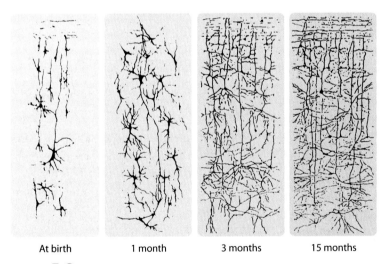

FIGURE **5.7**

THE VISUAL CLIFF. In a demonstration of depth perception, babies will stop at the edge of a clear sheet of plastic, rather than crawling over what appears to be a cliff.

individuals are biologically most receptive to a particular kind of input from the environment.

All babies who have normal vision in both eyes and have learned to crawl see the world in three dimensions. In a study that has become a classic, Gibson and Walk (1960) created the *visual cliff* to test depth perception in babies who have learned to crawl (see Figure 5.7). They placed clear Plexiglas over one end of a crawl area to make it look as though there was a steep drop in the middle. They put a baby on one end end of the crawl area and asked the mother to stand at the end with the drop. The mother's role was to encourage the baby to crawl across the Plexiglas to her. The baby would stop crawling when he or she reached the visual cliff, indicating that at least by the time babies learn to crawl, they can perceive depth.

Early Brain Development

After birth, the brain continues to grow new neurons (see Figure 5.8). Brain growth continues throughout the life span, but the rate of change slows down considerably after the age of 6 and then settles again after adolescence (Sakai, 2005).

After age 2, some neurons and synapses die off. During the first year of life, neural growth occurs, but it is somewhat random and disorganized.

| At birth | 1 month | 3 months | 15 months |

FIGURE **5.8**

NEURAL GROWTH DURING THE FIRST SIX MONTHS OF LIFE. Neural growth in the human brain, in this case the visual cortex, continues at a very rapid pace during the first year or two of life. After that, neurons and synapses that are not reinforced by learning die off by pruning. (*Source:* Reprinted by permission of the publisher from The Postnatal Development of the Human Cerebral Cortex, Vols. I–VIII by Jesse LeRoy Conel, Cambridge, Mass.: Harvard University Press, Copyright © 1939, 1975 by the president and Fellows of Harvard College.)

Musical Training Changes the Brain

The brain develops throughout life, and yet it is most responsive to stimulation during infancy and childhood. In other words, early in life there is more opportunity for experience to leave its mark on the brain (Cicchetti, 2001).

Learning to play a musical instrument, such as guitar, is a good example. You must learn fingering on the neck, how to hold your fingers and press the strings firmly enough to get a clear sound, and the fingering movements that represent the relationship between notes on different musical scales.

In Chapter 3 we discussed how monkeys trained in a finger-tapping task showed substantial increases in the amount of somatosensory cortex devoted to the fingertips compared to before training and compared to untrained monkeys (Jenkins et al., 1990). Do the brains of string instrument players also devote more resources to the fingers of the fingering hand than to the nonfingering hand? To answer this question, researchers applied a slight pressure to each finger on each hand of right-handed musicians and nonmusicians. Using fMRI, they mapped the brain's

responses to this pressure. For musicians, the area on the somatosensory cortex devoted to those fingers on the side of the brain that controls the fingering left hand was bigger than the area that controls the nonfingering right hand. The somatosensory maps did not differ between sides in the brains of nonmusicians (Elbert et al., 1995). Musicians who started playing before the age of 12 showed the most pronounced effects. So musical training may change brain organization, especially for people who start training as children.

Brain imaging studies also suggest that musical training molds the structure of the brain. People who have had intensive musical training have a thicker corpus callosum and increased brain growth in regions associated with music-related skills than do nonmusicians, even more so if they started their training before age 7 (Schlaug et al., 1995). A thicker corpus callosum means that there is greater communication between the two sides of the brain in musicians than in people who have not had such training. Also, musicians have larger cerebellums (an area involved in motor coordination) than do nonmusicians (Hutchinson et al., 2003). Other research shows that the earlier musical training begins, the greater the degree of activation of the

connection

Experience is crucial in the formation of synaptic connections and the growth of neurons in the brain throughout the life span. Pruning is nature's way of making the brain more efficient.

See Chapter 3, p. 108.

With learning and experience, as discussed in Chapter 3, certain synaptic connections become stronger, whereas those that do not receive stimulation from the environment die off. This process, known as **pruning,** is nature's way of making the brain more efficient (Baltes, Reuter-Lorenz, & Rösler, 2006; Greenough, Volkmar, & Juraska, 1973; Perry, 2002). By adolescence up to half of the synapses that existed in early childhood have been pruned (Chechik, Meilijson, & Ruppin, 1999).

The quality of the environments in which we are raised influences how our brains develop. Normal and enriched environments create more complex neural connections, while abusive, neglectful, and impoverished environments create less developed neural connections and fewer of them (Mirescu & Gould, 2006). Neglect exists when caregivers fail to provide basic sensory experience and stimulation to a child during key periods of development (Perry, 2002). Again, timing is critical. A dramatic instance of the

pruning
the degradation of synapses and dying off of neurons that are not strengthened by experience.

music-processing areas of the brain (left auditory cortex) when listening to music (Ohnishi et al., 2001).

The findings discussed so far are correlational. They suggest that musical training can shape the brain, but do not lead to the conclusion that musical training *causes* brain growth. One way to address the problem of correlation is to do an experiment. Pascual-Leone taught people who had never before played piano a one-hand five-finger exercise. They repeated the exercise in 2-hour practice sessions for 5 days, and then they were given a test. The test involved 20 repetitions of the exercise (responses measured by computer for speed, etc.). As skill improved, cortical representation for the finger muscles involved in the task increased (Pascual-Leone, 2001). Next, participants were randomly assigned to either continue daily practice of the exercise for four more weeks or to stop practicing. For those who stopped practicing, brain maps returned to the way they were before training within one week. For those who continued practicing, brain map changes continued. If you don't use it, you lose it!

Learning to play an instrument may foster the development of other skills too. Music training is positively correlated with intelligence test scores in children and college students, and this relationship is strongest for people who have trained longer (Schellenberg, 2006). It is also correlated with improved performance on verbal memory tasks. Moreover, the ability to detect pitch changes in music correlates with accuracy of perception of pitch changes in language processing (Ho, Cheung, & Chan, 2003; Moreno & Besson, 2006). In another study, Elizabeth Spelke (2008) found that children with more intensive musical training performed better on various spatial tasks, which is important in mathematics, a subject in which child musicians often excel. As always, we must use caution in interpreting these correlations: All we know is that music training and intelligence increase together.

effect of neglect and abuse on the development of the human brain comes from research on children who spent their early years in Romanian orphanages, where they were confined much of the time to cribs and had very limited stimulation. Figure 5.9 on page 184 shows a PET scan from one of the orphans alongside one from a typically developing child. The red to yellow areas in Figure 5.9a represent the active regions in the brain of a normal child. In Figure 5.9b, you see the brain activity of a Romanian orphan who was neglected from birth. As you can see, brain activity is greatly diminished in the orphan (Cicchetti, 2001).

Similarly, research shows decreases in brain size in children raised in severely neglectful homes. These deficits can be made up if the children are removed from the neglectful environment—sooner rather than later, however. The longer they stay in the deprived environment, the less likely it is that they will recover (Perry, 2002). As this study suggests, the young brain is uniquely responsive to changes in environment. "Psychology in the Real

nature & nurture

Musicians have better communication between the two sides of the brain than do people who have not had musical training.

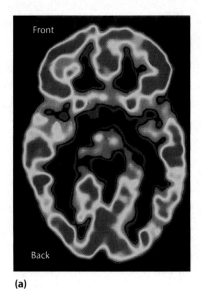

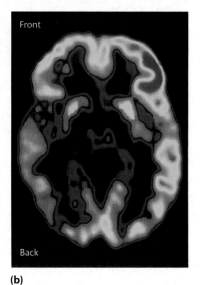

(a)   (b)

FIGURE **5.9**

BRAIN DEVELOPMENT IN A NORMAL CHILD COMPARED TO A DEPRIVED AND NEGLECTED CHILD. (a) In this PET scan of a typically developing child, the red and yellow areas indicate regions of high and moderate activity, respectively. (b) This PET scan of a child who experienced significant deprivation and neglect in a Romanian orphanage shows very little red and much more blue and black, indicating low activity. (*Source:* Cichetti, 2001.)

World" looks at another type of experience—musical training—that influences brain growth and cognitive development.

Findings in neuroscience suggest why children's brains are more plastic and more sensitive to stimulation from the outside world than are the brains of older people. In Chapter 3 we noted that many axons are covered with a myelin sheath, the fatty insulation that makes nerve impulses travel faster. Few neurons are myelinated at birth: With age, more and more neurons become myelinated (Fields, 2008). Figure 5.10 shows the relative increases in myelin over time from age 4 to age 20. In addition, myelination starts in the back of the brain and proceeds to the frontal lobes. This pattern of growth may partially explain why vision develops before language and abstract thinking. The visual cortex is in the back of the brain. The language centers are in the middle.

With age, more of the brain, especially the frontal lobes, becomes myelinated. More myelin increases processing speed, but it may also limit a neuron's ability to grow and change by strengthening commonly used neural connections. Young brains are more flexible because they have less myelin. Myelination may close the window on the critical periods for such skills as learning language

Back   Forehead

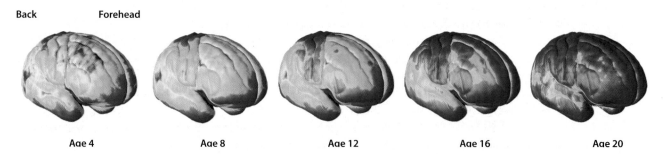

Age 4   Age 8   Age 12   Age 16   Age 20

FIGURE **5.10**

MYELINATION IN THE DEVELOPING BRAIN. At birth the human brain has very little myelin around the neurons' axons. Over time, axons become more and more myelinated. Unmyelinated neurons appear yellow and orange. Myelinated neurons appear purple. (*Source:* Fields, 2008.)

(Fields, 2008). In other words, brains are built in childhood, and those who wish to become musicians or athletes would do well to start young. Putting skills in place when the brain is most flexible and most open to change is important.

EARLY COGNITIVE DEVELOPMENT

Jean Piaget

With growth, especially brain growth, comes cognitive development—advances in the ability to think, reason, remember, learn, and solve problems. What are the principles of cognitive development from birth throughout childhood? The person who addressed this question most extensively was Jean Piaget.

Relying primarily on observations of his own three children, Piaget outlined four phases of cognitive development from birth through adolescence, which he called the sensorimotor, preoperational, concrete operational, and formal operational stages. Figure 5.11 summarizes Piaget's theory of cognitive development.

Piaget called the first stage of cognitive development the **sensorimotor stage** because it characterizes the way infants learn about the world through their senses and their own movements. Young children sense more than they "think." They come to understand the world by manipulating and moving through it. Piaget observed that during the first 8 or 9 months, a child has no concept of **object permanence,** which is the ability to realize that objects still exist when they are not being sensed (Piaget, 1954). In other words, it is "out of sight, out of mind" for young infants. When an object is hidden from them, they will not look for it, even if they see someone hide it. Around 9 months of age, however, infants will move a cloth or look under something to find the hidden object. They have begun to remember that objects continue to exist even when they are not directly sensed. Mastering object permanence is a hallmark of the sensorimotor stage.

object permanence
the ability to realize that objects still exist when they are not being sensed.

sensorimotor stage
Piaget's first stage of cognitive development (ages 0–2), when infants learn about the world by using their senses and by moving their bodies.

	Approximate age (years)	Core cognitive capacities (years)
Sensorimotor	0–2	Knowledge is through senses (tasting, seeing, smelling, touching, hearing) Object permanence develops between 4 and 9 months
Preoperational	2–5	Verbal and egocentric thinking develop Can do mentally what once could only do physically Conservation of shape, number, liquid not yet possible
Concrete operational	6–11	Conservation of shape, number, liquid are now possible Logic and reasoning develop, but are limited to appearance and what is concretely observed
Formal operational	12 and up	Abstract reasoning—principles and ideals develop Systematic problem solving is now possible (no longer just trial and error) Ability to think about and reflect upon one's thinking (metacognition) Scientific reasoning

FIGURE **5.11**
PIAGET'S STAGES OF COGNITIVE DEVELOPMENT.

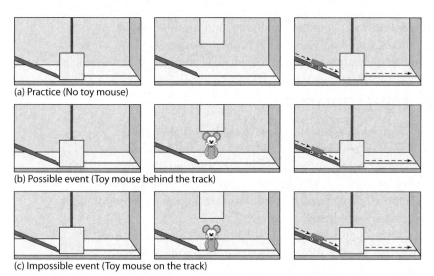

(a) Practice (No toy mouse)

(b) Possible event (Toy mouse behind the track)

(c) Impossible event (Toy mouse on the track)

FIGURE **5.12**

OBJECT PERMANENCE AT 4–5 MONTHS OF AGE. To measure a baby's response to an impossible event, Baillargeon devised three scenarios. In (a) the screen is raised to show that there's nothing behind it and a toy car rolls down the track behind the screen and appears on the other side. In (b), there's a toy mouse behind the car track, and again the car rolls down the track and keeps going. In (c) the impossible event occurs. The screen is raised to reveal the mouse sitting on the track, but again the car keeps going. By 4 months, most infants will stare at the impossible event longer than at the other two scenarios, as if surprised by what they saw. This behavior indicates that they have developed the concept of object permanence.

Rene Baillargeon and colleagues conducted research using a different technique to demonstrate that infants develop object permanence at about 4 or 5 months, which is earlier than Piaget thought (Baillargeon & DeVos, 1991). Their research design, depicted in Figure 5.12, measured infants' responses to expected and impossible events. First, infants are shown an inclined track and a screen that can be lowered or raised in front of the track. They learn that when a car rolls down the track, the car keeps rolling behind the lowered screen and appears on the other side of it. They are not surprised to see the car, even though it was hidden for a short time by the lowered screen. They are shown this event many times, until they get used to it. In the next sequence, everything is the same except that the researchers place a toy mouse *behind* the track while the babies watch. Again, they are not surprised to see the car roll behind the lowered screen and appear on the other side of it.

Then something impossible happens. The researchers place the mouse *on* the track while the infants watch. When the screen is down, hiding the mouse from the infants' view, the experimenters remove the mouse. When the car rolls down the track and keeps rolling, the infants are quite surprised. How do we know that four-month-old infants who cannot talk are surprised? We can study their eyes. When things go as they expected, infants stop looking at the event—they get bored. But when they witness an impossible event—namely a car rolling through a solid object and continuing to move—their eyes widen and they keep looking at it.

Thus, the infants knew the mouse still existed, even though they could not see it or, for that matter, say that they knew of its existence. This research suggests that knowledge of object permanence is present in 4-month-old infants, at half the age when Piaget said it would first appear. The way this knowledge was measured offers a clue as to why Piaget would say 9 months and these researchers would say 4 months.

Babies who have mastered object permanence love games like peek-a-boo, in which people seem to disappear and then reappear.

Piaget measured object permanence by whether the infant picked up a cloth that hid an object or looked underneath something for a hidden object. At 4 months, infants cannot pick up objects very well. In the Baillargeon studies, eye gaze was the indicator of the child's knowledge about the hidden object. Eye movement develops before hand movement, and as discussed in Chapter 2, the methods scientists use sometimes influence their findings.

At around age 2, with the emergence of symbolic thought, children move into Piaget's second stage of cognitive development—the **preoperational stage**, a period that lasts until about age 5 or 6. Symbolic thinking involves using symbols such as words or letters to represent ideas or objects. Other qualities of preoperational thinking include animistic thinking, egocentrism, and lack of conservation.

preoperational stage
the second major stage of cognitive development (ages 2–5), which begins with the emergence of symbolic thought.

Animistic thinking refers to the idea that inanimate objects are alive. For example, Piaget reported on a child in this stage who was asked whether the sun moved. The child answered, "Yes, when one walks, it follows." When the child was asked why it moves, he responded, "Because when one walks, it goes too." Finally, when the child was asked whether the sun was alive, he responded, "Of course, otherwise it wouldn't follow us; it couldn't shine" (Piaget, 1972b, p. 215).

animistic thinking
belief that inanimate objects are alive.

Egocentrism is the tendency to view the world from one's own perspective and not see things from another person's perspective. Piaget and Inhelder (1967) designed the *three mountains task* to measure young children's egocentrism (see Figure 5.13). For this demonstration, three mountains are placed on a small table. The child sits on one side of the table and a doll is placed in a chair on the other side of the table. The experimenter asks the child to describe how the doll sees the three mountains. Typically, the three possible perspectives are drawn on a board and the child has to choose the correct perspective. Egocentric, preoperational children will choose the perspective from which *they* see the mountains—they cannot visualize them from the doll's point of view.

egocentrism
viewing the world from one's own perspective and not being capable of seeing things from another person's perspective.

FIGURE **5.13**
PIAGET'S THREE MOUNTAINS TASK: EGOCENTRIC PERCEPTION OF PREOPERATIONAL CHILDREN. When asked to describe what the doll could see from the other side of the table, children in the preoperational stage can't visualize the scene from any perspective other than their own.

conservation
recognition that when some properties (such as shape) of an object change, other properties (such as volume) remain constant.

Conservation is the ability to recognize that when some properties (such as shape) of an object change, other properties (such as volume) remain constant. During preoperational thinking, the child cannot yet recognize that amounts stay the same when shapes change. They are unable to conserve. Piaget used many different objects and situations to examine conservation. Figure 5.14 shows a number of them.

Let's look at the conservation of liquid as an example. This task involves filling two glasses of the same shape and size with equal amounts of water. The child confirms they are the same amount of water. Then the child pours one of the glasses of water into a third container that is taller and thinner than the first two. One of the original glasses still has the same amount of water in it. When asked whether the two glasses contain the same amount of water, the child will say no if he or she lacks the ability to conserve. Usually, the child will say the tall, thin container has more water than the short, wide one.

	Original setup	Alter as shown	Ask child	Usual answer
conservation of liquid			Which has more liquid?	Has more
conservation of mass			Do they both weigh the same, or does one weigh more than the other?	Weighs more
conservation of number			Are there still as many pennies as nickels, or more of one than the other?	More
conservation of length			Are they the same length, or is one longer?	Is longer
conservation of length			Is one pencil as long as the other, or is one longer?	Is longer

FIGURE **5.14**

DIFFERENT KINDS OF CONSERVATION TASKS. Children in the preoperational stage don't realize that the quantity of something doesn't change if it is rearranged. (*Source:* Seifert et al., 2000.)

concrete operational stage
Piaget's third stage of cognitive development, which spans ages 6–11, during which the child can perform mental operations—such as reversing—on real objects or events.

During Piaget's third stage, called the **concrete operational stage** (ages 6–11), children can perform mental operations—on real, or concrete, objects and events—but they still have trouble with abstract ideas and reasoning. Reversing events is one type of operation a child masters in this stage. One of the yardsticks that measures whether a child has moved from preoperational to concrete operational thinking is the ability to conserve. For example, the child can mentally pour the liquid back into the original container in the conservation of liquid task and realize that pouring liquid from one container into another doesn't change the amount. Notice that this conclusion is also a logical conclusion: "It has to be same—the amount of liquid does not change when the shape of the container changes." In this stage, logic remains concrete and limited to objects that a child directly observes. The child can reason that the amount of liquid she or he sees go from one glass into the other must remain the same, but would have trouble solving a problem of this type: "If Susan is half

Conservation of liquid. Children in Piaget's pre-operation stage of cognitive development typically say that there is more liquid in the taller container even though they saw that was the same amount in the short wide container before it was poured into the taller glass. Only when they reach the concrete operational stage do they understand conservation of liquid.

as old as Robert, and Robert is twice as old as Samantha, then Samantha is _____ compared to Susan."

With the onset of adolescence, children gain the ability to reason about abstract concepts and problems. Piaget called this phase of cognitive development the **formal operational stage** (Inhelder & Piaget, 1958; Piaget, 1972a). During this stage, formal logic becomes possible. An example of formal logic is "If Maria is a woman, and all women are mortal, then Maria is mortal." In addition, adolescents develop scientific reasoning and hypothesis-testing skills. We'll go into more detail about this stage of cognitive development in the section on adolescence (see p. 200).

formal operational stage
Piaget's final stage of cognitive development, from age 11 or 12 on through adulthood, when formal logic is possible.

Theory of Mind

The term **theory of mind** refers to our knowledge and ideas of how other people's minds work. Knowing and understanding what other people are thinking, wanting, or feeling is a critical skill in human society. Not that we are or can be mind-readers, but in fact, we do recognize many verbal and nonverbal cues about other people's inner thoughts and feelings. The important questions from a development perspective are when and how does such a skill emerge, and how does it change with age?

theory of mind
ideas and knowledge about how other people's minds work.

Children under the age of 4 do not realize that people may believe things that are not true. Adults know that people believe things—such as superstitions—that are untrue all the time. Psychologists created the *false-belief* task to determine when children develop theory of mind and come to know that others can believe something that is false (Wimmer & Perner, 1983).

For the false-belief task, a child between the ages of 3 and 5 sits with an experimenter at a table. The experimenter has cardboard cutouts of a story (see Figure 5.15). In the first cutout, Sally puts her marble in a basket. In the next picture, Sally goes away. In the next scene, Anne takes the marble from the basket and puts it in a box. In the final scene, Sally returns. The researcher asks this critical false-belief question: Where will Sally look for her marble, in the box or the basket? A 3-year-old will say that Sally will look in the box because a 3-year-old cannot distinguish what she or he knows compared to what Sally knows. Around age 4, however, children can disentangle their own beliefs from other people's beliefs and say "Sally will look in the basket," because they understand that Sally doesn't know that Anne moved the marble (Gopnik, Meltzoff, & Kuhl, 1999; Sullivan, Zaitchik, & Tager-Flusberg, 1994; Wimmer & Perner, 1983). Research on false

connection
Autism is a childhood disorder characterized by severe language and social impairment combined with repetetive habits and inward-focused behaviors. How is autism related to theory of mind?
See Chapter 15, p. 603.

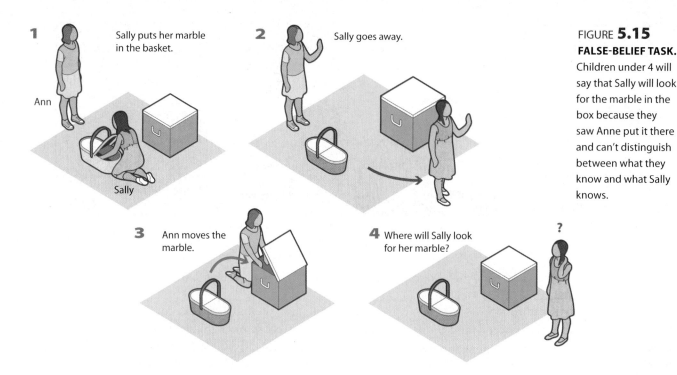

1 Sally puts her marble in the basket.

Ann

Sally

2 Sally goes away.

3 Ann moves the marble.

4 Where will Sally look for her marble?

?

FIGURE **5.15**
FALSE-BELIEF TASK.
Children under 4 will say that Sally will look for the marble in the box because they saw Anne put it there and can't distinguish between what they know and what Sally knows.

beliefs suggests that theory of mind, the ability to know what other people are thinking, especially when it is different from what you are thinking, develops around age 4.

DEVELOPMENT OF MORAL REASONING

As children develop cognitive and social skills, they also develop a sense of right and wrong. Piaget (1932) described stages of such *moral* development, pointing out differences in how preschoolers reasoned about morality compared to older children and adults. But the most well known account of the development of moral reasoning comes from Lawrence Kohlberg.

Kohlberg (1981) studied the development of moral reasoning in children and adults by giving them a moral dilemma and recording the reasons they provided for their responses. Their responses were less important to him than was the reasoning behind them.

The dilemma Kohlberg commonly presented to his participants was the "Heinz Dilemma," as follows:

A woman was near death from a special kind of cancer. There was one drug that the doctors thought might save her. It was a form of radium that a druggist in the same town had recently discovered. The drug was expensive to make, but the druggist was charging ten times what the drug cost him to produce. He paid $200 for the radium and charged $2,000 for a small dose of the drug. The sick woman's husband, Heinz, went to everyone he knew to borrow the money, but he could only get together about $1,000, which is half of

what it cost. He told the druggist that his wife was dying and asked him to sell it cheaper or let him pay later. But the druggist said: "No, I discovered the drug and I'm going to make money from it." So Heinz got desperate and broke into the man's store to steal the drug for his wife. Should Heinz have broken into the laboratory to steal the drug for his wife? Why or why not? (Kohlberg, 1981)

After analyzing the reasoning that people of different ages gave, Kohlberg proposed a three-stage theory of moral reasoning. He found that moral reasoning moves from being focused on the self to being increasingly focused on others, with a basis in clear personal principles of morality and ethics (see Figure 5.16). In the first and least-developed level of moral reasoning, the **preconventional level,** the responses tend to be something like this: "Heinz should not steal the drug because he will get in trouble and go to jail." The reasoning behind the answer has to do with avoiding punishment or maximizing reward. Children obey rules because their parents tell them to comply. In the second level, the **conventional level,** the person might respond with "Heinz should not steal the drug because stealing is wrong. Society cannot function if people steal all the time." At this level, the person values caring, trust, and relationships as well as social order and lawfulness. In the third level of moral reasoning—the **postconventional level**—a person might respond, "Although it is legally wrong, Heinz should steal the drug to save his wife's life. But he also has to be willing to suffer the consequences and go to jail if need be." In this case, the person acknowledges both the norm and the law, but argues that there are universal moral rules that may trump unjust or immoral local rules. Therefore, disobeying the more local rule or law may be necessary. This is the principle of *civil disobedience* embraced by great moral leaders from Henry David Thoreau to Mahatma Gandhi to Martin Luther King, Jr. These individuals exhibited well-developed moral codes for which they were willing to sacrifice their lives, if need be, to set right unjust and immoral laws and societies. For example, when Rosa

preconventional level
the first level in Kohlberg's theory of moral reasoning, focusing on avoiding punishment or maximizing rewards.

postconventional level
the third level in Kohlberg's theory of moral reasoning, in which the person recognizes universal moral rules that may trump unjust or immoral local rules.

conventional level
the second level in Kohlberg's theory of moral reasoning, during which the person values caring, trust, and relationships as well as the social order and lawfulness.

	Motive–reasoning
pre-conventional	To avoid punishment Judgments are based on personal needs
conventional	Rules are rules and they are not to be broken Judgments are based on needs of society; individual needs serve group needs
post-conventional	Willing to break law—and suffer the consequences—if it is perceived as unjust or immoral Judgments balance needs of society with personal convictions

FIGURE **5.16**
SUMMARY OF KOHLBERG'S STAGES OF MORAL REASONING. Kohlberg saw a possible progression through three stages of moral reasoning, but not everyone reaches the postconventional stage.

Parks refused to take a seat in the back of the bus and to violate local law, she exhibited postconventional moral reasoning.

Research supports Kohlberg's argument that children tend to reason preconventionally and adults conventionally (Carroll & Rest, 1981; Lapsley, 2006). Moreover, research on moral reasoning in different cultures from all over the world offers support for the first two stages of Kohlberg's model, but not for the third. Snarey (1985) reviewed 45 studies on the development of moral reasoning in 27 different countries and found universal support for the preconventional and conventional levels of moral reasoning. The postconventional level, however, appears to be limited more to Western cultures. When one realizes that Western cultures place a strong emphasis on individualism and individual values, this finding makes sense, because postconventional moral reasoning is heavily based in a personal moral code. In contrast, many non-Western cultures emphasize the group and community, and so the highest level of moral reasoning would be likely to involve compassion and caring for others, altruism, and family honor, values that Kohlberg did not measure (Matsumoto & Juang, 2004). Other scholars say that Kohlberg's theory is a male-oriented perspective that values justice above caring. Women the world over tend to put more emphasis on caring than men, and Kohlberg's theory, in effect, penalizes such an emphasis by including care for others in the conventional level, rather than in the higher postconventional level (Carlo, 2006; Gilligan, 1982).

EARLY SOCIOEMOTIONAL DEVELOPMENT

Even before children develop a sense of right and wrong, they have to learn about their social world. This learning starts at day 1, with the first touch. All mammals need warmth and contact to survive and flourish. Human babies, born in a very immature state, need constant care in order to survive to early childhood. They seem programmed from birth to form close relationships with their primary caregivers. Thanks to some pioneering research that began in the mid–20th century, we know that the quality of those relationships can have lifelong implications. Here we examine the nature of young children's social and emotional development, focusing especially on the relationship between the caregiver and the infant, but also on peer interactions among older children.

Attachment Some animals, especially birds, follow and imitate the first large creature they see immediately after birth. This behavior is called **imprinting**. The newborn sees this creature as a protector. Usually this creature also happens to *be* the protector (mom or dad), so it is a good strategy (Lorenz, 1935, 1937). Newborn humans cannot follow around the first large creature they see, so they do not imprint. They *attach* (Kirkpatrick, 2005).

imprinting
the rapid and innate learning of the characteristics of a caregiver very soon after birth.

In everyday usage, *attachment* means "connectedness." In human development, **attachment** refers to the strong emotional connection that develops early in life to keep infants close to their caregivers. Attachment is a way to describe the relationship between infant and caregiver. This relationship shapes the child's social and emotional development and may form the foundation for social relationships later in life.

attachment
the strong emotional connection that develops early in life between infants and their caregivers.

John Bowlby (1969) described how infants become emotionally attached to their caregivers and emotionally distressed when separated from them. He proposed that the major function of this affection-based bonding system is to protect infants from predation and other threats to survival. In his observations of human infants and primates, Bowlby noted that they went through a clear sequence of reactions—from protest, to despair, to detachment—when separated from their caregiver. Bowlby defined **separation anxiety** as the distress reaction shown by babies when they are separated from their primary caregiver (typically shown at around 9 months of age).

On the basis of such observations, Bowlby developed his attachment theory, which rests on two fundamental assumptions (1969, 1973, 1980). First, a responsive and accessible caregiver (usually the mother) must create a secure base for the child. The infant needs to know that the caregiver is accessible and dependable. With a dependable caregiver, the child can develop confidence and security in exploring the world. The bonding relationship serves the critical function of attaching the caregiver to the infant, thereby making survival of the infant, and ultimately the species, more likely.

A second assumption of attachment theory is that infants internalize the bonding relationship, which provides a mental model on which they build future friendships and love relationships. Therefore, attachment to a caregiver is the most critical of all relationships. In order for bonding to take place, infants must be more than a mere passive receptor to the caregiver's behavior. It is a bidirectional relationship—the infant and the caregiver respond to each other and influence each other's behavior.

nature & nurture

Human attachment is based on an affection-based bonding system that protects an infant from threats to survival.

"During the next stage of my development, Dad, I'll be drawing closer to my mother—I'll get back to you in my teens."

Influenced by Bowlby's work, Mary Ainsworth and her associates (1978) developed a technique for measuring the attachment of infant and caregiver. This procedure, known as the *strange situation*, consists of a 20-minute laboratory session in which a mother and her 12-month-old infant are initially alone in a playroom. Then a stranger comes into the room, and after a few minutes the stranger begins a brief interaction with the infant. The mother then leaves for two separate 2-minute periods. During the first period, the infant is left alone with the stranger. During the second period, the infant is left completely alone. The critical behavior that Ainsworth and colleagues rated was how the infant reacted when the caregiver returned. They presumed that the infant's reaction would reflect the way the baby learned to respond to his or her caregiver and that these reactions would be based on the history of comfort and reassurance the caregiver provided.

connections

Attachment styles are stable throughout life and may set the blueprint for love relationships in adulthood.
See Chapter 14, p. 564.

Ainsworth and her associates (1978) described three attachment styles: secure, anxious-resistant, and avoidant. In a **secure attachment**, infants are happy and initiate contact when the mother returns. They will go over to her and want to be held. After they've been reunited with their mothers, they may return to their play. Securely attached infants are confident in the accessibility and responsiveness of their caregiver, and this security and dependability provides the child with the foundation for play and exploration when the caregiver is absent.

secure attachment
attachment style characterized by infants who will gradually explore new situations when the caregiver leaves and initiate contact when the caregiver returns after separation.

The other two types of attachment represent insecure attachment. In an **anxious-resistant attachment** style, infants are ambivalent. When their mother leaves the room, they become unusually upset, and when their mother returns they seek contact with her but reject attempts at being soothed. These infants give very conflicted messages. On the one hand, they seek contact with their mother; on the other hand, they squirm to be put down and may throw away toys that their mother has offered them. In **anxious-avoidant attachment,** infants stay calm when their mother leaves; they accept the stranger, and when their mother returns, they ignore and avoid her. In both kinds of insecure attachment, infants lack the ability to engage in effective play and exploration.

The infant–caregiver relationship provides the first context for the development of love in the baby's life. Some research suggests that this initial relationship helps shape adult romantic love relationships (Hazan & Shaver, 1987) in that the attachment style from infancy brings something to bear on the ways one connects with a romantic partner (or not).

breaking new ground
How Touch and Comfort Influence Development

One of the surest ways to soothe a crying newborn is to pick her up and cuddle her close. Aside from its calming effect, how important is contact for a developing infant? And what purpose does it serve? Breakthrough research by Harry Harlow (1958) in the 1950s overturned traditional notions of the importance of touch and comfort in human development and, in particular, changed the way special needs infants are cared for.

DO BABIES' NEEDS EXTEND BEYOND HUNGER AND THIRST?

In the early part of the 20th century, psychologists assumed that all babies needed to survive was to have their internal biological needs met—hunger, thirst, and temperature regulation, for example. Physiological psychologists who studied motives and drives before the mid–20th century focused on the primary drives of hunger, thirst, pain, and sex, drives that they considered necessary for survival. External needs, including love, affection, and social contact, were considered secondary. According to this view, babies liked being held by their mothers because they had come to associate mom with the ability to satisfy their primary hunger needs. Psychoanalysts held a similar view on this issue, despite having very different views from the physiological psychologists generally. Freud argued that babies are so attached to their mothers because they wanted their breasts: Mom has breasts, the breasts give food, and so mom becomes the most desired object in the world. But is the connection to a caregiver really all a result of mom's link with food?

THE IMPORTANCE OF COMFORT AND PHYSICAL CONTACT

Harry Harlow thought there might be more to infants' desire for contact than a need for nourishment. In his early work, Harlow (1958) noticed that baby monkeys whom he had separated from their mothers became very attached to cloth diapers that lined their cages. This strong attachment to cloth made Harlow think that a baby primate needs something soft to cling to. It reminded him of the attachment babies have for their blankets.

To test his hunch that the need for something soft to hold is as fundamental as the need for nutrition, Harlow and his colleagues carried out a series of studies with newborn monkeys whom they separated from their mothers. They housed them with surrogate mothers constructed of wire and wood (see Figure 5.17). One was just a wire frame with a crude head. The other was a wire frame covered with soft terry cloth. Both mothers were heated and either could be hooked up to a bottle of milk.

In the first study, Harlow removed eight monkeys from their mothers shortly after birth. Cloth and wire mothers were housed in cubicles attached to the infants' cages. Half the monkeys were randomly assigned to get milk from the wire monkey; the other half got their milk from the cloth monkey. Harlow used the amount of time spent with a surrogate mother as a measure of the affection bond. He found that contact comfort was much more important than the source of food in determining which surrogate mother the monkeys preferred. Regardless of whether a baby monkey nursed from the cloth mother or the wire mother, it spent most of its time with the cloth mom (see Figure 5.18). Monkeys fed by wire surrogates would quickly get milk from the wire mom and then run over to the cloth mom to cuddle. Harlow's findings suggested that the view that babies preferred being with their moms because the mothers provided food was at least partially incorrect. Harlow went so far as to say that a primary function of nursing in humans was contact as much as nutrition.

Harlow's work was pivotal in showing the importance of comfort in primate development. That is not to say, however, that having a cloth surrogate is as good as having a real mother. In follow-up research, Harlow found that monkeys raised without mothers (including some raised with cloth surrogates) were negligent and abusive mothers when they had their own babies. They failed to give their babies proper contact or even to feed them correctly (Arling & Harlow, 1967). We can conclude that they did not know how to behave with their offspring because they hadn't had a live mother themselves. So real-life moms are more than a source of physical contact and nutrition. It seems they are role models for future social relationships, especially caregiving.

Because of Harlow's work, physical contact came to be considered central to optimal human development. Yet, as researcher Tiffany Field noted, preterm human babies might spend weeks or months in special hospital beds where they were kept warm, protected from infection, and monitored by the lat-

FIGURE **5.17**
THE CLOTH AND WIRE MOTHERS FROM HARLOW'S RESEARCH. The baby monkeys always spent more time on the cloth surrogate, going to the wire surrogate only for food.

FIGURE **5.18**
TIME MONKEYS SPENT ON CLOTH VERSUS WIRE SURROGATE "MOTHERS." Whether or not the baby monkeys were fed by the wire mother or the cloth mother, all of them preferred the comfort of the cloth mother. (*Source:* Harlow, 1958.)

est technology, but rarely *touched.* For these infants, touch may have been a crucial but missing part of their care.

What might be the effects of depriving the neediest babies of human contact? Field and her colleagues (1986) decided to test whether regular touch might help tiny premature infants. She randomly assigned 40 preterm infants from a hospital's newborn intensive care unit to either receive touch therapy (experimental group) or not (control group). All of the premature infants lived in isolettes, plastic-covered bassinets designed to prevent infection. This touch therapy involved gently stroking the baby with warmed hands (no gloves) through portholes in the isolette for 15 minutes, three times a day for 10 days. Over the treatment period, babies who received touch therapy gained significantly more weight than those who did not, even though they did not eat more (see Figure 5.19). Weight gain is crucial for preterm infants as they struggle to adjust to life outside the womb. Later research showed the same effect in weight gain when mothers touched their preterm infants (Field et al., 2004). Touch also leads to reduced stress levels in premature babies and to less diarrhea (Diego, Field, Hernandez-Reif, 2007; Jump, Fargo, & Akers, 2006). Touch, then, is more than just comforting—it makes for better health.

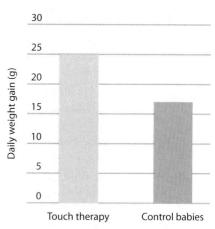

FIGURE **5.19**

WEIGHT GAIN IN PREMATURE INFANTS WHO DID OR DID NOT RECEIVE TOUCH THERAPY. Note that the graph shows the amount of weight gained per day, in grams. Over time, the difference in the weights of the two groups could be expected to increase. Along with the added weight, the massaged babies gained better overall health. (*Source:* Field et al., 1986.)

EXTENDING THE BENEFITS OF TOUCH THERAPY

The benefits of touch therapy for infants extend to older children with special needs, including children with neurological problems. Maria Hernandez-Reif and colleagues (2005) used massage therapy on toddlers with *cerebral palsy,* a movement disorder caused by brain damage that occurs during the birth process. The children received massage therapy twice a day for 12 weeks. The massaged children (compared to a control group who received no massage) experienced improved motor movements, better muscle control, and improved fine motor coordination. They also showed substantial cognitive and social improvements.

Massage therapy also helps people with developmental disorders, such as autism (a disorder characterized by drastic deficits in communication and language, social interaction, emotional expression and experience, and imaginative play as well as repetitive behaviors; see Chapter 15). A study of Qigong (a Chinese touch therapy) showed improvements in sensory, social, and basic living skills in autistic children (Silva et al., 2007). Massage improves well-being, motor dexterity, sleeping, and overall health in kids with other disabilities (Barlow et al., 2008). This work helps us further appreciate the importance of touch for healthy human development. It is a fine example of the difference nurture can make for individuals whose biological limitations preclude typical development.

Future work might explore the role of touch in broader developmental contexts. For example, if contact and touch are so crucial to infants, might there be differences

The benefits of touch and massage therapy for children with cerebral palsy include cognitive and social improvements as well as increased muscle control.

in social and emotional health among older kids who are touched and hugged a lot compared to those who are not?

Developing Social Relationships and Emotions

It is no doubt frustrating at times to be a baby. Think about it: There are things you need and want, and you are not yet able to ask for them, other than by crying. Yet babies learn other ways to communicate their needs to their caregivers, even before they can talk. One way in which they do so is by facial expression. Newborn babies as young as 7 hours old can imitate simple adult facial expressions (Meltzoff & Moore, 1977, 1983). By imitating others, infants learn to make certain facial expressions that help them to communicate their needs (Iacoboni & Mazziota, 2007; Lepage & Théoret, 2007).

connections

One way we learn is by imitating someone else's behavior. Imitation also contributes to aggressive behavior. See Chapter 8, p. 319, and Chapter 15, p. 597.

Babies also seem to know at a very young age what the facial expressions of others mean. Four-month-olds show different patterns of visual attention to angry, fearful, and sad facial expressions in a peek-a-boo game (Montague & Walker-Andrews, 2001). Older babies know how to look to their primary caregiver, whom they know they can trust, for information about emotion and situations. For example, is it safe to go here or crawl there? The visual cliff that we discussed earlier as a way of testing babies' depth perception has also been used to study whether babies look to their caregivers for information about safety.

Developmental psychologist James Sorce and his colleagues (1985) studied 1-year-old babies and their mothers' reactions to the visual cliff. In his study, the mom would place her baby on the visual cliff. She would stand at the other end, put a toy down, and pose one of five facial expressions of emotion: fear, anger, sadness, interest, or happiness. She said nothing and did nothing else. When mom's facial expression said fear or anger, the baby did not move to the deep side. But most babies went willingly over the cliff when the mom smiled. What this means is that by the age of 1, children can make sense of their mother's emotional facial expressions and use them to know what to do. This ability to make use of social and emotional information from another person, especially a caregiver, is known as **social referencing** (Campos & Stenberg, 1981). Babies also rely on parental vocal information (such as changes in the pitch and loudness of a voice) for social referencing (Vaish & Striano, 2004).

social referencing the ability to make use of social and emotional information from another person—especially a caregiver—in an uncertain situation.

The research on social referencing shows that babies understand the meaning of some different facial expressions of emotion much earlier than age one. Researchers have measured how long infants look at objects or people to determine whether they know or are interested in them; they also use electrophysiological brain responses. On the basis of such measures, we know that by 7 months babies can discriminate between fearful and happy faces. Babies of this age also understand the emotional meaning of the voice (intonation changes) that tends to go with certain emotional states, such as happy, angry, or sad (Grossman, Striano, & Friederici, 2006). Well before one year of age, then, babies possess a basic ability to interpret other people's emotions.

Development of Emotions. Babies show their own emotions very early in life. At first they do not display the subtle variations that adults do. They start with pleasure and pain after birth, and somewhat later they express more socioemotional behavior—responding to mom's voice or face with a smile. This transition occurs between 2 and 3 months of age (Lavelli & Fogel, 2005). A month later, they begin laughing in response to playful social interaction.

Signs of anger in facial expression occur as early as 4 months. How do you make young babies angry? One way is to restrain their movement, simply by holding their arms firmly. Between the ages of 4 and 7 months, infants begin to show facial expressions similar to adult expressions of anger when restrained, and the more frustrated they get, the more they show it (Stenberg & Campos, 1980; Stenberg, Campos, & Emde, 1983).

Other studies tell us that babies may not be able to differentiate their emotions the way adults can (Bridges, 1932). There is evidence, for example, that babies use "anger faces" in situations where they might feel fear, such as when they see a noisy toy gorilla head. So it is not clear whether the anger faces at this age are specific to situations that provoke anger (Camras et al., 2007; Oster, 2005). With further development and experience, babies refine their emotional expressions.

All humans, including babies, respond to cues in their social environments. Exposure to aggressive conflict between parents, for example, changes babies' behavior. Specifically, 6-month-old babies who have witnessed aggressive conflict between their parents tend to withdraw when presented with a novel stimulus, such as a new toy (Crockenberg, Leerkes, & Lekka, 2007). The withdrawal response makes sense given the history of these very young children. If the setting is unpleasant—or even toxic—it is better to pull back as a way of regulating distress.

Learning to regulate and control emotion is not easy for most children. **Emotional competence** is the ability to control emotions and know when it is appropriate to express certain emotions (Saarni, 1999; Trentacosta & Izard, 2007). The development of emotional competence starts as early as preschool and continues throughout childhood (Feng et al., 2008; Grolnick, McMenamy, & Kurowski, 2006; Saarni, 1984). Moreover, the better children do in school and the fewer stressful and dysfunctional situations they have at home, the more emotionally skilled and competent they are (Feng et al., 2008; Spinrad et al., 2006).

One aspect of emotional competence is learning to regulate emotion. By the age of 9, children become more aware of the impact of their reactions on other people's feelings. Carolyn Saarni (1984) conducted a classic series of

emotional competence
the ability to control emotions and know when it is appropriate to express certain emotions.

studies to uncover how children learn to modify their emotional expressions in the presence of others. She gave first-grade (age 7), third-grade (age 9), and fifth-grade (age 11) children a task to complete and told them that afterward they would get a very desirable toy. The children, however, received a less-than-desirable toy either alone or in the presence of the experimenter. When alone, kids readily showed their disappointment. In the presence of the experimenter, the young children (age 7) readily showed their disappointment, but by the age of 9 they tried to inhibit facial expressions of negative emotion when receiving an undesirable gift so as not to hurt the experimenter's feelings. Such social smiling comes only with age and maturity (Simonds et al., 2007).

Peer Interaction. As children get older, their social world expands from the intimate environment of the home to include play with other children. Although attachment to the primary caregiver is important for the baby and young child, relations with other children have a big impact after early childhood (Harris, 1998). Indeed, in early childhood, children do not even interact much with other children, even if other children are playing nearby. Children begin to interact socially during play at about age 3 (Howes & Matheson, 1992).

Nothing influences the behavior of children like other children—their peers. **Peers** share equal standing or status. They are at the same level, in terms of age, gender, skill, or power. How early does peer pressure start? A study of over 100 British children shows that sensitivity to criticism occurs in 5-year-olds. Sensitivity is more likely to occur in kids who do better in tasks that require skill in using social and emotional information—tasks such as identifying facial expression of emotion or determining what a puppet in an acted-out scene or a character in a book might do or feel (Cutting & Dunn, 2002).

One can see gender differences in peer interaction at many ages. First, even when not pressured by adults to do so, children will flock to same-sex playmates (Maccoby & Jacklin, 1987). Second, these gender differences in play occur all over the world—in Europe, the United States, Asia, and Africa (Omark, Omark, & Edelman, 1973; Whiting & Edwards, 1988). Eleanor Maccoby (2000) has attributed this same-sex interaction preference to shared preferences for certain types of play. Boys prefer rough-and-tumble play, whereas girls opt for cooperative play (Green and Cillessen, 2008; Maccoby, 2000). Only in adolescence do boys and girls begin to move toward opposite-sex interactions.

peers
people who share equal standing or status and are at the same level, in terms of age, gender, skill, or power.

quick quiz 5.2: The Developing Infant and Child

1. In the newborn infant, the sense of _____ is almost fully developed, but the sense of _____ continues to change and improve over the first few years of life.
   a. taste; hearing
   b. vision; taste
   c. vision; hearing
   d. hearing; vision

2. With learning and experience, certain synaptic connections grow stronger, while those that are not strengthened by experience degrade and die off. This process is known as
   a. neural efficiency
   b. honing
   c. pruning
   d. reductionism

3. People who have had intensive musical training have _____ than nonmusicians.
   a. thicker finger pads
   b. a thicker corpus callosum
   c. a thicker cerebellum
   d. a thicker caudate nucleus

4. Piaget's _____ stage of cognitive development begins when the child can conserve—that is, knows that the amount of a liquid or substance stays the same even when it changes shape.
   a. sensorimotor
   b. abstract–ideational
   c. logical operations
   d. concrete operations

Answers can be found at the end of the chapter.

The Developing Adolescent

adolescence
the transition period between childhood and adulthood.

Adolescence is the transition period between childhood and adulthood, beginning at about age 11 or 12 and lasting until around age 18. Adolescence is a tumultuous time. What makes it so exciting and difficult is all the changes that have to take place in a relatively short period to turn a girl into a woman and a boy into a man.

PHYSICAL DEVELOPMENT IN ADOLESCENCE

puberty
the period when sexual maturation begins; it marks the beginning of adolescence.

Puberty, the period when sexual maturation begins, marks the beginning of adolescence. During puberty, major hormonal changes prepare the body for reproduction and stimulate changes in body size and proportions. On average, girls reach puberty at about age 11 and boys at about age 13. The changes that mark the beginning of puberty stem from the release of sex hormones. First, the pituitary gland sends hormonal signals to the sex glands, telling them to mature. The sex glands, or *gonads,* then release sex hormones (see Figure 5.20). The male gonads are called *testes;* the female gonads are the *ovaries.* The testes release the male sex hormone *testosterone,* which initiates the physical changes we associate with male maturation, such as facial and pubic hair, deepening of the voice, widening of the shoulders, and growth of the penis. The release of the female sex hormone *estradiol* from the ovaries transforms girls into women, with the growth of breasts, widening of hips, and an increase in body fat.

Girls start puberty about 2 years earlier than boys. In the United States, African American girls begin maturing somewhat earlier than European American girls.

menarche
the first menstrual period.

In girls, breast development can start as early as age 10. The next major change is the onset of menstruation, known as **menarche.** The age of menarche is highly variable, but it often occurs by age 12. In most Western cultures, the age of menarche has dropped from about age 16 during the 1800s to 12 or 13 today. (The beginning of menstruation marks the beginning of fertility for a young woman, so this is an important developmental milestone.)

spermarche
the first ejaculation.

In boys, the event that signals readiness to reproduce is **spermarche,** or the first ejaculation. Usually the first ejaculation is unexpected, and it occurs as a *nocturnal emission*

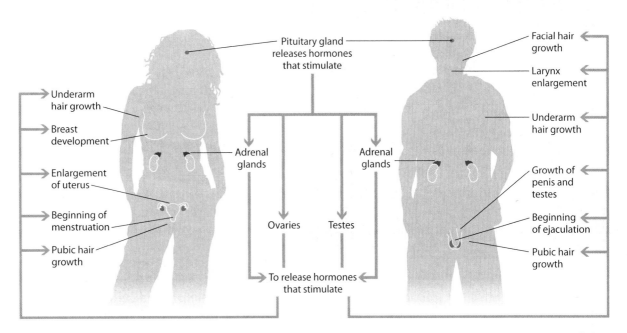

Pituitary gland
releases hormones
that stimulate

Facial hair
growth

Larynx
enlargement

Underarm
hair growth

Breast
development

Enlargement
of uterus

Beginning of
menstruation

Pubic hair
growth

Adrenal
glands

Adrenal
glands

Underarm
hair growth

Growth of
penis and
testes

Beginning
of ejaculation

Pubic hair
growth

Ovaries   Testes

To release hormones
that stimulate

FIGURE **5.20**
**PHYSICAL
DEVELOPMENT
OF MALES AND
FEMALES DUR-
ING PUBERTY.**

or "wet dream." Once a male has ejaculated, technically he can father a child. This presents a primary problem of adolescence: In boys and girls, the body is ready for parenthood far earlier than the mind is.

COGNITIVE AND BRAIN DEVELOPMENT

Meanwhile, changes continue to unfold in the brain. During adolescence, children gain the ability to reason about abstract concepts and problems. This is the stage of cognitive development that Piaget termed the **formal operational stage.** In this stage, teens may show the ability to engage in scientific reasoning and hypothesis testing. Adolescents and even adults do not all develop this reasoning ability to the same degree (Klahr, 2000; Kuhn & Pearsall, 2000; Kuhn, Amsel, & O'Loughlin, 1988). The extent to which people develop scientific reasoning skills is related to their ability to think and solve problems systematically, rather than relying on the trial-and-error method that children use. It is also related to the ability to distinguish one's thoughts about how the world works from the evidence for how it really works (Kuhn & Pearsall, 2000). For example, believing that the position of the planets affects human personality does not make it so. Good scientific thinkers realize the world may or may not operate the way they think it does, so they devise step-by-step ways of testing their ideas. This requires the ability to think about alternatives and to question their own thinking.

With adolescence and formal operations, young people begin to ask abstract philosophical, religious, and political questions and form their own beliefs. Moreover, with abstract thinking comes the ability to consider alternatives—not just how things are, but how they could be. For instance, science fiction and Internet gaming appeal to adolescents because they involve abstract, imaginative, and alternative forms of thinking.

Neuroscientists have only recently uncovered how changes in thinking correspond with changes in the adolescent brain. Indeed, many of the cognitive developments of adolescence, such as abstract reasoning and logical thinking, may be a consequence of brain development. In particular, the frontal lobes are the last areas of the brain to fully develop, and they continue to mature until

**formal
operational
stage**
Piaget's fourth
stage of cogni-
tive develop-
ment, consisting
of the ability to
reason abstractly,
scientifically, and
philosophically.

Many teens enjoy applying their developing abstract reasoning skills to computer games.

late adolescence or early adulthood (Fuster, 2002; Miller & Cummings, 1999; Sowell et al., 2001). The frontal lobes are involved in planning, attention, working memory, abstract thought, and impulse control. It is not so much that the frontal lobes are growing in size—they are growing in complexity. Specifically, the adolescent brain develops more myelin around the axons as well as more neural connections (Fields, 2008; Sabbagh, 2006; Sakai, 2005; Shaw et al., 2006). And as we saw in Figure 5.10, myelination proceeds from the back of the brain to the front, where the frontal lobes are, during the period from childhood to adolescence (Fields, 2008). The onset of formal operational and scientific thinking occurs after the frontal lobes have developed more fully (Kwon & Lawson, 2000). There appears to be a direct relationship, then, between cognitive development and brain development.

Because the teen brain is still developing, teens use more frontal lobe activity during complex and demanding tasks than do adults. Adults distribute the workload more evenly throughout their brain and do not overload the frontal lobes (Sabbagh, 2006). Moreover, although teenagers have the same basic reasoning skills as adults, more sophisticated cognitive skills, such as the ability to plan ahead or evaluate the possible consequences of a decision, do not develop until late adolescence or young adulthood (Steinberg, 2008). The tendency of teenagers to engage in impulsive and risky behavior, such as driving at excessive speeds and fighting, can be partly explained by these findings.

connection

Can Internet gaming and alternative realities and personalities (avatars) be an addiction for some people?

See Chapter 15, p. 580.

What is the association between brain development and intelligence? Researchers have known for decades that overall brain size is not correlated with overall intelligence. As it turns out, however, intelligence does seem to be associated with how the brain develops and, in particular, how the cortex develops. Philip Shaw and colleagues (2006) compared brain growth in very intelligent children and children of average intelligence. They periodically scanned the brains of more than 300 participants during childhood and adolescence and discovered something surprising. At age 7 the highly intelligent children had thinner frontal cortexes, but by mid-adolescence their cortexes had become thicker than those of the children of average intelligence. Moreover, by age 19 the thickness of the cortex in the two groups was the same (see Figure 5.21). These results suggest that the brains of highly intelligent people are more elastic and trace a different developmental path.

SOCIAL DEVELOPMENT IN ADOLESCENCE

An important part of social development in adolescence is the search for identity. Just as we try on clothes to see what fits, adolescents try on identities to see what fits. Although identity development occurs across the life span, teens are more self-conscious about the changes and experience them more intensely than do children or adults (Steinberg, 2008).

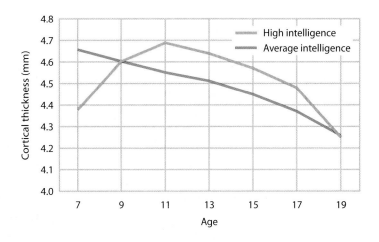

FIGURE **5.21**

THE DEVELOPING BRAIN: CORTICAL THICKNESS AND INTELLIGENCE. The cortex is thinner in highly intelligent 7-year-olds than in 7-year-olds of average intelligence. At age 9, cortical thickness is the same in the two groups, but thereafter the cortex is thicker in the highly intelligent group. By age 19, the two groups are once again equal in cortical thickness. The changes are quite small (less than half a millimeter), but in the context of brain development, they are significant. (*Source:* Shaw, 2006.)

Puberty brings profound changes not only in the body but also in relationships. Family becomes less central, and peer and sexual relationships become paramount. Having close, intimate friends during adolescence is associated with many positive social and emotional outcomes, such as self-confidence, better relationships with parents and authority figures, and better performance in school (Bagwell, Newcomb, & Bukowski, 1998). In contrast, feeling isolated and lacking close peer relationships during adolescence is associated with poorer performance in school, more conflict with parents and authority figures, and lower self-esteem. Moreover, the positive outcomes of peer acceptance and close relationships during adolescence predict better overall adjustment and feelings of self-worth in adulthood (Bagwell et al., 1998).

Compared to childhood, the most obvious change in adolescent social development is the emergence of sexual interest and sexual relationships. Teens not only become interested in sexual relationships, but sexual thoughts and feelings also occupy much of their attention and time. The average age for first sexual intercourse for men and women is around 17 years old, although there is quite a bit of variability in when people start having sex. A sexually mature body combined with a brain that is not fully developed can result in bad judgment, as the high rates of unplanned pregnancy and sexually transmitted diseases in teens attest (CDC, 2005).

Sexuality contributes to identity formation as well. Roughly 88 percent of teenagers describe themselves as predominantly heterosexual (interested only in the opposite sex), while about 1–2 percent see themselves as predominantly

Experimenting with different styles of dress appeals to adolescents in the midst of identity formation.

homosexual (interested only in the same sex) or bisexual (interested in both sexes). About 10 percent of teens say they are confused about their sexual orientation (Remafedi et al., 1992). Unfortunately, gay, lesbian, and bisexual youths are 2 to 3 times more likely to commit suicide than are heterosexual youths (Remafedi, 1999).

As adolescence draws to a close and people enter their 20s, much about development stabilizes. People move from high school to college and make the transition to increased independence. The phase from 18 to 25 has been called *emerging adulthood* (Arnett, 2006). This period is primarily a time of transition when individuals take full control of their own life. Young adults deal increasingly with financial responsibility, move away from home, become more self-focused, and contemplate the possibilities for their future (Arnett, 2006).

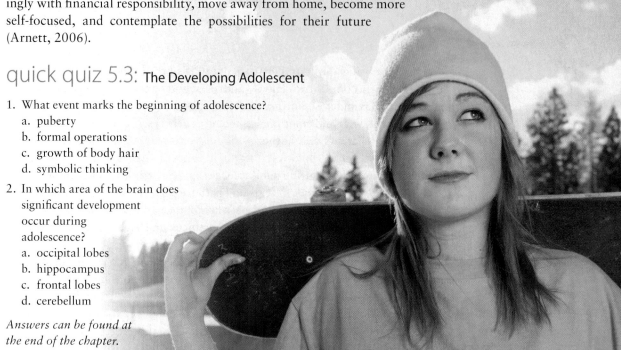

quick quiz 5.3: The Developing Adolescent

1. What event marks the beginning of adolescence?
   a. puberty
   b. formal operations
   c. growth of body hair
   d. symbolic thinking

2. In which area of the brain does significant development occur during adolescence?
   a. occipital lobes
   b. hippocampus
   c. frontal lobes
   d. cerebellum

Answers can be found at the end of the chapter.

The Developing Adult

As people enter their 30s, development has largely stabilized. This does not mean that adult mind, brain, and behavior are stagnant. Far from it—the brain and body continue to change throughout the life span. Such changes both emerge from and shape how we interact with the world.

SENSATION AND PERCEPTION IN ADULTHOOD

connection

Mosquito ringtones for cell phones were developed by young people to exploit older adults' decreasing ability to hear high-pitched sounds.
See Chapter 4, p. 152.

Many people experience some loss of vision or hearing or both by middle adulthood. Most people need reading glasses sometime in their 40s, as the lens of the eye loses flexibility (Goldstein, 2007). For those who already wear glasses or contacts as adults, bifocals may become necessary as they enter their late 40s.

Hearing declines, too, with age. A recent large-scale study found that as many as 50 percent of older adults (mean age of 67) experience some degree of hearing loss (Chia et al., 2007). Some hearing loss is preventable. Exposure to loud sounds throughout life, such as rock concerts, heavy machinery, and overuse of headphones accounts for many hearing problems in people over 40 (Wallhagen et al., 1997). Age-related hearing deficits can stem from problems with the ears, the auditory nerve, or various brain areas and are more common in men than women (Pearson et al., 1995; Tremblay & Ross, 2007). High-pitched, high-frequency sounds become harder to hear as people get older. Indeed, some people report that as they age, they can hear conversations but they cannot always understand them. This effect appears to result from age-related slowdown of the processing of auditory information in the brain (Tremblay & Ross, 2007).

Some people also experience a loss of sensitivity to taste and smell, though these changes vary considerably among individuals. Taste buds lose sensitivity, although the ones affected—sweet, salty, bitter, or savory—vary from person to person. These changes do not seem to adversely affect appetite, however (Kremer et al., 2007).

Losing one's sense of smell can dampen the sense of taste to the point that food no longer has much appeal, somewhat like what happens when you have a bad cold. It can also be a concern for elderly people who live alone and might be unable to detect gas leaks or smell smoke in case of fire. As many as half of the people over 65 demonstrate significant loss of smell (Doty et al, 1984).

COGNITIVE AND BRAIN DEVELOPMENT IN ADULTHOOD

The older brain does not change as rapidly as the younger brain (Baltes et al., 2006). Yet it remains dynamic. New experiences and mastery of new skills continue to give rise to neural branching and growth throughout life (Kemperman, 2006). Learning new skills, such as a new language, a new game, or a new computer activity can lead to new neural growth (Cotman et al., 2007). Taking up a musical instrument can also stimulate brain growth (Pascual-Leone, 2001; see "Psychology in the Real World").

nature & nurture
Mastering new skills stimulates neural growth and the formation of new synapses throughout the life span.

Physical activity has cognitive benefits as well. Research has shown that older people who were previously inactive improved significantly in a wide range of cognitive tasks after aerobic exercise training compared to a control group that did not exercise (Colcombe & Kramer, 2003). Similarly, engaging in meaningful, challenging work can make a huge difference for thinking and the brain.

One cognitive benefit of aging is *wisdom*, the ability to know what matters, to live well, to show good judgment (Baltes & Smith, 2008). Wisdom comes with learning from the situations in which we find ourselves. The more we experience, the more we learn about what is important and how to manage our time (Carstensen, 2006). Wisdom also comes from learning not to take things too seriously.

COGNITIVE DECLINE IN THE AGING BRAIN

People often complain about memory problems as they get older. Yet cognitive decline in adulthood is a complex topic. Some abilities, such as expertise in a given area, take time to develop and reach a peak in middle adulthood (Kim & Hasher, 2005). Verbal memory actually peaks after 50 (Schaie, 1996). Declines do occur in other kinds of memory, however, especially the kind involved in processing information and maintaining information while making decisions. The rate of decline does not become noticeable until people reach their 60s or

For these aging Japanese ball-players, an active lifestyle has cognitive and social benefits as well as physical benefits.

70s. Even then, healthy older people in their 70s who receive training in memory skills show improvements not only in cognitive performance, but also in their ability to manage tasks of daily living, such as shopping, food preparation, managing finances, and household tasks (Willis et al., 2006).

We used to think that the brain lost cells as part of normal aging, but this appears to be an overstatement. Nevertheless, normal changes in the brain occur with age. Just as body mass gradually decreases with age, so does brain mass (Enzinger et al., 2005). Age is a risk factor for dementia, but in and of itself, aging does not cause dementia (Fratiglioni, Winblad, & von Strauss, 2007). **Dementia** is a loss of cognitive functions and includes memory problems and difficulty reasoning, solving problems, making decisions, and using language.

Several neurological conditions, including stroke and **Alzheimer's disease,** can lead to dementia in the elderly. It may be impossible to determine which condition is responsible because they share symptoms. A *stroke* occurs when a blood vessel that serves the brain is blocked. As a result, the brain tissue served by that vessel does not receive the oxygen and nutrients it needs, and so the tissue dies. Multiple strokes are a common source of dementia in the elderly (Schneider, Arvanitakis, Bang, & Bennett, 2007). Elderly people may suffer multiple small strokes that may produce minor symptoms, such as dizziness or headaches. Yet these strokes leave many little places in the brain where tissue has died. This dead tissue makes for many little (or sometimes big) cognitive impairments, such as memory loss and confusion. Often the onset of dementia caused by stroke is sudden, but sometimes it can be more gradual, masquerading as Alzheimer's disease.

Alzheimer's disease is a degenerative disease marked by progressive cognitive decline and characterized by a collection of symptoms, including confusion, memory loss, mood swings, and eventual loss of physical function (Figure 5.22). Alzheimer's accounts for 60–70 percent of the cases of dementia among the elderly (Fratiglioni et al., 2007). Usually Alzheimer's affects older people, but not always. *Early-onset Alzheimer's* affects people younger than 65 (Alzheimer's Association, 2008).

Sadly, Alzheimer's can be diagnosed definitively only by examining brain tissue after death, although recent progress in brain imaging may help identify early risk factors (Wermke et al., 2008). For the most part, physicians diagnose

dementia
a loss of mental function, in which many cognitive processes are impaired, such as the ability to remember, reason, solve problems, make decisions, and use language.

Alzheimer's disease
a degenerative disease marked by progressive cognitive decline and characterized by a collection of symptoms, including confusion, memory loss, mood swings, and eventual loss of physical function.

Alzheimer's by noting a collection of symptoms that they cannot attribute to anything else.

The defining anatomical feature of Alzheimer's is the presence of patches of dead tissue in the brain, especially in the hippocampus and areas of the cortex (Kalat, 2007). As a result, the affected person experiences lapses in memory, confusion, and other cognitive impairments. In addition, low levels of the neurotransmitter acetylcholine inhibit memory formation in people with Alzheimer's (Akaike, 2006). Alzheimer's is progressive, which means that it worsens over time and eventually is fatal. Currently there is no cure for Alzheimer's, although some drugs do seem to slow the progression of the disease (Hansen et al., 2007).

Some evidence suggests that neurogenesis, the growth of new neurons, in the adult brain might offset or even prevent the kind of neural degeneration seen in Alzheimer's and other age-related brain disorders. One of the benefits of aerobic exercise—brisk physical activity that causes the heart and lungs to work harder to meet the body's increased need for oxygen—is that it appears to protect against a decline in higher mental processing and may actually make the brain grow (Colcombe et al., 2006; Colcombe & Kramer, 2003). Environmental enrichment is known to improve memory and learning, improve brain plasticity, and interact with genetic factors to reduce progressive degenerative diseases of the nervous system in rodents (Nithianantharajah & Hannan, 2006). It can also stimulate neurogenesis in humans (Kemperman, 2006). Can an enriched environment help to produce neurogenesis in people who suffer from degenerative brain disorders such as Alzheimer's? Neurogenesis in the adult brain might not repair damage due to a degenerative disease, but it might provide extra resources or "reserves" for cognitive function that might help counteract the cognitive effects of neural degeneration (Steiner, Wolf, & Kemperman, 2006).

nature & nurture

Aerobic exercise appears to protect against a decline in higher mental processing among aging adults and may actually make the brain grow.

SOCIOEMOTIONAL DEVELOPMENT IN ADULTS

In spite of the dramatic changes that can occur in cognitive functioning, there are fewer age-related changes in emotional functioning. In fact, there may be emotional gains with age, as people become motivated to develop more rewarding, meaningful relationships (Carstensen, Fung, & Charles, 2003). This motivation stems from awareness as people age that they have a limited amount of time left. According to socioemotional selectivity theory, as people age and become more aware of their limited time, they become more selective about where they expend their resources in personal and emotional relationships (Carstensen et al., 2003). They waste less time in superficial

- General confusion, disorientation to date, time or place
- Apathy, irritability, depression, anxiety
- Problems with language, math, abstract thinking, and judgment
- Personality changes with strange quirks or inappropriate behaviors
- Wandering, hiding objects, problems with eating and sleeping
- Late in the disease, paranoia and delusions possible
- Toward the end, total loss of self and inability to control bodily functions

FIGURE **5.22**

TYPICAL SIGNS AND SYMPTOMS OF ALZHEIMER'S DISEASE.
According to the Alzheimer's Association (2008), as many as 5.2 million people in the United States may be living with this fatal disease, most of them over 65.

Aerobic exercise can prevent mental decline in old age and may actually result in brain growth.

acquaintances and invest more in sustaining meaningful, fulfilling connections in their lives.

DEATH AND DYING

"What is death?" is a question without a simple answer. Physicians used to pronounce people dead when vital signs, such as heart rate and breathing, ceased. Today modern medical technology can keep a body alive when the brain is no longer functioning. *Brain death* occurs when no measurable electrical activity in the brain is evident, but life support equipment may maintain vital signs long after the brain has stopped functioning.

Family relationships become a central focus for the elderly as they approach the end of life.

In psychological terms, death is a complex event that marks the end of life. Western culture does not place much emphasis on talking about death. Some Eastern cultures take a different view. In Buddhism, for example, acceptance of death and of the fact that life is not a permanent condition is a touchstone against which life is evaluated. Knowing one has limited time on earth helps give meaning to daily life (Rinpoche, 1992). Some people with terminal illnesses report that knowing their time is limited helps them find meaning in their lives. Accessing such meaning seems to lessen their despair about dying (McClain, Rosenfeld, & Breibart, 2003).

People may move through a series of stages in dealing with the end of life. Based on her extensive talks with dying patients, Elizabeth Kübler-Ross (1969) detailed the stages people may move through after learning they are going to die. Initially they experience *denial,* a sense of utter disbelief that they are going to die. Next comes *anger,* in which the dying person feels the injustice of it all. At this stage, the dying person asks, "Why me?" In the *bargaining* stage, people start negotiating with God or whatever forces of nature they feel may control their fate to try to buy more time. Once the certainty of death sets in, *depression* may ensue. Finally, there is *acceptance* of death and the end of life. During this final stage people often come to terms with their own passing.

Increasingly, people in the United States and other Western countries prepare for death by resolving differences with family and friends and accomplishing their life goals. Some people prepare special rituals or events to mark the final stage of life or to say good-bye to friends and family (Bourgeois & Johnson, 2004). We have only so much control over when we die, but by preparing psychologically for it, not just for oneself but also for the loved ones who will be left behind, we can bring comfort to many people. Palliative care and hospice are growing branches of medicine that are devoted to end-of-life care (Morrison et al., 2005). The main goal of palliative care is to ease suffering and to make the dying person as comfortable as possible rather than to cure or treat the patient. Similarly, hospice focuses on the overall needs of the patient and family members, such as physical comfort, emotional care, and a dignified death.

quick quiz 5.4: The Developing Adult

1. Which of the following enhances neural growth in adulthood?
   a. gingko biloba
   b. diet
   c. caffeine
   d. physical exercise

2. What is necessary for a definitive diagnosis of Alzheimer's disease?
   a. an fMRI
   b. an autopsy
   c. EEG
   d. psychological testing

3. As people age and become more aware of their limited time on earth, they become more _____ about how they expend their resources in personal and emotional relationships.
   a. selective
   b. anxious
   c. regretful
   d. concerned

Answers can be found at the end of the chapter.

making connections
in development

Personality Across the Life Span

One thing that stays with us our entire lives is our personality. It may change a bit, but for the most part personality tends to be a fairly stable part of who we are. As such, it is an ideal topic for connecting the key ideas in this chapter.

Some of us are naturally shy, and others are outgoing; some of us are anxious and nervous; others are calm, cool, and relaxed. Some of us are warm and friendly; others are hostile, cold, and aloof. The biologically based tendency to behave in specific ways from the beginning of life is what psychologists call **temperament** (Gonzalez, Hynd, & Martin, 1994; Rothbart, Ahadi, & Evans, 2000). As we discuss in more detail in Chapter 14, *personality* is the consistently unique way in which an individual behaves over time and in many different situations. Temperament lays the foundation for personality in childhood, adolescence, and adulthood (A. Buss & Plomin, 1984; Rothbart et al., 2000).

temperament
the biologically based tendency to behave in particular ways from very early in life.

Many aspects of temperament and personality, including sociability and a cheerful disposition, are relatively stable throughout life.

Temperament and Personality in the Fetus and Infant

Evidence tells us that temperament and personality differences are present before birth. For instance, in one study, Janet DiPietro and her colleagues (1996) showed that fetal activity and fetal heart rate predict temperament differences over the first year of life. In particular, a high heart rate in a 36-week-old fetus foreshadowed less predictable eating and sleeping habits at 3 and 6 months after birth and would be less emotional at 6 months after birth.

What happens to the mother while pregnant may affect not only the temperament of the fetus, but the temperament and personality of the infant as well. Research shows that mothers who are depressed or anxious or who experience a lot of stress during pregnancy are more likely to have infants who are temperamentally "difficult" and "fussy" (Austin et al., 2004; Gutteling, et al., 2005). Inborn temperament and sensitivity to stress, then, are set not just by our genes but also by our mother's experiences.

nature & nurture

Infants born to mothers who experienced an unusual amount of stress during pregnancy tend to be more sensitive to stress throughout childhood and beyond.

After birth, some infants soon settle into a predictable routine. Others do not. Some are generally happy, and others aren't. And some infants have lower thresholds for stimulation than others. Based on their classic study of such differences, Alexander Thomas and Stella Chess (1977) developed a model of temperament with three general categories that is still widely accepted: the easy child, the difficult child, and the slow-to-warm-up child. The *easy child* is predictable in daily functions, is happy most of the time, and is adaptable. About 40% of children fell into this category. The *difficult child* is unpredictable in daily functions, is unhappy most of the time, and is slow to adapt to new situations. About 10% fell into this category. The *slow-to-warm-up child* is mildly intense in his or her reactions to new situations and mildly irregular in the daily patterns of eating, sleeping, and eliminating. Although his or her first response to new situations might be negative, after repeated exposures, he or she develops an approaching style. About 15% of the children fell into this category. About 35% of the children were not classified by these three dimensions.

Childhood Temperament and Personality

What does early childhood temperament predict about adult personality and behavior? One longitudinal study—a research design that tracks the same people over a period of time—periodically evaluated 1,000 New Zealand children over 18 years to try to answer this question. The children were assessed on many temperamental, cognitive, medical, and motor dimensions at age 3 and then again about every 2 to 2.5 years until they were 21 years old (Caspi, 2000). Ratings by parents at age 3 revealed three basic types of temperament: well-adjusted, undercontrolled, and inhibited.

Eighteen years after the initial assessment, the individuals whose parents had classified them as "undercontrolled" (impulsive and prone to temper tantrums) at age 3 were impulsive and likely to engage in thrill-seeking behaviors. Compared to well-adjusted kids, this group was also much more likely to be aggressive and hostile, to have more relationship conflict, and to abuse alcohol.

At age 21, "inhibited" children were less likely to have social support and were more likely to avoid risk and harm, to be nonassertive and overcontrolled, and to suffer from prolonged depression. They also were somewhat more likely than well-adjusted individuals to attempt suicide or have problems with alcohol. Further, they were about as likely as well-adjusted types (and less likely than the "undercontrolled" individuals) to have committed a criminal offense. Finally, as adults, "inhibited" children reported the least amount of social, emotional, and financial support from others. In sum, our temperament age 3 seems to have power over our personalities into adulthood (Kagan, 2003).

Adolescent and Adult Personality Development

Erik Erikson

Although many aspects of temperament and personality are stable over time, our personalities also grow and change as we age. Erik Erikson proposed a model of personality development with eight stages, each defined by an identity crisis or conflict (Erikson, 1968; see Figure 5.23). According to Erikson, an identity crisis is an opportunity for adaptive or

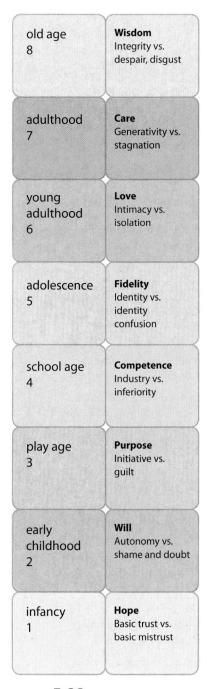

FIGURE **5.23**

ERIKSON'S EIGHT STAGES OF PERSONALITY DEVELOPMENT. Each stage has a core strength (shown in bold type) and a crisis to resolve. (*Source:* Feist & Feist, 2009.)

maladaptive adjustment. Each stage consists of a conflict from which a person may develop a strength.

Erikson's theory offers a rich account of adolescent and adult personality development. With the onset of puberty and adolescence, children begin to focus on the questions of who they are, what kinds of careers they want to pursue, what they believe, and what kinds of relationships they want to have. Erikson saw *identity versus identity confusion* as the conflict during adolescence. Testing, experimenting, and trying on identities is the norm during adolescence. Experimenting allows a person to find out which identities work and which ones don't. Dating and sexual orientation, as well as testing of different belief systems, allow adolescents to resolve the identity conflict of this stage. The basic strength that develops in adolescence is *fidelity,* a sense of faith and commitment to a belief system.

Having a solid sense of self and identity is important for early adulthood— the period during one's 20s. In this stage, the conflict is between *intimacy and isolation.* Erikson defined intimacy as the ability to fuse one's identity with another's without the fear of losing it (Erikson, 1963). If an individual does not form a relatively secure sense of identity as an adolescent, it may not be possible to form intimate relationships during young adulthood. For example, people may develop very close love relationships when they are adolescents, before they have completely figured out who they are. The relationship then shapes identity, which means individuals' identities may get lost in the relationship. Then, years later, the relationship may end—because as each person develops his or her own identity, differences surface. The core strength to emerge in young adulthood is *love,* which involves commitment, passion, cooperation, competition, and friendship (Erikson, 1982).

In adulthood, from about 30 to 60 or 65 years of age, the conflict is what Erikson called *generativity versus stagnation.* He defined **generativity** as the creation of new ideas, products, or people (Erikson, 1982). Parenting, starting a business, and creating a work of art are different ways of being generative. Stagnation occurs when the adult becomes more self-focused than oriented toward others and does not contribute in a productive way to society or family. The core strength of adulthood is *care,* being committed to and caring for the people, ideas, and products one has generated.

generativity
a term Erik Erikson used to describe the process in adulthood of creating new ideas, products, or people.

The final stage of personality development is old age, starting around age 60 or 65. The conflict of old age is between *integrity and despair.* Integrity is the feeling of being whole and integrated. It is the sense that all one's life decisions are coming together. The core strength of old age is *wisdom.* Erikson defined wisdom as being informed and knowledgeable about life and yet having a detachment from it that comes only with old age, when one is no longer in the throes of establishing a family and career.

In sum, personality develops and changes over our lifetime, and yet who we are tends to be quite stable. Infant temperament, for instance, predicts the kind of personality we develop later in life. In a very real sense, our personalities stay with us our entire lives.

quick quiz 5.5: Making Connections in Development

1. The biologically based tendency to behave in a specific way is what psychologists call
   a. temperament
   b. personality
   c. response bias
   d. aptitude

2. According to Erikson, the identity crisis during middle adulthood is between
   a. identity and identity confusion
   b. integrity and despair
   c. intimacy and isolation
   d. generativity and stagnation

Answers can be found at the end of the chapter.

chapter **review**

- Human development is the study of change and continuity in the individual across the life span.

THE DEVELOPING FETUS

- Life before birth is divided into the germinal, embryonic, and fetal stages.

- Prenatal programming refers to a change in developmental trajectory for certain health outcomes that are established in the womb.

- Two common sources of prenatal programming are maternal nutrition and substances known as teratogens, which can harm the developing infant. Mild to profound changes in the brain and body of the fetus can result from diet and chemicals the pregnant mother takes into her body.

THE DEVELOPING INFANT AND CHILD

- The five major senses develop at different rates. Hearing is almost fully developed at birth, but vision is not.

- Learning and experience strengthen certain synaptic connections. Synaptic connections that are not reinforced and strengthened by experience degrade and ultimately die off. This process is known as pruning.

- Piaget proposed four major stages of cognitive development. The first stage of cognitive development is the sensorimotor stage. The major accomplishment during the sensorimotor stage is object permanence. In the second stage, the preoperational stage, young children begin to think symbolically. The third stage is the concrete operational stage, when school-age children master conservation, the knowledge that the total amount of something stays the same even when its shape or arrangement changes. The fourth stage is the formal operational stage. In this stage, adolescents begin to think logically and abstractly.

- The ability to know and understand what other people are thinking, wanting, or feeling is called theory of mind. Typically this skill develops around age 4, when children recognize that other people's beliefs may be different from their own.

- In human development, attachment refers to the strong emotional connection that develops early in life to keep infants close to their caregivers. Comfort and touch in infancy are crucial to healthy development.

THE DEVELOPING ADOLESCENT

- For girls, a major change during adolescence is the first menstrual period, known as menarche. For boys, the equivalent change is spermarche, the first ejaculation.

- Brain development continues in adolescence, with the frontal lobes being the last part of the brain to mature.

- Social relationships become paramount in adolescence. Girls tend to have one or two deep friendships and more intimate relationships than boys. Sexual maturity brings sexual behavior, with most adolescents being sexually active by age 18.

THE DEVELOPING ADULT

- Most sensory systems (for example, vision and hearing) gradually decline after middle age.

- Cognitive decline is complex and not inevitable in adults. Most decline begins in the late 60s or early 70s.

- Age is a risk factor for dementia, a loss of mental function in which many cognitive processes, such as the ability to remember, reason, solve problems, make decisions, and use language, are impaired.

- Alzheimer's disease is a degenerative condition marked by progressive cognitive decline, confusion, memory loss, mood swings, and eventual loss of physical function.

- Healthy aging is possible through physical exercise and cognitive training.

- One cognitive benefit of aging is wisdom, or the ability to know what matters, to live well, and to show good judgment.

MAKING CONNECTIONS IN DEVELOPMENT

- Personality is the consistently unique way that individuals behave over time and in many different situations.

- Thomas and Chess identified three types of temperament in children: the easy child, the difficult child, and the slow-to-warm-up child.

- Erikson described eight stages of personality development. Each stage has a crisis and a core strength. For example, the crisis of adolescence is between identity and identity confusion and is a time when people explore their possible beliefs, partners, and occupational goals. Fidelity is the core strength that may emerge from the formation of a healthy identity in adolescence.

key **terms**

adolescence, p. 200

Alzheimer's disease, p. 206

animistic thinking, p. 187

anxious-avoidant, p. 194

anxious-resistant attachment, p. 194

attachment, p. 192

concrete operational stage, p. 188

conservation, p. 187

conventional level, p. 191

critical period, p. 180

dementia, p. 206

egocentrism, p. 187

embryo, p. 172

embryonic stage, p. 172

emotional competence, p. 198

fetal alcohol spectrum disorder (FASD), p. 177

fetal stage, p. 173

formal operational stage, p. 189

generativity, p. 211

germinal stage, p. 171

human development, p. 171

imprinting, p. 192

menarche, p. 200

neural migration, p. 173

object permanence, p. 185

peers, p. 199

personality, p. 209

preconventional level, p. 191

prenatal programming, p. 176

preoperational stage, p. 187

postconventional level, p. 191

pruning, p. 182

puberty, p. 200

secure attachment, p. 193

sensorimotor stage, p. 185

separation anxiety, p. 193

social referencing, p. 197

spermarche, p. 200

temperament, p. 209

teratogens, p. 176

theory of mind, p. 189

zygote, p. 171

quick quiz **answers**

Quick Quiz 5.1: 1. c 2. b 3. a   Quick Quiz 5.2: 1. d 2. c 3. b 4. d

Quick Quiz 5.3: 1. a 2. c   Quick Quiz 5.4: 1. d 2. b 3. a

Quick Quiz 5.5: 1. a 2. d

consciousness

On Super Bowl Sunday, January 30, 1994, our lives changed forever. David, the brother of one of your authors, was hit by a car while riding his bicycle home from work. He first crashed onto the windshield and then landed on the street. He was not wearing his helmet. Fortunately for David, within just a few minutes emergency workers whisked him off to one of the top trauma centers in the country. David had suffered a severe traumatic brain injury.

When we arrived at the hospital, David was in a coma. We asked the trauma nurse to explain just how comatose he was. She explained that they use a special scale to rate the degree of coma and nonresponsiveness. Scores range from 3 to 15. "Where was David on this scale?" we asked. She said David was a "4." We asked what a "4" meant in practical ▶

▶ terms. The nurse picked up the small bottle of saline solution (basically saltwater) from David's bedside table. "You see this?" she asked. "This is a 3." David was barely alive.

Two weeks after the accident, David opened his eyes. Five months later, he emerged from his vegetative state and began responding to input from the outside world. Witnessing David's near miraculous recovery over the next year not only pushed the limits of our concepts of life and death but also illustrated just how delicate states of consciousness can be.

For a long time, the topic of consciousness—something that occupies the center of our psychological experience—was a neglected area in psychology. Thanks to the cognitive revolution, evolutionary psychology, and neuroscience—which returned mental phenomena to the forefront of psychological research—the scientific study of consciousness is back. In this chapter, we review what the science of psychology has to say about consciousness. In particular, we'll explore what consciousness is, examine how we know the contents of our

chapter
outline

own minds, look at how psychologists have studied the conscious mind, and consider how meditation, sleep, drugs, and mental exercises can modify consciousness. Finally, we take a look at hypnosis (What is it and how is it different from other levels of consciousness?) before returning to the consciousness-altering effects of brain injury. ∎

What Is Consciousness?

Consider what happens if you walk out of a dark house onto a sunny porch. Many signals assault your brain: The bright light from the sky hits your eyes, which send information to visual processing areas in the thalamus and occipital cortex. The heat from the sun bathes your skin, and temperature sensors there send impulses to the thalamus, somatosensory cortex, and brain stem areas that regulate body temperature. The aroma from the orange blossoms in the yard wafts through your nostrils, quickly moving to the olfactory bulb and emotional centers in the brain, perhaps triggering pleasant memories of the orange trees that grew in front of your grandmother's house. The brain processes these signals instantaneously and simultaneously, and they come together into the experience of right now being on the front porch in the sun. They come together in your consciousness.

In spite of its central role in our experience, consciousness is not easily defined. Most simply, **consciousness** is an awareness of one's surroundings and of what is in one's mind at a given moment. It is our experience of a moment as we move through it. But consciousness also involves the capacity to take in and

consciousness
an awareness of one's surroundings and of what's in one's mind at a given moment; includes aspects of being awake and aware.

217

process information briefly before sending it to specialized areas for further use or storage. Consciousness can change very quickly and dramatically whenever new information arrives. Imagine the change in your experience if you step off the porch into a pile of dog droppings.

Consciousness acts as a stage for the "main event" of your brain at a given moment in time. Consider again the example of standing on the front porch with your brain receiving and processing sensory information from all around you. When the connections among the various processing areas of the brain areas become strong enough, a conscious experience occurs (Engel, Debener, & Kranczioch, 2006). The various sensory elements are brought together in what has been called the *global workspace* of consciousness (Baars, 1997; Baars & Franklin, 2003).

Many studies have examined the processes of consciousness, including sleeping, dreaming, wakefulness, perception, sensation, responsiveness, and awareness. The subjective aspect of being a conscious human—*what it feels like* to be in love, see red, or have an idea—has eluded science. The focus of this chapter is psychology's contribution to understanding conscious processes, and to the development of methods that may bring the subjective aspect of consciousness into clearer view.

connection

How much information can we hold in consciousness before it is processed further, stored, or forgotten?

See Chapter 7, p. 260.

Two Dimensions of Consciousness: Wakefulness and Awareness

We defined consciousness as the extent to which we are aware of our surroundings and of what's in our mind at a given moment. But consciousness really has two aspects to it: the degree to which we are awake and the degree to which we are aware. **Wakefulness** refers to the degree of alertness, whether a person is awake or asleep. **Awareness** refers to the monitoring of information from the environment and from one's own thoughts (Brown & Ryan, 2003). It might make sense that

wakefulness
degree of alertness reflecting whether a person is awake or asleep.

awareness
monitoring of information from the environment and from one's own thoughts.

FIGURE **6.1**

TWO DIMENSIONS OF CONSCIOUSNESS.
Consciousness exists on a continuum from low to high wakefulness and from little to high awareness. Each state of consciousness exists somewhere in this two-dimensional space. Coma is one extreme of consciousness and is characterized by very low wakefulness and awareness. Conscious mindful wakefulness is the other extreme, characterized by high wakefulness and awareness. The vegetative state, in contrast, is wakeful but not very aware. (*Source:* Laureys, 2007.)

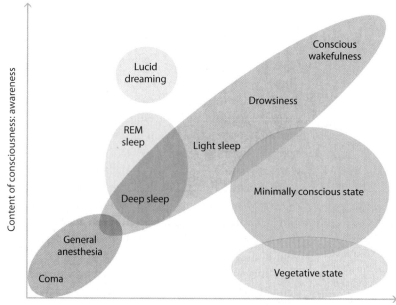

wakefulness and awareness go hand in hand, but in fact, they do not always work together. A person can be awake but not very aware, as is true in vegetative states or extreme drunkenness.

Variations in consciousness can be explained in terms of degrees of wakefulness and awareness (Laureys, 2007). Figure 6.1 shows that each component ranges from low to high and that all states of consciousness exist somewhere in this two-dimensional space. Coma, for example, is one extreme of consciousness and is characterized by very low wakefulness and awareness. The other extreme of consciousness is characterized by high wakefulness and awareness. In contrast, the vegetative state is wakeful but not very aware. Let's look at each level of consciousness in a little more detail, starting with minimal consciousness and moving to moderate and full consciousness.

MINIMAL CONSCIOUSNESS

If you have ever fainted, you have experienced a loss of consciousness. **Coma,** in which the eyes are closed and the person is unresponsive, is a much more severe and enduring loss of consciousness than fainting. People cannot be roused from a coma as they can be roused from sleep. Coma generally results from illness or brain injury that damages areas of the brain that control wakefulness—in particular, the reticular formation (Bernat, 2006). In fact, comatose people whose brains show normal sleep patterns are more likely to regain consciousness than are those who do not exhibit these patterns (Fischer, 2004).

coma
a state of consciousness in which the eyes are closed and the person is unresponsive and unarousable.

The medical community distinguishes different degrees of coma with the Glasgow Coma Scale (Teasdale & Jennett, 1976), the instrument used to assess David's level of consciousness (see Figure 6.2). The scale classifies people as suffering from severe, moderate, or mild brain injury based on their degree of eye opening, verbal responsiveness, and motor responsiveness. The scores are used to predict an individual's chances of recovery (Jain, Dharap, & Gore, 2008). Recall that David's initial score (from a total of his score on the three subscales) was a 4. His chances of any kind of meaningful recovery were slim.

Eye opening	
spontaneous	4
to speech	3
to pain	2
no reponse	1
Verbal response	
alert and oriented	5
disoriented conversation	4
speaking but nonsensical	3
moans/unintelligible sounds	2
no response	1
Motor response	
follows commands	6
localizes pain	5
withdraws from pain	4
decorticate flexion	3
decerebrate extension	2
no response	1

FIGURE **6.2**
GLASGOW COMA SCALE.
This scale is used to classify brain injuries as severe, moderate, or mild. Scores on each of the three sections are summed to provide a total score, which is used to predict chances of recovery in people with traumatic brain injury. (Source: Teasdale & Jennett, 1976.)

In another form of minimal consciousness, the **vegetative state,** the eyes might be open, but the person is otherwise unresponsive (Owen et al., 2006). The vegetative state has been defined as "wakefulness without awareness" (Bernat, 2006, p. 1181). Physicians used to think that anyone who was vegetative did not react to stimuli from the environment, primarily because of the lack of a behavioral response. We now know that this is not always the case.

vegetative state
a state of minimal consciousness in which the eyes might be open, but the person is otherwise unresponsive.

A highly publicized case study offers insight into the responsiveness of the brain in a vegetative state (Owen et al., 2006). Researchers asked a young woman who was in vegetative state to imagine a few things, such as walking through her house and playing tennis. As they asked her to imagine these things, they scanned her brain using fMRI. Surprisingly, her brain showed activation in the same areas as did the brains of people who were conscious and asked to imagine the same things. Not only does this mean that this woman was responsive while in a vegetative state—she was responding with her brain—but it also showed that she could exhibit intentional thought because she followed the researchers' instructions. Clearly, the absence of behavioral responses does not guarantee that people in vegetative states cannot process information from the outside world. The fact that one person in a so-called vegetative state could be this responsive forces a rethinking of the ethical implications of labeling someone vegetative.

This patient may have been in transition from a vegetative state to a *minimally conscious* state in which the person is barely awake or aware but shows some deliberate movements (Laureys, 2007). People who are minimally conscious show signs of intentional behavior, but cannot communicate (Laureys, 2007). For example, whereas a vegetative person cannot intentionally track a person with the eyes, a minimally conscious person can.

Personally, we are reminded of the time we spent with David when the doctors said he was vegetative. We asked whether David could hear us; they said probably not, but they did not know. We tried to reach him anyway. We played music for him, told him about our days, and moved his arms and legs. Was his brain taking in some of it? We always thought so, but we couldn't be certain.

MODERATE CONSCIOUSNESS

A great deal of mental activity occurs in the areas between a complete lack of consciousness and full consciousness. Freud used the term *preconscious* to refer to material that is potentially accessible but not currently available to awareness (Freud, 1933/1964). An example is the so-called *tip-of-the-tongue phenomenon* (Galin, 1994). We know a person's name, for example. We know we know it, but we can't come up with it. The experience of knowing that we know a name is conscious, even if we cannot bring the name into awareness. This state can be thought of as *moderate consciousness*.

When we sleep and dream we are moderately conscious. We may be roused by sounds that are important to us, while ignoring others. But while we sleep there is a perceptual wall in our consciousness that prevents us from perceiving most sensations of the outer world. Psychologists study many other processes that operate at the boundaries of awareness, several of which we discuss in Chapter 7.

FULL CONSCIOUSNESS

We spend most of our waking lives relatively alert and aware. Still, alertness waxes and wanes throughout the day. Sometimes we are sharp, and other times we lose focus. Some of these fluctuations in alertness stem from a normal daily rhythm, which we will discuss later in the chapter. But even normal wakefulness ranges from drowsiness to full focus. When people are awake but understimulated and not very aroused by their environment, they may be *bored*. When they are awake but have the impulse and need to sleep, they are *drowsy*. Ask your professors: They know only too well that not everyone who is awake is fully present and paying attention. As we will see in the sleep section, when we are drowsy our brains exhibit a unique pattern of brain wave activity that is different from a fully awake and alert brain.

There are also periods when we are more alert and present than normal. We may be stimulated and even excited. Or we may become so involved in what we are doing that we lose a sense of time and forget where we are. Some psychologists have called this state *flow* (Csikszentmihalyi, 1990). Flow exists when we thrive in our ability to rise to the occasion of challenging tasks. Think of a sport or craft you really love to do and do well. Think of the times when you were involved in such an activity and everything "clicked" all at once—everything you did was just right. This is the flow state. Our attention is so focused and everything goes so smoothly that an hour may feel like a minute or a minute like an hour. We are so engaged with the experience that time does not matter at all.

mindfulness
a heightened awareness of the present moment, whether of events in one's environment or in one's own mind.

Another state of full consciousness is **mindfulness**, a heightened awareness of the present moment, of events in one's environment and events in one's own mind. For example, when you are talking with a friend, you can be aware of what your friend is saying, how he looks, and how his words and tone of voice affect how you feel (Brown & Ryan, 2003). The more mindful person attends to all of these things; the less mindful person might notice only the friend's words. People vary considerably in how mindful they are, just as they differ in their personalities (Baer et al., 2006; Brown & Ryan, 2003). In addition, as we will discuss later in the chapter, people can develop their mindfulness skills using techniques such as meditation.

quick quiz 6.1: Two Dimensions of Consciousness: Wakefulness and Awareness

1. The two main dimensions of consciousness are
   a. unconsciousness, consciousness
   b. preconsciousness, consciousness
   c. wakefulness, sleepiness
   d. wakefulness, awareness

2. _____ is a heightened awareness of the present moment, which can be applied to events in one's environment and events in one's own mind.
   a. Wakefulness
   b. Attention
   c. Mindfulness
   d. Optimism

Answers can be found at the end of the chapter.

Attention: Focusing Consciousness

Being conscious—that is, being awake and aware—involves attending to particular parts of our world. So attention is a key aspect of consciousness; it is how we direct the spotlight of awareness.

We can be aware of only a finite amount of material at a time. **Attention** is the limited capacity to process information that is under conscious control (Styles, 2006). For example, when you are in class, it is not possible to type a text message to your friend and also to pay attention to the lecture. If you are typing your thoughts to a friend, you cannot also hear what the professor is saying. There are several different types of attention. We will examine two attentional processes that help determine the contents of consciousness at any given moment in time: selective attention and sustained attention.

attention
the limited capacity to process information that is under conscious control.

SELECTIVE ATTENTION

Imagine being in a crowded room where several people are talking, although you want to listen to just one person. You filter out unwanted noise to focus on the person you want to hear. If attention is a general process, then focusing conscious attention even more narrowly is selective attention. **Selective attention** is the ability to focus awareness on specific features in the environment while ignoring others. When your professor asks for your "undivided attention," then, she is really interested in your selective attention.

connection

The psychological disorder schizophrenia is marked by an inability to selectively attend to only the most relevant information in one's surroundings.

See Chapter 15, p. 591.

selective attention
the ability to focus awareness on specific features in the environment while ignoring others.

The classic scientific evidence for selective attention came from research on the dichotic listening task (Broadbent, 1954). In these studies, a participant received one message in one ear and another message in the other ear. Typically, researchers presented several messages to both ears and then told the participant to pay attention to just one ear (the attended ear). They then measured recall for items presented to both ears. Recall was much better for the attended ear. If, for example, people were instructed to attend to the left ear message, they showed little to no memory of the message presented to the right (unattended) ear (Broadbent, 1954; Styles, 2006).

Later studies showed that if the material presented to the unattended ear is meaningful in some way, it can make its way into consciousness (Treisman, 1964). For instance, if you were at a large party trying to listen to a conversation in spite of a lot of background noise and someone in another part of the room mentioned your name, you would immediately become aware of the other conversation. Somehow you tuned out the background noise so that you could follow the first conversation, but now you cannot push that background information out of your awareness. The ability to filter out auditory stimuli and then to refocus attention when you hear your name is called the *cocktail party effect* (see Figure 6.3; Moray, 1959).

Selective attention creates gaps in attention and perception. When we selectively attend, we focus so much on certain things that we are blind to other things. As a result of paying attention to some parts of our environment, we may miss other parts. Focusing attention can create gaps in attention and perception. In one study that clearly demonstrates gaps in attention, researchers showed people a video of two basketball teams, with one team dressed in white T-shirts and the other in black shirts. They asked participants simply to count the number of times the players on the team wearing white T-shirts passed the ball. About half the participants were dumbfounded to learn afterward that they completely missed seeing a person dressed in a gorilla suit walk into the game, pause for a second to beat his chest, and then walk off screen. They were so focused on counting passes made by people wearing white shirts that they ignored

FIGURE **6.3**

THE COCKTAIL PARTY EFFECT. The cocktail party effect is the ability to filter out auditory stimuli and then to refocus attention when you hear your name. This often occurs in noisy social situations, such as parties.

everything else (see Figure 6.4). Attending closely to one thing can blind us to other events, even gorillas walking into a basketball game (Simons & Chabris, 1999). This phenomenon by which we fail to notice unexpected objects in our surroundings is referred to as *inattentional blindness*.

If we can be inattentive in spite of efforts to attend, does that mean we can prevent the intrusion of unwanted information during concentration? For example, if you are reading an engrossing novel, is it possible to tune out the sounds of your roommate's TV? Can you apply your attention so intensely that nothing else can get in? The *perceptual load model* states that we do not notice potential distract-

FIGURE **6.4**

MISSING THE OBVIOUS. How could anyone miss the gorilla in the middle of this picture? If you were asked to watch a video and count the number of people wearing white shirts, you might be one of the 50% who wouldn't notice the gorilla.

ers when a primary task consumes all of our attentional capacity (Lavie et al., 2004). When a primary task is minimally demanding, however, distracters can capture your awareness. In a laboratory experiment on this phenomenon, participants were asked to view a drawing of a cross on a computer screen. The two arms of the cross were different colors, and one arm was subtly shorter than the other. In the low perceptual load condition, participants had to name the color of the arm. In the high perceptual load condition, participants had to say which arm was longer, a more difficult task. The researchers then introduced an irrelevant stimulus (a square) and looked at which group was more likely to see it. Those who were less busy—that is, the people in the low perceptual load condition—were more likely to see the square than those in the high perceptual load condition (Lavie, 2007). Perceptual load theory might explain why it is easier to ignore the TV when you are lost in an engrossing novel than when you are reading a boring chapter in a textbook. It might also explain why we might miss certain things when our mind is too busy. What might happen if you missed seeing a pedestrian while driving because you were involved in a cell phone conversation? Tuning out information is not always a good thing. See "Psychology in the Real World" for a discussion of the effects of cell phone use on attention in drivers.

Likewise, conscious attention occurs when neurons from many distinct brain regions work together—a process referred to as synchronization. Imaging techniques such as fMRI reveal synchronization in brain regions that are equally active. When synchronization occurs, we might have a conscious experience (Kranczioch et al., 2005). Imagine that you see an apple: Before you experience "apple," several areas of your brain are active, such as those responding to the object's shape (round) and color (red) and where the object is in your visual field. The synchrony of cell assemblies may be what binds together these separate experiences (of round and red, etc.) into the experience of an apple. This process harkens back to our earlier discussion of consciousness as a global workspace, and it shows how neuroscience is beginning to address how a moment of conscious experience actually occurs (Engel et al., 2006).

Hazards of Cell Phone–Induced Driver Distraction

People generally acknowledge the potential hazards of cell phone use while driving, yet the practice is widespread. Many states restrict cell phone use by drivers, but the laws vary. Some allow phone use on a hands-free device, others completely prohibit use among young drivers, and still others have no regulations at all (Governors Highway Safety Association, 2008).

In the view of psychologists, phone conversations while driving are distracting, even when the hands are free. Talking on the phone while driving diverts attention from the demanding tasks of safely operating and navigating a car. With such distraction, performance declines and safety is compromised. Think of all the things one has to manage while driving: scanning the road, operating the pedals and gears, watching for other cars and pedestrians, and remembering directions. There is much to attend to without the added task of having a phone conversation.

Recently a number of studies have been published on cell phone use in the car. Most employ hands-free devices, based on the fact that most states approve the use of these tools and imply they are safe. In fact, a recent analysis of studies looking at cell phone use during driving showed that the dangers to driving are similar for handheld and hands-free phones (Horrey & Wickens, 2006).

Strayer and Drews (2007) did several experiments with people in a driving simulator (see Figure 6.5). Some of the participants wore a hands-free headset and engaged in a conversation while doing a driving task; the others had no cell phone and simply drove. In the first study, the researchers inserted into the driving scene several objects that drivers were not told they'd need to attend to. Later they tested them on recognition of these objects. People talking on a cell phone saw half as many objects as those not on the phone. This suggests that they were not fully paying attention to the driving situation. In another study, the researchers varied the objects inserted into the driving scene in terms of how important they were for driving safety. The hypothesis was that people talking on the phone simply do not attend to things that have little relevance to safety, but they do attend to things that matter.

Some of the objects inserted into the driving scene were irrelevant to safety (such as billboards), and others were quite relevant (traffic signs, pedestrians). Later, when drivers were tested on memory for seeing the objects, they were just as likely to miss safety-relevant objects as safety-irrelevant objects.

SUSTAINED ATTENTION

Staying focused on a task is difficult, especially if the task both requires a high degree of concentration and can have life-and-death consequences. For example, as we discussed in Chapter 4, air traffic controllers must focus on an airplane on a visual display. To do so, they must coordinate with other airplanes, controllers, and pilots to make sure that each plane lands where it should without crossing the paths of other planes that are landing or taking off. This ability to maintain focused awareness on a target is known as **sustained attention.**

What are the limits of people's abilities to sustain their focused attention on one task? The airlines need to know this, as do many other industries that require careful attention on the part of their employees. Researchers study sustained attention using the Continuous Performance Test (CPT). Imagine having

sustained attention
the ability to maintain focused awareness on a target or idea.

An fMRI study of people driving in a simulator while using a hands-free device showed that activity in regions of the brain involved in processing spatial information (the parietal lobe) decreased by 37% when people listened to sentences while driving, whereas activity in areas associated with language processing increased. Their driving was also worse. This result suggests that conversations divert attentional resources from the task of the driving (Just, Kellar, & Cynkar, in press).

Is a cell phone conversation, even a hands-free one, any more distracting than having a conversation with someone in the car? At least two studies have shown that people talking with a friend in the car perform better in a simulator than can those on the phone. Why would real-life conversation be significantly less distracting than phone conversation? Passengers also attend to the driving environment and understand pauses in conversation due to driving demands, and they may assist the driver with directions, road obstacles, and other driving tasks (Strayer & Drews, 2007, Strayer, Drews, & Couch, 2006).

Clearly, talking on the phone while driving, even with a hands-free device, seriously impairs driver performance (Beede & Kass, 2006). Such effects may be particularly problematic for new drivers, who are less experienced, have more accidents, and tend to engage in more distracting

FIGURE **6.5**

RESEARCH PARTICIPANT IN A COMPUTERIZED DRIVING SIMULATOR. The simulator provides a 180-degree city street interactive driving display in a realistic car interior. The "driver" is wearing a hands-free cell phone headset.

activities while driving (Neyens & Boyle, 2007). In fact, using a cell phone while driving is similar to drunk driving in that the drivers follow other cars too closely, show slower braking reactions, and have more accidents (Strayer et al., 2006). This is one area in which psychological science has clarified a problem for the real world. It might make you think twice about using a phone while driving. Remember these studies all used hands-free devices. We can only imagine how much worse the problem would be if drivers were using handheld phones—or if they were texting while driving!

to detect the letter Y, among other letters shown very rapidly, one by one on a computer screen. The CPT requires that the participant maintain attentional focus for an extended period of time. Most people cannot perform well on CPT tasks for more than about 15 minutes, and their accuracy in detecting targets declines considerably after 5 to 7 minutes (Nuechterlein & Parasuraman, 1983; Parasuraman, 1998).

quick quiz 6.2: Attention: Focusing Consciousness

1. What term best describes not perceiving a person in a gorilla suit when asked to count the number of people playing basketball?
   a. inattentional blindness
   b. not paying attention
   c. absent-mindedness
   d. minimally conscious state

For air traffic controllers the ability to sustain attention for long stretches of time is fundamental to the safety of air travelers. Yet research suggests that most people have difficulty focusing attention on a continuous performance task for more than 15 minutes. What does this suggest about highly focused occupations like air traffic controller?

2. You are at a loud party talking to a friend. The noise of the chatter is nearly deafening, but all of sudden you hear your name rise above the noise. This is known as the
   a. self-recognition effect
   b. cocktail party effect
   c. attentional effect
   d. divided attention effect

Answers can be found at the end of the chapter.

Training Consciousness: Meditation

Any time you read, reason, solve problems, or learn something new, you are sharpening your mental skills. Some age-old techniques, however, are designed specifically to train the conscious mind. **Meditation** refers to a wide variety of practices that people use to calm the mind, stabilize concentration, focus attention, and enhance awareness of the present moment.

connection
Every time you make a memory or learn something new, you change your brain by strengthening synaptic connections or growing new neurons.
See Chapter 8, p. 325.

There are many different types of meditation techniques with different goals. To improve concentration, for example, meditators might spend minutes or even hours sitting still, relaxed yet alert, focusing their attention on the breath moving in and out of their mouths and noses, noticing how it moves in and out. This simple, but powerful ancient practice calms the mind and stabilizes attention (Wallace, 2006).

Psychologists and neuroscientists have begun to study the effects of such meditative practices on mental processes, emotion, and brain function. This research illustrates the dynamic relationship between mental life and neural structure and illustrates how experience and biology modify each other. Taken together, these studies show that meditation enhances mindfulness and well-being, improves perceptual sensitivity, and is associated with changes in brain anatomy and activation.

meditation practices that people use to calm the mind, stabilize concentration, focus attention, and enhance awareness of the present moment.

MEDITATION AND CONSCIOUS EXPERIENCE

Many forms of meditation develop mindfulness, a fully conscious state of heightened awareness of the present moment. Unlike concentration techniques, mindfulness meditation encourages attention to the details of momentary experience, such as all the thoughts, feelings, and sensations available in the moment (Baer et al., 2006).

People with high scores on questionnaire measures of mindfulness have higher scores on measures of well-being and optimism, are more in tune with their emotional states, and are less self-conscious and anxious. Also people who practice meditation consistently have higher mindfulness scores than those who do not (Brown & Ryan, 2003). Mindfulness meditation training appears to enhance well-being, reduce stress, decrease depression, and improve physical health (Anderson et al., 2007; Kabat-Zinn et al., 1998; Teasdale et al., 2000).

Meditation can also improve attentional skills (Jha, Krompinger, & Baime, 2007). In the first true experiment on this question, 64 experienced meditators were randomly assigned to a control group or to receive intensive training in concentration meditation (similar to the breathing technique described at the beginning of this section), which they practiced for several hours a day for 3 months straight. They were assessed before, during, and after the 3-month training. One of the questions the researchers asked was whether concentration meditation practices improve attention. Figure 6.6 illustrates one of their experiments on attention (MacLean et al., in press). The results suggest that concentration meditation makes people perceive visual objects—lines at least—with greater sensitivity. It is akin to having sharper vision or better hearing. In this case, meditation sharpened attention to detail.

Geek meditation session.

MEDITATION TRAINING AND THE BRAIN

Meditation may also change brain function and structure. For instance, after 8 weeks of mindfulness meditation training, people who had no previous meditation experience showed significant increases in EEG activity in the left frontal cortex (an area associated with positive mood) and decreases in negative mood, compared to those who received no training (Davidson et al., 2003). These EEG changes persisted for at least 4 months after training. In another study, MRI revealed thicker brain tissue in areas of the cortex associated with attention, sensitivity to bodily sensations, and the processing of external sensory information, in experienced meditators versus a comparison group of nonmeditators (Lazar et al., 2005). Also, those who had meditated the longest showed the greatest cortical thickness in certain areas. These correlational findings *suggest* that meditation can grow the brain and that the more one medi-

connection
What aspects of experimental designs allow for conclusions about cause and effect?
See Chapter 2, p. 52.

Buddhists practice meditation at a spiritual gathering. Meditation, an integral part of the Buddhist faith for thousands of years, develops concentration and mindfulness.

tates, the more the brain grows. A true experimental design is needed, however, to uncover a causal link between meditation training and brain thickness.

quick quiz 6.3: Training Consciousness: Meditation

1. Which of the following does meditation appear to improve?
   a. mindfulness
   b. attention
   c. well-being
   d. all of the above

2. A study of brain images of experienced meditators and a comparison group of nonmeditators found that the experienced meditators' brains showed evidence of
   a. thicker cortex in brain areas associated with attention and sensitivity to sensory information
   b. more diverse synaptic connections throughout the cerebellum
   c. cortical thinning throughout motor areas, but thickening in frontal areas
   d. less synaptic death than nonmeditators

Answers can be found at the end of the chapter.

Sleeping and Dreaming

Meditation offers specific practices for working with consciousness. Yet consciousness varies constantly on a daily basis without much intervention, by virtue of our degree of wakefulness or our moods. In this section, we discuss two major sources of variation of consciousness: sleeping and dreaming.

SLEEPING

A 5-year-old boy once described sleep as "when I go to my bed and I think about nothing." Typically, we think of sleep as a time of rest and relaxation, when we put out of our minds the day's events. Although our conscious experience of sleep may be of nothing and no time passing, it is in fact a very active process. We behave while we sleep—we move, we dream, sometimes we even

1 research question

Does intensive meditation training improve perception? MacLean and her colleagues (2008) hypothesized that by learning to train their attention, highly-trained meditators should be more sensitive than others to slight changes in perceptual stimuli.

Study participant wearing EEG cap

2 method

Participants were randomly assigned to receive intensive meditation training in a 3-month retreat (retreat group) or to have no training until a later date (control group). All participants performed various tasks pre-, mid-, and post retreat. In one key task, the line length task, participants viewed a series of lines on a computer screen. A long line was presented first as a reference line, and the participants were told to click the mouse whenever they saw a shorter line. They saw only one line at a time. In every trial the long reference line was the same length. The short line changed in length across trials, but was never as long as the long reference line. The longest short line that they perceived as different from the long line was their limit of perceptual sensitivity. Researchers also measured brain activity in participants using EEG.

Longest "short" line meditators perceived pre-retreat

Reference line

Longest "short" line meditators perceived post-retreat

3 results

The longer the line participants perceived as shorter than the reference line, the greater their perceptual sensitivity. Both groups (retreat and control) showed improved sensitivity across testing points. After 3 months, however, the participants who received the meditation training showed a greater increase in sensitivity to line length differences than the control group. The reference line shown above was the long line all participants used as a reference for the comparisons. The others show what meditators perceived as the longest "short" lines before and after the retreat, respectively. They indicate enhanced sensitivity to differences in line length as a function of meditation training.

Perceptual sensitivity

Length of short line in degrees of visual angle

- Control
- Retreat

Pre-retreat   Post-retreat

4 conclusion

Concentration meditation increases sensitivity to subtle changes in visual stimuli.

FIGURE **6.6**

HOW CONCENTRATION MEDITATION AFFECTS ATTENTION. A controlled experiment shows that intensive meditation training can improve attention to visual stimuli. (*Source:* MacLean, K., Saron, C., Aichele, S., Bridwell, D., Jacobs, T., Zanesco, A., & Mangun, G. R. (in press). Improvements in perceptual threshold with intensive attention training through concentration meditation. *Journal of Cognitive Neuroscience* [Suppl].)

FIGURE 6.7

HUMAN CIRCADIAN CYCLES. Our body temperature (a), melatonin levels (b), and alertness (c) fluctuate regularly on 24-hour circadian cycles.

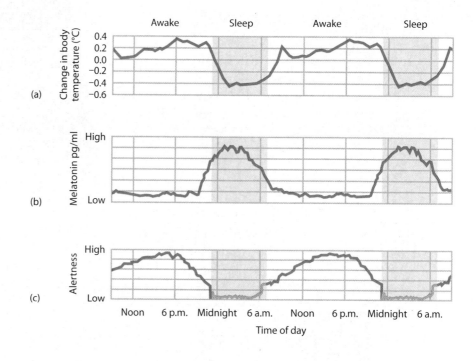

talk and walk. The sleeping brain is very active, but it is only partially processing information from the outside world. Sleep has two essential features: There is a perceptual wall between the conscious mind and the outside world, and the sleeping state can be immediately reversed (Dement, 1999). Awareness of the outside world is greatly diminished in sleep, but not completely. The mind is still able to filter relevant from irrelevant stimuli: a baby's cry may awaken a parent, but much louder sounds (like a TV blaring in the room) may not. Moreover, because sleep is reversible, it is different from being in a coma.

Sleep and Circadian Rhythms

Sleep occurs in the context of a daily sleep–wake cycle, which follows a pattern known as a circadian rhythm. **Circadian rhythms** are the variations in physiological processes that cycle within approximately a 24-hour period. Many physiological systems, including the sleep–wake cycle, feeding, hormone production, and cellular regeneration, vary on a circadian basis (Refinetti, 2006). In Figure 6.7 we see how three different bodily processes—body temperature, the hormone melatonin, and alertness—each fluctuate on a circadian cycle. Body temperature, for instance, peaks a few hours before bed and soon after waking up and then drops during sleep. That our bodies go through 24-hour cycles is the reason why we are sharper at some times of the day than others and why we experience jet lag. Shortening or lengthening our days by traveling across time zones throws the circadian cycles off, and it takes time for the body to readjust to the new daily cycle.

The body has an internal timekeeper located in the hypothalamus, called the suprachiasmatic nucleus. The *suprachiasmatic nucleus (SCN)* regulates physiological activity on daily cycles (Moore & Eichler, 1972; Weaver, 1998). When the retina in the eye senses light in the morning, it stimulates the SCN, which in turn signals the nearby *pineal gland* to decrease the amount of melatonin it releases (Itri et al., 2004). *Melatonin* is a hormone that plays a role in relaxation

circadian rhythms
the variations in physiological processes that cycle within approximately a 24-hour period, including the sleep–wake cycle.

and drowsiness. In the evening, decreased activity in the SCN prompts the secretion of melatonin, which increases relaxation. Because of its role in relaxation, melatonin can be taken as a drug to combat the effects of jet lag. Research suggests for some people it can be effective in reducing these disruptive effects of jet travel, but more when we travel ahead in time (east) than backward in time (west) (Atkinson, Reilly, & Waterhouse, 2007).

Sleep and the Brain

Until the 1950s people assumed the brain was relatively inactive during sleep, except for dreaming. In the 1950s, Nathaniel Kleitman and Eugene Aserinsky were studying attention in children and noticed that when children lost attention and fell asleep, their eyes moved rapidly underneath their eyelids (Bulkeley, 1997). They suspected these movements were important in sleep and, after further research, discovered that they occurred in everyone throughout the night. Kleitman and Aserinksy coined the phrase **rapid eye movements (REM)** to describe these eye movements (Dement, 1999). Their discovery revolutionized the study of sleep and dreaming. The brain, as it turns out, is very active during sleep. With EEG technology, scientists have learned that sleep changes throughout the night and that distinct patterns of brain activity characterize these changes (Bulkeley, 1997; Dement, 1999). Let's consider what they've learned.

Each state of wakefulness and sleep has its own pattern of brain activity. When we are awake, brain activity is characterized by rapid, low-energy waves known as **beta waves.** When we are awake but relaxed and drowsy, our brain activity switches to slower and slightly higher energy waves known as **alpha waves.**

The second major form of sleep, called **non-REM,** has relatively few eye movements; those that occur are slow rather than fast. There are four stages of non-REM sleep, each marked by unique brain wave patterns (see Figure 6.8).

beta waves
pattern of brain activity when one is awake; a rapid, low-energy wave.

non-REM
form of sleep with few eye movements, which are slow rather than fast.

rapid eye movements (REM)
quick movements of the eye that occur during sleep, thought to mark phases of dreaming.

alpha waves
pattern of brain activity when one is relaxed and drowsy; slower, higher-energy waves than beta waves.

FIGURE **6.8**

TYPES OF BRAIN WAVES AND DIFFERENT STAGES OF CONSCIOUSNESS AND SLEEP. Each stage of wakefulness and sleep is marked by a unique pattern of brain wave. For the typical 7-hour night of sleep for an adult, there are about five cycles of sleep.

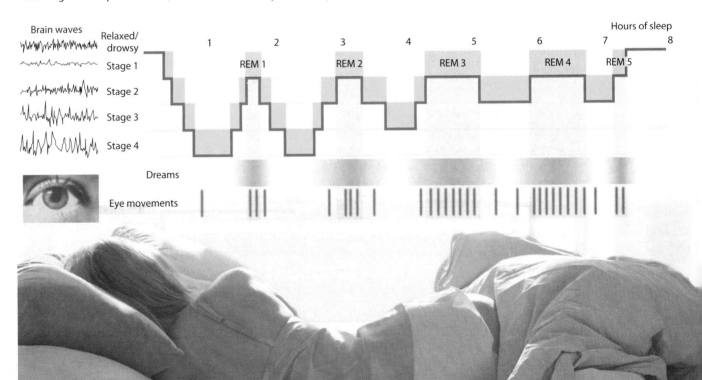

Relaxed-drowsy (alpha waves)　　　　　　　　Stage 1 sleep (theta waves)

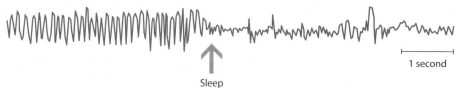

|—— 1 second ——|

↑
Sleep

FIGURE **6.9**

THE ONSET OF SLEEP. An EEG shows the abrupt transition from higher-energy alpha waves typical of the drowsy but awake state to the lower-energy alpha waves of Stage 1 sleep. This transition occurs in a period of less than 10 seconds.

When we enter Stage 1 of sleep, our brain waves change to **theta waves,** which are slower and lower in energy than alpha waves. The precise moment when we fall asleep is readily apparent on an EEG readout—we move from alpha to slower and lower-energy theta wave activity (see Figure 6.9). Stage 1 sleep starts when the sensory curtain drops and we are no longer responsive to the outside world. However, Stage 1 sleep is a light sleep, and not much stimulation is needed to awaken us. After about 5–7 minutes, we move to Stage 2 sleep, and the theta waves now show short periods of extremely fast and somewhat higher energy *sleep spindles.* The other unique markers of Stage 2 sleep are sudden high-energy *K-complexes.* After a short period of time, we move from Stage 2 to Stage 3 sleep. Stage 3 initially consists of theta waves with some higher-energy **delta waves.** As we progress through Stage 3, more and more delta waves appear and fewer and fewer sleep spindles and K-complexes. When the latter disappear completely, we have entered our deepest stage of sleep, Stage 4. Shortly after entering Stage 4 sleep, we start going back to sleep spindles and K-complexes of Stage 3 and then theta waves of Stages 2 and 1. When we return to Stage 1, our eyes begin to move rapidly underneath the eyelids. We are now in REM sleep and are actively dreaming. The night's first episode of REM sleep lasts for only about 8–10 minutes before the whole process starts over. With each progressive cycle, the non-REM periods are shorter and the REM periods longer (Dement, 1999). Adults move through about four to six different cycles of non-REM and REM sleep every night. Each cycle lasts roughly 90 minutes.

Full-blown dreams are less common during non-REM than REM sleep, but they do occur regularly during non-REM stages. Up to 70% of non-REM periods may involve dreaming. The dreams during non-REM sleep are different from REM dreams: They tend to be less detailed, less active, and more like regular thinking (Bulkeley, 1997; Foulkes, 1996; Kahan, 2001).

theta waves
pattern of brain activity during Stage 1 sleep; slower, lower-energy waves than alpha waves.

delta waves
type of brain activity that dominates Stage 3 sleep; higher energy than theta wave.

The Development of Sleep Over the Life Span　　Newborns of many species, especially humans, spend more time in REM sleep than in non-REM sleep. In humans, REM sleep declines rapidly over the life span (see Figure 6.10). Although newborns typically sleep for only a few hours at a time, they might spend a total of 8 hours in REM sleep and another 8 hours in non-REM sleep *per day.* The percentage of total sleep that is REM stays close to 50% for the first three months of life. By 8 months it falls to 33%, and by age 1 it drops to about 28%. During adolescence and adulthood, the amount of sleep that involves REM steadily decreases.

The fact that newborns and infants spend so much more time in REM sleep than adults has led some researchers to hypothesize that the main function

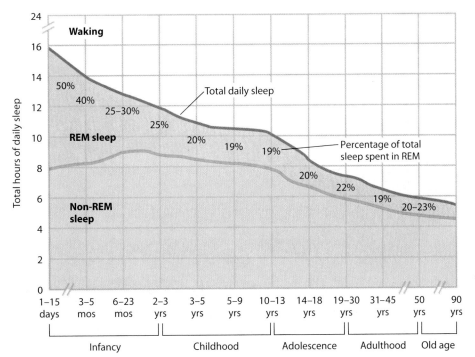

FIGURE **6.10**

SLEEP ACROSS THE LIFE SPAN. As this graph shows, infants and young children not only need more hours of sleep than do older children and adults, but also spend significantly more time in REM sleep. It may be that REM sleep supports brain growth and development.

of REM sleep is to assist in brain growth and development. The amount of REM sleep over the life span does correspond to the degree of brain plasticity and neural growth (Dement, 1999). Our brains are most plastic in infancy and childhood and less so in adulthood—precisely the pattern we see in REM sleep. REM sleep, just like new neural growth, continues throughout our lives—it just decreases with age.

The Function of Sleep

Sleep supports three major restorative processes: neural growth, memory consolidation, and protection against cellular damage (see Figure 6.11). First, sleep deprivation has been shown to inhibit the growth of new neurons in rats (Guzman-Marin et al., 2003)—something to think about next time you consider staying up all night to cram for a test.

nature & nurture

Sleep increases neural growth and helps us remember things.

Second, sleep helps us learn and remember things (Karni et al., 1994; Payne & Nadel, 2004; Stickgold & Walker, 2007). In a study of the effects of sleep deprivation on performance in a perceptual skills task, participants who had normal amounts of REM sleep performed better on the task afterward than did participants who were roused during REM sleep and missed some normal REM cycles (Karni et al., 1994). Neuroimaging studies of people learning to navigate a virtual maze show increases in activation in the hippocampus, the brain structure that is central to memory formation and learning (see Chapters 3, 6, and 7). If people sleep after this training, the same kind of hippocampal activity resurfaces during slow-wave sleep. The more hippocampal activation shown during slow-wave sleep, the better the person performs on the task the next day (Peigneux et al, 2004; Stickgold & Walker, 2007). In short, task learning is replayed in the brain during sleep, and then this brain practice helps performance the next day.

FIGURE **6.11**

THE FUNCTIONS OF SLEEP.
A good night's sleep before
an exam may do more for your
performance than an all-night
cram session.

to restore neural growth

to consolidate memory

to produce enzymes that protect
against cellular damage

Third, sleep appears to fight cell damage. When our bodies use energy through the process of metabolism, some cells are damaged. Specifically, when we metabolize oxygen, by-products of this process known as free radicals damage cells, including brain cells (Harmon, 2006). Sleep aids cell function by triggering the production of enzymes that fight cell damage (Ramanathan et al., 2002). Similarly, sleep slows metabolism itself, thereby slowing the rate of cellular damage (Wouters-Adriaens & Westerterp, 2006).

Sleep Deprivation and Sleep Debt

Not only does sleep facilitate learning and memory; it is also necessary for everyday functioning. Yet, 40 percent of adults in the United States suffer from sleep deprivation (Dement, 1999). Are you one of them? You might be sleep deprived if you need an alarm clock to wake up, if you sleep longer on the weekends than on weekdays, or if you fall asleep during lectures (Maas, 1998).

Recent surveys show that the typical adult gets only about 6 hours and 40 minutes of sleep on weekdays and 7 hours and 25 minutes on weekends (National Sleep Foundation, 2008). Sleep expert William Dement (1999) developed the concept of *sleep debt* to represent the amount of sleep our brains owe our bodies. It is like a monetary debt that must be "paid back." Simply put, if you get 2 hours less sleep one night, then you owe your body 2 hours additional sleep the next night (or within a few days). Sleeping longer on weekends is a way to pay back a little bit of sleep debt accumulated during the week.

Most people don't pay back their sleep debt, however, so they pay in other ways: daytime drowsiness, use of stimulants such as caffeine and nicotine, lack of focused attention, and impaired learning and memory. The most serious and dangerous payback comes in the form of accidents. A high percentage of all automobile, airplane, boating, and job-related accidents are caused by sleep deprivation and sleep debt. As many as 30% of all automobile accidents can be attributed to drowsiness (Dement, 1999). When you realize that roughly 40,000 people die every year in this country from automobile accidents, that means more than 10,000 lives are lost due to sleep deprivation. (See Figure 6.12 for tips on how to get a good night's sleep.)

Disorders of Sleep

For most people, sleeping 6 to 8 hours a day is a relaxing experience, notwithstanding the occasional nightmare or restless night. For an estimated 20 percent of the U.S. population, however, nighttime is often fraught with problems (Dement, 1999). Let us consider five disorders of sleep: insomnia, sleep apnea, sleepwalking, narcolepsy, and hypersomnia.

Insomnia is defined as taking more than 20 minutes to fall asleep, having trouble staying asleep, and/or not feeling rested after a night's sleep for two or more consecutive weeks (Krystal, 2005). Somewhere between 15 and 20 percent of U.S. adults suffer from insomnia (Pearson, Johnson, & Nahin, 2006). Some sleep experts consider insomnia more a symptom of other maladies than a disorder in its own right, although there is some debate on this matter (Dement, 1999). There are many possible causes of insomnia—for instance, restless leg syndrome, erratic hours, medical conditions, psychological disorders such as depression, and excessive use of alcohol (Dement, 1999; Roehrs, Zorick, & Roth, 2000). Iron deficiency may also cause insomnia. This fact might explain why women, who are more likely to be iron deficient, show higher rates of insomnia than men (Lee, 2006; Mizuno et al., 2005). Drug treatments for insomnia, such as the popular sleep aid Ambien, work by increasing the effects of GABA (gamma-aminobutyric acid), the neurotransmitter that decreases central nervous system activity. In this way, sleep aids produce a general feeling of relaxation.

Loud snoring may be due to **sleep apnea,** a temporary blockage of the airway (Dement, 1999). In sleep apnea, the person literally stops breathing for a short amount of time. (*Apnea* means "without breath.") It is more common in men than women (4% versus 2%) and in obese people. Because people with apnea seldom fall into deep and REM sleep, they are consistently sleep-deprived and often suffer from insomnia. Not only can apnea be disruptive, but in some cases it is also fatal. Apnea sufferers are at increased risk for automobile accidents, diabetes, and heart disease. Treatments for apnea aim to reduce throat blockage either by weight loss, surgery, or devices that keep the throat open. The most effective treatment is use of a device during sleep that pushes air into the throat at high enough pressure to keep the throat open (American Sleep Apnea Association, 2006).

Sleepwalking occurs when a person gets out of bed during sleep, usually during the first third of the sleep cycle, and engages in activities that normally occur during wakefulness, such as walking, eating, dressing, or bathing. People who sleepwalk are difficult to rouse and do not remember having been up after waking in the morning. Because sleepwalking occurs during non-REM sleep, the sleepwalker is not likely to be acting out a dream. Sleepwalking occurs in about 4–15% of children and about 1.5–2.5% of adults (Guilleminault et al., 2005).

The main feature of **narcolepsy,** another sleep disorder, is excessive daytime sleepiness. People with this condition may fall asleep at inopportune times throughout the day, often with little to no warning. They may also experience *cataplexy,* a weakness of facial muscles and muscles in limbs (Nishino, 2007). The origin of narcolepsy may lie in disrupted nighttime sleep patterns. Narcolepsy is often a function of insomnia; EEG studies reveal that people who suffer from narcolepsy show some abnormality in sleep spindles and disruption

Sleepwalking is more common in children than in adults, possibly because it occurs during non-REM sleep and adults spend less time in non-REM sleep than children do.

insomnia
a sleep difficulty characterized by difficulty falling and staying asleep, as well as not feeling rested.

sleep apnea
sleep difficulty that results from temporary blockage of the air passage.

sleepwalking
sleep difficulty characterized by activities occurring during non-REM sleep that usually occur when one is awake, such as walking and eating.

narcolepsy
sleep disorder characterized by excessive daytime sleepiness and weakness in facial and limb muscles.

of REM sleeping patterns. Narcolepsy appears to have a genetic basis. It is most often treated with amphetamines, which help prevent daytime sleepiness, and anti-depressants, which can help with cataplexy. Neither treatment addresses the nighttime sleep disruptions (Nishino, 2007; Tafti, Dauvilliers, & Overeem, 2007).

hypersomnia
sleep difficulty characterized by sleeping more than 10 hours a day for 2 weeks or more; includes urge to nap during inappropriate times.

Hypersomnia exists when a person sleeps more than 10 hours a day for 2 weeks or more. Hypersomnia involves strong urges to nap throughout the day, often at inappropriate times such as during meals or in the middle of conversations. It can be caused by other sleep disorders such as apnea, brain injury, or depression. Adolescents who commit suicide are more likely to have suffered from hypersomnia than those who do not commit suicide (Goldstein, Bridge, & Brent, 2008).

tips for better sleep

- Go to bed and get up at the same time each day.
- Avoid caffeine, nicotine, beer, wine and liquor in the 4 to 6 hours before bedtime.
- Don't exercise within 2 hours of bedtime.
- Don't eat large meals within 2 hours of bedtime.
- Don't nap later than 3 p.m.
- Sleep in a dark, quiet room that isn't too hot or cold for you.
- If you can't fall asleep within 20 minutes, get up and do something quiet.
- Wind down in the 30 minutes before bedtime by doing something relaxing.

DREAMING

dreams
images, thoughts, and feelings experienced during sleep.

Dreams are one of the most fascinating and curious features of consciousness. But what are dreams exactly? **Dreams** are the succession of images, thoughts, and feelings we experience while asleep. The succession of images is loosely connected by unusual associations and not well recalled afterward. Most of us dream numerous times each night, and yet we rarely recall our dreams on waking. When people in sleep labs are awakened, they report dreaming almost always if they were in REM sleep and somewhat regularly if they were in non-REM sleep (Bulkeley, 1998; Dement, 1999).

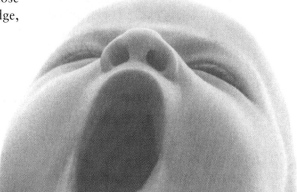

FIGURE **6.12**

SLEEP BETTER. Everyone has trouble falling asleep occasionally. Following these simple suggestions can help you avoid persistent problems with sleeplessness.

Do dreams have real meaning or do they simply reflect random activity of a complex brain? Psychologists from different perspectives disagree on what dreams are and what they mean. Let's look at these perspectives more closely.

Psychoanalytic Theory   In *The Interpretation of Dreams*, Sigmund Freud wrote that dreams are "the royal road to the unconscious" (1900/1953, p. 608). He argued that impulses, thoughts, feelings, and drives that threaten the waking mind are released in distorted and disguised form by the sleeping mind. In this view, each dream is an attempt to fulfill unacceptable desires or satisfy unconscious wishes.

According to Freud's theory, dreams operate on two distinct levels of consciousness. The dream that we consciously recall after waking up is only the surface level, which Freud called the **manifest level.** The deeper, unconscious level, where the true meaning of a dream lies, he labeled the **latent level.** In his clinical practice, Freud used

connection
Free association is another therapeutic technique used in Freudian psychoanalysis.
See Chapter 16, p. 625.

manifest level
Freud's surface level of dreams, recalled upon waking.

latent level
Freud's deeper, unconscious level of dreams; their meaning is found at this level.

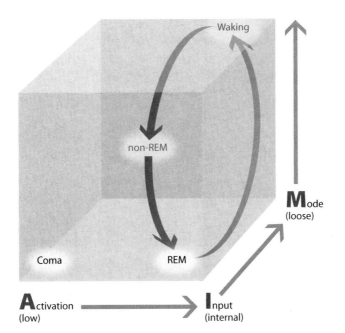

FIGURE **6.13**

HOBSON'S A-I-M MODEL OF CONSCIOUS-NESS. According to Hobson, the three dimensions of consciousness are activation, input, and mode. Activation ranges from low to high neural activation. Input ranges from internal to external, and mode ranges from loose to logical. All states of consciousness occupy a unique place in this three-dimensional space. Our days normally cycle between waking, non-REM, and REM sleep states of consciousness. (*Source:* Hobson, 2001.)

psychoanalysis to uncover the latent meaning of his clients' dreams, in order to help them resolve the hidden conflicts from which their problems arose.

Biological Theory   One influential biological theory of dreams has been AIM theory (Hobson, 2001, 2002). **AIM** stands for three biologically based dimensions of consciousness: Activation, Input, and Mode. *Activation* refers to the amount of neural activation and ranges from low to high activation. *Input* refers to whether stimulation is internal or external. Finally, *mode* refers to the mental state—from logical (wakeful) to loose-illogical (dreaming). These three dimensions (A-I-M) make up a cube, and all states of consciousness occupy a different space in this cube (see Figure 6.13). For example, waking is a highly active, external, and logical mode of consciousness residing in the upper back right portion of the cube. Non-REM sleep is moderately active, external, and logical and resides in the middle of the cube. By contrast, REM sleep is highly active, internal, and loose and therefore occupies the lower front right portion of the cube.

AIM
three biologically based dimensions of consciousness—Activation, Input, and Mode

Cognitive Theory   According to cognitive psychologists, dreams are not that different from everyday thinking. Research shows that some of the standard processes that we use during our waking life, such as imagery, memory, speech, and problem solving, operate in a similar manner during dreaming (Cavallero & Foulkes, 1993; Kahan, 2001). For instance, some people develop an ability to know when they are dreaming (lucid dreaming) and can therefore control the events and outcomes of the dreams (LaBerge, 1985). Others are able to reflect on and evaluate their experiences while dreaming (Kahan, 2001; Kahan & LaBerge, 1994). Also, recall that dreaming occurs during both REM and non-REM periods. Dreaming that occurs during non-REM sleep is closer to waking thought than is REM sleep dreaming—it is less visual, more verbal, and not as loose and unusual in its associations (Dement, 1999; Kahan, 2001).

1. When a perceptual wall between our conscious mind and the outside world emerges and we are in a state that is immediately reversible, we are
   a. asleep
   b. unconscious
   c. vegetative
   d. minimally conscious

2. Research shows that sleep functions to
   a. give our cells some energy
   b. facilitate learning and memory
   c. facilitate neural growth
   d. both b and c

3. Dreaming is most active during what kind of sleep?
   a. non-REM
   b. REM
   c. Stage 3
   d. Stage 4

4. In lucid dreaming, people become aware that they are dreaming and can sometimes even control their dreams. Lucid dreaming is most consistent with which theory of dreams?
   a. psychoanalytic
   b. biological
   c. cognitive
   d. none of the above

Answers can be found at the end of the chapter.

Hypnosis

Although the Greek word root *hypnos* means "sleep," hypnotized people are very much awake. Yet they have little voluntary control over their own behavior. **Hypnosis** is a state of mind that occurs in compliance with instructions and is characterized by focused attention, suggestibility, absorption, lack of voluntary control over behavior, and suspension of critical faculties of mind (Raz & Shapiro, 2002; Stewart, 2005). People may be more easily hypnotized if they are relaxed, but they can be hypnotized without relaxation (Raz & Shapiro, 2002).

People vary considerably in the degree to which they can be hypnotized, largely because they are not equally suggestible. About 65% of the population is mildly to

hypnosis
state characterized by focused attention, suggestibility, absorption, lack of voluntary control over behavior, and suspension of critical faculties; occurs when instructed by someone trained in hypnosis.

Hypnosis therapy has helped people to quit smoking. This group of smokers is being hypnotized to believe that cigarettes taste like vomit.

moderately responsive to hypnotic suggestion with about 15% being highly hypnotizable (Song, 2006; Hilgard, 1965). The rest are resistant to hypnosis.

The mention of hypnosis conjures up images of a performer putting audience volunteers into sleeplike trances and then instructing them to behave in ways that are out of character. Yet hypnosis is a clinical tool and should not be confused with stage techniques. Numerous studies support the effectiveness of hypnosis for pain relief during childbirth, dental procedures, and surgery. Further, hypnosis may be effective in treating nicotine addiction, nausea and vomiting related to chemotherapy, and anxiety associated with certain medical procedures (Lang et al., 2006; Montgomery, DuHamel, & Redd, 2000; Patterson, 2004; Stewart, 2005). The therapeutic benefits of hypnosis are not fully understood, but the availability of brain imaging techniques has motivated efforts to document its effectiveness and to learn how it works to reduce pain (Flammer & Bongartz, 2003; Stewart, 2005).

It is not easy to offer a general explanation for how hypnosis works. Even studies of brain activation and brain function during hypnosis cannot reveal whether the way hypnosis works to relieve pain is different from how it works to decrease anxiety. Recent research in cognitive neuroscience offers new insight into how the brain operates during hypnosis, however, and in the process expands our understanding of basic mechanisms of attention and consciousness. Let's consider what these researchers are finding.

breaking new ground
The Cognitive Neuroscience of Hypnosis

Is hypnosis a special psychological state? Or is it a role people adopt in reaction to situational demands? The groundbreaking research of a few pioneers shows that hypnosis may provide a model for understanding attention and the brain.

PREVIOUS RESEARCH ON HYPNOSIS

Some theorists consider hypnosis to be a state in which one part of the brain operates independently. Ernest Hilgard (1977) showed that under hypnosis one aspect of a person's mind can remain aware and open to stimulation from the outside (such as the hypnotist's voice), while other parts are cut off from external input. Hilgard hypnotized a man and told him he was deaf. While in the hypnotic state, the man did not respond to loud noises nearby. Next, Hilgard told the man to raise a finger if he could hear him. The man raised his finger! The man demonstrated both responsiveness to the hypnotic instruction (he was "deaf" as he did not respond to noises) and an ability to attend selectively to important external input. Hilgard called this phenomenon the *hidden observer effect*.

A second theory maintains that hypnosis does not alter consciousness, nor do hypnotized individuals give up control of their behavior. Instead, they behave the way they think a hypnotized person would behave. In short, they are role-playing (Orne, 1959). For decades, this was the prevailing scientific view on hypnosis. New research suggests a different explanation.

HOW HYPNOSIS AFFECTS THE BRAIN

Neuroscientist Amir Raz and his colleagues have studied whether hypnosis might help to eliminate the Stroop effect (Raz, Fan, & Posner, 2005). The Stroop task tests visual

FIGURE **6.14**

THE STROOP EFFECT. Participants will name the color of the letters more rapidly when their color matches the meaning of the word compared to when there is a mismatch.

YELLOW   BLUE

selective attention; it measures how people deal with conflicting verbal and color information. In a typical Stroop test, participants view the names of colors, such as *green, red,* and *blue,* printed in different colors and must name the color in which the word is printed. People are slower to identify the color of words that are printed in a different color from the meaning of the word (such as when the word *blue* is printed in yellow ink) than words that are printed in the same color (*blue* printed in blue). The delay in reaction time caused by mismatching color words and the color in which the words are printed is known as the **Stroop effect** (Stroop, 1935; see Figure 6.14).

Raz and his colleagues hypnotized 16 people—8 who were highly hypnotizable and 8 less hypnotizable (Raz et al., 2005). While hypnotized, the participants received instruction on a Stroop test that they would perform a few days later in an fMRI scanner. After the hypnosis session, all participants received a posthypnotic suggestion, which is a suggestive statement that a particular behavior will occur sometime in the future. Participants were told that during the test they would see gibberish words in different colors and they would have the task of pushing a button corresponding to the actual color of the letters. In fact, the words they saw during the test were names of colors.

Highly hypnotizable people who received the "gibberish" suggestion identified the colors faster than the less hypnotizable people who received the same suggestion. Brain scans taken during the Stroop test showed that highly hypnotizable people had turned off the areas of the brain that normally process word meaning, and so these areas did not interfere with color recognition. The anterior cingulate cortex (see Figure 4.27) is an area that is usually activated when people experience the conflict in the Stroop test (Carter et al., 1997). In highly hypnotizable people, there was less activation in the anterior cingulate cortex during the Stroop test than in the less hypnotizable people, who were not able to suppress the Stroop effect. It is important to emphasize that participants were not in a hypnotic state while in the brain scanner. In response to the posthypnotic suggestion, the highly hypnotizable people saw real words as gibberish and therefore attended only to identifying the color of the letters.

The studies on the Stroop effect lend support to the idea that consciousness can be divided in hypnosis. They don't address the issue of role-playing, but another set of studies does. In these studies, a group of researchers used brain imaging techniques to compare perceptions of hypnotically induced pain, physically induced pain, and imagined pain in highly hypnotizable people (Derbyshire et al., 2004; Raij et al., 2005). The researchers induced real pain by touching participants' skin with a hot metal rod, activating a well-known pain brain circuit. They contrasted this pattern of activation with that of participants who imagined pain. The imagined pain did not activate the same brain areas. However, hypnotically induced pain activated the same brain circuit as the real pain did. Also, participants reported actually feeling pain for both real and hypnotically induced pain, but not for imagined pain. So hypnotic and real pain activate the same brain regions and produce the same subjective feelings. Imagining pain does not have the same effects. Hypnotic pain, then, is not just an imitation of the real thing. It is more like real pain.

Where do these studies leave us? The study of hypnotically induced pain contradicts the view of hypnosis as role-playing, and the Stroop test study shows that

Stroop effect
delay in reaction time when color of words on a test and their meaning differ.

hypnosis can enable some people to override automatic processes. The possibility of using suggestion to deprogram automatic behaviors offers promise for the treatment of problematic behavior that has become automatic, such as drug abuse and eating disorders.

Smoking is another behavior that might be overcome with hypnosis. The behavior of smoking has become automatic for smokers. They need a cigarette and reach for it without thinking. Perhaps the results of Raz's work can be applied more deliberately to train smokers to see a cigarette as something they would not be interested in smoking—say, a snake.

quick quiz 6.5: Hypnosis

1. Scientific research has demonstrated that hypnosis
   a. is a real phenomenon
   b. is not real but learned
   c. is only an imagined state of mind
   d. is something everyone experiences

2. A groundbreaking area of research has recently demonstrated that under hypnosis
   a. hypnotically induced pain creates a subjective experience similar to real pain
   b. people had turned off the areas of the brain that normally process the meaning of words
   c. hypnotically induced pain activated the same brain circuit as real pain did
   d. all of the above

Answers can be found at the end of the chapter.

Altering Consciousness with Drugs

Hypnosis creates profound alterations in consciousness for some people. Drugs can change consciousness too. In this section, we will focus on the type of drugs known as psychoactive drugs. **Psychoactive drugs** are naturally occurring or synthesized substances that, when ingested or otherwise taken into the body, reliably produce qualitative changes in conscious experience.

Psychoactive drug use is universal among humans. Every culture in every recorded age has used mind-altering substances. People use psychoactive drugs for many reasons: to aid in spiritual practice, to improve their health, to explore the self, to regulate mood, to escape boredom and despair, to enhance sensory experience, to stimulate artistic creativity and performance, and to promote social interaction (Weil & Rosen, 1998). Whatever the reason, habitual use of psychoactive drugs can lead to abuse.

Problems arise when people develop a *physical dependence* on the drug to maintain normal function and to cope with the challenges of daily life. For some drugs, repeated use causes tolerance, meaning people require more and more of the drug to get the effect from it that they desire. Withdrawal symptoms are the adverse effects people with physical dependence experience if they stop using a drug. The drugs that lead to physical dependence create the most severe withdrawal symptoms. Alcohol withdrawal for an alcoholic, for example, creates many unpleasant side effects—such as delirium tremens (often referred to as the DTs), the symptoms of which may include tremors, insomnia, irritability, seizures, confusion, hallucinations, nausea and vomiting, and agitation. In some cases the DTs lead to death.

psychoactive drugs
naturally occurring or synthesized substances that, when ingested or otherwise taken into the body, reliably produce qualitative changes in conscious experience.

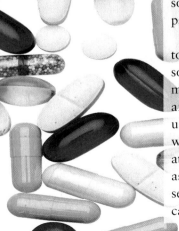

Drug classification	Short-term effects	Risks
Depressants		
Alcohol	Relaxation, depressed brain activity, slowed behavior, reduced inhibitions	Accidents, brain damage, liver damage, blackouts, birth defects
Sedatives	Relaxation, sleep	Accidents, slowed heart rate, possible death
Opioids	Euphoria, pain relief, bodily relaxation	Slowed heart rate and breathing, death
Stimulants		
Caffeine	Alertness, nervousness, increased heart rate	Anxiety, insomnia
Nicotine	Arousal, stimulation, increased heart rate	Cardiovascular disease, lung cancer risk with smoking
Cocaine	Exhilaration, euphoria, irritability	Insomnia, heart attack, paranoia
Amphetamines	Increased alertness, excitability, difficulty concentrating	Insomnia, paranoia, accelerated heart rate
Ecstasy (MDMA)	Mild amphetamine and hallucinogenic effects, high body temperature and dehydration; sense of well being and social connectedness	Depression, mental deficits, cardiovascular problems
Hallucinogens		
Marijuana	Euphoric feelings, relaxation, mild hallucinations, time distortion, attention and memory impairment, fatigue	Memory problems, respiratory illness, immune system impairment
LSD	Strong hallucinations, distorted time perception, synesthesia	Accidents, insomnia

FIGURE **6.15**

COMMON PSYCHOACTIVE DRUGS, THEIR PRIMARY EFFECTS ON CONSCIOUSNESS, AND RISKS.
Only caffeine, nicotine, and marijuana do not carry a risk of overdose resulting in death.

Psychological dependence occurs when people compulsively use a substance to alleviate boredom, regulate mood, or cope with the challenges of everyday life. For example, people who regularly take sleeping aids to help them fall asleep at night may be unable to sleep without them even though they may not be physically dependent on them. The essence of a compulsive behavior is the inability to control or regulate it. *Addiction* results from sustained use and physical or psychological dependence on a substance (Taylor, 2006). People who are addicted continue to use a given substance in spite of knowing that it is harmful and often in spite of attempts to quit.

In this section we survey the behavioral, psychological, and neurological effects of the major classes of psychoactive drugs: depressants, stimulants, and hallucinogens (Figure 6.15). We will consider illegal substances as well as the most commonly used and abused legal ones.

connection

How do compulsive behaviors become a problem for normal functioning?
See Chapter 15, p. 579.

DEPRESSANTS

Depressants decrease or slow down central nervous system activity. Alcohol, sedatives, and opioids (narcotics) are all depressants. In low doses, these drugs generally calm the body and mind; in high doses, they can slow down heart rate and brain activity to dangerously low levels. Alcohol and sedatives increase the activity of GABA, the main inhibitory neurotransmitter in the brain, and decrease the activity of glutamate, the main excitatory neurotransmitter in the brain. If taken during pregnancy, alcohol and sedatives can destroy developing neurons in the fetus's brain, leading to learning disabilities, poor judgment, or mental retardation (Farber & Olney, 2003). Additionally, combining alcohol with sedatives can be lethal. The opioids work differently, as we will see, but they can be equally dangerous. Let's look in more detail at each type of depressant.

depressants substances that decrease or slow down central nervous system activity.

Alcohol   Alcohol is the most widely used depressant. How quickly alcohol is absorbed in the bloodstream depends on a variety of factors, including how much food is in the stomach and how much body mass a person has. The amount of alcohol in the bloodstream is the common measure of inebriation known as blood alcohol concentration (BAC). BAC is measured in milligrams of alcohol per 100 milliliters of blood (milligrams %), so a BAC of .10 means that one tenth of 1 percent, or 1/1000th of one's blood content is alcohol. Figure 6.16 shows the amount of alcohol one must consume to reach .08 BAC, which is currently the legal limit for driving in all states in the United States, for various body weights. The figure includes various effects for different BACs.

The more alcohol a person consumes, the more obvious the depressant effects become, sometimes leading to blackouts. These effects are counterintuitive to the loose feeling that many people get in the early stages of drinking alcohol. This apparently stimulating effect occurs because alcohol suppresses the higher social regulatory functions of the cerebral cortex, thereby lowering inhibitions.

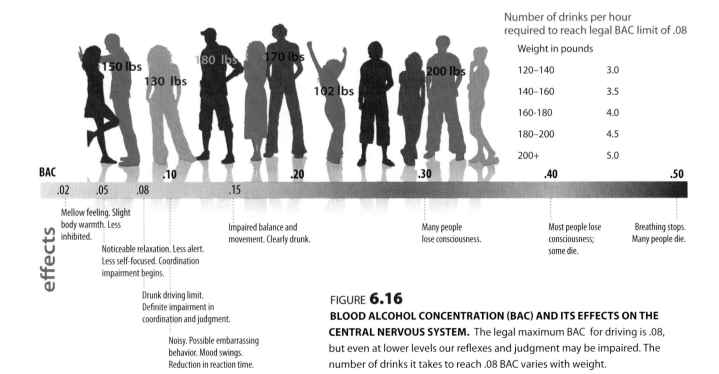

Number of drinks per hour required to reach legal BAC limit of .08	
Weight in pounds	
120–140	3.0
140–160	3.5
160-180	4.0
180–200	4.5
200+	5.0

BAC effects:

Mellow feeling. Slight body warmth. Less inhibited.

Noticeable relaxation. Less alert. Less self-focused. Coordination impairment begins.

Drunk driving limit. Definite impairment in coordination and judgment.

Noisy. Possible embarrassing behavior. Mood swings. Reduction in reaction time.

Impaired balance and movement. Clearly drunk.

Many people lose consciousness.

Most people lose consciousness; some die.

Breathing stops. Many people die.

FIGURE **6.16**

BLOOD ALCOHOL CONCENTRATION (BAC) AND ITS EFFECTS ON THE CENTRAL NERVOUS SYSTEM. The legal maximum BAC for driving is .08, but even at lower levels our reflexes and judgment may be impaired. The number of drinks it takes to reach .08 BAC varies with weight.

Alcohol consumption can result in numerous health hazards: accidents resulting in injury or death, usually caused by drunk driving; sudden death from binge drinking; blackouts; and increased risk of liver and throat cancers. Liver damage is one of the better-known health effects of drinking alcohol. Over time, heavy drinking, which is defined as more than five drinks per day, leads to fat accumulation and blocked blood flow in the liver. Without an adequate blood supply, liver tissue cannot function properly and dies. Chronic alcoholism is one of the most common causes of cirrhosis, the accumulation of nonfunctional scar tissue in the liver, an irreversible and eventually fatal condition.

Perhaps the most startling and most devastating physical effect of alcoholism, however, is that heavy drinking over a prolonged period actually shrinks the brain. Brain tissue is lost, creating widespread deficits in cognition and behavior (Mechtcheriakov et al., 2007; Oscar–Berman, & Marinkovic, 2003) (see Figure 6.17). For example, frontal lobe damage leads to deficits in planning, working memory, and abstract reasoning; and damage to the hippocampus leads to deficits in learning and memory. Neurons die from excessive alcohol. How exactly excessive alcohol shrinks the brain is unclear, but malnutrition and cirrhosis of the liver are two likely candidates. With abstinence from alcohol the brain recovers much of its lost volume, especially in the first month of abstinence (Gazdzinski, Durazzo, & Meyerhoff, 2005; Kubota et al., 2001). Research indicates that the risks of brain shrinkage from drinking may be greater for adolescents than adults, given the amount of development still occurring in the frontal cortex and other areas (Clark, Thatcher, & Tapert, 2008). As we have discussed elsewhere, the brain undergoes substantial development in adolescence, and that process can be disturbed by any kind of substance abuse. Brain shrinkage due to alcoholism is a serious reminder of how the brain not only affects behavior but also is affected by behavior.

Binge drinking is usually defined as at least five drinks in a row for men and four for women (Jackson, 2008; Wechsler, Lee, & Kuo, 2002). Some researchers argue, however, that not all binge drinkers are alike and that a distinction should be made between binge drinkers and heavy binge drinkers (seven or more drinks in a row for men and six or more for women) (Read et al., 2008). However defined, frequent episodes of consuming many drinks in a short period of time is an unhealthy pattern of behavior, and one that is becoming increasingly common in college students. How prevalent is it?

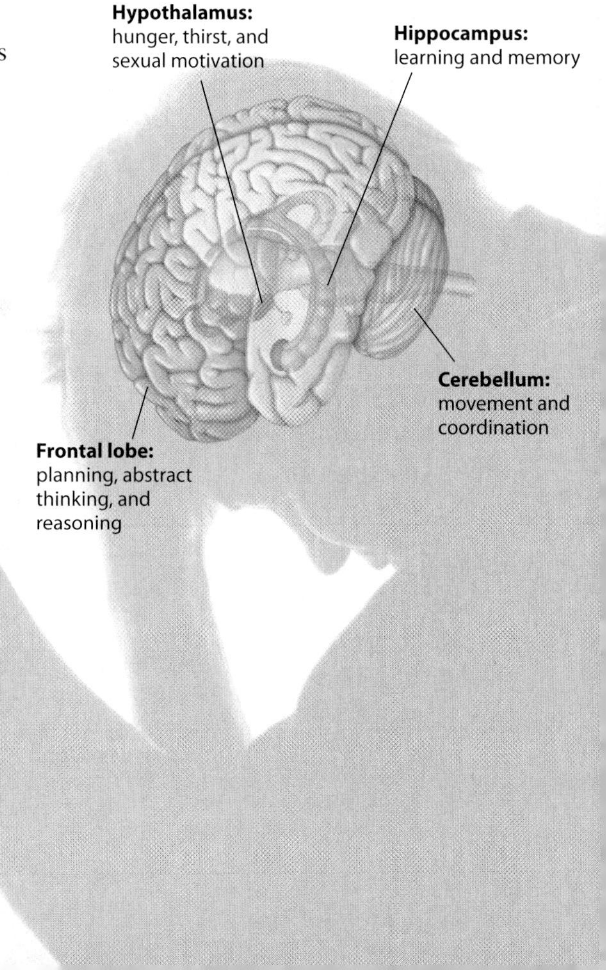

nature & nurture
Excessive drinking can shrink the brain.

connection
What is special about the adolescent brain?
See Chapter 5, p. 201.

Hypothalamus: hunger, thirst, and sexual motivation

Hippocampus: learning and memory

Cerebellum: movement and coordination

Frontal lobe: planning, abstract thinking, and reasoning

FIGURE **6.17**

BRAIN REGIONS MOST EFFECTED BY EXCESSIVE DRINKING. The main regions of the brain most effected by long-term and excessive drinking include the frontal lobes (planning and abstract thinking and reasoning); the hippocampus (learning and memory); the hypothalamus (hunger, thirst, and sexual motivation); and the cerebellum (movement and coordination).

About 40% of college students binge drink, and the numbers are rising (National Institute on Alcohol Abuse and Alcoholism, 2005; Wechsler et al., 2002).

One of the more serious risks of binge drinking is blacking out (Wechsler et al., 2002). *Blacking out* is a loss of memory of specific events. If anyone has ever told you of something you did the night before at a party when you were drunk and you have absolutely no recollection whatsoever of having done that, then you have blacked out.

As dangerous and deadly as alcohol can be, numerous studies show that mild to moderate alcohol intake provides protective effects for cardiovascular health. Moderate alcohol consumption is generally defined as no more than two drinks a day. Moderate alcohol use raises the amount of the beneficial form of cholesterol (HDL) in the blood, which has protective effects on the cardiovascular system (King, Mainous, & Geesey, 2008). Although these cardiovascular benefits were initially linked to red wine only, research now shows that many forms of alcohol convey the same advantages (Hines & Rimm, 2001; Sacco et al., 1999).

Sedatives   Sedatives create a feeling of stupor similar to that of alcohol intoxication. Prescription sedatives such as barbiturates and benzodiazepines slow the heart rate, relax skeletal muscles, and tranquilize the mind. Medically, barbiturates are used in anesthesia to calm people down during certain medical procedures and as a temporary sleeping aid. Examples of barbiturates are secobarbital (Seconal), pentobarbital (Nembutal), diazepam (Valium), and chlordiazepoxide (Librium). All these drugs have the potential for both physical and psychological dependence, can be lethal at high doses, and should be used only under strict medical supervision.

Opioids   Another class of depressants is the opioids (also called narcotics), a term that applies to all drugs derived from opium or chemicals similar to opium. Such drugs may be derived from natural sources (like morphine), may be partially synthetic (like heroin), or may be entirely synthetic (such as codeine). Modern synthetic opioids include oxycodone (Percocet or Percodan), which is prescribed for moderate to severe pain, and hydrocodone (Vicodin), which is prescribed for milder pain.

The effects of specific opioids vary, depending on the form and strength of the substance. Opioids depress central nervous system activity, slowing heart rate, respiration, digestion, and suppressing the cough center. In fact, pharmaceutical companies marketed heroin as a cough suppressant in the early 20th century. Prescription cough medicines today often include codeine, a safer alternative to heroin.

Opioids have been used for centuries as pain relievers. These drugs make use of the body's own naturally occurring opioid systems. Our own bodies produce *endorphins,* opioid-like proteins that bind to opioid receptors in the brain and act as natural painkillers. The stronger opioids— opium, morphine, and heroin—produce feelings of overwhelming bliss, euphoria, and bodily relaxation. The feeling is so good that nothing else

Actor Heath Ledger died in January 2008 of an accidental overdose of prescription drugs, including opioid painkillers.

matters. As one intravenous heroin user said, "It's so good. Don't even try it once" (Weil & Rosen, 1998).

Generally opioids have a high potential for abuse. Even some of the newer, widely prescribed synthetic opioids have become drugs of abuse (Paulozzi, 2006). Contrary to the popular image, not all addicts are junkies on the street. Some people inadvertently develop an addiction to opioids while being treated for chronic pain (Gallagher & Rosenthal, 2008). Opioids slow the heart and breathing; high doses can kill by stopping the heart and breathing (Hayes, Klein-Schwartz, & Doyon, 2008). For many of these drugs, the amount required to feel an effect may not be that much less than the amount that can be deadly, especially in people who have developed tolerance. Some newer therapeutic opioids, such as buprenorphine, can be taken at higher doses with less risk of overdose (Johnson, Fudala, & Payne, 2005).

STIMULANTS

stimulants
substances that activate the nervous system.

Stimulants activate the nervous system. Two of the most widely used psychoactive drugs are the stimulants caffeine and nicotine.

Caffeine   If you drink coffee, tea, cocoa, or certain soft drinks (including energy drinks), you are a stimulant user (see Figure 6.18). Caffeine is the world's most commonly consumed psychoactive drug, ingested by 90% of North American adults on a daily basis (Lovett, 2005). The effects of mild to moderate caffeine intake are increased alertness, increased heart rate, loss of motor coordination, insomnia, and nervousness. Too much caffeine can make people jittery and anxious. Caffeine is also a diuretic, which means it increases urine output.

If regular caffeine users stop consuming caffeine, they can experience withdrawal symptoms, the most common of which is headache. Giving up caffeine can also lead to fatigue and decreased energy, depressed mood, and difficulty concentrating (Juliano & Griffiths, 2004). These withdrawal effects show that caffeine creates physical dependence. To eliminate these negative

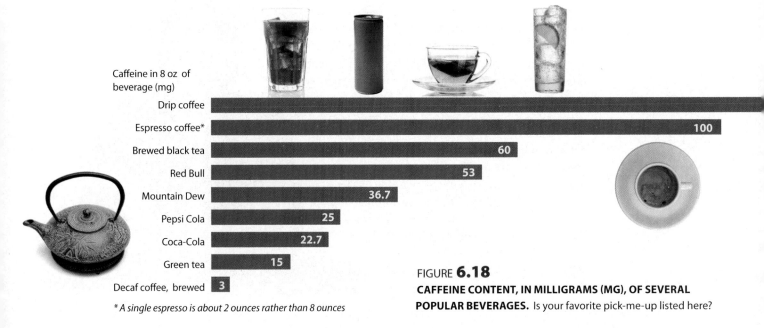

Caffeine in 8 oz of beverage (mg)

Beverage	mg
Drip coffee	
Espresso coffee*	100
Brewed black tea	60
Red Bull	53
Mountain Dew	36.7
Pepsi Cola	25
Coca-Cola	22.7
Green tea	15
Decaf coffee, brewed	3

*A single espresso is about 2 ounces rather than 8 ounces

FIGURE **6.18**
CAFFEINE CONTENT, IN MILLIGRAMS (MG), OF SEVERAL POPULAR BEVERAGES. Is your favorite pick-me-up listed here?

While their owners sleep, nervous little dogs prepare for their day.

withdrawal effects, people who want to stop using caffeine should gradually reduce their consumption.

Nicotine   The active drug in tobacco, nicotine is a powerful stimulant. Tobacco is used throughout the world. In 2006, approximately 21% (45.1 million) of American adults smoked cigarettes regularly (Centers for Disease Control and Prevention, 2006).

Smoking tobacco puts nicotine in the bloodstream almost immediately; within 8 seconds of inhalation it reaches the brain. As a stimulant, nicotine increases heart rate and rate of respiration, and it creates a feeling of arousal. Over time, the cardiovascular arousal associated with nicotine use increases the risk of high blood pressure and heart disease. Ironically, many nicotine users report that cigarettes calm them down. This perception may stem from the fact that nicotine relaxes the skeletal muscles even as it arouses the autonomic nervous system.

Nicotine is extremely addictive. It creates high tolerance, physical dependence, and unpleasant withdrawal symptoms. The high that heroin creates is more intense than the feeling of arousal from cigarettes, and the disruption to daily life of the heroin addict is more extreme than that of the smoker; but in terms of how difficult it is to quit, nicotine ranks higher than heroin (Keenan et al., 1994).

There are many known health risks of smoking. Cigarette smoking reduces life expectancy on average by 10 years, increases the risk for lung cancer more than 10-fold, and triples the risk of death from heart disease in both men and women (CDC, 2001; Doll et al., 2004). The U.S. Surgeon General has reported that smoking is also conclusively linked to leukemia, cataracts, pneumonia, and cancers of the cervix, kidney, pancreas, and stomach. Tobacco smoke contains many cancer-causing agents that trigger severe damage to DNA and can inhibit DNA repair in lung cells. Tobacco smoke also contains carbon monoxide, a toxic substance that displaces oxygen in the bloodstream, depriving tissues of needed oxygen. This is one reason why smokers often feel out of breath (Centers for Disease Control, 2001; Doll et al., 2004; Feng et al., 2006; Health & Human Services, 2004). Carbon monoxide from smoking also makes people look older than they are, because it reduces the blood supply to skin tissue. Tobacco smoking increases skin wrinkles even in young smokers (Koh et al., 2002).

115–175

Cocaine   For centuries, South American Indians have chewed the coca leaf for its stimulant and digestion-aiding properties (Weil & Rosen, 1998). The most notable component in the coca plant is cocaine, a psychoactive substance that when isolated from the coca leaf is a much stronger stimulant than chewed coca. When snorted, cocaine increases heart rate and produces a short-lived, but intense rush of euphoria. It also can lead to a sense of invulnerability and power. Physiologically, cocaine induces a sense of exhilaration by increasing the availability of the neurotransmitters dopamine and serotonin (Mateo et al., 2004).

connection
Dopamine is released when we feel good, and serotonin affects how sociable and affectionate we feel.
See Chapter 3, p. 92.

The brevity of the cocaine high helps explain why people abuse it—they keep chasing after a short-lived euphoria with even more cocaine. Some people inject (free-base) cocaine or smoke crack cocaine, a form of cocaine that is sold on the streets in pellets. Along with being extremely addictive, cocaine can cause other health problems, including increased heart rate and irregular heartbeat, increased risk of heart attack, and, occasionally, death (Weil & Rosen, 1998).

Amphetamines   Amphetamines are synthetically produced compounds that produce long-lasting excitation of the sympathetic nervous system, the part of the nervous system that keeps us ready for action. There are three main forms, all of which are pills: methamphetamine (Meth), dextroamphetamine (Dexedrine), and amphetamine sulfate (Benzedrine or "speed"). Methamphetamine is highly addictive. The street drug called crystal meth is a crystallized form of methamphetamine that is smoked. Most people who abuse amphetamines get them from health care providers. Common medical uses of amphetamines are to suppress appetite and to treat symptoms of attention deficit hyperactivity disorder.

Amphetamines raise heart rate, increase motivation, and elevate mood. The effects vary with dosage and manner of use, but other short-term effects may include insomnia, stomach distress, headaches, decreased libido, and difficulty concentrating. Long-term use can lead to severe depression, paranoia, loss of control over one's behavior, and, in some cases, amphetamine psychosis, a condition marked by hallucinations. Withdrawal from chronic amphetamine use creates unpleasant symptoms, such as fatigue, anxiety and depression, hunger, overeating, and disordered thought and behavior.

Ecstasy   The psychoactive drug MDMA, also known as ecstasy, is chemically similar to both methamphetamine and the active ingredient in hallucinogenic mushrooms, making it both a stimulant and a mild hallucinogen. At moderate to high doses, MDMA produces mild sensory hallucinations as well physiological arousal. It is sometimes called "the love drug" because it produces feelings of euphoria, warmth, and connectedness with others. Among friends, it dissolves interpersonal barriers and produces feelings of affection and a desire to touch and hug. This effect may be why MDMA became popular in dance clubs.

The dangers of MDMA include increased risk of depression with repeated use, slower processing times on cognitive tasks, and greater impulsivity (Halpern et al., 2004). Long-term effects include persistent mental deficits, low mood, and serotonin deficiencies in certain areas of the brain (Thomasius et al., 2006).

hallucinogens
substances that create distorted perceptions of reality ranging from mild to extreme.

HALLUCINOGENS

The third major class of psychoactive drugs is the hallucinogens. As the name implies, **hallucinogens** create distorted perceptions of reality ranging from mild to extreme. Sometimes, they also alter thought and mood. There are numerous hallucinogens, but we will discuss only marijuana and LSD.

In light of marijuana's known effectiveness in treating certain medical conditions, a number of states have decriminalized marijuana use for medical purposes. California, where Jeff Braun runs a cannibis dispensary, allows patients with a doctor's recommendation to obtain marijuana for personal use.

Marijuana

Marijuana Marijuana comes from the blossoms and leaves of the *Cannabis sativa* plant. People use the hemp fibers for clothing and other practical goods. They use the blossoms to alter consciousness and for medicinal properties. The active ingredient in cannabis is tetrahydrocannibinol (THC), a plant cannabinoid, which affects the brain and body when people eat or smoke it. Marijuana alters mood to create euphoria and changes perception, especially one's perception of time and food. It makes time appear to slow down and makes food more desirable (Crystal, Maxwell, & Hohmann, 2003; Nicoll & Alger, 2004). Marijuana is classified as a hallucinogen, although people rarely experience hallucinations when using low or moderate doses. Such experiences occur more readily when people eat it.

Marijuana is not addictive in the physiological sense; that is, it does not lead to physical dependence and withdrawal symptoms the way that nicotine and heroin do. But in the course of long-term habitual use, people develop cravings for marijuana when they are without it and this craving has a physiological basis (Wölfling, Flor, & Grüsser, 2008). People can become psychologically dependent on marijuana or use it compulsively.

Many researchers have argued that regular marijuana smoking increases risk for lung cancer, as marijuana smoke contains many of the same cancer-causing agents as cigarette smoke (Tashkin et al., 2002). A recent large-scale study, however, found no increased risk of lung cancer among heavy marijuana smokers compared to nonsmokers, but researchers need to conduct more research on this topic (Tashkin, 2006). Heavy marijuana smoking does increase the likelihood of a variety of respiratory illnesses, can cause immune system impairment, and appears to lead to memory problems (Kanayama et al., 2004; Tashkin et al., 2002). Regular marijuana use is common in adolescents who later develop schizophrenia, which has led some people to suggest a link between marijuana use and schizophrenia in people who might be genetically predisposed to this disorder (Arseneault et al., 2004).

endo-cannabinoids
natural, marijuana-like substances produced by the body.

Contrary to government reports that marijuana has no medical value, marijuana and the **endocannabinoids,** a class of marijuana-like chemicals produced by our own body, offer promise for medical treatment of various physical and even some psychological disorders ("Marijuana Research," 2004; Nicoll & Alger, 2004). For instance, marijuana is known for its effective prevention and treatment of nausea. As such, it has been recommended and prescribed for people who suffer chemotherapy-related nausea or the involuntary weight loss due to AIDS. Research shows that marijuana may help people eat not by increasing appetite, but by making food appear more appealing (Nicoll & Alger, 2004). Additionally, marijuana and its derivatives may be helpful for the treatment of pain. Marijuana-activated receptors in brain areas modulate pain and may work more safely and more effectively than opioids (Hohmann et al., 2005).

LSD LSD (lysergic acid diethylamide-25), or "acid," is a synthesized form of lysergic acid, which is derived from the grain fungus ergot. People notice dramatic changes in conscious experience when they ingest LSD. These experiences include altered visual perceptions (such as seeing the tracks that your hand makes when you move it through the air or the lines dance about on a page), enhanced color perception, hallucinations, and synesthesia, which is when we "see" sounds or "hear" visual images. Neurochemically, LSD appears to work by increasing the levels of the neurotransmitters dopamine and serotonin. Serotonin activity, in turn, increases the excitatory neurotransmitter glutamate, which may play a role in creating hallucinations (Marek & Aghajanian, 1996; Scruggs, Schmidt, & Deutch, 2003).

The known side effects from LSD include increased body temperature, increased blood pressure, insomnia, and psychosis-like symptoms in some people. Because it can temporarily separate a person from reality, for some people LSD use can lead to panic and negative experiences, known as bad trips. For other people, it can have the opposite effect and lead to very profound, life-altering experiences (Strassman, 1984; Weil & Rosen, 1998).

quick quiz 6.6: Altering Consciousness with Drugs

1. Even though it can make people feel more aroused in social settings, this popular drug is a depressant:
   a. alcohol
   b. heroin
   c. cocaine
   d. marijuana

2. This stimulant can be as addictive as heroin:
   a. caffeine
   b. ecstasy
   c. nicotine
   d. morphine

Answers can be found at the end of the chapter.

making connections
in consciousness

Brain Injury Revisited

Remember David? Today, more than a decade after his brain injury, David functions pretty well. His most profound deficits are problems with consciousness that affect attention, memory, and learning. By revisiting David's situation and the effects of brain injury on consciousness in general, we can integrate many of the topics addressed in this chapter.

David moved through various stages of conscious awareness in his first year of recovery. He went from comatose to vegetative to responsive in 5 months, but even when he was responding to the outside world, he was minimally conscious. In some cases of brain injury this is a transitional state to full consciousness; sometimes it is a permanent state. Fortunately, in David's case, minimal consciousness eventually led to full consciousness. His brain gradually became more and more responsive. How does this happen? We do not know for sure. What we do know is that people with damage to lower brain regions that control basic functions, such as sleep-wake cycles, are less likely to regain consciousness than are people with damage to the cerebral cortex (Laureys, 2007). David had cortical damage.

David's consciousness bears permanent scars from his injury. For example, when he is working on a task, David can suddenly become distracted and forget what he is doing. We all experience this kind of distraction from time to time, but for David it can be disabling. He might be emptying the dishwasher and overhear someone saying something about baseball. Hearing the word *baseball*, David might look up and—as a fanatic about baseball statistics—suddenly have some thought about baseball. He will then ask Greg if he knew, say, that Joe DiMaggio had a lifetime fielding percentage of .978. Then he'll head to his room to send an e-mail to his other brother about the same topic. Meanwhile, the dishwasher remains unemptied. By the time he's finished sending the e-mail, David has forgotten all about the dishwasher.

Some researchers attribute such distractibility to problems with selective attention. Indeed, David has a hard time staying on task and filtering out or setting aside information to deal with at a later time. As soon as he heard "baseball," David thought of Joe DiMaggio and simply had to talk about him. He couldn't set the topic aside briefly. As a result, he lost the ability to continue unloading the dishwasher. Distractibility is a common problem for people with brain injury. People with brain damage, especially to the frontal lobes, have trouble blocking out extraneous information and using selective attention to stay on task (Ries & Marks, 2005). Some studies show that such individuals perform poorly on the Stroop test, for example, possibly because it takes them longer to process information overall (Mathias & Wheaton, 2007). For David, a related problem is an inability to concentrate on one thing for any extended period of time. That is, he shows deficits in sustained attention. Research confirms that, in general, people with traumatic brain injury have deficits in sustained attention (Mathias & Wheaton, 2007).

Sleeping and dreaming may also change with brain injury. In fact,

how people sleep while comatose or vegetative may be an important predictor of recovery. People in coma, who show more organized EEG patterns during sleep, have less disability later and a greater likelihood of survival than those whose brain patterns are less organized while sleeping (Valente et al., 2002). After they have regained consciousness, sleep and wakefulness may be disrupted. David's sleep is not normal. He suffers from hypersomnia, or excessive sleeping. Sometimes he sleeps 14 hours a day; other times he has trouble sleeping at night and naps frequently throughout the day. Insomnia and chronic fatigue are also common in people with traumatic brain injury (Ouellet & Morin, 2006; Ouellet, Beaulieu-Bonneau, & Morin, 2006).

Brain injury can also lead to disruptions in dreaming, probably as a consequence of disordered sleep, though this doesn't seem to be a problem for David. It may depend on the location of the brain injury. Some people who sleep normally following traumatic brain injury nevertheless have problems with dreaming, indicating that different areas of the brain may be responsible for sleeping and dreaming. People with damage to the association cortex and the limbic system and areas around it or the links between these areas show the greatest dreaming deficits and, in some cases, a total absence of dreaming (Domhoff, 2001; Solms, 2000). Although not dreaming might seem insignificant, often people who experience a total lack of dreaming due to brain injury also lack "initiative, curiosity, and fantasy" in waking life (Domhoff, 2001, p. 16).

Lastly, drug use and abuse can occur in people who are coping with the challenges of a brain injury. It is most common among those who experience depression and anxiety (Anson & Ponsford, 2006).

quick quiz 6.7: Making Connections in Consciousness

1. Since his accident, David, like many people with brain injury, experiences an overwhelming need for sleep called
   a. somnambulism
   b. night terrors
   c. circadian flux
   d. hypersomnia

2. People with brain damage, especially to the frontal lobes, have trouble with selective attention. This problem leads to much _____ in daily life.
   a. fatigue
   b. distractibility
   c. amnesia
   d. confabulation

Answers can be found at the end of the chapter.

chapter **review**

WHAT IS CONSCIOUSNESS?

- Consciousness is an awareness of one's surroundings and of what's in one's mind at a given moment. It is also that limited portion of the mind of which we are aware at any given moment, sometimes called a global workspace.

TWO DIMENSIONS OF CONSCIOUSNESS: WAKEFULNESS AND AWARENESS

- Consciousness has two aspects: the degree to which we are awake and the degree to which we are aware.

- Three levels of consciousness stem from these two dimensions. First, minimal consciousness refers to states when people are barely awake or aware, such as coma and vegetative states. Second, moderate consciousness includes phenomena such as being preconscious, having words on the tip of the tongue, and sleeping and dreaming. Third, full consciousness is a high degree of wakefulness and awareness and ranges from normal waking states to states of flow and mindfulness.

ATTENTION: FOCUSING CONSCIOUSNESS

- Attention is focused awareness. Selective attention is the process by which we filter out unwanted stimuli while focusing on other stimuli. Selective attention can result in inattentional blindness, the failure to notice the unexpected. Sustained attention is the ability to stay focused on one thing.

TRAINING CONSCIOUSNESS: MEDITATION

- Meditation is a form of mental training that can be used to calm the mind, stabilize concentration, or enhance awareness of the present moment.

- Evidence from brain-imaging studies suggests that meditation has lasting effects on mood, concentration, and learning.

SLEEPING AND DREAMING

- Four stages of sleep are characterized by different EEG patterns. We move through sleep stages 1–4 roughly once every 90 minutes during the night. Rapid eye movement (REM) sleep occurs only during Stage 1 sleep, when most dreaming occurs. Most sleep consists of non-REM sleep.

- Sleep is important for three major restorative processes: neuronal growth, memory consolidation, and the formation of enzymes that protect against cellular damage.

- Sleep disorders affect about 20% of the U.S. population. Insomnia, apnea, sleepwalking, and hypersomnia are the most common sleep disorders.

- Dreams consist of images, thoughts, and feelings that we experience while we sleep. Freud maintained that dreams are attempts to fulfill unconscious wishes. A biological theory of dreams, AIM, argues that dreaming is the result of moderate levels of brain activation and internal focus, coupled with looseness of thought. The cognitive view argues that dreams do not differ greatly from normal waking forms of thinking, as seen most clearly in lucid dreaming.

HYPNOSIS

- Hypnosis is a state of mind that occurs naturally and is established by compliance with instructions. It is characterized by focused attention, suggestibility, absorption, lack of voluntary control over behavior, and suspension of critical faculties of mind.

- Research not only shows that hypnosis has a real physiological and neurological basis, but also points to ways that hypnosis may serve as a model for understanding attention.

ALTERING CONSCIOUSNESS WITH DRUGS

- A psychoactive drug is a naturally occurring or synthesized substance that produces qualitative changes in conscious experience. The three major categories of psychoactive drugs are depressants, stimulants, and hallucinogens.

- Depressants decrease central nervous system activity. Alcohol, sedatives, and opioids are all depressants. Typically, people develop tolerance for these drugs quickly, withdrawal is unpleasant, and the risk of overdose is high.

- Stimulants increase central nervous system activity. The most commonly used stimulants are caffeine and nicotine. Cocaine, amphetamines, and ecstasy all have stronger stimulant properties than caffeine and nicotine and carry a high risk of abuse and physical and psychological problems.

- Hallucinogens create altered sensations and perceptions. The two most widely known examples are marijuana and LSD. Heavy marijuana smoking increases the risk of respiratory ailments, impairs immune system functioning, and can lead to memory problems. Marijuana mimics the effects of endocannabinoids, pain-relieving substances produced in the body.

MAKING CONNECTIONS IN CONSCIOUSNESS

- Brain injury can affect many different aspects of consciousness, depending on the location and extent of the damage.

- As happened to David, brain damage interferes with selective attention, creating difficulties with staying on task, as well as with sleep and dreaming.

key **terms**

AIM, p. 237

alpha waves, p. 231

attention, p. 221

awareness, p. 218

beta waves, p. 231

circadian rhythms, p. 230

coma, p. 219

consciousness, p. 217

delta waves, p. 232

depressants, p. 243

dreams, p. 236

endocannabinoids, p. 249

hallucinogens, p. 248

hypersomnia, p. 236

hypnosis, p. 238

insomnia, p. 235

latent level, p. 236

manifest level, p. 236

meditation, p. 226

mindfulness, p. 221

narcolepsy, p. 235

non-REM, p. 231

psychoactive drugs, p. 241

rapid eye movements (REM), p. 231

selective attention, p. 222

sleep apnea, p. 235

sleepwalking, p. 235

stimulants, p. 246

Stroop effect, p. 240

sustained attention, p. 224

theta waves, p. 232

vegetative state, p. 219

wakefulness, p. 218

quick quiz **answers**

Quick Quiz 6.1: 1. d   2. c   Quick Quiz 6.2: 1. a   2. b   Quick Quiz 6.3: 1. d   2. a
Quick Quiz 6.4: 1. a   2. d   3. b   4. c   Quick Quiz 6.5: 1. a   2. d   Quick Quiz 6.6: 1. a   2. b
Quick Quiz 6.7: 1. d   2. b

memory

preview
questions

1 *Why can you remember your first date but not the phone number you heard 5 minutes ago?*

2 *Where and how does your brain store memories?*

3 *Why do different people have different memories of the same event?*

4 *How can studying this chapter help you get good grades?*

Many of us have vivid memories from when we were very young. Jean Piaget, the renowned child psychologist whose work is discussed in Chapter 5, recalled a harrowing experience from when he was only two. This is his recollection:

I was sitting in my pram [carriage], which my nurse was pushing in the Champs-Élysées, when a man tried to kidnap me. I was held by the strap fastened around me while my nurse bravely tried to stand between me and the thief. She received various scratches, and I can still see vaguely those on her face. Then a crowd gathered, a policeman with a short cloak and a white baton came up, and the man took to his heels. I can still see the whole scene. . . . (Piaget, 1962, p. 187)

Piaget recalled this event from his childhood clearly, but it never happened. No one ever tried to kidnap him. Apparently, Piaget had been told about this situation by his parents and his nurse (who was like a nanny). When Piaget was 15, the nurse confessed that she ▶

▶ had made up the whole thing; she had told his parents the story to improve their opinion of her. Meanwhile, Piaget had made it part of his own recollections, with vivid sensory details of the sights and sounds of the event, as though he had experienced every moment of it.

How is it that we can remember something that probably never happened? Furthermore, if memory can fool us into thinking we had an experience we didn't have, how reliable are our memories of real events and important information? In this chapter, as we discuss different types of memory, how we form memories, and the nature of forgetting, we also examine some of the research directed at answering these questions about memory. We will come to understand, as Piaget's false memory attests, that memory is not like a photographic image of the things we have experienced.

Without memory we would be stuck forever in the present, unable to learn anything or to adapt to a changing

chapter
outline

environment. The ability to remember not only makes us who we are, but is also the foundation of intelligence, learning, and thought. Although there is still much to learn about memory and the mechanisms involved in making and retaining memories, researchers agree on at least three attributes of memory:

1. There are three types of memory (sensory, short-term, and long-term) that last for different amounts of time.
2. Different memory systems involve different areas of the brain.
3. We reconstruct memories from our past experiences, rather than recording accurate images of what has happened.

We will explore each of these attributes in turn. ▪

Three Types of Memory

When he was 9 years old, a boy known as H. M. was hit by a bicyclist. He suffered a brain injury that resulted in severe epileptic seizures. To stop these seizures, doctors removed the hippocampus on both sides of H. M.'s brain as well as the adjoining brain structures. The seizures stopped, but at quite a cost: H. M. lost the ability to form new memories. He lived forever in the present. Brenda Milner, the neuropsychologist who examined H. M. regularly for more than 30 years, had to introduce herself each time they met! What makes H. M.'s story even more remarkable is that most of the memories he had formed prior to the surgery remained intact.

Milner's (1962) work with H. M. provided the first documented evidence of distinct kinds of memory in operation. For example, she gave H. M. a standard learning task, in which he had to trace inside the outline

Brenda Milner

1 **research question**

Can a person who cannot form new long-term memories learn to do a new task?

2 **method**

As part of her case study of H.M., who lost the ability to form new memories following the removal of his hippocampus, the neuropsychologist Brenda Milner (1962) asked H.M. to perform a mirror tracing task. The goal was to trace within the two lines of the star, while viewing only the reverse image of the star in a mirror. In other words, the image was inverted, so each time H.M. moved his hand in one direction, the movement of his hand in the mirror went in the opposite direction. H.M. was asked to perform this task up to 10 times each day for three days. An error was counted each time H.M. went outside the lines. H.M.'s drawings improved with time, even though he could not recall ever doing the task before.

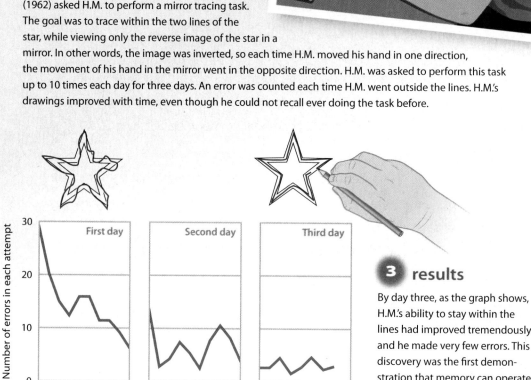

3 **results**

By day three, as the graph shows, H.M.'s ability to stay within the lines had improved tremendously, and he made very few errors. This discovery was the first demonstration that memory can operate outside conscious awareness.

4 **conclusion**

Many different parts of our brain are involved in learning, and conscious awareness is not required for all learning.

FIGURE **7.1**

A CASE STUDY OF MEMORY WITHOUT RECOLLECTION. Although H. M.'s memory problems prevented him from recalling ever having completed this star tracing task, some part of his brain clearly did "recall" the task. He got better and better at it over time. (*Source:* Kandel, Kupferman, & Iverson [2000]. Learning and memory. In E. Kandel, J. H. Schwartz, & T. M. Jessell [Eds.]. *Principles of neural science* [4th ed.] [pp. 1227–1246] McGraw-Hill.)

of a star while looking at the star in a mirror (see Figure 7.1). This task is particularly difficult because the mirror image of every movement is reversed. True to Milner's expectations, H. M. had no recollection of doing this task even though he had been trained on it for days and even though he did it up to 10 times in one day. Each time he did it, H. M. said that it was a completely new task. Yet some

memory
the ability to store
and use informa-
tion; also the
store of what has
been learned and
remembered.

**three-stage
model of
memory**
classification of
memories based
on duration as sen-
sory, short-term,
and long-term.

sensory memory
the part of memory
that holds informa-
tion in its original
sensory form for a
very brief period of
time, usually about
a half a second or
less.

**short-term
memory**
the part of memory
that temporar-
ily (for 2 to 30
seconds) stores a
limited amount
of information
before it is either
transferred to
long-term storage
or forgotten.

**long-term
memory**
the part of memory
that has the capac-
ity to store a vast
amount of informa-
tion for as little as
30 seconds and as
long as a lifetime.

part of his brain knew and remembered the task, because the drawings improved the more often he worked on them. Although H. M. may have lost the ability to form new memories of his experiences, some type of memory formation had to have occurred, or he would not have improved on the task.

How might one explain this contradictory finding? As H. M.'s case illustrates, being unable to consciously recall experiences doesn't mean there is no memory of an event. In fact, we humans are incapable of intentionally bringing into awareness much of what we remember, such as memories that have been put away for some time or memories for how to do things, like tie one's shoes or ride a bike. Many things we know are outside of conscious awareness. Most generally, **memory** is simply the ability to store and use information. It need not be a conscious recollection.

Some memories last much longer than others. The **three-stage model of memory** classifies three types of memories based on how long the memories last: sensory memory, short-term memory, and long-term memory (Atkinson & Shiffrin, 1971). **Sensory memory** holds information in its original sensory form for a very brief period of time, usually about a half a second or less. **Short-term memory** temporarily stores a limited amount of information before it is either transferred to long-term storage or forgotten. Information stays in short-term memory for 2 to 30 seconds—about long enough to remember a phone number before you dial it. **Long-term memory** has the capacity to store a vast amount of information for as little as 30 seconds and as long as a lifetime. This is where memories of your first pet and how to read reside. As the three-stage model suggests, memory formation is an active, dynamic process. Let's look at the stages of memory in more depth.

SENSORY MEMORY

As we interact with the world, our sensory systems are stimulated—we may smell, taste, feel, see, or hear an experience. In fact, two or more sensory systems may contribute information about a single experience, as when we dig into a bag of buttery popcorn while watching a scary movie. In Chapter 4, we saw that sensory neurons respond to sensory stimuli by sending signals to the brain for processing. Sensory memory is made up of the brief traces of a sensation left by the firing of neurons in the brain. These traces last from less than a half a second up to 2 or 3 seconds. Sensation is the first step toward the creation of a long-term memory.

Because seeing and hearing are key sources of information for humans, the two kinds of sensory memory that have received the most attention from memory researchers are iconic and auditory memory (Craik, 1979). *Iconic memory* is a brief visual record left on the retina of the eye, whereas *echoic memory* is short-term retention of sounds.

In a simple laboratory demonstration of iconic memory, four digits, such as 5 4 7 1, are flashed on a computer screen for 30 milliseconds. (A millisecond is a thousandth of a second.) Then the screen goes blank. At 30 milliseconds, the information is barely perceived at all. Yet, when a blank screen follows the numbers, most people have no trouble recalling them. However, if the same four digits are followed on the screen by # # # #, people have a lot of trouble recalling any digits and often report that they did not see any digits at all (Thompson & Madigan, 2005). The presentation of the symbols interferes with the

nature & nurture

What we hear, see, touch, taste, and smell forms brief traces in our brain. If we attend to these sensory traces, they make lasting changes in our brain by becoming either short- or long-term memories.

How good are you at remembering names of people after meeting them for the first time? Unless you rehearse them, names often don't make the transition to long-term memory.

Without working memory, we wouldn't be able to keep in mind the information needed to solve puzzles and other problems at hand.

ability to recall the digits. This demonstration suggests that all sensory memory traces are preserved for very short periods of time and yet are very fragile.

SHORT-TERM OR WORKING MEMORY

We often need to stay focused on something temporarily to solve a problem or perform a task, such as getting to a restaurant after just hearing the directions on the phone. To do so, we put our short-term memory to work. Because short-term memory is a place to temporarily store information we need while working on a problem, psychologists also refer to it as working memory. **Working memory** is the part of memory required to attend to and solve a problem at hand. When we no longer need the information, we forget it. Although we will use the terms *short-term memory* and *working memory* interchangeably, bear in mind that *short-term memory* emphasizes the duration of this type of memory, while the phrase *working memory* emphasizes its function.

Examples of tasks that involve short-term or working memory are reading, talking, and listening to someone speak. We use working memory to keep track of what we have just read or what we are about to say, but for only a brief period of time. Working memories can be transferred to long-term memory if they are practiced; otherwise, they are lost.

working memory
the part of memory required to attend to and solve a problem at hand; often used interchangeably with *short-term memory.*

Short-Term Memory Capacity Most of us hear someone's phone number, repeat it a few times, and then place the call. The number of items that can be held in short-term memory is called short-term memory capacity, and it is limited to about 7 items (Feldman-Barrett, Tugade, & Engle, 2004; Miller 1956). It is not a coincidence that local phone numbers in this country contain 7 digits. The short-term memory capacity of most people is between 5 and 9 units of letters, digits, or chunks of information, but there are substantial individual differences in this capacity. Some people struggle with 3 or 4 bits of information, whereas others easily handle 11 or 12 (Baddeley, 2003).

One of the best ways to increase short-term memory capacity is to transform what you want to remember into a smaller set of meaningful units or chunks, a process known as **chunking** (Thompson & Madigan, 2005). For example, 4155557982 is much more difficult to remember than the chunks of (415) 555-7982. Social Security numbers follow the same idea: 555-66-8888 is easier to remember than 555668888.

How Short-Term Memory Works
One researcher, Alan Baddeley (2003, 2007), has suggested that working memory consists of three distinct processes: *attending* to a stimulus, *storing* information about the stimulus, and *rehearsing* the stored process to help solve a problem. In Baddeley's model, the first process, focusing and switching attention, is carried out by a master attentional control system. This attention system is supported by three temporary storage systems, one for sounds and language (phonological), one for images and spatial relations (visuospatial), and one that connects the two storage systems, interacts with long-term memory, and provides temporary storage for specific events (buffer) (see Figure 7.2).

The *central executive* decides where to focus attention and selectively hones in on specific aspects of a stimulus. Attention allows us to focus on the task at hand and develop a plan for solving a problem. We are bombarded by dozens of sensations every second. How do we know which are important and deserve our attention and which we can ignore? According to Baddeley's model, children and people with brain injuries (at least those with frontal lobe damage) have a difficult time screening out irrelevant information because they lack well-developed or fully functioning central executives.

THE KIND OF THING YOU DON'T WANT TO HEAR HALFWAY THROUGH AN EXPERIMENTAL GAME OF MEMORY CHESS BETWEEN TWO OF THE WORLD'S MOST NOTED MEMORY EXPERTS

KING'S KNIGHT TO QUEEN THREE

AM I BLACK OR WHITE?

www.mrboffo.com

Joe Martin. Used with permission.

Once information is taken in and we attend to it, it is sent to a temporary store: the *phonological loop* if it is sound or linguistic information, the *visuospatial sketch pad* if it is visual or spatial information, or the *episodic buffer* if it is a specific event or experience. The *phonological loop* assists the central executive by providing extra storage for a limited number of digits or words for up to 30 seconds at a time. The storage system allows us to hold memory traces for a few seconds before they fade.

The *visuospatial sketch pad,* as the name implies, briefly provides storage for visual and spatial sensations, such as images, photos, scenes, or three-dimensional objects. Like verbal information stored in the phonological loop, a visual image created on the visuospatial sketch pad lasts only seconds before it fades—unless we attend to it and process it more deeply. Normally we can hold a small number of images (three or four) in short-term storage. An example would be a cognitive map that you visualize while someone is giving you directions to an unfamiliar location. If you are going to actually find your way there, however, you have to move this map from sensory memory to short-term memory by verbalizing and rehearsing the directions ("left at the stop sign, right at the Quicki-

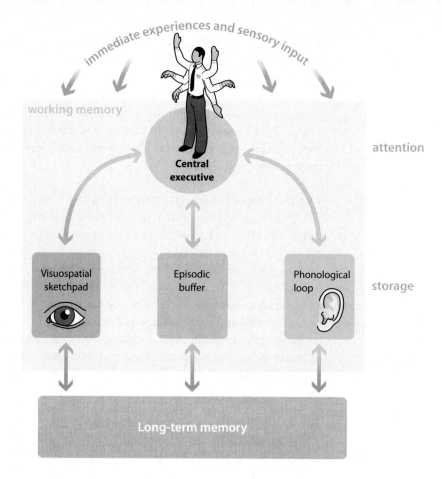

FIGURE **7.2**

BADDELEY'S MODEL OF SHORT-TERM MEMORY. The four components of short-term memory are the central executive, which focuses attention, and three storage systems (visuospatial sketchpad, episodic buffer, and phonological loop). Once our attention is focused on something, we need short-term places to store the relevant information. Images and spatial relations are stored in one storage center; events and experiences in another; and language and sounds in another. (*Source:* Baddeley, 2003.)

Mart . . ."). Depending on how complex the directions are, you might even move them to long-term memory. The *episodic buffer* is a temporary store for information that will become long-term memories of specific events. You can think of the episodic buffer like a buffer in your computer software. When you type something in a word processing program like Microsoft Word, the letters typed reside in a temporary store until you save the material. That temporary store is a buffer. It will not be saved to your hard disk unless you tell Word to save it. Saving it transfers the material from the buffer into long-term memory.

The three storage systems each require rehearsal if the information is to be remembered for any length of time. **Rehearsal** is the process of reciting or practicing material repeatedly. In contrast to the storage function of short-term memory, the rehearsal system enables us to repeat the information to ourselves as long as we need to retain it. Storing and recalling a shopping list is an everyday example of the function of the phonological loop. When we want to remember the list long enough to use it, we typically rehearse it by repeating it to ourselves. As long as we keep rehearsing it, we will be able to recall it. If we continue rehearsing it, after more than a minute or two, the information might make the transition to long-term memory. Otherwise, it will be lost.

The Serial Position Effect   In the late 19th century, Mary Whiton Calkins observed an interesting phenomenon of short-term memory. When learning a list

rehearsal
the process of repeatedly practicing material so that it enters long-term memory.

of items, people are better able to recall items at the beginning and end of the list; they tend to forget the items in the middle (Calkins, 1898; Madigan & O'Hara, 1992). This effect is known as the **serial position effect.**

In studies of the serial position effect, participants might be presented with a list of 15 words read at 1-second intervals. They would be told in advance that they would be asked to recall as many as they could, in any order. Typically, about 50% of the participants recall the first 2 words on the list, about 50–75% recall words near the end of the list, and about 90–95% of participants recall the last 2 words on the list. So recall for the beginning and end of the list is pretty good, but only about 25% of the participants recall words in the middle of the list. The tendency to preferentially recall items at the beginning of a list is known as the *primacy effect;* whereas recall for items at the end of a list is known as the *recency effect* (see Figure 7.3).

The main explanation offered for the primacy effect is that the items in the beginning of the list are quickly rehearsed and transferred to long-term memory storage. So they are remembered. The items in the middle of the list haven't made that trip to long-term memory yet. The recency effect results from those items at the end still being held in short-term memory. They are therefore accessible. The items in the middle cannot be rehearsed as more and more items are being added to the list. These new items interfere with rehearsal of those presented before, which can prevent long-term storage. For instance, if people hear 15 words and are asked to say three digits immediately after the 15th word is read, then words in the 10th through 15th places are no better recalled than words in the 5th through 9th places (about 25% recall). Recall is superior without the interfering task (Thompson & Madigan, 2005). Recent neuroimaging data support the idea that the serial position effect results from both short-term and long-term memory processes (Talmi et al., 2005).

Because of the serial position effect, we are more likely to remember the first and last parts of a book, TV program, movie, or commercial than to recall the middle. Writers, directors, and politicians all know about this tendency, either

serial position effect
the tendency to have better recall for items in a list according to their position in the list.

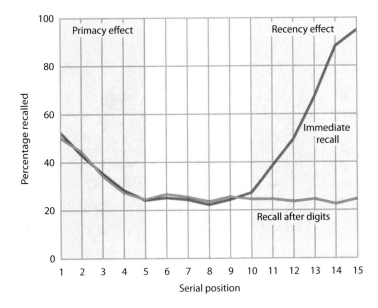

FIGURE **7.3**

SERIAL POSITION EFFECTS AND RECALL. People have the best recall of items that are in the beginning of a series (primacy) or at the end of a series (recency). The recency effects go away if people are given a distracting task such as having to recall digits before recalling the words in a list. (*Source:* Thompson & Madigan, 2005.)

consciously or not, and try to place the most important information near the beginning and end of their works.

LONG-TERM MEMORY

In April 2006, on the centennial of the 1906 San Francisco earthquake, a 109-year-old survivor reported these two memories from that disaster: "I remember the smell of the smoke [from the fires afterward] . . . and the cow running down California Street with its tail in the air" (Nolte & Yollin, 2006). Memories that are 100 years old definitely qualify as long-term memories! Yet, recalling our definition of long-term memory as "any information that is stored for at least 30 to 40 seconds and up to a lifetime," things that you remember from earlier today—the topic of a psychology lecture, for example—are also in long-term storage. So is information you remember for only a few weeks, such as material for your next midterm exam. Will you remember the material you learned in this course 20 years from now? That depends on a number of factors, but primarily it depends on how often you use or rehearse the information.

Long-term memory is what most people think of when they think of memory. Long-term memory is also the most complex form of memory: there are two distinct kinds and four distinct stages of processing.

Types of Long-Term Memory People often forget specific things, but they typically do not forget how to tie their shoes, ride a bike, or how even to add 6 to 12. How is it possible that a person could forget names but almost never forget skills such as simple arithmetic? The short answer is that there is more than one type of memory, and the types operate differently. At the broadest level, there are two types: implicit and explicit memory. How to ride a bike or add is implicit; where you left your car keys is explicit. H. M.'s case, described at the beginning of the chapter, is important partly because it helped psychologists see the distinction between implicit and explicit memory.

Implicit Memory. When we know or remember something but don't consciously know we remember it, we are tapping into **implicit memory.** Implicit memory is also known as *nondeclarative memory*, because we cannot directly recall this type of memory. Instead, implicit memory is based on prior experience, and it is the place where we store knowledge of previous experience, such as skills that we perform automatically once we have mastered them—how to ride a bicycle, for instance. If asked to describe how we perform these skills, we can't do so very well. Although we can perform many skills automatically, we don't have ready access

implicit memory kind of memory made up of knowledge based on previous experience, such as skills that we perform automatically once we have mastered them; resides outside conscious awareness.

Once learned, skills for riding a bicycle become implicit memories that we recall without effort.

procedural memory
kind of memory made up of implicit knowledge for almost any behavior or physical skill we have learned.

priming
a kind of implicit memory that arises when recall is improved by earlier exposure to the same or similar stimuli.

to the memory of the many steps they require (Kandel, Kupfermann, & Iversen, 2000).

Implicit memory includes procedural memory and priming. **Procedural memory** refers to knowledge we hold for almost any behavior or physical skill we learn, whether it is how to play golf, ride a bike, drive a car, or tie a shoe. The star-tracing task that H. M. worked on (Figure 7.1) is another example of procedural memory. Part of his brain remembered the mirror task because his performance improved each time he did it. The part of his brain responsible for conscious recall did not remember the task, however.

Priming is a kind of implicit memory that occurs when recall is improved by prior exposure to the same or similar stimuli. In one laboratory demonstration of priming, people with memory problems (amnesia group) were compared to individuals without such problems (comparison group) on a word-learning task. When asked to recall a list of words they were exposed to, people in the amnesia group demonstrated much less recall than the comparison group (see Figure 7.4). But when they were given the first three letters of the words as a prime, or memory aid, the amnesia group performed at least as well as the comparison group (Squire, 1987). What is intriguing about this outcome is that the amnesia group had no conscious recollection of having seen the words before. Like H. M., who was primed by his previous learning of the star-tracing task, people with severe long-term memory problems show a remarkable ability to recall words if they have been primed.

Explicit Memory. **Explicit memory** is the conscious recall of facts and events. Explicit memory is sometimes called *declarative memory* because it refers to memories that can be deliberately accessed or *declared*. There are two distinct kinds of explicit memory: semantic and episodic (Tulving, 1972, 1985).

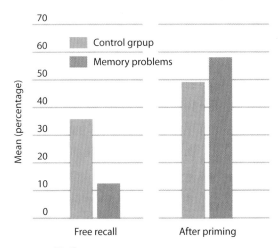

FIGURE **7.4**

RECALL OF WORDS WITH AND WITHOUT PRIMING. With no priming, recall by people with memory problems is impaired. They recall only about 10% of the words compared to about 35% for those without memory problems. Those with memory problems, however, outperform those without memory problems after they have been primed (given the first three letters of the word). (*Source:* Squire, 1987.)

connection
Besides the ability to consciously recall a memory, what other forms of consciousness affect our behavior without our knowing it?
See Chapter 6, p. 218.

explicit memory
knowledge that consists of the conscious recall of facts and events; also known as declarative memory.

How do you spell . . . ? This spelling bee contestant is relying on her semantic memory to spell challenging words correctly.

semantic memory
form of memory that recalls facts and general knowledge, such as what we learn in school.

episodic memory
form of memory that recalls the experiences we have had.

Semantic memory is our memory for facts and knowledge, such as what we learn in school. **Episodic memory** is our memory for the experiences we have had. Remembering that Baton Rouge is the capital of Louisiana is an example of semantic memory, whereas remembering your high school graduation would be an episodic memory. Episodic memories are more personal than semantic memories.

Stages in Long-Term Memory For sensory input to make the transition from sensory memory to short-term memory and then to long-term memory, it must go through four processing stages: encoding, consolidation, storage, and retrieval. Relatively few experiences survive this process, but those that do can become lifelong memories. These four stages occur for implicit and explicit memories alike, but they are more typical of explicit long-term memory, because we more consciously rehearse and retrieve this type of memory.

Images associated with events like high school graduation are stored temporarily by the visuospatial sketch pad in short-term memory before making the trip to long-term memory. The emotions that accompany such occasions increase the likelihood that our memories of them will last a lifetime.

encoding
the process by which the brain attends to, takes in, and integrates new information; the first stage of long-term memory formation.

Encoding. **Encoding** is the means by which we attend to, take in, and process new information. This phase is absolutely crucial for storage in long-term memory. Attention drives the encoding process. If we fail to pay attention or try to multitask, an experience is not going to be processed deeply enough to be stored for a long period. In general, we remember visual images more easily than verbal descriptions (Craik, 1979). Why? One explanation is that visual images create a richer and more detailed representation in memory than words and therefore are more deeply encoded (Craik, 1979).

Psychologists describe two kinds of encoding processes: one that happens with little effort and one that takes significant effort (Hasher & Zacks, 1979). **Automatic processing** happens with little effort or conscious attention to the task. Because these experiences are automatic, our recall of them does not improve much with practice. Furthermore, they are often not processed as deeply and are less likely to be recalled later. For instance, you most likely encoded what you ate for breakfast this morning without trying, but by this evening you may have trouble recalling what you ate hours earlier. Episodic memory involves this kind of automatic processing.

automatic processing
encoding of information that occurs with little effort or conscious attention to the task.

Now think about what you learn in college. You read the textbook, attend lectures, take notes, and study those notes, usually multiple times. Before an exam, you then go over these materials again and again. Needless to say, this

Associating images with information we want to remember, such as vocabulary words, helps to encode the material more deeply.

effortful processing
encoding of information that occurs with careful attention and conscious effort.

kind of learning takes work. **Effortful processing** occurs when we carefully attend to and put conscious effort into remembering information. Effortful processing is the basis of semantic memory. Effortful processing usually involves rehearsal of the information, so that it goes from short-term to long-term memory. Interestingly, advancing age tends to lessen recall for events and experiences that require effortful processing but not automatic processing (Hasher & Zacks, 1979).

To review, memory formation starts with sensory input from the outside world (see Figure 7.5). If we do not pay attention to it, the sensation vanishes and the information is lost. If we pay attention to it, the sensation becomes a short-term memory. Once the sensation enters short-term memory, either it makes the transition to long-term memory within about 30 seconds or it disappears. If we repeat or rehearse the information actively, if we apply some other memory-enhancing technique, or if we experience a strong emotion and the information at the same time, the original sensation becomes a long-term memory.

The connection between encoding and remembering is at the core of the levels-of-processing approach to memory (Craik & Lockhart, 1972). The idea behind **levels of processing** is that the more deeply people encode information, the better they will recall it. Thomas Hyde and James Jenkins (1973) created a standard procedure for manipulating depth of processing in which they typically presented a list of about 28 words with a 5-second interval between words. To eliminate primacy and recency effects, the researchers ignored participants' recall of the first two and the last two words on the list. Excluding these 4 words left 24 possible words to be recalled. Participants heard beforehand that they would be given a list of words and should focus on a specific aspect of the words. Participants were not told that they would be asked to recall as many words as possible,

levels of processing
the concept that the more deeply people encode information, the better they will recall it.

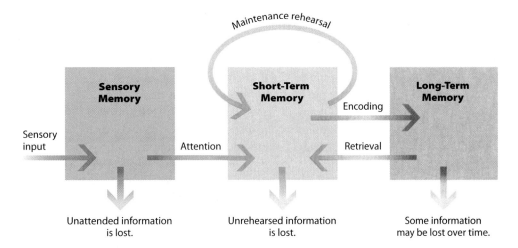

FIGURE **7.5**

THREE TYPES OF MEMORY. When our sense organs are stimulated, the nervous system forms a very brief image or trace of what we saw, heard, tasted, felt, or smelled (sensory memory). If we don't attend to it, we forget it immediately. If we do pay attention, the information is passed on to short-term memory. Here, if we attend to it only briefly, it will remain in short-term memory as long as we need it, but then will be forgotten. If we rehearse it over and over, the information is processed more deeply and passed on to long-term memory. If we encode the information deeply, it becomes a long-term memory. Some long-term memories fade or are forgotten over time. (*Source:* Atkinson & Schiffrin, 1971.)

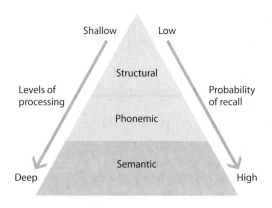

FIGURE **7.6**

**LEVELS-OF-PROCESSING MODEL OF MEMORY
AND RECALL.** The level at which we process information affects the probability of recall. The deeper we process information, the more likely we are to recall it. Structural processing is the shallowest level of processing and also the least likely to be recalled. Semantic processing is both the deepest and the most likely to be recalled. (*Source:* Craik & Lockhart, 1972.)

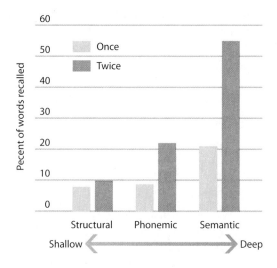

FIGURE **7.7**

RESULTS OF LEVELS OF PROCESSING AND RECALL.
These results show that the more deeply people process information, the better they recall it. If people are presented the word list twice, the effect of depth of processing on recall is even stronger. (*Source:* Craik & Tulving, 1975.)

so they were somewhat surprised when they were asked to name them.

Based on word-recall studies, researchers have identified three different levels of processing: structural, phonemic, and semantic (Craik & Tulving, 1975; Hyde & Jenkins, 1973; see Figure 7.6). *Structural processing* is the shallowest level of processing. When studying structural processing, researchers might have directed participants to focus on the structure of the word by asking questions such as "Is the word in capital letters?" To study *phonemic processing,* or midlevel processing, they asked questions to focus participants' attention on the sound of the word, such as "Does the word rhyme with _____?" *Semantic processing* is the deepest level of processing. Participants in studies of semantic processing were asked to think about the meaning of the words and answer questions such as "Would the word fit the sentence: 'He met a _____ in the street'?"

Results across many studies find the best recall when words are encoded more deeply and worse recall for words that are processed less deeply (Craik & Tulving, 1975; Hyde & Jenkins, 1973; Lockhart & Craik, 1990). Craik and Tulving (1975) conducted 10 different experiments in which they manipulated the participants' level of processing with target words (between 48 and 60 words) and found that the deeper the level of processing became, the better the recall was (see Figure 7.7). The take-away message here is that the more deeply you process material, the better you will remember it. We will come back to this point in our discussion of the role of memory in studying at the end of this chapter.

A common way to encode information deeply is to devise mnemonic (pronounced neh'-mon-ik) devices. A **mnemonic device** is a scheme that helps people remember information. Rhyming, chunking, and rehearsal are types of mnemonic devices. Others include imagery and acronyms. For example, imagery can be used to remember a set of words or a list of objects in a set order. Simply form a mental image of each word or object in a specific place along a route you know very well, such as from your home to your school. Rehearse this a few times. Then when you need to recall the word or object list, take a mental stroll along the familiar path and the visual images of the list should be relatively easy to recall (Thompson & Madigan, 2005).

mnemonic device
a method devised to help remember information, such as a rhyme or acronym.

Daniel Tammet, who can recall pi to 22,514 digits, is a mnemonist (someone who displays extraordinary memory skills). Like most mnemonists, Daniel uses his own mnemonic device: For him it is the ability to see each number as a shape in a landscape. He then simply "strolls" through that landscape and reads off the numbers, such as the digits of pi, as he sees them.

Acronyms are a type of mnemonic device. We usually create acronyms by combining the first letters of each word or object we need to remember. Acronyms work best when they form a word we can pronounce or some other meaningful unit. For example, the acronym RADAR is easier to remember than "**Ra**dio **D**etection **a**nd **R**anging" and "ROY G. BIV" is easier to remember than the colors of the rainbow "red, orange, yellow, green, blue, indigo, and violet." (And remember OPTIC from Chapter 2? That's another mnemonic device.)

You might have your own favorite mnemonic devices to help you encode material that you need to know for an exam. If you have never tried this approach to studying, you might be surprised at how much it improves memory.

Consolidation. The second stage of long-term memory formation is **consolidation,** the process of establishing, stabilizing, or solidifying a memory (Kandel, 2006; McGaugh, 2000). A consolidated memory is resistant to distraction, interference, and decay (Dubai, 2004). As we'll discuss in some detail shortly, new proteins are manufactured in the brain during long-term memory formation, and consolidation provides time for these proteins to develop. Once the proteins needed for consolidation have formed, a memory is beyond the effects of interference and decay.

consolidation
the process of establishing, stabilizing, or solidifying a memory; the second stage of long-term memory formation.

Sleep plays an important role in memory consolidation. Psychologists have long known that we recall information better after we "sleep on it" than after the same amount of time if we stay awake. Recent findings indicate that not only does sleep stabilize the memory, but it also enhances memory and makes it stronger (Walker & Stickgold, 2006). Moreover, sleep deprivation has been shown to have a detrimental effect on memory (Stickgold, 2005). We can conclude, then, that cramming all night before an exam is not the best study strategy. (We'll consider better alternatives in the "Making Connections in Memory" section at the end of this chapter.) In fact, research shows that learning over long periods of time and evenly spaced sessions leads to better recall (Kornell & Bjork, 2007).

Storage. Once memories have been encoded and consolidated, they are ready to be stored. Storing a memory is akin to putting something—say, a birthday gift purchased months ahead of time—away in a special place where you can find it later. **Storage,** the retention of memory over time, is the third stage of long-term memory formation. We organize and store memories in at least three distinct ways: in hierarchies, schemas, and networks.

storage
the retention of memory over time; the third stage of long-term memory formation.

hierarchies
a way of organizing related pieces of information from the most specific feature they have in common to the most general.

We use **hierarchies** to organize related information from the most specific feature they have in common to the most general. An example is the hierarchy human (specific), hominid (less specific), primate, mammal, and animal (general). Each step moves to a more general category in a hierarchy.

Schemas are mental frameworks that develop from our experiences with particular objects or events. They act as a filter through which we encode and organize information about our world. Once formed, schemas tell us how people, objects, or events are most likely to look or act. Because schemas help us organize and understand experiences they can also aid memory and recall. For instance, if your favorite childhood pet was a Chihuahua, your schema of Chihuahuas would be a very positive one that predisposes you to expect other Chihuahuas to act as friendly and fun-loving as yours did. Because you had so many happy experiences with your Chihuahua as a child, when you see one now you are able to most easily remember the fun experiences you had with your own pet. Likewise, because they do not fit your schema of the happy Chihuahua, you are less likely to remember the negative and aggressive experiences you may have had with your dog. For better and for worse, schemas bias our memory and perception.

schemas
mental frameworks that develop from our experiences with particular people, objects, or events.

Hierarchies and concepts bring order and organization to our perceptions and experiences. The psychological process that binds concepts together is *association*. Associations are linked together in networks by their degree of closeness or relatedness (Hopfield, 1982). An **associative network** is a chain of associations between related concepts. Each concept or association in a network is referred to as a *node*. The links between the nodes are associations. When people think of a concept, and its node is activated, they are primed and more likely to make an association to a nearby concept or node (Collins & Loftus, 1975). Figure 7.8 illustrates an associative network for the concept of fire engine. "Fire engine" activates both vehicle and color networks of association, and it may well activate others not shown here (such as emergency).

Neural networks also use networks to explain how memory works. Unlike associative networks, *neural networks* are computer models that imitate the way neurons talk to each other (Chappell & Humphreys, 1994). Neural networks have nodes too, but their nodes are not single concepts like a color or a vehicle. Rather, these nodes are information processing units. Based on the analogy of the nervous system, the nodes in a network of neurons are single cells (neurons) that can process information. The more the nodes in a neural network communicate with each other, the stronger the link between nodes. As we will discuss later in this chapter and in the next, repeated connection between neurons leads to stronger connections, and stronger memories and learning (Hebb, 1949).

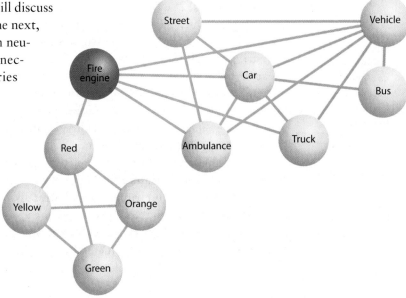

FIGURE **7.8**

ASSOCIATIVE NETWORK. Associative networks are chains of association between related concepts or nodes that get activated. The closer concepts are to each other, the more directly related they are and the more likely they are to activate the other node. The network for "fire engine" consists of a rich associative network of related concepts. (*Source:* Collins & Loftus, 1975.)

A well-known model of memory storage that integrates associative and neural networks is parallel distributed processing. *Parallel distributed processing (PDP)* models propose that associations involve the simultaneous activity of many nodes (McClelland, 1988; McClelland & Rogers, 2003; McClelland & Rumelhart, 1985). Many nodes can fire at the same time, spreading or distributing activation to other nodes in the network. This spread of activation can serve a priming function, making certain memories more likely than others to be stored. Recent work in neuroscience reveals that such PDP models may do a good job of explaining how neurons and genes actually work together to store new long-term memories (Miyashita et al., 2008).

Retrieval. The work of encoding, consolidating, and storing memories would be wasted if we could not retrieve information when we needed it. **Retrieval** is the recovery of information stored in memory. It's remembering where you put that birthday gift that you bought early—or that you even bought one—when it comes time to present it to your friend. The ease of retrieval and the time frame over which we can recall a particular event or piece of knowledge is determined by the previous stages of memory. How did we encode it? Did we consolidate it? Did we store it where we can access it? Additionally, whenever we retrieve a memory, we need to focus our attention on remembering, which requires working memory. Retrieval, attention, and working memory are related activities.

Implicit memories, such as how to ride a bicycle, are retrieved without conscious effort. Explicit memories are the ones that require conscious effort for retrieval. An example would be the date of a friend's birthday—factual information that is encoded and stored for later recall. But factual information is not always properly encoded and stored, and we cannot always retrieve it at will. A common retrieval problem is the inability to remember the name of a person only minutes after meeting him, even if we repeated his name immediately after hearing it. What most likely happens in this situation is that we fail to pay enough attention to the person's name when we first hear it and focus instead on the whole social interaction. Consequently, we do not encode, consolidate, and store the name very deeply. When we try to retrieve it, we cannot. We'll explore retrieval problems in more detail when we talk about forgetting, and later the "Making Connections in Memory" section outlines some strategies for improving retrieval.

retrieval
the recovery of information stored in memory; the fourth stage of long-term memory.

quick quiz 7.1: Three Types of Memory

1. H. M. had damage to which structure crucial for memory?
   a. hypothalamus
   b. hippocampus
   c. insula
   d. amygdala

2. The brief traces of a touch or a smell left by the firing of neurons in the brain are examples of
   a. perceptual memory
   b. long-term potentiation
   c. implicit memory
   d. sensory memory

3. What kind of memory do we use to keep someone's phone number in mind right after we've learned it?
   a. working memory
   b. iconic memory
   c. long-term memory
   d. sensory memory

4. What sort of memory allows us to perform skills such as tying our shoes automatically once we have mastered them?
   a. explicit memory
   b. declarative memory
   c. procedural memory
   d. echoic memory

5. For sensory input to make the transition from sensory memory to short-term memory to long-term memory, it must go through four processing stages:
   a. encoding, consolidation, storage, and retrieval
   b. encoding, reconstruction, storage, and retrieval
   c. encoding, consolidation, storage, and remembering
   d. encoding, reconstruction, storage, and remembering

Answers can be found at the end of the chapter.

The Biological Basis of Memory

At the beginning of this chapter we introduced H. M., who lost the ability to make new long-term memories after having his hippocampus removed. Why was he still able to retrieve memories stored before the surgery? And how was he able to learn the star-tracing task more and more rapidly each time it was presented, even though he didn't remember learning it before? The reason is that the hippocampus processes short-term memories, whereas other areas of the brain handle sensory and long-term memories.

In general, sensory memories are processed in the various sensory cortexes, short-term memory is processed in the hippocampus and frontal lobes, and long-term memories are stored in and retrieved with the help of areas associated with the **prefrontal cortex**. The prefrontal cortex is the front-most region of the frontal lobes. It plays an important part in attention, appropriate social behavior, impulse control, and working memory. Now that we know something about the three types of memory, we can explore the neuroscience of memory.

prefrontal cortex the front-most region of the frontal lobes that plays an important role in attention, appropriate social behavior, impulse control, and working memory.

THE SENSORY CORTEXES

Our sensory memory system is fairly straightforward. As we saw in Chapter 4, sensory neurons carry information about external stimuli from our sense organs to different parts of the brain. First, the sensation travels to the thalamus, which then relays the sensory information to the cerebral cortex for further processing. Three of the five sensory systems have a dedicated sensory cortex for processing sensory stimuli. The visual cortex is located in the occipital lobes, the auditory cortex is in the temporal lobes, and the somatosensory cortex (touch) is in the parietal lobes. Taste and smell do not have their own processing regions, although a particular smell can elicit a very strong and immediate memory even if it's been decades since you were exposed to that particular scent.

connection
Why do smells evoke particularly strong and specific memories?
See Chapter 4, p. 158.

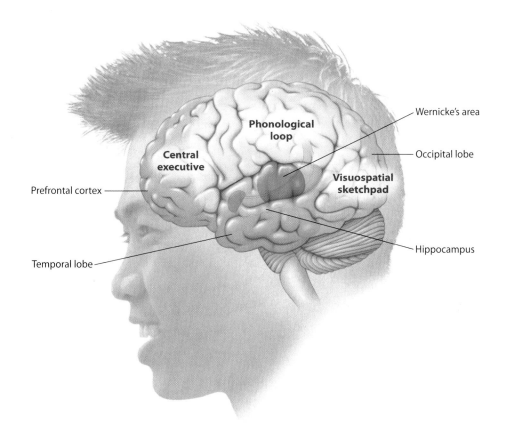

FIGURE **7.9**

BRAIN REGIONS INVOLVED IN WORKING MEMORY. The prefrontal cortex focuses attention on sensory stimuli and holds information long enough for us to solve a problem and transfers information to the hippocampus for memory consolidation. The temporal and occipital lobes, as well as Wernicke's area, are active in rehearsal of auditory and visuospatial information needed by working memory.

PATHWAYS OF SHORT-TERM MEMORY IN THE HIPPOCAMPUS AND PREFRONTAL CORTEX

The prefrontal cortex determines what information in the environment is worthy of our attention. Only then does a sensory memory make its way from the prefrontal cortex to the hippocampus. In other words, the encoding stage of memory formation activates the prefrontal cortex as well as the hippocampus, where the memory is consolidated through rehearsal and repetition (Fields, 2005; Kandel et al., 2000). The repeated firing of neural impulses necessary to convert a short-term memory to a long-term one occurs mostly in the hippocampus. Memory consolidation in the hippocampus may take hours, days, or sometimes weeks before the memory is transferred back to the cortex for permanent storage.

The hippocampus does not do all of the work in working memory, however. Attention and focus require the prefrontal cortex. Remember that a key function of working memory is to focus attention and to plan action. When we speak, read, solve problems, or make some other use of working memory, we rely on the prefrontal cortex to keep the crucial information accessible (Baddeley, 1998; Kandel, 2006; Miller & Cummings, 1999; Miyake et al., 2000).

The other main function of working memory is rehearsal. Auditory input is processed and rehearsed via the phonological loop from the prefrontal cortex to the language comprehension center (Wernicke's region) in the rear of the left parietal lobes (Paulesu, Frith, & Frackowiak, 1993; Schacter, 2001). The processing pathway for visual information and the visuospatial sketch pad goes from the prefrontal cortex to the temporal lobes (for spatial information) and then to the occipital lobes (for visual information; Baddeley, 2003). Figure 7.9 highlights the regions of the brain that play a role in short-term (working) memory.

LONG-TERM MEMORY STORAGE IN THE CORTEX

Most memories begin and end in the cortex, but in between, as we have seen, they are processed in the hippocampus, where some are converted to long-term memory. Because long-term memory is the most permanent form of memory, it is also the most complex when it comes to brain activity and location.

We store the different types of long-term memory in different places in the brain. Explicit long-term memories are stored in the cortex, specifically in the area where the original sensation was processed (Ji & Wilson, 2007). Implicit memories are stored in structures in the subcortex, specifically in the striatum (part of the basal ganglia), amygdala, and cerebellum (Kandel, 2006; see Figure 7.10).

When we actively try to recall information, especially words, from long-term memory, we use the prefrontal cortex (Gershberg & Shimamura, 1995; Mangels et al., 1996; Thompson & Madigan, 2005). Retrieving information requires attention and focus, and hence involves working memory, which is predominantly an activity of the prefrontal cortex.

Implicit memories are also processed and stored in different parts of the brain. Priming, for example, occurs mostly in the cortex. Procedural memories for skills and habits involve the striatum. The amygdala is crucial for associating particular events with emotional responses such as happiness or fear. So when we learn to associate a neighbor's house with a mean dog and we become afraid of going there, the amygdala is the part of our brain that is most involved.

Much of what psychologists have learned about memory and the brain has come from studying people who have suffered brain injury. The different functions of the cortex and hippocampus in memory explain why some brain-injured people can remember skills and behaviors, but not knowledge, events, and facts. As we have mentioned, memories for behaviors and skills are implicit, and we process them mostly in the subcortex. Explicit memories for events and facts we process

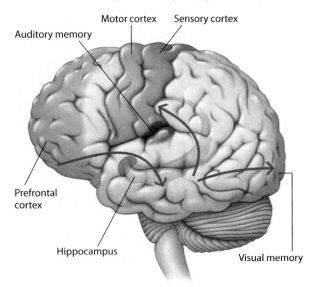

Explicit Memory Storage

Auditory memory — Motor cortex — Sensory cortex

Prefrontal cortex

Hippocampus

Visual memory

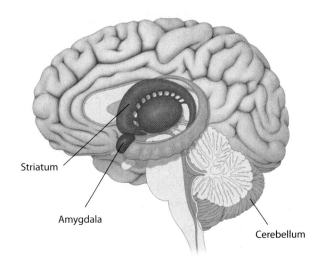

Implicit Memory Storage

Striatum

Amygdala

Cerebellum

FIGURE **7.10**

BRAIN REGIONS INVOLVED IN LONG-TERM MEMORY.
Many different brain areas are involved in memory. The hippocampus is involved in laying down and retrieving memories, particularly personal ones and those related to finding your way about. After being processed in the hippocampus, explicit long-term memories are returned to the cortex for storage in the area where the sensory information was processed originally. Implicit memories are processed and stored in the cortex, the striatum, and the amygdala. (*Source:* Kandel, 2006.)

and store mostly in the cortex. This can occur only if the hippocampus is intact and can pass them on for long-term cortical storage. Even if part of the hippocampus is removed, we cannot easily form new long-term memories.

Damage to areas of the cortex involved in processing particular kinds of information can lead to deficits in that knowledge system. For instance, damage to the temporal lobe often results in problems with one's sense of direction—that is, spatial problems. In Chapter 6 we introduced David, who suffered a major brain injury when hit by a car. David's injury involved portions of the left temporal lobe of his brain. Since his accident, David can get lost easily in almost any location except his immediate neighborhood, which he sees daily. Even there, if he wanders more than a few blocks down the street he knows he may become disoriented and lose his way.

So specialized knowledge in certain brain regions plays a role in memory for that kind of knowledge, such as spatial skills. This is just one example of the ways in which anatomy and function guide memory. Another example is emotion. Brain regions involved in memory are anatomically linked to those involved in emotion. Not surprisingly, emotion and memory are intimately connected.

EMOTION, MEMORY, AND THE BRAIN

Why is it that you can remember in great detail the events of your first date but cannot recall what you ate for breakfast yesterday morning? Generally speaking, emotional memories are easier to recall than are factual ones. Emotions help us encode and retrieve memories. When emotions occur—especially negative ones—attention is focused and details are noted, because emotions usually are connected with events that have important implications for the individual. As such, these events may be important to recall. From an evolutionary perspective, it makes sense for creatures to have better recall of anything that may have significance for well-being (as emotional events do).

connection

Do positive and negative emotions affect attention in the same way?

See Chapter 11, p. 435.

How does emotion help memory? One way, as we'll see in more detail in the next section, is through biochemical and genetic processes. Emotional events switch on genes that build proteins that strengthen the synaptic connections between neurons. These proteins also stimulate the formation of new synapses and even new neurons (Kandel, 2006). All of these structures make the memory "stick" for a long period of time.

Additionally, emotion helps memory by way of anatomy. Important structures for memory, namely, the amygdala and hippocampus, are linked to key structures for emotion. These two structures lie next to each other in the brain and are connected by many nerve fibers. The amygdala is involved in assigning emotional significance to events and is crucial in encoding information relevant to fear (Phelps & LeDoux, 2005). People remember the visual details of an object better if negative emotions were aroused while viewing it (Kensinger, Garoff-Eaton, & Schacter, 2007). It is in this way that the amygdala facilitates the encoding of a memory.

In a study that demonstrates the role of emotion in both the encoding and retrieval of memories, researchers brought nine women into the lab and showed them a series of pictures. Some pictures had potentially emotional content—such as spiders, snakes, graphic violence, nudes, nature, beauty—while others were neutral, such as a picture of a city street. A year later they saw the same images.

Both times their brains were scanned. One year later, the women showed better recognition of the pictures with emotional content than the neutral pictures. Also, their scans showed activity in the amygdala and hippocampus when they saw the emotional, remembered items (Dolcos, LeBar, & Cabeza, 2005). What is interesting about these findings is that there was activity in these two regions during both encoding and retrieval of the memories, indicating that emotion helped both stages of the memory process.

nature & nurture

Thanks to the amygdala, memories of scary things are hard to shake, and so we might behave in certain ways in order to avoid things that have scared us in the past.

The relationship between emotion and memory is far from perfect. Sometimes, emotions distort our memories. In terms of autobiographical memories, when people look back over their lives they recall pleasant times rather than the negative. So there is a positive bias in autobiographical memory recall. The "good ole' days" are good partly because we remember the good more readily than we remember the bad (Walker, Skowronski, & Thompson, 2003).

People with damaged amygdalas do not recall emotional events better than non-emotional events (Adolphs et al., 1997). In fact, there is evidence that amygdala damage can also impair memories for the overall feeling of an event, but not for details. The details are still there, but the emotional accent is gone (Adolphs, Tranel, & Buchanan, 2005). These findings attest to the importance of the amygdala in emotion and memory.

We do not have normal recall of traumatic events—those that are extremely stressful or horrifying. Such events may be relived quite vividly or completely lost, or they may alternate between both. Post-traumatic stress disorder (PTSD) is a condition in which a person who has experienced an extremely traumatic event, such as being a crime victim or a solider in a war, relives the event over and over. But stress may both enhance the encoding of information and impair the retrieval of emotional memories (Buchanan & Tranel, 2008). Refugees who have endured extreme emotional stress show impaired recall of specific episodic memories; cancer survivors with PTSD show impaired semantic memory (Moradi et al., 2008). It is possible that loss of autobiographical memory is a way of regulating or coping with extreme emotional stress.

Not all battle scars are physical. Post-traumatic stress disorder (PTSD), a condition that forces sufferers to relive terrifying events over and over, makes readjusting to civilian life difficult for an increasing number of war veterans. After returning to the United States from Iraq, this soldier was diagnosed with PTSD.

breaking new ground
The Remembering Brain

Memory is a complex process. How does the brain do it? What neural mechanisms enable us to remember the name of our first-grade teacher or a song that we haven't heard for years or how to calculate our GPA? It took a few decades and research by several people to begin answering these questions.

HEBB'S LAW: NEURONS THAT WIRE TOGETHER FIRE TOGETHER

In the first half of the 20th century, much of psychology ignored the biological basis of memory and learning, but not all psychologists did. Based on his studies of brain anatomy and behavior, Donald Hebb (1949) developed a theory of how neural connections form and how synaptic connections change with learning and memory. Hebb proposed

long-term potentiation
strengthening of a synaptic connection that results when synapse of one neuron repeatedly fires and excites another neuron.

that when the synapse of one neuron repeatedly fires and excites another neuron, there is a permanent change in the receiving neuron, the excitatory neuron, or both, which strengthens the synaptic connection. This strengthening process is called **long-term potentiation (LTP)** (Malenka & Nicoll, 1999). When synapses fire more readily, learning becomes easier and more efficient.

Hebb further suggested that repeated stimulation of a group of neurons leads to the formation of *cell assemblies,* networks of nerve cells that persist even after stimulation has stopped. The more times synapses in these assemblies fire together, Hebb asserted, the stronger the network becomes, increasing the likelihood that they will fire together again. Simply put, *neurons that fire together, wire together.* What is now referred to as Hebb's law led to another important conclusion from his theory: *Use it or lose it.* If the cell assemblies are not stimulated repeatedly, eventually the synaptic connections weaken and we forget.

When Hebb introduced his model, little was known about the inner workings of the human brain, and there was no way to test the model in humans. But by integrating ideas from psychology and biology, Hebb paved the way for a clearer understanding of memory. No one suspected a link between the hippocampus and memory formation, however, until a student of Hebb's, Brenda Milner, reported clinical observations of H. M. Her observations supported Hebb's theories (Milner, 1962; Milner, Corkin, & Teuber, 1968; Penfield & Milner, 1958). Research testing Hebb's ideas more directly came from Eric Kandel.

HOW PRACTICE MAKES PERFECT

Kandel decided to study memory and learning in the neurologically simplest animal he knew, the sea slug *(Aplysia).* Sea slugs have far fewer neurons than humans and their neurons can also be seen with the naked eye. When Kandel's group administered a

shock to the tail of the sea slug, it responded with a defensive posture. If the researchers administered the shock only once, the sea slug's defensive response persisted for only about 10 minutes. If administered four or five times in close succession, the sea slug exhibited the same defensive response to the shock days later. The sea slug had created a long-term memory of how to react to a shock (Pinsker et al., 1973). Kandel's conclusion: "Conversion from short-term to long-term memory storage requires spaced repetition—practice makes perfect, even in snails" (Kandel, 2001, p. 294).

In Kandel's study, the sea slug *(Aplysia)* created a long-term memory of how to react to shock.

Following up on these findings, Kandel set out to learn just how repeated experience changes the brain. What he found provides an intriguing example of the interaction of nurture and nature. Kandel and his colleagues discovered that repeated stimulation of a neuron actually sends signals to the nucleus of the cell, where its DNA is stored. These signals trigger the production of *CREB,* a protein that switches on genes responsible for the development of new synapses. Repetition brings about the growth of new synapses that stabilize a new memory (see Figure 7.11). Both the timing and frequency of neural firing are crucial in making a memory permanent. By repeatedly pulling away from a shock, the sea slug rehearsed and remembered a defensive behavior. Thus, experience from the outside world (repeated stimulation) changes genes and the way in which they are expressed (Kandel, 2006).

nature & nurture
Experience can change the brain by strengthening and forming new synapses.

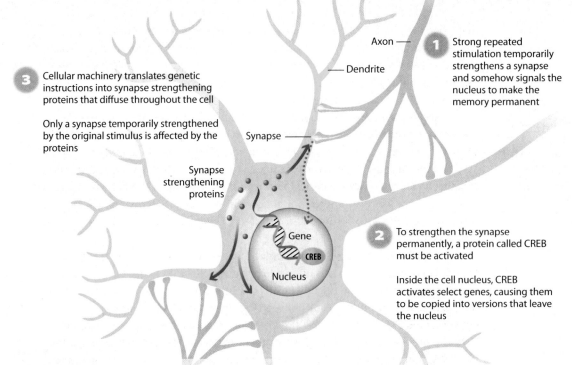

3 Cellular machinery translates genetic instructions into synapse strengthening proteins that diffuse throughout the cell

Only a synapse temporarily strengthened by the original stimulus is affected by the proteins

Synapse strengthening proteins

Axon

Dendrite

1 Strong repeated stimulation temporarily strengthens a synapse and somehow signals the nucleus to make the memory permanent

Synapse

Gene

CREB

Nucleus

2 To strengthen the synapse permanently, a protein called CREB must be activated

Inside the cell nucleus, CREB activates select genes, causing them to be copied into versions that leave the nucleus

FIGURE **7.11**

HOW MEMORIES STICK. When we experience something emotionally important or an experience is repeated over and over, synapses fire repeated neural impulses as if to say "this is important; remember this event." (1) These repeatd neural firings in turn strengthen the synapse by activating a protein called CREB (2). CREB then turns on certain genes that set into motion a process that builds other proteins that strengthen the synaptic connection (3). This process makes memories last in our minds, in effect "tattooing" the event in our brain. So timing and frequency of neural firings are crucial in making a memory permanent—an idea or thought needs to be rehearsed many times if it is to pass from short-term to long-term memory. (*Source:* Fields, 2005.)

People, too, need to rehearse an idea or thought many times in order to create a long-term memory. Strong emotions also make memories stick. In the process, our brain literally grows more synapses, thereby strengthening the neural connections—it becomes a different brain. Experience changes our brain, and these changes then change how we respond to our environment.

connection

Kandel's findings explain how and why the brains of mice reared in enriched environments are heavier and have more dendrites than the brains of mice reared in impoverished environments. See Chapter 3, p. 110.

HELP FOR MEMORY DISORDERS?

Kandel found the link between behavior and long-term memory that Hebb had speculated about in his model. This work was so significant that Kandel was awarded the 2000 Nobel Prize in Physiology and Medicine. In the words of the Nobel Committee, "Since we now understand important aspects of the cellular and molecular mechanisms which make us remember, the possibilities to develop new types of medication to improve memory function in patients with different types of dementia may be increased." Kandel agreed: he helped start a pharmaceutical company to develop drugs for the treatment of Alzheimer's disease, an application described in this chapter's "Psychology in the Real World."

1. When we actively try to recall information, especially words, from long-term memory, we use the
   a. occipital cortex
   b. prefrontal cortex
   c. parietal cortex
   d. parahippocampal gyrus

2. Rehearsal makes memories stick. So does this kind of experience:
   a. drunkenness
   b. storage
   c. emotion
   d. fatigue

3. Complete this phrase: Neurons that _____ together, _____ together.
   a. grow; sow
   b. lie; die
   c. synapse; degrade
   d. fire; wire

4. Both the timing and _____ of neural firing are crucial in making a memory permanent.
   a. frequency
   b. intensity
   c. location
   d. distance

5. CREB is a(n) _____ that switches on genes responsible for the development of new synapses.
   a. amino acid
   b. protein
   c. neurotransmitter
   d. enzyme

Answers can be found at the end of the chapter.

Forgetting and Memory Loss

So far we have discussed two of the three principles of memory: There are three types of memory, and different types of memory involve different areas of the brain. Here we examine the third principle: Memory and forgetting are much more of a subjective and reconstructive process than an objective one. It is all too easy to think of the mind as an objective recorder of events. But human memory is not an objective recorder of experience. In the process of remembering we select, distort, bias, and forget events.

One reason why we forget is **interference**, which occurs when other information competes with the information we are trying to recall. Interference can happen in one of two ways (Jacoby, Hessels, & Bopp, 2001). First, **retroactive interference** occurs when new experiences or information causes people to forget previously learned experiences or information. Memory's vulnerability to interference from information that follows immediately after an event has profound applications in the real world. For example, recall of a crime by an eyewitness, even if testimony is given only minutes after the event (which it usually is not), will be distorted by the events that occurred in those few minutes (or hours or days or weeks) after the crime occurred. A second type of interference, **proactive interference,** occurs when previously learned information interferes with

retroactive interference
disruption of memory because new experiences or information cause people to forget previously learned experiences or information.

interference
disruption of memory because other information competes with the information we are trying to recall.

proactive interference
disruption of memory because previously learned information interferes with the learning of new information.

psychology in the real world

Memory in a Pill

Have you ever wished for a better memory? Forgetting things we once had no trouble recalling, especially as we age, is one of the more frustrating experiences in life. The transience of most memory is inevitable, but for some people memory loss represents the loss of identity, the loss of self, and ultimately the loss of life. Alzheimer's disease, for instance, robs people in their later years of their most valued treasure—their memories. Ultimately, this fatal disease destroys the brain's ability to maintain basic functioning. Therefore, there is a real medical need, as well as a psychological need, for therapeutic help for people with Alzheimer's and other severe memory deficits.

A number of memory-oriented biotech companies have started developing memory-enhancing drugs. In fact, the Food and Drug Administration (FDA) has approved two drugs for the treatment of Alzheimer's disease: Aricept and Reminyl. Both of these drugs boost levels of *acetylcholine,*

a memory-enhancing neurotransmitter that is deficient in Alzheimer's patients.

Memory researchers Eric Kandel and Timothy Tully have joined the quest for new drugs to treat memory loss. Tully, a former academic researcher who became a pharmaceutical entrepreneur, and his colleagues demonstrated the power of the CREB protein in fruit flies. Flies bred to have an excess of CREB demonstrated super powers of memory: Instead of needing 10 trials to learn to avoid a scented room, they needed only one trial (Yin et al., 1995). Currently, Tully's team is researching drugs that stimulate the production of CREB and other memory-enhancing proteins in the brain. Clinical trials with humans are still at least a few years away.

Herbal preparations that do not require or rely on the laborious, time-consuming, expensive, and bureaucratic process of developing drugs that require FDA approval are readily available now. Some of these alternative medicines have been in use for thousands of years.

the learning of new information. Perhaps the serial position effect occurs because the process of remembering the first words interferes proactively with recall of the middle words.

THE SEVEN SINS OF MEMORY

One major memory researcher, Daniel Schacter, wrote a book titled *The Seven Sins of Memory* (2001) in which he summarizes the imperfections of memory. In his list of seven sins, Schacter labels the first three imperfections as errors of omission because they are failures of recall. The last four imperfections are errors of commission, which occur when we recall distorted, incorrect, or unwanted memories. Schacter calls the errors of omission *transience, absent-mindedness,* and *blocking,* and the errors of commission *misattribution, bias, persistence,* and *suggestibility.*

forgetting
the weakening or loss of memories over time.

"Sins of Omission": The Act of Forgetting What we generally think of as **forgetting** is the weakening or loss of memories over time. **Transience,**

transience
most common type of forgetfulness due to the fleeting nature of some memories.

One herbal medication, the ground-up leaves of the ginkgo biloba tree, does have a moderate amount of empirical support indicating that it is effective in mild to moderate cases of Alzheimer's disease. The effectiveness of gingko biloba seems limited to people with actual memory problems, such as early to midlevel stages of Alzheimer's disease (Le Bars et al., 1997). It is not yet completely clear why and how ginkgo biloba enhances cognitive functioning, but one reason may be that it increases blood flow to the brain. Gingko biloba seems to have no effect on people with no memory problems (Solomon et al., 2002).

Ginkgo biloba is a derivative of the leaves of the Ginkgo tree.

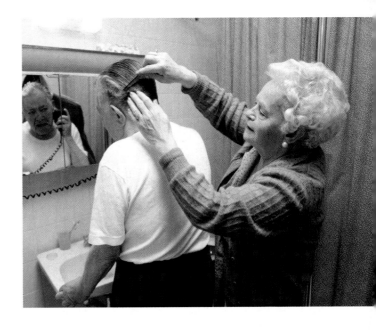

The science of memory has led to some promising treatments for problems with memory. Yet all "memory pills" are not equally effective. Be leery of pills that claim to "increase your mental power." One day, however, Alzheimer's disease and other memory problems may be a thing of the past.

Schacter's first sin of omission and the most common type of forgetting, simply refers to the fleeting nature of some memories. Another term often used to describe how memories fade with time is *decay*. Decay almost certainly happens because the connection between synapses weakens and degrades due to lack of use and repetition.

Research on forgetting began in the 1880s with Herman Ebbinghaus, who found that recall shows a steady decline over time. This decline is what we now call Ebbinghaus's **forgetting curve**. A modern demonstration of the forgetting curve comes from the work of Norman Slamecka and Brian McElree (1983). Participants in their research were given a long list of words to learn. Some saw the list once and others saw it three times. Moreover, some were asked to recall the list either immediately or one, two, three, or four days later. When Slamecka and McElree plotted the results, they produced the classic forgetting curve. Recall was between 70 and 80% immediately, but it declined steadily for each additional day between learning and recalling the word list (see Figure 7.12). It is noteworthy that seeing the list three times, compared to once, increased recall only a little bit.

forgetting curve a graphic depiction of how recall steadily declines over time.

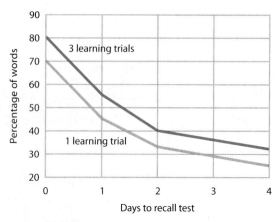

FIGURE **7.12**

THE FORGETTING CURVE. Forgetting happens in a predictable way over time, known as the "forgetting curve." With each passing day, we remember less, but the rate of decline slows. (*Source:* Slameck & McElree, 1983.)

Most normal forgetting occurs because we don't pay close attention when we first learn or experience something, and therefore we never encode or consolidate the memory very well. In contrast, **absent-mindedness,** Schacter's second sin of omission, is a form of forgetfulness that involves attention as well as memory. Consider this: Sandra is distraught over not being able to find her keys. After spending 10 minutes looking all over the house in all of the obvious places, she finally goes out the front door to the car only to discover the keys are still in the lock to the house. Such experiences happen when we do not pay close attention or divide our attention among different tasks.

Divided attention is likely to lead to absent-mindedness. Talking on your cell phone while writing an e-mail can only lead to poor encoding of either the phone conversation or the e-mail or both. You are much less likely to remember things if you try to multitask. Paying attention is crucial to long-term recall.

Absent-mindedness increases with age, but it typically is not a problem until people reach their 70s (Schacter, 2001). Some degree of dementia or age-related memory decline is common in people in their 60s and 70s, but as is true with all cognitive capacities, there are vast differences among individuals. Some people show little decline into their 90s, and others begin to experience it in their 60s.

Education seems to have a positive effect on age-related decline. Schmand and colleagues (1997) discovered that when trying to recall a list of words 30 minutes after learning them, people in their early- to mid-80s with low education recalled less than 50% of the words, whereas those in the same age group with high education recalled about 60% of the words. One of the few cross-cultural studies to compare age-related memory decline across different cultures found no cultural differences in the effect (Crook et al., 1992). Age-related memory decline, in other words, appears to be universal (Matsumoto & Juang, 2004).

The third of Schacter's "sins of omission" is **blocking,** the inability to retrieve some information that we once stored—say, a person's name or an old phone number. It simply won't resurface despite our efforts. One example of blocking is the frustrating *tip-of-the-tongue* phenomenon in which we can almost recall something but the memory eludes us. We might even know that the word begins with a particular letter. We say to ourselves: "I know it! It's right there. I can even see the person's face. Her name begins with _____." More often than not, it does begin with that letter.

Another form of blocking is **repression,** in which retrieval of memories that have been encoded and stored is actively inhibited. Memories of a traumatic

absent-mindedness
a form of forgetfulness that results from inattention.

connection

Can we really multitask? How does talking on the cell phone affect your attention to driving?

See Chapter 6, p. 224.

blocking
the inability to retrieve some information once it is stored.

repression
a form of blocking, in which retrieval of memories that have been encoded and stored is actively inhibited.

nature & nurture

Forgetting is a normal part of the aging process and is quite natural. It also appears to be universal.

experience are more likely to be repressed than other memories. The implication is that under the right circumstances—during psychotherapy, for instance—the person may suddenly remember the repressed event. We come back to this topic in the next section when we discuss "recovered memories."

"Sins of Commission": Memories as Reconstructions of the Past

Whereas sins of omission consist of forgetting, absent-mindedness, and blocking, sins of commission consist of distorting, reconstructing, or falsely remembering events. The first sin of commission is **misattribution,** which occurs when we wrongly believe the memory came from one source when in fact it came from another—for instance, when we believe a friend told us something that we actually read in the newspaper.

misattribution
belief that a memory came from one source when in fact it came from another.

What often happens in cases of misattribution is that we confuse both sources or we bind different memories into one unified memory. *Memory binding* can be seen clearly in a study reported by Schacter and his colleagues (1996) in which participants were shown a list of words, such as *thread, pin, eye, point, prick, thimble, haystack, hurt,* and *injection.* Most people had good recall of words on the list, but they also recalled a word that was not on the list yet was strongly implied: needle. It's clear that the word "needle" is associated with each word on the list, and so people's brains activated that word. They insisted—sometimes with great conviction—that this word was on the list.

In another form of misattribution, dubbed *cryptomnesia* by Schacter (2001), a person unintentionally plagiarizes someone else's (or even one's own!) ideas, believing that an idea is original or new when in fact it originated with someone else. Writers sometimes plagiarize other writers, but in cryptomnesia the writer is truly convinced he or she is the author of those words, having long forgotten the original source. Cryptomnesia, therefore, is unwitting and unconscious—which may or may not avoid legal problems involving plagiarism. A relatively widely publicized example of cryptomnesia occurred not long ago when a 19-year-old Harvard student unconsciously lifted text from a book she had known well—not for a class paper, but rather for a novel published by a major publishing house. Kaavya Viswanathan published her novel *How Opal Mehta Got Kissed, Got Wild and Got a Life* a few years after she had read Megan McCafferty's book *Sloppy Firsts.* Viswanathan was very impressed by McCafferty's book and so internalized the dialogue that a few years later when she wrote her own book, she used almost identical situations and language, not recalling that she had first read these situations in McCafferty's book (Smith, 2006).

consistency bias
selective recall of past events to fit our current beliefs.

Another of Schacter's "sins of commission" is **consistency bias,** or selective recall of past events to fit our current beliefs, such as when we edit or rewrite our memories of past events based on what we now know or believe. These revisions often tell us more about who we are now than who we were then. When people, for example, are asked to recall their political views from 10 years ago, they often remember them in ways that are more consistent with their current beliefs than with their beliefs as they were 10 years earlier (Schacter, 2001).

persistence
the repeated recall of pleasant or unpleasant experiences even when we actively try to forget them.

A third sin of commission is **persistence,** which is the repeated recall of pleasant or unpleasant experiences even when we actively try to forget them. Persistence explains how some of the effects of emotion on memory work. For example, persistent memories may play over and over in our mind some embarrassing or traumatic event that we'd really rather forget. Pleasant experiences—an unexpected great first date, being accepted to one's first-choice university—can pop into our minds over and over, against our will. Because they are so pleasant, they aren't at all problematic. When the event is negative or traumatic, then persistence becomes a problem. The most extreme form of persistence is PTSD, wherein the person might relieve a traumatic experience over and over again. More often persistence takes a milder form, as when we awake in the middle of the night thinking about an embarrassing blunder we made or when we think about how a former lover rejected us. What these kinds of memories have in common—the pleasant and unpleasant, the mild and the traumatic—is that they are created with strongly felt emotions.

Persistent memories make crystal clear the close connection between emotion and memory. The brain structure most involved with emotion, the amygdala, lies very close to the brain structure most involved with memory, the hippocampus. The two structures also have direct neural connections between them. It's not surprising therefore that memory and emotion are closely associated with each other. We experience emotions when important events happen to us or when our well-being is threatened. Most memories that last a lifetime are emotional ones—pleasant or unpleasant. Seldom do we recall some relatively neutral event years later.

The final sin of commission is **suggestibility,** which occurs when memories are implanted in our minds based on leading questions, comments, or suggestions from someone else or some other source. The Schacter study in which people recalled words from a list and mistakenly included a word that was not on the list but was suggested by the other words is an example of suggestibility. We are most prone to suggestions present in the interval between our original experience and when we are asked to recall it.

suggestibility
problem with memory that occurs when memories are implanted in our minds based on leading questions, comments, or suggestions by someone else or some other source.

Elizabeth Loftus has conducted the most systematic research on two major types of memory distortion: eyewitness testimony and false and recovered memories. Eyewitness testimony may be the deciding evidence presented at a trial, and so the reliability of eyewitnesses' recall of what they saw is a central concern for judges, lawyers, and jurors. Historically, lawyers and jurors have been prone to believe the testimony of eyewitnesses unless it was contradicted by firm, hard evidence. Loftus and her colleagues, however, were among the first memory researchers to demonstrate that people's memories of events, even under the best of circumstances, are not very accurate and are susceptible to suggestion (Loftus, 1996, 2003). In one classic study, Loftus and her colleagues showed participants an event on videotape and then asked them to answer questions, some of which contained misleading suggestions about the event they had just witnessed. A misleading suggestion, for instance, might be about what a person on the tape was wearing. After answering these questions, participants were asked to recall specific details about the event they saw on videotape. Results showed that participants are likely to incorporate suggestions about the wrong clothing into their memory and even elaborate on them.

Leading questions might influence how an eyewitness recalls a car accident.

Another classic study from Loftus's lab indicates how changing the wording of a question impacts people's recall for events. People will estimate higher speeds of travel when asked "How fast were the cars going when they *smashed* into each other?" rather than "How fast were the cars going when they *hit* each other?" (Loftus, 2003). With the first question, people also are more likely to report seeing broken glass than with the second question, simply because one word in the question was different. This effect is unconscious: People have no idea and will even deny that they responded differently to the different wording in the questions.

The most fascinating, if not the most disturbing, example of suggestibility comes from research on false memories and recovered memories. **False memories** are memories for events that never happened, but were suggested by someone or something. The person develops an actual memory, sometimes very elaborate and detailed, based on false information. The chapter-opening example of Piaget's mistaken memory of being kidnapped as a child is an example of a false memory. Loftus pioneered the technique of suggesting falsely that subjects in her studies experienced some event and then later asking them about their memories of that event. To be sure, a majority of the subjects never recalled anything. But across eight studies, on average 31% of the participants did create false memories (Lindsay et al., 2004).

A **recovered memory** is one supposedly from a real event, which was encoded and stored and not retrieved for a long period of time, but then is retrieved after some later event brings it suddenly to consciousness. Recovered memories have been blocked or repressed for years. The reason recovered memories are so controversial is that sometimes they are triggered while a person is under the care of a psychotherapist. The controversy arises when it is not clear whether a psychotherapist has helped a patient to recover a memory of an actual event or has unwittingly suggested an event that the client "remembers." If the event involves traumatic experiences such as physical or sexual abuse and people's lives are at stake, you can see why recovered memory became such an explosive topic when the phenomenon first came to light in the early 1990s.

false memories memories for events that never happened, but were suggested by someone or something.

recovered memory a memory from a real event that was encoded, stored, but not retrieved for a long period of time until some later event brings it suddenly to consciousness.

The 1990s saw the peak of the controversy over recovered memories. The so-called memory wars often pitted academic memory researchers against psychotherapists. The debate has died down somewhat, partly because everyone recognizes the truths on both sides: A large segment of the population really did experience abuse in childhood, and unprofessional suggestions by therapists can also lead to falsely recovered memories (Ost, 2003).

MEMORY LOSS CAUSED BY BRAIN INJURY AND DISEASE

When people forget due to injury or disease to the brain, we refer to the condition as **amnesia.** Two types of amnesia associated with organic injury or disease are anterograde amnesia and retrograde amnesia. **Anterograde amnesia** is the inability to remember events and experiences that occur *after* an injury or the onset of a disease. People with anterograde amnesia fail to make new long-term memories. They recall experiences for only a short period of time, perhaps 10 minutes or less. H. M., whose case we recounted earlier in the chapter, had anterograde amnesia after his hippocampus had been removed. **Retrograde amnesia** is an inability to recall events or experiences that happened *before* the onset of the disease or injury. The memory loss in this type of amnesia might involve only the incident that preceded it or might include years of memories. Accidents almost always result in retrograde amnesia of the event itself. Car accident victims, for instance, will usually say that they do not remember the accident.

David Feist's brain injury (from Chapter 6) resulted in problems with both anterograde and retrograde amnesia. A typical example of David's anterograde amnesia is that upon meeting friends who visit infrequently, David will forget having met them at all and say, "Have I told you about my memory problem?"

An example of the retrograde amnesia that David experiences is that he cannot remember anything that happened in the months before his accident, which includes completing a very difficult bicycle ride that he would have considered a "memory of a lifetime." His accident erased this memory from his long-term memory. This likely happened because the region of his cortex that stored those memories was permanently damaged or destroyed.

A severe form of age-related memory loss occurs in the organic brain disease known as Alzheimer's disease. Although it can affect people in their 40s or 50s, Alzheimer's disease usually strikes people in their 60s, 70s, and 80s. It results in progressive memory loss, ending with complete memory loss. In people who suffer from Alzheimer's disease, both transience and absent-mindedness are evident. For instance, forgetting the death of a spouse is common among people who suffer from moderate to severe forms of Alzheimer's. They may go through the whole grieving process over and over, as if each time someone reminds them that their loved one is gone, they are hearing the news for the first time. In Alzheimer's disease, experiences are lost due to anterograde amnesia, which can be caused by retroactive interference and absent-mindedness.

Savage Chickens   by Doug Savage

I HAVE AN IRRATIONAL FEAR OF AMNESIA

I KNOW. YOU TOLD ME LAST WEEK.

© 2008 BY DOUG SAVAGE

www.savagechickens.com

amnesia
memory loss due to brain injury or disease.

anterograde amnesia
the inability to remember events and experiences that occur after an injury or the onset of a disease.

retrograde amnesia
an inability to recall events or experiences that happened before the onset of a disease or injury.

quick quiz 7.3: Forgetting and Memory Loss

1. The most common type of forgetting, the fleeting nature of some memories, is known as
   a. absent-mindedness
   b. decay
   c. transience
   d. blocking

2. _____ occurs when we wrongly believe the memory came from one source when it fact it came from another.
   a. Misattribution
   b. Interference
   c. Decay
   d. Consistency bias

3. The fact that changing the wording of a question impacts people's recall for events illustrates which sin of memory?
   a. persistence
   b. traceability
   c. rephrasing
   d. suggestibility

4. Selective recall of past events to fit our current beliefs is known as
   a. memory binding
   b. consistency bias
   c. faulty rendering
   d. persistence

5. _____ is the inability to remember events and experiences that occur *after* an injury or the onset of a disease.
   a. Anterograde amnesia
   b. Retrograde amnesia
   c. Post-traumatic amnesia
   d. Selective amnesia

Answers can be found at the end of the chapter.

making connections
in memory

How to Study

One of the most common questions students have while learning about memory in Introductory Psychology is, "How can I use this material to study more efficiently?" This question may come up after the first exam, especially from students who expected an A but got a C. "What did I do wrong? I re-read my notes, highlighted the book; how come I didn't do better?" It turns out that the things that worked for you in high school might not work anymore. To really master a lot of complex new material, you may have to adopt new study strategies. You can make psychological science work for you by using the years of research about memory to optimize how to learn new material and prepare for exams (Bjork, 2001; Kornell & Bjork, 2007).

Consider that anything you hear in lecture or read in the book—after a brief stint in sensory memory—is in that vulnerable place called short-term memory. Your job is to move this information into long-term memory and to then retrieve it for an exam. In particular, the material you learn

in any class—new facts, terms, processes, and so on—is semantic memory. Like all long-term memories, how well you remember this material begins with encoding.

1. *Go to class and pay attention.* Attending and paying attention in lecture is a first, very important step. If there is something you don't understand when the instructor first mentions it, ask a question about it right away. If you are too shy to do so in class or you can't get a word in edgewise with your instructor, note it in the margin of your notes so you can come back to it later. Consider that if you do not attend to it now, you will forget it by the end of class. Why? Interference of new material presented afterward, the fact that your stomach is growling, and thoughts of getting to your next class in time will make it difficult for you to remember what you wanted to ask. If you do not rehearse or work with the material in some way—in this case, just the fact that you have a question about X and need to revisit it later—it will be gone. Then, by being in class and hearing in more detail what was posted on the lecture outline and what you read in the book, you give yourself another context in which to work with the material: engaging your attention. Avoid creating sources of interference, like talking with a friend, text messaging, or e-mailing during lecture. These activities will interfere with encoding and make it likely that you are not paying attention. If you start optimizing how you encode material in class, you will be ahead of the game. If you can do this, you are much more likely to store the information in long-term memory and be able to retrieve it easily during the exam. Who knows, some of the information might even stay with you longer than that.

2. *Read the book before class.* To increase the odds of learning and remembering the material for a long period of time, it is important to read the material in the book. Reading the chapter before class helps you to establish a network of associations in which to fit the new material, so that when you hear your instructor talk about it, you have a place to put the information—you can make the associations. A related encoding tool is relating the new material you learn to things you have already experienced, so you begin to build more associations. What else can help at the encoding stage? Many professors post lecture outlines electronically before class, which, like reading the book in advance, gives you the opportunity to begin encoding and storing material from the upcoming lecture before you get there. Reading through both lecture material and book assignments before going to class *primes* you to process the lecture material in a deep and meaningful way.

3. *Study deep, not shallow.* In addition to the lecture and book information, you can improve the way you study the material outside of class. What you have learned from levels of processing theory can help you learn how to approach studying. According to depth of processing theory and research, the more deeply you process material, the better it is recalled. Re-reading notes and highlighting the book are both examples of shallow processing. They involve rote rehearsal. You want to process the material semantically, to work with the meaning of the material, which enhances your depth of processing and memory. Simply reading a definition of a term like *storage* over and over again is not all that different from repeating a list of nonsense words over and over. But if you attempt to work with the meaning of the material, you will remember it better. Think about it. *Storage* is a word we use a lot, and you only recently saw it related to memory. What does it mean in our everyday speech? To put something away and keep it there. Like storing your memorabilia from high school in the attic of your parents' house. You put your yearbooks, varsity jacket, and track trophies into a box and bring them to the attic. You label the box and make a mental note—maybe even a cognitive map—of where you put the box, so that you will be able to retrieve it later. Memory storage is just like this. It is the process of putting something away and leaving it there for future use. If you can elaborate your understanding of concepts like storage in this way, you don't have to remember the word-for-word definition, because you understand what it means. That's good semantic processing. Add a few salient visual images to the mix—like the old bicycle and Darth Vader costume in the attic—and your depth of processing increases.

Also, the more different ways you work with material, the better you learn it. Connecting the concept of storage with your own experience—storing your high school things in a box—places *storage* into a semantic network of associations, with meaningful nodes in other networks: high school (friends, sports, classes, graduation), your parents' attic (and all the attic junk you know is up there), boxes and other forms of storage (file cabinets, closets). By making the material personally relevant—linking the concept of storage to fond memories from high school—you are adding the element of emotional significance, which research shows strengthens the associations. Moreover, every time you succeed in getting information stored deeply and permanently in long-term memory, you are actually changing your brain. Proteins in your neurons are activating genes that promote the growth of new dendrites and synapses.

Recent research on student study habits shows that spacing out study activities is also important. Students tend to cram right before an exam, and they often think this is the most effective approach to learning. Yet spacing things out and covering topics or chapters in separate study sessions, using both studying and self-testing of that material, is much more effective for long-term memory (Kornell & Bjork, 2007).

4. *Form a study group.* Another way to increase depth of processing is to form a study group. Getting together with a few other students to review and discuss material before an exam can be enormously helpful, as long as you prepare before getting together. Meeting with your peers to discuss course material adds new information, fills in gaps, and helps build up new semantic networks, but most importantly, it offers a context in which to talk about the material. This is an excellent opportunity to see if you know the material—by

talking about it with others. You might also have a peer who can explain a concept in a way that your instructor did not. Study groups foster discourse, social interaction, and the need to make another person understand you. This requires semantic processing, preparation, and some emotional charge, because you don't want to look like an idiot in study group. It is also important to have time between meeting with the study group and taking the test, so that you can go over any lingering questions that may have arisen during study group and consolidate your learning. To be sure that the material you are studying becomes consolidated or firmly established, make a point of sleeping well after studying.

5. *Devise meaningful mnemonics.* Will you be able to access the information you learned when you need it? What can you do while studying to facilitate retrieval? Reviewing material with the study group is like a practice test, which is a nice evaluation of retrieval ability. Also, using an easy-to-remember mnemonic device during encoding may make it easier to retrieve information later. If you make a concept personally relevant and integrate it into a semantic network, you can provide yourself with labels or tags as memory prompts. So, for example, to remember the meaning of memory *storage,* you can just think *attic* and you will activate that whole network of associations.

quick quiz 7.4: Making Connections in Memory: How to Study

1. In terms of studying your course material, re-reading notes and highlighting the book are both examples of _____ processing.
   a. depth of
   b. staged
   c. shallow
   d. retroactive

2. Which of the following study approaches is most effective for long-term memory?
   a. rote rehearsal
   b. studying large amounts of material in a few sessions
   c. re-reading the chapter
   d. spacing out your study sessions to cover different topics in several sessions

3. Which of the following helps you process new material more deeply?
   a. making the material personally relevant
   b. building up associations with new concepts
   c. discussing the material
   d. all of the above

Answers can be found at the end of the chapter.

chapter **review**

- Memory, the ability to store and recall information, is the foundation of all intelligence, learning, and thought.

- Three major principles of memory state that (1) memories persist for different lengths of time; (2) memories are processed and stored in different parts of the brain; and (3) memory is very much a reconstructive process.

THREE TYPES OF MEMORY

- Memory systems are classified as sensory, short-term (working), and long-term.

- Sensory memory is the brief trace of a sensory experience that lasts from less than a half a second to 2 or 3 seconds. Iconic memory is the trace memory of a visual sensation. Echoic memory is short-term retention of sounds.

- Short-term memory holds a limited amount of information for between about 2 seconds and 30 seconds, or as long as we continue to rehearse it, before we either transfer it to long-term memory or forget it. Baddeley's model of working memory describes how we are able to hold information in short-term memory while solving a problem.

- The serial position effect is a phenomenon of short-term memory whereby we most likely remember information that comes first and last in a series. It may be due to retroactive or proactive interference.

- Long-term memory is the repository of any material that we retain for between 30 seconds and a lifetime. It includes implicit memory, where skills, behaviors, and procedures that we don't consciously retrieve are stored, and explicit memories of events and facts stored for conscious recall.

- Long-term memory is divided into four stages: encoding, consolidation, storage, and retrieval.

- Encoding results from automatic processing or from effortful processing, such as rehearsal. The more deeply we encode information, the more likely we are to recall it. Mnemonic devices such as acronyms aid the encoding process.

- During consolidation, memory becomes firmly established and resistant to distraction, interference, and decay.

- Storage is the retention of information over time. Information can be stored via hierarchies, schemas, or association networks. According to parallel distributive processing (PDP) models, associations and neural processing result from the synchronized activity of many units or nodes.

- Retrieval is the recall of stored information from long-term memory.

THE BIOLOGICAL BASIS OF MEMORY

- Different memories are processed in different areas of the brain. Sensory memories are processed primarily by their respective sensory cortexes. Short-term memories are processed mostly by the hippocampus and frontal lobes. Long-term memories are stored for the most part in the areas of the cortex where they were processed as sensory memories.

- Repetition and sometimes strong emotion initiate neural activity that converts short-term memories to long-term memories. In long-term memory formation, proteins activate genes that turn on the production of new dendrites and synapses.

- In short-term memory, existing synapses grow stronger with rehearsal, but no new ones form.

FORGETTING AND MEMORY LOSS

- Daniel Schacter's "seven sins of memory" are categorized as sins of omission or sins of commission. Sins of omission include forgetting or transience, absent-mindedness, and blocking. The sins of commission are misattribution, consistency bias, persistence, and suggestibility, all of which can distort the way we recall past events.

- The two most serious effects of suggestibility are false memories and recovered memories. A false memory is a recollection of an event that never happened, whereas a recovered memory resurfaces after it was completely forgotten.

MAKING CONNECTIONS IN MEMORY

- Going to class and paying attention to lectures help you to encode lecture material deeply.

- Reading the book before a lecture will help build a richer network of associations of the lecture material.

- You can process the material deeply by rehearsing and spacing out your studying.

- Forming a study group also facilitates deeper processing of the material because you have to learn by generating information, not simply reading or hearing it.

key **terms**

absent-mindedness, p. 282
amnesia, p. 286
anterograde amnesia, p. 286
associative network, p. 270
automatic processing, p. 266
blocking, p. 282
chunking, p. 261
consistency bias, p. 283
consolidation, p. 269
effortful processing, p. 267
encoding, p. 266
episodic memory, p. 266
explicit memory, p. 265
false memories, p. 285
forgetting, p. 280
forgetting curve, p. 281

hierarchies, p. 269
implicit memory, p. 264
interference, p. 279
levels of processing, p. 267
long-term memory, p. 259
long-term potentiation, p. 277
memory, p. 259
misattribution, p. 283
mnemonic device, p. 268
persistence, p. 284
prefrontal cortex, p. 272
proactive interference, p. 279
procedural memory, p. 265
priming, p. 265
recovered memory, p. 285
rehearsal, p. 262

repression, p. 282
retrieval, p. 271
retroactive interference, p. 279
retrograde amnesia, p. 286
schemas, p. 270
semantic memory, p. 266
sensory memory, p. 259
serial-position effect, p. 263
short-term memory, p. 259
storage, p. 269
suggestibility, p. 284
three-stage model of memory, p. 259
transience, p. 280
working memory, p. 260

quick quiz **answers**

Quick Quiz 7.1:   1. b   2. d   3. a   4. c   5. a   Quick Quiz 7.2:   1. b   2. c   3. d   4. a   5. b
Quick Quiz 7.3:   1. c   2. a   3. d   4. b   5. a   Quick Quiz 7.4:   1. c   2. d   3. d

learning

preview **questions**

1 *What is learning and how does it occur?*

2 *How does learning change your brain?*

3 *How does learning change your behavior?*

I t was a beautiful August morning at the Santa Cruz Yacht Harbor, and I (Erika) was about to embark on an ocean adventure. This time I would conquer my motion sickness. I had, after all, cutting-edge medical knowledge on my side. My doctor had given me a scopolamine patch. Scopolamine is a drug that sometimes prevents or relieves nausea. (Astronauts use scopolamine for motion sickness in space.)

I was so sure I would not get seasick that I had agreed to go on a deep-sea fishing trip with my boyfriend and his coworkers. At 9 a.m. we boarded the boat. Someone had brought a big box of doughnuts. I grabbed an old-fashioned chocolate doughnut, my favorite kind, and downed it in a few seconds. About 30 minutes later we set sail. Before our boat had even cleared the harbor, I was turning green. Soon I was vomiting off the side of the boat. ▶

▶ The remaining 3 or 4 hours of the trip seemed like an eternity, as the sickness continued. I thought about jumping overboard, because surely death would have been better than this. Finally the boat returned to the harbor. For 10 years afterward, I could not eat chocolate doughnuts.

What happened? Exactly how did a chocolate doughnut, which had not caused my seasickness, become a source of queasiness for years to come? Why did I suddenly associate the taste and smell of chocolate doughnuts with the conditions that had made me sick? By associating the doughnut with nausea, I had *learned* to avoid chocolate doughnuts.

chapter
outline

Later we will see why this one experience made such an impression on me. First we need to understand what learning is. In this chapter, we will discuss three major theories of learning—classical conditioning, operant conditioning, and social learning theory—as well as the role of evolution in learning. We will also explore how learning both emerges from and changes the brain. ■

Basic Processes of Learning

Psychologists define **learning** as enduring changes in behavior that occur with experience. This definition sounds simple, but there are many forms of learning—from making a connection between motion sickness and a chocolate doughnut to mastering a musical instrument or a foreign language. As we try things out in the world, changes in sensation, perception, behavior, and brain function alter who we are, what we know, and what we can do.

Learning and memory work together. Without learning and memory, we could not process, retain, or make use of new information. Learning occurs when information moves from short-term to long-term memory. During this process, new knowledge is stored in networks in the brain. For this reason, we don't have to learn to ride a bicycle every time we want to go for a spin. Once we have mastered the skill of riding a bicycle, that knowledge can be retrieved from memory, and we can pedal away without thinking about it.

learning
enduring changes in behavior that occur with experience.

HABITUATION AND THE ORIENTING RESPONSE

Some phenomena fit the definition of learning as "enduring changes in behavior that occur with experience" much more clearly than others. For example, if a dim light were presented to you in a dark room, you would look at it immediately. This automatic shift of attention toward a new stimulus is known as the *orienting response*. After a while, if the brightness and location of the light remained the same, you would no longer respond to it. In fact, you might not notice it at all. This phenomenon, called *habituation,* is a sensory process by which organisms adapt to constant stimulation. The result is a change in your response (from seeing a spot of light to not seeing it) stemming from experience. The change is a fairly short-lived one, however. As soon as the stimulus is varied even slightly, the orienting response occurs, and the process begins again.

Habituation is a change in behavior due to experience, but is it learning? An argument can be made that neither habituation nor the orienting response fits our definition of learning, because each disappears immediately with a slight change in the stimulus. Still, habituation is often regarded as learning in its simplest form (Carew & Kandel, 1973).

connection
Right now you are habituated to dozens of stimuli—including the feel of clothing on your skin. Now you are sensitized to it. How so?
See Chapter 4, p. 126.

ASSOCIATION

Every time we feed our cat, Spalding, we first take the can opener out of the drawer in the kitchen. As a kitten, Spalding would hear the sound of someone opening a drawer at feeding time. So the sound of the drawer opening signaled to Spalding that he was going to be fed. Now, every time anyone opens a kitchen drawer, Spalding comes running and meowing eagerly. Frequently it is a false alarm (sometimes the drawer is opened for other reasons), but the connection, or association, between the sound of a drawer opening and being fed are very strong for him.

An **association** occurs when one piece of information from the environment is linked repeatedly with another and the organism begins to connect the two sources of information. Associations form simply as a result of two events occurring together, whether or not the relationship between them makes any sense. Eventually, the repeated association results in the events becoming linked in the individual's memory. By virtue of their association, one event may come to suggest that the other will occur. Learning by association is a simple but powerful form of learning.

association
process by which two pieces of information from the environment are repeatedly linked so that we begin to connect them in our minds.

Conditioning Models of Learning

conditioning
a form of associative learning in which behaviors are triggered by associations with events in the environment.

Conditioning is a form of associative learning in which a behavior becomes more likely because the organism links that behavior with certain events in its environment. Spalding the cat, for example, is *conditioned* to the sound of the drawer opening because he has come to associate the sound with food. Sometimes the sound means that food will come; sometimes it does not. But the association is strong because feeding is always preceded by the sound of a drawer opening.

Psychologists distinguish between two types of conditioning: classical and operant. Both are forms of associative learning. In classical conditioning, organisms learn from the relations between stimuli. In operant conditioning, organisms learn from the consequences of their behavior. Let us look at these two forms of learning in more detail.

CLASSICAL CONDITIONING

In **classical conditioning**, learning occurs when a neutral stimulus becomes associated with a stimulus to which the learner has an automatic, inborn response. Exactly how this works will become clearer if we consider the pioneering example of Ivan Pavlov and his dogs.

Pavlov's Dogs Ivan Pavlov received the Nobel Prize in Medicine in 1904 for his research on saliva and digestion. While he was studying digestion in dogs, Pavlov (1906, 1928) discovered classical conditioning quite accidentally. As often happens, luck, keen observation, and serendipity (making important discoveries by accident) led to this important scientific discovery.

In order to examine digestive enzymes in the dogs' saliva, Pavlov and his technicians placed tubes in their mouths to collect their saliva. Then they placed meat powder in their mouths, which naturally produces salivation. After doing this for a while, he noticed that the dogs would begin to salivate even before the meat powder was presented, when the laboratory technician who fed them prepared the apparatus to collect their saliva. It was as though the sounds of the technician manipulating the apparatus signaled to the dogs that meat powder was about to come (Fancher, 1996). Pavlov guessed that the dogs had formed an association between the sounds of the apparatus and the meat powder, just as Spalding formed an association between the sounds of a drawer opening and being fed.

Pavlov reasoned that the dogs had formed an association between a stimulus that had no inherent food value (the sound of the apparatus) and one that did (the meat powder). Could he teach a dog to salivate to something else? He designed a laboratory experiment that mimicked the conditions in which the dogs salivated to sounds made by the technician. Working with different dogs, Pavlov presented a neutral stimulus (a bell sound) just before showing them the meat powder. The dogs had no previous experience with the bell, but they salivated to the meat powder, because dogs always salivate to meat powder, from the first time they smell it. Salivation is a reflex, an automatic response to a particular stimulus (food) that requires no learning.

Pavlov and his dogs.

Pavlov presented the bell along with the meat powder to the dogs over and over again. The dogs salivated. Then he tried presenting the bell alone to see if the dogs might now link the bell with the meat powder in the way the first dogs linked the noise of the apparatus with the meat powder. Bingo! The dogs salivated to the bell alone. By virtue of the association made during repeated pairings with meat powder, the nonappetizing bell had come to signal "meat powder" to the dogs. The dogs had learned that they would get meat powder after the bell sounded.

How Classical Conditioning Works

unconditioned response (UCR) the automatic, inborn reaction to a stimulus.

unconditioned stimulus (UCS) the environmental input that always produces the same unlearned response.

Pavlov called the kind of learning he'd observed the *conditioning of reflexes,* and we now call it *classical conditioning.* He coined the term **unconditioned response (UCR)** to describe the automatic, inborn response to a stimulus. In this case, salivation is the UCR. *Unconditioned* simply means "unlearned." Pavlov used the term **unconditioned stimulus (UCS)** to refer to the environmental input (meat powder) that always produced the same unlearned response (salivation). Without learning, the UCS always produces the UCR; in Pavlov's experiment, meat powder—the UCS—always leads to salivation—the UCR.

Food makes you salivate, pressure on your eye makes you blink, and a tap just below your kneecap will cause your leg to jerk forth. These reflexes are unlearned, fixed responses to specific types of environmental stimuli. Pavlov defined reflexes, such as salivation in response to food, as fixed stimulus–response patterns. Classical conditioning is the modification of these stimulus–response (S–R) relationships with experience.

nature & nurture
Through classical conditioning, innate responses—like salivation—can become associated with and changed by almost any experience.

Pavlov presented the neutral stimulus (bell) right before the UCS (meat powder). Salivation in the presence of meat powder was the UCR. After repeated pairings of the bell with meat powder, when the bell alone led to salivation, the bell would be called a conditioned stimulus. A **conditioned stimulus (CS)** is a previously neutral stimulus that an organism learns to associate with the UCS. If salivation occurred in response to the CS (as it did in Pavlov's experiment), it would then be called a conditioned response. A **conditioned response (CR)** is a behavior that an organism learns to perform when presented with the CS alone. Figure 8.1 shows how classical conditioning works.

conditioned stimulus (CS) a previously neutral input that an organism learns to associate with the UCS.

conditioned response (CR) a behavior that an organism learns to perform when presented with the CS.

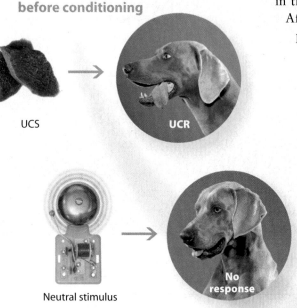

before conditioning

UCS → UCR

Neutral stimulus → No response

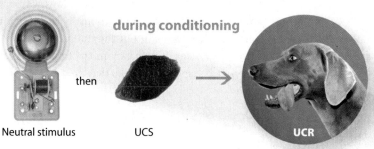

during conditioning

Neutral stimulus then UCS → UCR

Notice that Figure 8.1 shows the neutral stimulus being presented just before the UCS. This process is known as *forward conditioning*. One can also present the neutral stimulus and the UCS simultaneously. When the neutral stimulus follows the UCS, a process called *backward conditioning*, conditioning is less successful. An example of backward conditioning would be sounding the bell after presenting the food to Pavlov's dogs. Based on repeated, painstakingly careful experimentation, Pavlov laid out certain criteria for stimulus–response conditioning to succeed (Pavlov, 1906, 1928). Two of the most fundamental criteria are as follows:

1. Multiple pairings of UCS and neutral stimulus (CS) are necessary for an association to occur and for the CS to produce the conditioned response.
2. The UCS and CS must be paired or presented very close together in time in order for an association to form.

When a behavior has been conditioned to occur in the presence of a given stimulus (such as Spalding's meowing whenever he hears the kitchen drawer opening), it may also increase in the presence of similar stimuli. Spalding comes running to the kitchen not only when he hears the kitchen drawer opening, but also when he hears us open a cabinet or make almost any sound related to food preparation. This phenomenon, known as **stimulus generalization**, is the extension of the association between UCS and CS to a broad array of similar stimuli. The opposite of stimulus generalization is **stimulus discrimination**, which occurs when a CR (such as salivation) occurs only to the exact CS to which it was conditioned. For example, if Pavlov's dogs did not salivate to a buzzer but only to a bell, they would discriminate the conditioned stimulus (bell) from other stimuli (buzzers, clicks, and so on). Or take Erika's aversion to chocolate doughnuts: She was only unable to eat chocolate doughnuts. Glazed or sprinkle doughnuts were fine. Her conditioning was specific to chocolate doughnuts.

Can a conditioned response be unlearned? Would you expect Pavlov's dogs to continue salivating indefinitely in response to the bell alone? It turns out that the dogs gradually stopped salivating to the bell (CS) once they learned that the bell wasn't accompanied by meat powder (UCS). This weakening and disappearance of a conditioned response is called **extinction**, and it occurs when the UCS is no longer paired with the CS. It can be difficult to extinguish behaviors. Sometimes it takes 100 or more presentations of a CS without the UCS to achieve extinction, and still the behavior might return. For example, consider the case of a young man who had a bad experience with a bee sting when he was 4 years old. Thereafter, he had an extreme reaction to the sight of bees. Psychologists can treat this kind of abnormal fear reaction using extinction. Exposing the man

stimulus generalization
extension of the association between UCS and CS to include a broad array of similar stimuli.

stimulus discrimination
restriction of a CR (such as salivation) to the exact CS to which it was conditioned.

extinction
the weakening and disappearance of a conditioned response, which occurs when the UCS is no longer paired with the CS.

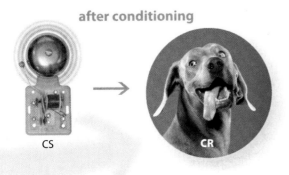

after conditioning

CS

CR

FIGURE **8.1**

CLASSICAL CONDITIONING. A dog's natural reflex is to salivate to food. The food is an unconditioned stimulus (UCS), and salivation is an unconditioned response (UCR). Before conditioning, a dog will not salivate when a bell rings. During conditioning, the bell is presented right before the food appears. The dog salivates (UCR) because of the food (UCS). After repeatedly hearing the ringing bell right before being presented with the food, the dog will begin to salivate. Now the ringing bell has become a conditioned stimulus (CS), and salivation to the sound of the bell alone has become a conditioned response (CR).

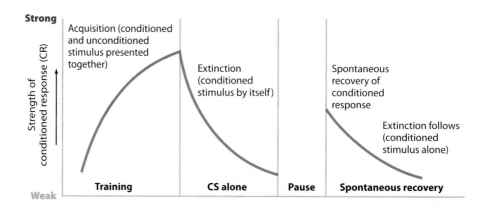

Unconditioned
stimulus:
bee sting

FIGURE **8.2**

CLASSICAL CONDITIONING IN THE REAL WORLD. A person who suffered a painful bee sting continues to fear all bees for a long time. After enough exposure to bees without being stung, however, the person can learn to not react with fear. At this point, the conditioned response (fear) is extinguished.

spontaneous recovery
the sudden reappearance of an extinguished response.

repeatedly to bees in situations in which he does not get stung helps him learn that they will not always sting. This experience reduces the extreme fear reaction he has to bees (see Figures 8.2 and 8.3).

The sudden reappearance of an extinguished response is known as **spontaneous recovery** (see Figure 8.3). One real example of spontaneous recovery comes from a colleague who was involved in a car accident. His car was sideswiped as he was making a blind turn from a campus parking lot. After the accident, he would have a panic attack whenever he passed that parking lot, and so he couldn't park there. Several months later the attacks stopped, and he started parking in the lot again. Then, one day as he approached the parking lot, he had an unexpected panic attack. A learned response he thought had been extinguished suddenly came back. It is clear from recent research on spontaneous recovery that extinction never completely eliminates the response, only suppresses it (Moody, Sunsay, & Bouton, 2006). After the response has been extinguished, it is quite common for the response to reappear spontaneously if a person returns to the original setting where the conditioning took place.

Why does classical conditioning—the ability to associate innate stimulus–response patterns with novel stimuli—work? It may be adaptive in an evolutionary sense. We need to be able to associate certain types of stimuli with potential harm and to respond quickly to new stimuli that present threats. For instance, we might not be hardwired to see long, sharp metal objects as dangerous; but once we see that pressing one of them against the skin causes bleeding, then we know it is dangerous. Most animals can learn such things readily, and it helps them survive and reproduce. It is by virtue of experience and association that many objects acquire their meaning for us. That knives are dangerous is

FIGURE **8.3**

ACQUISITION, EXTINCTION, AND SPONTANEOUS RECOVERY IN CLASSICAL CONDITIONING. The graph shows how a conditioned response (CR) gradually becomes stronger during conditioning, then weakens when the conditioned stimulus (CS) is no longer paired with the UCS, and disappears (extinction). Following a pause during which the CS is not presented, spontaneous recovery of the CR may occur briefly before it is extinguished again.

Strong

Strength of conditioned response (CR)

Acquisition (conditioned and unconditioned stimulus presented together)

Extinction (conditioned stimulus by itself)

Spontaneous recovery of conditioned response

Extinction follows (conditioned stimulus alone)

Weak

Training   **CS alone**   **Pause**   **Spontaneous recovery**

Unconditioned response: Pain, which can lead to fear

2

3

Conditioned response: fear of bees

4

Extinction: Repeated exposure to bees without getting stung may reduce fear of bees.

something we learn. The fact that classical conditioning is a powerful learning device for nearly all creatures suggests that it has advantages for survival.

The Conditioning of Little Albert

Pavlov's work caught the attention of young psychologists in the United States in the early 20th century. They saw in Pavlov's research the first systematic account of a scientific procedure for studying behavior. One American psychologist, John Watson, felt strongly that classical conditioning could be used to shape human behavior:

> Give me a dozen healthy infants, well-formed, and my own specified world to bring them up in and I'll guarantee to take any one at random and train him to become any type of specialist I might select—doctor, lawyer, artist, merchant-chief, and yes, even beggarman and thief, regardless of his talents, penchants, tendencies, abilities, vocations, and race of his ancestors. (Watson, 1925, p. 82)

Watson's complete faith in the ability to mold human behavior seems naïve today, and some would even call it dangerous. Yet Watson and his view of the infant as a blank slate helped push psychology—which Watson defined as "the

Little Albert with Rosalie Rayner and John B. Watson.

study of behavior"—forward as a science. To Watson, classical conditioning offered a model for transforming the field.

In a classic study of the power of conditioning techniques, Watson conditioned a baby known as Little Albert to fear white rats and other white fluffy objects. When Watson and his colleague Rosalie Rayner first met Albert, they brought out a white rat and showed it to Albert. He was curious, but not afraid of it. Then Watson and Rayner (1920) paired the presentation of the rat with a very loud noise

(the sound of a hammer striking a steel bar right behind Albert's head). Naturally, the loud sound (a UCS) startled Albert (the UCR), and he got very upset.

After repeated pairings of the loud sound with the rat, seeing the rat alone (the CS) upset Albert. Upon further testing, Albert's fear grew to include an intense emotional response not only to white rats but also to many other white, fluffy items, including John Watson's fake white beard. This is an example of stimulus generalization.

connection

Could Watson do research on Little Albert in today's world?

See Chapter 2, p. 66.

Regrettably, Little Albert did not undergo deconditioning (Watson & Rayner, 1920). Controversy surrounded this case for years, and it is still not clear what happened to Little Albert. We see in this case that psychology in its infancy lacked clear ethical guidelines for research. Watson's "experiment" raised many ethical issues, particularly about the need to safeguard the rights of individuals who cannot give informed consent to participate in research. Still, Watson is remembered as the father of behaviorism for his role in establishing psychology as the study of behavior.

OPERANT CONDITIONING

Unlike Little Albert's fear of white rats and other reactions that people can elicit from others, some behaviors occur spontaneously. In the late 19th century, Edward L. Thorndike (1905) noted that rewarding consequences can make a spontaneous behavior more likely to occur again. He found, for example, that a cat would escape from a specially designed cage if left to its own devices for a while, not necessarily because it figured out how to get out, but because certain motions eventually were rewarded by the door opening (see Figure 8.4). This reward made it more likely that the specific behavior that led to the door opening would happen again if the cat were again confined in the same cage. In the same way, you might come back to a café you casually walked into if you found out that it had free wireless Internet service and gave out tasty samples of its pastries. Thorndike labeled this principle the **law of effect**. Briefly, the law of effect means

law of effect

the consequences of a behavior increase (or decrease) the likelihood that the behavior will be repeated.

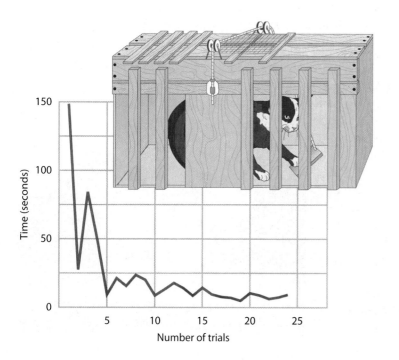

FIGURE **8.4**

THE LEARNING CURVE. Depicted here is the box from which Thorndike's cats learned to escape. Thorndike found that a cat would escape from a specially designed cage if left to its own devices for a while, not necessarily because it figured out how to get out, but because certain motions eventually were rewarded by the door's opening. This reward of the opening door made it more likely that the specific behavior that led to the opening door would happen again if the cat were again confined in the same cage. The graph shows the amount of time it would take the cat to escape. Initially, it took more than two minutes, but after just a few trials, the cat could consistently escape in about 10 seconds.

	Behavior	Consequence	Outcome
operant conditioning	Texting during class	Receive a reply that is more interesting than the lecture	Keep on texting
	Checking e-mail	Receive a desired message	Check e-mail more often
	Drinking coffee one morning	Feel more awake	Have coffee every morning

FIGURE **8.5**

THREE EXAMPLES OF HOW CONSEQUENCES CAN INCREASE OR REINFORCE BEHAVIOR.

that the consequences of a behavior increase (or decrease) the likelihood that the behavior will be repeated.

Like Thorndike, B. F. Skinner viewed the consequences of an individual's actions as the most important determinants of behavior (Skinner, 1938, 1953). Skinner set out to explain the environmental factors that led Thorndike's cat to learn to open the cage (or you to return to the Internet café). Skinner wanted to know how disorganized, spontaneous behavior becomes organized. And exactly what role do the consequences of an action play in the organization of the response? Figure 8.5 shows how consequences may increase behavior in real-life examples.

B. F. Skinner

Skinner (1938) coined the term *operant* to refer to behavior that acts—or operates—on the environment to produce specific consequences. **Operant conditioning** is the process of modifying behavior by manipulating the consequences of that behavior. According to Skinner, a behavior that is rewarded is more likely to occur again. For example, if a hungry animal does something that is followed by the presentation of food, then the animal is more likely to repeat the behavior that preceded the food presentation. If a café gives you free wireless access, you might come back. In contrast to classical conditioning, which modifies an involuntary behavior (such as salivation), operant conditioning works when voluntary behavior is made more likely by its consequences.

operant conditioning
the process of changing behavior by manipulating the consequences of that behavior.

Reinforcement and Punishment

When the consequences of a behavior increase the likelihood that a behavior will occur again, the behavior is reinforced, or strengthened. A **reinforcer** is any internal or external event that increases a behavior. When a baby sees he can get a big smile from his mother when he smiles at her, he is likely to smile more often (Adamson & Bakeman, 1985). The mother's smile in response to the infant's is a reinforcer that increases the frequency of smiling by the baby, because parental smiles are inherently rewarding to babies. This is a key point. Reinforcers have to be things that the learner wants in order for them to influence the likelihood that a behavior will occur again. For example, you will continue getting paid on a regular basis if you do your job. You want the money, so you keep working hard. But if your employer gave you paper clips for your hard work, you'd quit. Similarly, if your credit card company suddenly offered iTunes credits for using your card, you might use it more often. This last case shows how corporations apply principles of operant conditioning to make a profit. All of these examples differ from classical conditioning in which two things become linked because they occur together, whether or not they are inherently rewarding.

There are two kinds of reinforcers: primary and secondary. **Primary reinforcers** are not learned. They are innate and satisfy biological needs. Food, water, and sex are primary reinforcers. **Secondary (or conditioned) reinforcers** are learned by association, usually via classical conditioning. Money, grades, and peer approval are secondary reinforcers. A potential reinforcer may acquire pleasant characteristics if it is associated with something that is inherently reinforcing (such as food or sex). Advertisers regularly take advantage of this fact. Consider ads for sports cars, for instance. If a sports car is always shown in commercials or photo advertisements with attractive individuals, then it becomes linked in memory with something that is inherently desirable. The car itself becomes a secondary reinforcer due to its association with sex.

Reinforcement can be positive or negative—not in terms of being good or bad, but in terms of whether a stimulus is added to a situation (positive) or taken away (negative). **Positive reinforcement** occurs when the presentation or addition of a stimulus to a situation increases the likelihood of a behavior. Giving extra credit points for turning in homework on time would be positive reinforcement if it led to students submitting their assignments on time. We use the term **negative reinforcement** to refer to the removal of a stimulus to *increase* behavior. Frequently, the stimulus removed is something unpleasant. As an example, consider the beeper that sounds in your car until you fasten your seat belt. Those beepers are designed to be

reinforcer
an internal or external event that increases the frequency of a behavior.

secondary (or conditioned) reinforcers
reinforcers that are learned by association, usually via classical conditioning.

positive reinforcement
the presentation or addition of a stimulus after a behavior occurs that increases how often that behavior will occur.

primary reinforcers
innate, unlearned reinforcers that satisfy biological needs (such as food, water, or sex).

negative reinforcement
removal of a stimulus after a behavior to increase the frequency of that behavior.

A smile is inherently rewarding for babies. According to the principles of operant conditioning, the more often the baby is rewarded with a smile for smiling at mom, the more likely he will continue to smile at her.

result:	(+) add a stimulus	(−) take away a stimulus
increase in behavior using reinforcement	**Positive reinforcement** You exercise a few times and feel better. **Result:** You exercise more often.	**Negative reinforcement** You buckle your seat belt and the annoying buzzer sound is removed. **Result:** You continue using your seat belt.
decrease in behavior using punishment	**Positive punishment** You park in the faculty parking lot. You then receive a fine. **Result:** You stop parking in the faculty lot.	**Negative punishment** You talk back to your mom. She takes away TV and videos for a week. **Result:** You stop talking back to your mom.

FIGURE **8.6**

POSITIVE AND NEGATIVE REINFORCEMENT AND PUNISHMENT IN OPERANT CONDITIONING. It is the actual result, *not* the intended result that matters.

annoying, and fastening the seat belt stops the beeping noise. So in this case, the *removal* of the beeping is negative reinforcement for fastening the seat belt.

Is the distinction between positive and negative reinforcement important? Some behavioral psychologists have argued that it is unnecessary and, at times, difficult to make (Baron & Galizo, 2006; Michael, 1975). Here is an illustration of how this distinction can be confusing. Let's say you drink coffee to wake up. From one perspective, the wakefulness induced by the caffeine is positive reinforcement for drinking coffee. But are you really increasing wakefulness or decreasing fatigue (which would be negative reinforcement for drinking coffee)? Either way, the consequence for behavior is the same—you drink more coffee.

Negative reinforcement is often confused with **punishment**, which is any stimulus that *decreases* the frequency of a behavior. Like reinforcement, punishment can be positive or negative. Remember, however, that punishers *decrease* the frequency of behavior. By definition, negative reinforcers *increase* desired behaviors, and so they cannot be punishers.

Typically, when most people think of punishment, they think of **positive punishment**, the addition of a stimulus that decreases behavior. A classic example of a positive punisher is spanking. Spanking a child (adding a stimulus) is positive punishment if it decreases the undesirable behavior. Similarly, if you are fined for parking in the faculty lot and stop parking there, you have received positive punishment. **Negative punishment** decreases behavior by removing a stimulus, usually a desirable stimulus. For example, revoking a child's TV-watching privileges for repeatedly hitting a sibling is a form of negative punishment if it stops the hitting. Figure 8.6 summarizes positive and negative forms of punishment and reinforcement.

punishment
stimulus, presented after a behavior, that decreases the frequency of the behavior.

negative punishment
the removal of a stimulus to decrease behavior.

positive punishment
the addition of a stimulus that decreases behavior.

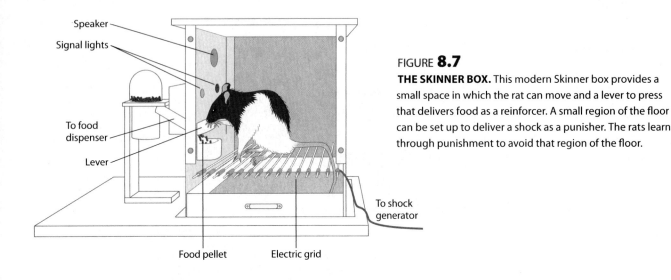

Speaker

Signal lights

To food
dispenser

Lever

Food pellet

Electric grid

To shock
generator

FIGURE **8.7**

THE SKINNER BOX. This modern Skinner box provides a
small space in which the rat can move and a lever to press
that delivers food as a reinforcer. A small region of the floor
can be set up to deliver a shock as a punisher. The rats learn
through punishment to avoid that region of the floor.

Skinner emphasized that reinforcement is a much more effective way of
modifying behavior than is punishment (Skinner, 1953). Specifically, using reinforcement to increase desirable behaviors works better than using punishment
in an attempt to decrease undesirable behaviors. Let's say a girl hit her brother
because she said he took away her toy. Instead of punishing the girl for hitting
her brother, the parents could reinforce more desirable behaviors for dealing
with the stolen toy—such as the girl's telling her brother that it upset her that he
took the toy and suggesting that if he would please give it back, they could share
it for a while. When the little girl acts in this preferable way, the parents could
commend her, perhaps give her special privileges (like more play time). This, in
turn, would increase the likelihood of the girl's using something more appropriate than physical retaliation to deal with theft. Punishment, as it focuses on
decreasing or eliminating behaviors, doesn't tell kids what they should be doing,
only what they shouldn't be doing. Reinforcement offers them an alternative.

How Operant Conditioning Works   In classical conditioning, organisms learn about the relationships between stimuli; in operant conditioning,
organisms learn from the consequences of their behavior. The basic idea behind
operant conditioning is that any behavior that is reinforced becomes strengthened and is more likely to occur in the future. Behaviors are reinforced because
they are instrumental in obtaining particular results.

Substance use and abuse can be learned through operant conditioning.
When someone tries a substance such as alcohol or nicotine for the first time and
it makes him feel elated (a positive reinforcer) or removes his fears (a negative
reinforcer), he will be more likely to use that drug again in the future. The problem with many drugs (especially alcohol and nicotine) is that the body adjusts
to their presence, and more and more of the drug is required to get the desired
effect. When increasing amounts of the drug are required to obtain reinforcement—to get "high"—then the behavior of taking the drug increases even more.
This is one reason why drug addictions are so powerful and hard to overcome.

To test his conditioning principles, Skinner created the **Skinner box**, a simple chamber in which a small animal can move around, with a food dispenser
and a response lever to trigger food delivery (see Figure 8.7). The Skinner box has
been modified in recent years to allow for computer collection of responses, but
many laboratories still use chambers very similar to Skinner's original device.

Skinner box
simple chamber
used for operant
conditioning of
small animals.

How exactly does someone do operant conditioning? How can you get a rat to press a lever? Rats have no inherent interest in lever pressing. You might give the rat a food pellet for pressing the lever, but how do you get the animal to press the lever in the first place?

Skinner trained a rat to perform a desired behavior (such as lever pressing) by reinforcing behaviors that occurred when the rat came closer and closer to pressing the lever. If you put a rat in a Skinner box, sooner or later—as a function of its random movements—it will come closer to the lever. When it does, you reinforce that behavior by giving it some food. Eventually the rat makes an association between getting closer to a particular region of the chamber and food appearing. More specifically, the rat learns that the appearance of food seems to be contingent on getting over to that region of the chamber. The researcher then increases the requirements for food presentation. Now brushing up against the lever will be reinforced with a food pellet. Finally, the rat has to press the lever to get the food.

Through shaping and reinforcement, pigeons can learn to discriminate colors.

Gradually reinforcing behaviors that come closer and closer to the target behavior will eventually produce the target behavior. The reinforcement of successive approximations of a desired behavior is called **shaping**. Shaping behavior is a bit like shaping clay, for the idea really is that an organism can be molded to do things that it typically wouldn't do. Professional trainers rely on shaping to get animals to perform tricks or to assist people with handicaps.

shaping
the reinforcement of successive approximations of a desired behavior.

Does shaping work with humans? Let's say you are trying to teach your friend how to drive a car with a stick shift. The first time he tries, even if he makes a few mistakes and stalls a few times, you might give him lots of encouragement and praise. Later, when you are trying to get him to master changing gears smoothly, you give praise only when each movement is done correctly. You are reinforcing successive approximations of the desired behavior, and as your student gets closer and closer to the desired behavior, the criteria for reinforcement become more stringent. By the 15th attempt, bucking forward a few feet before stalling gets no praise.

Operant conditioning also offers a powerful method for modifying behavior in the treatment of clinical disorders in humans, such as phobias (severe, specific fears), smoking cessation, and learning disabilities (Anthonisen et al., 2005; Lamb et al., 2004; Lovaas, 1987). A notable and beneficial application of operant conditioning is in the treatment of autism. (See "Psychology in the Real World.")

In operant conditioning, extinction occurs when a behavior stops being reinforced. So if a rat presses the lever and repeatedly gets no food, the lever-pressing behavior will decrease and eventually disappear. If you keep leaving phone messages for someone you want to ask on a date, but he or she never returns your calls, eventually you will stop calling. The phone calling behavior has been extinguished. Figure 8.8 compares classical and operant conditioning.

Schedules of Reinforcement Reinforcers can be arranged (or scheduled) to follow behavior under a variety of conditions or rules that

	Classical conditioning	**Operant conditioning**
basic principle	Learning to associate a conditioned stimulus (CS) and a conditioned response (CR).	Reinforcement increases the frequency of a behavior. Punishment decreases the frequency of a behavior.
nature of behavior	The behavior is based on an organism's involuntary behavior: its reflexes. The behavior is elicited by the unconditioned stimulus (UCS) or conditioned stimulus (CS).	The behavior is based on an organism's voluntary action. The consequence of the behavior creates the likelihood of its increasing or decreasing the behavior.
order of events	Before conditioning occurs, a UCS leads to a UCR. After conditioning, a CS leads to a CR.	Reinforcement leads to an increase in behavior. Punishment leads to a decrease in behavior.

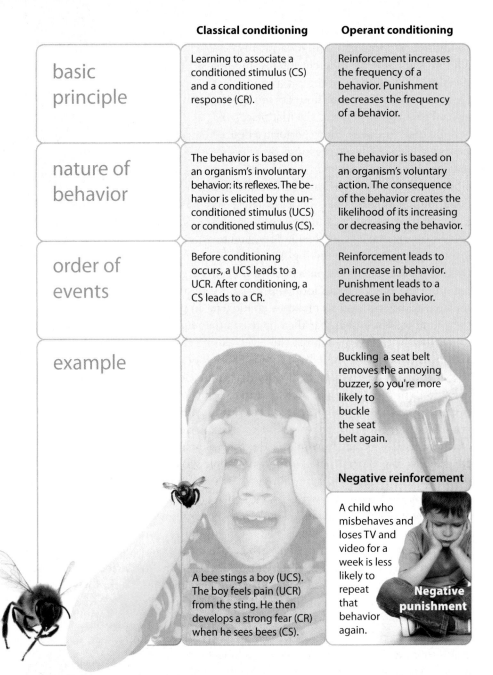

example

A bee stings a boy (UCS). The boy feels pain (UCR) from the sting. He then develops a strong fear (CR) when he sees bees (CS).

Buckling a seat belt removes the annoying buzzer, so you're more likely to buckle the seat belt again.

Negative reinforcement

A child who misbehaves and loses TV and video for a week is less likely to repeat that behavior again.

Negative punishment

FIGURE **8.8**
DIFFERENCES BETWEEN CLASSICAL AND OPERANT CONDITIONING.

can be termed *schedules of reinforcement*. Although schedules of reinforcement are a powerful tool in the laboratory, it is sometimes difficult to describe complex human behavior in terms of simple reinforcement schedules. Nonetheless, there are some parallels that we will describe below.

Reinforcers may be presented every time a behavior occurs or only occasionally. **Continuous reinforcement** means rewarding a behavior every time it occurs. Giving a dog a biscuit every time he jumps is continuous reinforcement. **Intermittent reinforcement** does not occur after every response.

Intermittent reinforcement produces a stronger behavioral response than continuous reinforcement does. Why? The explanation has to do with memory

continuous reinforcement reinforcement of a behavior every time it occurs.

intermittent reinforcement reinforcement of a behavior—but not after every response.

and expectation. If an animal gets a food pellet every time it hits the lever, it will remember and expect that food will appear each time it presses the lever. But if it sometimes receives food after one lever press and other times it takes 5 or 10 presses, the animal will not learn a predictable pattern. It will keep responding as fast as possible in hope that eventually it will receive food, because it is not sure when food will come.

It is well documented that intermittent reinforcement produces stronger responses—both in terms of rate of responding and resistance to extinction—than does continuous reinforcement (Ferster & Skinner, 1957). Think about your own behavior: How often do you check e-mail each day? Maybe you check it several times a day. Some people are essentially "addicted" to e-mail and check it dozens of times a day. This behavior is very easy to explain in terms of operant conditioning. Occasionally a very important or interesting (reinforcing) e-mail arrives. But we don't know when the next one will come (intermittent), so we check and we check, each time hoping for that important e-mail. This behavior is shaped by intermittent reinforcement.

Skinner identified four patterns of intermittent reinforcement, which he called **schedules of reinforcement** (see Figure 8.9). These schedules can be distinguished on the basis of whether reinforcement occurs after a set number of responses or after a certain amount of time has passed since the last reinforcement.

In a **fixed ratio (FR) schedule**, reinforcement follows a set number of responses. The pattern becomes predictable, and so the response rate is not steady. Typically, there will be a pause in response immediately after reinforcement occurs, and then the response rate will increase. The FR schedule produces a steep, stepwise pattern of response, as shown in Figure 8.10. An example is being paid by the number of units a worker produces, whether the units are pajama sets or pizzas delivered. A worker whose wages or tips depend on the number produced will work faster, possibly risking injury, to make more money.

A **variable ratio (VR) schedule,** in which the number of responses needed for reinforcement varies, produces a very steady rate of response, because the individual is not quite sure how many responses are necessary to obtain

schedules of reinforcement
patterns of reinforcement distinguished by whether reinforcement occurs after a set number of responses or after a certain amount of time has passed since the last reinforcement.

fixed ratio (FR) schedule
pattern of intermittent reinforcement in which reinforcement follows a set number of responses.

variable ratio (VR) schedule
pattern of intermittent reinforcement in which the number of responses needed for reinforcement changes.

FIGURE **8.9**
SCHEDULES OF REINFORCEMENT. Workers who are paid for the number of units produced are reinforced on a fixed ratio schedule. Winnings from playing slot machines vary in amount and in the interval between payoffs (variable ratio). An example of fixed interval reinforcement would be going to class right before a scheduled exam and not attending lecture after taking an exam. Continuing to redial a friend who doesn't respond to "call waiting" until you get an answer illustrates a variable interval reinforcement schedule, because the number of times you have to redial varies over time.

Treating Autism with Applied Behavior Analysis

Autism is a debilitating developmental disorder that usually appears in the first few years of life. It is characterized by drastic deficits in communication and language, social interaction with others, emotional expression and experience, and imaginative play (Kanner, 1943). At one time, autism was considered relatively rare, but with greater awareness and diagnosis, it has become a major mental health concern. Recent estimates suggest that autism affects anywhere from 41 to 45 out of every 10,000 children between the ages of 5 and 8 and that the rate is four times higher in boys than in girls (Fombonne, 2003).

It was long assumed that autism was untreatable. Because most children with autism are unresponsive to social interaction, psychotherapy is largely ineffective. Yet certain behavioral strategies offer the promise of modifying inappropriate social responses. The best-known behavioral treatment for autism is applied behavioral analysis (ABA), developed by Ivar Lovaas at UCLA.

Based on operant conditioning theory, ABA uses reinforcement to increase the frequency of adaptive behaviors in autistic children and, in some cases, punishment to decrease the likelihood of maladaptive behaviors. The intensive program involves ignoring harmful or undesirable behaviors such as hand flapping, twirling, or licking objects, as well as aggressive behaviors. It also involves reinforcing desirable behaviors, such as contact with others, simple

reinforcement (see Figure 8.10). VR schedules produce reinforcement around a mean number of responses, but the exact ratio differs for each trial. So the mean may be set at 10 responses, but some trials may require 10 responses for reinforcement, some 20, some 5, some 7, and so on. An example of a device that delivers reinforcement on a VR schedule is the slot machine. The player cannot know how many pulls of the slot machine arm it will take to win. On one occasion it might take just one pull to win a small jackpot. Other times dozens of quarters might be spent before winning. Casinos make a lot of money capitalizing on the steady rate of response produced by a variable ratio schedule—gamblers do not.

In a **fixed interval (FI) schedule,** reinforcement always follows the first response after a set amount of time, say, every 4 seconds. This produces a response pattern in which the rate of response immediately following reinforcement is low. The response rate accelerates as the time of reinforcement approaches. A graph of the FI schedule produces a scalloped pattern, as seen in Figure 8.10. An example of the effects of a fixed interval schedule of reinforcement might be studying behavior before and after a test. If tests are given every four weeks, students learn that immediately after the test their performance will not be evaluated, so we would expect to see a drop in rate of studying at that time. The same is true of class attendance before and after exams.

In a **variable interval (VI) schedule,** the first response is reinforced after time periods of different duration have passed. The researcher sets a mean interval length around which the intervals will vary. For example, the mean interval may be 5 seconds, but sometimes reinforcement occurs after 10 seconds, sometimes after 1 second, sometimes after 5 seconds, and so on. The variable nature

fixed interval (FI) schedule
pattern of intermittent reinforcement in which responses are always reinforced after a set period of time has passed.

variable interval (VI) schedule
pattern of intermittent reinforcement in which responses are reinforced after time periods of different duration have passed.

speech, appropriate toy play, and interaction with others. Typically, the program involves at least 2 years of treatment for 35–40 hours per week.

In his original study of ABA in 39 children, Lovaas (1987) found that almost half of the autistic children who started treatment at about 30 months of age went on to perform normally in first grade. Only 2% of the controls did. Also, intelligence test scores of children in the experimental group were significantly higher by age 7 than in the control group. Follow-up studies of these children at about 13 years of age showed that these gains endured (McEachin, Smith, & Lovaas, 1993). Apparently, ABA can produce long-lasting beneficial effects for young autistic children.

The behavior strategies taught in ABA have been most effective in improving language skills and communication,

reducing violent behaviors, and enhancing school performance. Recent reports suggest, however, that behavioral programs for autism such as ABA and others do not effectively treat the social and emotional deficits of autism (Lord & McGee, 2001). Nevertheless, ABA remains the most effective treatment for autism, especially in terms of school performance and life skills (Beadle-Brown, Murphy, & Wing, 2006).

of the interval makes it difficult for the subject to predict when reinforcement will occur. Variable interval schedules therefore produce a steady, moderate rate of response (see Figure 8.10). Suppose, for example, you are trying to reach a good friend on the phone, but every time you call you get her voice mail. You can tell she is on the line already. So you keep calling back every few minutes to see if she is off. Her conversation can last only so long. Eventually, she will pick up the phone (your reward), but the wait time is unpredictable. In other words, reinforcement follows a variable interval schedule.

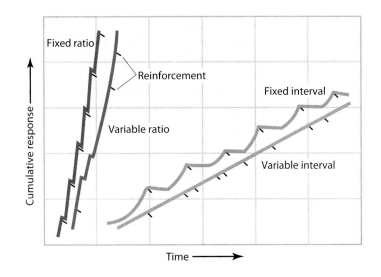

FIGURE **8.10**

EFFECT OF DIFFERENT SCHEDULES OF REINFORCEMENT ON LEARNING. Different schedules of reinforcement lead to different rates of response. Each hatch mark indicates when a reinforcer is administered. Ratio schedules of reinforcement result in more of the reinforced behavior being performed over a given amount of time (the two steep slopes) than interval schedules of reinforcement (the two flatter slopes). Also, the fixed interval schedule leads to the classic "scallop" effect, which indicates that responses decrease immediately after the reinforcer is administered and then increase again as the next reinforcer draws near.

Looking again at Figure 8.10, we can see that fixed schedules show pauses in response after reinforcement. (Note the scalloped pattern for FI and stepwise pattern for FR.) In contrast, variable schedules tend to yield a steadier rate of responding and greater resistance to extinction. (Note the smoother lines for the VR and VI schedules on the right.) Also, ratio schedules tend to produce more rapid responses than interval schedules, as seen in the steep slopes of the FR and VR curves.

Success! The variable interval schedule paid off.

CHALLENGES TO CONDITIONING MODELS OF LEARNING

Traditional learning theory assumes that the principles of conditioning are universal. That is, classical conditioning and operant conditioning each work pretty much the same way in different species of animals. In fact, Skinner maintained that given the proper reinforcement, almost any animal could be taught to do almost anything.

Skinner's faith in universal principles of learning was so strong that he was convinced that what he learned about a rat or pigeon in a conditioning chamber was representative of most species' learning in any context. In one sense Skinner was correct. The biochemical processes involved in learning and memory are the same in slugs as in humans (Kandel, 2006). Skinner was also suggesting that we could understand learning by training behavior, not because it is inherently interesting to us or to the animal, but rather because trained behavior is easily observed. The specific species or the behavior does not make a difference. As we are about to see, however, some of the basic assumptions of conditioning models of learning did not go unchallenged.

Biological Constraints on Conditioning Are species really interchangeable? And is learning to press a bar equivalent to learning to play the piano? Over many years, it has become clear that the notion of the equivalence of species and tasks is problematic. As it turns out, there are limits to what different species will learn and how they will learn it.

Ironically, this conclusion first appeared from the research of two of Skinner's students, Keller Breland and Marian Breland. Initially, the Brelands (1961) successfully applied traditional operant conditioning principles to shaping all kinds of behaviors in many kinds of animals. In fact, they successfully conditioned 38 different species and more than 6,000 animals. When they turned their attention to species whose learning behavior had not been studied, however, they began to experience failures. For example, when they tried to condition different animal species to insert poker chips into a vending machine, raccoons rubbed them instead of putting them in the slot machine, pigs rooted them with their snouts, and chickens

pecked at them. When describing the raccoons' "problematic behavior," Breland and Breland wrote, "The rubbing behavior became worse and worse as time went on, in spite of non-reinforcement. . . . These egregious failures came as a rather considerable shock to us, for there was nothing in our background in behaviorism to prepare us for such gross inabilities to predict and control the behavior of animals with which we had been working for years" (Breland & Breland, 1961, p. 683).

Initially the Brelands considered such behavior misguided and even titled their article "The Misbehavior of Organisms." Eventually, however, they became convinced that these behaviors were not "misbehaviors" but normal expressions of innate instincts. It seems that raccoons naturally wash, pigs root, and chickens peck. Breland and Breland (1961) called this effect **instinctive drift**, which they defined as learned behavior that shifts toward instinctive, unlearned behavior tendencies.

Instinctive drift challenges the behaviorist conviction that learning always results either from associating an event with an unconditioned stimulus or from shaping by reinforcement or punishment. The Brelands' findings imply that there are biological limitations, or constraints, on learning. According to the **biological constraint model** of learning, some behaviors are inherently more likely to be learned than others (Garcia, McGowan, & Green, 1972; Seligman & Hager, 1972). In other words, biology constrains, or limits, options so that the adaptive ones are more likely to occur than the maladaptive ones.

Constraints on learning have positive evolutionary implications: They guide organisms in a direction that speeds up learning and aids survival or reproductive success. This model serves to explain instinctive drift. Humans are geared to learn language—one could say we "instinctively drift" toward speaking. It is very easy for us to learn to speak, assuming we are simply exposed to language early in infancy and childhood. Reading, writing, and arithmetic, however, are not so easily learned, which is one reason why we need to go to school to learn these skills. We do not need to go to school to learn to speak. School might help with teaching us formal grammar and syntax, but we all use a grammar and kind of syntax.

Biological constraints provide an excellent example of the limits nature places on nurture. Biology makes it possible for humans, but not chimpanzees, to talk. Experience interacting with the capacity for speech determines not only whether an individual learns to talk, but also the language learned. Later in the chapter, we explore some groundbreaking research that revises traditional thinking about classical conditioning within the limits of biology.

Latent Learning   Even before the Brelands studied biological constraints and learning, other psychologists challenged some of the basic assumptions of learning theory. One was Edward Tolman. Like many other learning researchers, Tolman ran rats through mazes. In one key study, hungry rats were randomly assigned to one of three groups (Tolman & Honzick, 1930). Rats in Group 1 were rewarded with food if they reached the end of the maze. Rats in this group became better and better at maze running, thanks to the reliable reinforcement of a food reward. Rats in Group 2 received no food for their work, and not surprisingly, they never ran the maze very well. They had no reinforcement. These results are what standard behaviorism would predict.

The rats in Group 3, however, received no reinforcement for running the maze—at least not at first. Like Group 2, they did not run the maze very well.

instinctive drift
learned behavior that shifts toward instinctive, unlearned behavior tendencies.

biological constraint model
view on learning proposing that some behaviors are inherently more likely to be learned than others.

connection
What is innate about language learning?
See Chapter 9, p. 340.

nature & nurture
Animals are primed from birth to readily learn some things and not others. Humans, for example, are primed to talk.

But after a set of nonreinforced trials, they started being reinforced with food for their maze running. Suddenly, these rats started running the maze really well. It was as if they had been learning all along. In fact, the Group 3 rats even started performing better than the rats in Group 1.

How might we explain this outcome? Tolman argued that the rats in Group 3 had been learning all along—they just didn't show it before they started being reinforced. This type of learning is called **latent learning**, which is learning that occurs in the absence of reinforcement and is not demonstrated until later, when reinforcement occurs. Tolman reasoned that these rats had formed internal *cognitive maps*—like pictures in their minds—of the maze from all the practice they had received. When they finally had rewards waiting for them, the rats could use these maps to run the maze more efficiently. It is difficult to know whether the rats really had maps of the maze in their minds. What is clear from these findings is that some learning can occur in the absence of reinforcement. Running the maze, even without rewards, helped the rats in Group 3 run much better when reinforcement was available.

connection
How can people with severe long-term memory problems learn if they cannot remember?
See Chapter 7, p. 258.

latent learning learning that occurs in the absence of reinforcement and is not demonstrated until later, when reinforcement occurs.

Tolman's work was very important because it set the stage for future work on the role of thought in learning, something that Skinner (1990) and other behaviorists deemed irrelevant. Tolman's work also showed that prior experience—whether reinforced or not—aids future learning. Further, it suggested that motivation plays a part in learning. The idea of latent learning implies that learning sometimes stays hidden until the learner is motivated to perform.

quick quiz 8.1: Basic Processes and Conditioning Models of Learning

1. Using the definition provided in the text, which is the best example of learning?
   a. A plant moves toward the sun in order to get the best sunlight.
   b. A newborn baby automatically grabs a finger that is placed in its palm.
   c. A cat perks up its ears and looks toward the sound after a bell has rung.
   d. 10-year-old Jerry can snowboard down the mountain after practicing for a week.

2. Because we always use a can opener to open his food, Spalding the cat runs into the kitchen each time he hears someone open the drawer where the can opener is kept. According to the text, Spalding has _____.
   a. remembered what cat food is.
   b. made an association between the drawer opening and being fed.
   c. habituated to noises in the kitchen.
   d. none of the above.

3. A rat presses a lever, resulting in food delivery. The rat then presses the lever more frequently. This is an example of
   a. punishment
   b. higher-order conditioning
   c. reinforcement
   d. extinction

4. In a typical classical conditioning experiment, a neutral stimulus is
   a. repeatedly paired with the UCR
   b. not paired with any other stimulus
   c. repeatedly paired with the CS
   d. repeatedly paired with the UCS

5. A reinforcer is anything that _____; a punisher is anything that _____.
   a. makes a behavior less likely; makes a behavior more likely
   b. makes a behavior more likely; makes a behavior less likely
   c. is positive; is negative
   d. is shaped; is extinguished

6. A slot machine player cannot know how many pulls of the slot machine arm it will take to win. On one occasion it might take just 1 pull to win a small jackpot. Other times dozens of quarters might be spent before winning. This payout schedule is what kind of schedule of reinforcement?
   a. fixed interval
   b. fixed ratio
   c. variable interval
   d. variable ratio

Answers can be found at the end of the chapter.

breaking new ground

Conditioned Taste Aversion

Remember our story about an aversion to chocolate doughnuts caused by an episode of seasickness after eating a doughnut? This was a case of **conditioned taste aversion,** the learned avoidance of a particular taste when nausea occurs at about the same time as the food. Whether or not the food actually causes the sickness, it is experienced that way in future encounters. In the 1960s, experimental psychologist John Garcia made a remarkable discovery. His groundbreaking research went beyond the limits of conditioning to explain how we learn aversion to tastes.

conditioned taste aversion
the learned avoidance of a particular taste or food.

THE TRADITIONAL LEARNING MODEL

Traditional learning theory would explain conditioned taste aversion as a special case of classical conditioning, in which a neutral or even pleasant taste is linked with the unconditioned causes of nausea. This learned association (say, between a doughnut and nausea) is not much different from the one made by Pavlov's dogs (see Figure 8.11). The catch is that classical conditioning requires repeated pairings of the CS and the UCS to create and maintain a conditioned response. But in the case of the chocolate doughnut, the doughnut (the CS) acquired the ability to induce nausea (CR) after a brief pairing with the motion of the boat (UCS), more than 30 minutes after the doughnut was

FIGURE **8.11**
CLASSICAL CONDITIONING MODEL OF TASTE AVERSION.

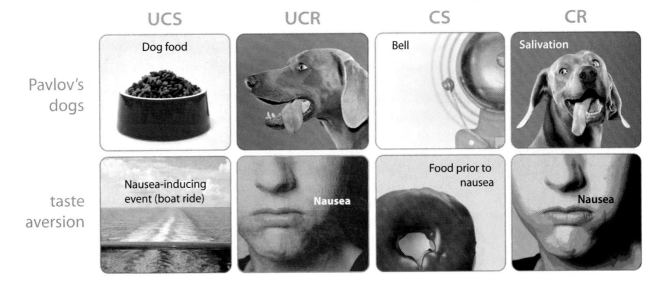

eaten. Garcia's work helped explain how the CR could last for years without repeated pairings of the CS with the UCS.

REFINING THE LEARNING MODEL

John Garcia

Garcia had always been curious about taste aversion because his mother had a lifelong aversion to chocolate due to one bad experience (Garcia, 2003). Yet he began studying taste aversion almost by accident. In research designed for other purposes, he noticed that rats receiving frequent low doses of radiation ate and drank less than normal. Garcia wondered whether the rats had developed a taste aversion for the food and water they had consumed during the radiation period. He and his colleagues (1955) at the U.S. Naval Laboratory decided to look more closely at this phenomenon. They would try to condition rats to develop an aversion to a taste they liked—saccharin water. They began with the following questions:

1. Could taste aversion to saccharin water occur by pairing the taste with radiation (a UCS for nausea)?

2. How long would the taste aversion last without repeated exposure to radiation (the UCS)?

Garcia's team varied the type of fluid presented during a radiation period (plain water or saccharine water) and the radiation exposure level (none, low, or moderate dose). One control group had access to plain water during a 6-hour period of exposure to radiation (irradiation). Another control group received saccharin water and no radiation. In the experimental conditions, rats received saccharin water during periods of low or moderate irradiation. According to traditional classical conditioning, UCS and CS must be paired very closely in time—typically no more than a few seconds apart. But in some cases, several minutes passed between the time when the rats were irradiated (UCS) and when they drank the fluid (CS).

Following the conditioning period in which rats were irradiated or not, all rats were housed in cages with two drinking bottles, one containing plain water and one with saccharin water. At this time, taste aversion was measured, and the dependent variable was how much saccharin water the rats consumed.

There were no changes in the control groups' water preferences, but in the two experimental groups aversion occurred. Regardless of radiation level, rats that had been drinking saccharin water during irradiation consumed significantly less saccharin water after conditioning. This result answered the first question the researchers posed: Rats could be conditioned to avoid a taste they previously liked. Also, the drop in intake of saccharin water lasted for at least 30 days. This finding answered the second question about how long such conditioning might last.

Garcia's subsequent research derailed another assumption of traditional learning theory: that reflexive responses (such as nausea) could be conditioned to any kind of stimulus. Garcia and Koelling (1966) varied the type of aversive stimulus (UCS) to which rats were exposed and the type of neutral stimulus (CS). Nausea (the UCR) was induced by exposure to X-rays, whereas pain (the other UCR) was induced by electrical shocks sent through the floor of the cage. When the rat licked the drinking tube, it received the CS of either saccharin water or "bright-noisy water" (plain water accompanied by a light and

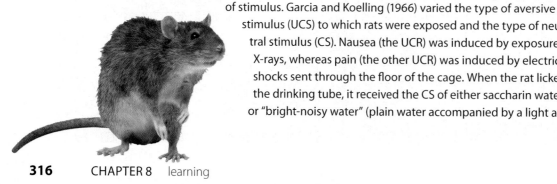

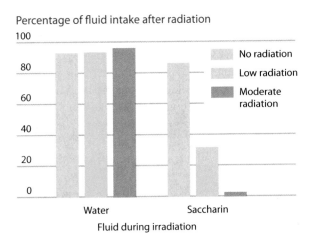

Percentage of fluid intake after radiation

Fluid during irradiation

Legend: No radiation, Low radiation, Moderate radiation

FIGURE **8.12**

CONDITIONED TASTE AVERSION. Compared to rats that received no radiation, rats exposed to radiation (UCS) while drinking saccharin water (CS), developed a long-lasting aversion to saccharin water (CR). Water intake did not vary much among the control and experimental groups, but the amount of saccharin water consumed by the irradiated rats was significantly less than the amount consumed by the control group. (*Source:* Garcia, Kimeldorf, & Koelling, 1955)

a buzzer that went on when the rat touched the drinking tube). The UCS for half the rats was irradiation-induced nausea. The other half received a shock. The irradiated rats avoided the sweet water but not the bright-noisy water (Figure 8.13), whereas rats that received a mildly painful shock avoided the bright-noisy water but not the sweet water (Figure 8.13). The researchers described the first response as "conditioned nausea" and the second as "conditioned fear."

The key finding here is that contrary to the predictions of traditional learning theory, an organism cannot be conditioned to respond to just any "neutral" stimulus paired with an unconditioned stimulus. We can learn certain things only under certain conditions. In other words, nausea can be conditioned to a taste but not to a light, because taste is relevant to eating and light is not.

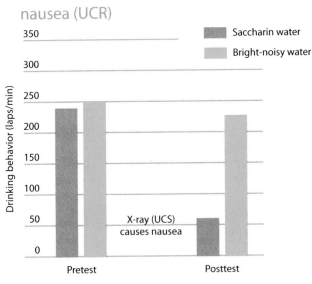

nausea (UCR)

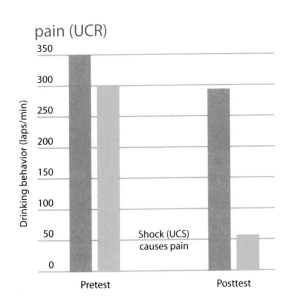

pain (UCR)

FIGURE **8.13**

LIMITS ON CONDITIONED TASTE AVERSION. Contrary to predictions from traditional learning theory, taste aversion conditioning depends on the stimulus. Conditioned taste aversion occurs only to the kind of stimulus that makes biological sense. For example, nausea produces aversion to taste, but not to noise and light, as shown in the graph on the left. Pain produces aversion to frightening stimuli, such as noise and bright lights, but not to saccharin water, as shown in the graph on the right. (*Source:* Garcia & Koelling, 1966).

In sum, Garcia's research on taste aversion undermined two key assumptions of classical conditioning: (1) that conditioning could happen only if an organism was exposed repeatedly within a brief time span to the UCS and CS together and (2) that organisms can learn to associate any two stimuli. With respect to the first assumption, Garcia showed in other research that the CS and UCS could be separated by as much as 75 minutes and still lead to conditioned taste aversion (Garcia, Ervin, & Koelling, 1966). With respect to the second assumption, the "bright noisy water" findings showed that only certain stimuli could be conditioned to produce nausea (Garcia & Koelling, 1966). More specifically, you cannot make someone be nauseated by a sound or a sight as easily as by a taste.

Garcia's findings fit with an evolutionary perspective on taste aversion. In this view, it is very important for organisms to learn which tastes might make them sick. Nausea may follow ingestion of a food by several minutes, even hours. It is valuable to learn quickly to associate that food with nausea in order to avoid contact with the potentially harmful substance again. From this perspective, taste aversion is a distinct evolutionary adaptation (Jacobson et al., 2006; Profet, 1992).

LIMITATIONS OF CONDITIONED TASTE AVERSION

Other researchers have built on Garcia's work and found further limitations on taste aversion and traditional learning theory. One example concerns the application of conditioned taste aversion to the treatment of alcoholism. The drug disulfiram suppresses an enzyme that breaks down alcohol in the bloodstream (Bhagar & Schmetzer, 2006). If people drink alcohol while on disulfiram, they get very sick. The idea is that the repeated pairing of alcohol with nausea should create an aversion to alcohol (Kristenson, 1995). In fact, when people take disulfiram they do drink less (Fuller & Gordis, 2004). Unfortunately, alcohol does not become a CS for nausea when the disulfiram is discontinued. So no conditioning occurs.

Why is it tough to condition alcohol to become a CS for nausea? The intoxication produced by drinking alcohol is such a positive reinforcer, especially for alcoholics, that it might not acquire aversive characteristics in the absence of UCS—disulfiram in this case (Nizhnikov, Molina, & Spear, 2007).

Social Learning Theory

We all look to others for clues on how to behave. Think about how you first learned to tie your shoes or even to swim. Did someone just explain the way to do it? Or did you try random motions and then get praise from your teacher every time you did something that was right? There may have been some random success, but chances are you learned the right movements by copying what your swim teacher or parent did. There is more to learning than associating one thing with another or doing something and then being reinforced for it. Classical and operant conditioning explain many aspects of learning, but they neglect the powerful role of modeling in the learning process.

Obviously, people learn from their own experience, from their own successes and failures, and from trial and error. But if we had to learn everything that way, not only would the process take much, much longer, but it would also require reinventing what others have already learned, over and over again. Learning by observing others is much more efficient. Albert Bandura proposed that we learn both by doing and by observing. Bandura (1986) called learning by doing **enactive learning** and learning by watching the behavior of others **observational learning.**

enactive learning
learning by doing.

observational learning
learning by watching the behavior of others.

Albert Bandura

Bandura's **social learning theory** (1986) goes beyond traditional conditioning approaches to include observation and modeling as major components of learning. **Modeling** is Bandura's term for the process of observing and imitating behaviors performed by others. Modeling is everywhere. Younger children mimic the behavior of their older siblings. We pick up figures of speech and mannerisms from our closest friends. Modeling is more likely to occur in some people than in others, more likely after some behaviors than others, and more likely after some consequences than others.

social learning theory
a description of the kind of learning that occurs when we model or imitate the behavior of others.

modeling
the imitation of behaviors performed by others.

Modeling is only one aspect of social learning theory. According to Bandura (1986), social learning also works through reinforcement. Remember from operant conditioning that the consequences of our behavior influence whether we repeat those behaviors. People learn best those things they are rewarded for doing, whether the rewards are external (such as praise, money, candy) or internal (such as joy and satisfaction). Bandura noted that reinforcement matters not only for the person carrying out the behavior, but also for those who watch. Advertisers make use of this phenomenon all the time. For example, when teenagers see young adults getting a lot of attention and having fun while they are drinking beer, they might be more likely to want to drink beer themselves. People will do things they see others doing, especially if the model's behavior is rewarded.

connection

Do you think watching violence in movies and TV leads to aggressive behavior? Overwhelmingly, the answer seems to be yes.

See Chapter 14, p. 555.

Bandura and his colleagues demonstrated the power of observational learning in a series of classic studies in the 1960s. They came up with clever experiments to show how two key elements of social learning—modeling and reinforcement—affect behavior. The first study focused on the power of observational learning on aggressive behavior (Bandura, Ross, & Ross, 1961). Children observed an adult either being aggressive or not with an inflatable doll, called a Bobo doll. Half saw the adult play politely with the Bobo doll. The others saw the adult sock the Bobo doll hard, hit it with a rubber mallet, and kick it around. Afterwards, one at a time the kids entered a room filled with toys (including the ones the model played with) and were allowed free play. Children who saw the adults act aggressively with the doll were much more likely to be aggressive when they had the chance to play with the Bobo than those who saw the adults play pleasantly with the doll. In fact, they adopted many of the same actions the adults used. So these initial studies demonstrated the power of modeling in the learning of aggression.

Children who observed an adult model being aggressive with a Bobo doll (top) in a study by Bandura tended to behave aggressively when given the opportunity to play with the doll (bottom).

Another key study showed how reinforcement works with modeling to lead to learning (Bandura, Ross, & Ross, 1963). Again using an experimental design, this time the researchers introduced another variable: What happened to the models after they behaved aggressively? Here's how they set it up. The children saw one of four films: one with no models, one with two adult men who interacted in a nonaggressive manner, and two films with adult men who played aggressively with each other, but in one the aggressive man was punished whereas in the other he was rewarded. The first two films (no model and nonaggressive models) were control conditions, whereas the last two (aggression) were experimental conditions. In

FIGURE 8.14

EXPERIMENTAL DESIGN FOR BANDURA'S STUDY OF OBSERVATIONAL LEARNING AND AGGRESSION. Children viewed one of four films: one with no model, one with nonaggressive adult models, or one of two with an aggressive adult model where the model is either rewarded for being aggressive or punished for it. (*Source:* Bandura, Ross, & Ross, 1963)

control films		experimental films	
No model	Nonaggressive model	Punished for aggression	Rewarded for aggression

Aggressive model

the films shown to the experimental groups, one man was aggressive toward the other man. The aggressive man hit the nonaggressive man with a rubber mallet and shot darts at him. He also roughed up the inflatable Bobo doll. A key element of this study is that the films also showed what happened to the aggressive adult after the interaction. There were two possibilities. The aggressive adult was either punished (he lost the conflict and ended up cowering in the corner) or rewarded (he won the conflict and got to play with all the toys) for his aggression. The research design is summarized in Figure 8.14.

After seeing the film, the children had an opportunity to play with the Bobo doll and other toys they saw in the film. Just as in the previous set of studies, how the kids acted with the doll and other toys was the main dependent variable. The primary finding from the previous study was replicated: Those who viewed aggression were more aggressive with the doll than those who did not see aggression (see Figure 8.15). But the consequences for the model also mattered. The children who saw the aggressive adult rewarded for his aggression were more violent with the toys and Bobo doll than those who saw the aggressive adult get punished. Those who did not see an aggressive model did not show much aggression with the toys, nor did those who saw the adult punished. These studies show how modeling and reinforcement can work together to influence behavior. Kids are more likely to copy behavior that they see others being rewarded for.

The Bobo doll studies were pivotal in showing how children learn aggression and other violent behaviors from viewing aggression in others. The results, of course, have implications for the effect of violence on television, in movies, and in

Too much violent TV?

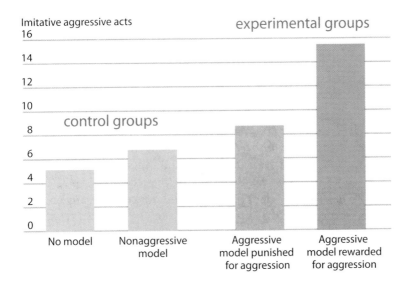

FIGURE **8.15**

EFFECT OF MODELING AND REWARD ON LEARNED AGGRESSIVE BEHAVIOR. This graph depicts the number of imitative aggressive acts by children who viewed one of four film conditions. The children who saw the aggressive adults get rewarded for their aggression showed more aggressive acts, such as hitting the Bobo doll with a hammer or punching it, than did the children in the other three categories. (*Source:* Bandura, Ross, & Ross, 1963)

video games on children and teens. Numerous studies have demonstrated that kids behave more violently after exposure to violence in the media (Bushman & Anderson, 2001). Consider this startling real example: Two teenage lovers, Ben Darras and Sarah Edmondson, apparently under the influence of drugs and Oliver Stone's movie *Natural Born Killer* went on a killing spree. The movie depicted two young lovers, on a wild and drug-filled rampage, callously killing and robbing people. After the copycat killers were arrested they claimed they had also taken drugs and played Stone's movie in a continuous loop all night ("Natural Born Copycats," 2002).

quick quiz 8.2: Social Learning Theory

1. Barbara just started a new job, and she watches how her colleagues dress and act. The type of learning Barbara is doing is known as
   a. observational learning
   b. enactive learning
   c. operant conditioning
   d. reinforcement

2. The major finding(s) from Bandura's so-called Bobo doll experiments were that
   a. children learn to be aggressive by watching other people be aggressive
   b. children learn to be aggressive by observing whether aggression in others is reinforced
   c. children learn to be aggressive only if they see someone of the same sex be aggressive
   d. both A and B are correct

3. Research generally shows that children
   a. are not at all likely to be aggressive after watching aggression on TV or in movies
   b. are likely to be aggressive after watching aggression on TV or in movies
   c. are more aggressive after watching aggression on TV or in movies only if they are from impoverished backgrounds
   d. know the difference between movies and real life and are not influenced by movie violence

Answers can be found at the end of the chapter.

The Interaction of Nature and Nurture in Learning

The early behaviorists refused to study anything that could not be directly observed, including mental processes and any potentially relevant biological structures. Watson and Skinner, in particular, took the position that all learning was a function of either stimuli (classical conditioning) or consequences (operant conditioning), both of which come from the outside environment. Although Skinner acknowledges the role of genetics in behavior, he and Watson ignored the role of cognitive and brain processes in learning, because these could not be observed (Skinner, 1938, 1990). Likewise, the behaviorists did not consider any form of instinctive behavior worthy of scientific study.

As we have seen, behaviorism sprang in part from a desire to study behavior in a measurable way. In behaviorism's heyday, there simply was no technology available for observing brain function or measuring its activity. When such technologies began to appear in the 1950s, the behaviorist model was challenged from various angles. Learning, it turns out, is not just an environmental process. It results from the constant interaction of the brain and the environment. Biology makes learning possible and learning changes biology. Extreme forms of behaviorism paint a picture of learning resulting primarily from the experiences one has. It is an extreme environmental, or nurture-only, view. Few modern behaviorists agree with such a one-sided view. Here we will look at four learning processes that illustrate the dynamic interplay between nature and nurture in learning: imprinting, imitation, synaptic change, and brain growth with enrichment.

IMPRINTING

Not all forms of learning depend on reward and reinforcement. A good example is **imprinting,** the rapid and innate learning of the characteristics of a caregiver within a very short period of time after birth (Lorenz, 1935, 1937). Mammals and birds, which are born helpless, need to form a strong bond to a caregiver almost immediately after birth to avoid getting lost or being killed by a predator. We know this from **ethology,** the scientific study of animal behavior, and especially from the work of Austrian ethologist and winner of the 1973 Nobel Prize in medicine, Konrad Lorenz. Lorenz studied imprinting extensively in birds. He observed that soon after they hatched, ducklings and goslings (baby geese) would learn to follow whomever they saw most, be it a mother duck or goose or, surprisingly, a human. This parent figure tends to be the first moving object the young

imprinting
the rapid and innate learning of the characteristics of a caregiver very soon after birth.

ethology
the scientific study of animal behavior.

Konrad Lorenz and goslings.

animal sees within the first few days of life. Usually this figure is the animal's mother, but it need not be, as Lorenz found out when he became an imprinted parent to a flock of goslings.

Imprinting provides clear evidence of a *sensitivity period* in learning: a period when a particular type of learning occurs very readily if an animal is exposed to a particular stimulus or situation. The brain seems to be primed at a particular time for a particular kind of learning. Once the animal has moved beyond that sensitivity period, it becomes much harder, if not impossible, to learn certain skills or make use of certain kinds of information. Once a "parent" has been imprinted on young ducks or geese, that learning is permanent and cannot be unlearned. Imprinting, in other words, can be learned soon after birth—or not at all. After a certain age, imprinting cannot be learned, unlearned, or relearned—it cannot be modified at all.

Although imprinting does not occur in humans, young babies do develop an important bond with their primary caregivers that serves much the same function (see Chapter 5). Imprinting and sensitivity periods in learning remind us that the mind is not a blank slate, able to learn anything at any time, given the right reinforcers and stimuli. The brain is structured in such a way that certain kinds of experiences are more or less easily learned at different periods in life; language learning by humans is one example, as discussed in Chapter 9.

connections

Do mirror neurons explain newborns' ability to imitate grown-ups who stick out their tongue?
See Chapter 5, p. 197.

Are mirror neurons behind much imitation seen in social interaction?
See Chapter 15, p. 605.

IMITATION, MIRROR NEURONS, AND LEARNING

Humans imitate one another. Imitation is fundamental to the way in which human and nonhuman primates learn. As we discussed in the section on social learning theory, classical and operant conditioning do not take into account the powerful role of imitation in the learning process. Infants begin copying the behavior of adults and other children almost immediately. Babies as young as 7 hours old imitate simple adult facial expressions (Meltzoff & Moore, 1977, 1983).

Imitation by infants may be a result of mirror neuron systems in the brain (Lepage & Théoret, 2007). As discussed in

Like father, like son. We learn by observing and imitating others.

1 **research question**

Rizzolatti and colleagues (1996) were studying neurons involved in hand movements in monkeys, when they made an accidental discovery: the same motor neurons fired when the monkey observed an experimenter grabbing an object as when the monkey made a similar action itself. It made the researchers wonder: Does the brain contain neurons that rehearse motor actions during observational learning?

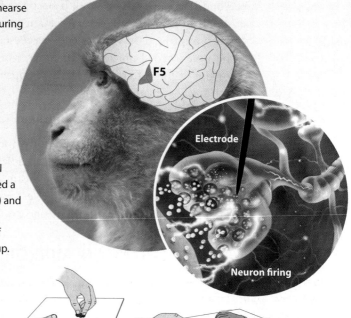

2 **method**

In a descriptive study of two monkeys, the researchers monitored activity of individual neurons in the motor cortex. They implanted a wire electrode in the motor cortex (area F5) and measured the firing rate of a single neuron while the monkey either grasped a piece of food itself or saw the experimenter pick it up.

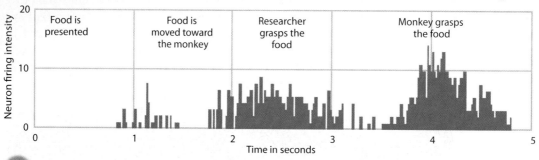

3 **results**

The graph shows the results of firing patterns in area F5 when food is presented, when it is moved toward the monkey, when the researcher grasps food, and when the monkey grasps food. The peaks of the graph are taller when the firing rate in area F5 is faster. They are shorter when the firing rate is slower. Notice that there is minimal firing when the monkey simply looks at the food. The firing rates increase during observation of grasping and during grasping itself. More importantly, the pattern of firing is similar when action is observed and when action is made by the monkey itself. Neurons that fire during action and observation of similar actions are called mirror neurons.

4 **conclusions**

Mirror neurons support the function of rehearsal during learning. By watching others' actions, we "exercise" the motor regions of the brain involved in making those actions. This, in turn, allows us perform the same behavior more readily.

FIGURE **8.16**

THE DISCOVERY OF MIRROR NEURONS. Mirror neurons in the brain respond in much the same way while watching an action as they do when performing an action. (*Source:* Rizzolatti, G., Fadiga, L., Gallese, V., & Fogassi, L. (1996). Premotor cortex and the recognition of motor actions. *Cognitive Brain Research, 3,* 131–141.)

Chapter 3, humans and other primates have mirror neurons that respond in much the same way while watching an action as they do while performing an action (Iacoboni & Mazziota, 2007; Rizzolatti et al., 1996; see Figure 8.16).

Simply put, for some neurons in the frontal lobe of the cerebral cortex, the experience of watching someone else do something is like doing it yourself. When a monkey observes another monkey or a human grab a peanut, the same neurons fire in the frontal lobe as fire when the observing monkey actually grabs a peanut (Fogassi & Ferrari, 2006). It is likely that mirror neuron systems are involved in imitation and social learning (Filimon et al., 2007; Iacoboni et al., 1999). Autistic children, who have trouble imitating others' gestures, may have deficits in mirror neuron systems (Oberman & Ramachadran, 2007; Williams et al., 2006).

nature & nurture
Thanks largely to mirror neurons, we cry along with characters in a sad movie.

SYNAPTIC CHANGE DURING LEARNING

If you've ever tried to learn a second language, you know that if you don't use it for a while, you forget what you've learned. Similarly, you will probably forget much of the material you learn in this class soon after the exam, even if it is learned well to begin with. Why is that?

In Chapter 7 we saw what Hebb's work on learning and memory revealed about the plasticity of the brain: "Neurons that fire together wire together" and "Use it or lose it." We also discussed Kandel's studies on the sea slug *Aplysia*. Both areas of research provided experimental evidence of the neural basis of learning and memory (Kadel, 2006; Pinsker et al., 1973). Specifically, certain proteins become activated in short- and long-term memory formation and learning. These proteins change preexisting synaptic connections and cause the growth of new synapses (Fields, 2005; Kandel, 2001). What this means is that learning, in a real sense, *is* the growth of new synapses. Synaptic connections between neurons become stronger and even grow during long-term associative learning. The brain literally grows and changes as we learn. The development and frequent use of new synaptic connections in response to stimulation from the environment strengthens the associated memories and makes learning easier. So having experiences repeated over a short period of time is often essential for moving an experience from short-term to long-term memory—that is, for learning to take place. The saying "practice makes perfect" is quite relevant here. To learn and become proficient at something requires repeating the behavior over and over. Synapses need to grow and strengthen.

Yet these same synaptic connections will weaken if they aren't used regularly, resulting in forgetting and the loss of learning. So when we stop using learned information, the synapses that support our knowledge weaken and ultimately degrade—and we forget what we once knew. Practice, use, and rehearsal are important in retaining what we have learned. If you play a musical instrument, you have experienced this phenomenon directly. The more you practice the scales on your piano or guitar, for example, the more synaptic connections you build and the stronger they become. The scales become easier and easier to play. The sensations and movements associated with the increased experience of playing occupy a greater area of your motor cortex and, in effect, change the mapping of touch information in your brain (Pascual-Leone, 2001). If you stop practicing, those connections weaken, the brain map changes, and the scales are harder to recall the next time you try to play.

nature & nurture
When we stop using what we've learned, the synapses that support that knowledge weaken and ultimately we forget what we once knew.

Practice makes perfect synaptic connections.

EXPERIENCE, ENRICHMENT, AND BRAIN GROWTH

As we have seen again and again, experience changes the brain. Recall the discussion in Chapter 2 of the classic work demonstrating that rats reared in enriched or normal environments grow more neural connections and learn to run mazes faster than genetically identical rats raised in impoverished environments (Bennett et al., 1964; Rosenzweig et al., 1962).

Building on this research, later experiments showed that animals did not have to be raised from birth in an enriched environment to benefit. Laboratory mice, for example, can have identical "childhoods" (the first 21 days of their lives) and then be randomly assigned to three different environments: no enrichment, short enrichment (68 days), and long enrichment (6 months). The longer they live in an enriched environment, the more neural growth there is in the hippocampus (Kempermann & Gage, 1999). More importantly, however, simply being in an enriched environment is not even the best way to stimulate the growth of new neurons: Being in an enriched environment that continues to have new and novel forms of stimulation is even better (Kempermann & Gage, 1999). Other research, in an effort to learn what it was about an enriched environment that caused the growth of new neurons (neurogenesis), compared the effects of social interaction, swimming, running, and maze learning (van Praag, Kempermann, & Gage, 1999). Only the running condition led to neurogenesis. Similar enrichment effects on neuron growth occur in other species besides rats, including birds, primates, and humans (Doetsch & Scharff, 2001; Eriksson et al., 1998; Gould et al., 1994).

connection

Can experience generate new neurons in an elderly person?

See Chapter 5, p. 205.

quick quiz 8.3: The Interaction of Nature and Nurture in Learning

1. Because Konrad Lorenz was the first and only animal they knew for the first few weeks of their life, baby geese thought Lorenz was their "mother." This kind of association is known as
   a. reinforcement
   b. imprinting
   c. learning
   d. conditioning

2. What biological structure best explains why we cry readily along with characters in a sad movie?
   a. mirror neurons
   b. sensory neurons
   c. frontal lobes
   d. hypothalamus
3. Research on learning and the brain has shown that rats raised in impoverished environments
   a. learn just as quickly as rats raised in enriched environments
   b. have the same number of neurons in the hippocampus as the rats raised in enriched environments
   c. learn more slowly but have the same number of neurons and synaptic connections as rats raised in enriched environments
   d. learn more slowly and have fewer neurons and synaptic connections as rats raised in enriched environments

Answers can be found at the end of the chapter.

making connections
in learning

Why Do People Smoke?

As you have probably figured out by now, human behavior is complex. So it should be no surprise that any given behavior may be acquired and maintained by means of several types of learning (classical, operant, and/or social), all operating in the context of a human being who has a personality and history. Consider, for example, cigarette smoking (see Figure 8.17). The acquisition of smoking behavior—how people become smokers in the first place—is perhaps best explained by social learning theory (Bandura, 1969, 1986). Think about it: The actual sensory qualities of cigarette smoking on first experience are anything but pleasant—coughing, dizziness, and nausea. But most smokers start smoking as teenagers, and most teens start smoking because they seek some of the rewards that appear to come with smoking: coolness, peer acceptance, looking like an adult. (All of these rewards are secondary reinforcers, which acquire their reinforcing characteristics by means of classical conditioning and operant conditioning.) Kids see that others who smoke get some of these rewards for smoking. Thus they might model smoking behavior in order to obtain these rewards themselves. They might view "being seen as cool"—a form of peer acceptance—as desirable, and so being seen as cool becomes a reinforcer for the smoking behaviors of others. "Whenever Mom gets stressed, she smokes a cigarette to relax—maybe that will work for me, too" is another example of social learning.

Once someone has become an established smoker, operant conditioning helps maintain smoking behavior. Smoking is bolstered by a number of positive reinforcers: arousal of the sympathetic nervous system (the "rush" of smoking), mild relaxation of the muscles, and, in some cases, increased peer acceptance. Smoking also has a number of negative reinforcers, such as the removal of stress, the removal of social isolation for some smokers, and a reduced appetite. The power of these reinforcers, combined with the physiologically addictive properties of nicotine, make it very difficult to quit smoking. Moreover, the potential punishers of smoking—a substantially increased risk of lung cancer and heart disease—are threats that are so far off in the future for teens that they tend to ignore them. It is for this reason that some psychologists who are concerned with preventing smoking by teens have tried to link smoking with unpleasant images and effects (such as ugliness and social rejection). The hope is that by using both classical and operant conditioning, they can make smoking appear less rewarding. For example, in order to discourage smoking, some public health campaigns show pictures of diseased lungs or smokers who look older than they are. The idea is that by means of classical conditioning people might

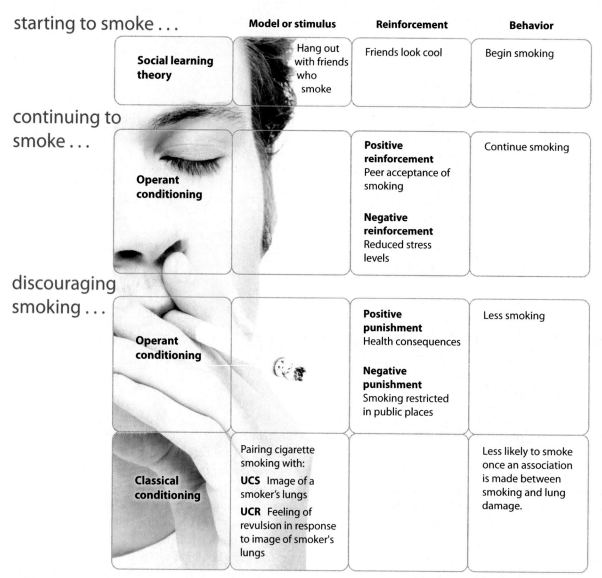

starting to smoke . . .	Model or stimulus	Reinforcement	Behavior
Social learning theory	Hang out with friends who smoke	Friends look cool	Begin smoking
continuing to smoke . . .			
Operant conditioning		**Positive reinforcement** Peer acceptance of smoking **Negative reinforcement** Reduced stress levels	Continue smoking
discouraging smoking . . .			
Operant conditioning		**Positive punishment** Health consequences **Negative punishment** Smoking restricted in public places	Less smoking
Classical conditioning	Pairing cigarette smoking with: **UCS** Image of a smoker's lungs **UCR** Feeling of revulsion in response to image of smoker's lungs		Less likely to smoke once an association is made between smoking and lung damage.

FIGURE **8.17**

HOW LEARNING THEORIES EXPLAIN SMOKING BEHAVIOR. Different theories of learning can explain why people start smoking and continue smoking. In addition, they provide treatment models for helping people to quit smoking. Here are some examples.

associate smoking with negative outcomes. It is an effort to teach people to have an unpleasant association with a cigarette and therefore stop smoking.

But smoking, like many complex human behaviors, derives from numerous other influences besides conditioning. Gender, personality, and sociocultural characteristics are some of the factors that may interact with conditioning and biology to influence people to start smoking and affect whether or not they successfully quit.

Although numerous studies have found no evidence for gender differences in factors related to smoking, one large-scale study found that gender influences susceptibility to smoking, the way people work with their urges to smoke,

and the ability to successfully quit (Ellickson, Tucker, & Klein, 2001). Whether or not friends smoke plays a stronger role in whether adolescent girls attempt and succeed at quitting smoking than it does in boys. In a study of the effects of smoking abstinence (and therefore nicotine withdrawal) on craving and cognitive performance in male and female adolescent smokers, girls reported greater tobacco cravings and symptoms of nicotine withdrawal than boys, but boys performed worse on two cognitive tasks during nicotine withdrawal than did girls (Jacobsen et al., 2005). Taken together, these studies suggest that gender may interact with social and cognitive factors to maintain smoking, both by influencing whether teens decide to attempt to quit (girls have more social pressures to try to quit) and the extent to which the effects of nicotine withdrawal are debilitating (the adverse effects on performance are worse for boys). These are just some of the factors that may explain why more boys smoke than girls, although the gap is narrowing (Robinson & Kleseges, 1997).

Other research shows that personality style predicts whether people start smoking and whether they try to stop, introducing yet another variable into this complex behavior. A study of personality and smoking found that people who are more sociable, impulsive, rebellious, hostile, and sensation-seeking are more likely to start smoking and less likely to quit successfully than those who do not have these personal characteristics (Lipkus et al., 1994). This finding fits with established theory that extraverts are more likely to be smokers than introverts because extraverts have a physiological need for stimulation and therefore seek experiences that are physiologically arousing, such as smoking, drinking, and thrill-seeking feats (Eysenck, 1980). Furthermore, the lack of certain cognitive skills, including long-term thinking and planning abilities, in some adolescents may predispose them to smoke. Not having a long-term perspective, they fail to understand the negative effects of smoking on health (Dinn, Aycicegi, & Harris, 2004). This explanation makes sense if we consider the prevalence of health promotion efforts designed to discourage people from smoking. The urges or need for stimulation may combine with cognitive factors and social learning (modeling peer behavior) to make it very difficult for some people to resist smoking.

The presence of models for smoking (such as parents and friends) figure among the environmental factors that influence smoking behavior. A study of more than 6,000 seventh-grade girls and boys reported differences between African Americans and European Americans in their exposure to peer and parent role models for smoking, which may account for discrepancies in smoking rates in these groups (Robinson & Kleseges, 1997). Specifically, African American children were less likely to smoke than European American children, and they had fewer family members and friends who smoked. They also believed that smoking was less common than did European American children. These findings indicate that cultural variables (ethnic group), social factors (availability of roles models), and basic principles of learning (observational learning) can all interact to influence whether young people start smoking (Ellickson et al., 2004).

Given the role that reinforcement plays in the acquisition of smoking behavior, it is not surprising that operant conditioning has been used to help people kick the smoking habit. **Behavior modification** techniques, which apply principles of operant conditioning to changing behavior, have been particularly effective in helping people quit

Having friends who smoke increases the likelihood of smoking.

smoking, especially when combined with nicotine replacement therapies (such as gum or the patch), which ease the symptoms of withdrawal. Smokers who participate in such programs are likely to live longer than those who don't (Anthonisen et al., 2005).

quick quiz 8.4:
Making Connections in Learning

1. Which model of learning best explains why people might start smoking?
   a. classical conditioning
   b. operant conditioning
   c. latent learning
   d. observational learning

2. Which model of learning best explains why people continue to smoke?
   a. classical conditioning
   b. operant conditioning
   c. latent learning
   d. both b and c

3. Which model of learning best explains how campaigns attempt to discourage smoking?
   a. classical conditioning
   b. sensitization
   c. latent learning
   d. observational learning

Answers can be found at the end of the chapter.

behavior modification
the application of operant conditioning principles to change behavior.

chapter **review**

BASIC PROCESSES OF LEARNING

- Learning is an enduring change in behavior that results from experience. It involves changes in sensation, perception, behavior, and brain function.

- Learning by association is a simple form of learning that links two pieces of information from the environment with one another because, in our experience, they repeatedly occur together.

CONDITIONING MODELS OF LEARNING

- Classical conditioning centers on stimulus–response (S–R) relationships. It involves the modification of reflexes with experience. A conditioned response occurs when a neutral stimulus (such as a bell) elicits what was previously an unconditioned response (such as salivation) to an unconditioned stimulus (such as food) when it is presented alone. After conditioning, the neutral stimulus is called a conditioned stimulus.

- In operant conditioning the consequences of spontaneous behavior are manipulated in order to elicit the desired behavior. According to Skinner, certain consequences make a behavior more likely to occur again. When the consequences of a behavior increase the likelihood that a behavior will occur again, we say that the behavior has been reinforced. Reinforcement can be positive (something added) or negative (something subtracted). In contrast, punishment decreases the likelihood that a behavior will occur again. The stimuli used for reinforcement and punishment are unrelated to the target behavior. Shaping is the reinforcement of successive approximations of a desired behavior.

- Reinforcement may be presented every time a behavior occurs or only occasionally. Intermittent reinforcement, reinforcement that does not occur after every response, produces a stronger behavioral response than does continuous reinforcement. There are four schedules of reinforcement that dictate how an intermittent

reinforcement might be implemented: fixed ratio, variable ratio, fixed interval, and variable interval.

- Biology limits behavioral options in order to make the adaptive ones more likely. The biological constraint model of learning suggests that some behaviors are inherently more likely to be learned than others. Instinctive drift, in which an organism fails to learn the target behavior because it conflicts with a stronger instinctive behavior, is a type of biological constraint.

- Latent learning occurs in the absence of reinforcement and is not demonstrated until later, when reinforcement occurs.

BREAKING NEW GROUND: CONDITIONED TASTE AVERSION

- Conditioned taste aversion, the learned avoidance of a particular taste or food if sickness occurs at the same time as or shortly after exposure to it, can develop after only one exposure. The time lapse between exposure and getting sick may be an hour or more.

- Biological constraints limit the development of a conditioned response to a neutral stimulus that is relevant to the situation. For example, you cannot make someone be nauseated by a sound or a sight as easily as by a taste.

SOCIAL LEARNING THEORY

- Social learning theory takes into account the role of social influence in learning. Imitation or modeling plays a key role in how we learn, and it can work together with reinforcement to shape behavior. Bandura proposed that reinforcement makes learning more likely not only for the person doing the behavior but also for observers.

- Modeling is the process of observing and imitating behaviors performed by others, particularly behaviors that are rewarded in others.

THE INTERACTION OF NATURE AND NURTURE IN LEARNING

- Examples of the bidirectional relationship between learning and the brain include imprinting, the rapid and innate learning of the characteristics of a caregiver within a very short period of time after birth; sensitivity periods, when the brain is most receptive to learning certain skills; imitation; the growth and strengthening of synaptic connections in response to environmental stimuli; and environmental enrichment.

MAKING CONNECTIONS IN LEARNING

- All of the major learning perspectives, as well as other factors, are needed to fully explain behaviors such as smoking.

- Applications derived from models of learning, such as behavior modification, may help people unlearn unwanted or undesirable behaviors, such as smoking.

key **terms**

association, p. 296

behavior modification, p. 329

biological constraint model, p. 313

classical conditioning, p. 297

conditioned taste aversion, p. 315

conditioned response (CR), p. 298

conditioned stimulus (CS), p. 298

conditioning, p. 296

continuous reinforcement, p. 308

enactive learning, p. 318

ethology, p. 322

extinction, p. 299

fixed ratio (FR) schedule, p. 309

fixed interval (FI) schedule, p. 310

imprinting, p. 322

instinctive drift, p. 313

intermittent reinforcement, p. 308

latent learning, p. 314

law of effect, p. 302

learning, p. 295

modeling, p. 319

negative punishment, p. 305

negative reinforcement, p. 304

observational learning, p. 318

operant conditioning, p. 303

positive punishment, p. 305

positive reinforcement, p. 304

primary reinforcers, p. 304

punishment, p. 305

reinforcer, p. 304

schedules of reinforcement, p. 309

secondary (or conditioned) reinforcers, p. 304

shaping, p. 307

Skinner box, p. 306

social learning theory, p. 319

spontaneous recovery, p. 300

stimulus discrimination, p. 299

stimulus generalization, p. 299

unconditioned response (UCR), p. 298

unconditioned stimulus (UCS), p. 298

variable interval (VI) schedule, p. 310

variable ratio (VR) schedule, p. 309

quick quiz **answers**

Quick Quiz 8.1: 1. d 2. b 3. c 4. d 5. b 6. d   Quick Quiz 8.2: 1. a 2. d 3. b

Quick Quiz 8.3: 1. b 2. a 3. d   Quick Quiz 8.4: 1. d 2. b 3. a

language and

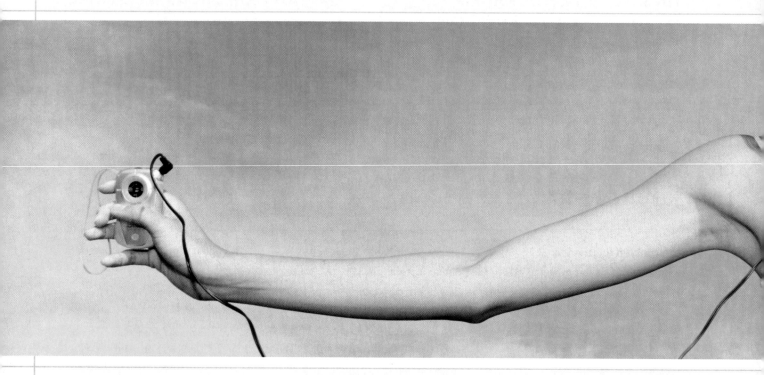

thought

preview
questions

1 *What are the theories behind language acquisition?*

2 *What would our thinking be like if we did not have spoken language?*

3 *How does the brain store and manipulate thoughts and ideas?*

4 *How does learning a second language affect the brain and the way we think?*

H ow many languages can you speak? Most likely you speak just one, or at most two. North Americans who can speak a second language fluently are somewhat unusual. Many Europeans, in contrast, speak two or three languages as a matter of course. Occasionally we hear about people who can speak up to five or six languages. But that's nothing compared to the achievement of Ziad Fazah. A Lebanese native who lives in Brazil, Fazah can speak 56 different languages (*World's Greatest Living Polyglot,* n.d.)! Suppose for a moment that you could speak several languages fluently. Would that change how you think? Would you think differently in each language? Would your thoughts alternate between the languages?

Language is so much a part of being human that we forget it is possible to think without words. Yet when we dream, visually imagine something, or experience a strong ▶

▶ sensation such as a touch or a smell, our thoughts are not initially word-bound. And surely the thoughts of young babies are not verbal. Still, most of our thoughts are translated into words. Even a smell is quickly labeled as a rose or a cake in the oven, and so it becomes a verbal experience as well as a sensory one. Language and thought develop side by side with few exceptions. One is not possible without the other, at least in adult humans.

This chapter introduces the psychology of language and thought, both separately and together. First we look at language by exploring its nature, evolution, and development in humans. Then we turn to current psychological research and theory concerning how we represent our thoughts visually and verbally. We will look at how people reason, form judgments, and make decisions. Finally, we bring all these topics together by examining how and

chapter
outline

when learning a second language changes our brain and affects our ability to reason, solve problems, and think flexibly. We will continue the discussion of thought in Chapter 10, where we discuss the nature of intelligence, problem solving, and creativity. ■

Language

If you lived 300,000 years ago, before language was fully developed, how would you think? How would you communicate if everyone you met could only grunt and groan? Much like the other primates on the planet, you would communicate with other humans only about immediate, concrete states. Everything you knew would be experienced directly through smell, taste, hearing, sight, or touch. Your memory would be limited chiefly to events in the recent past; you would have no language with which to process events and store them in long-term memory. Culture and civilization as we know it could not exist without language. Without language, your ways of thinking, understanding, and transmitting knowledge would be limited to the here and now.

THE NATURE OF LANGUAGE

human language
a communication system specific to *Homo sapiens*; it is open and symbolic, has rules of grammar, and allows its users to express abstract and distant ideas.

Linguists define **human language** as an open and symbolic communication system that has rules of grammar and allows its users to express abstract and distant ideas (Bickerton, 1995). *Open* means that the system is dynamic and free to change. *Symbolic* means that there is no real connection between a sound and the meaning or idea associated with it. Sounds are parts of words that symbolize meaning and ideas. Words, in turn, are put together in ways that follow the rules of syntax and grammar. **Syntax** refers to the rules for arranging words and symbols in sentences (or parts of sentences), whereas **grammar** comprises the entire set of rules for combining symbols and sounds to speak and write a particular language and includes such things in English as subject–verb agreement, plurals, and use of possessives.

syntax
the rules for arranging words and symbols to form sentences or parts of sentences in a particular language.

grammar
the entire set of rules for combining symbols and sounds to speak and write a particular language.

The easiest way to demonstrate the arbitrary nature of the connection between sound and meaning is to point out that we can say the exact same sentence in almost every language in the world, of which there are 5,000 to 6,000. For example, "I am reading the book" can also be "*Ich lese das Buch*" in German," "*Estoy leyendo el libro*" in Spanish, "*Je lis le livre*" in French, and "*Я читаю книгу*" in Russian. Each language has its own distinct sounds for saying the same thing. Because this is true, ideas can often be directly translated—more or less—from one language to another, an idea we return to in "Making Connections in Language and Thought."

Human language is unique because it is the only system capable of transmitting abstract ideas. Although most animals communicate, for the most part they are able to signal to other members of their species only their immediate and concrete states, such as being angry, threatened, hungry, hurt, or eager to reproduce (Deacon, 1997). Yet humans using language can discuss not only immediate feelings and needs but also abstract and remote ideas or states of being such as infinity, God, the afterlife, the universe—or whether Macs are better than PCs.

THE EVOLUTION OF LANGUAGE IN HUMANS

Although it is easy to take for granted, language is one of the most unique, amazing, and complex characteristics of the human species. How else but with language

If bonobos (pygmy chimps) could speak, what would these two be talking about? Bonobos do communicate with one another—not with words, but by leaving trail markers on the floor of the tropical forests where they live.

could Shakespeare have created *Macbeth*? How, without language, would we have ever traveled to the moon or invented the Internet?

As far as we know, earlier species of humans, such as *Homo erectus* and *Homo neanderthalensis,* had, at most, very rudimentary language, called **protolanguage,** or pre-language (Givón & Malle, 2002). No one knows for sure when fully grammatical language first appeared, but archaeologists and linguists suggest that probably only our species *(Homo sapiens)* has used grammatical and syntactical language. If so, language is less than 150,000 to 200,000 years old.

protolanguage
very rudimentary language, also known as pre-language, used by earlier species of *Homo.*

Because the development of fully grammatical language is such a big and unusual step, scientists think that evolution of language and evolution of the brain were intertwined. Anthropologists and psychologists suggest that the complexity of the human brain and the human ability to use language co-evolved. That is, as our ancestors moved from protolanguage to grammatical language, they required brains with greater working memory and the ability for abstract thought (Deacon, 1997; Dunbar, 2001). As the human brain, and especially the frontal lobes, grew larger and larger, people became capable of thinking and communicating more and more complex and abstract thoughts. Increases in the size of human social groups may have triggered increased brain size as well. The more complex a group is, the greater the need for its members to communicate (Dunbar, 2001).

nature & nurture
The development of language, the evolution of the brain, and the development of culture are all connected.

LANGUAGE DEVELOPMENT IN INDIVIDUALS

If you have ever traveled to a country where you don't speak the language, you know that a foreign language can seem like a single, continuous string of sounds. It is hard to know where one word ends and the next one begins unless you have been hearing and speaking that language since early childhood. As young children develop their understanding of language, they learn that the sounds coming from the mouths of the people around them are meaningful units that form words.

In a child's language development, the ability to understand words develops before the ability to produce words (Fenson et al., 1994). We can easily observe that comprehension comes first because babies can do many things that are asked of them, such as pointing to their nose, long before they can say the words associated with those actions. Language comprehension, as we saw in Chapter 3, occurs in the left hemisphere of the brain, in the region called Wernicke's area, whereas language production is associated with the left-hemisphere region called Broca's area (see Figure 9.1). The fact that infants understand language before they start speaking suggests that Wernicke's area develops earlier than Broca's area.

Stages of Language Development The first speech sounds humans make consist almost exclusively of vowels, such as "aah, ee, ooh." Most infants

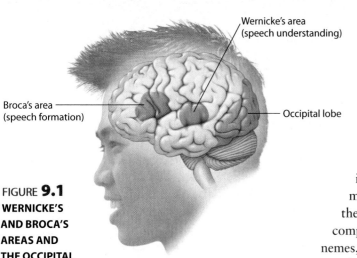

FIGURE **9.1**
WERNICKE'S AND BROCA'S AREAS AND THE OCCIPITAL LOBES. The occipital lobes are home to the visual cortex. As we'll see later, thinking involves both verbal and visual representations.

babbling
sounds made as a result of the infant's experimentation with a complex range of phonemes, which include consonants as well as vowels; starts around 5–6 months.

one-word utterances
single words, such as "mama," "dada," "more," or "no!"; occurs around 12 months of age.

begin uttering repeated vowel sounds, called **cooing**, during the first six months. Cooing sounds are universal: They vary little from hearing to deaf babies or among babies from all over the world.

Babbling overlaps with cooing, and it starts at around 5 or 6 months of age. **Babbling** refers to the infant's experimentation with a complex range of sounds, called phonemes, which include consonants as well as vowels. In babbling, however, the sounds are not yet recognizable as words. At first babies babble single syllables, such as "buh" and "duh"; later they utter "gibberish," which is simply a string of single syllables, such as "da, buh, ma, wee. . . ."

At first, babbling babies make many more sounds than they hear in their native language. Before babies' brains have been fully shaped by their native language, they can make many more sounds than their parents can. They can also hear more sounds than their parents (Jusczyk, 1997; Plunkett, 1997). Adults who speak Asian languages, which do not distinguish between "r" and "l" for example, do not perceive a difference between these two sounds. Their toddler children do. As children progress through the babbling stage, and with repeated exposure to the subset of sounds in their native language, they "prune" away sounds that are not used in that language and lose the ability to say or perceive nonnative sounds (Goto, 1971; Kuhl, Stevens, & Hayashi, 2006).

At the end of the babbling stage, usually at around 12 months, **one-word utterances** emerge. Now children first speak such classic words as "mama," "dada," "more," and the all-important "no!" One-word utterances are likely descended from protolanguage. Like toddlers, our ancestors probably made up sounds for objects (nouns) and actions (verbs) before they developed more complex sentences (Goldfield, 2000).

Whether a word is at the beginning, middle, or end of a sentence seems to be related to how likely young children are to learn that word. Children tend to acquire words that are spoken at the ends of sentences first. For example, in languages that are structured in the order of subject-verb-object, such as English, children acquire nouns earlier than verbs because objects are nouns. In languages that are structured subject-object-verb, such as Japanese and Mandarin, children acquire verbs earlier than nouns (Clancy, 1985; Tardif, Gelman, & Xu, 1999). In English, for example, we say, "Maria read the book," whereas in Japanese people say, "Maria the book read." English-speaking children learn *book* before *read*, whereas Japanese-speaking children learn the Japanese version of *read* before *book*. This tendency to learn the last word in a sentence first may reflect the memory phenomenon called the *recency effect* discussed in Chapter 8.

cooing
the first sounds humans make other than crying, consisting almost exclusively of vowels; occurs during first 6 months of life.

By age 3, children begin to speak in full grammatical sentences. Their brains are also nearly adult size.

Starting around 18 months, children make **two-word utterances** such as "my ball," "mo wawa" (more water), or "go way" (go away). During this phase of language development, parents often find themselves serving as translators because their children create unique ways of saying things. For instance, our youngest son, Evan, would say "ba" for any kind of water. Why? Because he had learned to say "ba" to mean "bottle of water." He extended "ba" to other types of water, such as a lake, pool, or bathtub, which we easily understood. Our babysitters did not, however, so we had to translate "Evanese" for them.

By age two and a half or three, most children enter the third phase of language development—the **sentence phase**—in which they begin speaking in fully grammatical sentences. This transition happens so quickly that linguists usually have a tough time studying it. Linguist Steven Pinker uses Adam as an example. At age 2, Adam would say, "Play checkers. Big drum. I got horn." Less than a year later, at age 3, he would say, "I going come in fourteen minutes. You dress me up like a baby elephant. You know how to put it back together" (Pinker, 1994, pp. 273–274). These sentences may not always be what adults consider grammatically correct, but they are grammatical sentences.

In sum, children go through a very predictable sequence in acquiring language: from cooing to babbling, one-word utterances, two-word utterances, and finally adultlike sentence structure, a stage that is reached around age 3. These stages in speech development map remarkably well onto the growth in the child's overall brain size (see Figure 9.2). There is a steep rise in both brain growth and language between the ages of 1 and 3. The brain of a 3-year-old child has reached about 80% of adult size. At about this age children can form adultlike sentences.

The Sensitivity Period An important principle of language development is that if children are not exposed to any human language before a certain age, their language abilities never fully develop (Lenneberg, 1967; Newport, 2003; Uylings, 2006). This sensitivity period for language acquisition begins in the

two-word utterances
phrases children put together, starting around 18 months, such as "my ball," "mo wawa," or "go way."

sentence phase
stage when children begin speaking in fully grammatical sentences; usually age 2½ to 3.

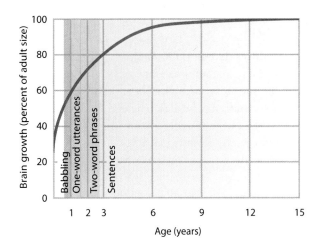

FIGURE **9.2**

ASSOCIATION BETWEEN BRAIN GROWTH AND LANGUAGE DEVELOPMENT. As the child's brain approaches its final adult size, the onset and rapid development of language matches the rapid growth of the brain. At age 1, when the child's brain is less than 50% of its adult size, the infant is babbling and perhaps saying a few words. By age 3, when the brain is 75–80% of its adult size, the child has progressed to two-word phrases and short sentences. (*Source:* Sakai, 2005.)

first years of life and ends at about age 12. It is the optimal time for learning language. Severe neglect and lack of exposure during this period cause permanent problems in language development. As Uylings (2006) points out, sensitivity periods end after neural pruning and neural wiring have reached their peak, at which point the plasticity of neural connections becomes less flexible.

One of the most dramatic examples of the importance of the sensitivity period in language development is the case of an abused and severely neglected girl known as "Genie." When she was 2 years old, a family doctor diagnosed Genie as being mildly retarded (Rymer, 1993). Her father, who was mentally unstable, interpreted this to mean that she was severely retarded and needed "protection." He tied her to a chair all day long and caged her in a crib at night. Moreover, he beat her every time she tried to speak and barked at her like a dog. This abuse lasted until Genie was 13½, when her mother finally ran away, taking Genie with her. The local social worker whose help they sought thought Genie was 6 or 7 years old because she was only 4 feet 6 inches tall and weighed 59 pounds. The social worker arranged for the state of California to take temporary custody of the child. At that time, Genie could speak only a few words, such as *stopit* or *nomore*.

At age 17, after 4 years of language training, Genie's language skills were still extremely delayed. She could communicate simple ideas, but her speech was limited mainly to ungrammatical sentences. She would say things like "Spot chew glove" or "Applesauce buy store" (*Transcripts*, 1997). In this sense, her language ability was on par with that of a young child. Her language comprehension, however, was much better than her language production. She understood much of what was said to her. Brain imaging revealed something most unusual about Genie's brain activity while speaking or listening: The activity was located mostly in her right hemisphere (Curtiss, 1977). Recall that language ability is located in the left hemisphere. The case of Genie suggests that left hemisphere speech development requires stimulation from the environment during a certain sensitivity period if it is to develop properly.

As tragic as Genie's story is, it reveals something very important about language: We need verbal stimulation from others, and we need it while we are young children if we are to develop fully and completely the ability to speak. Now in her early 50s, Genie lives in supportive foster care. The movie *Mockingbird Don't Sing*, released in 2001, is based on her life.

THEORIES OF LANGUAGE ACQUISITION

Unless they suffer from some sort of disease or deficit, all humans learn to speak, including those who were born deaf. Many children who can't hear learn spoken language in order to communicate with hearing individuals, but many rely heavily on sign language as well. Sign language is every bit as complex and communicative as spoken language. This suggests that we have innate, genetically based structures in the brain that enable us to learn language. Yet the vast differences in how well each of us learns to speak illustrate the importance of environmental stimulation. Different theories of language acquisition emphasize contributions of nature and nurture to language differently, but they all agree that both are involved.

Imitating family members helps shape language and vocabulary development of children.

Sociocultural Theories We learn language from the people around us. We acquire vocabulary by hearing others speak, and we figure out what they mean by the context (Hoff, 2006). In a review of the evidence for how environment shapes and molds language acquisition, Erika Hoff (2006) provides a partial list of the environmental influences on language. They include culture, socioeconomic status, birth order, school, peers, television, and parents. Each of these influences has a rich research history demonstrating how sociocultural forces shape language development, particularly the timing of vocabulary development.

Much of what we learn comes from imitating family members. Imitation is doing exactly what you see someone else do, and with certain behaviors imitation is evident immediately after birth. Newborns as young as 50 minutes old will stick out their tongues or open their mouths when they see an adult do so (Meltzoff & Moore, 1983). At a slightly older age babies try to imitate the speech sounds they hear (Kuhl & Meltzoff, 1997). Adults, in turn, do many things to encourage imitation. For example, they speak in a higher pitch, raise and lower the volume of their voice, use simpler sentence structures, emphasize the here and now, and use emotion to communicate their messages (Fernald & Morikawa, 1993; Rice, 1989). These changes in adult speech patterns—which appear to be universal—are referred to as **child-directed speech.**

The richness of verbal stimulation from family members affects the timing of a child's vocabulary development (Hoff, 2006). For instance, the children of very verbally responsive mothers reach the 50-word vocabulary milestone a full 5 months earlier than do children of less verbally responsive mothers. More generally, much of the differences in the timing of the child's vocabulary development can be explained by three characteristics of the mother: her socioeconomic status, her vocabulary use, and her personality characteristics.

Although these are very social processes we have been discussing, they also demonstrate profound interdependence with brain processes, which is yet another example of the interplay between nature and nurture. Mirror neurons, the clusters of brain cells that fire not only when an individual performs some task (such as

child-directed speech changes in adult speech patterns—apparently universal—when speaking to young children or infants; characterized by higher pitch, changes in voice volume, use of simpler sentences, emphasis on the here and now, and use of emotion to communicate messages.

sticking out one's tongue), but also when an individual observes another person do the same task, facilitate social learning and imitation (Rizzolatti & Craighero, 2004; Rizzolatti & Arbib, 1998). Many human social skills, including speech, develop because our brains allow and foster such social learning.

connections

One reason newborn infants are capable of imitating behavior immediately after birth is that humans and other animals have "mirror neurons." These were detected first after a chance observation in laboratory monkeys. See Chapter 3, p. 88, and Chapter 8, p. 324.

Conditioning and Learning Theory

B. F. Skinner (1957) believed that language is like any other behavior: something that exists because it is reinforced and shaped. He proposed that we speak not because we want to convey an idea or a feeling, but rather because we have been reinforced for doing so. What are the conditions that bring about or reinforce verbal behavior? According to Skinner, children learn to speak a particular language because when they say anything that even comes close to a word, the parents smile and say things like "Wow! She said 'mama'!" The parents' reaction has a reinforcing effect, making the child more likely to say that word; that is, the reaction shapes her behavior.

As we just discussed, young children begin language development by cooing, then babbling, then uttering one and two words until they begin to say short phrases and sentences. Skinner explained this progression in terms of shaping, successive approximations, and reinforcement: The first approximation of a complex behavior will be reinforced. When, for instance, a toddler utters "mama," she gets more of her mother's attention and smiles than she does when she utters "baba." The child learns first that the word *mama* matters and soon thereafter learns what it means. In a short while the child is saying "mama go bye-bye." Each step is subsequently reinforced until the child reaches the final behavior, which, in this case, would be speaking in fully grammatical sentences—"Mommy is going away."

Nativist Theory

There is little doubt that language development, such as the acquisition of certain words, is shaped partly by parental responses. When a child correctly names an object for the first time—such as "doggy"—the parents lavish much praise and encouragement: "Yes, that's right! Spot is a doggy!" However, such reinforcement does not as consistently occur for other aspects of language development, such as syntax and grammar rules. Still, children seem to learn these aspects with little difficulty. In fact, children tend to overgeneralize language rules; for example, they may add *ed* to *run* to form the past tense because adding *ed* is the typical way of forming the past tense in English. Instead of saying "Spot ran," then, the child says "Spot runned." Reinforcement cannot explain this formation, because children most likely have never heard "runned" from their parents and so have not been reinforced for using it. In other words, it is impossible to learn novel utterances through imitation and reinforcement. One cannot use shaping to teach someone to say something no one has ever said. So Skinner's explanation of language acquisition cannot fully explain how we learn language.

Some linguists contend that we discover language rather than learn it, that language development is "native," or inborn. This is the main assumption of the **nativist view of language.** In this view, the brain is structured, or "wired," for language learning; indeed, as we saw earlier, Broca's and Wernicke's areas are dedicated to speech production and comprehension, respectively. The linguist Noam Chomsky (1972, 1986) has argued that humans are born with a **language acquisition device (LAD)**—an innate, biologically based capacity to acquire

nativist view of language
the idea that we discover language rather than learn it, that language development is inborn.

language acquisition device (LAD)
an innate, biologically based capacity to acquire language, proposed by Noam Chomsky as part of his nativist view of language.

language. Just as birds are biologically built to fly, humans are biologically built to speak. It is part of our nature; hence the term "nativist." Further, Chomsky (1972, 2000) has suggested that there is essentially a single universal grammar underlying all human languages; each individual language is simply a specific expression of this universal grammar.

Noam Chomsky

Chomsky argues for a built-in language acquisition device partly because of how easily and automatically humans learn to do this most complex and difficult thing: speak in complete and grammatical sentences. It is universal. Moreover, it develops in children in about the same way and at the same time all over the world, regardless of which language they learn. Indeed, any child can learn equally easily any language as her or his native language. If you grew up in certain regions of Africa, you would be speaking Swahili; certain parts of Asia, Mandarin; certain parts of Europe, German. Where we are born and what language we are exposed to is the one we learn, and we have no trouble learning it.

Chomsky also argues that our biologically based language acquisition device must have *principles* of universal grammar that allow a child to learn any language as her or his native language (Chomsky, 2000; Radford, 1997). Universal grammar follows universal principles. For instance, a universal grammar principle might be, "Languages have subjects, objects, and verbs." All languages have these components of speech, but they vary in where they can be put in sentences. As we have seen, English, for instance, is a subject-verb-object (S-V-O) language, whereas Japanese is a subject-object-verb (S-O-V) language. So when an English speaker says "Maria read the book" and a Japanese speaker says "Maria the book read," the principles are the same, but the rules or word order are different.

Chomsky calls these different rules of what is allowed and what is not in different languages *parameters*. So although there are universal principles for language, each specific language sets limits, or parameters, for what is correct. We

According to Noam Chomsky, regardless of where we are born or what language we are exposed to, we have no trouble learning it.

Studies of twins, like these fraternal twins, suggest that grammar is more influenced by genetics than the environment, whereas vocabulary is more influenced by the environment than genetics.

learn these parameters as we learn to speak: Verbs go before objects in English but after them in Japanese. Limits, or parameters, make clear why it is relatively easy for a child to learn a particular language: Every language has rules that limit possible word orders and other aspects of language. Once children learn those rules, or limits, of their particular language, forming grammatically correct sentences becomes relatively easy (Dunbar, 2001; Pinker, 1994). And they learn these rules easily because of a built-in language acquisition device.

Nature, Nurture, and Language Learning

As we have seen, different theorists emphasize different contributions of nature and nurture. Social and learning theorists argue for the importance of social input and stimulation, whereas nativist theorists argue for the importance of brain structures and genetic factors. Yet, once again, both perspectives are needed to fully explain language. Most scholars of language agree that acquiring language involves natural abilities that are modified by the language learner's environment (Hoff, 2006; Lidz & Gleitman, 2004; MacWhinney, 1999). Indeed, the phrase *innately guided learning* captures the interaction between nature and nurture very well (Elman et al., 1996). We learn to speak, but in doing so we are guided by our innate capacity for language learning. The importance of both nature and nurture is starkly illustrated by the case of Genie: She could speak, and even learned a few words as a child, but her environment was so barren that her language development was severely stunted.

nature & nurture
The fact that you speak a language fluently means you made use of innately guided learning as a child.

Still, genetic factors and innate structures have a stronger influence on some aspects of language development, while environmental conditions have a greater influence on other aspects. For instance, grammar is more innate and genetically influenced than vocabulary, which is more strongly shaped by input from the environment (Dale et al., 2000; Hoff, 2006). Recall that one common way to determine how much of a trait is due to genetic influence is by comparing identical twin pairs to fraternal twin pairs (see Chapter 3). If a trait is strongly genetically influenced, it will show much stronger correlations in identical twins than in fraternal twins because identical twins are more genetically alike than fraternal twins. Dale and colleagues (2000) compared vocabulary and grammar skills in 1,008 identical twin pairs to those same skills in 1,890 fraternal twin pairs; all were about 2 years old. The children's parents assessed their vocabulary and grammar skills by completing questionnaires dealing with the kinds of words and sentences their children could say. Identical twin pairs were more similar in vocabulary and grammar than were fraternal twin pairs. Figures from the study show us that about 25% of vocabulary development and about 40% of learning about grammar are genetically influenced (Dale et al., 2000).

Animals of all kinds communicate with members of their own species. Birds sing songs to tell other birds where they are, that they want to mate, or that a predator is nearby; sometimes they sing just for the fun of it (Rothenberg, 2005). Whales sing long, melancholic (to human ears) tones that other whales hear from miles away. Bees dance to tell other bees where nectar can be found. But do these forms of animal communication represent the ability to use language as humans do?

CAN OTHER SPECIES LEARN HUMAN LANGUAGE?

For centuries it was argued that the capacity for language is what separates humans from other animals. Yet, if humans share almost all of their genes with chimps, and humans and apes share a common ancestor from roughly 6 million years ago, an obvious question is, Is it possible for apes to learn human language?

Chimps do not have a vocal apparatus that allows them to speak, so they are physically incapable of making the same range of sounds that humans can (see Figure 9.3). The only way humans can teach apes to communicate is to use a nonvocal sign language, most often American Sign Language (ASL). A number of captive apes have learned ASL to different degrees and have been able to communicate with humans. Allen and Beatrix Gardner, for instance, have compiled more than 400 ASL signs that three chimps named Dar, Tatu, and

Moja acquired in the course of extensive training (Gardner, Gardner, & Van Cantfort, 1989). Their first chimp, Washoe, learned to sign almost 200 distinct words. Another chimp, Sarah, developed a vocabulary of about 100 words (Premack, 1971). Perhaps the most linguistically gifted ape to date is Kanzi, a bonobo chimp (Rumbaugh, Beran, & Savage-Rumbaugh, 2003).

Kanzi was the son of Matata, who had been caught wild in Zaire. When Matata was an adult, linguist Sue Savage-Rumbaugh attempted to teach her sign language, with limited success. Kanzi was present during these training sessions but was not formally taught any signs. Savage-Rumbaugh soon discovered, however, that Kanzi had been paying attention to the signs they were teaching his mother. Moreover, he learned more quickly and developed a larger vocabulary than his mother. The research team decided to compare Kanzi's language comprehension to

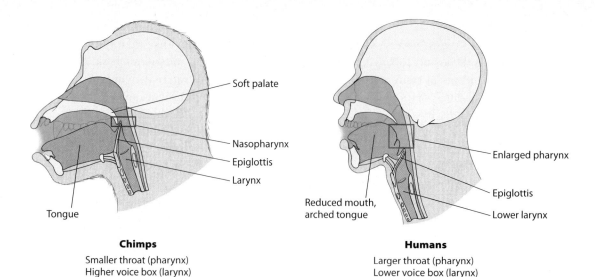

Soft palate

Nasopharynx

Epiglottis

Larynx

Tongue

Enlarged pharynx

Reduced mouth, arched tongue

Epiglottis

Lower larynx

Chimps

Smaller throat (pharynx)
Higher voice box (larynx)

Humans

Larger throat (pharynx)
Lower voice box (larynx)

FIGURE **9.3**

VOCAL ANATOMY OF CHIMPS AND HUMANS. Vocal structures (throat, voice box, tongue) determine the kinds of sounds chimps and humans are capable of making. (*Source:* Deacon, 1997.)

that of a 2½-year-old human child, Alia. At the time, Kanzi was 7 years old. Both Kanzi and Alia were given 660 spoken requests to see whether they understood them well enough to carry them out. The requests were things like "Take the shoe to the bathroom," "Give Karen an apple," or "Put the pine needles in the refrigerator," and reversals such as "Make the doggie bite the snake" then "Make the snake bite the doggie" (Rumbaugh, Beran, & Savage-Rumbaugh, 2003, p. 411). Alia and Kanzi performed these commands at very similar levels of success— about 70%. Since then, Kanzi, now 27 years old, has learned to comprehend as many as 3,000 English words (Raffaele, 2006).

If apes can learn sign language, do they use it to talk with each other? The answer seems to be: Sometimes, in some circumstances, and in some species of ape. So what do apes sign to one another about? Fouts and colleagues (1984) analyzed the types of conversations five signing chimpanzees had among themselves.

Kanzi, a bonobo who understands at least 3,000 English words, uses symbols to communicate with his teacher, linguist Sue Savage-Rumbaugh.

They found that 88% of the conversations were about social interaction, play, and reassurance, whereas the other 12% were about feeding, grooming, cleaning, discipline, and chimps signing, or "talking," to themselves (just as we humans talk to ourselves) (Fouts, Fouts, & Schoenfeld, 1984). More incredibly, one chimp, also named Washoe, spontaneously began teaching her adopted son Loulis how to sign (Fouts, 1997). Human trainers were careful not to sign around Loulis to ensure that he would learn only from Washoe. After just 8 weeks with Washoe, Loulis would regularly sign with humans, and after 18 months he had learned about 20 signs.

Taken together, even the most linguistically talented apes are limited compared to humans. First, the developmental sequence in which they acquire signs is slower than the sequence in which humans do so. For instance, a gorilla named Koko acquired signs at about half the speed of very young human children (Parker & McKinney, 1999), and Loulis learned only about one sign a month during his first 18 months of learning. In addition, apes seldom progress beyond two- or three-word combinations, which means that their highest level of language learning is equivalent to the level achieved by a toddler in terms of vocabulary and sentence structure. Adult apes may have vocabularies of 100 to 300 words, whereas an average high school student knows 60,000 words (Hauser, Chomsky, & Fitch, 2002; Parker & McKinney, 1999). Finally, primates seldom either understand or consistently use correct word order (syntax). For example, one chimp, named Nim Chimsky after linguist Noam Chomsky, would alternate among "Banana give Nim," "Give Nim banana," and "Banana Nim give" (Terrace, 1987).

Given the successes and limits of language acquisition by apes, the scientific community is split on the question of whether apes really can use language to communicate with humans. On the one hand, some researchers emphasize the linguistic abilities of apes. Often they have raised these apes like children of their own and taught them language. Such close relationships can also bias their perceptions—causing them to see things that may or may not be there. On the other hand, others, often linguists with little direct experience with apes, emphasize the linguistic limitations of apes. The main conclusion to draw from these opposing views is that the capacity for learning language in rudimentary form evolved from our early ancestors—ancestors common to both humans and apes (Deacon, 1997).

LANGUAGE, CULTURE, AND THOUGHT

Does the language we speak cause us to see the world in a particular way? Can people who speak vastly different languages communicate effectively, even in translation? After we learn our native language, can we still learn about concepts that do not exist in our language but only in other languages?

According to the *Whorf-Sapir hypothesis,* language creates thought as much as thought creates language (Whorf, 1956). Anthropologists Benjamin Whorf and Edward Sapir, the authors of the Whorf-Sapir hypothesis, suggested that language shapes our thoughts and perceptions to such an extent that people who speak languages that lack a common foundation, such as English and Chinese, have difficulty directly communicating and translating their ideas from one language to the other. Taken to its logical conclusion, the Whorf-Sapir view leads to the **linguistic determinism hypothesis**, which states that our language determines our way of thinking and our perceptions of the world. In this view, if there are no words for certain objects or concepts in one's language, it is not possible to think about those objects or concepts.

linguistic determinism hypothesis
the proposition that our language determines our way of thinking and our perceptions of the world; the view taken by Sapir and Whorf.

An example offers support for the linguistic determinism hypothesis. The Pirahã, a very small tribe of only about 200 people that lives in the Amazon area of Brazil, are challenging some of science's most basic notions of language, numbers, memory, perception, and thought (Everett, 2005). The Pirahã have no words for the numbers higher than 2. As a result, it is nearly impossible for them to learn concepts such as 9 or 10. They even have difficulty learning simple arithmetic relationships, such as 3 + 1 (Gordon, 2004). This difficulty occurs not because they are unintelligent, but rather because their language so strongly works against such concepts. They function very well without these concepts and by adulthood learning them is rather difficult.

Support for the linguistic determinism hypothesis comes from studies of the Pirahã tribe in Brazil. The language of the Pirahã has no words for numbers higher than 2, and they have difficulty learning simple arithmetic relationships because they don't need them in their daily life.

The most radical claim made by linguists studying the Pirahã is that the Pirahã have no way to include one clause within another. They can construct only independent clauses. For example, they cannot say something like, "When I finish eating, I want to speak to you." Instead, they must say two things: "I finish eating. I speak to you" (Bower, 2005). This claim is radical because it is directly challenges the concept of a universal grammar. According to Chomsky, a cornerstone of universal grammar is that all languages embed clauses within clauses. The Pirahã, however, do not do this; they do not construct sentences that start with words like *when, before,* or *after,* and as a result they are limited to talking about the here and now and only about what is directly observable. Not surprisingly, they lack stories about the ancient past—they have no stories, for instance, of how the world began, and they refer only to known, living relatives.

The view that language determines our thinking is almost certainly overstated. Most research on the topic does not support the strong view that language determines our thinking, but rather that it influences our thinking (Newcombe & Uttal, 2006). This position is known as *linguistic relativism.* A good example of linguistic relativism was recently reported in a study on how language affects color perception (Winawer et al., 2007). Russian has distinct words for lighter blues (*goluboy*) and darker blues (*siniy*). English has only "blue." When researchers presented 20 different shades of blue to both Russian and English speakers, they discovered Russian speakers were faster—by milliseconds—at discriminating between these two shades of blue that came from within the same category (*goluboy* or *siniy*) than when they came from different categories of blue (see Figure 9.4). For English speakers, however, who have no words for the different categories of blue, the category of blue made no difference. This is a typical finding on how language influences but does not determine thinking and perception.

1 research question

Is people's ability to discriminate colors altered by language? Unlike English, Russian has two distinct words for lighter blues (*goluboy*) and darker blues (*siniy*); English does not. Does knowledge of these different color categories affect how quickly a person can discriminate between different shades of blue?

English speakers

Russian speakers

2 method

Winauer and colleagues (2007) designed a quasi-experiment to measure color discrimination performance in native English and Russian speakers in a simple perceptual task. Twenty color stimuli spanning the Russian *siniy/goluboy* range were used. The participants viewed colors arranged in a triad as shown above. Their task was to indicate as quickly and accurately as possible which of the two bottom color squares was identical to the top square.

The prediction was that for the Russian speakers the time it takes them to identify the color as matching the target would depend on whether the color was in the same category or a different one. For English speakers there would be no real difference in reaction times for blues that were in the same or a different Russian color category.

FIGURE **9.4**
LANGUAGE AND COLOR DISCRIMINATION Words for color influence our perception of and thinking about those colors. (*Source:* Winawer, J., Witthoft, N., Frank, M. C., Wu, L., Wade, A. R., & Boroditsky, L. (2007). Russian blues reveal effect of language on color discrimination. *Proceedings of the National Academy of Science, 104,* 7780–7785.)

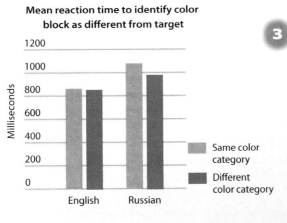

Mean reaction time to identify color block as different from target

3 results

Russian speakers were faster at discriminating blues that came from different color categories than at discriminating blues that came from within the same category. For English speakers, response time did not differ for same versus different category of blue, because there is only one category of blue in English.

4 conclusion

Knowledge of words for different categories of blue does affect how quickly people can discriminate between examples of blue. Notice, however, that the English speakers performed very well overall—in fact, they were faster than Russian speakers—but their performance was not affected by the different language categories. Language knowledge can influence thought.

As these examples illustrate, thought, memory, number, and perception are all tied to language. In fact, language is a close cousin to thought—humans rely on language for organizing, storing, and communicating ideas. Our ability to think, reason, and make decisions often takes verbal form. Let's therefore turn our attention to human thought, reasoning, and decision making.

quick quiz 9.1: Language

1. A language's particular rules for arranging words and symbols in a sentence or parts of a sentence is called
   a. grammar
   b. lexicon
   c. syntax
   d. representation

2. During which stage of language development do babies make many more sounds than they hear in their native languages?
   a. babbling
   b. cooing
   c. one-word utterances
   d. telegraphic speech

3. According to Skinner, children learn to speak a particular language because
   a. they possess an inherent ability to speak
   b. they engage in imitation of what they hear
   c. they have a language acquisition device
   d. they get reinforcement from their parents for various utterances

4. Which theory of language argues that if there are no words for certain objects or concepts in one's language, one is unable to think about those objects or concepts?
   a. nativist theory
   b. theory of innately guided learning
   c. linguistic determinism hypothesis
   d. Skinnerian theory of language

Answers can be found at the end of the chapter.

Among other things, humans rely on language to communicate ideas about who we are and how we feel.

Thinking, Reasoning, and Decision Making

What does it mean to know something? For instance, if our bodies just do something automatically, like breathing or digesting food, could we say that we know how to breathe and digest or that we just do it?

These questions and examples suggest that knowledge is distinct from instinct, and certainly it is. In this section we explore some questions about mental processes, such as how we come to know anything as well as how we know that we know anything. Psychologists use the word **cognition**, which means "to know," to refer to mental processes involved in acquiring, processing, and storing knowledge. **Cognitive psychology** is the science of how people think, learn, remember, and perceive (Sternberg, 2006). Humans are unique in their ability to represent ideas and think abstract and symbolic thoughts.

cognition
mental processes involved in acquiring, processing, and storing knowledge.

cognitive psychology
the science of how people think, learn, remember, and perceive.

In this section, we will consider three fundamental questions about cognition and reasoning:

1. How do we represent thoughts in our minds?
2. How do we reason about evidence?
3. How do we make judgments and decisions?

HOW DO WE REPRESENT THOUGHTS IN OUR MINDS?

Have you ever wondered, "Where exactly in my brain is a thought?" Cognitive psychologists and neuroscientists have and have even conducted research to find an answer. Cognitive psychologists, however, frame the question this way: How do we store or represent thoughts in our mind?

How does the brain store and maintain mental processes?

Even with the most up-to-date brain imaging technology we cannot actually see inside the brain as it conjures up an image or comes up with a solution to a problem. Imaging techniques can only measure changes in blood flow, which suggest brain activity. We cannot and probably never will be able to actually *see* thoughts and ideas. Yet it is clear that we all have thoughts, memories, and ideas, so the question arises: How do we use our brains to store and maintain these mental processes?

Cognitive psychologists approach this question by proposing that we represent ideas, knowledge, or memories as *mental representations*. A **mental representation** is a structure in our mind—such as an idea or image—that stands for something else, such as the external object or thing (Thagard, 1995). In general, mental representations are frequently not about things we are currently sensing (seeing, touching, or smelling, for instance), but rather about things we sensed in the past. Mental representations, therefore, allow us to think about and remember things in the past or imagine things in the future. They also allow us to think about abstract ideas that have no physical existence, such as love, truth, beauty, or justice. For the most part, we represent ideas and thoughts in our minds visually and verbally.

mental representation
a structure in our mind—such as an idea or image—that stands for something else, such as an external object or thing sensed in the past or future, not the present.

connection
The occipital and parietal lobes of the brain develop before the temporal and frontal lobes. This pattern of growth partly explains why we see before we can talk.
See Chapter 5, p. 184.

Visual Representation We think both in images and in words. The visual system, located mostly in the occipital lobes (see Figure 9.1), is older in evolutionary terms than the verbal system. It also develops before verbal ability (Givón, 2002): We see before we talk. Consider how babies respond to picture books before they learn to talk.

Every animal with eyes perceives visual images, but only those animals with significant cortex are better able to keep and store visual sensations in mind after the sensory stimulation stops. Indeed, visual perception occurs while the stimulus is still present, as we learned in Chapter 4. **Visual imagery**, however, involves visual representations created by the brain after the original

visual imagery
visual representations created by the brain after the original stimulus is no longer present.

stimulus is no longer present (Kosslyn, 2005). The brain is active much the same way during visual imagery as it is during visual perception. Thus, you would have a hard time distinguishing between a brain image of someone actually perceiving something and a brain image of someone imagining seeing the same thing (Thompson & Kosslyn, 2000).

Being able to imagine things that are not currently being perceived is a very useful and complex skill, although about 2% of the population cannot do it at all (Kosslyn 2002). People clearly differ in their ability to imagine an event or object in their "mind's eye" (Kosslyn, Van Kleeck, & Kirby, 1990). If you have the ability to imagine outcomes, you can make them more likely to happen. For instance, if you first form a mental image of an ideal performance, such as hitting a home run or playing a piece of music without errors, you are more likely to perform that activity better (Hale, Seiser, & McGuire, 2005). Performance may be improved because the brain is primed by the images of success; that is, the pathways are activated in advance. Neuroscientists have shown that the brain is activated in much the same way while imagining a task as it is while performing that task (Bonnet et al., 1997). So, next time you are getting ready to play a game of tennis or perform a Mozart sonata, imagine doing your best. It can help you succeed.

Many successful athletes use visual imaging to improve their performance. Visualizing success can help to make it happen.

Visual imagery and visual imagination can also be critical to many creative accomplishments, in both art and science (A. Miller, 1996). For example, Albert Einstein made it quite clear that words were not involved or came after the fact when he was developing his most creative ideas: "The words of the language, as they are written or spoken, do not seem to play any role in my mechanism of thought" (quoted in Calaprice, 2005, p. 279). When describing how he came up with his ideas for the theory of relativity, Einstein said, "These thoughts did not come in any verbal formulation. I rarely think in words at all. A thought comes and I may try to express it in words later" (quoted in Wertheimer, 1959, p. 228). He would often visually imagine certain thought experiments, such as riding on a light beam or traveling at the speed of light in an elevator. Other physicists have argued that Einstein's great creativity dried up when he could no longer produce such visual images (Feist, 2006).

mental rotation
process of imagining an object turning in three-dimensional space.

The process of imagining an object rotating in three-dimensional space is known as **mental rotation**. Look at the shapes in Figure 9.5. The pairs are either the same or different, and your task is to decide which is which. If you are

FIGURE **9.5**

MENTAL ROTATION. In this example, figures on the right are always rotated 80 degrees compared to the figures on the left. It takes most people about 2.5 seconds to mentally rotate the figures. The pairs in (a) and (b) are the same, whereas the pair in (c) is different. (*Source:* Shepard & Metzler, 1971)

 (a)

like most people, it will take you about 2.5 seconds for each pair to determine whether it is the same (a and b) or different (c).

Researchers examining gender differences in the performance of mental rotation tasks have reported moderate to large gender effects, with boys and men doing better than girls and women (Halpern, 2004; Hyde, 1990). Recent cross-cultural research has shown that these effects also appear in Ecuador, Ireland, and Japan (Flaherty, 2005).

One cause of this gender difference in spatial ability appears to be levels of the male sex hormone testosterone (Kimura, 2007). Men, women born with unusually high levels of testosterone, and female rats injected with testosterone during development all perform better than female rats and women with normal levels of testosterone at spatial tasks like mental rotations (for humans) and maze running (for rats) (Berenbaum, Korman, & Leveroni, 1995).

The fact that artificial increases in testosterone levels (caused by drugs, for instance) lead to improved spatial ability is another example of the intimate interaction between the forces of nature and nurture in shaping our thought and behavior.

nature & nurture
High levels of testoster-one, in men and women, are associated with the ability to perform spatial and mental rotation tasks such as finding one's way around a new building or playing a three-dimensional video game.

Verbal Representation   A major function of thought is to organize and classify our perceptions into categories. One way in which humans organize their environment is by naming things and giving them labels. We organize our sensory experience by putting like with like and then distinguishing that group of things from other groups of things. We do this by first finding similar features and then forming concepts and building categories based on those similarities. Indeed, the most basic unit of knowledge is a **concept,** which is a mental grouping of objects, events, or people. The concept *fruit* includes yellow, red, blue, orange, and green fruit, and large and small fruit, but what an apple and banana have in common defines the concept *fruit:* the edible part of a plant that contains seeds.

concept
a mental grouping of objects, events, or people.

Concepts help us organize our perceptions of the world. We can store and process these concepts in at least two ways: in a hierarchy and by parallel distributed processing, which we discussed in Chapter 7. A **concept hierarchy** lets us know that certain concepts are related in a particular way, with some being general and others specific. In so doing, it helps us order and understand our world. A particular dog, Goldie, is a "Golden Retriever," which is a "dog," which is an "animal," which is a "living thing."

concept hierarchy
arrangement of related concepts in a particular way, with some being general and others specific.

A more complex model of how we store and organize knowledge in our brain is *parallel distributive processing* (PDP). Recall from Chapter 7 that the PDP model

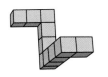

(b)

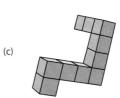

(c)

thinking, reasoning, and decision making   **353**

proposes that associations between concepts activate many networks or nodes at the same time (McClelland, 1988; McClelland & Rogers, 2003; McClelland & Rumelhart, 1985). The nodes are neuronlike and involve patterns of activation over the network. Concepts are activated in the network based on how strongly associated or connected they are to each other. They are also arranged by similarity as well as hierarchy. For instance, animals such as *bird* and *fish* are closer to each other and farther away from plants such as trees and flowers. The location of a concept is based on its relation to other concepts. In the example in Figure 9.6, "living thing" is the most general conceptual category, of which there are two particular examples, "plants" and "animals." The relationship between nodes takes the form of "CAN," "HAS," or "IS A." An animal, for instance, CAN move, HAS skin, and IS A bird or fish, whereas a plant HAS roots and IS A flower or tree. A fish, in turn, HAS scales and gills, IS A salmon, and CAN swim. We can use these relationships and networks to reason about things: If a bird can fly and a robin is a bird, then a robin can fly.

A **category** is a concept that organizes other concepts around what they all share in common. For instance, all things that move and eat can belong to the category "animals," whereas all living things that grow out

connection

Parallel processing of concepts help us establish, maintain, and retrieve memories.
See Chapter 7, p. 271.

category
a concept that organizes other concepts around what they all share in common.

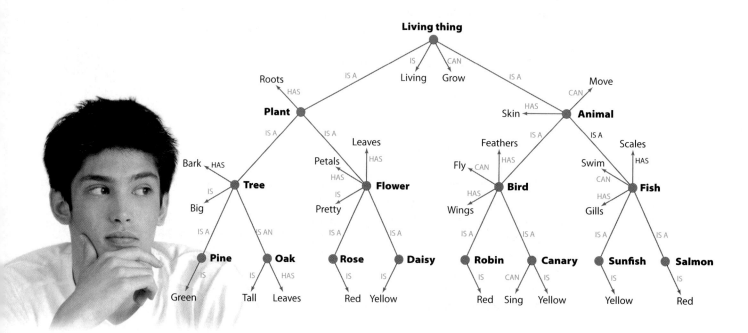

FIGURE **9.6**

PARALLEL DISTRIBUTED NETWORK OF THE VERBAL CONCEPT "LIVING THING." Concepts, printed in **bold** type, are represented by circles, or nodes, and are interconnected. Properties of concepts are depicted by arrows, which represent statements. Relationships are shown in CAPS. The concept **Flower,** for instance, HAS petals and leaves, IS pretty, IS a plant, and IS a rose or a daisy. The concept **Plant** is a more general concept, whereas **Rose** and **Daisy** are more specific ones. (*Source:* McClelland & Rogers, 2003.)

of the earth and do not eat are in the category "plants." Categories can be either *well-defined* (e.g., triangles, cars) or *fuzzy* (e.g., good, consciousness). In addition, some examples of a category fit that category better than others. "Robin," for example, fits and represents the category "bird" better than does "ostrich," as ostriches cannot fly, are big, and have long legs. We refer to the best-fitting examples of a category as **prototypes** (Rosch, 1973). Thus, a robin is a better prototype for the category "bird" than an ostrich is.

prototypes
the best-fitting examples of a category.

Now that we have developed concepts and categories to help organize our mind's representations, how do we use them to make sense of our world and to reason about them? In the next section we'll consider an answer to this question as we talk about humans' reasoning ability.

HOW DO WE REASON ABOUT EVIDENCE?

"He must like me because he always smiles when he talks to me." This is an example of **reasoning,** the process of drawing inferences or conclusions from principles and evidence (Sternberg, 2006). Sometimes reasoning allows us to draw sound, correct conclusions, yet this is not always the case. Consider the statement, "The FBI and CIA are both out to get me because I always see people looking at me." The conclusion is not a sound one, for it is based only on the evidence that people are looking at you. In fact, it's probably not correct, either.

reasoning
the process of drawing inferences or conclusions from principles and evidence.

Cognitive psychologists distinguish between two kinds of reasoning drawn from formal logic: deductive and inductive. **Deductive reasoning** occurs when we reason from general statements of what is known to specific conclusions. The specific conclusion is always correct if the general statement is true. For instance:

deductive reasoning
reasoning from general statements of what is known to specific conclusions.

All humans are mortal (premise A).
Socrates is human (premise B).
Therefore, Socrates must be mortal (conclusion).

That Socrates is mortal is a logical conclusion that has to be true if the two premises are true. This form of reasoning, of course, leads to correct conclusions only when the general premises on which they are based are true. Consider the following:

All humans are green (premise A).
Socrates is a human (premise B).
Therefore, Socrates must be green (false conclusion).

This reasoning obviously leads to a false conclusion because it is based on false premise A. Even though the structure of the two arguments is exactly the same, one leads to a correct conclusion and the other does not. When scientists make specific predictions from their general theories, they are engaging in deductive reasoning.

The second kind of reasoning is known as **inductive reasoning,** which is defined as drawing general conclusions from specific evidence. Conclusions drawn from inductive reasoning are less certain than those drawn from deductive reasoning because many different conclusions might be consistent with a specific fact. With deduction we can reach certain and necessarily correct conclusions. With induction, however, the best we can hope for are highly likely conclusions. An example of inductive reasoning is "All peaches I have eaten have been sweet; therefore, all peaches are sweet." All it takes is one unsweet peach to undermine that conclusion. A better inductive conclusion would be that *most*

inductive reasoning
reasoning to general conclusions from specific evidence.

peaches are sweet. When scientists develop theories, they employ inductive reasoning because they offer general statements that explain many specific facts or observations. When we use inductive reasoning we often use **causal inferences,** judgments about whether one thing causes another thing (Koslowski, 1996). "Every time I get chilled, I catch a cold. So getting chilled must cause colds."

Inductive reasoning and causal inferences are related to a phenomenon that is often seen in most people, including scientists: confirmation bias. **Confirmation bias** is the tendency to selectively attend to information that supports one's general beliefs while ignoring information or evidence that contradicts one's beliefs. In the 1960s, Peter Wason conducted classic research to demonstrate the pervasiveness of the confirmation bias. Wason (1960) decided to find out whether people propose and test hypotheses systematically and, more to the point, whether they would be more likely to falsify or to confirm their own theories.

Wason gave students the task of determining the hidden rule behind a sequence of three numbers, known as a *triplet*. The students were asked to guess at the rule by writing down triplets that they thought conformed to it and the reason they selected them. They could make as many guesses and explanatory statements as they wished, until they thought they knew the rule. Then they wrote down what they thought the rule actually was. The experimenter, who knew the hidden rule, could answer only "yes" or "no" to the students' guesses, and was not allowed to say whether their reasons were correct or incorrect. For instance, if the experimenter gave the students the triplet "2–4–6," the students might guess a triplet of "6–8–10" and state that the hidden rule is "continuous series of even numbers." In this case, the guess is right but the rule is incorrect, so the experimenter would say "yes" to the guess but "no" to the rule. The students would then have to keep proposing triplets to test other reasons until they come up with the specific rule.

Out of frustration, students might throw out a triplet with seemingly no pattern to it, such as "1-10-21." Imagine their surprise when the experimenter said "yes" to that seemingly nonsensical triplet! Yet the triplet "1-10-21" conformed to the rule the experimenter had in mind, because that rule was simply "three numbers that must ascend in order of magnitude." As this experiment shows, people are so inclined to test only ideas that confirm their beliefs that they forget that one of the best ways to test an idea is to try to tear it down—that is, disconfirm it. This is the foundation of the scientific method. Most people, though, look only for information that confirms what they already believe and seldom look for information that disconfirms what they think; that is, they fall prey to confirmation bias.

CRITICAL THINKING

You've probably heard about "critical thinking" quite often, first in high school and now in college. Teachers are always talking about getting their students to think critically. So what exactly is critical thinking?

We can answer this question in part by examining the origin of the word *critical*. It comes from the ancient Greek word *kritikos* and means "to question, to make sense of, and to be able to analyze; or to be skilled at judging" (Chaffee, 1999, p. 32). Educator Paul Chance has provided a more complete definition of **critical thinking:** "The ability to analyze facts, generate and organize ideas, defend opinions, make comparisons, draw inferences, evaluate arguments, and solve problems"

(Chance, 1986, p. 6). The core traits of critical thinking are sound analysis, evaluation, and formation of ideas based on the evidence at hand.

In the late 1980s a group of educators, philosophers, psychologists, and biological and physical scientists organized a conference around the topic of critical thinking in education, and there they arrived at a consensus on what it means to be a good critical thinker. They were almost unanimous in identifying three qualities that define critical thinking, and more than three-quarters of them agreed on the next three qualities (Facione, 1990):

Qualities of Critical Thinking Most Agreed Upon by Experts

- Analyze
- Evaluate
- Make Inferences

- Interpret
- Explain
- Self-Regulate

If you become skilled in these qualities, or at least in most of these qualities, you will be able to think critically. In particular, you will be able to counter assertions that have little basis in reality, and you will know the difference between sound and faulty reasoning. For instance, the following argument was made by Charles Johnson, a former president of the International Flat Earth Research Society: "Nobody knows anything about the true shape of the world. The known, inhabited world is flat. Just as a guess, I'd say that the dome of heaven is about 4,000 miles away, and the stars are about as far as San Francisco is from Boston."

Instead of simply saying, "That's silly" or "That's stupid" or "That's just wrong," a critical thinker would examine the claim by analyzing, evaluating, and drawing conclusions based on the facts and evidence at hand. A great deal of evidence directly and clearly contradicts the belief that the earth is flat. Just consider these two pieces of evidence: (1) The top of a ship is the last thing we see as it sails out to sea because it is sailing on a sphere rather than on a flat surface (see Figure 9.7), and (2) images and photographs taken from spaceships and satellites show Earth as a round sphere with half of it shining in the light of the sun.

FIGURE **9.7**
EVIDENCE THAT THE EARTH IS NOT FLAT. The drawing on the left shows how a ship would appear as it comes into view if Earth were flat. On the right we see the ship coming into view on a round Earth. Which view is correct?

scientific thinking
process using the cognitive skills required to generate, test, and revise theories.

metacognitive thinking
process that includes the ability first to think and then to reflect on one's own thinking.

Critical thinking is closely related to scientific thinking and reasoning (Koslowski, 1996; Kuhn, Amsel & O'Loughlin, 1988). **Scientific thinking** involves the cognitive skills required to generate, test, and revise theories (Zimmerman, 2007). What we believe or theorize about the world and what the world is actually like, in the form of evidence, are two different things. Scientific thinking keeps these two things separate, whereas nonscientific thinking confuses them. In other words, scientists keep in mind that belief is not the same as reality. Nonscientists, on the other hand, tend to assume that what they believe is true. Remember from Chapter 2 the phrase "Don't believe everything you think."

Critical and scientific reasoning also involves being able to think metacognitively. **Metacognitive thinking** requires the ability first to think and then to reflect on one's own thinking (Feist, 2006; Kuhn & Pearsall, 2000). People

psychology in the real world

Applying Critical Thinking Beyond the Classroom

Critical thinking is a necessary skill in almost every walk of life. We can apply it to any domain in which we form beliefs and opinions. Here is just a partial list: deciding whether someone committed a crime; evaluating the claims of a company advertising a product; deciding whether what we read or hear in the classroom, in the newspaper, in politics, or in our work environment is valid and what evidence it is based on.

To apply critical thinking skills we should ask ourselves, What is the evidence for this conclusion, and is it valid? Let's take just one example. Suppose you are on a jury in a murder trial. The primary evidence on which the case is based is eyewitness testimony: two people picked out the defendant from a lineup. The prosecutor offers no other concrete evidence, such as DNA findings, fingerprints, bloodstains, or ballistic (bullet) matching. Your job is to decide whether the defendant committed the murder. You will want to draw on your critical thinking skills, because in this situation ignoring evidence and basing judgments on bias can have costly, even deadly, consequences.

Unfortunately, many people, including adults, sometimes are lacking in critical and scientific reasoning. Deanna Kuhn studied the connection between scientific and informal (everyday) reasoning in adults (Kuhn, 1993). She asked 160 people (teenagers and people in their 20s, 40s, and 60s) their theories on three topics: what causes prisoners to return to a life of crime, what causes children to fail in school, and what causes unemployment. After stating their theories, participants were asked for evidence on which they based their ideas. Only 40 percent of the participants could give actual evidence, that is, is information that is based on actual observations that bear on the theory's correctness. For instance, a man in his 20s who theorized that poor nutrition causes children to fail in school answered the question, "What would show that?" with "[They would get poor grades because] they are lacking

who can think metacognitively are able to question their own thinking. This ability is not universal, however. Without specific training, many people find it difficult to question their own thinking. If one were able to do so as a matter of course, one could more readily dismiss a line of thinking as wrong when it is not supported by evidence.

HOW DO WE MAKE JUDGMENTS AND DECISIONS?

Should I wear the red shirt or the brown one? Paper or plastic? Should I go to class or not? Can I make it across the street without getting hit by that car? Should I have a glass of water or a soda? We make hundreds of decisions every day, and each of those decisions is based on many different assumptions, judgments, and estimates. We also make judgments countless times each day. Every time we say things like "I decided . . . ," "Chances are . . . ," "It is unlikely . . . ," or "She probably did that because . . . ," we are judging how likely something is to happen.

something in their body." This is false evidence because it does not explain why poor nutrition might affect school failure. When asked to come up with reasons their thinking may be wrong, many actively resisted. As one participant said, "If I knew from the evidence that I'm wrong, I wouldn't say what I am saying." Others were even more stubborn, saying things like, "They'll never prove me wrong." Critical thinking requires that we be open to evidence that bears on whether our ideas are correct or not, even if we are not happy with the evidence.

Developing critical thinking has consequences beyond the classroom and even beyond studies in psychology. To summarize:

> The ideal critical thinker is habitually inquisitive, well-informed, trustful of reason, open-minded, flexible, fair-minded in evaluation, honest in facing personal biases, prudent in making judgments, willing to reconsider, clear about issues, orderly in assessing complex matters, diligent in seeking relevant information, reasonable in the selection of criteria, focused

Political debates afford candidates like Barack Obama and Hillary Rodham Clinton the opportunity to persuade voters that they are the best people to represent their interests. They also give voters a chance to think critically about the issues and evaluate the candidates' positions.

> in inquiry, and persistent in seeking results that are as precise as the subject and the circumstances of inquiry permit. Thus, becoming good critical thinkers means working toward this ideal. It combines developing critical thinking skills with nurturing those dispositions that consistently yield useful insights and that are the basis of a rational and democratic society. (Facione, 1990, p. 2)

heuristics
mental shortcuts; methods for making complex and uncertain decisions and judgments.

As it turns out, most often we use shortcuts to make decisions. These shortcuts, known as **heuristics**, are methods for making complex and uncertain decisions and judgments (Kahneman & Tversky, 1972). Consider, for example, the thought processes involved in deciding how to avoid being hit by a car when crossing a busy street. Instead of reasoning out each step systematically, we check oncoming traffic in both directions and quickly judge how fast the cars are moving and how fast we can get across. We base the decision of whether to step off the curb on our quick judgment of the pace of the oncoming cars. We usually don't debate with ourselves for very long before making that decision. Heuristics allow us to come to quick and efficient decisions.

We use many types of heuristics. Here we look briefly at the two most common types: the representativeness heuristic and the availability heuristic.

The Representativeness Heuristic
We use the **representativeness heuristic** when we estimate the probability of one event based on how typical or representative it is of another event (Tversky & Kahneman, 1974). For example, consider this information about Joe: He is not overweight, wears glasses, and reads poetry. Now we ask you to answer this question: Is Joe more likely to be a truck driver or a professor of English at an Ivy League university? It's simply

representative-ness heuristic
a strategy we use to estimate the probability of one event based on how typical it is of another event.

Finding one item in a large supermarket is made easier by heuristics. If you're looking for cold juice, you can narrow your search to a few places where cold beverages are stored and ignore all the other aisles. Deciding on a specific juice drink might be harder.

an *either-or* decision that most people get wrong: Joe is more likely to be a truck driver!

To understand why this is so, we need to be aware of base rates, or how common something is in the population as a whole. The concept of a base rate can be applied to people, events, or things. For example, 6 out of 100,000 people contract brain cancer in a given year; that is the base rate for brain cancer. Taking the four descriptors *truck driver, not overweight, wears glasses,* and *reads poetry,* let's consider the base rates for those segments of the U.S. population. First (assuming that by "truck driver" we mean drivers of semis), there are about 3 million truck drivers in the United States (*Trucking Stats and FAQ's,* n.d). Second, because about two-thirds of adults in the U.S. population are overweight (see Chapter 11), we could use the figure 67% to determine how many truck drivers are overweight—about 2 million. This leaves us 1 million truck drivers who are not overweight. Third, about 50% of adults wear corrective lenses (National Eye Institute, 2002). Fifty percent of 1 million leaves us with 500,000 not-overweight glasses-wearing truck drivers. Last, it is difficult to estimate how many people read poetry, but even a very conservative figure of 1% of the population leaves us with 5,000 truck drivers who wear glasses, are not overweight, and read poetry. Once we have established that figure, we can simply ask ourselves whether there are more than 5,000 professors of English at the eight Ivy League universities. There are approximately 50 professors of English at each of the eight schools, meaning there are about 400 Ivy League English professors. So in fact, Joe is more likely to be a truck driver than a professor of English at an Ivy League university. The information (not overweight, glasses, poetry) is so *representative* of an English professor and not a truck driver that we ignored the base-rate differences when we made our initial decision. There are simply many more truck drivers than there are English professors. This type of error is not unusual when many of us make quick decisions.

The Availability Heuristic   The second major type of heuristic is the availability heuristic, which is a strategy we use when we make decisions based on the ease with which estimates come to mind or how available they are to our awareness (Tversky & Kahneman, 1974). One example of the availability heuristic occurs when people are asked whether they are more likely to be killed while flying in an airplane or while driving in a car. Some might answer that they are more likely to be killed in plane crashes, even though statistics show that far more fatalities are caused by auto accidents than by plane crashes. According to the National Safety Council (2003), the odds of any one person dying in a car accident in 2003 were 1 in 6,498, whereas the odds of any one person dying in a plane crash that year were 1 in 391,981—a ratio of about 60 to 1. We may think we have a greater chance of dying in a plane crash because the thought of such a death conjures up dramatic images, which we refer to as *vividness*. Thoughts of large numbers of people dying violent deaths in plane crashes, therefore, are readily available because they are vivid. Vividness and availability lead us to overestimate how likely certain events are.

Heuristics and their importance in decision making and judgments are relatively new concepts in psychology. These notions developed from research in the early 1970s by Daniel Kahneman and Amos Tversky. How they came up with the idea for carrying out this research provides an interesting glimpse into how they broke new ground with their studies of human decision making.

availability heuristic
a device we use to make decisions based on the ease with which estimates come to mind or how available they are to our awareness.

quick quiz 9.2: Thinking, Reasoning, and Decision Making

1. Structures in our mind—such as an idea or image—that stand for something else, such as the external object or thing are known as
   a. memories
   b. mental representations
   c. mental rotation
   d. visions

2. Which of the following would be considered a prototype for fruit?
   a. kiwi
   b. tomato
   c. avocado
   d. apple

3. When we reason from general statements of what is known to specific conclusions, we are engaging in
   a. hypothesis testing
   b. inductive reasoning
   c. deductive reasoning
   d. logic

4. What distinguishes scientific thinking from nonscientific thinking?
   a. the ability to separate belief from evidence
   b. the ability to reason
   c. concept formation
   d. the use of heuristics

5. _____ are mental shortcuts for making complex and uncertain decisions and judgments.
   a. Categories
   b. Schemas
   c. Calculations
   d. Heuristics

6. Which of the following makes people believe they are more likely to die in a plane crash than while driving a car?
   a. the fear schema
   b. the availability heuristic
   c. concept formation
   d. the representativeness heuristic

Answers can be found at the end of the chapter.

breaking new ground
Nonrational Decision Making

Are the mental processes you use to make decisions based on reasonable, rational thought? Are you sure? Most of us like to think we are always reasonable and rational, and yet a Nobel Prize was awarded in 2002 for findings showing that not all decisions are rational and reasonable, especially economic decisions.

RATIONAL CHOICE THEORY

For much of the 20th century, cognitive scientists and economists who studied human decision making believed that people generally make rational decisions. Specifically, it was thought that when given a choice between two or more options, humans will choose the one that is most likely to help them achieve their particular goals—that is, the rational choice. Economists called this *rational choice theory* (Scott, 2000). They based this theory on principles of behaviorism. For decades, theorists held that people base financial decisions on a *cost-benefit analysis*. They ask themselves, "Do the costs outweigh the benefits? If yes, we don't buy; if no, we do buy." Think, however, about how you actually purchase items. How often do you buy things when you know you shouldn't because you really can't afford them—that is, the cost outweighs the benefits? If the rising levels of credit card debt are any indication, many of us are not rational consumers. But what does research tell us about how rational our decisions and judgments are?

EVIDENCE AGAINST RATIONAL CHOICE THEORY

David Kahneman

As we saw in the case of confirmation bias, not all reasoning is rational. In the 1970s, Amos Tversky and Daniel Kahneman began to challenge rational choice theory with their research on human judgment and decision making. Their collaboration began when both were at the Hebrew University in Israel, where Kahneman was teaching a graduate seminar in applied psychology. "In what turned out to be a life-changing event," Kahneman writes, "I asked my younger colleague Amos Tversky to tell the class about what was going on in his field of judgment and decision-making" (Kahneman, 2002). In the seminar, Tversky demonstrated how people make

Many of us are not rational consumers. The fact that we cannot afford to buy three pairs of shoes at a time does not mean that we do not buy them.

Amos Tversky

judgments about the probability of events. He combined red and white poker chips in two different bags and in two different ratios as an example. He explained that people are generally rational in their judgments; that is, they take into account differences in base rates. Using his bags of poker chips, he demonstrated that the odds are higher that a red chip will come from a bag with a base rate of 70/30 red to white chips than from a bag with a base rate of 30/70 red to white chips.

Tversky's conclusion that people are rational and make use of base rate information, however, started a lively debate in the seminar, as Kahneman later described: "The idea . . . did not seem to fit with the everyday observation of people commonly jumping to conclusions. [Tversky] went in to the seminar believing in his findings that people are relatively rational judges but left with that belief shaken" (Kahneman, 2002). This seminar exchange was the beginning of the research collaboration between Kahneman and Tversky.

In 1974 they published a paper that summarized the results of 13 of their studies on "judgments under uncertainty" (Tversky & Kahneman, 1974). In it, they presented several principles that would change the fields of psychology, economics, and even philosophy. We have already discussed two of them: the availability and representativeness heuristics.

Additional research by Kahneman and Tversky revealed other areas in which people are less than rational in their decision making and judgments. For example, if people were rational they would realize that the odds of two events can never be higher than the odds of one of those events alone. To put it most simply, the odds of A and B occurring together can never exceed the odds of either A or B occurring separately. Let's consider a specific example: The odds of your both (A) winning the lottery

Would you have predicted that Cate Blanchett (or any other actress) was likely to be nominated for an Oscar in the Best Actress category, in the Best Supporting Actress category, or in both categories for films released in a single year? Recall the conjunction fallacy before you answer! In 2008, Blanchett was coincidentally nominated in both categories (and didn't win for either role).

and (B) getting a promotion on the same day can never be greater than the odds of either one of these events happening alone. Sometimes, though, we get information that can be so representative of a stereotype that it biases us and we are likely to forget this simple rule of logic and make an error in our judgment. Take the classic example of Linda offered by Tversky and Kahneman (1983):

> Linda is 31 years old, single, outspoken, and very bright. She majored in philosophy. As a student, she was deeply concerned with issues of discrimination and social justice, and participated in anti-nuclear demonstrations.

Now you are asked the odds of each of the following: (A) that Linda is active in the feminist movement, (B) that Linda is a bank teller, and (C) that Linda is a bank teller and is active in the feminist movement. It is clear that A is more likely than B. But what about B compared to C? Remember that the combination of two events cannot be more likely than either event separately. Yet because what we are told about Linda is representative of feminists (A) and not of bank tellers (B), we are likely to say what 85% of the participants said—namely, that (C) is more likely than (B). In this case, the representativeness heuristic has led to an error known as the *conjunction fallacy,* which occurs when people say the combination of two events is more likely than either event alone.

These findings and others like them point to the conclusion that people sometimes ignore base rates, sometimes are biased by stereotypes, and sometimes use shortcuts to arrive quickly, but not completely rationally, at their decisions and conclusions. In short, Kahneman and Tversky demonstrated that people bypass fully rational decision making and make use of automatic shortcuts in their reasoning and judgments.

HOW THESE FINDINGS CHANGED PEOPLE'S MINDS

To some psychologists, these conclusions about less than rational reasoning were not surprising—after all, psychologists know just as much as anyone else about irrational thought and biased behavior. Yet to others, as well as to many economists and philosophers, Kahneman and Tversky's findings were nothing short of revolutionary, although not everyone appreciated them. A well-known American philosopher once told Kahneman, who had started to describe some of his findings at a dinner party, "I am not really interested in the psychology of stupidity" and walked away (Kahneman, 2002).

As a sign of how revolutionary their research was, in 2002 Kahneman won the Nobel Prize in Economics (Tversky had died in 1996). In so honoring Kahneman, the Nobel committee wrote in its press release:

> Traditionally, much of economic research has relied on the assumption of a "homo-economicus" [economic human] motivated by self-interest and capable of rational decision-making. Daniel Kahneman has integrated insights from psychology into economics, thereby laying the foundation for a new field of research. Kahneman's main findings concern decision-making under uncertainty, where he has demonstrated how human decisions may systematically depart from those predicted by standard economic theory. Kahneman has also discovered how human judgment may take heuristic shortcuts that systematically depart from basic principles of probability. His work has inspired a new generation of researchers in economics and finance to enrich economic theory using insights from cognitive psychology into intrinsic human motivation. (*The Prize,* 2002)

making connections
in language and thought

Learning a Second Language

Learning a second language involves many of the linguistic and cognitive principles we reviewed in this chapter. Bilingualism, or fluency in more than one language, is common, especially in India and Europe. As we consider bilingualism and how we can apply it to the topics in this chapter, we'll think about these questions: Is learning a second language essentially the same as learning one's first language? How much does it matter how old we are when we learn the second language? Finally, does learning a second language actually make you more creative?

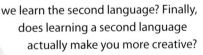

Sensitivity Periods and Second-Language Acquisition

There is a sensitive period for second-language acquisition: Children learn second languages more quickly than adults do and speak them more fluently (Birdsong, 2006; Kim et al., 1997; Sakai, 2005; Uylings, 2006). By around age 7, learning

a second language starts to become more difficult, and proficiency is reduced (Sakai, 2005). The sensitive period for learning to speak a second language without an accent appears to end in early adolescence (around age 13 to 15) (Flege, Munro, & MacKay, 1995; Long, 1990; Oyama, 1976). For example, native English speakers evaluated the strength of the accent in English spoken by Italian immigrants to the United States (Oyama, 1976). The length of time the immigrants had been in the United States did not affect the strength or thickness of their accent, but the age at which they had moved to the United States did. If they were six when they immigrated and had been in the country for only 2 years, they had much less of an accent than if they were 30 years old when they learned the language but had been in the United States for 10 years. A systematic review of the literature by Long (1990) confirmed this finding from dozens of studies. Thus, as a time for learning to speak a second language without an accent, childhood is better than adolescence and adolescence is better than adulthood.

Second-Language Learning and the Brain
People who are fluent in two languages apparently are capable of more efficient cognitive processing than those who speak only one language. Psychologists examined the ability of speakers of one and two languages to perform cognitive tasks (Bialystok, Craik, & Ryan, 2006). They found

that those who spoke two languages performed better on these cognitive tasks and continued to do so later in life.

Learning another language may also have a long-term beneficial effect on the brain. When matched for age, gender, and other qualities, elderly speakers of two languages develop dementia more than 4 years later than do elderly speakers of only one language (Bialystok, Craik, & Freedman, 2007). What is most interesting about these results is they once again support the view that stimulation from the environment—in this case, learning another language—can enrich our brains and enable them to process information more efficiently.

Neuroscientists have begun to demonstrate the long-lasting effects of learning two languages even more directly. First, compared to those of single-language speakers, bilingual speakers have a greater density of neurons in the language centers of the brain (Mechelli et al., 2004). Not only that, but neural density is proportional to the age at which the person learned the second language. The earlier the second language is learned, the greater the neural density (Mechelli et al., 2004). These findings demonstrate yet again how the brain is shaped by experience.

Second, bilingual people exhibit differences in brain activation depending on when they learned their second language (Kim et al., 1997). What is most fascinating is that the brains of people who learn a second language early in life are more efficient at language processing and more similar when speaking in both languages than are the brains of

people who learn a second language late in life. If someone learns a second language early in life, essentially at the same time that they learn their first language, the brain regions that are active during speech (production) overlap almost completely. On the other hand, if a person learns a second language years after learning the first language, the brain regions that are active during speech (production) are next to each other but hardly overlap (see Figure 9.8).

What is equally fascinating is that the same pattern does not hold for comprehension or listening. The Wernicke's area of people who learn a second language at a young age show nearby—yet not completely overlapping—cortical regions being activated when listening to the different languages, a phenomenon that does not appear in people who learn a second language later in life (Kim et al., 1997). Thus, the age at which a person learns a second language is reflected in differences in the brain, but only in areas involved in producing rather than understanding speech.

Concept Formation and Translation Into Foreign Languages

Linguists have demonstrated that the more prototypical an idea is, the more easily it can be translated from one language to another (Gass, 1984; Kellerman, 1979). Recall that a robin is a more prototypical example of bird than is an ostrich. Ideas and concepts that are prototypical are easier to understand in a second language. For example, consider the phrases *to kick the ball* and *to kick the bucket.* With *to kick the ball,* the use of the verb *to kick* is prototypical and easily translated. The phrase *to kick the bucket,* which means "to die," does not yield an accurate literal translation because the use of the verb *to kick* in this phrase does not represent the prototypical concept of *to kick,* meaning "to use your leg and foot in such a way as to move an object quickly." Many such **idioms**—expressions that are unique to a particular language—do not make sense when they are literally translated.

idioms

expressions unique to a particular language; usually their meaning cannot be determined by decoding the individual meanings of the words.

Reasoning in a Second Language

It is difficult enough to get through a college entrance exam, such as the Scholastic Aptitude Test (SAT), in one's native language. Imagine doing it in a second language in which you are not perfectly fluent. Each year thousands of foreign students seeking admission to American universities undertake this challenge. The SAT includes questions that require deductive reasoning, such as analogies. In research that compared students' deductive reasoning in their native language and their deductive reasoning in a second language, not surprisingly the students performed better

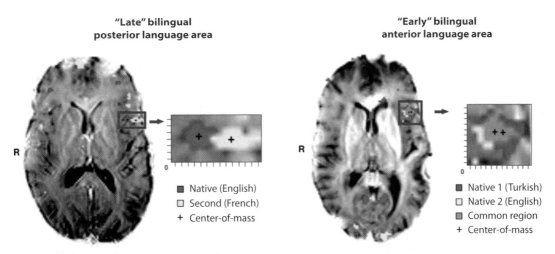

"Late" bilingual posterior language area

"Early" bilingual anterior language area

R

R

■ Native (English)
□ Second (French)
+ Center-of-mass

■ Native 1 (Turkish)
□ Native 2 (English)
▨ Common region
+ Center-of-mass

FIGURE **9.8**

ACTIVATION IN BROCA'S AREA FOR LATE LEARNERS AND EARLY LEARNERS OF A SECOND LANGUAGE. People who learn a second language later in life (after the age of 16), use different areas of the brain to produce speech in two languages, as shown by the images on the left. People who learn a second language in childhood show activation in overlapping areas of the brain when producing speech in two languages, as shown on the right. In other words, the brain of the early learner responds almost identically when speaking either language. Perhaps the reason why late learners are less fluent is that the brain treats the two languages differently. (*Source:* Kim et al., 1997.)

in their native language (D'Anglejan, 1979). Therefore, it is quite possible that the validity of these tests for nonnative speakers is somewhat questionable and that the scores do not accurately portray the aptitude of the test takers.

Second Language Acquisition and Metacognition

Accurately knowing what you do and do not know and the ability to monitor your thinking as you work on a problem are two hallmarks of metacognition. Because learning a second language requires one to think about one's thinking, some linguists and psychologists have proposed that bilingual children should be better at knowing what they know and monitoring their thinking than monolingual children (Jimenez, Garcia, & Pearson, 1994; Ruan, 2004; Tobias & Everson, 2002; Wenden, 1998). The findings of research on this question are mixed. It may be, however, that metacognitive thinking is more pronounced when one is first learning a second language than later, when one is rather fluent (Tobias & Everson, 2002).

Other studies have also reported at least partial support for the idea that speaking two languages facilitates creative, flexible, and original problem solving (Landry, 1973; Lasagabaster 2000; Ricciardelli, 1992). In a quantitative review (meta-analysis) of the research, Ricciardelli reported that 20 out of 24 published studies found that bilingual students scored higher on creativity tasks than did monolingual students. Flexible and creative thinking thus are closely aligned with metacognitive thinking (Sternberg, 2004).

quick quiz 9.3: Making Connections in Language and Thought

1. Kahneman and Tversky broke new ground in psychology by showing that people
   a. are not always rational in their decision making
   b. are almost always rational in their decision making
   c. often act like scientists in their decision making
   d. are motivated by self-interest and rational decision making

2. The sensitive period for learning to speak a second language without an accent appears to end at what stage of life?
   a. early childhood
   b. early teens
   c. young adulthood
   d. middle age

3. Compared to those of single-language speakers, the brains of bilingual speakers have
   a. greater density of neurons in the brain
   b. higher income
   c. higher intelligence
   d. fewer axons in the corpus callosum

4. Expressions that are unique to a particular language and do not make sense when literally translated are called
   a. axiomatic phrases
   b. tangential clauses
   c. idioms
   d. conjunctions

Answers can be found at the end of the chapter.

chapter **review**

LANGUAGE

- Human language is an open symbolic communication system that follows rules of syntax and grammar.

- Individuals develop language in a four-stage sequence, beginning with cooing and babbling in infancy. At about 12 months of age, toddlers start making their first one-word utterances. At around 18 months, babies progress to two-word utterances. By age 2½ to 3, most children enter the short-sentence phase. Continued language development requires stimulation from other people during a sensitive period between about the first 6 years of life and age 12.

- There are three major theories of language. Social-cultural theories propose that we learn vocabulary by hearing others speak and figure out what they mean by the context. Conditioning and learning theories argue that language is like any other learned behavior, something that occurs because it is reinforced and shaped. Nativist theories argue that humans possess a language acquisition device (LAD), an innate, biologically based capacity to acquire language that comes with a general and universal grammar.

THINKING, REASONING, AND DECISION MAKING

- Cognitive psychology is the scientific study of how people think, learn, remember, and perceive.

- We use visual and verbal representations in our mind as mental structures or processes for an image or idea. Concepts and categories are mental representations that we use to organize our world. Prototypes are the best-fitting examples of a category.

- We use reasoning to draw inferences or conclusions from principles and evidence. In deductive reasoning, we start with a general statement of what is known and draw specific conclusions from it. We use inductive reasoning to draw general conclusions from specific evidence. These conclusions are less certain because many different conclusions might be consistent with a specific fact.

- Confirmation bias is the tendency to selectively attend to information that confirms one's general beliefs while ignoring information or evidence that contradicts one's beliefs.

- Critical thinking uses sound reasoning when analyzing facts, generating and organizing ideas, defending opinions, making comparisons, drawing inferences, evaluating arguments, and solving problems.

- Scientific thinking is metacognitive thinking that is used to generate, test, reflect upon, and revise theories.

- Heuristics are shortcuts that we use in making judgments. We use the representativeness heuristic when we estimate the probability of one event based on how typical it is of another event. We use the availability heuristic to make estimates based on the ease with which we can bring an event or object to mind.

MAKING CONNECTIONS IN LANGUAGE AND THOUGHT

- Children who learn a second language early, during a sensitive period that ends around age 7, speak it more fluently and with greater proficiency than do older children or adults.

- Bilingualism appears to enhance cognitive processing and is associated with a lower rate of dementia in the elderly.

- People who learn a second language in childhood process both languages in roughly the same area of the brain, whereas in later learners, processing of the two languages occurs in two scarcely overlapping areas.

- At least initially, learning a second language may enhance metacognition, knowledge of what we know and don't know, and foster flexible thinking and creative problem solving.

key **terms**

availability heuristic, p. 361

babbling, p. 338

category, p. 354

causal inferences, p. 356

child-directed speech, p. 341

cognition, p. 350

cognitive psychology, p. 350

concept, p. 353

concept hierarchy, p. 353

confirmation bias, p. 356

cooing, p. 338

critical thinking, p. 356

deductive reasoning, p. 355

grammar, p. 336

heuristics, p. 359

human language, p. 336

idioms, p. 366

inductive reasoning, p. 355

language acquisition device (LAD), p. 342

linguistic determinism hypothesis, p. 348

mental representation, p. 351

mental rotation, p. 352

metacognitive thinking, p. 357

nativist view of language, p. 342

one-word utterances, p. 338

protolanguage, p. 337

prototypes, p. 355

reasoning, p. 355

representativeness heuristic, p. 359

scientific thinking, p. 357

sentence phase, p. 339

syntax, p. 336

two-word utterances, p. 339

visual imagery, p. 351

quick quiz **answers**

Quick Quiz 9.1:   1. c   2. a   3. d   4. c
Quick Quiz 9.2:   1. b   2. d   3. c   4. a   5. d   6. b
Quick Quiz 9.3:   1. a   2. b   3. a   4. c

intelligence,
problem-solving,

and creativity

1 *What are the characteristics of intelligence?*

2 *How is it possible to know something that you never learned?*

3 *How can a person be considered intelligent in one culture and below average in another?*

4 *What makes someone a good problem solver?*

5 *What characteristics do highly creative people have in common?*

In high school, Vanessa Liu was a competitive ice-skater, soccer player, award-winning debater, accomplished pianist, and A+ student. She scored 780 on her math SAT and 670 on her verbal SAT (each out of 800). At age 17, she designed and conducted an impressive study on how dendrites form and develop in response to stimulation, a project for which she became a finalist in the prestigious Westinghouse Science Talent Search competition (now known as the Intel Science Talent Search). Her friends wondered if there was anything she did not do exceptionally well (Berger, 1994).

Most people would agree that Vanessa is smart and talented. Vanessa may be exceptionally gifted, hardworking, or both. Her parents will tell you that Vanessa's exceptional abilities showed up at an early age. By the time of her first birthday, Vanessa knew all the letters ▶

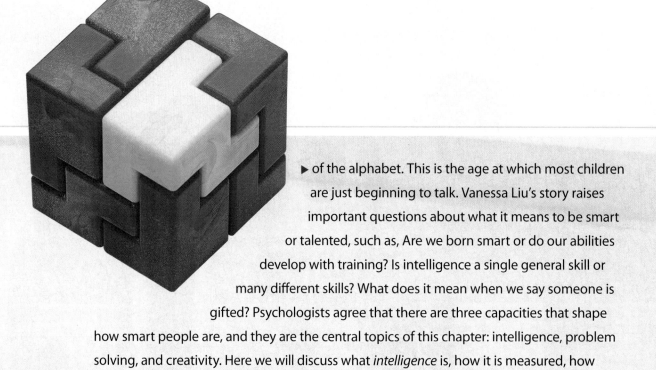

▶ of the alphabet. This is the age at which most children are just beginning to talk. Vanessa Liu's story raises important questions about what it means to be smart or talented, such as, Are we born smart or do our abilities develop with training? Is intelligence a single general skill or many different skills? What does it mean when we say someone is gifted? Psychologists agree that there are three capacities that shape how smart people are, and they are the central topics of this chapter: intelligence, problem solving, and creativity. Here we will discuss what *intelligence* is, how it is measured, how nature and nurture both contribute to and interact to mold intelligence, and how it

chapter
outline

is the same or differs among different groups and cultures. Then we will look at a practical ability called *problem solving*. Finally, we will examine the capacity for solving problems in unique and useful ways, a process known as *creativity*. Throughout the chapter, we will see how these topics overlap considerably, yet also reveal distinct capabilities of the human mind. At the end of the chapter, we connect all of these topics by looking at the achievements of talented young scientists like Vanessa Liu. ■

Intelligence

Many people consider intelligence the primary trait that sets humans apart from other animals. But what is intelligence? Is it the same as being generally smart, or is it more complicated than that? Is it a single ability or many different abilities, as Vanessa's case might suggest? Intelligence can be defined in a number of ways, and even the experts cannot agree on a definition. Over the years, groups of intelligence experts have convened for the purpose of defining intelligence (Neisser et al., 1996; Snyderman & Rothman, 1987; Sternberg & Detterman, 1986). Let's see what they have come up with.

DEFINING INTELLIGENCE

Intelligence may be our inherent potential for learning, how fast we are able to learn, or the body of knowledge we possess. It may also include the ability to do things in ways that other people have never tried. The definition of intelligence

FIGURE 10.1
**THEORIES OF
INTELLIGENCE.**
There are two
principal views of
intelligence. One
considers intelligence
as a single, measur-
able ability. The other
looks at intelligence
as comprising several
distinct abilities.

Question	Theory	Summary
How intelligent are you?	Spearman's general intelligence (g)	Intelligence is a single general capacity.
How are you intelligent?	Thurstone's multiple factors	Intelligence consists of 7 primary mental abilities, including spatial ability, memory, perceptual speed, and word fluency.
How are you intelligent?	Cattell–Horn–Carroll (CHC) hierarchical intelligence	Intelligence can be broken down into 3 levels of ability: general, broad, and narrow.
How are you intelligent?	Sternberg's triarchic theory	Intelligence is made up of 3 abilities (analytical, creative, and practical) necessary for success.
How are you intelligent?	Gardner's multiple intelligences	Intelligence includes at least 8 distinct capacities, including musical intelligence, interpersonal intelligence, and bodily-kinesthetic intelligence.

intelligence
a set of cognitive
skills that include
abstract thinking,
reasoning, problem
solving, and the
ability to acquire
knowledge.

that we will use in this book encompasses all these qualities. According to the experts, **intelligence** is a set of cognitive skills that include abstract thinking, reasoning, problem solving, and the ability to acquire knowledge. Other less-agreed-on qualities of intelligence include mathematical ability, general knowledge, and creativity (see Figure 10.1).

THEORIES OF INTELLIGENCE

Theories of intelligence started sprouting up in the early 1900s, soon after the first modern intelligence tests appeared. Two distinct views of intelligence have come to dominate these theories. One view says that intelligence is a single, general ability; the other says that intelligence consists of multiple abilities.

Intelligence as One General Ability
Charles Spearman (1904, 1923) developed the first theory of intelligence. He proposed that human intelligence is best thought of as a single general capacity, or ability. Spearman came to this conclusion after research consistently showed that specific dimensions, or factors, of intelligence—namely, spatial, verbal, perceptual, and quantitative factors—correlated strongly with one another, suggesting that they were all measuring much the same thing. In other words, people who achieve high scores on the verbal section of an intelligence test are also likely to have high scores on the spatial, perceptual, and quantitative sections.

Spearman's theory is now known as a **g-factor theory** of intelligence because it describes intelligence as a single *general* factor made up of specific components. This theory strongly influenced intelligence test construction for most of the 20th century. A person's overall intelligence score is determined by his or her specific scores on subtests. Thus, the g-factor theory implies that a single number can accurately reflect a person's intelligence. A person who scores 115 on an intelligence test is generally more intelligent than a person who scores 100, for example. This perspective is illustrated by the question, "How intelligent are you?" (see Figure 10.1).

Intelligence as Multiple Abilities   Critics of Spearman's theory argue that it does not do justice to the complexity of intelligence. They do not dispute that moderately high correlations among subtests of intelligence exist, but they disagree on how they should be interpreted. Early critics noted that the correlations are low enough to support arguments that verbal, quantitative, and other abilities are distinct dimensions of intelligence (Thurstone, 1938). Moreover, they insisted that test scores by themselves ignore important aspects of intelligence that the traditional tests don't measure. This view, the **multiple-factor theory of intelligence,** holds that the different aspects of intelligence are distinct enough that multiple abilities must be considered, not just one. This perspective is illustrated by the question, "*How* are you intelligent?" (see Figure 10.1). The key difference, then, between g-factor and multiple-factor theorists is that g-factor theorists say a single test score accurately reflects a person's overall intelligence, whereas multiple-factor theorists say that it doesn't.

One of the first people to "break intelligence in two" was Raymond Cattell, with his notion of fluid and crystallized intelligence (Horn & Cattell, 1966). **Fluid intelligence** involves raw mental ability, pattern recognition, and abstract reasoning and is applied to a problem that a person has never confronted before. Problems that require finding relationships, understanding implications, and drawing conclusions all require fluid intelligence. Neither culture nor vocabulary influence fluid intelligence. One commonly used measure of fluid intelligence is the *Raven's Progressive Matrices Test* (see Figure 10.2). Matrix reasoning is fluid intelligence because it does not depend on acquired knowledge and involves the ability to find patterns. Fluid intelligence measures are *culture-free* because their solutions do not require culturally acquired experience.

Knowledge that we have gained from experience and learning, education, and practice, however, is called **crystallized intelligence**. This form of intelligence is influenced by how large your vocabulary is as well as your knowledge of your culture. Being asked, for example, whether Dalmatian is to dog as oriole is to bird is an example of a problem that requires crystallized intelligence.

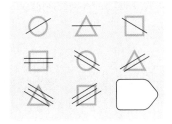

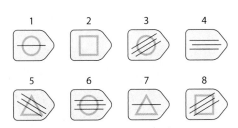

FIGURE 10.2
EXAMPLE FROM RAVEN'S PROGRESSIVE MATRICES TEST. This sample problem requires fluid intelligence. It is nonverbal and requires pattern recognition, not prior acquired knowledge. For this reason, this test is often considered a "culture-free" test of intelligence. Can you figure out which of the numbered bottom figures would be next in the series of nine above? Simulated items similar to those in the Raven's Progressive Matrices. Copyright © 1998 by NCS Pearson, Inc. Reproduced with permission. All rights reserved.

John Carroll (1993) further subdivided intelligence when he reviewed and integrated more than 450 sets of intelligence data published from the 1930s to the mid-1980s and concluded that the Cattell–Horn model of fluid and crystallized intelligence best fit the existing evidence. Carroll extended the model, however, arguing that intelligence actually consists of *three* levels, arranged in a hierarchy. At the top of the hierarchy is general intelligence, at the middle is broad intelligence, and at the bottom is narrow intelligence. **General intelligence** is very similar to Spearman's concept of "g." **Broad intelligence** consists of abilities such as crystallized and fluid intelligence, as well as memory, learning, and processing speed. **Narrow intelligence** consists of nearly 70 distinct abilities, such as speed of reasoning and general sequential reasoning for fluid intelligence and reading, spelling, and language comprehension for crystallized intelligence (see Figure 10.3). Because this model includes Cattell and Horn's crystallized and fluid intelligences, it has become known as the *Cattell–Horn–Carroll (CHC) model of intelligence.*

Robert Sternberg and Howard Gardner have proposed even more radical theories of multiple intelligence. Sternberg argues for a broader view of intelligence than is found in traditional g-factor theories. Most important, he focuses not simply on intelligence but on **successful intelligence,** which he defines as an integrated set of information-processing and cognitive abilities needed for life success (Sternberg, 2005, p. 104). Three interrelated but distinct abilities make up successful intelligence: analytic, creative, and practical intelligence (Sternberg, 1985, 2006).

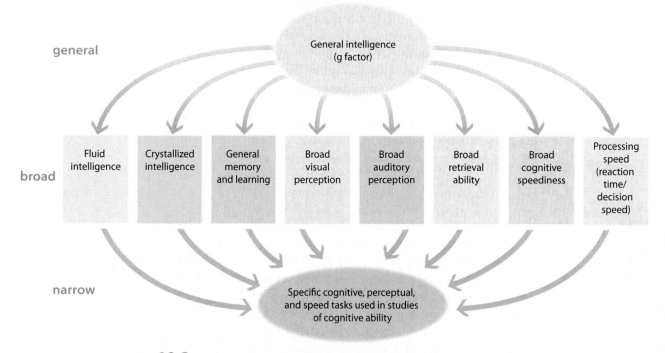

FIGURE 10.3

THE CATTELL–HORN–CARROLL (CHC) MODEL OF INTELLIGENCE. This hierarchical model integrates the concept of a general intelligence with several broadly defined abilities, including fluid and crystallized intelligence. The broad categories consist of more specific abilities, such as speed of reasoning (fluid intelligence) and language comprehension (crystallized intelligence).

triarchic theory of intelligence
Sternberg's three-part model of intellligence, including analytic, creative, and practical intelligence.

Sternberg's three-part theory is known as the **triarchic theory of intelligence.**

The first type of intelligence, *analytic intelligence,* involves judging, evaluating, or comparing and contrasting information (Sternberg, 1998). Analytic intelligence resembles the kind of academic intelligence that leads to high scores on tests of intelligence. For example, an analytic problem might require a person to figure out an uncommon word from its context in a sentence, or it might ask the person to determine the next number in a series of numbers (Sternberg, 2003). The second form of intelligence is *creative intelligence.* Creative intelligence is involved in coming up with fresh and useful ideas for solving problems. For example, a person might be given a number of cartoon images and then be asked

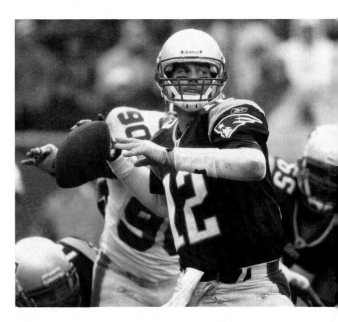

Athletes use practical intelligence to solve problems on the field.

to come up with a caption for each (Sternberg, 2006). Traditional measures of intelligence do not measure creative intelligence well. The third processing skill, *practical intelligence,* is the ability to solve problems of everyday life efficiently. Practical intelligence plays a role in knowing how to do one's job well and requires knowledge and skills that one learns "on the street" rather than in the classroom. A practical intelligence problem, for example, might ask people to come up with three solutions to a real everyday problem they are currently experiencing in their life (Sternberg, 2003).

Howard Gardner

Another scholar who has focused on the multifaceted view of intelligence is Howard Gardner. Gardner (1983, 1993) argues that intelligence comprises at least eight distinct capacities: linguistic, mathematical–logical, musical, bodily–kinesthetic, spatial, intrapersonal, interpersonal, and naturalistic. *Naturalistic intelligence,* for instance, is the ability to recognize, classify, and understand the plants and animals in one's environment. In cultures that have formal science, highly skilled people in this domain of intelligence are likely to become biologists, botanists, and animal scientists or veterinarians. In cultures without formal science, they are the most talented hunters, gatherers, and farmers. *Interpersonal intelligence* is the ability to perceive and understand other people's intentions, motives, and behaviors. Interpersonally intelligent people therefore work well with others and know how to get along with others. See Figure 10.4 on page 378 for a complete listing and definitions of Gardner's eight intelligences.

Scholars are strongly divided, however, over Gardner's theory. Those who have the most problems with it tend to be psychologists. They see little value in calling skills like music, movement, and social skills "intelligence" and argue that Gardner has not provided tests of these intelligences. Moreover, there have been few direct empirical tests on Gardner's theory, and therefore some argue his ideas are more theory than science. For some psychologists and more educators, however, Gardner's ideas address two real problems: (1) Different students learn in different ways, and (2) some students who have demonstrated ability in

FIGURE 10.4

GARDNER'S MULTIPLE INTELLIGENCES. The far-right column lists professions that are well served by each ability.

Intelligence	Definition	Representative Professions
linguistic	Ability to learn, understand, and use both spoken and written language	Poets, writers, lawyers, politicians
logical-mathematical	Ability to analyze information and problems logically and to perform mathematical operations	Scientists, engineers, accountants
musical	Ability in performing, composing, or appreciating musical patterns	Musicians, dancers, song-writers
bodily-kinesthetic	Ability to use one's body or parts of it to solve problems or create products	Athletes, dancers, mechanics, craftspeople
spatial	Ability to think about and solve problems in three-dimensional space	Navigators, pilots, architects, sculptors
interpersonal	Ability to understand and be aware of other people's intentions, motivations, thoughts, and desires; also the ability to work well with and get along with others	Psychologists, social workers, teachers, politicians
intrapersonal	Ability to be aware of, understand, and regulate one's own behavior, thoughts, feelings, and motivations	Psychologists, monks, priests
naturalistic	Ability to recognize, classify, and understand the plants and animals in one's environment	Naturalists, biologists, botanists, veterinarians, hunters, farmers

some areas fail academic subjects and do poorly on traditional intelligence tests (Kornhaber, Fierros, & Veenema, 2004). They may even drop out of school.

How should teachers nurture and teach these failing students—indeed, all students—given the fact that different students learn different material differently? Entire schools have been designed to enhance the "intelligences" of students. We describe a few of these programs in "Psychology in the Real World."

MEASURES OF INTELLIGENCE

Like different theories of intelligence, tests of intelligence, commonly called IQ tests, are controversial. Some of the questions they raise are "How does someone interpret a person's score on an intelligence test?" "Where does a person stand compared to everyone else?" and "How do we know that a given test is any good at all?" There have been numerous attempts to answer these questions over the years. All of them have been based on the way intelligence was understood at the time the tests were devised, and so we begin our discussion with a bit of history.

Bringing Multiple Intelligences to School

The chief motivation behind bringing multiple intelligences (MI) to the school setting is to avoid some of the limitations of traditional testing and teaching that discourage students who do not do well. Gardner (1999) realized that testing in the usual sense would have to be abandoned and classrooms would have to be arranged and equipped with materials that stimulate and foster each of the different forms of intelligence. Under this model, classrooms may be arranged with areas meant for dance, exercise, and construction. The materials may include board games, art and music materials, nature specimens (e.g., a fish tank), and natural objects.

An educational principle based on MI theory is that children should have some freedom to choose activities on their own. If they ignore certain kinds of activities, their teachers provide encouragement and "bridges" for them to try the neglected activities. For instance, if students are reluctant to tell stories, a teacher might encourage them to build a diorama (a three-dimensional model). The teacher would then ask the students to tell a story about what is happening to the people and animals in the diorama.

More than 40 schools in the United States have been designed to put into practice the development of all Gardner's forms of intelligences (Kornhaber et al., 2004). One example is The Key Learning Community in Indianapolis, Indiana. It opened in 1987 as a public elementary and middle school. Assessment takes place at the end of the school year, when each student presents a project based on any or all of the intelligences on which he or she has focused during the year. Students often present their project as a performance, such as a play, poetry reading, or artistic interpretation. They may also write papers on what they have learned. These presentations are videotaped and put into the student's portfolio, which serves as a record of each student's cognitive and emotional development. Students in these schools still must take the local school district's standardized tests, and when they do, they do at least as well as students from other schools (*Key Learning Community,* n.d.; Kornhaber et al., 2004). Moreover, most of the schools adopting this model reported that the MI approach helped decrease disciplinary problems and increase parent participation. Finally, the performance of students with learning disabilities improved markedly when they attended MI schools.

In short, the MI schools teach to different learning styles and to their students' different intellectual talents. For some students at least, this alternative fosters academic achievement that might not occur in a traditional setting.

According to Gardner, naturalistic intelligence should be nurtured in the same way as mathematical skills, verbal ability, and at least 5 other kinds of intelligence.

The development and history of intelligence testing has been marked by three distinct periods. For the first period of 70 years or so, from about 1910 to about 1980, people constructed tests around practical and clinical concerns rather than any theory and understanding of intelligence. That began to change during the second period in the 1980s, when the first theory-driven intelligence tests were developed. Then, during the third period in the 1990s, in a major shift, some creators of intelligence tests acknowledged that intelligence may be many things rather than just one. Integrating theory and measurement, they developed intelligence tests that assess several aspects of intelligence.

Intelligence tests were among the first psychological tests. The person who deserves the most credit for developing the first true test of intelligence is the French scholar Alfred Binet. In the early 1900s, the government hired Binet to identify students who would benefit most from special instruction techniques. For this purpose, Binet and a colleague, Theodore Simon, developed a test containing 30 problems of increasing difficulty. Their idea that ability to solve increasingly difficult problem depends on age became widely influential and has since become known as mental age. **Mental age** is the equivalent chronological age a child has reached based on his or her performance on an intelligence test. Children are given a mental age not according to how old they are in years, but rather according to the level or age group at which they can solve problems. Mental age is a norm or average because it is based on what most children at a particular age level can do.

mental age
the equivalent chronological age a child has reached based on his or her performance on an IQ test.

A few years after Binet developed the concept of mental age, a German psychologist, William Stern, introduced the *intelligence ratio*, in which mental age (MA) is divided by chronological age (CA) and multiplied by 100 to determine an intelligence score. The ratio of mental age over chronological age is commonly known as a person's *intelligence quotient* or IQ. In other words, if a child had a mental age of 10 and was 10 years old, she had an IQ of 100 ($10 \div 10 \times 100$). But if she had a mental age of 12 and was only 10 years old, she had an IQ of 120, whereas if she had a mental age of 8 and was 10 years old, her IQ was 80. This ratio was very useful in the early years of IQ testing with children, but it is no longer used. Today IQ scores are based on how well a child does on tests relative to norms or standards established by testing children of the same age.

About 10 years after Binet published his first test, Lewis Terman, an American psychologist, translated the test for American students. Because Terman taught at Stanford University, he named the test the *Stanford-Binet test*. The most significant changes Terman made were to establish national norms and to adopt and apply the ratio score of MA $\div$ CA to a widely used IQ test.

In the 1930s, David Wechsler created new intelligence tests to measure adult intelligence. Wechsler's test became known as the *Wechsler Adult Intelligence Scales (WAIS,* Wechsler, 1944, 1958). Later he developed a test for children, the *Wechsler Intelligence Scales for Children (WISC)*. At present, these two tests are the ones most frequently administered in the United States (Wasserman & Tulsky, 2005). To sample the kinds of problems included on one of these IQ tests, see Figure 10.5. The current versions of both the Stanford-Binet and the WAIS are based on modern theories about intelligence, which we discuss next.

Similarities

An individual must think logically and abstractly to answer a number of questions about how things might be similar.

Example: "In what ways are boats and trains the same?"

Comprehension

This subscale is designed to measure an individual's judgment and common sense.

Example: "Why do individuals buy automobile insurance?"

Picture Arrangement

A series of pictures out of sequence is shown to an individual, who is asked to place them in their proper order to tell an appropriate story. This subscale evaluates how individuals integrate information to make it logical and meaningful.

Example: "The pictures below need to be placed in an appropriate order to tell a story."

Block Design

An individual must assemble a set of multicolored blocks to match designs that the examiner shows. Visual-motor coordination, perceptual organization, and the ability to visualize spatially are assessed.

Example: "Use the four blocks on the left to make the pattern at the right."

FIGURE 10.5

IQ TEST PROBLEMS SIMILAR TO THE ONES IN THE WECHSLER ADULT INTELLIGENCE SCALES (WAIS). The WAIS and the Wechsler Intelligence Scale for Children are the most widely administered intelligence tests in the United States. Simulated items similar to those found in the Wechsler Adult Intelligence Scale—Revised (WAIS-R). Copyright © 1981, 1955 by NCS Pearson, Inc. Reproduced with permission. All rights reserved.

breaking new ground
Changing Intelligence Tests

Because IQ tests were first created for practical purposes in the early part of the 20th century, they were not based on a clear understanding of the nature of human intelligence. In the 1980s, however, there was a shift in the way intelligence tests were developed. Now all major IQ tests have some basis in theories of intelligence.

OLD ASSUMPTIONS ABOUT THE NATURE OF INTELLIGENCE

For 50 years IQ tests were based on the assumption that intelligence is a single quality. The developers of both the Stanford-Binet and Wechsler tests failed to take into account Jean Piaget's work on cognitive development and newer findings from neuroscience.

As discussed in Chapter 5, Piaget found that the cognitive abilities of young children and adolescents are fundamentally different and that cognitive development occurs in stages rather than gradually over time. Adolescents can reason abstractly, for example, but young children cannot. Yet IQ tests continued to give very similar problems to young children, teenagers, and adults, changing only the level of difficulty.

Moreover, until the 1980s, IQ test developers ignored advances in neuroscience indicating that the two hemispheres of the brain process information differently, with the right hemisphere integrating the overall message and the left hemisphere analyzing the specific pieces of information in a message (Kaufman, 1979). Consistent with these findings, new evidence showed that some children learn best when information is taught piece-meal, one step at a time, whereas others learn best when information is presented visually all at once. In the late 20th century, a new approach to intelligence testing incorporated Piaget's ideas, findings from neuroscience, and learning style differences.

INTELLIGENCE TESTS BASED ON MODERN PSYCHOLOGICAL THEORY

Nadeen & Alan Kaufman

Advances in neuroscience led to greater understanding of how the brain solves problems, psychologists became increasingly aware of the limits of existing IQ tests. In the late 1970s, when Alan and Nadeen Kaufman were on a family outing with their young children, they found themselves discussing the need for an intelligence test that would reflect current neuroscientific theories of the brain and information processing. They talked about what such a test would look like. By the time they reached their destination, they agreed that their plan was unrealistic and they wouldn't attempt it. As luck would have it, however, a test developer telephoned the next day to ask Alan, "Would either you, or Nadeen, or both of you want to develop a new intelligence test to challenge the Wechsler?" In this way the Kaufman-Assessment Battery for Children (K-ABC) was born (*Test Developer Profiles*, 2001).

The K-ABC differed from the Stanford-Binet and Wechsler tests in four ways. First, it was the first IQ test to be guided by theories of intelligence, in particular Cattell and Horn's concepts of fluid and crystallized intelligence and Piaget's theory of cognitive development. Second, influenced by Piaget, the Kaufmans included fundamentally different kinds of problems for children of different ages, as well as problems at varied levels of difficulty. Third, unlike older tests, the K-ABC measured several distinct aspects of intelligence. Finally, influenced by neuroscience and information processing theory, the K-ABC assessed different types of learning styles. In this sense, the K-ABC was the first of many intelligence tests informed by contemporary ideas about how the brain worked and developed (Kaufman & Kaufman, 1983).

The K-ABC test was the first theory-based IQ test and one of two major shifts in the field of intelligence testing that took place in the 1980s. Raymond Cattell, John Horn, and John Carroll (who developed the CHC model of intelligence) led the second one (the "CHC shift"). The ground-breaking event that started the second shift was a 1985 conference where Horn presented the theory of crystallized and fluid intelligence. For Richard Woodcock and his team of test developers, Horn's paper was too abstract and not grounded in actual tests. Then Carroll applied the Cattell–Horn theory to the test that Woodcock and colleagues had developed, and "a collective 'Ah ha!' engulfed the room as Carroll . . . provided a meaningful link between the theoretical terminology of Horn and the concrete world of the . . . tests." (McGrew, 2005, p. 144) Now the test makers knew how they could create an intelligence test that measured intelligence on more than one dimension.

THE AFTERMATH OF THE SHIFT IN INTELLIGENCE TESTS

Both the Kaufman and CHC shifts led to fundamental changes, first in the minds of intelligence test developers and then in the tests themselves, including the Stanford-Binet and the Wechsler scales. Carroll's analysis of all known intelligence tests and his extension of the Cattell–Horn model led to a rapid shift in all major intelligence tests. The power of the CHC model comes from the fact that it connects theory with testing and also links models of intelligence as a single quality with multidimensional models (see Figure 10.3; McGrew, 2005).

connection
How much information can most people keep in mind while working on a problem? Is working memory the same as short-term memory?
See Chapter 7, p. 260.

Tests may still produce an overall IQ score, but now they also yield scores on as many as seven dimensions of intelligence. Influenced by the CHC model, the newest versions of both the WAIS (WAIS-III) and the WISC (WISC-IV) include scores on four dimensions: Verbal Comprehension, Perceptual Reasoning, Working Memory, and Processing Speed (Hogan, 2007). Working memory, which holds information in mind for a short period so that it can be used to solve a problem at hand, is one of the dimensions that were missing before 1985. For examples of working memory tasks included in the Wechsler scales, see Figure 10.6.

Also influenced by the CHC model, the fifth edition of the Stanford-Binet assesses five different factors of general intelligence, each with verbal and nonverbal dimensions (Roid & Pomplun, 2005). In addition to assessing fluid and crystallized intelligence, the newest version of the Stanford Binet assesses quantitative reasoning, visual–spatial processing, and working memory.

In sum, current intelligence tests reflect contemporary thinking about intelligence as a general quality with many dimensions. Since the development of the CHC model and publication of the first version of the K-ABC, all other major IQ tests have followed suit and developed more theory-driven and complex tests of at least five aspects of intelligence rather than just two or three.

Reliability and Validity of IQ Tests

Tests are meaningful only if they are both reliable and valid. **Reliability** refers to consistency of results. If a test is reliable, a person who takes the same test on two

reliability
consistency of a measurement, such as an intelligence test.

FIGURE 10.6

SIMULATED EXAMPLES OF WORKING MEMORY TASKS ON THE WECHSLER SCALES OF INTELLIGENCE. The latest version of the WISC and the WAIS also assess verbal comprehension, perceptual reasoning, and processing speed. Simulated items similar to those in Wechsler Intelligence Scale for Children—Fourth Edition (WISC-IV). Copyright © 2003 by NCS Pearson, Inc. Reproduced with permission. All rights reserved. "Wechsler Intelligence Scale for Children" and "WISC" are trademarks, in the US and/or other countries, of Pearson Education, Inc. or its affiliates.

Digit span

| Examiner says: 6 - 2 - 9 | Examinee repeats it back |
| Examiner says: 7 - 4 - 6 - 1 - 4 - 8 - 3 - 9 | Examinee repeats it back |

Letter-number sequencing

| Examiner says: L - 7 - C - 3 | Examinee has to repeat the sequence with numbers in ascending order and then letters in alphabetical order 3 - 7 - C - L |

different occasions will obtain very similar scores on both occasions. IQ tests tend to be extremely reliable. Questions on a given subtest also tend to correlate very highly with other items on the subtest, meaning that the test's internal consistency is very high. So, overall, test makers have done a good job of creating reliable IQ tests (Gregory, 2007).

Validity requires that the tests really measure intelligence and not something else, and that test scores predict real-world outcomes. The validity of a test is more difficult to establish than is its reliability. Although there is a great deal of evidence that the Wechsler and Stanford-Binet tests, among others, do provide valid measures of intelligence, many intelligence experts, notably Sternberg and Gardner, have argued that they measure only verbal, spatial, and mathematical forms of intelligence. The other forms that Gardner identified—social, emotional, musical, bodily, practical, and natural history—are not measured at all.

There are at least two distinct forms of validity: construct and predictive. **Construct validity** refers to what we have just discussed: that a test measures the concept, or *construct,* it claims to measure. **Predictive validity** addresses the question of whether the construct is related positively to real-world outcomes, such as school achievement or job success. IQ tests do predict certain real-world outcomes, the first and foremost being academic performance. IQ scores predict students' grades, school performance, and class rank in high school quite well. That is, after all, what they were meant to predict. For example, preschool scores on two IQ tests taken by children in the Head Start Program accurately predicted the children's academic achievement scores from kindergarten to sixth grade (Lamp & Krohn, 2001). Moreover, scores from the WAIS predict both one's academic class rank in high school and one's college grade point average (Gregory, 2007). Even though IQ can predict the kind of job you get and how much money you make, it cannot predict how happy and satisfied you are with your life or how well you will do in your job (Gow et al., 2005).

Are IQ Tests Biased?   Given the differences among groups in average IQ scores, it is tempting to conclude that IQ tests are biased and unfair. Whether a test is either biased or unfair or both involves two separate, though related, issues.

Are IQ tests unfair to a particular group of individuals?

Let's first be clear about what each term means and then examine the evidence for each. The general public attaches a different meaning to *bias* than scientists do. The general public may use the term *bias* to refer to the notion that group differences in IQ scores are caused by different cultural and educational backgrounds, not by real differences in intelligence. This view is expressed in the **cultural test bias hypothesis** (Reynolds, 2000). Scientists, however, distinguish between test bias and test fairness. When scientists refer to **test bias** in an IQ test, they refer to whether a test predicts outcomes equally well for different groups. A test is biased if it is a more valid measure for one group than for another. For example, if an IQ test predicts academic achievement better for Hispanics than for Asians, it is biased. Researchers have found, however, very little evidence for the existence of this kind of bias in IQ tests (Brown, Reynolds, & Whitaker, 1999; Hunter & Schmidt, 2000; Reynolds, 2000). Intelligence tests are developed using norms that reflect the makeup of the general population. Just because different groups score differently on a given test does not automatically mean that it is biased. If the test is equally valid for different groups and they still score differently on it, the test is not biased. It may be unfair, but it's not biased.

Test fairness, on the other hand, reflects values, philosophical differences, and the ways in which test results are applied (Gregory, 2007). Test results, especially IQ test results, are meant to be applied—often by people in education, the military, and business. Problems arise when people use IQ test results unfairly to deny certain groups access to universities or jobs. So test fairness, in this sense, concerns the application of the test results rather than the test itself. An unbiased test result could be applied unfairly.

cultural test bias hypothesis
the notion that group differences in IQ scores are caused by different cultural and educational backgrounds, not by real differences in intelligence.

test fairness
judgment about how test results are applied to different groups based on values and philosophical inclinations.

test bias
characteristic of a test that produces different outcomes for different groups.

EXTREMES OF INTELLIGENCE

Intelligence varies in a very predictable way, which is most easily seen in the frequency of different IQ scores in the population. When one plots the scores on a graph, one sees a very clear bell curve, with most people falling in the middle and a few people at the high and low ends of the curve. This shape is referred to as a *bell curve* because it is shaped like a bell. Looking at the bell curve for IQ scores in Figure 10.7, we can see that 68% of test-takers will score between 85 and 115 and almost all—99.7%—will score between 55 and 145. It is at the two ends of the curve, or distribution, that we find "extremes of intelligence"—specifically, mental retardation and giftedness.

FIGURE 10.7

NORMAL DISTRIBUTION OF IQ TEST SCORES (BELL CURVE). The vast majority of people (95%) achieve scores between 70 and 130 on the Wechsler IQ scales. The norm is 100. The higher the standard score is, whether positive or negative, the further away the scores are from the norm. Only a small percentage are found at the extremes.

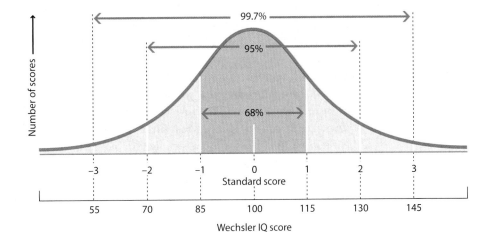

mental retardation

significant limitations in intellectual functioning as well as in everyday adaptive behavior, which start before age 18.

adaptive behavior

adjustment to and coping with everyday life.

Mental Retardation To meet the criteria for **mental retardation,** an individual must show significant limitations in intellectual functioning as well as in everyday adaptive behavior, and these deficits must start before age 18 (AAMR, 2002; American Psychiatric Association, 2000). Historically, retardation was defined and diagnosed solely on the basis of IQ, with 70 being the most common cutoff score. There are four levels of retardation, depending on how adaptive the behavior or thinking is: mild (IQ of 50–70), moderate (35–50), severe (20–35), and profound (below 20). More recently, however, a different criterion, adaptive behavior, has been added to IQ as a determinant of mental retardation. **Adaptive behavior** is defined as how well a person adjusts to and copes with everyday life (Hogan, 2007). For example, how well can the person feed or dress himself or herself? Does the person have the ability to understand the time, make change, or read simple words? At a more complex level, one might ask whether the person can take a bus or subway or follow the news on TV. Most current diagnoses of retardation emphasize adaptive functioning over IQ scores. They therefore measure a person's everyday abilities more than their academic performance.

The origins of mental retardation vary. In about 50 percent of cases, the cause or mental retardation is *organic*, meaning that it is genetic or the result of brain damage. **Down syndrome,** a disorder that results from a condition known as trisomy-21, in which a person has three rather than two number 21 chromosomes, is an example of organic retardation. The genetic cause of Down syndrome is not fully known, but it is related to maternal age. Children born to older women are

Down syndrome

a chromosomal disorder characterized by mild to profound mental retardation.

more likely to develop trisomy-21 and Down syndrome (*What Causes Down Syndrome,* 2007). In other cases, in which the cause is not clearly biological, environmental factors, such as neglect and poor nutrition, may be to blame. Sometimes called *familial-cultural retardation*, this type is more prevalent among people of low socioeconomic status, tends to occur in more than one family member, and tends to be mild (Kerig & Wenar, 2006).

Like this happy couple, many people with Down syndrome have full, productive lives in spite of their intellectual limitations.

Giftedness. Giftedness lies at the high end of the intelligence spectrum. Starting in about the third grade in the United States, students who do very well in school and also do well on standardized tests of intelligence are sometimes placed in "gifted" programs. In most schools, children are admitted to such a program if they score 130–140 or above on a standardized IQ test like the WISC or Stanford-Binet. Extreme giftedness takes various forms, two of which are prodigies and savants.

Prodigies. A **prodigy** is a young person who is extremely gifted and precocious in one area, such as math, music, art, or chess, and is at least average in intelligence (Feldman, 2004). Most often, prodigies are people under the age of 20. Sometimes they possess extreme talent in more than one domain, such as math and language. Probably the world's most famous child prodigy was Wolfgang Amadeus Mozart, who was playing keyboard by age 3 and composing symphonies by age 8. A more recent example is Tiger Woods, who started playing golf at age 3 and was winning tournaments and making holes-in-one by age 6.

prodigy

a young person who is extremely gifted and precocious in one area and at least average in intelligence.

Akiane Kramarik is a gifted young artist who has been painting and drawing since she was a small child. With her parents' encouragement, Akiane has developed her natural creative abilities to an extraordinary level. She also writes poetry.

Although they are relatively rare, some people display extreme early talent in visual arts. Akiane Kramarik is an example. She was sketching incredibly lifelike drawings by age 4 and producing world-class paintings by age 9. She loves drawing and painting so much that she wakes each morning at 4 a.m. to express herself on canvas (Kramarik, 2006). What makes Kramarik even more unusual is that she is also an accomplished and published poet. In short, she is both visually and verbally gifted.

In addition to documenting individual cases of intellectual prodigies, researchers have conducted large-scale studies of mathematical prodigies. The best-known of these is the Study for Mathematically Precocious Youth (SMPY; Stanley, 1996). Begun in 1971, the SMPY is a 50-year longitudinal study of extremely talented people, especially in math. One of the main criteria for participation is a score of 500 or higher (out of 800) on the SAT-Quantitative test before age 13. A score of 500 by age 13 occurs in about 1 in 100 cases, meaning that the person scores higher than 99% of his or her peers.

A subset of the study focuses on an even more select group: those who score 700 on the SAT-Quantitative and 630 or higher on the SAT-Verbal *before* their thirteenth birthday. Only about one in every 10,000 test-takers achieves a score this high (Lubinski et al., 2006). Students in this precocious group go on to have very successful careers. Follow-up research 25–35 years later shows that many of them attended top universities at both the undergraduate and graduate levels and then went on to become successful scientists, mathematicians, engineers, and doctors (Lubinski & Benbow, 2006).

Savants. Since at least the 1700s, there have been reports of people with **savant syndrome,** a very rare condition characterized by serious mental handicaps and isolated areas of ability or remarkable giftedness (Treffert, 2006). Savants (the word *savant* comes from the French word for "knowing") have low overall intelligence, typically with an IQ below 70, and an incredible ability for calculating numbers, recalling events, playing music, or drawing. Often these individuals cannot speak at all or speak poorly.

savant syndrome
a very rare condition in which people with serious mental handicaps also show isolated areas of ability or brilliance.

By some estimates, there are only about 100 savants in the world today, about 50% of whom suffer from autism and the other 50% from some other kind of psychological disorder, such as brain injury, epilepsy, or mental retardation (Treffert, 2006). Savant syndrome occurs most often in five major areas of talent: music (usually piano), art, math, calendar calculations, and spatial/mechanical skills (Treffert, 2006). A relatively common form is seen in individuals who can immediately calculate the day of the week on which a particular date in history fell. For example, if asked what day of the week June 15, 1899, was, they would correctly answer "Thursday." Others with savant syndrome can take apart clocks, toys, bicycles, and other machines and rebuild them with expert precision.

In Chapter 8, we met Daniel Tammet, whose uncanny memory skills enable him to recall pi to 22,514 digits and calculate complex mathematical problems almost instantaneously. Tammet has savant syndrome as well as synesthesia, which, as you might recall from Chapter 4, occurs when a person experiences sensations in one sense when a different sense is stimulated. In Tammet's case, he sees each number as a distinct color and shape, and this is the secret behind his uncanny memory for numbers and calculations. For example, when he is reciting pi out to 22,500 digits he does not think in numerals but rather he simply sees in his mind's eye a rolling landscape of colored shapes.

Another person with savant syndrome is Kim Peek. Although Peek may be most famous as the inspiration for the movie *Rain Man*, starring Dustin Hoffman, his abilities go much further than the movie suggests. He is one of the world's only true speed-readers—he can read a page in about 3 seconds and retain essentially every word. Incredibly, Peek has memorized about 9,000 books after reading them only *once*. He can immediately provide biographical information about any of the U.S. presidents; tell you the zip code of any city or borough in the United States; and identify who composed almost any piece of classical music, where it was composed, and when it was first performed. Like some other savants, he also can tell you more or less instantly the day of the week on which any date in history fell.

Given his phenomenal abilities, it is easy to forget that Peek is unable to do many basic things—such as dress himself. Indeed, his tested IQ is 73, which is in the range for people with autism. Socially he is very awkward, and he likes to repeat certain phrases, saying over and over again how great is the person he has just met. He also does not understand metaphors like "get hold of yourself." Instead, he interprets everything literally. His adaptive functioning skills are poor, and his father continues to take care of him on a daily basis. A scan of his brain revealed that Peek, like some other savants, has no corpus callosum and very little cerebellum (Treffert & Christensen, 2005). The absence of a corpus callosum means that information processed in one of the brain's hemispheres cannot be communicated to the other hemisphere. Lacking a functional cerebellum also means that Peek lacks coordinated movement and balance.

connection

Daniel Tammet used mnemonic devices, a memory tool, to help him remember the value of pi. How do mnemonic devices aid memory?

See Chapter 7, p. 268.

THE NATURE AND NURTURE OF HUMAN INTELLIGENCE

If you want to start an argument, all you need to do is take a strong stance on one of the following positions: (1) A person's intelligence is determined almost completely by genetics, or (2) a person's intelligence is determined almost completely by the environment in which he or she is raised. Most people realize that intelligence results from a combination of "being born that way" and "being brought up that way" by our family and teachers. What is most remarkable is the complexity of the interaction between these two forces.

One way we see the interaction between environment and biological forces is in how the brain responds differently to different kinds of problems, intelligence problems among them. The region most often involved in various IQ tasks is the prefrontal cortex (Duncan et al., 2000; Haier et al., 2004). For instance, when a person is working on verbal tasks, only the left prefrontal region of the brain is activated. When an individual is working on spatial tasks, however, the prefrontal cortexes of both the left and right hemispheres, as well as the occipital cortex, are activated (see Figure 10.8; Duncan et al., 2000; Haier et al., 2004). Moreover, the frontal lobe is more involved when an individual is performing fluid intelligence tasks, such as pattern recognition, than when the person is performing tasks that involve crystallized intelligence and learned experiences (Gray & Thompson, 2004).

Furthermore, twin-adoption and family studies demonstrate the interconnectedness of nature and nurture in intelligence. As we saw in Chapter 3, these kinds of studies allow researchers to hold one factor constant, while varying the other one. The more genetically related people are, the more similar they are in IQ, even if reared apart (see Figure 10.9 on page 390). Identical twins reared apart are

Spatial Task

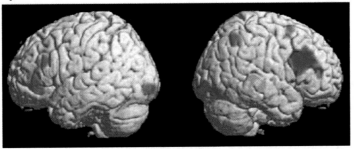

Left Hemisphere   Right Hemisphere

Verbal Task

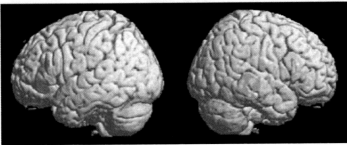

Left Hemisphere   Right Hemisphere

FIGURE 10.8

BRAIN ACTIVATION WHILE WORKING ON IQ PROBLEMS. Red areas show activation during two different IQ tasks, a verbal task and a spatial task. The spatial task activates the frontal lobe in both the right and left hemispheres, whereas the verbal task activates only the left frontal lobe region (Broca's area). (*Source:* Duncan et al., 2000.)

more similar in their levels of intelligence than fraternal twins reared together. Similarly, dozens of studies have shown that adopted children's overall intelligence is more similar to that of their biological parents than to that of their adoptive parents (Munsinger, 1975). Yet adoption—hence, the environment—can also enhance a child's IQ (van IJzendoorn & Juffer, 2005). Compared to orphans not adopted, adopted children tend to have higher IQs. In sum, genetic factors ("nature") account for about 50% of the variability in intelligence among individuals; environment ("nurture") accounts for about 40%; the remaining 10% is, as yet, unexplained (Grigorenko, 2000; Lynn, 2006; Plomin & Petrill, 1997).

Separated at birth, the Malifert twins meet accidentally.

(© Charles Addams. With permission by Tee and Charles Addams Foundation.)

The concept of reaction range provides further evidence for the interaction of biology and environment in determining a person's intelligence. A **reaction range** is the genetically determined range within which a given trait, such as intelligence, may fall; that trait's exact value, however, depends on the quality of the individual's environment (Scarr, 1981; Weinberg, 1989). For most people in most environments, the reaction range for IQ is about 25 points—meaning that a given person may end up scoring anywhere in a 25-point range on an IQ test, depending on the kind of environment in which he or she is raised (Weinberg, 1989). Being raised in an enriched environment means someone is likely to obtain an IQ score near the upper limit of his or her reaction range; being raised in an impoverished environment means one is likely to obtain a score near the lower limit;

reaction range for a given trait, such as IQ, the genetically determined range of responses by an individual to his or her environment.

nature & nurture
The concept of reaction range describes how biology and environment work together to produce a person's overall level of intelligence.

FIGURE 10.9

GENETIC AND ENVIRONMENTAL EFFECTS ON IQ.

Numbers in orange represent genetic relatedness. Genetic relatedness of 1 means 100% genetic similarity; .5 means 50% genetic similarity; and 0 means no genetic similarity.

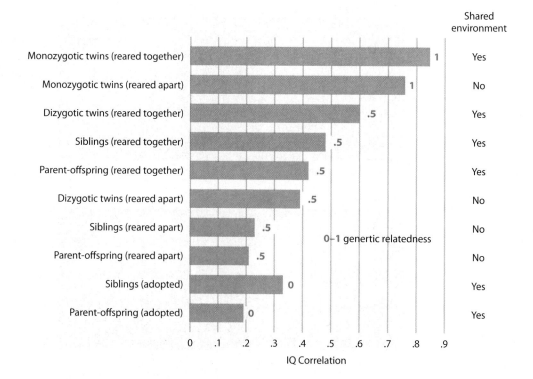

Reading to children regularly from the time they are very young as part of an enriched environment may actually enhance their IQ.

and being raised in a normal environment means one is likely to obtain a score in the middle of his or her reaction range (see Figure 10.10). The important point here is that genes do not determine behavior but, rather, establish the range of possible behaviors.

Environment, however, is a complex thing. Only part of the environmental influence on intelligence comes from being in the same household and sharing experiences. The other part comes from experiences that are not shared by family members—that is, the individual's unique environmental experiences. One such experience is the prenatal environment and what happens to the fetus during pregnancy. Toxins ingested by the mother, either intentionally or unintentionally, may influence the child's intelligence. Alcohol, drugs, and viral infections in a pregnant woman can seriously lower her child's overall intelligence (Jacobson & Jacobson, 2000; Ruff, 1999; Steinhausen & Spohr, 1998). For example, heavy alcohol consumption during pregnancy can lead to mental retardation in the child (Streissguth et al., 1989). Prenatal exposure to high levels of lead, mercury, or manganese may lead to serious impairments in a child's intelligence (Dietrich et al., 1991; Jacobson & Jacobson, 2000).

nature & nurture

What happens in the womb can permanently affect a person's measured intelligence.

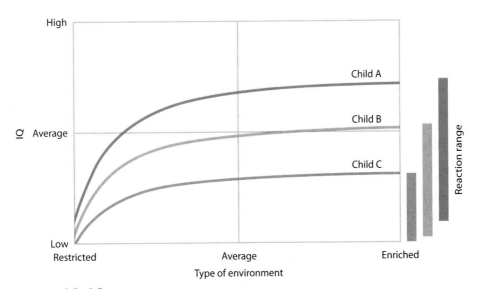

FIGURE 10.10

REACTION RANGE AND INTELLIGENCE. The concept of reaction range suggests that heredity places upper and lower limits on an individual's potential, but environment determines whether the individual reaches the upper limit or a point somewhere between the upper limit and the lower limit. This graph shows hypothetical reaction ranges for three children (A, B, and C) and how their surroundings could shape their IQs. With enriched environments, all three could reach their individual upper limit, as shown on the right side of the graph. (*Source:* Seifert et al., 2000.)

Another environmental effect on intelligence is *birth order*. Recent research has reported that first-born children have a slight advantage over second-born children, who have a smaller advantage over third-born children (Kristensen & Bjerkedal, 2007). Analysis of these results showed that these advantages must be caused by birth order, not prenatal environment, because the effect held only in situations in which no older sibling died in infancy. In other words, if a biological second-born has an older sibling who dies in infancy, that second-born child becomes, in effect, a first-born and displays a slight increase in IQ.

GROUP DIFFERENCES IN INTELLIGENCE SCORES

Given the importance of intelligence to success in life, the question of whether there are group differences in intelligence is bound to stir up controversy (Fancher, 1985). Research on this topic necessarily has political and social implications, and from time to time scientists who have studied group differences in intelligence have been harassed or threatened. If there are differences in intelligence between racial–ethnic groups or genders, what should we do as a society to compensate for those differences to level the playing field? Can that even be done?

Race–Ethnicity and Intelligence In the 1960s and 1970s Arthur Jensen received death threats for publishing research that not only reported differences in IQ among racial–ethnic groups, but also argued that because IQ is under genetic influence, racial–ethnic differences in IQ must be at least partly genetic in origin (Jensen, 1969). But it was another highly controversial book, published in the mid-1990s, that most recently ignited an academic, political, and cultural firestorm over intelligence. The book was called simply *The Bell Curve*, but its subtitle hinted at the more controversial contents: *Intelligence and Class Structure in American Life*. The book's authors, Richard Herrnstein and Charles Murray (1994), summarized the results of a study on racial–ethnic group differences, social class, and intelligence among 12,000 individuals. They concluded what many others had before and since: First, racial–ethnic groups vary on IQ scores; second, differences in IQ contribute to a large extent to differences in education and income (Gottfredson, 1997). Their carefully worded conclusion suggested that group differences in IQ, and hence in education and income, can be explained in part by genetics. Herrnstein and Murray tried to avoid some of the more blatant racial–ethnic arguments of Jensen, but to little avail. The controversy swept through universities and social circles very quickly (Sternberg, 1995).

When all of the smoke cleared and tempers settled down, there was still no widely accepted and agreed-on explanation for racial–ethnic differences on IQ scores. There are a few schools of thought (in addition to a partly genetic one). Some experts maintain that racial–ethnic differences in IQ result from biases in IQ tests that favor people from certain cultural backgrounds over others (Reynolds, 2000). Others have argued that a finding of differences in IQ scores according to race–ethnicity is meaningless because race is mostly a social construct with little scientific support or biological foundation (Sternberg, Grigorenko, & Kidd, 2005). In addition, these psychologists also point out that heritability findings apply only within the group of people studied, not between groups. So it is a misinterpretation of heritability to argue that group differences are due to genetics even if IQ is heritable. Moreover, most of the research conducted on heritability and IQ has come from European Americans and therefore is not applicable among the different racial–ethnic groups (Sternberg et al., 2005).

The conclusion that genetics influence intelligence is often interpreted—or misinterpreted—as implying that IQ levels are determined at birth or conception. If this were so, then trying to change IQ levels with intervention programs such as Head Start would likely be unsuccessful (Herrnstein & Murray, 1994). Yet, such a conclusion is faulty for two reasons. First, genes interact with environmental forces, and therefore environment can shape gene expression. We saw this in Chapter 3 with the concept of epigenesis. Similarly, the concept of a reaction range makes clear the connection between genes and environment. Second, interventions have succeeded in changing IQ levels. As we will see in more detail in Chapter 15, children raised under conditions of severe neglect and abuse who are adopted within the first few years of life showed tremendous growth in brain size and gains in IQ scores. Those adopted later in life or not adopted at all do not show increases in IQ scores (Perry, 2002). Moreover, one longitudinal study randomly assigned infants to either an early educational intervention program or to a control group. All children were from socially disadvantaged households. The intervention program lasted up until age 5 and focused on language, social, emotional, and cognitive stimulation. The children from both groups were studied again at ages 12, 15, and 21. The findings were clear: During adolescence and early adulthood, those who had been in the intervention program had higher IQ scores, performed better in school, and obtained higher-paying jobs than those in the control condition (Campbell & Ramey, 1995; Campbell et al., 2002). In short, both genetic and environmental forces play important roles in determining IQ scores.

Men and women may have their differences, but intelligence isn't one of them.

Gender and Intelligence

Larry Hedges and Amy Nowell (1995) reviewed six nationally representative sets of IQ scores. Each set ranged in size from 12,000 to 73,000 participants altogether. They concluded that there are relatively few real differences between the sexes in cognitive ability; men and women are equally intelligent. Indeed, most research on overall intelligence and gender has reported no difference between men and women on average.

The one consistent difference shows more variability in intelligence among men than among women. This difference is illustrated in Figure 10.11 on page 394. Men are more likely than women to score at either end of the range, especially in some areas. Men more frequently score at the high or low end of the scale on tests of science, math, spatial reasoning and social studies (Ceci & Williams, 2007; Gallagher & Kaufman, 2005). Women, however, tend to consistently do better than men in

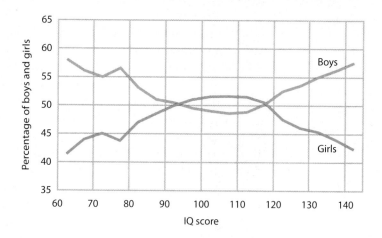

FIGURE 10.11

GENDER VARIABILITY IN INTELLIGENCE. Results from more than 80,000 Scottish children found mean IQ scores were nearly identical. Mean IQ was 100.5 for boys and 100.6 for girls. Boys were much more likely to be at the two extreme ends of intelligence, however. They made up 58% of the scores at 60 and 140, whereas girls made up only about 42% of those scores. (*Source:* Deary et al., 2003.)

writing, reading comprehension, perceptual speed, and associative memory (Deary et al., 2003; Hedges & Nowell, 1995; Maccoby & Jacklin, 1974).

NON-WESTERN VIEWS OF INTELLIGENCE

Ask people in the United States or Europe what it means to be intelligent. Then ask people in Kenya, China, Malaysia, and Bolivia. No doubt you will get very different answers. Western cultures emphasize verbal and cognitive skills first, whereas many African cultures see social skills, such as being socially responsible, cooperative, and active in family and social life, to be crucial aspects of intelligence (Ruzgis & Grigorenko, 1994; Serpell, 1982). Asian cultures have traditionally emphasized humility, awareness, doing the right thing, and mindfulness as important qualities of intelligence (Sternberg, 2000). Doing well in school and being quick to learn are not universally acknowledged to be essential qualities of intelligence. Sternberg and his colleagues have examined practical intelligence in cultures where academic intelligence is not valued as highly as it is in Western cultures. They have found that children in Kenya and Tanzania, for example, may not do well at solving "bookish" analytic problems but do very well at solving everyday, practical problems (Sternberg, 1998).

Problems that require intelligence are just one kind of problem we face. Problem solving pervades almost everything we do, from our choice of a major in college to our choice of friends, where we live, how we vote, and so on. Next we look at the psychology of problem solving.

quick quiz 10.1: Intelligence

1. Which of the following skills is NOT part of the definition of intelligence?
   a. abstract reasoning
   b. problem solving
   c. acquiring knowledge
   d. remote associations

2. Historically, a child's IQ was calculated by dividing _____ by chronological age and multiplying by _____. (Pick the best pair of words/numbers.)
   a. perceptual skill; 100
   b. mental age; 50
   c. perceptual skill; 50
   d. mental age; 100

3. The Kaufmans broke new ground in intelligence testing by developing an IQ test that
   a. could be universally applied
   b. was grounded in psychological theory and knowledge of the brain
   c. was reliable and valid
   d. was culture-free and fair

4. _____ involves raw mental ability, pattern recognition, and abstract reasoning and is applied to a problem that a person has never confronted before.
   a. crystallized intelligence
   b. narrow intelligence
   c. fluid intelligence
   d. general intelligence

5. Someone who is good at detecting whether or not a person is lying would be said to have high _____.
   a. interpersonal intelligence
   b. naturalistic intelligence
   c. practical intelligence
   d. creative intelligence

Answers can be found at the end of the chapter.

Problem Solving

None of us goes through a day without having to solve a problem, because every time we face a task that we do not know how to carry out, we are confronted with a problem (Simon, 1978). On any given day, you may have to budget your time so that you can study for your test and go to a party with friends or figure out the most efficient route to drive to a place you have never visited.

Psychologists have examined how people go about solving problems, often by presenting research participants with problems and studying how they solve them. Take a few minutes to work on each of the following problems. Some are easy and others not so easy, but give them a try. We will return to each problem later in the section.

- How are a dog and a lion alike?

- How would you solve the problem of rising world temperatures?

FIGURE 10.12

PROBLEM SOLVING. (a) Remove one match to make seven squares. (b) Connect all 9 dots with 4 straight lines—without lifting your pencil. (*Answer to b appears at the end of the chapter.*)

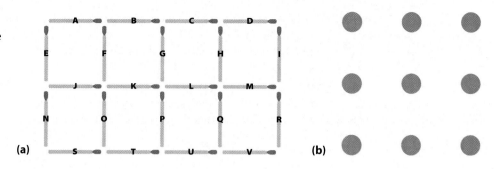

(a)   (b)

- In Figure 10.12a, remove one match to make 7 squares.

- Look at the 9 dots in Figure 10.12b. Connect all the dots using only 4 straight lines without lifting up your pen or pencil from the paper once you've started.

- Figure 10.13 is a picture of a person in a room with two strings hanging from the ceiling. Also in the room are a book of matches, a pair of pliers, and some cotton. The task is to tie the two pieces of string together. The strings are too short for the person to hold on to one and grab the other. How would you go about tying the strings together?

- Pretend you have three jars (A, B, and C), each containing a set amount of water. Add or subtract the given amounts in each jar to come up with a set final amount. For instance, Jar A holds 21 units of water, Jar B 127 units, and Jar C 3 units. Using any of the jars, discard or add water as needed to end up with 100 units of water. Figure 10.14 shows some variations you can try.

TYPES OF PROBLEMS

convergent thinking problems

problems that have known solutions and require analytic thinking and crystallized intelligence to come up with the correct answer.

Convergent thinking problems have known solutions, which can be reached by narrowing down a set of possible answers. Intelligence tests and college entrance exams include convergent problems. Figuring out how to operate a new coffee maker is another convergent problem. There is one right way to brew coffee with a given machine. Convergent problems require analytic thinking and crystallized intelligence—the problem solver has to analyze the problem and then apply learned strategies and knowledge to come up with the answer.

Some problems, however, may not have a known solution. Consider the problem: "How would you solve the problem of rising world temperatures?" There are many possible solutions to these problems, some of which work better than others. These kinds of problems are known as **divergent thinking problems**. To solve them, we must break away from our normal problem-solving strategies and make unusual associations to arrive

divergent thinking problems

problems that have no known solutions and require novel solutions.

FIGURE 10.13

TWO STRING PROBLEM.
How do you connect two strings if you can't reach the second one without dropping the first one? (Answer appears at the end of the chapter.)

FIGURE 10.14

WATER JAR PROBLEMS AND MENTAL SET. The task is to use any combination of jars A, B, and C, subtracting or adding jars of "water" to obtain the desired amount. Try it. (*Source:* Luchins & Luchins, 1970.)

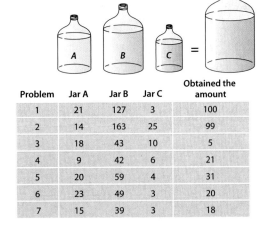

Problem	Jar A	Jar B	Jar C	Obtained the amount
1	21	127	3	100
2	14	163	25	99
3	18	43	10	5
4	9	42	6	21
5	20	59	4	31
6	23	49	3	20
7	15	39	3	18

at novel ways of thinking about a problem. Imagine that your new dorm-mate snores so loudly you can't sleep. How would you solve this problem? Divergence may lead to redefining the problem in a way that makes finding a solution more likely. These kinds of problems require fluid and creative intelligence.

SOLUTION STRATEGIES

Psychologists describe three kinds of strategies that people use to solve different kinds of problems: algorithms, insight, and thinking outside the box. When you were solving the water jug problems in Figure 10.14, did you realize that the last two could be solved much more easily than the first five? If you are like about 75% of the population, you continued to use the solution pattern or algorithm you may have discovered in solving the first few problems. **Algorithms** are step-by-step formulas or procedures for solving problems. In this case, the algorithm is "Jar B – Jar A – Jar C (twice)." For this problem, this algorithm also helped you create a **mental set,** which is a tendency to continue to use problem-solving strategies that have worked in the past, even if better solutions are available (Luchins & Luchins, 1970). This mental set probably made you miss the easier solutions to Problems 6 and 7: Jar A – Jar C and Jar A + Jar C, respectively. Luchins and Luchins (1970) found that if Problems 1 to 5 were not given first, 100% of adults saw the direct solution. In contrast, if they first received Problems 1 to 5 and had to develop an algorithm, only 24% found the more direct solutions to Problems 6 and 7. Figure 10.15 on page 398 depicts the research process for a jar study that demonstrated that groups are better able to break out of their mental set than individuals (Luchins & Luchins, 1969).

Not all solutions involve algorithms. Some occur with a flash of insight. One of the best-known examples of insight occurred in ancient Greece, when the philosopher-scientist Archimedes solved the problem of how to determine whether a crown contained anything besides gold. The solution came to him in a flash when he saw the water level rise as he entered the public baths. Because gold is heavier than other metals, it will displace more water, so by seeing how much water it displaced, Archimedes would be able to determine whether the crown was pure gold without melting it down. The insight excited him so much that without pausing to dress, he ran out of the baths yelling *"Eureka!"* (in Greek, "I have found it!"). In honor of Archimedes, these kinds of sudden solutions are referred to as either **Eureka insights** or **insight solutions.**

mental set
a tendency to continue to use problem-solving strategies that have worked in the past, even if better solutions are available.

algorithms
a step-by-step procedure or formula for solving a problem.

Eureka insight or **insight solutions**
sudden solutions that come to mind in a flash.

1 research question

Are individuals or small groups better at breaking out of their mental sets to solve the water jar problem?

2 method

As with the jar problem presented in Figure 10.14, participants were given cards representing three jars (A, B, C). Each card had different amounts of water and they had to add or subtract any combination of the cards to obtain a final amount. The problems were identical to those in Figure 10.14, with two exceptions. First, a fourth jar was added, and second, two additional problems were administered that could be solved without the mental set algorithm established by the first five problems (B– A – 2C). In this study there were four problems (problems 6 through 9) that gave participants an opportunity to break their mental set and solve the problem more directly. In addition to being tested individually, some participants were assigned to be tested in small groups of four people. In the group condition, each group member was given only one jar amount and the group then had to work together to solve the problem. As was true of individuals, each group had 2.5 minutes to solve the problem.

3 results

In all of the last six problems, groups outperformed individuals in the ability to solve the problem by breaking out of the mental set algorithm suggested by the first three problems (B - A – 2C). More than 80% of individuals, however, had figured out how to break out of the mental set by the time they were given the last two problems (8 and 9), but groups still outperformed individuals.

Percentage of participants who solved by breaking out of mental sets

4 conclusion

Mental sets are ways of thinking that help in some situations but blind us to simpler ways of solving problems in other situations. Because each person in the group received only one jar amount, the group had to cooperate in order to solve the problems. All jars had to be considered in the group in a way that was not true for individuals working on the problem.

FIGURE 10.15

GROUP VERSUS INDIVIDUAL SOLUTIONS TO THE JAR PROBLEM. Group problem solving takes advantage of the group's "collective intelligence" and people are better able to break out of a mental set when solving a simple quantitative problem. All it takes is one person to come up with the more direct solution and the whole group benefits. (*Source:* Luchins, A. S., & Luchins, E. H. (1969). Einstellung effect and group problem solving. *The Journal of Social Psychology, 77,* 79–89.)

A modern version of such a "Eureka solution" happened to George de Mestral, a Swiss engineer (*How a Swiss invention hooked the world*, 2007). De Mestral would often go on hikes in the Alps with his dog. When they came home he noticed that his clothes and his dog's fur caught thistle burrs, which he found on close inspection to have hooks on the ends. The dog's fur and his clothes contained loops that snagged the plants. In a flash, de Mestral realized that a fastener could be made to connect to loops. The best part about the hook and loop system was it was easily reversible and could be fastened over and over again. De Mestral invented Velcro, which is now a common fastener of such things as shoe straps, backpacks, and clothing.

The solution to the two-string problem in Figure 10.13 often comes as a Eureka insight (Maier, 1931). You might have suddenly realized that the screwdriver could be used as a weight at the end of one string and then swung into motion. As you stand holding the other string, the weighted string swings over and you grab it and tie the two together.

The third problem-solving strategy is turning a problem around and thinking about it from a different perspective. If you have ever heard the phrase "thinking outside the box," you now know where it comes from—the 9-dot problem (Figure 10.12b). **Thinking outside the box** requires you to break free of self-imposed conceptual constraints and think about a problem differently in order to solve it. If you came up with a solution, it required that you go outside the self-imposed "box" that the 9 dots create in your mind. There is no such box there in reality, but you perceive one. Once you think outside the box, a couple of solutions may come to you rather easily (see the end of the chapter for the solution). Creative thinkers regularly think flexibly and differently about problems (Feist, 1999).

thinking outside the box
approach to problem solving that requires breaking free of self-imposed conceptual constraints and thinking about a problem differently in order to solve it.

"*Never, ever, think outside the box.*"

OBSTACLES TO SOLUTIONS

The difficulties people encounter in solving the 9-dot problem point to some of the common obstacles we face in solving all kinds of problems. One of the biggest blocks to solving a problem is **fixation,** or the inability to break out of a particular mind-set in order to think about a problem from a fresh perspective. Fixation prevents many people from seeing possible solutions to the 7-square match problem (Figure 10.12a). It is difficult, for example, to see that one can simply remove match B, C, T, or U. If one takes away match B, for instance, there are only 7 squares but the continuity in the upper row of squares is broken. This solution may not be obvious because people become fixated on a self-imposed mental set in which "all the squares must continue to touch each other." Note that the instructions do not require this—people unconsciously impose such rules themselves.

fixation
the inability to break out of a particular mind-set in order to think about a problem from a fresh perspective.

As we saw earlier, mental sets are a kind of fixation. A mental set provides solutions to problems but can also stand in the way of new ideas and novel solutions. Education and training create mental sets. When we learn solution

connection

Heuristics are mental short-cuts we use in making decisions and judgments.

See Chapter 9, p. 359.

functional fixedness

mind-set in which one is blind to unusual uses of common everyday things or procedures.

strategies in school and in the workplace, we learn how to solve problems. Sometimes these solutions are algorithms, sometimes insights, and sometimes they are heuristics. But strategies can blind us to more novel, efficient, and even creative solutions. It becomes hard to step back and see the problem from a fresh perspective.

Another obstacle to successful problem solving is our tendency to be blind to unusual uses of common everyday things or procedures: This is known as **functional fixedness** (Duncker, 1945). A good example of functional fixedness occurs when people try to solve the two-string problem. People are used to thinking of screwdrivers as tools for driving screws into wood or metal. But a screwdriver can also be used as a weight at the end of a string that causes it to swing like a pendulum. Figuring out a new way to use a screwdriver is an example of thinking outside the box to find a creative solution to a problem. As mentioned earlier, creative thinkers often think differently about how to solve a problem. We discuss this type of creative thinking and creativity in general next.

quick quiz 10.2: Problem Solving

1. In what kind of problems must the person trying to solve them narrow down the range of possible solutions to arrive at the correct answer?
   a. simple problems
   b. convergent thinking problems
   c. algorithms
   d. divergent thinking problems

2. A child discovers that 2 × 2 is the same as 2 + 2. He therefore wrongly concludes that 3 × 3 is the same as 3 + 3. What tendency is affecting this child's problem-solving strategies?
   a. mental set
   b. divergent thinking
   c. test bias
   d. response bias

3. An inability to break out of a particular frame of mind in order to think about a problem from a fresh perspective is known as
   a. perpetuation
   b. mental set
   c. fixation
   d. functional fixedness

Answers can be found at the end of the chapter.

Creativity

What was it about Leonardo da Vinci that made him so versatile as an artist and inventor? What was going on in the mind of Isaac Newton when he realized the significance of the apple falling from a tree? Why are some people able to paint magnificent landscapes while others can hardly draw a straight line? The answer is that these individuals are more creative than the average person.

The ability to think or act creatively is highly prized in our society (Feist, 1999; Sawyer, 2006; Simonton, 1999). All of society's advances—artistic, musical, industrial, governmental, legal, and scientific—happen because a person or group of people came up with a creative idea. Creative thinking is related to, yet distinct from, both intelligence and problem solving. To fully appreciate the nature of human creativity, we define what psychologists mean by it, discuss its connection to genius and intelligence, define its stages, review the brain systems involved in creative thought, and finally discuss the cognitive mechanisms involved in creative thinking.

WHAT IS CREATIVITY?

Read the following two paragraphs, written by different people, and think about what each one means and whether they are equally "creative":

> They're all so different Boylan talking about the shape of my foot he noticed at once even before he was introduced when I was in the DBC with Poldy laughing and trying to listen I was waggling my foot we both ordered 2 teas and plain bread and butter I saw him looking with his two old maids of sisters when I stood up and asked the girl where it was what do I care with it dropping out of me and that black closed breeches he made me buy takes you half an hour to let down wetting all myself always with some brand new fad every other week. . . .

> This creation in which we live began with the Dominant Nature as an Identification Body of a completed evolutionary Strong Material creation in a Major Body Resistance Force. And is fulfilling the Nature Identification in a like Weaker Material Identification creation in which Two Major Bodies have already fulfilled radio body balances, and embodying a Third Material Identification Embodiment of both.

The first paragraph is an excerpt from James Joyce's great novel *Ulysses*. The second paragraph was written by a person who is schizophrenic and is an example of what is called *word salad*, a collection of words that are mixed up

For the New Zealand duo Flight of the Conchords, creativity meant combining acoustic folk rock with parody, a novel approach to comedy that won them a radio series, a TV series, and in 2008, a Grammy award for best comedy album.

in sentences with no real meaning (White, 1964). These two paragraphs demonstrate an essential point about what creativity is and what it is not. It is not simply original thinking, for the paragraphs are equally original. They are both unusual, and both give voice to sentences that probably had not been uttered or written before these writers penned them. For something to be deemed creative, however, it not only has to be original but must also be useful or adaptive and solve a problem. Joyce's paragraph does that because it's part of solving the problem of telling a story. The second paragraph is not creative because it is not useful and it does not solve a problem.

creativity
thinking and/ or behavior that is both novel– original and useful–adaptive.

Creativity, then, is thought or behavior that is both novel-original and useful-adaptive (Amabile, 1996; Feist, 1999; MacKinnon, 1970; Simonton, 1999). The usefulness criterion requires that someone at some time sees real value and usefulness in the creative accomplishment. Truly creative works are often appreciated in the creator's lifetime, but not always. For instance, Vincent van Gogh sold very few of his paintings while alive. But his creative genius is now fully appreciated by novices and experts alike, and his paintings are worth millions.

STAGES OF CREATIVE PROBLEM SOLVING

Creative problem solving is a process that has distinct stages. Long ago, Graham Wallas (1926) identified four such stages of creative problem solving: preparation, incubation, insight, and elaboration-verification. The first stage of creative problem solving is *preparation,* or discovering and defining the problem and then attempting to solve it. This leads to the second stage, *incubation,* or putting the problem aside for a while and working on something else. The third stage, *insight,* is a Eureka insight in which the solution comes immediately to mind. The fourth and final stage of creative problem solving is *verification–elaboration.* The solution, even if it has the feel of certainty, still needs to be confirmed. How it is confirmed depends on what kind of task is involved. The verification process is different for an everyday problem, such as problems in art, literature, music, science, technology, invention, or philosophy.

WHERE EARL GETS HIS IDEAS

GENIUS, INTELLIGENCE, AND CREATIVITY

What makes someone a genius? Is superior intelligence enough? Consider Marilyn vos Savant. Most people have not heard of her, although she does write a weekly nationally syndicated column for *Parade* magazine. She has the world's highest recorded IQ ever—an off-the-chart 228. Yet she has not created master works of note. Genius is not, as some have claimed, simply being smart or having a very high IQ (Simonton, 1999). Having an IQ of 130 or 140, which puts one in the top 1% or higher of the population, does not guarantee producing creative works of lasting influence.

Something other than intelligence must go into the making of a genius. **Genius** is high intelligence combined with creative accomplishments that have a tremendous impact on a given field (Simonton, 1999). The paintings, plays, buildings, novels, or scientific discoveries of geniuses change their respective fields. Literature was never the same after Shakespeare or Virginia Woolf. Physics has not been the same since Newton, Einstein, and Marie Curie. Art has not been the same since van Gogh and Picasso. Music has not been the same since Bach and Beethoven. And art, medicine, anatomy, and invention have not been the same since da Vinci. If people's accomplishments change their field, other people appreciate their importance sooner or later. Indeed, having a major impact on a field and being appreciated for the accomplishments is what distinguishes genius from geniuslike IQ. For every Shakespeare, Beethoven, da Vinci, and Einstein, there are many more people with equally high intelligence who make no significant contributions to society. Moreover, there have been people of truly monumental creative accomplishment whose intelligence was only somewhat above average. Charles Darwin, for example, was reputed to be—by his own admission—of only modestly high intelligence (Simonton, 1999). Yet his accomplishments have had as much impact on science and culture as those of just about any other person. By this standard, he was a genius.

Genius, by definition, and creativity are closely related. Suprisingly, however, IQ and creativity are not very strongly related (Albert & Runco, 1989; Sternberg & O'Hara, 1999). For example, a meta-analysis of 21 studies that included more than 45,000 participants reported an average correlation between creativity and intelligence of only +.17 (Kim, 2005). That is, knowing an IQ score tells us only a little bit about how creative someone may be. In addition, the relationship between IQ and creativity is not stronger for IQs below 120 than for IQs above 120, as researchers once proposed (Kim, 2005; Preckel, Holling, & Wiese, 2006).

CREATIVITY AND THE BRAIN

Imagine what was going on in Newton's brain when he "discovered" gravity or in Einstein's when he came up with the theory of relativity. Of course, we'll never know what was going on in the minds of these geniuses from the past. But neuroscientists are beginning to uncover what happens in the brain when a typical person has a Eureka insight or when creative people solve problems compared to less creative people. The research has revealed two consistent findings: Insights occur in the right hemisphere rather than the left, and creative people solving creative problems show more balanced activity between their right and left frontal lobes.

Creative Insight and the Right Hemisphere   It's not easy to undertake brain research related to creativity. The main way to study creativity and the brain is to administer a creativity problem to a person while she or he is either lying down in a brain scanner or sitting down hooked up to an EEG machine. One kind of problem that has been used in such research is a *remote associate*

William Shakespeare

Virginia Woolf

Leonardo da Vinci

Isaac Newton

Albert Einstein

word problem (Mednick & Mednick, 1967). Remote associate problems display three words at one time to the participant, who must then come up with a single word that could be used with all three of the words. The single word could be added to each of the words to create a compound word or it could be modify one of the displayed words in some way. This requires the participant to form a non-obvious or "remote" association in order solve the problem. For example, if the three words were *French, shoe,* and *car,* what one word could you think of that could be used with the other three? What if the three words were *pine, crab,* and *sauce*? (The answers appear at the end of the chapter.) Interestingly, people often solve these kinds of problems with Eureka insights.

In one set of studies, researchers presented remote association tests to either the right or left visual fields of participants. These participants were not selected for high or low levels of creativity. The researchers presented the information to the individual visual fields because they wanted to control which hemisphere of the brain processed the information. Recall from Chapter 3 that information presented to the left visual field is processed in the right hemisphere of the brain and information presented to the right visual field is processed in the left hemisphere of the brain. When the problem was presented in the left visual field and processed in the right hemisphere, insight into the problems occurred much more frequently than when the problem was presented to the right visual field and processed in the left hemisphere (Beeman & Bowden, 2000; Bowden & Jung-Beeman, 2003). Moreover, when researchers took brain images using fMRI and EEG while people were solving insight problems, they found that sudden insights consistently activated the right hemisphere more than the left (Bowden et al., 2005). Similarly, patients with damage to the frontal region of their right hemisphere are less able to solve problems requiring insight than people without damage to their right hemisphere (Miller & Tippett, 1996).

connection

People who have had their corpus callosum severed cannot say what they see if the information is presented to their left visual field but can verbally label it if it is presented to their right visual field. Why?

See Chapter 3, p. 106.

Creativity and Balanced Activity Between the Hemispheres

The second consistent finding from the neuroscience of creativity is that when solving problems, creative people have more balanced brain activity between the hemispheres than less creative people. In particular, while solving problems they show equally active areas in their right and left frontal lobes, which translates

Marie Curie

J. S. Bach

Ludwig van Beethoven

Vincent van Gogh

Pablo Picasso

into a widening rather than a narrowing of attention and a greater flexibility in moving from one way of thinking to another (Carlsson, Wendt, & Risberg, 2000; Goel & Vartanian, 2005). Widening attention and being able to shift ways of thinking easily and flexibly are hallmarks of creative thinking (Feist, 2004; Martindale, 1999). Let's take one study as an example: Carlsson and colleagues (2000) selected participants who during earlier testing scored either high or low on creativity problems. Participants in each of these two groups were each given a noncreative and creative task to complete while in a brain scanner. Brain scans compared the two conditions. Results showed more left than right frontal lobe activity in the less-creative participants. Highly creative participants, however, showed a balance in right and left frontal lobe activity. See the orange regions in Figure 10.16.

This finding may appear to contradict what we just said about the importance of the right hemisphere in creative problem solving, but it does not. The

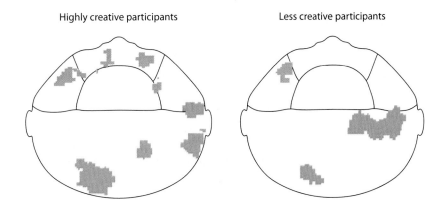

Highly creative participants

Less creative participants

FIGURE 10.16

BRAIN ACTIVITY WHILE SOLVING CREATIVE PROBLEMS. Orange regions show areas of increased activity while solving creative problems compared to noncreative problems. Green regions show areas of decreased activity. The more creative participants use both left and right hemispheres (frontal region) while working on creative problems, while the less creative participants show increased activity only in their right frontal lobe. (*Source:* Carlsson et al., 2000).

right hemisphere findings are from noncreative participants who are coming up with insight solutions. The balanced hemisphere result comes from comparing creative to less creative people. In both cases, right hemisphere activity is more pronounced in creative people than in less creative ones.

COGNITIVE PROCESSES IN CREATIVE THINKING

Creative thinking entails unique cognitive processes. Psychologists who study the cognitive aspects of creative thought have focused on visual thinking, fluency, flexibility, and originality. Visual imagery occurs when we see a solution in our "mind's eye." Many scientists, artists, and writers solve problems by using creative mental images (A. Miller, 1996). Einstein, for example, often visualized a situation, such as riding in an elevator traveling at the speed of light. Imagining such a scenario and then thinking about what would happen to a light beam he emitted led to his discovery of the theory of relativity.

Cognitive psychologists have developed clever experiments to test people's ability to come up with creative mental images. They display images of letters or geometric shapes and ask participants to combine some of them in a creative way (Finke, Ward, & Smith, 1992). Figure 10.17a contains a set of such objects. Three of these images are chosen at random during each trial, and the participant's task is to assemble them in such a way as to create a recognizable shape or pattern. Various solutions are presented in Figure 10.17b.

The ability to produce many ideas is central to creative thought. This ability is termed **ideational fluency** (Guilford, 1967). Highly creative people usually come up with more ideas for a given problem than less creative people do. Not all the ideas will be equally useful, but having a large number of ideas increases the chance that any one of them will be a useful or adaptive solution to the problem at hand. J. P. Guilford developed the *Alternate Uses* test to measure creativity. In this test, participants are given a common object such as a brick or a pencil and asked to write down all the possible uses they can think of for the object within a limited amount of time. An ideationally fluent person can list many alternate uses for the object within a short period.

The ability to produce many ideas does not by itself guarantee that one can break out of one's mental set and think of unusual uses. A creative person can also come up with many different categories of ideas and think of other

ideational fluency
the ability to produce many ideas.

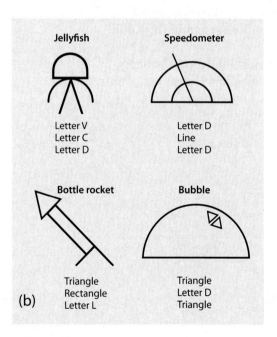

FIGURE 10.17
CREATIVE PROBLEM SOLVING USING MENTAL IMAGERY. (a) Three stimulus shapes at a time are presented to a person, whose task it is to combine them in any way to produce a single image or object. (b) These are some of the solutions created using shapes in (a). (*Source:* Finke et al., 1992.)

responses besides the obvious one. This ability is called **flexibility of thought** (Guilford, 1967). In the *Alternate Uses* test, flexibility of thought is gauged by the number of categories of response a person offers. For instance, if all the answers for the uses of a brick involve building something, the person is not displaying flexible thinking but remaining within one rather obvious category. In contrast, coming up with uses that involve building, painting, writing, weights, step stools, and ballasts means a person is a flexible thinker because those uses cut across many different categories. As we saw with the 9-dot problem, creative people "think outside the box" and break out of mental sets more easily than less creative people do.

flexibility of thought
the ability to come up with many different categories of ideas and think of other responses besides the obvious one.

A third cognitive process involved in creative thought is **originality,** which means thinking of unusual and novel ideas. In the *Alternate Uses* test, the test taker's originality is scored by comparing his or her responses to a set of norms developed from the answers given by thousands of respondents who have taken the test previously. A person's answer is scored as original if it is rare or uncommon compared to the norms. Again using the brick as an example, a higher originality score is given to "step stool" than to "paperweight" because there are fewer instances of "step stool" in the norms. In this sense, an original response is the same as an infrequent response. But originality in itself is not enough to explain creative thought. Creative thinking occurs when a person combines all three cognitive processes at once—fluency, flexibility, and originality.

originality
the ability to come up with unusual and novel ideas.

THE CREATIVE PERSONALITY

We have seen how creative people differ from others by their brain activity and cognitive style. What about their personalities? Do creative people tend to have unique personalities, and if so what personality characteristics tend to be found in highly creative people? The best way to answer this question is by looking at what all of the published studies on the topic say—that is, by conducting a meta-analysis.

Feist (1998) conducted such a meta-analysis by locating all of the published studies that reported personality qualities of artists and scientists (see also Batey & Furnham, 2008). Twenty-six studies on almost 5,000 participants had reported personality traits of scientists compared to norms and twenty-nine studies on almost 4,400 participants had reported the personality traits of artists compared to norms. Creative artists and scientists do share some common personality traits (see Figure 10.18). To highlight some of the most pronounced personality traits of creative artists and scientists: Openness to experience is the

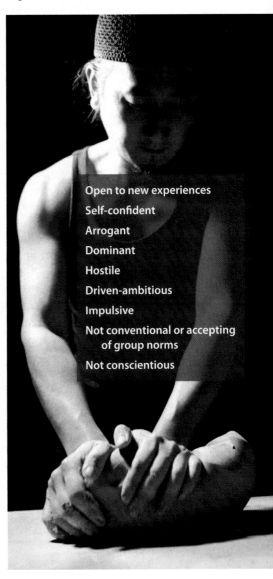

Open to new experiences
Self-confident
Arrogant
Dominant
Hostile
Driven-ambitious
Impulsive
Not conventional or accepting of group norms
Not conscientious

FIGURE 10.18
PERSONALITY TRAITS SHARED BY CREATIVE ARTISTS AND SCIENTISTS.

tendency to enjoy and seek out new experiences, new foods, new places, and new ideas. Highly creative people have this quality, which is not surprising given that creativity involves novel thoughts and behavior. Also, they are unconventional and tend to have a firm belief that they possess a better way of doing things. In some, this comes off as self-confidence and in others as arrogance (Feist, 1993). Also, artists are more emotionally sensitive and unstable than scientists (Feist, 1998; Ludwig, 1995).

connection

Is there a connection between mental illness and creativity?

See Chapter 15, p. 605.

As you see from this discussion, intelligence, creativity, and problem solving are abilities used by people in every walk of life, including art, science, cooking, teaching, parenting, inventing, and engineering. Indeed, humans are distinguished from other animals by our well developed intellectual, problem solving, and creative abilities. Next we connect the topics explored in this chapter by focusing on one group that exhibits the three abilities in abundance, namely extremely talented young scientists.

quick quiz 10.3: Creativity

1. Creative thinking or behavior is both novel and _____.
   a. interesting
   b. artistic
   c. useful
   d. unusual

2. The four stages of creative problem solving include preparation, incubation, insight, and _____.
   a. elaboration–verification
   b. validation
   c. discrimination
   d. resolution

3. When compared to less creative people, creative people show what pattern of brain activity while solving problems?
   a. asymmetry between the hemispheres
   b. balance between the hemispheres
   c. parietal lobe activation
   d. occipital lobe activation

4. What is measured by the task in which participants are asked to think of as many different uses for a brick as they can?
   a. originality
   b. flexibility of thought
   c. functional fixedness
   d. both a and b

Answers can be found at the end of the chapter.

making connections
in intelligence, problem solving, and creativity

Whiz Kids in Science

Perhaps you participated in science fairs in elementary or high school. Projects for these events might have been something you did because it was required. For some students, however, science fairs provide a means of expressing their interest in and passion for science, as well as an outlet for creativity. Especially creative teens who participate in science fairs may become finalists in the prestigious Intel Science Talent Search. A look at some of the characteristics of finalists in this contest brings together topics we have explored in this chapter.

The Intel Science Talent Search (STS) competition attracts 1,500 to 1,700 high school applicants annually. Only the top 40 (2%) become finalists. STS finalists are among the top high school science students in the nation. Indeed, six finalists have gone on to win Nobel Prizes, and many others have had illustrious careers in science, math, and medicine (Kaye, 2001). Moreover, the finalists are at or near the top of

their high school class, and a very high percentage of them gain entrance to elite universities (Berger, 1994; Feist, 2006; Subotnik, Duschl, & Selmon, 1993).

The academic performance and test scores of STS finalists leave little doubt that they are a highly intelligent group of young people. Many finalists score in the top 1 or 2% in the quantitative portion of the SAT, and approximately 25% of the finalists score perfect scores on the SAT overall (*Teen Scientists,* 2005).

Becoming an STS finalist takes more than a high level of intelligence. It also requires an aptitude for solving difficult problems creatively. This involves devising a solution to a novel task that is both original and useful. For example, Mary Masterman, first-prize winner in 2007, stated a real problem: How can a $300 machine be made to do what is normally done by a $20,000 to $100,000 machine? Solving this problem required intelligence and a great deal of creativity, but Masterman was up to these tasks. She designed and built a spectrograph—a machine that identifies the structure of molecules. "I wanted to build one that was lower costing so it would be more available to anyone interested in spectrography," she said. "The most challenging part was trying to get it to work. I had to keep coming up with creative ways to adjust or change something. It took three months to build and another three months before it actually functioned properly" (Carr, 2007).

quick quiz 10.4: Making Connections in Intelligence, Problem Solving, and Creativity

1. Thinking back to Sternberg's model of intelligence and applying it to the Science Talent Search finalists, we would predict they are unusually talented in their
   a. analytic intelligence
   b. creative intelligence
   c. practical intelligence
   d. both a and b
2. A high percentage of STS finalists
   a. leave science careers
   b. have productive and creative careers in science, engineering, or math
   c. have unremarkable careers
   d. win Nobel prizes

Answers can be found at the end of the chapter.

In 2006, Intel STS finalist Elyse Hope, 18, presented the results of her space science research at the National Academy of Sciences.

chapter **review**

INTELLIGENCE

- Intelligence is a set of cognitive skills that include abstract thinking, reasoning, problem solving, and the ability to acquire knowledge.

- There are two major theories of the nature of intelligence. The single-factor or general-factor theory argues that intelligence at its core is one overall ability. The other theory, the multifactor theory, says that intelligence consists of multiple abilities.

- Some of the factors of intelligence in the multifactor theory are crystallized and fluid intelligence, as well as analytic, practical, musical, and bodily–kinesthetic intelligence.

- Measures of intelligence, including the Stanford-Binet and the Wechsler Adult Scales of Intelligence (WAIS), tend to be reliable and predictive of certain outcomes (school achievement), but not others (happiness or satisfaction with one's job).

- Intelligence ranges widely on a continuum from very low to very high. On the extreme low end is mental retardation and on the extreme high end is giftedness.

- Group differences in IQ do exist for race and gender, and yet there is much debate concerning possible explanations for these differences.

PROBLEM SOLVING

- Two distinct kinds of problem exist. Convergent thinking problems have known solutions, which can be reached by narrowing down a set of possible answers. Divergent thinking problems have no known solution, and require breaking away from our normal problem-solving strategies and making unusual associations to arrive at novel ways of thinking about a problem.

- People use different kinds of strategies to solve problems. Algorithms are formulas that guarantee correct solutions to particular problems. Thinking outside the box requires one to break free of self-imposed conceptual constraints

and think about a problem differently in order to solve it. Eureka insights involve a sudden understanding of a solution.

- Obstacles to solutions include fixation, or inability to break out of a particular mind-set in order to think about a problem from a fresh perspective, and functional fixedness, which is the tendency to be blind to unusual uses of common everyday things or procedures.

CREATIVITY

- Creativity is thought or behavior that is both novel and useful or adaptive.

- Genius is closely related to creativity in that it combines high intelligence with achievements that change entire fields (art, music, science, technology, business).

- Researchers have uncovered two principles of creative thinking and the brain: Insights occur more in the right hemisphere than the left, and creative people solving creative problems show more balanced activity between their right and left frontal lobes than less creative people.

- Cognitive processes commonly associated with creative thinking are visual imagery, flexibility (coming up with many different categories of ideas), ideational fluency (the ability to produce many ideas), and originality (thinking of novel solutions).

- Creative people tend to be open to new experiences, self-confident, arrogant, and nonconventional.

MAKING CONNECTIONS IN INTELLIGENCE, PROBLEM SOLVING, AND CREATIVITY

- Science research, as exemplified by the Intel Science Talent Search, requires not just intelligence, but also the ability to identify and solve problems in a novel and useful way.

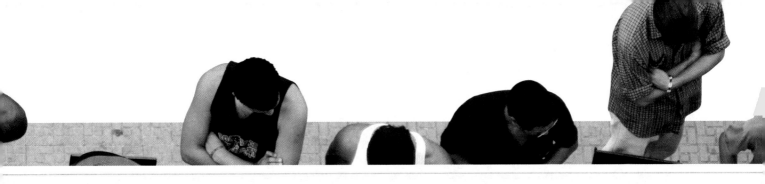

key **terms**

adaptive behavior, p. 386

algorithm, p. 397

broad intelligence, p. 376

construct validity, p. 384

convergent thinking problems, p. 396

creativity, p. 402

crystallized intelligence, p. 375

cultural test bias hypothesis, p. 385

divergent thinking problems, p. 396

Down syndrome, p. 386

Eureka insight or insight solutions, p. 397

fixation, p. 399

flexibility of thought, p. 407

fluid intelligence, p. 375

functional fixedness, p. 400

general intelligence, p. 376

genius, p. 403

g-factor theory, p. 375

ideational fluency, p. 406

intelligence, p. 374

mental age, p. 380

mental retardation, p. 386

mental set, p. 397

multiple-factor theory of intelligence, p. 375

narrow intelligence, p. 376

originality, p. 407

predictive validity, p. 384

prodigy, p. 386

reaction range, p. 390

reliability, p. 383

savant syndrome, p. 387

successful intelligence, p. 376

test bias, p. 385

test fairness, p. 385

thinking outside the box, p. 399

triarchic theory of intelligence, p. 377

validity, p. 384

quick quiz **answers**

Quick Quiz 10.1: 1. d   2. d   3. b   4. c   5. a   **Quick Quiz 10.2:** 1. b   2. a   3. c

Quick Quiz 10.3: 1 c   2. a   3. b   4. d   **Quick Quiz 10.4:** 1. d   2. b

Solution to first remote association on p. 404 is "horn" and the second is "apple."

SOLUTIONS TO FIGURES 10.12b AND 10.13. Can you think of any others?

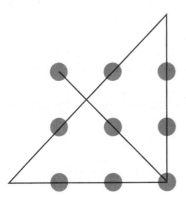

motivation and

emotion

preview **questions**

1 *Why do people seek stimulation and arousal?*

2 *Why is it so difficult to keep from gaining weight?*

3 *What is an emotion?*

4 *What cultural differences exist in expressions of emotion?*

5 *What makes a person happy?*

Many countries measure their wealth in terms of a statistic called the *Gross National Product* (GNP). GNP reflects the value in goods, services, and income produced by a country in one year. Often evaluated on a per person basis, a high GNP is considered a sign of a country's economic success. So why, in 1972, did the King of Bhutan decide to measure the wealth of his nation differently? In response to criticism that his country was poor, King Jigme Singye Wangchuk argued that, on the contrary, Bhutan is rich. This tiny Himalayan kingdom is steeped in spiritual practices that promote happiness and freedom from suffering for all beings. Although the king didn't intend to discount the role of economic growth, he emphasized that wealth also ought to be measured in terms of happiness as well. ▶

As an alternative to the GNP, King Wangchuk created a new metric, the *GNH*. GNH is an indicator of *Gross National Happiness*. It reflects things like access to health care, a clean non-polluted environment, the amount of free time available for family, and other nonmonetary measures of well-being. GNH per person is measured by having people complete a survey to measure their sense of well-being in different contexts, from the workplace to the home.

The concept of GNH may seem peculiar to many people. But researchers who study well-being and life satisfaction are finding that money cannot buy happiness, except for the very poor, in which case making more money does bring some happiness for a while (Diener & Seligman, 2004). Maybe, then, GNH is a better measure of well-being than GNP, although GNP more accurately reflects a country's economic achievements.

What makes people happy? Food? Achievement? Sex? Friends? This chapter addresses two concepts related to happiness, motivation and emotion. Motivation encompasses the forces that move us to behave or think the way we do. Hunger, sex, the need to belong, and achivement are the primary motives we explore in this chapter. Emotions are short-term changes in our bodies in response to meaningful and important experiences. Emotions—fear, anger, sadness, disgust, and happiness—can also motivate us. We are driven to seek pleasure and avoid feeling bad, for example. Happiness and satisfaction in life encompass more than a brief feeling of joy, however. They entail an enduring state of being content with one's life. We will revisit this topic at the end of the chapter. ■

Motivation

Consider what the following situations have in common:

a baby seeking a nipple
a boy studying for a math exam
a homeless person searching for food in a garbage can
a scientist conducting research
a musician learning a new piece
a couple making love

These are all examples of motivated behaviors. **Motivation** can be defined as the urge to move toward one's goals, whatever they may be. Motivation gives us an energetic push toward accomplishing tasks, such as getting dinner, getting rich, and getting lucky. Babies seek the nipple because they need nutrition; a boy might study for a test because he finds the material fascinating. There might be various reasons for a behavior, but each involves motivation.

motivation
the urge to move toward one's goals; to accomplish tasks.

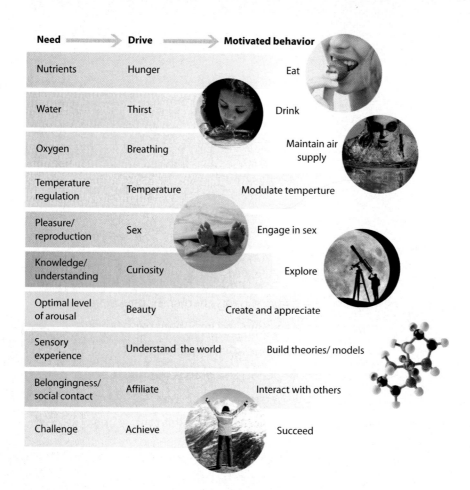

FIGURE **11.1**
NEEDS, DRIVES, AND MOTIVATED BEHAVIORS.

Need	Drive	Motivated behavior
Nutrients	Hunger	Eat
Water	Thirst	Drink
Oxygen	Breathing	Maintain air supply
Temperature regulation	Temperature	Modulate temperture
Pleasure/ reproduction	Sex	Engage in sex
Knowledge/ understanding	Curiosity	Explore
Optimal level of arousal	Beauty	Create and appreciate
Sensory experience	Understand the world	Build theories/ models
Belongingness/ social contact	Affiliate	Interact with others
Challenge	Achieve	Succeed

drives
the perceived states of tension that occur when our bodies are deficient in some need, creating an urge to relieve the tension.

Needs, drives, and incentives all contribute to motivation. **Needs** are states of cellular or bodily deficiency that compel drives. They are inherently biological. Examples include the needs for water, food, and oxygen. **Drives** are the perceived states of tension that occur when our bodies are deficient in some need. Such a deficiency creates a drive (thirst or hunger) to alleviate the state—to drink or eat. In this way, needs and drives push us. On a very hot day when we are extremely thirsty, we simply *must* get a drink of water! All our physiological needs have drive components. Figure 11.1 shows the drive components associated with various physiological and psychological needs. Motivated *behaviors*, therefore, result from needs and drives.

If drives *push* us into action, then incentives *pull* us into action. An **incentive** is any external object or event that motivates behavior. In general, drives come from the body, whereas incentives come from the environment. For some people, money is a primary incentive, but for others winning a gold medal at the Olympics or getting a college diploma might be the main incentive behind their training or studying.

needs
inherently biological states of deficiency (cellular or bodily) that compel drives.

incentive
any external object or event that motivates behavior.

MODELS OF MOTIVATION

Psychologists propose many models, or explanations, for motivation. Some models of motivation focus more on internal drives, some more on external incentives, and others on both.

416 CHAPTER 11 motivation and emotion

The Evolutionary Model

Evolutionary theory looks at internal drives to explain why people do what they do. Biologically speaking, the purpose of any living organism is to perpetuate itself. The processes of natural and sexual selection have shaped motivation over time to make all animals, including humans, want those things that help them survive and reproduce (Buss, 2003). As a result, the major motives all involve basic survival and reproduction needs and drives: hunger, thirst, body-temperature regulation, oxygen, and sex. Our bodies "know" they want food, water, oxygen, and—after adolescence—sex.

Desires, wants, and needs have been shaped over the course of human evolution to guide behavior either toward adaptive or away from maladaptive actions (Buss, 2003; Miller, 2000). In most cases, we are unaware that our behavior is related to these drives. We know only that we do something because it feels good and that we stop doing something if it feels bad. So one answer to the question of why we do what we do is that we do it to please ourselves or to remove some undesirable state. Often we are unaware of why we want what we do, but we are aware of what feels good or bad.

The Drive Reduction Model

Other psychologists argue that when our physiological systems are out of balance or depleted, we are driven to reduce this depleted state (Hull, 1943; McKinley et al., 2004; Weisinger et al., 1993). That's what drive is—the perceived internal state of tension that arises when our bodies are lacking in some basic physiological capacity. Central to drive reduction is the idea of maintaining physiological balance, or **homeostasis** (Cannon, 1929). The term implies that all organisms are motivated to maintain physiological equilibrium around an optimal **set point,** defined as the ideal fixed setting of a particular physiological system. We have set points for hunger, thirst, respiration, and many other drives. For example, compare the normal human body temperature of 98.6° F to a thermostat that is set to keep a temperature in a room constant (see Figure 11.2). When the thermometer in the

homeostasis

the process by which all organisms work to maintain physiological equilibrium or balance around an optimal set point.

set point

the ideal fixed setting of a particular physiological system, such as internal body temperature.

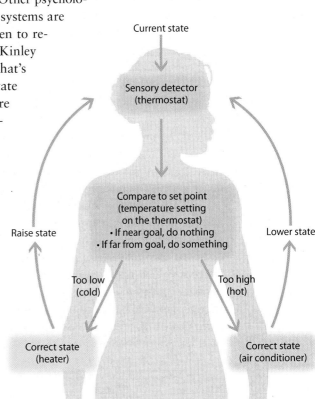

FIGURE **11.2**

MODELS OF HOMEOSTASIS. Detectors in the brain stabilize the body's psychological state by comparing the current state (for example, blood sugar level, body fluids, body temperature) to a set point. If the body is far from the set point, the organism is motivated to correct the imbalance (for example, by seeking food or putting on a sweater). Sensory feedback to the brain tells it when the set point has been achieved, and the brain then tells the body to stop correcting. This feedback system keeps the body's physiological systems at their ideal set point. (*Source:* Berridge, 2004.)

thermostat senses that the temperature in the room has fallen more than a degree or two lower than the set point, it switches on the heater. If it senses that it's too hot, the air conditioner comes on. Once the temperature has been brought back within the ideal set-point range, the thermostat turns off the heater or air conditioner. Our body behaves in a similar fashion: If we get too hot, we sweat to cool off. If we get too cold, we shiver to warm up.

For this system to work, our bodies must have sensors that detect its current state and any changes that cause it to deviate from the set point. Most of these sensory detectors are mechanisms in the brain. If our bodily states move too far from the set point, these mechanisms motivate us to take action—to raid the refrigerator, for example. In other words, certain brain mechanisms evaluate the options and decide what to do to meet a biological need based on the information the brain is getting from our organs and tissues. *Homeostasis* is the term we use to describe this feedback loop.

The Optimal Arousal Model   Another model of motivation proposes that we function best at an "optimal level of arousal." This model rests on classic research by Yerkes and Dodson (1908), who showed that both low arousal and high arousal lead to poor performance, whereas moderate levels of arousal lead to optimal performance (Yerkes & Dodson, 1908). The finding is so common that it is now referred to as the **Yerkes–Dodson law** (see Figure 11.3).

The optimal arousal model of motivation argues that humans are motivated to be in situations that are neither too stimulating nor not stimulating enough. We know this, for instance, from research on sensory deprivation. Sensory deprivation research involves having a person lie down on a bed or in a sensory deprivation (salt water) tank. Classic research from the 1950s demonstrated that people could not remain in sensory deprivation for more than 2 to 3 days even if they were paid double their daily wage for each day they remained in the tank (Bexton, Heron, & Scott, 1954). Moreover, when they stayed for only a few days, "pathology of boredom" developed (Heron, 1957). After long periods of sensory deprivation, people begin to hallucinate, their cognitive ability and concentration suffer, and they develop childish emotional responses. Sensory deprivation in rats actually shrinks the brain regions most involved in the senses that have been deprived—yet another example of the plasticity of the brain (Cheetham et al., 2007; Finnerty, Roberts, & Connors, 1999).

Yerkes–Dodson law
the principle that moderate levels of arousal lead to optimal performance.

FIGURE **11.3**

YERKES–DODSON LAW. The Yerkes–Dodson law states that performance is best when we are optimally aroused. To be optimally aroused is to be moderately aroused. Performance is worst when we are not very aroused (asleep or not paying attention) or overly aroused (highly excited or anxious). (*Source:* Smith, 1999.)

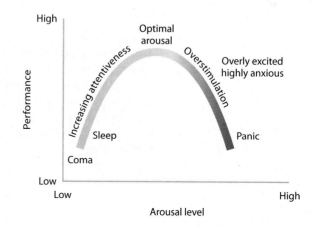

In the 1990s, Mihaly Csikszentmihalyi introduced the concept of *flow* to describe the fact that people perform best and are most creative when they are optimally challenged relative to their abilities (Csikszentmihalyi, 1990, 1996). Others have applied a similar model to explain learning and motivation (Day, 1982). According to this school of thought, needs such as curiosity, learning, interest, beauty-aesthetics, competence, challenge, flow states, and optimal experiences are motivated by the desire to be optimally aroused (Berlyne, 1960; Csikszentmihalyi, 1990; Deci & Ryan, 1985; Silvia, 2006).

The Hierarchical Model

Another model of motivation, which combines drives and incentives, is Abraham Maslow's hierarchy of needs (Maslow, 1970). The essence of Maslow's hierarchy is simple: Needs range from the most basic physiological necessities to the highest, most psychological needs for growth and fulfillment (see Figure 11.4). At the lowest level of the hierarchy are *physiological needs*, such as the needs for food, water, oxygen, and adequate body temperature. The next level are *safety needs*, which include the needs for physical security, stability, dependency, protection, and freedom from threats such as war, assault, and terrorism. We need to be fed and out of danger's way before we can pay attention to higher-level needs.

connection
What are some of the qualities of self-actualizing people?
See Chapter 13, p. 510.

The third level in the hierarchy consists of the *love and belongingness needs*, including the desire for friendship, sex, a mate, and children, as well as the desire to belong to a family or social group. The fourth level in Maslow's hierarchy of needs is the *need for esteem*, that is, the need to appreciate oneself and one's worth and to be appreciated and respected by others. The top level in the hierarchy is the need for self-actualization. Maslow defined **self-actualization** as the full realization of one's potentials and abilities in life. Only when lower-level needs have been satisfied can people focus on higher-level needs. For example, hunger and safety needs must be met before self-actualization needs can be fulfilled.

self-actualization
the inherent drive to realize one's full potential.

Now we are ready to turn our attention to two very basic drive states: hunger and sex. In evolutionary terms, there is nothing more basic than the survival of the individual and the species.

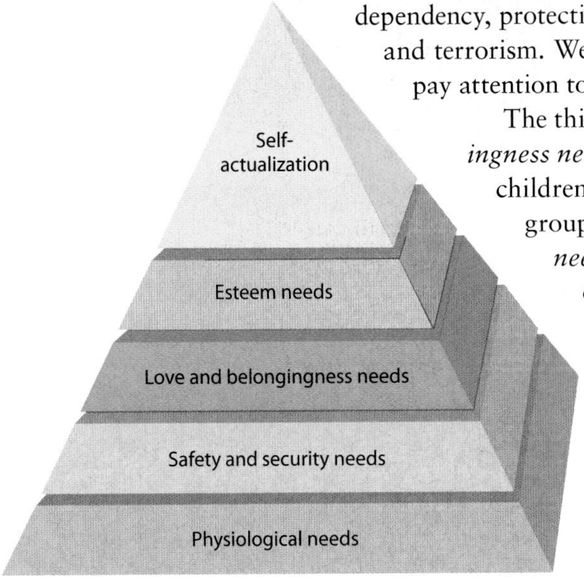

FIGURE **11.4**
MASLOW'S HIERARCHY OF NEEDS. Lower level needs must be satisfied before we can focus on achieving self-actualization.

HUNGER: SURVIVAL OF THE INDIVIDUAL

All animals need to replenish the energy continuously being used by their bodies. The rate at which we consume energy is known as *metabolism*. When our energy has been depleted, hunger drives us to replenish it by eating. Hunger is not just an internal biological process, however. It is the product of biological processes interacting with external, environmental ones.

The Biology of When We Eat

Internal signals control the desire to eat or stop eating. From a drive reduction perspective, being hungry depends not only on how much food we have consumed recently but also on how much energy is available for organ function. Hunger has four biological components: the stomach, the blood, the brain, and hormones and neurochemicals.

We've all noticed that when we get hungry, our stomach starts to growl. "Growling" results from gastric secretions that are activated by the brain when we think of, see, or smell food. Hunger can also cause the stomach to contract. Contractions occur when the stomach and small intestine have been relatively empty for about two hours. Although stomach contractions correspond with hunger pangs, they do not cause hunger: Humans who have their stomachs removed for medical reasons still feel hunger, as do rats in whom the nerves between the stomach and the brain have been severed (Brown & Wallace, 1980; Cannon & Washburn, 1912). So the stomach does not act by itself to produce feelings of hunger.

nature & nurture

Hunger involves internal biological processes interacting with external, environmental ones.

Blood is another important player in hunger. The most important source of energy for the body is cellular glucose. **Glucose** is a simple sugar in the blood that provides energy for cells throughout the body, including the brain. Although fat and protein provide their own forms of energy, some organs, including the brain, can use only glucose. Our blood sugar level drops when we go without eating for long periods. If this happens, the hypothalamus, which monitors glucose levels, triggers the drive to obtain food.

glucose

a simple sugar that provides energy for cells throughout the body, including the brain.

As with almost all behavior, many regions of the brain are involved in eating behavior. The hypothalamus regulates all basic physiological needs, including hunger. The body signals the hypothalamus about the nutritional needs of cells. In this way it acts as hunger's sensory detector. Different parts of the hypothalamus, in turn, send signals to different brain regions to either start or stop eating (Berthoud, 2002; Stellar, 1954).

Hormones and neurochemicals also play a role in hunger. Some of these substances stimulate appetite and others suppress it (Rowland, Li, & Morien, 1996; Williams, et al., 2004). At least four major hormones stimulate appetite: neuropeptide Y (NPY), orexin, ghrelin, and melanin (Williams et al., 2004). *Neuropeptide Y (NPY)* is released in the hypothalamus when an animal is hungry or underfed, and it stimulates appetite. *Ghrelin* sends signals of hunger to the brain and thereby stimulates hunger. Ghrelin levels rise when we are hungry and fall drastically after we eat. The endocannabinoids are naturally occurring neurochemicals that can increase appetite. Blocking receptor sites for endocannabinoids leads to a decrease in eating and to weight loss (Kirkham, 2005; Nicoll & Alger, 2004).

connection

Endocannabinoids and their relative, marijuana, are used medically to treat cancer patients who are on chemotherapy, because they stimulate appetite.

See Chapter 6, p. 249.

At least four hormones suppress appetite: insulin, leptin, peptide YY (PYY), and cholecystokinin (CCK; Williams et al., 2004). For example, one of the most important hormonal effects on hunger comes from *insulin*, which is produced by the pancreas. Rising glucose levels stimulate insulin production; insulin, in turn, transports glucose out of the blood and into the cells. As a result, hunger decreases.

nature & nurture

Our preferences for particular foods have a biological basis, but are shaped by experience and cultural preferences.

The Psychology of What We Eat
Our body's internal signals concerning eating and hunger dictate *when* we eat. *What* we eat, however, is influenced by external factors, including the sight

and smell of food and cultural preferences, or both. Much of what we eat is psychological—either we don't think about what we are eating or we are not bothered by it. That some people eat cows and others worms is, for the most part, culturally determined.

Different cultures expose children to different flavors. Exposure does not immediately lead to preference, however (Pliner, 1982; Rozin, 1996). It often takes multiple exposures, perhaps 8 to 10, before children will come to like a food that they initially disliked (Birch & Fischer, 1996; Birch & Marlin, 1982). Different cultures expose children to their unique flavor combinations, which means that different cultures shape food preferences while people are young. For instance, people in very cold climates commonly eat raw animal fat: Icelanders eat raw whale blubber pickled in whey; the Inuit eat raw seal fat. In contrast, cow brains and tongue are commonly eaten in Mexico. The more often people eat certain foods, the more they like them. Once people develop a preference for a kind of food, they are motivated and even driven to eat that kind of food. If, for example, you develop a strong liking for Mexican food, but then spend a year studying in Europe or Asia, where there is little Mexican food, you will probably be driven to seek out and find any kind of burrito.

The Motive to Be Thin and the Tendency Toward Obesity

Fat provides a store of energy for future use. In our evolutionary past, this was important, in case food became scarce. But in modern industrialized societies with abundant food, fat is a liability. We no longer need to consume large quantities of food against the day when there isn't enough to eat.

Moreover, because our lifestyle is sedentary compared with earlier times, we need less food to be healthy. Even our ideas about beauty have been transformed as a result of having more food available than we need. Thinness has come to define attractiveness, and being thin has become a cultural obsession. For example, 70 percent of girls between the ages of 14 and 21 in the United States say they are on a diet (Hamer & Copeland, 1998). The obsession with thinness sometimes leads to the development of eating disorders.

At the same time, rates of obesity have increased dramatically over the last 50 years. How do we define obesity? Any definition of being overweight must consider both height and weight. Therefore, in evaluating an individual's weight we use a measure termed the *body mass index (BMI)*. BMI is determined by dividing weight by height to yield a weight-to-height ratio (see Figure 11.5 on page 422). The ideal BMI range is between 20 and 25, with 26 to 29.9 considered overweight and 30 or above considered obese. As of 2004, the Centers for Disease Control and Prevention (CDC) reported that roughly one-third of adult Americans were obese, one-third were overweight, and

connection

Anorexia nervosa and bulimia nervosa are the most common eating disorders in more affluent nations.

See Chapter 12, p. 484.

Actress America Ferrera downplays her own looks for her role in the TV series *Ugly Betty*. Her character presents a different kind of role model for U.S. girls growing up in a culture in which being thin defines attractiveness.

FIGURE 11.5

BODY MASS INDEX (BMI). To determine your body mass index, find your height in the left column and go across to your body weight. Then, at the top of the chart, locate the BMI for your height and weight.

	Normal						Overweight					Obese									
BMI	**19**	**20**	**21**	**22**	**23**	**24**	**25**	**26**	**27**	**28**	**29**	**30**	**31**	**32**	**33**	**34**	**35**	**36**	**37**	**38**	**39**
Height (inches)																					
58	91	96	100	105	110	115	119	124	129	134	138	143	148	153	158	162	167	172	177	181	186
59	94	99	104	109	114	119	124	128	133	138	143	148	153	158	163	168	173	178	183	188	193
60	97	102	107	112	118	123	128	133	138	143	148	153	158	163	168	174	179	184	189	194	199
61	100	106	111	116	122	127	132	137	143	148	153	158	164	169	174	180	185	190	195	201	206
62	104	109	115	120	126	131	136	142	147	153	158	164	169	175	180	186	191	196	202	207	213
63	107	113	118	124	130	135	141	146	152	158	163	169	175	180	186	191	197	203	208	214	220
64	110	116	122	128	134	140	145	151	157	163	169	174	180	186	192	197	204	209	215	221	227
65	114	120	126	132	138	144	150	156	162	168	174	180	186	192	198	204	210	216	222	228	234
66	118	124	130	136	142	148	155	161	167	173	179	186	192	198	204	210	216	223	229	235	241
67	121	127	134	140	146	153	159	166	172	178	185	191	198	204	211	217	223	230	236	242	249
68	125	131	138	144	151	158	164	171	177	184	190	197	203	210	216	223	230	236	243	249	256
69	128	135	142	149	155	162	169	176	182	189	196	203	209	216	223	230	236	243	250	257	263
70	132	139	146	153	160	167	174	181	188	195	202	209	216	222	229	235	243	250	257	264	271
71	136	143	150	157	165	172	179	186	193	200	208	215	222	229	236	243	250	257	265	272	279
72	140	147	154	162	169	177	184	191	199	206	213	221	228	235	242	250	258	265	272	279	287
73	144	151	159	166	174	182	189	197	204	212	219	227	235	242	250	257	265	272	280	288	295
74	148	155	163	171	179	186	194	202	210	218	225	233	241	249	256	264	272	280	287	295	303
75	152	160	168	176	184	192	200	208	216	224	232	240	248	256	264	272	279	287	295	303	311
76	156	154	172	180	189	197	205	213	221	230	238	246	254	263	271	279	287	295	304	312	320

one-third were of ideal weight (Ogden et al., 2006). Moreover, rates of obesity have climbed rapidly over the last 20 years—from 12% in 1991, to 18% in 1998, to 32% in 2004 (Mokdad et al., 1999; Ogden et al., 2006).

Weight gain is clearly subject to environmental influence. This is not to say, however, that biological factors play no role in being overweight or obese. They do, as genes appear to be responsible for about 70% of adult weight (Allison et al., 1994; Hamer & Copeland, 1998). One study found that adults who had been adopted as children were much closer in weight to their biological parents than to their adoptive parents (Maes, Neale, & Eaves, 1997). In addition, in some obese people the gene that produces the leptin hormone, which normally suppresses appetite, has suffered a mutation and therefore does not function properly (Hamer & Copeland, 1998).

Genes also control the number of fat cells a person has: The number of fat cells a person has is set by childhood and adolescence and does not change much after that (Spalding et al., 2008). Each year about 10% of our fat cells die, but they are replaced by roughly the same number of new fat cells (Spalding et al., 2008). Dieting does not change this. When people diet, they are not decreasing the number of fats cells they have, but rather how much fat each cell stores. The stable number of adult fat cells may explain why it is so difficult to keep off weight that has been lost. Indeed, a recent meta-analysis of 31 studies reported that losing weight is relatively easy, but keeping it off is very difficult (Mann et al., 2007).

Fat cells.

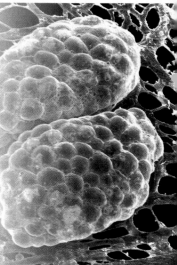

SEX: SURVIVAL OF THE SPECIES

Without food, we would starve to death. Without sex, individuals would not die, but if everyone went without sex, our species would die. So the simplest answer to the question "Why do we have sex?" would be "To propagate the species." Such an answer is useful at the species level but not at the individual level. As individuals we have sex for the simple reason that it is enjoyable and feels good.

Human Sexual Response   Like many basic questions, "What is sex?" is more complex than it would appear. For the sake of clarity, we define **sexual behavior** as actions that produce arousal and increase the likelihood of orgasm.

Masters and Johnson (1966) were the first scientists to study the human sexual response systematically and directly. One of their major findings was that men and women go through four phases of sexual arousal, but do so somewhat differently (see Figure 11.6). The four phases are excitement, plateau, orgasm, and resolution. The major signs of the initial excitement phase are vaginal lubrication in the female and erection in the male. In the second phase, plateau, excitement level remains high but is preorgasmic. In men, the plateau phase might be rather short, but orgasm almost always follows. In women, the plateau phase often lasts longer than in men and is not necessarily followed by orgasm. In fact, some women stay in the plateau phase for a while and then pass to the resolution phase without achieving orgasm. These women also have a gradual resolution phase. An even more striking gender difference is the ability of women to have multiple orgasms. Men always have a refractory period immediately following orgasm in which erection is lost and orgasm is not possible, but women may go on to have multiple orgasms.

Updated models of female sexual arousal suggest that the initial sexual response in women involves more psychological processes than simply arousal and desire (Basson, 2001). Desire and arousal do not happen spontaneously in

sexual behavior actions that produce arousal and increase the likelihood of orgasm.

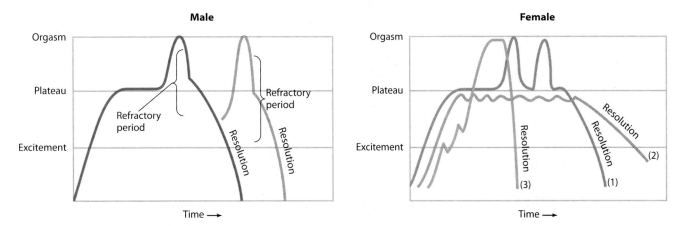

FIGURE **11.6**

THE SEXUAL RESPONSE CYCLE IN MEN AND WOMEN. The four phases are excitement, plateau, orgasm, and resolution. Women are more varied in their sexual response than men. There are at least three distinct types of response in women. In (1) we see a response pattern much like men's, except that there is the possibility of multiple orgasm. In (2) we see a woman who gets aroused and stays at the plateau level, never reaching orgasm. In (3) we see a pattern where the woman gets aroused and excited, skips the plateau phase and has a quick resolution phase. In men, there is only one pattern, though sometimes second orgasm can occur after a refractory period. (*Source:* Masters et al., 1986.)

many women, who often require the right balance of thoughts and feelings dealing with intimacy, closeness, trust, and lack of fear and anxiety. Only if these conditions are met will arousal happen. These thoughts and feelings play off and feed arousal, which in turn leads to deeper feelings of intimacy and closeness. Arousal continues to increase and may or may not lead to orgasm, but arousal and excitement are important and meaningful even without orgasm (Basson, 2001).

The Biology of Sexual Behavior

This newer model of sexual response matches well with brain imaging research on sexual arousal, including orgasm. Many brain regions involved in emotion, which we will discuss shortly, are also involved in the earlier stages of sexual arousal, prior to orgasm. As is true of many physiological drives, such as hunger, the hypothalamus plays a crucial role in sexual behavior (Dominguez & Hull, 2005; Melis & Argiolis, 1995). In humans, lesions to the back portion of the hypothalamus lead to a decrease in sexual behavior, whereas electrically stimulating the same region leads to an increase in sexual behavior, especially in males (Dominguez & Hull, 2005). In addition, the part of the hypothalamus involved in sexual behavior is larger in men than in women (Allen & Gorski, 2007).

As you might expect, brain activity changes during orgasm—surprisingly, certain brain regions actually shut down. Gert Holstege and colleagues from the Netherlands took brain images of women while they were having an orgasm (being manually stimulated by their partners) and while they were faking it (Georgiadis et al., 2006). Achieving a real orgasm always involved deactivation of brain regions involved with fear and anxiety in the amygdala and hippocampus as well as parts of the cortex involved in consciousness. During faked orgasms, however, these brain regions remained activated. Men too show brain deactivation during orgasm, but only in the left amygdala (Holstege et al., 2003).

Testosterone, the primary male sex hormone, also controls women's sex drive.

Testosterone, the major male sex hormone, controls sex drive in both men and women (Morris et al., 1987; Persky et al., 1978). The role of testosterone in the female sex drive was discovered accidentally when women whose adrenal glands were removed lost their sex drive (Waxenberg, Drellich, & Sutherland, 1959). The adrenal glands produce testosterone. Moreover, younger women have both higher levels of male sex hormones and more frequent sexual activity than do older women (Persky et al., 1982). Indeed, males and females with high baseline levels of testosterone are more sexually active at earlier ages and engage in sex more frequently than those with low baseline levels of testosterone. Similarly, testosterone treatments appear to increase sex drive in women (Bolour & Braunstein, 2005).

In most species, females are not continually receptive to males. Although women are not nearly as cyclical in their sexual desire as are females of other species, there is, in fact, some regular cyclical activity and interest in the course of the 28-day menstrual cycle. Female-initiated sexual behavior peaks around ovulation and again before and after menstruation (Bullivant et al., 2004; Ford & Beach, 1951; Udry, Morris, & Waller, 1973). The strongest cyclical effect for women, however, occurs in relation to their fantasies involving men other than their regular sex partner (Buss, 2003). As women approach ovulation, the frequency and intensity of their fantasies involving sex with men other than their partner increase (Bullivant et al., 2004). Such an increase in sex drive makes sense from an evolutionary perspective, because a woman is most likely to become pregnant during ovulation.

Culture and Sexual Behavior   What is acceptable and normal sexual behavior varies from culture to culture. In a classic study of sexual behavior and culture, Clellan Ford and Frank Beach (1951) studied attitudes toward sex before and after marriage in 190 different cultures. They identified three kinds of societies in terms of sexual attitudes: *restrictive societies* restrict sex before and outside of marriage; *semirestrictive societies* place formal prohibitions on pre- and extramarital sex that are not strictly enforced; and *permissive societies* place few restrictions on sex. Thirty years later, Broude and Greene (1980) conducted a similar study of 141 non-Western cultures and found that for women, premarital sex was mildly to moderately disapproved of in 30% of the societies and strongly disapproved of in 26%. Extramarital sex was common among men in 69% of the cultures and among women in 57% of the cultures.

Gender and the Drive for Casual Sex   The belief that men are more promiscuous than women is widespread, but is it true? In a word, yes. Research consistently shows that men are more willing and interested in casual sex than are women (see, for example, Bailey, Kirk, et al., 2000; Buss, 2003; Clark & Hatfield, 1989; Maticka-Tyndale, Harold, & Opperman, 2003). For instance, in a meta-analysis of 177 studies of gender and sexual attitudes and behavior published between 1966 and 1990, Oliver and Hyde (1993) reported that men, on average, have much more positive attitudes toward casual sex and are slightly more likely to approve of premarital or extramarital sex. Russell Clark III and Elaine Hatfield (1989, 2003) conducted a classic study on the question of gender differences and casual sex. Research assistants approached strangers of the opposite sex and asked them whether they would be willing to either go on a date, come over, or go to bed with them. As you can see in Figure 11.7 on page 426, the results were striking. Three-quarters of the men responded that they were willing to have sex with a stranger of the opposite sex, but not one woman was willing to do so!

Parental investment theory offers an explanation for the gender difference in attitude toward casual sex. If pregnancy results, the cost of having sex is quite different for men and women (Trivers, 1972). Biologically speaking, for men the only assured contribution to parenthood is the act of sex itself. If a woman becomes pregnant, however, her contribution includes nine months of carrying the fetus, a good portion of which might involve pregnancy sickness; then there is the painful labor and delivery; and finally, there are approximately 18 years of caring for the child. It follows, therefore, that women would be less motivated to have sex with little emotional commitment—a single sexual encounter could have consequences that endure a lifetime.

research process

1 research question

Are there differences between men and women in their interest in casual sex? The researchers hypothesized that men are more eager for casual sex than are women.

2 method

Clark and Hatfield (1989) developed a brief survey to address the research question. Research assistants who were college students approached students of the opposite sex. After a brief introduction, the research assistant would ask each student one of these questions: "Would you go out with me tonight?" "Would you come over to my apartment tonight?" or "Would you go to bed with me tonight?"

Question	Said "Yes" Men	Women
"Would you go out with me tonight?"	56%	50%
"Would you come over to my apartment tonight?"	69%	6%
"Would you go to bed with me tonight?"	75%	0%

3 results

This table gives responses to the various questions, by gender.

4 conclusion

Men and women were equally likely to agree to go on a date with someone they didn't really know. As the proposal became increasingly intimate, however, women backed off. Consistent with the hypothesis, men were much more likely than women to agree to have sex. This finding would be predicted by parental investment theory, which states that the cost of having sex is quite different for men and women.

FIGURE **11.7**

GENDER AND CASUAL SEX. A simple survey revealed gender differences in the interest in casual sex. When approached, most men will agree to casual sex with an opposite-sex stranger, while most women will not. (*Source:* R. D. Clark III & E. Hatfield. 1989. Gender differences in willingness to engage in casual sex. *Journal of Psychology and Human Sexuality, 2,* 39–55.)

Sexual Orientation   What drives most people to be attracted predominantly to the opposite sex, yet a significant minority to be attracted to the same sex? **Sexual orientation** is our disposition to be attracted to either the opposite sex (heterosexual), the same sex (homosexual), or both sexes (bisexual). Historically, sexual orientation was thought of as an either–or proposition—a person was either heterosexual or homosexual. But in the 1940s Alfred Kinsey proposed a now-standard view of sexual orientation: It exists on a continuum from exclusively heterosexual to exclusively homosexual (Kinsey, Pomeroy, & Martin, 1948). After interviewing thousands of individuals, Kinsey and his colleagues realized that sexual orientation was not either–or and devised a 7-point scale extending from 0 to 6. Zero was exclusively heterosexual and 6 exclusively homosexual. Most people fall between 0 and 2 but a consistent minority of people exist on the homosexual end of the scale. Between 1% and 5% of the adult male population and 1% and 3.5% of the adult female population classify themselves as predominantly homosexual (LeVay & Hamer, 1994; Tarmann, 2002). For men, sexual orientation tends to be either–or, producing a dip between 2 and 4 on Kinsey's 7-point scale (the "bisexual" range). For women, however, there is a more gradual decrease from exclusively heterosexual to exclusively homosexual, with more women than men identifying themselves as bisexual (Diamond, 2008; Hamer & Copeland, 1998; Rahman, 2005).

Many people wonder what causes a person to be sexually attracted to someone of the opposite sex or the same sex. The age-old nature–nurture question inevitably arises: Is sexual orientation more a result of biology or of upbringing and environment? Both are involved in sexual orientation, and in complex ways (Bailey, Dunne, & Martin, 2000). There is evidence that our first biological environment—the womb—exerts a long-term effect on our sexual orientation. Research has revealed that, to some extent, individuals exposed to relatively high levels of testosterone in the womb are more likely to be attracted to women, whereas those exposed to relatively low levels of testosterone are more likely to be attracted to men (Cohen, 2002; Ellis & Ames, 1987; Rahman, 2005). These findings are not fully replicated and more research is needed before people can draw conclusions about the role of prenatal testosterone exposure in sexual orientation.

Sexual orientation is influenced by both nature and nurture.

Another influence on sexual orientation is the hypothalamus. Intrigued by research showing that a small region in the hypothalamus involved in sexual behavior is about twice as large in men's brains as in women's, Simon LeVay (1991) decided to examine this structure in the brains of gay and straight men. He found that this region is substantially smaller in gay men than in straight men—it's about the size of women's.

Genetic research suggests that sexual orientation is partly under genetic influence, at least in men. Studies of twins indicate that genetics plays a bigger role in determining sexual orientation in men than in women. For women, environmental factors seem to have a strong influence on sexual orientation. Female twins raised in the same household are much more likely to have the same sexual orientation than are females twins raised in different households, regardless of whether they are identical or fraternal twins. For males, degree of genetic relationship seems to matter most in twin sexual orientation (Bailey, Dunne, & Martin, 2000; Demir & Dickson, 2005; Hamer & Copeland, 1998; Hyde, 2005; Rahman, 2005).

nature & nurture
Sexual orientation depends on both biological and social factors.

Scholars have also proposed a number of social-environmental theories to explain the origins of sexual orientation. These theories argue that sexual orientation is a social construction (Bell, Weinberg, & Hammersmith, 1981; Van Wyk & Geist, 1984). Some social-environmental theories of sexual orientation have argued, for example, that child play, early peer relations, differences in how parents treat boys and girls, and gender identity are important factors in the development of sexual orientation, both heterosexual and homosexual. For instance, many studies report that engaging in play more typical of the opposite sex early in childhood predicts a homosexual orientation later in life, in both men and women (Bailey & Zucker, 1995; Cohen, 2002). These environmental theories are quite consistent with biological ones. Biology could start the development of sexual orientation, which in turn would be strengthened or discouraged by environmental factors. The two sets of explanations work best in cooperation rather than competition.

THE NEEDS TO BELONG AND TO EXCEL

As we saw in Maslow's hierarchy of needs, human needs extend beyond the physiological needs of hunger and sex. The need for social contact and belonging is a powerful and universal need. Psychologists call this the *need for affiliation*. The need to excel, achieve, and be competitive with others is also a powerful and universal one. Psychologists call this the *need for achievement*.

The Need to Belong: Affiliation Humans are inherently social creatures. We depend on other people our entire lives, especially at life's beginning and end. It is not surprising, therefore, that our need to belong and to be accepted by others is one of the strongest of all human needs (Adler, 1956; Baumeister &

Leary, 1995; Murray, 1938/1962). Almost every close relationship in our lives is driven by this need.

connections
Affiliation with others is so important that social exclusion physically hurts and activates pain regions in the brain involved in physical pain.
See Chapter 14, p. 544.

The opposite of being accepted is being rejected, which can be one of the more painful experiences in life. Baumeister and Leary (1995) reviewed evidence that lack of belongingness and being rejected lead to both physical health and psychological problems, ranging from having more health problems to developing eating disorders, from being more depressed to being more likely to commit suicide. Moreover, being rejected also makes people more prone to get angry and lash out and be aggressive toward others (Leary et al., 2006). Many explosive violent episodes are preceded by the person's being fired from work or being rejected by peers, a lover, or a spouse (Williams & Zudro, 2001). For example, many of the school shootings over the last 10 years, such as Columbine and Virginia Tech, have been carried out by boys and men who were teased and rejected by their peers (Leary et al., 2003).

The Need to Excel: Achievement

Some people have a tremendous need to excel and to be the best at what they do. Many successful athletes, businesspeople, and politicians, for example, are driven by such a need. But in truth, almost everyone strives to overcome shortcomings and imperfections (Adler, 1956). In the process, some people compete fiercely with other people, whereas others compete more with themselves simply to do the best they can.

achievement motivation
a desire to do things well and overcome obstacles.

The motivation to succeed raises the question of how to define achievement and success. McClelland and his colleague Atkinson emphasized that **achievement motivation** is a desire to do things well and overcome difficulties and obstacles (McClelland, 1985). However, those obstacles can be measured only in terms of one's goals. When David (the brother of one of the authors, whom you met in Chapter 6) was coming out of his vegetative state following his bicycle accident, lifting a finger was a tremendous achievement. Yet, for a highly driven, accomplished, and motivated athlete, a silver medal at the Olympics might be a crushing defeat.

Atkinson (1964) argued that the tendency to achieve success is a function of three things: motivation to succeed, expectation of success, and the incentive value of the success (see also McClelland, 1985). Let's apply Atkinson's model to a familiar example: your motivation to obtain a good grade in this introductory psychology course. Your *motivation to succeed* is the extent to which you really want to be successful. In a course such as introductory psychology, success will have different meanings for different students. For some, an A– might be a horrible failure, whereas for others a B+ might be a great accomplishment.

Expectation of success is an individual's evaluation of the likelihood of succeeding at a task. Your evaluation of your performance in this course consists of two different beliefs: whether you have the ability to do well and what the actual outcome is likely to be. These two beliefs may not match. For instance, some students may see themselves as quite capable, but due to other circumstances, such as missing several classes, they may not obtain a high grade for the course.

What makes Oscar run? Oscar Pistorius, a double amputee sprinter from South Africa, won 3 gold medals at the 2008 Paralympics in Beijing. Determined to race against able-bodied runners in the Olympics, Pistorius competed in the 2008 Olympic trials, breaking a personal record but falling short of the qualifying time.

Incentive value stems from two factors. First, success at the task has to be important to you. Second, the more difficult the task and the lower the odds of succeeding at it, the more it will mean to you if you do succeed. Applied to taking this course, the incentive value for doing well differs depending on what a good grade in the course means to you. If you are a psychology major and the GPA in your major plays an important role in your class standing or whether you keep your scholarship, the grade in Intro Psych might have a higher incentive value than it would if you were a physics major taking the course to satisfy a general education requirement. In addition, the difficulty of a task plays a role in its incentive value. Succeeding at something that is very difficult means more to most people than succeeding at something they consider easy, because the easier task does not provide much feedback about ability. Likewise, failing at a difficult task may not provide much useful feedback concerning your abilities. Intuitively most people shy away from tasks that they perceive as very easy or very difficult and seek to tackle tasks that are moderately challenging.

quick quiz 11.1: Motivation

1. Which model of motivation can be compared to the thermostat in your house?
   a. evolutionary
   b. drive reduction
   c. optimal arousal
   d. hierarchical

2. In addition to blood sugar (glucose) and the hypothalamus, and as discussed in this chapter, what is another important biological system involved in regulating hunger?
   a. adrenaline
   b. the liver
   c. hormones
   d. protein

3. Most research on weight loss has reported that
   a. losing weight is very difficult for most people
   b. losing weight is relatively easy, but keeping it off is very difficult
   c. keeping weight off is relatively easy for most people
   d. losing weight is relatively easy and so too is keeping it off

4. Brain imaging research has found that during orgasm
   a. some parts of the brain "shut down" and become deactivated
   b. most of the brain becomes very active
   c. only the brain stem is active
   d. the insula becomes very active

5. Researchers have found that a small part of the _____ is about the same size in homosexual men and heterosexual women.
   a. amygdala
   b. hippocampus
   c. hypothalamus
   d. prefrontal cortex

Answers can be found at the end of the chapter.

Emotion

Not all of our actions stem from basic drives or higher motivations. Sometimes we are motivated to do something simply because it makes us happy. In this sense, emotions are motivators too.

Basic drives such as hunger and sex differ from emotions in important ways. First, drives are linked with very specific needs, whereas emotions are not (Tomkins, 1962; 1981). Hunger comes from a need for food, thirst from a need for water, lust from a need for sex. But joy can be associated with just about anything: smelling a rose, visiting a friend, reading a good book, or seeing a beautiful sunset. Also, emotions can override biological drives (Tomkins, 1962). We saw that sexual orgasm cannot occur unless the areas of the brain involved in fear and anxiety are shut down. Another example is how the emotion of disgust can easily override the fundamental drive of hunger. A sandwich is less appealing after a fly lands on it or if, on closer contact, it smells bad.

How can the emotion of disgust override a drive as strong as hunger? Disgust is important for survival. It arises when we have come across something that is potentially toxic or harmful. Sometimes disgust can override drives if we just think something is disgusting, even if we know it is not. Consider how you would react if you were asked to hold a piece of rubber that is joke vomit between your lips. How about a rubber eraser? Studies show that most people are disgusted by the fake vomit but would willingly put the eraser between their lips (Rozin & Fallon, 1987). We know they are made of the same substance and are equally sanitary, but the basic need to avoid contamination overwhelms our sense of reason. This fear of contagion appears in cultures all over the world (Nemeroff & Rozin, 1994; Rozin & Fallon, 1987).

Disgust is one of several basic emotions (Ekman, 1992; Rozin, Haidt, & McCauley, 2000). In this part of the chapter we explore what emotions are, why we have them, and how they affect our thoughts and bodily systems.

DEFINING EMOTION

Emotions emerge from our interactions with the world around us. They are triggered by situations that are relevant to our personal goals, physical safety, or well-being. Because emotions stem from situations that are important to us, they reveal much about what makes us tick.

Types of Affect   Psychologists use the term *affect* to refer to a variety of emotional phenomena, including emotions, moods, and affective traits. **Emotions** are brief, acute changes in conscious experience and physiology that occur in response to meaningful situations in the person's environment. Emotions make us pay attention, forcing us to set priorities and deal with life-relevant situations (Ekman, 1992; Lazarus, 1991; Levenson, 1994). They occupy the foreground of our consciousness, often dominating our awareness. In fact, emotions can impact memory, perception, attention, and decision making (Cohen, 2005; Phelps, 2006).

Moods are transient changes in affect that fluctuate throughout the day or over several days. We experience moods both physiologically and psychologically, and they tend to last longer than most emotions (Ekman, 1984; Davidson, 1994; Hedges, Jandorf,

emotions
brief, acute changes in conscious experience and physiology that occur in response to a personally meaningful situation.

moods
affective states that operate in the background of consciousness and tend to last longer than most emotions.

& Stone, 1985). Moods make certain emotions more likely to occur than others. An irritable mood, for instance, makes people more easily angered than usual. A slight inconvenience that would not ordinarily bother you, such as having to wait in line at the supermarket checkout, might cause you to act rudely toward the clerk.

connection

We tend to remember emotional events better than nonemotional events.

See Chapter 7, p. 275.

Affective traits are enduring aspects of our personalities that set the threshold for the occurrence of particular emotional states (Ekman, 1984; Lazarus, 1991; Rosenberg, 1998). Consider the example of being cut off in traffic. People who have the affective trait of hostility are most likely to feel anger. They aren't always angry, but they have hair triggers. For several minutes or likely even longer, these people will continue focusing on the event—how they were wronged—and they feel the emotion of anger. Then the event recedes from consciousness, and the feelings of anger go with it. Nonetheless, they may remain in a more diffuse, less focused, less pressing irritable mood. By the end of the day, they may still be in a bad mood but not even realize it.

affective traits
stable predispositions toward certain types of emotional responses such as anger.

Emotions, Basic Emotions, and the Dimensions of Affect

A small set of emotions seems to be common to all humans and a product of our evolutionary past (Ekman, 1992). These **basic emotions** are anger, disgust, fear, happiness, sadness, and surprise (see Figure 11.8). These emotions reflect fundamental emotional states that play a role in essential life tasks, such as protecting oneself and loved ones from harm (fear), progressing toward the realization of a goal (happiness), or experiencing irrevocable loss (sadness) (Ekman, 1992; Lazarus, 1991). Basic emotions are only a small set of the infinite variety of emotional states humans can experience.

basic emotions
set of emotions that are common to all humans; includes anger, disgust, fear, happiness, sadness, and surprise.

The basic emotions are not single states; rather, they are categories or groups of related emotions. Ekman (1992) describes such a grouping as an *emotion family*. For instance, the fear family may arise in response to a threat to physical safety. This family includes such emotions as anxiety, trepidation, and nervousness. The happiness family of emotions includes joy, contentment, elation, amusement, and exhilaration, among others.

Other theorists argue that all emotions are states that vary in their degree of pleasantness and arousal (Clark, Watson, & Leeka, 1989; Russell, 1980; Watson & Tellegen, 1985; Woodworth & Schlossberg, 1954). Figure 11.9 shows how these underlying dimensions of pleasantness and arousal might explain a number of emotions.

Basic emotions

Anger
Disgust
Fear
Happiness
Sadness
Surprise

Self-conscious emotions

Embarrassment
Guilt
Humiliation
Pride
Shame

FIGURE **11.8**
BASIC AND SELF-CONSCIOUS EMOTIONS.
(*Source:* Ekman, 1992; Tracy, Robins, & Tangney, 2007.)

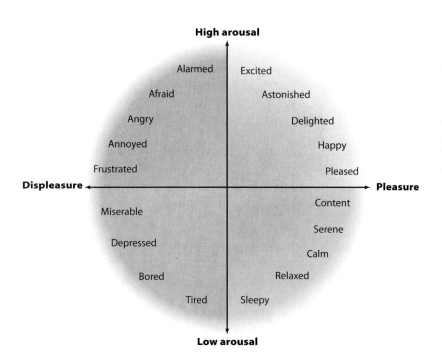

High arousal

Alarmed	Excited
Afraid	Astonished
Angry	Delighted
Annoyed	Happy
Frustrated	Pleased

Displeasure ←——————→ **Pleasure**

	Content
Miserable	Serene
Depressed	Calm
Bored	Relaxed
Tired	Sleepy

Low arousal

FIGURE **11.9**

MODEL OF EMOTIONS AS COMBINATIONS OF AROUSAL AND PLEASURE. According to Russell's (1980) model of emotion, all emotions can be placed in two dimensions, arousal and pleasure–displeasure. For example, being afraid is a state of high arousal and displeasure, whereas being happy is a pleasant and moderately aroused state. (*Source:* Russell, 1980.)

Self-Conscious Emotions   The feeling of pride a child feels at learning how to ride a bike and the shame of being caught in a lie are examples of **self-conscious emotions,** which are emotions that occur as a function of how well we live up to our expectations, the expectations of others, or the rules set by society (see Figure 11.8; Tracy, Robins, & Tangney, 2007; Tangney, Stuewig, & Mashek, 2007). These emotions require a sense of self and the ability to reflect on one's own actions. They include shame, guilt, humiliation, embarrassment, and pride. Let's look at pride and embarrassment in detail.

Jessica Tracy and Rick Robins (2007) distinguish between two kinds of pride: *authentic pride* and *hubristic pride*. Authentic pride is the pride we feel in some sense of accomplishment, like finishing a task, completing a marathon, and the like. It is pride due to success in situations with controllable causes. It applies to a specific accomplishment. Hubristic pride is a more general sense of pride in oneself, such as "I won because I am great." It is the more puffed up, slightly arrogant version of pride.

Pride· has a recognizable expression, which involves body movements, a smile, head tilted upward, with slightly expanded chest (see Figure 11.10). This expression is recognized as pride by children and adults in America and by people in a preliterate, socially isolated tribe in West Africa (Tracy & Robins, 2008). This cross-cultural recognition data from very diverse groups suggest that this pride expression may be common across the globe, but more data are needed to be sure. People show elements of this behavior when in situations that produce pride, such as winning medals at the Olympics (Tracy & Matsumoto, 2008).

self-conscious emotions

types of emotion that require a sense of self and the ability to reflect on actions; they occur as a function of meeting expectations (or not) and abiding (or not) by society's rules.

FIGURE **11.10**

THE EXPRESSION OF PRIDE. U.S. swimmer Michael Phelps shows the typical pride display after winning one of his 8 gold medals at the 2008 Olympic Games in Beijing, China.

FIGURE **11.11**

THE FACIAL EXPRESSION OF EMBARRASSMENT. The display of embarrassment involves a sequence of actions, each of which might serve a social function. After an initial look down, which may indicate an attempt to escape the situation, there is a smile. The smile may reflect amusement at one's own transgression. Muscular actions to control the smile ("smile controls") dampen the amusement responses. Finally, the person will look away and perhaps look downward, as a kind of retreat from the embarrassing situation. (*Source:* Keitner, 1995.)

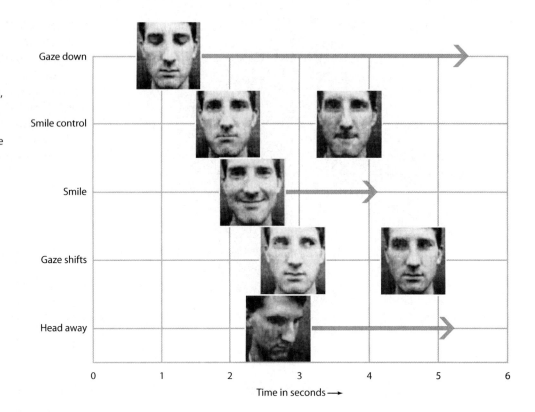

We all know quite well what it feels like to be embarrassed. You are admiring yourself in the mirror when you realize your roommate has walked in and caught you preening. Embarrassment involves unintentionally revealing something about yourself to someone else. Being embarrassed makes you feel self-conscious, as if you have violated some social rule (such as not admiring yourself in the mirror). People often get giggly when embarrassed and act as if they want to make amends for some sort of social transgression (Keltner, 1995; Tangney et al., 2007). Keltner (1995) describes the facial expression of embarrassment, which he argues serves to appease and placate those who have seen one's mistake. The embarrassment expression involves a sequence of facial and gestural actions, each of which may correspond to some sort of social function (see Figure 11.11).

Emotions as Evolutionary Adaptations Why do we have emotions? From an evolutionary perspective, emotions are adaptations. That is, they evolved because they solved a particular problem in our ancestral past and thus contributed to survival and reproductive success (Tooby & Cosmides, 1990). According to one evolutionary view, emotions bring our physiological systems together to help us deal efficiently with critical situations (Levenson, 1988; Mauss et al., 2005; Rosenberg & Ekman, 1994). For example, when danger approaches, the heart pumps blood to the skeletal muscles to enable quick movement in case escape is necessary, the respiratory system works harder to bring in more oxygen, and the brain prioritizes attention so that we can figure out what we need to do to escape the dangerous situation. This view of emotions as *organized responses* illustrates the adaptive value of negative emotions, which enable people to respond efficiently to a significant challenge or obstacle.

Positive emotions, such as contentment, happiness, love, and amusement, solve different kinds of adaptive problems. According to the **broaden-and-build model**, positive emotions widen our cognitive perspective, making our thinking more expansive and enabling the acquisition of new skills (Fredrickson, 1998, 2001). Compared to negative emotions, which promote a narrow, vigilant way of looking at the world, positive emotions help us see the possibilities for new ways of responding to situations, which helps us to *build* new skills (Derryberry & Tucker, 1994). Play, for example, especially the rough-and-tumble play of animals and young children, helps develop physical and strategic skills that may be useful for hunting, escaping, or defensive fighting.

broaden-and-build model Fredrickson's model for positive emotions, which posits that they widen our cognitive perspective and help us acquire useful life skills.

Several studies show that positive emotions broaden one's focus (Fredrickson & Branigan, 2005). For instance, when people are in positive moods they perform poorly on tasks of selective attention that require a narrow focus compared to people in sad or neutral moods, and they perform better on tasks that require a broader attentional focus (Rowe, Hirsch, & Anderson, 2007). For instance, in a task in which people were instructed to think of as many uses as they could for a brick, people who had been put in a positive mood thought of more uses and more creative uses than those experiencing negative emotion (Rowe et al, 2007; Isen, Daubman, & Nowicki, 1987). In a perceptual task, positive emotions also enhance attention to visual information in the outer edges of a visual display, compared to the center (Wadlinger & Isaacowitz, 2006). This finding indicates that positive emotions might enable people to take more information from any given visual scene.

EMOTION AS A PROCESS

Emotions create changes in experience, thought, physiology, and behavior. For decades psychologists debated which component of emotion best defines or exemplifies what an emotion is, be it a facial expression, an experience, or a physiological change. Researchers now recognize that we can best understand emotions by considering how the various aspects of emotion unfold—that is, by viewing emotion as a *process* (Lazarus, 1991; Levenson, 1994).

An emotion begins with an **antecedent event**, a situation that may lead to an emotional response (see Figure 11.12). We use the word *may* because not everyone responds to the same situation in the same way. The person evaluates the event to determine whether it is potentially harmful or beneficial. Depending on the results of that appraisal, he or she may experience an emotional response. The emotional response, in turn, produces changes in physiology, behavior and

antecedent event a situation that may lead to an emotional response.

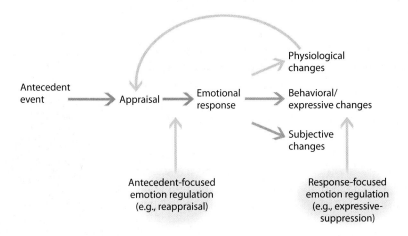

FIGURE **11.12**

THE EMOTION PROCESS. Emotions start with an event that is appraised as relevant to one's goals. If deemed relevant, an emotional response begins, which consists of physiological changes, behavioral and expressive changes, and subjective changes in feelings. Changes in the body's physiology, behavior, and subjective feelings then feed back to the appraisal process and become inputs for experiencing new emotions. Attempts to regulate (modify, change, or suppress) emotion can occur early or late in the emotion process.

expressions, and subjective experience of the event. The direction of the arrows moving from left to right in Figure 11.12 is only part of the story. As the reverse-curved arrow suggests, the process can move in the other direction as well. That is, the activation of facial and physiological responses might enhance the emotion, becoming yet another kind of input for a new emotional experience. Levenson (2003) points out that in addition to the antecedent events that are external to us, there may be internal inputs into the emotion process, inputs provided by facial and physiological changes. In addition, once we generate emotions, we sometimes attempt to modify them, regulate them, or make them go away, which in turn involves new appraisals and new responses. To some extent, then, the emotion process moves in a loop rather than in a single direction.

Appraisal in the Emotion Process

Whether an event or situation leads to an emotion depends on how the person appraises it. **Appraisal** is the evaluation of a situation with respect to how relevant it is to one's own welfare (Lazarus, 1991). Appraisal need not be a conscious, deliberate thought process. Most of the time it probably occurs automatically, well outside awareness, and it may occurr in an instant (Barrett, Ochsner, & Gross, 2007).

Appraisal drives the process by which emotions are elicited (Roseman, 1984; Scherer, Dan, & Flykt, 2006). It explains why, for example, the level of happiness expressed by Olympic athletes can be greater for winners of the bronze medals (third place) than for winners of the silver medal (second place) (Medvec, Madey, & Gilovich, 1995). Bronze medalists could easily imagine an alternative outcome: They may not have even placed. Compared to that outcome, third is great. Silver medalists, on the other hand, could easily imagine and hope for an alternative outcome: Winning first place! Compared to that outcome, second is somewhat disappointing. Our own beliefs clearly influence the way in which we appraise our situation, as do our personalities, personal histories, and goals.

The type of appraisal that occurs determines the type of the emotion generated. Fear, for instance, comes from situations of uncertainty and over which we feel we have little control (Ekman, 2003; Lazarus, 1991). In one study, students completed appraisal and emotion questionnaires before and immediately after taking a midterm exam. Students who reported appraisals of unfairness and uncertainty and the idea that others were in control of the situation after the exam were more likely to experience fear than those who did not report such appraisals (Ellsworth & Smith, 1988; Smith & Ellsworth, 1987). Although it might be impossible to study automatic appraisals as they happen, research on people's understanding of situations and their responses to them can inform us indirectly about appraisal.

Regulation of Emotion

People can intentionally or unintentionally change their emotions or the extent to which they experience certain emotions. The term **emotion regulation** refers to the cognitive and behavioral efforts people use to modify their emotions.

Looking at the emotion process as depicted in Figure 11.12, you can see that attempts to regulate emotions may occur at the beginning or end of the emotion process (Gross, 1998; Gross, Richards, & John, 2006). An example of emotion regulation that can occur early in the emotion process is **reappraisal,** in which people reevaluate their views of an event so that a different emotion results. For example, rather than seeing your next midterm as an opportunity for failure,

appraisal

the evaluation of a situation with respect to how relevant it is to one's own welfare; it drives the process by which emotions are elicited.

emotion regulation

the cognitive and behavioral efforts people make to modify their emotions.

reappraisal

an emotion regulation strategy in which one reevaluates an antecedent event so that a different emotion results.

nature & nurture

Our appraisal of events leads to emotional experiences, which in turn influence how we respond to new situations.

an outlook that might create fear or anxiety, you might reappraise the exam as a challenging opportunity to prove to yourself and others how much you have learned, an outlook that would lead to eager anticipation.

Another kind of emotion regulation operates when people want to make an unpleasant feeling go away. An example of this kind of strategy for regulating emotion is **expressive-suppression,** the deliberate attempt to inhibit the outward display of an emotion (Gross et al., 2006). For instance, in order to avoid a confrontation, you might literally bite your lip rather than tell your roommates that they are slobs for letting the dishes pile up and waiting for you to wash them. Instructing people to suppress their negative emotions like this can decrease the experience of negative emotion, but it increases activation of the sympathetic nervous system and sustains the emotional response (Gross & Levenson, 1997).

In an important application of emotion research to the real world, researchers have taught schoolchildren strategies for regulating emotion in order to reduce maladaptive behavior and improve academic performance (see "Psychology in the Real World"; Conduct Problems Prevention Research Group, 1999a, 1999b; Kam, Greenberg, & Kusché, 2004). The idea that emotional skills are linked to success in life was popularized in the mid-1990s by Daniel Goleman (1995). Goleman's book, *Emotional Intelligence,* summarizes research on how the ability to recognize emotions in oneself and others, the development of empathic understanding, and skills for regulating emotions in oneself and others may be at least as important to one's success in life as academic achievement. Goleman drew heavily on research by Peter Salovey and John Mayer, who introduced the concept of emotional intelligence in 1990 (Salovey & Mayer, 1990).

> **expressive-suppression**
> a response-focused strategy for regulating emotion that involves the deliberate attempt to inhibit the outward manifestation of an emotion.

The Emotional Response

Whether processed consciously or automatically, emotional responses emerge from events appraised as relevant to one's safety or personal goals. As shown in Figure 11.12, the **emotional response** includes physiological, behavioral/expressive, and subjective changes. Here we will discuss each type of change.

Physiological Changes. Emotions produce physiological changes, such as increases in heart rate and rate of respiration. The physiological system responsible for changes during an emotional response is the autonomic nervous system (ANS). The ANS governs structures and processes over which we have little conscious control, such as changes in heart rate and blood pressure and the release of hormones. The ANS plays a crucial role in emotional response because it activates other systems that are needed for action, including the circulatory system and the respiratory system.

Once elicited, emotions engage the ANS almost immediately. For emotions that are concerned with survival and protection from harm, such as fear, the sympathetic branch of the ANS is activated. Sympathetic activity mobilizes

> **emotional response**
> the physiological, behavioral/expressive, and subjective changes that occur when emotions are generated.

Social and Emotional Learning in Schools

If you ask most people what you are supposed to learn in elementary school, they might say, "Reading, writing, math, science, history. . . ." How many people would say "I learned how to regulate my anger"? Yet today many schools are teaching just that. Psychologists and educators argue that the development of skills for recognizing and regulating emotions is just as important to success in life as is academic achievement. And new research backs up this assertion. The past decade or so has seen the development and implementation of programs designed to teach young children skills for managing their emotions and promoting social adjustment. These social-emotional learning (SEL) programs constitute an important application of the psychology of emotion to the real world.

Mark Greenberg, director of the Prevention Research Center for the Promotion of Human Development at Penn State University, initiated much of the research on SEL. Through applied psychological research, he and his colleagues have evaluated the effectiveness of the prevention programs developed by the center. One of those programs is PATHS (Providing Alternative THinking Strategies), a ground-breaking program developed by Greenberg and Carol Kusché (Greenberg & Kusché, 1998; Kusché & Greenberg, 1994). The PATHS program gives teachers a detailed curriculum for improving children's emotional awareness and regulation skills and enhancing their social competence.

An example of an exercise in the PATHS program is the turtle story and lesson, which is aimed at developing self-control. Children are told about a turtle that gets into trouble with other turtles in various situations because he does not stop to think. He gets some help from "wise old turtle," who tells him that when he just can't handle his anger and feels aggressive, he should go into his shell and consider what the best way to respond might be.

The PATHS program uses a modified version of the turtle story to teach children the technique of pulling back and mulling over options when they are upset in order to

body resources into an organized response to a real or imagined environmental threat. The heart pumps blood rapidly to the muscles; oxygen intake in the lungs increases; and processes that are not immediately necessary for action, such as digestion, shut down so that energy is conserved for more urgent body functions.

The patterns of ANS activity can vary, depending on the emotion elicited. Anger increases heart rate more than fear does; disgust slows the heart (Ekman, Levenson, & Friesen, 1983; Levenson, Ekman, & Friesen, 1990). Such autonomic nervous system changes appear to be common to people all over the world (Levenson et al., 1992; Tsai et al., 2002; Tsai, Levenson, & Carstensen, 2000). Such cross-cultural data on the physiology of emotion supports the view of emotions as evolutionarily old, as does evidence of emotion in nonhuman primates, other mammals, birds, and even fish (Paul, Harding, & Mendl, 2005).

Positive emotions engage the parasympathetic branch of the ANS. They apparently serve to return the body to a more relaxed, responsive state (Levenson, 2003). For example, Fredrickson and Levenson (1998) showed participants a fear-eliciting film and followed it with film clips known to elicit sadness, amusement, or contentment—or no emotions at all. They measured cardiovascular activity while participants viewed the films and again afterward. Cardiovascular

gain self-control and reduce aggressive behaviors. Kids learn to time themselves out when they get upset by "playing turtle" and thinking about what to do next. Other exercises are designed to help children identify their feelings, develop empathic understanding, and recognize that it's okay to have all feelings but that not all behaviors are okay.

Research using controlled intervention trials in which classrooms were randomly assigned to receive the PATHS curriculum or not (thereby continuing as usual) has shown that PATHS leads to improvements in social and emotional skills in high-risk children, reduction of aggressive behaviors in both normal and special-needs children, fewer depressive symptoms in special-needs kids, and improvements in classroom functioning (Conduct Problems Prevention Research Group, 1999a, 1999b; Kam, Greenberg, & Kusche, 2004). Other prevention programs, such as Head Start, have also applied the theory and methods of emotion research to decrease behavior problems in schools, and initial results are promising (Izard et al., 2004).

Now, more than a decade after the implementation of major SEL programs, it is possible to see how the development of socioemotional learning might be linked to academic success. A large-scale meta-analysis of more than 500 studies shows that SEL programs significantly improve children's academic performance (Durlak et al., 2007). Specifically, children who participate in these programs have better attendance and less disruptive classroom behavior; they like school more and have higher GPAs.

activation elicited by the negative film returned to baseline levels more quickly in people who saw a pleasant film (amusement or contentment) after the fear film, than in those who saw films leading to sad or nonemotional conditions. This ability of positive emotions to "undo" the effects of negative emotional arousal by helping to return the body to a state of relaxation may result from parasympathetic nervous system activation.

Behavioral-Expressive Changes. Emotions create expressive changes in the face and voice, as well as behavioral tendencies toward particular types of action (Frijda, 1986). People show their emotions—knowingly or not—through both verbal and nonverbal means, such as changes in facial behavior and vocal intonation. Although researchers have studied both facial and vocal expressions of emotion, the most extensive body of research has focused on facial expressions.

Humans are predisposed to respond to faces. Newborn babies mimic the facial expressions of adults; at five months they can discriminate between different types of facial expressions of emotion; and by one year of age they rely on the faces of their caregivers to convey important information about how they might

connection
The autonomic nervous system both activates and relaxes physiological systems.
See Chapter 3, p. 84.

act (Meltzoff & Moore, 1977; Schwartz, Izard, & Ansul, 1985; Sorce et al., 1985). There are specialized neurons in the brain for responding to faces, and certain brain areas are specialized for particular facial expressions, such as fear (Adolphs et al., 1994, 2005; Kanwisher, 2000).

How do psychologists study spontaneous facial expressions? The **Facial Action Coding System (FACS)** is a widely used method by which coders score all observable muscular movements that are possible in the human face (Ekman & Friesen, 1978). Using FACS, researchers have found that many different facial expressions recognized across cultures—such as anger, disgust, fear, happiness, sadness, and surprise—are also shown when people spontaneously experience emotions (Ekman & Rosenberg, 2005).

Facial Action Coding System (FACS)
a widely used method for measuring all observable muscular movements that are possible in the human face.

The most recognizable facial expression of emotion is the smile of happiness. Yet research using FACS shows that not all smiles are created equal. Only certain smiles indicate truly felt enjoyment. Other smiles are used for a variety of interpersonal reasons, such as to be polite in conversation, to mask negative emotions, or to pretend that one is feeling happy when, in fact, one is not. A smile that both pulls up the lip corners diagonally and contracts the band of muscles that circle the eye to create crow's feet and raise the cheeks is known as a **Duchenne smile**. A Duchenne smile is a genuine smile that expresses true enjoyment. When we smile for social reasons and are not genuinely happy, we use only the lips and not the band of muscles around the eye, which is called a non-Duchenne smile (Davidson et al., 1990; Ekman, Davidson, & Friesen, 1990). Figure 11.13 shows a Duchenne smile and a non-Duchenne smile.

Duchenne smile
a smile that expresses true enjoyment, involving both the muscles that pull up the lip corners diagonally and those that contract the band of muscles encircling the eye.

The human voice also expresses emotion. Have you ever noticed how your voice can betray you? Consider the first time you ever gave a speech. You may have had your hair and clothes in fine order; perhaps your facial expressions showed great composure; and you knew your speech well, having practiced it many times. But when the time came to start speaking, your voice quivered or even squeaked! Why did this happen? The voice is very sensitive to emotional fluctuations because the vocal cords are innervated by the autonomic nervous

Is Leonardo da Vinci's *Mona Lisa* smiling out of pleasure or merely posing a smile in her portrait?

FIGURE **11.13**
DUCHENNE SMILE VERSUS NON-DUCHENNE SMILE. Both photos depict a smile of the same intensity, but they differ in the involvement of muscles around the eye. Which one is a Duchenne, or true enjoyment, smile?

system. So nervousness leaks through the voice (Bachorowski, 1999; Scherer et al., 1991).

The same vocalization can sound different, depending on the speaker's facial expression. This happens because lip movements affect vocal characteristics. For example, you can actually hear a smile or a frown. When listening to recordings people can reliably distinguish between laughs produced while smiling and while frowning (Bachorowski, 1999).

Subjective Changes in Emotion. The third component of the emotional response is referred to as the **subjective experience of emotion,** which is the quality of our conscious experience during an emotional response. When people talk about how an emotion *feels,* they are referring to subjective experience. Each emotion creates a unique feeling: Anger feels different from sadness, which feels different from happiness. The subjective aspect of emotion draws on a person's experience of body changes as well as the effects emotions have on cognition, for emotions can activate associations with images and memories of significant events.

What produces subjective feelings of emotion? Perhaps the most influential theory was proposed by William James (1884) and Carl Lange (1885/1992). The **James-Lange theory of emotion** says that it is our perception of the physiological changes that accompany emotions that creates the subjective emotional experience. Without the perception of body changes, they argued, there is no emotional experience. Moreover, these changes that accompany different emotional states are unique. We experience fear as feeling different from sadness, for example, because we perceive different body changes for each emotion. In short, "I am trembling, and therefore I am afraid; or I feel a lump in my throat, therefore I am sad."

Several lines of evidence support the James-Lange view. First, when people in many cultures are asked to identify the body sensations associated with emotions, they differentiate among several emotional states. For instance, "stomach sensations" are associated most strongly with disgust, far more so than with other emotions, and sadness with a lump in the throat (Breugelmans et al., 2005). Figure 11.14 presents an overview of the sensations that people participating in research studies report are associated with each emotion. In support of the idea that feedback from body sensations creates the subjective experience of emotion, people who pose on their faces the muscular movements of some emotion

  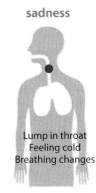 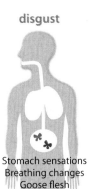  

happiness	anger	sadness	disgust	surprise	fear
Feeling warm Heart beats faster	Heart beats faster Breathing changes Feeling hot	Lump in throat Feeling cold Breathing changes	Stomach sensations Breathing changes Goose flesh	Heart beats faster Breathing changes Feeling hot	Heart beats faster Breathing changes Weak in the knees

FIGURE **11.14**

BODILY SENSATIONS ASSOCIATED WITH DIFFERENT EMOTIONS. People in different cultures report experiencing somewhat different sensations in different emotional states, as shown here. These findings are based on self-reports, however, and not on external measures of physiological changes. Studies on external measures of emotion (e.g., Levenson et al., 1990) reveal slightly different patterns. (*Source:* Breugelmans et al., 2005.)

expressions report feeling that emotion (Strack, Martin, & Stepper, 1988). Additionally, the better people pose facial expressions of emotion, the more intense the feeling (Ekman et al., 1983; Levenson et al., 1990).

quick quiz 11.2: Emotion

1. The fact that sexual orgasm cannot occur unless the areas of the brain involved in fear and anxiety are shut down illustrates what basic feature of emotions versus drives?
   a. drives have supremacy over emotions
   b. emotions can override biological drives
   c. emotions and drives serve similar masters
   d. drive must be resolved before emotions can motivate behavior

2. Which of the following is *not* a self-conscious emotion?
   a. pride
   b. embarrassment
   c. resentment
   d. shame

3. According to the view of emotions as a process, _____ drive(s) the process by which emotions are elicited.
   a. emotional responses
   b. expressive changes
   c. physiological changes
   d. appraisal

Answers can be found at the end of the chapter.

breaking new ground
The Universality of Facial Expressions of Emotion

If you were to visit an exotic place, such as the Amazon rain forest, could you expect your smile to be greeted with a smile from the local inhabitants? Or might they do something else? More generally, can we expect facial expressions of emotion to mean the same thing to people from different cultures? In the late 1960s, Paul Ekman went to a remote culture to find out whether facial expressions of emotion were universal or culturally specific. His research broke new ground, not just in our understanding of expression, but in helping launch the field of emotion research in psychology as well.

EMOTION EXPRESSION: CULTURALLY DETERMINED OR UNIVERSAL?

cultural relativism
the idea that behavior varies across cultures and can be understood only within the context of the culture in which they occur.

In the 1960s, most social scientists believed that behavior was strongly determined by a person's environment. Anthropologists, for instance, proposed that facial expressions of emotion were **culturally relative;** that is, expressions varied across cultures and could be understood only in their cultural context. After all, anthropologists in the field had observed cultures in which people acted playfully at funerals and those in

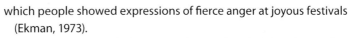

which people showed expressions of fierce anger at joyous festivals (Ekman, 1973).

Trained as a behaviorist who emphasized the effects of environment on behavior, a young psychologist named Paul Ekman thought the anthropologists were right. By the mid-1960s, however, he was beginning to question that view. Ekman's mentor, Silvan Tomkins, showed research participants numerous photographs of European Americans posing different emotions and asked them to decide which emotion the person in the picture may have been feeling. He obtained pretty strong evidence of agreement on the emotional meaning of those facial expressions (Tomkins & McCarter, 1964). Then Ekman and his colleague, Wallace Friesen, showed Tomkins's pictures to people in the United States, Japan, Argentina, and Chile and found a high degree of consensus on the meanings of a core set of facial expressions of emotion (Ekman & Friesen, 1969). At about the same time, Carroll Izard (1969) did a similar study and obtained similar results. Such high level of consensus on the meaning of facial expressions of emotion across numerous cultural groups in several studies supported Darwin's (1872) assertion that the facial expressions of certain "basic" emotions are **universal,** that is, common to all human beings (see Figure 11.15).

One problem with these studies on emotion recognition, however, is that all participants lived in literate, industrialized cultures. Maybe the findings of cross-cultural consistency in facial expression recognition reflected the spreading influence of the popular media rather than the existence of a universal human skill. That is, people in Japan and the United States might have agreed on the emotional meaning of certain expressions because they had seen portrayals of actors in movies. About this time Ekman (Ekman, 1972; personal communication, March 28, 2006) read Charles Darwin's (1872) book *The Expression of the Emotions in Man and Animals,* in which Darwin described in detail how people and animals display emotions through their faces and bodies and offered a theory for the evolution of emotion expression. Ekman knew he needed to collect data from preliterate people who were isolated from Western culture, if he wanted to show that consistency in certain facial expressions of emotion occurred universally and was not a product of culture. This approach to disproving a rival hypothesis in order to rule out an alternative explanation of one's findings represents an important step in the process of doing science. In this case, the rival hypothesis was that cross-cultural consistency in the understanding of facial expressions reflected the spread of media influence.

universal
term referring to something that is common to all human beings and can be seen in cultures all over the world.

EVIDENCE OF UNIVERSALITY IN EMOTION EXPRESSION

Thanks to an anthropologist friend, Ekman had the chance to study just such an isolated, preliterate group: the Fore tribe from Papua New Guinea. His plan was to show members of this tribe pictures of facial expressions of emotion and find out which emotions, if any, they saw in those faces. But how could he gather such data from a culture without a written language? He decided to ask the people to make up stories to explain why the person in a picture would make such a face. To Ekman's dismay, the New Guineans found it very difficult to make up stories about the pictures, so he was not able to get a large sample of data. Ekman says that after collecting these data, he sat alone on a hill,

FIGURE **11.15**
DRAWINGS AND PHOTO-GRAPHS OF ANGER/AGGRESSION ACROSS SPECIES FROM DARWIN'S 1872 BOOK. Darwin asserted that expressions of emotion are universal across human cultures. His book *The Expression of the Emotions in Man and Animals* influenced Ekman's research. (*Source:* Darwin, 1998.)

Paul Ekman with children in Papua New Guinea, circa 1967. The boys are wearing western clothing that they accepted as gifts for participating in Ekman's research.

listening to "The Fool on the Hill" by the Beatles, and felt disappointed. Nonetheless, the data were promising, and he published them, but they did not yield the high consensus he had expected (Ekman, Sorenson, & Friesen, 1969).

Ekman was fairly convinced that the people in New Guinea knew what the expressions meant, but he believed that his method was flawed. Instead of giving up, Ekman decided to try another approach. He chose a technique that had been used in studies of children's ability to recognize emotion in facial expressions. The method involved presenting stories about emotional situations to New Guineans and showing them a set of three photographed faces per story. Examples of stories include "He [she] is angry and about to fight" (which should lead participants to pick an "angry" face) or "She [he] is looking at something that smells bad" (for disgust). Then the experimenter would ask the listener which of the three faces matched the story. When Ekman used this method, the degree of consensus was much higher. Both children and adult New Guineans consistently discriminated the "correct" face from other faces; that is, they consistently matched a given story with the face that would have been predicted, and the results matched the data from studies of people in literate cultures (Ekman & Friesen, 1971). Results of these two early studies from both literate and preliterate cultures show that the range of agreement was relatively high for five of the six basic emotions (Ekman et al., 1969; Ekman & Friesen, 1971). Follow-up research conducted 20 years later showed similar high-level agreement across 10 literate cultures (Ekman et al., 1987). For summaries of facial recognition data across several studies see Figure 11.16.

FIGURE **11.16**

CONSISTENCY IN EXPRESSIONS OF BASIC EMOTION ACROSS LITERATE AND PRELITERATE CULTURES.

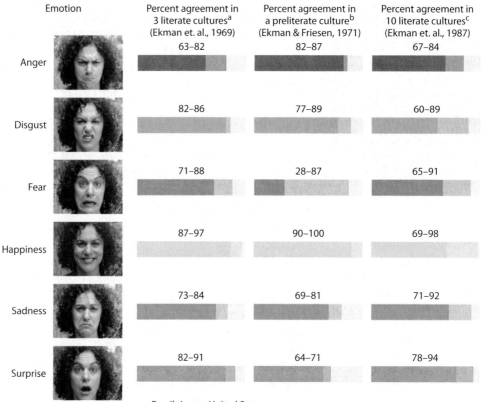

Emotion	Percent agreement in 3 literate cultures[a] (Ekman et. al., 1969)	Percent agreement in a preliterate culture[b] (Ekman & Friesen, 1971)	Percent agreement in 10 literate cultures[c] (Ekman et. al., 1987)
Anger	63–82	82–87	67–84
Disgust	82–86	77–89	60–89
Fear	71–88	28–87	65–91
Happiness	87–97	90–100	69–98
Sadness	73–84	69–81	71–92
Surprise	82–91	64–71	78–94

a = Brazil, Japan, United States
b = Papua New Guinea (Fore)
c = Estonia, Germany (West), Greece, Hong Kong, Italy, Japan, Scotland, Sumatra, Turkey, United States

EMOTION RESEARCH AFTER THE FINDINGS ON UNIVERSALITY

Ekman's findings showed that the face contained reliable information about emotion that was common to all humans. It brought the subjective state of emotion into the realm of science and made it a topic of objective study. By the late 1980s and throughout the 1990s, emotion became one of the most widely studied topics in all of psychology (Rosenberg, 2005). Moreover, spurred by the knowledge that the face contained reliable information about emotion, Ekman and his colleagues developed the objective coding system of the face, FACS, that we discussed earlier in the chapter (Ekman & Friesen, 1978). And finally, the findings from New Guinea led to an integration of the two competing perspectives, culture differences and universality. Soon after returning from New Guinea, Ekman (1972) proposed the **neurocultural theory of emotion** to account for the fact that certain aspects of emotion, such as the facial expressions and physiological changes of basic emotions, are similar in all humans, whereas other aspects, such as how people appraise situations and regulate their emotional expressions in front of others, vary from one culture to another.

neurocultural theory of emotion
Ekman's explanation that some aspects of emotion, such as facial expressions and physiological changes associated with emotion, are universal and others, such as emotional regulation, are culturally derived.

display rules
learned norms or rules, often taught very early, about when it is appropriate to express certain emotions and to whom one should show them.

HOW CULTURE IMPACTS EMOTION EXPRESSION

Anthropologists have offered numerous examples of cultural variability in emotion expression—such as the case of Samurai women who smiled broadly after learning that their husband or son had died in battle (Ekman, 1973). Such examples suggest that facial expressions of happiness and sadness are not universal. How can the findings on universality of facial expressions jibe with the fact that there are cultural differences in emotions? Friesen and Ekman (1972; Friesen, 1972) proposed the concept of display rules to address this dilemma. **Display rules** are learned norms or rules, often taught very early, about when it is appropriate to show certain expressions of emotion and to whom one should show them. As it turns out, Samurai women were expected to be proud of a son or husband who had been killed in battle, and the society required them to display joy at the news. More mundane examples from daily life in the United States include the requirements that winners should not boast, losers should not mope, and men should not cry in public (although this last norm is changing).

In some cultures, men are expected to refrain from crying in public. Sometimes, though, strong emotions can override display rules, as they apparently have for the man in this picture.

The first empirical support for display rules came from a study comparing disgust expressions in American and Japanese students (Ekman, 1972; Friesen, 1972). Both groups viewed a film showing a very graphic medical procedure, but in two different conditions: in the presence of an authority figure and alone. When alone, both groups felt perfectly comfortable expressing the obvious response—disgust. When in the presence of an authority figure, however, the Japanese students did not show disgust, and they masked their responses with non-Duchenne (fake) smiles. American students, however, showed about the same level of disgust in both conditions. The expressive differences between groups emerged in a situation in which the cultures had very different norms about expression, but not in the solo viewing condition. More recent research on display rules and expression support and extend these original findings (Matsumoto et al., in press). Overwhelmingly, however, people across many cultures show remarkably similar emotion displays in highly emotional situations—in the Olympics, for example (Matusmoto & Willingham, 2006).

Another recent finding on universality goes back to Darwin (1872), who asserted that facial expressions evolved due to their functional role in survival. For instance, the expression of fear, with its raised brows and widely opened eyes, increased the scope of vision for someone looking for options for escape. Recent research shows that people posing fear faces actually see better in terms of tests of peripheral vision and quickness of eye movements. These changes may actually fulfill the function of the fear face hypothesized by Darwin—to enable people to respond more quickly to danger (Susskind et al., 2008).

nature & nurture
When and how we express emotion is a function of both biological and cultural forces.

In sum, when and how we express emotion on our face is determined both by innate, biologically determined factors and by learned influences, such as display rules, that may vary from one culture to another. The evidence strongly suggests that all humans share a core set of basic facial expressions of emotion.

EMOTION AND THE BRAIN

So far we have examined the emotion process in detail, from the eliciting event to the appraisal mechanisms that bring forth the emotional response to the resulting changes in physiology, expression, and experience. Missing from this picture is the brain, which participates in every aspect of the emotion process.

Affective neuroscience, the field devoted to studying the brain's role in emotion, is a rapidly growing area of research. Most current evidence tells us that emotional information is processed in brain circuits that involve several brain structures, and emotional processing is highly interlinked with cognitive processing (Pessoa, 2008). Although there is no main emotion center in the brain, we can identify some key areas for emotion processing, including the amygdala and the prefrontal cortex, as well as other brain regions (see Figure 11.17).

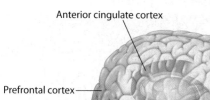

Anterior cingulate cortex
Prefrontal cortex
Hypothalamus
Amygdala

FIGURE **11.17**

FOUR MAIN REGIONS OF THE EMOTIONAL BRAIN. No single area of the brain is responsible for emotion, but the amygdala, prefrontal cortex, anterior cingulate cortex, and the hypothalamus play key roles in the way we experience emotion and remember emotional experiences.

The Amygdala Anatomically, the amygdala has connections with many important brain regions, including structures that appear to be involved in emotion and memory: the hypothalamus, which controls the ANS; the hippocampus, which plays a crucial role in memory; the thalamus, which receives information from the sense organs; and the cerebral cortex. The amygdala appears to play a very important role in appraisal of the emotional significance of stimuli, with a specialized function for noticing fear-relevant information (Öhman, 2002; Phelps & LeDoux, 2005).

Much of the research on the amygdala has centered on its pivotal role in quick appraisals during threatening or fear-inducing situations (LeDoux, 1996, 2000). Along these lines, Joseph LeDoux and his colleagues have used classical conditioning of fear in rats as a model for studying emotion in the human brain (Wilensky et al., 2006). In their experiment, a rat is exposed to a tone, which is emotionally neutral at first. Then the tone is repeatedly paired

with an aversive stimulus, an electric shock (the unconditioned stimulus, or UCS). After repeated pairings with the shock, the tone itself becomes a fear-eliciting stimulus (the conditioned stimulus or CS). When the researchers examined the circuitry of fear conditioning in the rat brain, they found that the side and middle of the amygdala are most active in learning to be afraid of the tone (Wilensky et al., 2006).

A number of studies of the amygdala's role in fear in humans have yielded findings consistent with those of studies using rats. People with damaged amygdalas do not show normal physiological reactions under fear conditioning. They tend to trust faces that most people find to be untrustworthy and have trouble recognizing facial expressions of fear, especially in the eyes (Adolphs et al., 1994, 2005; Adolphs, Tranel, & Damasio, 1998; Phelps & LeDoux, 2005). Brain imaging studies of people with intact brains reveal increased amygdala activation when they are exposed to fear faces, while the amygdala is not active when people view other facial expressions of emotion (Breiter et al., 1996). Finally, although certain regions of the amygdala are more involved in fear, other regions are more involved in anger and rage (Panksepp, 2000). In fact, tumors of the amygdala have been found in violent criminals, such as in Charles Whitman, who climbed the tower at the University of Texas in 1966 and in a 90-minute shooting spree killed 19 people and wounded 38 (Charles J. Whitman Catastrophe, Medical Aspects. Report to Governor, September 8, 1966).

The Prefrontal Cortex Phineas Gage, whose case is described in Chapter 3, was a 19th century railroad worker who survived a severe injury to his prefrontal cortex, only to be transformed from a relatively mild-mannered man into an impatient, easily enraged individual. This was the first indication to scientists of the importance of the prefrontal cortex in emotion and personality. Since then, researchers have discovered that the prefrontal cortex is one of the more active regions of the brain in the experience and appraisal of emotions. Damage to the left prefrontal cortex results in depression (Morris et al., 1996; Sackheim et al., 1982). According to EEG studies that measure cortical activity, clinically depressed people show less activity in the left prefrontal cortex than do nondepressed people (Davidson, 2001).

Moreover, due to its involvement in planning, impulse control, and working memory, the prefrontal cortex plays a role in the appraisal and reappraisal of emotion (Miller & Cummings, 1999; Miyake et al., 2000). Kevin Ochsner and his colleagues (2002) reported that the amygdala is more involved in determining whether a situation merits an emotional response at all, while the prefrontal cortex may be more involved in determining options for response or reappraisal.

connection

The prefrontal cortex plays a key role in working memory by evaluating sensory information and designating it for storage or disposal.

See Chapter 7, p. 273.

Given that there are neural connections between the prefrontal cortex and the amygdala, this finding and others like it may indicate that certain regions of the prefrontal cortex influence the emotional responses produced by the amygdala (Davidson, 2004; Pessoa, Padmala, & Morland, 2005; Pessoa, 2008).

Other Brain Regions in Emotion Other regions of the brain are involved in emotions as well (Dalgleish, 2004). A meta-analysis of more than 55 brain imaging studies reports that the *anterior cingulate cortex* (ACC) is active when people either recall or imagine emotional experiences (Phan et al., 2002; also see Figure 11.17). The ACC is also the region of the brain that is active both in physical pain and in the pain of rejection or exclusion (Eisenberger et al., 2003).

What areas of the brain are active when we experience positive emotions? Several studies suggest that the left prefrontal cortex is more involved in positive emotions than the right (Davidson, 2004; Davidson et al., 1990). Other work suggests that these regions are primarily involved in emotions that have approach components (emotions that impel the organism to move toward something or someone), which includes the negative emotion of anger as well as positive emotions (Harmon-Jones, 2003). The hypothalamus also appears to be a pleasure or reward center, because animals will forgo food and drink to receive stimulation there (Olds & Milner, 1954). Similarly, humans report feeling pleasure when this region is stimulated (Heath, 1975).

Finally, the insula is the brain structure most involved in *interoception*, or the perception of sensations arising within the body. As such, it plays an important role in emotional experience. In fMRI studies, the insula is active during the experience of pain and empathy for another's pain (Singer et al., 2004). Visualizing disgusting scenes also leads to activation of the insula as well as the ACC (Schienle, Shafer, & Vaitl, 2008). Insular activity is reduced when women attempt to regulate their disgust with reappraisal (Goldin et al., 2008).

connection
When you see another person you care about get hurt physically, it creates activity in the insula similar to what you experience with feelings of your own physical pain.
See Chapter 14, p. 560.

GENDER AND EMOTION

Are there sex differences in emotion? People all around the world think women are more emotional than men (Fischer & Manstead, 2000). Women do outperform men in accurately recognizing facial expressions of emotion (Brody & Hall, 2000; Hall & Matsumoto, 2004; Merten, 2005). But if you study emotions as they are actually happening, men and women's ratings of their emotional experience look similar (Barrett et al., 1998). The sexes differ most in how they describe their emotional experiences in words and in the frequency of smiling.

Women talk more about emotions than men do. In a study of older married couples discussing an area of conflict in their marriage, women were more likely to use words expressing distress and anger, whereas men were more likely to withdraw from conflict (Levenson, Carstensen, & Gottman, 1994). Women are more likely to describe their reactions to a particular experience with more refinement than men, using phrases such as

Women tend to talk about emotions more than men do, but there is little difference in the facial expressions of men and women during emotional experiences.

"I felt angry and upset" rather than the more general phrase "I felt bad" (Barrett et al., 2000).

In general, women smile more often than men (LaFrance, Hecht, & Paluk, 2003). And exposure to pictures of animal or human attacks provokes greater amygdala activation in men than in women, possibly reflecting a greater tendency toward aggressive action in men (Scheinle et al., 2008). Otherwise, studies of facial behavior during emotional experiences find no consistent differences between men and women (Gross & John, 1998). Likewise, the similarities between the sexes in terms of emotion and the brain are far more impressive than the differences (Wagner & Ochsner, 2005).

quick quiz 11.3: Culture, the Brain, and Gender in Emotion

1. Which of the following is *not* a basic emotion?
   a. fear
   b. happiness
   c. disgust
   d. shame

2. The social norm set forth by our culture which says that winners should not gloat is an example of a(n)
   a. display rule
   b. human universal
   c. affective trait
   d. antecedent event

3. The _____ appears to play a very important role in appraisal of the emotional significance of stimuli, with a specialized function for noticing fear-relevant information.
   a. amygdala
   b. hypothalamus
   c. prefrontal cortex
   d. insula

4. Which kind of emotion phrases are women more apt to use than men?
   a. more general comments, such as "I feel bad"
   b. more specific comments, such as "I am upset and angry."
   c. more affective imagery, such as "my fear is blue and cold"
   d. phrases such as "I will blow my top!"

Answers can be found at the end of the chapter.

life satisfaction the overall evaluation we make of our lives and an aspect of subjective well-being.

subjective well-being state that consists of life satisfaction, domain satisfactions, and positive and negative affect.

making connections
in motivation and emotion

Living a Satisfied Life

The word *happiness* often refers to a brief emotion, but it can also be used to mean a long-term sense of satisfaction with life. **Life satisfaction** is the overall evaluation we have of our lives (Diener et al., 1999). Psychologists consider life satisfaction to be a subset of **subjective well-being,** which also includes satisfaction in different domains, such as career, family, finances, and social networks. In this section we discuss the pursuit of life satisfaction in the context of motivation and emotion.

Motivation and Happiness

Maslow's hierarchical model of motivation offers a useful framework for a discussion of motivation and happiness. Both basic and higher-level needs contribute to life satisfaction.

Basic Needs and Happiness

Basic needs must be met for a person to be relatively satisfied with life. Accordingly, industrialized countries have higher levels of well-being than nonindustrialized countries (see Figure 11.18). After all, basic needs are met with money to buy food, clothes, and shelter. But more and more money does not lead to more and more happiness. At a national level, in the early stages of a country's development, increased income makes people happier with their lives. After a relatively modest level of increased income, however, money makes little difference and may even be a hindrance to happiness. In general, the higher a country's GNP, the higher its well-being. But there are many exceptions, especially in Latin America. Countries like Mexico and Colombia are just as happy as countries like Denmark, Iceland, and Switzerland, in spite of having only half their per person GNP. Moreover, when absolute income rose in the United States from the late 1940s to the late 1990s, well-being and life satisfaction stayed constant (Diener & Seligman, 2004).

At the individual level, there is a modest and complex relationship between income and overall life satisfaction as well. Having more money does make people slightly happier, but this is true only for those driven by money (Diener et al., 1999; Nickerson et al., 2003). Diet and weight also relate to overall happiness in various ways. First, having a healthy diet is associated with high life satisfaction (Due et al., 1991; Valois et al., 2003). On the other hand, being overweight—having a body mass index higher than 25—is associated with low life satisfaction (Ball, Crawford, & Kenardy, 2004; Nieman et al., 2000; Sarlio-Lähteenkorva,

2001; Zullig, Pun, & Huebner, 2007). Second, long-term weight loss, which less than 10% of dieters are able to maintain, is related to increases in life satisfaction (Korkeila et al., 1998; Valois et al., 2003).

Having a satisfying sex life can also be a source of overall happiness and well-being for people, just as problems in one's sex life can lead to overall problems in one's well-being. A worldwide survey of more than 27,000 men and women from 29 countries found a positive relationship between how happy people were in their lives in general and how happy they were in their sexual lives (Laumann et al., 2006). In general, subjective well-being and sexual satisfaction were highest in European and European-based cultures (e.g., Germany, Austria, Spain, Canada, and the United States).

Higher Needs and Happiness

Once a person or a country crosses the $12,000 per person per year GNP, close relationships matter most for overall levels of happiness (Headey, 2008). This would explain why the Danes are consistently the happiest people on the planet. Like people in Bhutan, the Danish are a happy people who are more interested in fostering healthy relationships than in increasing their personal wealth or climbing the career ladder (Christensen et al., 2006).

Bruce Headey (2008) reported in a 20-year longitudinal study that people who value noncompetitive goals, such as spending time with a spouse, children, and friends, tend to become happier and more satisfied with life over time. People, however, who most value competitive achievement goals, such as career advancement and material gains, actually decrease in happiness over time. Headey argues that when the main goal is monetary or advancing a career, all people have to look forward to after they achieve their goals is more competition and a greater pressure to achieve at an even higher level—not a recipe for happiness and well-being.

"I've got the bowl, the bone, the big yard. I know I *should* be happy."
© 1992 Mike Twohy: The New Yorker.

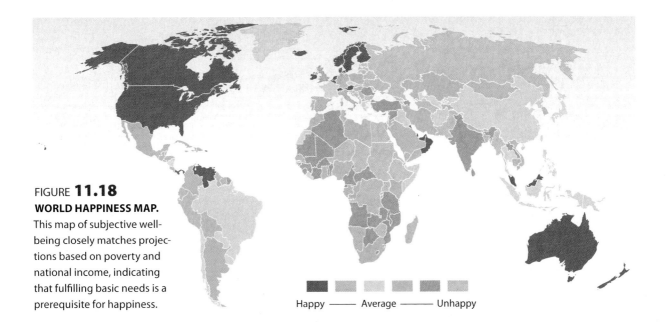

FIGURE **11.18**

WORLD HAPPINESS MAP.
This map of subjective well-being closely matches projections based on poverty and national income, indicating that fulfilling basic needs is a prerequisite for happiness.

Happy ———— Average ———— Unhappy

Another higher-level need is the cognitive need to explore and understand the world. People who are curious and interested in exploring novel and challenging situations tend to be happier than people who would rather stick with what they know and not challenge themselves with new tasks and experiences (Diener et al., 1999; Gallagher & Lopez, 2007; Headey, 2008). This finding is consistent with the broaden-and-build model of positive emotion we discussed earlier, which assumes that positive emotional states lead to expansive thoughts and behavior rather than to a narrow focus. The connection between curiosity, openness to novel experiences, and life satisfaction is also consistent with the optimal arousal theories of motivation , which assert that people seek out challenging and moderately arousing situations for optimal performance.

Emotions, Happiness, and Meaning in Life

A sense of well-being and satisfaction in life consists of the right balance of many different positive and negative emotions. In particular, the positive emotions can act as a buffer against long-term negative emotions. Happiness and life satisfaction are not about avoiding negative emotions, but rather about not dwelling on them. Sadness, anger, disgust, and even depression happen to everyone. Psychological science shows that if we bring some degree of life satisfaction and positive emotions with us as we go through our more challenging life experiences, we are more likely to emerge happier and healthier than if we don't. For example, after the terrorist attacks in the United States on September 11, 2001, people who were resilient and prone to experience positive emotion and life satisfaction six months prior to

9/11 experienced more positive emotion in the weeks after the attacks and less depression in the months after the attacks (Fredrickson et al., 2003). Fostering positive emotion, even in the face of tragic and trying experiences, can reap long-term psychological and emotional benefits (Fredrickson & Joiner, 2002).

Similarly, people who find meaning in their lives in general and even in negative and tragic experiences are likely to be happier in life than those who do not see meaning and purpose in life's difficult and unpleasant experiences (King et al., 2006). Psychologists propose that positive emotion can enhance meaning in life by broadening one's way of thinking and connecting experiences. The broaden-and-build model of positive emotion would predict just such an effect (Fredrickson, 1998).

quick quiz 11.4: Living a Satisfied Life

1. Which of the following contribute to subjective well-being?
   a. negative emotions
   b. fulfillment of basic needs
   c. sexual satisfaction
   d. all of the above

2. People who are curious and interested in exploring novel and challenging situations tend to be _____?
   a. about as smart as everyone else
   b. happier than those who have a narrow perspective
   c. smarter than narrow-minded people
   d. alienated from others

Answers can be found at the end of the chapter.

chapter **review**

MOTIVATION

- The psychology of motivation addresses the question of why people do what they do.

- Motivation encompasses needs, drives, and motivated behavior. Motives involve anything that energizes or directs behavior.

- Needs are states of cellular or bodily deficiency that compel drives, such as the need for water, food, and oxygen, while drives are the perceived state of tension that occurs when our bodies are deficient in some need—thirst, hunger, breathing.

- Maslow organized the various forces that drive human behavior in a vertical fashion, creating a hierarchy in which lower-level biological needs are subordinate to higher-level needs.

- Hunger is a basic drive that ensures that we take in sufficient nutrition to survive.

- Internal signals of hunger include sensations of the stomach and blood glucose levels, both of which are coordinated by sensors in the brain; external signals for hunger include the sight and smell of food as well as culturally influenced preferences.

- Eating disorders are complex and dangerous outcomes of a culture obsessed with thinness. At the same time, rates of obesity have increased dramatically over the last 50 years.

- Like all human motives, sexual desire results from a complex interplay of both biological and social forces.

- The hypothalamus plays an important role in sexual arousal.

- Hormones, especially testosterone, regulate sexual drive.

- Research on gender differences and casual sex tends to consistently find that males are more likely than females to engage in casual sex.

- Sexual orientation is a motive that involves both biological and social influences.

- One's tendency to achieve success is a function of three things: motivation to succeed, expectation of success, and the incentive value of the success.

EMOTION

- Unlike the longer-lasting moods and affective traits, emotions are acute, multifaceted responses to important events in our environment. Emotion can best be understood as a process that unfolds over time, beginning with exposure to an antecedent event, then appraisal. Appraisals determine whether an emotion occurs. Emotional responses include changes in behavior/expression, physiology, and subjective experience.

- Emotion regulation is an umbrella term for anything we do to try to change or otherwise manipulate the emotions we experience.

- From an evolutionary perspective, emotions function to organize body systems for a quick and efficient response to an important environmental event. This model applies best to negative emotions. Positive emotions, according to the broaden-and-build model, expand our thinking and help us develop knowledge and skills.

- The facial expressions of a set of basic emotions—anger, disgust, fear, happiness, sadness, and surprise—are recognized universally and appear to have evolutionary significance.

- Self-conscious emotions are a function of how well we live up to our expectations, the expectations of others, or the rules set by society and require a sense of self and the ability to reflect on one's own actions. Shame, guilt, humiliation, embarrassment, and pride are examples of self-conscious emotions.

- Display rules show how cultural factors can lead to differences in expression of emotion. Cultural variability is less apparent in the physiological changes associated with emotions.

- Physiological changes of negative emotions tend to be associated with higher arousal and activation of the sympathetic branch of the autonomic nervous system. Many physiological changes of positive emotions engage the parasympathetic nervous system to relax the body.

- Scientists are not sure what produces the subjective experience of emotion. The James-Lange theory holds that the perception of body changes plays an important role in a person's emotional experience.

- The brain is involved in every aspect of the emotion process, from appraisal to regulation. Although many brain structures appear to be crucial to emotions, the amygdala and the prefrontal cortex are major players.

- Men and women differ in how they talk about their emotional experiences, and women tend to smile more than men. The sexes, however, are much more similar than different in their emotionality.

MAKING CONNECTIONS IN MOTIVATION AND EMOTION

- Happiness, life satisfaction, and subjective well-being are not directly related to income. People who find meaning in their lives in general and even in negative and tragic experiences are likely to be happier in life.

key terms

achievement motivation, p. 429

affective traits, p. 432

antecedent event, p. 435

appraisal, p. 436

basic emotions, p. 432

broaden-and-build model, p. 435

cultural relativism, p. 442

display rules, p. 445

drives, p. 416

Duchenne smile, p. 440

emotion regulation, p. 438

emotional response, p. 438

emotions, p. 431

expressive-suppression, p. 438

Facial Action Coding System (FACS), p. 440

glucose, p. 420

homeostasis, p. 417

incentive, p. 416

James-Lange theory of emotion, p. 441

life satisfaction, p. 449

moods, p. 431

motivation, p. 415

needs, p. 416

neuro-cultural theory of emotion, p. 445

reappraisal, p. 438

self-actualization, p. 419

self-conscious emotions, p. 433

set point, p. 417

sexual behavior, p. 423

sexual orientation, p. 427

subjective experience of emotion, p. 441

subjective well-being, p. 449

universal, p. 443

Yerkes–Dodson law, p. 418

quick quiz answers

Quick Quiz 11.1: 1. b   2. c   3. b   4. a   5. c   **Quick Quiz 11.2:** 1. b   2. c   3. d

Quick Quiz 11.3: 1. d   2. a   3. a   4. b   **Quick Quiz 11.4:** 1. d   2. b

stress

and health

preview
questions

1 *What is stress?*

2 *How can stress make me physically ill?*

3 *Why do some people get stressed out by too many demands and others seem to thrive on multiple challenges?*

4 *What effect does exercise have on the brain?*

5 *How does behavior change health, and how does health change behavior?*

The most stressful daily challenges are the severe night and day sweats that John gets. . . . I bring John back upstairs around 10 p.m. I settle him in and within minutes he begins; it's beyond sweating. Night sweats doesn't describe what's going on, the word that comes to mind is that . . . he is leaking. For the next 2, 5, 8 hours he sweats through a long sleeve shirt and a terry cloth bathrobe and also through a pillow and the sheets. This process can take 20 minutes to a half an hour at which point I disturb him but he's appreciative of getting out of these wet things and into a dry shirt and bathrobe. He'll settle down and relax a little and I take a cold cloth to his forehead and wrists and wait anywhere for 20 to 30 minutes until the next episode and we repeat the process. On a good night it's four times; last night we did it 10 times. The thought that comes to mind is that I'm glad we have a heavy duty washer and dryer on the premises. . . . Personally I feel proud, pleased that I can comfort him and have the energy and God knows where it comes from to cope. The event shows our tremendous love for each other. We are still making our love for each other the focal point. (Folkman, Chesney, & Christopher-Richards, 1994, p. 48, cited in Folkman, 1997). ▶

▶ This was the response of the caregiver for a man dying of AIDS (acquired immunodeficiency syndrome), who was asked to describe the most stressful event he'd experienced in the last week.

Life is full of major threats, challenges, and tasks that burden us on a daily basis. Sometimes these stresses are minor, such as balancing the demands of work, school, and social relationships. In other cases, like the one just described, the stress is immense. What causes stress, and what effects does stress have on us? How is it that some people manage to find hope in the midst of anguish while others cannot?

In this chapter we examine the psychological and physiological nature of stress and the related topic of coping. We then briefly survey

chapter
outline

some major topics in the field of health psychology, a discipline that emerged from an interest in the effects of stress on physical health. Few other topics in psychology illustrate as clearly the interdependence of nature and nurture. Throughout this chapter we will highlight how stress emerges from and modifies mental and physical processes, how differences in people's ability to deal with life's challenges influence the functioning of their bodies, and how these bodily responses can affect how people think and feel. ■

What Is Stress?

We all know what it means to be stressed. But the term *stress* can refer to a wide variety of phenomena. We speak of having a stressful life when we consider the pressures or demands that make our lives difficult or interfere with our ability to maintain a feeling of well-being. Sometimes people talk about "feeling stressed," as if stress were an emotional state, one that involves anxiety and exhaustion. Some people are "stressed" by minor events such as a parking ticket or a missed train, whereas others seem to sail through life amid a great number of demands—work, family, school—all the while maintaining a sense of well-being and balance.

Stress is part of a dynamic interplay between people's interpretations of events in their lives and their reactions to those interpretations. **Stress** occurs when a situation overwhelms a person's perceived ability to meet the demands of that situation. As with emotions, we continually evaluate our experiences of

stress
A response elicited when a situation overwhelms a person's perceived ability to meet the demands of a situation.

stressful situations and attempt to cope with the challenges they pose. Suppose, for example, you are doing poorly in a class, and you have the final in one week. You feel stressed at first, but then you realize that with more review of the material, meeting with a study group, and more sleep, you could do better. You resolve to make these changes to improve your chances for a good final exam grade.

STRESS AS STIMULUS OR RESPONSE

Stress has different meanings in different contexts. Stress can be external to us. We can think of stress as something that happens *to* us—that is, as situations that push us to the limit or threaten our safety or well-being. Or stress can be the relentless onslaught of difficulties, such as being late on a term paper, the car breaking down, realizing there is no money in the checking account, and then getting into a fight with a roommate all in one week. We call these events that push us to the limit or exceed our ability to manage the situation at hand **stressors**. The focus on the situations that cause stress is known as the *stimulus view of stress.*

stressors
events that trigger a stress response.

In contrast, stress can be internal to us; we can think of it as the feeling we experience when events are too much to handle. The *response view of stress* has focused on the physiological changes that occur when someone encounters an excessively challenging situation. Later we will explore Hans Selye's work on looking at stress as a physiological response.

Clearly stress is much more than being in certain situations, and it is much more than physiological responses. It exists within the relationship between the external events and the internal responses. Stress emerges from people's interpretations of the relevance of certain stressors to their lives and their ability to deal with them. This *relational view of stress* holds that stress is a particular relationship between the people and the situations in which they find themselves.

Driving, particularly in high-traffic urban areas, can elicit a stress response.

We will look briefly at the view of stress as a stimulus, which has dominated psychological research for many years. Then we will explore the relational view, before turning to the research on stress as a physiological response, which sets a foundation for our understanding of how stress can affect health.

Stress as a Stimulus   Certain events demand an overwhelming amount of our energy and time. Any number of things can be stressors: unpleasant situations, such as divorce, financial troubles, or being sick; or pleasant situations, such as a wedding or the birth of a child.

Psychologists measure stress as a stimulus by quantifying the number of stressors a person experiences during a given period. Two major categories of stressors are major life events and daily hassles.

Any situation that creates a major upheaval in a person's life could potentially lead to stress. Indeed, one approach to measuring stress as a stimulus focuses

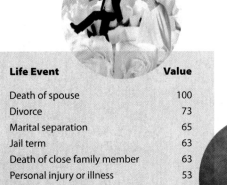

Life Event	Value
Death of spouse	100
Divorce	73
Marital separation	65
Jail term	63
Death of close family member	63
Personal injury or illness	53
Marriage	50
Fired from job	47
Marital reconciliation	45
Retirement	45
Change in health of family member	44
Pregnancy	40
Sex difficulties	39
Gain of a new family member	39
Business readjustment	39
Change in financial state	38
Death of a close friend	37
Change to a different line of work	36
Foreclosure of mortgage	30
Change in responsibilities at work	29
Son or daughter leaving home	29
Trouble with in-laws	29
Outstanding personal achievement	28
Wife begins or stops work	26
Begin or end school	26
Change in living conditions	25
Revision of personal habits	24
Trouble with boss	23
Change in residence	20
Change in school	20
Change in recreation	19
Change in church activities	19
Change in social activities	18
Change in sleeping habits	16
Change in eating habits	15
Vacation	13
Christmas	12
Minor legal violations	11

on major life events. In the late 1960s, Holmes and Rahe developed an instrument called the "Social Readjustment Rating Scale" (SRRS) to quantify stress in terms of major life changes. The scale, shown in Figure 12.1, consists of a list of events that might be considered life-changing; each is assigned a corresponding life change value.

After a person has responded to the questions on the scale, a researcher can calculate the total amount of stress the respondent is experiencing by adding up relative stress values, which were derived on the basis of previous research, known as Life Change Units (Holmes & Rahe, 1967).

The SRRS is easy to administer and score, but it has some drawbacks. First, it ignores the fact that people view similar events differently, and while some people might find marriage more stressful than a major work change, for others it may be vice versa (Scully, Tosi, & Banning, 2000). Second, by measuring stress in terms of life events, the SRRS fails to consider differences in people's emotional responses to stressors. Nevertheless, the SRRS is still widely used in research on stress and health, showing positive correlations with measures of mental and physical health (Gottlieb & Green, 1984).

Sometimes, little things really bother us. The accumulation of minor irritations—traffic, too much homework, relationship troubles—might wear us down, both mentally and physically. These daily hassles can be measured as well (Kanner et al., 1981). The "Hassles and Uplifts Scale" measures the frequency and intensity of minor irritations (hassles) and positive events of daily life that may counteract their damaging effects.

A number of studies report positive correlations between the frequency of daily hassles and self-reported health symptoms (DeLongis, Folkman, & Lazarus, 1988; Feist et al., 1995;

FIGURE **12.1**

SOCIAL READJUSTMENT RATING SCALE. Developed by Holmes and Rahe, this scale quantifies stress in terms of major life changes. The higher the value, the greater the stress associated with an event.

Kohn, Lafreniere, & Gurevich, 1991). Some data indicate that hassles are more strongly related to health outcomes than are major life events (Kohn, et al., 1991; Weinberger, Hiney, & Tierney, 1987).

But we have said that stress is complex, involving situations, interpretations, and physiological responses. Given such a perspective, what are the limitations of measuring stress only in terms of stressors, or situations? A major limitation to measuring both major life events and hassles is that not all people view situations in the same way. What is a stressor to one person might not be a stressor at all to another. For example, a poorly prepared student might dread an exam, but a student who has studied thoroughly might welcome it as a challenge. This example points to the ways in which people differ in how they respond to situations. Using this logic, Lazarus and Folkman (1984) argued that because people do not view similar situations in the same way, it is misleading to examine stress solely in terms of the situations that may call it forth. We have to look at the person in relation to the situation.

connection

Like stress, emotions are generated by our appraisals of events in our lives.

See Chapter 11, p. 436.

Relationship Between Person and Situation As we saw with emotion, when we first encounter a situation in our environment, we quickly appraise what it means for us. Lazarus and Folkman (1984) talk about two kinds of appraisal. **Primary appraisal** is an assessment of what a situation means to us. The outcome of this appraisal determines whether an emotional response might occur. If we view the event as not personally relevant, we feel no emotion. If we consider it personally relevant, we appraise its significance as either contrary to or consistent with our goals or welfare. If we appraise it as contrary to our well-being, we feel a negative emotion, which might cause stress. If we appraise it as consistent with our well-being, we feel a positive emotion. Figure 12.2 depicts the process by which different appraisals lead to different emotional outcomes. Even though both pleasant and unpleasant events might lead to stress, stress emerges from negative emotional responses to events that we cannot get under control.

primary appraisal

quick assessment of the meaning of a given environmental event for the individual.

FIGURE **12.2**

THE EMOTION/STRESS PROCESS. When events are appraised as threatening, negative emotions occur. In this model, stress occurs only when negative emotion is sustained.

Any kind of event—pleasant or unpleasant—might be fodder for such emotional reactions. For example, a wedding is a pleasant event that can be stressful, as is a new relationship or a busy social calendar.

Emotional events may escalate into stress when we cannot deal with the demands that the event entails. According to Lazarus and Folkman, we assess the resources available to cope with stress in a process they term **secondary appraisal.** When we find ourselves in a stressful situation, we try to figure out what to do about that situation, how to resolve it, or how to make the unpleasant feeling it creates go away.

secondary appraisal
self-assessment of the resources available to cope with stress.

THE PHYSIOLOGY OF STRESS

When stressful situations lead to negative emotions, physiological changes occur in the autonomic nervous system (ANS), the endocrine system, and the brain.

The ANS, as discussed in Chapter 3, consists of all the neurons that serve the organs and the glands. Because it is linked to the body systems that support action, it plays a crucial role in the responses of stress and emotion. These systems include the circulatory system, to pump blood to large muscle groups during times of emergency, and the respiratory system, to provide the oxygen required so that those muscles can function.

connections
The sympathetic branch of the ANS activates the body; the parasympathetic branch calms the body. Both play a role in stress and emotion.
See Chapter 3, p. 84, and Chapter 11, p. 437.

The second major system involved in stress is the endocrine system, which consists of the major hormone-releasing glands. The term **neuroendocrine system** refers to the hormonal systems involved in emotions and stress. The interactions among various organs, glands, and nervous system chemicals lay the groundwork for the dynamic interplay between psychological experience and physiological functioning.

neuroendocrine system
the hormonal systems involved in emotions and stress.

Physiological changes that enable us to respond quickly during an emergency can take a toll on our bodies if stress persists.

The key structures involved in the neuroendocrine regulation of stress responses include the hypothalamus, the pituitary gland, and the adrenal glands. The hypothalamus serves as a major link between the nervous system and the parts of the endocrine system relevant to emotions: It releases chemicals that stimulate the release of hormones from the pituitary gland, which sits just beneath it, and it is connected to brain stem structures that control the ANS. The pituitary releases hormones that play a key role in the stress response. The adrenal glands sit atop the kidneys, and they release several stress-related hormones: the

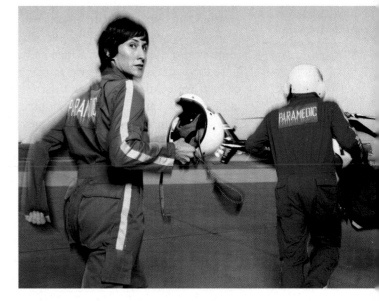

catecholamines
hormones that control ANS activation.

catecholamines, which control ANS activation, and the **glucocorticoids,** which are responsible for maintaining the activation of physiological systems during emergencies.

When activated by an emotional event, the hypothalamus initiates a series of endocrine events that have a profound effect on the body. Two major neuroendocrine pathways are stimulated: the adrenal-medullary system and

glucocorticoids
hormones responsible for maintaining the activation of physiological systems during emergencies.

FIGURE **12.3**

**THE HPA AXIS AND THE ADRENAL-
MEDULLARY SYSTEM.** During emotional
arousal and stress, the hypothalamus activates
the neuroendocrine system to prepare the
body's response. The hypothalamus releases
CRF, which stimulates the pituitary to release
ACTH. ACTH then stimulates the cortex of the
adrenal gland to release the "stress hormone"
cortisol.

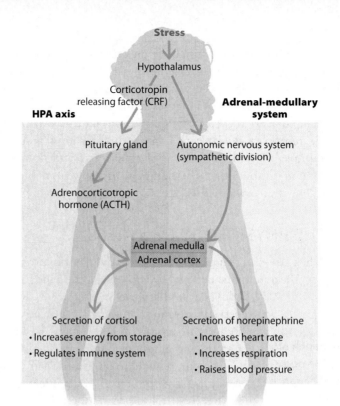

norepinephrine
a neurotransmit-
ter that activates
the sympathetic
response to stress,
increasing heart
rate, rate of respira-
tion, and blood
pressure in support
of rapid action.

the hypothalamus-pituitary-adrenal axis (see Figure 12.3). First in line is the **adrenal-medullary system,** in which the hypothalamus sends instructions to the brain stem to activate sympathetic neurons. Then, sympathetic neurons tell the adrenal gland to release the important catecholamine **norepinephrine.** Norepinephrine activates the sympathetic response, increasing heart rate, rate of respiration, and blood pressure in order to support rapid action by the body.

The sympathetic response evolved because rapid mobilization of the body's resources in emergency situations had clear survival and reproductive benefits. In cases of stress, however, we cannot regulate this emergency response. Moreover, if we continually live with stress-inducing situations, our body remains in "emergency mode" for long periods. Thus, a response that is adaptive in the short term can take a toll on the body in the long term, leading, for example, to sustained increases in blood pressure and heart rate. Think about how you feel when something startles you: Your heart races; you start breathing heavily; you're in a state of high alert. Now imagine what it would be like to remain in that condition for a period of days.

**hypothalamic-
pituitary-adrenal
(HPA) axis**
a major neuro-
endocrine pathway
relevant to the
stress response
involving the hypo-
thalamus, pituitary
gland, and the
adrenal cortex.

The other major neuroendocrine pathway that is relevant to the stress response is known as the **hypothalamic-pituitary-adrenal (HPA) axis.** Recall that the hypothalamus releases substances, called releasing factors, which tell the pituitary when to release various hormones. During emotional arousal and stress, the hypothalamus releases a substance called corticotropin releasing factor (CRF), which stimulates the pituitary to release adrenocorticotropic hormone (ACTH). ACTH then stimulates the cortex of the adrenal gland to release **cortisol,** the major glucocorticoid produced in humans, which is commonly known as the "stress hormone." When the level of cortisol in the blood adequately meets the body's metabolic needs, the hypothalamus stops releasing CRF, thereby reducing the release of cortisol. This kind of negative feedback occurs throughout the neuroendocrine system.

**adrenal-
medullary
system**
a major neuro-
endocrine pathway
stimulated during
stress in which
the hypothalamus
activates the sym-
pathetic nervous
system.

cortisol
the stress
hormone; it is
produced by the
body to mobilize
the body's energy
resources during
stressful situations.

Cortisol has many important functions. It plays a role in the breakdown of complex molecules into simpler ones to release energy and so plays an important role in ensuring that more glucose is available for fuel in the bloodstream. Cortisol also has a regulatory effect on the immune system. It often acts to reduce the number of immune cells in the bloodstream, thus suppressing the immune system's ability to protect the body against infection. (Segerstrom & Miller, 2004).

The General Adaptation Syndrome (GAS)   Austrian physiologist Hans Selye was fascinated by what happens to the body when it cannot cope with extreme stressors. In 1946 he proposed a three-stage model to explain the changes in physiology that occur during exposure to severe stressors. Selye believed that attempts to adapt to overwhelming stressors cause the body to wear down and eventually get sick. He used homeostasis as his starting point, and he viewed the changes that the body goes through when confronted with extreme situational demands as manifestations of adaptation to stress. He exposed animals to a range of stressors such as extreme temperature change, severe electrical shock, radiation, or heavy exercise (Selye, 1976).

Selye proposed that although an infinite range of circumstances elicit stress, all stress causes a generalized, nonspecific set of changes in the body. He measured hormones, metabolism, organ function, and other variables that respond to stressors and observed a consistent pattern of responses regardless of the stressor. Selye coined the term **general adaptation syndrome** (GAS) to describe this general pattern of responses. In Selye's words, "The general adaptation syndrome is the sum of all the nonspecific, systemic reactions of the body which ensue upon long continued exposure to stress" (1946, p. 119).

The GAS consists of three stages: alarm, resistance, and exhaustion (see Figure 12.4). Upon exposure to a stressor, an animal enters into a state of physiological shock, called the **alarm stage,** which is the body's emergency response to an environmental threat. The alarm stage mobilizes the body's resources to act via the effects of adrenal-medullary activation of the sympathetic nervous system. During this stage the HPA axis is active as well, and the sustained release of cortisol from the adrenal glands may move from being helpful (by making more fuel available) to being harmful in the long run (by suppressing certain aspects of immune function).

connection

Do you think an ethics review board would allow Selye to conduct his research on extreme stressors in animals today?

See Chapter 2, p. 66.

general adaptation syndrome (GAS) as defined by Hans Selye, a generalized, nonspecific set of changes in the body that occur during extreme stress.

alarm stage the phase of the general adaptation syndrome in which all of the body's resources respond to a perceived threat.

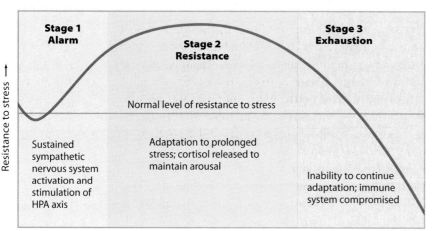

FIGURE **12.4**

SELYE'S GENERAL ADAPTATION SYNDROME (GAS). In the alarm stage, the body's resources are mobilized in response to a stressor. Resistance occurs when the body can no longer sustain the emergency response, and the organism must find other ways to ward off the threat. If the threat persists, eventually the body's resources become depleted, physical exhaustion occurs, and illness becomes much more likely.

Animals, however, can persist in the alarm stage for only so long. With continued exposure to the stressor, they eventually either die or find other ways of coping with the enduring threat. When they develop other ways to cope, they enter the second stage of adaptation, the **resistance stage**. Resistance implies that the organism maintains efforts to fight off or manage the threat. This extended effort, however, takes its toll physically and psychologically by diverting resources from maintenance of normal body functions.

Resistance cannot be maintained indefinitely. With repeated or continuous exposure to a stressor, animals enter the **exhaustion stage**. At this stage, their resources for fighting off threats have been depleted, and illness becomes much more likely. Have you ever come down with a cold or other illness a week or so after final exams?

resistance stage in the general adaptation syndrome, extended effort by the body to deal with a threat.

exhaustion stage the phase of the general adaptation syndrome when all resources for fighting the threat have been depleted and illness is more likely.

Selye's model laid the groundwork for research on the physiology of stress, but it soon became clear that his GAS model did not apply to all stress responses. First, Selye studied extreme physical stressors, such as nearly freezing an animal to death or repeatedly exposing it to severe electrical shock, and subjected animals to these stressors for prolonged periods. Questions arose as to whether the body changes that occurred in response to such severe demands provided a good model for enduring the stress of, say, divorce or financial troubles. Second, some researchers questioned the idea that a syndrome of body responses to stress occurred regardless of the type of stressor.

In the 1970s, John Mason conducted research that seriously challenged Selye's assumption that the stress response is a general one. Mason (1971, 1975) showed that an animal's response to a stressor differed depending on its psychological state. If the animal could anticipate a stressor, for example, it showed a less severe physiological response than an animal that could not anticipate a stressor (Mason, 1971). Further, research conducted during the 1980s showed that different emotions produce different patterns of ANS activation, casting further doubt on Selye's idea of a generalized physiological response to any environmental demand (Ekman, Levenson, & Friesen, 1983).

Stress isn't unique to humans. Other species, like this oil-covered survivor of Hurricane Katrina, also experience a physiological reaction in response to stressful situations.

How We Adapt to Stress   In addition to disputing the notion of stress as a general physiological response, researchers have updated other ideas in the physiology of stress. Most accounts of the physiology of stress (such as Selye's) think of stress as a deviation from balance. Recovery from stress occurs when all systems return to normal. This view is based on the notion of homeostasis—the idea that unless we are being provoked by something, we are operating at a state of balance, humming along at an even-keeled *baseline* state, and we return to that same state after the stress. Moreover, homeostasis implies that just one system in the body struggles to return to baseline at a time (*homeo-* means "same"). For example, suppose you are walking in a desert: The homeostasis view says that you would sweat to cool your body to return to an ideal temperature. In doing so, you would also become dehydrated (Sapolsky, 1998). If you think about it for a minute, you'll realize that it's not just your sweat glands that need to adapt to the desert. So a new concept was needed to explain the more complex and dynamic changes that occur when the body is stressed.

Yet some researchers have offered an alternative explanation: Rather than a state of balance, our normal state is one of actively responding to the world around us. This more dynamic, responsive "resting" state is known as **allostasis,** which means that the body achieves stability through change (Schulkin, 2005; Sterling & Eyer, 1988). *Allo* means "different" or "changing."

connection

The concept of homeostasis is key to drive theories of motivation.

See Chapter 11, p. 417.

allostasis
process by which the body achieves stability through physiological change.

If we think of the baseline state as one of dynamic responsiveness, it is easier to understand the effects of stressful challenges on the body. To return to the example of walking in the desert: The concept of allostasis emphasizes that your body would respond in many ways, not simply by sweating. Your kidneys would start producing less output; mucous membranes in your eyes and skin would dry out; even your veins and arteries would constrict to maintain blood pressure with a smaller volume of blood. The concept of allostasis makes clear that our bodies can adaptively respond to challenge for only a short period of time. If we are pushed too long, and the kinds of active attempts the body makes to adapt are sustained, we are taxed, and the body starts to wear down. This is how stress causes illness.

Stress and the Brain   So far we have emphasized how stress affects a wide array of physiological responses, most of which involve systems outside the central nervous system. But what about the brain? We tend to think of stress as being caused by processes within the brain, for it is our interpretations of the events in the world around us that trigger emotions. In another example of the bidirectional relationship between nature and nurture, the physiological activation triggered by stress also affects the brain. Cortisol has a profound effect on the hippocampus, a brain structure that plays a pivotal role in memory. It turns out that the hippocampus contains one of the greatest concentrations of cortisol receptors in the brain (McEwen, De Kloet, & Rostene, 1986).

connections

The hippocampus, located deep inside the brain, is critical for memory formation.

See Chapter 3, p. 101, and Chapter 7, p. 272.

Why? Because this brain structure—which plays a crucial role in the transformation of short-term to long-term memories—also plays a part in terminating the activation of the HPA axis via a negative feedback mechanism (Kim & Yoon, 1998). Unfortunately, stress-related cortisol release can cause dendrites to wither and shrink, and this can interfere with several types of memory. Stress reduces neurogenesis in the hippocampus, and it may inhibit the synaptic plasticity in the hippocampus and neocortex, impacting learning and memory formation (Artola, 2008; Wang et al., 2008).

If a person clearly cannot cope with the demands created by a situation, stress escalates to the point where it wears down body systems. Whether or not a person can cope depends on how well he or she adapts psychologically to the situation by modifying either the situation, his or her interpretation of the situation, or the feelings it creates. Such is the domain of coping. Coping plays a big role in the duration of stress responses and whether they develop sufficiently to become harmful.

1. According to the definition provided in the text, which of the following is the best example of stress?
   a. Maria is studying for one exam.
   b. Maria is studying for three exams on the same day, but she has a handle on all three.
   c. Maria is studying for two exams on the same day and feels unprepared for both of them.
   d. Maria is angry at her boyfriend.

2. The _____ view of stress focuses on the physiological changes that occur when someone encounters an excessively challenging situation.
   a. stimulus
   b. response
   c. relational
   d. situational

3. The model of adaptation that says there is stability through change is the
   a. functional view
   b. physiological view
   c. homeostatic view
   d. allostatic view

4. Which part of the nervous system becomes most involved when we are feeling stressed?
   a. hypothalamic-pituitary-adrenal (HPA) axis
   b. temporal lobes
   c. hippocampus
   d. frontal lobes

Answers can be found at the end of the chapter.

Coping

Even though stress results from situations in which we feel that we cannot manage or cope with the challenges we face, we are probably coping with those challenges in some way whether we realize it or not. Generally, **coping** refers to anything people do to deal with or manage stress or emotions. When we walk away from someone who is making us angry, or complain about our boss to a friend, we are coping with stresses in our lives. In this section we explore various ways people cope with stress.

coping
act of dealing with stress or emotions.

COPING STRATEGIES

People don't like feeling bad. So they try to get out of situations that create unpleasantness or look for ways to change their negative feelings. Psychologists Richard Lazarus and Susan Folkman (1984) differentiated between these two types of coping strategies, labeling them *problem-focused* and *emotion-focused* coping. Social support combines problem-focused and emotion-focused coping strategies. Figure 12.5 provides an overview of these three coping strategies.

problem-focused coping
way of dealing with stress that aims to change the situation that is creating stress.

Problem-Focused Coping Problem-focused coping involves strategies that aim to change the situation that is creating stress. For example, if your roommate plays a stereo loudly while you are sleeping, you might choose to discuss it with her, buy earplugs, or cut the speaker wires. Each of these choices is a

problem-focused strategy	Solve the problem Seek social support Take assertive action	Roommate's stereo too loud: Focus on how to make it quiet. An assertive act might be to cut the stereo speaker wires.	
emotion-focused strategy	Reappraise Distancing Use escape-avoidance Seek social support Exercise self-control Emotional disclosure	Break up with a partner: Focus on how to feel better. An escape-avoidance act may be to take a vacation to get away from the former partner. Write about it to unburden emotions.	
social support strategy	Combines problem-focused and emotion-focused strategies Develop social connectedness Seek advice from or talk with friends and loved ones	Support groups: Giving and showing support to other people may increase longevity.	

FIGURE **12.5** **COPING STRATEGIES.** We tend to apply problem-focused coping strategies to change a stressful situation and emotion-focused coping strategies in situations that we feel we cannot control.

form of problem-focused coping, as each is geared toward changing the situation that created the stress. Examples of problem-focused coping strategies include devising a plan to solve the problem, seeking social support as a way to gather information, and taking assertive action. Problem-focused coping tends to focus attention on the stress-provoking situation, and we are most likely to use it when we feel that we can do something to change the situation.

Emotion-Focused Coping
In contrast, **emotion-focused coping** aims to regulate the experience of distress. Lazarus and Folkman describe several forms of emotion-focused coping, including *reappraisal*, the emotional regulation strategy of reevaluation of a situation in light of new information or additional thought; *distancing*, or attempting to separate oneself from an emotional experience; *escape-avoidance*, wishful thinking or doing something to get one's

emotion-focused coping
way of dealing with stress that aims to regulate the experience of distress.

467

mind off the situation (such as going to the movies); *seeking social support* by talking with friends for purposes of emotional support; *self-control,* or trying to regulate one's feelings or actions regarding the problem; and *accepting responsibility,* acknowledging one's role in the stress-eliciting situation (Lazarus & Folkman, 1984).

connection

Emotion regulation is another term for the strategies we use to alter our emotional state and is similar to emotion-focused coping.

See Chapter 11, p. 436.

Emotion-focused coping may be beneficial when a situation is beyond one's control, and certain types of emotion-focused coping—especially reappraisal—can be helpful in regulating the emotional aspects of stress. But it can also be problematic. Willful suppression of upsetting emotions, which is a form of self-control, can lead to chronic physiological arousal and is associated with poor psychological adjustment (Gross & Levenson, 1993; Gross, Richards, & John, 2006). Moreover, some strategies that we use to reduce the experience of distress, such as drinking, smoking, and other forms of drug use, may be maladaptive (Hien & Miele, 2003).

It is widely believed that a good way to cope with stress is to vent, or "let it all out." The implication is that relieving ourselves of a burden can be beneficial. James Pennebaker has developed and tested a technique known as **emotional disclosure** that enables people to unburden (Pennebaker, 1995). In a typical emotional disclosure task, people are instructed to write for about 15 minutes about a recent emotional experience—in particular, one that they have found troubling, that still bothers them from time to time, and that they haven't discussed much with other people. Participants in the control condition write for a similar amount of time about nonemotional events, such as what they did the day before. Emotional disclosure consistently improves a number of health outcomes, including health variables related to HIV/AIDS, immune function, and cancer (O'Cleirigh et al., 2008; Petrie et al., 2004; Smyth, 1998; Stanton et al., 2002).

emotional disclosure

way of coping with stress through writing or talking about the situation.

Writing about a stressful experience is one way of working through the negative emotions associated with it.

How might writing about one's emotional experiences, especially traumatic ones, benefit health? There are several possible explanations. People in both Western and non-Western cultures believe that confession is beneficial. For the Ndembu of West Africa, for instance, public confession allows for the transformation of negative feelings into positive ones in the community, thereby promoting social harmony (Georges, 1995). It is also thought that *not* working through difficult emotions taxes the body, as research on the association between emotional suppression and ANS arousal suggests (Gross & Levenson, 1993). When confession or disclosure occurs, then, one should observe a decrease in sympathetic nervous system activation or a return to a more relaxed state. In fact, numerous laboratory studies have found that just talking about a traumatic event creates noticeable reductions in autonomic measures such as blood pressure and sweating (Pennebaker, 1995).

Social Support A coping strategy that combines problem- and emotion-focused coping is seeking social support. Our friends and loved ones provide advice, give hugs, or simply listen when we are under stress. Social support not only is one of the most frequently used ways of coping but also can benefit physical health. The *direct effects hypothesis* states that social support is beneficial to mental and physical health whether or not the person is under stress. Cohen (2004) has pointed out that being part of a social network guarantees the availability of certain resources. Our social network may offer guidelines for health-related behaviors, help us regulate our emotions, and give us a sense of identity. We may learn from friends, for instance, that running or jogging can help us feel better when we're stressed. Examples of social connectedness include being married, belonging to social groups such as churches or clubs, and having many friends. Friends provide an outlet for sharing emotional distress, offering comfort as well as advice.

connection

If you have a Facebook page, you are in an electronic social network.

See Chapter 1, p. 29.

Alternatively, social support may serve as a buffer against the impact of stress. This is known as the *buffering hypothesis,* which states that social support works as a buffer only under certain conditions, such as a highly stressful life. In fact, one influential study found that regular participation in a support group in which members talked about their emotional difficulties improved well-being and extended survival in women with advanced breast cancer (Spiegel et al., 1989), though this finding has not replicated consistently (Edelman et al., 1999; Edmonds, Lockwood, & Cunningham, 1999; Goodwin, 2004; Goodwin et al., 2001).

The extent to which a person is integrated into a *social network* influences whether social resources are beneficial to health. A social network is simply a cluster of related people, such as family members, spouses, friends, coworkers, or neighbors. When people are well integrated into a social network, social support can buffer the effects of stress by providing interpersonal resources for emotional support and problem solving (Cohen & Wills, 1985). This is why people with close friendships have an easier time dealing with stressful events than do "loners," who have no one to turn to when they feel overwhelmed.

The health benefits of social connectedness include longer life and reduced susceptibility to colds (Berkman & Glass, 2000; Cohen et al., 2003). A recent study that followed more than 12,000 people over 32 years examined the influence of social networks on quitting smoking (Christakis & Fowler, 2008). Social networks influenced the likelihood that a person would stop smoking, but not all social connections had the same effect. If a spouse stopped smoking, the chance the other spouse would also stop went up by 67%; if a friend stopped smoking, the chance another friend stopped went up by 36%; and if a coworker stopped smoking, the chance another worker stopped went up by 34%. So the effect of the other person's behavior on any given person depended to some extent on how close they were to each other.

Social networks may be harmful to health as well. For instance, researchers looked at the influence of obesity in the same social network study of 12,000 people. The risk of obesity spread among people who were socially connected. In other words, if a person became obese (body mass index [BMI] > 30), his or her friends, family members, spouse, or neighbors were more likely to become obese. As was true with smoking, however, not all social connections had the same effect. For instance, if a person's friend became obese over a given period of time, that person's chance of becoming obese increased 57%; if a sibling became obese, the chance increased 40%; and if a spouse became obese, the chance increased 37% (Christakis & Fowler, 2007). Moreover, gender mattered. Individuals of the same gender in a social network influenced same-sexed individuals more than opposite-sexed individuals.

Social resources clearly play a role in health-related behavior and how we manage stress, but so do our own personal resources. Life is not just a course in stress management, but rather a daily journey through a series of joys as well as challenges.

THE POSITIVE PSYCHOLOGY OF COPING

Traditionally, research on stress and coping has focused on how people respond to threatening situations and manage the distress associated with them. For years, however, some psychologists have argued that it is an oversimplification to assume that stress involves only negative emotions and their management (Folkman & Moskowitz, 2000; Lazarus, Kanner, & Folkman, 1980; Seligman & Csikszentmihalyi, 2000). This section discusses various ways in which positive psychological states have been studied in relation to stress and coping.

Positive Traits, Positive Emotions Some people approach the world in a positive way, and as a result their interpretation or experience of distress is reduced compared to that of others. *Optimists* tend to emphasize the positive, see the glass as "half full" rather than "half empty," and believe that things will turn out well (Scheier, Weintraub, & Carver, 1989). *Pessimists*, by contrast, emphasize the negative; for them, the glass is always half empty and the future uncertain. Optimists are less likely to feel helpless or depressed, adjust better to

negative life events than do pessimists, and show better general mental health than pessimists (Chang, 1998; Smith, Young, & Lee, 2004). Optimism may also benefit physical health (Kubzansky et al., 2001). By seeing the world positively, optimists may appraise events in such a way that negative emotions are less likely and positive emotions more likely. They may be more likely to see potentially stressful situations as challenges rather than threats.

Surprisingly, believing that you have some control over situations in life, especially traumatic situations, can improve your psychological health (Taylor, 1989). Health psychologist Shelley Taylor has studied various groups of people suffering from chronic, debilitating, and often fatal diseases such as breast cancer, heart disease, and HIV/AIDS. She has found that people who believe they have some control over their illness—in spite of medical evidence to the contrary—are actually happier and less stressed than less optimistic people with the same diseases (Hegelson & Taylor, 1993; Reed et al., 1994; Taylor, 1989). As it turns out, these perceptions of control provide the greatest benefits in situations that are severe or uncontrollable (Taylor et al., 2000).

Positive emotions may facilitate recovery from the physiological effects of negative emotions. For example, Fredrickson and Levenson (1998) showed participants a fear-eliciting film and followed it with either a sad, a pleasant, or a neutral film. The researchers measured cardiovascular activity throughout the film-viewing and post-film-viewing period. Cardiovascular activation elicited by the fear film returned to baseline levels more quickly in people who saw the pleasant film after the fear film, but not in people in the sad or neutral conditions. So positive emotions may help the body return to a state of calmness. Tugade and Fredrickson (2004) looked at how resilience affected people's ability to recover from stress. *Resilience* is a personality trait that means being more flexible and able to bounce back from difficult situations. Resilient people experience quicker recovery from stress-induced cardiovascular arousal, in part because they are more likely to find some positive meaning in a difficult situation (Tugade & Fredrickson, 2004).

Finding Meaning   Perhaps the key to psychological health is to be open enough to notice the other things going on in life, even in the midst of tragedy. Positive psychological traits and states do play a big role in whether people are able to find meaning in stressful and tragic events (Folkman, 1997; Folkman & Moskowitz, 2000; Park & Folkman, 1997; Tugade & Fredrickson, 2004). People with terminal illnesses who notice beauty amidst their pain and find opportunities for positive experience in their lives are happier than those who don't, and they may even live longer (Folkman, 1997; Moskowitz, 2003). As we mentioned in Chapter 11, resilient people who managed to experience positive moods amidst their despair in the wake of the September 11, 2001, terrorist attacks were more likely to thrive and less likely to fall into depression than those who were less resilient (Fredrickson et al., 2003).

A fascinating set of studies by Elissa Epel and her colleagues reveals some of the connections between biology and environment that play a role in people's responses to stress and their effects on health. In the next "Psychology in the Real World," we describe how Epel and her colleagues (2004) demonstrated that stress can literally affect aging at the cellular level.

nature & nurture
Stress makes your cells age more rapidly.

quick quiz 12.2: Coping

1. You buy earplugs so you can sleep when your roommate plays loud music at 1:00 a.m. You have used what kind of coping?
   a. problem-focused
   b. emotion-focused
   c. stimulus-focused
   d. meaning-focused

2. Research has found that having a well-connected social network of friends, family, neighbors, and coworkers is _____ for health outcomes
   a. never beneficial
   b. sometimes beneficial
   c. sometimes beneficial and sometimes harmful
   d. always beneficial

Effects of Chronic Stress on Aging

Stress often makes people look worn out. As mentioned earlier, this is one of Selye's main ideas: Physiologically, long-term stress wears out or wears down the body, making a person more vulnerable to illness (the exhaustion stage). People often refer to the stresses of life as wearing them out or causing gray hairs. Is there any evidence, however, that this everyday logic has any basis in the physiology of aging? Can stress actually make you age more quickly?

In an innovative study of the physiological effects of stress, psychologist Elissa Epel and her colleagues examined indicators of cellular aging in healthy women who were biological mothers of either normal or chronically ill children. The mothers reported on the amount of stress they perceived in their daily lives, using a standard questionnaire.

The researchers derived indicators of cellular aging from tests on blood samples collected from each woman. In particular, they examined the telomeres of chromosomes in the DNA of certain white blood cells. *Telomeres* are part of the chromosome involved in replication during the process of cell division. With age, telomeres shorten; moreover, the activity of telomerase, an enzyme that protects telomeres, decreases with age. Both of these variables are good measures of aging.

Epel and her colleagues measured stress not in terms of life conditions per se but in terms of the duration of

3. Seeing the "glass as half full," or being optimistic, is likely to have what kind of an effect on a person's response to stress and illness?
   a. no real effect
   b. negative effect
   c. a positive effect
   d. the same effect as being pessimistic would

4. Who would be most likely to bounce back quickly from a very stressful experience?
   a. a young person
   b. a pessimist
   c. someone who holds in his or her feelings and pretends the event did not happen
   d. a resilient person

Answers can be found at the end of the chapter.

How Stress and Coping Affect Health

psychosomatic theory
the idea that emotional factors can lead to the occurrence or worsening of illness.

Our discussion so far has implied that stress increases a person's susceptibility to disease. This idea is one of the oldest expressions of the interplay between nature and nurture, and it forms the central tenet of **psychosomatic theory.** Even though people tend to use the term *psychosomatic* to refer to an illness that is "all in the head" or, by implication, "made up," this is a misconception of the actual theory. Rather, *psychosomatics* deal with how emotional factors can increase the likelihood of certain disorders occurring or worsening.

stress and the perceived severity of stress experienced by the women. They found that the more stress a woman perceived in her life, the shorter the telomeres and the lower the level of telomerase activity in her blood, conditions that imply older cells. In practical terms, these women's cells were "the equivalent of 9–17 additional years" older than those of women who perceived less stress (Epel et al., 2004, p. 17314). A different analysis of the same sample found a positive relationship between measures of cellular aging and the stress-relevant hormones norepinephrine and cortisol (Epel et al., 2006). Even though we do not yet know how cellular aging translates into body age and health changes, this research provides a fascinating example of how stress can wear down the body.

Ask any mother of young children how she feels. Chances are she'll tell you she's exhausted. Long-term stress that is perceived as severe can speed up the process of cellular aging.

Eating in response to stress may make us feel good, but it may also make us more susceptible to certain diseases.

The field of health psychology grew out of psychosomatic medicine. **Health psychology** is the study of psychological factors related to health and illness. It includes disease onset, prevention, treatment, and rehabilitation and involves clinical practice as well as research. Research in health psychology ranges from studies of how psychological variables enhance health or increase susceptibility to disease to the role of social factors in doctor–patient communication.

There are two primary ways of explaining the relationship between stress and illness: Both illustrate the dynamic interplay among environmental situations, people's interpretations of them, and changes in body functioning. The **physiological reactivity model** examines how the sustained physiological activation associated with the stress response can affect body systems in such a way as to increase the likelihood that illness or disease occurs. As such, this model is rooted in psychosomatic medicine. By contrast, the **health behavior approach** focuses on the behaviors in which people engage, such as diet, exercise, or substance abuse, that may make them more susceptible to illness or may enhance health. These explanations are not mutually exclusive. For example, a person

health psychology
the study of psychological factors related to health and illness.

physiological reactivity model
explanation for the causal role of stress-related bodily changes in illness.

health behavior approach
explanation for illness or health that focuses on the role of behaviors such as diet, exercise, and substance abuse .

how stress and coping affect health **473**

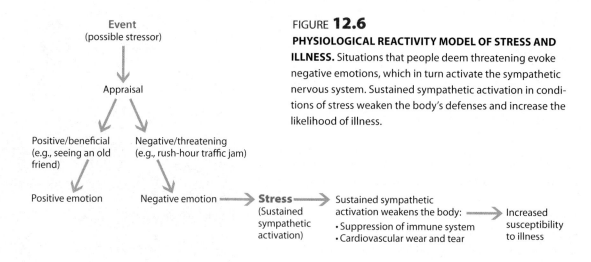

Event
(possible stressor)

↓

Appraisal

↙ ↘

Positive/beneficial
(e.g., seeing an old
friend)

Negative/threatening
(e.g., rush-hour traffic jam)

↓ ↓

Positive emotion

Negative emotion → **Stress** → Sustained sympathetic
(Sustained activation weakens the body: → Increased
sympathetic • Suppression of immune system susceptibility
activation) • Cardiovascular wear and tear to illness

FIGURE **12.6**

PHYSIOLOGICAL REACTIVITY MODEL OF STRESS AND ILLNESS. Situations that people deem threatening evoke negative emotions, which in turn activate the sympathetic nervous system. Sustained sympathetic activation in conditions of stress weaken the body's defenses and increase the likelihood of illness.

might experience sustained blood pressure elevation due to stress and drink heavily during a time of intense stress, both of which would affect the person's health.

Figure 12.6 depicts the physiological reactivity model. (We discuss the health behavior approach later in the chapter.) You will notice similarities between this and the emotion/stress process diagram in Figure 12.2: Each begins with the elicitation of negative emotion and stress. In the physiological reactivity model, however, the activation of the sympathetic nervous system persists and creates sustained physiological arousal. Recall Selye's notion that the physiological effects of sustained stress contribute to the wearing out of the body. This is the exhaustion stage, which may create a greater susceptibility to illness.

A wide array of body systems may be affected by sustained stress, but a few key systems have been the focus of much research.

Let's consider what we mean by sustained physiological arousal and why it can be harmful to health. Earlier we said that the sympathetic branch of the autonomic nervous system activates organ systems to enable an animal to respond to emergency situations. So the effects of sympathetic arousal on the heart and lungs (increasing pumping and oxygen intake) help the animal act quickly and thus survive. From an evolutionary perspective, these physiological effects were advantageous because of their ability to enable a quick and efficient response. However, the same type of emotional response occurs in daily life, in most cases without an outlet for action—for example, when you are stuck in traffic or annoyed with a coworker. So the activation persists for hours or days, or is elicited repeatedly in similar situations over many years. Under such conditions, you can become ill as a result of the recurring arousal produced by stress-related body changes (Sapolsky, 1998).

Especially susceptible to the effects of sustained arousal is the **cardiovascular system,** which consists of the heart and all the blood vessels of the body. During activation of the sympathetic nervous system, heart rate and blood pressure increase. In sustained physiological activation, heart rate and blood pressure remain elevated or are activated repeatedly over extended periods. Frequent blood pressure elevations can damage arteries by reducing their elasticity and increasing the likelihood of fatty buildup. These processes set the stage for heart disease.

Also subject to the effects of sustained arousal is the immune system—whose impaired function increases susceptibility to many kinds of disease. Sustained activation of the HPA axis leads to sustained release of cortisol, which inhibits the production of certain immune cells. In the short term, suppression of immune cell production makes sense, because in an emergency these immune cells might not be immediately necessary. Over the long term, however, immune suppression makes a person more susceptible to certain diseases. Interest in this possibility, and its implications for health care, has given rise to a field of study known as **psychoneuroimmunology (PNI),** the science of how psychological factors relate to immune changes. The story of the birth of PNI illustrates groundbreaking work that showed for the first time the link between psychological states and immune function.

psychoneuro-immunology (PNI)
the science of how psychological factors relate to changes in the immune system.

One way of assessing the risk of heart disease is to take a stress test, aptly named because it subjects the cardiovascular system to increasing physiological activation.

breaking new ground
Psychological Processes and the Immune System

With the general adaptation syndrome, Hans Selye provided a framework for thinking about how stress might make the body vulnerable to disease, and he suggested that this vulnerability might be due to the effects of stress on the immune system. As we will see, however, no one knew if psychological factors could affect the immune system until some groundbreaking research of the 1970s.

IMMUNE SYSTEM AS AN AUTONOMOUS DEFENSE SYSTEM

The job of the immune system is to defend the body against foreign substances. Before the 1970s, the prevailing view was that the immune system operated quite independently of the central nervous system. In other words, everyone believed the immune system was invulnerable to thoughts, feelings, and stress. As far as anyone knew at the time, there were no anatomical or chemical connections between immune system structures and any aspect of the nervous system that would allow them to communicate. Even though most physicians believed that stress could make people sick, or at least sicker, they did not consider it physiologically possible for psychological conditions to have any effect on the immune system. But that was about to change.

CONNECTING THE BRAIN AND THE IMMUNE SYSTEM

Robert Ader was replicating some classic experiments on conditioned taste aversion. Recall from Chapter 8 that conditioned taste aversion is a form of classical conditioning in which a neutral taste, after repeated pairing with an agent that can induce nausea and vomiting, will come to produce those characteristics when it is presented alone. In the early research, saccharin water was paired with radiation, which causes nausea (Garcia, Kimeldorf, & Koelling, 1955). In his work, Ader paired a chemical that induces nausea with saccharin water to create taste aversion to the saccharin water. Some rats were exposed to a lot of saccharin water even after they had learned to associate it with nausea. And something unusual was happening to those rats. They were dying! But why? Ader remembered that the toxin he was using to induce nausea also happened to be an immunosuppressant; that is, something that suppresses immune system function. Perhaps, he reasoned, in addition to learning to avoid saccharin water, the rats were acquiring conditioned immunosuppression from the repeated pairing of the saccharin solution with the immunosuppressant.

connection
Conditioned taste aversion is a type of learning similar to what happened when Pavlov's dogs learned to salivate to the sound of a bell (classical conditioning).
See Chapter 8, p. 315.

To suggest any connection between psychological processes and immune system functioning ran counter to the view in medicine that the immune system operates independently of the central nervous system (Boorboor, 2002). Nevertheless, Ader and his colleague, Nicholas Cohen, embarked on a series of experiments to determine whether immunosuppression could be classically conditioned in rats (Ader & Cohen, 1975). They conditioned nausea or "illness-induced" taste aversion in an experimental group by pairing saccharin water with injections of the immunosuppressant. They also created two control groups: a group that was injected with a placebo around the time they drank saccharin water (which served as a control for the stress-inducing effects of injection in the absence of conditioning) and a group that received the immunosuppressant and plain water (a nonconditioning control group).

Ader and Cohen needed a way to test whether the immune system was suppressed in rats with immunosuppressant-induced conditioned taste aversion. They reintroduced the conditioned stimulus, in this case saccharin, and then introduced an **antigen**, a substance foreign to the body. They injected the antigen, sheep blood cells, into the bloodstreams of all the rats. In healthy animals, exposure to a foreign substance like this should cause certain immune cells to release chemicals called antibodies. If immune suppression had been conditioned to the taste of saccharin water, the taste of saccharin water should impair the antibody response to the antigen. Because it takes a while for the body to manufacture an antibody response to an antigen, the experimenters waited a few days and then sacrificed the rats to collect their blood. They found that the blood of rats that had been conditioned to avoid saccharin via the immunosuppressant showed a much weaker antibody response to the sheep blood cells than did rats injected with the placebo. That is, the blood from rats with conditioned immunosuppression showed a weaker defense against a foreign substance.

antigen
any foreign substance that triggers an immune response.

THE BIRTH OF PSYCHONEUROIMMUNOLOGY

Some scientists were amazed by these results. By demonstrating that one could classically condition the suppression of an antibody response to an antigen, Ader and Cohen had shown that there must be connections between the CNS and the immune system. How else could a change in immune system functioning be learned?

Not long after Ader and Cohen published their results, some important findings in biomedical science gave increased credibility to the finding of conditioned immunosuppression. In the late 1970s and early 1980s, scientists discovered that the ANS is linked to immune system structures such as the thymus gland and that immune cells have receptors for and can produce certain stress hormones (Smith & Blalock, 1988). There was now solid behavioral and biological evidence for what Selye and others had believed all along—that psychological processes and immune processes interact. In this way, the field of psychoneuroimmunology was born.

STRESS AND IMMUNE FUNCTION

Today, the field of psychoneuroimmunology (PNI) examines the relationships among the brain, thought, feeling, endocrine changes, and immune system functioning. As a discipline, PNI is concerned with any kind of connection between psychological processes and the immune system. For instance, there are chemical linkages between psychological processes and immune system changes. Chemicals involved in the stress response, such as cortisol and norepinephrine, influence the number of immune cells produced in the body. This is a means by which stress can affect the immune system.

Furthermore, connections between the central nervous system and immune system are bidirectional. That is, just as stress can change immune function, certain immune changes (such as the release of chemicals called *cytokines*, which regulate immune response) can feed back and influence brain areas involved in mood regulation (Nishida et al., 2002; Miller, Capuron, & Raison, 2005).

A newborn's immune system is still developing. Antibodies present in the mother's breast milk protect the baby from infection until her own immune system has matured.

Overview of the Immune System.
The human immune system defends the body against invasion by disease, inspects the body for cells that may take on dangerous mutations, and performs basic housekeeping functions such as cleaning up cellular debris after an injury. There are two basic lines of defense: natural immunity and acquired immunity. **Natural immunity** consists of a number of inborn processes that help remove foreign substances from the body. These responses typically are very quick, and they provide the first line of defense upon exposure to antigens. Forms of natural immunity include phagocytosis and inflammation. *Phagocytosis* is a process by which a white blood cell engulfs a substance (usually an antigen or another cell) and digests it or moves it to a place where it will be destroyed. *Inflammation* is a process by which tissues are restored following injury. After you cut your finger, for example, blood vessels at the injured area contract and dilate to increase blood flow to the area, creating warmth and redness. The dilated vessels then release inflammatory chemicals, and damaged cells release enzymes to destroy invading microorganisms.

natural immunity
form of immunity that is the first response to antigens.

acquired immunity
immunity provided by antibodies or cells produced in the body in response to specific antigens.

The immune system depends on several kinds of white blood cells, including those responsible for phagocytosis. Other white blood cells, called *lymphocytes*, control acquired immunity. **Acquired immunity** involves a number of endocrine and cellular processes that recognize specific antigens and then reproduce specialized cells or circulating proteins to fight those antigens. Acquired immunity is so called because it involves experience—an effective immune response occurs only after prior exposure to a particular antigen. For instance, every cold we have leads to a learned or acquired immune response, and as a result we are less likely to get sick if we are exposed to that particular virus again. Acquired immune responses take longer to initiate than natural immune responses because the former involve recognition processes and duplication of cells. On subsequent exposure to a specific antigen, however, acquired immune responses can be rapid and efficient. This latter fact forms the basis for how vaccination protects against disease.

Acquired immunity involves two classes of lymphocytes, called B and T lymphocytes. In response to specific antigens, *B lymphocytes* release antibodies into the bloodstream. Antibodies destroy antigens directly. The *T lymphocytes*, or "T cells," fight antigens not by releasing antibodies but by means of cellular processes, collectively known as **cellular immunity**.

cellular immunity
the immune response that occurs when the T lymphocytes (T cells) fight antigens.

Research on Stress, Immune Function, and Health

The physiological reactivity model predicts that the physiological effects of stress, when sustained over time, will eventually weaken the immune system. Theorists have extended the model a step further, reasoning that *immunosuppression* increases susceptibility to disease by reducing the body's ability to fight invading bacteria or viruses or its ability to fight off potentially cancerous cells, or both. This is why psychologists, in collaboration with medical researchers, began conducting studies of stress and immune function. The basic idea is simple: If researchers can show that stress affects immune variables, it should follow that such immune system changes would leave the organism more susceptible to disease. In reality, many studies have shown linkages between stress and numerous immune system measures, but very few have shown that these reductions actually affect susceptibility to disease. Let's look at some of the major research on stress and immune function in both animals and humans.

Results from animal research show that a variety of stressors can weaken responses to antigens, reduce the numbers of certain immune cells, and impair immune cell functions such as responses to vaccines (Glaser & Kiecolt-Glaser, 2005). Some of the stressors tested in animal studies are maternal separation, inescapable shock, abrupt temperature change, and loud noise. A few studies have manipulated stress in humans by randomly assigning people to participate in a stressful task, such as public speaking, or an emotion-evoking task, such as writing about a traumatic event (Pennebaker, Kiecolt-Glaser, & Glaser, 1988). The more common approach in human research, however, is to rely on naturally occurring stressors such as final exams, sleep deprivation, loud noise, bereavement, divorce, and caring for an Alzheimer's or AIDS patient.

Research on the effects of stress on the human immune system often makes use of natural stressors, such as exam time.

In these studies, different measures of immunity are dependent variables. Among these measures are numbers of certain lymphocytes; tests of how effectively certain lymphocytes function either in a test tube or in a living person; the toxicity of tumor-fighting cells called *natural killer cells;* and the quantities of chemicals that regulate lymphocytes.

Although the major finding in studies of humans is that stressors are associated with changes in various kinds of immune function, it is often difficult to know whether the observed immune changes have meaningful effects on health. A few studies address this concern by including measures of illness that are controlled by immune mechanisms. In a study of people caring for Alzheimer's patients, the caregivers and a matched comparison group (all volunteers for the study) received small puncture wounds. They then returned to the laboratory for wound healing assessments and blood tests to measure immune variables. Compared to the comparison group, the caregivers exhibited substantially slower healing of puncture wounds and reductions in chemicals involved in healing (Kiecolt-Glaser et al., 1995).

Stress has also been studied in relation to the common cold, which is an infectious illness mediated by the immune system. In particular, Sheldon Cohen and his colleagues (1993, 2003) have studied the interplay of stress and social connectedness in people's susceptibility to the common cold. They have actually exposed people to the common cold, measured whether they acquired a cold, and, especially, looked at how the experience of stress or people's social resources in managing stress influence whether or not people got sick, using clever dependent measures such as weighing tissues to approximate how much mucous people created! Susceptibility, however, is the key issue here, as exposure to the cold virus does not guarantee a person will get sick. For example, you and your roommate might both spend time with a friend who is sick, but only one of you might catch the cold. In these studies, Cohen and his colleagues exposed people to a virus; measured perceived stress in some participants, external stressors; and social networks; and clinically verified whether or not people got sick. They found that perception of stress—rather than the number of stressors to which people had been exposed—predicted whether or not they develop a cold (Cohen, Tyrell, & Smith, 1993). Further, having more meaningful social interactions in one's daily life reduces susceptibility to colds (Cohen et al., 2003). Perceiving oneself as lower in socioeconomic status also predicts susceptibility to the common cold in people exposed to the virus, independent of one's actual socioeconomic status (Cohen et al., 2008).

In terms of the relationship between stress and illness, then, it is not the situation as much as how the individual evaluates that situation that drives the stress and its effects. Notice that in terms of susceptibility to the common cold, *perceived* stress mattered more than actual exposure to stressors; *perceived* low socioeconomic status mattered more than actual socioeconomic status. These results remind us of the importance of defining and measuring stress not just as a stimulus (number of stressors), but also in terms of how people respond to the stressors and

nature & nurture

Having plenty of meaningful social relationships can protect you from the common cold.

cope with possible stress. As discussed earlier, social support and social connectedness might buffer the effects of stress by providing interpersonal resources for emotional support and problem solving (Cohen & Wills, 1985).

PSYCHOLOGICAL RISK FACTORS FOR HEART DISEASE

Heart disease is the number one killer of both men and women in the United States (American Heart Association, 2005; Lethbridge-Cejku & Vickerie, 2005). We saw earlier that the physiological changes associated with negative emotions and stress influence the cardiovascular system. Research has identified a number of psychological risk factors for heart disease. In this section we tell the story of how this research began and describe the main areas of research on psychology and cardiovascular health.

Type A and Anger   For centuries scientists have argued that personality and emotion might play a role in the development of heart disease, but research on this topic did not begin until the middle of the 20th century. In fact, it began in the waiting room of cardiologist Meyer Friedman's office in San Francisco. A janitor pointed out to Friedman that the upholstery on the chairs in his waiting room was wearing out much more quickly than that on chairs in other waiting rooms. He wondered whether Friedman's patients fidgeted a lot. Friedman said "yes." In fact, he had noticed that many of his patients were tense and impatient. Friedman and his colleague Ray Rosenman decided to study the effects of such an emotional style on a person's risk of developing heart disease. They described a set of psychological characteristics that they believed put people at risk for heart disease: impatience, competitiveness, hostility, and time urgency. They named it the **Type A Behavior Pattern (TABP)** and explained that this pattern emerges when under conditions of challenge or stress. That is, Type A people are not always impatient and hostile, but when they find themselves in high-pressure situations they exhibit this pattern of behavior. Friedman and Rosenman hypothesized that people who exhibit the TABP *under provocation* are at greater risk for heart disease than those who do not.

Friedman and Rosenman embarked on an ambitious research program to see if they could measure the Type A pattern and determine whether it increases a person's risk for heart disease. They developed an interview to measure Type A behavior and distinguish it from Type B behavior, which is a more relaxed, laid-back style. Then they designed a study in which healthy people were evaluated on psychological and health-related variables at some initial baseline point and then assessed periodically over a period that spanned more than 20 years. This long-term study would make it possible to see whether certain personality characteristics

Time urgency is a component of the Type A behavior pattern that does not predict heart disease after all.

Type A Behavior Pattern
a way of responding to challenge or stress, characterized by hostility, impatience, competitiveness, and time urgency.

predicted changes in an individual's health status. Their sample consisted of 3,000 healthy white men, whom they tracked for 8 years in their original study (Rosenman et al., 1964). They found that Type A behavior predicted the incidence of coronary heart disease, over and above such traditional risk factors as blood pressure, cholesterol, and age. This finding shocked the medical world, for no one had anticipated that something psychological could affect heart disease.

Soon other major studies replicated the finding that the presence of Type A behavior predicted the incidence of heart disease and extended it to women (French-Belgian Collaborative Group, 1982; Haynes et al., 1978). Twenty-two years later, Rosenman and Friedman conducted a follow-up study on their original participants. Surprisingly, Type A did *not* predict death from heart disease in this group. Then another major study of men and women produced null findings (Shekelle et al., 1985). People began to question whether psychological factors could put anyone at greater risk for heart disease.

But could it really be that Type A did not affect the incidence of heart disease after all? Karen Matthews wondered if the concept just needed to be refined. After all, Type A is a collection of various characteristics. She took a closer look at the follow-up interviews from Friedman and Rosenman's original sample to see how each component of the Type A pattern (hostility, time urgency, competitiveness, and impatience) related to coronary outcomes (Matthews et al., 1977). She found that *hostility* was the only component that predicted death from heart disease at a 22-year follow-up. As a result of Matthews's findings, the measurement of global Type A has been abandoned, for the most part, in favor of more specific measures of hostility.

Matthews's findings stimulated numerous studies on the relationship between hostility and a number of measures of cardiovascular health. Redford Williams and his colleagues (1980) measured Type A behavior, hostility, and other psychological variables in 400 patients who were about to undergo angiography, a procedure that enables physicians to see the inside of the coronary arteries, which supply the heart muscle with oxygen-rich blood. As coronary artery disease develops, the openings of these arteries narrow due to the accumulation of fatty deposits, and the risk of coronary heart disease increases. Measures of hostility positively correlated with the degree of arterial blockage in those patients, much more so than Type A behavior did. Hostility also correlates with a number of other cardiovascular conditions that are relevant to coronary health, such as blood pressure reactivity in situations that provoke anger (Suarez et al., 1993; Suarez & Williams, 1989) and increases in fats in the bloodstream (Suarez, Bates, & Harralson, 1998).

How might having a hostile personality put someone at greater risk for heart disease? Hostility is an affective trait, which some emotion theorists say sets a threshold for the likelihood of particular emotional responses (Ekman, 1984; Rosenberg, 1998). By this logic, hostile people would have a lower threshold for the elicitation of anger. To link hostility and anger to heart disease, we need to look at a special version of physiological reactivity model known as the cardiovascular reactivity model (see Figure 12.7).

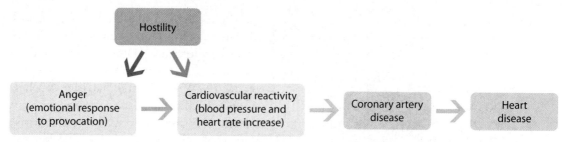

FIGURE **12.7**

CARDIOVASCULAR REACTIVITY MODEL OF STRESS AND ILLNESS. This version of the physiological reactivity model links hostility and anger to heart disease. Repeated cardiovascular reactivity leads to coronary artery disease and heart disease.

In the **cardiovascular reactivity (CVR) model,** hostility can increase the likelihood of heart disease through at least two different causal routes. On one route, hostility makes the elicitation of anger more likely and more frequent. Frequent episodes of anger lead to frequent cardiovascular reactivity (this route starts with the red arrow in Figure 12.7). Over time, repeated cardiovascular reactivity sets the stage for the development of coronary artery disease. As coronary artery disease develops, the narrowed arteries deprive the heart of the blood it needs to function properly; thus, progressive coronary artery disease can lead to coronary heart disease. The yellow arrows in the diagram designate the transition between repeated cardiovascular reactivity and coronary artery disease and the later development of coronary heart disease. It is also possible that hostility has a direct connection to how much cardiovascular reactivity certain people experience, without the need for anger; this path is indicated by the blue arrow in Figure 12.7.

Research indicates that anger affects health-relevant cardiovascular outcomes. Anger can lead to heightened and prolonged blood pressure reactivity (Schuler & O'Brien, 1997; Siegman, et al., 1992). In coronary patients, the risk of heart attack increases significantly during the hour following an outburst of anger (Moller et al., 1999). A study of coronary patients undergoing the Type A Structured Interview found that episodes of insufficient blood supply to the muscle of the heart were more likely to occur when those patients displayed facial expressions of anger (Rosenberg et al., 2001). More research addressing all the stages of the cardiovascular reactivity model is needed. A better understanding of how anger and hostility lead to heart disease can help health psychologists develop programs to help people reduce their risk for heart disease.

Depression   A hostile disposition is not the only characteristic that can harm cardiac health. Depression, a mood disorder involving sadness and lethargy, is associated with increased severity of symptoms and increased risk of death from coronary heart disease (Geerlings, et al., 2002; Glassman & Shapiro, 1998). A large-scale meta-analysis reported that for people with diagnosed coronary heart disease, being clinically depressed more than doubles the risk of death from the disease (Barth, Schumacher, & Hermann-Lingen, 2004). Also, chemicals involved in inflammation that present a risk for coronary heart disease are present at higher levels in people who are depressed than in others (Barth et al., 2004; Empana et al., 2005). Studies such as these make it hard to know which comes first—the

cardiovascular reactivity (CVR) model
hypothesis that hostility can increase the likelihood of heart disease through at least two different pathways.

heart disease or the depression. As both of these diseases represent major health problems in the United States, further work is needed to better understand the causal pathways linking heart disease and depression.

RESEARCH ON HEALTH-RELEVANT BEHAVIOR

Earlier we mentioned another pathway to illness called the *health behavior approach*. People engage in behaviors that increase risk for disease or help to prevent disease. Some health behaviors are conscious lifestyle choices, such as how and what to eat or whether or not to exercise. Others may begin as conscious choices but over time become habits that have serious health implications, such as smoking, drinking alcohol, and taking other drugs. Sometimes, when under stress, people drink or take drugs to change their mood. This is emotion-focused coping. They may turn to tobacco, alcohol, or food to calm themselves down or cheer themselves up. Long-term use of some of these substances can create health problems and may increase the likelihood of major, sometimes fatal, illnesses.

Smoking   Many smokers say that they have a cigarette when they are stressed because it calms them down. Yet nicotine, the drug component of cigarette smoke, is not a relaxant. Nicotine is a stimulant that activates the sympathetic nervous system, increasing heart rate and blood pressure. Nicotine relaxes the skeletal muscles, however, which is probably why some people find it calming. This calming effect is one reason that smokers tend to have a cigarette when stressed—they use nicotine for emotion regulation. But cigarette smoking is harmful to health in many ways. In fact, it is the single most preventable cause of death in the United States (U.S. Department of Health and Human Services [USDHHS], 2004). Cigarette smoking reduces life expectancy by an average of 10 years, increases one's risk for lung cancer more than 10-fold, and triples the risk of death from heart disease in both men and women (Centers for Disease Control and Prevention [CDC], 2001; Doll et al., 2004). Smoking is also a risk factor for many other cancers, stroke, lung disease, emphysema, and male impotence (USDHHS, 2004). The increased risk of mortality associated with smoking occurs in several cultures (Jacobs, et al., 1999).

Drinking Alcohol   People often drink alcohol to calm down or loosen up. Alcohol is a depressant, which means it slows down central nervous system functions. Alcohol can cause liver damage, and severe alcoholism can lead to a serious liver condition known as cirrhosis. Heavy alcohol consumption also increases the likelihood of liver cancer and cancers of the digestive tract, not to mention an increased risk for accidents due to alcohol's effect on motor and cognitive performance. Not all the news regarding alcohol is bad, however. Considerable data indicate that regular but moderate alcohol consumption (one to two drinks), especially with food, may reduce the risk of coronary heart disease, the number one killer in the developed world (Guiraud et al., 2008; Renaud & de Lorgeril, 1992).

connection

Binge drinking can lead to sudden death.

See Chapter 6, p. 244.

Diet and Eating   Eating well promotes health. Eating saturated fats, such as those found in meats and dairy products, increases risk for heart disease, while eating other essential fats, such as those found in certain kinds of fish and nuts, may have protective effects (Schaefer, Gleason, & Dansinger, 2005). The consumption of ample high-fiber, less fatty foods, such as whole grains and plenty of leafy green vegetables, may help protect against cancers of the colon and rectum, although the data are somewhat inconclusive (Cummings et al., 1992). It is well known, however, that excessive weight gain is risky. Obesity increases a person's risk for heart disease, high blood pressure, adult-onset diabetes, and certain cancers (McTiernan, 2005).

Eating and Stress. Some people eat as a way of coping with stress. In fact, sugary foods in particular actually help some people feel better and calm down. Research now supports the connection between eating and stress reduction: Stress increases eating and, in turn, eating reduces stress reactivity in the HPA axis (Dallman, Pecoraro, & la Fleur, 2005). When a person eats in response to stress, stress-related physiological activity decreases. So eating relieves stress for some people, which makes it likely they will continue to do such eating. When people eat in response to stress (especially sugary foods), reward pathways in the brain are stimulated. These areas release endorphins that make people feel better. So people eat under stress because they get a "good feeling" reward—like a drug high—from the brain (Adam & Epel, 2007).

A healthy diet rich in fruits, vegetables, and whole grains and low in fat may protect against heart disease and certain cancers and prevent conditions associated with obesity, such as adult-onset diabetes.

But stress-induced eating is risky, as it increases fat in the abdominal area (compared to other places), which is a predictor of heart disease in men and women (Epel et al., 2000; Rexrode et al., 1998; Rexrode, Buring, & Manson, 2001). This is especially true if the stress-induced eating includes sugary junk foods (Kuo et al., 2007).

Eating Disorders. Sometimes a person's relationship with food can become maladaptive. The two most prevalent eating disorders are anorexia nervosa and bulimia nervosa. People diagnosed with **anorexia nervosa** cannot maintain 85% of their ideal body weight for their height, have an intense fear of eating, and a distorted body image (American Psychiatric Association, 2000). Moreover, they do not recognize that they are unusually thin or that they have an eating disorder. The other major eating disorder is bulimia. A person suffering from **bulimia nervosa** is prone to binge eating and feeling a lack of control during the eating session. Binge eating involves eating much more food at one time than the average person would, such as having a half gallon of ice cream as a late-night snack. A person with bulimia regularly engages in either self-induced vomiting, use of laxatives or diuretics, strict dieting or fasting, or vigorous exercise in order to prevent weight gain.

The causes of anorexia are unknown, although a number of factors have been identified that put people at risk for this disorder, such as reactivity to stress, genetics, and personality. Women are much more likely than men to develop anorexia or bulimia (Nolen-Hoeksema, 2008). Women with eating disorders show higher physiological reactivity to stress. A study of more than 31,000 fraternal

anorexia nervosa an eating disorder in which people cannot maintain 85% of their ideal body weight for their height, have an intense fear of eating, and have a distorted body image.

bulimia nervosa an eating disorder characterized by binge eating and a perceived lack of control during the eating session.

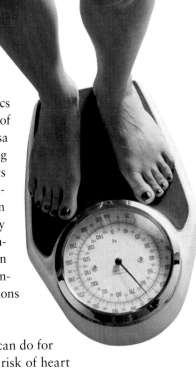

and identical twin pairs (both male and female) from Sweden examined the genetics of anorexia nervosa (Bulik et al., 2006). By comparing twins raised apart to twins raised together, one can calculate how much of a trait is attributable to genetics and how much to environment. This study reported that 56% of the variability in whether or not people develop anorexia nervosa is attributable to genetic influence, with most of the remaining influence (38%) being attributable to the common environments shared by family members. Moreover, people who had demonstrated a proneness to anxiety, depression, and low self-esteem (as measured by the trait of neuroticism) later were more likely to develop anorexia. Other studies have found that many personality traits distinguish anorexics from other people: in addition to being higher in neuroticism, anorexics are also more conscientious, more introverted, and less open to new and novel situations than are non-anorexics (Bollen & Wojciechowski, 2004).

Exercise   Besides not smoking, one of the best things you can do for your health is exercise regularly. Regular exercise reduces the risk of heart disease, stroke, and certain types of cancer (Noda et al., 2005; Thune & Furberg, 2001). Exercise helps keep diabetes under control and also slows the rate of bone loss in older women (Cussler et al., 2005). Recent data show that moderate exercise, even as little as walking 20–25 minutes a day 3 or 4 times per week, can extend life by 3 to 4 years (Franco, et al., 2005). In addition, exercise offers a healthy way to regulate mood, as it reduces anxiety and depression (Barbour & Blumenthal, in press; Binder et al., 2004).

Exercise can also help your brain. One correlational study found that third- and fifth-grade children who were the most physically fit also performed the highest on standardized math and reading tests (Hillman, Erickson, & Kramer, 2008).

Other research more directly suggests exercise promotes the growth of new neurons (neurogenesis) in the hippocampus, the area of the brain most involved in learning and memory (Pereira et al., 2007). Compared to mice that did not exercise, mice that exercised had increased

nature & nurture
Physical exercise causes new neurons to grow in brain areas devoted to learning and memory.

brain activity in their hippocampus after exercising for two weeks. They also developed new neurons in the same region of the hippocampus. Increased activity is directly related to neural growth. Similar effects have been found with humans as well (see Figure 12.8 on page 486). Being physically fit appears to make the brain fit, too.

Meditation for Stress Reduction   We have already discussed how positive emotions can reduce the physiological activation caused by negative emotions and how higher positive affect may help people with diseases like AIDS live longer (Moskowitz, 2003). Given the harmful effects of stress, strategies designed to reduce stress can benefit both mental and physical health. One such strategy is meditation.

1 research question

Will exercise increase brain activity and stimulate neural growth in humans?

2 method

Having found that exercise was correlated with neural growth in the hippocampus of mice, Pereira and colleagues (2007) conducted a study to look for the same effects in humans. They recruited eleven adults (ages 21–45) with below-average cardiovascular fitness to take part in an exercise program 4 times a week for 12 weeks. Each session lasted about 1 hour and consisted of a combination of stretching, aerobic training, and cooling down. Brain images were made before and after the training with MRI to measure changes in blood volume, an indirect measure of neural growth.

The hippocampus is the brain region most involved in learning and memory, so participants' memories were tested before and after the program with a list of 20 words read by the experimenter, to find out whether there was any change in memory capacity. Participants were distracted with another word list and were then asked to recall as many words from the original list as they could.

Hippocampus

FIGURE **12. 8**
EFFECTS OF EXERCISE ON THE BRAIN.
Physical exercise is as good for the brain as it is the body. (*Source:* A. C. Pereira, D. E. Huddleston, A. M. Brickman, A. A. Sosunov, R. Hen, G. M. McKhann, R. Sloan, F. H. Gage, T. R. Brown, & S. A. Small (2007). An in vivo correlate of exercise-induced neurogenesis in the adult dentate gyrus. *Proceedings of the National Academy of Sciences, 104,* 5638–5643.)

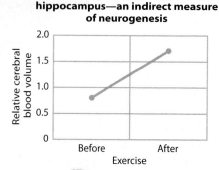

Brain activity (blood volume) in the hippocampus—an indirect measure of neurogenesis

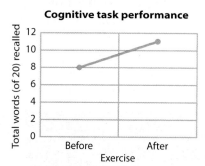

Cognitive task performance

3 results

MRIs performed before and after the exercise program revealed that cerebral blood flow increased after the program. In addition, participants improved their performance on a cognitive test after 12 weeks of exercise.

4 conclusion

After exercising regularly, people who had been out of shape showed improvement in memory. This improvement is correlated with—and perhaps a consequence of—new neural growth in the region of the brain most involved in learning and memory, the hippocampus. Although we cannot conclude from the correlations revealed by this study that physical exercise causes improvements in memory, these findings suggest that exercise not only makes the body more fit, but it also makes the brain more fit.

connection

Mindfulness meditation can improve well-being, cognition, and brain function.

See Chapter 6, pp. 226–228.

Mindfulness meditation involves both paying attention to the present moment and being aware that everything that may arise in one's mind, be it a thought, an emotion, or a sensation, will eventually fade away. The meditator is trained to note experiences as they occur, without clinging to or ascribing value to them. These skills allow one to keep thoughts and emotions in perspective and help prevent an unhealthy obsession with negative emotions (Kabat-Zinn, 1990).

Researchers have applied mindfulness meditation training to the treatment of stress reduction, pain relief, and physical disorders. Kabat-Zinn and his colleagues have examined the effectiveness of a program called Mindfulness-Based Stress Reduction (MBSR) for treating a variety of physical and psychological conditions. MBSR training reduces self-reported pain and pain-related behaviors in people suffering from chronic pain (Kabat-Zinn, Lipworth, & Burney, 1985). Also, Kabat-Zinn and colleagues (1992) found that MBSR training led to significant and substantial reductions in anxiety, depression, and fear in people who have various types of anxiety disorders.

Mindfulness training also improves the rate of skin healing in people with psoriasis (Kabat-Zinn et al., 1998). Psoriasis is an annoying and often painful rash that can be exacerbated by stress. Mindfulness meditation techniques appear to be effective in reducing the stress-related immune changes underlying skin outbreaks. Mindfulness meditation has also been linked to enhanced immune response to a vaccine (Davidson et al., 2003).

quick quiz 12.3: How Stress and Coping Affect Health

1. If a psychologist studies how diet and sleep affect overall health, which view would best match her research?
   a. physiological reactivity
   b. general adaptation syndrome
   c. health behavior approach
   d. homeostasis view

2. Martin is very prone to anger, impatient, and competitive; he is always in a hurry and feeling rushed. We would say Martin probably suffers from
   a. Type A behavior pattern
   b. Type B behavior pattern
   c. hostility
   d. high drive disorder

3. Which personality trait is most strongly related to the development of heart disease?
   a. anxiety
   b. hostility
   c. depression
   d. introversion

4. Exercise helps
   a. improve cardiovascular health
   b. decrease stress
   c. stimulate neural growth
   d. all of the above

Answers can be found at the end of the chapter.

making connections
in stress and health

The Health Psychology of HIV and AIDS

HIV/AIDS is a chronic and often fatal disease. The progression from infection to management of the illness to possible death presents a series of major psychological challenges. The course of HIV offers a good model for examining the psychological and physiological correlates of coping in a real-life context. Living with HIV is a serious challenge involving enormous stressors such as managing the symptoms of a chronic illness, dealing with the threat of death, and carrying out a complex treatment regimen. Those who care for people suffering from AIDS also endure the extreme stress of caring for loved ones who are dying.

How does this disease work? The human immunodeficiency virus (HIV) enters the bloodstream and, latching on to T lymphocytes, inserts its own genetic information into the lymphocytes and then turns them into HIV replication factories (see Figure 12.9). If untreated, HIV wipes out the infected person's cellular immunity, making him or her vulnerable to many kinds of infections. AIDS is the disease that results from living with such an extremely deficient immune system. It may be characterized by a host of irritating infections; ultimately, the victim may die of rare forms of pneumonia or

Susan Folkman

cancer. New drug treatments for HIV, however, have transformed it from a death sentence into a chronic, manageable disease for many people. But adhering to the complex drug regimen and dealing with the side effects are often stress provoking. Those who care for people suffering from AIDS also endure extreme stress.

In the early to mid-1990s, Folkman and her colleagues (1997) interviewed caregivers of men dying with AIDS. Many of the caregivers were themselves infected with HIV. The researchers were surprised to find that some of the caregivers managed to find beauty or meaning in the details of daily life despite the stress of caring for a partner who was dying of AIDS. Folkman argued that traumatic experiences often motivate people to find sources of positive emotion. This coping strategy may provide mental and physical health benefits, for we know that positive emotions can alleviate negative emotional arousal (Fredrickson & Levenson, 1998). According to Folkman, "The negative psychological state associated with significant and enduring stress may actually motivate people—consciously or unconsciously—to search for and *create* positive psychological states in order to gain relief, if only momentary, from distress" (Folkman, 1997, p. 1216).

Choosing to use a particular coping strategy in times of stress is also an indicator of coping ability. Reappraisal, especially reframing a situation in a positive light, is an adaptive coping strategy in chronic stress situations. Reappraisal can be thought of as any strategy that helps people see something difficult or unpleasant in a positive light. A study of people coping with the loss of a partner to AIDS found that engaging in reappraisal correlated with increases in positive mood (Moskowitz et al., 1996).

Before effective drug therapies became available, some HIV-infected people did not manifest AIDS for years, while others died within months (Rutherford et al., 1990). How could this be? The physiological reactivity model would predict that people with HIV who experienced greater distress might be more vulnerable to disease progression than people who experienced less distress. Many researchers have investigated the role of emotions and coping in this general context. One study of men infected with

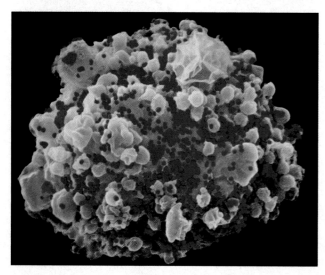

FIGURE **12.9**

T LYMPHOCYTE INFECTED WITH THE HUMAN IMMUNO-DEFICIENCY VIRUS (HIV). The virus (red) uses the lymphocyte (green) to reproduce and prevents it from functioning normally.

Once a week these women distribute condoms and educational leaflets about safe sex and AIDS in the Gauteng Province of South Africa. The AIDS epidemic has hit South Africa particularly hard, in part because of social instability, high levels of poverty, the low status accorded women, and the government's reluctance to acknowledge the extent of the problem and its causes.

HIV found slower disease progression in those who were happier (Moskowitz, 2003). Other research has found that depression appears to alter the functioning of certain T cells in both men and women infected with HIV (Kemeny et al., 1994; Evans et al., 2002, respectively). Also, chronic depression increases the risk of mortality in men infected with HIV (Mayne et al., 1996).

Even in the presence of the highly effective medications, psychosocial factors influence immune variables and disease progression in both men and women. In a longitudinal study of psychological factors in men and women infected with HIV, baseline self-reports of stress, depression, hopelessness, and avoidant coping predicted significant reductions in the kinds of T lymphocytes that are most dramatically targeted by HIV (Ironson et al., 2005). More stressful life events, more depressive symptoms, and less social support all correlated with a faster progression to AIDS in gay men infected with HIV (Leserman et al., 1999).

Certain ways of coping with emotional trauma or distress appear to affect the progression of disease symptoms in people infected with HIV. Faster disease progression is also associated with denial as a form of coping and with less satisfactory social support (Leserman et al., 2000). In an experiment in which patients with HIV were either asked to write about an emotional topic (disclosure condition) or assigned to a control condition, those in the disclosure condition showed a drop in HIV viral load (an indication of improved immune function) and an increase in T lymphocytes that are crucial to combating the virus (Petrie et al., 2004).

Becoming infected with HIV is largely a function of health-related behavior. Whether or not you engage in safe sex practices is probably the single biggest determinant of HIV risk, with intravenous drug use the next. Nevertheless, many people continue to practice unsafe behaviors (Weinhardt, 2005).

quick quiz 12.4: Making Connections in Stress and Health

1. Human immunodeficiency virus (HIV) replicates by latching on to
   a. T lymphocytes
   b. B lymphocytes
   c. red blood cells
   d. antibodies
2. Which of the following reduces disease progression in men with HIV?
   a. depression
   b. optimism
   c. hostility
   d. happiness

Answers can be found at the end of the chapter.

chapter **review**

WHAT IS STRESS?

- Stress results when we appraise the demands of a situation as exceeding our ability to cope with or manage those demands. Researchers often define stress in terms of events or our physiological responses to certain events.

- Primary appraisal is the initial evaluation of how threatening a situation is. Secondary appraisal involves evaluation of resources to manage the stressful situation or the feelings it generates.

- Most stress-related physiological changes are observed in the autonomic nervous system (ANS), especially the sympathetic branch.

- The adrenal-medullary system controls the release of catecholamines, chemicals that activate heart rate, respiration, and other responses that prepare the organism to deal with emergency situations.

- The hypothalamic-pituitary-adrenal (HPA) axis releases the hormone cortisol, which frees up glucose as a source of energy.

- The stress response is beneficial in short-term, emergency situations but not over the long term. When sustained over time, the stress response can weaken the body.

- Hans Selye proposed a three-stage model, the general adaptation syndrome (GAS), to describe how the body reacts and adapts to chronic, extreme stress. In the alarm stage, the body is in emergency mode and all body systems are activated for quick response. In the resistance stage, the body gradually adjusts to the high level of stress created by the demands of its environment. In the exhaustion stage the body is unable to sustain the response and becomes more susceptible to illness.

- Mason and others argued that Selye had overlooked the fact that people respond to different situations with different emotions and made a case for greater specificity in the stress response. Research shows that different emotions are indeed associated with different patterns of ANS response.

COPING

- Some strategies for coping are problem-focused, in that they address how to remedy or change the situation that called forth the stress response. Others are emotion-focused, aimed at reducing the emotional distress or unpleasant experience created by a stressful situation.

- Social support can profoundly improve mental and physical health. Social networks influence health behavior, both positively and negatively.

- Some people are more likely than others to believe that they have control over situations, and this belief may make them healthier.

- Some people experience positive affect, even in dramatically stressful situations. Positive affect, in turn, may facilitate recovery from the negative emotional arousal of stress.

HOW STRESS AND COPING AFFECT HEALTH

- There are two major approaches to studying how stress leads to illness: the physiological reactivity model and the health behavior model.

- The physiological reactivity model examines how the psychological effects of sustained stress make illness more likely.

- Psychoneuroimmunology (PNI) encompasses research on any type of connection between the CNS and the immune system.

- The work of Ader and Cohen on classically conditioned immunosuppression showed a relationship between psychological processes and changes in immune function.

- The immune system defends the body against disease. Immunity consists of natural and acquired aspects. When antigens are present, lymphocytes either release antibodies into the blood or bind directly with the antigen to disable it.

- Numerous studies have demonstrated the effects of stress on regulation of the immune system. The most convincing argument for a meaningful stress-immune connection comes from studies that measure the experience of stress, immune measures, and related illness outcomes.

- The Type A behavior pattern, a characteristic way of responding to demanding situations with hostility, time urgency, and competitiveness, can predict the later development of heart disease. The hostility component of the Type A pattern best predicts coronary heart disease.

- The cardiovascular reactivity model offers a perspective for understanding how hostility might increase risk for heart disease. Hostility increases the likelihood and frequency of the physiological effects of anger, which, over time, increases the likelihood of hardened arteries and, eventually, coronary heart disease.

- People engage in behaviors that enhance health as well as those that make them more susceptible to illness. Behaviors such as smoking and drinking alcohol increase risk for major illness such as heart disease, cancer, and liver disease. Eating in response to stress also imposes risks.

- Healthy diet and exercise can extend life and enhance brain function.

MAKING CONNECTIONS IN STRESS AND HEALTH

- Living with HIV and possibly developing AIDS present enormous challenges for patients and caregivers alike. Psychosocial variables, such as depression and coping, influence immune measures, disease progression, and mortality in people infected with HIV.

key **terms**

acquired immunity, p. 478

adrenal-medullary system, p. 462

alarm stage, p. 463

allostasis, p. 465

anorexia nervosa, p. 484

antigen, p. 476

bulimia nervosa, p. 484

cardiovascular reactivity (CRV) model, p. 482

cardiovascular system, p. 475

catecholamines, p. 461

cellular immunity, p. 478

coping, p. 466

cortisol, p. 462

emotional disclosure, p. 468

emotion-focused coping, p. 467

exhaustion stage, p. 464

general adaptation syndrome (GAS), p. 463

glucocorticoids, p. 461

health behavior approach, p. 473

health psychology, p. 473

hypothalamic-pituitary-adrenal (HPA) axis, p. 462

natural immunity, p. 477

neuroendocrine system, p. 461

norepinephrine, p. 462

primary appraisal, p. 460

problem-focused coping, p. 466

psychological reactivity model, p. 473

psychoneuroimmunology (PNI), p. 475

psychosomatic theory, p. 472

resistance stage, p. 464

secondary appraisal, p. 461

stress, p. 457

stressors, p. 458

Type A Behavior Pattern, p. 480

quick quiz **answers**

Quick Quiz 12.1: 1. c 2. b 3. d 4. a **Quick Quiz 12.2:** 1. a 2. c 3. c 4. d
Quick Quiz 12.3: 1. c 2. a 3. b 4. d **Quick Quiz 12.4:** 1. a 2. d

personality:
the **uniqueness**

of the **individual**

preview
questions

1 *How has your personality changed since you were 3 years old? In what ways has your personality stayed the same?*

2 *Why are some people anxious and others calm, some extraverted and others introverted?*

3 *How do psychologists explain personality?*

4 *What can psychology tell us about the personalities of horses, octopuses, and other nonhuman species?*

S till at the hospital and in only his second day of life, Jerry received a needle stick in his heel for a routine blood test. As the needle pricked his skin, Jerry let out a typical newborn cry. Almost four years later, Jerry's new brother, Evan, went through the same procedure. He hardly flinched, at which the nurse predicted, "He's going to be a tough one!" The two brothers differ physically in other ways besides their response to pain, even though they share obvious similarities in eyes, face, and physical size.

Jerry and Evan also have similar yet distinct personalities. Both are curious, intelligent, verbal, full of energy, and active. Jerry, however, is rule-bound, bothered by adult anger, socially skilled, gentle, and afraid of spiders and the dark. He is assertive and competitive, but never aggressive with peers, and incredibly friendly. Evan, by contrast, is mischievous, energetic, aggressive, fearless, and socially skilled but manipulative. He enjoys being ▶

▶ angry and making others angry, and he likes to dramatize. Often during play, even if alone, Evan will pose intense anger and scowl at pretend enemies. When playing with others, he dives right in, fearless of the consequences.

We, your authors, know these two children very well: they are our children! Although we highlight them here, Jerry and Evan could be any pair of brothers. This kind of contrast is more the rule than the exception among siblings. If you have brothers or sisters, this description, at least in outline form, probably rings true. How is it that two people—reared in similar environments by the same parents—can have such different personalities?

chapter **outline**

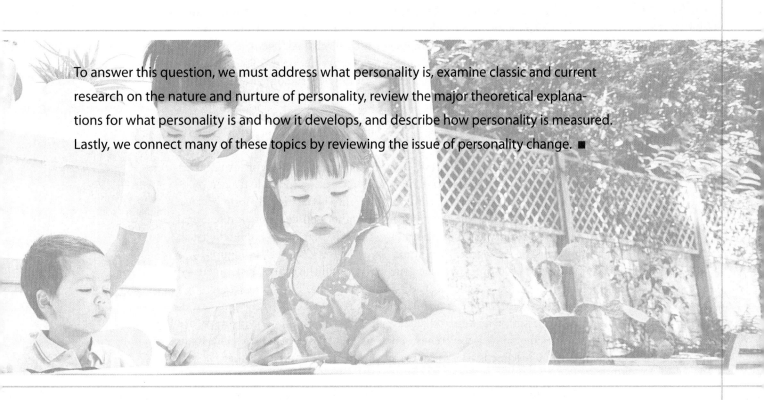

To answer this question, we must address what personality is, examine classic and current research on the nature and nurture of personality, review the major theoretical explanations for what personality is and how it develops, and describe how personality is measured. Lastly, we connect many of these topics by reviewing the issue of personality change. ■

Defining Personality

personality
the unique and relatively enduring set of behaviors, feelings, thoughts, and motives that characterize an individual.

When psychologists use the term **personality,** they are referring to the unique and relatively enduring set of behaviors, feelings, thoughts, and motives that characterize an individual (Feist & Feist, 2009; Roberts & Mroczek, 2008). There are two key components to this definition. First, personality is what distinguishes us from one another and makes us unique. Second, personality is relatively enduring, or consistent. Let's consider these key components in more detail.

The first major component of personality is the uniqueness of an individual's thoughts, feelings, and behavior. The fact is that in almost every situation, people will behave somewhat differently from each other. Consider what happens when one driver cuts in front of another. Some people react to such an incident with "road rage," while others are able to take it in stride. A characteristic of personality—hostility—may determine whether someone responds with road rage or not. Personality, therefore, is about uniqueness, or *individual differences.* The concept of personality would not exist if everyone acted and thought alike.

Research supports the strength of individual differences: Even when a strong authority figure creates extreme pressure to obey, not everyone will do so (Milgram, 1963). Personality psychology is concerned with the fact that some people do and some people don't act in a particular way in the same situation.

connection

Are there extreme situations that can push people to behave in ways we would not expect from their personalities?

See Chapter 14, pp. 534–540.

A second part of the definition of personality is its relatively enduring consistency, of which there are two kinds: consistency across different situations and consistency over time. *Consistency across situations* refers to the notion that people behave the same way in different situations and carry who they are into almost every situation. *Consistency over time*, in contrast, is the extent to which people behave the same way throughout their lives.

Bringing these two components of personality together, we label a person as "friendly" for example, only if we observe her behaving in a friendly manner in situations in which most others might not act friendly and she does so consistently over time and in many different situations. A friendly person might behave in a friendly manner at a party, while having coffee with friends, or when meeting someone for the first time. We would say that this person's friendly behavior is unique and consistent.

Friendliness is a personality **trait,** or a disposition to behave consistently in a particular way. Although traits make up a large part of an individual's personality, they are not quite synonymous with it. Personality is the broader term because it comprises not only traits but also motives, thoughts, self-concept, and feelings.

trait
a disposition to behave consistently in a particular way.

One important principle of personality traits is that they, like intelligence, are normally distributed in the population. Recall from Chapter 10 (Figure 10.7) that a normal distribution exists when the graph of all the scores is symmetrical and bell-shaped. A few people exist at both the extreme low and extreme high end of the distribution, but most people are average. Consider the traits of "anxiety" (or neuroticism), warmth, and extraversion. A few people, for instance, are barely anxious and a few are extremely anxious, but most people are somewhere in the middle. The same is true for extraversion, warmth, and any other personality trait.

Another important principle of traits is they are directly connected to behavior. They lower **behavioral thresholds,** or the point at which you move from not having a particular response to having one (Allport, 1937; Feist & Barron, 2003; Rosenberg, 1998). A low threshold means you are very likely to behave in a particular way, whereas a high threshold means you are not. To illustrate: Carlos is shy, which means he has a low threshold for feeling awkward. If he were introduced to a group of strangers, he would likely feel uncomfortable. In the same

behavioral thresholds
the point at which a person moves from not having a particular response to having one.

situation, however, Karen, who is outgoing, would probably feel comfortable because she has a much higher threshold for social awkwardness. Their optimal levels of arousal—or thresholds—are different. In short, traits lower behavioral thresholds and are directly connected to behavior.

quick quiz 13.1: Defining Personality

1. Two characteristics of personality include
   a. uniqueness and instability in behavior
   b. uniqueness and consistency in behavior
   c. consistency in behavior and identity formation
   d. uniqueness and change in behavior
2. A statistical property of most personality traits is that they are
   a. unreliably measured
   b. randomly distributed
   c. normally distributed
   d. skewed distributions

Answers can be found at the end of the chapter.

The Nature and Nurture of Personality

Personality is shaped by the forces of both nature and nurture. The interaction between the two can be seen in at least four lines of reasoning and research: evolutionary theory, genetics, temperament and fetal development, and cross-cultural universality.

THE EVOLUTION OF PERSONALITY TRAITS

Human personality traits evolved as adaptive behavioral responses to fundamental problems of survival and reproduction. Certain behaviors were useful for survival or reproductive success during early periods of human evolution, and these behaviors have been shaped by natural selection (Buss, 1990; Buss & Greiling, 1999; McCrae & Costa, 1999). The tendency to be sensitive to threats, for instance, may well have been adaptive in dangerous environments like those in which our ancestors lived. Heightened anxiety would provide a signal of danger and threat; its absence would quickly lead to extinction of the species. Consider a hunter on the savannah. He hears the growl of a large animal and becomes fearful. He drops back behind the bushes, before the animal becomes aware of his presence. If he did not feel anxious, he might not hide, with dire consequences for his safety and his likelihood of catching dinner. By the same token, the other extreme—hypersensitivity to threats— would be debilitating and disruptive to everyday functioning. If the same man who became fearful at hearing the growl of a large animal also became fearful with every rustling of leaves or every sound of the wind, he would have a hard time functioning in everyday life. Having some degree of fearfulness is adaptive, and people with that quality were more likely to survive, reproduce, and pass on that disposition.

nature & nurture

The evolution of personality traits demonstrates how our bodies, brain, and behavior can be shaped by environmental forces over long periods of time.

Naturally selected traits are favored if they increase one's chances of survival and reproductive success. Sexually selected traits, on the other hand, make one more attractive to the opposite sex. For example, a recent study of over

400 individuals, many of whom were creative artists and poets, revealed a positive correlation between creativity and sexual success. That is, more creative people were also more sexually active (Nettle & Clegg, 2005). The authors argue that this supports the theory, first proposed by Darwin and more recently by Geoffrey Miller (2000), that human creative ability is a sexually selected trait because it is a quality that increases one's attractiveness to members of the opposite sex.

GENETICS AND PERSONALITY

connection

Behavior and personality traits are not the result of single genes but are influenced by many genes.
See Chapter 3, pp. 77–82.

Recall from Chapter 3 that complex traits are almost never the result of a single gene and that our genome is the starting point, not the end point, for how our genes are expressed (our phenotype). There is no "smart" gene, "shy" gene, or "aggressive" gene. We discuss these two themes in detail later in this section, but first let's look at how *behavioral geneticists* study the relationship between genes and personality.

When studying behavioral genetics, researchers use two major methods to examine the relationship among genetics, behavior, and personality. With the first method they look for the location of specific bits of DNA on genes that might be associated with particular behaviors. In this sense, it is a search for "genetic markers" of behavior. This method is referred to as the **quantitative trait loci (QTL) approach.** The traits are quantitative because they are markers for behaviors that are expressed on a broad continuum, from very little to very much. For example, anxiety is a quantitative trait because some people are not at all anxious, most people are average, and a few are very anxious. The QTL method uncovers the location on particular genes that is associated with high or low levels of a trait. These locations are also known as "markers."

quantitative trait loci (QTL) approach
a technique in behavioral genetics that looks for the location on genes that might be associated with particular behaviors.

QTL research points to genetic markers for several basic personality traits, such as novelty- or thrill seeking, impulsivity, and neuroticism/anxiety (Benjamin et al., 1996; Hamer & Copeland, 1998; Lesch et al., 1996; Plomin & Caspi, 1999; Rutter, 2006). Consider the case of thrill seeking, a trait that entails risk taking. People with this trait may seek out highly exciting activities like bungee jumping, mountain climbing, or scuba diving. Thrill-seeking activities create a "rush" of excitement—a positive feeling that may be related to the release of dopamine, a neurotransmitter associated with physiological arousal. Given the possible connection between dopamine and thrill seeking, one theory suggests that people who are deficient in dopamine will tend to seek out exciting situations as a way of increasing their dopamine release. Thrill seeking increases dopamine release and therefore may be a way to make up for deficient levels of dopamine.

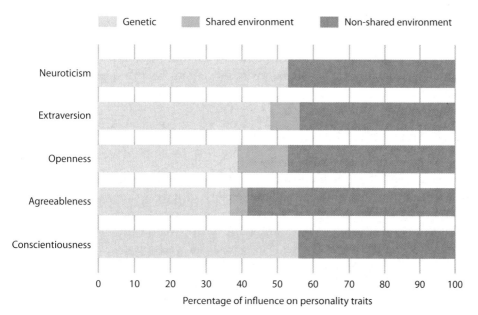

Legend: Genetic | Shared environment | Non-shared environment

Neuroticism
Extraversion
Openness
Agreeableness
Conscientiousness

0   10   20   30   40   50   60   70   80   90   100
Percentage of influence on personality traits

FIGURE **13.1**

NATURE AND NURTURE OF PER-SONALITY: HERITABILITY OF FIVE TRAITS. Twin studies indicate that heredity (genetics) accounts for 50% to 60% of most traits, slightly less for agreeableness and openness. What's surprising is that the influence of the shared environment (home and family) on these traits is small, compared with the influence of the non-shared environment. (*Source:* Plomin & Caspi, 1999.)

In the mid-1990s, researchers presented the first genetic evidence to support this theory. The gene DRD4 is involved in dopamine production in the limbic system, and the longer the gene sequence, the less efficient dopamine production is. In other words, long versions of the DRD4 gene are associated with less efficient dopamine production. If the theory is correct, people who seek out thrills should have the longer form of this gene, and that is exactly what the research has shown (Ebstein, et al., 1996; Hamer & Copeland, 1998). An exciting aspect of this finding is that it was the first to demonstrate a specific genetic influence on a normal (nonpathological) personality trait.

As discussed more fully in Chapter 3, the second method for examining the effect that genetics play in behavior and personality is the study of twins, both identical and fraternal, who have been raised together or apart. Twin studies have found that most basic personality traits have heritability estimates of between 40 and 60 percent. In other words, an individual's genetic makeup goes about halfway toward accounting for his or her basic traits. For instance, the trait of extraversion or outgoingness often correlates around .50 for identical twins and around .20 to .25 for fraternal twins, which leads to a heritability estimate of between 50% and 60% (see Figure 13.1). Likewise, between 50% and 55% of the differences in neuroticism and conscientiousness are due to genetics, and about 40% of differences in openness and agreeableness are due to genetics (Bouchard & Loehlin, 2001; Caspi, Roberts, & Shiner, 2003; Loehlin et al., 1998; Plomin & Caspi, 1999; Tellegen et al., 1988).

Such a figure leaves roughly 50% of the differences in personality to be explained by three nongenetic sources: shared environment, unshared environment, and error. Shared environment consists of what siblings share in common, such as parents or household, whereas unshared environment consists of things like birth order, different friends, different teachers, and different social groups. The surprising conclusion from research is that most of the environmental effects are of the unshared kind, and almost no variance is explained by shared environment (see Figure 13.1). The environment that seems to matter most is the "unshared" environment—differences in birth order or peer groups or even changes in parenting style and attitudes over time (Arseneault et al., 2003; Bouchard & Loehlin, 2001; Hamer & Copeland, 1998; Plomin & Caspi, 1999; Rutter, 2006). In short, personality is influenced by our environment, but more by the experiences we do not share in common with our family members, such as peer group influences.

TEMPERAMENT AND THE FETAL ENVIRONMENT

Recall from Chapter 5 that temperament is the biologically based disposition to behave in certain ways, which lays the foundation for later personality traits. Evidence suggests that temperament and personality differences are manifest even *before* birth. Apparently, fetal activity and heart rate can reveal something about temperament differences over the first year of life. In particular, a high heart rate at 36 weeks gestation (nearly full term) foreshadowed less predictable eating and sleeping habits 3 and 6 months after birth and less emotionality at 6 months after birth. Having high activity levels at 36 weeks' gestation predicted being slow to adapt to new people or situations and having more irregular eating and sleeping habits at 3 and 6 months and being more difficult or fussy at 6 months (DiPietro et al., 1996).

connection
Are some babies and toddlers temperamentally fussy and more difficult to care for than others?
See Chapter 5, p. 210.

nature & nurture
Fetal activity and heart rate can reveal something about temperament differences over the first year of life.

The prenatal environment may play an important role in shaping personality. In fact, the amount of stress the mother experiences during pregnancy changes the infant's permanent stress response. That is, infants born to mothers who have experienced an unusual amount of stress during pregnancy tend to have impaired stress function, higher baseline levels of stress hormones, and a faster, stronger, and more pronounced stress response, all of which persist into childhood (Barbazanges et al., 1996).

PERSONALITY AND CULTURE: UNIVERSALITY AND DIFFERENCES

Additional evidence that both nature and nurture shape personality comes from cross-cultural research on personality traits. If personality dispositions are part of our biology, we would expect the same personality dimensions or traits to appear in cultures all over the world. Environment and culture, however, might modify temperament and make certain traits more likely in some societies than in others. Indeed, there is evidence for both of these perspectives.

Researchers have investigated the personality traits of extraversion, neuroticism, agreeableness, openness to experience, conscientiousness, and psychoticism, which is a combination of warmth, impulse control, and conventional attitudes. Research confirms the existence of these personality traits not only in Western cultures (the United States, the United Kingdom, Germany, Australia, Iceland, Spain, Portugal), but also in Asian (China, Japan, South Korea), African (Zimbabwe), Middle Eastern (Iran, Israel), and Pacific Rim (Malaysia and the Philippines) cultures (McCrae, 2002; McCrae & Allik, 2002; McCrae & Costa, 1997). One measure of five major dimensions of personality, the NEO-Personality Inventory (PI), for example, has been translated into more than 40 languages and the same five personality dimensions have emerged in each and every one (Rolland, 2002). In other words, people from vastly different cultural backgrounds exhibit these traits—evidence of their universal and biological basis.

Yet people in different cultures also differ on certain dimensions of personality. In particular, people in Asian cultures exhibit qualities that fit a dimension of "interpersonal relatedness" that is rarely seen in Western cultures. Interpersonal relatedness includes such behaviors and attitudes as a respectful, obedient demeanor toward others, a belief in saving "face" (that is, allowing a "losing" party to suffer a loss and yet maintain esteem and reputation), and an emphasis on harmonious relationships. This dimension of personality reflects how people in Asian cultures tend to be more concerned about the impact of their behavior on their family, friends, and social groups (known as *collectivism*), whereas people in Western cultures are more concerned with how their behavior will affect their personal goals (known as *individualism*) (Cross & Markus, 1999; Hofstede, 2001). Thus, an Asian employee who is offered a promotion that would require relocating to another city may be concerned primarily with how the move would affect her family. On the other hand, the primary consideration of a Western employee might be how the move would increase her chances of someday becoming an executive in a major corporation.

quick quiz 13.2: The Nature and Nurture of Personality

1. The genetic marker for thrill seeking involves genetic differences in which neurotransmitter?
   a. dopamine
   b. acetylcholine
   c. serotonin
   d. norepinephrine

2. Researchers obtain estimates of how heritable personality traits are by
   a. studying biochemical markers of personality
   b. analyzing DNA in rats reared together
   c. documenting family histories
   d. studying twins

3. People in Asian cultures exhibit qualities that suggest a personality dimension of _____ that is rarely seen in Western cultures.
   a. anxiety
   b. interpersonal relatedness
   c. separation distress
   d. agreeableness

Answers can be found at the end of the chapter.

How Do Theorists Explain Personality?

Maria is calm most of the time and gets along well with most people. Emily is excitable, and the slightest thing can make her "blow up." Annie loves parties and chats animatedly with anyone she happens to meet. Dmitry is reclusive and is rarely seen anywhere except the office. How do we explain such differences in personality style? Many theorists have devoted much attention to answering this question. Let's take a look at the answers they have provided. The major explanations can be grouped into five distinct theoretical camps: psychoanalysis, humanism, social–cognitive learning, trait theory, and biological theory.

PSYCHOANALYTIC THEORIES

Psychoanalytic theories are all based on or are variations of Freud's ideas.

Sigmund Freud Undoubtedly the most famous individual in psychology is Sigmund Freud (1856–1939). Freud not only proposed an overarching theory of personality and psychotherapy but also founded the movement known as psychoanalysis and in the process of doing so essentially invented the field of psychotherapy.

As we mentioned in Chapter 1, the starting point for Freud's theory of psychoanalysis is the idea that the unconscious is the most powerful force in our personality. More generally, Freud described three layers of consciousness: unconscious, preconscious, and conscious. The *conscious* layer is simply what we are aware of at any given moment in time, whereas the *preconscious* is just below the surface of awareness. It is not currently conscious but can become so relatively easily. Because the conscious and preconscious layers are relatively unimportant in Freud's theory, we focus instead on the unconscious.

Theories of personality, like all scientific theories, are based on theorists' observations and are used to generate research hypotheses. What observations about personality does this photograph bring to mind?

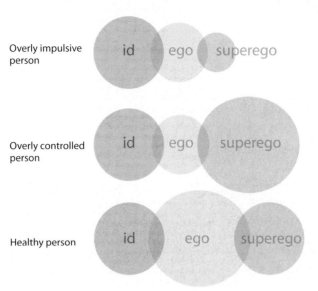

FIGURE **13.2**

THE RELATIVE INFLUENCES OF ID, EGO, AND SUPEREGO IN THREE TYPES OF PEOPLE. Freud argued that the relative sizes and strengths of the id, ego, and superego (as symbolized by the size of the circles) contributed to whether a person is overly impulsive, neurotically repressed and overcontrolled, or psychologically balanced and healthy. (*Source:* Feist & Feist, 2009.)

According to Freud, the **unconscious** contains all the drives, urges, or instincts that are outside awareness but nonetheless motivate most of our speech, thoughts, feelings, or actions. Before Freud, most people assumed that what we consciously think, feel, and believe is a relatively accurate and important source of information for explaining our behavior and personality. Freud believed that much of what we do and the reasons that we do it are hidden from our awareness and revealed to us only in distorted forms, such as slips of the tongue and dreams (Freud, 1900/1953, 1901/1960). He developed an elaborate system for interpreting the meaning of dreams, because they were the best way to understand a person's unconscious.

Freud also developed the notion that the human mind has three distinct "provinces," or regions, that involve control and regulation of impulses. The first province—developed in infancy—is the **id,** and it is the seat of impulse and desire. The id is the part of our personality that we do not yet own; it owns or controls us. Its sole function is to seek pleasure; it is therefore founded in the "pleasure principle" and operates on the "do it" principle. By the end of the first year of life, a sense of self, or **ego,** begins to emerge. It is the only part of the mind that is in direct contact with the outside world, and it operates on the "reality principle." If the id wants pleasure, the ego makes a realistic attempt to obtain it. The last part of the mind to develop, around age 2 or 3, is the **superego,** the part of the self that monitors and controls behavior. The superego "stands over us" and evaluates actions in terms of right and wrong; hence, it is our conscience. It operates on the "moralistic principle" and gives us a sense of what we should and should not do. Thus, the superego is the control center of the personality and frequently applies the brakes to impulses of the id.

In a healthy person, the ego mediates this conflict between impulse and control. In fact, Freud believed that some people are mostly id-driven, whereas others are mostly superego-driven. People who are overly impulsive and pleasure seeking have a highly developed id. People who are overly controlling and repress their impulses have a highly developed superego. The healthiest person is one in whom the ego is most developed and can control in a realistic and healthy way the conflict between impulse and control (see Figure 13.2).

connections

Cognitive psychologists refer to mental processes that occur outside awareness as "implicit" or "automatic." Much of what we learn and remember is implicit.
See Chapter 7, p. 274, and Chapter 8, p. 297.

ego
Freud's term for the sense of self; the part of the mind that operates on the "reality principle."

unconscious
the level of consciousness containing all drives, urges, and instincts that are outside awareness but nonetheless motivate most behavior.

id
Freud's term for the seat of impulse and desire; the pleasure-seeking part of our personality.

superego
Freud's term for the part of the mind that monitors behavior and evaluates it in terms of right and wrong; the conscience.

To honor Freud's contributions to psychology, his last home in London has been preserved as a museum. His patients would lie on this couch during treatment sessions.

defense mechanisms
unconscious strategies the mind uses to protect itself from anxiety by denying and distorting reality in some way.

Another of Freud's major contributions to psychology is the concept of psychological **defense mechanisms** (Freud, 1926/1959). Although Freud first described these mechanisms, his daughter, Anna, developed them further (A. Freud, 1946). Just as the physical body has the immune system to protect it from foreign substances, the mind also protects itself from harmful, threatening, and anxiety-provoking thoughts, feelings, or impulses. All defense mechanisms share two qualities: (1) They operate unconsciously; (2) they deny and distort reality in some way.

The most basic of all defense mechanisms is **repression;** it underlies all the other defense mechanisms. Repression is the unconscious act of keeping threatening or disturbing thoughts, feelings, or impulses out of consciousness. The impulses that are most likely to be repressed are sexual and aggressive impulses, because these are inherently the most threatening. Although repression may keep these impulses and thoughts out of awareness, they may be expressed in disguised or distorted form. In fact, they often reveal themselves—through dreams, slips of the tongue, or neurotic behavior.

repression
defense mechanism for keeping unpleasant thoughts, feelings, or impulses out of consciousness.

reaction formation
a defense mechanism that turns an unpleasant idea, feeling, or impulse into its opposite.

Reaction formation occurs when an unpleasant idea, feeling, or impulse is turned into its opposite. This often results in exaggerated or compulsive feelings and behavior (Freud, 1926/1959). For example, a woman may resent and even hate her mother, but because these feelings are not acceptable to her or to society, she turns them into showy, exaggerated love. Homophobia is another example: Hatred and aggression toward homosexuals might well be a reaction against fear of one's own latent homosexual impulses.

In **projection** we deny and repress particular ideas, feelings, or impulses but project them onto others. For example, a man may desire a married woman, but instead of recognizing his feelings, he projects his desire onto the woman and believes that she is seducing him. Another defense is **sublimation,** which involves expressing a socially unacceptable impulse in a socially acceptable and even desirable way. Freud believed that most creative achievements are motivated by sublimated impulses, usually sexual or aggressive. That is, unfulfilled sexual desire or aggressive impulses drive much creative output. Thus, for example, a man who is hopelessly in love with an unattainable woman may engage in sublimation, channeling his feelings into writing a novel whose main characters closely resemble him and the woman he desires.

projection
a defense mechanism in which people deny particular ideas, feelings, or impulses and project them onto others.

sublimation
a defense mechanism in which a socially unacceptable impulse is expressed in a socially acceptable way.

One of Freud's most important ideas was that adult personality stems from early childhood experiences. It is an idea so widespread today that you might find it difficult to believe that 100 years ago very few people, except Freud and his followers, agreed with it. How personality developed, however, is also without a doubt one of Freud's most controversial ideas. He called it a **psychosexual stage theory** because he believed that sexual feelings were key to each stage of personality development, even infancy. More specifically, Freud argued that as we move through each stage of life, a different region of our body is most erogenous, that is, a source of pleasure. He delineated four major stages of psychosexual development: oral, anal, phallic, and genital (see Figure 13.3).

The *oral stage* is the first 12 to 18 months of life when the mouth is the center of pleasure. Infants suck, bite, and chew as a means of obtaining nourishment and a way of exploring their world. The *anal stage* takes place during the second and third year of life and involves the pleasure gained from holding and releasing one's bladder and bowels. Toilet training is the crucial event during the anal stage, and children learn to control their bladder and bowels. The third stage occurs from approximately ages 3 to 6 and is the *phallic stage* because the child discovers that the genitals are a source of pleasure (note that Freud used the male term *phallic*, which means "penis-like, to apply to both boys and girls). The phallic stage, however, was the most complex and controversial of all of Freud's stages. He argued that children not only discover pleasure from manipulating their genitals, but also harbor unconscious feelings of attraction for their opposite-sex parent and hostility for their same-sex parent. Desire for the opposite-sex parent and hostility toward the same-sex parent is known as the *Oedipal complex*. As children move through the phallic stage, they resolve the Oedipal complex by identifying with their same-sex parent and choosing to be more like him or her.

After the phallic stage Freud argued that children go through a *latency stage* in which no region of the body is erogenous and the sense of sexuality goes beneath the surface (becomes latent). The last stage is the *genital stage*, which starts with puberty and lasts for the rest of one's life. The genital stage is where the source of pleasure is once again the genitals, but this time in a mature adult fashion. Sexual pleasure is interpersonal and exists between people outside

psychosexual stage theory Freud's stages of personality development; in different stages a different region of the body is most erogenous.

FIGURE **13.3**

FREUD'S THEORY OF PSYCHOSEXUAL DEVELOPMENT. Freud's theory focuses on distinct regions of the body being the main source of pleasure.

Stage	Pleasure comes from …	Fixations may result in …
Oral (0–18 months)	The mouth and sucking, biting, chewing	Smoking and sarcasm
Anal (18–36 months)	The anus and bowel and bladder elimination	Obsessive and compulsive cleaning behaviors
Phallic (3–6 years)	The genitals (self-focused) and attraction for opposite-sex parent	Attraction to people like one's opposite-sex parent
Latency (6–puberty)	Not applicable; sexual feelings remain latent and dormant	Not applicable
Genital (puberty and up)	The genitals (self- *and* other-focused) and mature sexual behavior (giving and receiving pleasure)	Immature sexuality that is either self- *or* other-focused

the family. Healthy sexuality is a balance between giving and receiving sexual pleasure, but unfortunately, Freud argued, few people are healthy and balanced. Some remain selfish and focus on their own pleasure, whereas others give up their own pleasure and focus only on their partner's satisfaction.

A key offshoot of Freud's psychosexual stages was his idea of **fixation**, which is a defense mechanism whereby a person continues to be concerned and even preoccupied with an earlier stage of development. For example, someone with an oral fixation may continue in adulthood to get oral gratification from smoking or from being "biting and sarcastic." An anal fixation might be expressed in adulthood as obsessive or compulsive focus on cleanliness. A phallic or Oedipal fixation, for example, might be expressed as a person's continuously being attracted to people who resemble the opposite-sex parent in some way.

connection
Clinical psychologists refer to anal fixations as obsessive–compulsive disorder.
See Chapter 15, p. 579.

fixation
a defense mechanism whereby a person continues to be concerned and even pre-occupied with earlier stages of development.

Although Freud's theory of psychosexual stages has been very influential, there is little empirical research to support his ideas. To Freud's credit, however, he was one of the first psychologists to acknowledge that children have sexual feelings and gain pleasure from their genitals, a fact that is now well-established. Moreover, the idea that adult personality has its origin in childhood is also now widely accepted, but not as fixations to earlier psychosexual stages. Even Freud's followers, as we see in the next section, did not agree with many of the details of his theory of psychosexual development.

Freud is one of the most complex figures in the history of psychology. His theories have had a significant and lasting influence on Western thought. Large segments of twentieth-century art and literature were directly or indirectly influenced by Freud's views of human nature, from James Joyce's use of stream of consciousness to Salvador Dali's surrealistic paintings (Adams & Szaluta, 1996; Brivic, 1980; Kimball, 2003). And yet over the last generation many research-oriented psychologists have dismissed Freud as a pseudoscientist, because he did not support his ideas with research that could be replicated. His status as a scientist is indeed questionable, but this does not mean that his insights as a clinician have no scientific merit. In fact, in the late 1990s a group of neuroscientists began to argue that the latest evidence from neuroscience confirms certain of Freud's ideas. Antonio Damasio, a well-known contemporary neuroscientist, has stated, "I believe we can say that Freud's insights on the nature of consciousness are consonant with the most advanced contemporary neuroscience views" (quoted in Solms & Turnbull, 2002, p. 93). Others argue that Freud's ideas about the power of the unconscious, the conflicting nature of motives, and the importance of early childhood experience on adult personality have had a lasting impact and have survived empirical testing (Weston, 1998).

For all of Freud's genius, however, he became dogmatic about his ideas after he had published them. If any of his followers seriously challenged them, they were often kicked out of Freud's inner circle or official society. Some of these followers went on to develop their own theories of psychoanalysis. Among them were Alfred Adler, Carl Jung, and Karen Horney.

striving for superiority
according to Adler, the major drive behind all behavior, whereby humans naturally strive to overcome their physical and psychological deficiencies.

Alfred Adler The first to break away from Freud, Alfred Adler (1870–1937) saw himself as Freud's colleague rather than follower. But when he disagreed with Freud on the major motives underlying behavior, he had to resign from the presidency of Freud's Vienna Psychoanalytic Society. Adler's first major assumption was that humans naturally strive to overcome their inherent inferiorities or deficiencies, both physical and psychological. This **striving for superiority,** not sex

Adler observed that people's personalities are shaped by their birth order.

or aggression, is the major drive behind all behavior (Adler, 1956). Adler introduced the term *compensation* to explain how this process unfolds. All people, he pointed out, begin life as young, immature, and helpless. As they grow, they strive toward growth and completion. In the process, they attempt to *compensate* for their feelings of weakness or inferiority. Although all people do this to some extent, some develop an unhealthy need to dominate or upstage others as a way of compensating for feelings of inferiority—that is, they develop an **inferiority complex.**

Another key idea in Adler's theory of individual psychology is the importance of birth order in influencing personality (Adler, 1931). Adler noticed consistent differences in the personalities of first-born, middle-born, and last-born individuals. First-born children tend to have strong feelings of superiority and power. After all, by definition, first-born children are older and more mature than their siblings. First-borns can be nurturing of others, but they are sometimes highly critical and have a strong need to be right. Second children tend to be motivated and cooperative, but they can become overly competitive. Youngest children can be realistically ambitious but also pampered and dependent on others. Finally, only children can be socially mature, but they sometimes lack social interest and have exaggerated feelings of superiority.

Carl Jung   Though younger, Carl Jung (1875–1961) became more widely known than Adler. Jung's signature idea was that the unconscious has two distinct forms: personal and collective (Jung, 1918/1964). The **personal unconscious** consists of all our repressed and hidden thoughts, feelings, and motives. This is similar to Freud's notion of the unconscious. Jung also believed, however, that there is a second kind of unconscious, one that belongs not to the individual but to the species. He called it the **collective unconscious,** and it consists of the shared experiences of our ancestors—God, mother, life, death, water, earth, aggression, survival—that have been transmitted from generation to generation. Jung decided that there must be some kind of collective unconsciousness that would explain the many instances in which dreams, religions, legends, and myths share the same content even though the people who created them have never directly or

inferiority complex
an unhealthy need to dominate or upstage others as a way of compensating for feelings of deficiency.

collective unconscious
according to Jung, the shared experiences of our ancestors that have been passed down from generation to generation.

personal unconscious
according to Jung, all our repressed and hidden thoughts, feelings, and motives.

even indirectly communicated with one another. The idea of a collective unconscious came naturally to Jung because he was extraordinarily well versed in world mythology, world religion, and archeology. However, he was less well versed in biological theory or genetics; thus, his understanding of the mechanisms involved was inconsistent and, at times, based on faulty assumptions, such as experiences being inherited from generation to generation.

The collective unconscious is made up of **archetypes**: ancient or archaic images that result from common ancestral experiences. Their content is made manifest most often in our dreams but also in fantasies, hallucinations, myths, and religious themes. Jung postulated many archetypes, including the shadow, anima, and animus. The *shadow* is the dark and morally objectionable part of ourselves. We all have impulses that are dark and disturbing; in fact, most often we project evil and darkness onto our enemies and deny that we ourselves are evil or capable of it. Shadow figures are found everywhere in politics, literature, and art, not to mention movies: Darth Vader of *Star Wars* clearly personifies the shadow figure.

The **anima** is the female part of the male personality, and the **animus** is the male part of the female personality. All people possess characteristics and traits—not to mention hormones—that are typical of both genders, but men tend to deny and repress their feminine side, or anima. Women likewise tend to deny or repress their masculine side, or animus. Full personality development requires acknowledging and being receptive to these unconscious or less-well-developed sides of one's personality.

archetypes
ancient or archaic images that result from common ancestral experiences.

anima
according to Jung, the female part of the male personality.

animus
according to Jung, the male part of the female personality.

Darth Vader, the villain from the movie *Star Wars*, epitomizes Jung's shadow archetype of the dark, morally repugnant side of human nature.

Karen Horney

One of the first major female voices in the psychoanalytic movement was that of Karen Horney (pronounced "horn-eye"; 1885–1952). Compared to Freud, Horney focused more on the social and cultural forces behind neurosis and the neurotic personality, and indeed her approach is labeled "psychoanalytic social theory." The essence of Horney's theory is that neurosis stems from basic hostility and basic anxiety. *Basic hostility* is anger or rage that originates in childhood and stems from fear of being neglected or rejected by one's parents. Because hostility toward one's parents is so threatening, however, it is often turned inward and converted into *basic anxiety*, which Horney defined as "a feeling of being isolated and helpless in a world conceived as potentially hostile" (1950, p. 18).

Although basic anxiety in itself is not neurotic—it can give rise to normal behaviors—in some people it can result in neurotic behaviors. Horney argued that all people defend themselves against basic anxiety (isolation and helplessness) by developing particular needs or trends (see Figure 13.4). If these needs become compulsive and the person is unable to switch from one need to another as the situation demands, that person is neurotic. The three *neurotic trends* or needs are

1. *moving toward others* (the compliant personality)
2. *moving against others* (the aggressive personality)
3. *moving away from others* (the detached personality)

FIGURE **13.4**

INTERACTION AMONG HOSTILITY, ANXIETY, AND DEFENSES IN HORNEY'S THEORY.
Hostility and anxiety mutually influence one another, and the person then defends him- or herself by developing either normal or neurotic defenses. Horney maintained that we all may develop defenses, but in neurotic individuals, these needs become compulsive.

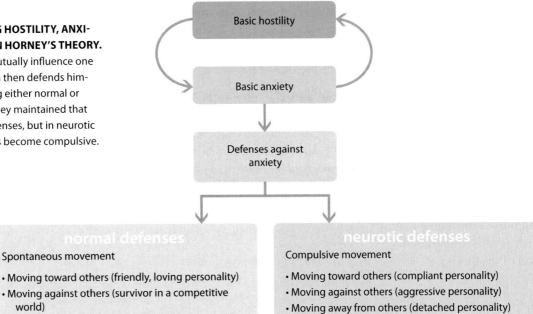

Neurotically moving toward others involves consistently needing or clinging to other people, belittling oneself, getting people to feel sorry for "poor little me," and almost completely repressing feelings of anger and hostility. Neurotically moving against others involves puffing oneself up in an obvious and public manner, "chest-beating," competing against others at almost everything, and being prone to hostility and anger. Finally, neurotically moving away from others involves developing a detached and "cool" demeanor—not responding emotionally, not caring, and being "above it all." One way to avoid feeling isolated and helpless is not to feel anything. Whenever someone tries to get close to a detached person and open up to him or her, the detached person withdraws and closes up. Detached individuals are unwilling to make commitments, especially to long-term relationships (Horney, 1945).

HUMANISTIC–POSITIVE PSYCHOLOGY THEORIES

A second major perspective explaining personality comes from a *humanistic approach,* which is optimistic about human nature, believing that humans are naturally interested in realizing their full potential. Humanists argue that psychology needs to study humans at their best as well as at their worst. As Abraham Maslow wrote (1968, p. 5), "Freud supplied us with the sick half of psychology, and we must now fill it with the healthy half." The term *humanism* is not commonly used today, mostly because many adherents of this approach did not conduct empirical research. Yet the movement has been rekindled since the late 1990s under a new label: *positive psychology.* Positive psychology embraces and generates empirical research, but its fundamental ideas come from two major thinkers in the humanistic tradition: Abraham Maslow and Carl Rogers.

Abraham Maslow We discussed one of Abraham Maslow's (1908–1970) major ideas in Chapter 11: his hierarchy of needs. An important concept that followed from his theory of needs was that of self-actualization, which stood at the top of the hierarchy. This term refers to people's inherent drive to realize their full potential (an idea that was influenced by Adler's notion of striving for superiority; Maslow, 1970). Only a very few people attain this highest level of the hierarchy of needs because only a very few are "fully human"—that is, living life at its fullest and achieving their full potential.

connection

Maslow's hierarchy of needs describes how the basic needs (such as hunger, thirst) must be satisfied before one can pursue the higher needs, such as self-actualization.

See Chapter 11, p. 419.

Based on an examination of historical figures whom he considered self-actualizing, Maslow identified a set of characteristics that he believed to be more common in self-actualizing individuals than in other people (Maslow, 1970). He listed 15 characteristics, 5 of which we summarize here:

1. *Spontaneity, simplicity, naturalness:* Self-actualizing people sometimes can appear quite childlike in their ability to be spontaneous and straightforward; they do not pretend to be what they are not.

2. *Problem-centered (have a "calling"):* Self-actualizing people often experience moments of profound personal importance or personal meaning (what Maslow called "peak experiences"), and these experiences shape the rest of their lives. A sense of what they were meant to do with their lives is suddenly revealed to them, and they devote the rest of their lives to it. These individuals are focused and secure in who they are and what matters most to them—and often their concerns have great philosophical, spiritual, political, artistic, or scientific meaning.

3. *Creativity (self-actualizing rather than specialized):* Problems confront us dozens, if not hundreds, of times each day. Self-actualizing people are able to readily solve problems with originality and novelty. By *creativity*, Maslow does not mean creativity as expressed in art or science (specialized creativity) but rather the kind of creativity that can be found in everyday life (self-actualizing creativity). Practical, everyday creativity is more important than professional achievement—although self-actualized people may be creative in their work as well.

4. *Deep interpersonal relations:* Self-actualizing individuals are likely to have few but profound relationships. They do not call 10 or 15 people their "best friends" or even "friends" but instead may have close relationships with only one or two people. These relationships, however, are intensely intimate—they share deep thoughts and feelings about themselves, each other, and the world.

Does Bill Gates (center, with his wife Melinda Gates and a patient at a clinic in South Africa) fit Maslow's profile of a self-actualizing individual? In 1975 Gates founded the Microsoft Corporation and revolutionized the computing industry. Having left the day-to-day management of Microsoft to others, he now dedicates his efforts to eradicating AIDS and other diseases throughout the world, providing college scholarships for minority students, and other philanthropic endeavors through the Bill and Melinda Gates Foundation.

Carl Rogers (second from right) leads a group therapy session. His client-centered therapy approach is discussed in Chapter 16.

5. *Resistance to enculturation:* Self-actualizing people are less likely than most people to be influenced by the ideas and attitudes of others. Their ideas are solidly their own; because they have a clear sense of direction in life, they don't look to others for guidance on what to think or how to behave.

unconditional positive regard acceptance of another person regardless of his or her behavior.

Carl Rogers   Another key figure in the humanistic–positive psychology tradition was the psychotherapist Carl Rogers (1902–1987). Rogers developed a unique form of psychotherapy based on the assumption that people naturally strive toward growth and fulfillment and need unconditional positive regard for that to happen (Rogers, 1980). **Unconditional positive regard** is the ability to respect and appreciate another person unconditionally—that is, regardless of their behavior. This may sound easy, but in fact it is very difficult. It means that even if someone violates our basic assumptions of what it means to be a good, decent, and moral person, we still appreciate, respect, and even love him or her as a person. It requires that we separate person from behavior—which can be difficult even for parents and their children. To love people only when they do things that we want and like is to love them conditionally.

In contrast to Maslow, Rogers had a specific, measurable way of defining the self-actualizing tendency and psychological adjustment. To Rogers, all of us have two distinct ways of seeing and evaluating ourselves: as we really are and as we ideally would like to be. The first he called the *real self* and the second the *ideal self* (Rogers, 1959). Rogers then defined psychological adjustment as congruence between the real and ideal selves.

SOCIAL–COGNITIVE LEARNING THEORIES

A third major category of personality theory is based on the social–cognitive learning perspective, exemplified by the research and writings of Walter Mischel. As we have seen, personality traits produce consistent behavior over time and across situations. A hostile person, for example, may be less hostile in one situation (for example, being run into by a child) than in another (for example, being cut off in traffic). Yet, compared to a nonhostile person he or she is likely to be more hostile in many—but not all—situations. Mischel says that people are not consistent across all situations (Mischel & Shoda, 1995, 1999), as it would be pathological not to change one's behavior when the situation changes. What

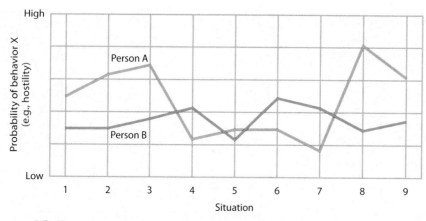

FIGURE **13.5**

HYPOTHETICAL PERSON–SITUATION–BEHAVIOR INTERACTION. People respond to different situations differently, producing unique personality–situation profiles. Here, Person A is more hostile than Person B in the first three situations. They are roughly the same in the middle four situations. So saying that Person A is more hostile than Person B would be misleading and simplistic. It depends on the situation. (*Source:* Mischel & Shoda, 1995.)

qualities a person brings to each situation interact with the situation to make one person act somewhat differently when the situation changes. Figure 13.5 above illustrates how people and situations interact according to Mischel's theory. The figure presents the probabilities of two individuals (A and B) acting in a hostile manner across nine different situations. As you can see, Person A is more likely to be hostile in six of the nine situations, so we would label this person "hostile." But notice two things: (1) There are a few situations in which Person B is more hostile, and (2) Person B is more stable and consistent across all nine situations, whereas Person A is sometimes *very* hostile but at other times not hostile at all. This hypothetical situation demonstrates how the person, situation, and behavior interact.

TRAIT THEORIES

A fourth general perspective that explains personality is the trait approach, which assumes that traits or dispositions are the major force behind personality. But which traits are most important? Between the 1930s and the 1980s, dozens of different measures of personality were developed, but almost none of them measured the same personality traits. Some psychologists argued for the central importance of hostility, authoritarianism, introversion, intelligence, repression, and impulsivity, while others cited psychopathic deviance, tolerance, or psychological insight. But until personality psychologists could reach a consensus on a set of traits that make up personality across cultures, no progress could be made in the study of personality, as it would mean different things to different people.

As far back as the 1930s, Gordon Allport (1897–1967) tried to figure out how many personality traits existed (Allport & Odbert, 1936). He began with the idea that language would be a good place to start looking. His argument was simply that if a word exists for a trait, it must be important. He approached the problem by taking

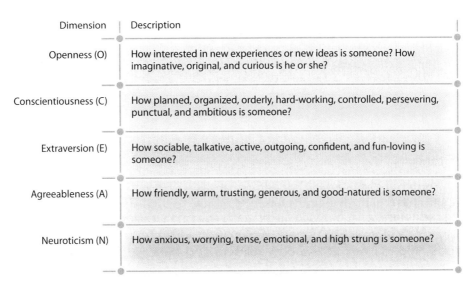

Dimension	Description
Openness (O)	How interested in new experiences or new ideas is someone? How imaginative, original, and curious is he or she?
Conscientiousness (C)	How planned, organized, orderly, hard-working, controlled, persevering, punctual, and ambitious is someone?
Extraversion (E)	How sociable, talkative, active, outgoing, confident, and fun-loving is someone?
Agreeableness (A)	How friendly, warm, trusting, generous, and good-natured is someone?
Neuroticism (N)	How anxious, worrying, tense, emotional, and high strung is someone?

FIGURE **13.6**
BIG FIVE DIMEN-SIONS OF PER-SONALITY. The acronym OCEAN (or CANOE) will help you remember the five dimensions.

an English dictionary and combing through it page by page and counting each time a term described a person. After going through and counting all the personally descriptive words, he came away with nearly 18,000 words in English. A few problems arose, however. First, some of these terms—such as *sad, angry, bored,* or *annoyed*—described temporary states. Others were personal evaluations (*wonderful, unhelpful*) or described physical traits (*tall, heavy*). And finally, others were essentially synonyms, such as *friendly* and *nice*. When he fixed these problems, he still ended up with more than 4,000 English words that were personally descriptive. He went on to argue, however, that most individuals could typically be described with only about 10 or so central traits.

By the 1980s, personality researchers amassed evidence for the existence of five universal and widely agreed upon dimensions of personality (Costa & McCrae, 1992; Digman, 1990; John & Srivastava, 1999). This perspective is known as the **Big Five** or **five-factor model;** the five dimensions are openness to experience, conscientiousness, extraversion, agreeableness, and neuroticism (see Figure 13.6). An easy way to remember these is to use the acronym O-C-E-A-N or C-A-N-O-E.

The Big Five dimensions are more of a taxonomy, or categorization scheme, than a theory. They describe but do not explain personality. In the 1990s, Robert McCrae (1949–) and Paul Costa (1942–) proposed a theory around the Big Five personality dimensions. The two major components of their theory are basic tendencies and characteristic adaptations (McCrae & Costa, 1996, 1999). The Big Five personality dimensions, along with our talents, aptitudes, and cognitive abilities, are referred to as **basic tendencies** and they have their origin in biological forces. In fact, McCrae and Costa take a clear but somewhat controversial stance in arguing that these basic tendencies are due solely to internal or biological factors such as genes, hormones, and brain structures.

Big Five or **five-factor model** a theory of personality, that includes five dimensions: **o**penness to experience, **c**onscientiousness, **e**xtraversion, **a**greeableness, and **n**euroticism (OCEAN).

basic tendencies the essence of personality: the Big Five personality dimensions plus talents, aptitudes, and cognitive abilities.

BIOLOGICAL THEORIES

The fifth way of explaining personality theoretically, biological theory, does provide explanations for McCrae and Costa's scheme. The biological theories of personality assume that differences in personality are partly based in differences

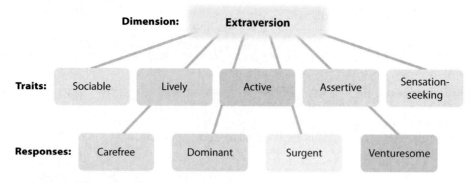

FIGURE **13.7**

EYSENCK'S HIERARCHY OF PERSONALITY TRAITS FOR EXTRAVERSION. For each of the three dimensions of personality, Eysenck developed a hierarchy of related traits and responses. (*Source:* Eysenck, 1990.)

in structures and systems in the central nervous system, such as genetics, hormones, and neurotransmitters. Among the most important of these theories for personality is the one proposed by Hans Eysenck (1916–1997), who argued for the fundamental importance of biology in shaping personality (Eysenck, 1947, 1982, 1990). Eysenck proposed three, rather than five, fundamental dimensions of personality. Two are included in the Big Five, neuroticism and extraversion. The third, psychoticism, is a combination of the three other traits from the Big Five of openness, conscientiousness, and agreeableness. Psychoticism consists of traits such as "aggressive," "cold," "antisocial," "impulsive," "egocentric," "nonconforming," and "creative." All three personality dimensions are hierarchical; that is, neuroticism, extraversion, and psychoticism each comprise more specific traits, which in turn comprise even more specific traits (see Figure 13.7).

Eysenck developed a model in which differences in personality are caused by the combined influences of genes, neurochemistry, and certain characteristics of the central nervous system (Eysenck, 1997). The main idea behind Eysenck's model is that differences in individuals' genome (DNA) create a different level of arousal and sensitivity to stimulation. These differences in genetics and levels of arousal and sensitivity lead to differences in the three major dimensions of personality: psychoticism, extraversion, and neuroticism (P-E-N). Personality differences in dimensions, in turn, lead to differences in learning, conditioning, perception, and memory. These cognitive-perceptual-learning differences lead to differences in social behaviors such as sociability, criminality, sexual behavior, and creativity.

Evidence supports the connection between central nervous system arousal and personality traits, especially extraversion–introversion. Specifically, differences in cortical arousal and sensory thresholds lead to differences in extraversion–introversion. **Cortical arousal** refers to how active the brain is at a resting state as well as how sensitive it is to stimulation (Eysenck, 1997; Gale, 1983). Because they have higher baseline levels of cortical arousal, introverts require a lower stimulus level to arouse them and reach their "comfort zone" than do extraverts. Eysenck argued that lower thresholds to arousal imply greater sensitivity to stimuli. Stimulation, whether it is a new place or new people, can easily become overwhelming for an introvert. Therefore,

nature & nurture
Eysenck's model attributes personality to biological as well as social factors.

cortical arousal level of activation in the brain.

introverts consistently shy away from or withdraw from stimulating environments. By the same token, extraverts, with low cortical arousal and high thresholds of arousal, seek out and enjoy highly stimulating experiences (Eysenck, 1990, 1997). Introversion or inhibition can thus be seen as a way of coping with an inherently aroused and sensitive central nervous system.

As you see, a number of different approaches have been proposed by different theorists. The primary assumptions and key ideas of each of the five approaches is presented in Figure 13.8.

	Assumptions	Theorist	Key ideas
Psychoanalytic	Our personality resides in the unconscious and early childhood experiences lay the foundation for adult personality.	Freud	Unconscious, Preconscious, Conscious Id, Ego, Superego, Psychosexual Development
		Adler	Striving for superiority, Compensation Inferiority complex Birth order
		Jung	Personal unconscious, Collective unconscious Archetypes: shadow, anima, animus
		Horney	Basic hostility, basic anxiety, defenses against anxiety
Humanistic	We have a natural interest in becoming the best person possible.	Maslow	Strive to become the best possible person Self-actualization
		Rogers	Strive toward growth and fulfillment through unconditional positive regard Real self, Ideal self
Social-Cognitive	A person's behavior changes in different situations.	Mischel	Behavior results from the interaction of the cognitive and emotional qualities of the person and the particular situation he or she is in.
Traits	Traits are the major force behind personality.	McCrae/Costa	**O**penness to experience **C**onscientiousness **E**xtraversion **A**greeableness **N**euroticism Five-factor Model includes: Basic tendencies—biologically based Characteristic adaptations—culturally based
Biological	We have a biological foundation for our personality traits.	Allport	Personality is a product of both heredity and environment.
		Eysenck	**P**sychoticism **E**xtraversion **N**euroticism Differences in genetics, neurochemistry, and CNS cause personality differences.

FIGURE **13.8**
SUMMARY OF FIVE APPROACHES TO PERSONALITY.

quick quiz 13.3: How Do Theorists Explain Personality?

1. Hatred and aggression toward homosexuals as a reaction to fear of one's own homosexual impulses would be an example of which Freudian defense mechanism?
   a. reaction formation
   b. psychosexual stages
   c. repression
   d. projection

2. According to Jung, the collective unconscious is made up of ancient or archaic images that result from common ancestral experiences called
   a. core-relational themes
   b. the animus
   c. the inferiority complex
   d. archetypes

3. The key assumption of humanistic theorists, such as Maslow or Rogers, is that people
   a. are driven by unconscious motives
   b. strive toward growth and fulfillment
   c. learn from observing others
   d. none of the above

4. The Big Five dimensions of personality are openness to experience, conscientiousness, extraversion, _____, and _____.
   a. depression; neuroticism
   b. agreeableness; neuroticism
   c. agreeableness; introversion
   d. anxiousness; introversion

Answers can be found at the end of the chapter.

breaking new ground
Animal Personality

The question of whether animals have personality might seem to be stretching the definition of personality too far. If we claim that animals have personality, might we simply be projecting human qualities onto them, what scientists term *anthropomorphizing?* Most people who have owned more than one cat or dog can identify differences in the personalities of their pets. Some pets are calm, while others are excitable; some are friendly and readily approach strangers, whereas others are more reserved and wary. But even if we can see evidence of personality in animals such as dogs and cats, can we see it in other animals? Do mice have personality? birds? reptiles? fish? worms? What do you think? At what point does the term *personality* become meaningless?

ONLY HUMANS HAVE PERSONALITY

Until the 1990s, most psychologists would have argued that the term *personality* made sense only as a term applied to humans. But a graduate student at the University of California, Berkeley, changed this view. In the early 1990s Samuel Gosling was attending his required graduate seminar on personality psychology, which involved detailed discussion, readings, and debate about what personality means and how it should be defined. Here is what happened:

> My undergraduate degree had been in philosophy and psychology so in the service of understanding what personality means, I tried to adopt a *reductio ad absurdum* [reduction to absurdity] strategy, pushing the term *personality* until it no longer made sense. I thought I'd take a case where it clearly made no sense to use personality and then work backward to find out where the limits of personality lay. Animals seemed like a good example of something that clearly didn't have personality so I decided to start there. But the more I thought about it the less I could generate arguments for why personality could not be applied to animals. (Gosling, personal communication, November 9, 2005)

If Gosling had accepted his own assumption of the absurdity of animal personality, he would have never gone on to make important contributions to the field.

EVIDENCE FOR PERSONALITY IN OTHER ANIMALS

Gosling and his colleague Oliver John (1999) reported findings from 19 studies across 12 nonhuman species. Along with other researchers, they provided evidence for at least 14 major nonhuman species in which personality traits exist. They can be categorized along the same dimensions as human personality. The summary of these findings is presented in Figure 13.9 on page 518. Keep in mind that the labels from the Big Five are general labels and the specific ones used in these studies vary somewhat. For instance, *neuroticism* is sometimes called *emotional stability, excitability, fearfulness, emotional reactivity, fear–avoidance,* or *emotionality. Agreeableness* is sometimes labeled *aggression, hostility, understanding, opportunistic, sociability, affection,* or *fighting–timidity.* In addition, *dominance–submission* is a trait that is often seen and measured in nonhuman animals, but it does not fit into any of the Big Five categories. These ratings of animal personality were made by one of two behavioral observation techniques: either by animal trainers who had extensive knowledge of the individual animals or by trained observers with no history with the animals but who were trained until they could reliably evaluate the dimensions in question.

It may not surprise you that primates and other mammals tend to share the largest number of personality traits with humans. However, chimpanzees, our closest relative, share with humans a distinct "conscientiousness" dimension. Such a finding suggests that conscientiousness—which involves impulse control and therefore requires highly developed brain regions capable of controlling impulses—is the most recently evolved personality trait. Thus, with the exception of chimps and horses, animals other than humans do not possess the required brain structures to control impulse and organize and plan their activities in advance. Even with chimps, the conscientiousness dimension was somewhat narrowly defined as lack of attention, goal directedness, and disorganized behavior.

It may be surprising, however, to see wild birds, fish, and even octopus on a list of animals that possess humanlike personality traits. For instance, in a study of a European bird resembling a chickadee, when researchers placed a foreign

	Neuroticism	Extraversion	Agreeableness	Openness	Conscientiousness
chimpanzee	✔	✔	✔	✔	✔
horse[a]	✔	✔	✔	?	✔
rhesus monkey	✔	✔	✔	✔	
gorilla	✔	✔	✔		
dog	✔	✔	✔	✔	✔[b]
cat	✔	✔	✔		✔[b]
hyena	✔		✔	✔	
pig		✔	✔	✔	
vervet monkey		✔	✔		
donkey		✔	✔		
rat	✔		✔		
guppy	✔	✔			
octopus	✔	✔			
chickadee[c]				✔	

[a] Based on Morris, Gale and Duffy (2002).
[b] Competence/learning is a mixture of openness and conscientiousness.
[c] Based on Dingemanse, Both, Dent, Van Oers and Van Noordwijk (2002).

FIGURE **13.9**

PERSONALITY DIMENSIONS ACROSS SPECIES. Ratings by trainers who know the animals or by trained observers produced these results, which suggest that animals do have personalities and that they share some of the same traits as humans. Note that domestic dogs and cats have a "competence" or "learning" dimension that is a mixture of openness and conscientiousness. Where no check mark appears, there is no evidence for that trait in that species. (*Source:* Gosling & John, 1999.)

object into the cage, such as a battery or a Pink Panther doll, some birds were consistently curious and explored the novel object while others consistently withdrew and avoided the object (Zimmer, 2005; cf. Dingemanse et al., 2002). The researchers called these differences in birds "bold" and "shy." These differences are much like those psychologists observe when they place an infant in a room with a stranger. Approach–boldness and shyness–avoidance are also dimensions of human temperament.

connection

Psychologists have used the Strange Situation to measure attachment styles in infants.
See Chapter 5, p. 192.

In another experiment, the researchers placed a bowl of worms in the room and then startled the birds by lifting a metal plate nearby. They then observed the amount of time it took for the birds to return to the worms. Once again, there were consistent individual differences: Some birds returned very quickly (bold) and others very slowly (shy). Even more interesting from the standpoint of personality is that these behavioral differences are consistent over long periods and appear to have a strong genetic component. It took, for instance, only four generations of breeding to produce noticeably bolder or shyer birds.

Moreover, these behaviors are influenced by the same gene (DRD4) that is involved in thrill seeking and openness to novel experiences in humans. If the same individual differences in traits (behavioral tendencies) exist in humans and other animals, they must share a common evolutionary history. In other words, these similarities between human and animal personality lend support to the argument that human personality is the product of evolutionary forces.

HOW THESE STUDIES CHANGED PEOPLE'S MINDS

Many researchers dismissed research about animal personality as anthropomorphic— merely projecting human ideas and values onto animals. When Gosling and others began this research in the early 1990s, there was considerable resistance to the idea that animals have personalities. Gosling himself began with the assumption that the idea of animal personality was absurd.

Yet top research journals are now publishing research on animal personality. More importantly, the potential benefits are being recognized. Research on genetics, health, and the biological and evolutionary basis of personality all benefit from an understanding of how animals differ in their personalities. Much of the early and current work on animal personality has a distinctly applied purpose—for example, selecting seeing-eye dogs or dogs that are suitable for bomb-detection tasks. As a result of ongoing research, it has become clear that individuals in most every species exhibit consistent differences in behavior in a specific situation and that these differences remain constant over time. As such, the evidence very much fits the definition of personality: consistency of individual differences over time and across situations.

quick quiz 13.4: Breaking New Ground: Animal Personality

1. Which of the human Big Five personality characteristics appears only in humans, chimpanzees, and horses?
   a. openness
   b. extraversion
   c. conscientiousness
   d. agreeableness
2. What is one real-world application of the work on animal personality?
   a. animal therapy
   b. dog show training
   c. selection of pets
   d. selection of seeing-eye dogs

Answers can be found at the end of the chapter.

How Is Personality Measured?

Defining and explaining personality are of prime importance, but you can only define and explain what you can measure. So how do psychologists measure and study personality? There are at least four distinct methods: behavioral observation, interviewing, projective tests, and questionnaires.

BEHAVIORAL OBSERVATION

The most direct and objective method for gathering personality data is to observe behavior and simply count specific behaviors that are associated with particular traits, such as aggression, hostility, friendliness, anxiety, or conscientiousness. However, collecting valid data is more difficult than it might seem. For instance, choosing to rate the fairly straightforward example of "aggression" raises many questions. What specific behaviors will count as aggression? Hitting? Insulting? Sarcasm? How does a researcher quantify each behavior—on a continuum from none to a great deal, or simply on the basis of whether it is present or not? Over what time period will the behavior be observed? Will the people who are being observed see the raters? If so, will this affect their behavior? Where will the behavior take place: in a real-world setting or in a laboratory? Who will rate the behavior? How do we know that different observers will view a given behavior in the same way?

These questions address the issue of measurement in general and reliability in particular. If two or more raters are to accurately rate and agree upon their ratings, there must be **inter-rater reliability.** The researchers must first establish an exact definition of the trait they wish to measure, identify the behaviors that make up that trait, and practice rating it against experienced, expert, and reliable raters. The new raters are deemed "reliable" if their ratings compare well with established norms or expert ratings, usually with a correlation of .80 or higher.

When children or others, such as animals, who cannot evaluate or report on their own personalities are being assessed, behavioral observations are required. Advantages to behavioral observations do not depend on people's view of themselves, as self-report measurements do, and they are direct and relatively objective.

Despite these strengths, behavioral observations are costly and time-consuming. Moreover, not all personality traits can be observed by other people. Anxiety and depression, for instance, although they can be expressed through behavior, are often experienced internally and subjectively—external observations can't tell the whole story. It is for these kinds of personality traits that a person's own reporting—that is, a self-report—is more reliable. Self-reports can be obtained in three ways: interviewing, projective tests, and questionnaires.

inter-rater reliability
measure of how much agreement there is in ratings when using two or more raters or coders to rate personality or other behaviors.

INTERVIEWING

Sitting down with another person face-to-face is probably the most natural and comfortable of all personality assessment techniques. Interviewing is an ideal way to gather important information about a person's life. In fact, from the participant's perspective, interviewing is usually more engaging and pleasant than, for example, filling out a questionnaire. The clear advantage for participants is the open-ended nature of the interview, in which they can say anything they wish in response to a question. Of course, this is also a drawback of interviewing. What does a response mean? How are responses scored and by whom? What criteria are used? These issues are similar to those associated with behavioral ratings, but with interviews the "behavior" is a verbal response to a question that must be coded reliably and accurately. Thus, the ease of interviews from the participant's perspective is offset by the difficulty of scoring responses reliably.

PROJECTIVE TESTS

Projective tests present an ambiguous stimulus or situation to participants and ask them to give their interpretation of or tell a story about what they see. These techniques are based on the assumption, stemming from psychoanalysis, that unconscious wishes, thoughts, and motives will be "projected" onto the task. By interpreting an entire series of such answers, a psychologist can identify consistent unconscious themes. The two most widely used projective tests are the Rorschach Inkblot Test and the Thematic Apperception Test (TAT).

In the **Rorschach Inkblot Test,** a series of ambiguous inkblots are presented one at a time, and the participant is asked to say what he or she sees in each one (see Figure 13.10). The responses are recorded and then coded by a trained coder (most often a psychologist or psychotherapist) as to how much human and nonhuman "movement," color, form, and shading the participant sees in each card (Exner, 1974; Masling & Borenstein, 2005). Not only is the test used to measure unconscious motives, but its supporters also claim that responses can help them diagnose various psychological disorders, such as depression, suicidal thoughts, pedophilia, post-traumatic stress disorder, or anxiety disorders (Guarnaccia et al., 2001; Nash et al., 1993; Ryan, Baerwald, & McGlone, 2008; Sloan, Arsenault, & Hilsenroth, 2002).

Similarly, the **Thematic Apperception Test** consists of a series of hand-drawn cards depicting simple scenes that are ambiguous. The participant's task is to make up a story about what he or she thinks is going on in the scene. For instance, a TAT card might depict a male and female sitting next to each other on a sofa, with the woman talking on the phone. One person might tell a story of how this is a couple going through a stormy period in their relationship. The woman in fact is talking with one of her other male friends. Another person might tell a story of how the couple is trying to figure out what do that evening, and the woman is calling another couple about going to a movie tonight.

Like Rorschach responses, TAT answers are scored by trained raters. No interpretation of personality is ever based on just one inkblot or one TAT story. Rather, over a series of inkblots or TAT cards, a set of themes may emerge. One person might consistently see sexual objects in the inkblots; another might consistently make up stories that reveal conflict and aggression toward parents or authority in general. Although projective tests provide fascinating information, as with interviews their open-ended responses create difficulties in scoring. Inter-rater reliability is not as high as it should be, making conclusions drawn from projective techniques questionable (Huprich, 2008; Petot, 2000; Wood & Lilienfeld, 1999).

PERSONALITY QUESTIONNAIRES

Because of the expense and time behavioral ratings and interviews require, along with the relative unreliability of projective tests, the most common way of measuring personality is asking participants to summarize their own behavioral tendencies by means of questionnaires. **Personality questionnaires**

projective tests
personality assessment in which the participant is presented with a vague stimulus or situation and asked to interpret it or tell a story about what they see.

Rorschach Inkblot Test
a projective test in which the participant is asked to respond to a series of ambiguous inkblots.

Thematic Apperception Test (TAT)
a projective test in which the participant is presented with a series of picture cards and asked to tell a story about what is going on in the scene.

personality questionnaires
self-report instruments on which respondents indicate the extent to which they agree or disagree with a series of statements as they apply to their personality.

FIGURE **13.10**
AN INKBLOT SIMILAR TO THOSE FOUND ON A RORSCHACH INKBLOT CARD. In the Rorschach Inkblot test, a person is asked to interpret the inkblot however he or she wishes. After the participant has done this with a dozen or more cards, psychologists can form ideas about what kinds of thoughts, feelings, and motives are consistently being "projected."

Screening and Selecting Police Officers

As they devise personality questionnaires, researchers in university settings often examine questions such as these: What is the structure of personality? How consistent is personality over the life span? Does personality have a biological basis? In addition to these academic questions, however, measures of personality have numerous real-world applications. Therapists use them when they are trying to understand destructive bickering and hostility between spouses (Atkins, Berns, et al., 2005; Atkins, Yi, et al., 2005). Career guidance counselors use them in advising students on their career choices (Costa, 1996; Mount et al., 2005). Government and business organizations rely on them to select the right people for particular jobs (Carless, 1999; De Fruyt & Murvielde, 1999).

Let's look more closely at the last example. Imagine that you are the chief of police in your town and part of your job involves hiring police officers. In police work it is of the utmost importance to have officers who are conscientious and dependable, can handle stress, and can control their impulses—especially violent ones. An officer who is not in control and hurts or even kills someone out of anger is not acceptable.

How will you make sure that you select the right kind of person to handle the job? In addition to references, background checks, criminal history investigations, training performance, and other kinds of testing, personality testing is crucial to your decision to hire or not to hire. In fact, most major police departments routinely include personality assessments in their selection process. Personality tests are more useful in screening than in selecting. In other words, they alert those making hiring decisions to candidates who

consist of individual statements, or *items*; respondents indicate the extent to which they agree or disagree with each statement as it applies to their personality. Responses are usually arranged on a *Likert scale*, which attaches numbers to descriptive responses, such as 1 "completely disagree," 3 "neither agree nor disagree," and 5 "completely agree."

The development of a personality questionnaire takes years of research and data collection before items are selected for the final version. The items first must meet the requirements of validity and reliability. That is, they must measure the trait or traits they claim to measure and must do so consistently over time and across questions dealing with the same traits.

Questions are based on either the rational or the empirical method. The **rational, or face valid method,** involves using reason or theory to come up with a question. For instance, if we wanted to develop a new measure of anxiety, we might include an item like "I feel anxious much of the time." This is a "face valid" item because what it measures, anxiety, is clear and can be taken at face value. A frequently used personality questionnaire that uses the face valid method is the NEO-PI (Costa & McCrae, 1992). The problem with such questionnaires, however, is that because the questions are transparent, participants might give *socially desirable* or false answers rather than honest ones. For example, for the item "I am anxious much of the time," the person might not want to admit to frequently feeling anxious and hence might not answer honestly.

rational (face valid) method a method for developing questionnaire items that involves using reason or theory to come up with a question.

might be better suited to another line of work rather than indicating which ones will perform best as police officers.

For example, authorities used a cluster of personality scales from the widely used California Psychological Inventory (CPI; Gough & Bradley, 1996) to reliably identify police officers who consistently used excessive force and provided drugs to inmates (Hargrave & Hiatt, 1989). More specifically, the problematic officers scored unusually low on the CPI's Self-control, Socialization, and Responsibility scales. These dimensions tap into what some psychologists refer to as conscientiousness—the tendency to plan and to be organized, controlled, and careful. Sarchione and colleagues (1998) replicated this study by selecting case histories of 109 officers from 13 police agencies who had been formally disciplined by the agency. That is, they had engaged in various "dysfunctional" behaviors: excessive force, sexual misconduct, substance abuse, insubordination, embezzlement, lying to superiors, and multiple motor vehicle violations.

The "disciplinary group" was then matched in terms of gender, ethnicity, and age with 109 officers who had not committed any of these dysfunctional behaviors. The two groups scored very differently on Self-control, Socialization, and Responsibility. The disciplinary group was significantly lower on all three dimensions. These findings suggest that low scores on these personality dimensions would be red flags against hiring certain applicants as police officers.

A second technique for selecting questions uses the **empirical method,** which disregards theory and face validity and focuses instead simply on whether a question distinguishes groups it is supposed to distinguish (Gough & Bradley, 1996). For instance, if the statement "I prefer baths to showers" distinguishes anxious from non-anxious people, it is used in a measure of anxiety. We would have to have an outside criterion of who is anxious or not, such as a therapist's evaluation of the anxiety levels. A standard way to empirically validate questions on an anxiety measure would be to develop a series of questions and then administer them to people known to suffer from anxiety disorders (as diagnosed by a therapist) and to people known to not suffer from anxiety disorders. If the questions are answered differently by the two groups, they are valid and should be included in the questionnaire. If they are not answered differently, they do not distinguish anxious from non-anxious people and should be discarded. For example, if we discover in initial testing that anxious people are more likely than non-anxious people to endorse the statement "I prefer baths to showers," we should include this item in our questionnaire on anxiety. We would include it even if we did not really understand why the two groups answer it differently. The evidence shows that it does distinguish the two groups, so it is used. This is the essence of the empirical method of making personality inventories.

Two of the most commonly used personality questionnaires in existence each were made using the empirical method: the Minnesota Multiphasic Personality

empirical method
a method for developing questionnaire items that focuses on including questions that characterize the group the questionnaire is intended to distinguish.

Inventory (MMPI) and the California Personality Inventory (CPI). The MMPI is used by psychotherapists to assess the degree and kind of a person's psychiatric personality traits, such as depression, paranoia, or psychopathic deviance (antisocial personality; Tellegen et al., 2003). The CPI, however, is a measure of nonpathological or normal personality traits such as sociability, responsibility, dominance, or self-control (Gough & Bradley, 1996). Both the MMPI and CPI consist of questions that target groups answer differently than the general population. In "Psychology in the Real World" we describe how measures like the CPI have been used in screening potentially dangerous police officers from police departments.

quick quiz 13.5: How Is Personality Measured?

1. The most objective method for gathering information about personality traits is to
   a. observe behavior
   b. conduct interviews
   c. administer questionnaires
   d. do genetic testing

2. The Rorschach inkblot test is an example of which type of personality measurement?
   a. structure interview
   b. questionnaire
   c. projective test
   d. standardized test

3. Scales that use response categories ranging from 1 to 5 (with labels ranging from 1 for "completely agree" to 5 for "completely disagree") are called
   a. ratio scales
   b. Likert scales
   c. face valid
   d. dichotomous

Answers can be found at the end of the chapter.

making connections
in personality

Does Personality Change Over Time?

Personality is at the center of who we are. Recall our definition of personality at the beginning of the chapter: Personality is the unique and enduring manner in which a person thinks, feels, and behaves. Although it shows considerable stability over our lifetime, it also changes and develops between our infant and adult years. Hundreds of studies have looked at how personality traits change or don't change over the course of individuals' lives. Personality consistency and change illustrate many of the principles discussed in this chapter. Indeed, all definitions, theories,

and measures of personality confront the question of consistency and change of personality.

Personality Consistency

When we talk about personality consistency, we mean relative consistency. In fact, that is one of the lessons learned from Walter Mischel's work on how qualities and traits interact with the specific situations to bring about different behavior across different situations (Kammrath et al., 2005; Mischel & Shoda, 1999). No one is consistent all of the time or in all situations. Consistency is a matter of degree.

Longitudinal studies, those that examine the same people over a period of time, reveal high levels of stability of personality traits. Early in their collaboration, Costa and

McCrae (1976) conducted a longitudinal study of personality, expecting to find that personality traits change over time. To their surprise, they found a high degree of stability over a 10-year period. Another set of longitudinal studies revealed very small changes in neuroticism, extraversion, and openness over a period of 6 to 9 years (Costa et al., 2000; McCrae & Costa, 2003).

Most parents or observers of infants and toddlers are quick to project subtle signs of their children's interest or talent into the future. But do our personality and traits at age 3 portend future outcomes such as employment, mental illness, criminal behavior, and quality of interpersonal relationships? Jack and Jeanne Block conducted some of the first long-term studies of human temperament and personality. They used most of the methods for assessing personality discussed in this chapter: interviews, behavioral observations, and personality questionnaires. They found, for instance, that children who were impulsive, aggressive, and tended to cry at age 3 were most likely to use drugs during adolescence (Block, Block, & Keyes, 1988).

connection

Children who are rated by their parents as being undercontrolled at age 3 are more likely than other children to have drinking problems, get in trouble with the law, and even attempt suicide at age 21.
See Chapter 5, p. 210.

Research from behavior genetics has demonstrated that personality stability between adolescence and adulthood is largely due to genetic factors (Blonigen et al., 2006; Takahashi et al., 2007). More specifically, genetics contribute to the personality consistency we see from adolescence to adulthood, whereas environmental factors contribute to both stability and change in personality traits (Takahashi et al., 2007).

Personality Change
We all like to think we can change—that we have the power to change our destructive habits and become a better person. But can we? Research does support some degree of personality change as we move from adolescence through adulthood and as we adapt to changes in life circumstances. First, we consider changes across the life span.

Typical Personality Change Across the Life Span
Recent research confirms that some degree of change in personality occurs normally from adolescence to adulthood and into old age (Allemand, Zimprich, & Hendricks, 2008; Roberts & Mroczek, 2008). The most impressive evidence comes from a meta-analysis of 92 studies that assessed personality change in over 50,000 individuals on the Big Five dimensions of personality (Roberts, Walton, & Viechtbauer, 2006). In general, people become steadily more agreeable

and conscientious from adolescence to late adulthood (see Figure 13.11 on page 000). In addition, people tend to become more assertive or dominant and emotionally stable from adolescence to middle adulthood and then level off on these personality dimensions. Finally, people generally become more sociable (social vitality) and open to new experiences from adolescence to early adulthood. These traits level off in adulthood and then decline in older adulthood. The same pattern of change is seen in cross-sectional research that examines personality differences in different age groups at the same time (Allemand et al., 2008). Together, these results make clear that personality is not set in plaster once we reach adulthood.

Personality Change After Changes in Life Circumstances
Not only does personality show some degree of change during normal life-span development, but it also is open to change when we experience drastic changes in our lives, such as becoming a parent, suffering a brain injury, or developing Alzheimer's disease. Let's consider each of these circumstances.

Parenting and Personality Change. Few events change a person as much as becoming the primary caregiver for a totally helpless infant. How does such a major transition affect one's personality? The answer seems to be that it depends on many factors. Paris and Helson (2002) conducted a longitudinal study of female college seniors in their early 20s and followed them until they reached their 50s and 60s. They found that becoming a mother affected personality differently, depending on the woman's evaluation of motherhood. That is, if a woman liked being a full-time mother, then having children led to an increase in her flexibility, self-esteem, adjustment, resourcefulness, and control and a decrease in her dependence and fearfulness. If, however, she did not especially enjoy being a full-time mother, the opposite personality changes were observed.

FIGURE **13.11**

PERSONALITY CHANGE FROM ADOLESCENCE TO LATE ADULTHOOD. This graph shows the results of a meta-analysis of personality change on the Big Five dimensions across 92 studies and involving more than 50,000 individuals. The scale of change is measured in standardized units. 0 units means no change. Emotional stability is the opposite end of neuroticism. (*Source:* Roberts, Walton, & Viechtbauer, 2006.)

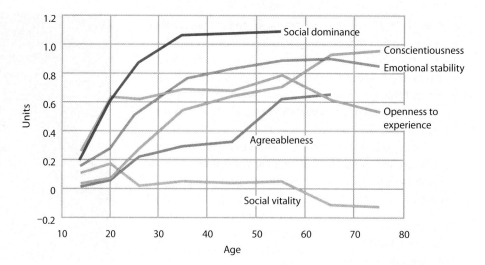

Other researchers report that parenthood affects the personalities of mothers and fathers differently. For example, although self-concept in general seems to stay the same for both mothers and fathers, self-esteem goes down and irritability goes up in mothers but not in fathers (Onodera, 2003). Similarly, the gender of the parent interacts with the temperament of the child. Compared to having a child with an "easy temperament," having one with a "difficult temperament" is more likely to increase the father's but not the mother's anxiety (Sirignono & Lachman, 1985). The biggest personality change seems to come from increases in a personal sense of control and mastery if parents have an "easy" child and decreases on these dimensions if they have a "difficult" child (Sirignono & Lachman, 1985). Having a child who is difficult undermines the belief that parents can truly control the life and behavior of their children.

Brain Injury and Personality Change. Do you remember Phineas Gage from Chapter 3? He was the railroad foreman who had a tamping iron shoot through his cheek and out the top of his skull, forever changing his personality (Macmillan, 2000).

Current recent research on damage to the same part of the frontal lobes where Gage's injury occurred shows similar kinds of personality change. Based on ratings of personality (behavioral observations, Rorschach Inkblots, and semi-structured interviews), children and adults who suffer brain injury often lose the ability to control impulses, are socially inappropriate, have a temper, and are more prone to anger (Mathiesen, Förster, & Svendsen, 2004; Max, Robertson, & Lansing, 2001; Max et al., 2006; Parker, 1996; Rao et al., 2008).

Alzheimer's Disease and Personality Change. Alzheimer's disease is a major degenerative brain disease whose hallmarks are severe dementia and memory loss. It eventually affects personality and ultimately leads to death. Using the NEO-PI as a measure of the Big-Five personality dimensions, various studies have shown that neuroticism increases and openness and conscientiousness decrease after the onset of Alzheimer's disease (Chatterjee et al., 1992; Clark et al., 2000; Strauss, Pasupathi, & Chatterjee, 1993). Two studies have also reported a decrease in extraversion (Strauss et al., 1993; Williams, Briggs, & Coleman, 1995), and at least one study has reported a decrease in agreeableness (Chatterjee et al., 1992; see Figure 13.12). Most studies, however, report no change on the agreeableness dimension. Research using other measures of personality have reported that Alzheimer's patients became less kind, generous, enthusiastic, and self-reliant and more irritable and out-of-touch (Petry et al., 1989; Talassi et al., 2007). In other words, there is a biological basis for our personality. Changes in the brain are often accompanied by personality changes.

quick quiz 13.6: Making Connections in Personality

1. Which personality trait tends to increase sharply from adolescence to adulthood but then taper off in late adulthood?
   a. sociability (social vitality)
   b. neuroticism
   c. openness to experience
   d. repression

2. People who suffer brain injury, especially to the frontal lobes, often show which kind of personality change? They become
   a. more agreeable.
   b. less able to control their impulses.
   c. lower self-esteem.
   d. more neurotic.

Answers can be found at the end of the chapter.

1 research question

Does Alzheimer's disease change an individual's personality? Do different observers agree on the nature of personality change after a person develops Alzheimer's disease?

Jack and Lucy before Alzheimer's diagnosis

2 method

Eleven elderly men and 11 elderly women (mean age = 72) who met the criteria for Alzheimer's disease, based on cognitive testing and brain images, participated in this correlational study by Strauss and colleagues (1993). The primary caregiver (most often a spouse) and a secondary good friend or family member each rated the patient's personality using the NEO-PI. The NEO-PI measures the "Big Five" personality dimensions of neuroticism, extraversion, openness, agreeableness, and conscientiousness. Raters were asked to remember when the symptoms of Alzheimer's first started and then pick a period of a few years prior to that and rate the person's personality at that time. Approximately two to three months later, each rater was asked to evaluate the patient's personality again, but this time as he or she was then--after the onset of Alzheimer's.

Lucy after diagnosis

research process

Personality rating by Jack and his daughter

3 results

Personality ratings of the person showed changes in three of the Big Five dimensions of personality after the onset of Alzheimer's disease. People were rated higher in neuroticism (anxiety) and lower in extraversion, openness, and conscientiousness. Agreeableness did not change. Independent ratings by secondary raters matched those of the primary raters and showed the same pattern.

NEO personality rating

Bar chart. Y-axis: Mean, from 20 to 70. X-axis categories: Neuroticism, Extraversion, Openness, Agreeableness, Conscientiousness. Legend: Before (dark), After (light).
- Neuroticism: Before ≈47, After ≈65
- Extraversion: Before ≈47, After ≈34
- Openness: Before ≈38, After ≈34
- Agreeableness: Before ≈54, After ≈50
- Conscientiousness: Before ≈55, After ≈32

4 conclusion

Primary and secondary raters agreed that after the onset of the Alzheimer's disease people became more anxious, less extraverted, less open, and less conscientious. Other studies have replicated these general findings (Clark et al., 2000; Williams et al., 1995). Alzheimer's changes personality in predictable ways.

FIGURE **13.12**

PERSONALITY CHANGE AFTER ALZHEIMER'S DISEASE. (*Source:* M. E. Strauss, M. Pasupathi, & A. Chatterjee. (1993). Concordance between observers in descriptions of personality change in Alzheimer's disease. *Psychology and Aging, 8,* 475–480.)

chapter **review**

DEFINING PERSONALITY

- Personality is the essence of who we are—both our uniqueness and our consistency. Personality traits function to change behavioral thresholds and make certain behaviors more likely and others less likely.

THE NATURE AND NURTURE OF PERSONALITY

- Personality is an expression of both nature and nurture. Personality traits have evolved through natural and sexual selection, in which genetic and environmental forces work in tandem in shaping an individual's personality.

- Studies of infant temperament offer another line of evidence for a biological basis for adult personality. Infants make their way into the world with different and unique ways of behaving. Children may be temperamentally easy, difficult, or slow to warm up.

HOW DO THEORISTS EXPLAIN PERSONALITY?

- Theories of personality organize and explain observations and also stimulate testable hypotheses. There are five perspectives that explain personality differences and development.

- The first theory, Freud's psychoanalytic theory, assumes distinct levels of consciousness. The most important of these is the unconscious, the level at which most thoughts, feelings, motives, and images reside.

- Freud developed the idea of psychological defense mechanisms, which defend us against psychological threats by unconsciously denying or distorting reality. Repression, for example, is the unconscious process of keeping disturbing thoughts, feelings, or impulses out of consciousness.

- Three followers of Freud broke their ties with him to establish their own views. Alfred Adler argued that striving for superiority is the primary motive underlying almost all behavior. Carl Jung introduced the idea of the personal unconscious and the collective unconscious. Karen Horney developed a psychoanalytic social theory centered on three neurotic trends: moving toward others, moving against others, and moving away from others.

- Second, humanistic theory emphasizes psychological growth and health. Abraham Maslow developed a detailed concept of self-actualization—that is, the inherent tendency to strive to realize one's full potential. Carl Rogers developed the concept of unconditional positive regard to help people achieve self-fulfillment.

- Third, the social–cognitive learning theory of Walter Mischel is based on the belief that consistent personality characteristics interact with the environment to produce a person's unique behaviors.

- Fourth, trait theory argues for a universal and stable personality structure that consists of five dimensions of personality: openness, conscientiousness, extraversion, agreeableness, and neuroticism (O-C-E-A-N). These traits are normally distributed in the population, with most people falling somewhere between the two extremes on each trait.

- Fifth, biological theories such as those of Hans Eysenck are another perspective. Eysenck argued for three fundamental dimensions of personality: psychoticism, extraversion, and neuroticism (P-E-N). Eysenck's theory holds that differences in individuals' cortical arousal and sensitivity threshold lead to differences in introversion and extraversion.

- Confirming the importance of the biological basis of personality, personality psychologists and animal behaviorists have begun to explore the nature of animal personality. They have found not only that other primates and mammals exhibit many consistent and unique personality qualities but also that birds,

fish, octopi, and even insects have personality traits that distinguish one individual from another.

HOW IS PERSONALITY MEASURED?

- Personality is measured in four major ways: observing and coding behavior; interviewing; administering projective tests; and administering structured personality questionnaires.

MAKING CONNECTIONS IN PERSONALITY

- Most of the major topics in this chapter can be connected by highlighting research demonstrating the stability and change in personality over time. Genetic forces contribute to personality stability, whereas environmental factors contribute to both stability and change.

key **terms**

anima, p. 508

animus, p. 508

archetypes, p. 508

basic tendencies, p. 513

behavioral thresholds, p. 496

Big Five or five-factor model, p. 513

collective unconscious, p. 507

cortical arousal, p. 514

defense mechanisms, p. 504

ego, p. 503

empirical method, p. 523

fixation, p. 506

id, p. 503

inferiority complex, p. 507

inter-rater reliability, p. 520

personal unconscious, p. 507

personality, p. 495

personality questionnaires, p. 521

projection, p. 504

projective tests, p. 521

psychosexual stage theory, p. 505

quantitative trait loci (QTL) approach, p. 498

rational (face valid) method, p. 522

reaction formation, p. 504

repression, p. 504

Rorschach Inkblot Test, p. 521

striving for superiority, p. 506

sublimation, p. 504

superego, p. 503

Thematic Apperception Test (TAT), p. 521

trait, p. 496

unconditional positive regard, p. 511

unconscious, p. 503

quick quiz **answers**

Quick Quiz 13.1:   1. b   2. c   Quick Quiz 13.2:   1. a   2. d   3. b   Quick Quiz 13.3:   1. a   2. d   3. b   4. b
Quick Quiz 13.4:   1. c   2. d   Quick Quiz 13.5:   1. a   2. c   3. b   Quick Quiz 13.6:   1. c   2. b

social
behavior

preview
questions

1 *Why does it hurt to be left out?*

2 *What effect does the presence of other people have on our behavior?*

3 *How can we anticipate what other people might do?*

4 *Why do people risk their own lives to help others?*

W hen Shaundra was in third grade she spent most of her time with two friends, Lindi and Tara. In Shaundra's mind, they were all best friends, although sometimes it seemed to her that Lindi and Tara spent more time together than either of them did with Shaundra. One afternoon the three girls were running on the playground. Lindi and Tara ran a bit ahead of Shaundra. Suddenly Lindi stopped, turned around and screamed at Shaundra: "Shaundra, you're such a tagalong. Would you just leave us alone?" Shaundra—stunned—felt as if she had been kicked in the stomach.

Being rejected hurts. In fact, social exclusion creates physical pain. In one study on the neural basis for social pain, participants were brought into a lab with an fMRI scanner and were told they would be involved in an electronic ball tossing game called "Cyberball" (Eisenberger et al., 2003). Once inside the scanner, they could see, on a screen, a ▶

▶ Cyberball game that was apparently in progress between two other research participants in scanners in different rooms. Actually, unknown to the participant, there were no other people playing the game. After watching the "others" play for a few throws, the participant joined in. For a while, the three players continued playing Cyberball together. After seven throws, however, the other players stopped throwing the ball to the participant and went on about their game. In effect, the participant was left out, like Shaundra. Participants reported being upset about being excluded. What's more, the fMRI scans showed that the brain circuitry activated immediately after exclusion maps very well onto known brain circuitry for physical pain.

chapter
outline

Why does it hurt to be excluded? Like other mammals, humans form important bonds with other members of our species. We depend on other people to raise us and to cooperate with us in the presence of threats (Neuberg & Cottrell, 2006). As a result, the ways in which we relate to others play a huge role in our lives. In this chapter we will discuss why belonging to a group matters to us, as well as other key aspects of social behavior, such as how the presence of others influences our behavior, how we perceive our social world, how we form attitudes, and how we relate to others. These topics are the focus of **social psychology,** which is the study of the effects of the real or imagined presence of others on people's thoughts, feelings, and actions. Exclusion is one of the topics we'll explore. ■

social psychology
study of how living among others influences thought, feelings, and behavior.

Group Living and Social Influence

The social nature of human beings stems from the importance of group living in our evolutionary history. We are not solitary animals. Group living offered many advantages in the evolution of our species, such as increased safety in the presence of danger, cooperation with others to complete challenging tasks (such as hunting), and child rearing (Brewer & Caporael, 2006). This is why people work to preserve group membership and why they modify their behavior when in the presence of others. In this section we examine how the presence of other people influences performance and one's willingness to go along with the group. As we will see, social factors may push people to do things they might not otherwise do.

You may have noticed that sometimes you perform a task better with others around and sometimes you do worse. Such effects are seen in animals as diverse as humans, chimps, birds, and even cockroaches (Gates & Allee, 1933; Klopfer, 1958). The effect of having others present can depend on the situation or task at hand, how easy or difficult the task is, and how excited you are. For example, some joggers find that they run faster in groups than they do when running alone. **Social facilitation** occurs when the presence of others improves our performance. Over a century ago, Norman Triplett (1898) noticed that he rode his bike faster when he rode with others. In a laboratory test of the idea that the presence of others improves performance, Triplett asked children to wind a fishing reel as fast as they could. He tested them when alone and when in groups of other kids doing the same thing. Sure enough, they wound faster when other kids were present—they showed social facilitation. Social facilitation usually occurs for tasks that are easy, we know well, or we can perform well (Zajonc, 1965).

Social loafing is the opposite of social facilitation. **Social loafing** occurs when the presence of others causes individuals to relax their standards and slack off (Harkins, 1987). For example, if you are singing in a choir and there are dozens of other voices supporting yours, you are less likely to sing your heart out. You alone are not responsible for the sound, so the diffusion of responsibility alters your behavior (you loaf). If you were singing a solo, you would belt it out—because all responsibility would rest on your shoulders.

social facilitation
phenomenon in which the presence of others improves one's performance.

social loafing
phenomenon in which the presence of others causes one to relax one's standards and slack off.

connection
Our level of arousal also affects our performance, according to the Yerkes-Dodson law.
See Chapter 11, p. 418.

CONFORMITY

Social facilitation is a subtle way in which the presence of others changes our actions. More direct social factors also pressure us to act in certain ways. Society, for instance, imposes rules about acceptable behavior, called **social norms.**

social norms
rules about acceptable behavior imposed by the cultural context in which one lives.

In nomadic cultures, such as Mongolia, extended family groups have traditionally stayed together, sharing food, shelter, livestock, childrearing, and all other aspects of daily life. How might communal living in isolated surroundings affect an individual's behavior?

Examples of social norms include "Boys don't cry," "Don't pick your nose in public," and "Don't be a sore loser." Norms vary by culture, too. Burping at the dinner table is considered rude in the United States, but in some parts of East Asia, belching is seen as a compliment to the chef.

Most of the time we abide by, or conform to, the social norms of our culture. **Conformity** occurs when people adjust their behavior to what others are doing or adhere to the norms of their culture. The reasons for conformity vary, depending on the situation. **Informational social influence** occurs when people conform to the behavior of others because they view them as a source of knowledge about what they are supposed to do. A familiar example is the tendency for incoming freshmen to look to other students for information about how to dress, how to behave in class, and the like. This type of conformity is most pronounced in ambiguous or novel situations. This is informational social influence. We do this all the time, especially as children. Chimps even look to other chimps to learn how to use unfamiliar tools (Whiten, Horner, & de Waal, 2005).

Sometimes we do things that go against our better judgment in an effort to preserve group membership. **Normative social influence** occurs when people go along with the behavior of others in order to be accepted by them. A classic example is peer pressure, in which people engage in certain behaviors, such as drinking or trying drugs, in order to be accepted as a member of a particular social group. This phenomenon is widespread. Look at yourself and your peers. Do you wear the same kinds of clothes? How many of you have similar hairstyles? A more subtle example of normative social influence occurs when you emerge from the theater after going to a movie with friends, not sure whether you liked the movie or not, although everyone else in the group loved the film and is talking about it. By the end of the evening you may also be talking about what a great film it was and may have actually convinced yourself that it was great. This example shows that we are not always aware of how other people shape our behavior and beliefs.

One of the classic studies of social psychology, conducted by Solomon Asch in 1951, demonstrates the power of normative social influence. Asch devoted his career to the study of perception, specifically to investigating the fact that perception is not a direct function of the physical properties of stimuli. For example, our perceptions of the angle of a line can be influenced by the frame around it (Witkin & Asch, 1948). Asch wondered if the social world could shape our perceptions as well. If pressured by the opinions of others, would people say they saw something that clearly wasn't there? He didn't think they would, but he was wrong.

Asch assembled several groups of six to seven people in the lab and told them he was researching visual acuity. Asch was really interested in conformity, but did not want to tell his participants the real object of the study in case that information changed their behavior. Asch then showed the participants two cards—one with a standard line, the other displaying three lines of varying length. The participant's job was to pick the one line out of the three that matched the standard

conformity
tendency of people to adjust their behavior to what others are doing or to adhere to the norms of their culture.

informational social influence
conformity to the behavior of others because one views them as a source of knowledge about what one is supposed to do.

normative social influence
conformity to the behavior of others in order to be accepted by them.

FIGURE **14.1**

STIMULUS LINES PRESENTED TO PARTICIPANTS IN THE ASCH CONFORMITY STUDIES. Each participant was asked to say which of the comparison lines (1, 2, or 3) matched the length of the standard line. The answers were always clear-cut; in this case, the answer is "2." The conformity manipulation involved the confederates in the group giving an obviously wrong answer (such as "1") and then seeing how the participant answered.

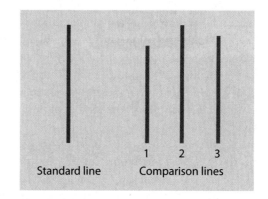

Standard line   Comparison lines

line. As you can see in Figure 14.1, the task was easy. This comparison process was repeated 18 times and, on each occasion, participants gave their answers out loud.

So where is the conformity? What the one real participant didn't know was that all of the other so-called participants were *confederates,* people who actually worked for the experimenter. The one real participant was always seated in the last chair and so heard the judgments of all of the other group members before making a choice. The trick was that on the first 6 trials everyone gave the obvious and correct answer. Starting on trial 7, however, the confederates started giving wrong answers. On the first of the rigged trials, the first confederate would glance at the cards and confidently say, "The answer is line 1," even when it clearly was not correct. The next confederate would nod in agreement and say, "Yes, it is line 1." After 5 or 6 people in a row gave the wrong answers—remember, this is a *very* easy task—it was the real participant's turn. Participants faced a choice: Agree with everyone else's clearly erroneous judgments or give the answer that they personally thought was correct.

While none of the participants agreed with the group all of the time, 76% of them went along with the group at least once when a group answer was clearly wrong. On average, participants answered incorrectly 37% of the time. Yet when left alone to do the task, participants made errors less than 1% of the time.

How does the design of this study make it a test of normative social influence rather than informational social influence? The answer is the lack of ambiguity in the task. Judging the lengths of the lines was really easy—there was no need for participants to look to others for information about what the right answer was. When participants worked alone, they rarely made errors. But in the situation just described, after all the confederates had given the same wrong answer, many participants conformed by also giving the clearly wrong answer.

Indeed, sometimes people go to great lengths to do what the group is doing, when it does not make sense, especially when the group is required to make a decision. This phenomenon, called **groupthink,** occurs when the thinking of the group takes over, so much so that group members forgo logic or critical analysis in the service of reaching a decision (Janis, 1983). Groupthink can occur in juries that are hard-pressed to reach a verdict or in governments under pressure. According to the Senate Intelligence Committee's report on intelligence failures leading up to the 2003 invasion of Iraq, the erroneous CIA assertion that Iraq possessed weapons of mass destruction—the primary justification for the invasion—was based on groupthink by an administration invested in finding a reason to attack Iraq (U.S. Senate, 2004).

groupthink
situation in which the thinking of the group takes over, so much so that group members forgo logic or critical analysis in the service of reaching a decision.

Another factor that affects conformity is culture. In collectivist cultures, groups matter more than the individual, so any group-preserving behavior (such as conformity) would be valued and encouraged. In Japan, for example, the company that one works for is elevated to the status of family. One is expected to make personal sacrifices for the company to preserve group unity (Miller & Kanazawa, 2000). Cross-cultural replications of the Asch experiments reveal that people in collectivist cultures like Japan are more likely to conform than are people in individualistic cultures (Bond & Smith, 1996).

connection
In an individualistic culture, behavior is determined more by personal goals than by group goals, whereas in a collectivist culture, behavior is determined more by shared goals.
See Chapter 13, p. 501.

MINORITY SOCIAL INFLUENCE

At times a single individual or small number of individuals can influence an entire group. In social psychology, a single person or small group within a larger group is termed a *minority*, while the larger group is referred to as the *majority*. Just as the majority pushes for group unity, the minority can push for independence and uniqueness. After all, if people always conformed, how would change occur (Moscovici, 1985)? In order to change the majority view, however, the minority must present a consistent, unwavering message.

Most often, minority opinion shifts majority opinion by means of informational social influence. If a group encounters a situation in which the members are unsure about what to do and a minority carefully presents a well–thought out position to the majority, then the majority might accept it. In this way juries can change course. Juries must provide unanimous decisions, and sometimes only one voice disagrees with the majority. If that minority of one offers a logical argument for the dissenting opinion, the majority might change their views.

OBEDIENCE

Obedience is a kind of conformity in which people yield to the social pressure of an authority figure. Social psychological research on obedience emerged in response to real-life concerns in the aftermath of World War II. The horrific events of the Holocaust raised troubling questions: How could an entire nation endorse the extermination of millions of people? Were all Germans evil? Sure, Adolf Hitler did not act alone. A supporting cast of thousands was necessary to annihilate so many people. Former Nazi officers who testified in war trials after the war said they were "following orders." The same rationale was offered in 2004 by U.S. soldiers who humiliated and tortured Iraqi prisoners at Abu Ghraib.

obedience
a type of conformity in which a person yields to the will of another person.

Will people really do horrible things if an authority figure orders them to do so? One psychologist spurred into action by the Nazi atrocities was Stanley Milgram. A Jew whose family left Europe before Hitler's rise to power, Milgram spent much of his early academic life trying to make sense of the Holocaust (Blass, 2004). With the support of his graduate advisor, Solomon Asch, Milgram decided to investigate whether people would conform even when their actions might harm others.

Stanley Milgram

Milgram recruited people from the community to participate in an experiment at Yale University. A participant arrived at the lab and sat down next to another supposed participant, who was a confederate. The experimenter, who looked very official in a white lab coat, then told both individuals that they would be participating in a study on the effects of mild punishment on memory. He then assigned them to be either a teacher or learner by asking them to pull a note that said either "teacher" or "learner" from a bowl. The drawing was rigged so that the real participant always landed the "teacher" role and the confederate got the "learner" role. Then the experimenter showed both the teacher and learner to the room where the learner would sit. The learner's task involved learning and repeating lists of words. The learner was told that every time he made an error he would receive a mild electric shock, delivered by the teacher. With each mistake the shocks would increase in intensity. Both teacher and learner were shown the chair where the learner would sit, which had restraints to make sure the electrodes had a good contact when he received the shock. The teacher then received a sample shock of very low voltage to get a sense of what the learner would experience. In actuality, this was the only real shock administered during the entire experiment.

Then they went to the teacher's room. The teacher sat at a table behind a panel of little switches. Under each switch was a label indicating voltage level. The levels started at 15 volts ("mild shock") and increased in 15-volt increments all the way up to 450, with 315 volts designated as "danger: severe shock" and 435–450 (end of scale) as "XXX" (see Figure 14.2). The teacher was reminded that if the learner made mistakes he or she would have to deliver a shock, and with each mistake would have to increase the level.

The experiment began uneventfully. Then the learner made occasional mistakes. At lower levels of shock, the learner gave no real response to the shocks. As the teacher moved up the shock scale and the learner supposedly made more errors, the teacher and experimenter could hear a yelp of pain come from the learner with each shock. (In fact, the learner played a prerecorded tape of his responses to the shock.) At this point, many teachers would ask the experimenter if they should go on, and he would say, "The experiment requires that you go on."

Before beginning the experiments, Milgram polled experts to see how many "teachers" they thought would go along with the experimenter's demands to administer high levels of shock. One group of experts, psychiatrists, predicted that only about 30% would administer shocks as high as 150 volts, less than 4% would go to the 300-volt level, and only 1 person in 1,000 would go all the way to 450 volts. How far do *you* think most people would go in administering shocks?

The results differed drastically from these predictions. As shown in Figure 14.2b, at 150 volts, the point at which the learner yelled, "Get me out of here! My heart's starting to bother me! I refuse to go on! Let me out!" there was a drop in obedience—from 100% to about 83%. Some participants stopped, but many, although visibly uncomfortable, continued with the experiment. What is alarming is how many people went all the way up to the end of the shock scale, despite the yells and protests (and eventual silence) of the learner. Twenty-six of the 40 participants in the original experiment (65%) went all the way to 450 volts (Milgram, 1963, 1974). Men and women were equally likely to reach the 450-volt level.

Milgram's experiments show how powerful situations can make reasonable people do things that seem cruel and unusual. In fact, several "teachers" did protest and yet went on when the experimenter urged them to continue. When asked, "Who is going to take responsibility if that guy gets hurt?" the experimenter would say, "I have full responsibility, please continue." Somehow, the belief that someone else (the authority figure) was responsible for their actions

connection
What are the obligations of researchers to ensure the ethical treatment of participants in research?
See Chapter 2, p. 66.

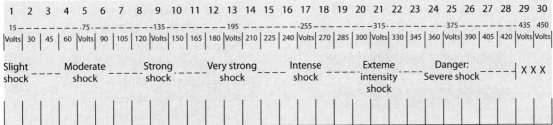

| 1 | 2 | 3 | 4 | 5 | 6 | 7 | 8 | 9 | 10 | 11 | 12 | 13 | 14 | 15 | 16 | 17 | 18 | 19 | 20 | 21 | 22 | 23 | 24 | 25 | 26 | 27 | 28 | 29 | 30 |

15————————75——————————135———————195 ———————255———————315————————375—————————435 450

| Volts | 30 | 45 | 60 | Volts | 90 | 105 | 120 | Volts | 150 | 165 | 180 | Volts | 210 | 225 | 240 | Volts | 270 | 285 | 300 | Volts | 330 | 345 | 360 | Volts | 390 | 405 | 420 | Volts | Volts |

Slight shock — Moderate shock — Strong shock — Very strong shock — Intense shock — Exteme intensity shock — Danger: Severe shock — X X X

(a) Control panel seen by the "teacher."

FIGURE **14.2**

MILGRAM'S STUDY OF OBEDIENCE. (a) This is the control panel seen by the "teacher." (b) Experts consulted by Milgram prior to the study predicted that at higher voltages, participants would refuse to administer further shocks to the "learner." As the graph shows, the experts were wrong. At the highest voltages, when the experimenter told them the experiment must continue in spite of the "learner's" protests, 60 percent of the "teachers" continued to administer "shocks." (c) The "learner" is strapped in for Milgram's study. (*Source:* Milgram, 1974.)

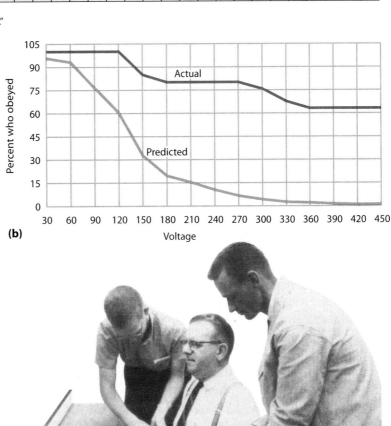

alleviated feelings of guilt or concern in some of the participants. This is akin to former Nazi officers saying, "I was just following orders." But who really has the final responsibility?

Because participants clearly experienced mental anguish while taking part in the study, it sparked a fierce debate about ethics in research. Milgram contacted his participants later and asked whether they regretted having participated. Less than 2% did (see Figure 14.3 on page 540).

You might think that you would never administer those shocks or that people today would know better. Not so. In 2006, social psychologist Jerry Burger conducted a modified version of Milgram's original study with college students. An important change from the original study was that when the participants

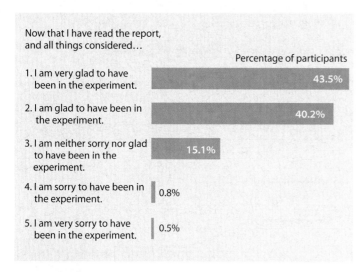

Now that I have read the report, and all things considered…

Percentage of participants

1. I am very glad to have been in the experiment. **43.5%**

2. I am glad to have been in the experiment. **40.2%**

3. I am neither sorry nor glad to have been in the experiment. **15.1%**

4. I am sorry to have been in the experiment. 0.8%

5. I am very sorry to have been in the experiment. 0.5%

FIGURE **14.3**

QUESTIONNAIRE RESPONSES OF PARTICIPANTS IN MILGRAM'S OBEDIENCE STUDY. Despite the distress they experienced during the experiment, the majority of the respondents did not regret their involvement.

began to protest, they were told to continue rather than told that they *had* to continue. Also, once participants passed the 150-volt range, the experiment stopped. By making these changes, the researchers were able to obtain permission from the American Psychological Association to conduct the experiment, which otherwise would not meet current standards for ethical treatment of human participants. As in Milgram's experiment, Burger reported that two-thirds of participants obeyed the authority figure and continued to administer shocks after the "learner" began protesting.

quick quiz 14.1: Group Living and Social Influence

1. Sometimes people perform better—for example, ride a bike faster—when they are in groups than when alone. Social psychologists call this
   a. the Yerkes–Dodson principle
   b. social loafing
   c. social facilitation
   d. conformity

2. People who are of a minority opinion in a group are most likely to change the opinion of the majority by
   a. getting them to conform to group pressure
   b. reason and logic
   c. trying to shame them
   d. presenting a well-formed persuasive argument

3. When put in a situation where an individual has to say something about the length of a line that goes against what everyone else in the group has said, most people
   a. eventually conform at least once and go along with the group
   b. always conform and go along with the group
   c. never conform and go along with the group
   d. pretend not to be paying attention

4. In Milgram's study on obedience, under pressure from an authority figure, approximately what percentage of the participants gave the maximum punishment of 450 volts to the learner's incorrect answers?
   a. 25%
   b. 50%
   c. 65%
   d. 90%

Answers can be found at the end of the chapter.

Social Perception

Social processes not only influence our behavior but also guide our perceptions of the behavior of others. For example, we wonder why people do what they do. (Why does Maria wear her hair like that?) We wonder whether we can believe what people say. (Can we reliably tell when someone is lying to us?) And how do we form attitudes about others? These are all matters of *social perception*, the way in which we make sense of our social world.

ATTRIBUTION

We often wonder why people do the things that they do (Kelley & Michela, 1980), and we try to explain their actions. **Attributions** are the inferences we make about the causes of other people's behavior.

Pioneering social psychologist Fritz Heider (1958) made an important distinction between two types of attributions. Internal or *dispositional attributions* ascribe other people's behavior to something within them, such as their personality, motives, or attitudes. For example, let's say that Chris flunked a test. A dispositional attribution would be "Chris flunked the test because he is too lazy to study." The person making this attribution assumed that Chris's flunking is a result of something about him, about his personal character or skills. But it is also possible that Chris's failing grade resulted from some external factor. Perhaps the test was too hard. People make an external or *situational attribution* when they think that something outside the person, such as the nature of the situation, is the cause of his or her behavior. If Jake says that Chris failed because the exam was too hard, Jake has made a situational attribution for Chris's grade.

We tend to evaluate our own behavior in different ways depending on whether we have succeeded or failed. For instance, it is likely that Chris would attribute his failure on a test to something about the situation—say, the test was too hard or the professor unfair—rather than to his own abilities. If Chris had aced the test, however, it is likely he'd attribute his success to his own skills. This tendency to make situational attributions for our failures but dispositional attributions for our successes is known as a **self-serving bias.**

People tend to explain other people's behavior in terms of dispositional attributions rather than situational ones, a bias in judgment known as the

attributions
inferences made about the causes of other people's behavior.

self-serving bias
the tendency to make situational attributions for our failures but dispositional attributions for our successes.

Meeting potential mates in a group of singles might make some people seem shy. Would you make the fundamental attribution error in a situation like this and assume that shyness is a personality trait?

connection
Cultural differences in big-picture versus detailed processing are seen in performance on visual perception tasks too.
See Chapter 4, p. 162.

fundamental attribution error (Ross, 1977). This is not to say that dispositions don't matter, but rather that when making attributions of other people's behavior, we tend to think that dispositional or personal characteristics matter the most. People living in Asian cultures, such as India and Japan, are much less likely to make the fundamental attribution error than are European Americans (Choi, Nisbett, & Norenzayan, 1999). This seems to be due to a cultural tendency for Asians to explain behaviors—even things as extreme as murder—in situational or big-picture terms (Morris & Peng, 1994; Norenzayan & Nisbett, 2000).

fundamental attribution error the tendency to explain others' behavior in dispositional rather than situational terms.

DETECTING DECEPTION

One way that we try to figure out others is by judging whether or not they are being truthful. Most people think that they can tell when people lie to them. According to the research, however, most of us are not effective lie detectors. Most people perform no better than chance—which means no better than randomly guessing between the two alternatives of lying or truthfulness—in detecting deception from the way people act (Ekman & O'Sullivan, 1991).

Why are we unsuccessful at catching liars? Most of us rely on misleading cues. We put too much weight on what people are saying, overinterpret ambiguous nonverbal cues (thinking any sign of nervousness means a person is lying), ignore relevant nonverbal information, and get fooled by signs of warmth and competence (Ekman & O'Sullivan, 1991). If people learn to focus instead on inconsistent behaviors (shaking the head while saying yes) and signs of emotion that don't match what people are saying, then they become better "lie detectors." There are no foolproof ways of detecting deception, however.

The best lie detectors attend to nonverbal information more than verbal information (Frank & Ekman, 1997). In a study of experts who should be good at catching liars, such as U.S. Secret Service agents, FBI agents, CIA agents, police, judges, and psychiatrists, only the Secret Service agents performed significantly better than if they had been guessing (Ekman & O'Sullivan, 1991). Psychologists with a special interest in deception have also been shown to do much better than others in detecting deceit (Ekman, O'Sullivan & Frank, 1999).

The only foolproof way to tell if someone is bluffing may be to look at his cards.

SCHEMAS

Whether we are trying to determine if people are lying or simply trying to make sense of simple actions, our own notions of how the world works influence our perceptions of it. People develop models, or *schemas*, about the social world, which are like lenses through which one filters perceptions. We first discussed schemas in Chapter 7 and defined them broadly as ways of knowing that we develop from our experiences with particular objects or events. In the area of social perception, schemas are ways of knowing that affect how we view our social world.

We rely on schemas when forming impressions of other people, especially when we encounter ambiguous information. Imagine you are invited to dinner and notice that one of the guests has slurred speech and walks shakily across the room. You assume—reasonably—that she is drunk. Later you learn that she has Parkinson's disease, a neurological condition that affects motor coordination. Slurred speech and shaky walking are common symptoms of this disorder. You assumed that the woman was drunk because the schema of drunkenness was much more *accessible* to you than that of Parkinson's disease.

STEREOTYPES

Schemas of how people are likely to behave based simply on the groups to which they belong are known as **stereotypes**. When we resort to stereotypes, we form conclusions about people before we even interact with them just because they are of a certain ethnicity or live in a certain place. As a result, we end up judging people not by their actions, but by our notions of how they are likely to act.

stereotypes schemas of how people are likely to behave based simply on groups to which they belong.

connection
Another name for mental shortcuts we use in decision making is *heuristics*. Heuristics often lead to flawed thinking. See Chapter 9, p. 359.

One of the reasons people resort to stereotypes is that they allow us to form quick—but often inaccurate—impressions, especially if we do not know someone very well. The human mind has a tendency to categorize and understand all members of a group in terms of characteristics that are typical of the group (Rosch, 1975). So if we meet someone new and learn that they belong to a particular (ethnic, social, political, or religious) group, we rely on what we think we know about the characteristics of that group so that we can anticipate how this new person might behave. When people avoid stereotyped thinking, fMRI scans show that the prefrontal cortex—an area involved in inhibiting inappropriate responses—is activated (De Neys, Vartanian, & Goel, 2008). This suggests that when you rely on stereotypes, you are not thinking carefully.

Take a look at a few of the common stereotypes that exist in U.S. culture:

Jocks are dumb.

Jews are cheap.

Middle Eastern men with beards are probably terrorists.

With stereotypes, we have formed conclusions about people even before we interact with them. Stereotypes are often linked to something that is indeed factual but that does not characterize a whole group. The terrorists involved in the September 11, 2001, attacks in the United States, for example, were Middle Eastern men, many of whom had beards—but

Overcoming stereotypes associated with his name, race, and educational background, Barack Obama, shown in an old photo with his mother, was elected president of the United States in 2008.

not all Middle Eastern men with beards are terrorists. Most serial killers in the United States have been young, white men. Does that mean all young, white men are serial killers (Apsche, 1993)?

During his 2008 run for the presidency, Barack Obama faced numerous stereotypes associated with his name (which has Muslim roots), his mixed race, and his education. People who did not know much about him were more likely to believe rumors that he was a Muslim (although he is not). The implication of being a Muslim activated the terrorist stereotype we just discussed. Another stereotype applied to Obama was that he was an elitist because he went to Harvard Law School. Rivals tried to link him with stereotypical notions of well-educated people as being out of touch with average people, in spite of the fact that he grew up in a low-income household and right out of college worked with the poor and unemployed in Chicago.

Stereotypes paint dividing lines between people. They support notions of belonging and exclusion that can lead to unfair actions.

EXCLUSION AND INCLUSION

As a result of having evolved for group living, we humans tend to judge others and ourselves—judgments that stem from defending ourselves against other groups and competing with them for limited resources (Neuberg & Cottrell, 2006). That is, the machinery is in place for using cognitive and emotional processes to separate "us" from "them." Perceiving others as different from us has several consequences:

1. We sometimes evaluate and treat people differently because of the group they belong to.
2. Our actions are based on in-group/out-group distinctions ("us" versus "them").

What stereotypes do these images bring to mind?

3. It hurts to be excluded from our group.

When we show positive feelings toward people in our own group and negative feelings toward those in other groups, we are displaying **in-group/out-group bias.** Think back to the rivalry between your high school and its crosstown rival. Everyone who went to your school was part of your in-group, and you identified with them and felt pride belonging to that group. Everyone who went to the other school was part of the out-group, and you felt competitive whenever the two schools interacted. Moreover, you likely made many distinctions between students and groups at your school, but categorized everyone who went to the other school into one group: "them." This or the tendency to see all members of an out-group as the same is known as **out-group homogeneity.** For example, people tend to use category labels ("Black" "White" "young" "old") as shortcuts for getting to know each person as an individual.

out-group homogeneity the tendency to see all members of an out-group as the same.

One result of the human tendency to include and exclude others is that sometimes we get left out. As our chapter-opening scenario illustrated, rejection hurts. One possible reason it hurts to be left out is that our social connections are as important to us as our physical safety—so important, in fact, that the brain's physical pain circuits evolved to signal also when we have been excluded

in-group/out-group bias tendency to show positive feelings toward people who belong to the same group as we do, and negative feelings toward those in other groups.

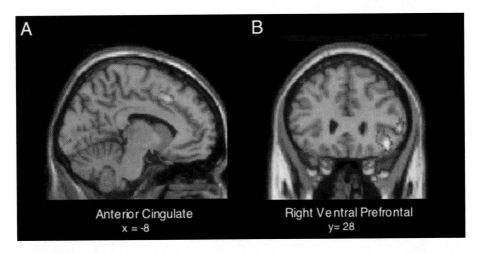

FIGURE **14.4**

BRAIN REGIONS ACTIVATED BY SOCIAL PAIN. Exclusion from an electronic ball-tossing game increased blood flow to the same areas of the brain activated by physical pain. The increase in activity in the anterior cingulate cortex (A) and in the right front section of the prefrontal cortex (B) shows up in these fMRI images as patches of orange and yellow. (*Source:* Eisenberger et al., 2003.)

from the group (see Figure 14.4; Eisenberger et al., 2003; MacDonald, Kingsbury, & Shaw, 2005; MacDonald & Leary, 2005). In modern life, we separate physical from social needs. But in early human evolution, these two needs were often intertwined. To be included in a social group meant you were fed, you were secure, and you could reproduce. Being excluded threatened not only survival but also the chance to reproduce (MacDonald et al., 2005).

nature & nurture

Social rejection activates the same brain circuitry that is activated by physical pain.

PREJUDICE AND DISCRIMINATION

We have discussed many processes that affect how we act in a group and how we view others. Unfortunately, as we try to make sense of each other and rely on schemas to decide who is like us or who is different, we often use stereotypes to unfairly categorize others, which can fuel prejudice and discrimination.

A **prejudice** is a biased attitude toward a group of people or an individual member of a group based on unfair generalizations about what members of that group are like (Allport, 1954). Prejudicial thinking often stems from stereotypes rather than from careful observation of people's behavior. They are generally negative and are often based on insufficient information as well. Prejudices based on race-ethnicity are called *racism;* those based on sex are called *sexism.* If a business executive does not seriously consider a highly qualified female applicant for a high-level management job because he is convinced that women are not capable of leading a company, his thinking is prejudicial. More precisely, it is sexist thinking. Not offering her an interview—even if she is the best-qualified applicant in the pool—is discrimination. **Discrimination** is the preferential treatment of certain people that is usually driven by prejudicial attitudes. Discrimination can also result from institutionalized rules, such as a requirement that firefighters must be at least 6 feet tall.

prejudice
a biased attitude toward a group of people or an individual member of a group based on unfair generalizations about what members of that group are like.

discrimination
preferential treatment of certain people, usually driven by prejudicial attitudes.

Prejudicial attitudes are learned early in life (when people are presented with racial-ethnic stereotypes, for example); and even if they are formally abandoned later in life, these reactions can become quite automatic (Banaji & Greenwald, 1995). Consider the case of Edith, a 21-year-old European American college student who is politically liberal and an activist for progressive causes. Yet, when Edith walks to her car at night, if an African American man is on the other side of the street, she becomes nervous without knowing why. She is not a racist! Why does this happen? Prejudices can operate outside conscious awareness, and they sometimes stand in stark contrast to one's conscious beliefs (Devine, 1989). Even a person who works hard at being fair may have a hard time overcoming biases that are automatic and deeply learned. There may also be an evolutionary basis for our automatic responses: The mechanism of recognizing group members may have evolved to preserve group harmony, cohesion, and close alliances, which could have been a means to enhance the survivability of individuals (Neuberg & Cottrell, 2006).

breaking new ground
The Study of Implicit Bias

Prejudice operates both inside and outside a person's awareness. As in Edith's case, much racial-ethnic bias is unconscious. How can psychologists measure such unconscious attitudes and their effects on behavior? Asking people directly about their racial-ethnic preferences provides information on their conscious beliefs at best; at worst, it provides answers that people think the researchers want to hear. Two social psychologists, Anthony Greenwald and Mahzarin Banaji, came up with a solution that has changed the way attitudes are measured.

TRADITIONAL APPROACHES TO THE STUDY OF PREJUDICE

For years studying prejudice meant surveying people about their conscious attitudes toward individuals from different racial-ethnic backgrounds. But over time, as it became less socially acceptable to display overt racism or show ethnic bias, people became less willing to openly acknowledge their prejudices. Prejudicial attitudes have actually declined steadily since the 1950s in the United States. Still, when questionnaire respondents appear to be less prejudiced, it's impossible to know whether they are truly less prejudiced, are prejudiced but are hiding their biases due to social unacceptability, or have deeply rooted biases that are not accessible to conscious awareness.

Social psychologists now distinguish between *explicit* and *implicit* prejudice. Explicit ideas are plainly stated. Implicit views are indirect. An explicit reference to a

Mahzarin Banaji

desire to have sex with someone is "I want to go to bed with you." An implicit reference would be "Why don't you come by my place and watch a movie with me?" Measuring implicit knowledge and beliefs presents a challenge.

Mahzarin Banaji had been interested in the relationship between explicit and implicit memory. She drew upon earlier research on *priming*, which showed that prior exposure to a word or image, even if it is not consciously recalled, leads to better recall of that word or image. Prior exposure leaves memory "traces" that can affect how we respond to information we encounter later (Jacoby & Dallas, 1981; Schacter, 1987).

connection
Priming is a kind of implicit memory that stems from prior exposure to the same or similar stimuli.
See Chapter 7, p. 265.

Banaji reasoned that this principle might apply to social cognition as well; that is, prior exposure—say from growing up in a racist society or from values at home—could ingrain certain biases. We may develop racist attitudes unknowingly (these are implicit) and later in life work to overcome them (these are explicit) (Baron & Banaji, 2006). The challenge for Banaji, then, was to disentangle the explicit and implicit sources of racism empirically.

INNOVATIONS IN MEASURING IMPLICIT BIAS

Banaji's graduate school advisor, Anthony Greenwald, developed a technique for mea-

Anthony Greenwald

suring implicit biases and decided to apply it to racial words. He took European American and African American names and paired them with both pleasant and unpleasant words. He then took his own test to see how long it took to form associations between pairs of words. He was shocked at the difficulty he had pairing African American names with pleasant words (Vedantum, 2005). When Banaji took the same test, she, too, was upset by the results, which looked about the same as Greenwald's. Banaji and Greenwald knew they were on to something. They dubbed the new test the *Implicit Associations Test (IAT)*.

Greenwald and Banaji have applied the IAT to race concepts. Faster response times on the test indicate that people more readily associate two concepts; slower response times indicate a less automatic association. European Americans tend to respond more slowly to pairings of "Black" (words or faces) with positive words than they do to pairings of "Black" with negative words (Dasgupta et al., 2000; Greenwald, McGhee, & Schwartz, 1998). This is true even for people whose questionnaire responses seem to indicate that they do not hold racist attitudes. The reverse is true for African Americans. They respond more slowly to pairings of "White American" with positive words than they do to pairings of "White American" with negative words. Banaji and Greenwald (1995) have also reported evidence of implicit gender bias using the IAT; female and male college students more readily associated "fame" with male names than with female names.

REDUCING IMPLICIT BIAS

When social scientists heard about the IAT, their enthusiasm for the technique was immediate. The power of the findings was obvious: Even those of us who are convinced that we are not biased may harbor prejudices of which we are unaware. It became evident that researchers and the general population alike must deal with their own implicit prejudice and racism. In just over 15 years more than 300 published research papers, in areas ranging from marketing to neuroscience, have used the IAT technique.

Their experience has made Banaji and others interested in efforts to reduce racial bias in people in all walks of life—which means changing not only their conscious

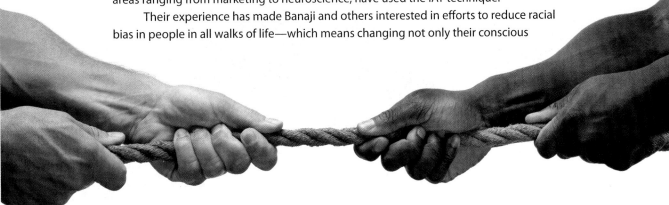

opinions but their unconscious and implicit ones as well. Indeed, the IAT is an excellent teaching tool for anyone confronting his or her own implicit prejudice. Results from the test can be used to reduce prejudice and sensitize individuals and groups to the fact that these prejudices operate in subtle yet powerful ways. Banaji, Greenwald, and Nosek are setting up a nonprofit organization to help people apply the IAT technique.

Banaji lives by her own advice. She was so dismayed by her own performance on race- and gender-based IATs—in spite of being a minority woman herself—that she changed her behavior. In addition to the nonprofit work, she does little things to help undo her deeply held biases, such as displaying pictures of prominent black men and women from history in her office. You can try the IAT yourself at https://implicit.harvard.edu/implicit/demo/.

quick quiz 14.2: Social Perception

1. Our tendency to conclude that Alex must have an aggressive personality because we see him hit Bobby once on the playground is an example of
   a. a stereotype
   b. prejudice
   c. deception
   d. the fundamental attribution error

2. "College professors are absent minded" is an example of
   a. an attitude
   b. an attribution
   c. a stereotype
   d. a prejudice

3. Out-group homogeneity is the tendency to
   a. see people outside our group as looking or acting alike
   b. see people inside our group as looking or acting alike
   c. believe people outside our group think the same way we do
   d. believe people inside our group think the same way we do

4. Brandon believes women are not very good at math. However, as a computer scientist, he has always been able to treat women the same way he treats men at work.
   a. Brandon is prejudiced toward women
   b. Brandon's behavior is an example of discrimination
   c. Brandon's beliefs are based on stereotypes
   d. both a and c are correct

5. Measuring how long it takes a person to pair positive or negative terms with particular ethnic groups is used in social psychology as a measure of
   a. explicit racism
   b. implicit racism
   c. stereotypes
   d. reaction time

Answers can be found at the end of the chapter.

Attitudes and Behavior

People use the word *attitude* frequently, but what does it mean? Social psychologists define **attitudes** as a person's favorable or unfavorable feelings, beliefs, or actions toward an object, idea, or person (Olson & Zanna, 1993). Thus attitudes have affective, cognitive, and behavioral components. The *affective* component includes the feelings or emotions associated with the belief; the *cognitive* component consists of the rational thoughts and beliefs that make up the attitude; and the *behavioral* component includes the motive to act in a particular way toward the person or object of the attitude. Consider Elizabeth, who is a huge Giants fan (see Figure 14.5). She loves the team (affective), knows all about each starting player (cognitive), and has bought season tickets to their home games (behavioral).

Attitudes differ by how heavily each component is weighted. Some attitudes are more cognitive, such as your beliefs about the best way to slice a mango. Others may be more affective, such as your attitude about the death penalty. Our attitudes and beliefs stem from our history as a species as well as our history as individuals.

attitude
an individual's favorable or unfavorable beliefs, feelings, or actions toward an object, idea, or person.

Attitude: Giants fan

Affective component:	Enthusiasm about the Giants team
Cognitive component:	Knowledge about the players
Behavioral component:	Goes to all Giants home games

FIGURE **14.5**
ATTITUDE COMPONENTS. For a sports fan, a positive attitude is sometimes the only way to get through a losing season.

THE NATURE AND NURTURE OF ATTITUDES

Some of our most basic attitudes may be instinctive, while others are learned. Certain negative attitudes and emotional responses, such as fear of snakes or the nearly universal human revulsion for bodily waste and decaying matter, may be so important for human survival that they are part of our genetic heritage (Buss, 1999). Evolutionary pressures to preserve group membership favor in-group bias (fear of those who are different). Because humans evolved in small social groups in threatening environments, it made sense for people to trust those who were most like them. Also, there are evolutionary pressures to perform quick evaluations. The tendency to automatically make quick good–bad and like–dislike assessments is a fundamental cognitive process with clear evolutionary benefits: It helps people make quick decisions in life-threatening situations (Cunningham & Zelazo, 2006; Neuberg & Cottrell, 2006).

nature & nurture
Evolutionary forces may explain certain inborn attitudes, but many of our attitudes come from experience.

On the other hand, many of our attitudes come from experience. In some cases, we learn attitudes through both direct and indirect instruction by others. We may adopt the musical preferences of our friends, for example. Sometimes we like ideas or objects simply because they are familiar. *Mere exposure,* or direct experience with an object, idea, or person, increases our overall preference for it (Zajonc, 1968). The things that we come to like from exposure can be trivial, such as abstract symbols, or very meaningful, such as human faces. For example, Zajonc (1968) showed people nonsense words 5, 10, or 25 times; the more often they saw a word, the more they reported liking it.

Strong attitudes about controversial issues, such as abortion, often reflect longstanding beliefs and consequently are difficult to change.

ATTITUDE CHANGE

Are people willing to switch attitudes based on evidence or a persuasive argument? What role do personality and persuasion play in our willingness to change attitudes? These are just some of the questions asked by social psychologists interested in attitude change. We examine two major reasons for changes in attitude: cognitive dissonance and persuasion.

Cognitive Dissonance One explanation for why and how we change our attitudes is cognitive dissonance. **Cognitive dissonance** is the feeling of discomfort caused by information that is at odds with one's conception of oneself as a reasonable and sensible person (Festinger, 1957). Because we don't like feeling uncomfortable, we are motivated to try to reduce the discomfort. There are three options for decreasing the discomfort created by dissonance:

cognitive dissonance
the feeling of discomfort caused by information that is different from a person's conception of himself or herself as a reasonable and sensible person.

1. We can change our behavior to make it consistent with dissonant cognition.
2. We can attempt to justify our behavior by changing one of the cognitions to make it more consistent with our behavior;
3. We can add new cognitions that are consistent with the behavior and that therefore support it.

When we experience cognitive dissonance, we may go extreme lengths to reduce it. In this way, we reduce our discomfort and we maintain our self-esteem, meaning we justify ourselves to ourselves. We often end up behaving very irrationally in order to reduce cognitive dissonance. For instance, we might end up rationalizing our not-so-adaptive behavior.

Smoking offers a classic example of an irrational behavior in which many people engage. Smoking can cause lung cancer, emphysema, and heart disease. Still, many people continue to smoke. Are they stupid? No. They are addicted. Smokers have to deal with the conflict between their notion of themselves as rational and intelligent beings and the fact that they smoke, which is not a smart thing to do. To reduce the unpleasant feeling these dissonant thoughts and behaviors cause, people who smoke may behave in one of the three ways that we just listed, as seen in Figure 14.6. People will work hard to defend behaviors or strongly held positions in order to reduce the dissonance—the uncomfortable feeling—produced by opposing arguments. When we do these things, we are *rationalizing* our behavior. Otherwise, people have to change their behavior, which can be tough.

Persuasion.   People can also use persuasion to change attitudes. **Persuasion** is an attempt by a person or group to change our opinions, beliefs, or choices by explaining or arguing their position. Persuasion is all around us all the time; friends, family, teachers, politicians, salespeople, and advertisers often want to change our minds about something. They attempt to talk us into something or convince us of their point of view. How successful they will be depends on three things: who they are (source), the method they use to convey the message, and who we are (audience) (Lippa, 1994).

First, how trustworthy, prestigious, and likeable is the persuader? The more prestigious and trustworthy the persuader, the more likely he or she is to succeed in persuading us. If the persuader is also attractive and familiar, so much the better. This is why people want to buy pain relievers promoted in commercials

persuasion
the act of attempting to change the opinions, beliefs, or choices of others by explanation or argument.

change behavior

Quit smoking.

justify smoking by changing cognitions associated with it

"Smoking is not that harmful."

"Results of research on smoking and cancer are not as conclusive as people think they are."

change cognitions so as to justify smoking

"It makes me feel good, so it's worth it, whatever the risk."

FIGURE **14.6**

COGNITIVE DISSONANCE AND SMOKING. People smoke even though they know it's unhealthy. To reduce their cognitive dissonance, smokers might try one of these approaches, including quitting.

Which persuasion criteria are represented by this GAP ad featuring actress Penelope Cruz? At what audience do you think it is aimed?

by famous TV doctors rather than unknown figures. The credibility of the character enhances the credibility of the product.

Second, what methods of persuasion are used? Politicians often rely on fear to convince us to support their policies or candidacy. An example is the "Willie Horton" ad shown during the 1988 U.S. presidential campaign. When Democratic presidential candidate Michael Dukakis was governor of Massachusetts, he had supported a weekend release program for prisoners. Willie Horton committed armed robbery and rape during such a weekend. A group supporting the Republican candidate, George H. W. Bush, ran a TV ad showing prisoners walking out of a prison yard with a voice-over about Horton. It ran regularly on stations across the country. It played on people's fears of dangerous criminals, and it linked that fear with Dukakis. That one commercial is thought to have played a major role in Dukakis's loss to Bush.

Fear campaigns work only if they actually create fear in the audience (Witte & Allen, 2000). Most ads meant to scare us don't actually do so. Simply citing statistics, for instance—such as the fact that smoking increases one's risk of lung cancer 20-fold—often does not instill fear in people and is not very effective at getting people to change their behavior. People rarely believe that they will suffer the negative consequences implied by the ads.

Last, who is the targeted audience or receiver of the message? People are not equally malleable in their opinions or behavior. The more people know about a topic and the firmer their prior opinions are, the less likely they are to change their attitudes (Eagly & Chaiken, 1998). Political campaigners know this well. Candidates often focus their efforts, especially near election day, on swing states that either have not consistently voted one way in the past or have a mix of party preferences. In regions that have voted Republican for years, say, campaigning by Democratic candidates may be a waste of time.

We now move from how we view other people to how we relate to other people. The next section considers human social relationships.

quick quiz 14.3: Attitudes and Behavior

1. Janice is a college student who is active in politics. She considers voting to be very important for everyone, especially young people. So she volunteers 5 hours a week to staff a table at the student union encouraging students to register to vote, for any political party. Her stance toward voting would best be described as a(n)
   a. belief
   b. attitude
   c. attribution
   d. bias

2. LeBron considers himself to be a healthy person. He eats a healthy diet and exercises four days a week. Yet he is a smoker. His attitude toward smoking before he became a smoker was very negative. Now that he is a smoker, however, his attitude is not so negative. The change in his attitude is best explained by _____.
   a. attribution
   b. persuasion
   c. mere exposure
   d. cognitive dissonance

3. Social psychologists have demonstrated that three things matter most in whether an argument will persuade other people or not. The three things are _____.
   a. source, method, and audience
   b. source, believability, and audience
   c. logic, believability, and audience
   d. pressure to conform, source, and authority

Answers can be found at the end of the chapter.

Social Relations

We constantly interact with other people. Sometimes these interactions lead to special connections with others that grow into friendship or even love. Other times we clash and find ourselves in conflict with others. In this section we discuss three different kinds of social interaction: aggression, helping, and attraction.

THE NATURE AND NURTURE OF AGGRESSION

Aggression is part of life. All animals compete with others, both within and outside their species, for survival. Almost every animal can be aggressive, and many animals kill others in order to survive. Humans are unique in that they often engage in aggression and violent behavior when their survival is not at issue.

aggression
violent behavior that is intended to cause psychological or physical harm, or both, to another being.

Aggression refers to violent behavior that is intended to cause psychological or physical harm, or both, to another being. By definition, aggression is deliberate. A dentist who performs a root canal may hurt a patient, but we hardly would call that behavior aggressive. Aggression is often provoked by anger, but not always.

There are several types of aggression. When aggression stems from feelings of anger, it is called *hostile aggression*. When aggression is a means to achieve some goal, it is called *instrumental aggression*. The hostile type of aggression is easy to understand. While you are driving, someone cuts you off on the road. You honk, and in response, the other driver makes an obscene hand gesture toward you (the hand gesture is an aggressive action).

An example of instrumental aggression occurs in football when a defensive

connection
How does hostility differ from anger? Hostility is a personality characteristic that sets the threshold for the emotion of anger.
See Chapter 11, p. 432.

Does violence in video games and other visual media increase the likelihood of aggressive behavior?

lineman smashes down a ball carrier to prevent the opponent from scoring. The goal is to prevent scoring by the other team, not to hurt the ball carrier. In this case, the aggressive action is considered to be justified by its instrumental goal.

Where does aggression come from, and why are people aggressive? Some people are more prone to violence than others. An individual's genetic disposition often plays a role, but genes by themselves are seldom enough to cause violent behavior (Miczek et al., 2007). Caspi and colleagues (2002) found that when genetic factors combine with an abusive and neglectful environment, the likelihood of committing violence increases dramatically.

Moreover, research on murderers has identified a cluster of traits shared by most of these individuals: being male, growing up in an abusive and neglectful household, having at least one psychological disorder, and having experienced some kind of injury to the head or brain (Pincus, 1999, 2001; Strueber, Lueck, & Roth, 2006–2007). Having only one of these traits is not enough—all must be present for a person to become antisocial and prone to violence. In other words, the person's disposition interacts with certain environmental influences to make aggressive behavior more likely.

Internal factors can explain why some people are more aggressive than others. Several brain areas are involved in aggression, including the hypothalamus, the amygdala, and the prefrontal cortex (Pincus, 1999). More specifically, the part of the prefrontal cortex responsible for impulse control often is functionally impaired in aggressive and violent people (Grafman et al., 1996). Similarly, as a result of head injuries or living in a constant state of fear and abuse, murderers may have moderate to severe problems with frontal lobe functioning, which involves impulse control, emotional intelligence, working memory, and attention (Strueber et al., 2006–2007). Living in a constant state of fear can lead to neural systems being primed for unusually high levels of anxiety, impulsive behavior, and vigilance, or a constant state of alertness (Bishop, 2007). These are all conditions that bring about violent or criminal behaviors.

nature & nurture

Aggression stems from the interaction between genetic and social forces.

In addition to certain brain structures, two hormones are consistently related to high levels of aggression: testosterone and serotonin. Testosterone, the primary male sex hormone, may account for the finding that boys are consistently more aggressive than girls at most ages (Maccoby & Jacklin, 1974). In adults, the great majority of people arrested for criminal offenses are men (Strueber et al., 2006–2007). Relatively high levels of testosterone, whether in men or women, correlate positively with a propensity toward violence. Among both male and female prisoners, naturally occurring testosterone levels are higher in criminals convicted of violent crimes than in those convicted of nonviolent crimes (Dabbs, Carr, & Frady, 1995; Dabbs & Hargrove, 1997). Serotonin has a broad range of effects on behavior, one of which is keeping anger and anxiety in check. Also, low levels of serotonin make aggression more likely in humans and animals (Moffitt et al., 1998; Raleigh et al., 1991).

Social Influences on Aggression Situations that frustrate us and prevent us from reaching our goals are likely to make us aggressive. Moreover, the closer we are to our goal when we become frustrated, the more aggressive we are likely to be. A classic study by Harris (1974) demonstrated this effect. Confederates of the researchers cut in front of people in lines for movies or crowded restaurants. Sometimes they cut in front of the second person in line and other times they cut in front of someone farther back in line. The response of the person standing behind the intruder was much more aggressive when the confederate cut in front of the person second in line—closest to the goal.

connection

Social learning theory offers an explanation of modeling, the kind of learning in which we imitate the behavior of others.

See Chapter 8, p. 318.

Similarly, situations that lead to anger stimulate aggression, especially hostile aggression. Threats to our safety or the safety of our family fall into this category. Aggressive responses may be motivated by anger and/or fear. Road rage is a good example of such a situation, and aggressive driving is most likely to happen when people are angry (Nesbit, Conger, & Conger, 2007).

Observing aggressive people and the consequences of their actions can make us more aggressive. This is the fundamental idea behind Albert Bandura's *social learning theory*. Bandura's research demonstrated repeatedly that if children see adults punching an inflatable Bobo doll, they will do it too, especially if they see the adult being rewarded for the aggressive behavior.

How does the Bobo doll research apply to real-life aggression? According to longitudinal studies of men and women, the more violence people watch on TV when they are children, the more violent behavior they exhibit as adults (Huesmann, Moise-Titus, & Podolski, 2003). This correlational result does not tell us for sure that TV is the cause of the aggressive behavior. However, more controlled experiments also suggest that watching TV violence leads to aggressive behavior in children. Liebert and Baron (1972) showed a violent TV program to a group of children. The control group saw an exciting but nonviolent sporting event that had the same running time. Children were randomly assigned to the two groups. After viewing the programs, each child was allowed to play in another room with a group of children. Those who had watched the violent program were far more aggressive in their play than those who saw the nonviolent show. The evidence of a connection between exposure to violence in the media and violent behavior is becoming harder to ignore. See "Psychology in the Real World" for a discussion of the problem of media violence and aggression in children in contemporary society.

PROSOCIAL BEHAVIOR

Just as people can harm others through aggression, sometimes people can be extraordinarily kind to others. **Prosocial behavior** is behavior that benefits others. In this section we will explore social processes that benefit others: altruism and empathy.

Sometimes humans do extraordinary things that benefit others at great cost to themselves. Consider the case of Wesley Autrey. One morning in January 2007, Autrey and his two daughters were waiting for the subway in New York City. Suddenly a teenager standing nearby began convulsing and collapsed on the platform. Among the dozens of people there, only Autrey and a few women stopped to help the young man. They thought they had stabilized him, but the young man got up,

prosocial behavior
action that is beneficial to others.

Violent Media, Violent World

Social learning research paints a convincing picture of the role observation plays in the development of aggression. Moreover, Bushman and Anderson (2001) have argued that the level of violence on TV greatly exaggerates the level of violence in society. The media have ignored this relationship or denied that there is one, but consider these statistics:

About 87% of the crimes occurring in the real world are nonviolent crimes, whereas only 13% of crimes occurring in reality-based TV programs are nonviolent crimes.... Only 0.2% of the crimes reported by the FBI are murders, whereas about 50% of the crimes shown in reality-based TV programs are murders (Oliver, 1994). (quoted in Bushman & Anderson, 2001, p. 479)

Bushman and Anderson used meta-analysis to objectively assess the relationship between TV violence and aggression. Figure 14.7 shows that numerous scientific studies have found a much stronger relationship between TV violence and aggression than is reported by the media (Bushman & Anderson, 2001, p. 486).

The effect of media violence on children is of particular concern in the United States, where many children watch TV or play video games for hours daily. Young children are most often exposed to violence in TV cartoons, which

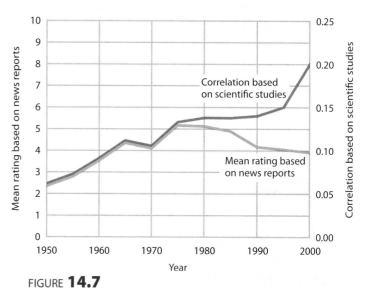

FIGURE **14.7**

EFFECT OF MEDIA VIOLENCE ON AGGRESSION. This analysis by Bushman and Anderson shows that the news media have played down the relationship between violence in the media and aggression since the 1980s. A positive mean rating based on news reports indicates that journalists reported a positive correlation between media violence and aggression. For the scientific studies, the higher the correlation is, the more positive the relationship between media violence and aggression is. (*Source:* Bushman & Anderson, 2001.)

tottered, and fell onto the tracks. The headlights of an oncoming train appeared, and in an instant Autrey jumped onto the tracks to help the young man. When Autrey realized that he could not pull the teen off the tracks before the train hit them, he lay on top of him and pressed him down firmly in a bear hug. The train went over both men without touching them.

Autrey heard the screams of onlookers. "We're okay down here," he yelled, "but I've got two daughters up there. Let them know their father's okay." He heard cries of wonder and applause (Buckley, 2007). When interviewed later, Autrey said he had done nothing heroic. He had simply decided to help someone in need. "I didn't want the man's body to get run over," he said. "Plus, I was with my daughters and I didn't want them to see that" (CBS News, 2007).

Repeated exposure to violence on TV and in video games may desensitize people to real violence, making us less likely to help in an emergency and perhaps more prone to aggressive behavior.

appear to increase aggression in those who watch them (Kirsh, 2006). Older children play violent video games.

Another way of looking at the effects of exposure to violence in the media is to ask whether repeated exposure actually makes one less responsive to violence, rather than whether it increases aggression (or its emotional precursor—anger). The logic of such an approach is this: By repeatedly seeing and even participating in violent action (albeit in a virtual world), young people may become desensitized to violence. In a study of desensitization to violence in kids who play violent video games, the researchers randomly assigned more than 250 male and female college students to play either a violent or a nonviolent video game for 20 minutes (Carnagey, Anderson, & Bushman, 2007). Then they measured the participants' physiological responses to films of real-life violence, such as courtroom outbursts, police confrontations, shootings, and prison fights. The students who had played the violent video games showed less evidence of physiological arousal (as measured by heart rate and sweating) while watching films of real people being stabbed and shot than did the students who had played the nonviolent games. A similar study showed that young men who had a history of playing video games showed reduced brain activation to real-life violence and that this reduced brain activation correlated with aggression in a behavioral task (Bartholow, Bushman, & Sestir, 2006). Such nonreaction to violence is disturbing.

What does this finding mean? Some psychologists argue that desensitization to violence can increase aggression by reducing the perceived seriousness of a real situation people encounter and decreasing the likelihood of helping in an emergency (Carnagey et al., 2007). People are more likely to help when they are physiologically aroused by an emergency; in other words, they are more likely to help when they have an emotional reaction to a situation (Dovidio et al., 1991). Normally, people react to violence with fear and disgust, emotions that motivate us to avoid contact with the stimulus (Cantor, 1998). If people can get so used to violence that it does not arouse these negative, avoidance-relevant emotions, then they may be more willing to behave aggressively themselves (Bartholow et al., 2006).

Would you jump in front of an oncoming train to help a complete stranger? How many people do you think would? What makes people help other people? Most evidence, both from real life and from laboratory studies, indicates that most people would not help a stranger, especially when many others are present and are doing nothing. Social psychologists have studied various factors that influence whether people will help others or not.

The Bystander Effect

Late one night Kitty Genovese was walking from her parked car to her apartment building in New York City after coming home from her job as a bar manager. As she approached the building, a man accosted her and stabbed her in the back. She screamed, "Oh my God, he stabbed me!

Help me!" Fearing that her cries for help would be heeded, her attacker ran away. Lights went on in the apartment building, and a few people looked out, but no one called the police or came to help her. The man returned and renewed his attack. Genovese's screams were heard by numerous people, but still no one came to help. The 28-year-old Genovese died from her wounds before someone summoned the police.

How could so many people have ignored the screams of a young woman who was being so brutally attacked? What kind of attribution—either dispositional or situational—best explains this behavior?

The Kitty Genovese case received tons of publicity, and it spurred a great deal of research in social psychology. John Darley and Bibb Latané (1968) used the scientific method to try to understand why no one came to Genovese's rescue. First, they did an experiment in which research participants heard another participant choking over an intercom (what they actually heard was an audiotape). The researchers led some of the participants to believe that they were the only ones hearing the person choking, while others thought many participants heard it. Of the participants who thought they alone heard the choking man, 85% tried to help. Of those who thought many other people also heard the man choking, only 62% tried to help. The researchers concluded there is no safety in numbers. Specifically, the greater the number of bystanders who witness an emergency, the less likely any one of them will help. Latané and Darley called this phenomenon the

bystander effect
phenomenon in which the greater the number of bystanders who witness an emergency, the less likely any one of them is to help.

bystander effect.

In 1964, Kitty Genovese was attacked and killed while residents of her Queens neighborhood, shown in this photo taken after the murder, ignored her screams. Subsequent research has shown that the more people who witness an emergency, the less likely someone will offer help.

One explanation of the bystander effect involves *diffusion of responsibility;* that is, when there are many people around, an individual's responsibility to act seems decreased. It makes sense when you think about it. When you alone witness an emergency, you know that you are the only source of aid. If several people are present, however, you might not regard it as your responsibility to help the person in need. Someone else might take care of it. Indeed, this is probably why no one helped poor Kitty Genovese. A lot of people were around, so everyone assumed "somebody else must have called the police!"

A number of factors influence whether or not someone will intervene in an emergency. One is whether people actually notice the event. When people are in a hurry they are less likely to notice an emergency (Darley & Batson, 1973). Moreover, when many people are present and doing nothing, a person is less likely to interpret an event as an emergency. This is an example of informational social influence, because in this ambiguous situation people look to others for clues as to what should be done. If everyone else is doing nothing, then maybe there's no emergency after all.

Even if we notice an event and interpret it as an emergency, we must decide that it is our responsibility to do something. In addition to a diffusion of responsibility, people often do a cost-benefit analysis to determine whether helping is worth the cost. Sometimes it is dangerous to be helpful. If you get to this step and decide it is worth helping, you still might not know how to help. For example, if you witness someone having a heart attack and want to help, you might not know CPR. Even if you've passed all the previous hurdles, you may not be able to help after all, though you could still call 911.

Altruism   The term **altruism** refers to a selfless concern for and giving of aid to others. Because altruists often expose themselves to greater danger than those who selfishly protect themselves, helping poses risks to personal survival. For this reason, altruism makes no sense from an evolutionary perspective (Dawkins, 1989). So why do humans and other animals sometimes engage in altruistic behavior?

Evolutionary theory offers two explanations for altruistic behavior: kin selection and reciprocal altruism. **Kin selection** is the evolutionary mechanism that prompts individuals to help their close relatives or kin so that they will survive to reproduce and pass on related genes to their offspring (Hamilton, 1964). For instance, a dominant macaque monkey will share food with a subordinate monkey only if the two are close relatives (Belisle & Chapais, 2001; Furuichi, 1983). Individuals who help close relatives may be risking their lives, but they are also increasing the chances that if they do not survive, at least some of their genes will survive in their relatives.

Kin selection is more common in social animals, such as bees. Greenberg (1979) bred bees to have varied degrees of genetic relatedness and then released them near a nest watched by guard bees. Because the nest was crowded, not everyone could get in. Guard bees were much more likely to let in the bees that were closely related than those that were distantly related. There is evidence for kin selection in humans too. Burnstein and colleagues (1994) asked people to specify whom they would be most likely to help in life-and-death situations and non-life-and-death situations. People reported they would be more likely to help a relative in life-and-death situations, but not in non-life-and-death situations. In fact, when people are rescuing others from a burning building, they are much more likely to look for relatives first (Sime, 1983).

Another evolutionary explanation for altruistic behavior is **reciprocal altruism,** helping others in the hope that they will help you in the future (Trivers, 1971, 1985). It is easier for humans to survive when group members cooperate, and reciprocal altruism promotes such cooperation. That is, you might help another member of your group if you believe that you might benefit in some way as a result. From an evolutionary perspective, reciprocal altruism should be most common in species that are social, for only animals that live in groups have opportunities to benefit from reciprocal helping.

Some people have argued that these evolutionary mechanisms do not adequately explain all altruistic behavior. After all, what about Wesley Autrey?

altruism
selfless attitudes and behavior toward others.

kin selection
the evolutionary favoring of genes that prompts individuals to help their relatives or kin.

reciprocal altruism
the act of helping others in the hope that they will help us in the future.

social exchange theory
the idea that we help others when we understand that the benefits to ourselves are likely to outweigh the costs.

Some social psychologists argue that in our relations with others we try to maximize our gains and minimize our losses (Thibaut & Kelly, 1959). This is the essence of **social exchange theory,** a nonevolutionary explanation of altruistic behavior that says we help others because such behavior can be rewarding, but we will help only if the rewards will outweigh the costs. How can helping be rewarding? For one thing, helping someone in need relieves our own distress at witnessing suffering. Also, helping someone is an investment in the future, because it is possible that they will help us when we need help. In this sense, social exchange is essentially the same as reciprocal altruism.

According to social exchange theory, truly selfless altruism does not exist. What about Wesley Autrey? Were his actions representative of selfless altruism? He did say that he didn't want his daughters to see the man die. Perhaps by helping, Autrey was protecting the psychological well-being of his kids (which is kin selection after all).

Empathy   C. Daniel Batson (1991) has proposed that true selfless helping occurs only when there is empathy. **Empathy** can be defined as sharing feeling and understanding about another person's situation. According to Batson's **empathy-altruism hypothesis,** people will offer selfless help only when they truly empathize with the victim. Consider the following example: A professor is talking with a student in his office. While pleading with the professor to postpone an upcoming test, the student begins to cry. Reacting to the student's distress, the professor becomes upset as well. The professor decides to help the student by postponing the test. Batson and his colleagues believe that two different motivations may underlie the professor's behavior.

empathy-altruism hypothesis
the idea that people help others selflessly only when they feel empathy for them.

empathy
the ability to share the feelings of others and understand their situations.

The first motivation Batson calls the *egoistic motivation.* The professor may help the student in order to relieve the professor's own distress. This is not true altruism and would fit with social exchange theory, where the reward is reduction of distress. A second motivation, *empathic motivation,* may be that the professor's behavior may spring from an altruistic desire to reduce the distress of the person in need. Unlike the person who is the egoistic helper, the empathic helper is serving another with the primary goal of helping the student through the crisis.

Clearly empathy plays an important role in helping. But what do we really know about empathy? In order to understand the brain mechanisms of empathy, Singer and colleagues examined brain activation during a person's real pain experience and when witnessing the pain of a loved one (Singer et al., 2004). They created an experiment to study the response to a loved one's pain in the confines of an MRI scanner. Singer obtained measures of functional brain activity in the female partner of a couple while the woman herself received a painful stimulus to her hand and then while she witnessed her male partner receiving the same painful stimulus (see Figure 14.8). The actual pain stimulus was a mild electric shock delivered by an electrode attached to the hand. The actual pain stimulus activated a well-known pain circuit in the brain, involving the somatosensory cortex, insula, anterior cingulate cortex (ACC), thalamus, and cerebellum. When her partner was experiencing pain, only those structures in the pain circuit that are triggered by the emotional aspect of pain showed activation, most notably the front region of the insula and the ACC. So, when a partner experiences pain, people truly do feel it *with* their loved ones.

nature & nurture
Watching someone you love experience pain activates components of physical pain circuitry in the brain.

1 research question

If empathy really is feeling what another person is feeling, are pain circuits in the brain activated similarly when someone feels pain and when empathizing with a loved one's pain?

2 method

In a quasi-experimental study, Tania Singer and colleagues (2004) used fMRI to measure brain activation in women when they received a mild shock to the hand and also while they witnessed their partner receiving the same painful stimulus.

The partner sat next to the MRI scanner. The woman and her partner placed their right hands on a tilted board, which allowed the woman to see her and her partner's right hand with help of a mirror. On a large screen the woman saw visual cues that indicated whether she or her partner would get low pain or high pain. When administered, the shock lasted for 2 seconds.

The experimental set up

3 results

A mild shock was administered 3.5 seconds after the scan began, lasting for 2 seconds. The scans showed that self-pain activated all the structures in the pain circuit, while the partner's pain (the empathic pain condition) mainly activated the structures typically involved only in the emotional aspect of pain (anterior cingulate cortex, or ACC, and the insula). The graphs show brain activation for the women as a change from a baseline (pain-free) state.

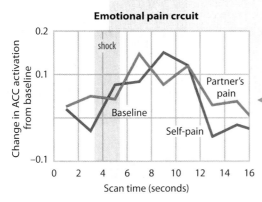

Emotional pain crcuit

The similarity in patterns of activation in the ACC across these two conditions suggests that the women empathized with– that is *felt* – their partner's pain.

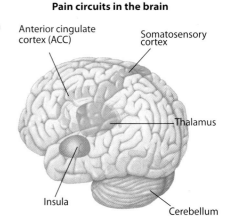

Pain circuits in the brain

Anterior cingulate cortex (ACC)
Somatosensory cortex
Thalamus
Insula
Cerebellum

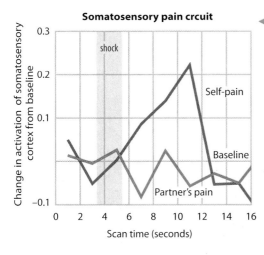

Somatosensory pain crcuit

The difference in patterns of activation in the somatosensory cortex suggests that the women did not experience the same sensory aspects of pain when their partners received the shock as when they received the shock themselves.

4 conclusion

Experienced pain activates all pain networks in the brain (emotional and sensory), but empathic pain activates only the emotional pain network. When a loved one experiences pain, people truly do feel their loved one's pain, but that feeling may be more emotional than sensory.

FIGURE **14.8**

FEELING ANOTHER'S PAIN. Empathy for a loved one's pain involves brain circuitry that is activated by real pain. (*Source:* T. Singer, B. Seymour, J. O. O'Doherty, H. Kaube, R. J. Dolan, and C. D. Frith. 2004. Empathy for pain involves the affective but not sensory components of pain. *Science, 303,* 1157–1162.)

LIKING, ATTRACTION, AND LOVE

What makes one person want to be with another? Is this process different for friends and lovers? What is love, anyway? In this section we will see how psychologists tackle questions of the human heart. Let's first examine how we come to like and be attracted to other people, and then we'll take a look at love.

Familiarity, Similarity, and Attraction As we have seen throughout this chapter, research in social psychology shows that merely being exposed to an object, idea, or person causes you to like it more (Zajonc, 1968). Therefore, the more often we see a face, the more we like it.

People with similar ideas, values, and interests are more likely to like one another and share satisfying, long-lasting relationships (Keller, Thiessen, & Young, 1996). For example, researchers randomly assigned male college students to be roommates in a certain dorm at the beginning of the year. Those roommates who became real friends had common backgrounds, similar majors, and similar political viewpoints (Newcomb, 1961). People report that they like and want to help others who have similar personalities, attitudes, or beliefs (Wakimoto & Fujihara, 2004; Westmaas & Silver, 2006). Finally, people also tend to be attracted to and partner with people of a similar level of attractiveness to themselves—a phenomenon known as *assortative mating* (Buss, 2004). There is a moderately strong correlation between the personality of a person's ideal partner and their own personality, and married couples also have strongly correlated age, levels of intelligence, and imaginativeness (Botwin, Buss, & Shackelford, 1997; Keller et al., 1996).

Do we choose our pets the same way we select our human mates?

Physical Attractiveness Humans worldwide value physical attractiveness in partners (Buss, 1999; Etcoff, 1999; Miller, 2000). But what, exactly, is considered to be attractive? In research on attractiveness, people rate average and symmetrical faces as more attractive than less average and less symmetrical faces. *Average,* in this case, does not mean "common." Rather, *average* means that the

FIGURE **14.9**

RATING PHYSICAL ATTRACTIVENESS. The more faces that are morphed into one image, the more they move toward having average features. As they become more average in features, the faces are perceived as increasing in attractiveness.

4 face composite

8 face composite

16 face composite

32 face composite

size, location, and shape of each feature of the face—nose, eyes, mouth, cheek-bones—are mathematically average in the population. They are neither too big nor too small, neither too far apart nor too close together. Look, for example, at the faces in Figure 14.9. These faces were produced by using computer technology to morph images of several real faces together. As more and more faces were averaged, people rated the faces as more and more attractive. People rated the 8-face composite as more attractive than the 4-face composite; the 16-face composite as more attractive than the 8; and the 32-face composite as more attractive than the 16 (Langlois & Roggman, 1990; Langlois, Roggman, & Musselman, 1994). Although exact standards for beauty vary by culture, average faces are preferred and rated as most attractive all over the world (Langlois & Roggman, 1990). Furthermore, infants as young as 6 or 9 months of age also tend to prefer average faces over others, although they are too young for other people to have had much influence over their face preferences (Hoss & Langlois, 2003).

Averaged faces tend to be more symmetrical, and people seem to prefer symmetry when they rate faces for attractiveness (Etcoff, 1999). Moreover, symmetry is a rough indicator of genetic fitness; that is, symmetrical faces and bodies are signs of fewer genetic mutations (Miller, 2000).

Sexual Attraction and Mate Selection

What qualities do you look for in a prospective sexual partner? **Sexual strategies theory** suggests that men and women often approach relationships differently (Buss & Schmitt, 1993). In virtually all societies, men and women engage in both short-term matings (affairs, one-night stands) and long-term matings (marriages, extended companionships). Both are effective ways to increase one's reproductive fitness, but each strategy has strengths and weaknesses.

Sex differences in attraction arise because *parental investment* is greater for women than for men (Trivers, 1972). Consequently, men devote a larger portion of their total mating effort to short-term mating than do women (Buss, 1999).

Buss (1999) found that men report wanting an average of 18 different partners throughout their lifetime, whereas women report only wanting 4 or 5. Men value qualities that may signal fertility and accessibility (e.g., large breasts, wide hips compared to waist, youth), especially in short-term partners. This is less true in evaluating long-term partners. Women, in contrast, value men who can provide resources to support their offspring.

connection

Men are more likely than women to be interested in casual sex.

See Chapter 11, p. 425.

sexual strategies theory
the idea that men and women face different problems when they seek out mates, and so they often approach relationships in very different ways.

4 face composite

8 face composite

16 face composite

32 face composite

social relations **563**

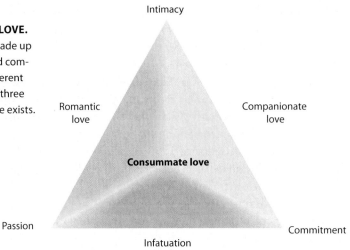

FIGURE **14.10**
STERNBERG'S TRIANGULAR THEORY OF LOVE.
In Sternberg's model, all types of love are made up of three components: intimacy, passion, and commitment. Each type of love consists of a different balance of the three components. When all three exist in equal proportions, consummate love exists. (*Source:* Sternberg, 1986.)

Mate selection factors might drive sexual partnerships, but these evolutionary pressures operate outside conscious awareness. Once people mate, it is the love that may develop between two people that keeps them together. But what is love?

Love As a concept, love is not easy to define. It takes many different forms and means different things to different people at different times in their lives.

Types of Love. Humans love in many different ways. We love our parents, lovers, friends, brothers and sisters, children, dogs, lattes, and music. How do we account for the variations? One well-known theory is Robert Sternberg's **triangular theory of love** (Sternberg, 1986). Sternberg proposed that three components—intimacy, passion, and commitment, in various combinations—can explain all the forms of human love (see Figure 14.10). *Intimacy* refers to close, connected, and bonded feelings in loving relationships. *Passion* refers to the drives that lead to romance, physical attraction, and sexual consummation and is accompanied by physiological changes and arousal. *Commitment* refers to both the decision to love someone—or not—and the decision to commit to love for the long term.

These three components are present in different amounts for different kinds of love. *Companionate love* exists when intimacy and commitment are high and passion is low. In *passionate love,* intimacy and passion are high and commitment is low. *Lust* is characterized by a lot of passion but no intimacy or commitment. For example, arranged marriages are all about commitment, at least in the beginning, with no intimacy or passion.

Love as Attachment. Love is also closely connected to a well-known psychological phenomenon: attachment. Attachment, an important concept in human development, is an affection-based bond between infants and their primary caregivers that serves to protect infants from threats to their survival (Bowlby, 1969). Attachment researchers distinguish among secure, avoidant, and anxious/ambivalent attachment styles (Ainsworth et al., 1978).

The attachment system established when we are infants forms a template for our adult relationships with others, including our intimate partners, according to Cynthia Hazan and Phillip Shaver (1987). Hazan and Shaver argued that the infant-caregiver attachment system underlies the important dynamics and individual

triangular theory of love
Sternberg's idea that three components (intimacy, passion, and commitment), in various combinations, can explain all the forms of human love.

connection
Attachment is a bidirectional relationship requiring the active participation of infants and caregivers.
See Chapter 5, p. 192.

differences in adult romantic relationships. By categorizing people's infant-caregiver attachment style based on an adult attachment interview, they found that securely attached adults report that they easily get close to others, readily trust others, and have more satisfying romantic relationships. Anxious/ambivalent adults tend to have less satisfying relationships, are more preoccupied with them, and fear that their partners do not want the intimacy they desire. Avoidant adults are uncomfortable being close to others and have less satisfying relationships (Hazan & Shaver, 1987).

As you can see, we have a partial understanding of how liking, attraction, and love work, but psychological science has yet to explain how these elements come together. Evolutionary psychology offers one integrative framework. In this view, for example, liking and loving both evolved to help ensure survival of the species.

making connections
in social behavior

Analysis of the Jonestown Cult

The tragic mass suicide of hundreds of members of the People's Temple in Jonestown, Guyana, illustrates many of the social-psychological concepts discussed in this chapter. In late November 1978, under the direction of the Rev. Jim Jones, members of this cult fed a poison-laced drink to their children and then drank it themselves. More than 900 adults and children died; most were found lying together, arm in arm.

Most of the members of the People's Temple went willingly to their deaths. Why? After years of indoctrination and isolation from mainstream society, they had been led into complete commitment to Jones and the People's Temple. Jonestown had all the hallmarks of a cult. A **cult** is

cult
an extremist group led by a charismatic, totalitarian leader who uses coercive methods to prevent members from leaving the group.

an extremist group led by a charismatic, totalitarian leader in which coercive methods are used to prevent members from leaving the group.

If we apply social-psychological theory to an analysis of these events, they become more comprehensible because we can see that the members of the People's Temple were not very different from us. Four principles of social psychology—persuasion, conformity, obedience, and cognitive dissonance—can shed light on the tragedy of Jonestown (Osherow, 1999).

Jim Jones and the People's Temple
Jim Jones founded the People's Temple in Indiana in 1958, preaching a message of brotherhood, racial integration, and

Jim Jones

freedom from poverty. His group helped feed and employ the poor. Jones presented a public image of a beloved leader who promoted a vision of racial harmony.

Throughout the 1960s, the group grew in size and popularity. Rumors surfaced that Jones used coercive methods to keep people from leaving the People's Temple. In the mid-1970s, after a great deal of bad publicity, Jones and his followers moved to a jungle outpost he called Jonestown in

These are some of the victims of a mass suicide at Jonestown, Guyana, in 1978. People's Temple leader Jim Jones used his status as an authority figure to persuade, intimidate, and indoctrinate his followers over several years, apparently convincing them that death was the only alternative to being captured and separated from the group.

Guyana, South America. In 1978, U.S. Congressman Leo Ryan heard reports that the People's Temple was holding members against their will. He led a delegation of government officials, reporters, and concerned relatives to Jonestown to talk with residents about how they liked living there. Two families secretly informed Ryan that they wanted out. As Ryan's party and these two "defector" families tried to board their plane for the United States, Temple gunmen ambushed and killed five people, including Congressman Ryan. This ambush precipitated the mass suicide, an act that Jones and his followers had practiced and rehearsed many times. It was their final act of rebellion against the system that they believed had forced them into exile.

The Role of Persuasion
Jones was a charismatic figure. He sought out people who needed to hear his message: the urban poor, minorities, the elderly, ex-addicts, and convicts. Potential members of the People's Temple first encountered an almost idyllic scene in which Blacks and Whites lived, worked, and worshiped together in total harmony. Guests were greeted warmly and invited to share a meal. Jones also gave them miracles. He cured diseases; he made predictions that came true with uncanny frequency. Members were motivated to believe in Jones; they appreciated the racial harmony, sense of purpose, and relief from feelings of worthlessness that the People's Temple provided.

Jones carefully managed his public image. He used letter writing and the political clout of hundreds of cult members to praise him and impress the politicians and reporters who supported the People's Temple as well as to criticize and intimidate its opponents. Most important, Jones limited the information available to members.

The Role of Conformity and Obedience
Conformity played a role in the People's Temple from the outset. Even getting into the group was not easy. People underwent a strict initiation process that actually drew members more firmly into the group. As they became increasingly involved in the People's Temple, they committed themselves more strongly to the group because they were required to donate their property and 25% of their income to the church. Before they entered the meeting room for each service, they wrote self-incriminating letters that were turned over to the church. If anyone objected, the refusal was interpreted as a "lack of faith" in Jones. All of these rules functioned to make the group more important than individuals, which according to social impact theory, makes conformity to the group all the more likely.

As he gradually increased his demands, Jones also exposed cult members to the concept of a "final ritual," mass suicide. Rehearsals of this ritual served to test followers and their faith in Jones. In essence, Jones was making use of what social psychologists call the *foot-in-the-door* technique by getting people to agree to a moderate request (i.e., rehearsal). Once cult members had agreed to engage in frequent rehearsals of mass suicide, it became easier for them to go through with the real thing.

The suicides at Jonestown can be viewed as the product of obedience—people complying with the orders of a leader and reacting to the threat of force. In the People's Temple, whatever Jim Jones commanded, the members did. Jones was a forceful authority. By the early 1970s, the members of the People's Temple lived in constant fear of severe punishment—brutal beatings coupled with public humiliation—for committing trivial or even inadvertent offenses. Milgram's experiments show us that the power of authority need not be so explicitly threatening to create compliance with demands. Nor does the consensus of the group need to be coercive, as Asch's experiments on conformity indicate. Yet Jones' power was both threatening and coercive.

Jones used threats to impose the discipline and devotion he demanded, and he took steps to eliminate any behavior that might encourage resistance among his followers. As Solomon Asch found in his experiments on conformity, if just one confederate expressed an opinion different from that of the majority, the rate of conformity drastically declined. This is minority social influence. In the People's Temple, Jones tolerated no dissent, made sure that members had no allegiance more powerful than their loyalty to him, and tried to make the alternative of leaving the church unthinkable. Anyone who dared to dissent was terrorized as a traitor, thereby squelching the possibility of minority social influence.

How did Jones do this? He used informers who reported indiscretions, split families to prevent allegiances, and forced parents to give over their children to the Temple. He thereby created conditions in which kin selection could not promote helping between members. Similarly, Jones worked to dissolve marital bonds by forcing couples into extramarital relations (sometimes with Jones himself). "Families are part of the enemy system," Jones said, because they weakened the individual's dedication to the cause. Not surprisingly, it was very hard to leave the cult. Not being able to defect or escape from the group, people had little choice but to conform.

The Role of Cognitive Dissonance

Cognitive dissonance helps explain why cult members believed Jones to the end and why so few defected. People did not become cult members all at once. Rather, the process of justifying their choice and becoming committed to Jones unfolded slowly over the course of weeks and months, sometimes years. Jones knew what he was doing. Starting the process with harsh acts of initiation is a perfect way to get people to rationalize their otherwise embarrassing behavior. If people don't see the group they are about to join very positively, how could they possibly justify going through such humiliation in order to get in?

Even so, how could members not seek to escape and accept killing themselves and their children so easily? These acts were the product of a situation that made dissent impossible and faith in Jones and the Temple absolute. Once they were isolated from the rest of the world at Jonestown, escape was impossible. When escape is impossible, people rationalize their predicament. The members of the People's Temple reduced their cognitive dissonance by changing their attitude to conform with their behavior. In this case, they told themselves that Jones was great and his message was wonderful. When the time to commit suicide finally arrived, most of the members clearly drank the juice quite willingly and by their own choice, so strong was their belief in Jones and his message.

quick quiz 14.4: Social Relations

1. Sam was driving his car and recklessly caused an accident that seriously injured a driver in another car. Susan insulted an acquaintance because she believed the acquaintance had questioned her honesty. According to the definition of aggression in the book, who behaved aggressively?
   a. Sam
   b. Susan
   c. both Sam and Susan
   d. neither Sam nor Susan

2. The bystander effect says
   a. the more people who observe a person in need of help, the less likely any one person will help
   b. the fewer people who observe a person in need of help, the less likely any one person will help
   c. people stand by and wait for help when they need it
   d. people are more likely to rescue people who are most closely related to themselves

3. The world over, faces that have _____ are perceived as the most attractive
   a. the smallest nose
   b. blue eyes
   c. features that are average in their dimensions
   d. eyes furthest apart

4. The tragedy of Jonestown, where more than 900 committed mass suicide, can be explained by four principles of social psychology: persuasion, conformity, _____ and _____.
   a. attraction; aggression
   b. obedience; cognitive dissonance
   c. obedience; empathy
   d. discrimination; prejudice

Answers can be found at the end of the chapter.

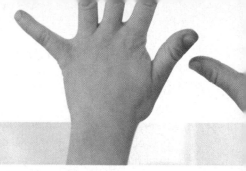

chapter **review**

GROUP LIVING AND SOCIAL INFLUENCE

- Social psychology is the study of the effects of the real or imagined presence of others on people's thoughts, feelings, and actions.

- We act differently when other people are present than we do when we are alone. Sometimes our performance is improved when we are with other people; sometimes it is hindered. In addition, people adjust their behavior in order to conform to what others are doing or to adhere to the rules of their culture.

- An individual can change the majority opinion of a group, but doing so takes perseverance and consistency.

- Obedience to authority can and has led to numerous instances of people doing things they otherwise would not, from soldiers in Nazi Germany and Abu Ghraib prison in Iraq to participants in Milgram's studies.

SOCIAL PERCEPTION

- We are constantly drawing conclusions about why people do what they do; that is, we make attributions. Sometimes we say internal qualities of the person were the cause of their behavior. Other times we see outside forces in the environment as the cause of a person's behavior.

- When forming opinions about others, we use schema about individuals based on what they are like or are likely to do based simply on the group they belong to. Opinions formed this way are stereotypes. Similarly, a prejudice is an attitude toward a group of people or an individual member of a group based on unfair generalizations about that group. Finally, discrimination is preferential treatment of certain people that is driven by prejudicial attitudes.

- Applying stereotypes, prejudices, and discrimination to people based on their racial-ethnic group affiliations is racism. Racism operates both inside (explicitly) and outside (implicitly) our awareness.

ATTITUDES AND BEHAVIOR

- Psychologists define attitudes as a person's favorable or unfavorable beliefs, feelings, or actions toward an object, idea, or person. People's attitudes and behaviors do not always match and are often resistant to change.

- One explanation for why and how people change their attitudes is cognitive dissonance, which is the feeling of discomfort caused by information that differs from one's conception of oneself as a reasonable and sensible person.

- Persuasion is another way in which attitudes can be changed.

SOCIAL RELATIONS

- People hurt other people, help other people, and are attracted to and love other people.

- Aggression refers to violent behaviors that are intended to cause psychological and/or physical harm to another being. Aggression stems from a complex interplay of genetic and social forces.

- The more people who witness an accident or crime, the more likely it is that no one will call for help or intervene. This phenomenon is the bystander effect.

- People also act in prosocial ways to help others in need. In life-and-death situations, kin selection explains why people are most willing to help those who are most closely related to them.

- Relationships that are bound by similarities in personality, attitude, intelligence, and attractiveness tend to last the longest.

- People all over the world rate as most attractive those faces that possess average and symmetrical features. Sexual strategies theory suggests that men and women face different problems when they seek out mates, so they often approach relationships in very different ways.

- Sternberg's triangular theory of love states that all of the different forms of love each have three components: intimacy, passion, and commitment. Romantic love, for example, exists when intimacy and passion are present but commitment is absent.

MAKING CONNECTIONS
IN SOCIAL PSYCHOLOGY

- The People's Temple was considered to be a cult, which is an extremist group led by a charismatic, totalitarian leader who uses coercive methods to prevent members from leaving the group.

- Methods used by Jim Jones to ensure obedience and conformity by his followers included persuasion, rigid discipline and punishment of dissent, isolation, separation from family, and forced marital infidelity. Cult members resolved cognitive dissonance brought on by their situation through rationalization, telling themselves that Jones was a great leader with a wonderful message.

key **terms**

aggression, p. 553

altruism, p. 559

attitude, p. 549

attributions, p. 541

bystander effect, p. 558

cognitive dissonance, p. 550

conformity, p. 535

cult, p. 565

discrimination, p. 545

empathy, p. 560

empathy-altruism hypothesis, p. 560

fundamental attribution error, p. 542

groupthink, p. 536

informational social influence, p. 535

in-group/out-group bias, p. 544

kin selection, p. 559

normative social influence, p. 535

obedience, p. 537

out-group homogeneity, p. 544

persuasion, p. 551

prejudice, p. 545

prosocial behavior, p. 555

reciprocal altruism, p. 559

self-serving bias, p. 541

sexual strategies theory, p. 563

social exchange theory, p. 560

social facilitation, p. 534

social loafing, p. 534

social norms, p. 534

social psychology, p. 533

stereotypes, p. 543

triangular theory of love, p. 564

quick quiz **answers**

Quick Quiz 14.1:   1. c   2. d   3. a   4. c   **Quick Quiz 14.2:**   1. d   2. c   3. a   4. d   5. b
Quick Quiz 14.3:   1. b   2. d   3. a   **Quick Quiz 14.4**   1. b   2. a   3. c   4. b

psychological disorders

preview
questions

1 *How do we know whether or not someone's behavior is disordered?*

2 *What causes mental illness?*

3 *Should I be concerned about my roommate, who is tired all the time and doesn't feel like doing anything?*

4 *What is the chance that my friend who has an identical twin sister with bipolar disorder will also develop this disorder?*

I t was a Sunday evening in the middle of winter—December 23, 1888. The artists Vincent van Gogh and Paul Gauguin, who were close friends, had had an intense argument. Over what, we do not know. What we do know is how it ended: Van Gogh, in a fit of rage, took a razor and cut off the lower portion of his left ear. He then wrapped the earlobe in a newspaper and gave it to a prostitute named Rachel, telling her to "keep this object carefully" (Runyan, 1981).

Why Van Gogh might have committed such a bizarre act has been the subject of much speculation. We do know, however, that he was not well either mentally or physically; diagnoses of his mental disorder have ranged from epilepsy to schizophrenia to alcohol poisoning. It is difficult to know for sure what he suffered from, but we know that his younger brother committed suicide and his sister spent 40 years in an insane asylum, diagnosed ▶

▶ with "chronic psychosis." We also know that Van Gogh walked into a field near his home, shot himself in the chest, and died two days later at the age of 37. His last words were "the sadness will last forever."

What distinguished van Gogh from most others, of course, was his incredible gift for expressing his inner world and vision in artistic form. Van Gogh's searing, intense, and powerful paintings offer a glimpse into both his mental anguish and his genius. At the very least, his paintings and his life, fraught with psychological disorder, are fascinating to study.

Indeed, psychological disorders are compelling. They demand our attention, care, understanding, and treatment. But

chapter
outline

what are these disorders and how do they come about? In this chapter, we describe many psychological disorders and explain some of what is known about how they develop. As we discuss the causes of these disorders, we will focus on explanations that intertwine the biological with the environmental (Kendler, 2005; Moffitt, Caspi, & Rutter, 2005). We will begin by considering what it means for behavior to be disordered and how disorders are diagnosed. At the end of the chapter we will explore the topic of creativity and psychological disorders and consider whether artists are more likely than the general population to suffer from a psychological disorder. ■

Defining Psychological Disorders

Creative artists such as Van Gogh and Gauguin are different from most people. So are spelling bee champs and class valedictorians. Yet *different* does not mean *disordered*. How do psychologists distinguish behavior that is simply different from behavior that is disordered? Does a young boy who has more than 5,000 baseball cards and can tell you something about every one of them suffer from a psychological disorder? What about someone who washes his hands

Van Gogh painted *Self-Portrait with Bandaged Ear* (1889) after cutting off part of his ear following a violent disagreement with his friend and fellow painter Paul Gauguin.

for 45 minutes 10 times a day? How do psychologists distinguish behavior that is simply different from behavior that is disordered?

Most psychologists agree on three criteria that distinguish disordered from healthy, or just different, behavior: It must be deviant, distressing, and dysfunctional (APA, 2000). Deviant literally means "different from the norm," or different from what most people do. This criterion allows for the fact that behavior which is considered deviant in one culture might be considered normal in others. Distressing behavior leads to real discomfort or anguish, either in the person directly or in others. The distressing element is one reason we say a person is "suffering" from a disorder. It causes pain to the person and/or other people, especially family members. Dysfunctional behavior interferes with everyday functioning and occasionally can be a risk to oneself or others. Dysfunctional also implies it prevents one from participating in everyday social relationships, holding a regular job, or being productive in other ways. In sum, deviant behavior can be classified as disordered only if it is also both distressing and dysfunctional. Albert Einstein was deviant in his intelligence and creativity, but he was not suffering from a psychological disorder. Behaviors that possess only one or even two of these qualities are not typically classified as disordered.

Most people suffering from psychological disorders do not pose a risk to others, but some do. For instance, people who are sexually attracted to children (pedophiles) and individuals with violent impulse disorder could be a very real danger to others.

How do mental health professionals determine whether someone is suffering from a psychological disorder? A major tool for diagnosing psychological disorders is the *Diagnostic and Statistical Manual (DSM)* published by the American Psychiatric Association (APA). Beginning with the third edition and continuing in the fourth edition, the *DSM-IV-TR* (for "Text Revision"; APA, 2000), the *DSM* places disorders in one of two diagnostic classifications, or axes. **Axis I disorders** are the major clinical **syndromes,** or clusters of related symptoms

Axis I disorders in the *DSM-IV-TR,* the major clinical syndromes that cause significant impairment.

syndromes groups or clusters of related symptoms that are characteristic of a disorder.

Looking at this photograph, we might think this person has a psychological disorder. However, behavior must be deviant, distressing to the individual, and dysfunctional to be classified as disordered.

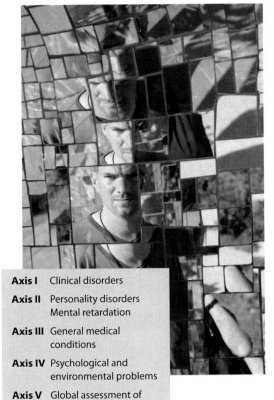

FIGURE **15.1**

DSM-IV-TR **AXES.** Axes I and II describe the disorders and their symptoms. Axes III, IV, and V take into account factors in an individual's background and environment that might affect the diagnosis or treatment of a psychological disorder. (*Source:* APA, 2000.)

Axis I	Clinical disorders
Axis II	Personality disorders Mental retardation
Axis III	General medical conditions
Axis IV	Psychological and environmental problems
Axis V	Global assessment of functioning

that cause significant impairment: anxiety, depression, bipolar disorder, and schizophrenia. These disorders tend to develop after adolescence, can wax and wane, and are not always permanent. **Axis II disorders** include personality disorders and mental retardation, which tend to appear in childhood or adolescence and are more difficult to treat than Axis I disorders. One final difference between Axis I and Axis II disorders is that Axis I disorders tend to be viewed by people suffering from them as inconsistent with their personality and therefore cause some degree of subjective stress. Axis II disorders are viewed as consistent with an individual's personality and therefore do not cause as much subjective stress as Axis I disorders. They are simply part of the person (APA, 2000).

Axis II disorders in *DSM-IV-TR*, the more long-standing personality disorders as well as mental retardation.

The *DSM-IV-TR* includes three additional axes, which list medical conditions and environmental factors that may contribute to an individual's psychological state or affect treatment. Figure 15.1 lists the five axes of the *DSM* classification system.

Psychological disorders are not uncommon (see Figure 15.2). Almost half of the adults in the United States will suffer from at least one psychological disorder in their lifetime, and more than half of those will suffer from two or more disorders (Kessler et al., 2005). The existence of two or more disorders at the same time is termed **comorbidity**.

comorbidity coexistence of two or more disorders.

connections

Dementia and Alzheimer's disease are cognitive disorders related to age. Other disorders, such as sleep disorders, can occur at any time in a person's life. See Chapter 5, p. 206, and Chapter 6, p. 235.

The *DSM* describes more than 250 Axis I disorders and more than 100 Axis II disorders. Figure 15.3 on page 576 lists the major ones. In this chapter, we examine anxiety disorders, mood disorders, schizophrenia, dissociative disorders, personality disorders, and childhood disorders.

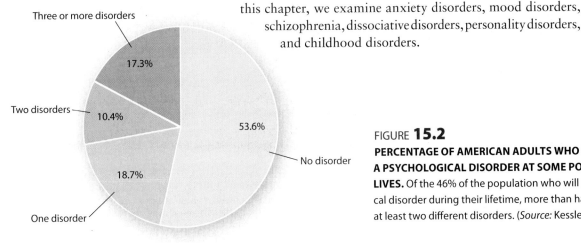

FIGURE **15.2**

PERCENTAGE OF AMERICAN ADULTS WHO WILL EXPERIENCE A PSYCHOLOGICAL DISORDER AT SOME POINT DURING THEIR LIVES. Of the 46% of the population who will suffer a psychological disorder during their lifetime, more than half will suffer from at least two different disorders. (*Source:* Kessler et al., 2005.)

FIGURE **15.3**

**MAJOR PSY-
CHOLOGICAL
DISORDERS.**
Although
DSM-IV-TR
describes more
than 250 Axis I
disorders and
100 Axis II dis-
orders, these are
the most com-
mon. (*Source:* APA,
2000.)

Axis I disorders	Description
Disorders usually first diagnosed in infancy, childhood, or adolescence	Attention deficit hyperactivity disorder, autistic spectrum disorders, learning disorders, conduct and oppositional disorder, separation anxiety disorder, and feeding, tic, and elimination disorders.
Anxiety disorders	Characterized by motor tension, hyperactivity and apprehensive expectation/thoughts. Include generalized anxiety disorder, panic disorder, phobic disorder, obsessive-compulsive disorder, and post-traumatic stress disorder.
Somatoform disorders	Occur when psychological symptoms take a physical form even though no physical causes can be found. Include hypochondriasis and conversion disorder.
Factitious disorders	Characterized by the individual's deliberate fabrication of a medical or mental disorder to gain medical attention.
Dissociative disorders	Involve a sudden loss of memory or change of identity.
Delirium, dementia, amnestic, and other cognitive disorders	Disorders involving problems in consciousness and cognition, such as substance-induced delirium or dementia related to Alzheimer's disease.
Mood disorders	Characterized by a primary disturbance in mood; include depressive disorders and bipolar disorder (sometimes called manic depression).
Schizophrenia and other psychotic disorders	Characterized by distorted thoughts and perceptions, odd communication, inappropriate emotion, and other unusual behaviors.
Substance-related disorders	Characterized by abuse or dependence on drugs, such as alcohol, cocaine, and hallucinogens.
Sexual and gender-identity disorders	Consist of three main types of disorders: gender-identity disorders (person is not comfortable with identity as a female or male), paraphilias (person has a preference for unusual sexual acts to stimulate sexual arousal), and sexual dysfunctions (impairments in sexual functioning).
Eating disorders	Include anorexia nervosa and bulimia nervosa (see Chapter 12).
Sleep disorders	Consist of primary sleep disorders, such as insomnia and narcolepsy, and sleep disorders due to a general medical condition, such as sleep apnea (see Chapter 6).
Impulse-control disorders not elsewhere classified	Include kleptomania, pyromania, and compulsive gambling.
Adjustment disorders	Characterized by distressing emotional or behavioral symptoms in response to an identifiable stressor.

Axis II disorders	
Mental retardation	Low intellectual functioning and an inability to adapt to everyday life (see Chapter 10).
Personality disorders	Develop when personality traits become inflexible and maladaptive.
Other conditions that may be a focus of clinical attention	Include relational problems (with a partner, sibling, and so on), problems related to abuse or neglect (physical abuse of a child, for example), or additional conditions (such as bereavement, academic problems, and religious or spiritual problems).

Anxiety Disorders

For most of us, anxiety and fear are occasional, distressing, but necessary emotions that tell us something is wrong. For about 29% of the U.S. population, however, anxiety is out of proportion to the situation and interferes with everyday functioning. We discuss seven types of anxiety disorder: generalized anxiety disorder, panic disorder, agoraphobia, post-traumatic stress disorder (PTSD), social phobia, specific phobias, and obsessive–compulsive disorders (see Figure 15.4).

GENERALIZED ANXIETY DISORDER

generalized anxiety disorder (GAD)
state of pervasive and excessive anxiety lasting at least six months.

Generalized anxiety disorder (GAD) is a common anxiety disorder, characterized by a pervasive and excessive state of anxiety lasting at least six months (APA, 2000). More women than men experience GAD (Kessler et al., 2005). Moreover, unlike those suffering from other anxiety disorders, people with GAD often have been anxious throughout their lives and cannot recall when they began to feel that way (Barlow, 2004). In everyday language, we might call such people "worrywarts"—someone who worries about anything and everything, often out

FIGURE **15.4**

MAJOR SYMPTOMS AND CRITERIA OF SPECIFIC ANXIETY DISORDERS. All of these disorders share the symptom of intense anxiety. (*Source:* APA, 2000.)

Disorder	Major symptoms	Behaviors
Generalized anxiety disorder (GAD)	Pervasive/excessive anxiety lasting at least 6 months	Inability to relax
Panic disorder	Persistent worry about having a panic attack	*Panic attack:* Heart palpitations, trembling, dizziness, intense dread, and fear of dying *Panic disorder:* Prone to panic attacks, concerned about having a panic attack and about embarrassment of having a panic attack
Agoraphobia	Fear of not being able to escape or of help not being available if panic attack should occur in public place	Unwilling to leave home so as to avoid panic attacks
Post-traumatic stress disorder (PTSD)	Anxiety disorder triggered by a traumatic experience	(1) Possible flashbacks; nightmares about the traumatic event (2) Emotional numbness and avoidance of thoughts, feelings, and activities associated with the trauma (3) Irritability or outbursts of anger; hypervigilance and trouble sleeping
Social phobia	Persistent fear of humiliation in the presence of others	Highly anxious, extremely self-conscious about appearance or behavior or both, possibly housebound
Specific phobias	Undue anxiety response to particular objects or situations	Intense fear or panic when confronted with particular situations or objects or even when thinking about them
Obsessive–compulsive disorder	Preoccupation with unwanted thoughts and repetitive behaviors to control the anxiety caused by the distressing thoughts, which are often understood to be irrational	Cleaning and checking behaviors that may help to control the obsessive thoughts but that interfere with daily life

Filmmaker Woody Allen uses writing, acting, and directing as a distraction from his own anxiety.

of proportion to the actual threat. The writer, director, and actor Woody Allen has made a career out of his pervasive tendency to worry. Allen says he uses filmmaking and writing as a creative distraction from his anxiety (Briggs, 2005). However, the constant anxiety of GAD can be debilitating.

PANIC DISORDER WITH OR WITHOUT AGORAPHOBIA

Panic attacks are associated with perceptions of threat and can occur for a number of reasons: fear of danger, inability to escape, fear of embarrassment, or fear of a specific category of objects. Attacks usually last about 10 minutes but sometimes come and go over an hour or more. They are characterized by an overwhelming sense of impending doom, accompanied by heart palpitations, trembling, dizziness, intense dread, and even fear of dying. Panic attacks often result in people believing they are having a heart attack or are "going crazy." People with **panic disorder** get panic attacks and experience persistent worry, embarrassment, and concern about having more attacks (APA, 2000). Preoccupation with the threat of another attack creates an anxious mood, which increases the likelihood of more worrisome thoughts. Panic disorder hijacks the body's emergency response system and catapults it out of control.

People who have only occasional panic attacks without intense anxiety or fear about the possibility of future panic attacks do not qualify for the diagnosis of panic disorder. Approximately 10% of the U.S. population has experienced a panic attack in the past 12 months, whereas only about 2% to 5% of the population has panic disorder (Grant et al., 2006).

Panic attacks lead to agoraphobia in about one-third of cases. **Agoraphobia** is intense anxiety and panic about being in places from which escape might be difficult or in which help might not be available should a panic attack occur (APA, 2000). It is the most severe of all phobias (Bouton, Mineka, & Barlow, 2001). Contrary to popular belief, the primary "fear" in agoraphobia is not of being out in public but rather of being in an inescapable situation. The fear of being unable to escape keeps people at home, where they feel safe. Agoraphobia typically begins when a person experiences a panic attack in a public place, such as a park or a crowd of people, and feels trapped and unable to escape.

POST-TRAUMATIC STRESS DISORDER

Post-traumatic stress disorder (PTSD) is an anxiety disorder triggered by exposure to a catastrophic or horrifying event that caused serious harm or posed a threat to the person—such as experiences of war, attempted murder, rape, natural disasters, sudden death of a loved one, or physical or sexual abuse. Symptoms of PTSD are grouped into three categories: (1) reexperiencing the trauma; (2) avoiding thoughts, feelings, and activities associated with the trauma; emotional numbing and distancing from loved ones; and (3) increased arousal, such as irritability, difficulty sleeping, or exaggerated startle response (Duke & Vasterling, 2005). War veterans are at increased risk not only for PTSD but also for depression, drug abuse, and suicide after returning home. For example, upwards of 20% of the veterans from Iraq have developed PTSD (Roehr, 2007).

panic attack
sudden, short period of extreme anxiety involving physiological and psychological symptoms and intense fear.

panic disorder
an anxiety disorder characterized by panic attacks and persistent anxiety about having more attacks.

agoraphobia
an anxiety disorder involving intense fear of being in places from which escape might be difficult or in which help might not be available should a panic attack occur.

post-traumatic stress disorder (PTSD)
a type of anxiety disorder triggered by exposure to a catastrophic or horrifying event that poses serious harm or threat.

SOCIAL PHOBIA (SOCIAL ANXIETY DISORDER)

phobia
an anxiety disorder marked by ongoing and irrational fear of a particular object, situation, or activity.

A **phobia** is a persistent and unreasonable fear of a particular object, situation, or activity (APA, 2000). Some people suffer extreme anxiety associated with interacting with other people. **Social phobia** or **social anxiety disorder,** a pronounced fear of humiliation in the presence of others, is marked by severe self-consciousness about appearance or behavior or both. People with social phobia are afraid of embarrassing or humiliating themselves, of being evaluated negatively by others, and of having their faults continually observed by everyone. Consider the case of "Sarah," who hates going to the grocery store: She would not dare ask anyone working there how to find an item, for she might look as if she is stupid for not being able to find it herself. She doesn't want anyone to know she is anxious about being in the grocery store. She is concerned that her voice might quiver when forced to say the obligatory "hello" to the cashier. This would make her seem really foolish and everybody would stare at her foolishness.

Fear like Sarah's can be paralyzing, making it very difficult to go out into public situations, even though in most cases the person recognizes that these fears are irrational. Unfortunately, the high degree of anxious arousal produced by social phobia may lead the person to act very nervously and thus, in a self-fulfilling way, exhibit behaviors that do indeed attract other people's attention.

social phobia (social anxiety disorder)
fear of humiliation in the presence of others, characterized by intense self-consciousness about appearance or behavior or both.

People with social anxiety disorder are extremely self-conscious and fearful of embarrassing themselves in front of others.

SPECIFIC PHOBIAS

Only a few of us enjoy spiders, snakes, or heights, but most of us feel only mild levels of fear about such objects or experiences. Some of us, however, go beyond mild levels of fear. As many as 1 in 8 people will develop a *specific phobia* for a particular object or situation, such as spiders (arachnophobia), heights, flying, enclosed spaces (claustrophobia), doctors and dentists, or snakes (Kessler et al., 2005). A specific phobia is a persistent, irrational fear of a particular situation or object; even thinking about the situation or object may set off the fear reaction. People with specific phobias are not generally anxious people, but they will do almost anything to avoid coming into contact with the feared object or experiencing the feared event. Football announcer John Madden, for example, who travels tens of thousands of miles a year for his job, always travels by bus or train, despite the inconvenience, because of his intense fear of flying.

obsession
an unwanted thought, word, phrase, or image that persistently and repeatedly comes into a person's mind and causes distress.

OBSESSIVE–COMPULSIVE DISORDER

obsessive– compulsive disorder (OCD)
an anxiety disorder in which compulsive thoughts lead to obsessive behaviors.

Obsessive–compulsive disorder (OCD) is an anxiety disorder that is manifested in both thought and behavior. An **obsession** is an unwanted thought, word, phrase, or image that persistently and repeatedly comes into a person's mind and causes distress. People with OCD have thoughts that they cannot dismiss, especially negative thoughts that most people can disregard (APA, 2000). A **compulsion** is a repetitive behavior performed in response to uncontrollable urges or according

compulsion
a repetitive behavior performed in response to uncontrollable urges or according to a ritualistic set of rules.

Can Internet Use Become an Addiction?

Some people just can't stay off-line. This, in itself, may not be a great problem. In some cases, however, people are online all day, cannot continue their work or activities around the home without logging on, and think about the Internet whenever they are not online. For them, Internet use has become so intrusive that it adversely affects their professional and personal lives.

Mental health professionals do not agree on whether Internet abuse is an addiction, a compulsion, or an impulse disorder. The word *addiction* is problematic, as it suggests a physiological dependence in which the body cannot function without a particular substance, such as with heroin or nicotine. It is more likely that problems of Internet use are compulsions or impulse disorders. As you've read, compulsions are uncontrollable behaviors that serve to control the anxiety created by the obsessions. Although Internet abuse can be viewed as compulsive, the possibility that it is a

problem of impulse control has received the most empirical support (Aboujaoude et al., 2006).

It is clear that, for a minority of people, Internet use does interfere with everyday functioning and activities. A large-scale telephone survey found that 4%–13% of 2,500 adults in the United States answered at least one question in a way that indicated problematic Internet use (Aboujaoude et al., 2006). About 1% met proposed diagnostic criteria for Internet-based impulse disorder. Recent surveys of teenagers indicate that about 5% have problems of excessive Internet use (Pallanti, Bernardi, & Quercoli, 2006).

Figure 15.5 lists the types of Internet activities that people are most likely to engage in, according to a recent survey (Meerkerk, van den Eijnden, & Garretsen, 2006). Almost 15% of the respondents spent more than 21 hours a week (3 hours per day) on e-mail, and about 11% spent that much

to a ritualistic set of rules. In short, obsessions are thought disturbances whereas compulsions are repetitive behaviors.

Obsessive–compulsive disorder most often involves either cleaning, checking, or counting behaviors that interfere with everyday functioning. A man who is obsessed with security might check that the front door is locked 15 or 20 times before being able to drive away; a woman who is obsessed with germs might wash her hands dozens or even hundreds of times throughout the day. A famous example of OCD is the case of billionaire businessman and airplane innovator Howard Hughes, portrayed in the film *The Aviator*. Here, for example, are the explicit instructions Hughes gave his staff for removing his hearing aid cord from a cabinet:

The young Howard Hughes prior to becoming an obsessive-compulsive recluse.

> First use six or eight thicknesses of Kleenex pulled one at a time from the slot in touching the door knob to open the door to the bathroom. The door is to be left open so there will be no need to touch anything when leaving the bathroom. The same sheaf of Kleenex may be employed to turn on the spigots so as to obtain a good force of warm water. (quoted in Ludwig, 1995, p. 128)

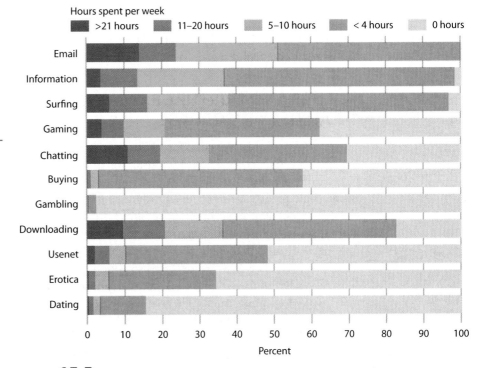

Hours spent per week

■ >21 hours ■ 11–20 hours ■ 5–10 hours ■ < 4 hours □ 0 hours

Email
Information
Surfing
Gaming
Chatting
Buying
Gambling
Downloading
Usenet
Erotica
Dating

Percent

FIGURE **15.5**

TIME SPENT ON INTERNET ACTIVITIES. Participants were Dutch adults who used the Internet for at least 16 hours a week and had home Internet access. Of the 1,000 e-mail users who received a request to participate, 447 completed the online survey. (*Source:* Meerkerk et al., 2006.)

time chatting. But how do we measure whether spending excessive amounts of time online is a disorder or not?

For one thing, Internet abuse is common in the workplace, where it reduces worker productivity when people use the Internet obsessively and/or impulsively for non-work-related purposes, such as talking with friends, surfing news sites and blogs, and perusing adult video sites. These activities waste company resources and can interfere with everyday work-related functioning (Chen, Chen, & Yang, 2007; Stewart, 2000). Also, in a study of Internet use in college students, those who spend excessive amounts of time online are more likely to report depressive symptoms and to engage in less face-to-face social interaction (Forsten et al., 2007). The bottom line is that Internet-related behavior that meets the criteria of being deviant, distressing, and dysfunctional also meets the standards for being a disorder. If it does not meet those criteria, it is not a disorder. Evidence suggests for a small percent of the population, Internet-related behavior may become a disorder.

People with OCD often know that their thoughts are irrational, or at least that their compulsive behaviors are excessive, but they cannot stop themselves. In some cases, compulsive behaviors stem from superstitions. For example, a person might feel the need to tap the wall 65 times before leaving a room for fear that not doing so will result in his or her parents dying. The person knows rationally that there is no connection between wall tapping and the death of one's parents, but performs the ritual nevertheless.

There may be a close link between some compulsive and some *impulsive* behaviors. *DSM-IV-TR* defines **impulse control disorder** as involving those behaviors that people cannot control and feel an intense, repetitive desire to perform (APA, 2000). Moreover, the behavior must interfere with everyday functioning. The behavior is experienced as pleasurable in the moment but has repercussions that are unpleasant or create impairments. Behaviors that develop into impulse control disorders in some individuals include gambling, shopping, hair pulling, and substance abuse. Recently, mental health professionals have pointed to a great deal of similarity between OCD and impulse disorders, even to the point of suggesting that OCD spectrum disorders should be a separate category in *DSM*

impulse control disorder

an anxiety disorder related to obsessive–compulsive disorder in which a person feels an intense, repetitive desire to perform certain behaviors.

(Storch, Abramowitz, & Goodman, 2008). For a recent manifestation of a possible impulse control disorder, see "Psychology in the Real World."

NATURE AND NURTURE EXPLANATIONS OF ANXIETY DISORDERS

How do anxiety disorders develop? Like all animals, humans have evolved fear mechanisms to determine whether a situation is safe or not and whether we need to try to fight or flee (LeDoux, 2000). Additionally, as is true for most complex traits, some people are more genetically disposed to anxiety than others. Anxiety disorders—and most other psychological disorders—result from the interplay between biological and environmental factors.

Historically, this explanation has been called the **diathesis–stress model.** *Diathesis* is the Greek word for "predisposition," so the diathesis–stress view is that biological predispositions plus stress or abusive environments together produce psychological disorders. The diathesis–stress model is becoming more fully developed and refined based on the findings of research in such areas as behavioral genetics, epigenetics, and brain plasticity.

diathesis–stress model
explanation for the origin of psychological disorders as a combination of biological predispositions (diathesis) plus stress or an abusive environment.

connection

How does our first environment—the womb—shape the expression of our genes?
See the discussion of epigenetics in Chapter 3, p. 82.

Three biological factors that make people vulnerable to anxiety disorders are deficiencies in the neurotransmitter GABA, their genetic heritage, and their personality. Researchers have discovered that people who are prone to anxiety are deficient in receptors for GABA, a major inhibitory neurotransmitter (Charney, 2004; Lydiard, 2003). Deficiencies in GABA lead to excessive activation in certain brain regions, especially the limbic structures associated with fear. Moreover, the fact that major medications for treating anxiety disorders work on GABA receptors is further evidence for GABA's role in anxiety. Genetic heritability estimates for generalized anxiety, panic disorder, and agoraphobia range from 30% to 40% (Hettema, Neale, & Kendler, 2001). As for personality, people who are high in neuroticism—prone to worry, anxiety, and nervousness—are more likely to develop anxiety disorders than are people who are low in neuroticism (Eysenck, 1982; Hamer & Copeland, 1998).

In summary, people who have the bad luck of having a genetic predisposition to anxiety, low levels of GABA, or the personality trait of neuroticism *and* who also experience chronic stress or abuse are most likely to develop anxiety disorders. Those who have the biological predispositions *or* experience abuse are next most likely to develop these disorders, whereas those who have *neither* biological vulnerability nor chronically stressful experiences are least likely to develop these disorders.

nature & nurture

People who have a genetic predisposition to anxiety, low levels of GABA, or the personality trait of neuroticism *and* who also experience chronic stress or abuse are most likely to develop anxiety disorders.

connection

Classical conditioning is the means by which Pavlov's dogs learned to salivate to a tone.
See Chapter 8, p. 297.

Another kind of biological predisposition may be present in OCD. The repetitive links between thought and behavior in OCD have been linked to hyperactivity in certain brain structures, including the anterior cingulate cortex (ACC) and the *caudate nucleus* (Fitzgerald et al., 2005; Guehl et al., 2008). The caudate nucleus is part of the basal ganglia, which controls voluntary behavior. The ACC plays an important role in monitoring conflicting information or detecting errors.

How is hyperactivity in the brain related to OCD? Some scientists argue that the brain circuit that connects the caudate, the ACC, and limbic structures (such as the amygdala and hypothalamus) is working overtime in OCD (Aouizerate et al., 2004; Schwartz, 1999a, 1999b). The overactive ACC creates a perpetual feeling that something is wrong, which the limbic system structures translate into anxiety. In turn, anxiety stimulates more intrusive thoughts, which sometimes become compulsive actions. These actions occur as behavioral responses aimed at reducing the tensions or anxiety generated by the situation (from the caudate nucleus). Relief may be experienced, but only briefly, before the anxiety returns. The cycle goes on endlessly, due to the hyperactivity of the brain circuit—which is stuck in the "on" position. So this circuit involving the ACC, caudate nucleus, and limbic structures supports the obsessive thinking and compulsive responding (Fitzgerald et al., 2005; Guehl et al., 2008).

connections
Implicit memory differs from explicit memory in terms of whether we are consciously aware of remembering. Similarly, implicit learning is learning without conscious effort. See Chapter 7, p. 264, and Chapter 8, p. 297.

In OCD, too many thoughts are held in awareness, too much importance is ascribed to all thoughts (rational or irrational), and thinking about one's thoughts is excessive (Janeck at al., 2003). Research on cognitive performance in people with OCD reveals a preoccupation with conscious thinking; it is hard for people with this disorder to keep certain ideas or information out of awareness. Consequently, people with OCD have trouble with implicit learning but not with explicit learning (Goldman et al., 2008; Marker et al., 2006). Figure 15.6 on page 584 shows how one research team studied this problem.

quick quiz 15.1: Anxiety Disorders

1. The occurrence of two or more disorders at the same time is known as _____.
    a. bipolar disorder
    b. comorbidity
    c. dipolarity
    d. syndrome

2. Maya is preoccupied with fears of embarrassing herself in public, so much so that she avoids going shopping or out for walks in town. What disorder best describes this set of symptoms?
    a. agoraphobia
    b. specific phobia
    c. panic disorder
    d. social phobia

3. People who are prone to anxiety are deficient in receptors for _____, a major inhibitory neurotransmitter.
    a. GABA
    b. glutamate
    c. serotonin
    d. dopamine

Answers can be found at the end of the chapter.

Mood Disorders

Approximately half of the individuals who suffer from an anxiety disorder also suffer from a mood disorder (Cairney et al., 2008; Löwe et al., 2008). **Mood disorders** are disturbances in emotional behavior that prevent people from functioning effectively in everyday life. The two major forms of mood disorder are depression and bipolar disorder.

mood disorders
category of psychological disorder characterized by severe disturbances in emotional behavior.

1 research question

People with OCD don't discriminate between rational and irrational thoughts. Marker and colleagues (2006) asked whether implicit learning might be impaired and explicit learning might be superior in people with OCD when compared with a control group.

2 method

The participants included 43 people who had been diagnosed with OCD and 41 people without OCD (the control group). (This was a quasi-experimental study because the participants could not be randomly assigned to the OCD and control group.) All participants completed an implicit learning task and a related explicit learning task on a computer.

For both tasks, an asterisk appeared on the screen in one of 4 locations. The first task (implicit learning) was to press a key on the computer keyboard corresponding to the asterisk's location as quickly as possible. The locations were varied in a repeating pattern, although the participants were not informed about this. The dependent variable was reaction time—how long it took to hit the key identifying the location of the asterisk. To do this task well, participants had to notice the pattern of locations and anticipate where the next asterisk would appear. If they did, their reaction time would decrease.

In the second, explicit learning task, participants again saw the asterisk at different locations in repeated patterns. This time they were told to press a key corresponding to where they thought the next asterisk would appear. This change in instruction made it explicit to participants that they should pay attention to the pattern. The dependent variable in this task was the number of correct responses regarding the location of the next asterisk.

3 results

Task 1: Implicit pattern learning The performance of all participants got better (faster) with each trial, which is an expected learning effect. But overall the OCD group was measurably slower. This means that the OCD group did not implicitly pick up on the pattern as readily as the comparison group.

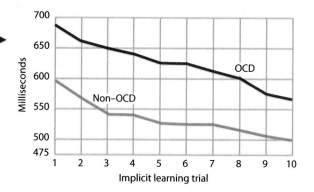

Task 2: Explicit pattern learning On the explicit learning task, the OCD group did a superior job, showing a significantly higher percentage of correct responses than the nonclinical comparison group.

4 conclusion

People with OCD perform less well on an implicit learning task and better on an explicit learning task than people without the disorder. This result supports the hypothesis that people with OCD have an overactive conscious awareness of their thoughts, which makes obsessions more likely.

FIGURE 15.6

IMPLICIT AND EXPLICIT LEARNING IN OBSESSIVE COMPULSIVE DISORDER (OCD). Research on cognitive performance in people with OCD reveals a preoccupation with conscious thinking. If this is so, then treatments for OCD that focus on quieting the overabundance of thoughts in awareness will be most effective. (*Source:* C. D. Marker, J. E. Calamari, J. L. Woodard, & B. C. Riemann. 2006. Cognitive self-consciousness, implicit learning, and obsessive–compulsive disorder. *Journal of Anxiety Disorders, 20,* 389–407.)

DEPRESSION AND ITS CAUSES

Like feeling anxious, occasionally feeling depressed is a normal part of everyday life. Feeling despondent after being rejected by a lover or failing an exam is a normal response to real setbacks. The clinical form of depression, however, is different and occurs in about 10% of adults in the United States at some point in their life. **Major depressive disorder**—often referred to simply as *depression*—is characterized by pervasive low mood, lack of motivation, low energy, and feelings of worthlessness and guilt that last for at least two consecutive weeks (APA, 2000). Sleep is often disturbed in depression, resulting sometimes in insomnia and sometimes hypersomnia (excessive sleep). Major depressive disorder sometimes is a single event in a person's life, but more often than not it is recurring. In either case, depression is more than just "the blues." It is a life-altering change in behavior accompanied by a lack of desire to do much of anything. It is also a major risk factor for suicide. A milder form of depression, however, does exist and is called **dysthymia.** Most of the symptoms are the same as in a major depressive disorder, only they are less intense in dysthymia.

Depression manifests itself differently in different people. For some, it takes the form of eating less or eating more; others alternate between intense anxiety and intense sadness; still others feel flat and have no sense of connection to other people; and many people exhibit combinations of these symptoms. The Pulitzer Prize–winning novelist William Styron, who went through a major depressive episode in his 60s, left one of the more poignant accounts of the experience in his book *Darkness Visible*. For Styron, as for many seriously depressed people, the feelings of despair reached a point at which ending his life seemed to be the only guaranteed source of relief:

> I had not as yet chosen the mode of my departure, but I knew that that step would come next, and soon, as inescapable as nightfall. . . . Late one bitterly cold night, when I knew that I could not possibly get myself through the following day, I sat in the living room of the house bundled up against the chill. . . . I had forced myself to watch the tape of a movie. . . . At one point in the film . . . came a contralto voice, a sudden soaring passage from the Brahms *Alto Rhapsody.*
>
> This sound, which like all music—indeed, like all pleasure—I had been numbly unresponsive to for months, pierced my heart like a dagger, and in a flood of swift recollection I thought of all the joys the

major depressive disorder
mood disorder characterized by pervasive low mood, lack of motivation, low energy, and feelings of worthlessness and guilt that last for at least two consecutive weeks.

dysthymia
form of depression that is milder in intensity than major depressive disorder.

Major depressive disorder can be a chronic, recurrent condition that robs people of the joys of living.

Stressful life events, such as the death of a loved one, can trigger a major depressive episode in people who have a genetic predisposition for depression.

house had known; the children who had rushed through its rooms, the festivals, the love and work, the honestly earned slumber, the voices and the nimble commotion. . . . All this I realized was more than I could ever abandon, . . . I drew upon some last gleam of sanity to perceive the terrifying dimensions of the mortal predicament I had fallen into. I woke up my wife and soon telephone calls were made. The next day I was admitted to the hospital. (1990, pp. 63–67)

Depression is not often caused solely by an external life event, such as physical or sexual abuse. For some people, depression just comes on, like using a switch to turn on a light. To the extent that this is true, the reason some people and not others develop depression stems from a combination of brain chemistry and life circumstance—the diathesis–stress model again. Consider a recent study showing how genetic vulnerability interacts with life events to make some people more vulnerable to depression than others.

Caspi and colleagues followed a group of nearly 1,000 people from age 3 until age 26 (Caspi et al., 2003). The investigators measured life events experienced by the participants at different ages. They obtained data on the presence of long and short forms of the serotonin gene in the participants' genotypes. One form (allele) comes from each parent. They found that people who had inherited two short forms (s/s) of the serotonin gene were more likely to exhibit depressive symptoms following stressful life events than were those who had inherited the long form (l/l). For example, in Figure 15.7, we see that if people experience a few major stressful events (no more than two), their risk of having a major depressive episode does not increase, regardless of which form of the serotonin gene they carry. But if they experience three or four stressful events, the likelihood that they will have a major depressive episode nearly doubles or triples in those with the short form compared to those with the long form. These findings have been independently replicated (Kendler

nature & nurture
Different forms of the serotonin gene and stressful events work together to increase the risk of depression.

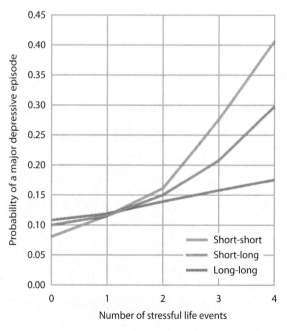

FIGURE **15.7**

INTERACTION BETWEEN SEROTONIN GENE AND STRESS ON RISK FOR DEPRESSION. Individuals with at least one short allele of the serotonin gene are more likely to experience depression than those with two long alleles. Those with two short forms of the gene are most vulnerable to depression if they experience at least three stressful life events. (*Source:* Caspi et al., 2003.)

connection

A person can inherit one form of a gene, or allele—say, for red hair—from one parent and a different form—maybe for brown hair—from the other parent.

See Chapter 3, p. 78.

et al., 2005; Wilhelm et al., 2006). In sum, depression is most likely in individuals who carry the short form of the gene *and* experience many severe life stressors. Neither condition by itself is likely to lead to depression.

The role of stress in the development of depression is not trivial. Animal research shows that stress kills neurons in the hippocampus, which can lead to symptoms of depression (Jacobs, 2004; Jacobs, van Praag, & Gage, 2000; Kendler, Karkowski, & Prescott 1999). Medications that make more serotonin available in the brain stimulate neural growth, which mitigates the symptoms of depression (Jacobs & Fornal, 1999; Malberg et al., 2000).

BIPOLAR DISORDER AND ITS CAUSES

In some cases, periods of depression alternate with highly elevated mood and intense activity. These extreme swings of mood are symptoms of bipolar disorder. People who suffer from **bipolar disorder** experience severe mood fluctuations, cycling between very low (depressive) and very high (manic) episodes. (At one time, this disorder was called "manic depression.") **Manic episodes** typically involve increased energy, sleeplessness, euphoria, irritability, delusions of grandeur, increased sex drive, and "racing" thoughts. A useful mnemonic for remembering the symptoms of mania is D-I-G-F-A-S-T (Carlat, 1998):

bipolar disorder
mood disorder characterized by substantial mood fluctuations, cycling between very low (depressive) and very high (manic) moods.

manic episode
one mood cycle in bipolar disorder, typically involving increased energy, sleeplessness, euphoria, irritability, delusions of grandeur, increased sex drive, and "racing" thoughts.

D = Distractibility
I = Indiscretion
G = Grandiosity
F = Flight of ideas
A = Activity increased
S = Sleep (decreased need for)
T = Talkativeness

People with bipolar disorder often find the initial onset of the manic phase pleasant, especially compared to the dullness and despair of the depressive phase. Unfortunately, the symptoms quickly become quite unpleasant and frightening. The manic upswing spirals out of control, often leading to frenetic activity, excessive energy, and grandiose thinking, in which sufferers think they have relationships with important people or have expertise in areas where they have none. Indiscretion occurs when a person says things that are somewhat inappropriate or gets involved in promiscuous sexual relationships. Figure 15.8 lists the characteristics and symptoms of depression and mania.

FIGURE **15.8**
MAJOR SYMPTOMS AND BEHAVIORS OF MOOD DISORDERS. (*Source:* APA, 2000.)

	Major Symptoms	Behaviors
major depressive disorder	Low mood, lack of motivation, low energy, feelings of worthlessness and guilt that last for at least two weeks	Change in eating behavior, intense anxiety or sadness, feeling of being disconnected, and/or inability to take pleasure in enjoyable experiences
bipolar disorder	Extreme swings in mood between depressive and manic episodes	Manic episodes characterized by distractibility, increased activity, euphoria, grandiosity, decreased need for sleep, talkativeness, flight of ideas, and indiscretion

"Gina" is a young woman with bipolar disorder. During one of her manic phases, Gina came up with the idea that she could create a cookie recipe to end all cookie recipes; once people tasted her cookies, no other dessert would do:

Completely taken with this idea, Gina got in her car and spent several days buying as much flour, sugar, butter, and eggs as she could from the stores in her neighborhood, both to corner the market on ingredients and to get busy mass-producing the cookies right away. Gina ultimately purchased several hundred pounds of products and spent the next few days mixing and baking, a process she carried out on only a couple of hours sleep each night. At one point, the young woman received a phone call from her mother who, upon hearing her daughter's confused recitation of her "ingenious" plan, knew that she was once again manic. Racing over to Gina's apartment, her mother found her in the kitchen, looking like a creature from another planet—white as a ghost. Covered from head to toe with a thick coating of flour, her hair a tangled mess of sugar, butter, and eggs. The kitchen itself was piled high with mounds of malformed cookies, and the stove was sending out billows of smoke. (Gorenstein & Comer, 2001, pp. 67–68)

Bipolar disorder affects men and women in roughly equal proportions. The manic episodes are less frequent than the depressive episodes, and the nature and frequency of the manic episodes varies considerably (APA, 2000). In a milder form of bipolar disorder called **cyclothymia**, both the manic and depressive episodes are less severe than they are in bipolar disorder.

What causes bipolar disorder? The environment shapes the brain in bipolar disorder much as it does in other disorders. The first example of the dynamic relationship between the environment and brain in bipolar disorder may be seen in the development of fetuses in women who abuse alcohol. Fetuses exposed to large amounts of alcohol suffer permanent effects, including increased risks for bipolar disorder as well as depression, schizophrenia, alcoholism, mental retardation, and drug abuse (Famy, Streissguth, & Unis, 1998; O'Conner & Paley, 2006).

Bipolar disorder also has a genetic component. If one identical twin develops bipolar disorder, there is a 40–70% chance that the other twin will also develop the disorder (Müller-Oerlinghausen, Berghöfer, & Bauer, 2002; Shastry, 2005). But even if the chance is 70% that both twins will have the disorder, that still suggests that life events, such as stress and trauma, also play a role in the development of bipolar disorder (Müller-Oerlinghausen et al., 2002; Shastry, 2005). The genetics of the disorder are complex, as researchers have identified several genes that may play a role, but they do not know which of those genes are most critical (Comer, 2007; Shastry, 2005).

Many brain regions consistently seem to malfunction in people who suffer from bipolar disorder, including the prefrontal cortex, the amygdala, the hippocampus, and the basal ganglia (Müller-Oerlinghausen et al., 2002; Shastry, 2005). Overactivity in many of these regions is evident in the PET scan images displayed in Figure 15.9, showing up as red areas compared to the blue regions that indicate depressed mood.

Neurochemistry is also important to bipolar disorder. In both the manic and depressed phases, serotonin levels are low, but low serotonin may be coupled with high levels of norepinephrine in the manic phase and with low levels in the

cyclothymia
a relatively mild form of bipolar disorder.

nature & nurture
The chance that if one identical twin has bipolar disorder so will the other is 40%–70%, indicating that life events, such as stress and trauma, also play a role in the development of this disorder.

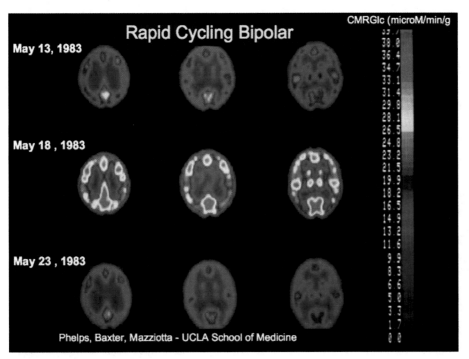

FIGURE 15.9

THE BIPOLAR BRAIN. PET scan images show the brain of someone with bipolar disorder over the course of 10 days. Blue and green indicate low levels of brain activity, and red and yellow indicate high levels of brain activity. The top and bottom images show the low activity of depression, whereas the middle images show an increased level of brain activity during mania.

depressed phase (Comer, 2007; Müller-Oerlinghausen et al., 2002). In addition, thyroid hormones, which control metabolism, are sometimes present in either abnormally high or low levels in people with bipolar disorder (Bauer & Why-brow, 2001; Müller-Oerlinghausen et al., 2002).

quick quiz 15.2: Mood Disorders

1. Latresha is not hungry, is extremely tired, and doesn't feel like doing much of anything. She might be coming down with a cold, or she might be suffering from which mood disorder?
   a. generalized anxiety disorder
   b. bipolar disorder
   c. major depressive disorder
   d. obsessive–compulsive disorder

2. David went home for Christmas break and he found that his mother, who was usually depressed, had just purchased dozens of bird houses from a local gift store. She'd had each custom wrapped and was planning to give them to all extended members of the family and all her neighbors, whom she claimed to love like family. She had spent thousands of dollars. What might be going on with David's mom?
   a. She won the lottery.
   b. She has bipolar disorder.
   c. She has an overactive hypothalamus.
   d. She is just depressed.

3. Which neurotransmitter is reduced in both the manic and depressed phases of bipolar disorder?
   a. acetylcholine
   b. dopamine
   c. norepinephrine
   d. serotonin

Answers can be found at the end of the chapter.

Schizophrenia

psychotic disorders psychological disorders of thought and perception, characterized by inability to distinguish between real and imagined perceptions.

Mood and anxiety disorders are mainly impairments of affect. In contrast, the **psychotic disorders** are primarily disorders of thought and perception and are characterized by an inability to distinguish real from imagined perceptions. One very serious psychotic disorder is **schizophrenia,** which involves profound disturbances in thought and emotion—in particular, impairments in perception, such as hallucinations. Emil Kraepelin, who coined the term schizophrenia (literally "split mind") in the 1890s, viewed the disorder as a split from reality, not a split attitude or split personality as is sometimes mistakenly assumed. Approximately 1% of the American population is afflicted with this disorder at any given time, making schizophrenia much less common than depression (National Institute of Mental Health, [NIMH], 2007). Genetically, however, if a first-degree relative (biological parent, sibling, or child) has the disorder, the odds of a person having the disorder rise to 10% (NIMH, 2007).

schizophrenia psychotic disorder characterized by significant disturbances in thought and emotion, specifically problems with perception.

MAJOR SYMPTOMS OF SCHIZOPHRENIA

For a diagnosis of schizophrenia, at least one of the following symptoms must persist for six months, and at least two must be present sometime during those six months (APA, 2000):

- delusions
- hallucinations
- disorganized speech
- grossly disorganized or catatonic behavior (immobile and unresponsive, though awake)
- negative symptoms (such as not speaking or being unable to experience emotion)

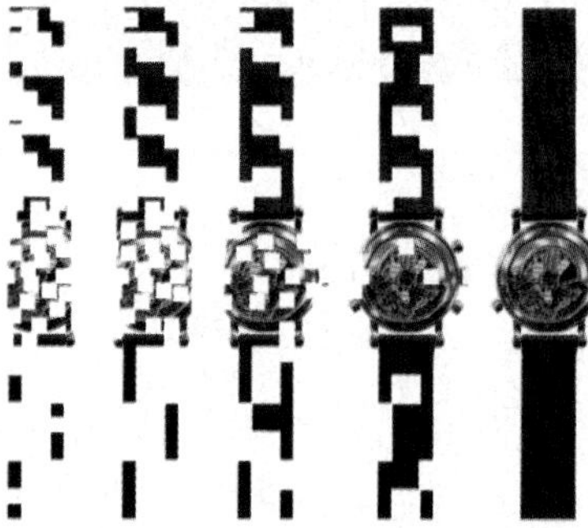

FIGURE **15.10**
INABILITY TO PERCEIVE FRAGMENTS IN SCHIZOPHRENIA. Perceiving fragments as parts of a whole can be difficult for people with schizophrenia. When normal subjects view fractured images like those above in sequence, they identify the object quickly, but individuals with schizophrenia often cannot make that leap swiftly. (*Source:* Javitt & Coyle, 2004.)

positive symptoms (of schizophrenia) the perceptual experiences associated with schizophrenia, including hallucinations, delusional thinking, and disorganized thought and speech.

Symptoms of schizophrenia fall into three major categories: positive, negative, and cognitive. The bizarre perceptual experiences associated with schizophrenia are known as **positive symptoms.** These include hallucinations, delusional thinking, and disorganized thought and speech. Typically, perception is poorly integrated as well. Look, for instance, at the pictures of watches in Figure 15.10. People with schizophrenia have more trouble putting the fragmented image together and perceiving it as a watch.

hallucinations convincing sensory experiences that occur in the absence of an external stimulus.

Hallucinations are convincing sensory experiences that occur in the absence of an external stimulus—in other words, the brain receives false sensory input. Auditory hallucinations are the most common form of hallucination in schizophrenia, typically taking the form of hearing voices in one's head. The following account from a person with schizophrenia describes an auditory hallucination:

> Recently my mind has played tricks on me, creating The People inside my head who sometimes come out to haunt me and torment me. They surround me in rooms, hide behind trees and under the snow outside. They taunt me and scream at me and devise plans to break my spirit. The voices come and go, but The People are always there, always real. ("I feel I am trapped," *New York Times,* March 18, 1986)

Schizophrenia	Major symptoms	Behaviors	FIGURE **15.11**
Subtypes: Paranoid Catatonic Undifferentiated Disorganized	Distortions in thought and perception plus the inability to distinguish real from imagined perceptions	**Positive symptoms:** Delusions, auditory and visual hallucinations, disorganized speech, poor integration of perception **Negative symptoms:** Non-responsiveness, grossly disorganized or catatonic behavior, flattened affect **Cognitive symptoms:** Problems with working memory, attention, verbal/visual learning and memory, reasoning, and processing speed	

The important point about hallucinations is that patients experience them as real. It is not *as if* someone is talking to them; rather, they hear voices and are convinced that someone is living inside them. Indeed, this is a defining feature of psychosis (Nolen-Hoeksema, 2007). Similar to but distinct from hallucinations, **delusions** are false beliefs, often exaggerated claims, that a person holds in spite of evidence to the contrary, such as the idea that one is Jesus Christ.

Other patients experience less flamboyant, but no less disabling, symptoms that are characterized by an absence of what would be considered appropriate behavior. These **negative symptoms** include nonresponsiveness, emotional flatness, immobility or the striking of strange poses (catatonia), reduction of speaking, and inability to complete tasks. Traditionally, negative symptoms have been harder to diagnose and treat than positive symptoms.

The **cognitive symptoms** exhibited by people with schizophrenia include problems with working memory, attention, verbal and visual learning and memory, reasoning and problem solving, speed of processing, and disordered speech (Barch, 2005). For example, the speech of a person with schizophrenia often follows grammatical rules, but the content makes little sense. Such utterances are referred to as **word salad.** Similarly, patients sometimes make up new words. In the following example, a woman who believed she was the only female professor at the "University of Smithsonian" (no such place) in England uses new words to produce a word salad.

> I am here from a foreign university. . . . and you have to have a "plausity" of all acts of amendment to go through for the children's code . . . and it is no mental disturbance or "putenance." . . . it is an "amorition" law. . . . It is like their "privatilinia" and the children have to have this "accentuative" law so they don't go into the "mortite" law of the church. (Vetter, 1968, p. 306)

Figure 15.11 shows the main characteristics and symptoms of schizophrenia and its subtypes, which we discuss next.

SUBTYPES OF SCHIZOPHRENIA

The major symptoms of schizophrenia—disordered thought, hallucinations, and disorganized speech—are characteristics of most, but not all, types of schizophrenia. **Paranoid schizophrenia** consists of persistent preoccupation with one or more delusions or frequent auditory hallucinations, but the person must be free of disorganized speech, catatonic behavior, and flat and inappropriate affect. The most common delusions are those of being persecuted, followed, slandered, or

delusion in people with schizophrenia, a false belief or exaggeration held despite evidence to the contrary.

negative symptoms (of schizophrenia) symptoms that include non-responsiveness, emotional flatness, immobility, catatonia, problems with speech, and the inability to complete tasks.

cognitive symptoms (of schizophrenia) problems with working memory, attention, verbal and visual learning and memory, reasoning and problem solving, processing, and speech.

word salad term for the speech of people with schizophrenia, which may follow grammatical rules but be nonsensical in terms of content.

paranoid schizophrenia subtype of schizophrenia characterized by preoccupation with delusions and auditory hallucinations.

catatonic schizophrenia subtype of schizophrenia characterized by two of the following symptoms: extreme immobility, excessive activity, peculiar posturing, mutism, or parroting what other people say.

discriminated against. Delusions of grandeur, also characteristic of bipolar disorder, are false beliefs that one is God, Napoleon, or some other very important figure. In **catatonic schizophrenia** the person exhibits at least two of the following symptoms: extreme immobility, excessive activity, peculiar posturing, mutism, or parroting what other people say. People who are diagnosed with **undifferentiated schizophrenia** exhibit the general symptoms discussed at the beginning of the section (delusions, hallucinations, disorganized speech, and so on), but do not fit any of the specific subtypes. Patients with **disorganized schizophrenia** show no signs of catatonia but exhibit both disorganized speech and behavior and flat or inappropriate affect, such as laughter in a serious situation.

NATURE AND NURTURE EXPLANATIONS OF SCHIZOPHRENIA

Schizophrenia offers a perfect, though tragic, illustration of the dynamic interplay between biology and experience in the development of a psychological disorder. Some researchers describe the diathesis–stress interaction between biological dispositions and environmental forces as a two-stage model (Kandel, 2000). Stage one is the biological–genetic foundation or disposition, and stage two is an environmental event that occurs at some point after conception, such as maternal infection, chronic stress, or using certain drugs (such as marijuana or amphetamines) at certain critical points in development (Fergusson, Horwood, & Ridder, 2005).

Although genetic factors play an important role in the development of schizophrenia, they do not make it inevitable. The heritability rates are 80% to 85%, suggesting the disorder is due largely to genetic influences (Cardno & Gottesman, 2000; Harrison & Owen, 2003; Kandel, 2000). Scientists have identified as many as 19 genes that contribute to schizophrenia, but the mechanisms they regulate are not yet well understood (Harrison & Owen, 2003). The fact that one identical twin can develop schizophrenia while the other, genetically identical, twin does not develop it indicates that genes alone do not cause schizophrenia. Instead, genes are turned on or off by environmental experiences during brain development to produce the disorder (Grossman et al., 2003; Moffitt et al., 2005; Petronis, 2004).

Although we may not yet know their causes or how exactly they interact with environmental forces, certain biological and brain abnormalities are hallmarks of schizophrenia. We consider some of the better-known ones: maternal infection, dysfunctional prefrontal and hippocampus activity, enlarged ventricles, an excess of dopamine activity in the basal ganglia, and a deficiency in the neurotransmitter glutamate.

undifferentiated schizophrenia subtype of schizophrenia characterized by the general symptoms of delusions, hallucinations, and disorganized speech.

disorganized schizophrenia subtype of schizophrenia characterized by disorganized speech and behavior and flat or inappropriate affect.

connection
During the first six months of fetal development, the brain is extremely vulnerable to all kinds of toxins.
See Chapter 5, p. 174.

Maternal Infections and Schizophrenia During fetal development, neural growth can occur at a rate of 250,000 new neurons per minute and peak at approximately *3 million* per minute (Purves & Lichtman, 1985)! Consequently, what happens to both the mother and the fetus is crucially important; any kind of disease or toxic substance experienced by the mother may dramatically affect neural growth in the fetus. If a woman contracts an infection during pregnancy, the risk of the child's developing schizophrenia later in life increases dramatically (Brown, 2006; Koenig, 2006). Prenatal exposure to infections and diseases such as influenza, rubella, toxoplasmosis, and herpes has been linked to increased risk of schizophrenia (Brown, 2006).

Schizophrenia and the Brain   Abnormal brain development before birth may be responsible for many of the brain dysfunctions that are characteristic of schizophrenia. One mechanism by which maternal infections, for instance, may increase the risk of schizophrenia is by affecting the path neurons take when they migrate during fetal brain growth (Kandel, 2000; Koenig, 2006). One of the most widely recognized brain abnormalities is a dysfunctional prefrontal cortex; in people with schizophrenia, there is evidence of both reduced and excessive activity in that area (Andreasen et al., 1997; Barch, 2005; Goldman-Rakic, 1999; Weinberger et al., 2001). Similarly, while using working memory—which requires prefrontal activity—people with schizophrenia process information less efficiently and less automatically than other people do (Barch, 2005; Weinberger et al., 2001). In most individuals, regions of the brain that are necessary for working on a problem are activated only when needed. In people with schizophrenia, some regions stay very active even when not needed. Moreover, considerable research has found that the hippocampus is smaller in people with schizophrenia, compared to those without the disorder (Barch, 2005; Harrison, 2004). See Figure 15.12 for an overview of these and other areas of the brain affected by schizophrenia.

FIGURE **15.12**

AREAS OF THE BRAIN IMPAIRED BY SCHIZOPHRENIA. The structures highlighted here do not function normally in people with schizophrenia. Limbic system structures not shown here are the hypothalamus, amygdala, and cingulate gyrus. (*Source:* Javitt & Coyle, 2004.)

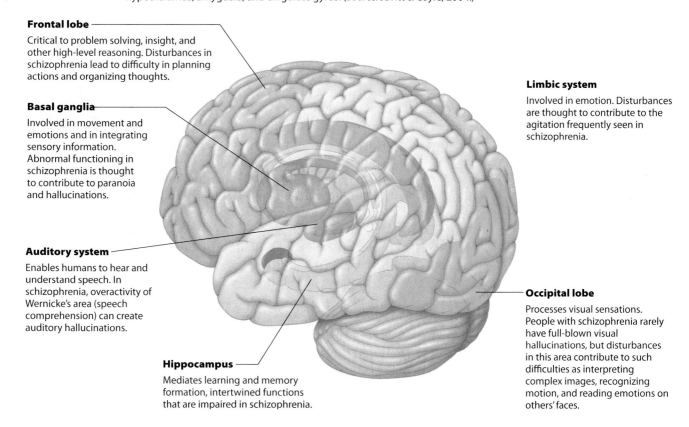

Frontal lobe
Critical to problem solving, insight, and other high-level reasoning. Disturbances in schizophrenia lead to difficulty in planning actions and organizing thoughts.

Basal ganglia
Involved in movement and emotions and in integrating sensory information. Abnormal functioning in schizophrenia is thought to contribute to paranoia and hallucinations.

Auditory system
Enables humans to hear and understand speech. In schizophrenia, overactivity of Wernicke's area (speech comprehension) can create auditory hallucinations.

Hippocampus
Mediates learning and memory formation, intertwined functions that are impaired in schizophrenia.

Limbic system
Involved in emotion. Disturbances are thought to contribute to the agitation frequently seen in schizophrenia.

Occipital lobe
Processes visual sensations. People with schizophrenia rarely have full-blown visual hallucinations, but disturbances in this area contribute to such difficulties as interpreting complex images, recognizing motion, and reading emotions on others' faces.

schizophrenia   **593**

An obvious positive symptom of schizophrenia is hallucinations. What is going on in the brain during a hallucination? Brain imaging studies show that hallucinations activate the brain in ways similar, but not identical, to real external stimulation (Shergill et al., 2000; Shergill et al., 2003; Silbersweig et al., 1995). For example, activity in the auditory cortex of the temporal lobe and the visual cortex of the occipital lobe during visual and auditory hallucinations shows striking similarities to the kind of brain activity that occurs when visual and auditory stimuli are present. Also noteworthy, however, is the lack of activity in the frontal lobes during the hallucination, which suggests that the person is unable to monitor and determine the source of the images or sounds (Shergill et al., 2003).

One of the oldest findings on the brain and schizophrenia is the tendency of people with schizophrenia to have enlarged ventricles (the fluid-filled spaces in the brain) (Lieberman et al., 2001). Enlarged ventricles can be a result of abnormalities in other brain structures, however, so it is unclear whether enlarged ventricles are a cause or an effect of schizophrenia.

Neurochemistry of Schizophrenia   In addition to structural differences in the brain, there are neurochemical differences in the brains of people with and without schizophrenia. For decades, the prevailing view on the neurochemistry of schizophrenia was the *dopamine hypothesis,* which states that people with schizophrenia have an excess of dopamine in certain areas of the brain (Javitt & Coyle, 2004). The dopamine hypothesis was based on two findings. First, Nobel laureate Arvid Carlsson discovered that amphetamines stimulate dopamine release and therefore may mimic the hallucinations and delusions of schizophrenia (Javitt & Coyle, 2004). Second, early antipsychotic drugs that block dopamine receptors were somewhat effective at treating positive symptoms.

There are, however, some problems with the dopamine hypothesis. As we discuss in more detail in the next chapter, dopamine-specific medications (major tranquilizers) effectively treat only positive symptoms and even then are not entirely effective. In addition, only a minority of the people who receive the traditional drug treatment find it effective in managing their symptoms (Javitt & Coyle, 2004). When researchers became aware that another set of recreational drugs led to schizophrenia-like symptoms that did not directly involve dopamine, they turned their attention to these drugs. These drugs, PCP ("angel dust") and ketamine (an animal anesthetic, used recreationally as "Vit K" or "Special K"), do not affect dopamine production; instead, they impair the functioning of a different neurotransmitter, glutamate, and one of its receptors, NMDA. Glutamate is a major excitatory neurotransmitter that regulates the release of dopamine. PCP and ketamine block the action of glutamate, thus producing the same kinds of disturbances that we see in schizophrenia (Harrison & Owen, 2003; Moghaddam, 2003). Glutamate deficiencies, then, may explain many of the symptoms of schizophrenia (Javitt & Coyle, 2004).

These findings stimulated researchers to explore the role of glutamate in schizophrenia more fully. Not only is it crucial in learning, memory, neural processing, and brain development, but it also amplifies certain neural signals, making some stimuli more important than others (Goff & Coyle, 2001; Javitt & Coyle, 2004; Mayer, 2004). This process is crucial to selective attention—that is, focusing attention on some items of information while ignoring others. Thus, dysfunction in glutamate action would explain why people with schizophrenia have trouble with selective attention, cognitive control, and working memory.

quick quiz 15.3: Schizophrenia

1. Which of the following is a negative symptom of schizophrenia?
   a. hallucinations
   b. delusions of grandeur
   c. catatonia
   d. fatigue

2. The heritability rate for schizophrenia is roughly:
   a. 100%
   b. 60%
   c. 80%
   d. 25%

3. Low levels of the neurotransmitter _____ might explain why people with schizophrenia have trouble with selective attention, cognitive control, and working memory.
   a. acetylcholine
   b. glutamate
   c. norepinephrine
   d. GABA

Answers can be found at the end of the chapter.

Dissociative Disorders

dissociative disorders
psychological disorders characterized by extreme splits or gaps in memory, identity, or consciousness.

Daydreaming and being caught up in a great novel or movie are common everyday experiences in which we may lose our sense of time, space, and ourselves. **Dissociative disorders** magnify this effect: They produce extreme splits or gaps in memory, identity, or consciousness. These disorders lack a clear physical cause, such as brain injury, and often stem from extreme stress or abusive experiences, especially during childhood. We focus on the most dramatic dissociative disorder, dissociative identity disorder.

DISSOCIATIVE IDENTITY DISORDER

People with **dissociative identity disorder (DID)** develop at least two distinct personalities, each with a unique set of memories, behaviors, thoughts, and emotions. Consider the case of Eric, 29, who was found wandering around a shopping mall in Daytona Beach, Florida:

dissociative identity disorder (DID)
dissociative disorder in which a person develops at least two distinct personalities, each with its own memories, thoughts, behaviors, and emotions.

> Eric began talking to doctors in two voices: the infantile rhythms of "young Eric," a dim and frightened child, and the measured tones of "older Eric," who told a tale of terror and child abuse. According to "older Eric," after his immigrant German parents died, a harsh stepfather and his mistress took Eric from his native South Carolina to a drug dealers' hideout in a Florida swamp. Eric said he was raped by several gang members and watched his stepfather murder two men. (quoted in Comer, 2007, p. 208)

Eric had 27 distinct personalities, three of whom were female. Among these personalities were Dwight, who was middle-aged and quiet; Michael, an arrogant jock; Phillip, an argumentative lawyer; and Jeffrey, who was blind and mute and rather hysterical.

Eric is a classic example of what used to be called "multiple personalities" but is now referred to as dissociative identity disorder. Although it may not be diagnosed until adolescence, DID often first develops in childhood (Comer, 2007). Women are about three times more likely to suffer from DID than are men (APA, 2000). In one study, more than 90% of people with DID report having been either sexually or physically abused (Ellason, Ross, & Fuchs, 1996).

Symptoms of dissociative identity disorder include amnesia, self-destructive behaviors, and auditory hallucinations. People with dissociative identity disorder may not remember anything about an experience or a particular period of their life, may cut themselves or attempt suicide, and sometimes hear voices giving them orders that they feel compelled to obey. The diagnosis of DID is somewhat controversial, with some psychiatrists claiming the diagnosis is not real but rather is produced unintentionally by therapists themselves (Putnam & McHugh, 2005). In one survey, a majority of psychiatrists said they believed DID should be included in the *DSM* only with reservations and have questioned the scientific evidence for the diagnosis (Lalonde et al., 2002).

CAUSES OF DISSOCIATIVE DISORDERS

People who suffer from dissociative disorders have one characteristic in common: they lived through a highly traumatic experience. They may have suffered sexual or physical abuse or survived a terrible accident or natural disaster in which a loved one was killed. Most explanations of dissociative disorder view it as a coping strategy that has gone awry (Putnam, 2006). The experience was so traumatic that the individual disconnects or dissociates the self from the event as a way of having it happen not to "him" or "her" but rather to "someone else." Yet not everyone who experiences traumatic events develops a dissociative disorder. Some theorists, therefore, argue that particular personality traits, such as susceptibility to hypnotism, make some people more likely to develop dissociative disorders (Kihlstrom, 2005).

quick quiz 15.4: Dissociative Disorders

1. _____ produce extreme splits or gaps in memory, identity, or consciousness.
   a. Dissociative disorders
   b. Bipolar disorders
   c. Mood disorders
   d. Cognitive disorders

2. Years ago this disorder was known as multiple personality disorder:
   a. schizophrenia
   b. schizoid disorder
   c. schizotypal disorder
   d. dissociative identity disorder

3. A history of _____ appears to play a causal role in the development of dissociative disorders.
   a. physical or sexual abuse
   b. traumatic experiences
   c. both a and b
   d. neither a nor b

Answers can be found at the end of the chapter.

breaking new ground

Abuse, Disorders, and the Dynamic Brain

Childhood physical and sexual abuse are horrible not only because of the short-term trauma, but also because they inflict lasting effects. Early adverse experiences may increase the likelihood of developing psychological disorders by fundamentally altering the structure and function of the brain. Research in this area has changed the way psychologists have looked at the causes of psychological disorders. It may seem obvious to us, but for years, no one knew of the key role abuse plays in mental health.

EARLY VIEWS ON SEXUAL AND PHYSICAL ABUSE

Before the 1950s, medical and psychiatric professionals did not recognize the pervasiveness of childhood sexual and physical abuse. Most people assumed that the majority of parents cared for their children, although most people also seemed aware that some children were abused. Careful documentation of serious child abuse began with research on orphans and battered children (Kempe & Helfe, 1968; Spitz, 1945). Eventually, the prevalence of abuse could no longer be denied. Most researchers and clinicians viewed the long-term consequences of abuse for mental health as products of learned behaviors and bad environments. They did not know that serious abuse could change the brain and interact with genetic variability in such a way as to make certain psychological disorders more likely.

ABUSE AND NEGLECT CHANGE THE BRAIN

An ambitious study that is changing the way psychologists view the interaction between biology and environment in the development of psychological disorders is the Adverse Childhood Experiences (ACE) Study. For the ACE study, which began in the mid- to late 1990s, more than 17,000 participants have been interviewed about eight "adverse childhood experiences," including abuse, domestic violence, and serious household dysfunction (meaning that someone in the household abused drugs, had a psychological disorder, or committed criminal acts). Because participants had extensive medical histories on file at the hospital, researchers could correlate their adverse childhood experiences with health and mental health outcomes in adulthood.

The results were dramatic. The more adverse childhood experience participants reported, the worse the psychological outcomes. For example, someone who reported four or more adverse childhood experiences was almost four times as likely to be depressed and two and a half times as likely to suffer from anxiety disorder as someone who reported no adverse childhood experiences (Anda et al., 2006). Illness and disease, substance abuse, aggression and violence, and depression and schizophrenia all became more likely (Anda et al., 2006; Edwards et al., 2003; Whitfield et al., 2005).

In psychology, neglect means the absence of basic stimulation during the critical periods of growth and development. There are few more concrete examples of how abuse and neglect shape the brain than the images shown in Figure 15.13 on page 598 from ACE researcher Bruce Perry (2002). In the child who suffered extreme neglect, notice the much smaller overall brain size as well as the enlarged ventricles (butterfly shapes) in the middle of the brain. These features are two of the major brain abnormalities characteristic of schizophrenia.

connections

Brain development and language development, in particular, occur rapidly during critical periods, when we are biologically most receptive to a specific kind of input from the environment. See Chapter 5, p. 173, and Chapter 9, p. 337.

Perry (2002) found that when children were removed from neglectful home environments at age 1 or 2 and placed in caring foster homes, the size of their brains increased dramatically. If they were removed from the neglectful environment after age four, however, there was little increase in brain size (circumference). And if they were removed after age five there was almost no increase (see Figure 15.14). Thus, there is a critical period for brain growth. Generally, for a child's brain size to be anywhere near normal, the child needs regular environmental stimulation by about age 4.

In one study, researchers tracked more than 1,000 people to examine the role of heredity and environment in the development of psychological disorders (Cannon et al., 2002). Participants were first assessed at age 3 and then every two years until they were 15, and again at ages 18, 21, 26, and 28. The researchers obtained medical records of their births and used early life information to identify whether certain events that occurred between birth and 5 years predicted whether psychological disorders would occur later in life. An increased incidence of a brief psychotic disorder at age 26 occurred in people who had undergone birth complications (such as lack of oxygen), had shown childhood difficulties in understanding speech, had motor-movement problems, and had lower IQs. Finally, genetics interact with abusive experience to create psychological disorders. Different forms of one particular gene, for instance, when coupled with being abused as a child, make violent and antisocial behavior in adulthood more likely (Caspi et al., 2002).

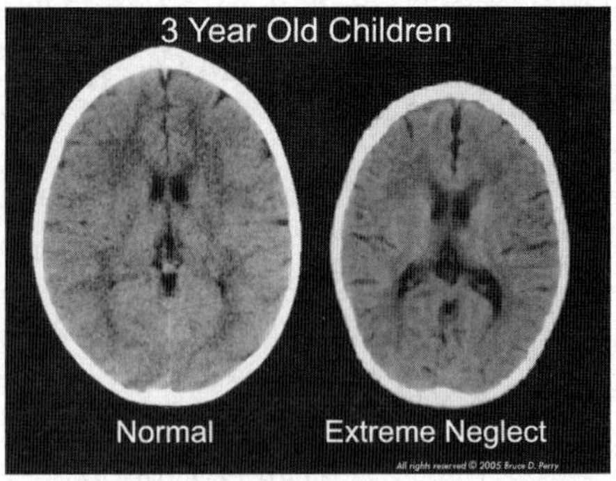

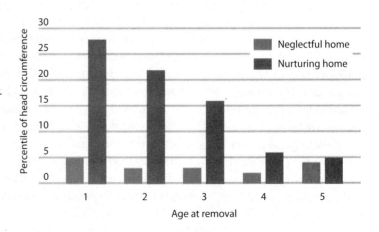

FIGURE **15.13**

EFFECT OF EXTREME NEGLECT ON BRAIN DEVELOPMENT. These MRI images show the brain of a typically developing 3-year-old child who has had a normal amount of cognitive, social, and linguistic stimulation (left), and that of a 3-year-old child who was deprived of regular social, linguistic, tactile, or cognitive stimulation (right). Growth is clearly stunted in the child who suffered from extreme neglect. Additionally, the dark butterfly-shaped structures (ventricles) are much larger in the child who suffered from extreme neglect. Enlarged ventricles are common in people with schizophrenia. (*Source:* Perry, 2002.)

HOW ACE RESEARCH CHANGED THE COURSE OF THE FIELD

In the 1960s most therapists and researchers focused on social and environmental explanations of the effects of child abuse on adult personality and behavior. The outcomes were said to be learned through modeling and shaping of behavior.

That view was correct, but limited. Abuse and neglect do shape long-term behavior, and dysfunctional behaviors are modeled and imitated. But this view does not explain exactly how abuse shapes the brain to produce disordered states of mind. It does not fully explain why some people who experience child abuse "break" while

FIGURE **15.14**

EFFECTS OF NEGLECT AND REMOVAL FROM NEGLECTFUL ENVIRONMENTS ON CHILDREN'S BRAIN SIZE. Percentile of head circumference means the percentage of people in the population who have heads that are a particular size or smaller. So 30th percentile means that only 30% of people have that size or smaller. The younger the child is when he or she is removed from a neglectful home, the larger the brain/head size is after one year in a nurturing foster home. (*Source:* Perry, 2002.)

others merely "bend"—that is, reach adulthood with less severe psychological disorders or none at all. It is now widely recognized that the interaction of genetic factors with exposure to abusive or neglectful environments plays a major role in the development of psychological disorders. Separating the influences of nature and nurture is impossible in abuse cases.

quick quiz 15.5: Breaking New Ground: Abuse, Disorders, and the Dynamic Brain

1. How might adverse childhood experiences increase the risk of psychological disorders?
   a. by depriving the child of physical contact
   b. by profoundly altering brain development
   c. by providing impoverished social stimulation
   d. all of the above

2. Perry's ACE research has shown that if children who are raised in neglectful home environments are placed in caring and stimulating foster care at age 5,
   a. their bodies recover but their brain size remain small the rest of their lives
   b. their brains can bounce back and become average size
   c. their brains show little increase in brain size
   d. their brains show little increase at first but by age 10 they are normal size

Answers can be found at the end of the chapter.

Personality Disorders

As we saw in Chapter 13, personality consists of an individual's unique, long-term behavior patterns. **Personality disorders** are maladaptive and inflexible patterns of cognition, emotion, and behavior that generally develop in late childhood or adolescence and continue into adulthood; they are more stable than clinical disorders such as schizophrenia, depression, and bipolar disorder. The distinction between clinical and personality disorders is somewhat arbitrary, however, and many people with personality disorders also suffer from clinical disorders. The *DSM* places the personality disorders on Axis II, meaning they are relatively permanent, may show up in childhood, and are viewed by the person as consistent with their personality and therefore do not cause much subjective distress. There are three distinct clusters of personality disorders: odd–eccentric, dramatic–emotional, and anxious–fearful (see Figure 15.15 on page 600).

personality disorders
maladaptive and inflexible patterns of cognition, emotion, and behavior that develop in late childhood or adolescence.

ODD–ECCENTRIC PERSONALITY DISORDERS

The three major forms of odd–eccentric personality disorder are schizoid, schizotypal, and paranoid (APA, 2000). A person with **schizoid personality disorder** does not want close relationships; is emotionally aloof, reclusive, and humorless; and wants to live a solitary life. Similarly, a person with **schizotypal personality disorder** is also isolated and asocial, but in addition has very odd thoughts and beliefs. For instance, people with schizotypal personality disorder may believe that stories on TV or in the newspaper were written directly about them or that people they don't know are saying things about them behind their backs. A person with **paranoid personality disorder** is extremely suspicious and mistrustful of other people, in ways that are both unwarranted and not adaptive. They may often test the loyalty of their friends and lovers because they regularly believe

schizoid personality disorder
odd–eccentric personality disorder characterized by a desire to avoid close relationships as well as by emotional aloofness, reclusivity, and a lack of humor.

schizotypal personality disorder
odd–eccentric personality disorder characterized by a desire to live an isolated and asocial life, but also by the presence of odd thoughts and beliefs.

paranoid personality disorder
odd–eccentric personality disorder characterized by extreme suspicions and mistrust of others in unwarranted and maladaptive ways.

FIGURE **15.15**
**THREE CLUSTERS OF PERSON-
ALITY DISORDERS AND THEIR
MAJOR SYMPTOMS.** (*Source:*
APA, 2000.)

Cluster	Major symptoms	Personality disorders
Odd–eccentric	Lack of interest in social relationships, inappropriate or flat emotion, thought, and coldness	Schizoid
	Isolated, odd, and bizarre thoughts and beliefs	Schizotypal
	Extreme, unwarranted, and maladaptive suspicion	Paranoid
Dramatic–emotional	Wild, exaggerated behaviors, extreme need for attention, suicidal, seductive, unstable relationships, shifting moods	Histrionic
	Shifting moods, dramatic, impulsive, self-injury (e.g., cutting)	Borderline
	Grandiose thoughts and sense of one's importance, exploitative, arrogant, lack of concern for others	Narcissistic
	Impulsive, violent, deceptive, and criminal behavior; no respect for social norms, ruthless	Antisocial
Anxious–fearful	Anxious and worrying, sense of inadequacy, fear of being criticized, nervousness, avoids social interaction	Avoidant
	Pervasive selflessness, need to be cared for, fear of rejection, total dependence on and submission to others	Dependent
	Extreme perfectionism and anxiety over minor disruption of routine, very rigid activities and relationships, pervades most aspects of everyday life	Obsessive–compulsive

other people are trying to harm them. If someone does slight them, they hold a grudge for an unusually long time. For example, if someone with this type of personality disorder discovers that a colleague has just been promoted to a position she had wanted, she might conclude that the boss does not appreciate her and is actively trying to sabotage her career. When she sees coworkers talking later that day, she might assume that they are talking about her in a disparaging manner.

DRAMATIC–EMOTIONAL PERSONALITY DISORDERS

There are four main kinds of dramatic–emotional personality disorders: histrionic, borderline, narcissistic, and antisocial (APA, 2000). People with **histrionic personality disorder** want very much to be the center of attention and often behave in very dramatic, seductive, flamboyant, and exaggerated ways. They can also be very emotional, intense, self-centered, and shallow in their emotions and relationships. Those with **borderline personality disorder** have out-of-control emotions, are very afraid of being abandoned by others, and vacillate between idealizing and despising those who are close to them. They are more likely than most to hurt themselves (cutting, burning, or attempting suicide) or suffer from eating disorders or substance abuse. Individuals with **narcissistic personality disorder** have an extremely positive and arrogant self-image, and most of their time and attention is self-focused. They have an exaggerated sense of self-importance and are grandiose, believing they are "God's gift to humanity." As a result, they often make unrealistic and unreasonable demands of others and ignore others' needs or wishes. They may be quite successful and climb the career ladder very quickly, but their narcissism often isolates them from others.

Perhaps the most captivating and intriguing of all personality disorders is antisocial personality. Formerly known as "sociopathic" or "psychopathic"

histrionic personality disorder
dramatic–emotional personality disorder characterized by the desire to be the center of attention and by dramatic, seductive, flamboyant and exaggerated behaviors.

narcissistic personality disorder
dramatic–emotional personality disorder characterized by having an extremely positive and arrogant self-image and being extraordinarily self-centered.

borderline personality disorder
dramatic–emotional personality disorder characterized by out-of-control emotions, fear of being abandoned by others, and a vacillation between idealizing and despising people who are close to the person with the disorder.

antisocial personality disorder
dramatic–emotional personality disorder characterized by extremely impulsive, deceptive, violent, ruthless, and callous behaviors; a serious and potentially dangerous disorder.

personality, **antisocial personality disorder** is marked by extremely impulsive, deceptive, violent, ruthless, and callous behaviors. People with antisocial personality disorder are most likely to engage in criminal, deceptive, and violent behaviors. Indeed, although only about 3% of the population has this disorder, between 45% and 75% of male prison inmates are diagnosed with the disorder (Fazel & Danesh, 2002; Hare, 1993). Only about 20% of female prisoners are diagnosed with antisocial personality disorder (Fazel & Danesh, 2002). Do not confuse antisocial with asocial. Antisocial personality is a serious and potentially dangerous disorder, whereas being asocial simply means being shy and not enjoying social situations.

ANXIOUS–FEARFUL PERSONALITY DISORDERS

The third cluster of personality disorders consists of the avoidant, dependent, and obsessive–compulsive personality disorders. Each of these is characterized by persistent, high levels of anxiety, nervousness, and fear.

avoidant personality disorder
anxious–fearful personality disorder characterized by extreme fear of being criticized, low self-esteem, and avoidance of social interaction.

People with **avoidant personality disorder** are so afraid of being criticized that they avoid interacting with others and become socially isolated. They often feel inadequate and have low self-esteem and therefore tend to choose professions that allow them to be alone. People with **dependent personality disorder** fear being rejected and have such a strong need to be cared for that they form clingy and dependent relationships with others. They feel safe only in relationships with others; ironically, however, they tend to drive others away because they are so demanding. People with **obsessive–compulsive personality disorder** are very rigid in their habits and extremely perfectionistic. This personality disorder is similar to the clinical disorder with the same name but is more general. For example, OCD is usually focused only on cleanliness or checking, whereas obsessive–compulsive personality disorder is focused on all aspects of a person's life, as illustrated in the following case study of a 32-year-old accountant:

dependent personality disorder
anxious–fearful personality disorder characterized by fear of being rejected and having a strong need to be cared for.

obsessive–compulsive personality disorder
anxious–fearful personality disorder characterized by rigid habits and extreme perfectionism; more general than obsessive–compulsive disorder.

> For many years he has maintained an almost inviolate schedule. On weekdays he arises at 6:47, has two eggs soft-boiled for 2 minutes, 45 seconds, and is at his desk at 8:15. Lunch is at 12:00, dinner at 6:00, bedtime at 11:00. He has separate Saturday and Sunday schedules, the latter characterized by a methodical and thorough trip through the *New York Times*. Any change in schedule causes him to feel varying degrees of anxiety, annoyance, and a sense that he is doing something wrong and wasting his time. . . . [His] major problems are with women and follow the same repetitive pattern. At first, things go well. Soon, however, he begins to resent the intrusion upon his schedule a woman inevitably causes. This is most strongly illustrated in the bedtime arrangements. He must spray his sinuses, take two aspirin, straighten the apartment, do 35 sit-ups and read two pages of the dictionary. (Spitzer and colleagues, quoted in Nolen-Hoeksema, 2007, pp. 451–452)

NATURE AND NURTURE EXPLANATIONS OF PERSONALITY DISORDERS

Because we have already discussed causes of the Axis I disorders that are similar to the schizotypal and obsessive–compulsive personality disorders, and less is known about the causes of dramatic–emotional disorders, in this section we focus on antisocial personality disorder.

Research on murderers has identified a cluster of traits possessed by most of these violent criminals: being male, coming from abusive and neglectful households, having at least one psychological disorder (often antisocial personality disorder), and having suffered some kind of injury to the head or brain (Pincus, 1999, 2001; Strueber, Lueck, & Roth, 2006–2007). Just being abused or having a psychological disorder or suffering a brain injury is not enough. To become antisocial and violent, a person usually has to experience all of these conditions.

Moreover, as a result of head injuries or living in a constant state of fear and abuse, or both, murderers almost always have moderate to severe problems of impulse control, social intelligence, working memory, and attention (Strueber et al., 2006–2007). Recall the principle of neuroplasticity from Chapter 3. Research on brain development suggests that living under a constant threat of abuse and stress changes the neural connectivity in the brain, making it less likely to develop many complex synaptic connections, especially in the frontal lobes. Being in a constant state of fear often leads to neural systems that are primed for unusually high levels of anxiety, impulsive behavior, and a state of constant alertness. These are all conditions that might lead to violent or criminal behaviors.

In the film *Monster*, Charlize Theron (above) portrayed Aileen Wuornos, a prostitute who confessed to killing several men. Abandoned by her parents in childhood, Wuornos later ran away from her grandparents' home and turned to prostitution to support herself. At one of her trials, a psychiatrist testified that she was mentally ill with borderline personality disorder. Nevertheless, she was convicted of murder and later executed.

quick quiz 15.6: Personality Disorders

1. People with _____ personality disorder are so afraid of being criticized that they stay away from others and become socially isolated.
   a. borderline
   b. avoidant
   c. dependent
   d. psychopathic

2. Individuals with which kind of personality disorder are most likely to commit crimes and end up in jail?
   a. histrionic
   b. narcissistic
   c. antisocial
   d. avoidant

Answers can be found at the end of the chapter.

Childhood Disorders

Although most clinical diagnoses are reserved for adults (older than 18), a number of disorders first show up in childhood (see Figure 15.3). We will discuss two of them: attention deficit hyperactivity disorder (ADHD) and autism. See Figure 15.16 for an overview of these two disorders.

SUBTYPES OF CHILDHOOD DISORDERS

attention deficit hyperactivity disorder (ADHD) childhood disorder characterized by inability to focus attention for more than a few minutes, to remain still and quiet, to do careful work.

Jade seldom can work more than a few minutes on any given task, whether it is homework, reading, or even watching television. At school, she is constantly fidgeting in her chair and blurts out whatever she is thinking. Jade's teacher regularly has to ask her to be quiet and stop disrupting others. Her homework is full of careless mistakes, even though she usually knows the answers. With these symptoms, psychologists would probably diagnose Jade as suffering from **attention deficit hyperactivity disorder (ADHD)**. To receive the diagnosis of ADHD, the child must have displayed these symptoms before age 7. From 5% to 10% of American school-age children and 3% to 5% of children worldwide meet the diagnostic criteria of ADHD (Kessler et al., 2005; Polanczyk et al., 2007).

In his first year of life, Antoine behaved relatively normally. At the end of that year, however, subtle signs that things were not right appeared: he did not babble or point to things, he made very little eye contact, and he was hardly speaking at 18 months. When he did speak he often simply repeated what someone else said and later he would say "you" when he meant "I." Moreover, he would regularly flap his hands. Finally, he became very interested in the details and sensory experience of objects. He often would smell and taste toys. Psychologists would diagnose Antoine with autistic disorder, or **autism** (from *autos*, meaning "self"). Autism is characterized by severe language and social impairment combined with repetitive habits and inward-focused behaviors. Evidence suggests that people with autism have an oversensitivity to sensory stimulation

autistic disorder or autism childhood disorder characterized by severe language and social impairment along with repetitive habits and inward-focused behaviors.

FIGURE **15.16 SYMPTOMS AND BEHAVIORS OF TWO CHILDHOOD DISORDERS.** (*Source:* APA, 2000.)

Disorder	Major symptoms	Behaviors
Attention deficit hyperactivity (ADHD)	Inattention	Often fails to give close attention to details or makes careless mistakes, cannot sustain attention, does not listen when spoken to, does not follow through on instructions
	Hyperactivity	Fidgets with hands or feet, leaves seat in classroom when sitting is expected, inappropriate and excessive running or climbing, talks excessively
	Impulsivity	Blurts out answers before question is complete, cannot wait turn, often intrudes or interrupts others
Autism	Impaired social interaction	Has impaired eye-to-eye gaze and facial expressions, fails to develop peer relationships, lacks sharing interests
	Impaired communication	Has impaired or severely delayed speech, language use is stereotypic or repetitive
	Repetitive and stereotypic behaviors	Shows preoccupation and repetitive interests or behaviors (such as finger or hand flapping), inflexible routines or rituals

or trouble integrating multiple sources of sensory information, such as sight, sound, and touch (Iarocci & McDonald, 2006; Reynolds & Lane, 2008). Compared to children without autism, those with autism also are more interested in things and inanimate objects than in people and social activities (Baron-Cohen et al., 2001). For example, researchers who were not aware of diagnoses and who closely examined eye contact made by autistic and nonautistic children on their first-birthday home videos were able to correctly classify children as autistic or not 77% of the time (Osterling & Dawson, 1994). Historically, approximately 5 to 6 children in 1,000 met the criteria for autism, but during the 1990s and 2000s the rate has increased at least 10 times to 60 per 1,000 (Rice, 2007). Some researchers believe the disorder may be overdiagnosed, and yet the evidence suggests the rise is mostly due to increased awareness of the disorder (Rutter, 2005; Wing & Potter, 2002).

People at the high-functioning end of the spectrum of autistic disorders may have independent, productive lives in spite of their social impairments and narrow interests. One such individual is Temple Grandin, who earned a PhD in animal science and became a professor at Colorado State University. A leading animal rights advocate, Grandin has designed humane facilities for livestock and written and spoken extensively about animal rights.

Asperger's syndrome
a childhood disorder at the high-functioning end of the autistic spectrum; characterized by impaired social interest and skills and restricted interests.

Autism is a spectrum of disorders, ranging from severe disability to high functioning. On the high-functioning end is **Asperger's syndrome.** Children with Asperger's syndrome have impaired social interest and skills and restricted interests, but are not at all delayed or deficient in language and often have above-average intelligence (APA, 2000). In fact, they often are quite advanced in their speech. Children with Asperger's syndrome, for instance, may engage adults in long-winded and "professorial" discussions on one rather narrow topic. The man after whom the disorder is named, Hans Asperger, referred to these children as "little professors" (Asperger, 1944/1992).

CAUSES OF CHILDHOOD DISORDERS

As is true of many psychological disorders, childhood disorders stem from genetic factors but often remain latent unless triggered by some environmental condition (Larsson, Larsson, & Lichtenstein, 2004). For ADHD, one of the environmental factors is whether the mother smokes while pregnant. Yet, even smoking while pregnant leads to conduct and impulse problems only if the child has one form of a dopamine gene but not another (Kahn, et al., 2003). Neither prenatal smoke exposure alone nor the dopamine genotype alone is significantly associated with increased behavior disorders. One environmental factor, long suspected to cause ADHD, was the child's consuming excessive amounts of sugar. Controlled clinical studies, however, do not bear out this belief (Krummel, Seligson, & Guthrie, 1996; Whalen & Henker, 1998).

One consistent finding regarding brain activity of those with ADHD is low levels of activation. Brain activity in general is less pronounced in people with ADHD than in those without it (Zametkin et al., 1990; Zang et al., 2005). An understimulated brain explains the "paradoxical" effects of giving children with ADHD a stimulant to calm them down. The stimulant elevates their abnormally low nervous system activity and they require less stimulation and activity from the outside.

In autism, the brain is smaller than normal at birth but grows much faster during the first few years of life than the brains of nonautistic children (Courchesne, Carper, & Akshoomoff, 2003). The brain of a 5-year-old with autism is the same size as that of a typical 13-year-old (Blakeslee, 2005). Head size, therefore, is a marker of possible autism. Although we do not yet know which genes are involved, this abnormal rate of brain growth is almost certainly due to genetic influences. In addition, the frontal lobes, where much processing of social information occurs, are less well connected in children with autism than in normal children (Belmonte et al., 2004).

A promising theory about the origins of autism is based on the mirror neurons (Ramachandran & Oberman, 2006). As we saw in earlier chapters, mirror neurons fire both when a person performs a particular behavior (such as reaching for an object) and when he or she simply watches someone else performing the same behavior. Mirror neurons are thought to be involved in many, if not most, social behaviors, such as observational learning, imitation, and even language learning. Because children with autism are deficient in these skills, neuroscientists predicted that mirror neurons malfunction in autistic children; research results show that this is indeed the case (Ramachandran & Oberman, 2006).

quick quiz 15.7: Childhood Disorders

1. Jolo is a 5-year-old boy who does not speak, waves his arms around a lot, does not make eye contact, and does not seem to connect with other kids or adults. Jolo may have which disorder?
   a. autistic disorder
   b. ADHD
   c. childhood depression
   d. theory of mind

2. Kelly fidgets a lot, blurts out what she is thinking, and makes many careless mistakes in her homework, even when she knows the answers. Kelly most likely would be diagnosed with which childhood disorder?
   a. low IQ
   b. autism
   c. Asperger's
   d. ADHD

Answers can be found at the end of the chapter.

making connections
in Psychological Disorders

Creativity and Mental Health

Recall the mental anguish of Vincent van Gogh, whom we described at the beginning of the chapter. Ludwig von Beethoven, Amadeus Mozart, Robert Schumann, Virginia Wolf, Ernest Hemingway, William Styron, Jackson Pollock, Howard Hughes, Sylvia Plath, Salvador Dali, and the Nobel Prize–winning mathematician John F. Nash Jr. are other creative geniuses who have suffered from a psychological disorder. So many creative individuals have experienced some psychological condition that many people think creativity and disorders of the mind are connected. The term *mad genius* reflects this belief.

Exploring the connection between psychological disorders and creativity offers an opportunity to look again at the topics discussed in this chapter. We address two questions: (1) What is the evidence that creative people suffer from psychological disorders at a higher rate than the rest of the population? (2) Which disorders are more likely to be linked with creativity?

Evidence for a Relationship Between Creativity and Psychological Disorders

To help us answer the first question, we can look at an impressive study of creativity and psychological disorder conducted by Arnold Ludwig. In a biographical study of 1,005 eminent people in 18 professions, Ludwig (1995) examined the lifetime rates of psychological disorder across the professions and over lifetimes. Lifetime rate simply means the likelihood that a person will suffer a disorder at some point in her or his lifetime. Lifetime rates for any psychiatric illness are remarkably high for people in the arts: 87% of poets, 77% of fiction writers, 74% of actors, 73% of visual artists, 72% of nonfiction writers, 68% of musical performers and 60% of musical composers (see Figure 15.17). Compare these figures with the 46% lifetime rate in the general population for any disorder is (Kessler et al., 2005). The data from this large scale study clearly indicate a higher prevalence of disorder in creative artists than people in the general population.

Which Disorders Affect Creative Individuals?

Not all disorders are associated with creative ability. There is evidence, however, for a connection between creativity and many of the disorders we discussed in this chapter.

Psychotic Symptoms and Creativity

Having unusual thoughts is common to both creative people and those with schizophrenia. For instance, much of the art of Salvador Dali, who claimed to be psychotic, consists of bizarre, dreamlike images—bordering on the kinds of delusions experienced by people with schizophrenia. John F. Nash Jr., the mathematician made famous by the book and movie *A Beautiful Mind,* is a creative person who also has schizophrenia (Nasar, 1998). He was creative despite, rather than because of, the psychotic episodes he has experienced; all of his creative work preceded his schizophrenic symptoms and stopped after they began.

It is the milder psychotic symptoms, however, that are most strongly associated with creativity (Kinney et al., 2000–2001; Nettle & Clegg, 2006; Schuldberg, 2000–2001). Each of the following groups manifest unusual thought processes that are milder than those of schizophrenia: first-degree relatives of individuals with schizophrenia, people with schizotypal personality disorder, and those who score high on the normal personality dimension of psychoticism (see Chapter 13). People in these groups are more likely to have unusual thought processes that develop into creative achievements that other people recognize to be significant (Burch et al., 2006; Fisher et al., 2004). Having a lot of ideas come to mind quickly can lead to many unusual associations that may be

connection

Creative thinking requires novelty and connections among ideas.
See Chapter 10, p. 401.

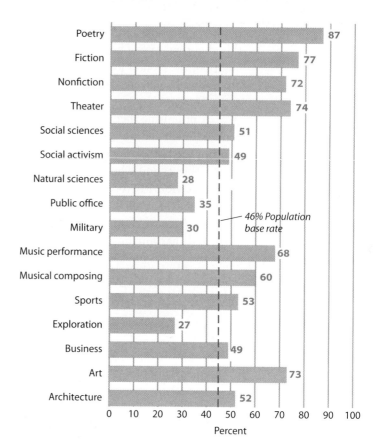

FIGURE **15.17**
LIFETIME RATES OF PSYCHOLOGICAL DISORDERS IN FAMOUS PEOPLE IN 16 DIFFERENT PROFESSIONS. (*Source:* Ludwig, 1995.)

creative, but they may also be so unusual as to be similar to the bizarre associations seen in people with schizophrenia (Carson, Peterson, & Higgins, 2003; Eysenck, 1995).

Depression and Creativity

Emotional distress is a familiar companion to creative people (Feist, in press). Many highly creative people have suffered from major depression (Ludwig, 1995). Across the 18 professions identified in Figure 15.17, the lifetime rate of depression was 30%, with poets (77%), fiction writers (59%), and visual artists (50%) having the highest rates. In addition, poets are 20 times more likely to commit suicide, a key indicator for depression, than most people (Ludwig, 1995).

Although highly creative artists and writers may have a higher rate of depression than the general population, depressive episodes themselves do not generate much creative output. Recall that a complete lack of motivation is a common symptom of depression, so lower productivity would follow. Still, the experiences one has while depressed might inspire and motivate the creation of works of art as a way of understanding it.

Bipolar Disorder and Creativity

For more than three decades, studies of the relationship between psychological disorder and creativity have devoted more attention to bipolar illness than to any other condition (Andreasen & Glick, 1988; Bowden, 1994; Fodor & Laird, 2004; Jamison, 1993; Ludwig, 1995). Actors (17%), poets (13%), architects (13%), and nonfiction writers (11%) all exceed a 10% lifetime rate of bipolar disorder—10 times the rate in the general population (Ludwig, 1995). There is a positive relationship between bipolar disorder and creative thought. For instance, some studies show that highly creative people are more likely than noncreative people to have bipolar disorder (Andreasen, 1987, 2006; Jamison, 1993; Jamison et al., 1980; Richards, 1994). Others report the other side of the coin: People with bipolar disorder are likely to be more creative than those without this condition (Fodor & Laird, 2004; Richards, 1994; Richards & Kinney, 1990). Indeed, many creative individuals throughout history have been bipolar (Jamison, 1993).

The manic phase is more likely than the depressive phase to generate creative behavior (Andreasen & Glick 1988; Jamison et al., 1980). Few artists and writers are creative during their depressed phases; rather, they are creatively inspired during a milder form of mania, known as the hypomanic phase. A tragic example is the composer Robert Schumann whose output and episodes of mania and depression are graphed in Figure 15.18.

Autism and Creativity

Some people who have autism or Asperger's syndrome are extremely gifted in one domain, such as music or math, a phenomenon known as savant syndrome (see Chapter 10). Most autistic savants do not produce great works of original genius because their amazing feats of calculation and recall are not original. Yet some savants do produce truly creative works of art, usually math analyses, musical compositions, drawings, or paintings (Fitzgerald, 2004). One of the 20th

century's greatest mathematicians, Srinivasa Ramanujan, showed clear signs of childhood autism (Fitzgerald, 2004). Composer Wolfgang Amadeus Mozart, also, may have been such a savant. A contemporary creative savant is Matt Savage (born in 1992), who was diagnosed with autism at the age of 3. He is a professional jazz musician and composer who recorded three CDs by the time he was 14.

Asperger's syndrome has been associated with creative ability in science, math, and engineering (Austin, 2005; Baron-Cohen et al., 2001). Baron-Cohen and his colleagues have shown that engineers, mathematicians, and physical scientists score much higher than nonscientists on measures of high-functioning autism and Asperger's syndrome and score higher than social scientists on a nonclinical measure of autism. Lastly, children with Asperger's are more than twice as likely as normal children to have a father or grandfather who was an engineer (Baron-Cohen et al., 1997; Baron-Cohen et al., 1998; Baron-Cohen et al., 2001).

quick quiz 15.8: Making Connections in Psychological Disorders

1. Research shows which psychotic disorder is most strongly associated with creativity?
   a. schizophrenia
   b. schizotypal
   c. schizoid
   d. split-personality

2. With respect to the relationship between bipolar disorder and creativity, the _____ phase is more likely to produce creative behavior than the _____ phase. (pick the best pair of words)
   a. depressive; manic
   b. cognitive; depressive
   c. manic; depressive
   d. manic; affective

Answers can be found at the end of the chapter.

FIGURE **15.18**

BIPOLAR DISORDER AND CREATIVITY IN THE WORK OF ROBERT SCHUMANN.

The composer's creative output coincided directly with the highs and lows of his disorder. His most productive years (1840 and 1849) were marked by his most hypomanic periods. (*Source:* Slater & Meyer, 1959.)

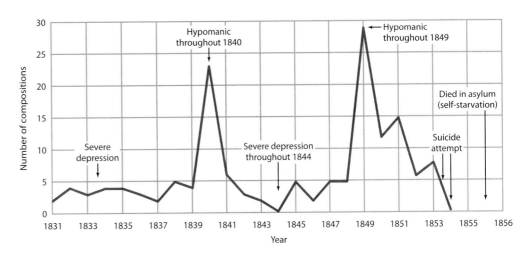

chapter **review**

DEFINING PSYCHOLOGICAL DISORDERS

- Psychologists agree on three general criteria for a psychological disorder: deviant, distressing, and dysfunctional.

- A major tool for diagnosing disorders is the *Diagnostic and Statistical Manual (DSM)*. Axis I disorders, the clinical syndromes, tend to develop after adolescence, come and go, and are not permanent. Axis II disorders tend to be lifelong and relatively permanent.

ANXIETY DISORDERS

- Anxiety disorders occur when fears and worrying are out of proportion to the situation and interfere with everyday functioning. There are numerous anxiety disorders. Generalized anxiety disorder is a pervasive state of anxiety lasting at least six months and consists of excessive worrying about relatively minor events of daily life. Panic disorder is extreme anxiety about having a panic attack. Social anxiety disorder, a pronounced fear of humiliation in the presence of others, is marked by severe self-consciousness about appearance, behavior, or both.

- Specific phobias involve an intense fear when confronted with particular situations or objects, such as spiders or heights. Obsessive–compulsive disorder is an anxiety disorder of thought and behavior. Compulsions are repetitive behaviors, which are often rituals that people have developed to control the anxiety created by the obsessions. Obsessions are anxiety-producing thoughts that can preoccupy a person throughout the day and are beyond the person's control.

MOOD DISORDERS

- Mood disorders are disturbances in emotional behavior that prevent people from functioning normally. People with major depressive disorder experience a pervasive low mood, lack of motivation, low energy, and feelings of worthlessness and guilt. Bipolar disorder, on the other hand, involves substantial mood fluctuation between depressive and manic episodes.

SCHIZOPHRENIA

- Schizophrenia is a psychotic disorder of profound disturbances in thought and emotion. Positive symptoms of schizophrenia include hallucinations, delusional

thinking, and disorganized thought and speech. Negative symptoms of schizophrenia include nonresponsiveness, flattened affect, immobility or strange poses, reduction of speaking, and inability to complete tasks. Cognitive symptoms of schizophrenia include disordered thinking, including impaired attention and profound difficulty in monitoring conflicting sources of information.

DISSOCIATIVE DISORDERS

- Dissociative disorders entail the loss of a sense of time and space but also involve extreme gaps in memories, identity, or consciousness. People with dissociative identity disorder (DID) develop at least two distinct personalities, each of whom has a unique set of memories, behaviors, thoughts, and emotions. Some experts have reservations about classifying DID as a disorder.

PERSONALITY DISORDERS

- Personality disorders differ from clinical disorders in being generally a more stable part of a person's personality than the clinical disorders (e.g., schizophrenia, depression, and bipolar disorder). The schizoid personality is very emotionally cold, reclusive, humorless, or uninteresting; someone with schizotypal personality disorder expresses very odd thoughts and behavior, is socially isolated, and has a restricted range of emotions. Paranoid personality disorder is marked by extreme suspiciousness and mistrust of other people, in ways that are both unwarranted and not adaptive.

- Those with borderline personality disorder suffer from out-of-control emotions, are very afraid of being abandoned by others, and vacillate between idealizing those close to them and despising them. People with dependent personality disorder fear rejection and have such a strong need to be cared for that they form very clingy relationships with others. Antisocial personality disorder is marked by extremely impulsive, deceptive, violent, and ruthless behaviors.

CHILDHOOD DISORDERS

- The most common disorders to affect children are attention deficit hyperactivity disorder (ADHD) and autism. ADHD consists of severe inattention, hyperactivity, and impulsivity. Children with autism show very inward-focused behaviors, with severe language and social impairment combined with repetitive habits and behaviors. They also have serious deficits in understanding other people's thoughts, feelings, and intentions. Asperger's syndrome is characterized by many of the same symptoms, with no impairments of language or intelligence.

MAKING CONNECTIONS IN PSYCHOLOGICAL DISORDERS

- Creativity and psychological disorder are related, especially in the arts. Disorders such as depression, bipolar disorder, anxiety disorders, substance abuse, and suicide occur at higher rates in creative artists than in members of other professions and in the general population.

key **terms**

agoraphobia, p. 578

antisocial personality disorder, p. 601

Asperger's syndrome, p. 604

attention deficit hyperactivity disorder (ADHD), p. 603

autistic syndrome disorder or autism, p. 603

avoidant personality disorder, p. 601

Axis I disorders, p. 574

Axis II disorders, p. 575

bipolar disorder, p. 587

borderline personality disorder, p. 600

catatonic schizophrenia, p. 592

cognitive symptoms, p. 591

comorbidity, p. 575

compulsion, p. 579

delusion, p. 591

dependent personality disorder, p. 601

diathesis–stress model, p. 582

disorganized schizophrenia, p. 592

dissociative disorders, p. 595

dissociative identity disorder (DID), p. 595

dysthymia, p. 585

generalized anxiety disorder (GAD), p. 577

hallucinations, p. 590

histrionic personality disorder, p. 600

impulse control disorder, p. 581

major depressive disorder, p. 585

manic episodes, p. 587

mood disorders, p. 583

narcissistic personality disorder, p. 600

negative symptoms, p. 591

obsession, p. 579

obsessive–compulsive disorder (OCD), p. 579

obsessive–compulsive personality disorder, p. 601

panic attack, p. 578

panic disorder, p. 578

paranoid personality disorder, p. 599

paranoid schizophrenia, p. 591

personality disorders, p. 599

phobia, p. 579

positive symptoms, p. 590

post-traumatic stress disorder (PTSD), p. 578

psychotic disorders, p. 590

schizoid personality disorder, p. 599

schizophrenia, p. 590

schizotypal personality disorder, p. 599

social phobia (social anxiety disorder), p. 579

undifferentiated schizophrenia, p. 592

word salad, p. 591

quick quiz **answers**

Quick Quiz 15.1: 1. b   2. d   3. a   Quick Quiz 15.2: 1. c   2. b   3. d   Quick Quiz 15.3: 1. c   2. c   3. b

Quick Quiz 15.4: 1. a   2. d   3. c   Quick Quiz 15.5: 1. d   2. c   Quick Quiz 15.6: 1. b   2. c

Quick Quiz 15.7: 1. a   2. d   Quick Quiz 15.8: 1. b   2. c

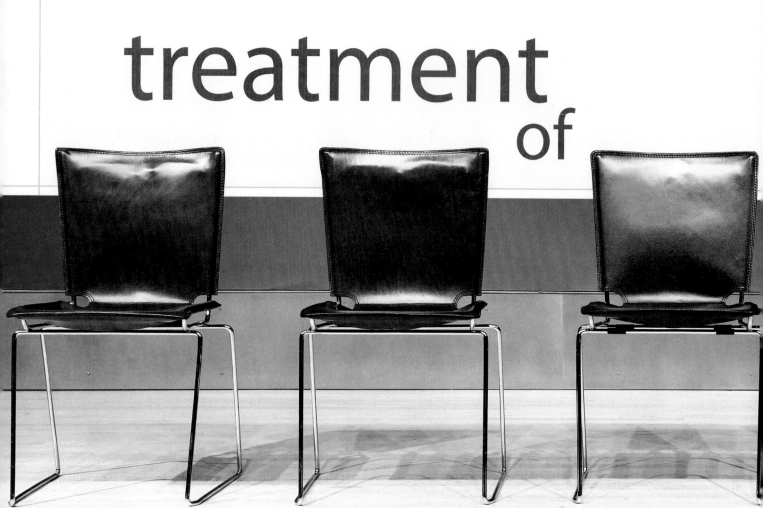

treatment of

psychological disorders

1 *How do mental health professionals treat different disorders?*

2 *When are drugs better than psychotherapy for treating psychological disorders?*

3 *Which treatment approach is most effective overall?*

Spending three years as a prisoner of war during World War II did not dampen John Cade's scientific curiosity. Shortly after the war ended, in the mid-1940s, this Australian psychiatrist began conducting experiments in an unused kitchen of the mental hospital where he was a superintendent. Cade was seeking a cure for mania, the state of high energy and euphoria experienced by some people with bipolar disorder. After studying the chemical composition of urine samples from manic patients, Cade had a hunch that mania might result from problems in protein metabolism. He manipulated many compounds, focusing briefly on urea, a product of protein metabolism that occurs in high concentrations in urine. While conducting controlled experiments on urea, he worked with a salt called lithium urate. Cade gave lithium urate to guinea pigs, initially just to test its toxicity. He noticed that the guinea pigs became quite lethargic. Upon further experimentation, it became clear ▶

▶ that the lithium itself, not urea, had a calming effect. Cade wondered if lithium might cure mania. After testing carefully modulated doses of lithium on himself, Cade tried it on manic patients. He witnessed gradual calming, and after about 10 days the mania had all but subsided (Johnson, 1998).

Cade had discovered the first effective drug treatment for a psychological disorder. Although concerns about its toxicity delayed the widespread adoption of lithium for treating mania in the United States, it was used successfully in Australia and Europe. In the 1970s the Food and Drug Administration, the government agency in the United States that evaluates the safety of drugs for public use, finally approved the use of lithium as a treatment for mania. As we will see later in the chapter, lithium is still widely used to regulate mania, although it is not a cure. Scientists are just beginning to understand how lithium works.

Nowhere can one see the complex interaction between biology and environment more profoundly than in the development and treatment of psychological disorders. As we

chapter
outline

describe in this chapter, a combination of psychological and drug therapies might offer the best treatment for anxiety disorders, in which both life experiences and biological predisposition clearly intertwine. We also explain that some psychological disorders are curable, while others are not. Psychiatrists, psychologists, and other mental health professionals draw on biologically based, psychological, and integrative treatments to help people with various kinds of disorders. Although we discuss the biological treatments and the psychological treatments separately for clarity, we must bear in mind that both categories of treatment can and do modify the brain. ■

Biological Treatments

Three major forms of treatment exist: biological, psychological, and integrative (see Figure 16.1 on page 614). Drugs, surgical treatments, and electric and magnetic treatments comprise the biological approaches. The psychological therapies include psychodynamic (psychoanalytic), humanistic, cognitive, and behavioral therapies. The integrative therapies combine either drugs and psychotherapies or different variations of psychotherapy. Let's first consider the biological treatments, specifically drug therapies.

DRUG THERAPIES

An overwhelming number of pharmaceutical drugs are available for the treatment of psychological disorders. Drugs can be

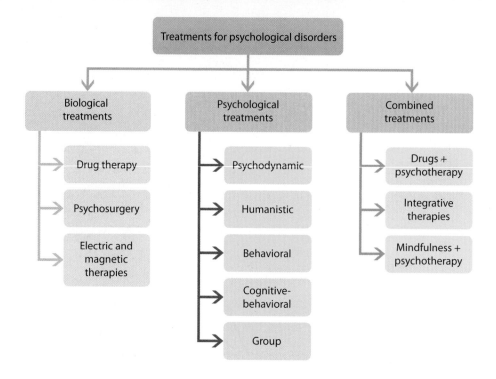

Treatments for psychological disorders

Biological treatments
→ Drug therapy
→ Psychosurgery
→ Electric and magnetic therapies

Psychological treatments
→ Psychodynamic
→ Humanistic
→ Behavioral
→ Cognitive-behavioral
→ Group

Combined treatments
→ Drugs + psychotherapy
→ Integrative therapies
→ Mindfulness + psychotherapy

used to treat, but usually not cure, everything from mild anxiety to schizophrenia. We examine some of these drug treatments next.

Drug Treatments for Mood and Anxiety Disorders

There are six major categories of drugs used to treat mood and anxiety disorders: monoamine oxidase (MAO) inhibitors, tricyclic antidepressants, selective serotonin reuptake inhibitors (SSRIs), benzodiazepines, barbiturates, and lithium.

The **monoamine oxidase (MAO) inhibitors** were among the first pharmaceuticals used to treat depression. These drugs reduce the action of the enzyme monoamine oxidase, which breaks down monoamine neurotransmitters (including norepinephrine, epinephrine, dopamine, and serotonin) in the brain. By inhibiting the action of this enzyme, MAO inhibitors allow more of these neurotransmitters to stay active in the synapse for a longer time, which presumably improves mood. Brand names of MAO inhibitors include Nardil and Parnate. Unfortunately, MAO inhibitors interact with many foods and common over-the-counter drugs such as antihistamines to produce undesirable, even dangerous, side effects, such as life-threatening increases in blood pressure. At present, therefore, they are not often prescribed for depression (Fiedorowicz & Swartz, 2004; Yamada & Yasuhara, 2004).

Tricyclic antidepressants such as imipramine and amitriptyline, marketed under the trade names Elavil and Anafranil, are still popular for treating depression. They are also used in chronic pain management, to treat ADHD, and as a treatment for bedwetting. These drugs appear to work by blocking the reuptake of serotonin and norepinephrine almost equally. Hence, they make more of these neurotransmitters available in the brain. However, the tricyclics produce unpleasant side effects such as dry mouth, weight gain, irritability, confusion, and constipation.

Many of the unpleasant side effects of the tricyclic antidepressants come from their effects on norepinephrine. People with depression have serotonin

monoamine oxidase (MAO) inhibitors
class of drugs used to treat depression; they slow the breakdown of monoamine neurotransmitters in the brain.

tricyclic antidepressants
drugs used for treating depression, as well as in chronic pain management and in the treatment of ADHD.

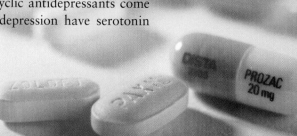

"Discouraging data on the antidepressant."
© 1997 Mike Twohy: *The New Yorker.*

deficiencies (Delgado et al., 1994; Drevets et al., 1999). Therefore, the development of new drugs that target only serotonin offered hope for treatments with fewer side effects. One class of drugs brought to the market in the 1990s, the **selective serotonin reuptake inhibitors (SSRIs)**, make more serotonin available in the synapse. Prozac (fluoxetine), Zoloft (sertraline), Paxil (paroxetine), and Celexa (citalopram) are some of the more widely used SSRIs and are among the most widely prescribed psychotherapeutic drugs in the United States today.

Here is how SSRIs work: Serotonin, like all neurotransmitters, is released from the presynaptic neuron into the synapse. It then binds with serotonin-specific receptor sites on the postsynaptic neuron to stimulate the firing of that neuron. Normally, neurotransmitters that do not bind with the postsynaptic neuron will be either taken back up into the presynaptic neuron, in a process called *reuptake*, or destroyed by enzymes in the synapse. The SSRIs inhibit the reuptake process, thereby allowing more serotonin to bind with the postsynaptic neuron (see Figure 16.2). By allowing more serotonin to be used, the SSRIs alleviate some of the symptoms of depression.

connection
Deficiencies in either the amount or the utilization of serotonin in certain parts of the brain are found in people with depression.
See Chapter 15, p. 586.

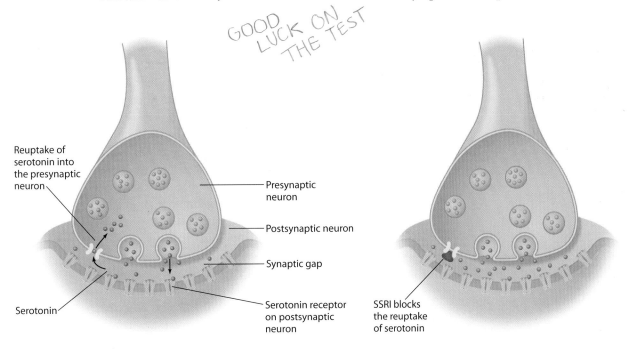

FIGURE **16.2**
THE EFFECT OF SSRIs ON REUPTAKE OF SEROTONIN. SSRIs increase serotonin levels by blocking the reuptake of serotonin into the presynaptic neuron. As a result, more serotonin stays in the synaptic cleft, where it can bind with receptors on the postsynaptic neuron.

SSRI medications create far fewer unpleasant side effects than do tricyclic antidepressants. For this reason they have become popular, even among people who are not particularly ill but want to feel happier. Although these drugs are prescribed primarily for depression, they are also prescribed for the treatment of certain anxiety disorders, especially OCD, as well as disorders of impulse control such as compulsive gambling (Vaswani, Linda, & Ramesh, 2003). SSRIs can have some side effects, such as agitation, insomnia, nausea, and difficulty in achieving orgasm. This last side effect has led some physicians to prescribe SSRIs to treat premature ejaculation (Waldinger et al., 2004). Another highly publicized but infrequent side effect of SSRI is an increased likelihood of attempting suicide compared to other treatments for depression (Fergusson et al., 2005). The recently publicized cases of teens on SSRIs committing suicide often neglect to report that adolescents are usually in severely depressed states when they are prescribed SSRIs, which suggests that they would be more likely to attempt or to commit suicide no matter which drug they were prescribed (Wessely & Kerwin, 2004).

Bupropione (trade name Wellbutrin) is another widely used antidepressant that is chemically unrelated to the tricyclics, MAO inhibitors, and SSRIs. It inhibits the reuptake of norepinephrine and dopamine, both of which are excitatory neurotransmitters involved in arousal and positive emotion. Bupropione is also marketed under the trade name of Zyban as a smoking cessation aid.

Two major classes of drugs, the **benzodiazepines** (Valium, Librium) and the **barbiturates**, are prescribed for anxiety. Both have calming effects and can be addictive, but barbiturates have the higher risk of overdose. People with anxiety disorders often take SSRIs as well. We will discuss the drug treatment of anxiety disorders in more detail later in this chapter's "Making Connections" section.

The treatment of bipolar disorder presents many challenges, as the manic episodes have to be regulated, the depressive episodes prevented, and the shifts from one type of episode to the other controlled. Because no one drug can manage all these effects, treatment often consists of a combination of drug therapies. As we saw in the chapter opening, thanks to John Cade, **lithium** has long been prescribed for its ability to stabilize the mania associated with bipolar disorder. We do not know how lithium works, although it appears to influence many neurotransmitter systems in the brain, including glutamate, the major excitatory neurotransmitter in the brain, which appears to play a substantial role in schizophrenia (Chuang, 2004; Jope, 1999). Taking lithium can be unpleasant and dangerous, as it can cause diarrhea, nausea, tremors, cognitive problems, kidney failure, brain damage, and even adverse cardiac effects (Aichorn et al., 2006). Also, because the amount of lithium required for effective treatment is not very different from the amount that can cause harm, it is difficult to determine the effective dosage. In addition, some people develop tolerance to lithium after years of treatment, making the drug less effective (Post et al., 1998). For these reasons, physicians need to monitor their

bupropione
a widely used antidepressant that inhibits the reuptake of norepinephrine and dopamine.

benzodiazepines
a class of anxiety-reducing drugs that can be addictive, but are less dangerous than barbiturates.

barbiturates
a class of anxiety-reducing sedatives that can be addictive and carry a risk of overdose.

lithium
a salt that is prescribed for its ability to stabilize the mania associated with bipolar disorder.

Actor Robert Downey, Jr., has struggled with symptoms of bipolar disorder and drug abuse for a number of years. Treating bipolar disorder is challenging and typically involves a combination of drugs to control mania and prevent depression. Lithium effectively regulates mania, but its use must be monitored carefully to avoid harmful side effects.

connection

Do you need a caffeinated beverage to get you going in the morning? And more throughout the day to stay alert? People who require more and more caffeine or other drugs, including prescription drugs, have developed a drug tolerance.

See Chapter 6, p. 241.

patients' lithium levels carefully by taking regular blood samples.

Due to toxicity concerns, physicians often favor other drugs to treat the mania phase, including drugs prescribed to prevent convulsions, either alone or in combination with lithium. Physicians prescribe various antidepressants to manage the depressive phase of bipolar disorder. They also use antipsychotic drugs, which we discuss in the next section on treatments for schizophrenia, to manage the psychotic symptoms of bipolar disorder (Bauer & Mitchner, 2004). Throughout the world, most physicians prescribe antipsychotic drugs to manage severe mania (Carney & Goodwin, 2005).

Drug Treatments for Schizophrenia

Drug therapies are typically the first choice for schizophrenia. In the 1950s, researchers discovered that a class of drugs, the **phenothiazines**, helped diminish hallucinations, confusion, agitation, and paranoia in people with schizophrenia. They made this discovery by accident. As you read in Chapter 15, the prevailing view for decades was that schizophrenia resulted from an excess of dopamine in the brain. This hypothesis emerged from the observation that people who were addicted to the stimulant amphetamine, also called "speed," experienced hallucinations and delusions of grandeur similar to those seen in schizophrenia. Amphetamine stimulates pathways that use dopamine in the brain. Maybe, they inferred, schizophrenia results from excess dopamine as well. Although the dopamine hypothesis has come into question, currently the major antischizophrenia drugs are those that reduce the availability of dopamine in the brain (Javitt & Coyle, 2004).

Phenothiazines block dopamine receptors in the brain. The best-known phenothiazine is chlorpromazine (marketed as Thorazine in the United States). Another drug, haloperidol (Haldol), discovered at about the same time, showed similar effects on schizophrenic symptoms. The phenothiazines and haloperidol are known as **traditional antipsychotics**, because they were the first medications used to manage psychotic symptoms. Unfortunately, they have many unpleasant side effects. These include fatigue, visual impairments, and a condition called **tardive dyskinesia**, which consists of repetitive, involuntary movements of jaw, tongue, face, and mouth (such as grimacing and lip smacking), and body tremors. Tardive dyskinesia is particularly problematic, as the effects often continue for months after the drugs are discontinued (Trugman, 1998).

Some newer antipsychotic drugs, called **atypical antipsychotics**, do not have these side effects. Clozapine (Clozaril), olanzapine (Zyprexa), and risperidone (Risperdal) are examples of atypical antipsychotics. Many physicians now consider the atypical antipsychotics the first line of treatment for schizophrenia. These drugs preferentially block a different type of dopamine receptor than the traditional antipsychotics do, which makes them less likely to create tardive dyskinesia (Potkin et al., 2003). Atypical antipsychotics also affect the activity of

phenothiazines drugs used to treat schizophrenia; help diminish hallucinations, confusion, agitation, and paranoia but also have adverse side effects.

traditional antipsychotics historically, the first medications used to manage psychotic symptoms.

atypical antipsychotics newer antipsychotic drugs, which do not create tardive dyskinesia.

connection

Schizophrenia and other disorders can be caused in part by genes that are expressed only under specific environmental circumstances.

See Chapter 15, p. 592.

tardive dyskinesia repetitive, involuntary movements of jaw, tongue, face, and mouth and body tremors resulting from the extended use of traditional antipsychotic drugs.

FIGURE **16.3** SUMMARY OF DRUGS USED TO TREAT PSYCHO- LOGICAL DISOR- DERS. Most of the major psychologi- cal disorders can be treated with some form of medication, to varying degrees of effectiveness and with various side effects.

Disorder	Class of drug treatment	Drug name	Side effects
Anxiety	SSRIs	Paxil, Prozac Zoloft, Celexa	Agitation, insomnia, nausea, difficulty achieving orgasm; rare cases of increased risk for suicide
	Benzodiazepines	Valium Librium	Can be addictive
	Barbiturates	Pentobarbitol	Slows breathing and heart rate; can lead to overdose
Depression	MAO inhibitors	Nardil Parnate	Dangerous increases in blood pressure
	Tricyclic antidepressants	Elavil Anafranil	Dry mouth, weight gain, irritability, confusion, constipation
	SSRIs	Paxil, Prozac Zoloft, Celexa	Agitation, insomnia, nausea, difficulty achieving orgasm; rare cases of increased risk for suicide
	Bupropione	Wellbutrin	
Bipolar disorder	Lithium	Lithobid	Diarrhea, nausea, tremors, kidney failure, cognitive effects, adverse cardiac effects
Schizophrenia	Chlorpromazine	Thorazine	Fatigue, visual impairment, tardive dyskinesia
	Haloperidol	Halodol	Fatigue, visual impairment, tardive dyskinesia
	Clozapine	Clozaril	Weight gain, increased risk of diabetes, reduction of white blood cells
	Risperidone	Risperdal	Weight gain, increased risk of diabetes, reduction of white blood cells

other neurotransmitters in the brain. In rare cases, an excess of serotonin occurs, which can lead to tremor, diarrhea, delirium, neuromuscular rigidity, and high body temperature (Dvir & Smallwood, 2008). Unfortunately, even these medi- cations can produce some unpleasant or dangerous side effects, such as weight gain, increased risk of diabetes, a reduction in the number of certain white blood cells, and, rarely, a particular kind of cancer (Javitt & Coyle, 2004; Lieberman et al., 2005). Figure 16.3 summarizes the major drug therapies, the names of the medications that are used to treat specific disorders, and the various side effects of each medication.

PSYCHOSURGERY

Recall from Chapter 1 the evidence from very early human history of attempts to cure insanity by trephining, which is drilling a hole in the skull to allow evil spirits to escape. Although psychological disorders are not now usually treated by surgical means, in the early 20th century physicians experimented with the use of surgery to disrupt the transmission of brain signals in people suffering from psy- chosis. In a procedure known as **prefrontal lobotomy,** they severed connections between the prefrontal cortex and the lower portion of the brain. Because the pre- frontal cortex is involved in thinking (and, we now know, are crucial for working memory and planned action) and the lower areas are more concerned with emo- tion, they believed the surgery would have the effect of modifying behavior and possibly disengaging disruptive thought patterns involved in hallucinations and confused thinking. Typically, however, prefrontal lobotomies produced profound personality changes, often leaving the patient listless or subject to seizures; some patients were even reduced to a vegetative state (Mashour, Walker, & Martuza, 2005).

prefrontal lobotomy a form of psycho- surgery in which the connections between the pre- frontal cortex and the lower portion of the brain are severed; no longer in use.

Rosemary Kennedy, the late President John F. Kennedy's younger sister, underwent a lobotomy when she was 23 years old to treat her erratic, often violent mood swings. Instead of producing the desired calming effect, the lobotomy left Rosemary mentally incapacitated. She would stare blankly at walls for hours on end and lost the ability to speak coherently (Lerner, 1996).

After the introduction of the traditional antipsychotic medications, lobotomy fell out of favor. Moreover, the practice was widely regarded as cruel and inhumane. Today a very few, highly constrained forms of brain surgery are occasionally performed, but only as a last resort after other forms of treatment have been unsuccessful (Mashour et al., 2005).

ELECTRIC AND MAGNETIC THERAPIES

Although brain surgery for psychological disorders is rare, there are other ways to stimulate or decrease brain activation. Bizarre as it seems, electrical current can be used to help ease the suffering caused by certain psychological disorders. The application of electrical current as a medical practice goes back centuries: Apparently the ancient Romans used electric fish to treat headaches (Abrams, 1997). One of the more innovative applications of electrical stimulation may well hold the key to unlocking the mystery of depression and is discussed later in the chapter.

Electroconvulsive Therapy The notion of "shock therapy" conjures up images of barbaric torture of psychiatric patients. Yet electroconvulsive therapy is still used and can be effective for severe cases of depression in people who have not responded to other therapies (Fink, 2006). **Electroconvulsive therapy (ECT)** involves passing an electrical current through a person's brain in order to induce a seizure. The origins of ECT stem from the observation that people who have seizures become calm after they have them (Abrams, 1997). Physicians thought that ECT could be an effective treatment for schizophrenia because the induced seizures would calm the patient. Research eventually demonstrated, however, that ECT did not treat the symptoms of schizophrenia effectively at all, and it disappeared as a viable therapy for years. It resurfaced later as a treatment for people with severe cases of depression.

Today, ECT is administered by placing electrodes to the patient's head and passing an electric current (ranging from 60 to 140 volts) through the brain for one-third to one-half second. The voltage is not lethal because it is administered only to the head—indeed, the same voltage to the chest would be lethal. The treatment is called electro*convulsive* because the procedure produces a brief seizure, including bodily convulsions. To minimize the convulsions, patients today are given an anesthetic and muscle relaxant prior to ECT.

Standard ECT treatment involves up to 12 sessions over the course of several weeks. Some people report immediate relief of their depressive symptoms after treatment, although scientists do not fully understand how ECT works

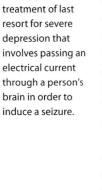

electro-convulsive therapy (ECT) treatment of last resort for severe depression that involves passing an electrical current through a person's brain in order to induce a seizure.

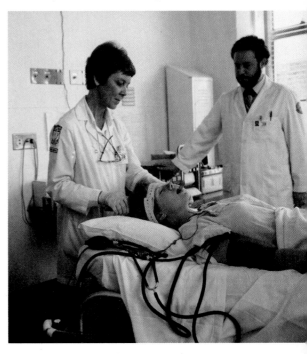

Repetitive transcranial magnetic stimulation exposes specific areas of the brain to bursts of high-intensity magnetic fields and may be used to treat people with severe depression when other options have failed.

to relieve them (Nolen-Hoeksema, 2008). The downside to ECT is that it creates some permanent memory loss and other types of cognitive damage because it actually destroys some brain tissue. Using ECT on one side of the brain rather than both appears to reduce the risk of memory loss (Squire, 1977).

Repetitive Transcranial Magnetic Stimulation

The idea of somehow stimulating or manipulating brain activity with an external application of energy has enduring appeal. Some practitioners have tried to find a way to do this without creating more harm. ECT was a good idea in some respects, but as just mentioned, it leaves people with memory damage and other negative effects. In **repetitive transcranial magnetic stimulation**, physicians expose particular brain structures to bursts of high-intensity magnetic fields instead of electricity. Like ECT, repetitive transcranial magnetic stimulation is usually reserved for people with severe depression who have not responded well to other forms of therapy. Although some people experience relief from this therapy, it is not yet clear how much magnetic stimulation is optimal and for what length of time (Fitzgerald et al., 2006; Turner-Shea, Bruno, & Pridmore, 2006).

Recently, innovative breakthroughs in neurology and psychiatry have led to the development of a very promising treatment for depression. This revolutionary approach has roots in both neurosurgery and the use of electricity to treat psychological disorders. We examine how it was discovered and how it works in "Breaking New Ground."

repetitive transcranial magnetic stimulation treatment for severe depression involving exposure of specific brain structures to bursts of high-intensity magnetic fields instead of electricity.

breaking new ground

Deep Brain Stimulation for the Treatment of Severe Depression

The treatment of depression remains a major challenge. Few people are cured, although many obtain some relief from drugs, psychotherapy, repetitive transcranial magnetic stimulation, or ECT. Others, however, find no relief in any of these treatments. For them, depression is severe, unrelenting, and debilitating.

Helen Mayberg

But there is hope. In her quest to understand the brain circuitry of depression, neurologist Helen Mayberg discovered what appears to be a neural switch that activates depression. In the process, she came upon a strikingly effective treatment for the disorder. The path that led Mayberg to discover how a brain region called Brodmann's Area 25 (we'll call it Area 25) may control depression is an interesting story of how scientific discovery depends on luck, creativity, vision, and hard work.

PREVAILING THINKING ABOUT BRAIN CIRCUITRY IN DEPRESSION

Most theories about the brain mechanisms of depression hypothesize deficiencies in various neurotransmitters, based on how the effective drugs work. For example, the SSRIs increase serotonin availability; the MAO inhibitors affect dopamine, norepinephrine, and serotonin. In terms of brain regions, depressed people show reduced activity in certain brain areas, especially the cortex and areas involved in mood (Drevets et al., 1997; Mayberg, 2003; Shestyuk et al., 2005). Researchers and therapists therefore believed that deficiencies in these neurotransmitters were most important for understanding depression.

MAYBERG'S BREAKTHROUGH RESEARCH

Helen Mayberg took a different approach. As a young scientist, she trained with a neurologist who studied how various areas of the human brain work together. Her early training helped her see the brain in terms of the interactions among various areas rather than in terms of their individual functions alone. Early in her career, Mayberg studied depression in people with Parkinson's disease. Using PET imaging of brain activation, she and her colleagues found that these patients had reduced activity in both frontal cortex thinking areas and limbic emotional areas. But they also stumbled on a surprising phenomenon: Area 25 was hyperactive in these patients. Rather than discounting this unexpected finding, Mayberg tested it further. She found this same pattern of overactivation in Area 25 in depressed people with Alzheimer's, epilepsy, and Huntington's disease (Mayberg, 1997). Perhaps it played a role in depression more generally.

Finding overactivation in any brain area of depressed people was surprising, since many researchers have found that depression is related to underactivity rather than overactivity of certain cortical areas (Shestyuk et al., 2005). But Mayberg found *depressed activity* in frontal cortex areas, which fit with current models of depression, along with *overactivity* in Area 25.

Area 25 is located in the cingulate region of the prefrontal cortex, and it is surrounded by the limbic system. As such, it has connections with emotional and memory centers of the brain (see Figure 16.4 on page 622). Mayberg reasoned that if Area 25 plays a key role in sustaining depressive thinking, one would see a reduction in activity

FIGURE **16.4**

BRODMANN'S AREA 25, THE PREFRON- TAL CORTEX, AND THE LIMBIC SYSTEM. Brodmann's Area 25 is located in the cingu- late region of the prefrontal cortex, where it is surrounded by the corpus callosum and structures of the limbic system (amygdala, hippocampus, thalamus). The limbic sys- tem is important in regulating emotion and motivation.

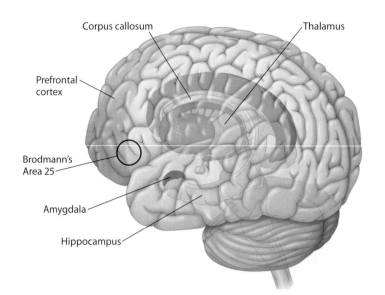

Corpus callosum

Thalamus

Prefrontal cortex

Brodmann's Area 25

Amygdala

Hippocampus

in this area after successful treatment for the disorder. She and colleagues performed PET scans of depressed people before and after a 15–20-week course of cognitive– behavioral therapy, an effective psychological treatment for depression. They did similar scans on people with depression taking an SSRI. Both groups of patients showed that reduced activity in Area 25 corresponded with clinical improvement of depressive symptoms (Goldapple et al., 2004; Kennedy et al., 2001). Mayberg also found activity in Area 25 when otherwise healthy people recalled sad memories (Mayberg et al., 1999).

Eventually, Mayberg and her colleagues amassed evidence that an overactive Area 25 is a general feature of depression. Moreover, successful treatment by an SSRI or cognitive–behavioral therapy reduced Area 25 activation. What seems most important about Area 25 is its connections with thinking areas of the prefrontal cortex and limbic structures involved in emotion (which are connected to each other). Area 25 thus may be a gateway between thinking and emotion. An overactive Area 25 may enable the type of negative thinking that feeds depressive states. Mayberg reasoned that if it were possible to close this gate, depression might cease. But how?

Mayberg knew scientists were implanting electrodes deep in the brains of people with Parkinson's disease to regulate activity in an area of the brain that produces the tremors (shaking) associated with that disease. Mayberg figured that she could apply the same technology, known as *deep brain stimulation,* to Area 25. She tried it with 12

FIGURE **16.5**

DEEP BRAIN ELECTRODES AND STIMULATOR FOR STIMULATION OF AREA 25 IN DEPRESSED PATIENTS. A pacemaker implanted in the person's chest sends electrical impulses to electrodes projecting down into Area 25 of the frontal cortex.

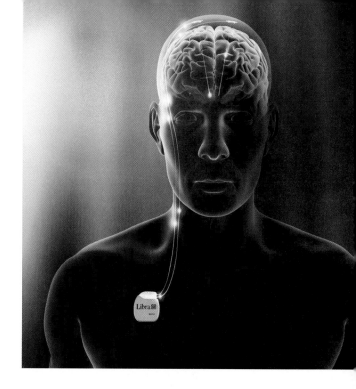

patients whose severe depression had failed to respond to anything else. They implanted electrodes in Area 25 and delivered voltage to that area from an external stimulator. For 11 of the patients, the depression ceased almost immediately (Mayberg et al., 2005). Shortly after activation of the electrodes, these patients said that they felt "sudden calmness or lightness," "disappearance of the void," or "connectedness." One of them described heightened awareness and greater perception of visual details and colors in the room.

Figure 16.5 illustrates the location of the implanted electrodes and the wearable pacemaker for stimulating them. Note that the treatment involves brain stimulation in the operating room as well as a method for stimulating the implants in daily life. Patients wear an external pacemaker that controls the delivery of electrical stimulation to Area 25.

In the following passage, Mayberg describes what happened when the stimulator was turned on to activate the electrode just implanted in Area 25 in the brain of a woman named Deanna. As the electrodes were being implanted in Area 25, Mayberg sat by Deanna's side and asked her to report, throughout the surgery, whatever she felt, however minor it might seem. What follows is Mayberg's account of what Deanna said when, unbeknownst to Deanna, the surgical team turned the stimulator on:

"So we turn it on," Mayberg told me later, "and all of a sudden she says to me, 'It's very strange,' she says, 'I know you've been with me in the operating room this whole time. I know you care about me. But it's not that. I don't know what you just did. But I'm looking at you, and it's like I just feel suddenly more connected to you.'"

Mayberg, stunned, signaled with her hand to the others, out of Deanna's view, to turn the stimulator off.

"And they turn it off," Mayberg said, "and she goes: 'God, it's just so odd. You just went away again. I guess it wasn't really anything.'

"It was subtle like a brick," Mayberg told me. "There's no reason for her to say that. Zero. And all through those tapes I have of her, every time she's in the clinic beforehand, she always talks about this disconnect, this closeness and sense of affiliation she misses, that was so agonizingly painful for her to lose. And there it was. It was back in an instant." (Dobbs, 2006, April 2)

Although most people who have had the procedure experience dramatic improvements or complete elimination of their depression, a few do not. A large-scale clinical trial is underway in which Mayberg and her colleagues are studying the effects of stimulation of Area 25 on a much larger group of people with treatment-resistant depression.

nature & nuture
Electrical stimulation of certain areas of the brain changes mood.

Mayberg made several choices that may have contributed to her revolutionary discovery. First, she pursued a phenomenon, not an idea. She had expectations about the role of frontal and limbic areas in depression, but then she noticed the high level of activity in Area 25. She then employed diverse approaches: studying depressed people with neurological conditions, depressed people without neurological conditions, and healthy people in sad moods. Consistent findings across these groups helped build her confidence that an overactive Area 25 was an indicator of depression. Last, Mayberg integrated diverse findings and devised a way of applying them, a hallmark of creativity (Sternberg, 1999).

quick quiz 16.1: Biological Treatments

1. The antidepressant medications known as the SSRIs work by
   a. inhibiting monoamine oxidase
   b. decreasing serotonin levels by inhibiting the reuptake of serotonin into the presynaptic neuron
   c. increasing serotonin levels by inhibiting the reuptake of serotonin into the presynaptic neuron
   d. reducing the activity of the neurotransmitter glutamate

2. Your Aunt Julia has been in treatment for years for schizophrenia. She often has jerky spastic movements, which she tells you are from her medication, not the disorder itself. What side effect is she experiencing?
   a. intolerance
   b. reactive dysphoria
   c. tardive dyskinesia
   d. insomnia

3. Electroconvulsive therapy (ECT) is still in limited use for people with which disorder?
   a. schizophrenia
   b. obsessive-compulsive disorder
   c. generalized anxiety disorder
   d. major depressive disorder

4. Helen Mayberg was surprised to find that brain images of Area 25 showed _____ in people with severe depression and helped devise a way to treat them with deep brain stimulation.
   a. reduced activity
   b. overactivity
   c. tumors
   d. reduced blood flow

Answers can be found at the end of the chapter.

psychotherapy
the use of psychological techniques to modify maladaptive behaviors or thought patterns, or both, and to help patients develop insight into their own behavior.

Psychological Treatments for Psychological Disorders

A number of psychological therapies have developed alongside the various medications and biologically based techniques for treating psychological disorders. **Psychotherapy** is the use of psychological techniques to modify maladaptive behaviors or

thought patterns, or both, and to help patients develop insight into their own behavior. In psychotherapy a therapist and a client work together, or a therapist works with a group of people.

People may engage in psychotherapy for self-development as well as for the treatment of psychological disorders. In this chapter, we will focus on the use of psychotherapeutic techniques in treating disorders. There are several types of psychotherapeutic approaches, as outlined in Figure 16.1: psychodynamic, humanistic, behavioral, cognitive, and cognitive–behavioral. Each type of psychotherapy has its own explanation of what causes different disorders as well as how they should be treated.

PSYCHODYNAMIC THERAPY

psychodynamic psychotherapy
therapy aimed at uncovering unconscious motives that underlie psychological problems.

Inspired by Freudian theory, **psychodynamic psychotherapy** aims to uncover unconscious motives that underlie psychological problems. The relationship between therapist and client in psychodynamic psychotherapy is that of a supportive partnership, in which the therapist listens to the client in a nonjudgmental manner. The therapist's role is to help the client gain insight into the unconscious influences behind unwanted behaviors. To help the client access these unconscious influences, the therapist may use techniques such as free association or examine processes that might reveal unconscious motives, such as transference and repression. We will discuss how therapists may use these techniques and processes to help clients access the unconscious.

One of Sigmund Freud's major contributions to psychology was his argument that "dreams are the royal road to the unconscious" (Freud, 1900/1953, p. 608). Freud's two major techniques for interpreting dreams in order to uncover their unconscious content were free association and symbols. In **free association**, the client recounts the dream and then takes one image or idea and says whatever comes to mind, regardless of how threatening, disgusting, or

free association
a psychotherapeutic technique in which the client takes one image or idea from a dream and says whatever comes to mind, regardless of how threatening, disgusting, or troubling it may be.

troubling it may be. After this has been done with the first image, the process is repeated until the client has made associations with all the recalled dream images. Ideally, somewhere in the chain of free associations is a connection that unlocks the key to the dream. The second technique for interpreting dreams is through *symbols;* that is, dream images are thought of as representing or being symbolic of something else. Classic examples of symbols are a snake symbolizing a penis and a cave representing a vagina. If the techniques just described are successful, the patient becomes aware of the disturbing thoughts in her or his unconscious and the problematic symptoms decrease.

In the process of **transference**, the client reacts to someone in a current relationship as though that person were someone from the client's past. While the client is in therapy, that person is the therapist, but it can be anyone in the person's present life circumstances. For example, a woman whose father was verbally abusive to her might find herself shirking her job responsibilities because she experiences extreme fear when her older male supervisor at work speaks with even a slightly raised voice. The supervisor thinks this is an overreaction, but he does not realize that the woman's response stems from her relating to him as if he were her father. If these reactions occur during a therapy session, as they often do, the therapist can use the transference to help the client understand how her behavior

transference
process in psychotherapy in which the client reacts to a person in a present relationship as though that person were someone from the client's past.

and emotions in current relationships are influenced by her relationship with her father. By working through the unconsciously transferred feelings in the therapeutic setting, a client might be freed from their powerful grip in other settings.

Like transference, defense mechanisms are also central to psychodynamic theory and therapy. Freud described many different **defense mechanisms,** but all of them operate unconsciously and involve defending against anxiety and threats to the ego. The most basic one is **repression,** which involves forcing threatening feelings, ideas, or motives into the unconscious. In psychodynamic therapy, dream interpretation and transference are used to uncover repressed defenses and unconscious wishes.

Some or all of these techniques may lead the client to catharsis. **Catharsis** is the process of releasing intense, often unconscious, emotions in a therapeutic setting.

Carl Rogers (far right) leads a group therapy session.

HUMANISTIC THERAPY

Humanistic therapies seek to help the client reach his or her greatest potential. The most prominent figure in humanistic therapy is Carl Rogers (1951), who developed **client-centered therapy.** The main idea of client-centered therapy is that people are not well because there is a gap between who they are and who they would ideally like to be. In client-centered therapy, the therapist must show **unconditional positive regard**—that is, genuine liking and empathy for the client, regardless of what he or she has said or done. The goal is to create an atmosphere in which clients can communicate their feelings with certainty that they are being understood rather than judged. If this unconditional positive regard is effective, the client will develop a strong sense of self-worth and the confidence to strive for self-fulfillment.

BEHAVIORAL TREATMENTS

In **behavior therapies,** therapists apply the principles of classical and operant conditioning to treat psychological disorders. They focus on changing behavior, rather than thoughts, feelings, or motives. The idea is to help clients eliminate undesirable behaviors and increase the frequency of desirable ones.

Behavioral therapists employ the basic principles of operant conditioning through the use of **token economies** to treat maladaptive behaviors. This technique is based on a simple principle: Desirable behaviors are reinforced with a token, such as a small chip or fake coin, which the client can then exchange for privileges. Parents can use this approach with their children—if their room is messy and they clean it, they get a token. The kids can turn in five tokens for candy or a toy. The more this happens, the more likely they are to clean their rooms, or so the logic goes. In the realm of mental health, the technique was used with some success in the 1950s and 1960s to reduce undesirable psychotic behaviors in patients in mental institutions (Nolen-Hoeksema, 2007). Recent uses include treatment of substance abuse by people with schizophrenia. Each time the

repression
the unconscious act of keeping threatening thoughts, feelings, or impulses out of consciousness.

defense mechanisms
ways in which the mind protects itself from anxiety by unconsciously distorting reality.

catharsis
the process of releasing intense, often unconscious, emotions in a therapeutic setting.

client-centered therapy
a form of humanistic therapy in which the therapist shows unconditional positive regard for the patient.

unconditional positive regard
basic tenet of client-centered therapy, the therapist's genuine liking and empathy for the client, regardless of what he or she has said or done.

behavior therapies
therapies that apply the principles of classical and operant conditioning in the treatment of psychological disorders.

token economies
a behavioral technique in which desirable behaviors are reinforced with a token, such as a small chip or fake coin, which can be exchanged for privileges.

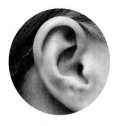

1. Hearing the word "spider"

2. Seeing the word "spider" in print

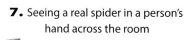

3. Imagining a spider

4. Seeing a photograph of a spider in a glass jar

5. Seeing a photograph of a spider in someone's hand

6. Seeing a real spider in a jar across the room

7. Seeing a real spider in a person's hand across the room

8. Holding a real spider in a glass jar

9. Holding a real spider in one's own hand

patients did not use drugs, they were rewarded with small amounts of money. Coupled with problem-solving and social-skills training, this token system helped control substance abuse in hospitalized patients with schizophrenia, who are generally very hard to treat (Bellack et al., 2006).

Systematic desensitization is a widely used application of behavioral treatment that is especially effective for treating simple phobias (Tyron, 2005). Systematic desensitization pairs relaxation with gradual exposure to a phobic object. First, the therapist generates a hierarchy of increasing contact with the feared object, ranging from mild to extreme. Figure 16.6 shows a possible hierarchy for a person with arachnophobia (a fear of spiders). In addition to increasing exposure, the therapist helps the client learn relaxation techniques that he or she can use when experiencing anxiety, especially anxiety related to the phobic object. The therapist works to help the client relax and then exposes the client to the phobic stimulus at gradually increasing levels of intensity. The idea is a clever one—to pair two incompatible body responses, relaxation and anxiety. People cannot be both relaxed and anxious at the same time. And it works! Systematic desensitization often successfully treats phobias and some other anxiety disorders (Tyron, 2005).

connection

Principles of classical and operant conditioning, including the powerful effect of reinforcement on learning, are the foundation of many behavioral therapies.

See Chapter 8, p. 303.

systematic desensitization a behavioral therapy technique, often used for phobias, in which the therapist pairs relaxation with gradual exposure to a phobic object, generating a hierarchy of increasing contact with the feared object.

FIGURE **16.7**
SYSTEMATIC DESENSITIZATION IN TREATMENT OF FLYING PHOBIA. Because it is impractical and expensive to do therapy while on an actual airplane, simulating flying in a virtual reality format is an effective and cost-efficient way of systematically desensitizing people who are afraid of flying.

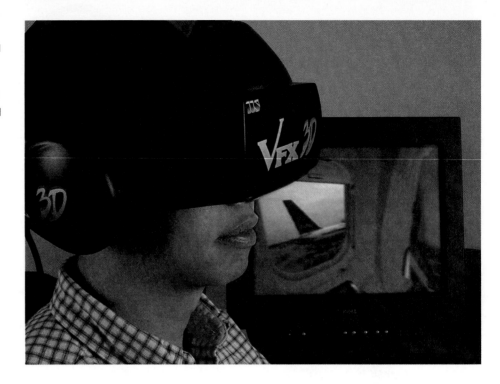

Systematic desensitization involves three levels of exposure to a phobic object: imagined, virtual, or real. In imagined exposure, people simply imagine contact with the phobic object. The next level is virtual reality exposure. At this stage, the individual may be shown photographs or exposed to a virtual reality computer simulation. For instance, one type of virtual reality software allows clients to simulate flying during treatment for flying phobia, as depicted in Figure 16.7 (Wiederhold & Wiederhold, 2005). The most realistic level of exposure is in vivo exposure, in which the client makes real-life contact with phobic object. Implosion therapy, or **flooding,** is an extreme form of in vivo exposure in which the client experiences extreme exposure to the phobic object, such as asking a person who is arachnophobic to hold three hairy tarantulas at once.

flooding
an extreme form of in vivo exposure in which the client experiences extreme exposure to the phobic object.

COGNITIVE AND COGNITIVE–BEHAVIORAL TREATMENTS

cognitive therapy
any type of psychotherapy that works to restructure irrational thought patterns.

Any type of psychotherapy that works to restructure irrational thought patterns is known as **cognitive therapy.** Typically, in cognitive therapy the therapist helps the client identify irrational thought patterns and then challenges these thoughts. Cognitive therapy is structured and problem-oriented, with the primary goal of fixing erroneous thought patterns, as we will illustrate with an example shortly. It is also time limited and involves a collaborative effort by the therapist and the client. In using cognitive therapy, the therapist relies on what is known as the Socratic method: The therapist poses questions that help the client recognize erroneous logic that may support problematic thinking (Beck & Emery, 1985).

Let's consider the real-life case of Carlos, a 39-year-old man suffering from major depressive disorder. Carlos had tried several medications for his depression and had undergone one voluntary hospitalization, without satisfactory effects.

His general practitioner (Dr. Hsu) recommended him for cognitive therapy. Many therapists believe that depressed people perceive events in such a way that they see only potentially adverse outcomes. Cognitive therapy for depression aims to point out the negative bias in such depressive thinking. Consider the following exchange between Carlos and his therapist, Dr. Walden (Gorenstein & Comer, 2002, pp. 54–55).

> **DR. WALDEN:** You say you are a "basket case" and can barely function. What leads you to those conclusions?
>
> **CARLOS:** Well, I've been hospitalized. That's how bad it's been. I just can't believe it.
>
> **DR. WALDEN:** . . . Tell me again what led to the hospitalization.
>
> **CARLOS:** I sort of panicked when the medicine didn't help, and I stopped going to work or anything else. Dr. Hsu figured that as long as I wasn't working, I might as well go into the hospital where I could try different drugs without having to manage all the side effects on my own. I also was pretty miserable at the time. I told Dr. Hsu my family might be better off without me.
>
> **DR. WALDEN:** Do you think they would be better off?
>
> **CARLOS:** I don't know. I'm not doing them much good.
>
> **DR. WALDEN:** What would life be like for them without you?
>
> **CARLOS:** It would be terrible for them. I suppose saying they'd be better off without me is going too far. As bad off as I am, I'm still able to do a few things.
>
> **DR. WALDEN:** What are you able to do?
>
> **CARLOS:** Well, I'm not in the hospital anymore. And I don't think I will be back either. . . . I mainly went in because I thought I could get better treatment or whatever. But it didn't pan out, so what would be the point of going back in?
>
> **DR. WALDEN:** So the fact that you were in the hospital isn't really a sign that you are now or were ever a "basket case," which I take to mean someone who is completely helpless and cannot function.
>
> **CARLOS:** . . . In looking back on it now, it was all basically voluntary. But that doesn't erase the fact that I am still a mess.
>
> **DR. WALDEN:** How much of a mess are you?
>
> **CARLOS:** I can't work, I can't help out at home. I can't even watch a television show. How much else do you want to know?
>
> **DR. WALDEN:** A couple of minutes ago you said you were still able to do a few things. What are those?
>
> **CARLOS:** I can drive to work and . . . I guess it's an exaggeration to say that I can't work at all. There are a few things I can do at the office.
>
> **DR. WALDEN:** Like what?

Cognitive behavioral therapy focuses on changing a client's way of thinking in order to avoid irrational thoughts. Asking the client to break down problems into steps that can be tackled one at a time illustrates this approach.

Notice how Dr. Walden helps Carlos use his own logic to point out errors in the thinking that supports his notion of being worthless. For instance, Dr. Walden helps Carlos see that in spite of being hospitalized for depression, he was neither useless to his family nor totally unable to do things. Carlos came to realize that he really wasn't a "basket case" after all (Gorenstein & Comer, 2002, pp. 54–55).

Often therapists integrate cognitive techniques for restructuring irrational thoughts with behavioral techniques to shape desirable behaviors in what is known as **cognitive–behavioral therapy** (CBT). As the name implies, the focus of CBT is to change both thoughts and behavior. CBT entails restructuring thoughts, loosening the client's belief in irrational thoughts that may perpetuate the disorder, and offering incentives for acquiring more adaptive thought and behavior patterns. Cognitive–behavioral therapy is a short-term psychological treatment that has been successfully applied to disorders as varied as depression, phobias, post-traumatic stress disorder (PTSD), obsessive–compulsive disorder, eating disorders, and substance abuse. One way to conceptualize CBT is to think of it as a tool for teaching skills that curtail *depressogenic thinking,* or thinking that tends to help generate or support depressed moods. CBT has revolutionized the treatment of many psychological disorders.

cognitive–behavioral therapy an approach to treating psychological disorders that combines techniques for restructuring irrational thoughts with operant and classical conditioning techniques to shape desirable behaviors.

CBT helps clients change the way they evaluate potential emotional threats. One way CBT does this is by encouraging reappraisal, which entails reexamining a situation that was previously seen as stressful. Through problem solving, clients can learn to adopt a new outlook on a situation. For example, a common depressogenic thought is that one is unable to do anything because all tasks seem insurmountable. A problem-solving approach to this kind of thinking would be to list the various steps in a given task and then work on each step until the task is completed. Not only will the client successfully accomplish the task, but that accomplishment may also have the further benefit of improving mood. Research on the cognitive processes involved in CBT in relation to treatment effectiveness show that people who engage in more problem solving during CBT reap more benefits (Chen, Jordan, & Thompson, 2006).

GROUP THERAPIES

group therapy therapeutic settings in which several people who share a common problem all meet regularly with a therapist to help themselves and one another.

In **group therapy,** several people who share a common problem all meet regularly with a therapist to help themselves and one another; the therapist acts as a facilitator. Group therapies often follow a structured process with clear treatment goals. The group serves as both a source of support and an aid to the therapeutic process, by allowing several people with a common problem to listen, discuss, and criticize one another. The interactions among participants become as much a part of the treatment as people's individual comments. These relationships become real-life contexts in which the various issues play out in front of the group. The presence of other people with the same problem also helps remove feelings of isolation. Groups can be very structured, as are groups that offer training in learning to overcome social anxiety disorder and groups that use CBT to treat eating disorders.

Groups can offer less structured therapeutic contexts as well. **Support groups** are meetings of people who share a common situation, be it a disorder, a disease, or coping with an ill family member. They meet regularly to share experiences, usually without programmatic treatment goals. They usually have a facilitator, a regular meeting time, and an open format. Support groups offer a sense of community, a forum for information exchange, and a place to share feelings for people who may have felt isolated by their situation. Support groups are widely available for people with all types of psychological disorders, as well as those living with chronic illnesses, such as diabetes and cancer.

Groups can be categorized in terms of their focus, such as eating disorders, substance abuse, treatment of OCD, or coping with bereavement and may be time limited or ongoing. Time-limited groups run for a set number of sessions, tend to follow a program of treatment, and usually do not add members after the first few meetings. Ongoing groups, in contrast, welcome new members as they appear. Alcoholics Anonymous and other substance abuse groups that follow AA's 12-step approach are examples of ongoing groups. Also in this category are "life support groups" offered by churches, where people who are coping with, say, a spouse with a brain tumor or a son with major depressive disorder can meet and share their feelings about what they are going through.

Psychological treatments have been used not only to alleviate psychological disorders but also to help prevent the development of such disorders. Given the difficulties in treating many psychological disorders and the costs to individuals and society of the large numbers of people suffering from such conditions, prevention programs are an increasing area of effort in psychology and medicine (see "Psychology in the Real World"). Figure 16.8 on page 634 summarizes the psychotherapies that we discussed in this section. It includes the causes addressed by each therapy, treatment goals, and techniques.

quick quiz 16.2: Psychological Treatments

1. José's therapist asks to hear about José's week. José tells him about some difficulty he is having with his wife and how he feels worthless in his marriage. The therapist expresses his empathy and understanding. He tells José he knows what it feels like to feel worthless and how uncomfortable that feeling is. What therapeutic approach is José's therapist taking?
   a. humanistic
   b. cognitive–behavioral
   c. cognitive
   d. psychodynamic

Preventing Depression

The best and safest form of treatment for psychological disorders is prevention. *Prevention* focuses on identifying risk factors for disorders, targeting at-risk populations, and offering training programs that decrease the likelihood of disorders occurring. Many prevention efforts are underway in this country, but the majority focus on the prevention of depression, the number one mental health concern in the United States (Kessler et al., 2005).

Just as a healthy diet and exercise program can help prevent heart disease, certain behaviors or coping skills may help stave off depression. Prevention programs train people to behave in ways that make depression less likely to develop. Many prevention programs focus on children, because catching people earlier in life increases the likelihood of making a difference. Also, teen depression is a growing problem and the major cause of suicide in young people (Wessely & Kerwin, 2004).

Van Voorhees and colleagues (2008) conducted a large-scale study of risk factors for adolescent depression. They conducted face-to-face interviews of teens in grades 7–12 in the home, obtained parent surveys, and measured depressive symptoms using a questionnaire. Several characteristics put teens at risk for a depressive episode: being female, being of a nonwhite race–ethnicity, having low-income status, being in poor health, and experiencing parental conflict. Teens who felt a connection among family members, warmth from their parents, and peer acceptance; who did better in school; and who participated in religious activities were less likely to have a depressive episode than others (Van Voorhees et al., 2008). Research on elementary school children reports similar findings (Dallaire et al., 2008).

In addition to poverty and unemployment, psychosocial factors increase the risk of depression, especially life stress and having a pessimistic outlook on life (Southwick, Vythilingam, & Charney, 2005). For this reason, some intervention programs for teens focus on teaching them skills for dealing with stress, including developing a more optimistic outlook. One after-school program for teens at risk for developing depression is based on CBT. Participants had already experienced mild to moderate symptoms of the disorder. This program involved retraining in ways of thinking about adversity in life. Compared to those who did not receive the training, those who had the training were significantly less likely to become clinically depressed 18 months later (Clarke et al., 1995).

Another program, the Penn Resiliency Program (PRP), is designed to prevent depression and other psychological

2. Which of the following methods is widely used for effective treatment of simple phobias?
   a. implosion therapy or flooding
   b. token economies
   c. client-centered therapy
   d. systematic desensitization

3. Often therapists integrate cognitive techniques for restructuring irrational thoughts with behavioral techniques to shape desirable behaviors in what is known as
   a. cognitive–behavioral therapy
   b. humanistic therapy
   c. psychodynamic therapy
   d. behavior modification

disorders by developing resilience and skills for coping with stress, problem solving (flexibility in the face of adverse or challenging circumstances), and cognitive restructuring (learning to change one's perspective on events). In a large-scale study of 697 middle school children, the PRP was administered in weekly 90-minute sessions over a 12-week period (Gillham et al., 2007). PRP significantly reduced depressive symptoms at follow-up compared to a control group and to another intervention, which was not aimed at resiliency, in two of the three schools. In a similar prevention program, students were assigned to a control group or to an 8-week training program, which consisted of a weekly, 90-minute workshop based on PRP. The group in the training program reported significantly fewer symptoms of anxiety and depression and significantly greater well-being than the control group. There were no differences between groups on depressive episodes 6 months later, however (Seligman, Schulman, & Tryon, 2007).

What is notable is that, compared to the control group, the students in the workshop group increased their ability to achieve an optimistic outlook (Seligman et al., 2007). This is a crucial skill, because depressive thinking is characterized by a tendency to see the negative in any given situation. For example, if a glass is filled halfway, someone who is thinking

negatively sees the glass as half empty. So helping people to look at things differently, in this case seeing the glass as half full, should help prevent the relapse into depression (Teasdale et al., 2000). Outlooks ingrained early in life ought to help offset a lifetime of depression. Interestingly, the researchers who set up PRP intervention trials will conduct a follow-up on the same group of people a year later, so we will be able to see if such skill development has a long-term protective effect on mental health.

4. What is the safest and best form of treatment for depression?
   a. Paxil
   b. prevention
   c. group therapy
   d. cognitive therapy

Answers can be found at the end of the chapter.

Combined Approaches

Some integrative approaches combine different types of psychotherapy or combine nontraditional practices with traditional approaches. Sometimes the optimal treatment for a psychological disorder may be to combine drugs with psychotherapy. We will look at combinations of drugs with psychotherapy, integrative

Therapy	Cause of problem	Goal of therapy	Techniques
Psychodynamic	Disorders are symptoms of unconscious and repressed thoughts, feelings, and motives.	Work to uncover repressed and unconscious thoughts, feelings, and motives (defense mechanisms).	Dream interpretation, free association, transference Catharsis
Humanistic	Conditions are blocking personal growth.	Create conditions for optimal growth.	Unconditional positive regard, empathic listening
Behavioral	Maladaptive behavior has been reinforced and rewarded.	Change reinforcers and rewards to change maladaptive behavior.	Classical and operant conditioning; token economies; systematic desensitization
Cognitive	Irrational thoughts lead to disordered behaviors.	Change emotions/irrational thoughts.	Critical questioning (Socratic method)
Cognitive–behavioral	Maladaptive behaviors have been reinforced and irrational thoughts have developed.	Change thoughts and behavior.	Restructure thoughts and offer incentives for acquiring more adaptive thoughts and behaviors; reappraisal
Group	Being isolated and unsupported makes disorders worse.	Facilitate support groups and sense of community so person realizes he or she is not alone.	Support groups; 12-step programs

FIGURE **16.8**

CAUSES, GOALS, AND TECHNIQUES OF PSYCHOLOGICAL THERAPIES. Each major psychological perspective has its own theory of what causes psychological disorders, as well as distinct goals and techniques of treatment.

psychotherapy, and the integration of mindfulness practices with psychotherapeutic techniques.

DRUGS AND PSYCHOTHERAPY

Given the dynamic interplay between biological and psychological influences in determining many psychological disorders, combining these two approaches might work better than either alone. The drugs can modify some of the debilitating effects of a disorder enough so that the patients can function sufficiently well to learn techniques that might help in changing their problematic thinking and behavior. This approach works best for mood and anxiety disorders, in which thinking is not severely impaired. For example, CBT combined with drugs has been used most effectively to manage depression. The drugs help manage the depressive state, and the CBT helps clients recognize and control the thought patterns that may push them into depressive states (Teasdale et al., 2000).

INTEGRATIVE THERAPIES

Some therapists take an *eclectic* approach to psychotherapy, which means that they draw on numerous techniques in their work with clients. These clinicians are typically trained in many methods and use those that seem most appropriate given the situation. They are not loyal to any particular orientation or treatment, but rather draw on those that seem most appropriate given the situation. This approach is

nature & nurture
Treatments that combine biological and psychotherapeutic approaches are often more effective than those based on a single approach.

integrative therapy
an eclectic approach in which the therapist draws on different treatment approaches and uses those that seem most appropriate for the situation.

known as **integrative therapy** (Prochaska & Norcross, 2007). For example, a client may show symptoms of simple phobia, which would argue for a behavioral therapy, but may also suffer from depression, which would best be treated by cognitive techniques. Problems of self-esteem might best be treated with a humanistic approach.

The vast majority of clinical psychologists practicing in the United States today say they take an integrative approach to treating disorders (Norcross, Karpiak, & Lister, 2005). These practitioners share the experience that no one therapeutic approach is effective for all psychological disorders.

Prolonged exposure therapy is an integrative treatment program for people who have post-traumatic stress disorder (PTSD) (Foa et al., 2005). It combines CBT with the imagined exposure form of systematic desensitization and relaxation. For clients with PTSD, this involves a course of individual therapy in which clients directly process traumatic events and thus reduce trauma-induced psychological disturbances. So a person with combat-related PTSD might revisit traumatic war scenes in her mind (such as the death of a compatriot) and also engage in cognitive approaches with the therapist to reduce irrational thinking about her role in that event (she could not have saved him). This technique has been used effectively for the treatment of combat- and rape-related PTSD (Cahill et al., 2006; Foa et al., 1999, 2005; Nacash et al., 2007). Sometimes drugs prescribed for anxiety disorders are used in combination with prolonged exposure therapy to treat PTSD (Rothbaum et al., 2006).

MINDFULNESS TRAINING AND PSYCHOTHERAPY

Some recently developed therapies integrate the nontraditional practice of mindfulness meditation with psychotherapeutic techniques to treat psychological disorders. In mindfulness meditation, the meditator is trained to note thoughts as they occur, without clinging to them. These skills allow one to keep such thoughts or emotions in perspective. We will explore three combined approaches in this vein: mindfulness-based cognitive therapy, dialectical behavior therapy, and the four steps, a treatment for obsessive–compulsive disorder.

John Teasdale and his colleagues applied mindfulness meditation to the treatment of major depressive disorder (Segal, Williams, & Teasdale, 2002; Teasdale et al., 2000). Their approach combines elements of CBT with mindfulness meditation to create a treatment known as **mindfulness-based cognitive therapy (MBCT)**. Both mindfulness meditation and cognitive therapy involve restructuring one's thoughts. Standard cognitive therapy helps depressed people recognize their depressogenic thought patterns and has been very effective in reducing relapse when administered during depressive episodes. Mindfulness meditation develops skills for approaching thoughts nonjudgmentally and enhances people's ability to realize that they are neither bound by their thoughts nor defined by them. To the extent that depression stems from recursive "negative" thought patterns in which the person becomes caught in a feedback loop that is reinforced by repeated episodes of depression, mindfulness meditation might help the patient break out of these loops (Teasdale et al., 1995).

connection
Mindfulness meditation practices help people become aware of everything that occurs in the mind and recognize it for what it is: a thought, an emotion, or a sensation that will arise and dissipate.
See Chapter 6, p. 226.

mindfulness-based cognitive therapy (MBCT)
an approach that combines elements of CBT with mindfulness meditation to help people with depression learn to recognize and restructure negative thought patterns.

nature & nurture
By restructuring thoughts, MBCT also restructures synaptic connections involved in learning, memory, and emotion.

dialectical behavior therapy (DBT)

treatment that integrates elements of CBT with exercises aimed at developing mindfulness without meditation and is used to treat borderline personality disorder.

Another combined treatment involving mindfulness is **dialectical behavior therapy (DBT)**, a program developed for the treatment of borderline personality disorder (Linehan, 1993). DBT integrates elements of CBT with exercises aimed at developing mindfulness without meditation. The training, which involves individual as well as group therapy, is designed to help clients develop a nonjudgmental attitude toward their emotions and to accept their current behavior. These skills and attitudes form the cornerstone of personality change, enabling the patient to learn how to regulate his or her own emotions (Linehan et al., 1991).

Jeffrey Schwartz (1997) has applied principles of mindfulness to the treatment of obsessive–compulsive disorder (OCD). Once again, the application is via a form of cognitive therapy that emphasizes the restructuring of maladaptive thought patterns. Schwartz's program, called the *Four Steps*, teaches people with OCD to use mindful thinking to break out of the rigid pattern of intrusive thoughts that plagues them. The Four Steps are self-instructional, although Schwartz uses them in conjunction with group therapy. The steps themselves involve a progression of cognitive and mindfulness exercises aimed at helping people with OCD to recognize intrusive thoughts as nothing but a symptom, and not a defining characteristic of the individual.

The Four Steps of Schwartz's approach are Relabel, Reattribute, Refocus, and Revalue (Schwartz, 1997). The goal of Step 1 is to learn to *relabel* intrusive thoughts and urges in one's own mind as obsessions and compulsions: "It's not me, it's the OCD" is how people describe it. Step 2, *reattribute*, involves ascribing the causes of those thoughts to the brain disorder involved in OCD, rather than one's own control. In Step 3, *refocus*, they learn to see that they can do something useful when an anxious thought occurs, rather than engage in a compulsive behavior such as hand washing. They learn to understand anxious feelings in an entirely new way. The feelings of anxiety may not change, but their interpretation of what those feelings mean does change. Step 4, *revalue*, involves not taking the obsessive thought to mean all that much—it is just an obsessive thought, and it too will fade away. This is where mindfulness comes in.

quick quiz 16.3: Combined Approaches

1. Combining drugs with psychotherapy works well for which of the following disorders?
   a. mood disorders
   b. anxiety disorders
   c. both a and b
   d. neither a nor b

2. Dialectical behavior therapy (DBT) is a combined treatment program developed for the treatment of
   a. schizophrenia
   b. borderline personality disorder
   c. bipolar disorder
   d. panic disorder

3. "It's not me, it's the OCD" is how people describe a stage of which integrative treatment for obsessive–compulsive disorder?
   a. the 12 Steps
   b. cognitive behavioral therapy
   c. systematic desensitization
   d. the Four Steps

Answers can be found at the end of the chapter.

Effectiveness of Treatments

Consider some important questions about these treatments: How effective are these different therapies? Are some more effective for certain disorders than others? What outcomes and criteria do we use for assessing effectiveness? Just because something is called a therapy doesn't automatically mean that it is effective. In this section we consider these questions, first for biological treatments, then for psychological therapies, and finally for integrative approaches.

EFFECTIVENESS OF BIOLOGICAL TREATMENTS

The SSRIs and tricyclics show comparable effectiveness in the treatment of depression (Kendrick et al., 2006). Both do a reasonable job of regulating depression and are preferable to the MAO inhibitors, given the undesirable, possibly dangerous, side effects of the latter. Of the various classes of antidepressants, the SSRIs have the fewest adverse side effects, and people seem to tolerate them better for long-term use (Nemeroff, 2007). Still, these drugs can take up to 4 weeks to take effect. Presumably, this is how long it takes synapses to produce enough new receptor sites to make use of the increased amounts of serotonin made available by SSRIs.

Lithium is still widely used for treatment of mania, although the evidence for lithium's effectiveness in treating "acute" phases of mania is weak in spite of its regular use for this purpose in the United States. Lithium does not appear to be superior to anticonvulsant or antipsychotic medications, or both, in regulating manic episodes. Moreover, these other medications have fewer toxic side effects than does lithium. Some research indicates that lithium may be most effective in preventing relapse and suicide in people with bipolar disorder, but many providers are not aware of this benefit (Carney & Goodwin, 2005).

The treatment of schizophrenia still presents a huge problem for mental health professionals. Both traditional and atypical antipsychotic drugs work best on the positive symptoms of schizophrenia, such as hallucinations and delusions, but are generally less effective on the negative symptoms, such as flattened affect, and the cognitive confusion that is characteristic of the disorder (Javitt & Coyle, 2004). One atypical antipsychotic, clozapine (Clorazil), does appear to be somewhat effective in treating the negative symptoms, but it also has a potentially serious side effect: diabetes (Javitt & Coyle, 2004). One of the major problems in treating schizophrenia, however, is persuading patients to continue taking the medication. Because of the unpleasant and often dangerous side effects of these drugs, patients often stop taking them. Up to 74% of people using traditional and atypical antipsychotics discontinue treatment (Lieberman et al., 2005; McEvoy, et al., 2006). Recent evidence that glutamate may drive the neurotransmitter system in schizophrenia offers hope for the development of more effective, less aversive drug therapies for the disorder (Patil et al., 2007).

ECT is regarded as a treatment of last resort for severely depressed people who have not responded to any other therapy. Although many patients report immediate relief with ECT treatment, its benefits usually last only as long as the treatments are maintained. Also, ECT can have severe side effects, including memory loss and confusion. ECT treatment to one hemisphere of the brain appears to work better than treatment to both hemispheres and creates fewer cognitive side effects (Sackheim et al., 1993). A recent controlled trial found that ECT and pharmacological therapy for depression were about equally effective in preventing relapse in people with major depressive disorder, but each form of treatment helped only about half the people studied (Kellner et al., 2006).

EFFECTIVENESS OF PSYCHOLOGICAL TREATMENTS

evidence-based therapies
treatment choices based on empirical evidence that they produce the desired outcome.

An increasingly prevalent view in psychiatry is that we need to make treatment choices based on the empirical evidence of their efficacy—that is, they need to be **evidence-based therapies** (APA Presidential Task Force, 2006). Yet very little research has addressed the issue of which psychotherapies work best for various disorders. Years ago, a review of the literature on the effectiveness of various types of psychotherapies showed that people who received any kind of therapy were better off on a number of outcomes relevant to mental status than most people who did not receive therapy (Smith & Glass, 1977). The study revealed no differences between behavioral therapies and psychodynamic ones. This meta-analysis, however, was conducted before the advent of cognitive–behavioral therapy. Also, these researchers were focused on general mental health outcomes, such as personality profile, social behaviors, achievement at work or in school, and physiological stress response. They were not interested in measuring the effectiveness of therapies in treating specific psychological disorders.

In general, then, the usefulness of psychotherapy depends on the nature of the disorder being treated and the state of the patient's mental health. Some conditions are more responsive to psychological intervention than others. For example, people with schizophrenia experience such disordered thinking that it may be very difficult to teach them to work with their feelings and thoughts in order to change their behavior. That said, long-term group therapy appears to improve the basic life skills of people with schizophrenia (Sigman & Hassan, 2006). People experiencing mood disorders are much more responsive to psychological approaches than are people suffering from schizophrenic disorders. But the approach needs to be matched up carefully with the disorder. Systematic desensitization, for example, is quite effective for treating a simple phobia but is inappropriate for treating depression. Length of treatment matters as well. As therapy continues, effectiveness declines (Howard et al., 1986; Kopta, 2003). Perhaps the potency of a psychological treatment begins to wear out after a certain point, or maybe only the harder-to-treat cases stay in therapy longer (Barkham et al., 2006).

Cognitive therapy (CT) and cognitive–behavioral therapy have shown perhaps the greatest effectiveness of any form of psychotherapy for treating various psychological disorders, but they are especially effective for certain cases of depression and anxiety disorders. Recent data suggest that cognitive therapy is as effective as antidepressants in treating severe depression (Hollon et al., 2005). In one study, depicted in Figure 16.9, experimental groups of individuals diagnosed with depression received either cognitive therapy or drug therapy while a control group was treated with a placebo. Cognitive therapy was as effective as drug therapy in treating depression, with fewer risks (DeRubeis et al., 2005). In the treatment of

1 research question

Is cognitive therapy as effective as antidepressant medication in treating people with depression?

2 method

An experimental study by DeRubeis and colleagues (2005) included 240 patients with moderate to serious depression. Half were randomly assigned to the antidepressant medication condition, and the other half were randomly assigned to either the cognitive therapy or placebo pill condition. The medication group received Paxil (paroxetine) for 16 weeks and no psychotherapy. The cognitive therapy group received individualized cognitive psychotherapy twice a week for the first 4 weeks, once or twice weekly for the next 8 weeks, and once a week for the last 4 weeks of the study. Those in the placebo pill condition received the placebo for 8 weeks and medication (Paxil) for the final 8 weeks.

Depression scores were measured twice a week for all 16 weeks using the Hamilton Depression Rating Scale, a standard depression questionnaire. A score of 12 and above is representative of depression. Participants had to have scores 20 or higher to be included in the study.

3 results

The criterion for the absence of depression was a score lower than 12 on the Hamilton Depression Rating Scale. After 8 weeks, 50% of the medication group, 43% of the cognitive therapy group, and 25% of the placebo group were no longer depressed, as the graph shows. After 16 weeks, 58% of both the medication and cognitive therapy groups were no longer depressed. There is no placebo group at 16 weeks, because those participants became part of the medication group after 8 weeks.

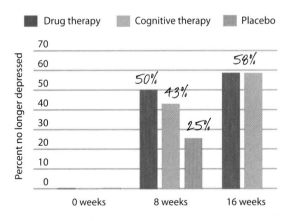

4 conclusion

At 8 weeks both cognitive and drug therapy were superior to a placebo condition in treating depression. After 16 weeks of treatment, cognitive therapy and drug therapy had been equally effective in treating depression.

FIGURE **16.9**

COMPARING COGNITIVE THERAPY TO DRUG THERAPY IN THE TREATMENT OF DEPRESSION. A controlled trial shows that cognitive therapy can be as effective as medication in the treatment of major depression. (*Source:* R. J. DeRubeis et al. 2005. Cognitive therapy vs medications in the treatment of moderate to severe depression. *Archives of General Psychiatry, 62,* 409–416.)

obsessive–compulsive disorder, CBT slows metabolism in the caudate nucleus, an area of the brain that is overactive in people suffering from this disorder (Linden, 2006). In short, psychotherapy can change the brain.

nature & nurture

Psychotherapy can change the brain.

Behavioral treatments such as systematic desensitization, are very effective for treatment of certain anxiety disorders, especially simple phobias, including performance anxiety and public speaking (Lazarus & Abramovitz, 2004; Tyron, 2005). In vivo exposure appears to offer the most effective treatment of simple phobias such as snake phobia, but people are more likely to drop out of such therapies than are people undergoing other forms of systematic desensitization (Choy, Fyer, & Lipsitz, 2007).

EFFECTIVENESS OF INTEGRATIVE APPROACHES

In spite of the logic for combining drugs with cognitive–behavioral therapy for both the treatment and the prevention of depression (Nolen-Hoeksema, 2008), few studies have systematically examined the relative benefits of drugs, psychotherapy, and the combination of the two. However, a 14-month study of mental health in more than 500 children examined the relative effectiveness of medication, behavioral treatment, and the combination of the two approaches in treating a variety of disorders. For ADHD, for example, the combination of drugs and behavioral therapy was superior to behavioral intervention and better than medication alone for most outcome measures (Edwards, 2002).

Clinical research shows that prolonged exposure therapy (an integrative CBT approach) is effective, substantially reducing symptoms of PTSD over extended periods of up to 18 months after treatment is complete (Foa et al., 1999). Also, prolonged exposure therapy shows substantial benefits compared to no therapy, supportive counseling, and other procedures designed to reduce stress, although it has still not been widely adopted by clinicians (Cahill et al., 2006).

The advantage of MBCT compared with standard cognitive therapy is that it works when the person is in a nondepressive state, and so it might help prevent relapse. One study shows that MBCT can prevent relapse in people who have had at least three previous depressive episodes. All participants had recently completed successful drug therapy for their most recent bout of depression. They were then randomly assigned to participate in MBCT or to continue with the treatment they otherwise would have received (treatment as usual), which included seeking help from other sources, such as family or doctor (Segal, Williams, & Teasdale, 2002). Figure 16.10 shows that those who practiced MBCT relapsed into depression only about half as often as those who received treatment as usual (Teasdale et al., 2000).

Borderline personality disorder has long been considered nearly untreatable, but DBT is quite effective in reducing the symptoms of this disorder. It has been shown to reduce self-inflicted harmful behaviors, to lower scores on depression questionnaires, to decrease dysfunctional patterns associated

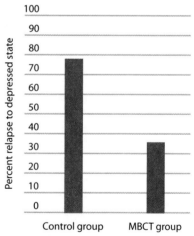

FIGURE **16.10**

EFFECTIVENESS OF MINDFULNESS-BASED COGNITIVE THERAPY (MBCT) FOR DEPRESSION. When people with depression were treated with mindfulness-based cognitive therapy, they were much less likely to experience a relapse compared to a comparison group of people with depression who received treatment as usual. (*Source:* Teasdale et al., 2000.)

with substance abuse, and to increase the likelihood of staying in treatment (Kröger, et al, 2006; Koerner & Linehan, 2000; Linehan, Heard, & Armstrong, 1993). Most important, DBT reduces the risk of suicide attempts—the most disastrous risk associated with borderline personality disorder—much more than does nonbehavioral psychotherapy (Linehan et al., 2006). Not only is DBT effective in treating borderline personality disorder, but it has also been adapted to treat eating disorders, conduct disorders, and domestic violence (Kristeller, Baer, & Quillian-Wolever, 2006; Nelson-Gray et al., 2006; Rathus, Cavuoto, & Passarelli, 2006).

nature & nurture
Used together, psychotherapy and mindfulness training can rewire brain circuits in people with OCD.

The last combined mindfulness technique is the Four Steps. It may take several months to progress through the Four Steps. But the treatment appears to work. In fact, Four Steps training not only helps break the thinking-behavioral cycles of OCD but also (or for this reason) changes the brain circuitry that appears to support repetitive thinking and behavior Schwartz (2000). People with OCD have dramatically increased activity in the areas of the frontal cortex and caudate nucleus.

connection
PET, a form of brain imaging predating fMRI, measures metabolism in the brain.
See Chapter 3, p. 115.

These areas tend to be active in healthy people when events in one's environment deviate from what is expected (Schwartz, 2000). As people with OCD are constantly checking their environment for things that could be wrong, overactivation in the caudate nucleus area seems consistent with this disorder. PET studies reveal decreases in caudate nucleus metabolism in people who respond to the Four Steps treatment (Schwartz, 1999). This is consistent with other findings that CBT reduces overactivation in the caudate nucleus of people with OCD (Linden, 2006).

quick quiz 16.4: Effectiveness of Treatments

1. Both traditional and atypical antipsychotic drugs work best on the _____ symptoms of schizophrenia, but are generally less effective on the _____ symptoms. (Pick the best pair of words to fill in the blanks.)
   a. negative; positive
   b. positive; negative
   c. cognitive; emotional
   d. emotional; cognitive

2. _____ exposure is a form of systematic desensitization that is very effective but has a high drop-out rate.
   a. Imagined
   b. Virtual reality
   c. Twelve-step
   d. In vivo

3. According to the research presented in Figure 16.9, which is more effective in decreasing depression, cognitive therapy (CT) or antidepressant medication (Paxil)?
   a. CT
   b. Paxil
   c. they are equally effective
   d. neither; the MAO inhibitors are best

Answers can be found at the end of the chapter.

making connections
in the Treatment of Psychological Disorders

Approaches to the Treatment of Anxiety Disorders

The anxiety disorders are a diverse group of conditions, and although they share the core symptoms of fear and anxiety, they differ in many ways. Because they are so diverse, mental health practitioners employ a wide variety of treatment strategies to help people with these disorders. Because of this diversity in symptoms and treatment, the anxiety disorders offer a useful context in which to illustrate the application of treatments discussed in this chapter.

Drug Therapies

Drug therapies play a major role in the management and treatment of anxiety disorders. The main categories of medications used for anxiety disorders include the antidepressants and the antianxiety drugs.

Antidepressants

Many doctors prescribe SSRIs for the treatment of anxiety disorders, especially for OCD, social phobia, post-traumatic stress disorder (PTSD), and panic disorder. People who take SSRIs for anxiety disorders report that these medications help them avoid getting caught up in certain thoughts that otherwise would snowball into anxiety. These drugs appear to help people disengage from the repetitive cycle of anxiety-provoking thoughts or simply not care as much about such thoughts. As a result, the SSRIs have been helpful to people with OCD and may aid in changing patterns of thinking when combined with the thought restructuring produced by CBT. As mentioned earlier, the drugs help loosen the grip of anxious thinking, allowing the patient to apply cognitive techniques to learn how to think differently. Recent findings that people with OCD who take SSRIs often relapse suggest that combining these drugs with psychological treatments might be more effective than the drugs alone (Catapano et al., 2006). The SSRIs are also considered the first line of treatment for generalized anxiety disorder (Baldwin & Polkinghorn, 2005).

Other antidepressants are prescribed for anxiety disorders, but much less often. Most tricyclic antidepressants apparently do not work for people with OCD, for example, but do work for other anxiety disorders. One tricyclic, CMI, however, is most effective on norepinephrine synapses and actually reduces symptoms of OCD. Because tricyclics have numerous side effects, medical professionals tend to prescribe SSRIs instead (Bleier, Habib, & Flament, 2006).

Antianxiety Medications

Drugs that soothe the agitation of anxiety are used to treat anxiety disorders, especially for people who suffer from panic attacks. Occasionally physicians prescribe beta-blockers—drugs that block the action of neurotransmitters such as norepinephrine—to quickly calm the aroused sympathetic nervous system. One such drug is propanolol, which is often used to treat high blood pressure and other cardiovascular conditions. These medications calm the physiological symptoms of anxiety by bringing down heart rate, blood pressure, and rate of breathing.

The benzodiazepines (for example, Valium) also calm the physiological arousal caused by anxiety and are widely prescribed for social phobias, panic disorder, and generalized anxiety disorder. They can also treat or prevent panic attacks in high-anxiety situations. Unfortunately, when regular users discontinue use of benzodiazepines they experience withdrawal symptoms such as insomnia, tremors, increased anxiety, tachycardia (rapid heartbeat), and sweating. Hence, the benzodiazepines are best used only occasionally. Newer antianxiety medications, such as a drug used for generalized anxiety disorder known as buspirone, are less likely to create withdrawal symptoms, but they require longer continuous usage to be effective.

Psychotherapeutic Treatments

As we have seen, cognitive–behavioral therapy helps people with anxiety disorder identify irrational thoughts and undo thinking patterns that support fear; it also helps them modify their responses to anxiety-provoking situations. Group CBT therapy is very effective for the treatment of social phobia (Hofman et al., 2006). Such contexts usually involve weekly meetings for about 12 weeks, as well as homework assignments each week. In addition to the normal benefits of CBT for reducing anxious thoughts and behaviors, the social factors involved in a group play a key role in the therapy's effectiveness. The group offers social support: All the participants have gone through similar situations and can share their experiences. This support helps prevent feelings of isolation and helplessness. Also, group members provide examples of success. For instance, if someone in a social phobia group managed to go to a deli, order a sandwich, and pay the cashier (simple social transactions) and it went well, this provides an example that it really can be done. Other group members might be inspired to try it themselves.

Traditional psychodynamic therapies for anxiety disorders viewed anxiety as the main symptom of what was then commonly called neurosis. Neuroses, according to Freud, most often stemmed from repressed thoughts, feelings, and impulses that usually originated in childhood experiences. Therefore, the main approach to treatment is to uncover the unconscious thoughts, feelings, and impulses that lead to neurotic symptoms. Most commonly, this is achieved through dream interpretation, free associations, uncovering defense mechanisms, and catharsis. Relieving neurotic symptoms requires insight, and insight requires emotional release of repressed feelings.

We have already discussed the use of systematic desensitization for the treatment of specific phobias. This process couples relaxation training with gradual exposure to the feared object and is very effective for the treatment of specific phobias such as fears of animals, flying, and heights (Aitken & Benson, 1984; Wiederhold & Wiederhold, 2005).

As we have seen, sometimes medication can help people get "over the hump" of crippling symptoms so that a nondrug therapy has a chance to work. Such is the case with the combination of either antidepressants or antianxiety medications and CBT or systematic desensitization. Often the course of medication treatment is short term, until the psychotherapeutic training begins to take effect. Alternatively, the medication may be decreased slowly during the course of psychological treatment. Although many people recommend combined therapies, a recent review of the treatment efficacy of combined therapies versus single therapy for anxiety disorders yielded little consistent evidence that combined therapy works better (Black, 2006).

Integrative Therapies and Anxiety

There is evidence that integrative psychotherapeutic approaches offer potential relief from a range of anxiety disorders. As already noted, OCD may be treated with mindfulness meditation practices and cognitive therapy. Mindfulness-based cognitive therapy shows promise in the treatment of generalized anxiety disorder (Evans et al., 2008). Also, dialectical behavior therapy (DBT), which was developed to treat borderline personality disorder, has been used effectively to treat post-traumatic stress disorder (Wagner & Linehan, 2006).

quick quiz 16.5: Making Connections in the Treatment of Psychological Disorders

1. These drugs appear to help people with OCD disengage from the repetitive cycle of anxiety-provoking thoughts:
   a. SSRIs
   b. MAO inhibitors
   c. benzodiazepines
   d. lithium salts

2. Group CBT therapy is very effective for the treatment of which anxiety disorder?
   a. generalized anxiety disorder
   b. social phobia
   c. panic disorder
   d. simple phobias

Answers can be found at the end of the chapter.

chapter **review**

BIOLOGICAL TREATMENTS

- Both biological and psychological approaches are used to treat psychological disorders. Drugs are the most commonly used biological treatment.

- Many different drugs are used to treat depression. The older antidepressants include the monoamine oxidase (MAO) inhibitors and the tricyclic antidepressants. The selective serotonin reuptake inhibitors (SSRIs) reduce reuptake of serotonin at the synapse and create far fewer unpleasant side effects than the older antidepressants.

- Lithium is prescribed to stabilize the mania associated with bipolar disorder. Due to the toxicity of lithium, medical professionals often prescribe other drugs to regulate manic episodes.

- Drug therapies for schizophrenia include the traditional antipsychotics, which are rarely prescribed these days due to their adverse side effects, and the atypical antipsychotics. The atypical antipsychotics do not lead to tardive dyskinesia, but they are somewhat better at treating negative symptoms.

- Psychosurgery is brain surgery performed to treat psychological disorders. Prefrontal lobotomy was once used to reduce psychotic behavior, but it is now considered an outdated and cruel procedure.

- Electroconvulsive therapy (ECT) involves passing electrical current through the brain to induce a seizure. Because ECT can lead to memory loss, the only currently acceptable clinical application of ECT is for cases of severe depression that fail to respond to any other treatment.

- Helen Mayberg discovered what may be a neural switch for depression, known as Area 25. Deep brain stimulation of Area 25 can provide sudden relief from depression in people who have failed to respond to all other treatments.

PSYCHOLOGICAL TREATMENTS

- Psychotherapy is the use of psychological techniques to modify maladaptive behaviors or thought patterns, or both, and develop insight into the patient's behavior.

- The aim of psychodynamic therapies is to uncover unconscious conflicts or motives underlying

psychological problems or symptoms. Psychodynamic therapists use several techniques, such as free association, to access the unconscious.

- Humanistic therapy, such as client-centered therapy, helps clients realize their full potential. Therapists create an atmosphere in which clients can communicate their feelings with the certainty that they are being understood rather than judged.

- Behavior therapies apply the principles of conditioning to the treatment of disorders. Systematic desensitization, a widely used behavioral method, pairs relaxation with gradual exposure to a phobic object.

- Cognitive therapies work to restructure irrational thought patterns. Often therapists combine cognitive techniques for changing irrational thoughts with behavioral techniques to shape desirable behaviors in what is known as cognitive–behavioral therapy (CBT). CBT is a short-term psychological treatment that has been successfully applied to many disorders.

COMBINED APPROACHES

- Combined treatments are increasingly common in practice. These include methods that combine drugs with psychotherapy or combine various forms of psychotherapy with each other. Mindfulness practices have also been added to traditional treatments.

- Many treatments, including CBT, are administered as group therapy. Group contexts serve both as a source of support and as an aid to the therapeutic process, allowing several people with similar problems to listen, discuss, and criticize one another.

EFFECTIVENESS OF TREATMENTS

- The SSRIs and tricyclics are equally effective in the treatment of depression. The SSRIs have the fewest adverse side effects, and seem to be tolerated better for long-term use.

- The evidence for lithium's effectiveness in treating bipolar disorder is weak in spite of its regular use for this purpose in the United States. It does not appear to be superior to less toxic anticonvulsants or antipsychotics in regulating manic episodes.

- Both traditional and atypical antipsychotic drugs work best on the positive symptoms of schizophrenia. Certain atypical antipsychotic drugs may relieve the negative symptoms.

- Although many patients report immediate relief with ECT, usually it is effective only as long as treatments are maintained. Also, the adverse effects of ECT on memory can be fairly severe.

- Psychotherapy is more effective for certain disorders than for others. CBT may be the most effective form of psychotherapy, especially for certain cases of depression and anxiety disorders.

- In some cases, the most effective treatments for many psychological disorders integrate one form of treatment with another.

MAKING CONNECTIONS IN THE TREATMENT OF DISORDERS

- The treatment of anxiety disorders illustrates how diverse approaches may be used to treat psychological disorders. Both psychological and biological therapies have been used, alone and together to treat anxiety disorders.

key terms

atypical antipsychotics, p. 617

barbiturates, p. 616

behavior therapies, p. 626

benzodiazepines, p. 616

bupropione, p. 616

catharsis, p. 626

client-centered therapy, p. 626

cognitive therapy, p. 628

cognitive–behavioral therapy, p. 630

defense mechanisms, p. 626

dialectical behavior therapy (DBT), p. 636

electroconvulsive therapy (ECT), p. 619

evidence-based therapies, p. 639

flooding, p. 628

free association, p. 625

group therapy, p. 630

integrative therapy, p. 634

lithium, p. 616

mindfulness-based cognitive therapy (MBCT), p. 635

monoamine oxidase (MAO) inhibitors, p. 614

phenothiazines, p. 617

prefrontal lobotomy, p. 618

psychodynamic psychotherapy, p. 625

psychotherapy, p. 624

repetitive transcranial magnetic stimulation, p. 620

repression, p. 626

selective serotonin reuptake inhibitors (SSRIs), p. 615

support groups, p. 631

systematic desensitization, p. 627

tardive dyskinesia, p. 617

token economies, p. 626

traditional antipsychotics, p. 617

transference, p. 625

tricyclic antidepressants, p. 614

unconditional positive regard, p. 626

quick quiz answers

Quick Quiz 16.1: 1. c 2. c 3. d 4. b   Quick Quiz 16.2: 1. a 2. d 3. a 4. b   Quick Quiz 16.3: 1. c 2. b 3. d
Quick Quiz 16.4: 1. b 2. d 3. c   Quick Quiz 16.5: 1. a 2. b

glossary

absent-mindedness a form of forgetfulness that results from inattention.

absolute threshold the lowest intensity level of a stimulus a person can detect half of the time.

accommodation the process by which the muscles control the shape of the lens to adjust to viewing objects at different distances.

acetylcholine (ACh) a neurotransmitter that controls muscle movement and plays a role in mental processes such as learning, memory, attention, sleeping, and dreaming.

achievement motivation a desire to do things well and overcome obstacles.

acquired immunity immunity provided by antibodies produced in the body in response to specific antigens.

action potential the impulse of positive charge that runs down an axon.

adaptations inherited solutions to ancestral problems that have been selected for because they contribute in some way to reproductive success.

adaptive behavior adjustment to and coping with everyday life.

adolescence the transition period between childhood and adulthood.

adoption studies research into hereditary influence in which adopted people are compared to their biological and adoptive parents.

adrenal glands endocrine structures that release hormones important in regulating the stress response and emotions.

adrenal-medullary system a major neuro-endocrine pathway stimulated during stress, in which the hypothalamus activates the sympathetic nervous system.

affective traits stable predispositions toward certain types of emotional responses.

afterimages visual images that remain after removal of or looking away from the stimulus.

aggression violent behavior that is intended to cause psychological or physical harm, or both, to another being.

agoraphobia an anxiety disorder involving fear of being in places from which escape might be difficult or in which help might not be available should a panic attack occur.

AIM three biologically based dimensions of consciousness—Activation, Input, and Mode.

alarm stage the phase of the general adaptation syndrome in which all of the body's resources respond to a perceived threat.

algorithms a step-by-step procedure or formula for solving a problem.

alleles different forms of a gene.

all-or-none principle the idea that once the threshold has been crossed, an action potential either fires or it does not; there is no halfway.

allostasis process by which the body achieves stability through physiological change.

alpha waves pattern of brain activity when one is relaxed and drowsy; slower, higher-energy waves than beta waves.

altruism selfless attitudes and behavior toward others.

Alzheimer's disease a degenerative disease marked by progressive cognitive decline and characterized by a collection of symptoms, including confusion, memory loss, mood swings, and eventual loss of physical function.

amnesia memory loss due to brain injury or disease.

amygdala a small, almond-shaped structure located directly in front of the hippocampus; has connections with many important brain regions and is important for processing emotional information, especially that related to fear.

anima according to Jung, the female part of the male personality.

animistic thinking belief that inanimate objects are alive.

animus according to Jung, the male part of the female personality.

anorexia nervosa an eating disorder in which people cannot maintain 85% of their ideal body weight for their height, have an intense fear of eating, and have a distorted body image.

antecedent event a situation that may lead to an emotional response.

anterograde amnesia the inability to remember events and experiences that occur after an injury or the onset of a disease.

antigen any foreign substance that triggers an immune response.

antisocial personality disorder dramatic–emotional personality disorder characterized by extremely impulsive, deceptive, violent, ruthless, and callous behaviors; a serious and potentially dangerous disorder.

anxious-avoidant attachment style characterized by infants who stay calm when their primary caregiver leaves and who ignore and avoid her when she returns.

anxious-resistant attachment attachment style characterized by infants who are ambivalent when separated and reunited with their caregiver.

aphasia deficit in the ability to speak or comprehend language.

appraisal the evaluation of a situation with respect to how relevant it is to one's own welfare; it drives the process by which emotions are elicited.

arborization the growth and formation of new dendrites.

archetypes ancient or archaic images that result from common ancestral experiences.

Asperger's syndrome a childhood disorder at the high-functioning end of the autistic spectrum; characterized by impaired social interest and skills and restricted interests; intelligence is usually above average and language is not delayed or deficient.

association process by which two pieces of information from the environment are repeatedly linked so that we begin to connect them in our minds.

asylums facilities for treating the mentally ill in Europe during the Middle Ages and into the 19th century.

attachment the strong emotional connection that develops early in life between infants and their caregivers.

attention the limited capacity to process information that is under conscious control.

attention deficit hyperactivity disorder (ADHD) childhood disorder characterized by inability to focus attention for more than a few minutes, to remain still and quiet, to do careful work.

attitude an individual's favorable or unfavorable beliefs, feelings, or actions toward an object, idea, or person.

attributions inferences made about the causes of other people's behavior.

atypical antipsychotics newer antipsychotic drugs, which do not create tardive dyskinesia.

auditory nerve the nerve that receives action potentials from the hair cells and transmits auditory information to the brain.

autistic disorder or autism childhood disorder characterized by severe language and social impairment along with repetitive habits and inward-focused behaviors. Symptoms may be a result of oversensitivity to sensory stimulation and problems integrating multiple sources of such stimulation.

automatic processing encoding of information that occurs with little effort or conscious attention to the task.

autonomic nervous system (ANS) all the nerves of the peripheral nervous system that serve involuntary systems of the body, such as the internal organs and glands.

availability heuristic a device we use to make decisions based on the ease with which estimates come to mind or how available they are to our awareness.

avoidant personality disorder anxious–fearful personality disorder characterized by extreme fear of being criticized, low self-esteem, and avoidance of social interaction.

awareness monitoring of information from the environment and from one's own thoughts.

Axis I disorders in the *DSM-IV-TR*, the major clinical syndromes that cause significant impairment.

Axis II disorders in the *DSM-IV-TR*, the more long-standing personality disorders as well as mental retardation.

axon a long projection that extends from a neuron's soma; it transmits electrical impulses toward the adjacent neuron and stimulates the release of neurotransmitters.

babbling sounds made as a result of the infant's experimentation with a complex range of phonemes, which include consonants as well as vowels; starts around 5–6 months.

barbiturates a class of anxiety-reducing sedatives that can be addictive and carry a risk of overdose.

basal ganglia a collection of structures surrounding the thalamus involved in voluntary motor control.

basic emotions set of emotions that are common to all humans; includes anger, disgust, fear, happiness, sadness, and surprise.

basic tendencies the essence of personality: the Big Five personality dimensions as well as talents, aptitudes, and cognitive abilities.

basilar membrane a membrane that runs through the cochlea; contains the hair cells.

behavior modification principles of operant conditioning used to change behavior.

behavior therapies therapies that apply the principles of classical and operant conditioning in the treatment of psychological disorders.

behavioral genetics the scientific study of the role of heredity in behavior.

behavioral measures measures based on systematic observation of people's actions either in their normal environment or in a laboratory setting.

behavioral neuroscience study of the links among brain, mind, and behavior.

behavioral thresholds the point at which a person moves from not having a particular response to having one.

behaviorism a school of psychology that proposed that psychology can be a true science only if it examines observable behavior, not ideas, thoughts, feelings, or motives.

benzodiazepines a class of anxiety-reducing drugs that can be addictive, but are less dangerous than barbiturates.

beta waves pattern of brain activity when one is awake; a rapid, low-energy wave.

Big Five or **five-factor model** a theory of personality that includes the following five dimensions: openness to experience, conscientiousness, extraversion, agreeableness, and neuroticism (OCEAN).

binocular depth cues aids to depth perception that rely on input from both eyes.

biological constraint model a view on learning which proposes that some behaviors are inherently more likely to be learned than others.

biological psychology the study of the relationship between bodily systems and chemicals and how they influence behavior and thought.

bipolar disorder mood disorder characterized by substantial mood fluctuations, cycling between very low (depressive) and very high (manic) moods.

blocking the inability to retrieve some information once it is stored.

bodily senses the senses based in the skin, body, or any membrane surfaces.

borderline personality disorder dramatic–emotional personality disorder characterized by out-of-control emotions, fear of being abandoned by others, and a vacillation between idealizing and despising people who are close to the person with the disorder.

bottom-up processing idea that perception is a process of building a perceptual experience from smaller pieces.

broad intelligence one of Carroll's three levels of intelligence that includes abilities such as crystallized and fluid intelligence, as well as memory, learning, and processing speed.

broaden-and-build model Fredrickson's model for positive emotions, which posits that they widen our cognitive perspective and help us acquire useful life skills.

Broca's area an area in the left frontal lobe responsible for the ability to produce speech.

bulimia nervosa an eating disorder characterized by binge eating and a perceived lack of control during the eating session.

bupropione a widely used antidepressant that inhibits the reuptake of norepinephrine and dopamine.

bystander effect phenomenon in which the greater the number of bystanders who witness an emergency, the less likely any one of them is to help.

cardiovascular reactivity (CVR) model hypothesis that hostility can increase the likelihood of heart disease through at least two different causal routes.

cardiovascular system the heart, blood, and all the blood vessels.

case study a study design in which a psychologist, often a therapist, observes one person over a long period of time.

catatonic schizophrenia subtype of schizophrenia characterized by two of the following symptoms: extreme immobility, excessive activity, peculiar posturing, mutism, or parroting what other people say.

catecholamines chemicals released from the adrenal glands that function as hormones and as neurotransmitters to control ANS activation.

category a concept that organizes other concepts around what they all share in common.

catharsis the process of releasing intense, often unconscious, emotions in a therapeutic setting.

causal inferences judgments about causation of one thing by another.

cellular immunity the immune response that occurs when the T lymphocytes (T cells) fight antigens.

central nervous system (CNS) the part of the nervous system that comprises the brain and spinal cord.

cerebellum a hindbrain structure involved in body movement, balance, coordination, fine-tuning motor skills, and cognitive activities such as learning and language.

cerebral cortex the thin outer layer of the cerebrum, in which much of human thought, planning, perception, and consciousness takes place.

cerebrum each of the large halves of the brain that are covered with convolutions, or folds.

child-directed speech changes in adult speech patterns—apparently universal—when speaking to young children or infants; characterized by higher pitch, changes in voice volume, use of simpler sentences, emphasis on the here and now, and use of emotion to communicate messages.

chromosomes a coiled-up thread of DNA.

chunking the process of breaking down a list of items to be remembered into a smaller set of meaningful units.

cingulate gyrus a beltlike structure in the middle of the brain that plays an important role in attention and cognitive control.

circadian rhythms the variations in physiological processes that cycle within approximately a 24-hour period, including the sleep–wake cycle.

classical conditioning form of associative learning in which a neutral stimulus becomes associated with a stimulus to which one has an automatic, inborn response.

client-centered therapy a form of humanistic therapy in which the therapist shows unconditional positive regard for the patient.

clinical psychology the treatment of mental, emotional, and behavioral disorders and the promotion of psychological health.

cochlea a bony tube of the inner ear, which is curled like a snail's shell and filled with fluid.

cognition mental processes involved in acquiring, processing, and storing knowledge.

cognitive dissonance the feeling of discomfort caused by information that is different from a person's conception of himself or herself as a reasonable and sensible person.

cognitive psychology the study of how people perceive, remember, think, speak, and solve problems.

cognitive symptoms (of schizophrenia) problems with working memory, attention, verbal and visual learning and memory, reasoning and problem solving, processing, and speech.

cognitive–behavioral therapy an approach to treating psychological disorders that combines techniques for restructuring irrational thoughts with operant and classical conditioning techniques to shape desirable behaviors.

cognitive therapy any type of psychotherapy that works to restructure irrational thought patterns.

collective unconscious according to Jung, form of consciousness that consists of the shared experiences of our ancestors—God, mother, life, death, water, earth, aggression, survival—that have been passed down from generation to generation.

coma a state of consciousness in which the eyes are closed and the person is unresponsive and unarousable.

comorbidity occurrence of two or more disorders at the same time.

compulsion a repetitive behavior performed in response to uncontrollable urges or according to a ritualistic set of rules.

concept a mental grouping of objects, events, or people.

concept hierarchy arrangement of related concepts in a particular way, with some being general and others specific.

concrete operational stage Piaget's third stage of cognitive development, which spans ages 6–11, during which the child can perform mental operations—such as reversing—on real objects or events.

conditioned response (CR) a behavior that an organism learns to perform when presented with the CS.

conditioned stimulus (CS) a previously neutral input that an organism learns to associate with the UCS.

conditioned taste aversion the learned avoidance of a particular taste or food.

conditioning a form of associative learning in which behaviors are triggered by associations with events in the environment.

conduct disorder childhood disorder characterized by aggression toward people and animals, destruction of property, lying and stealing, and serious violations of rules.

cones photoreceptors that are responsible for color vision and are most functional in conditions of bright light.

confirmation bias the tendency to selectively attend to information that supports one's general beliefs while ignoring information or evidence that contradicts one's beliefs.

conformity tendency of people to adjust their behavior to what others are doing or to adhere to the norms of their culture.

confounding variable variable whose influence on the dependent variable cannot be separated from the independent variable being examined.

consciousness an awareness of one's surroundings and of what's in one's mind at a given moment; includes aspects of being awake and aware.

conservation recognition that when some properties (such as shape) of an object change, other properties (such as volume) remain constant.

consistency bias selective recall of past events to fit our current beliefs.

consolidation the process of establishing, stabilizing, or solidifying a memory; the second stage of long-term memory formation.

construct validity the degree to which a test measures the concept it claims to measure, such as intelligence.

continuous reinforcement reinforcement of a behavior every time it occurs.

contralaterality the fact that one side of the brain controls movement on the opposite side.

control group a group of research participants who are treated in exactly the same manner as the experimental group, except that they do not receive the independent variable or treatment.

conventional level the second level in Kohlberg's theory of moral reasoning, during which the person values caring, trust, and relationships as well as the social order and lawfulness.

convergence a binocular depth cue: the way in which the eyes move inward as an object moves closer to you.

convergent thinking problems problems that have known solutions and require analytic thinking and the use of learned strategies and knowledge to come up with the correct answer.

cooing the first sounds humans make other than crying, consisting almost exclusively of vowels; occurs during first 6 months of life.

coping act of dealing with stress or emotions.

cornea the clear hard covering that protects the lens of the eye.

corpus callosum the nerve fibers that connect the two hemispheres of the brain.

correlation coefficient a statistic that ranges from –1.0 to +1.0 and assesses the strength and direction of association between two variables.

correlational designs studies that measure two or more variables and their relationship to one another; not designed to show causation.

cortical arousal level of activation in the brain.

cortisol the stress hormone produced by the body to ensure that the body gets enough fuel during emotional arousal and stress.

creativity thinking and/or behavior that is both novel–original and useful–adaptive.

critical period specific period in development when individuals are most receptive to a particular kind of input from the environment (such as visual stimulation and language).

critical thinking process by which one analyzes, evaluates, and forms ideas.

crystallized intelligence the kind of knowledge that one gains from experience and learning, education, and practice

cult an extremist group led by a charismatic, totalitarian leader in which coercive methods are used to prevent members from leaving the group.

cultural test bias hypothesis the notion that group differences in IQ scores are caused by different cultural and educational backgrounds, not by real differences in intelligence.

culturally relative term describing the idea that behavior varies across cultures and can only be understood within the social laws, rules, or norms of the culture in which they occur; refers to the concept of cultural relativism.

cyclothymia a relatively mild form of bipolar disorder.

dark adaptation process of adjustment to seeing in the dark.

debriefing the explanation of the purposes of a study following data collection.

deductive reasoning reasoning from general statements of what is known to specific conclusions.

defense mechanisms unconscious strategies the mind uses to protect itself from anxiety by denying and distorting reality in some way.

delta waves type of brain activity that dominates Stage 3 sleep; higher energy than theta wave.

delusion one of the symptoms of schizophrenia: a false belief or exaggeration held despite evidence to the contrary; such as the idea that one is a famous person.

dementia a loss of mental function, in which many cognitive processes are impaired, such as the ability to remember, reason, solve problems, make decisions, and use language.

dendrites fingerlike projections from a neuron's soma that receive incoming messages from other neurons.

dependent personality disorder anxious–fearful personality disorder characterized by fear of being rejected and having a strong need to be cared for.

dependent variable in an experiment, the outcome or response to the experimental manipulation.

depressants substances that decrease or slow down central nervous system activity.

depth perception the ability to see things in three dimensions and to discriminate what is near from what is far.

descriptive designs study designs in which the researcher defines a problem and variable of interest but makes no prediction and does not control or manipulate anything.

descriptive statistics measures used to describe and summarize research.

developmental psychology study of how thought and behavior change and remain stable across the life span.

dialectical behavior therapy (DBT) treatment that integrates elements of CBT with exercises aimed at developing mindfulness without meditation and is used to treat borderline personality disorders.

diathesis–stress model explanation for the origin of psychological disorders as a combination of biological predispositions (diathesis) plus stress or an abusive environment.

difference threshold the smallest amount of change between two stimuli that a person can detect half of the time.

discrimination preferential treatment of certain people, usually driven by prejudicial attitudes.

disorganized schizophrenia subtype of schizophrenia characterized by disorganized speech and behavior and flat or inappropriate affect.

display rules learned norms or rules, often taught very early, about when it is appropriate to express certain emotions and to whom one should show them.

dissociative amnesia an extensive form of amnesia that results from painful or traumatic experiences; it is a detachment from the experience, rather than a reliving of it, as is seen in post-traumatic stress disorder.

dissociative disorders psychological disorders characterized by extreme splits or gaps in memory, identity, or consciousness.

dissociative fugue form of dissociative disorder characterized not only by amnesia

but also by fleeing to a new location and establishing a new identity.

dissociative identity disorder (DID) dissociative disorder in which a person develops at least two distinct personalities, each with its own memories, thoughts, behaviors, and emotions. Some psychiatrists question the legitimacy of the disorder.

divergent thinking problems problems that have no known solutions and require novel solutions.

DNA (deoxyribonucleic acid) a large molecule that contains genes.

dominant genes genes that show their effect even if there is only one allele for that trait in the pair.

dopamine a neurotransmitter released in response to behaviors that feel good or are rewarding to the person or animal; also involved in voluntary motor control.

double-blind studies studies in which neither the participants nor the researchers administering the treatment know who has been assigned to the experimental or control group.

Down syndrome a chromosomal disorder characterized by mild to profound mental retardation.

dreams images, thoughts, and feelings experienced during sleep.

drives the perceived states of tension that occur when our bodies are deficient in some need, creating an urge to relieve the tension.

Duchenne smile a smile that expresses true enjoyment, involving both the muscles that pull up the lip corners diagonally and those that contract the band of muscles encircling the eye.

dysthymia form of depression that is milder in intensity than major depressive disorder.

educational psychology the study of how students learn, the effectiveness of particular teaching techniques, the social psychology of schools, and the psychology of teaching.

effect size a measure of the strength of the relationship between two variables or the extent of an experimental effect.

effortful processing encoding of information that occurs with careful attention and conscious effort.

ego one of Freud's provinces of the mind; a sense of self; the only part of the mind that is in direct contact with the outside world: operates on the "reality principle."

egocentrism viewing the world from one's own perspective and not being capable of seeing things from another person's perspective.

electroconvulsive therapy (ECT) treatment of last resort for severe depression that involves passing an electrical current through a person's brain in order to induce a seizure.

electroencephalography (EEG) a method for measuring brain activity in which the electrical activity of the brain is recorded from electrodes placed on a person's scalp.

embryo the term for the developing organism from 2 weeks until about 8 weeks after conception.

embryonic stage the second prenatal stage, from 2 weeks to 8 weeks after conception, when all of the major organs form.

emotion regulation the cognitive and behavioral efforts people make to modify their emotions.

emotional competence the ability to control emotions and know when it is appropriate to express certain emotions.

emotional disclosure way of coping with stress through writing or talking about the situation.

emotional response the physiological, behavioral/expressive, and subjective changes that occur when emotions are generated.

emotion-focused coping way of dealing with stress that aims to regulate the experience of distress.

emotions brief, acute changes in conscious experience and physiology that occur in response to a personally meaningful situation.

empathy the ability to share the feelings of others and understand their situations.

empathy-altruism hypothesis the idea that people help others selflessly only when they feel empathy for them.

empirical method a method for developing questionnaire items that focuses on including questions that characterize the group the questionnaire is intended to distinguish.

empiricism the view that all knowledge and thoughts come from experience.

enactive learning learning by doing.

encoding the process by which the brain attends to, takes in, and integrates new information; the first stage of long-term memory formation.

endocannabinoids natural, marijuana-like substances produced by the body.

endocrine system system of glands that secrete and regulate hormones in the body.

enzymatic degradation a way of removing excess neurotransmitter from the synapse, in which enzymes specific for that neurotransmitter bind with the neurotransmitter and destroy it.

epigenetics concerns changes in the way genes are turned on or off without a change in the sequence of DNA.

epinephrine also known as adrenaline, a neurotransmitter that arouses bodily systems (such as increasing heart rate).

episodic memory form of memory that recalls the experiences we have had.

ethics the rules governing the conduct of a person or group in general or in a specific situation—or more simply, standards of right and wrong.

ethology the scientific study of animal behavior.

Eureka insight or insight solutions sudden solutions that come to mind in a flash.

event-related potential (ERP) a special technique that extracts electrical activity from raw EEG data to measure cognitive processes.

evidence-based therapies treatment choices based on empirical evidence that they produce the desired outcome.

evolution the change over time in the frequency with which specific genes occur within a breeding species.

evolutionary psychology the branch of psychology that studies human behavior by asking what adaptive problems it may have solved for our early ancestors.

exhaustion stage the phase of the general adaptation syndrome when all resources for fighting the threat have been depleted and illness is more likely.

experiment a research design that includes independent and dependent variables and random assignment of participants to control and experimental groups or conditions.

experimental group a group consisting of those participants who will receive the treatment or whatever is predicted to change behavior.

experimenter expectancy effects result that occurs when the behavior of the participants is influenced by the experimenter's knowledge of who is in the control group and who is the experimental group.

explicit memory knowledge that consists of the conscious recall of facts and events; also known as declarative memory.

expressive-suppression a response-focused strategy for regulating emotion that involves the deliberate attempt to inhibit the outward manifestation of an emotion.

extinction the weakening and disappearance of a conditioned response in the absence of reinforcement.

Facial Action Coding System (FACS) a widely used method for measuring all observable muscular movements that are possible in the human face.

false memories memories for events that never happened, but were suggested by someone or something.

feature detectors neurons in the visual cortex that analyze the retinal image and respond to specific aspects of shapes, such as angles and movements.

fetal alcohol spectrum disorder a consequence of prenatal alcohol exposure that causes multiple problems, notably brain damage.

fetal stage the third prenatal stage, which begins with the formation of bone cells 8 weeks after conception and ends at birth.

fixation a defense mechanism whereby a person continues to be concerned and even preoccupied with earlier stages of development. Occurs when stages are left unresolved.

fixed interval (FI) schedule a pattern of intermittent reinforcement in which responses are always reinforced after a set period of time has passed.

fixed ratio (FR) schedule pattern of intermittent reinforcement in which reinforcement follows a set number of responses.

flexibility of thought the ability to come up with many different categories of ideas and think of other responses besides the obvious one.

flooding an extreme form of in vivo exposure in which the client experiences extreme exposure to the phobic object.

fluid intelligence raw mental ability, pattern recognition, abstract reasoning that can be applied to a problem one has never confronted before.

forensic psychology field that blends psychology, law, and criminal justice.

forgetting the weakening or loss of memories over time.

forgetting curve a graphic depiction of how recall steadily declines over time.

formal operational stage Piaget's final stage of cognitive development, from age 11 or 12 on through adulthood, when formal logic is possible.

fovea spot on the back of the retina that contains the highest concentration of cones in the retina; place of clearest vision.

fraternal twins twins that develop from two different eggs fertilized by two different sperm.

free association a psychotherapeutic technique in which the client takes one image or idea from a dream and says whatever comes to mind, regardless of how threatening, disgusting, or troubling it may be.

functional fixedness mind-set in which one is blind to unusual uses of common everyday things or procedures.

functional magnetic resonance imaging (fMRI) brain imaging technique that uses magnetic fields to produce detailed images of activity in areas of the brain and other soft tissues.

functionalism 19th-century school of psychology that argued it was better to look at why the mind works the way it does than to describe its parts.

fundamental attribution error the tendency to explain others' behavior in dispositional rather than situational terms.

GABA (gamma-aminobutyric acid) a major inhibitory neurotransmitter in the brain that tells postsynaptic neurons *not* to fire; it slows CNS activity and is necessary to regulate and control neural activity.

gate control theory of pain idea that the spinal cord regulates the experience of pain by either opening or closing neural channels, called *gates*, that transmit pain sensations to the brain.

gene-by-environment interaction research a method of studying heritability by comparing genetic markers that allows researchers to assess how genetic differences interact with environment to produce certain behaviors in some people but not in others.

general adaptation syndrome (GAS) as defined by Hans Selye, a generalized, nonspecific set of changes in the body that occur during extreme stress.

general intelligence one of Carroll's three levels of intelligence; very similar to Spearman's concept of "g."

generalized anxiety disorder (GAD) state of pervasive and excessive anxiety lasting at least six months.

generativity a term Erik Erikson used to describe the process in adulthood of creating new ideas, products, or people.

genes small segments of DNA that contain information for producing proteins.

genius high intelligence combined with creative accomplishments that have a tremendous impact on a given field.

genome all the genetic information in DNA.

germinal stage the first prenatal stage of development which begins at conception and lasts two weeks.

Gestalt law of closure the tendency to see a whole object even when complete information isn't available.

Gestalt law of continuity the tendency to see points or lines in such a way that they follow a continuous path.

Gestalt law of proximity the tendency to group objects together that are near one another.

Gestalt law of similarity the tendency to group like objects together in visual perception.

Gestalt psychology a theory of psychology that maintains that we perceive things as wholes rather than as a compilation of parts.

g-factor theory Spearman's theory that intelligence is a single general (g) factor made up of specific components.

glial cells central nervous system cells that provide structural support, promote efficient communication between neurons, and serve as scavengers, removing cellular debris.

glucocorticoids hormones responsible for maintaining the activation of physiological systems during emergencies.

glucose a simple sugar that provides energy for cells throughout the body, including the brain.

glutamate a major excitatory neurotransmitter in the brain that increases the likelihood that a postsynaptic neuron will fire; important in learning, memory, neural processing, and brain development.

graded potentials small changes in membrane potential that by themselves are insufficient to trigger an action potential.

grammar the entire set of rules for combining symbols and sounds to speak and write a particular language.

group therapy therapeutic settings in which several people who share a common problem all meet regularly with a therapist to help themselves and one another.

groupthink situation in which the thinking of the group takes over, so much so that group members forgo logic or critical analysis in the service of reaching a decision.

hair cells inner ear sensory receptors for sound that transduce sound vibrations into neural impulses.

hallucinations convincing sensory experiences that occur in the absence of an external stimulus.

hallucinogens substances that create distorted perceptions of reality ranging from mild to extreme.

health behavior approach explanation for illness or health that focuses on the role of behaviors such as diet, exercise, or substance abuse.

health psychologists scientists who examine the role that psychological factors play in regard to physical health and illness.

health psychology the study of the role psychological factors play in regard to health and illness.

heritability the extent to which a characteristic is influenced by genetics.

heuristics mental shortcuts; methods for making complex and uncertain decisions and judgments.

hierarchies a way of organizing related pieces of information from the most specific feature they have in common to the most general.

hippocampus a limbic structure that wraps itself around the thalamus; plays a vital role in learning and memory.

histrionic personality disorder dramatic–emotional personality disorder characterized by the desire to be the center of attention and by dramatic, seductive, flamboyant and exaggerated behaviors.

homeostasis the process by which all organisms work to maintain physiological equilibrium or balance around an optimal set point.

hormones chemicals, secreted by glands, that travel in the bloodstream and carry messages to tissues and organs all over the body.

human development the study of change and continuity in the individual across the life span.

human language a communication system specific to *Homo sapiens*; it is open and symbolic, has rules of grammar, and allows its users to express abstract and distant ideas.

humanistic psychology a theory of psychology that focuses on personal growth and meaning as a way of reaching one's highest potential.

hypersomnia sleep difficulty characterized by sleeping more than 10 hours a day for 2 weeks or more; includes urge to nap during inappropriate times.

hypnosis state characterized by focused attention, suggestibility, absorption, lack of voluntary control over behavior, and suspension of critical faculties; occurs when instructed by someone trained in hypnosis; may be therapeutic.

hypothalamic-pituitary-adrenal (HPA) axis a major neuroendocrine pathway relevant to the stress response involving the hypothalamus, pituitary gland, and the adrenal cortex.

hypothalamus a limbic structure; the master regulator of almost all major drives and motives we have, such as hunger, thirst, temperature, and sexual behavior; also controls the pituitary gland.

hypothesis a specific, informed, and testable prediction of the outcome of a particular set of conditions in a research design.

id one of Freud's provinces of the mind; the seat of impulse and desire; the part of our personality that we do not yet own; it owns or controls us.

ideational fluency the ability to produce many ideas.

identical twins twins that develop from a single fertilized egg that splits into two independent cells.

idioms expressions unique to a particular language; usually their meaning cannot be determined by decoding the individual meanings of the words.

implicit memory kind of memory made up of knowledge based on previous experience, such as skills that we perform automatically once we have mastered them; resides outside conscious awareness.

imprinting the rapid and innate learning of the characteristics of a caregiver very soon after birth.

impulse control disorder an anxiety disorder related to obsessive–compulsive disorder in which a person feels an intense, repetitive desire to perform certain behaviors.

incentive any external object or event that motivates behavior.

independent variable a property that is manipulated by the experimenter under controlled conditions to determine whether it causes the predicted outcome of an experiment.

inductive reasoning reasoning to general conclusions from specific evidence.

industrial/organizational (I/O) psychology application of psychological concepts and questions to work settings.

inferiority complex an unhealthy need to dominate or upstage others as a way of compensating for feelings of deficiency.

informational social influence conformity to the behavior of others because one views them as a source of knowledge about what one is supposed to do.

in-group/out-group bias tendency to show positive feelings toward people who belong to the same group as we do, and negative feelings toward those in other groups.

insomnia a sleep difficulty characterized by difficulty falling and staying asleep, as well as not feeling rested.

instinctive drift learned behavior that shifts toward instinctive, unlearned behavior tendencies.

institutional review boards (IRBs) organizations that evaluate research proposals to make sure research involving humans does not cause undue harm or distress.

insula a small structure inside the cerebrum that plays an important role in the perception of bodily sensations, emotional states, empathy, and addictive behavior.

integrative therapy an eclectic approach in which the therapist draws on different treatment approaches and uses those that seem most appropriate for the situation.

intelligence a set of cognitive skills that include abstract thinking, reasoning, problem solving, and the ability to acquire knowledge.

interference disruption of memory because other information competes with the information we are trying to recall.

intermittent reinforcement reinforcement of a behavior—but not after every response.

interneurons neurons that communicate only with other neurons.

inter-rater reliability measure of how much agreement there is in ratings when using two or more raters or coders to rate personality or other behaviors.

introspection the main method of investigation for structuralists; it involves looking into one's own mind for information about the nature of conscious experience.

ions chemically charged particles that predominate in bodily fluids; found both inside and outside cells.

iris the muscle that forms the colored part of the eye; it adjusts the pupil to regulate the amount of light that enters the eye.

James-Lange theory of emotion the idea that it is the perception of the physiological changes that accompany emotions that produces the subjective emotional experience.

kin selection the evolutionary favoring of genes that prompt individuals to help their relatives or kin.

language acquisition device (LAD) an innate, biologically based capacity to acquire language, proposed by Noam Chomsky as part of his nativist view of language.

latent learning learning that occurs in the absence of reinforcement and is not demonstrated until later, when reinforcement occurs.

latent level Freud's deeper, unconscious level of dreams; their meaning is found at this level.

law of effect the consequences of a behavior increase (or decrease) the likelihood that the behavior will be repeated.

learning enduring changes in behavior that occur with experience.

lens the structure that sits behind the pupil; it bends the light rays that enter the eye to focus images on the retina.

levels of processing the concept that the more deeply people encode information, the better they will recall it.

life satisfaction the overall evaluation we make of our lives and an aspect of subjective well-being.

Likert scales response categories on a questionnaire, in which answers are given on a numeric scale ranging from complete agreement on one end to complete disagreement on the other.

linguistic determinism hypothesis the proposition that our language determines our way of thinking and our perceptions of the world; the view taken by Sapir and Whorf.

lithium a salt that is prescribed for its ability to stabilize the mania associated with bipolar disorder.

long-term memory the part of memory that has the capacity to store a vast amount of information for as little as 30 seconds and as long as a lifetime.

long-term potentiation strengthening of a synaptic connection that results when synapse of one neuron repeatedly fires and excites another neuron.

magnetic resonance imaging (MRI) brain imaging technique that uses magnetic fields to produce detailed images of the structure of the brain and other soft tissues.

major depressive disorder mood disorder characterized by pervasive low mood, lack of motivation, low energy, and feelings of worthlessness and guilt that last for at least two consecutive weeks.

manic episode one mood cycle in bipolar disorder, typically involving increased energy, sleeplessness, euphoria, irritability, delusions of grandeur, increased sex drive, and "racing" thoughts.

manifest level Freud's surface level of dreams, recalled upon waking.

mean the arithmetic average of a series of numbers.

mechanoreceptors receptor cells in the skin that are sensitive to different tactile qualities, such as shape, grooves, vibrations, and movements.

median the score that separates the lower half of scores from the upper half.

meditation practices that people use to calm the mind, stabilize concentration, focus attention, and enhance awareness of the present moment.

medulla a hindbrain structure that extends directly from the spinal cord; regulates breathing, heart rate, and blood pressure.

memory the ability to store and use information; also the store of what has been learned and remembered.

menarche the first menstrual period.

mental age the equivalent chronological age a child has reached based on his or her performance on an IQ test.

mental representation a structure in our mind—such as an idea or image—that stands for something else, such as an external object or thing sensed in the past or future, not the present.

mental retardation significant limitations in intellectual functioning as well as in everyday adaptive behavior, which start before age 18.

mental rotation process of imagining an object turning in three-dimensional space.

mental set a tendency to continue to use problem-solving strategies that have worked in the past, even if better solutions are available.

meta-analysis research technique for combining all research results on one question and drawing a conclusion.

metacognitive thinking process that includes the ability first to think and then to reflect on one's own thinking.

mindfulness a heightened awareness of the present moment, whether of events in one's environment or in one's own mind.

mindfulness-based cognitive therapy (MBCT) an approach that combines elements of CBT with mindfulness meditation to help people with depression learn to recognize and restructure negative thought patterns.

minimal consciousness states or phases of consciousness when people are barely awake or aware.

mirror neurons nerve cells that are active when we observe others performing an action as well as when we are performing the same action.

misattribution belief that a memory came from one source when in fact it came from another.

mnemonic device a method devised to help remember information, such as a rhyme or acronym.

mode a statistic that represents the most commonly occurring score or value.

modeling the imitation of behaviors performed by others.

monoamine oxidase (MAO) inhibitors class of drugs used to treat depression; they slow the breakdown of monoamine neurotransmitters in the brain.

monocular depth cues aids to depth perception that do not require two eyes.

monogenic transmission the hereditary passing on of traits determined by a single gene.

mood disorders category of psychological disorder that is characterized by disturbances in emotional behavior that inhibit normal everyday functioning.

moods affective states that operate in the background of consciousness and tend to last longer than most emotions.

moral treatment 19th-century approach to treating the mentally ill with dignity in a caring environment.

motivation the urge to move toward one's goals; to accomplish tasks.

motor neurons nerve cells that carry commands for movement from the brain to the muscles of the body.

multiple-factor theory of intelligence idea that intelligence consists of distinct dimensions and is not just a single factor.

multiple measurement the use of several measures to acquire data on one aspect of behavior.

myelin sheath the fatty substance wrapped around some axons, which insulates the axon, making the nerve impulse travel more efficiently.

narcissistic personality disorder dramatic–emotional personality disorder characterized by having an extremely positive and arrogant self-image and being extraordinarily self-centered; other symptoms are an exaggerated sense of self-importance and grandiosity.

narcolepsy sleep disorder characterized by excessive daytime sleepiness and weakness in facial and limb muscles.

narrow intelligence one of Carroll's three levels of intelligence that includes many distinct abilities.

nativist view of language the idea that we discover language rather than learn it, that language development is inborn.

natural immunity form of immunity that is the first response to antigens.

natural selection a feedback process whereby nature favors one design over another because it has an impact on reproduction.

naturalistic observation a study in which the researcher unobtrusively observes and records behavior in the real world.

nature through nurture the position that the environment constantly interacts with biology to shape who we are and what we do.

needs inherently biological states of deficiency (cellular or bodily) that compel drives.

negative punishment the removal of a stimulus that decreases behavior. An example would be taking away a child's TV privilege for hitting her brother if it stops her from hitting her brother.

negative reinforcement removal of a stimulus after a behavior to increase the frequency of that behavior.

negative symptoms (of schizophrenia) symptoms that include nonresponsiveness, emotional flatness, immobility, catatonia, problems with speech, and inability to complete tasks.

neural migration the movement of neurons from one part of the fetal brain to their more permanent destination; occurs during months 3–5 of the fetal stage.

neurocultural theory of emotion Ekman's explanation that some aspects of emotion, such as facial expressions and physiological changes associated with emotion, are universal and others, such as emotion regulation, are culturally derived.

neuroendocrine system the hormonal systems involved in emotions and stress.

neurogenesis the development of new neurons.

neurons the cells that process and transmit information in the nervous system.

neuroplasticity the brain's ability to adopt new functions, reorganize itself, or make new neural connections throughout life, as a function of experience.

neurotransmitters chemicals that transmit information between neurons.

non-REM form of sleep with few eye movements, which are slow rather than fast.

norepinephrine a neurotransmitter that activates the sympathetic response to stress, increasing heart rate, rate of respiration, and blood pressure in support of rapid action.

normative social influence conformity to the behavior of others in order to be accepted by them.

obedience a type of conformity in which a person yields to the will of another person.

object permanence the ability to realize that objects still exist when they are not being sensed.

observational learning learning by watching the behavior of others.

obsession an unwanted thought, word, phrase, or image that persistently and repeatedly comes into a person's mind and causes distress.

obsessive–compulsive disorder (OCD) an anxiety disorder in which compulsive thoughts lead to obsessive behaviors.

obsessive-compulsive personality disorder anxious-fearful personality disorder characterized by rigid habits and extreme perfectionism; more general than obsessive-compulsive disorder.

olfactory bulb a forebrain structure that sends information either directly to the smell processing areas in the cortex or indirectly to the cortex by way of the thalamus.

olfactory sensory neurons the sensory receptors for smell that reside high up inside the nose.

one-word utterances single words, such as "mama," "dada," "more," or "no!"; occurs around 12 months of age.

operant conditioning the process of changing behavior by manipulating the consequences of that behavior.

opponent-process theory the theory that color vision results from cones linked together in three pairs of opposing colors, so that activation of one member of the pair inhibits activity in the other.

optic chiasm the point at which strands of the optic nerve from half of each eye cross over to the opposite side of the brain.

optic nerve structure composed of the axons of ganglion cells from the retina that carry visual information from the eye to the brain.

originality the ability to come up with unusual and novel ideas.

out-group homogeneity the tendency to see all members of an out-group as the same.

pain a complex emotional and sensory experience associated with actual or potential tissue damage.

panic attacks an anxiety disorder; associated with perceptions of threat and occurring because of fear of danger, inability to escape, embarrassment, or specific objects, for example.

panic disorder an anxiety disorder characterized by panic attacks and persistent anxiety about having more attacks.

papillae textured structures on the surface of the tongue; contain thousands of taste buds.

paranoid personality disorder odd–eccentric personality disorder characterized by extreme suspicions and mistrust of others in unwarranted and maladaptive ways.

paranoid schizophrenia subtype of schizophrenia characterized by preoccupation with delusions and auditory hallucinations; symptoms do not include disorganized speech, catatonia, and flat or inappropriate affect.

parasympathetic nervous system the branch of the autonomic nervous system that usually relaxes or returns the body to a less active, restful state.

peers people who share equal standing or status and are at the same level, in terms of age, gender, skill, or power.

perception a psychological process: the act of organizing and interpreting sensory experience.

perceptual constancy the ability of the brain to preserve perception of objects in spite of changes in retinal image when an object changes in position or distance from the viewer.

perceptual set the effect of frame of mind on perception; a tendency to perceive stimuli in a certain manner.

peripheral nervous system the part of the nervous system that comprises all the nerve cells in the body outside the central nervous system.

persistence the repeated recall of pleasant or unpleasant experiences even when we actively try to forget them.

personal unconscious according to Jung, form of consciousness that consists of all our repressed and hidden thoughts, feelings, and motives.

personality the unique and relatively enduring set of behaviors, feelings, thoughts, and motives that characterize an individual.

personality disorders patterns of cognition, emotion, and behavior that develop in late childhood or adolescence and are maladaptive and inflexible; they are more stable than clinical disorders.

personality psychology the study of what makes people unique and the consistencies in people's behavior across time and situations.

personality the consistently unique way that each individual behaves over time and in many different situations.

persuasion the act of attempting to change the opinions, beliefs, or choices of others by explanation or argument.

phenothiazines drugs used to treat schizophrenia; help diminish hallucinations, confusion, agitation, and paranoia, but also have adverse side effects.

phobia an anxiety disorder: an ongoing and irrational fear of a particular object, situation, or activity.

photoreceptors cells in the retina (called rods and cones) that convert light energy into nerve energy.

physiological measures measures of bodily responses, such as blood pressure or heart rate, used to determine changes in psychological state.

physiological reactivity model explanation for the role of the stress response in illness.

pituitary gland the master endocrine gland of the body that controls the release of hormones from glands throughout the body.

placebo a substance or treatment that appears identical to the actual treatment but lacks the active substance.

polygenic transmission the process by which many genes interact to create a single characteristic.

pons a hindbrain structure that serves as a bridge between lower brain regions and higher midbrain and forebrain activity.

population the entire group a researcher is interested in; for example, all humans, all adolescents, all boys, all girls, all college students.

positive psychology scientific approach to studying, understanding, and promoting healthy and positive psychological functioning.

positive punishment the addition of a stimulus that decreases behavior. An example would be that you stop parking in the faculty parking lot after you've received a ticket for doing so.

positive reinforcement the presentation or addition of a stimulus after a behavior occurs that increases how often that behavior will occur.

positive symptoms (of schizophrenia) the perceptual experiences associated with schizophrenia, including hallucinations, delusional thinking, and disorganized thought and speech.

positron emission tomography (PET) brain imaging technique that measures blood flow to active areas in the brain.

postconventional level the third level in Kohlberg's theory of moral reasoning, in which the person recognizes universal moral rules that may trump unjust or immoral local rules.

post-traumatic stress disorder (PTSD) a type of anxiety disorder triggered by exposure to a catastrophic or horrifying event that poses serious harm or threat.

preconventional level the first level in Kohlberg's theory of moral reasoning, focusing on avoiding punishment or maximizing rewards.

predictive validity the degree to which intelligence test scores are positively related to real-world outcomes, such as school achievement or job success, and thus have predictive value.

prefrontal cortex the front-most region of the frontal lobes that plays an important role in attention, appropriate social behavior, iimpulse control, and working memory.

prefrontal lobotomy a form of psychosurgery in which the connections between the prefrontal cortex and the lower portion of the brain are severed; no longer in use.

prejudice a biased attitude toward a group of people or an individual member of a group based on unfair generalizations about what members of that group are like.

prenatal programming the process by which events in the womb alter the development of physical and psychological health.

preoperational stage the second major stage of cognitive development (ages 2–5), which begins with the emergence of symbolic thought.

primary appraisal quick assessment of the meaning of a given environmental event for the individual.

primary reinforcers innate, unlearned reinforcers that satisfy biological needs (such as food, water, or sex).

priming a kind of implicit memory that arises when recall is improved by earlier exposure to the same or similar stimuli.

proactive interference disruption of memory because previously learned information interferes with the learning of new information.

problem-focused coping way of dealing with stress that aims to change the situation that is creating stress.

procedural memory kind of memory made up of implicit knowledge for almost any behavior or physical skill we have learned.

prodigy a young person who is extremely gifted and precocious in one area and at least average in intelligence.

projection a defense mechanism in which people deny particular ideas, feelings, or impulses and project them onto others.

projective tests personality assessment in which the participant is presented with a vague stimulus or situation and asked to interpret it or tell a story about what they see.

prosocial behavior action that is beneficial to others.

protolanguage very rudimentary language; also known as pre-language; used by earlier species of *Homo*.

prototypes the best-fitting examples of a category.

pruning the degradation of synapses and dying off of neurons that are not strengthened by experience.

pseudoscience claims presented as scientific that are not supported by evidence obtained with the scientific method.

psychoactive drugs naturally occurring or synthesized substances that, when ingested or otherwise taken into the body, reliably produce qualitative changes in conscious experience.

psychoanalysis a clinically based approach to understanding and treating psychological disorders; assumes that the unconscious mind is the most powerful force behind thought and behavior.

psychodynamic psychotherapy therapy aimed at uncovering unconscious motives that underlie psychological problems.

psychology the scientific study of thought and behavior.

psychoneuroimmunology (PNI) the science of how psychological factors relate to changes in the immune system.

psychophysics the study of how people psychologically perceive physical stimuli such as light, sound waves, and touch.

psychosexual stage theory Freud's stages of personality development; as people move through each of the stages of life (oral, anal, phallic, and genital), a different region of the body is most erogenous.

psychosomatic theory the idea that emotional factors can lead to the occurrence or worsening of illness.

psychotherapy the use of psychological techniques to modify maladaptive behaviors

or thought patterns, or both, and to help patients develop insight into their own behavior.

psychotic disorders psychological disorders of thought and perception, characterized by inability to distinguish between real and imagined perceptions.

puberty the period when sexual maturation begins; it marks the beginning of adolescence.

punishment stimulus that decreases the frequency of a behavior.

pupil the opening in the iris through which light enters the eye.

quantitative trait loci (QTL) approach a technique in behavioral genetics that looks for the location on genes that might be associated with particular behaviors.

quasi-experimental design research method similar to an experimental design except that it makes use of naturally occurring groups rather than randomly assigning subjects to groups.

questionnaires self-report instruments on which respondents indicate the extent to which they agree or disagree with a series of statements as they apply to their personality.

random assignment the method used to assign participants to different research conditions so that all participants have the same chance of being in any specific group.

rapid eye movements (REM) quick movements of the eye that occur during sleep, thought to mark phases of dreaming.

rational (face valid) method a method for developing questionnaire items that involves using reason or theory to come up with a question.

reaction formation a defense mechanism that occurs when an unpleasant idea, feeling, or impulse is turned into its opposite.

reaction range for a given trait, such as IQ, the genetically determined range of responses by an individual to his or her environment.

reappraisal an emotion regulation strategy in which one reevaluates an event so that a different emotion results.

reasoning the process of drawing inferences or conclusions from principles and evidence.

recessive genes genes that show their effects only when both alleles are the same.

reciprocal altruism the act of helping others in the hope that they will help us in the future.

recovered memory a memory from a real event that was encoded, stored, but not retrieved for a long period of time until some later event brings it suddenly to consciousness.

reflexes inborn and involuntary behaviors—such as coughing, swallowing, sneezing, or vomiting—that are elicited by very specific stimuli.

refractory period the span of time, after an action potential has been generated, when the neuron is returning to its resting state and the neuron cannot generate an action potential.

rehearsal the process of repeatedly practicing material so that it enters long-term memory.

reinforcer an internal or external event that increases the frequency of a behavior.

reliability consistency of a measurement, such as an intelligence test.

repetitive transcranial magnetic stimulation treatment for severe depression involving exposure of specific brain structures to bursts of high-intensity magnetic fields instead of electricity.

replication the repetition of a study to confirm the results; essential to the scientific process.

representative sample a research sample that accurately reflects the population of people one is studying.

representativeness heuristic a strategy we use to estimate the probability of one event based on how typical it is of another event.

repression the unconscious act of keeping threatening thoughts, feelings, or impulses out of consciousness.

research design plans of action for how to conduct a scientific study.

resistance stage in the general adaptation syndrome, extended effort by the body to deal with a threat.

resting potential the difference in electrical charge between the inside and outside of the axon when the neuron is at rest.

reticular formation a network of nerve fibers that runs up through both the hindbrain and the midbrain; it is crucial to waking up and falling asleep.

retina the thin layer of nerve tissue that lines the back of the eye.

retrieval the recovery of information stored in memory; the fourth stage of long-term memory.

retroactive interference disruption of memory because new experiences or information cause people to forget previously learned experiences or information.

retrograde amnesia an inability to recall events or experiences that happened before the onset of a disease or injury.

reuptake a way of removing excess neurotransmitter from the synapse, in which excess neurotransmitter is returned to the sending, or presynaptic, neuron for storage in vesicles and future use.

rods photoreceptors that function in low illumination and play a key role in night vision; responsive to dark and light contrast.

Rorschach Inkblot Test a projective test in which the participant is asked to respond to a series of ambiguous inkblots.

samples subsets of the population studied in a research project.

savant syndrome a very rare condition in which people with serious mental handicaps also show isolated areas of ability or brilliance.

schedules of reinforcement patterns of intermittent reinforcement distinguished by whether reinforcement occurs after a set number of responses or after a certain amount of time has passed since the last reinforcement.

schemas mental frameworks that develop from our experiences with particular people, objects, or events.

schizoid personality disorder odd–eccentric personality disorder characterized by a desire to avoid close relationships as well as by emotional aloofness, reclusivity, and a lack of humor.

schizophrenia psychotic disorder characterized by significant disturbances in thought and emotion, specifically problems with perception, including hallucinations.

schizotypal personality disorder odd–eccentric personality disorder characterized by a desire to live an isolated and asocial life, but also by the presence of odd thoughts and beliefs.

scientific method the procedures by which scientists conduct research, consisting of five basic processes: observation, prediction, testing, interpretation, and communication.

scientific thinking process using the cognitive skills required to generate, test, and revise theories.

secondary (or conditioned) reinforcers reinforcers that are learned by association, usually via classical conditioning (such as money, grades, and peer approval).

secondary appraisal self-assessment of the resources available to cope with stress.

secure attachment attachment style characterized by infants who will gradually explore new situations when the caregiver leaves and initiate contact when the caregiver returns after separation.

selective attention the ability to focus awareness on specific features in the environment while ignoring others.

selective serotonin reuptake inhibitors (SSRIs) drugs prescribed primarily for depression and some anxiety disorders that work by making more serotonin available in the synapse.

self-conscious emotions types of emotion that require a sense of self and the ability to reflect on actions; they occur as a function of meeting expectations (or not) and abiding (or not) by society's rules.

self-fulfilling prophecy a statement that affects events to cause the prediction to become true.

self-reports written or oral accounts of a person's thoughts, feelings, or actions.

self-serving bias the tendency to make situational attributions for our failures but dispositional attributions for our successes.

semantic memory form of memory that recalls facts and general knowledge, such as what we learn in school.

semicircular canals structure of the inner ear involved in maintaining balance.

sensation a physical process: the stimulation of our sense organs by features of the outer world.

sensorimotor stage Piaget's first stage of cognitive development (ages 0–2), when infants learn about the world by using their senses and by moving their bodies.

sensory adaptation the process by which our sensitivity diminishes when an object constantly stimulates our senses.

sensory memory the part of memory that holds information in its original sensory form for a very brief period of time, usually about a half a second or less.

sensory neurons nerve cells that receive incoming sensory information from the sense organs (eye, ear, skin, tongue, nose).

sentence phase stage when children begin speaking in fully grammatical sentences; usually age 2½ to 3.

separation anxiety the distress reaction shown by babies when they are separated from their primary caregiver (typically shown at around 9 months of age).

serial-position effect the tendency to have better recall for items in a list according to their position in the list.

serotonin a neurotransmitter with wide-ranging effects: involved in dreaming and in controlling emotional states, especially anger, anxiety, and depression.

set point the ideal fixed setting of a particular physiological system, such as internal body temperature.

sexual behavior actions that produce arousal and increase the likelihood of orgasm.

sexual orientation the disposition to be attracted to either the opposite sex (heterosexual), the same sex (homosexual), or both sexes (bisexual).

sexual strategies theory the idea that men and women face different problems when they seek out mates, and so they often approach relationships in very different ways.

shamans medicine men or women who treat people with mental problems by driving out their demons with elaborate rituals, such as exorcisms, incantations, and prayers.

shaping the reinforcement of successive approximations of a desired behavior.

short-term memory the part of memory that temporarily (for 2 to 30 seconds) stores a limited amount of information before it is either transferred to long-term storage or forgotten.

signal detection theory the viewpoint that both stimulus intensity and decision-making processes are involved in the detection of a stimulus.

single-blind studies studies in which participants do not know the experimental condition (group) to which they have been assigned.

Skinner box simple cage used for operant conditioning of small animals.

sleep apnea sleep difficulty that results from temporary blockage of the air passage.

sleepwalking sleep difficulty characterized by activities occurring during non-REM sleep that usually occur when one is awake, such as walking and eating.

social desirability bias the tendency toward favorable self-presentation that could lead to inaccurate self-reports.

social exchange theory the idea that we help others when we understand that the benefits to ourselves are likely to outweigh the costs.

social facilitation phenomenon in which the presence of others improves one's performance.

social impact theory idea that our likelihood of following either informational or normative social influence depends on three different aspects of the group: (1) how important the group is to us, (2) how close the group is

to us in space and time, and (3) how many people are in the group.

social learning theory a description of the kind of learning that occurs when we model or imitate the behavior of others.

social loafing phenomenon in which the presence of others causes one to relax one's standards and slack off.

social norms rules about acceptable behavior imposed by the cultural context in which one lives.

social phobia (social anxiety disorder) an anxiety disorder: fear of humiliation in the presence of others, characterized by intense self-consciousness about appearance or behavior or both.

social psychology the study of how living among others influences thought, feeling, and behavior.

social referencing the ability to make use of social and emotional information from another person—especially a caregiver—in an uncertain situation.

soma the cell body of the neuron.

somatic nervous system nerve cells of the peripheral nervous system that transmit sensory information to the central nervous system (CNS) and those that transmit information from the CNS to the skeletal muscles.

spermarche the first ejaculation.

spontaneous recovery the sudden reappearance of an extinguished response.

sports psychology the study of psychological factors in sports and exercise.

standard deviation a statistical measure of how much scores in a sample vary around the mean.

statistics collection, analysis, interpretation, and presentation of numerical data.

stereotypes schemas of how people are likely to behave based simply on groups to which they belong.

stimulants substances that activate the nervous system.

stimulus discrimination restriction of a CR (such as salivation) to only the exact CS to which it was conditioned.

stimulus generalization extension of the association between UCS and CS to include a broad array of similar stimuli.

storage the retention of memory over time; the third stage of long-term memory formation.

stress a response elicited when a situation overwhelms a person's perceived ability to meet the demands of a situation.

stressors events that trigger a stress response.

striving for superiority according to Adler, the major drive behind all behavior, whereby humans naturally strive to overcome their inherent inferiorities or deficiencies, both physical and psychological.

Stroop effect delay in reaction time when color of words on a test and their meaning differ.

structuralism 19th-century school of psychology that argued that breaking down experience into its elemental parts offers the best way to understand thought and behavior.

subjective experience of emotion the changes in the quality of our conscious experience that occur during emotional responses.

subjective well-being state that consists of life satisfaction, domain satisfactions, and positive and negative affect.

sublimation a defense mechanism that involves expressing a socially unacceptable impulse in a socially acceptable way.

successful intelligence according to Sternberg, an integrated set of abilities needed to attain success in life.

suggestibility problem with memory that occurs when memories are implanted in our minds based on leading questions, comments, or suggestions by someone else or some other source.

superego one of Freud's provinces of the mind; the part of the self that monitors and controls behavior; "stands over us" and evaluates actions in terms of right and wrong; hence, our conscience.

support groups meetings of people who share a common situation, be it a disorder, a disease, or coping with an ill family member.

sustained attention the ability to maintain focused awareness on a target or idea.

sympathetic nervous system the branch of the autonomic nervous system that activates bodily systems in times of emergency.

synapse the junction between an axon and the adjacent neuron, where information is transmitted from one neuron to another.

synaptic vesicles tiny sacs in the terminal buttons that contain neurotransmitters.

synaptogenesis the formation of entirely new synapses or connections with other neurons.

syndromes groups or clusters of related symptoms that are characteristic of a disorder.

synesthesia an unusual sensory experience in which a person experiences sensations in one sense when a different sense is stimulated.

syntax the rules for arranging words and symbols to form sentences or parts of sentences in a particular language.

systematic desensitization a behavioral therapy technique, often used for phobias, in which the therapist pairs relaxation with gradual exposure to a phobic object, generating a hierarchy of increasing contact with the feared object.

tardive dyskinesia repetitive, involuntary movements of jaw, tongue, face, and mouth resulting from the extended use of traditional antipsychotic drugs.

taste buds structures inside the papillae of the tongue that contain the taste receptor cells.

taste receptor cells sensory receptors for taste that reside in the taste buds.

temperament the biologically based tendency to behave in particular ways from very early in life.

teratogens substances that can disrupt normal prenatal development and cause lifelong deficits.

terminal buttons little knobs at the end of the axon that contain tiny sacs of neurotransmitters.

test bias characteristic of a test that produces different outcomes for different groups.

test fairness judgment about how test results are applied to different groups based on values and philosophical inclinations.

thalamus a forebrain structure that receives information from the senses and relays it to the cerebral cortex for processing.

Thematic Apperception Test (TAT) a projective test in which the participant is presented with a series of picture cards and asked to tell a story about what is going on in the scene.

theory a set of related assumptions from which scientists can make testable predictions.

theory of mind ideas and knowledge about how other people's minds work.

theta waves pattern of brain activity during Stage 1 sleep; slower, lower-energy waves than alpha waves.

thinking outside the box approach to problem solving that requires breaking free of self-imposed conceptual constraints and thinking about a problem differently in order to solve it.

three-stage model of memory classification of memories based on duration as sensory, short-term, and long-term.

token economies a behavioral technique in which desirable behaviors are reinforced

with a token, such as a small chip or fake coin, which can be exchanged for privileges.

top-down processing perception of the whole based on our experience and expectations, which guide our perception of smaller elemental features of a stimulus.

traditional antipsychotics historically, the first medications used to manage psychotic symptoms.

trait a disposition to behave consistently in a particular way.

transduction the conversion of physical into neural information.

transference process in psychotherapy in which the client reacts to a person in a present relationship as though that person were someone from the client's past.

transience most common type of forgetfulness due to the fleeting nature of some memories.

triangular theory of love Sternberg's idea that three components (intimacy, passion, and commitment), in various combinations, can explain all the forms of human love.

triarchic theory of intelligence Sternberg's three-part model of intelligence, including analytic, creative, and practical intelligence.

trichromatic color theory the theory that all color that we experience results from a mixing of three colors of light (red, green, and blue).

tricyclic antidepressants drugs used for treating depression as well as in chronic pain management and in the treatment of ADHD.

twin–adoption studies research into hereditary influence on twins, both identical and fraternal, who were raised apart (adopted) and who were raised together.

two-word utterances phrases children put together, starting around 18 months, such as "my ball," "mo wawa," or "go way."

tympanic membrane the eardrum.

Type A Behavior Pattern a way of responding to challenge or stress, characterized by hostility, impatience, competitiveness, and time urgency.

unconditional positive regard acceptance of another person regardless of his or her behavior.

unconditioned response (UCR) the natural automatic, inborn reaction to a stimulus.

unconditioned stimulus (UCS) the environmental input that always produces the same unlearned response.

unconscious one of Freud's three levels of consciousness; it contains all the drives,

urges, or instincts that are outside awareness but nonetheless motivate most of our speech, thoughts, feelings, or actions.

undifferentiated schizophrenia subtype of schizophrenia characterized by the general symptoms of delusions, hallucinations, and disorganized speech but not by any of the symptoms of specific subtypes.

universal term referring to something that is common to all human beings and can be seen in cultures all over the world.

validity the degree to which a test accurately measures what it purports to measure, such as intelligence, and not something else, and the degree to which it predicts real-world outcomes.

variable a characteristic that changes or "varies," such as age, gender, weight, intelligence, anxiety, and extraversion.

variable interval (VI) schedule a pattern of intermittent reinforcement in which responses are reinforced after time periods of different duration have passed.

variable ratio (VR) schedule a pattern of intermittent reinforcement in which the number of responses needed for reinforcement changes.

vegetative state a state of minimal consciousness in which the eyes might be open, but the person is otherwise unresponsive.

visual acuity the ability to see clearly.

visual imagery visual representations created by the brain after the original stimulus is no longer present.

wakefulness degree of alertness reflecting whether a person is awake or asleep.

Weber's law the finding that the size of a just noticeable difference is a constant fraction of the intensity of the stimulus.

Wernicke's area an area deep in the left temporal lobe responsible for the ability to speak in meaningful sentences and to comprehend the meaning of speech.

word salad term for the speech of people with schizophrenia, which may follow grammatical rules but be nonsensical in terms of content.

working memory the part of memory required to attend to and solve a problem at hand; often used interchangeably with short-term memory.

Yerkes–Dodson law the principle that moderate levels of arousal lead to optimal performance.

zygote the single cell that results when a sperm fertilizes an egg.

references

Aboujaoude, E., Koran, L. M., Gamel, N., Large, M. D., & Serpe, R. T. (2006). Potential markers for problematic Internet use: A telephone survey of 2,513 adults. *CNS Spectrum: The International Journal of Neuropsychiatric Medicine, 11,* 750–755.

Abrams, R. (1997). *Electroconvulsive therapy* (3rd ed.). New York: Oxford University Press.

Achter, J. A., Lubinski, D., Benbow, C. P., & Eftekhari-Sanjani, H. (1999). Assessing vocational preferences among intellectually gifted adolescents adds incremental validity to abilities: A discriminant analysis of educational outcomes over a 10-year interval. *Journal of Educational Psychology, 91,* 777–786.

Ackerman, D. (1990). *A natural history of the senses.* New York: Vintage Books.

Adam, T. C., & Epel, E. S. (2007). Stress, eating and the reward system. *Physiology & Behavior, 91,* 449–458.

Adams, L., & Szaluta, J. (1996). *Psychoanalysis and the humanities.* Philadelphia: Brunner/Mazel.

Adamson, L., & Bakeman, R. (1985). Affect and attention: Infants observed with mothers and peers. *Child Development, 56,* 582–593.

Ader, R., & Cohen, N. (1975). Behaviorally conditioned immunosuppression. *Psychosomatic Medicine, 37,* 333–340.

Adler, A. (1931). *What life should mean to you.* New York: Capricorn Books.

Adler, A. (1956). *The individual psychology of Alfred Adler: A systematic presentation in selections from his writings* (H. L. Ansbacher & R. R. Ansbacher, Eds.). New York: Norton.

Adler, J. (Ed.). (2004). *Forensic psychology: Concepts, debates and practice.* Cullupton, England: Willan.

Adolphs, R., Cahill, L., Schul, R., & Babinsky, R. (1997) Impaired declarative memory for emotional material following bilateral amygdala damage in humans. *Learning and Memory, 4,* 291–300.

Adolphs, R., Gosselin, F., Buchanan, T. W., Tranel, D., Schyns, P., & Damasio, A. R. (2005). A mechanism for impaired fear recognition after amygdala damage. *Nature, 433,* 68–72.

Adolphs, R., Tranel, D., & Buchanan, T. W. (2005) Amygdala damage impairs emotional memory for gist but not details of complex stimuli. *Nature Neuroscience, 8,* 512–518.

Adolphs, R., Tranel, D., & Damasio, A. R. (1998). The human amygdala in social judgment. *Nature, 393,* 470–474.

Adolphs, R., Tranel, D., Damasio, H., & Damasio, A. R. (1994). Impaired recognition of emotion in facial expressions following bilateral damage to the human amygdala. *Nature, 372,* 669–672.

Aichorn, W., Huber, R., Stuppaeck, C., & Whitworth, A. B. (2006). Cardiomyopathy after long-term treatment with lithium— more than a coincidence? *Journal of Psychopharmacology 20,* 589–591.

Ainsworth, M. D. S., Blehar, M. C., Waters, E., & Wall, S. (1978). *Patterns of attachment: A psychological study of the strange situation.* Hillsdale, NJ: Erlbaum.

Aitken, J. R., & Benson, J. W. (1984). The use of relaxation/desensitization in treating anxiety associated with flying. *Aviation Space and Environmental Medicine, 55,* 196–199.

Akaike, A. (2006). Preclinical evidence of neuroprotection by cholinesterase inhibitors. *Alzheimer Disease and Associated Disorders, 20*(Suppl. 1), S8–S11.

Albert, R. S., & Runco, M. A. (1989). Independence and the creative potential of exceptionally gifted boys. *Journal of Youth and Adolescence, 18,* 221–230.

Allemand, M., Zimprich, D., & Hendriks, A. A. J. (2008). Age differences in five personality domains across the life span. *Developmental Psychology, 44,* 758–770.

Allen, L., & Gorski, R. (2007). *Sex differences in the bed nucleus of the stria terminalis of the human brain* [e-book]. Cambridge, MA: MIT Press.

Allen, N. J., & Barres, B. A. (2005). Signaling between glia and neurons: Focus on synaptic plasticity. *Current Opinion in Neurobiology, 15,* 542–548. doi:10.1016/j.conb.2005.08.006

Allison, D. B., Heshka, S., Neale, M. C., Lykken, D. T., & Heymsfield, S. B. (1994). A genetic analysis of relative weight among 4,020 twin pairs, with an emphasis on sex effects. *Health Psychology, 13,* 362–365.

Allport, G. W. (1937). *Personality: A psychological interpretation.* New York: Holt, Rinehart & Winston.

Allport, G. W. (1954). *The nature of prejudice.* Cambridge, MA: Addison-Wesley.

Allport, G. W., & Odbert, H. W. (1936). Trait-names: A psycho-lexical study. *Psychological Monographs, 47,* 1–171.

Alt, K. W., Jeunesse, C., Buritrago-Tellez, C. H., Wächter, R., Boes, E., & Pichler, S. L. (1997). Evidence for stone-age cranial surgery. *Nature, 387,* 360.

Altman, J., & Das, G. D. (1966). Autoradiographic and histological studies of postnatal neurogenesis. I. A longitudinal investigation of the kinetics, migration and transformation of cells incorporating tritiated thymidine in neonate rats, with special reference to postnatal neurogenesis in some brain regions. *Journal of Comparative Neurology, 126,* 337–389.

Alzheimer's Association. (2008). *What is Alzheimer's?* Retrieved March 10, 2008, from http://www.alz.org/alzheimers_disease_what_is_alzheimers.asp#plaques

Amabile, T. (1996). *Creativity in context.* Boulder, CO: Westview.

Amaral, D. (2000). The anatomical organization of the central nervous system. In E. R. Kandel, J. H. Schwartz, & T. M. Jessell (Eds.). *Principles of neural science* (4th ed.; pp. 317–336). New York: McGraw-Hill.

Amedi, A., Merabet, L. B., Bermpohl, F., & Pascual-Leone, A. (2005). The occipital cortex in the blind. *Current Directions in Psychological Science, 14,* 306–311.

American Association on Mental Retardation (AAMR). (2002). *Mental retardation: Definition, classification, and systems of support* (10th ed.). Alexandria, VA: Author.

American Heart Association (2005). *Heart disease and stroke statistics—2005 update.* Dallas, TX: American Heart Association.

American Psychiatric Association. (2000). *Diagnostic and statistical manual of mental disorders* (4th ed.). Washington, DC: Author.

American Sleep Apnea Association (2006). *Sleep apnea information.* Washington, DC: Author.

Anda, R. F., Felitti, V. J., Bremner, J. D., Walker, J. D., Whitfield, C., Perry, B. D., et al. (2006). The enduring effects of abuse and related adverse experiences in childhood: A convergence of evidence from neurobiology and epidemiology. *European Archives of Psychiatry and Clinical Neuroscience, 256,* 174–186.

Anderson, N. D., Lau, M. A., Segal, Z. V., & Bishop, S. R. (2007). Mindfulness-based stress reduction and attentional control. *Clinical Psychology and Psychotherapy, 14,* 449–463.

Andreasen, N. C. (1987). Creativity and psychological disorder: Prevalence rates in writers and their first-degree relatives. *American Journal of Psychiatry, 144,* 1288–1292.

Andreasen, N. C. (2006). *The creative brain.* New York: Penguin Books.

Andreasen, N. C., & Glick, I. D. (1988). Bipolar affective disorder and creativity: Implications and clinical management. *Comprehensive Psychiatry, 29,* 207–216.

Andreasen, N. C., O'Leary, D. S., Flaum, M., Nopoulos, P., Watkins, G. L., Ponto, L. L. B., et al. (1997). Hypofrontality in schizophrenia: Distributed dysfunctional circuits in neuroleptic-naïve patients. *The Lancet, 349,* 1730–1734.

Anson, K., & Ponsford, J. (2006). Coping and emotional adjustment following traumatic brain injury. *Journal of Head Trauma Rehabilitation, 21,* 248–259.

Anthonisen, N. R., Skeans, M. A., Wise, R. A., Manfreda, J., Kanner, R. E., & Connett, J. E. (Lung Health Study Research Group). (2005). The effects of a smoking cessation intervention on 14.5-year mortality: A randomized clinical trial. *Annals of Internal Medicine, 142,* 233–239.

Aouizerate, B., Cuny, E., Martin-Guehl, C., Guehl, D., Rougier, A., Bioulac, B., et al. (2005). Deep brain stimulation for OCD and major depression. *Neurology, 64,* A223–A224.

Aouizerate, B., Guehl, D., Cuny, E., Rougier, A., Bioulac, B., Tignol, J., et al. (2004). Pathophysiology of obsessive-compulsive disorder: A necessary link between phenomenology, neuropsychology, imagery and physiology. *Progress in Neurobiology, 72,* 195–221.

APA Presidential Task Force on Evidence-Based Practice, US. (2006). Evidence-based practice in psychology. *American Psychologist, 61,* 271–285.

Apsche, J. (1993). *Probing the mind of a serial killer.* International Information Associates.

Arling, G. L., & Harlow, H. F. (1967). Effects of social deprivation on maternal behavior of rhesus monkeys. *Journal of Comparative and Physiological Psychology, 64,* 371–377.

Arnett, J. J. (2006). Emerging adulthood: Understanding the new way of coming of age. In J. J. Arnett and J. L. Tanner (Eds.). *Emerging adults in America: Coming of age in the 21st century* (pp. 3–19). Washington, DC: American Psychological Association.

Arseneault, L., Cannon, M., Witton, J., & Murray, R. M. (2004). Causal association between cannabis and psychosis: Examination of the evidence. *British Journal of Psychiatry, 184,* 110–117.

Arseneault, L., Moffitt T. E., Caspi A., Taylor, A., Rijsdijk F., Jaffee, S. R., et al. (2003). Strong genetic effects on cross-situational antisocial behaviour among 5-year-old children according to mothers, teachers, examiner-observers, and twins' self-reports. *Journal of Child Psychology and Psychiatry, 44,* 832–848.

Artola, A. (2008). Diabetes-, stress- and ageing-related changes in synaptic plasticity in hippocampus and neocortex—The same metaplastic process? *European Journal of Pharmacology, 585,* 153–162.

Asch, S. E. (1951). Effects of group pressure on the modification and distortion of judgments. In H. Guetzkow (Ed.), *Groups, leadership and men.* Pittsburgh: Carnegie Press.

Asch, S. E. (1952). *Social psychology.* New York: Prentice-Hall.

Asperger, H. (1991). "Autistic psychopathy" in childhood (U. Frith, Trans.). In U. Frith (Ed.), *Autism and Asperger syndrome* (pp. 37–62). New York: Cambridge University Press. (Original work published 1944)

Associated Press. (2006, Oct. 24). Man with amnesia reunited with family. Retrieved from http://www.msnbc.msn.com/id/15373503/

Atkins, D. C., Berns, S. B., George, W. H., Doss, B. D., Gattis, K., & Christensen, A. (2005). Prediction of response to treatment in a randomized clinical trial of marital therapy. *Journal of Consulting and Clinical Psychology, 73,* 893–903.

Atkins, D. C., Yi, J., Baucom, D. H., & Christensen, A. (2005). Infidelity in couples seeking marital therapy. *Journal of Family Psychology, 19,* 470–473.

Atkinson, G., Reilly, T., & Waterhouse, J. (2007). Chronobiological aspects of the sleep-wake cycle and thermoregulation. *Physiology & Behavior, 90(2),* 189.

Atkinson, J. W. (1964). *An introduction to motivation.* New York: Van Nostrand.

Atkinson, R. C., & Shiffrin, R. M. (1971). The control of short-term memory. *Scientific American, 225,* 82–90.

Austin, E. J. (2005). Personality correlates of the broader autism phenotype as assessed by the Autism Spectrum Quotient (AQ). *Personality and Individual Differences, 38,* 451–460.

Austin, M., Hadzi-Pavlovic, D., Leader, L., Saint, K., & Parker, G. (2004). Maternal trait anxiety, depression, and life-event stress in pregnancy: Relationships with infant temperament. *Early Human Development, 81,* 183–190.

Baars, B. J. (1997). In the theatre of consciousness: Global workspace theory, a rigorous scientific theory of consciousness. *Journal of Consciousness Studies, 4,* 292–309.

Baars, B. J., & Franklin, S. (2003). How conscious experience and working memory interact. *TRENDS in Cognitive Sciences, 7,* 166–172.

Bachorowski, J. (1999). Vocal expression and perception of emotion. *Current Directions in Psychological Science, 8,* 53–57.

Baddeley, A. (2007). *Working memory, thought, and action.* New York: Oxford University Press.

Baddeley, A. D. (1998). The central executive: A concept and some misconceptions. *Journal of the International Neuropsychological Society, 4,* 523–526.

Baddeley, A. D. (2003). Working memory: Looking back and looking forward. *Nature Reviews Neuroscience, 4,* 829–839.

Baer, R. A., Smith, G. T., Hopkins, J., Krietemeyer, J., & Toney, L. (2006). Using self-report assessment methods to explore facets of mindfulness. *Assessment, 13,* 27–45.

Bagwell, C. L., Newcomb, A. F., & Bukowski, W. M. (1998). Preadolescent friendship and rejection as predictors of adult adjustment. *Child Development, 69,* 140–153.

Bailey, D. S. (2004). Why accreditation matters. *gradPSYCH, 2.* Retrieved from http://gradpsych.apags.org/apr04/accreditation.cfm

Bailey, M. J., Dunne, M. P., & Martin, N. G. (2000). Genetic and environment effects on sexual orientation and its correlates in an Australian twin sample. *Journal of Personality and Social Psychology, 78,* 524–536.

Bailey, M. J., Kirk, K. M., Zhu, G., Dunne, M. P., & Martin, N. G. (2000). Do individual differences in sociosexuality represent genetic or environmentally contingent strategies? Evidence from the Australian twin registry. *Journal of Personality and Social Psychology, 78,* 537–545.

Bailey, M. J., & Zucker, K. J. (1995). Childhood sex-typed behavior and sexual orientation: A conceptual analysis and quantitative review. *Developmental Psychology, 31,* 43–55.

Baillargeon, R., & DeVos, J. (1991). Object permanence in young infants: Further evidence. *Child Development, 62,* 1227–1246.

Baird, J. C., Wagner, M., & Fuld, K. (1990). A simple but powerful theory of the moon illusion. *Journal of Experimental Psychology: Human Perception and Performance, 16,* 675–677.

Baldwin, D. S., & Polkinghorn, C. (2005). Evidence-based pharmacotherapy of generalized anxiety disorder. *International Journal of Neuropsychopharmacology, 8,* 293–302.

Ball, K., Crawford, D., & Kenardy, J. (2004). Longitudinal relationships among overweight, life satisfaction, and aspirations in young women. *Obesity Research, 12(6),* 1019–1030.

Baltes, P. B., Reuter-Lorenz, P. A., & Rösler, F. (Eds.). (2006). *Lifespan development and the brain: The perspective of biocultural co-constructivism.* New York: Cambridge University Press.

Baltes, P. B., & Smith, J. (2008). The fascination of wisdom: Its nature, ontogeny, and function. *Perspectives on Psychological Science, 3,* 56–64.

Banaji, M. R. (2007). Unraveling beliefs. Retrieved June 18, 2007, from http://www.edge.org/q2007/q07_13.html

Banaji, M. R., & Greenwald, A. G. (1995). Implicit gender stereotyping in judgments of fame. *Journal of Personality and Social Psychology, 68,* 181–198.

Bandura, A. (1969). *Principles of behavior modification.* New York: Holt, Rinehart & Winston.

Bandura, A. (1986). *Social foundations of thought and action: A social cognitive theory.* Englewood Cliffs, NJ: Prentice-Hall.

Bandura, A., Ross, D., & Ross, S. A. (1961). Transmission of aggression through imitation of aggressive models. *Journal of Abnormal and Social Psychology, 63,* 575–582.

Bandura, A., Ross, D., & Ross, S. A. (1963). Vicarious reinforcement and imitative learning. *Journal of Abnormal & Social Psychology, 67,* 601–608.

Banks, M. S., & Salapatek, P. (1983). Infant visual perception. In P. H. Mussen (Ed.)., *Handbook of child psychology* (4th ed., Vol. 2). New York: Wiley.

Barbazanges, A., Piazza, P. V., Le Moal, M., & Maccari, S. (1996). Maternal glucocorticoid secretion mediates long-term effects of prenatal stress. *Journal of Neuroscience, 16,* 3943–3949.

Barbour, K. A., & Blumenthal, J. A. (in press). Exercise training and depression in older adults. *Neurobiology of Aging.*

Barch, D. M. (2005). The cognitive neuroscience of schizophrenia. *Annual Review of Clinical Psychology, 1,* 321–353.

Barkham, M., Connell, J., Stiles, W. B., Miles, J. N. V., Margison, F., Evans, C., et al. (2006). Dose-effect relations and responsive regulation of treatment duration: The good enough level. *Journal of Consulting and Clinical Psychology, 74,* 160–167.

Barlow, J. H., Powell, L. A., Gilchrist, M., & Fotiadou, M. (2008). The effectiveness of the Training and Support Program for parents of children with disabilities: A randomized controlled trial. *Journal of Psychosomatic Research, 64,* 55–62.

Baron, A., & Galizio, M. (2006). The distinction between positive and negative reinforcement: Use with care. *Behavior Analyst, 296,* 141–151.

Baron, A. S., & Banaji, M. R. (2006). The development of implicit attitudes: Evidence of race evaluations from ages 6 and 10 and adulthood. *Psychological Science, 17,* 53–58.

Baron-Cohen, S., Bolton, P., Wheelwright, S., Short, L., Mead, G., Smith, A., et al. (1998). Autism occurs more often in families of physicists, engineers, and mathematicians. *Autism, 2,* 296–301.

Baron-Cohen, S., Wheelwright, S., Skinner, R., Martin, J., and Clubley, E. (2001). The Autism-Spectrum Quotient (AQ): Evidence from Asperger syndrome/high-functioning autism, males and females, scientists and mathematicians. *Journal of Autism & Developmental Disorders, 31,* 5–17.

Baron-Cohen, S., Wheelwright, S., Stott, C., Bolton, P., & Goodyer, I. (1997). Is there a link between engineering and autism? *Autism, 1,* 101–109.

Barr, C. L., Kroft, J., Feng, Y., Wigg, K., Roberts, W. Malone, M., et al. (2002). The norepinephrine transporter gene and attention-deficit hyperactivity disorder. *American Journal of Medical Genetics, 114,* 255–259.

Barrett, L. F., Lane, R. D., Sechrest, L., & Schwartz, G. E. (2000). Sex differences in emotional awareness. *Personality and Social Psychology Bulletin, 26,* 1027–1035.

Barrett, L. F., Ochsner, K. N., & Gross, J. J. (2007). On the automaticity of emotion. In J. Bargh (Ed.), *Social psychology and the unconscious: The automaticity of higher mental processes* (pp. 173–217). New York: Psychology Press.

Barrett, L. F., Robin, L., Pietromonaco, P. R., & Eysell, K. M. (1998). Are women the "more emotional" sex? Evidence from emotional experiences in social context. *Cognition & Emotion, 12,* 555–578.

Barth, J., Schumacher, M., & Herrmann-Lingen, C. (2004). Depression as a risk factor for mortality in patients with coronary heart disease: A meta-analysis. *Psychosomatic Medicine, 66,* 802–813.

Bartholow, B. D., Bushman, B. J., & Sestir, M. A. (2006). Chronic violent video game exposure and desensitization to violence: Behavioral and event-related brain potential data. *Journal of Experimental Social Psychology, 42,* 532–539.

Basbaum A. L., & Jessell, T. M. (2000). The perception of pain. In E. R. Kandel, J. H. Schwartz, & T. M. Jessell (Eds.), *Principles of neural science* (4th ed.; pp. 472–491). New York: McGraw-Hill.

Basson, R. (2000). The female sexual response: A different model. *Journal of Sex & Marital Therapy, 26,* 51–65.

Batey, M., & Furnham, A. (2008). Creativity, intelligence, and personality: A critical review of the scattered literature. *Genetic, Social, and General Psychology Monographs, 132,* 355–429.

Batson, C. D. (1991). *The altruism question: Toward a social psychological answer.* Hillsdale, NJ: Erlbaum.

Batson, C. D., Fultz, J., & Schoenrade, P. A. (1987). Distress and empathy: Two qualitatively distinct vicarious emotions with different motivational consequences. *Journal of Personality, 55,* 19–39.

Bauer, F., Korpert, K., Neuberger, M., Raber, A., & Schwetz, F. (1992). Risk-factors for hearing-loss at different frequencies in a population of 47388 noise-exposed workers. *Journal of Acoustic Society of America, 6,* 3086–3098.

Bauer, M., & Whybrow, P. C. (2001). Thyroid hormone, neural tissue and mood modulation. *World Journal of Biological Psychiatry, 2,* 57–67.

Bauer, M. S., & Mitchner, L. (2004). What is a "mood stabilizer"? An evidence-based response. *American Journal of Psychiatry, 161,* 3–18.

Baumeister, R., & Leary, M. (1995). The need to belong: Desire for interpersonal attachments as a fundamental human motivation. *Psychological Bulletin, 117,* 497–529.

Baumrind, D. (1964). Some thoughts on ethics of research: After reading Milgram's "Behavioral study of obedience." *American Psychologist, 19,* 421–423.

Bavelier, D., Tomann, A., Hutton, C., Mitchell, T., Corina, D., Liu, G., et al. (2000). Visual attention to the periphery is enhanced in congenitally deaf individuals. *Journal of Neuroscience, 20,* 1–6.

Beadle-Brown, J., Murphy, G., & Wing, L. (2006). The Camberwell cohort 25 years on: Characteristics and changes in skills over time. *Journal of Applied Research in Intellectual Disabilities, 19*(4), 317–329.

Beck, A. T. (1976). *Cognitive therapy and emotional disorders.* New York: International Universities Press.

Beck, A. T., & Emery, G. (1985). *Anxiety disorders and phobias.* New York: Basic Books.

Beede, K. E., & Kass, S. J. (2006). Engrossed in conversation: The impact of cell phones on simulated driving performance. *Accident Analysis and Prevention, 38,* 415–421.

Beeman, M. J., & Bowden, E. M. (2000). The right hemisphere maintains solution-related activation for yet-to-be solved insight problems. *Memory & Cognition, 28,* 1231–1241.

Begley, S. (2007). *Train your mind, change your brain.* New York: Ballantine Books.

Belisle, P., & Chapais, B. (2001). Tolerated co-feeding in relation to degree of kinship in Japanese macaques. *Behaviour, 138,* 487–509.

Bell, A. P., Weinberg, M. S., & Hammersmith, S. K. (1981). *Sexual preference: Its development in men and women.* Bloomington: Indiana University Press.

Bellack, A. S., Bennett, M. E., Gearon, J. S., Brown, C. H., & Yang, Y. (2006). A randomized clinical trial of a new behavioral treatment for drug abuse in people with severe and persistent mental illness. *Archives of General Psychiatry, 63,* 426–432.

Belmonte, M. K., Allen, G., Beckel-Mitchener, A., Boulanger, L. M., Carper, R. A., & Webb, S. J. (2004). Autism and abnormal development of brain connectivity. *Journal of Neuroscience, 24,* 9228–9231.

Bem, D. J., & Horonton, C. (1994). Does psi exist? Replicable evidence for an anomalous process of information transfer. *Psychological Bulletin, 115,* 4–18.

Benarroch, E. (2007). Neurosteroids: Endogenous modulators of neuronal excitability and plasticity. *Neurology, 68,* 945–947.

Benjamin, J., Li, L., Patterson, C., Greenburg, B. D., Murphy, D. L., & Hamer, D. H. (1996). Population and familial association between the D4 dopamine receptor gene and measures of novelty seeking. *Nature Genetics, 12,* 81–84.

Benjamin, L. T., Jr. (2007). *A brief history of modern psychology.* Malden, MA: Blackwell.

Bennett, E. L., Diamond, M. C., Krech, D., & Rosenzweig, M. R. (1964). Chemical and anatomical plasticity of brain. *Science, 146,* 610–619.

Bennett, P. J., Sekuler, R., & Sekuler, A. B. (2007). The effects of aging on motion detection and direction identification. *Vision Research, 47,* 799–809.

Berenbaum, S. A., Korman, K., & Leveroni, C. (1995). Early hormones and sex differences in cognitive abilities. *Learning and Individual Differences, 7,* 303–321.

Berger, J. (1994). *The young scientists: America's future and the winning of the Westinghouse.* Reading, MA: Addison-Wesley.

Berkman, L. F., & Glass, T. (2000). Social integration, social networks, social support and health. In L. F. Berkman & I. Kawachi (Eds.), *Social epidemiology* (pp. 137–173). New York: Oxford University Press.

Berlyne, D. (1960). *Conflict, arousal, and curiosity.* New York: McGraw-Hill.

Bernat, J. (2006). Chronic disorders of consciousness. *Lancet, 367,* 1181–1192.

Berridge, K. C. (2004). Motivation concepts in behavioral neuroscience. *Physiology and Behavior, 81,* 179–209.

Berthoud, H. R. (2002). Multiple neural systems controlling food intake and body weight. *Neuroscience and Biobehavioral Reviews, 26,* 393–428.

Bexton, W. H., Heron, W., & Scott, T. H. (1954). Effects of decreased variation in the sensory environment. *Canadian Journal of Psychology, 8,* 70–76.

Bhagar, H. A., & Schmetzer, A. D. (2006). The new antidipsotropics. *Annals of the American Psychotherapy Association, 9,* 29–30.

Bialystok, E., Craik, F. I. M., & Freedman, M. (2007). Bilingualism as a protection against the onset of symptoms of dementia. *Neuropsychologia, 45,* 459–464.

Bialystok, E., Craik, F. I. M., & Ryan, J. (2006). Executive control in a modified antisaccade task: Effects of aging and bilingualism. *Journal of Experimental Psychology: Learning, Memory, & Cognition, 32,* 1341–1354.

Bickerton, D. (1995). *Language and human behavior.* Seattle, WA: University of Washington Press.

Binder, E., Droste, S. K., Ohl, F., & Reul, J. M. (2004). Regular voluntary exercise reduces anxiety-related behavior and impulsiveness in mice. *Behavioural Brain Research, 155,* 197–206.

Biography, Esref Armagan (n.d.). Retrieved October 23, 2007, from http://www.esrefarmagan.com/bio.html

Birch, L. L., & Fisher, J. A. (1996). The role of experience in the development of children's eating behavior. In E. D. Capaldi (Ed.), *Why we eat what we eat: The psychology of eating* (pp. 113–141). Washington, DC: American Psychological Association.

Birch, L. L., & Marlin, D. W. (1982). I don't like it; I never tried it: Effects of exposure on two-year-old children's food preferences. *Appetite, 3,* 353–360.

Birdsong, D. (2006). Age and second language acquisition and processing: A selective overview. *Language Learning, 56,* 9–49.

Bishop, S. J. (2007). Neurocognitive mechanisms of anxiety: An integrative account. *Trends in Cognitive Sciences, 11,* 307–316.

Biss, W. J., & Horne, S. G. (2005). Sexual satisfaction as more than a gendered concept: The roles of psychological well-being and sexual orientation. *Journal of Constructivist Psychology, 18,* 25–38.

Bjork, R. A. (2001, March). How to succeed in college: Learn how to learn. *American Psychological Society Observer, 14,* 3, 9.

Black, D. W. (2006). Efficacy of combined pharmacotherapy and psychotherapy versus monotherapy in the treatment of anxiety disorders. *CNS Spectrums, 11,* 29–33.

Blakeslee, S. (2005, February 8). Focus narrows in search for autism's cause. *New York Times.* Retrieved from http://www.nytimes.com

Blakeslee, S., & Blakeslee, M. (2007). *The body has a mind of its own.* New York: Random House.

Blass, T. (2004). *The man who shocked the world: The life and legacy of Stanley Milgram.* New York: Basic Books.

Bleier, P., Habib, R., & Flament, M. F. (2006). Pharmacotherapies in the management of obsessive-compulsive disorder. *Canadian Journal of Psychiatry, 51,* 417–430.

Block, J., Block, J. H., & Keyes, S. (1988). Longitudinally foretelling drug usage in adolescence: Early childhood personality and environmental precursors. *Child Development, 59,* 336–355.

Blonigen, D. M., Hicks, B. M., Krueger, R. F., Patrick, C. J., & Iacono, W. G. (2006). Continuity and change in psychopathic traits as measured via normal-range personality: A longitudinal–biometric study. *Journal of Abnormal Psychology, 115,* 85–95.

Bollen, E., & Wojciechowski, F. L. (2004). Anorexia nervosa subtypes and the Big Five personality factors. *European Eating Disorders Review, 12,* 117–121.

Bolour, S., & Braunstein, G. (2005). Testosterone therapy in women: A review. *International Journal of Impotence Research, 17,* 399–408.

Bond, R., & Smith, P. B. (1996). Culture and conformity: A meta-analysis of studies using Asch's (1952b, 1956) line judgment task. *Psychological Bulletin, 119,* 111–137.

Bonnet, M., Decety, J., Jeannerod, M., & Requin, J. (1997). Mental simulation of an action modulates the excitability of spinal reflex pathways in man. *Cognitive Brain Research, 5,* 221–228.

Book, A. S., Starzyk, K. B., & Quinsey, V. L. (2001). The relationship between testosterone and aggression: A meta-analysis. *Aggression and Violent Behavior, 6,* 579–599.

Boorboor, S. (2002). Integrating the incompatible: The rise of the incorporated immune system. (University of Rochester) *Journal of Undergraduate Research, 1,* 10–26.

Botvinick, M. M., Cohen, J. D., & Carter, C. S. (2004). Conflict monitoring and anterior cingulate cortex: An update. *Trends in Cognitive Sciences, 8,* 539–546.

Botwin, M., Buss, D. M., & Shackelford, T. K. (1997). Personality and mate preferences: Five factors in mate selection and marital satisfaction. *Journal of Personality and Social Psychology, 65,* 107–136.

Bouchard, T. J., Jr., & Loehlin, J. C. (2001). Genes, evolution, and personality. *Behavioral Genetics, 31,* 243–273.

Bourgeois, S., & Johnson, A. (2004). Preparing for dying: Meaningful practices in palliative care. *Omega: Journal of Death and Dying, 49,* 99–107.

Bouton, M. E., Mineka, S., & Barlow, D. H. (2001). A modern learning theory perspective on the etiology of panic disorder. *Psychological Review, 108,* 4–32.

Bowden, C. L. (1994). Bipolar disorder and creativity. In M. P. Shaw & M. A. Runco (Eds.), *Creativity and affect* (pp. 73–86). Norwood, NJ: Ablex.

Bowden, E. M., & Jung-Beeman, M. (2003). Aha! Insight experience correlates with solution activation in the right hemisphere. *Psychonomic Bulletin & Review, 10*, 730–737.

Bowden, E. M., Jung-Beeman, M., Fleck, J., & Kounios, J. (2005). New approaches to demystifying insight. *Trends in Cognitive Sciences, 9*, 322–328.

Bower, B. (2005, December 10). The Piraha challenge: An Amazonian tribe takes grammar to a strange place. *Science News, 168*(24). Retrieved from http://www.sciencenews.org

Bowlby, J. (1969). *Attachment and Loss: Vol. 1. Attachment.* New York: Basic Books.

Bowlby, J. (1973). *Attachment and Loss: Vol. 2. Separation, anxiety, and anger.* New York: Basic Books.

Bowlby, J. (1980). *Attachment and Loss: Vol. 3. Loss, sadness, and depression.* New York: Basic Books.

Boyack, K. W., Klavans, R., & Börner, K. (2005). Mapping the backbone of science. *Scientometrics, 64*, 351–374.

Boyd, D. (2007). Why youth (heart) Social Network Sites: The role of networked publics in teenage social life. In D. Buckingham (Ed.), *MacArthur Foundation Series on Digital Learning—Youth, Identity, and Digital Media Volume* (pp. 1–26). Cambridge, MA: MIT Press.

Bradberry, C. W. (2007). Cocaine sensitization and dopamine mediation of cue effects in rodents, monkeys, and humans: Areas of agreement, disagreement, and implications for addiction. *Psychopharmacology, 191*, 705–717.

Bradley, R. M. (1972). Development of the taste bud and gustatory papillae in human fetuses. In J. F. Bosma (Ed.), *The third symposium on oral sensation and perception: The mouth of the infant.* Springfield, IL: Thomas.

Brand, G., & Millot, J-L. (2001). Sex differences in human olfaction: Between evidence and enigma. *The Quarterly Journal of Experimental Psychology B: Comparative and Physiological Psychology, 54B*, 259–270.

Breiter, H. C., Etcoff, N. L., Whalen, P. J., Kennedy, W. A., Rauch, S. L., Buckner, R. L., et al. (1996). Response and habituation of the human amygdala during visual processing of facial expressions. *Neuron, 17*, 875–887.

Breland, K., & Breland, M. (1961). The misbehavior of organisms. *American Psychologist, 16*, 681–684.

Breugelmans, S. M., Poortinga, Y. H., Ambadar, Z., Setiadi, B., Vaca, J. B., Widiyanto, B., et al. (2005). Body sensations associated with emotions in Rarámuri Indians, rural Javanese, and three student samples. *Emotion, 5*, 166–174.

Brewer, M. B., & Caporael, L. R. (2006). An evolutionary perspective on social identity: Revisiting groups. In M. Schaller, D. T. Kenrick, & J. A. Simpson (Eds.), *Evolution and social psychology* (pp. 143–161). New York: Psychology Press.

Brickman, P., Coates, D., & Janoff-Bulman, R. (1978). Lottery winners and accident victims: Is happiness relative? *Journal of Personality and Social Psychology, 36*, 917–927.

Bridges, K. (1932). Emotional development in infancy. *Child Development, 3*, 324–341.

Briggs, C. (2005). Allen uses films to avoid anxiety. *BBC News-Online.* Retrieved July 3, 2008, from http://news.bbc.co.uk/2/hi/entertainment/4539493.stm

Brivic, S. (1980). *Joyce between Freud and Jung.* Port Washington, NY: Kennikat Press.

Broadbent, D. E. (1954). The role of auditory localization in attention and memory span. *Journal of Experimental Psychology, 44*, 51–55.

Brody, L. R., & Hall, J. A. (2000). Gender, emotion, and expression. In M. Lewis and J. M. Haviland-Jones (Eds.), *Handbook of emotions* (2nd ed.; pp. 338–349). New York: Guilford Press.

Broude G., & Greene, S. (1980). Crosscultural codes on 20 sexual attitudes and practices. In H. Barry & A. Schlegel (Eds), *Cross-cultural samples and codes* (pp. 313–333). Pittsburgh: University of Pittsburgh Press.

Brown, A. S. (2006). Prenatal infection as a risk factor for schizophrenia. *Schizophrenia Bulletin, 32*, 200–202.

Brown, A. S., Begg, M. D., Gravenstein, S., Schaefer, C. A., Wyatt, R. J., Bresnahan, M., et al. (2004). Serologic evidence of prenatal influenza in the etiology of schizophrenia. *Archives of General Psychiatry, 61*, 774–780.

Brown, K. W., & Ryan, R. M. (2003). The benefits of being present: Mindfulness and its role in psychological well-being. *Journal of Personality and Social Psychology, 84*, 822–848.

Brown, R. T., Reynolds, C. R., & Whitaker, J. S. (1999). Bias in mental testing since Jensen's "Bias in Mental Testing." *School Psychology Quarterly, 14*, 208–238.

Brown, T. S., & Wallace, P. (1980). *Physiological psychology.* New York: Academic Press.

Brown/Grizzly Bear Facts (n.d.). Retrieved November 5, 2007 from http://www.bear.org/Grizzly/Grizzly_Brown_Bear_Facts.html

Bruner, J. S., & Minturn, A. L. (1955). Perceptual identification and perceptual organization. *Journal of General Psychology, 53*, 21–28.

Bryans, W. A. (1959). Mitotic activity in the brain of the adult white rat. *Anatomical Record, 133*, 65–71.

Buchanan, T. W., & Tranel, D. (2008). Stress and emotional memory retrieval: Effects of sex and cortisol response. *Neurobiology of Learning and Memory, 89*, 134–141.

Buck, L. B. (2000). Smell and taste: The chemical senses. In E. R. Kandel, J. H. Schwartz, & T. M. Jessell (Eds.), *Principles of neural science* (4th ed.; pp. 625–647). New York: McGraw-Hill.

Buckley, C. (2007, January 3). Man is rescued by stranger on subway tracks. *New York Times.* Retrieved from http://www.nytimes.com

Bulik, C. M., Sullivan, P. F., Tozzi, F., Furberg, H., Lichtenstein, P., & Pedersen, N. L. (2006). Prevalence, heritability, and prospective risk factors for anorexia nervosa. *Archives of General Psychiatry, 63*, 305–312.

Bulkeley, K. (1997). *An introduction to the psychology of dreaming.* Westport, CT: Praeger.

Bullivant, S. B., Sellergren, S. A., Stern, K. Spencer, N. A., Jacob, S., Mennella, J. A., & McClintock, M. K. (2004). Women's sexual experience during the menstrual cycle: Identification of the sexual phase by noninvasive measurement of luteinizing hormone. *Journal of Sex Research, 41*, 82–93.

Burch, G., Pavelis, C., Hemsley, D. R., & Corr, P. J. (2006). Schizotypy and creativity in visual artists. *British Journal of Psychology, 97*, 177–190.

Burd, L., Roberts, D., Olson, M., & Odendaal, H. (2007). Ethanol and the placenta: A review. *The Journal of Maternal-Fetal and Neonatal Medicine, 20*, 361–375.

Burnstein, E., Crandall, C., & Kitayama, S. (1994). Some neo-Darwinian decision rules for altruism: Weighing cues for inclusive fitness as a function of the biological importance of the decision. *Journal of Personality and Social Psychology, 67*, 773–789.

Burton, T. M. (2007, September 26). One doctor's lonely quest to heal brain injury. *The Wall Street Journal (online).* Retrieved from http://www.wsj.com

Bushman, B. J., & Anderson, C. A. (2001). Media violence and the American public: Scientific facts versus media misinformation. *American Psychologist, 56*, 477–489.

Buss, A. H., & Plomin, R. (1984). Temperament: Early personality traits. Hillsdale, NJ: Erlbaum.

Buss, D. M. (1990). Toward a biologically informed psychology of personality. *Journal of Personality, 58*, 1–16.

Buss, D. M. (1999). *Evolutionary psychology: The new science of the mind*. New York: Allyn & Bacon.

Buss, D. M. (2003). *The evolution of desire: Strategies of human mating* (Rev. ed.). New York: Basic Books.

Buss, D. M. (2004). Sex differences in human mate preferences. In H. T. Reis & C. E. Rusbuslt (Eds.), *Close relationships: Key readings* (pp. 135–151). Philadelphia: Taylor & Francis.

Buss, D. M., & Greiling, H. (1999). Adaptive individual differences. *Journal of Personality, 67*, 209–243.

Buss, D. M., & Schmitt, D. P. (1993). Sexual strategies theory: An evolutionary perspective on human mating. *Psychological Review, 100*, 204–232.

Cahill, S. P., Foa, E. B., Hembree E. A., Marshall, R. D., & Nacash, N. (2006). *Journal of Traumatic Stress, 19*, 597–610.

Cairney, J., Corna, L., Veldhuizen, S., Herrmann, N., & Streiner, D. (2008). Comorbid depression and anxiety in later life: Patterns of association, subjective well-being, and impairment. *American Journal of Geriatric Psychiatry, 16*(3), 201–208.

Calaprice, A. (Ed.) (2005). *The new quotable Einstein*. Princeton, NJ: Princeton University Press.

Calkins, M. W. (1898). Short studies in memory and in association from the Wellesley College Psychological Laboratory. I.: A study of immediate and delayed recall of the concrete and of the verbal. *Psychological Review, 5*, 451–456.

Campbell, F. A., & Ramey, C. T. (1995). Cognitive and school outcomes for high-risk African-American students at middle adolescence: Positive effects of early intervention. *American Educational Research Journal, 32*, 743–772.

Campbell, F. A., Ramey, C. T., Pungello, E. P., Sparling, J., & Miller-Johnson, S. (2002). Early childhood education: Young adult outcomes from the Abecedarian Project. *Applied Developmental Science, 6*, 42–57.

Campos, J. J., & Stenberg, C. (1981). Perception, appraisal, and emotion: The onset of social referencing. In M. E. Lamb & L. R. Sherrod (Eds.), *Infant social cognition: Empirical and theoretical considerations* (pp. 273–314). Hillsdale, NJ: Erlbaum.

Camras, L. A., Oster, H., Bakeman, R., Meng, Z., Ujiie, T., & Campos, J. J. (2007). Do infants show distinct negative facial expressions for fear and anger? Emotional expression in 11-month-old European American, Chinese, and Japanese infants. *Infancy, 11*, 131–155.

Cannon, M., Caspi, A., Moffitt, T., Harrington, H., Taylor, A., Murray, R. M., et al. (2002). Evidence for early childhood pandevelopmental impairment specific to schizophreniform disorder: Results from a longitudinal birth cohort. *Archives of General Psychiatry, 59*, 449–456.

Cannon, W. B. (1929). *Bodily changes in pain, hunger, fear, and rage: An account of recent researches into the function of emotional excitement*. New York: Appleton.

Cannon, W. B. (1939). *The wisdom of the body*. New York: W. W. Norton.

Cannon, W. B., & Washburn, A. L. (1912). An explanation of hunger. *American Journal of Physiology, 29*, 441–454.

Canter, R. R., & Hirsch, J. (1955). An experimental comparison of several psychological scales of weight. *American Journal of Psychology, 68*, 645–649.

Cantor, J. (1998). Children's attraction to violent television programming. In J. H. Goldstein (Ed.), *Why we watch: The attractions of violent entertainment* (pp. 88–115). New York: Oxford University Press.

Caramagno, T. C. (1992). *The flight of the mind: Virginia Woolf's art and manic-depressive illness*. Berkeley: University of California Press.

Cardno, A. G., & Gottesman, I. I. (2000). Twin studies of schizophrenia: From bow-and-arrow concordances to Star Wars Mx and functional genomics [Review]. *American Journal of Medical Genetics, 97*, 12–17.

Carew, T. J., & Kandel, E. R. (1973). Acquisition and retention of long-term habituation in *Aplysia*: Correlation of behavioral and cellular processes. *Science, 182*, 1158–1160.

Carlat, D. J. (1998). The psychiatric review of symptoms: A screening tool for family physicians. *American Family Physician, 58*, 1617–1624.

Carless, S. A. (1999). Career assessment: Holland's vocational interests, personality characteristics, and abilities. *Journal of Career Assessment, 7*, 125–144.

Carlo, G. (2006). Care-based and altruistically based morality. In M. Killen and J. G. Smetana (Eds.), *Handbook of moral development* (pp. 551–579). Mahwah, NJ: Erlbaum.

Carlsson, I. (2002). Anxiety and flexibility of defense related to high or low creativity. *Creativity Research Journal, 14*, 341–349.

Carnagey, N. L., Anderson, C. A., & Bushman, B. J. (2007). The effect of video game violence on physiological desensitization to real-life violence. *Journal of Experimental Social Psychology, 43*, 489–496.

Carney, S. M., & Goodwin, G. M. (2005). Lithium—a continuing story in the treatment of bipolar disorder. *Acta Psychiatrica Scandinavia, 111*(Suppl. 426), 7–12.

Carr, L. K. (2007, March 14). Teenager's science project wins $100,000 scholarship.

New York Times. Retrieved from http://www.nytimes.com

Carroll, J. B. (1993). *Human cognitive abilities*. New York: Cambridge University Press.

Carroll, J. L., & Rest, J. (1981, December). Development in moral judgment as indicated by rejection of lower-stage statements. *Journal of Research in Personality, 15*(4), 538–544.

Carson, S. H., Peterson, J. B., & Higgins, D. M. (2003). Decreased latent inhibition is associated with increased creative achievement in high-functioning individuals. *Journal of Personality and Social Psychology, 85*, 499–506.

Carstensen, L. L. (2006). The influence of a sense of time on human development. *Science, 312*, 1913–1915.

Carstensen, L. L., Fung, H. H., & Charles, S. T. (2003). Socioemotional selectivity theory and the regulation of emotion in the second half of life. *Motivation and Emotion, 27*, 103–123.

Carter, C. S., Mintun, M., Nichols, T. N. & Cohen, J. D. (1997). Anterior cingulate gyrus dysfunction and selective attention deficits in schizophrenia: [15O]H2O PET study during single-trial Stroop task performance. *American Journal of Psychiatry, 154*, 1670–1675.

Casey, B. J., Davidson, M., & Rosen, B. (2002). Functional magnetic imaging: Basic principles of and application to developmental science. *Developmental Science, 5*, 301–309.

Caspi, A. (2000). The child is father of the man: Personality continuities from childhood to adulthood. *Journal of Personality and Social Psychology, 78*, 158–172.

Caspi, A., McClay, J., Moffitt, T. E., Mill, J., Martin, J., Craig, I. W., et al. (2002). Role of genotype in the cycle of violence in maltreated children. *Science, 297*, 851–853.

Caspi, A., Roberts, B. W., & Shiner, R. L. (2003). Personality development: Stability and change. *Annual Review of Psychology, 56*, 453–484.

Caspi, A., Sugden, K., Moffitt, T. E., Taylor, A., Craig, I. W., Harrington, H., et al. (2003). Influence of life stress on depression: Moderation by a polymorphism in the 5-HTT gene. *Science, 301*, 386–389.

Catapano, F., Perris, F., Masella, M., Rossano, F., Cigliano, M., Magliano, L., & et al. (2006). Obsessive–compulsive disorder: A 3-year prospective follow-up study of patients treated with serotonin reuptake inhibitors. *Journal of Psychiatric Research, 40*, 502–510.

Cavallero, C., & Foulkes, D. (Eds.). (1993). *Dreaming as cognition*. New York: Harvester-Wheatsheaf.

CBS News. (2007, January 3). Bystander pulls off daring subway rescue. Retrieved from http://www.cbsnews.com/stories/2007/

01/03/national/main2324961.shtml?source =search_story

Ceci, S. J., & Williams, W. M. (2007). *Why aren't more women in science? Top researchers debate the evidence.* Washington, DC: American Psychological Association.

Centers for Disease Control and Prevention (CDC). (2001). *Cigarette-smoking related mortality.* Retrieved March 26, 2007, from http://www.cdc.gov/tobacco/research_data/ health_consequences/mortali.htm

Centers for Disease Control and Prevention (CDC). (2005). *Sexual behavior and selected health measures: Men and women 15–44 years of age, United States, 2002.* Retrieved March 12, 2008, from http://www.cdc.gov/ nchs/data/ad/ad362.pdf

Centers for Disease Control and Prevention (CDC). (2006). *Smoking and tobacco use fact sheet.* Retrieved May 16, 2008, from http://www.cdc.gov/tobacco/data_statistics/ Factsheets/cessation2.htm

Centers for Disease Control and Prevention (CDC). (2007, August 8). *Smoking during pregnancy.* Retrieved February 23, 2008, from http://www.cdc.gov/tobacco/health_ effects/pregnancy.htm

Centers for Disease Control and Prevention. (2007, May 31). *Fetal Alcohol Disorders* Retrieved April 25, 2008, from http://www .cdc.gov/ncbddd/fas/default.htm

Chaffee, J. (1999). *The thinker's guide to college success* (2nd ed.). Boston: Houghton Mifflin.

Chance, P. (1986). *Thinking in the classroom: A survey of programs.* New York: Teachers College, Columbia University.

Chang, E. C. (1998). Dispositional optimism and primary and secondary appraisal of a stressor: Controlling for confounding influences and relations to coping and psychological and physical adjustment. *Journal of Personality and Social Psychology, 74,* 1109–1120.

Chappell, M., & Humphreys, M. S. (1994). An auto-associative neural network for spares representations: Analysis and application to models of recognition and cued recall. *Psychological Review, 101,* 103–128.

Charney, D. S. (2004). Psychological mechanisms of resilience and vulnerability: Implications for successful adaptation to extreme stress. *American Journal of Psychiatry, 161,* 195–216.

Chatterjee, A., Strauss, M. E., Smyth, K. A., & Whitehouse, P. J. (1992). Personality changes in Alzheimer's disease. *Archives of Neurology, 49,* 486–491.

Chechik, G., Meilijson, I., & Ruppin, E. (1999). Neuronal regulation: A mechanism for synaptic pruning during brain maturation. *Neural Computation, 11,* 2151–2170.

Cheetham, C. E. J., Hammond, M. S. L., Edwards, C. J., & Finnerty, G. T. (2007). Sensory experience alters cortical connectivity and synaptic function site specifically. *The Journal of Neuroscience, 27,* 3456–3465.

Chen, J. V., Chen, C. C., & Yang, H-H. (2007). An empirical evaluation of key factors contributing to Internet abuse in the workplace. *Industrial Management & Data Systems, 108,* 87–106.

Chen, S. Y., Jordan, C., & Thompson, S. (2006). The effect of cognitive behavioral therapy (CBT) on depression: The role of problem-solving appraisal. *Research on Social Work Practice, 16,* 500–510.

Chia, E., Wang, J. J., Rochtchina, E., Cumming, R. R., Newall, P., & Mitchell, P. (2007). Hearing impairment and health-related quality of life: The Blue Mountains Hearing Study. *Ear & Hearing, 28,* 187–195.

Choi, I., Nisbett, R. E., & Norenzayan, A. (1999). Causal attribution across cultures: Variation and universality. *Psychological Bulletin, 125,* 47–65.

Chomsky, N. (1972). *Language and mind* (2nd ed.). New York: Harcourt Brace Jovanovich.

Chomsky, N. (1986). *Knowledge of language: Its nature, origins, and use.* New York: Praeger.

Chomsky, N. (2000). *New horizons in the study of language and the mind.* Cambridge: Cambridge University Press.

Choy, Y., Fyer, A. J., & Lipsitz, J. D. (2007). Treatment of specific phobia in adults. *Clinical Psychology Review, 27*(3), 266–286. Advance online publication. doi:10.1016/j .cpr.2006.10.002

Christakis, N. A., & Fowler, J. H. (2007). The spread of obesity in a large social network over 32 years. *New England Journal of Medicine, 357,* 370–379.

Christakis, N. A., & Fowler, J. H. (2008). The collective dynamics of smoking in a large social network. *New England Journal of Medicine, 358,* 2249–2258.

Christensen, K., Herskind, A. M., & Vaupel, J. W. (2006). Why Danes are smug: Comparative study of life satisfaction in the European Union. *British Medical Journal, 333,* 1289–1291.

Chuang, D. M. (2004). Lithium protection from glutamate excitotoxicity: Therapeutic implications. *Clinical Neuroscience Research, 4,* 243–252.

Churchill, J. D., Galvez, R., Colcombe, S., Swain, R. A., Kramer, A. F., & Greenough, W. T. (2002). Exercise, experience and the aging brain. *Neurobiology of Aging, 23,* 941–955.

Cichetti, D. (2001). How a child builds a brain. In W. W. Hartup & R. A. Weinberg (Eds.), *Child psychology in retrospect and prospect.* Mahwah, NJ: Erlbaum.

Clancy, P. M. (1985). The acquisition of Japanese. In D. Slobin (Ed.), *The crosslinguistic study of language acquisition: Vol. 1. The data.* Hillsdale, NJ: Erlbaum.

Clark, A. E., Georgellis, Y., Lucas, R. E., & Diener, E. (2004). Unemployment alters the set point for life satisfaction. *Psychological Science, 15,* 8–15.

Clark, D. B, Thatcher, D. L., & Tapert, S. F. (2008). Alcohol, psychological dysregulation, and adolescent brain development. *Alcoholism: Clinical and Experimental Research, 32,* 375–385.

Clark, L., Bosworth, H., Welsh-Bohmer, K., Dawson, D., & Siegler, I. (2000). Relation between informant-rated personality and clinician-rated depression in patients with memory disorders. *Neuropsychiatry, Neuropsychology, & Behavioral Neurology, 13,* 39–47.

Clark, L. A., Watson, D., & Leeka, J. (1989). Diurnal variation in the positive affects. *Motivation and Emotion, 13,* 205–234.

Clark, R. D., III, & Hatfield, E. (1989). Gender differences in willingness to engage in casual sex. *Journal of Psychology and Human Sexuality, 2,* 39–55.

Clark, R. D., III, & Hatfield, E. (2003). Love in the afternoon. *Psychological Inquiry, 14,* 227–231.

Clark, W. R., & Grunstein, M. (2000). *Are we hardwired? The role of genes in human behavior.* New York: Oxford University Press.

Clarke, G. N., Hawkins, W., Murphy, M., Sheeber, L. B., Lewinsohn, P. M., & Seeley, J. R. (1995). Targeted prevention of unipolar depressive disorder in an at-risk sample of high school adolescents: A randomized trial of group cognitive intervention. *Journal of the American Academy of Child & Adolescent Psychiatry, 34,* 312–321.

Coe, C. L., & Lubach, G. R. (2008). Fetal programming: Prenatal origins of health and illness. *Current Directions in Psychological Science, 17,* 36–41.

Cohen, J. D. (2005). The vulcanization of the human brain. *Journal of Economic Perspectives, 19,* 3–24.

Cohen, K. M. (2002). Relationships among childhood sex-atypical behavior, spatial ability, handedness, and sexual orientation in men. *Archives of Sexual Behavior, 31,* 129–143.

Cohen, S. (2004). Social relationships and health. *American Psychologist, 59,* 676–684.

Cohen, S., Alper, C. M., Doyle, W. J., Adler, N., Treanor, J. J., & Turner, R. B. (2008). Objective and subjective socioeconomic status and susceptibility to the common cold. *Health Psychology, 27,* 268–274.

Cohen, S., Doyle, W. J., Turner, R. B., Alper, C. M., & Skoner, D. P. (2003). Sociability and susceptibility to the common cold. *Psychological Science, 14,* 389–395.

Cohen, S., Tyrrell, D. A. J., & Smith, A. P. (1993). Negative life events, perceived stress, negative affect, and susceptibility to the common cold. *Journal of Personality and Social Psychology, 64,* 131–140.

Cohen, S., & Wills, T. A. (1985). Stress, social support, and the buffering hypothesis. *Psychological Bulletin, 98,* 310–357.

Colcombe, S. J., Erickson, K. I., Scalf, P. E., Kim, J. S., Praskash, R., McAuley, E., et al. (2006). Aerobic exercise training increases brain volume in aging humans. *Journal of Gerontology, 61,* 1166–1170.

Colcombe, S. J., & Kramer, A. F. (2003). Fitness effects on the cognitive function of older adults: A meta-analytic study. *Psychological Science, 14,* 125–130.

Collins, A., & Loftus, E. F. (1975). A spreading activation theory of semantic processing. *Psychological Review, 82,* 407–428.

Comer, R. J. (2007). *Abnormal psychology* (6th ed.). New York: Worth.

Comery, T. A., Stamoudis, C. X., Irwin, S. A., & Greenough, W. T. (1996). Increased density of multiple-head dendritic spines on medium-sized spiny neurons of the striatum in rats reared in a complex environment. *Neurobiology of Learning and Memory, 66,* 93–96.

Conduct Problems Prevention Research Group (1999a). Initial impact of the Fast Track prevention trial for conduct problems: I. The high-risk sample. *Journal of Consulting and Clinical Psychology, 67,* 631–647.

Conduct Problems Prevention Research Group (1999b). Initial impact of the Fast Track prevention trial for conduct problems: II. Classroom effects. *Journal of Consulting and Clinical Psychology, 67,* 648–657.

Correll, J., Park, B., Judd, C. M., & Wittenbrink, B. (2002). The police officer's dilemma: Using ethnicity to disambiguate potentially threatening individuals. *Journal of Personality and Social Psychology, 83,* 1314–1329.

Costa, P. T. (1996). Work and personality: Use of the NEO–PI–R in industrial/organizational psychology. *Applied Psychology: An International Review, 45,* 225–241.

Costa, P. T., Herbst, J. H., McCrae, R. R., & Siegler, I. C. (2000). Personality at midlife: Stability, intrinsic maturation, and response to life events. *Assessment, 7,* 365–378.

Costa, P. T., & McCrae, R. R. (1976). Age differences in personality structure: A cluster analytic approach. *Journal of Gerontology, 31,* 564–570.

Costa, P. T., & McCrae, R. R. (1980). Influences of extraversion and neuroticism on subjective well-being. *Journal of Personality and Social Psychology, 38,* 668–678.

Costa, P. T., & McCrae, R. R. (1992). *NEO PI-R professional manual.* Odessa, FL: Psychological Assessment Resources.

Cotman, C. W., Berchtold, N. C., & Christie, L. A. (2007). Exercise builds brain health: Key roles of growth factor cascades and inflammation. *Trends in Neurosciences, 30,* 464–472.

Couch, D., & Liamputtong, P. (2008). Online dating and mating: The use of Internet to meet sexual partners. *Qualitative Health Research, 18,* 268–279.

Courchesne, E., Carper, R., &, Akshoomoff, N. (2003). Evidence of brain overgrowth in the first year of life in autism. *Journal of American Medical Association, 290,* 337–344.

Coyne, J. C., Stefanek, M., & Palmer, S. C. (2007). Psychotherapy and survival in cancer: The conflict between hope and evidence. *Psychological Bulletin, 133,* 367–394.

Craik, F. I. M. (1979). The structure and organization of memory. *Annual Review of Psychology, 30,* 63–102.

Craik, F. I. M., & Lockhart, R. S. (1972). Levels of processing: A framework for memory research. *Journal of Verbal Learning and Verbal Behavior, 11,* 671–684.

Craik, F. I. M., & Tulving, E. (1975). Depth of processing and the retention of words in episodic memory. *Journal of Experimental Psychology: General, 104,* 268–294.

Crockenberg, S. C., Leerkes, E. M., & Lekka, S. K. (2007). Pathways from marital aggression to infant emotion regulation: The development of withdrawal in infancy. *Infant Behavior & Development, 30,* 97–113.

Crook, T. H., Youngjohn, J. R., Larrabee, G. J., & Salama, M. (1992). Aging and everyday memory: A cross-cultural study. *Neuropsychology, 6,* 123–136.

Cross, S. E., & Markus, H. (1999). The cultural constitution of personality. In L. A. Pervin & O. P. John (Eds.), *Handbook of personality theory and research* (pp. 378–396). New York: Guilford Press.

Crump, T. (2001). *A brief history of science.* New York: Carroll & Graf.

Crystal, J. D., Maxwell, K. W., & Hohmann, A. G. (2003). Cannabinoid modulation of sensitivity to time. *Behavioural Brain Research, 144,* 57–66.

Csikszentmihalyi, M. (1990). *Flow: The psychology of optimal experience.* New York: HarperPerennial.

Csikszentmihalyi, M. (1996). *Creativity: Flow and the psychology of discovery and invention.* New York: HarperCollins.

Cummings, J. H., Bingham, S. A., Heaton, K. W., & Eastwood, M. A. (1992). Fecal weight, colon cancer risk, and dietary intake of nonstarch polysaccharides (dietary fiber). *Gastroenterology, 103,* 1783–1789.

Cunningham, W. A., & Zelazo, P. D. (2006). Attitudes and evaluations: A social cognitive neuroscience perspective. *Trends in Cognitive Sciences, 11,* 97–104.

Curtiss, S. (1977). *Genie: A psycholinguistic study of a modern-day wild child.* New York: Academic Press.

Cussler, E. C., Going, S. B., Houtkooper, L. B., Stanford, V. A., Blew, R. M., Flint-Wagner, H. G., et al. (2005). Exercise frequency and calcium intake predict 4-year bone changes in postmenopausal women. *Osteoporosis International, 16,* 2129–2141.

Cutting, A. L., & Dunn, J. (2002). The cost of understanding other people: Social cognition predicts young children's sensitivity to criticism. *Journal of Child Psychology and Psychiatry, 43,* 849–860.

Cytowic, R. E. (1989). *Synaesthesia: A union of the senses.* New York: Springer-Verlag.

Czech, C., & Adessi, C. (2004). Disease modifying therapeutic strategies in Alzheimer's disease targeting the amyloid cascade. *Current Neuropharmacology, 2,* 295–307.

Dabbs, J. M., Jr., Carr, T. S., & Frady, R. L. (1995). Testosterone, crime, and misbehavior among 692 male prison inmates. *Personality and Individual Differences, 18,* 627–633.

Dabbs, J. M., Jr., & Hargrove, M. F. (1997). Age, testosterone, and behavior among female prison inmates. *Psychosomatic Medicine, 59,* 477–480.

Dabbs, J. M., Jr., & Mohammed, S. (1992). Male and female salivary testosterone concentrations before and after sexual activity. *Physiology & Behavior, 52,* 195–197.

Dale, P. S., Dionne, G., Eley, T. C., & Plomin, R. (2000). Lexical and grammatical development: A behavioural genetic perspective. *Journal of Child Language, 27,* 619–642.

Dallaire, D. H., Cole, D. A., Smith, T. M., Ciesla, J. A., LaGrange, B., Jacquez, F. M., et al. (2008). Predicting children's depressive symptoms from community and individual risk factors. *Journal of Youth and Adolescence, 37,* 830–846.

Dallman, M. F., Pecoraro, N. C., & la Fleur, S. E. (2005). Chronic stress and comfort foods: Self-medication and abdominal obesity. *Brain, Behavior, and Immunity, 19,* 275–280.

Damasio, A. R., (2000). *The feeling of what happens: Body and emotion in the making of consciousness.* Chicago: Harcourt.

D'Anglejan, A. (1979). Solving problems in deductive reasoning: Three experimental studies of adult second language earners. *Working Papers on Bilingualism, No. 17.*

Darke, P. R., & Ritchie, R. J. B. (2007). The defensive consumer: Advertising deception, defensive processing, and distrust. *Journal of Marketing Research, 44,* 114–127.

Darley, J. M., & Batson, C. D. (1973). "From Jerusalem to Jericho": A study of situational and dispositional variables in helping behavior. *Journal of Personality and Social Psychology, 27,* 100–108.

Darley, J. M., & Latané, B. (1968). Bystander intervention in emergencies: Diffusion of responsibility. *Journal of Personality and Social Psychology, 8,* 377–383.

Darwin, C. (1998). *The expression of the emotions in man and animals.* New York: Oxford University Press. (Original work published 1872)

Dasgupta, N., McGhee, D. E., Greenwald, A. G., & Banaji, M. R. (2000). Automatic preference for White Americans: Eliminating the familiarity explanation. *Journal of Experimental Social Psychology, 36,* 316–328.

Davidson, R. J. (1994). On emotion, mood, and related affective constructs. In P. Ekman & R. J. Davidson (Eds.), *The nature of emotion: Fundamental questions* (pp. 51–55). New York: Oxford University Press.

Davidson, R. J. (2001). Toward a biology of personality and emotion. *Annals of the New York Academy of Sciences, 935,* 191–207.

Davidson, R. J. (2004). What does the prefrontal cortex "do" in affect: Perspectives on frontal EEG asymmetry research. *Biological Psychology, 67,* 219–233.

Davidson, R. J., Ekman, P., Saron, C., Senulis, J., & Friesen, W. V. (1990). Approach-withdrawal and cerebral asymmetry: Emotional expression and brain physiology I. *Journal of Personality and Social Psychology, 58,* 330–341.

Davidson, R. J., Kabat-Zinn, J., Schumacher, J., Rosenkranz, M., Muller, D., Santorelli, S. F., et al. (2003). Alterations in brain and immune function produced by mindfulness meditation. *Psychosomatic Medicine, 65,* 564–570.

Dawkins, R. (1989). *The selfish gene* (New ed.). New York: Oxford University Press.

Day, H. I. (1982). Curiosity and the interested explorer. *Performance and Instruction, 21,* 19–22.

De Fruyt, F., & Murvielde, I. (1999). RAISEC types and Big Five traits as predictors of employment status and nature of employment. *Personnel Psychology, 52,* 701–727.

De Neys, W., Vartanian, O., & Goel, V. (2008). Smarter than we think: When our brains detect that we are biased. *Psychological Science, 19,* 483–489.

de Win, M. M. L., Reneman, L., Reitsma, J. B., den Heeten, G. J., Booij, J., & van den Brink, W. (2004). Mood disorders and serotonin transporter density in ecstasy users—the influence of long-term abstention, dose, and gender. *Psychopharmacology, 173,* 376–382.

Deacon, T. (1997). *Symbolic species: Co-evolution of language and the brain.* New York: Norton.

Deary, I. J., Graham, T., Wilson, V., Starr, J. M., & Whalley, L. J. (2003). Population sex differences in IQ at age 11: The Scottish mental survey 1932. *Intelligence, 31,* 533–542.

DeCasper, A. J., & Fifer, W. (1980). Of human bonding: Newborns prefer their mothers' voices. *Science, 208,* 1174–1176.

DeCasper, A. J., & Spence, M. J. (1986). Prenatal maternal speech influences newborns' perception of speech sounds. *Infant Behavior & Development, 9,* 133–150.

Delgado, P. L., Price, L. H., Miller, H. L., Salomon, R. M., Aghajanian, G. K., Heninger, G. R., et al. (1994). Serotonin and the neurobiology of depression—effects of tryptophan depletion in drug-free depressed patients. *Archives of General Psychiatry, 51,* 865–874.

Deci, E. L., & Ryan, R. M. (1985). *Intrinsic motivation and self-determination in human behavior.* New York: Plenum.

DeLongis, A., Folkman, S., & Lazarus, R. S. (1988). The impact of daily stress on health and mood: Psychological and social resources as mediators. *Journal of Personality and Social Psychology, 54,* 486–495.

Dembroski, T. M., MacDougall, J. M., Williams, R. B., Haney, T. L., & Blumenthal, J. A. (1985). Components of Type A, hostility, and anger-in: relationship to angiographic findings. *Psychosomatic Medicine, 47,* 219–233.

Dement, W. (1999). *The promise of sleep.* New York: Delacorte Press.

Demir, E., & Dickson, B. J. (2005). *Fruitless* splicing specifies male courtship behavior in *Drosophila. Cell, 121,* 785–794.

Derbyshire, S. W. G., Whalley, M. G., Stenger, A., & Oakley, D. A. (2004). Cerebral activation during hypnotically induced and imagined pain. *NeuroImage, 23,* 392–401.

Derry, G. (1999). *What is science and how it works.* Princeton: Princeton University Press.

Derryberry, D., & Tucker, D. M. (1994). Motivating the focus of attention. In P. M. Niedenthal & S. Kitayama (Eds.), *The heart's eye: Emotional influences in perception and attention* (pp. 167–196). San Diego, CA: Academic Press.

DeRubeis, R. J., Hollon, S., Amsterdam, J., Shelton, R., Young, P., Salomon, R., et al. (2005). Cognitive therapy vs medications in the treatment of moderate to severe depression. *Archives of General Psychiatry, 62*(4), 409–416.

Devine, P. (1989). Stereotypes and prejudice: Their automatic and controlled components. *Journal of Personality and Social Psychology, 56,* 5–18.

Diamond, L. M. (2008). Female bisexuality from adolescence to adulthood: Results from a 10-year longitudinal study. *Developmental Psychology, 44,* 5–14.

Diener, E., & Seligman, M. E. P. (2004). Beyond money toward an economy of well-being. *Psychological Science, 5,* 1–31.

Diener, E., Suh, E. M., Lucas, R. E., & Smith, H. L. (1999). Subjective well-being: Three decades of progress. *Psychological Bulletin, 125,* 276–302.

Dietrich, K., Succop, P., Berger, O., & Hammond, P. (1991). Lead exposure and the cognitive development of urban preschool children: The Cincinnati Lead Study cohort at age 4 years. *Neurotoxicology and Teratology, 13*(2), 203–211.

Digman, J. M. (1990). Personality structure: Emergence of the Five-Factor Model. *Annual Review in Psychology, 41,* 417–440.

Dingemanse, N. J., Both, C., Drent, P. J., Van Oers, K., & Van Noordwijk, A. J. (2002). Repeatability and heritability of exploratory behaviour in great tits from the wild. *Animal Behaviour, 64,* 929–938.

Dinn, W. M., Aycicegi, A., & Harris, C. L. (2004). Cigarette smoking in a student sample: Neurocognitive and clinical correlates. *Addictive Behaviors, 29,* 107–126.

DiPietro, J. A., Hodgson, D. M., Costigan, K. A., & Johnson, T. R. B. (1996). Fetal antecedents of infant temperament. *Child Development, 67,* 2568–2583.

Dobbs, D. (2006). Turning off depression. *Scientific American Mind, 2006, 17,* 26–31.

Dobbs, D. (2006, April 2). A depression switch? *New York Times Magazine.* Retrieved from http://www.nytimes.com

Doetsch, F., & Scharff, C. (2001). Challenges for brain repair: Insights from adult neurogenesis in birds and mammals. *Brain, Behavior & Evolution, 58,* 306–322.

Dolcos, F., LaBar, K. S., & Cabeza, R. (2005). Remembering one year later: Role of the amygdala and the temporal lobe memory system in retrieving emotional memories. *Proceedings of the National Academy of Sciences, 102,* 2626–2631.

Dolinoy, D., & Jirtle, R. L. (2008). Environmental epigenomics in human health and disease. *Environmental and Molecular Mutagenesis, 49,* 4–8.

Doll, R., Peto, R., Boreham, J., & Sutherland, I. (2004). Mortality in relation to smoking: 50 years' observations on male British doctors. *British Medical Journal, 328,* 1519–1528.

Domhoff, G. W. (2001). A new neuro-cognitive theory of dreams. *Dreaming, 11,* 13–33.

Dominguez, J. M., & Hull, E. M. (2005). Dopamine, the medial preoptic area, and male sexual behavior. *Physiology and Behavior, 86,* 356–368.

Doty, R. L., Applebaum, S., Zusho, H., & Settle, R. G. (1985). Sex differences in odor identification ability: A cross-cultural analysis. *Neuropsychologia, 23,* 667–672.

Dovidio, J. F., Piliavin, J. A., Gaertner, S. L., Schroeder, D. A., & Clark, R. D., III. (1991). The arousal: Cost-reward model and the process of intervention: A review of the evidence. In M. S. Clark (Ed.), *Prosocial behavior* (pp. 86–118). Newbury Park, CA: Sage.

Drevets W. C., Frank, E., Price, J. C., Kupfer, D. J., Holt, D., Greer, P. J., et al. (1999). PET imaging of serotonin 1A receptor binding in depression. *Biological Psychiatry, 46,* 1375–1387.

Drevets, W. C., Price, J. L., Simpson, J. R., Todd, R. D., Reich, T., Vannier, M., et al. (1997). Subgenual prefrontal cortex abnormalities in mood disorders. *Nature, 386,* 824–827.

Dubai, Y. (2004). The neurobiology of consolidations, or, How stable is the engram? *Annual Review of Psychology, 55,* 51–86.

Due, P., Holstein, B. E., Ito, H., & Groth, M. V. (1991). Diet and health behavior in Danish children aged 11–15 years. *Tandlaegernes Tidsskr, 6*(8), 232–237.

Duke, L. M., & Vasterling, J. J. (2005). Epidemiological and methodological issues in neuropsychological research on PTSD. In J. Vasterling & C. Brewin (Eds.)., *Neuropsychology of PTSD* (pp. 3–24). New York: Guilford Press.

Dunbar, R. (1996). *Grooming, gossip and the evolution of language.* London: Faber & Faber.

Dunbar, R. I. M. (2001). Brains on two legs: Group size and the evolution of intelligence. In F. B. M. deWaal (Ed.), *Tree of origin: What primate behavior can tell us about human social evolution* (pp. 173–191). Cambridge, MA: Harvard University Press.

Duncan, J., Seitz, R. J., Koldny, J., Bor, D., Herzog, H., Ahmed, A., et al. (2000). A neural basis for general intelligence. *Science, 289,* 457–460.

Duncker, K. (1945). On problem-solving. *Psychological Monographs, 58,* ix. (Whole No. 270).

Dunham, Y., Baron, A. S., & Banaji, M. R. (2006). From American city to Japanese village: A cross-cultural investigation of implicit race attitudes. *Child Development, 77,* 1268–1281.

Durlak, J. A., Taylor, R. D., Kawashima, K., Pachan, M. K., DuPre, E. P., Celio, C. I., et al. (2007). Effects of positive youth development programs on school, family, and community systems. *American Journal of Community Psychology, 39,* 269–286.

Dvir, Y., & Smallwood, P. (2008). Serotonin syndrome: A complex but easily avoidable condition. *General Hospital Psychiatry, 30,* 284–287.

Eagly, A. H., & Chaiken, S. (1998). Attitude structure and function. In D. T. Gilbert, S. T. Fiske, & G. Lindzey (Eds.), *The handbook of social psychology* (4th ed., Vol. 1, pp. 269–322). New York: McGraw-Hill.

Ebstein, R. P. (2006). The molecular genetic architecture of human personality: Beyond self-report questionnaires. *Molecular Psychiatry, 11,* 427–445.

Ebstein, R. P., Novick, O., Umansky, R., Priel, B., Osher, Y., Blaine, D., et al. (1996). Dopamine D4 receptor D4DR exon III polymorphism associated with the human personality trait Novelty Seeking. *Nature Genetics, 12,* 78–80.

Edelman, S., Lemon, J., Bell, D. R., & Kidman, A. D. (1999). Effects of group CBT on the survival time of patients with metastatic breast cancer. *Psychooncology, 8,* 474–481.

Edmonds, C. V., Lockwood, G. A., & Cunningham, A. J. (1999). Psychological response to long-term therapy: A randomized trial with metastatic breast cancer patients. *Psychooncology, 8,* 74–91.

Edwards, J. H. (2002). Evidenced-based treatment for child ADHD: "Real-world" practice implications. *Journal of Mental Health Counseling, 24,* 126–139.

Edwards, V. J., Holden, G. W., Felitti, V. J., & Anda, R. F. (2003). Relationship between multiple forms of childhood maltreatment and adult mental health in community respondents: Results from the adverse childhood experiences study. *American Journal of Psychiatry, 160,* 1453–1460.

Eisenberger, N. I., Lieberman, M. D., & Williams, K. D. (2003). Does rejection hurt? An fMRI study of social exclusion. *Science, 203,* 290–292.

Ekman, P. (1972). Universals and cultural differences in facial expressions of emotion. In J. Cole (Ed.), *Nebraska Symposium on Motivation 1971, Vol. 19,* (pp. 207–283). Lincoln: University of Nebraska Press.

Ekman, P. (1973). Cross-cultural studies of facial expression. In *Darwin and facial expression: A century of research in review* (pp. 169–222). New York: Academic Press.

Ekman, P. (1984). Expression and the nature of emotion. In K. R. Scherer & P. Ekman (Eds.), *Approaches to emotion* (pp. 319–343). Hillsdale, NJ: Lawrence Erlbaum.

Ekman, P. (1992). An argument for basic emotions. *Cognition & Emotion, 6,* 169–200.

Ekman, P. (2003). *Emotions revealed.* New York: Holt.

Ekman, P., Davidson. R. J., & Friesen, W. V. (1990). The Duchenne smile: Emotional expression and brain physiology II. *Journal of Personality and Social Psychology, 58,* 342–353.

Ekman, P., & Friesen, W. V. (1969). The repertoire of nonverbal behavior—categories, origins, usage, and coding. *Semiotica, 1,* 49–98.

Ekman, P., & Friesen, W. V. (1971). Constants across cultures in the face and emotion. *Journal of Personality and Social Psychology, 17,* 124–129.

Ekman, P., & Friesen, W. V. (1978). *The facial action coding system.* Palo Alto, CA: Consulting Psychologist's Press.

Ekman, P., Friesen, W. V., & Hager, J. (2002). *The Facial Action Coding System* (2nd ed.). Salt Lake City, UT: Research Nexus.

Ekman, P., Friesen, W. V., O'Sullivan, M., Chan, A., Diacoyanni-Tarlatzis, I., Heider, K., et al. (1987). Universals and cultural differences in the judgments of facial expressions of emotion. *Journal of Personality and Social Psychology, 53,* 712–717.

Ekman, P., Levenson, R. W., & Friesen, W. V. (1983). Autonomic nervous system activity distinguishes among emotions. *Science, 221,* 1208–1210.

Ekman, P., & O'Sullivan, M. (1991). Who can catch a liar? *American Psychologist, 46,* 913–920.

Ekman, P., O'Sullivan, M., & Frank, M. G. (1999). A few can catch a liar. *Psychological Science, 10,* 263–266.

Ekman, P., & Rosenberg, E. L. (Eds.). (2005). *What the face reveals: Basic and applied studies of spontaneous facial expression using the Facial Action Coding System (FACS)* (2nd ed.). New York: Oxford University Press.

Ekman, P., Sorenson, E. R., & Friesen, W. V. (1969). Pan-cultural elements in facial displays of emotion. *Science, 164,* 86–88.

Elbert, T., Pantev, C., Wienbruch, C., Rockstroh, B., & Taub, E. (1995). Increased cortical representation of the fingers of the left hand in string players. *Science, 270,* 305–307.

Ellason, J. W., Ross, C. A., & Fuchs, D. L. (1996). Lifetime Axis I and Axis II comorbidity and childhood trauma history in dissociative identity disorder. *Psychiatry, 59,* 255–266.

Ellickson, P. L., Orlando, M., Tucker, J. S., & Klein, D. J. (2004). From adolescence to young adulthood: Racial/ethnic disparities in smoking. *American Journal of Public Health, 94,* 293–299.

Ellickson, P. L., Tucker, J. S., & Klein, D. J. (2001). Sex differences in predictors of adolescent smoking cessation. *Health Psychology, 20,* 186–195.

Ellis, E., & Ames, M. A. (1987). Neuro-hormonal functioning and sexual orientation: A theory of heterosexuality–homosexuality. *Psychological Bulletin, 101*, 233–258.

Ellsworth, P. C., & Smith, C. A. (1988). Shades joy: Patterns of appraisal differentiating pleasant emotions. *Cognition & Emotion, 2*, 301–331. Elman, J. L., Bates, E. A., Johnson, M. H., Karmiloff-Smith, A., Parisi, D., & Plunkett, K. (1996). *Rethinking innateness: A connectionist perspective on development*. Cambridge, MA: MIT Press.

Elms, A. (1993). *Uncovering lives: The uneasy alliance between biography and psychology*. New York: Oxford University Press.

Empana, J. P., Sykes, D. H., Luc, G., Juhan-Vague, I., Arveiler, D., Ferrieres, J., et al. (2005). Contributions of depressive mood and circulating inflammatory markers to coronary heart disease in healthy European men: The Prospective Epidemiological Study of Myocardial Infarction (PRIME). *Circulation, 111*, 2299–2305.

Engel, A. K., Debener, S., & Kranczioch, C. (2006, August). Coming to attention. *Scientific American Mind, 17*, 46–53.

Enzinger, C., Fazekas, F., Matthews, P. M., Ropele, S., Schmidt, H., Smith, S., et al. (2005). Risk factors for progression of brain atrophy in aging: Six-year follow-up of normal subjects. *Neurology, 64*, 1704–1711.

Epel, E. S., Blackburn, E. H., Lin, J., Dhabhar, F. S., Adler, N. E., & Morrow, J. D. (2004). Accelerated telomere shortening in response to life stress. *Proceedings of the National Academy of Sciences, 101*, 17312–17315.

Epel, E. S., Lin, J., Wilhelm, F. H., Wolkowitz, O. M., Cawthon, R., Adler, N. E., et al. (2006). Cell aging in relation to stress arousal and cardiovascular disease risk factors. *Psychoneuroendocrinology, 31*, 277–287.

Epel, E. S., McEwen, B., Seeman, T., Matthews, K., Castellazzo, G., Brownell, K. D., et al. (2000). Stress and body shape: Stress-induced cortisol secretion is consistently greater among women with central fat. *Psychosomatic Medicine, 62*, 623–632.

Erikson, E. (1963). *Childhood and society*. New York: Norton.

Erikson, E. (1968). *Identity: Youth and crisis*. New York: Norton.

Erikson, E. (1982). *The life-cycle completed: A review*. New York: Norton.

Eriksson, P. S., Perfilieva, E., Bjork-Eriksson, T., Alborn, A. M., Nordborg, C., Peterson, D. A., et al. (1998). Neurogenesis in the adult human hippocampus. *Nature Medicine, 4*, 1313–1317.

Etcoff, N. (1999). *Survival of the prettiest*. New York: Anchor Books.

Evans, D. L., Ten Have, T. R., Douglas, S. D., Gettes, D. R., Morrison, M., Chiappini, M. S., et al. (2002). Association of depression with viral load, CD8 T lymphocytes, and natural killer cells in women with HIV infection. *American Journal of Psychiatry, 159*, 1752–1759.

Evans, S., Ferrando, S., Findler, M., Stowell, C., Smart, C., & Haglin, D. (2008). Mindfulness-based cognitive therapy for generalized anxiety disorder. *Journal of Anxiety Disorders, 22*, 716–721.

Everett, D. L. (2005). Cultural constraints on grammar and cognition in Piraha: Another look at the design features of human language. *Current Anthropology, 46*, 621–646.

Exaptations (2006). Retrieved November 28, 2007, from http://evolution.berkeley.edu/evosite/evo101/IIIE5cExaptations.shtml

Exner, J. E., Jr. (1974). *The Rorschach: A comprehensive system*. New York: Wiley.

Eysenck, H. J. (1947). *Dimensions of personality*. London: Routledge & Kegan Paul.

Eysenck, H. J. (1980). *The causes and effects of smoking*. London: Temple Smith.

Eysenck, H. J. (1982). *Personality, genetics, and behavior: Selected papers*. New York: Praeger.

Eysenck, H. J. (1990). Biological dimensions of personality. In L. A. Pervin (Ed.), *Handbook of personality: Theory and research* (pp. 244–276). New York: Guilford Press.

Eysenck, H. J. (1995). *Genius: The natural history of creativity*. Cambridge: Cambridge University Press.

Eysenck, H. J. (1997). Personality and experimental psychology: The unification of psychology and the possibility of a paradigm. *Journal of Personality and Social Psychology, 73*, 1224–1237.

Facione, P. A. (1990). *Critical thinking: A statement of expert consensus for purposes of educational assessment and instruction—The Delphi report*. Millbrae, CA: California Academic Press.

Famy, C., Streissguth, A. P., & Unis, A. S. (1998). Psychological disorder in adults with fetal alcohol syndrome or fetal alcohol effects. *Journal of Pediatric Psychology, 155*, 552–554.

Fancher, R. E. (1985). *The intelligence men: Makers of the IQ controversy*. New York: Norton.

Fancher, R. E. (1996). *Pioneers of psychology* (3rd ed.). New York: Norton.

Fantz, R. L. (1963). Pattern vision in newborn infants. *Science, 140*, 296–297.

Farber, N. B., & Olney, J. W. (2003). Drugs of abuse that cause developing neurons to commit suicide. *Developmental Brain Research, 147*, 37–45.

Fazel, S., & Danesh, J. (2002). Serious mental disorder in 23,000 prisoners: A systematic review of 62 surveys. *Lancet, 359*, 545–550.

Feist, G. J. (1993). A structural model of scientific eminence. *Psychological Science, 4*, 366–371.

Feist, G. J. (1998). A meta-analysis of the impact of personality on scientific and artistic creativity. *Personality and Social Psychological Review, 2*, 290–309.

Feist, G. J. (1999). Personality in scientific and artistic creativity. In R. J. Sternberg (Ed.), *Handbook of human creativity* (pp. 273–296). Cambridge: Cambridge University Press.

Feist, G. J. (2004). Creativity and the frontal lobes. *Bulletin of Psychology and the Arts, 5*, 21–28.

Feist, G. J. (2006). The development of scientific talent in Westinghouse finalists and members of the National Academy of Sciences. *Journal of Adult Development, 13*, 23–35.

Feist, G. J. (2006). *The psychology of science and the origins of the scientific mind*. New Haven, CT: Yale University Press.

Feist, G. J. (in press). Affective state and traits in creativity: Evidence for non-linear relationships. In M. Runco (Ed.). *Creativity research handbook* (Vol. 3). Cresskill, NJ: Hampton Press.

Feist, G. J., & Barron, F. X. (2003). Predicting creativity from early to late adulthood: Intellect, potential and personality. *Journal of Research in Personality, 37*, 62–88.

Feist, G. J., Bodner, T. E., Jacobs, J. F., Miles, M., & Tan, V. (1995). Integrating top-down and bottom-up structural models of subjective well-being: A longitudinal investigation. *Journal of Personality and Social Psychology, 68*, 138–150.

Feist, J., & Feist, G. J. (2009). *Theories of Personality* (7th ed.). New York: McGraw-Hill.

Feldman, D. H. (2004). Child prodigies: A distinctive form of giftedness. In R. J. Sternberg (Ed.), *Definition and conceptions of giftedness* (pp. 133–144). Thousand Oaks, CA: Corwin Press.

Feldman-Barrett, L., Tugade, M. M., & Engle, R. W. (2004). Individual differences in working memory capacity and dual-process theories of mind. *Psychological Bulletin, 130*, 553–573.

Feng, X., Shaw, D. S., Kovacs, M., Lane, T., O'Rourke, F. E., & Alarcon, J. H. (2008). Emotion regulation in preschoolers: The roles of behavioral inhibition, maternal affective behavior, and maternal depression. *Journal of Child Psychology and Psychiatry, 49*, 132–141.

Feng, Z., Hu, W., Hu, Y. & Teng, M. (2006). Acrolein is a major cigarette-related lung cancer agent: Preferential binding at *p53* mutational hotspots and inhibition of

DNA repair. *Proceedings of the National Academy of Sciences, 103,* 15404–15409.

Fenson, L., Dale, P., Reznick, J. S., Bates, E., Thal, D. J., & Pethick, S. (1994). Variability in early communicative development. *Monographs of the Society for Research in Child Development, 59* (5, Serial No. 242).

Fergusson, D., Doucette, S., Glass, K. C., Shapiro, S., Healy, D., Hebert, P., et al. (2005). Association between suicide attempts and selective serotonin reuptake inhibitors: Systematic review of randomized controlled trials. *British Medical Journal, 330,* 396–402.

Fergusson, L., Horwood, J., & Ridder, E. M. (2005). Tests of causal linkages between cannabis use and psychotic symptoms. *Addiction, 100,* 354–366.

Fernald, A., & Morikawa, H. (1993). Common themes and cultural variations in Japanese and American mothers' speech to infants. *Child Development, 64,* 637–656.

Ferster, C. B., & Skinner, B. F. (1957). *Schedules of reinforcement.* Englewood Cliffs, NJ: Prentice-Hall.

Festinger, L. (1957). *A theory of cognitive dissonance.* Stanford, CA: Stanford University.

Festinger, L., & Carlsmith, J. M. (1959). Cognitive consequences of forced compliance. *Journal of Abnormal and Social Psychology, 58,* 203–210.

Fiedorowicz, J., & Swartz, K. (2004). The role of monoamine oxidase inhibitors in current psychiatric practice. *Journal of Psychiatric Practice, 10,* 239–248.

Field, T. M., Hernandez-Reif, M., Diego, M., Feijo, L., Vera, Y., & Gil, K. (2004). Massage therapy by parents improves early growth and development. *Infant Behavior and Development, 27,* 435–442.

Field, T. M., Schanberg, S. M., Scafidi, F., Bauer, C. R., Vega-Lahr, N., Garcia, R., et al. (1986). Tactile/kinesthetic stimulation effects on preterm neonates. *Pediatrics, 77,* 654–658.

Fields, H. L. (2005). *Pain: Mechanisms and management.* New York: McGraw-Hill.

Fields, R. D. (2005). Making memories stick. *Scientific American, 292,* 75–81.

Fields, R. D. (2008). White matter matters. *Scientific American, 298,* 54–61.

Filimon, F., Nelson, J. D., Hagler, D. J., & Sereno, M. I. (2007). Human cortical representations for reaching: Mirror neurons for execution, observation, and imagery. *NeuroImage, 37,* 1315–1328.

Finger, S. (1994). *Origins of neuroscience: A history of explorations into brain function.* New York: Oxford University Press.

Fink, M. (2006). ECT in therapy-resistant mania: Does it have a place? *Bipolar Disorders, 8,* 307–309.

Finke, R. A., Ward, T. B., & Smith, S. M. (1992). *Creative cognition: Theory, research and applications.* Cambridge, MA: MIT Press.

Finnerty, G. T., Roberts, L. S. E., & Connors, B. W. (1999). Sensory experience modifies the short-term dynamics of neocortical synapses. *Nature, 400,* 367–371.

Fischer, A. H. & Manstead, A. S. R. (2000). Gender differences in emotion across cultures. In A. H. Fischer (Ed.), *Emotion and gender: Social psychological perspectives* (pp. 91–97). London: Cambridge University Press.

Fischer, G. G. (2004). Should I order an EEG? An overview of electroencephalography in the hospital setting at Gundersen Lutheran Medical Center. *Gundersen Lutheran Medical Journal, 3,* 26–29.

Fisher, J. E., Mohanty, A., Herrington, J. D., Koven, N. S., Miller, G. A., & Heller, W. (2004). Neuropsychological evidence for dimensional schizotypy: Implications for creativity and psychopathology. *Journal of Research in Personality, 38,* 24–31.

Fitzgerald, K. D., Welsh, R. C., Gehrig, W. J., Abelson, J. L., Himle, J. A., Liberzon, I., et al. (2005). Error-related hyperactivity of the anterior cingulated cortex in obsessive-compulsive disorder. *Biological Psychiatry, 57,* 287–294.

Fitzgerald, M. (2004). *Autism and creativity.* Hove, England: Brunner-Routledge.

Fitzgerald, P. B., Benitez, J., de Castella, A. R., Daskalakis, Z. J., & Kulkarni, J. (2006). Naturalistic study of the use of transcranial magnetic stimulation in the treatment of depressive relapse. *Australian and New Zealand Journal of Psychiatry, 40,* 764–768.

Flaherty, M. (2005). Gender differences in mental rotation ability in three cultures: Ireland, Ecuador and Japan. *Psychologia: An International Journal of Psychology in the Orient, 48,* 31–38.

Flammer, E., & Bongartz, W. (2003). On the efficacy of hypnosis: A meta-analytic study. *Contemporary Hypnosis, 20,* 179–197.

Flege, J. E., Munro, M. J., MacKay, I. R. A. (1995). Effects of age of second-language learning on the production of English consonants. *Speech Communication, 16,* 1–26.

Foa, E. B., Dancu, C. V., Hembree, E. A., Jaycox, L. H., Meadows, E. A., & Street, G. P. (1999). A comparison of exposure therapy, stress inoculation training, and their combination for reducing posttraumatic stress disorder in female assault victims. *Journal of Consulting and Clinical Psychology, 67,* 194–200.

Foa, E. B., Hembree, E. A., Cahill, S. P., Rauch, S. A., Riggs, D. S., Feeny, N. C., et al. (2005). Randomized trial of prolonged exposure for PTSD with and without cognitive

restructuring: Outcome at academic and community clinics. *Journal of Consulting and Clinical Psychology, 73,* 953–964.

Fodor, E. M., & Laird, B. A. (2004). Therapeutic intervention, bipolar inclination, and literary creativity. *Creativity Research Journal, 16,* 149–161.

Fogassi, L., & Ferrari, P. F. (2006). Mirror neurons and the evolution of embodied language. *Current Directions in Psychological Science, 16,* 136–141.

Folkman, S. (1997). Positive psychological states and coping with severe stress. *Social Science and Medicine, 45,* 1207–1221.

Folkman, S., & Moskowitz, J. T. (2000). Positive affect and the other side of coping. *American Psychologist, 55,* 647–654.

Fombonne, E. (2003). The prevalence of autism. *Journal of the American Medical Association, 289,* 87–89.

Ford, C., & Beach, F. (1951). *Patterns of sexual behavior.* New York: Harper & Row.

Forsten, B. L., Scotti, J. R., Chen, Y-C, Malone, J., Del Ben, K. S. (2007). Internet use, abuse, and dependence among students at a southeastern regional university. *Journal of American College Health, 56,* 137–144.

Foulkes, D. (1996). Dream research: 1953–1993. *Sleep: Journal of Sleep Research & Sleep Medicine, 19,* 609–624.

Fouts, R. S. (1997). *Next of kin: My conversations with chimpanzees.* New York: Avon.

Fouts, R. S., Fouts, D. H., & Schoenfeld, D. (1984). Sign language conversational interaction between chimpanzees. *Sign Language Studies, 42,* 1–12.

Franco, O. H., de Laet, C., Peeters, A., Jonker, J., Mackenbach, J., & Nusselder, W. (2005). Effects of physical activity on life expectancy with cardiovascular disease. *Archives of Internal Medicine, 165,* 2355–2360.

Frank, M. G., & Ekman, P. (1997). The ability to detect deceit generalizes across different types of high stakes lies. *Journal of Personality and Social Psychology, 72,* 1429–1439.

Fratiglioni, L., Winblad, B., & von Strauss, E. (2007). Prevention of Alzheimer's disease and dementia. Major findings from the Kungsholmen Project. *Physiology & Behavior, 92,* 98–104.

Fredrickson, B. L. (1998). What good are positive emotions? *Review of General Psychology, 2,* 300–319.

Fredrickson, B. L. (2001). The role of positive emotions in positive psychology: The broaden-and-build theory of positive emotions. *American Psychologist, 56,* 218–226.

Fredrickson, B. L., & Branigan, C. (2005). Positive emotions broaden the scope of attention and thought-action repertoires. *Cognition & Emotion, 19,* 313–332.

Fredrickson, B. L., & Joiner, T. (2002). Positive emotions trigger upward spirals toward emotional well-being. *Psychological Science, 13*, 172–175.

Fredrickson, B. L., & Levenson, R. W. (1998). Positive emotions speed recovery from the cardiovascular sequelae of negative emotions. *Cognition & Emotion, 12*, 191–220.

Fredrickson, B. L., Tugade, M. M., Waugh, C. E., & Larkin, G. R. (2003). What good are positive emotions in crises? A prospective study of resilience and emotions following the terrorist attacks on the United States on September 11th, 2001. *Journal of Personality & Social Psychology, 84*, 365–376.

French-Belgian Collaborative Group. (1982). Ischemic heart disease and psychological patterns: Prevalence and incidence studies in Belgium and France. *Advances in Cardiology, 29*, 25–31.

Freud, A. (1946). *The ego and the mechanisms of defense.* New York: International Universities Press.

Freud, S. (1953). *The interpretation of dreams.* In J. Strachey (Ed. & Trans.), *The standard edition of the complete works of Sigmund Freud* (Vols. 4 & 5). London: Hogarth Press. (Original work published 1900)

Freud, S. (1959). *Inhibitions, symptoms, and anxiety.* In J. Strachey (Ed. & Trans.), *Standard edition of the complete works of Sigmund Freud* (Vol. 20). London: Hogarth Press. (Original work published 1926)

Freud, S. (1960). *Psychopathology of everyday life.* In J. Strachey (Ed. & Trans.), *Standard edition of the complete works of Sigmund Freud* (Vol. 6). London: Hogarth Press. (Original work published 1901)

Freud, S. (1964). *New introductory lectures on psychoanalysis.* In J. Strachey (Ed. & Trans.), *The Standard edition of the complete works of Sigmund Freud* (Vol. 22). London: Hogarth Press. (Original work published 1933)

Friesen, W. V. (1972). *Cultural differences in facial expressions in a social situation: An experimental test of the concept of display rules.* Unpublished doctoral dissertation, University of California, San Francisco.

Frijda, N. H. (1986). *The emotions.* Cambridge, UK: Cambridge University Press.

Fruntes, V., & Limosin, F. (2008). Schizophrenia and viral infection during neurodevelopment: A pathogenesis model? *Medical Science Monitor, 14*, RA71–RA77.

Fuller, R. K., & Gordis, E. (2004). Does disulfiram have a role in alcoholism treatment today? *Addiction, 99*, 21–24.

Furster, J. M. (1999). Cognitive functions of the frontal lobes. In B. L. Miller & J. L. Cummings (Eds.), *The human frontal lobes: Functions and disorders* (pp. 187–195). New York: Guilford Press.

Furuichi, T. (1983). Interindividual distance and influence of dominance on feeding in a natural Japanese macaque troop. *Primates, 24*, 445–455.

Fuster, J. M. (2002). Frontal lobe and cognitive development. *Journal of Neurocytology, 31*, 373–385.

Gage, F. H. (2002). Neurogenesis in the adult brain. *The Journal of Neuroscience, 22*, 612–613.

Galanter, E. (1962). Contemporary psychophysics. In R. Brown (Ed.), *New directions in psychology* (pp. 87–157). New York: Holt, Rinehart & Winston.

Gale, A. (1983). Electroencephalographic studies of extraversion-introversion: A case study in the psychophysiology of individual differences. *Personality and Individual Differences, 4*, 371–380.

Galin, D. (1994). The structure of awareness: Contemporary applications of William James' forgotten concept of "The Fringe." *The Journal of Mind and Behavior, 15*, 375–402.

Gallagher, A. M., & Kaufman, J. C. (2005). *Gender differences in mathematics: An integrative psychological approach.* New York: Cambridge University Press.

Gallagher, M., & Lopez, S. (2007). Curiosity and well-being. *Journal of Positive Psychology, 2*(4), 236–248.

Gallagher, R. M., & Rosenthal, L. J. (2008). Chronic pain and opiates: Balancing pain control and risks in long-term opioid treatment. *Archives of Physical Medicine and Rehabilitation, 89*(Suppl. 1), S77–S82.

Galletti, C., & Fattori, P. (2003). Neuronal mechanisms for detection of motion in the field of view. *Neuropsychologia, 41*, 1717–1727.

Garcia, J. (2003). Psychology is not an enclave. In R. J. Sternberg (Ed.), *Defying the crowd: Stories of those who battled the establishment and won* (pp. 67–77). Washington, DC: American Psychological Association.

Garcia, J., Ervin, F. R., & Koelling, R. (1966). Learning with a prolonged delay of reinforcement. *Psychonomic Science, 5*, 121–122.

Garcia, J., Kimeldorf, D. J., & Koelling, R. A. (1955). A conditioned aversion towards saccharin resulting from exposure to gamma radiation. *Science, 122*, 157–159.

Garcia, J., & Koelling, R. A. (1966). The relation of cue to consequence in avoidance learning. *Psychonomic Science, 4*, 123–124.

Garcia, J., McGowan, B. K., & Green, K. F. (1972). Biological constraints on conditioning. In A. H. Black and W. F. Prokasy (Eds.), *Classical conditioning II: Current research and theory* (pp. 3–27). New York: Appleton-Century-Crofts.

Gardner, H. (1980). *Artful scribbles: The significance of children's drawings.* New York: Basic Books.

Gardner, H. (1983). *Frames of mind: The theory of multiple intelligences.* New York: Basic Books.

Gardner, H. (1987). *The mind's new science: A history of the cognitive revolution.* New York: Basic Books.

Gardner, H. (1993). *Frames of mind: The theory of multiple intelligences* (2nd edition). New York: Basic Books.

Gardner, H. (1999). *Intelligence reframed: Multiple intelligences for the 21st century.* New York: Basic Books.

Gardner, R. A., Gardner, B. T., & Van Cantfort, T. E. (Eds.). (1989). *Teaching sign language to chimpanzees.* Albany: SUNY Press.

Garrett, R. K., & Danziger, J. N. (2008). IM = Interruption management? Instant messaging and disruption in the workplace. *Journal of Computer-Mediated Communication, 13*, 23–42.

Gass, S. (1984). A review of interlanguage syntax: Language transfer and language universals. *Language Learning, 34*, 115–132.

Gates, M. F., & Allee, W. C. (1933). Conditioned behavior of isolated and grouped cockroaches on a simple maze. *Journal of Comparative Psychology, 15*, 331–358.

Gazdzinski, S., Durazzo, T. C., & Meyerhoff, D. J. (2005). Temporal dynamics and determinants of whole brain tissue volume changes during recovery from alcohol dependence. *Drug and Alcohol Dependence, 78*, 263–273.

Geerlings, S. W., Beekman, A., Deeg, D., Twisk, J., & van Tilburg, W. (2002). Duration and severity of depression predict mortality in older adults in the community. *Psychological Medicine, 32*, 609–618.

Georges, E. (1995). A cultural and historical perspective on confession. In J. W. Pennebaker (Ed.), *Emotion, disclosure, and health* (pp. 11–22). Washington, DC: American Psychological Association.

Georgiadis, J. R., Kortekaas, R., Kuipers, R., Nieuwenburg, A., Pruim, J., Simone Reinders, A. A. T., et al. (2006). Regional cerebral blood flow changes associated with clitorally induced orgasm in healthy women. *European Journal of Neuroscience, 24*, 3305–3316.

Gershberg, F. B., & Shimamura, A. P. (1995). The role of the frontal lobes in the use of organizational strategies in free recall. *Neuropsychologia, 13*, 1305–1333.

Gibson, E., & Walk, R. (1960). The visual cliff. *Scientific American, 202*, 64–71.

Gibson, J. J. (1950). *The perception of the visual world.* Boston: Houghton Mifflin.

Gibson, J. J. (1966). *The senses considered as perceptual systems.* Boston: Houghton Mifflin.

Gil, S. (2007). Body-image, well-being and sexual satisfaction: A comparison between heterosexual and gay men. *Sexual and Relationship Therapy, 22*(2), 237–244.

Gillham, J. E., Reivich, K. J., Freres, D. R., Chaplin, T. M., Shatté, A. J., Samuels, B., et al. (2007). School-based prevention of depressive symptoms: A randomized controlled study of the effectiveness and specificity of the Penn Resiliency Program. *Journal of Consulting and Clinical Psychology, 75,* 9–19.

Gilligan, C. (1982). *In a different voice.* Cambridge, MA: Harvard University Press.

Givón, T. (2002). The visual information-processing system as an evolutionary precursor of human language. In T. Givón & B. F. Malle (Eds.), *The evolution of language out of pre-language* (pp. 3–50). Amsterdam: John Benjamins.

Givón, T., & Malle, B. F. (Eds.). *The evolution of language out of pre-language.* Amsterdam: John Benjamins.

Glaser, R., & Kiecolt-Glaser, J. K. (2005). Stress-induced immune dysfunction: Implications for health. *Nature Reviews Immunology,4,* 243–251.

Glassman, A., & Shapiro, P. (1998). Depression and the course of coronary artery disease. *American Journal of Psychiatry, 155,* 4–11.

Goel, V., & Vartanian, O. (2005). Dissociating the roles of right ventral lateral and dorsal lateral prefrontal cortex in generation and maintenance of hypotheses in set-shift problems. *Cerebral Cortex, 15,* 1170–1177.

Goff, D. C., & Coyle, J. T. (2001). The merging role of glutamate in the pathophysiology and treatment of schizophrenia. *American Journal of Psychiatry, 158,* 1367–1377.

Goldapple, K., Segal, Z., Garson, C., Lau, M., Bieling, P., Kennedy, S., et al. (2004). Modulation of cortical-limbic pathways in major depression. *Archives of General Psychiatry, 61,* 34–41.

Goldfield, B. A. (2000). Nouns before verbs in comprehension vs. production: The view from pragmatics. *Journal of Child Language, 27,* 501–520.

Goldin, P., McRae, K., Ramel, W., & Gross, J. J. (2008). The neural bases of emotion regulation: Reappraisal and suppression of negative emotion. *Biological Psychiatry, 63,* 577–586.

Goldman-Rakic, P. S. (1999). The physiological approach: Functional architecture of working memory and disordered cognition in schizophrenia. *Biological Psychiatry, 46,* 650–661.

Goldsmith, T. H. (2006). What birds see. *Scientific American, 295,* 69–75.

Goldstein, E. B. (2007). *Sensation and perception* (7th ed.). New York: Thomson-Wadsworth.

Goldstein, T., Bridge, J., & Brent, D. (2008). Sleep disturbance preceding completed suicide in adolescents. *Journal of Consulting and Clinical Psychology, 76*(1), 84–91.

Goleman, D. P. (1995). *Emotional Intelligence: Why it can matter more than IQ for character, health and lifelong achievement.* New York: Bantam Books.

Gonzalez, J. J., Hynd, G. W., & Martin, R. P. (1994). Neuropsychology of temperament. In P. A. Vernon (Ed.), *The neuropsychology of individual differences* (pp. 235–256). San Diego: Academic Press.

Goodwin, P. J. (2004). Support groups in breast cancer: When a negative result is positive. *Journal of Clinical Oncology, 22,* 4244–4246.

Goodwin, P. J., Leszcz, M., Ennis, M., Koopmans, J., Vincent, L., Guther, H., et al. (2001). The effect of group psychosocial support on survival in metastatic breast cancer. *New England Journal of Medicine, 345,* 1719–1726.

Gopnik, A., Meltzoff, A. N., & Kuhl, P. K. (1999). *The scientist in the crib: Minds, brains, and how children learn.* New York: Morrow.

Gordon, P. (2004). Numerical cognition without words: Evidence from Amazonia. *Science, 306,* 496–499.

Gorenstein, E. E., & Comer, R. J. (2002). *Case studies in abnormal psychology.* New York: Worth.

Gosling, S. D. (1998). Personality differences in spotted hyenas (*Crocuta crocuta*). *Journal of Comparative Psychology, 112,* 107–118.

Gosling, S. D., & John, O. P. (1999). Personality dimensions in non-human animals: A cross-species review. *Current Directions in Psychological Science, 8,* 69–75.

Goto, H. (1971). Auditory perception by normal Japanese adults of the sounds "l" and "r." *Neuropsychologia, 9,* 317–323.

Gottfredson, L. (1997). Mainstream science on intelligence: An editorial with 52 signatories, history, and bibliography. *Intelligence, 24,* 13–23.

Gottlieb, N. H., & Green, L. W. (1984). Life events, social network, life-style, and health: An analysis of the 1979 National Survey of Personal Health Practices and Consequences. *Health Education Quarterly, 11,* 91–105.

Gough, H. G., & Bradley, P. (1996). *California Psychological Inventory Manual* (3rd ed.). Palo Alto, CA: Consulting Psychologists Press.

Gould, E. (2008, May 25). Exposed. *The New York Times Magazine.*

Gould, E., Vail, N., Wagers, M., and Gross, C. G. (2004). Adult-generated hippocampal and neocortical neurons in macaques have a transient existence. *Proceedings of the National Academy of Sciences, 98,* 10910–10917.

Gould, S. J., & Vrba, E. S. (1982). Exaptation: A missing term in the science of form. *Paleobiology, 8,* 4–15.

Governors Highway Safety Association. (2008). *Cell phone driving laws.* Retrieved April 1, 2008, from http://www.ghsa.org/html/stateinfo/laws/cellphone_laws.html

Gow, A., Whiteman, M., Pattie, A., Whalley, L., Starr, J., & Deary, I. (2005). Lifetime intellectual function and satisfaction with life in old age: Longitudinal cohort study. *BMJ: British Medical Journal, 331*(7509), 141–142. doi:10.1136/bmj.38531.675660.F7.

Grafman, J., Schwab., K., Warden, D., Pridgeon, A., Brown, H. R., & Salazar, A. M. (1996). Frontal lobe injuries, violence, and aggression: A report of a Vietnam head injury study. *Neurology, 46,* 1231–1238.

Graham, S., & Lowery, B. S. (2004). Priming unconscious racial stereotypes about adolescent offenders. *Law and Human Behavior, 28,* 483–504.

Grant, B. F., Hasin, D. S., Stinson, F. S., Dawson, D. A., Goldstein, R. B., Smith, S., et al. (2006). The epidemiology of *DSM-IV-TR* panic disorder and agoraphobia in the United States: Results from the National Epidemiologic Survey on Alcohol and Related Conditions. *Journal of Clinical Psychiatry, 67,* 363–374.

Graves, K. N. (2007). Not always sugar and spice: Expanding theoretical and functional explanations for why females aggress. *Aggression and Violent Behavior, 12,* 131–140.

Gray, J. L., & Thompson, P. (2004). Neurobiology of intelligence: Science and ethics. *Nature Reviews: Neuroscience, 5,* 471–482.

Green, D., & Swets, J. (1974). *Signal detection theory and psychophysics.* Oxford: Krieger.

Greenberg, L. (1979). Genetic component of bee odor in kin recognition. *Science, 206,* 1095–1097.

Greenberg, M. T., & Kusché, C. A. (1998). *Promoting alternative thinking strategies.* Boulder: Institute of Behavioral Sciences, University of Colorado.

Greenough, W. T., Volkmar, F. R., and Juraska, J. M. (1973). Effects of rearing complexity on dendritic branching in frontolateral and temporal cortex of the rat, *Experimental Neurology, 41,* 371–378.

Greenwald, A. G., & Banaji, M. R. (1995). Implicit social cognition: Attitudes, self-esteem, and stereotypes. *Psychological Review, 102,* 4–27.

Greenwald, A. G., McGhee, D. E., & Schwartz, J. L. K. (1998). Measuring individual differences in implicit cognition: The implicit association test. *Journal of Personality and Social Psychology, 74,* 1464–1480.

Gregory, R. J. (2007). *Psychological testing* (5th ed.). New York: Allyn & Bacon.

Grigorenko, E. (2000). Heritability and intelligence. In R. J. Sternberg (Ed.), *Handbook of intelligence* (pp. 53–91). New York: Cambridge University Press.

Grolnick, W. S., McMenamy, J. M., & Kurowski, C. O. (2006). Emotional self-regulation in infancy and toddlerhood. In L. Balter & C. S. Tamis-LeMonda (Eds.), *Child psychology: A handbook of contemporary issues* (2nd ed.; pp. 3–25). New York: Psychology Press.

Groome, L., Mooney, D., Holland, S., Smith, Y., Atterbury, J., & Dykman, R. (2000). Temporal pattern and spectral complexity as stimulus parameters for eliciting a cardiac orienting reflex in human fetuses. *Perception and Psychophysics, 62*(2), 313–320.

Gross, C. G. (2000). Neurogenesis in the adult brain: Death of a dogma. *Nature Reviews Neuroscience, 1,* 67–73.

Gross, J. J. (1998). The emerging field of emotion regulation: An integrative review. *Review of General Psychology, 2,* 271–299.

Gross, J. J., & John, O. (1998). Mapping the domain of expressivity: Multimethod evidence for a hierarchical model. *Journal of Personality and Social Psychology, 74,* 170–191.

Gross, J. J., & Levenson, R. W. (1993). Emotional suppression—Physiology, self-report, and expressive behavior. *Journal of Personality and Social Psychology, 64,* 970–986.

Gross, J. J., & Levenson, R. W. (1997). Hiding feelings: The acute effects of inhibiting positive and negative emotions. *Journal of Abnormal Psychology, 106,* 95–103.

Gross, J. J., Richards, J. M., & John, O. P. (2006). Emotion regulation in everyday life. In D. K. Snyder, J. A. Simpson, & J. N. Hughes (Eds.), *Emotion regulation in families: Pathways to dysfunction and health* (pp. 13–35). Washington, DC: American Psychological Association.

Grossman, A. W., Churchill, J. D., McKinney, B. C., Kodish, I. M., Otte, S. L., & Greenough, W. T. (2003). Experience effects on brain development: Possible contributions to psychopathology. *Journal of Child Psychology and Psychiatry, 44,* 33–63.

Grossman, T., Striano, T., & Friederici, A. D. (2006). Crossmodal integration of emotional information from face and voice in the infant brain. *Developmental Science, 9,* 309–315.

Guarnaccia, V., Dill, C. A., Sabatino, S., & Southwick, S. (2001). Scoring accuracy using the comprehensive system for the Rorschach. *Journal of Personality Assessment, 77,* 464–474.

Guarraci, F. A. & Benson, A. (2005). "Coffee, Tea and Me": Moderate doses of caffeine affect sexual behavior in female rats. *Pharmacology, Biochemistry and Behavior, 82,* 522–530.

Guehl, D., Benazzouz, A., Aouizerate, B., Cuny, E., Rotgé, J.-Y., Rougier, A., et al. (2008). Neuronal correlates of obsessions in the caudate nucleus. *Biological Psychiatry, 63,* 557–562.

Guilford, J. P. (1967). *The nature of human intelligence.* New York: McGraw-Hill.

Guilleminault, C., Kirisoglu, C., Bao, G., Arias, V., Chan, A., Li, K. K. (2005). Adult chronic sleepwalking and its treatment based on polysomnography. *Brain, 128,* 1062–1069.

Guiraud, A., deLorgeril, M., Zeghichi, S., Laporte, F., Salen, P., Saks, V., et al. (2008). Interactions of ethanol drinking with n-3 fatty acids in rats: Potential consequences for the cardiovascular system. *British Journal of Nutrition,* April 29, 1–8. Advance online publication. Retrieved July 10, 2008. doi:10.1017/S0007114508981472

Gunderson, E., Moline, J., & Catalano, P. (1997). Risks of developing noise-induced hearing loss in employees of urban music clubs. *American Journal of Industrial Medicine, 31,* 75–79.

Gupta, S., Agarwal, A., Banerjee, J., & Alvarez, J. G. (2007). The role of oxidative stress in spontaneous abortion and recurrent pregnancy loss: A systematic review. *Obstetrical, Gynecological Survey, 62,* 335–347.

Gutteling, B. M., de Weerth, C., Willemsen-Swinkles, S. H. N., Huizink, A. C., Mulder, E. J. H., Visser, G. H. A., et al. (2005). The effects of prenatal stress on temperament and problem behavior of 27-month-old toddlers. *European Child and Adolescent Psychiatry, 14,* 41–51.

Guzman-Marin, R., Suntsova, N., Methippara, M., Greiffenstein, R., Szymusiak, R., & McGinty, D. (2003). Sleep deprivation suppresses neurogenesis in the adult hippocampus of rats. *European Journal of Neuroscience, 22,* 2111–2116.

Haier, R. J., Jung, R. E., Yeo, R. A., Head, K., & Alkire, M. T. (2004). Structural brain variation and general intelligence. *NeuroImage, 23,* 425–433.

Hale, B., Seiser, L., & McGuire, E. J. (2005). Mental imagery. In J. Taylor & J. Wilson (Eds.), *Applying sport psychology: Four perspectives* (pp. 117–135). Champaign, IL: Human Kinetics.

Hall, J. A., & Matsumoto, D. (2004). Gender difference in the judgment of multiple emotions from facial expression. *Emotion, 4,* 201–206.

Halpern, D. (2004). A cognitive-process taxonomy for sex differences in cognitive abilities. *Current Directions in Psychological Science, 13,* 135–139.

Halpern, J. H., Pope, H. G., Sherwood, A. R., Barry, S., Hudson, J. I., & Yurgelun-Todd, D. (2004). Residual neuropsychological effects of illicit 3,4-methylenedioxymethamphetamine (MDMA) in individuals with minimal exposure to other drugs. *Drug and Alcohol Dependence, 75,* 135–147.

Hamann, S., Herman, R. A., Nolan, C. L., & Wallen, K. (2004). Men and women differ in amygdala response to visual sexual stimuli. *Nature Neuroscience, 7,* 411–416.

Hamer, D., & Copeland, P. (1998). *Living with our genes.* New York: Anchor Books.

Hamilton, W. D. (1964). The genetical evolution of social behaviour I and II. *Journal of Theoretical Biology, 7,* 1–16; 17–52.

Han, J. (2004). Acupuncture and endorphins. *Neuroscience Letters, 361,* 258–261.

Haney, C., Banks, W. C., & Zimbardo, P. G. (1973). Interpersonal dynamics in a simulated prison. *International Journal of Criminology and Penology, 1,* 69–97.

Hansen, R. A., Gartlehner, G., Lohr, K. N., & Daufer, D. (2007). Functional outcomes of drug treatment in Alzheimer's disease: A systematic review and meta-analysis. *Drugs & Aging, 24*(2): 155–167.

Hannigan, T. P. (1995). Body odor: The international student and cross-cultural communication. *Culture & Psychology, 1,* 497–503.

Hare, R. D. (1993). *Without conscience: The disturbing world of the psychopaths among us.* New York: Pocket Books.

Hargittai, E. (2008). Whose space? Differences among users and non-users of social network sites. *Journal of Computer-Mediated Communication, 13,* 276–297.

Hargrave, G. E., & Hiatt, D. (1989). Use of the California Psychological Inventory in law enforcement officer selection. *Journal of Personality Assessment, 53,* 267–277.

Harkins, S. G. (1987). Social loafing and social facilitation. *Journal of Experimental Social Psychology, 23,* 1–18.

Harlow, H. (1958). The nature of love. *American Psychologist, 13,* 573–685.

Harmon, D. (2006). Free-radical theory of aging: An update. *Annals of the New York Academy of Sciences, 1067,* 10–21.

Harmon-Jones. E. (2003). Clarifying the emotive functions of asymmetrical frontal cortical activity. *Psychophysiology, 40,* 838–848.

Harris, J. R. (1998). *The nurture assumption: Why children turn out the way they do.* New York: Free Press.

Harris, M. B. (1974). Mediators between frustration and aggression in a field experiment. *Journal of Experimental Social Psychology, 10,* 561–571.

Harrison, P. J. (2004). The hippocampus in schizophrenia: A review of the neuropathological evidence and its pathophysiological implications. *Psychopharmacology, 174,* 151–162.

Harrison, P. J., & Owen, M. (2003). Genes for schizophrenia? Recent findings and their pathophysiological implications. *The Lancet, 361,* 417–419.

Hasher, L., & Zacks, R. T. (1979). Automatic and effortful processes in memory. *Journal of Experimental Psychology: General, 108,* 356–388.

Hauser, M. D., Chomsky, N., & Fitch, W. T. (2002). The faculty of language: What is it, who has it, and how did it evolve? *Science, 298,* 1569–1579.

Hayes, B. D., Klein-Schwartz, W., & Doyon, S. (2008). Toxicity of buprenorphine overdoses in children. *Pediatrics, 121,* 782–786.

Haynes, S. G., Levine, S., Scotch, N., Feinleib, M., & Kannel, W. B. (1978). The relationship of psychosocial factors to coronary heart disease in the Framingham study. I. Methods and risk factors. *American Journal of Epidemiology, 107,* 362–383.

Hazan, C., & Shaver, P. (1987). Romantic love conceptualized as an attachment process. *Journal of Personality and Social Psychology, 52,* 511–524.

Headey, B. (2008). Life goals matter to happiness: A revision of set-point theory. *Social Indicators Research, 86,* 213–231.

Headey, B. W., & Wearing, A. J. (1992). *Understanding happiness: A theory of subjective well-being.* Melbourne: Longman Cheshire.

Health and Human Services. (2004). *New surgeon general's report expands the list of diseases caused by smoking.* Retrieved August 19, 2008, from http://www.hhs.gov/news/press/2004pres/20040527a.html

Heath, R. G. (1975). Brain function and behavior. *Journal of Nervous and Mental Disease, 160,* 159–175.

Hebb, D. O. (1949). *The organization of behavior: A neuropsychological theory.* New York: Wiley.

Hedges, L., & Nowell, A. (1995). Sex differences in mental test scores, variability, and numbers of high-scoring individuals. *Science, 269,* 41–45.

Hedges, S. M., Jandorf, L., & Stone, A. A. (1985). Meaning of daily mood assessments. *Journal of Personality and Social Psychology, 48,* 428–434.

Hegelson, V. S., & Taylor, S. E. (1993). Social comparisons and adjustment among cardiac patients. *Journal of Applied Social Psychology, 23,* 1171–1195.

Heider, F. (1958). *The psychology of interpersonal relations.* New York: Wiley.

Henderson, A. (2007). Sexual satisfaction among lesbian and heterosexual women: An ecological model. *Dissertation Abstracts International: Section B: The Sciences and Engineering, 67*(8-B), 4709.

Hering, E. (1878). *Zur Lehre vom Lichtsinn.* Vienna, Austria: Gerold.

Hernandez-Reif, M., Field, T., Largie, S., Diego, M., Manigat, N., Seoanes, J., et al. (2005). Cerebral palsy symptoms in children decreased following massage therapy. *Early Child Development and Care, 175,* 445–456.

Herrnstein, R. J., & Murray, C. (1994). *The bell-curve: Intelligence and class structure in American life.* New York: Free Press.

Herz, R. (2004). A naturalistic analysis of autobiographical memories triggered by olfactory visual and auditory stimuli. *Chemical Senses, 29,* 217–224.

Hettema, J. M., Neale, M. C., & Kendler, K. S. (2001). A review and meta-analysis of the genetic epidemiology of anxiety disorders. *American Journal of Psychiatry, 158,* 1568–1578.

Hien, D. A., & Miele, G. M. (2003). Emotion-focused coping as a mediator of maternal cocaine abuse and antisocial behavior. *Psychology of Addictive Behaviors, 17,* 49–55.

Hilgard, E. (1965). *Hypnotic susceptibility.* New York: Harcourt, Brace, & World.

Hilgard, E. (1977). *Divided consciousness: Multiple controls in human thought and action.* New York: Wiley.

Hillman, C. H., Erickson, K. I., & Kramer, A. F. (2008). Be smart, exercise your heart: Exercise effects on brain and cognition. *Nature Reviews Neuroscience, 9,* 58–65.

Hines, L. M., & Rimm, E. B. (2001). Moderate alcohol consumption and coronary heart disease: A review. *Postgraduate Medical Journal, 77,* 747–752.

Ho, Y-C, Cheung, M-C, & Chan, A. S. (2003). Music training improves verbal but not visual memory: Cross-sectional and longitudinal explorations in children. *Neuropsychology, 17,* 439–450.

Hobson, J. A. (2001). *The dream drugstore: Chemically altered states of consciousness.* Cambridge, MA: MIT Press.

Hobson, J. A. (2002). *Dreaming: An introduction to the science of sleep.* New York: Oxford University Press.

Hoff, E. (2006). How social contexts support and shape language development. *Developmental Review, 26,* 55–88.

Hofman, S. G., Schulz, S. M., Meuret, A. F., Moscovitch, D. A., & Suvak, M. (2006). Sudden gains during therapy of social phobia. *Journal of Consulting and Clinical Psychology, 74,* 687–697.

Hofstede, G. (1980). *Culture's consequences: International differences in work-related values.* Beverly Hills, CA: Sage.

Hofstede, G. (2001). *Culture's consequences: Comparing values, behaviors, institutions, and organizations across nations* (2nd ed.). Thousand Oaks, CA: Sage.

Hogan, T. P. (2007). *Psychological testing: A practical introduction.* (2nd ed.). New York: John Wiley.

Hohmann, A. G., Suplita, R. L., Bolton, N. M., Neely, M. H., Fegley, D., Mangieri R., et al. (2005). An endocannabinoid mechanism for stress-induced analgesia. *Nature, 435,* 1108–1112.

Hollon, S. D., DeRubeis, R. J., Shelton, R. C., Amsterdam, J. D., Salomon, R. M., O'Reardon, J. P., et al. (2005). Prevention of relapse following cognitive therapy vs medications in moderate to several depression. *Archives of General Psychiatry, 62,* 417–422.

Holmes, T. H., & Rahe, R. H. (1967). The social readjustment rating scale. *Journal of Psychosomatic Research, 11,* 211–218.

Holstege, G., Georgiadis, J., Paans, A., Meiners, L., van der Graaf, F., & Reinders, A. (2003). Brain activation during human male ejaculation. *Journal of Neuroscience, 23*(27), 9185–9193.

Hopfield, J. J. (1982). Neural networks and physical systems with emergent collective computational abilities. *Proceedings of the National Academy of Science, 79,* 2554–2558.

Hopson, J. L. (1998, September/October). Fetal psychology. *Psychology Today, 31,* 44. Retrieved from http://www.leaderu.com/orgs/tul/psychtoday9809.html

Horn, J. L., & Cattell, R. B. (1966). Refinement and test of the theory of fluid and crystallized general intelligences. *Journal of Educational Psychology, 57,* 253–270.

Horney, K. (1945). *Our inner conflicts: A constructive theory of neurosis.* New York: Norton.

Horney, K. (1950). *Neurosis and human growth: The struggle toward self-realization.* New York: Norton.

Horrey, W. J., & Wickens, C. D. (2006). Examining the impact of cell phone conversations on driving using meta-analytic techniques. *Human Factors, 48,* 196–205.

Hoss, R. A., & Langlois, J. H. (2003). Infants prefer attractive faces. In O. Pascalis & A. Slater (Eds.), *The development of face processing in infancy and early childhood: Current perspectives* (pp. 27–38). New York: Nova Science.

How a Swiss inventor hooked the world. (2007, January 4). Retrieved September 16, 2007, from http://www.swissinfo.org/eng/search/detail/How_a_Swiss_invention_hooked_the_world.html?siteSect=881&sid=7402384&cKey=1167927120000

Howard, K. I., Kopta, S. M., Krause, M. S., & Orlinsky, D. E. (1986). The dose-effect relationship in psychotherapy. *American Psychologist, 41*, 159–164.

Howes, C., & Matheson, C. C. (1992). Sequences in the development of competent play with peers: Social and social pretend play. *Developmental Psychology, 28*, 961–974.

Hubbard, E. M., & Ramachandran, V. S. (2005). Neurocognitive mechanisms of synesthesia. *Neuron, 48*, 509–520.

Hubel, D., & Wiesel, T. (1962). Receptive fields, binocular interaction and functional architecture in the cat's visual cortex. *Journal of Physiology of London, 160*, 106–154.

Hubel, D., & Wiesel, T. (1979). Brain mechanisms of vision. *Scientific American, 241*, 130–144.

Hudson, W. (1960). Pictorial depth perception in subcultural groups in Africa. *Journal of Social Psychology, 52*, 183–208.

Huesmann, L. R., Moise-Titus, J., & Podolski, C. (2003). Longitudinal relations between children's exposure to TV violence and their aggressive and violent behavior in young adulthood: 1977–1992. *Developmental Psychology, 39*, 201–221.

Huff, D. (1954). *How to lie with statistics.* New York: Norton.

Hull, C. L. (1943). *Principles of behavior: An introduction to behavior theory.* New York: Appleton-Century.

Hunter, J. E., & Schmidt, F. L. (2000). Racial and gender bias in ability and achievement tests: Resolving the apparent paradox. *Psychology, Public Policy and Law, 6*, 151–158.

Huprich, S. (2008). TAT oral dependency scale. *A handbook of clinical scoring systems for thematic apperceptive techniques* (pp. 385–398). Mahwah, NJ: Erlbaum.

Hutchinson, S., Lee, L. H., Gaab, N., & Schlaug, G. (2003). Cerebellar volume of musicians. *Cerebral Cortex, 13*, 943–949.

Hyde, J. S. (1990). Meta-analysis and the psychology of gender differences. *Signs: Journal of Women in Culture & Society, 16*, 53–73.

Hyde, J. S. (2005). The genetics of sexual orientation. In J. S. Hyde (Ed.), *Biological substrates of human sexuality* (pp. 9–20). Washington, DC: American Psychological Association.

Hyde, T. S., & Jenkins, J. J. (1973). Recall for words as a function of semantic, graphic, and syntactic orienting tasks. *Journal of Verbal Learning and Verbal Behavior, 12*, 471–480.

Hyman, S. E. (2005). Neurotransmitters. *Current Biology, 15*, R154–R158.

I feel I am trapped inside my head, banging against its walls, trying desperately to escape. (1986, March 18). *New York Times.* Retrieved from http://www.nytimes.com

Iacoboni, M., & Mazziotta, J. C. (2007). Mirror neuron system: Basic findings and clinical applications. *Annals of Neurology, 62*, 213–218.

Iacoboni, M., Woods R. P., Brass, M., Bekkering, H., Mazziotta, J. C., & Rizzolatti, G. (1999). Cortical mechanisms of human imitation. *Science, 286*, 2526–2528.

Iarocci, G., & McDonald, J. (2006). Sensory integration and the perceptual experience of persons with autism. *Journal of Autism and Developmental Disorders, 36*, 77–90.

Inhelder, B., & Piaget, J. (1958). *The growth of logical thinking: From childhood to adolescence.* New York: Basic Books.

Institutional Review Board Guidebook. (1993). U.S. Department of Health & Human Services. Retrieved January 10, 2008, from http://www.hhs.gov/ohrp/irb/irb _guidebook.htm

Ironson, G., O'Cleirigh, C., Fletcher, M. A., Laurenceau, J. P., Balbin, E., Klimas, N., et al. (2005). Psychosocial factors predict CD4 and viral load change in men and women with human immunodeficiency virus in the era of highly active antiretroviral treatment. *Psychosomatic Medicine, 67*, 1013–1021.

Isen, A. M., Daubman, K. A., & Nowicki, G. P. (1987). Positive affect facilitates creative problem solving. *Journal of Personality and Social Psychology, 52*, 1122–1131.

Itri, J., Michel, S., Waschek, J., & Colwell, C. (2004). Circadian rhythm in inhibitory synaptic transmission in the mouse suprachiasmatic nucleus. *Journal of Neurophysiology, 92*(1), 311–319.

Izard, C. E. (1969). The emotions and emotion constructs in personality and culture research. In R. B. Cattell (Ed.), *Handbook of modern personality theory.* Chicago: Aldine Press.

Izard, C. E., Trentacosta, C. J., King, K. A., & Mostow, A. J. (2004). An emotion-based prevention program for Head Start children. *Early Education & Development, 15*, 407–422.

Jablensky, A., & Woodbury, M. A. (1995). Dementia praecox and manic-depressive insanity in 1908: A Grade of Membership analysis of the Kraepelinian dichotomy. *European Archives of Psychiatry and Clinical Neuroscience, 245*, 202–209.

Jackson, K. M. (2008). Heavy episodic drinking: Determining the predictive utility of five or more drinks. *Psychology of Addictive Behaviors, 22*, 68–77.

Jacobs, B. L. (2004). Depression: The brain finally gets into the act. *Current Directions in Psychological Science, 13*, 103–106.

Jacobs, B. L., & Fornal, C. A. (1999). Chronic fluoxetine treatment increases hippocampal neurogenesis in rats: A novel theory of depression. *Society for Neuroscience Abstracts, 25*, 714.

Jacobs, B. L., van Praag, H., & Gage, F. H. (2000). Adult brain neurogenesis and psychiatry: A novel theory of depression. *Molecular Psychiatry, 5*, 262–269.

Jacobs, D. R., Jr., Adachi, H., Mulder, I., Kromhout, D., Menotti, A., Nissinen, A., et al. (1999). Cigarette smoking and mortality risk: Twenty-five-year follow-up of the Seven Countries Study. *Archives of Internal Medicine, 159*, 733–740.

Jacobsen, L. K., Krystal, J. H., Mencl, E., Westerveld, M., Frost, S. J., & Pugh, K. R. (2005). Effects of smoking and smoking abstinence on cognition in adolescent tobacco smokers. *Biological Psychiatry, 57*, 56–66.

Jacobson, A. L. (1963). Learning in flatworms and annelids. *Psychological Bulletin, 60*, 74–94.

Jacobson, L. H., Kelly, P. H., Bettler, B., Kaupmann, K., & Cryan, J. F. (2006). GABAB(1) receptor isoforms differentially mediate the acquisition and extinction of aversive taste memories. *Journal of Neuroscience, 26*, 8800–8803.

Jacobson, S., & Jacobson, J. (2000). *Teratogenic insult and neurobehavioral function in infancy and childhood.* Mahwah, NJ: Erlbaum.

Jacoby, L. L., & Dallas, M. (1981). On the relationship between autobiographical memory and perceptual learning. *Journal of Experimental Psychology: General, 110*, 306–340.

Jacoby, L. L., Hessels, S., & Bopp, K. (2001). Proactive and retroactive effects in memory performance: Dissociating recollection and accessibility bias. In H. Roediger, J. S. Nairne, I. Neath, & A. M. Suprenant (Eds.), *The nature of remembering: Essays in honor of Robert G. Crowder* (pp. 35–54). Washington, DC: American Psychological Association.

Jain, S., Dharap, S. B., & Gore, M. A. (2008). Early prediction of outcome in very severe closed head injury. *Injury: International Journal of the Care of the Injured, 39*, 598–603.

James, W. (1884). What is an emotion? *Mind, 9*, 188–205.

Jamison, K. R. (1993). *Touched with fire: Manic-depressive illness and the artistic temperament.* New York: Free Press.

Jamison, K. R., Gerner, R. H., Hammen, C., & Padesky, C. (1980). Clouds and silver linings: Positive experiences associated with primary affective disorders. *American Journal of Psychiatry, 137*, 198–202.

Janeck, A. S., Calamari, J. E., Riemann, B. C., & Heffelfinger, S. K. (2003). Too much thinking about thinking? Metacognitive differences in obsessive-compulsive disorder. *Journal of Anxiety Disorders, 17*, 181–195.

Janis, I. L. (1983). *Groupthink* (2nd ed., revised). Boston: Houghton-Mifflin.

Javitt, D. C., & Coyle, J. T. (2004). Decoding schizophrenia. *Scientific American, 290,* 48–55.

Jenkins, W. M., Merzenich, M. M., Ochs, M. T., Allard, T., & Guic-Roble, E. (1990). Functional reorganization of primary somatosensory cortex in adult owl monkeys after behaviorally controlled tactile stimulation. *Journal of Neurophysiology, 63,* 82–104.

Jensen, A. R. (1969). How much can we boost IQ and scholastic achievement? *Harvard Educational Review, 39,* 1–23.

Jerison, H. J. (2000). The evolution of intelligence. In R. J. Sternberg (Ed.), *The handbook of intelligence* (pp. 216–244). New York: Cambridge University Press.

Jha, A. P., Krompinger, J., & Baime, M. J. (2007). Mindfulness training modifies subsystems of attention. *Cognitive, Affective, & Behavioral Neuroscience, 7,* 109–119.

Ji, D., & Wilson, M. A. (2007). Coordinated memory replay in the visual cortex and hippocampus during sleep. *Nature Neuroscience, 10,* 100–107.

Jimenez, R. T., Garcia, G. E., & Pearson, P. D. (1994). *The metacognitive strategies of Latina/o students who read Spanish and English.* Center for the Study of Reading, Technical Report No. 601. Urbana-Champagne, IL: College of Education.

John, O. P., & Gross, J. J. (2004). Healthy and unhealthy emotion regulation: Personality processes, individual differences, and life span development. *Journal of Personality, 72,* 1301–1333.

John, O. P., & Srivastava, S. (1999). The Big Five trait taxonomy: History, measurement, and theoretical perspectives. In L. A. Pervin & O. P. John (Eds.), *Handbook of personality theory and research* (pp. 102–138). New York: Guilford Press.

Johnson, G. (1998). Lithium—Early development, toxicity, and renal function. *Neuropsychopharmacology 19,* 200–205.

Johnson, R. E., Fudala, P. J., & Payne, R. (2005). Buprenorphine: Considerations for pain management. *Journal of Pain and Symptom Management, 29,* 297–326.

Johnston, J. C., & McClelland, J. L. (1974). Perception of letters in words: Seek not and ye shall find. *Science, 184,* 1192–1994.

Jope, R. S. (1999). Anti-bipolar therapy: Mechanism of action of lithium. *Molecular Psychiatry, 4,* 117–128.

Juliano, L. M., & Griffiths, R. R. (2004). A critical review of caffeine withdrawal: Empirical validation of symptoms and signs, incidence, severity, and associated features. *Psychopharmacology, 176,* 1–29.

Jump, V. K., Fargo, J. D., & Akers, J. F. (2006). Impact of massage therapy on health outcomes among orphaned infants in Ecuador: Results of a randomized clinical trial. *Family & Community Health, 29,* 314–319.

Jung, C. G. (1918/1964). The role of the unconscious. In *Collected works* (Vol. 10; Trans. R. F. C. Hull). New York: Bollingen Foundation.

Jusczyk, P. W. (1997). *The discovery of spoken language.* Cambridge, MA: MIT Press.

Jussim, L., & Harber, K. D. (2005). Teacher expectations and self-fulfilling prophecies: Knowns and unknowns, resolved and unresolved controversies. *Personality and Social Psychology Review, 9,* 131–155.

Just, M. A., Kellar, T. A., & Cynkar, J. (in press). A decrease in brain activation associated with driving when listening to someone speak. *Brain Research.*

Kabat-Zinn, J. (1990). *Full catastrophe living.* New York: Delta.

Kabat-Zinn, J., Lipworth, L., & Burney, R. (1985). The clinical use of mindfulness meditation for the self-regulation of chronic pain. *Journal of Behavioral Medicine, 8,* 163–190.

Kabat-Zinn, J., Massion, A. O., Kristeller, J., Peterson, L. G., Fletcher, K. E., Pbert, L., et al. (1992). Effectiveness of a meditation-based stress reduction program in the treatment of anxiety disorders. *American Journal of Psychiatry, 149,* 936–943.

Kabat-Zinn, J., Wheeler, E., Light, T., Skillings, A., Scharf, M. J., Cropley, T. G., et al. (1998). Influence of a mindfulness meditation-based stress reduction intervention on rates of clearing in patients with moderate to severe psoriasis undergoing phototherapy (UVB) and photochemotherapy (PUVA). *Psychosomatic Medicine, 60,* 625–632.

Kagan, J. (2003). Biology, context, and developmental inquiry. *Annual Review of Psychology, 54,* 1–23.

Kahan, T. L. (2001). Consciousness in dreaming. A metacognitive approach. In T. Bulkeley (Ed.), *Dreams: A reader on religious, cultural, and psychological dimensions of dreaming* (pp. 333–360). New York: Palgrave Macmillan.

Kahan, T. L., & LaBerge, S. (1994). Lucid dreaming as metacognitions: Implications for cognitive science. *Consciousness and Cognition, 3,* 246–264.

Kahn, R. S., Khoury, J., Nichols, W. C., & Lanphear, B. P. (2003). Role of dopamine transporter genotype and maternal prenatal smoking in childhood hyperactive-impulsive, inattentive, and oppositional behaviors. *The Journal of Pediatrics, 143,* 104–110.

Kahneman, D. (2002). Autobiography—Nobel Prize for 2002 in Economics. Retrieved December 15, 2006 from http://nobelprize.org/nobel_prizes/economics/laureates/2002/kahneman-autobio.html.

Kahneman, D., & Tversky, A. (1972). Subjective probability: A judgment of representativeness. *Cognitive Psychology, 3,* 430–454.

Kalat, J. W. (2007). *Biological Psychology,* 9th ed. (Belmont, CA: Wadsworth).

Kam, C. M., Greenberg, M. T., & Kusché, C. A. (2004). Sustained effects of the PATHS curriculum on the social and psychological adjustment of children in special education. *Journal of Emotional and Behavioral Disorders, 12,* 66–78.

Kam, C. M., Greenberg, M. T., & Walls, C. T. (2003). Examining the role of implementation quality in school–based prevention using the PATHS curriculum. *Prevention Science, 4,* 55–63.

Kammrath, L. K., Mendoza-Denton, R., & Mischel, W. (2005). Incorporating *if . . . then . . .* personality signatures in person perception: Beyond the person–situation dichotomy. *Journal of Personality and Social Psychology, 88,* 605–618.

Kanayama, G., Rogowska, J., Pope, H. G., Gruber, S. A., & Yurgelun-Todd, D. A. (2004). Spatial working memory in heavy cannabis users: A functional magnetic resonance imaging study. *Psychopharmacology, 176,* 239–247.

Kandel, E. R. (2000a). Disorders of thought and volition: Schizophrenia. In E. R. Kandel, J. H. Schwartz, & T. M. Jessell (Eds.), *Principles of neural science* (4th ed.; pp. 1188–1208). New York: McGraw-Hill.

Kandel, E. R. (2000b). Nerve cells and behavior. In E. R. Kandel, J. M. Schwartz, & T. M. Jessell (Eds.). *Principles of neural science* (4th ed.; pp. 19–35). New York: McGraw-Hill.

Kandel, E. R. (2001). The molecular biology of memory storage: A dialogue between genes and synapses. *Science, 294,* 1030–1038.

Kandel, E. R. (2006). *In search of memory: The emergence of a new science of mind.* New York: Norton.

Kandel, E. R., Kupfermann, I., Iversen, S. (2000). Learning and memory. In E. R. Kandel, J. H. Schwartz, & T. M. Jessell (Eds.), *Principles of neural science* (4th ed.; pp. 1227–1246). New York: McGraw-Hill.

Kanner, A. D., Coyne, J. C., Schaefer, C., Lazarus, R. S. (1981). Comparison of two modes of stress measurement: Daily hassles and uplifts versus major life events. *Journal of Behavioral Medicine, 4,* 1–39.

Kanner, L. (1943). Autistic disturbances of affective contact. *Nervous Child, 2,* 217–250.

Kanwisher, N. (2000). Domain specificity in face perception. *Nature Neuroscience, 3,* 759.

Karama, S., Lecours, A. R., Leroux, J-M., Bourgouin, P., Beaudoin, G., Joubert, S., et al. (2002). Areas of brain activation in males and females during viewing of erotic film excerpts. *Human Brain Mapping, 16,* 1–13.

Karni, A., Tanne, D., Rubenstein, B. S., Askenasy, J. J. M., & Sagi, D. (1994). Dependence on REM sleep of overnight improvement of a perceptual skill. *Science, 265,* 679–682.

Kaufman, A. S. (1979). *Intelligent testing with the WISC-R.* New York: Wiley.

Kaufman, A. S., & Kaufman, N. L. (1983). *K-ABC interpretative manual.* Circle Pines, MN: American Guidance Service. (2nd ed., 2004, KABC-II).

Kawamura, Y., & Kare, M. R. (1987). *Umami: A basic taste.* New York: Dekker.

Kay, L. M., & Sherman, S. M. (2007). An argument for an olfactory thalamus. *Trends in Neurosciences, 30,* 47–53.

Kaye, G. T. (2001). *Celebrating 60 years of science.* Intel Corporation.

Keel, P. K., & Klump, K. L. (2003). Are eating disorders culture-bound syndromes? Implications for conceptualizing their etiology. *Psychological Bulletin, 129,* 747–767.

Keeler, R. F. (1983). Naturally occurring teratogens from plants. In R. F. Keeler & A. T. Tu (Eds.), *Handbook of natural toxins: Vol. 1. Plant and fungal toxins* (pp. 161–191). New York: Marcel Dekker.

Keenan, R. M., Jenkins, A. J., Cone, E. J., & Henningfield, J. E. (1994). Smoked and IV nicotine, cocaine and heroin have similar abuse liability. *Journal of Addictive Diseases, 13,* 259–269.

Keller, M. C., Thiessen, D., & Young, R. K. (1996). Mate assortment in dating and married couples. *Personality and Individual Differences, 21,* 217–221.

Kellerman, E. (1979). Transfer and non-transfer: Where we are now. *Studies in Second Language Acquisition, 2,* 37–57.

Kelley, H. H., & Michela, J. L. (1980). Attribution theory and research. *Annual Review of Psychology, 31,* 457–501.

Kellman, P. J., & Arterberry, M. E. (2006). Infant visual perception. In D. Kuhn & R. Siegler (Eds.), *Handbook of child psychology: Vol. 2, Cognition, perception, and language* (6th ed., 109–160). Hoboken, NJ: Wiley.

Kellner, C. H., Knapp, R. G., Petrides, G., Rummans, T. A., Husain, M. M., Rasmussen, K., et al. (2006). Continuation electroconvulsive therapy vs pharmacotherapy for relapse prevention in major depression. *Archives of General Psychiatry, 63,* 1337–1344.

Kelly, M. M., Tyrka, A. R., Andeson, G. M., Price, L. H., & Carpenter, L. L. (2008). Sex differences in emotional and physiological responses to the Trier Social Stress Test. *Journal of Behavior Therapy and Experimental Psychiatry, 39,* 87–98.

Keltner, D. (1995). Signs of appeasement: Evidence of distinct displays of embarrassment, amusement, and shame. *Journal of Personality and Social Psychology, 68,* 441–454.

Kemeny, M., Weiner, H., Taylor, S., Schneider, S., Visscher, B., & Fahey, J. (1994). Repeated bereavement, depressed mood, and immune parameters in HIV seropositive and seronegative gay men. *Health Psychology, 13,* 14–24.

Kempe, C. H., & Helfe, R. C. (1968). *The battered child.* Chicago: University of Chicago Press.

Kempermann, G. (2006). Adult neurogenesis. In P. B. Baltes, P. A. Reuter-Lorenz, & F. Rösler (Eds.). *Lifespan development and the brain: The perspective of biocultural co-constructivism* (pp. 82–107). New York: Cambridge University Press.

Kempermann, G., & Gage, F. H. (1999). Experience-dependent regulation of adult hippocampal neurogenesis: Effects of long-term stimulation and stimulus withdrawal. *Hippocampus, 9,* 321–332.

Kendler, K. S. (2005). "A gene for . . ." The nature of gene action in psychiatric disorders. *American Journal of Psychiatry, 162,* 1243–1252.

Kendler, K. S., Karkowski, L. M., & Prescott, C. A. (1999). Causal relationship between stressful life events and the onset of major depression. *American Journal of Psychiatry, 156,* 837–841.

Kendler, K. S., Kuhn, J. W., Vittum, J., Prescott, C. A., & Riley, B. (2005). The interaction of stressful life events and a serotonin transporter polymorphism in the prediction of episodes of major depression. *Archives of General Psychiatry, 62,* 529–535.

Kendrick, T., Peveler, R., Logworth, L., Baldwin, D., Moore, M., Chatwin, J., et al. (2006). Cost-effectiveness and cost-utility of tricyclic antidepressants, selective serotonin reuptake inhibitors and lofepramine: Randomized controlled trial. *British Journal Psychiatry, 188,* 337–345.

Kennedy, J. M., & Juricevic, I. (2006). Blind man draws using diminution in three dimensions. *Psychonomic Bulletin & Review, 13,* 506–509.

Kennedy, S. H., Evans, K. R., Krüger, S., Mayberg, H. S., Meyer, J. H., McCann, S., et al. (2001). Changes in regional brain glucose metabolism measured with positron emission tomography after paroxetine treatment of major depression. *American Journal of Psychiatry, 158,* 899–905.

Kensinger, E. A., Garoff-Eaton, R. J., & Schacter, D. L. (2007). How negative emotion enhances the visual specificity of a memory. *Journal of Cognitive Neuroscience, 19,* 1872–1887.

Kenyon, C. (2005). The plasticity of aging: Insights from long-lived mutants, *Cell, 120,* 449–460.

Kessler, R. C., Berglund, P., Demler, O., Jin, R., Merikangas, K. R., & Walters, E. E. (2005). Lifetime prevalence and age-of-onset distributions of *DSM-IV* disorders in the National Comorbidity Survey replication. *Archives of General Psychiatry, 62,* 593–602.

Kessler, R. C., Chiu, W. T., Demler, O., & Walters, E. E. (2005). Prevalence, severity, and comorbidity of twelve-month *DSM-IV-TR* disorders in the National Comorbidity Survey Replication (NCS-R). *Archives of General Psychiatry, 62,* 617–627.

Key Learning Community (n.d.). Retrieved July 13, 2007, from http://www.ncrel.org/sdrs/areas/issues/methods/assment/as7key.htm

Kiecolt-Glaser, J. K., Garner, W., Speicher, C., Penn, G., Holliday, J., Glaser, R. (1984). Psychosocial modifiers of immunocompetence in medical students. *Psychosomatic Medicine, 46,* 7–14.

Kiecolt-Glaser, J. K., Marucha, P. T., Malarkey, W. B., Mercado, A. M., & Glaser, R. (1995). Slowing of wound healing by psychological stress. *Lancet, 346,* 1194–1196.

Kiecolt-Glaser, J. K., McGuire, L., Robles, T. F., & Glaser, R. (2002). Psychoneuroimmunology and psychosomatic medicine: Back to the future. *Psychosomatic Medicine, 64,* 15–28.

Kihlstrom, J. F. (2005). Dissociative disorders. *Annual Review of Clinical Psychology, 1,* 227–253.

Kim, H. K. (2005). Can only intelligent people be creative? A meta-analysis. *Journal of Secondary Gifted Education, 16,* 57–66.

Kim, J. J., & Yoon, K. S. (1998). Stress: Metaplastic effects in the hippocampus. *Trends in Neuroscience, 21,* 505–509.

Kim, K. H. S., Relkin, N. R., Lee, K. M., & Hirsch, J. (1997). Distinct cortical areas associated with native and second languages. *Nature, 388,* 171–174.

Kim, S., & Hasher, L. (2005). The attraction effect in decision making: Superior performance by older adults. *Quarterly Journal of Experimental Psychology, 58A,* 120–133.

Kimball, J. (2003). *Joyce and the early Freudians.* Gainesville, FL: University Press of Florida.

Kimura, D. (2007). "Underrepresentation" or misinterpretation? In S. J. Ceci & W. M. Williams (Eds.). *Why aren't more women in science?: Top researchers debate the evidence* (pp. 39–46). Washington, DC: APA.

King, D. E., Mainous, A. G. III, & Geesey, M. E. (2008). Adopting moderate alcohol consumption in middle age: Subsequent cardiovascular events. *The American Journal of Medicine 121,* 201–206.

King, L. A., Hicks, J. A., Krull, J. L., Del Gaiso, A. K. (2006). Positive affect and the experience of meaning in life. *Journal* of *Personality and Social Psychology, 90,* 179–196.

Kinney, D. K., Richards, R., Lowing, P. A., LeBlanc, D., Zimbalist, M. E., & Harlan, P. (2000–2001). Creativity in offspring of schizophrenic and control parents: An adoption study. *Creativity Research Journal, 13,* 17–26.

Kinsey, A. C., Pomeroy, W. B., & Martin, C. E. (1948). *Sexual behavior in the human male.* Philadelphia: Saunders.

Kinsey, A. C., Pomeroy, W. B., Martin, C. E., & Gebhard, P. H. (1953). *Sexual behavior in the human female.* Philadelphia: Saunders.

Kirkham, T. C. (2005). Endocannabinoids in the regulation of appetite and body weight. *Behavioral Pharmacology, 16,* 297–313.

Kirkpatrick, L. A. (2005). *Attachment, evolution, and the psychology of religion.* New York: Guilford Press.

Kirsh, S. J. (2006). Cartoon violence and aggression in youth. *Aggression and Violent Behavior, 11,* 547–557.

Kisilevsky, B. S., Muir, D. W., & Low, J. A. (1992). Maturation of human fetal responses to vibroacoustic stimulation. *Child Development, 63,* 1497–1508.

Klahr, D. (2000). *Exploring science: The cognition and development of discovery processes.* Cambridge, MA: MIT Press.

Klein, R. G. (1999). *The human career: Human biological and cultural origins* (2nd ed.). Chicago: University of Chicago Press.

Klopfer, P. H. (1958). Influence of social interaction on learning rates in birds. *Science, 128,* 903.

Klüver, H., & Bucy, P. (1939). Preliminary analysis of functioning of the temporal lobes in monkeys. *Archives of Neurology and Psychiatry, 42,* 979–1000.

Knox, R. (2007, April 26). Kids' use of earbuds worries hearing experts. Retrieved from http://www. npr.org/templates/story/story.php?storyId=9797364

Kobayashi, M., Saito, S., Kobayakawa, T., Deguchi, Y., & Costanzo, R. M. (2006). Cross-cultural comparison of data using the odor stick identification test for Japanese (OSIT-J). *Chemical Senses, 31,* 335–342.

Koenig, J. I. (2006). Schizophrenia: A unique translational opportunity in behavioral neuroendocrinology. *Hormones and Behavior, 50,* 602–611.

Koerner, K., & Linehan, M. M. (2000). Research on dialectical behavior therapy for patients with borderline personality disorder. *Psychiatric Clinics of North America, 23,* 151–167.

Koh, J. S., Kang, H., Choi, S. W., & Kim, H. O. (2002). Cigarette smoking associated with premature facial wrinkling: Image analysis of facial skin replicas. *International Journal of Dermatology, 41,* 21–27.

Kohlberg, L. (1981). *Essays on moral development, Vol. I: The philosophy of moral development.* New York: Harper & Row.

Kohn, P. M., Lafreniere, K., & Gurevich, M. (1991). Hassles, health, and personality. *Journal of Personality and Social Psychology, 61,* 478–482.

Kopell, B. H., Rezai, A. R., Chang, J. W., & Vitek, J. L. (2006). Anatomy and physiology of the basal ganglia: Implications for deep brain stimulation for Parkinson's disease. *Movement Disorders, 21,* S238–S246.

Kopta, S. M. (2003). The dose-effect relationship in psychotherapy: A defining achievement for Dr. Kenneth Howard. *Journal of Clinical Psychology, 59,* 727–733.

Korkeila, M., Kaprio, J., Rissanen, A., Koshenvuo, M., & Sorensen, T. L. (1998). Predictors of major weight gain in adult Finns: Stress, life satisfaction and personality traits. *International Journal of Obesity Related Metabolic Disorders, 22*(10), 949–957.

Kornell, N., & Bjork, R. A. (2007). The promise and perils of self–regulated study. *Psychonomic Bulletin & Review, 14,* 219–224.

Kornhaber, M. L., Fierros, E., & Veenema, S. (2004). *Multiple intelligences: Best ideas from research and practice.* Boston, MA: Pearson.

Koslowski, B. (1996). *Theory and evidence: The development of scientific reasoning.* Cambridge, MA: MIT Press.

Kosslyn, S. M. (2002, July 15). What shape are a German shepherd's ears: A talk with Stephen Kosslyn. *Edge,* Retrieved from http://www.edge.org/3rd_culture/kosslyn/kosslyn_index.html

Kosslyn, S. M. (2005). Mental images and the brain. *Cognitive Neuropsychology, 22,* 333–347.

Kosslyn, S. M., Van Kleeck, M. H., & Kirby, K. N. (1990). A neurologically plausible model of individual differences in visual mental imagery. In P. J. Hampson, D. F. Marks, & J. T. E. Richardson (Eds.), *Imagery: Current developments* (pp. 39–77). Florence, KY: Taylor & Frances/Routledge.

Kounios, J., Frymiare, J. L., Bowden, E. M., Fleck, J. I., Subramaniam, K., Parrish, T. B., et al. (2006). The prepared mind: Neural activity prior to problem presentation predicts subsequent solution by sudden insight. *Psychological Science, 17,* 882–890.

Kramarik, A. (2006). *Akiane: Her life, her art, her poetry.* Nashville, TN: W. Publishing Group.

Kramer, P. D. (1993). *Listening to Prozac.* New York: Penguin Books.

Kranczioch, C., Debener, S., Schwarzbach, J., Goebel, R. & Engel, A. K. (2005). Neural correlates of conscious perception in the attentional blink. *Neuroimage, 24,* 704–714.

Kremer, S., Bult, J. H., Mojet, J., & Kroeze, J. H. (2007). Food perception with age and its relationship to pleasantness. *Chemical Senses, 32,* 591–602.

Kring, A. M., & Gordon, A. H. (1998). Sex differences in emotion: Expression, experience, and physiology. *Journal of Personality and Social Psychology, 74,* 686–703.

Kristeller, J. L., Baer, R. A., & Quillian-Wolever, R. (2006). Mindfulness-based approaches to eating disorders. In R. A. Baer (Ed.), *Mindfulness-based treatment approaches: Clinician's guide to evidence base and applications* (pp. 75–91). San Diego: Elsevier Academic Press.

Kristensen, P., & Bjerkedal, T. (2007). Explaining the relation between birth order and intelligence. *Science, 316,* 1717.

Kristenson, H. (1995). How to get the best out of Antabuse. *Alcohol and Alcoholism, 30,* 775–783.

Kroeber, A. L. (1948). *Anthropology.* New York: Harcourt Brace Jovanovich.

Kröger, C., Schweiger, U., Sipos, V., Arnold, R., Kahl, K. G., Schunert, T., et al. (2006). Effectiveness of dialectical behavior therapy for borderline personality disorder in an inpatient setting. *Behaviour Research and Therapy, 44,* 1211–1217.

Krummel, D., Seligson F., & Guthrie, H. (1996). Hyperactivity: Is candy causal? *Critical Review of Food Science and Nutrition, 36,* 31–47.

Krystal, A. D. (2005). The effect of insomnia definitions, terminology, and classifications on clinical practice. *Journal of American Geriatrics Society, 53,* S255–S263.

Kübler-Ross, E. (1969). *On death and dying.* New York: Macmillan.

Kubota, M., Nakazaki, S., Hirai, S., Saeki, N. Yamaura, A., & Kusaka, T. (2001). Alcohol consumption and frontal lobe shrinkage: Study of 1432 non-alcoholic subjects. *Journal of Neurology, Neurosurgery, and Psychiatry, 71,* 104–106.

Kubzansky, L. D., Sparrow, D., Vokonas, P., & Kawachi, I. (2001). Is the glass half empty or half full? A prospective study of optimism and coronary heart disease in the Normative Aging Study. *Psychosomatic Medicine, 63,* 910–916.

Kuhl, P. K., & Meltzoff, A. N. (1997). Evolution, nativism, and learning in the development of language and speech. In M. Gopnik (Ed.), *The inheritance and innateness of grammars* (pp. 7–44). New York: Oxford University Press.

Kuhl, P. K., Stevens, E., & Hayashi, A. (2006). Infants show a facilitation effect for native language phonetic perception between

6 and 12 months. *Developmental Science, 9,* F13–F21.

Kuhn, D. (1993). Connecting scientific and informal reasoning. *Merrill-Palmer Quarterly, 39,* 74–103.

Kuhn, D., Amsel, E., & O'Loughlin, M. (1988). *The development of scientific thinking skills.* Orlando FL: Academic Press.

Kuhn, D., & Pearsall, S. (2000). Developmental origins of scientific thinking. *Journal of cognition and development, 1,* 113–129.

Kuo, L. E., Kitlinska, J. B., Tilan, J. U., Li, L., Baker, S. B., Johnson, M. D., et al. (2007). Neuropeptide Y acts directly in the periphery on fat tissue and mediates stress-induced obesity and metabolic syndrome. *Nature Medicine, 13,* 803–811.

Kupfermann, I., Kandel, E. R., & Iversen, S. (2000). Motivational and addictive states. In E. R. Kandel, J. H. Schwartz, & T. M. Jessell (Eds.), *Principles of neural science* (4th ed.; pp. 998–1013). New York: McGraw-Hill.

Kurdek, L. (2004). Are gay and lesbian co-habiting couples really different from heterosexual married couples? *Journal of Marriage and Family, 66*(4), 880–900.

Kurson, R. (2007). *Crashing through: The true story of risk, adventure and the man who dared to see.* New York: Random House.

Kusché, C. A., & Greenberg, M. T. (1994). *The PATHS Curriculum.* Seattle: Developmental Research and Programs.

Kwon, Y., & Lawson, A. E. (2000). Linking brain growth with the development of scientific reasoning ability and conceptual change during adolescence. *Journal of Research in Science Teaching, 37,* 44–62.

LaBerge, S. (1985). *Lucid dreaming.* Los Angeles: Tarcher.

LaFrance, M., Hecht, M. A., & Paluk, B. L. (2003). The contingent smile: A meta-analysis of sex differences in smiling. *Psychological Bulletin, 129,* 305–334.

Lagopoulos, J. (2007). Functional MRI: An overview. *Acta Neuropsychiatrica, 19,* 64–65.

Lalonde, J., Hudson, J., Gigante, R., & Pope, H. (2001). Canadian and American psychiatrists' attitudes toward dissociative disorders diagnoses. *The Canadian Journal of Psychiatry / La Revue canadienne de psychiatrie, 46*(5), 407–412.

Lamb, R. J., Morral, A. R., Kirby, K. C., Iguchi, M. Y., & Galbicka, G. (2004). Shaping smoking cessation using percentile schedules. *Drug and Alcohol Dependence, 76,* 247–259.

Lamp, R., & Krohn, E. (2001). A longitudinal predictive validity investigation of the SB:FE and K-ABC with at-risk children. *Journal of Psychoeducational Assessment, 19,* 334–349.

Landry, R. G. (1973). The relationship of second language learning and verbal creativity. *Modern Language Journal, 57,* 110–113.

Lang, E., Berbaum, K., Faintuch, S., Hatsiopoulou, O., Halsey, N., Li, X., Berbaum, M., et al. (2006). Adjunctive self-hypnotic relaxation for outpatient medical procedures: A prospective randomized trial with women undergoing large core breast biopsy. *Pain, 126,* 155–164.

Lange, C. (1922). *The emotions* (I. A. Haupt, Trans.). Baltimore: Williams & Wilkins. (Original work published 1885)

Lange, P. G. (2008). Publicly private and privately public: Social networking on YouTube. *Journal of Computer-Mediated Communication, 13,* 361–380.

Langlois, J. H., & Roggman, L. A. (1990). Attractive faces are only average. *Psychological Science, 1,* 115–121.

Langlois, J. H., Roggman, L. A., & Musselman, L. (1994). What is average and what is not average about attractive faces? *Psychological Science, 5,* 214–220.

Lapsley, D. K. (2006). Moral stage theory. In M. Killen & J. G. Smetana (Eds.), *Handbook of moral development* (pp. 37–66). Mahwah, NJ: Erlbaum.

Larsson, J., Larsson, H., & Lichtenstein, P. (2004). Genetic and environmental contributions to stability and change of ADHD symptoms between 8 and 13 years of age: A longitudinal twin study. *Journal of American Academy of Child and Adolescent Psychiatry, 43,* 1267–1275.

Lasagabaster, D. (2000). The effects of three bilingual education models on linguistic creativity. *International Review of Applied Linguistics in Language Teaching, 38,* 213–228.

Laschet, J., Kurcewicz, I., Minier, F., Trottier, S., Khallou-Laschet, J., Louvel, J., et al. (2007). Dysfunction of GABA-sub(A) receptor glycolysis-dependent modulation in human partial epilepsy. *Proceedings of the National Academy of Sciences, 104*(9), 3472–3477. doi:10.1073/pnas.0606451104

Latané, B. (1981). The psychology of social impact. *American Psychologist, 36,* 343–356.

Latané, B., & Wolf, S. (1981). The social impact of majorities and minorities. *Psychological Review, 88,* 438–453.

Laumann, E., Paik, A., Glasser, D., Kang, J., Wang, T., Levinson, B., et al. (2006). A cross-national study of subjective sexual well-being among older women and men: Findings from the global study of sexual attitudes and behaviors. *Archives of Sexual Behavior, 35*(2), 145–161.

Laureys, S. (2007). Eyes open, brain shut. *Scientific American, 296,* 84–89.

Lavelli, M., & Fogel, A. (2005). Developmental changes in the relationship between the infant's attention and emotion during early face-to-face communication: The 2-month transition. *Developmental Psychology, 41,* 265–280.

Lavie, N. (2007). The role of perceptual load in visual awareness. *Brain Research, 1080,* 91–100.

Lavie, N., Hirst, A., De Fockert, J. W., & Viding, E. (2004). Load theory of selective attention and cognitive control. *Journal of Experimental Psychology: General, 133,* 339–354.

Lawless, H. T., Schlake, S., Smythe, J., Lim, J., Yang, H., Chapman, K., et al. (2004). Metallic taste and retronasal smell. *Chemical Senses, 29,* 25–33.

Lazar, S. W., Kerr, C., Wasserman, R. H., Gray, J. R., Greve, D., Treadway, M. T., et al. (2005). Meditation experience is associated with increased cortical thickness. *NeuroReport, 216,* 1893–1897.

Lazarus, A. A., & Abramovitz, A. (2004). A multimodal behavioral approach to performance anxiety. *Journal of Clinical Psychology, 60,* 831–840.

Lazarus, R. S. (1991). *Emotion and adaptation.* New York: Oxford University Press.

Lazarus, R. S. (1993). From psychological stress to the emotions: A history of changing outlooks. *Annual Review of Psychology, 44,* 1–21.

Lazarus, R. S., & Folkman, S. (1984). *Stress, appraisal, and coping.* New York: Springer.

Lazarus, R. S., Kanner, A. A., & Folkman, S. (1980). Emotions: A cognitive-phenomenological analysis. In R. Plutchik & H. Kellerman (Eds.), *Emotion: Theory, research, and experience: Vol. 1. Theories of emotion* (pp. 189–217). New York: Academic Press.

Le Bars, P. L., Katz, M. M., Berman, N., Itil, T. M., Freedman, A. M., & Schatzberg, A. F. (1997). A placebo-controlled, double-blind, randomized trial of an extract of ginkgo biloba for dementia. North American EGb Study Group. *Journal of the American Medical Association, 278,* 1327–1332.

Leary, M. R., Kowalski, R. M., Smith, L., & Phillips, S. (2003). Teasing, rejection, and violence: Case studies of the school shootings. *Aggressive Behavior, 29,* 202–214.

Leary, M. R., Twenge, J. M., & Quinlivan, E. (2006). Interpersonal rejection as a determinant of anger and aggression. *Personality and Social Psychology Review, 10,* 111–132.

LeDoux, J. (1996). *The emotional brain: The mysterious underpinnings of emotional life.* New York: Simon & Schuster.

LeDoux, J. (2003). *Synaptic self.* New York: Penguin.

LeDoux, J. E. (2000). Emotion circuits in the brain. *Annual Review of Neuroscience, 23,* 155–184.

Lee, K. A. (2006). Sleep dysfunction in women and its management. *Current Treatment Options in Neurology, 8,* 376–386.

Lenneberg, E. (1967). *The biological foundations of language.* New York: Wiley.

Lennie, P. (2000). Color vision. In E. R. Kandel, J. H. Schwartz, & T. M. Jessell (Eds.), *Principles of neural science* (4th ed.; pp. 572–589). New York: McGraw-Hill.

Lepage, J-F., & Théoret, H. (2007). The mirror neuron system: Grasping others' actions from birth? *Developmental Science, 10,* 513–523.

Lerner, L. (1996). *The Kennedy women: The saga of an American family.* New York: Random House.

Lesch, K. P., Bengel, D., Heils, A., Sabol, S. Z., Greenburg, B. D., Petri, S., et al. (1996). Association of anxiety-related traits with a polymorphism in the serotonin transporter gene regulatory region. *Science, 274,* 1527–1531.

Leserman, J., Jackson, E. D., Petitto, J. M., Golden, R. N., Silva, S. G., Perkins, D. O., et al. (1999). Progression to AIDS: The effects of stress, depressive symptoms, and social support. *Psychosomatic Medicine, 61,* 397–406.

Leserman, J., Petitto, J. M., Golden, R. N., Gaynes, B. N., Gu, H., Perkins, D. O., et al. (2000). Impact of stressful life events, depression, social support, and cortisol on progression to AIDS. *American Journal of Psychiatry, 157,* 1221–1228.

Lethbridge-Cejku, M., & Vickerie, J. (2005). Summary health statistics for U.S. adults: National Health Interview Survey, 2003. National Center for Health Statistics, *Vital Health Statistics, 10.*

LeVay, S. (1991). A difference in hypothalamic structure between heterosexual and homosexual men. *Science, 253,* 1034–1037.

LeVay, S., & Hamer, D. (1994). Evidence for a biological influence in male homosexuality. *Scientific American, 270,* 44–49.

Levenson, R. W. (1988). Emotion and the autonomic nervous system: A prospectus for research on autonomic specificity. In H. Wagner (Ed.), *Social psychophysiology and emotion: Theory and clinical applications* (pp. 17–42). London: Wiley.

Levenson, R. W. (1994). Human emotion: A functional view. In P. Ekman & R. J. Davidson (Eds.), *The nature of emotion* (pp. 123–126). New York: Oxford.

Levenson, R. W. (2003). Blood, sweat, and fears: The autonomic architecture of emotion. *Annals of the New York Academy of Sciences, 1000,* 348–366.

Levenson, R. W., Carstensen, L. L., & Gottman, J. M. (1994). The influence of age and gender on affect, physiology, and their interactions: A study of long-term marriages.

Journal of Personality & Social Psychology, 67, 56–68.

Levenson, R. W., Ekman, P., & Friesen, W. V. (1990). Voluntary facial action generates emotion-specific autonomic nervous system activity. *Psychophysiology, 27,* 363–384.

Levenson, R. W., Ekman, P., Heider, K., & Friesen, W. V. (1992). Emotion and autonomic nervous system activity in the Minangkabau of West Sumatra. *Journal of Personality & Social Psychology, 62,* 972–988.

Levine, D., McCright, J., Dobkin, L., Woodruff, A. J., & Klausner, J. D. (2008, March). SEXINFO: A sexual health text messaging service for San Francisco Youth. *American Journal of Public Health, 98,* 393–395.

Lewis, K., Kaufman, J., & Christakis, N. A. (in press). The taste for privacy: An analysis of college student privacy settings in the Facebook.com social network. *Journal of Computer-Mediated Communication.*

Lidz, J., & Gleitman, L. R. (2004). Argument structure and the child's contribution to language learning. *Trends in Cognitive Sciences, 8,* 157–161.

Lieberman, J. A., Chakos, M., Wu, H., Alvir, J., Hoffman, E., Robinson, D., et al. (2001). Longitudinal study of brain morphology in first episodes of schizophrenia. *Biological Psychiatry, 49,* 487–499.

Lieberman, J. A., Stroup, T. S., McEvoy, J. P., Swartz, M. S., Rosenheck, R. A., Perkins, D. O., et al. (2005). Effectiveness of antipsychotic drugs in patients with chronic schizophrenia. *New England Journal of Medicine, 353,* 1209–1223.

Liebert, R. M., & Baron, R. A. (1972). Some immediate effects of televised violence on children's behavior. *Developmental Psychology, 6,* 469–475.

Linden, D. E. J. (2006). How psychotherapy changes the brain—the contribution of functional neuroimaging. *Molecular Psychiatry, 11,* 528–538.

Lindsay, D. S., Hagen, L., Read, J. D., Wade, K. A., & Garry, M. (2004). True photographs and false memories. *Psychological Science, 15,* 149–154.

Linehan, M. M. (1993). *Skills training manual of treating borderline personality disorder.* New York: Guilford Press.

Linehan, M. M., Armstrong, H. E., Suarez, A., Allmon, D., & Heard, H. L. (1991). Cognitive–behavioral treatment of chronically parasuicidal borderline patients. *Archives of General Psychiatry, 48,* 1060–1064.

Linehan, M. M., Comtois, K. A., Murray, A. M., Brown, M. Z., Gallop, R. J., Heard, H. L., et al. (2006). Two-year randomized controlled trial and follow-up of dialectical behavior therapy vs therapy by experts for suicidal behaviors and borderline personality disorder. *Archives of General Psychiatry, 63,* 757–766.

Linehan, M. M., Heard, H. L., & Armstrong, H. E. (1993). Naturalistic follow-up of a behavioral treatment for chronically parasuicidal borderline patients. *Archives of General Psychiatry, 50,* 971–974.

Lipkus, I. M., Barefoot, J. C., Williams, R. B., & Siegler, I. C. (1994). Personality measures as predictors of smoking initiation and cessation in the UNC alumni heart study. *Health Psychology, 13,* 149–155.

Lippa, R. (1994). *Introduction to social psychology.* Pacific Grove, CA: Brooks/Cole.

Locke, J. (1690/1959). *An essay concerning human understanding: Vol. 1.* New York: Dover.

Lockhart, R. S., & Craik, F. I. M. (1990). Levels of processing: A retrospective commentary on a framework for memory research. *Canadian Journal of Psychology, 44,* 77–112.

Loehlin, J. C., McCrae, R. R., Costa, P. T., & John, O. P. (1998). Heritabilities of common and measure specific components of the Big Five personality factors. *Journal of Research in Personality, 32,* 431–453.

Loeser, J. D., & Melzack, R. (1999). Pain: An overview. *Lancet, 353,* 1607–1609.

Loftus, E. (1996). *Eyewitness testimony.* Cambridge, MA: Harvard University Press.

Loftus, E. (2003). Make-believe memories. *American Psychologist, 58,* 864–873.

Logothetis, N. K., Pauls, J., Augath, M., Trinath, T., & Oeltermann, A. (2001). Neurophysiological investigation of the basis of the fMRI signal. *Nature, 412,* 150–157.

Long, M. (1990). Maturational constraints on language development. *Studies in Second Language Acquisition, 12,* 251–285.

Lord, C., & McGee, J. P. (2001). *Educating children with autism.* Washington, DC: National Academy Press.

Lorenz, K. (1935). Der Kumpan in der Umwelt des Vogels. *Journal of Ornithology, 83,* 137–215.

Lorenz, K. (1937). The companion in the bird's world. *Auk, 54,* 245–273.

Lovaas, O. I. (1987). Behavioral treatment and normal educational and intellectual functioning in young autistic children. *Journal of Consulting and Clinical Psychology, 55,* 3–9.

Lovett, R. (2005, September 24). Coffee: The demon drink? *New Scientist.* Löwe, B., Spitzer, R., Williams, J., Mussell, M., Schellberg, D., & Kroenke, K. (2008). Depression, anxiety and somatization in primary care: Syndrome overlap and functional impairment. *General Hospital Psychiatry, 30(3),* 191–199.

Lozoff, B., Beard, J., Connor, J., Felt, B., Georgieff, M., & Schallert, T. (2006). Long-lasting neural and behavioral effects of iron deficiency in infancy. *Nutrition Reviews, 64*(Suppl.), S34–S43.

Lubinski, D., & Benbow, C. P. (2006). Study of mathematically precocious youth after 35 years: Uncovering antecedents for the development of math-science expertise. *Perspectives on Psychological Science, 1,* 316–345.

Lubinski, D., Benbow, C. P. Webb, R. M., & Bleske-Rechek, A. (2006). Tracking exceptional human capital over two decades. *Psychological Science, 17,* 194–199.

Luchins, A. S., & Luchins, E. H. (1969). Einstellung effect and group problem solving. *The Journal of Social Psychology, 77,* 79–89.

Luchins, A. S., & Luchins, E. H. (1970). *Wertheimer's seminars revisited: Problem solving and thinking.* Albany: SUNY Press.

Ludwig, A. M. (1995). *The price of greatness.* New York: Guilford Press.

Lutman, M. E., & Spencer, H. S. (1991). Occupational noise and demographic factors in hearing. *Acta Otolaryngologica, Suppl. 476,* 74–84.

Lutz, A., Greischar, L. L., Rawlings, N. B., Ricard, M., & Davidson, R. J. (2004). Long-term meditators self-induce high-amplitude gamma synchrony during mental practice. *Proceedings of the National Academy of Sciences, 101,* 16369–16373.

Lydiard, R. B. (2003). The role of GABA in anxiety disorders. *Journal of Clinical Psychiatry, 64,* 21–27.

Lykken, D. (1999). *Happiness: What studies on twins show us about nature, nurture and the happiness set point.* New York: Golden Books.

Lynn, R. (2006). *Race differences in intelligence: An evolutionary analysis.* Augusta, GA: National Summit.

Maas, J. (1998). *Power sleep.* New York: Villard.

Maccoby, E. E. (2000). Perspectives on gender development. *International Journal of Behavioral Development, 24,* 398–406.

Maccoby, E. E., & Jacklin, C. N. (1974). *The psychology of sex differences.* Stanford, CA: Stanford University Press.

Maccoby, E. E., & Jacklin, C. N. (1987). Gender segregation in childhood. In H. Reese (Ed.), *Advances in child behavior and development.* New York: Academic Press.

MacDonald, G., Kingsbury, R., & Shaw, S. (2005). *Adding insult to injury: Social pain theory and response to social exclusion.* New York: Psychology Press.

MacDonald, G., & Leary, M. R. (2005). Why does social exclusion hurt? The relationship between social and physical pain. *Psychological Bulletin, 131,* 202–23.

MacKinnon, D. W. (1970). Creativity: A multi-faceted phenomenon. In J. Roslanksy

(Ed.), *Creativity* (pp. 19–32). Amsterdam: North-Holland.

MacKinnon, D. W., & Hall, W. (1972). Intelligence and creativity. *Proceedings of the XVIIth International Congress of Applied Psychology,* Liege, Belgium (Vol. 2, 1883–1888). Brussels: EDITEST.

MacLean, K., Saron, C., Aichele, S., Bridwell, D., Jacobs, T., Zanesco, A., et al. (in press). Improvements in perceptual threshold with intensive attention training through concentration meditation. *Journal of Cognitive Neuroscience (Suppl).*

Macmillan, M. (2000). *An odd kind of fame: Stories of Phineas Gage.* Cambridge, MA: MIT Press.

MacWhinney, B. (1999). *The emergence of language.* Mahwah, NJ: Erlbaum.

Madigan, S., & O'Hara, R. (1992). Short-term memory at the turn of the century: Mary Whiton Calkins's memory research. *American Psychologist, 47,* 170–174.

Maes, H. M. M., Neale, M. C., & Eaves, L. J. (1997). Genetic and environmental factors in relative body weight and human adiposity. *Behavior Genetics, 27,* 325–351.

Maestripieri, D., Higley, J. D., Lindell, S. G., Newman, T. K., McCormack, K. M., & Sanchez, M. M. (2006). Early maternal rejection affects the development of monoaminergic systems and adult abusive parenting in rhesus macaques (*Macaca mulatto*). *Behavioral Neuroscience, 120,* 1017–1024.

Maguire, E. A., Woollett, K., & Spiers, H. J. (2006). London taxi drivers and bus drivers: A structural MRI and neuropsychological analysis. *Hippocampus, 16,* 1091–1101.

Maier, N. R. F. (1931). Reasoning in humans: II. The solution of a problem and its appearance. *Journal of Comparative and Physiological Psychology, 12,* 181–194.

Maier, S. F., Watkins, L. R., & Fleshner, M. (1994). Psychoneuroimmunology: The interface between brain, behavior, and immunity. *American Psychologist, 49,* 1004–1017.

Malberg, J. E., Eisch, A. J., Nestler, E. J., & Duman, R. S. (2000). Chronic antidepressant treatment increases neurogenesis in adult rat hippocampus. *Journal of Neuroscience, 20,* 9104–9110.

Malenka, R. C., & Nicoll, R. A. (1999). Long term potentiation—A decade of progress? *Science, 285,* 1870–1874.

Mangels, J. A., Gershberg, F. B., Shimamura, A. P., & Knight, R. T. (1996). Impaired retrieval from remote memory in patients with frontal lobe damage. *Neuropsychology, 10,* 32–41.

Mann, T., Tomiyama, A. J., Westling, E., Lew, A-M., Samuels, B., & Chatman, J. (2007). Medicare's search for effective obesity treatments: Diets are not the answer. *American Psychologist, 62,* 220–233.

Marek, G. J., & Aghajanian, G. K. (1996). LSD and the phenethylamine hallucinogen DOI are potent partial agonists at 5-HT2A receptors on interneurons in the rat piriform cortex. *Journal of Pharmacology and Experimental Therapeutics, 278,* 1373–1382.

Marijuana research. (2004, December 8). [Editorial]. *Scientific American, 291,* 8.

Marker, C. D., Calamari, J. E., Woodard, J. L., & Riemann, B. C. (2006). Cognitive self-consciousness, implicit learning, and obsessive-compulsive disorder. *Journal of Anxiety Disorders, 20,* 389–407.

Marks, R. (2006). The superlative, sensitive shark. Retrieved November 5, 2007 from http://www.pbs.org/kqed/oceanadventures/episodes/sharks/indepth-senses.html

Markus, H., & Kitayama, S. (1991). Culture and the self: Implications for cognition, emotion, and motivation. *Psychological Review, 98,* 224–253.

Martindale, C. (1999). Biological bases of creativity. In R. J. Sternberg (Ed.), *Handbook of creativity* (pp. 137–152). Cambridge: Cambridge University Press.

Maschi, S., Clavenna, A., Campi, R., Schiavetti, B., Bernat, M., & Bonati, M. (2008). Neonatal outcome following pregnancy exposure to antidepressants: A prospective controlled cohort study. *BJOG—An International Journal of Obstetrics and Gynaecology, 115,* 283–289.

Mashour, G. A., Walker, E. E., & Martuza, R. L. (2005). Psychosurgery; past, present, and future. *Brain Research Reviews, 48,* 409–419.

Masling, J. M., & Bornstein, R. F. (2005). *Scoring the Rorschach: Retrospect and prospect.* Mahwah, NJ: Erlbaum.

Maslow, A. (1968). *Toward a psychology of being* (2nd ed.). New York: Van Nostrand.

Maslow, A. (1970). *Motivation and personality* (2nd ed.). New York: Harper & Row.

Mason, J. W. (1971). A re-evaluation of the concept of "non-specificity" in stress theory. *Journal of Psychiatric Research, 8,* 323–333.

Mason. J. W. (1975). A historical view of the stress field. *Journal of Human Stress, 1,* 6–12.

Masters, W. H., & Johnson, V. E. (1966). *The human sexual response.* Boston: Little & Brown.

Masuda, T., & Nisbett, R. E. (2001). Attending holistically versus analytically: Comparing the context sensitivity of Japanese and Americans. *Journal of Personality and Social Psychology, 81,* 922–934.

Mateo, Y., Budygin, E. A., John, C. E., & Jones, S. R. (2004). Role of serotonin in cocaine effects in mice with reduced dopamine transporter function. *Proceedings of the National Academy of Sciences, 101,* 372–377.

Mathias, J. L., & Wheaton, P. (2007). Changes in attention and information-processing speed following severe traumatic brain injury: A meta-analytic review. *Neuropsychology, 21,* 212–223.

Mathiesen, B. B., Förster, P. L. V., Svendsen, H. A. (2004). Affect regulation and loss of initiative in a case of orbitofrontal injury. *Neuro-psychoanalysis, 6,* 47–62.

Maticka-Tyndale, E., Harold, E. S., & Opperman, M. (2003). Casual sex among Australian schoolies. *The Journal of Sex Research, 40,* 158–169.

Matsumoto, D., & Juang, L. (2004). *Culture and psychology* (3rd ed.) Belmont, CA: Thomson-Wadsworth.

Matsumoto, D., & Willingham, B. (2006). The thrill of victory and the agony of defeat: Spontaneous expressions of medal winners of the 2004 Athens Olympic Games. *Journal of Personality and Social Psychology, 91,* 568–581.

Matsumoto, D., Yoo, S. H., et al. (in press). Mapping expressive differences around the world: The relationship between emotional display rules and Individualism v. Collectivism. *Journal of Cross-Cultural Psychology.*

Matthews, K. A., Glass, D. C., Rosenman, R. H., & Bortner, R. W. (1977). Competitive drive, Pattern A, and coronary heart disease: A further analysis of some data from the Western Collaborative Group Study. *Journal of Chronic Diseases, 30,* 489–498.

Mauss, I. B., Levenson, R. W., McCarter, L., Wilhelm, F. H., & Gross, J. J. (2005). The tie that binds? Coherence among emotion experience, behavior, and physiology. *Emotion, 5,* 175–190.

Max, J. E., Levin, H. S., Schachar, R. J., Landis, J., Saunders, A. E., Ewing-Cobbs, L., et al. (2006). Predictors of personality change due to traumatic brain injury in children and adolescents six to twenty-four months after injury. *Journal of Neuropsychiatry and Clinical Neurosciences, 18,* 21–32.

Max, J. E., Robertson, B. A. M., & Lansing, A. E. (2001). The phenomenology of personality change due to traumatic brain injury in children and adolescents. *Journal of Neuropsychiatry and Clinical Neurosciences, 13,* 161–170.

May, P. A., & Gossage, J. P. (2001). Estimating the prevalence of fetal alcohol syndrome. A summary. *Alcohol Research & Health, 25,* 159–167.

May, P. A., Gossage, J. P., Marais, A-S, Hendricks, L. S., Snell, C. L., Tabachnik, B. G., et al. (2008). Maternal risk factors for fetal alcohol syndrome and partial fetal alcohol syndrome in South Africa: A third study. *Alcoholism: Clinical and Experimental Research, 32,* 738–753.

Mayberg, H. S. (1997). Limbic-cortical dysregulation: A proposed model of depression. *Journal of Neuropsychiatry and Clinical Neuroscience, 9,* 471–481.

Mayberg, H. S. (2003). Modulating dysfunctional limbic-cortical circuits in depression: Towards development of brain-based algorithms for diagnosis and optimized treatment. *British Medical Bulletin, 65,* 193–207.

Mayberg, H. S., Liotti, M., Brannan, S. K., McGinnis, S., Mahurin, R. K., Jerabek, P. A., et al. (1999). Reciprocal limbic-cortical function and negative mood: Converging PET findings in depression and normal sadness. *American Journal of Psychiatry, 156,* 675–682.

Mayberg, H. S., Lozano, A. M., Voon, V., McNeely, H. E., Seminowicz, D., Hamani, C., et al. (2005). Deep brain stimulation for treatment-resistant depression. *Neuron, 45,* 651–660.

Mayer, M. (2004). Structure and function of glutamate receptors in the brain. *Annals of the New York Academy of Sciences, 1038,* 125–130.

Mayne, T. J., Vittinghoff, E., Chesney, M. A., Barrett, D. C., & Coates, T. J. (1996). Depressive affect and survival among gay and bisexual men infected with HIV. *Archives of Internal Medicine, 156,* 2233–2238.

McCabe, C., & Rolls, E. T. (2007). Umami: A delicious flavor formed by convergence of taste and olfactory pathways in the human brain. *European Journal of Neuroscience, 25,* 1855–1864.

McClain, C. S., Rosenfeld, B., Breitbart, W. (2003). Effect of spiritual well-being on end-of-life despair in terminally-ill cancer patients. *Lancet, 361,* 1603–1607.

McClelland, D. C. (1985). How motives, skills, and values determine what people do. *American Psychologist, 40,* 812–825.

McClelland, J. L. (1988). Connectionist models and psychological evidence. *Journal of Memory and Language, 27,* 107–123.

McClelland, J. L., & Rogers, T. (2003). The parallel distributed processing approach to semantic knowledge. *Nature Reviews Neuroscience, 44,* 310–322.

McClelland, J. L., & Rumelhart, D. (1985). Distributed memory and the representation of general and specific information. *Journal of Experimental Psychology: General, 114,* 159–188.

McCrae, R. R. (2002). NEO-PI-R data from 36 cultures: Further intercultural comparisons. In R. R. McCrae & J. Allik (Eds.), *The Five-Factor Model of personality across cultures* (pp. 105–125). New York: Kluwer Academic/Plenum.

McCrae, R. R., & Allik, J. (Eds.). (2002). *The Five-Factor Model of personality across cultures.* New York: Kluwer Academic/Plenum.

McCrae, R. R., & Costa, P. T. (1996). Toward a new generation of personality theories: Theoretical contexts for the five-factor model. In J. S. Wiggins (Ed.), *The Five-Factor model of personality: Theoretical perspectives* (pp. 51–87). New York: Guilford Press.

McCrae, R. R., & Costa, P. T. (1997). Personality trait structure as a human universal. *American Psychologist, 52,* 509–516.

McCrae, R. R., & Costa, P. T. (1999). A Five-Factor theory of personality. In L. A. Pervin and O. P. John (Eds.), *Handbook of personality theory and research* (pp. 139–153). New York: Guilford Press.

McCrae, R. R., & Costa, P. T. (2003). *Personality in adulthood: A five-factor theory perspective* (2nd ed.). New York: Guilford.

McCrae, R. R., and John, O. P. (1992). An introduction to the Five-Factor Model and its applications. *Journal of Personality, 60,* 175–215.

McEachin, J. J., Smith, T., & Lovaas, O. I. (1993). Long-term outcome for children with autism who received early intensive behavioral treatment. *American Journal on Mental Retardation, 97,* 359–372.

McEvoy, J. P., Lieberman, J. A., Stroup, T. S., Davis, S. M., Meltzer, H. Y., Rosenheck, R. A., et al. (2006). Effectiveness of clozapine versus olanzapine, quetiapine, and risperidone in patients with chronic schizophrenia who did not respond to prior atypical antipsychotic treatment. *American Journal of Psychiatry, 163,* 600–610.

McEwen, B. S. (1998). Protective and damaging effects of stress mediators. *The New England Journal of Medicine, 338,* 171–179.

McEwen, B. S., De Kloet, E. R., & Rostene, W. (1986). Adrenal steroid receptors and actions in the nervous system. *Physiological Review, 66,* 1121–1188.

McGaugh, J. L. (2000). Memory—a century of consolidation. *Science, 287,* 248–251.

McGrew, K. S. (2005). The Cattell-Horn-Carroll theory of cognitive abilities: Past, present and future. In D. P. Flanagan & P. L. Harrison (Eds.), *Contemporary intellectual assessment: Theories, tests, and issues* (pp. 136–181). New York: Guilford Press.

McKinley, M., Cairns, M., Denton, D., Egan, G., Mathai, M., Uschakov, A., et al. (2004). Physiological and pathophysiological influences on thirst. *Physiology & Behavior, 81*(5), 795–803.

McTiernan, A. (2005). Obesity and cancer: The risks, science, and potential management strategies. *Oncology (Williston Park), 19,* 871–881.

Mechelli, A., Crinion, J. T., Noppeney, U., O'Doherty, J, Ashburner, J., Frackowiak, R. S., et al. (2004). Neurolinguistics: Structural plasticity in the bilingual brain. *Nature, 431,* 757.

Mechtcheriakov, S., Brenneis, B., Koppel-staetter, F., Schocke, M., & Marksteiner, J. (2007). A widespread distinct pattern of cerebral atrophy in patients with alcohol addiction revealed by voxel-based morphometry. *Journal of Neurology, Neurosurgery, and Psychiatry, 78,* 610–614.

Medina, A. E., & Krahe, T. E. (2008). Neocortical plasticity deficits in fetal alcohol spectrum disorders: Lessons from barrel and visual cortex. *Journal of Neuroscience Research, 86,* 256–263.

Mednick, S. A., & Mednick, M. T. (1967). *Remote Associates Test: Experimenter's manual.* Boston: Houghton Mifflin.

Medvec, V., Madey, S., & Gilovich, T. (1995, October). When less is more: Counterfactual thinking and satisfaction among Olympic medalists. *Journal of Personality and Social Psychology, 69*(4), 603–610.

Meerkerk, G., van den Eijnden, R. J. J. M., & Garretsen, H. F. L. (2006). Predicting compulsive Internet use: It's all about sex! *CyberPsychology and Behavior, 9,* 95–103.

Melis, M. R., & Argiolis, A. (1995). Dopamine and sexual behavior. *Neuroscience and Biobehavioral Reviews, 19,* 19–38.

Mellon, S. (2007). Neurosteroid regulation of central nervous system development. *Pharmacology & Therapeutics, 116,* 107–124.

Meltzoff, A. N., & Moore, M. K. (1977). Imitation of facial and manual gestures by human neonates. *Science, 198,* 75–78.

Meltzoff, A. N., & Moore, M. K. (1983). Newborn infants imitate adult facial gestures. *Child Development, 54,* 702–709.

Melzack, R., & Wall, P. D. (1965). Pain mechanisms: A new theory. *Science, 150,* 971–979.

Melzack, R., & Wall, P. D. (1988). *The challenge of pain* (revised edition). New York: Penguin.

Mennella, J. A., Johnson, A., & Beauchamp, G. K. (1995). Garlic ingestion by pregnant women alters the odor of amniotic fluid. *Chemical Senses, 20,* 207–209.

Mennella, J. A., & Beauchamp, G. K. (1996). The early development of human flavor preferences. In E. D. Capaldi (Ed.), *Why we eat what we eat: The psychology of eating* (pp. 83–112). Washington, DC: APA Books.

Merskey, H., & Bogduk, N. (1994). *Classification of chronic pain.* Seattle: International Association for the Study of Pain Press.

Merten, J. (2005). Culture, gender and the recognition of the basic emotions. *Psychologia, 48,* 306–316.

Meunier, M., & Bachevalier, J. (2002). Comparison of emotional responses in monkeys with rhinal cortex or amygdala lesions. *Emotion, 2,* 147–161.

Michael, J. (1975). Positive and negative reinforcement, a distinction that is no longer necessary; or a better way to talk about bad things. *Behaviorism, 3,* 33–45.

Miczek, K. A., de Almeida, R. M. M., Kravitz, E. A., & Rissman E. F. (2007). Neurobiology of escalated aggression and violence. *Journal of Neuroscience, 27,* 11803–11806.

Milgram, S. (1963). Behavioral study of obedience. *Journal of Abnormal and Social Psychology, 67,* 371–378.

Milgram, S. (1974). *Obedience to authority: An experimental view.* New York: Harper.

Miller, A. (1996). *Insights of genius: Imagery and creativity in science and art.* New York: Springer Verlag.

Miller, A. (1996). *Insights of genius: Imagery and creativity in science and art.* New York: Springer Verlag.

Miller, A. H., Capuron, L., & Raison, C. L. (2005). Immunologic influences on emotion regulation. *Clinical Neuroscience Research, 4,* 325–333.

Miller, A. S., & Kanazawa, S. (2000). *Order by accident: The origins and consequences of conformity in contemporary Japan.* Boulder, CO: Westview Press.

Miller, B. L., & J. L. Cummings (Eds.). (1999). *The human frontal lobes: Functions and disorders.* New York: Guilford Press.

Miller, G. (2000). *The mating mind.* New York: Doubleday.

Miller, G. A. (1956). The magical number seven, plus or minus two: Some limits on our capacity for processing information. *Psychological Review, 63,* 81–97.

Miller, G. F. (2000). *The mating mind: How sexual choice shaped the evolution of human nature.* New York: Doubleday.

Miller, L. A., & Tippett, L. J. (1996). Effects of focal brain lesions on visual problem-solving. *Neuropsychologia, 34,* 387–398.

Milner, B. (1962). Les troubles de la mémoire accompagnant des lésions hippocampiques bilatérales. In *Physiologie de l'hippocampe* (pp. 257–272). Paris: Centre National de la Recherche Scientifique. English translation: P. M. Milner & S. Glickman (Eds.). (1965). *Cognitive processes and the brain: An enduring problem in psychology. Selected readings* (pp. 97–111). Princeton: Van Nostrand.

Milner, B., Corkin, S., & Teuber, H. L. (1968). Further analysis of the hippocampal amnesic syndrome: 14-year follow-up study of H. M. *Neuropsychologia, 6,* 215–234.

Mirescu, C., & Gould, E. (2006). Stress and adult neurogenesis. *Hippocampus, 16,* 233–238.

Mirescu, C., Peters, J. D., Noiman, L., & Gould, E. (2006). Sleep deprivation inhibits adult neurogenesis in the hippocampus by elevating glucocorticoids. *Proceedings of the National Academy of Sciences, 103,* 19170–19175. doi:10.1073/pnas.0608644103

Mischel, W., & Shoda, Y. (1995). A cognitive-affective system theory of personality: Reconceptualizing situations, dispositions, dynamics, and invariance in personality structure. *Psychological Review, 102,* 246–268.

Mischel, W., & Shoda, Y. (1999). Integrating dispositions and processing dynamics within a unified theory of personality: The cognitive-affective personality system. In L. A. Pervin & O. P. John (Eds.), *Handbook of personality: Theory and research* (pp. 197–218). New York: Guilford Press.

Mitchell, K. J., Finkelhor, D., & Wolak, J. (2001). Risk factors for and impact of online sexual solicitation of youth. *Journal of American Medical Association, 285,* 3011–3014.

Miyake, A., Friedman, N. P., Emerson, M. J., Witzki, A. H., & Howerter, A. (2000). The unity and diversity of executive functions and their contributions to complex "frontal lobe" tasks: A latent variable approach. *Cognitive Psychology, 41,* 49–100.

Miyashita, T., Kubik, S., Lewandowski, G., & Guzowski, J. F. (2008). Networks of neurons, networks of genes: An integrated view of memory consolidation. *Neurobiology of Learning and Memory, 89,* 269–284.

Mizuno, S., Mihara, T., Miyaoka, T., Inagaki, T., & Horiguchi, J. (2005, March). CSF iron, ferritin and transferrin levels in restless legs syndrome. *Journal of Sleep Research, 14*(1), 43–47.

Moffitt, T. E., Brammer, G. L., Caspi, A., Fawcett, J. P., Raleigh, M., Yuwiler, A., et al. (1998). Whole blood serotonin relates to violence in an epidemiological study. *Biological Psychiatry, 43,* 446–457.

Moffitt, T. E., Caspi. A., & Rutter, M. (2005). Strategy for investigating interactions between measured genes and measured environments. *Archives of General Psychiatry, 62,* 473–481.

Moghaddam, B. (2003). Bringing order to the glutamate chaos in schizophrenia. *Neuron, 40,* 881–884.

Mokdad, A. H., Serdula, M. K., Dietz, W. H., Bowman, B. A., Marks, J. S., & Koplan, J. P. (1999). The spread of the obesity epidemic in the United States, 1991–1998. *Journal of American Medical Association, 282,* 1519–1522.

Moller, J., Hallqvist, J., Diderichsen, F., Theorell, T., Reuterwall, C., & Ahblom, A. (1999). Do episodes of anger trigger myocardial infarction? A case-crossover analysis in the Stockholm Heart Epidemiology Program (SHEEP). *Psychosomatic Medicine, 61,* 842–849.

Montague, D. P. F., & Walker-Andrews, A. S. (2001). Peekaboo: A new look at infants perception of emotion. *Developmental Psychology, 37,* 826–838.

Montgomery, G. H., DuHamel, K. N., & Redd, W. H. (2000). A meta-analysis of hypnotically induced analgesia: How effective is hypnosis? *International Journal of Clinical and Experimental Hypnosis, 48,* 138–153.

Moore, E. S., Ward, R. E., Wetherill, L. F., Rogers, J. L., Autti-Rämö, I., Fagerlund, A., et al. (2007). Unique facial features distinguish fetal alcohol syndrome patients and controls in diverse ethnic populations. *Alcoholism: Clinical and Experimental Research, 31,* 1707–1713.

Moore, R. Y., & Eichler, V. B. (1972). Loss of a circadian adrenal corticosterone rhythm following suprachiasmatic lesions in the rat. *Brain Research, 42,* 201–206.

Moradi, A. R., Herlihy, J., Yasseri, G., Shahraray, M., Turner, A., & Dalgleish, T. (2008). Specificity of episodic and semantic aspects of autobiographical memory in relation to symptoms of posttraumatic stress disorder (PTSD). *Acta Psychologica, 127,* 645–653.

Moray, N. (1959). Attention in dichotic listening: Affective cues and the influence of instructions. *Quarterly Journal of Experimental Psychology, 11,* 56–60.

Moreno, S., & Besson, M. (2006). Musical training and language-related brain electrical activity in children. *Psychophysiology, 43,* 287–291.

Morris, J. S., Frilt, C. D., Perrett, D. I., Rowland, D., Yong, A. N., Calder, A. J., & Dolan, R. J. (1996). A different neural response in the human amygdala in fearful and happy facial expressions. *Nature, 383,* 812–815.

Morris, M. W., & Peng, K. (1994). Culture and cause: American and Chinese attributions for social and physical events. *Journal of Personality and Social Psychology, 67,* 949–971.

Morris, N. M., Udry, J. R., Khandawood, F., & Dawood, M. Y. (1987). Marital sex frequency and midcycle female testosterone. *Archives of Sexual Behavior, 16,* 27–37.

Morris, P. H., Gale, A., & Duffy, K. (2002). Can judges agree on the personality of horses? *Personality and Individual Differences, 33,* 67–81.

Morris, P. L., Robinson, R. G., Raphael, B., & Hopwood, M. J. (1996). Lesion location and post-stroke depression. *Journal of Neuropsychiatry and Clinical Neurosciences, 8,* 399–403.

Morrison, R. S., Maroney-Galin, C., Kralovec, P. D., & Meier, D. E. (2005). The growth of palliative care programs in United States hospitals. *Journal of Palliative Medicine.* December 1, 2005, 8(6): 1127–1134.

Moruzzi, G., & Magoun, H. W. (1949). Brain stem reticular formation and activation of the EEG. *Electroencephalography and Clinical Neurophysiology, 1,* 455–473.

Moscovici, S. (1985). Social influence and conformity. In G. Lindzey & E. Aronson (Eds.), *The handbook of social psychology* (3rd ed., Vol. 2; pp. 347–412). New York: Random House.

Moses-Kolko, E. L., Bogen, D., Perel, J., Bregard, A., Uhl, K., Levin, B., et al. (2005). Neonatal signs after late in utero exposure to serotonin reuptake inhibitors: Literature review and implications for clinical applications. *JAMA, 293,* 2372–2383.

Moskowitz, J. (2003). Positive affect predicts lower risk of AIDS mortality. *Psychosomatic Medicine, 65,* 620–626.

Moskowitz, J., Folkman, S., Collette, L., & Vittinghoff, E. (1996). Coping and mood during AIDS related caregiving and bereavement. *Annals of Behavioral Medicine, 18,* 49–57.

Motluk, A. (2005, January 29th). Senses special: The art of seeing without sight. *New Scientist, 2484,* p. 37. Retrieved from http://www.newscientist.com

Mount, M. K., Barrick, M. R., Scullen, S. M., & Rounds, J. (2005). Higher-order dimensions of the Big Five personality traits and the Big Six vocational interest types. *Personnel Psychology, 58,* 447–478.

Müller-Oerlinghausen, B., Berghöfer, A., & Bauer, M. (2002). Bipolar disorder. *The Lancet, 359,* 241–247.

Munsinger, H. (1975). The adopted child's IQ: A critical review. *Psychological Bulletin, 82,* 623–659.

Murray, H. A. (1938/1962). *Explorations in personality.* New York: Science Editions.

Nacash, N., Foa, E. B., Fostick, L., Polliack, M., Dinstein, Y., Tzur, D., et al. (2007). Prolonged exposure therapy for chronic combat-related PTSD: A case report on five veterans. *CNS Spectrums, 12,* 690–695.

Nadarajah, B., & Parnavelas, J. (2002). Modes of neuronal migration in the developing cerebral cortex. *Nature Reviews Neuroscience, 3,* 423–432.

Naqvi, N. H., Rudrauf, D., Damasio, H., & Bechara, A. (2007). Damage to the insula disrupts addiction to cigarette smoking. *Science, 315,* 531–534.

Nasar, S. (1998). *A beautiful mind.* New York: Touchstone.

Nash, M. R., Hulsey, T. L., Sexton, M. C., Harralson, T. L., Lambert, W., & Lynch, G. V. (1993). Adult psychopathology associated with a history of childhood sexual abuse: A psychoanalytic perspective. Washington, DC: American Psychological Association.

National Eye Institute. (2002). *Vision problems in the U.S.: Prevalence of adult vision impairment and age-related eye disease in America, 2002.* Retrieved January 20, 2007, from http://www.nei.nih.gov/eyedata/pdf/VPUS.pdf

National Institute of Mental Health (NIMH). (2007). *Schizophrenia.* Washington, DC: NIMH Publication # 06-3517.

National Institute on Alcohol Abuse and Alcoholism. (2005). *Heavy episodic consumption of alcohol.* Retrieved April 4, 2008, from http://www.collegedrinkingprevention.gov/NIAAACollegeMaterials/TaskForce/HeavyEpisodic_00.aspx

National Safety Council. (2003). *What are the odds of dying?* Retrieved January 20, 2007, from http://www.nsc.org/lrs/statinfo/odds.htm.

National Science Foundation. (2002). Science and technology: Public attitudes and public understanding. In *Science and Engineering Indicators—2002* (Chapter 7). Arlington, VA: National Science Foundation.

National Sleep Foundation. (2008). *2008 Sleep in America poll.* Retrieved April 2, 2008, from http://www.sleepfoundation.org/site/c.huIXKjM0IxF/b.3933533/

Natural born copycats. (2002, December 20). *The Guardian.* Retrieved from http://www.mediaknowall.com/violence/nbk.html

Nauta, W. J. H., & Feirtag, M. (1979). The organization of the brain. *Scientific American, 241,* 88–111.

Neisser, U., Boodoo, G., Bouchard, T. J., Boykin, A. W., Brody, N., Ceci, S. J., et al. (1996). Intelligence: Knowns and unknowns. *American Psychologist, 51,* 77–101.

Nelson-Gray, R. O., Keane, S. P., Hurst, R. M., Mitchell, J. T., Warburton, J. B., Chok, J. T., et al. (2006). A modified DBT skills training program for oppositional defiant adolescents: Promising preliminary findings. *Behaviour Research and Therapy, 44,* 1811–1820.

Nemeroff, C., & Rozin, P. (1994). The contagion concept in adult thinking in the United States: Transmission of germs and of interpersonal influence. *Ethos, 22,* 158–186.

Nemeroff, C. B. (2007). The burden of severe depression: A review of diagnostic challenges and treatment alternatives. *Journal of Psychiatric Research, 41,* 189–206.

Nesbit, S. M., Conger, J. C., & Conger, A. J. (2007). A quantitative review of the relationship between anger and aggressive driving. *Aggression and Violent Behavior, 12,* 156–176.

Nettle, D., & Clegg, H. (2005). Schizotypy, creativity, and mating success in humans. *Proceedings of the Royal Society (B).* doi:10.1098/rspb.2005.3349

Neuberg, S. L., & Cottrell, C. A. (2006). Evolutionary bases of prejudices. In M. Schaller, J. A. Simpson, & D. T. Kenrick (Eds.). *Evolution and social psychology* (pp. 163–187). New York: Psychology Press.

Neugebauer, R., Hoek, H. W., & Susser, E. (1999). Prenatal exposure to wartime famine and development of antisocial personality disorder in early adulthood. *Journal of the American Medical Association, 282*, 455–462.

New York Academy of Sciences. (2003). *Adolescent brain development: Vulnerabilities and opportunities.* [E-briefing]. Retrieved March 13, 2008 from http://www.nyas.org/ebriefreps/main.asp?intSubSectionID=570#02

Newcomb, T. M. (1961). *The acquaintance process.* Oxford, England: Holt, Rinehart & Winston.

Newcombe, N. S., & Uttal, D. H. (2006). Whorf versus Socrates, round 10. *Trends in Cognitive Sciences, 10*, 394–396.

Newport, E. L. (2003). Language development, critical periods in. In L. Nadel (Ed.), *Encyclopedia of cognitive science* (Vol. 2; pp. 733–740). London: Nature Group Press.

Neyens, D. M., & Boyle, L. N. (2007). The effect of distraction on the crash types of teenage drivers. *Accident Analysis and Prevention, 39*, 206–212.

Nickerson, C., Schwarz, N., Diener, E., & Kahneman, D. (2003). Zeroing in on the dark side of the American dream: A closer look at the negative consequences of the goal for financial success. *Psychological Science, 14*, 531–536.

Nicoll, R. A., & Alger, B. E. (2004). The brain's own marijuana. *Scientific American, 291*, 69–75.

Nieman, D. C., Custer, W. F., Butterworth, D. E., Utter, A. C., & Henson, D. A. (2000). Psychological response to exercise and/or energy restriction in obese women. *Journal of Psychosomatic Research, 48*(1), 23–29.

Nisbett, R. E., Peng, K., Choi, I., & Norenzayan, A. (2001). Culture and systems of thought: Holistic versus analytic cognition. *Psychological Review, 108*, 291–301.

Nisbett, R. E., & Wilson, T. D. (1977). Telling more than we can know: Verbal reports on mental processes. *Psychological Review, 84*, 231–259.

Nishida, A., Hisaoka, K., Zensho, H., Uchitomi, Y., Morinobu, S., & Yamawaki, S. (2002). Antidepressant drugs and cytokines in mood disorders. *International Immunopharmacology, 2*, 1619–1626.

Nishino, S. (2007). Clinical and neurobiological aspects of narcolepsy. *Sleep Medicine, 8*, 373–399.

Nithianantharajah, J., & Hannan, A. (2006). Enriched environments, experience dependent plasticity and disorders of the nervous system. *Nature Reviews Neuroscience, 7*, 697–709.

Nizhnikov, M. E., Molina, J. C., & Spear, N. E. (2007). Central reinforcing effects of alcohol are blocked by catalase inhibition. *Alcohol, 41*, 525–534.

Noble, R. E. (2001). Waist-to-hip ratio versus BMI as predictors of cardiac risk in obese adult women. *Western Journal of Medicine, 174*, 240.

Noda, H., Iso, H., Toyoshima, H., Date, C., Yamamoto, A., Kikuchi, S., et al. (2005). Walking and sports participation and mortality from coronary heart disease and stroke. *Journal of the American College of Cardiology, 46*, 1761–1767.

Nolen-Hoeksema, S. (2007). *Abnormal psychology* (4th ed). New York: McGraw-Hill.

Nolte, C., & Yollin, P. (2006, April 19). Officials salute city's majestic rise from rubble of '06—and the survivors. *San Francisco Chronicle*, pp. A1, A12.

Norcross, J. C., Karpiak, C. P., & Lister, K. M. (2005). What's an integrationist? A study of self-identified integrative and (occasionally) eclectic psychologists. *Journal of Clinical Psychology, 61*, 1587–1594.

Norcross, J. C., Sayette, M. A., Mayne, T. J., Karg, R. S., & Turkson, M. A. (1998). Selecting a doctoral program in professional psychology: Some comparisons among PhD counseling, PhD clinical, and PsyD clinical psychology programs. *Professional Psychology: Research and Practice, 29*, 609–614.

Norenzayan, A., & Nisbett, R. E. (2000). Culture and causal cognition. *Current Directions in Psychological Science, 9*, 132–135.

Nottebohm, F. (1985). Neuronal replacement in adulthood. *Annals of the New York Academy of Sciences, 457*, 143–161.

Novak, M. A. (2003). Self-injurious behavior in Rhesus monkeys: New insights into its etiology, physiology, and treatment. *American Journal of Primatology, 59*, 3–19.

Nuechterlein, K., & Parasuraman, R. (1983). Visual sustained attention: Image degradation produces rapid sensitivity decrement over time. *Science, 220*, 327–329.

Oberman, L. M., & Ramachadran, V. S. (2007). The simulating social mind: The role of mirror neuron system and simulation in the social and communicative deficits of autism spectrum disorders. *Psychological Bulletin, 133*, 310–327.

Ochsner, K. N., Bunge, S. A., Gross, J. J., & Gabrieli, J. D. E. (2002). Rethinking feelings: A fMRI study of the cognitive regulation of emotion. *Journal of Cognitive Neuroscience, 14*, 1215–1229.

O'Cleirigh, C., Ironson, G., Fletcher, M. A., & Schneiderman, N. (2008). Written emotional disclosure and processing of trauma are associated with protected health status and immunity in people living with HIV/AIDS. *British Journal of Health Psychology, 13*, 81–84.

O'Conner, M. J., & Paley, B. (2006). The relationship of prenatal alcohol exposure and the postnatal environment of child depressive symptoms. *Journal of Pediatric Psychology, 31*, 50–64.

O'Connor, C. A., Cernak, I., & Vink, R. (2005). Both estrogen and progesterone attenuate edema formation following diffuse traumatic brain injury in rats. *Brain Research, 1062*, 171–174.

Ogawa, H., Wakita, M., Hasegawa, K., Kobayakawa, T., Sakai, N., Hirai, T., et al. (2005). Functional MRI detection of activation in the primary gustatory cortices in humans. *Chemical Senses, 30*, 583–592.

Ogden, C. L., Carroll, M. D., Curtin, L. R., McDowell, M. A., Tabak, C. J., & Flegal, K. M. (2006). Prevalence of overweight and obesity in the United States, 1999–2004. *Journal of the American Medical Association, 295*, 1549–1555.

Öhman, A. (2002). Automaticity and the amygdala: Nonconscious responses to emotional faces. *Current Directions in Psychological Science, 11*, 62–66.

Ohnishi, T., Matsuda, H., Asada, T., Aruga, M., Hirakata, M., Nishikawa, M., et al. (2001). Functional anatomy of musical perception in musicians. *Cerebral Cortex, 11*, 754–760.

Olds, J., & Milner, P. (1954). Positive reinforcement produced by electrical stimulation of septal area and other regions of rat brain. *Journal of Comparative and Physiological Psychology, 47*, 419–427.

Oliver, M. B., & Hyde, J. S. (1993). Gender differences in sexuality: A meta-analysis. *Psychological Bulletin, 114*, 29–51.

Olson, J. M., & Zanna, M. P. (1993). Attitudes and attitude change. *Annual Review of Psychology, 44*, 117–154.

Omark, D., Omark, M., & Edelman, M. (1973). Formation of dominance hierarchies in young children. In T. R. Williams (Ed.), *Physical anthropology*. The Hague: Mouton.

Onodera, A. (2003). Changes in self-concept in the transition to parenthood. *Japanese Journal of Developmental Psychology, 14*, 180–190.

Orne, M. T. (1959). The nature of hypnosis: Artifact and essence. *Journal of Abnormal and Social Psychology, 58*, 277–299.

Oscar–Berman, M., & Marinkovic, K. (2003). Alcoholism and the brain: An overview. *Alcohol Research & Health, 27*, 125–133.

Osherow, N. (1999). Making sense of the nonsensical: An analysis of Jonestown. In E. Aronson (Ed.), *Readings about the social animal* (8th ed.; pp. 71–88). New York: Worth/Freeman.

Ost, J. (2003). Seeking the middle ground in the "memory wars." *British Journal of Psychology, 94*, 125–139.

Oster, H. (2005). The repertoire of infant facial expressions: An ontogenetic perspective. In J. Nadel & D. Muir (Eds.), *Emotional development* (pp. 261–292). New York: Oxford University Press.

Osterling, J., & Dawson, G. (1994). Early recognition of children with autism: A study of first birthday home videotapes. *Journal of Autism and Developmental Disorders, 24*, 247–257.

Ouellet, M-C., Beaulieu-Bonneau, S., & Morin, C. M. (2006). Insomnia in patients with traumatic brain injury: Frequency, characteristics, and risk factors. *Journal of Head Trauma Rehabilitation, 21*, 199–212.

Ouellet, M-C., & Morin, C. M. (2006). Fatigue following traumatic brain injury: Frequency, characteristics, and associated factors. *Rehabilitation Psychology, 51*, 140–149.

Owen, A. M., Coleman, M. R., Boly, M., Davis, M., Laureys, S., & Pickard, J. D. (2006). Detecting awareness in the vegetative state. *Science, 313*, 1402.

Oyama, S. (1976). A sensitive period for the acquisition of a nonnative phonological system. *Journal of Psycholinguistic Research, 5*, 261–283.

Pallanti, S., Bernardi, S., & Quercoli, L. (2006). The shorter PROMIS questionnaire and the Internet addiction scale in the assessment of multiple addictions in a high school population: Prevalence and related disability. *CNS Spectrum, 11*, 966–974.

Panksepp, J. (2000). Emotions as natural kinds within the mammalian brain. In M. Lewis and J. M. Haviland-Jones (Eds.), *Handbook of emotions* (2nd ed.; pp. 137–156). New York: Guilford.

Panksepp, J. (2005). Why does separation distress hurt? Comment on MacDonald and Leary (2005). *Psychological Bulletin, 131*, 224–230.

Pantev, C., Engelien, A., Candia, V., & Elbert, T. (2001). Representational cortex in musicians: Plastic alterations in response to musical practice. In R. J. Zatorre & I. Peretz (Eds.), *The biological foundations of music: Annals of the New York Academy of Sciences* (pp. 300–314). New York: New York Academy of Sciences.

Parasuraman, R. (1998). *The attentive brain.* Cambridge, MA: MIT Press.

Paris, R., & Helson, R. (2002). Early mothering experience and personality change. *Journal of Family Psychology, 16*, 172–185.

Park, C. L., & Folkman, S. (1997). Meaning in the context of stress and coping. *Review of General Psychology, 1*, 115–144.

Parker, R. S. (1996). The spectrum of emotional distress and personality changes after

minor head injury incurred in a motor vehicle accident. *Brain Injury, 10*, 287–302.

Parker, S. T., & McKinney, M. L. (1999). *Origins of intelligence: The evolution of cognitive development in monkeys, apes, and humans.* Baltimore: Johns Hopkins University Press.

Pascual-Leone, A. (2001). The brain that plays music and is changed by it. *Annals of the New York Academy of Sciences, 930*, 315–329.

Patil, S. T., Zhang, L., Martenyi, F., Lowe, S. L., Jackson, K. A., Andreev, B. V., et al. (2007). Activation of mGlu2/3 receptors as a new approach to treat schizophrenia: A randomized Phase 2 clinical trial. *Nature Medicine, 13*, 1102–1107.

Patterson, C. J. (2008). *Child development.* New York: McGraw-Hill.

Patterson, D. R. (2004). Treating pain with hypnosis. *Current Directions in Psychological Science, 13*, 252–255.

Paul, E. S., Harding, E. J., & Mendl, M. (2005). Measuring emotional processes in animals: The utility of a cognitive approach. *Neuroscience and Biobehavioral Reviews, 29*, 469–491.

Paulesu, E., Frith, C. D., & Frackowiak, R. S. J. (1993). The neural correlates of the verbal component of working memory. *Nature, 362*, 342–345.

Paulozzi, L. J. (2006). Opioid analgesia involvement in drug abuse deaths in American metropolitan areas. *American Journal of Public Health, 96*, 1755–1757.

Pavlov, I. P. (1906). The scientific investigation of the psychical faculties or processes in the higher animals. *Science, 24*, 613–619.

Pavlov, I. P. (1928). *Lectures on conditioned reflexes: Twenty-five years of objective study of the higher nervous activity (behaviour) of animals* (W. H. Gantt, Trans.). New York: Liveright.

Payne, J. D., & Nadel, L. (2004). Sleeps, dreams, and memory consolidation: The role of the stress hormone cortisol. *Learning & Memory, 11*, 671–678.

Pearson, J. D., Morrell, C. H., Gordon-Salant, S., Brant, L. J., Metter, E. J., Klein, L., et al. (1995). Gender differences in a longitudinal study of age-associated hearing loss. *Journal of the Acoustical Society of America, 97*, 1197–1205.

Pearson, N. J., Johnson, L. L., & Nahin, R. L. (2006). Insomnia, trouble sleeping, and complementary and alternative medicine: Analysis of the 2002 National Health Interview Survey data. *Archives of Internal Medicine, 166*, 1775–1782.

The peculiar institution. (2002). [Editorial]. *Scientific American, 286*, 8.

Pedersen, D. M., & Wheeler, J. (1983). The Müller–Lyer illusion among Navajos. *Journal of Social Psychology, 121*, 3–6.

Peigneux, P., Laureys, S., Fuchs, S., Collette, F., Perrin, F., Reggers, J., et al. (2004). Are spatial memories strengthened in the human hippocampus during slow wave sleep? *Neuron, 44*, 535–545.

Pelli, D. G., Farell, B., & Moore, D. C. (2003). The remarkable inefficiency of word recognition. *Nature, 423*, 752–756.

Penfield, W., & Milner, B. (1958). Memory deficit produced by bilateral lesions in the hippocampal zone. *Archives of Neurology & Psychiatry (Chicago), 79*, 475–497.

Pennebaker, J. W. (1995). *Emotion, disclosure, and health.* Washington, DC: American Psychological Association.

Pennebaker, J. W., Kiecolt-Glaser, J. K., & Glaser, R. (1988). Disclosure of traumas and immune function: Implications for psychotherapy. *Journal of Consulting and Clinical Psychology, 56*, 239–245.

Pereira, A. C., Huddleston, D. E., Brickman, A. M., Sosunov, A. A., Hen, R., McKhann, et al. (2007). An *in vivo* correlate of exercise-induced neurogenesis in the adult dentate gyrus. *Proceedings of the National Academy of Sciences, 104*, 5638–5643.

Perry, B. D. (2002). Childhood experience and the expression of genetic potential: What childhood neglect tells us about nature and nurture. *Brain and Mind, 3*, 79–100.

Perry, R., & Zeki, S. (2000). The neurology of saccades and covert shifts in spatial attention: An event-related fMRI study. *Brain, 123*, 2273–2288.

Persky, H., Dreisbach, L., Miller, W. R., O'Brien, C. P., Khan, M. A., Lief, H. I., et al. (1982). The relation of plasma androgen levels to sexual behaviors and attitudes of women. *Psychosomatic Medicine, 44*, 305–319.

Persky, H., Lief, H. I., Strauss, D., Miller, W. R, & O'Brien, C. P. (1978). Plasma testosterone level and sexual behavior of couples. *Archives of Sexual Behavior, 7*, 157–173.

Pessoa, L. (2008). On the relationship between emotion and cognition. *Nature Reviews Neuroscience, 9*, 148–158.

Pessoa, L., Padmala, S., & Morland, T. (2005). Fate of unattended fearful faces in the amygdala is determined by both attentional resources and cognitive modulation. *Neuroimage, 28*, 249–255.

Petot, J. (2000). Interest and limitations of projective techniques in the assessment of personality disorders. *European Psychiatry, 15*, 11–14.

Petrie, K. J., Fontanilla, I., Thomas, M. G., Booth, R. J., & Pennebaker, J. W. (2004). Effect of written emotional expression on immune function in patients with human immunodeficiency virus infection: A randomized trial. *Psychosomatic Medicine, 66,* 272–275.

Petronis, A. (2004). Schizophrenia, neurodevelopment, and epigenetics. In M. S. Keshavan, J. L. Kennedy, & R. M. Murray (Eds.). *Neurodevelopment and schizophrenia* (pp. 174–190). New York: Cambridge University Press.

Petry, S., Cummings, J. L., Hill, M. A., & Shapiro, J. (1989). Personality alterations in dementia of the Alzheimer type: A three-year follow-up study. *Journal of Geriatric Psychiatry and Neurology, 2,* 203–207.

Pettigrew, T. F. (1979). The ultimate attribution error: Extending Allport's cognitive analysis of prejudice. *Personality and Social Psychology Bulletin, 5,* 461–476.

Pfrieger, F. W. (2002). Role of glia in synapse development. *Current Opinion in Neurobiology, 12,* 496–490.

Phan, K. L., Wager, T., Taylor, S. F. & Liberzon, I. (2002). Functional neuroanatomy of emotion: A meta-analysis of emotion activation studies in PET and fMRI. *Neuroimage, 16,* 331–348.

Phelps, E. A. (2006). Emotion and cognition: Insights from the study of the human amygdala. *Annual Review of Psychology, 57,* 27–53.

Phelps, E. A., & LeDoux, J. E. (2005). Contributions of the amygdala to emotional processing: From animal models to human behavior. *Neuron, 48,* 175–187.

Piaget, J. (1954). *The construction of reality in the child.* New York: Basic.

Piaget, J. (1962). *Plays, dreams and imitation in childhood.* New York: Norton.

Piaget, J. (1972a). Intellectual evolution from adolescence to adulthood. *Human Development, 15,* 1–12.

Piaget, J. (1972b). *The child's conception of the world.* Totowa, NJ: Littlefield, Adams.
Piaget, J., and Inhelder, B. (1967). *The child's conception of space.* New York: Norton.

Pincus, J. H. (1999). Aggression, criminality, and the frontal lobes. In B. L. Miller and J. L. Cummings (Eds.). *The human frontal lobes: Functions and disorders* (pp. 547–556). New York: Guilford Press.

Pincus, J. H. (2001). *Base instincts: What makes killers kill?* New York: Norton.

Pinker, S. (1994). *The language instinct: How the mind creates language.* New York: HarperPerennial.

Pinker, S. (2002). *The blank slate.* New York: Viking.

Pinker, S. (2004, Fall). Why nature and nurture won't go away. *Daedalus,* 1–13.

Pinsk, M. A., DeSimone, K., Moore, T., Gross, C. G., & Kastner, S. (2005). Representations of faces and body parts in

macaque temporal cortex: A functional MRI study. *Neuroscience, 102,* 6996–7001.

Pinsker, H. M., Hening, W. A., Carew, T. J., & Kandel, E. R. (1973). Long-term sensitization of a defensive withdrawal reflex in *Aplysia. Science, 182,* 1039–1042.

Plassart-Schiess, E., & Baulieu, E. (2001). Neurosteroids: Recent findings. *Brain Research Reviews, 37,* 133–140.

Pliner, P. (1982). The effects of mere exposure on liking for edible substances. *Appetite, 3,* 283–290.

Plomin, R., & Caspi, A. (1999). Behavioral genetics and personality. In L. A. Pervin and O. P. John (Eds.), *Handbook of personality theory and research* (pp. 251–276). New York: Guilford Press.

Plomin, R., & Petrill, S. A. (1997). Genetics and intelligence: What's new? *Intelligence, 24,* 53–77.

Plum, F., & Posner, J. (1980). *Diagnosis of stupor and coma* (3rd ed.). Philadelphia, PA: F. A. Davis.

Plunkett, K. (1997). Theories of early language acquisition. *Trends in Cognitive Sciences, 1,* 146–153.

Polanczyk, G., de Lima, M. S., Horta B. L., Biederman J., Rohde, L. A. (2007). The worldwide prevalence of ADHD: A systematic review and metaregression analysis. *American Journal of Psychiatry, 164,* 942–948.

Popper, K. (1965). *Conjectures and refutations: The growth of scientific knowledge.* New York: Harper.

Post, R. M., Frye, M. A., Denicoff, K. D., Leverich, G. S., Kimbrell, T. A., & Dunn, R. T. (1998). Beyond lithium in the treatment of bipolar illness. *Neuropsychopharmacology, 19,* 206–219.

Potkin, S. G., Saha, A. R., Kujawa, M. J., Carson, W. H., Ali, M., Stock, E., et al. (2003). Aripirazole, an antipsychotic with a novel mechanism of action, and risperidone vs placebo in patients with schizophrenia and schizoaffective disorder. *Archives of General Psychiatry, 60,* 681–690.

Preckel, F., Holling, H., Wiese, M. (2006). Relationship of intelligence and creativity in gifted and non-gifted students: An investigation of threshold theory. *Personality and Individual Differences, 40,* 159–170.

Premack, D. (1971). Language in chimpanzees? *Science, 172,* 808–822.

The prize in economics, 2002. (2002). Retrieved November 15, 2006, from http://nobelprize.org/nobel_prizes/economics/laureates/2002/press.html

Prochaska, J. O., & Norcross, J. C. (2007). *Systems of psychotherapy* (6th ed.). Belmont, CA: Wadsworth.

Prochazka, A. (2000). New developments in smoking cessation. *Chest, 117,* 169–175.

Profet, M. (1992). Pregnancy sickness as adaptation: A deterrent to maternal ingestion of teratogens. In J. Barkow, L. Cosmides, & J. Tooby (Eds), *The adapted mind* (pp. 327–365). New York: Oxford University Press.

Ptito, M., & Desgent, S. (2006). Sensory input-based adaptation and brain architecture. In P. B. Baltes, P. A. Reuter-Lorenz, & F. Rösler (Eds.), *Lifespan development and the brain: The perspective of biocultural co-constructivism* (pp. 111–133). New York: Cambridge University Press.

Purves, D., & Lichtman, J. W. (1985). *Principles of neural development.* Sunderland, MA: Sinauer.

Putnam, F., & McHugh, P. (2005). Issue 3: Is multiple personality disorder a valid diagnosis? In R. P. Halgin (Ed.), *Taking sides: Clashing views on controversial issues in abnormal psychology* (3rd ed.; pp. 42–53). New York: McGraw-Hill.

Putnam, F. W. (2006). Dissociative disorders. In D. Cicchetti & D. J. Cohen (Eds.), *Developmental psychopathology: Vol. 3. Risk, disorder, and adaptation* (pp. 657–695). Hoboken, NJ: John Wiley.

Quiroga, R. Q., Reddy, L., Kreiman, G., Koch, C., & Fried, I. (2005). Invariant visual representation by single neurons in the human brain. *Nature, 435,* 1102–1107.

Radeau, M., & Colin, C. (2004). On ventriloquism, audiovisual neurons, neonates, and the senses. *Behavioral and Brain Sciences, 27,* 889–890.

Radford, A. (1997). *Syntactic theory and the structure of English: A minimalist approach.* New York: Cambridge University Press.

Raffaele, P. (2006, November). Speaking bonobo. *Smithsonian.* Retrieved from http://www.smithsonianmagazine.com

Rahman, Q. (2005). The neurodevelopment of human sexual orientation. *Neuroscience and Biobehavioral Reviews, 29,* 1057–1066.

Raij, T. T., Numminen, J., Närvänen, S., Hiltunen, J., & Hari, R. (2005). Brain correlates of subjective reality of physically and psychologically induced pain. *Proceedings of the National Academy of Sciences, 102,* 2147–2151.

Raleigh, M. J., McGuire, M. T., Brammer, G. L., Pollack, D. B., & Yuwiler, A. (1991). Serotonergic mechanisms promote dominance in adult male vervet monkeys. *Brain Research, 559,* 181–190.

Ramachandran, V. S., & Hubbard, E. M. (2003, May). Hearing colors, tasting shapes. *Scientific American, 288,* 52–59.

Ramachandran, V. S., & Oberman, L. M. (2006). Broken mirrors: A theory of autism. *Scientific American, 295,* 63–69.

Ramanathan, L., Gulyani, S., Nienhuis, R., & Siegel, J. M. (2002). Sleep deprivation decreases superoxide dismutase activity in rat hippocampus and brainstem. *Neuroreport, 13*, 1387–1390.

Rao, V., Spiro, J. R., Handel, S., & Onyike, C. U. (2008). Clinical correlates of personality changes associated with traumatic brain injury. *Journal of Neuropsychiatry and Clinical Neurosciences, 20*, 118–119.

Rathus, J. H., Cavuoto, N., & Passarelli, V. (2006). Dialectical behavior therapy (DBT): A mindfulness-based treatment for intimate partner violence. In R. A. Baer (Ed.), *Mindfulness-based treatment approaches: Clinician's guide to evidence base and applications* (pp. 333–358). San Diego: Elsevier Academic Press.

Raz, A., Fan, J., & Posner, M. I. (2005). Hypnotic suggestion reduces conflict in the human brain. *Proceedings of the National Academy of Sciences, 102*, 9978–9983.

Raz, A., & Shapiro, T. (2002). Hypnosis and neuroscience. *Archives of General Psychiatry, 59*, 85–90.

Read, J. P., Beattie, M. Chamberlain, R., & Merrill, J. E. (2008). Beyond the "binge" threshold: Heavy drinking patterns and their association with alcohol involvement indices in college students. *Addictive Behaviors, 33*, 225–234.

Reed, G. M., Kemeny, M. E., Taylor, S. E., Wang, H. Y. J., & Visscher, B. R. (1994). Realistic acceptance as a predictor of decreased survival time in gay men with AIDS. *Health Psychology, 13*, 299–307.

Refinetti, R. (2006). *Circadian Physiology* (2nd ed.). Boca Raton, FL: CRC Press.

Remafedi, G. (1999). Sexual orientation and youth suicide. *JAMA: Journal of the American Medical Association, 282*(13), 1291–1292.

Remafedi, G., Resnick, M., Blum, R., & Harris, L. (1992). Demography of sexual orientation in adolescents. *Pediatrics, 89*, 714–721.

Renaud, S., & de Lorgeril, M. (1992). Wine, alcohol, platelets, and the French paradox for coronary heart disease. *Lancet, 339*, 1523–1526.

Rexrode, K. M., Buring, J. E., & Manson, J. E. (2001). Abdominal and total adiposity and risk of coronary heart disease in men. *International Journal of Obesity, 25*, 1047–1056.

Rexrode, K. M., Carey, V. J., Hennekens, C. H., Walters, E. E., Colditz, G. A., Stampfer, M. J., et al. (1998). Abdominal adiposity and coronary heart disease in women. *Journal of the American Medical Association, 280*, 1843–1848.

Reynolds, C. R. (2000). Why is psychometric research on bias in mental testing so often ignored? *Psychology, Public Policy, and Law, 6*, 144–150.

Reynolds, S., & Lane, S. J. (2008). Diagnostic validity of sensory over-responsivity: A review of the literature and case reports. *Journal of Autism and Developmental Disorders, 38*, 516–529.

Ricciardelli, L. A. (1992). Creativity and bilingualism. *Journal of Creative Behavior, 26*, 242–254.

Rice, C. (2007). Prevalence of autism spectrum disorders: Autism and developmental disabilities monitoring network, six sites, United States, 2000. *Morbidity and Mortality Weekly Report, CDC, 56*, 1–11.

Rice, M. L. (1989). Children's language acquisition. *American Psychologist, 44*, 149–156.

Richards, R. L. (1994). Creativity and bipolar mood swings: Why the association? In M. P. Shaw & M. A. Runco (Eds.), *Creativity and affect* (pp. 44–72). Norwood, NJ: Ablex.

Richards, R. L., & Kinney, D. K. (1990). Mood swings and creativity. *Creativity Research Journal, 3*, 202–217.

Ridley, M. (2003). *Nature via nurture: Genes, experience, and what makes us human*. New York: Harper Collins.

Ries, M., & Marks, W. (2005). Selective attention deficits following severe closed head injury: The role of inhibitory processes. *Neuropsychology, 19*, 476–481.

Riis, J. L., Chong, H., Ryan, K. K., Wolk, D. A., Rentz, D. M., Holcomb, P. J., & Daffner, K. R. (2008). Compensatory neural activity distinguishes different patterns of normal cognitive aging. *Neuroimage, 39*, 441–454.

Rinpoche, S. (1992). *The Tibetan book of living and dying*. New York: HarperCollins.

Rizzolatti, G., & Arbibb, M. A. (1998). Language within our grasp. *Trends in Neuroscience, 21*, 188–194.

Rizzolatti, G., & Craighero, L. (2004). The mirror-neuron system. *Annual Review of Neuroscience, 27*, 169–192.

Rizzolatti, G., Fadiga, L., Fogassi, L., & Gallese, V. (1996). Premotor cortex and the recognition of motor actions. *Brain Research: Cognitive Brain Research, 3*, 131–141.

Roberts, B. W., & Mroczek, D. (2008). Personality trait change in adulthood. *Current Directions in Psychological Science, 17*, 31–35.

Roberts, B. W., Walton, K. E., & Viechtbauer, W. (2006). Patterns of mean-level change in personality traits across the life course: A meta-analysis of longitudinal studies. *Psychological Bulletin, 132*, 1–25.

Robinson, D. N. (1995). *An intellectual history of psychology* (3rd ed.). Madison: University of Wisconsin Press.

Robinson, G. E. (2004). Beyond nature and nurture. *Science, 304*, 397–399.

Robinson, L. A., & Kleseges, R. C. (1997). Ethnic and gender differences in risk factors for smoking onset. *Health Psychology, 16*, 499–505

Röder, B. (2006). Blindness: A source and case of neuronal plasticity. In P. B. Baltes, P. A. Reuter-Lorenz, & F. Rösler (Eds.), *Lifespan development and the brain* (pp. 134–157). New York: Cambridge University Press.

Roehr, B. (2007). High rate of PTSD in returning Iraq war veterans. *Medscape Medical News*. Retrieved July 5, 2008, from http://www.medscape.com/viewarticle/565407

Roehrs, T., Zorick, F. J., & Roth, T. (2000). Transient and short-term insomnias. In M. H. Kryger, T. Roth, and W. C. Dement (Eds.), *Principles and practice of sleep medicine*. Philadelphia: Saunders.

Rogelberg, S. G., & Gill, P. M. (2006). The growth of industrial and organizational psychology: Quick facts. Retrieved December 6, 2007, from http://www.siop.org/tip/backissues/july04/05rogelberg.aspx

Rogers, C. R. (1951). *Client-centered counseling*. Boston: Houghton Mifflin.

Rogers, C. R. (1959). A theory of therapy, personality, and interpersonal relationships, as developed in the client-centered framework. In S. Koch (Ed.), *Psychology: A study of a science* (Vol. 3). New York: McGraw-Hill.

Rogers, C. R. (1980). *A way of being*. Boston: Houghton Mifflin.

Rogers, C. R., & Dymond, R. G. (Eds.). (1954). *Psychotherapy and personality change: Co-ordinated research studies in the client-centered approach*. Chicago: University of Chicago Press.

Roid, G. H., & Pomplun, M. (2005). Interpreting the Stanford-Binet Intelligence Scales, fifth edition. In D. P. Flanagan & P. L. Harrison (Eds.), *Contemporary intellectual assessment: Theories, tests, and issues* (pp. 325–343). New York: Guilford Press.

Rolland, J. P. (2002). Cross-cultural generalizability of the Five-Factor Model of personality. In R. R. McCrae & J. Allik (Eds.), *The Five-Factor Model of personality across cultures* (pp. 7–28). New York: Kluwer Academic/Plenum.

Rolls, E. T. (2000). The orbitofrontal cortex and reward. *Cerebral Cortex, 10*, 284–294.

Rolls, E. T. (2004). The functions of the orbitofrontal cortex. *Brain and Cognition, 55*, 11–29.

Rolls, E. T. (2006). Brain mechanisms underlying flavour and appetite. *Philosophical Transactions of the Royal Society of London, 361*, 1123–1136.

Roof, R. L., Duvdevani, R., Braswell, L., & Stein, D. G. (1994). Progesterone facilitates recovery and reduces secondary neuronal loss caused by cortical contusion. *Experimental Neurology, 129,* 64–69.

Roof, R. L., Duvdevani, R., Heyburn, J. W., & Stein, D. G. (1996). Progesterone rapidly decreases brain edema: Treatment delayed up to 24 hours is still effective. *Experimental Neurology, 138,* 246–251.

Rosch, E. (1973). Natural categories. *Cognitive Psychology, 4,* 328–350.

Rosch, E. (1975). Cognitive representations of semantic categories. *Journal of Experimental Psychology: General, 104,* 192–223.

Roseman, I. J. (1984). Cognitive determinants of emotion: A structural theory. *Review of Personality & Social Psychology, 5,* 11–36.

Rosenberg, E. L. (1998). Levels of analysis and the organization of affect. *Review of General Psychology, 2,* 247–270.

Rosenberg, E. L. (2005). The study of spontaneous facial expressions in psychology. In P. Ekman & E. L. Rosenberg (Eds.), *What the face reveals: Basic and applied studies of spontaneous expression using the Facial Action Coding System (FACS)* (2nd ed.; pp. 3–17). New York: Oxford University Press.

Rosenberg, E. L., & Ekman, P. (1994). Coherence between expressive and experiential systems in emotion. *Cognition & Emotion, 8,* 201–229.

Rosenberg, E. L., & Ekman, P. (2000). Emotion: Methods of study. In A. Kasdan (Ed.), *Encyclopedia of psychology* (pp. 171–175). Washington, DC: American Psychological Association and Oxford University Press.

Rosenberg, E. L., Ekman, P., Jiang, W., Coleman, R. E., Hanson, M., O'Connor, C., et al. (2001). Linkages between facial expressions of anger and transient myocardial ischemia in men with coronary artery disease. *Emotion, 1,* 107–115.

Rosenman, R. H., Friedman, M., Straus, R., Wurm, M., Kositchek, R., Hahn, W., & Werthessen, N. T. (1964). A predictive study of coronary artery disease. *Journal of the American Medical Association, 189,* 113–124.

Rosenthal, R. (1976). *Experimenter effects in behavioral research enlarged edition.* New York : Irvington.

Rosenthal, R. (1986). Meta-analytic procedures and the nature of replication: The debate. *Journal of Parapsychology, 50*(4), 315–336.

Rosenthal, R. (1994). On being one's own case study: Experimenter effects in behavioral research—30 years later. In W. Shadish and S. Fuller (Eds.), *The social psychology of science* (pp. 214–229). New York: Guilford Press.

Rosenthal, R., & Fode, K. L. (1963). The effect of experimenter bias on the performance of the albino rat. *Behavioral Science, 8,* 183–189.

Rosenthal, R., & Jacobson, L. (1968). *Pygmalion in the classroom.* New York: Holt, Rinehart & Winston.

Rosenthal, R., & Jacobson, L. (1992). *Pygmalion in the classroom* (Rev. ed.). New York: Irvington.

Rosenthal, R., & Rubin, D. B. (1978). Interpersonal expectancy effects: The first 345 studies. *The Behavioral and Brain Sciences, 3,* 377–386.

Rosenzweig, M. R., & Bennett, E. L. (1969). Effects of differential environments on brain weights and enzyme activities in gerbils, rats and mice. *Developmental Psychobiology, 2,* 87–95.

Rosenzweig, M. R., Krech, D., Bennett, E. L., and Diamond, M. C. (1962). Effects of environmental complexity and training on brain chemistry and anatomy: A replication and extension. *Journal of Comparative and Physiological Psychology, 55,* 429–437.

Rosenzweig, S. (1933). The experimental situation as a psychological problem. *Psychological Review, 40,* 337–354.

Ross, L. (1977). The intuitive psychologist and his shortcomings: Distortions in the attribution process. In L. Berkowitz (Ed.), *Advances in experimental social psychology* (Vol. 10), pp. 173–220. New York: Academic Press.

Rothbart, M. K., Ahadi, S. A., & Evans, D. E. (2000). Temperament and personality: Origins and outcomes. *Journal of Personality and Social Psychology, 78,* 122–135.

Rothbaum, B. O., Cahill, S. P., Foa, E. B., Davidson, J. R. T., Compton, J., Connor, K. M., et al. (2006). Augmentation of sertraline with prolonged exposure in the treatment of posttraumatic stress disorder. *Journal of Traumatic Stress, 19,* 625–638.

Rothenberg, D. (2005). *Why birds sing: A journey through the mystery of bird song.* New York: Basic Books.

Rowe, G., Hirsch, J. B., & Anderson, A. K. (2007). Positive affect increases the breadth of attentional selection. *Proceedings of the National Academy of Sciences, 104,* 383–388.

Rowland, N. E., Li, B-H., & Morien, A. (1996). Brain mechanisms and the physiology of feeding. In E. D. Capaldi (Ed.), *Why we eat what we eat: The psychology of eating* (pp. 173–204). Washington, DC: American Psychological Association.

Rozin, P. (1996). Sociocultural influences on human food selection. In E. D. Capaldi (Ed.), *Why we eat what we eat: The psychology of eating* (pp. 233–263). Washington, DC: American Psychological Association.

Rozin, P., Haidt, J., & McCauley, C. R. (2000). Disgust. In M. Lewis and J. M. Haviland-Jones (Eds.), *Handbook of emotions* (2nd ed.; pp. 637–653). New York: Guilford Press.

Rozin, P., & Fallon, A. E. (1987). Perspectives on disgust. *Psychological Review, 94,* 23–41.

Ruan, J. (2004). Bilingual Chinese/English first-graders developing metacognition about writing *Literacy, 38,* 106–112.

Ruff, H. (1999). Population-based data and the development of individual children: The case of low to moderate lead levels and intelligence. *Journal of Developmental & Behavioral Pediatrics, 20*(1), 42–49.

Rumbaugh, D. M., Beran, M. J., & Savage-Rumbaugh, S. (2003). Language. In D. Maestripieri (Ed.), *Primate psychology* (pp. 395–423). Cambridge, MA: Harvard University Press.

Runyan, W. M. (1981). Why did Van Gogh cut off his ear? The problem of alternative explanations in psychobiography. *Journal of Personality and Social Psychology, 40,* 1070–1077.

Runyan, W. M. (1982). *Life histories and psychobiography.* New York: Oxford University Press.

Rushton, W. A. H. (1961). Rhodopsin measurement and dark adaptation in a subject deficient in cone vision. *Journal of Physiology, 156,* 193–205.

Russell, J. A. (1980). A circumplex model of affect. *Journal of Personality and Social Psychology, 39,* 1161–1178.

Rutherford, G. W., Lifson, A. R., Hessol, N. A., Darrow, W. W., O' Malley, P. M., Buchbinder, S. P., et al. (1990). Course of HIV-1 infection in a cohort of homosexual and bisexual men: An 11-year follow-up study. *British Medical Journal, 301,* 1183–1188.

Rutter, M. (2002). Nature, nurture, and development: From evangelism through science toward policy and practice. *Child Development, 73,* 1–21.

Rutter, M. (2005). Incidence of autism disorders: Changes over time and their meaning. *Acta Paediatrica, 94,* 2–15.

Rutter, M. (2006). *Genes and behavior: Nature-nurture interplay explained.* Malden, MA: Blackwell.

Ruzgis, P. M., & Grigorenko, E. L. (1994). Cultural meaning systems, intelligence and personality. In R. J. Sternberg & P. Ruzgis (Eds.), *Personality and intelligence* (pp. 248–270). New York: Cambridge University Press.

Ryan, G., Baerwald, J., & McGlone, G. (2008). Cognitive mediational deficits and the role of coping styles in pedophile and ephebophile Roman Catholic clergy. *Journal of Clinical Psychology, 64,* 1–16.

Ryan-Harshman, M., & Aldoori, W. (2008). Folic acid and prevention of neural tube defects. *Canadian Family Physician, 54,* 36–38.

Rymer, R. (1993). *Genie: A scientific tragedy.* New York: HarperPerennial.

Saarni, C. (1984). An observational study of children's attempts to monitor their expressive behavior. *Child Development, 55,* 1504–1513.

Saarni, C. (1999). *The development of emotional competence.* New York: Guilford Press.

Sabbagh, L. (2006, August/September). The teen brain, hard at work: No, really. *Scientific American Mind, 17,* 21–25.

Sacco, R. L., Elkind, M., Boden-Albala, B., Lin, I-F., Kargman, D. E., Hause, W. A., et al. (1999). The protective effect of moderate alcohol consumption on ischemic stroke. *Journal of American Medical Association, 281,* 53–60.

Sackeim, H. A., Greenberg, M. S., Weiman, A. L., Gur, R. C., Hungerbuhler, J. P., & Geschwind, N. (1982). Hemispheric asymmetry in the expression of positive and negative emotions: Neurologic evidence. *Archives in Neurology, 39,* 210–218.

Sackeim, H. A., Prudic, J., Devanand, D. P., Kiersky, J. E., Fitzsimons, L., Moody, B. J., et al. (1993). Effects of stimulus intensity and electrode placement on the efficacy and cognitive effects of electroconvulsive therapy. *New England Journal of Medicine, 328,* 839–846.

Sagan, C. (1987). The burden of skepticism. *Skeptical Inquirer, 12,* 38–46.

Sakai, K. (2005). Language acquisition and brain development. *Science, 310,* 815–819.

Salovey, P., and Mayer, J. D. (1990). Emotional intelligence. *Imagination, Cognition, and Personality, 9,* 185–211.

Sapolsky, R. (1998). *Why zebras don't get ulcers: An updated guide to stress, stress-related disease and coping.* New York: Freeman.

Sarchione, C. D., Cuttler, M. J., Muchinsky, P. M., & Nelson-Gray, R. O. (1998). Prediction of dysfunctional job behaviors among law enforcement officers. *Journal of Applied Psychology, 83,* 904–912.

Sarlio-Lähteenkorva, S. (2001). Weight loss and quality of life among obese people. *Social Indicators Research, 54*(3), 329–354.

Sawyer, R. K. (2006). *Explaining creativity: The science of human innovation.* New York: Oxford University Press.

Scarr, S. (1981). *Race, social class, and individual differences in I. Q.* Hillsdale, NJ: Erlbaum.

Schaal, B., Marlier, L., & Soussignan, R. (2002). Human fetuses learn odors from their pregnant mother's diet. *Chemical Senses, 25,* 729–737.

Schacter, D. L. (1987). Implicit memory: History and current status. *Journal of Experimental Psychology: Learning, Memory, and Cognition, 12,* 432–444.

Schacter, D. L. (2001). *The seven sins of memory.* Boston: Houghton Mifflin.

Schacter, D. L., Reiman, E., Curran, T., Yun, L. S., Bandy, D., McDermott, K. B., et al. (1996). Neuroanatomical correlates of veridical and illusory recognition memory: Evidence from positron emission tomography. *Neuron, 17,* 267–274.

Schaefer, E. J., Gleason, J. A., & Dansinger, M. L. (2005). The effects of low-fat, high-carbohydrate diets on plasma lipoproteins, weight loss, and heart disease risk reduction. *Current Atherosclerosis Reports, 7,* 421–427.

Schaie, K. W. (1996). *Intellectual development in adulthood: The Seattle Longitudinal Study.* New York: Cambridge University Press.

Scheier, M. F., Weintraub, J. K., & Carver, C. S. (1989). Coping with stress: Divergent strategies of optimists and pessimists. *Journal of Personality and Social Psychology, 51,* 1257–1264.

Schein, E., & Bernstein, P. (2007). *Identical strangers: A memoir of twins separated and reunited.* New York: Random House.

Schellenberg, E. G. (2006). Long-term positive associations between music lessons and IQ. *Journal of Educational Psychology, 98,* 457–468.

Scherer, K. R., Banse, R., Wallbott. H. G., & Goldbeck. T. (1991). Vocal cues in emotion coding and decoding. *Motivation and Emotion, 15,* 123–148.

Scherer, K. R., Dan, E., & Flykt, A. (2006). What determines a feeling's position in affective space? A case for appraisal. *Cognition & Emotion, 20,* 92–113.

Schienle, A., Schäfer, A., Stark, R., Walter, B., & Vaitl, D. (2005). Gender differences in the processing of disgust- and fear-inducing pictures: An fMRI study. *NeuroReport, 16,* 277–280.

Schienle, A., Schäfer, A., & Vaitl, D. (2008). Individual differences in disgust imagery: A functional magnetic resonance imaging study. *NeuroReport, 19,* 527–530.

Schlaug, G., Jäncke, L., Huang, Y., Staiger, J. F., & Steinmetz H. (1995). Increased corpus callosum size in musicians. *Neuropsychologia, 33,* 1047–1055.

Schmand, B., Smit, J., Lindeboom, J., Smits, C., Hooijer, C., Jonker, C., et al. (1997). Low education is a genuine risk factor for accelerated memory decline and dementia. *Journal of Clinical Epidemiology, 50,* 1025–1033.

Schneider, J. A., Arvanitakis, Z., Bang, W., & Bennett, D. A. (2007). Mixed brain pathologies account for most dementia cases in community-dwelling older persons. *Neurology, 69,* 2197–2204.

Schuldberg, D. (1990). Schizotypal and hypomanic traits, creativity, and psychological health. *Creativity Research Journal, 3,* 218–230.

Schuldberg, D. (2000–2001). Six subclinical spectrum traits in normal creativity. *Creativity Research Journal, 13,* 5–16.

Schuler, J. L. H., & O' Brien, W. H. (1997). Cardiovascular recovery from stress and hypertension risk factors: A meta-analytic review. *Psychophysiology, 34,* 649–659.

Schulkin, J. (Ed.) (2005). *Allostasis, homeostasis, and the costs of physiological adaptation.* New York: Cambridge University Press.

Schultz, W. T. (2005). *Handbook of psychobiography.* New York: Oxford University Press.

Schwartz, G. M., Izard, C. E., & Ansul, S. E. (1985). The 5-month-old's ability to discriminate facial expressions of emotion. *Infant Behavior and Development, 8,* 65–77.

Schwartz, J. H. (2000). Neurotransmitters. In E. R. Kandel, J. M. Schwartz, & T. M. Jessell (Eds.), *Principles of neural science* (4th ed.; pp. 280–297). New York: McGraw-Hill.

Schwartz, J. M. (1997). *Brain lock: Free yourself from obsessive-compulsive behavior.* New York: Harper.

Schwartz, J. M. (1999a). A role for volition and attention in the generation of new brain circuitry: Toward a neurobiology of mental force. *Journal of Consciousness Studies, 6,* 115–142.

Schwartz, J. M. (1999b). First steps toward a theory of mental force: PET imaging of systematic cerebral changes after psychological treatment of obsessive-compulsive disorder. In S. R. Hameroff, A. W. Kaszniak, & D. J. Chalmers (Eds.), *Toward a science of consciousness III: The third Tucson discussions and debates.* Boston: MIT Press.

Schwartz, J. M. (2000). The use of mindfulness in the treatment of obsessive compulsive disorder (OCD). Invited address presented at the Youth Mental Health Conference, New Zealand.

Schwerdtfeger, A. (2007). Individual differences in auditory, pain, and motor stimulation. *Journal of Individual Differences, 28,* 165–177.

Scott, J. (2000). Rational choice theory. In G. Browning, A. Halcli, and F. Webster (Eds.), *Understanding contemporary society: Theories of the present* (pp. 126–138). New York: Sage.

Scott, T. H., Bexton, W. H., Heron, W., & Doane, B. K. (1959). Cognitive effects of perceptual isolation. *Canadian Journal of Psychology, 13,* 200–209.

Scruggs, J. L., Schmidt, D., & Deutch, A. Y. (2003). The hallucinogen 1-[2,5-dimethoxy-4-iodophenyl]-2-aminopropane (DOI) increases cortical extracellular glutamate levels in rats. *Neuroscience Letters, 346*, 137–140.

Scully, J. A., Tosi, H., & Banning, K. (2000). Life event checklists: Reevaluating the social readjustment rating scale after 30 years. *Educational and PsychologicalMeasurement, 60*, 864–876.

Segal, Z. V., Williams, J. M. G., & Teasdale, J. D. (2002). *Mindfulness-based cognitive therapy for depression*. New York: Guilford Press.

Segerstrom, S. C., & Miller, G. E. (2004). Psychological stress and the human immune system: A meta-analytic study of 30 years of inquiry. *Psychological Bulletin, 130*, 601–630.

Seifert, K. L., Hoffnung, R. J., & Hoffnung, M. (2000). *Lifespan development* (2nd ed.). Boston, MA: Houghton Mifflin.

Seligman, M. E. P., & Csikszentmihalyi, M. (2000). Positive psychology: An introduction. *American Psychologist, 55*, 5–14.

Seligman, M. E. P., & Hager, J. L. (Eds.). (1972). *The biological boundaries of learning*. New York: Appleton.

Seligman, M. E. P., Schulman, P., & Tryon, A. M. (2007). Group prevention of depression and anxiety symptoms. *Behaviour Research and Therapy, 45*, 1111–1126.

Selkoe, D. (2002). Alzheimer's disease is a synaptic failure. *Science, 298*(5594), 789–791.

Selye, H. (1946). The general adaptation syndrome and diseases of adaptation. *The Journal of Clinical Endocrinology, 6*, 117–230.

Selye, H. (1976). *The stress of life*. New York: McGraw-Hill.

Selye, H. (1982). History and present status of the stress concept. In L. Goldberger and S. Breznitz (Eds.), *Handbook of Stress: Theoretical and Clinical Aspects* (pp. 7–20). New York: Free Press.

Sen, B., & Swaminathan, S. (2007). Maternal prenatal substance use and behavior problems among children in the U.S. *The Journal of Mental Health Policy and Economics, 10*, 189–206.

Serpell, R. (1982). Measures of perception, skills, and intelligence. In W. W. Hartup (Ed.), *Review of child development research* (Vol. 6, pp. 392–440). Chicago: University of Chicago Press.

Shastry, B. S. (2005). Bipolar disorder: An update. *Neurochemistry International, 46*, 273–279.

Shaw, P., Greenstein, D., Lerch, J. Clasen, L., Lenroot, R., Gogtay, N., et al. (2006). Intellectual ability and cortical development in children and adolescents. *Nature, 440*, 676–679.

Shea, D. L., Lubinski, D., & Benbow, C. P. (2001). Importance of assessing spatial ability in intellectually talented young adolescents: A 20-year longitudinal study. *Journal of Educational Psychology, 93*, 604–614.

Shekelle, R. B., Hulley, S. B., Neston, J. D., Billings, J. H., Borboni, N. O., Gerace, T. A., et al. (1985). The MRFIT behavior pattern study: Type A behavior and incidence of coronary heart disease. *American Journal of Epidemiology, 122*, 559–570.

Shepard, M. (1995). Kraepelin and modern psychiatry. *European Archives of Psychiatry and Clinical Neuroscience, 245*, 189–195.

Shergill, S. S., Brammer, M. J., Fukuda, R., Williams, S. C. R., Murray, R. M., & McGuire, P. K. (2003). Engagement of brain areas implicated in processing inner speech in people with auditory hallucinations. *British Journal of Psychiatry, 182*, 525–531.

Shergill, S. S., Brammer, M. J., Williams, S. C. R., Murray, R. M., & McGuire, P. K. (2000). Mapping auditory hallucinations in schizophrenia using functional magnetic resonance imaging. *Archives of General Psychiatry, 57*, 1033–1038.

Shermer, M. (1997). *Why people believe weird things: Pseudoscience, superstition, and other confusions of our time*. New York: W. H. Freeman.

Shestyuk, A. Y., Deldin, P. J., Brand, J. E., & Deveney, C. M. (2005). Reduced sustained brain activity during processing of positive emotional stimuli in major depression. *Biological Psychiatry, 57*, 1089–1096.

Siegman, A. W., Anderson, R., Herbst, J., Boyle, S., & Wilkinson, J. (1992). Dimensions of anger-hostility and cardiovascular reactivity in provoked and angered men. *Journal of Behavioral Medicine, 15*, 257–272.

Sigman, M., & Hassan, S. (2006). Benefits of long-term group therapy to individuals suffering schizophrenia: A prospective 7-year study. *Bulletin of the Menninger Clinic, 70*, 273–282.

Silbersweig, D. A., Stern, E., Frith, C., Cahill, C., Holmes, A., Grootoonk, S., et al. (1995). A functional neuroanatomy of hallucinations in schizophrenia. *Nature, 378*, 176–179.

Silva, L. M., Cignolini, A., Warren, R., Budden, S., & Skowron-Gooch, A. (2007). Improvement in sensory impairment and social interaction in young children with autism following treatment with an original Qigong massage methodology. *American Journal of Chinese Medicine, 35*, 393–406.

Silvia, P. J. (2006). *Exploring the psychology of interest*. New York: Oxford University Press.

Sime, J. D. (1983). Affiliative behavior during escape to building exits. *Journal of Environmental Psychology, 3*, 21–41.

Simon, H. A. (1978). Information-processing theory of human problem solving. In W. K. Estes (Ed.), *Handbook of learning and cognitive processe: Vol. 5. Human information processing* (pp. 271–295). Hillsdale, NJ: Erlbaum.

Simonds, J., Kieras, J. E., Rueda, M. R., & Rothbart, M. K. (2007). Effortful control, executive attention, and emotional regulation in 7–10-year-old children. *Cognitive Development, 22*, 474–488.

Simons, D. J., & Chabris, C. F. (1999). Gorillas in our midst: Sustained inattentional blindness for dynamic events. *Perception, 28*, 1059–1074.

Simonton, D. K. (1984). *Genius, creativity & leadership: Historiometric inquiries*. Cambridge, MA: Harvard University Press.

Simonton, D. K. (1999). *Origins of genius*. New York: Oxford University Press.

Simpson, K. (2001). The role of testosterone in aggression. *McGill Journal of Medicine, 6*, 32–40.

Singer, T., Seymour, B., O' Doherty, J. O., Kaube, H., Dolan, R. J., & Frith, C. D. (2004). Empathy for pain involves the affective but not sensory components of pain. *Science, 303*, 1157–1162.

Sirignono, S. W., & Lachman, M. E. (1985). Personality change during the transition to parenthood: The role of perceived infant temperament. *Developmental Psychology, 21*, 558–567.

Skinner, B. F. (1938). *The behavior of organisms*. New York: Appleton.

Skinner, B. F. (1953). *Science and human behavior*. New York: Free Press.

Skinner, B. F. (1957). *Verbal behavior*. New York: Appleton-Century-Crofts.

Skinner, B. F. (1979). *The making of a behaviorist*. New York: Knopf.

Skinner, B. F. (1990). Can psychology be a science of mind? *American Psychologist, 45*, 1206–1210.

Slamecka, N. J., & McElree, B. (1983). Normal forgetting of verbal lists as a function of their degree of learning. *Journal of Experimental Psychology: Learning, Memory, & Cognition, 9*, 384–397.

Slater, E., & Meyer, A. (1959). Contributions to a pathography of the musicians: Robert Schumann. *Confinia Psychiatrica, 2*, 65–94.

Sloan, P., Arsenault, L., & Hilsenroth, M. (2002). *Use of the Rorschach in the assessment of war-related stress in military personnel*. Ashland, OH: Hogrefe & Huber.

Smith, C. A., & Ellsworth, P. C. (1987). Patterns of appraisal and emotion related to taking an exam. *Journal of Personality and Social Psychology, 52*, 475–488.

Smith, D. (2006, April 25). Harvard novelist says copying was unintentional. *New York Times*. Retrieved from http://www.nytimes.com

Smith, E. M., & Blalock, J. E. (1988). A molecular basis for interactions between the immune and neuroendocrine systems. *International Journal of Neuroscience, 38,* 455–464.

Smith, M., & Glass, G. (1977). Meta-analysis of psychotherapy outcome studies. *American Psychologist, 32,* 752–760.

Smith, M., & Kollock, P. (Eds). (1999). *Communities in cyberspace.* London: Routledge.

Smith, N., Young, A., & Lee, C. (2004). Optimism, health-related hardiness and well-being among older Australian women. *Journal of Health Psychology, 9,* 741–752.

Smyth, J. M. (1998). Written emotional expression, effect sizes, outcome types, and moderating variables. *Journal of Consulting & Clinical Psychology, 66,* 174–184.

Snarey, J. R. (1985). Cross-cultural universality of social-moral development: A critical review of Kohlbergian research. *Psychological Bulletin, 97,* 202–232.

Snyderman, M., & Rothman, S. (1987). Survey of expert opinion on intelligence and aptitude testing. *American Psychologist, 42,* 137–144.

Solms, M. (2000). Dreaming and REM sleep are controlled by different brain mechanisms. *Behavioral and Brain Sciences, 23,* 843–850.

Solms, M., & O. Turnbull. (2002). *The brain and the inner world: An introduction to the neuroscience of subjective experience.* New York: Other Press.

Solomon, P. R., Adams, F., Silver, A., Zimmer, J., & DeVeaux, R. (2002). Ginkgo for memory enhancement: A randomized controlled trial. *Journal of the American Medical Association, 288,* 835–840.

Song, S. (2006, March 27). Mind over medicine. *Time, 167,* 13.

Sorce, J. F., Emde, R. N., Campos, J., & Klinnert, M. D. (1985). Maternal emotional signaling: Its effect on the visual cliff behavior of 1-year-olds. *Developmental Psychology, 21,* 195–200.

Southwick, S. M., Vythilingam, M., & Charney, D. S. (2005). The psychobiology of depression and resilience to stress: Implications for prevention and treatment. *Annual Review of Clinical Psychology, 1,* 255–291.

Sowell, E. R., Thompson, P. M., Tessner, K. D., & Toga, A. W. (2001). Mapping continued brain growth and gray matter density reduction in dorsal frontal cortex: Inverse relationships during postadolescent brain maturation. *The Journal of Neuroscience, 21,* 8619–8829.

Spalding, K. L., Arner, E., Westermark, P. O., Bernard, S., Buchholz, B. A., Bergmann, O., et al. (2008, June 5). Dynamics of fat cell turnover in humans. *Nature, 453,* 783–787. doi:10.1038/nature06902

Spearman, C. (1904). "General intelligence," objectively determined and measured. *The American Journal of Psychology, 15,* 201–292.

Spearman, C. (1923). *The nature of 'intelligence' and the principles of cognition.* London: Macmillan.

Sperry, R. W., Gazzaniga, M. S., & Bogen, J. E. (1969). Interhemispheric relationships: The neocortical commissures: syndromes of hemisphere disconnection. In P. J. Vinken & G. W. Bruyn (Eds.), *Handbook of clinical neurology* (pp. 273–290). Amsterdam: North-Holland.

Spiegel, D., Bloom, J. R., Kraemer, H. C., & Gottheil, E. (1989). Effect of psychosocial treatment on survival of patients with metastatic breast cancer. *Lancet, 8668,* 88–91.

Spinrad, T. L., Eisenberg, N., Cumberland, A., Fabes, R. A., Valiente, C., Shepard, S. A., et al. (2006). Relation of emotion-related regulation to children's social competence: A longitudinal study. *Emotion, 6,* 498–510.

Spitz, R. A., (1945). Hospitalism: An inquiry into the genesis of psychiatric conditions in early childhood. *Psychoanalytic Study of the Child, 1,* 53–74.

Squire, L. R. (1977). ECT and memory loss. *American Journal of Psychiatry, 134,* 997–1001.

Squire, L. (1987). *Memory and brain.* New York: Oxford University Press.

Stanley, J. (1996). In the beginning: The Study of Mathematically Precocious Youth. In C. P. Benbow & D. Lubinski (Eds.), *Intellectual talent* (pp. 225–235). Baltimore: Johns Hopkins University Press.

Stanton, A. L., Danoff-Burg, S., Sworowski, L. A., Rodriguez-Hanley, A., Kirk, S. B., & Austenfeld, J. L. (2002). Randomized, controlled trial of written emotional expression and benefit finding in breast cancer patients. *Journal of Clinical Oncology, 20,* 4160–4168.

Starr, C., & Taggart, R. (2004). *Biology: The unity and diversity of life* (10th edition). Belmont, CA: Thomson–Brooks Cole.

Stein, D. G., Wright, D. W., & Kellerman, A. L. (in press). Does progesterone have neuroprotective properties? *Annals of Emergency Medicine.*

Steinberg, L. (2008). *Adolescence,* 8th ed. New York: McGraw-Hill.

Steiner, B., Wolf, S., & Kempermann, G. (2006). Adult neurogenesis and neurodegenerative disease. *Regenerative Medicine, 1,* 15–28.

Steinhausen, H., & Spohr, H. (1998). Long-term outcome of children with fetal alcohol syndrome: Psychopathology, behavior, and intelligence. *Alcoholism: Clinical and Experimental Research, 22*(2), 334–338.

Stellar, E. (1954). The physiology of motivation. *Psychological Review, 61,* 5–22.

Stenberg, C. R., Campos, J. J., & Emde, R. (1983). The facial expression of anger in seven-month-old infants. *Child Development, 54,* 178–184.

Sterling, P., & Eyer, J. (1981). Allostasis: A new paradigm to explain arousal pathology. In S. Fisher & H. S. Reason (Eds.), *Handbook of life stress, cognition and health* (pp. 629–649). New York: John Wiley.

Sternberg, R. J. (1985). *Beyond IQ: A triarchic theory of human intelligence.* New York: Cambridge University Press.

Sternberg, R. J. (1986). A triangular theory of love. *Psychological Review, 93,* 119–135.

Sternberg, R. J. (1995). For whom The Bell Curve tolls: A review of *The Bell Curve. Psychological Science, 6,* 257–261.

Sternberg, R. J. (1998). Principles of teaching for successful intelligence. *Educational Psychologist, 55,* 65–72.

Sternberg, R. J. (Ed.). (1999). *Handbook of human creativity.* Cambridge, England: Cambridge University Press.

Sternberg, R. J. (2000). The concept of intelligence. In. R. J. Sternberg (Ed.), *The handbook of intelligence* (pp. 3–15). Cambridge: Cambridge University Press.

Sternberg, R. J. (2003). A broad view of intelligence: A theory of successful intelligence. *Consulting Psychology Journal: Practice and Research, 55,* 139–154.

Sternberg, R. J. (Ed.). (2004). *Definitions and conceptions of giftedness.* Thousand Oaks, CA: Corwin Press.

Sternberg, R. J. (2005). The triarchic theory of successful intelligence. In D. P. Flanagan & P. L. Harrison (Eds.), *Contemporary intellectual assessment: Theories, tests, and issues* (pp. 103–119). New York: Guilford Press.

Sternberg, R. J. (2006a). *Cognitive psychology* (4th ed.). Belmont: CA: Thomson-Wadsworth.

Sternberg, R. J. (2006b). The Rainbow Project: Enhancing the SAT through assessments of analytical, practical, and creative skills. *Intelligence, 34,* 321–350.

Sternberg, R. J., & Detterman, D. K. (Eds.). (1986). *What is intelligence? Contemporary viewpoints on its nature and definition.* Norwood, NJ: Ablex.

Sternberg, R. J., Grigorenko, E. L., & Kidd, K. K. (2005). Intelligence, race, and genetics. *American Psychologist, 60,* 46–59.

Sternberg, R. J., & O'Hara, L. (1999). Creativity and intelligence. In R. J. Sternberg (Ed.), *Handbook of creativity* (pp. 251–272). New York: Cambridge University Press.

Stevens, S. B., & Morris, T. L. (2007). College dating and social anxiety: Using the

Internet as a means of connecting to others. *CyberPsychology & Behavior, 10,* 680–688.

Stewart, F. (2000). Internet acceptable use policies: Navigating the management, legal, and technical issues. *Information Systems Security, 9,* 46–53.

Stewart, J. H. (2005). Hypnosis in contemporary medicine. *Mayo Clinic Proceedings, 80,* 511–524.

Stewart, R. A., Rule, A. C., & Giordano, D. A. (2007). The effect of fine motor skill activities on kindergarten attention. *Early Childhood Education Journal, 35,* 103–109.

Stewart, V. M. (1973). Tests of the "carpentered world" hypothesis by race and environment in America and Zambia. *International Journal of Psychology, 8,* 83–94.

Stickgold, R. (2005). Sleep-dependent memory consolidation. *Nature, 437,* 1272–1278.

Stickgold, R., & Walker, M. P. (2007). Sleep-dependent memory consolidation and reconsolidation. *Sleep Medicine, 8,* 331–343.

Storch, E. A., Abramowitz, J., & Goodman, W. K. (2008). Where does obsessive-compulsive disorder belong in DSM-V? *Depression and Anxiety, 25,* 336–347.

Strack, F., Martin, L. L., & Stepper, S. (1988). Inhibiting and facilitating conditions of the human smile: A nonobtrusive test of the facial feedback hypothesis. *Journal of Personality and Social Psychology, 54,* 768–777.

Strassman, R. J. (1984). Adverse reactions to psychedelic drugs. A review of the literature. *Journal of Nervous and Mental Disease, 172,* 577–595.

Strauss, M. E., Pasupathi, M., & Chatterjee, A. (1993). Concordance between observers in descriptions of personality change in Alzheimer's disease. *Psychology and Aging, 8,* 475–480.

Strayer, D. L., & Drews, F. A. (2007). Cell-phone-induced driver distraction. *Current Directions in Psychological Science, 16,* 128–131.

Strayer, D. L., Drews, F. A., & Couch, D. J. (2006). A comparison of the cell phone driver and the drunk driver. *Human Factors, 48,* 381–391.

Streissguth, A., Barr, H., Sampson, P., Darby, B., & Martin, D. (1989). IQ at age 4 in relation to maternal alcohol use and smoking during pregnancy. *Developmental Psychology, 25*(1), 3–11.

Stroop, J. R. (1935). Studies of interference in serial-verbal reaction. *Journal of Experimental Psychology, 18,* 643–662.

Strueber, D., Lueck, M., & Roth, G. (2006–2007). The violent brain. *Scientific American Mind, 17,* 20–27.

Styles, E. A. (2006). *The psychology of attention* (2nd ed.). Hove, England: Psychology Press.

Styron, W. (1990). *Darkness visible: A memoir of madness.* New York: Vintage.

Suarez, E. C., Harlan, E., Peoples, M. C., Williams, R. B., Jr. (1993). Cardiovascular reactivity and emotional responses in women: The role of hostility and harassment. *Health Psychology, 12,* 459–468.

Suarez, E. C., & Williams, R. B., Jr. (1989). Situational determinants of cardiovascular and emotional reactivity in high and low hostile men. *Psychosomatic Medicine, 51,* 404–418.

Suarez, E. C., Bates, M. P., & Harralson, T. L. (1998). The relation of hostility to lipids and lipoproteins in women: Evidence for the role of antagonistic hostility. *Annals of Behavioral Medicine, 20,* 59–63.

Subotnik, R. F., Duschl, R. A., & Selmon, E. H. (1993). Retention and attrition of science talent: A longitudinal study of Westinghouse Science Talent winners. *International Journal of Science Education, 15,* 61–72.

Subrahmanyam, K., & Greenfield, P. (2008). Online communication and adolescent relationships. *The Future of Children, 18,* 119–146.

Sullivan, K., Zaitchik, D., & Tager-Flusberg, H. (1994). Preschoolers can attribute second-order beliefs. *Developmental Psychology, 30,* 395–402.

Suomi, S. (2005). Genetic and environmental factors influencing the expression of impulsive aggression and serotonergic functioning in rhesus monkeys. In R. E. Tremblay, W. W. Hartup, & J. Archer (Eds.), *Developmental origins of aggression* (pp. 63–82). New York: Guilford Press.

Susskind, J. M., Lee, D. H., Cusi, A., Feiman, R., Grabski, W., & Anderson, A. K. (2008). Expressing fear enhances sensory acquisition. *Nature Neuroscience, 11,* 843–850.

Swets, J. A. (1964). *Signal detection and recognition by human observers.* New York: Wiley.

Tafti, M., Dauvilliers, Y., & Overeem, S. (2007). Narcolepsy and familial advanced sleep-phase syndrome: Molecular genetics of sleep disorders. *Current Opinion in Genetics & Development, 17,* 222–227.

Takahashi, Y., Yamagata, S., Kijima, N., Shigemasu, K., Ono, Y., & Ando, J. (2007). Continuity and change in behavioral inhibition and activation systems: A longitudinal behavioral genetic study. *Personality and Individual Differences, 43*(6), 1616–1625.

Talassi, E., Cipriani, G., Bianchetti, A., & Trabucchi, M. (2007). Personality changes in Alzheimer's disease. *Aging & Mental Health, 11,* 526–531.

Talmi, D., Grady, C. L., Goshen-Gottstein, Y., & Moscovitch, M. (2005). Neuroimaging the serial position curve: A test of single-store versus dual-store models. *Psychological Science, 16,* 717–723.

Tambs, K., Hoffman, H. J., Borchgrevink, H. M., Holmen, J., & Engdahl, B. (2006). Hearing loss induced by occupational and impulse noise: Results on threshold shifts by frequencies, age and gender from the Nord-Trøndelag Hearing Loss Study. *International Journal of Audiology, 45,* 309–317.

Tammet, D. (2006). *Born on a blue day: A memoir.* New York: Free Press.

Tangney, J. P., Stuewig, J., & Mashek, D. J. (2007). Moral emotions and moral behavior. *Annual Review of Psychology, 58,* 345–372.

Tardif, T., Gelman, S., & Xu, F. (1999). Putting the "noun bias" in context: A comparison of English and Mandarin. *Developmental Psychology, 70,* 620–635.

Tarmann, A. (2002, May/June). Out of the closet and onto the Census long form. *Population Today, 30,* 1, 6.

Tashkin, D. (2006, May 23). *Marijuana smoking not linked to lung cancer.* Paper presented at the annual meeting of the American Thoracic Society, San Diego, CA.

Tashkin, D. R., Baldwin, G. C., Sarafian, T., Dubinett, S., Roth, M. D. (2002). Respiratory and immunologic consequences of marijuana smoking. *Journal of Clinical Pharmacology, 42,* S71–S81.

Taylor, S. E. (1989). *Positive illusions: Creative self-deception and the healthy mind.* New York: Basic Books.

Taylor, S. E. (2006). *Health psychology* (6th ed.). New York: McGraw-Hill.

Taylor, S. E., Kemeny, M. E., Reed, G. M., Bower, J. E., & Gruenewald, T. L. (2000). Psychological resources, positive illusions, and health. *American Psychologist, 55,* 99–109.

Teasdale, G., & Jennett, B. (1976). Assessment and prognosis of coma after head injury. *Acta Neurochirurgica, 34,* 45–55.

Teasdale, J. D., Segal, Z. V., & Williams, J. M. G. (1995). How does cognitive therapy prevent depressive relapse and why should attentional control (mindfulness) training help? *Behaviour Research and Therapy, 33,* 25–39.

Teasdale, J. D., Segal, Z., Williams, M. G., Ridgeway, V. A., Soulsby, J. M., & Lau, M. A. (2000). Prevention of relapse/recurrence in major depression by mindfulness-based cognitive therapy. *Journal of Consulting and Clinical Psychology, 68,* 615–623.

Teen Scientists Move to Finals in Prestigious Competition (2005, January 26). Retrieved August 2, 2007, from http://www.sciserv .org/sts/press/20050126.asp

Tellegen, A., Ben-Porath, Y. S., McNulty, J. L., Arbisi, P. A., Graham, J. R., & Kaemmer, B. (2003). *The MMPI-2 Restructured*

Clinical Scales: Development, validation, and interpretation. Minneapolis: University of Minnesota Press.

Tellegen, A., Lykken, D. T., Bouchard, T. J., Wilcox, K. J., Segal, N. L., & Rich, S. (1988). Personality similarity in twins reared apart and together. *Journal of Personality and Social Psychology, 54,* 1031–1039.

Terrace, H. S. (1987). *Nim: A chimpanzee who learned sign language.* New York: Columbia University Press.

Test Developer Profiles (2001). Retrieved July 15, 2007, from http://www.mhhe.com/mayfieldpub/psychtesting/profiles/karfmann.htm

Thagard, P. (2005). *Mind: An introduction to cognitive science* (2nd ed.). Cambridge, MA: MIT Press.

Thibaut, J. W., & Kelley, H. H. (1959). *The social psychology of groups.* New York: Wiley.

Thomas, A., & Chess, S. (1977). *Temperament and development.* New York: Brunner/Mazel.

Thomasius, R., Zapletalova, P., Petersen, K., Buchert, R., Andresen, B., Wartberg, L., et al. (2006). Mood, cognition and serotonin transporter availability in current and former ecstasy (MDMA) users: The longitudinal perspective. *Journal of Psychopharmacology, 20,* 211–225.

Thompson, P. M., Giedd, J. N., Woods, R. P., MacDonald, D., Evans, A. C., & Toga, A. W. (2000). Growth patterns in the developing brain using continuum mechanical tensor maps. *Nature, 404,* 190–193.

Thompson, R. F., & Madigan, S. A. (2005). *Memory: The key to consciousness.* Washington, DC: Joseph Henry Press.

Thompson, W. L., & Kosslyn, S. M. (2000). Neural systems activated during visual mental imagery. In A. W. Toga & J. C. Mazziotta (Eds.), *Brain mapping: The systems* (pp. 535–560). San Diego: Academic Press, 2000.

Thorndike, E. L. (1905). *Elements of psychology.* New York: Seiler.

Thune, I., & Furberg, A. S. (2001). Physical activity and cancer risk: Dose-response and cancer, all sites and site specific. *Medicine and Science in Sports and Exercise, 33,* S530–S550.

Thurstone, E. L. (1938). *Primary mental abilities.* Chicago: University of Chicago Press.

Tobias, S., & Everson, H. T. (2002). *Knowing what you know and what you don't: Further research on metacognitive knowledge monitoring.* New York: College Entrance Examination Board.

Todd, P. M., & Gigerenzer, G. (2007). Environments that make us smart. *Current Directions in Psychological Science, 16,* 167–171.

Tolman, E. C., & Honzik, C. H. (1930). Introduction and removal of reward, and maze performance in rats. *University of California Publications in Psychology, 4,* 257–275.

Tomkins, S. S. (1962). *Affect, imagery, consciousness: Vol. 1. The positive affects.* New York: Springer.

Tomkins, S. S. (1981). The quest for primary motives: Biography and autobiography of an idea. *Journal of Personality and Social Psychology, 41,* 306–329.

Tomkins, S. S., & McCarter, R. (1964). What and where are the primary affects? Some evidence for a theory. *Perceptual and Motor Skills, 18,* 119–158.

Tooby, J., & Cosmides, L. (1990). The past explains the present: Emotional adaptations and the structure of ancestral environments. *Ethology and Sociobiology, 11,* 375–424.

Tooby, J., & Cosmides, L. (1992). The psychological foundations of culture. In J. H. Barkow, L. Cosmides, & J. Tooby (Eds.), *The adapted mind: Evolutionary psychology and the generation of culture* (pp. 19–136). New York: Oxford University Press.

Tracy, J. L., & Matsumoto, D. M. (2008). The spontaneous display of pride and shame: Evidence for biologically innate nonverbal displays. *Proceedings of the National Academy of Science, 105,* 11655–11660.

Tracy, J. L., & Robins, R. W. (2007). Emerging insights into the nature and function of pride. *Current Directions in Psychological Science, 16,* 147–150.

Tracy, J. L., & Robins, R. W. (2008). The nonverbal expression of pride: Evidence for cross-cultural recognition. *Journal of Personality and Social Psychology, 94,* 516–530.

Tracy, J. L., Robins, R. W., & Tangney, J. P. (2007). *The self-conscious emotions: Theory and research.* New York: Guilford Press.

Transcripts of "Secrets of the Wild Child." (1997). Retrieved from http://www.pbs.org/wgbh/nova/transcripts/2112gchild.html

Treffert, D. A. (2006). *Extraordinary people: Understanding savant syndrome.* Updated version. Lincoln, NE: iUniverse Inc.

Treffert, D. A., & Christensen, D. D. (2005). Inside the mind of a savant. *Scientific American, 293,* 108–113.

Treisman, A. (1964). Verbal cues, language and meaning in selective attention. *American Journal of Psychology, 77,* 206–209.

Tremblay, K., & Ross, B. (2007). Effects of age and age-related hearing loss on the brain. *Journal of Communication Disorders, 40,* 305–312.

Trentacosta, C. J., & Izard, C. E. (2007). Kindergarten children's emotion competence as a predictor of their academic competence in first grade. *Emotion, 7,* 77–88.

Triandis, H. C. (1990). Cross-cultural studies of individualism and collectivism. In J. J. Herman (Ed.), *Nebraska Symposium on Motivation 1989, 37,* 41–133.

Triplett, N. (1898). The dynamogenic factors in pacemaking and competition. *American Journal of Psychology, 9,* 507–533.

Trivers, R. L. (1971). The evolution of reciprocal altruism. *Quarterly Review of Biology, 46,* 35–57.

Trivers, R. L. (1972) Parental investment and sexual selection. In B. Campbell (Ed.), *Sexual selection and the descent of man, 1871–1971* (pp. 136–179). Chicago: Aldine.

Trivers, R. L. (1985). *Social evolution.* Menlo Park, CA: Benjamin/Cummings.

Troisi, A. (2003). Psychopathology. In D. Maestripieri (Ed.), *Primate psychology* (pp. 451–470). Cambridge, MA: Harvard University Press.

Tronick, E., Morelli, G. A., & Ivey, P. K. (1992). The Efe forager infant and toddler's pattern of social relationships: Multiple and simultaneous. *Developmental Psychology, 28,* 568–577.

Trucking stats and FAQ's. (n.d.). Retrieved January 20, 2007, from http://www.geocities.com/TheTropics/1608/stats.htm

Trugman, J. M. (1998). Tardive dyskinesia: Diagnosis, pathogenesis, pathogenesis, and management. *Neurologist, 4,* 180–187.

Tsai, J. L., & Chentsova-Dutton, Y. (2003). Variation among European Americans in emotional facial expression. *Journal of Cross-Cultural Psychology, 34,* 650–657.

Tsai, J. L., Chentsova-Dutton, Y., Friere-Bebeau, L., & Przymus, D. E. (2002). Emotional expression and physiology in European Americans and Hmong Americans. *Emotion, 2,* 380–397.

Tsai, J. L., Levenson, R. W., & Carstensen, L. L. (2000). Autonomic, expressive, and subjective responses to emotional films in older and younger Chinese American and European American adults. *Psychology and Aging, 15,* 684–693.

Tsakiris, M., Hesse, M. D., Boy, C., Haggard, P., & Fink, G. R. (2007). Neural signatures of body ownership: A sensory network for bodily self-consciousness. *Cerebral Cortex 17,* 2235—2244.

Tseng, W. S. (1973). The development of psychiatric concepts in traditional Chinese medicine. *Archives of General Psychiatry, 29,* 569–575.

Tugade, M. M., & Fredrickson, B. L. (2004). Resilient individuals use positive emotions to bounce back from negative emotional experiences. *Journal of Personality and Social Psychology, 86,* 320–333.

Tulku, T. (1984). *Knowledge of freedom.* Berkeley, CA: Dharma.

Tulving, E. (1972). Episodic and semantic memory. In E. Tulving & W. Donaldson (Eds.), *Organization of memory* (pp. 381–403). New York: Academic Press.

Tulving, E. (1985). How many memory systems are there? *American Psychologist, 40,* 385–398.

Turner-Shea, Y., Bruno, R., & Pridmore, S. (2006). Daily and spaced treatment with transcranial magnetic stimulation in major depression: A pilot study. *Australian and New Zealand Journal of Psychiatry, 40,* 759–763.

Tversky, A., & Kahneman, D. (1974). Judgment under uncertainty: Heuristics and biases. *Science, 185,* 1124–1131.

Tversky, A., & Kahneman, D. (1983). Extensional versus intuitive reasoning: The conjunction fallacy in probability judgment. *Psychological Review, 90,* 293–315.

Tyron, W. W. (2005). Possible mechanisms for why desensitization and exposure therapy work. *Clinical Psychology Review, 25,* 67–95.

Udry, J. R., Morris, N. M., & Waller, L. (1973). Effect of contraceptive pills on sexual activity in the luteal phase of the human menstrual cycle. *Archives of Sexual Behavior, 2,* 205–214.

U.S. Department of Health and Human Services (USDHHS). (2004). *The health consequences of smoking: A report of the Surgeon General.* Atlanta, GA: Author.

U.S. Senate. (2004). Report of the Select Committee on Intelligence on the U.S. Intelligence Community's Prewar Intelligence Assessments on Iraq. Retrieved from http://www.gpoaccess.gov/serialset/creports/iraq.html

Uylings, H. B. M. (2006). Development of the human cortex and the concept of "critical" or "sensitive" periods. *Language Learning, 56,* 59–90.

Vaish, A., & Striano, T. (2004). Is visual reference necessary? Contributions of facial versus vocal cues in 12-month-olds' social referencing behavior. *Developmental Science, 7,* 261–269.

Valente, M., Placid, F., Oliveira, A. J., Bigagli, A., Morghen, I., Proietti, R., & Gigli, G. L. (2002). Sleep organization pattern as a prognostic marker at the subacute stage of post-traumatic coma. *Clinical Neurophysiology, 113,* 1798–1805.

Valkenburg, P. M., & Peter, J. (2007). Who visits online dating sites? Exploring some characteristics of online daters. *Cyber-Psychology & Behavior, 10,* 849–852.

Valois, R. F., Zullig, K. J., Huebner, E. S., & Drane, J. W. (2003). Dieting behaviors, weight perceptions, and life satisfaction among public high school adolescents. *Eating Disorders, 11,* 271–288.

van IJzendoorn, M., & Juffer, F. (2005). Adoption is a successful natural intervention enhancing adopted children's IQ and school performance. *Current Directions in Psychological Science, 14,* 326–330.

van Praag, H., Kempermann, G., & Gage, F. H. (1999). Running increases cell proliferation and neurogenesis in the adult mouse dentate gyrus. *Nature Neuroscience, 2,* 266–270.

Van Voorhees, B. W., Paunesku, D., Kuwabara, S. A., Basu, A., Gollan, J., Hankin, B. L., et al. (2008). Protective and vulnerability factors predicting new-onset depressive episode in a representative of U. S. adolescents. *Journal of Adolescent Health, 42,* 605–616.

van Vugt, M., & van Lange, P. A. M. (2006). The altruism puzzle: Psychological adaptations for prosocial behavior. In M. Schaller, D. T. Kenrick, & J. A. Simpson (Eds.), *Evolution and social psychology* (pp. 237–261). New York: Psychology Press.

Van Wyk, P. H., & Geist, C. S. (1984). Psychosocial development of heterosexual, bisexual and homosexual behavior. *Archives of Sexual Behavior, 13,* 505–544.

Vaswani, M., Linda, F. K., & Ramesh, S. (2003). Role of selective serotonin reuptake inhibitors in psychiatric disorders: A comprehensive review. *Progress in Neuro-Psychopharmacology and Biological Psychiatry, 2,* 85–102.

Vazire, S., & Gosling, S. D. (2004). E-perceptions: Personality impressions based on personal websites. *Journal of Personality and Social Psychology, 87,* 123–132.

Vedantum, S. (2005, January 23). See no bias. *The Washington Post.*

Veith, I. (1965). *Hysteria: The history of a disease.* Chicago: University of Chicago Press.

Vetter, H. J. (1968). New-word coinage in the psychopathological context. *Psychiatric Quarterly, 42,* 298–312.

Vitello, P. (2006, June 12). A ringtone meant to fall on deaf ears. *New York Times.* Retrieved from http://www.nytimes.com

Wadlinger, H. A., & Isaacowitz, D. M. (2006). Positive mood broadens visual attention to positive stimuli. *Motivation & Emotion, 30,* 89–101.

Wagner, A. W., & Linehan, M. M. (2006). Applications of dialectical behavior therapy to posttraumatic stress disorder and related problems. In V. M. Folette & J. I. Ruzek (Eds.), *Cognitive–behavioral therapies for trauma* (2nd ed.; pp. 117–145). New York: Guilford Press.

Wagner, T. D., & Ochsner, K. N. (2005). Sex differences in the emotional brain. *Neuro-Report, 16,* 85–87.

Wahlbeck, K., Forsen, T., Osmond, C., Barker, D. J. P., & Erikkson, J. G. (2001). Association of schizophrenia with low maternal body mass index, small size at birth, and thinness during childhood. *Archives of General Psychiatry, 58,* 48–55.

Wakimoto, S., & Fujihara, T. (2004). The correlation between intimacy and objective similarity in interpersonal relationships. *Social Behavior and Personality, 32,* 95–102.

Waldinger, M. D., Zwinderman, A. H., Schweitzer, D. H., & Olivier, B. (2004). Relevance of methodological design for the interpretation of efficacy of drug treatment of premature ejaculation: A systematic review and meta-analysis. *International Journal of Impotence Research, 16,* 369–381.

Walker, M. P., & Stickgold, R. (2006). Sleep, memory and plasticity. *Annual Review of Psychology, 57,* 139–166.

Walker, R. W., Skowronski, J. J., Thompson, C. P. (2003). Life is pleasant—and memory helps to keep it that way. *Review of General Psychology, 7,* 203–210.

Wallace, B. A. (2006). *The attention revolution: Unlocking the power of the focused mind.* Boston: Wisdom.

Wallas, G. (1926). *The art of thought.* New York: Harcourt & Brace.

Wallhagen, M. I., Strawbridge, W. J., Cohen, R. D., & Kaplan, G. A. (1997). An increasing prevalence of hearing impairment and associated risk factors over three decades of Alameda County Study. *American Journal of Public Health, 87,* 440–442.

Walther, E., Bless, H., Strack, F., Rackstraw, P., Wagner, D., & Werth, L. (2002). Conformity effects in memory as a function of group size, dissenters, and uncertainty. *Applied Cognitive Psychology, 16,* 793–810.

Wang, S., Zhang, Z., Guo, Y., Teng, G., & Chen, B. (2008). Hippocampal neurogenesis and behavioural studies on adult ischemic rat response to chronic mild stress. *Behavioural Brain Research, 189,* 9–16.

Warga, C. (1987). Pain's gatekeeper. *Psychology Today, 21,* 50–59.

Wason, P. C. (1960). On the failure to eliminate hypotheses in a conceptual task. *Quarterly Journal of Experimental Psychology, 12,* 129–140.

Wasserman, J. D., & Tulsky, D. S. (2005). A history of intelligence assessment. In D. P. Flanagan & P. L. Harrison (Eds.). *Contemporary intellectual assessment: Theories, tests, and issues* (pp. 3–38). New York: Guilford Press.

Waterland, R., & Jirtle, R. L. (2003). Transposable elements: Targets for early nutritional effects on epigenetic gene regulation. *Molecular and Cellular Biology, 23,* 5293–5300.

Watkins, L. R., & Maier, S. F. (2003). When good pain turns bad. *Current Directions in Psychological Science, 12,* 232–236.

Watson, D., & Tellegen, A. (1985). Toward a consensual structure of mood. *Psychological Bulletin, 98,* 219–235.

Watson, J. B. (1925). Behaviorism. New York: Norton.

Watson, J. B., & Rayner, R. (1920). Conditioned emotional reactions. *Journal of Experimental Psychology, 3,* 1–14.

Watters, E. (2006, November 22). DNA is not destiny. *Discover.* Retrieved from http://discovermagazine.com

Waxenberg, S. E., Drellich, M. G., & Sutherland, A. M. (1959). The role of hormones in human behavior: I. Changes in female sexual after adrenalectomy. *Journal of Clinical Endocrinology and Metabolism, 19,* 193–202.

Weaver, D. (1998). The suprachiasmatic nucleus: A 25-year retrospective. *Journal of Biological Rhythms, 13,* 100–112.

Weaver, I. C. G., Cervoni, N., Champagne, F. A. (2004). Epigenetic programming by maternal behavior. *Nature Neuroscience, 7,* 847–854.

Weber, J., & Wahl, J. (2006). Neurological aspects of trepanations from Neolithic times. *International Journal of Osteoarchaeology, 16,* 536–545.

Wechsler, D. (1944). *Measurement of adult intelligence* (3rd ed.). Baltimore: Williams & Wilkins.

Wechsler, D. (1958). *The measurement and appraisal of adult intelligence* (4th ed.). Baltimore: Williams & Wilkins.

Wechsler, H. L., Lee, J. E., & Kuo, M. (2002). Trends in college binge drinking during a period of increased prevention efforts. *Journal of American College Health, 50,* 203–217.

Weil, A., & Rosen, W. (1998). *From chocolate to morphine.* New York: Houghton Mifflin.

Weinberg, R. A. (1989). Intelligence and IQ: Issues and great debates. *American Psychologist, 44,* 98–104.

Weinberg, R. S., & Gould, D. (1999). *Foundations of sport and exercise psychology* (2nd ed.). Champaign, IL: Human Kinetics.

Weinberger, D. R., Egan, M. F., Bertolino, A., Callicott, J. H., Mattay, V. S., Lipska, B. K., Berman, K. F., & Goldberg, T. E. (2001). Prefrontal neurons and the genetics of schizophrenia. *Biological Psychiatry, 50,* 825–844.

Weinberger, M., Hiner, S. L., Tierney, W. M. (1987). In support of hassles as a measure of stress in predicting health outcomes. *Journal of Behavioral Medicine, 10,* 19–31.

Weinhardt, L. S. (2005). Changing HIV and AIDS-related behavior: Promising approaches at the individual, group, and community levels. *Behavior Modification, 29,* 219–226.

Weisinger, R., Denton, D., McKinley, M., & Miselis, R. (1993, November). Forebrain lesions that disrupt water homeostasis do not eliminate the sodium appetite of sodium deficiency in sheep. *Brain Research, 628*(1), 166–178.

Weissberg, R. P. (2005, August 20). *Social and emotional learning for school and life success.* Talk presented at the 113th Annual Convention of the American Psychological Association, Washington, DC.

Wenden, A. L. (1998). Metacognitive knowledge and language learning. *Applied Linguistics, 19,* 515–537.

Wermke, M., Sorg, C., Wohlschläger, A. M., & Drzezga, A. (2008, February 26). A new integrative model of cerebral activation, deactivation and default mode function in Alzheimer's disease. *European Journal of Nuclear Medicine and Molecular Imaging.* Advance online publication. doi:10.1007/s00259-007-0698-5

Wertheimer, M. (1959). *Productive thinking.* New York: Harper.

Wessely, S., & Kerwin, R. (2004). Suicide risk and the SSRIs. *Journal of the American Medical Association, 292,* 379–381.

Westmaas, J. L., & Silver, R. C. (2006). The role of perceived similarity in supportive responses to victims of negative life events. *Personality and Social Psychology Bulletin, 32,* 1537–1546.

Weston, D. (1998). The scientific legacy of Sigmund Freud: Toward a psychodynamically informed psychological science. *Psychological Bulletin, 124,* 333–371.

Whalen, C. K., & Henker, B. (1998). Attention-deficit/hyperactivity disorder. In T. H. Ollendick & M. Hersen (Eds.), *Handbook of child psychopathology* (pp. 181–212). New York: Plenum Press.

What causes Down syndrome. (2007). National Down Syndrome Society. Retrieved July 20, 2007, from http://www.ndss.org/index.php?option=com_content&task=category&sectionid=23&id=56&Itemid=234

White, A. M. (2003, Spring). What happened? Alcohol, memory blackouts, and the brain. *Alcohol Research & Health,* 186–196.

White, P. (2006). A background to acupuncture and its use in chronic painful musculoskeletal conditions. *Journal of the Royal Society of Health, 126,* 219–227.

White, R. (1964). *The abnormal personality.* New York: Ronald Press.

Whiten, A., Horner, V., & de Waal, F. B. M. (2005). Conformity to cultural norms of tool use in chimpanzees. *Nature, 437,* 737–740.

Whitfield, C. L., Dube, S. R., Felitti, V. J., & Anda, R. E. (2005). Adverse childhood experiences and hallucinations. *Child Abuse and Neglect, 29,* 797–810.

Whiting, B., & Edwards, C. (1988). *Children of different worlds: The formation of social behavior.* Cambridge, MA: Harvard University Press.

Whorf, B. L. (1956). *Language, thought, and reality: Selected writings of Benjamin Lee Whorf* (J. B. Carroll, Ed.). Cambridge, MA: MIT Press.

Wiederhold, B. K., & Wiederhold, M. D. (2005). Specific phobias and social phobia. In B. K. Wiederhold & M. D. Wiederhold (Eds.), *Virtual reality therapy for anxiety disorders: Advances in evaluation and treatment* (pp. 125–138). Washington, DC: American Psychological Association.

Wilensky, A., Schafe, G., Kristensen, M., & LeDoux, J. (2006). Rethinking the fear circuit: The central nucleus of the amygdala is required for the acquisition, consolidation, and expression of Pavlovian fear conditioning. *Journal of Neuroscience, 26*(48), 12387–12396.

Wilhelm, K., Mitchell, P. B., Niven, H., Finch, A., Wedgewood, L., Scimone, A., et al. (2006). Life events, first depression onset and the serotonin transporter gene. *British Journal of Psychiatry, 188,* 210–215.

Williams, G., Cai, X. J., Elliot, J. C., & Harrold, J. A. (2004). Anabolic neuropeptides. *Physiology and Behavior, 81,* 211–222.

Williams, J. H. G., Waiter, G. D., Gilchrist, A., Perrett, D. I., Murray, A. D., & Whiten, A. (2006). Neural mechanisms of imitation and "mirror neuron" functioning in autistic spectrum disorder. *Neuropsychologia, 44,* 610–621.

Williams, K. D., & Zudro, L., (2001). Ostracism: On being ignored, excluded, and rejected. In M. R. Leary (Ed.), *Interpersonal rejection* (pp. 21–53). New York: Oxford University Press.

Williams, R., Briggs, R., & Coleman, P. (1995). Carer-rated personality changes associated with senile dementia. *International Journal of Geriatric Psychiatry, 10,* 231–236.

Williams, R. B., Jr., Haney, T. L., Lee, K. L., Kong, Y., Blumenthal, J. A., & Whalen, R. (1980). Type A behavior, hostility, coronary atherosclerosis. *Psychosomatic Medicine, 42,* 539–549.

Willis, S. L., Tennstedt, S. L., Marsiske, M., Ball, K., Elias, J., Koepke, K. M., et al. for the ACTIVE Study Group. (2006). Long-term effects of cognitive training on everyday functional outcomes in older adults. *Journal of the American Medical Association, 295,* 2805–2814.

Wimmer, H., & Perner, J. (1983). Beliefs about beliefs: Representation and constraining function of wrong beliefs in young children's understanding of deception. *Cognition, 13,* 103–128.

Winawer, J., Witthoft, N., Frank, M. C., Wu, L., Wade, A. R., & Boroditsky, L. (2007). Russian blues reveal effect of language on color discrimination. *Proceedings of the National Academy of Science, 104,* 7780–7785.

Wing, L., & Potter, D. (2002). The epidemiology of autistic spectrum disorders: Is the prevalence rising? *Mental Retardation and Mental Disabilities Research Review, 8,* 151–161.

Witkin, H. A., & Asch, S. E. (1948). Studies in space orientation. IV. Further experiments on perception of the upright with displaced visual fields. *Journal of Experimental Psychology, 38,* 762–782.

Witte, K., & Allen, M. (2000). A meta-analysis of fear appeals: Implications for effective public health campaigns. *Health Education & Behavior, 27,* 591–615.

Wölfling, K., Flor, H., & Grüsser, S. M. (2008). Psychophysiological responses to drug-associated stimuli in chronic heavy cannabis use. *European Journal of Neuroscience, 27,* 976–983.

Wood, J. M., & Lilienfeld, S. O. (1999). The Rorschach inkblot test: A case of overstatement? *Assessment, 6,* 341–351.

Woodworth, R. S., & Schlosberg, H. (1954). *Experimental psychology* (Rev. ed.). New York: Henry Holt.

World's greatest living polyglot. (n.d.). Retrieved May 31, 2007, from http://www.spidra.com/fazah.html

Wouters-Adriaens, M., & Westerterp, K. (2006). Basal metabolic rate as a proxy for overnight energy expenditure: The effect of age. *British Journal of Nutrition, 95,* 1166–1170.

Wright, D. W., Kellerman, A. L., Hertzberg, V. S., Clark, P. L., Frankel, M., Goldstein, F. C., et al. (2007). ProTECT: A randomized clinical trial of progesterone for acute traumatic brain injury. *Annals of Emergency Medicine, 49,* 391–402.

Wurtz, R. H., & Kandel, E. R. (2000a). Central visual pathways. In E. R. Kandel, J. H. Schwartz, & T. M. Jessell. (2000). *Principles of Neural Science* (4th ed.; pp. 523–545). New York: McGraw-Hill.

Wurtz, R. H., & Kandel, E. R. (2000b). Perception of motion, depth, and form. In E. R. Kandel, J. H. Schwartz, & T. M. Jessell (Eds.). *Principles of neural science* (4th ed.; pp. 548–571). New York: McGraw-Hill.

Yamada, M., & Yasuhara, H. (2004). Clinical pharmacology of MAO inhibitors: Safety and future. *NeuroToxicology, 25,* 215–221.

Yerkes, R. M., & Dodson, J. D. (1908). The relation of strength of stimulus to rapidity of habit-formation. *Journal of Comparative Neurology and Psychology, 18,* 459–482.

Yin, J. C. P., Del Vecchio, M., Zhou, H., & Tully, T. (1995). CREB as a memory modulator: Induced expression of a dCREB2 activator isoform enhances long-term memory in Drosophilia. *Cell, 81,* 107–115.

Zajonc, R. B. (1965). Social facilitation. *Science, 149,* 269–274.

Zajonc, R. B. (1968). Attitudinal effects of mere exposure. *Journal of Personality and Social Psychology, 9,* 1–27.

Zametkin, A. J., Nordahl, T. E., Gross, M., King, A. C., Semple, W. E., Rumsey, J., et al. (1990). Cerebral glucose metabolism in adults with hyperactivity of childhood onset. *New England Journal of Medicine, 15,* 1361–1366.

Zang, Y. F., Jin, Z., Weng, X. C., Zhang, L., Zeng, Y. W., Yang, L., et al. (2005). Functional MRI in attention-deficit hyperactivity disorder: Evidence for hypofrontality. *Brain Development, 27,* 544–550.

Zanna, M. P., Kiesler, C. A., & Pilkonis, P. A. (1970). Positive and negative attitudinal affect established by classical conditioning. *Journal of Personality and Social Psychology, 14,* 321–328.

Zatorre, R. J., Evans, A. C., & Meyer, E. (1994). Neural mechanisms underlying melodic perception and memory for pitch. *Journal of Neuroscience, 14,* 1908–1919.

Zigler, E. F., Finn-Stevenson, M., & Hall, N. W. (2002). *The first three years and beyond.* New Haven: Yale University Press.

Zimbardo, P. G. (2007). *The Lucifer effect: Understanding how good people turn evil.* New York: Random House.

Zimmer, C. (2005, March 1). Looking for personality in animals, of all people. *New York Times.* Retrieved from http://www.nytimes.com

Zimmerman, C. (2007). The development of scientific thinking skills in elementary and middle school. *Developmental Review, 27,* 172–223.

Zullig, K., Pun, S., & Huebner, E. (2007). Life satisfaction, dieting behavior, and weight perceptions among college students. *Applied Research in Quality of Life, 2*(1), 17–31.

credits

Copyright © 2008 The McGraw-Hill Companies. Used with permission.

Figure 9.2: From Sakai, 2005. "Language Acquisition and Brain Development," *Science*, 310, 810–819. Reprinted with permission from AAAS.

Figure 9.3: From *The Symbolic Species: Co-Evolution of Language and the Brain* by Terrence W. Deacon. Copyright © 1997 by Terrence W. Deacon. Used by permission of W. W. Norton & Company, Inc.

Figure 9.4: From J. Winawer et al., 2007. "Russian Blues Reveal Effect of Language on Color Discrimination," *Proceedings of the National Academy of Science*, 104, 7785–7789. Used with permission.

Figure 9.5 a, b, c: From R. N. Shepard and J. Metzler, 1971. "Mental Rotation of Three-Dimensional Objects," *Science*, 171, 701–703. Reprinted with permission from AAAS.

Figure 9.6: From James L. McClelland and Timothy T. Rogers (2003). "The Parallel Distributed Processing Approach to Semantic Cognition," *Nature Reviews Neuroscience*, 4, 4, 310–322. Reprinted by permission from Macmillan Publishers Ltd.

Chapter 10

Figure 10.3: Adapted from J. B. Carroll (1993). *Human Cognitive Abilities*, New York: Cambridge University Press. Used with the permission of Cambridge University Press.

Figure 10.10: From E. Grigorenko, 2000. "Heritability and Intelligence," in R.J. Sternberg (ed.). *Handbook of Intelligence*, pp. 53–91. Reprinted with the permission of Cambridge University Press.

Figure 10.12: From Ian J. Deary et al., "Population Sex Differences in IQ at Age 11: The Scottish Mental Survey 1932," *Intelligence*, 31, 533–542. Copyright © 2003 with permission from Elsevier.

Figure 10.14: Adapted from Laura King, *The Science of Psychology: An Appreciative View*, 1st ed., Figs. 9.3 and 9.4, p. 330. Copyright © 2008 The McGraw-Hill Companies. Used with permission.

Figure 10.15a: From Vinod Goel et al. "Dissociating the Roles of Right Ventral Lateral and Dorsal Lateral Prefrontal Cortex in Generation and Maintenance of Hypotheses in Set-Shift Problems," *Cerebral Cortex*, 15, 1170–1171. Used with permission by Oxford University Press.

Figure 10.18: From Carlsson I., Wendt, P. E. & Risberg, J. 2000. "On the Neurobiology of Creativity: Differences in Frontal Activity between High and Low Creative Subjects." *Neuropsychologia*, 38, 873–885. Copyright © 2000 with permission from Elsevier.

Figure 10.19: Finke, Ronald A., Thomas B. Ward, and Steven M. Smith, *Creative Cognition: Theory, Research, and Applications.* Figure: "Creative Problem Solving Using Mental Imagery," Copyright © 1992 Massachusetts Institute of Technology, by permission of The MIT Press.

Chapter 11

Figure 11.2: After Kent C. Berridge (2004). "Motivation Concepts in Behavioral Neuroscience," *Physiology and Behavior*, 81, 179–209. Copyright © 2004 with permission from Elsevier.

Figure 11.3: From B. Smith, *Psychology: Science and Understanding*, 1st ed., Fig. 11.1. Copyright © 1998 The McGraw-Hill Companies. Used with permission.

Figure 11.6: From Michael Passer and Ronald Smith, *Psychology: The Science of Mind and Behavior*, 4th ed., Fig. 11.14, p. 377. Copyright © 2008 The McGraw-Hill Companies. Used with permission.

Figure 11.9: From J. A. Russell, 1980. "A Circumplex Model of Affect," *Journal of Personality & Social Psychology*, 39, 1161–1178. American Psychological Association.

Chapter 12

Figure 12.1: Reprinted from T. H. Holmes and R. H. Rahe. "The Social Readjustment Rating Scale," *Journal of Psychosomatic Research*, 11, 213–218. Copyright © 1967 with permission from Elsevier.

Figure 12.4: From H. Seyle, *The Stress of Life*, Fig. 12.4, p. 476. Copyright © 1976 The McGraw-Hill Companies. Used with permission.

Chapter 13

Figure 13.1: From Plomin and Caspi (1990). In L. A. Pervie (ed.), *Handbook of Personality: Theory and Research* 251–276. New York: The Guilford Press. Used with permission by Guilford Publications, Inc.

Figure 13.2: From Gregory Feist, *Theories of Personality*, 6th ed. Copyright © 2006 The McGraw-Hill Companies. Used with permission.

Figure 13.5: From W. Mischel and Y. Shoda, 1995. "A Cognitive-Affective System Theory of Personality," *Psychological Review*, 102, 246–268. American Psychological Association.

Fig. 13.7: From Eysenck, 1990. In L. A. Pervin (ed.), *Handbook of Personality: Theory and Research*, 224–276. New York: The Guilford Press. Used with permission by Guilford Publications, Inc.

Figure 13.12: From B. W. Roberts, K. E. Walton, and W. Viechtbauer, 2006, "Patterns of Mean-Level Change in Personality Traits Across the Life Course," *Psychological Bulletin*, 132, 1–25. American Psychological Association.

Chapter 14

Figure 14.1: From Michael Passer and Ronald Smith, *Psychology: The Science of Mind and Behavior*, 4th ed., Fig. 11a, p. 635. Copyright © 2008 The McGraw-Hill Companies. Used with permission.

Figure 14.2a: From *Obedience to Authority: An Experimental View*, Figure 4, p. 28, by Stanley Milgram. Copyright © 1974 by Stanley Milgram. Reprinted by permission of HarperCollins Publishers and Pinter & Martin.

Figure 14.3: From *Obedience to Authority: An Experimental View*, Appendix 1, p. 195, by Stanley Milgram. Copyright © 1974 by Stanley Milgram. Reprinted by permission of HarperCollins Publishers and Pinter & Martin.

Figure 14.7: From B. J. Bushman and C. A. Anderson (2001). "Media Violence and the American Public," *American Psychologist*, 56, p. 486. American Psychological Association.

Figure 14.10: From R. J. Sternberg (1986). "A Triangular Theory of Love," *Psychological Review*, 93, 119–135. Used with permission by Dr. Robert Sternberg.

Chapter 15

Figure 15.1: Reprinted with permission from the *Diagnostic and Statistical Manual of Mental Disorders*, Text Revision, Fourth Edition (Copyright 2000). American Psychiatric Association.

Fig. 15.2: Adapted from R. C. Kessler, W. T. Chiu, O. Dealer, & E. E. Walters (2005). Prevalence, severity, and comorbidity of twelve-month DSM-IV-TR disorders in the National Comorbidity Survey Replication (NCS-R). *Archives of General Psychiatry*, 62, 617–627. With permission from the American Medical Association.

Figure 15.3: From Laura King, *The Science of Psychology: An Appreciative View*, 1st ed., Fig. 14.2, p. 529. Copyright © 2008 The McGraw-Hill Companies. Used with permission.

Figure 15.5: Adapted from G. Meerkert, van den Eijnden, & H. F. L. Garretsen (2006). "Predicting Compulsive Internet Use: It's All About Sex," *Cyber-Psychology and Behavior*, 9, 95-103. Reprinted with permission by Mary Ann Liebert, Inc.

Figure 15.6: Reprinted from C. D. Market at al,. "Cognitive Self-Consciousness, Implicit Learning, and Obsessive-Compulsive Disorder," *Journal of Anxiety Disorders*, 20, 389–407. Copyright © 2006 with permission from Elsevier.

Figure 15.7: From A. Caspi et al., 2003. "Influence of Life Stress on Depression: Moderation by a Polymorphism in the 5-HTT Gene," *Science*, 301, 386–389. Reprinted with permission from AAAS.

Figure 15.14: From B. D. Perry, 2002, "Childhood Experience and the Expression of Genetic Potential: What Childhood Neglect Tells Us About Nature and Nurture," *Brain and Mind*, 3, p. 94. With kind permission of Springer Science and Business Media.

Figure 15.15: Reprinted with permission from the *Diagnostic and Statistical Manual of Mental Disorders*, Text Revision, Fourth Edition (Copyright 2000). American Psychiatric Association.

Figure 15.16: Reprinted with permission from the *Diagnostic And Statistical Manual of Mental Disorders*, Text Revision, Fourth Edition (Copyright 2000). American Psychiatric Association.

Figure 15.18: From Ludwig, 1995, *The Price of Greatness*. Used with permission by Guilford Publications, Inc.

Figure 15.19: From E. Slater and A. Meyer, 1959, "Contributions to a Pathography of the Musicians: Robert Schumann," *Confinia Psychiatrica*, 2, 65–94. Used with permission by S. Karger AG.

Chapter 16

p. 623: From David Dobbs, "A Depression Switch?" from *The New York Times*, April 2, 2006, p. 50. Used with permission of PARS International Corp., Inc.

p. 629: From *Case Studies in Abnormal Psychology* by Ethan E. Gorenstein and Ronald J. Comer. Copyright © 2002 by Worth Publishers. Used with permission.

PHOTOGRAPHS

Front Matter

p. i: Victor Albrow/FoodPix/Jupiter Images; **pp. ii–iii:** Bob Garas/Jupiter Images; **p. v:** Thom Lang/Corbis; **p. viii:** Marc O. Finley/Getty Images; **p. xxiiT:** Brand X Pictures/Getty Images; **pp. xxii–xxiii:** Jupiter Images; **p. xxiv:** Mark Andersen/Getty Images; **p. xxix:** Mike Kemp/Rubberball; **p. xxxi:** istockphoto.com/Pavel Lebedinsky; **p. xxxiR:** Photodisc/Getty Images; **p. xxxii:** Dev Carr/ Getty Images; **p. xxxvi:** Getty Images/Digital Vision; **p. xxxvii:** Polka Dot Images/Jupiter Images; **p. xl:** Digital Vision/Punchstock.

Chapter 1

pp. 2–3: Masterfile; **p. 4–5:** Martin Holtkamp/Getty Images; **p. 5T:** Brad Wilson/Getty Images; **p. 6:** Sonya Farrell/Digital Vision/Getty Images; **p. 7:** Duangkamon Khattiya/ Getty Images; **p. 9:** Image Source/Getty Images; **p. 10:** Matthias Rietschel/AP Images; **p. 11:** Redchopsticks/Getty Images; **p. 12:** Canadian Museum of Civilization, Artifact VII-C-1758, image S95-3306/Corbis; **p. 13:** SSPL/The Image Works; **p. 14:** Bettmann/ Corbis; **p. 15:** David Buffington/ Blend Images/Punchstock; **p. 16:** Bloomimage/Corbis; **p. 18:** Goodshoot/Alamy; **p. 19:** Petty Officer First Class Brien Aho/AP Images; **p. 20TL:** Hulton Archive/Getty Images; **p. 20BM:** istockphoto.com/Kurt Holter; **p. 20TM:** Squared Studios/Getty Images; **p. 20BL:** SSPL/The Image Works; **p. 21L.:** Bettmann/Corbis; **p. 21BR:** Tetra Images/Jupiter Images; **p. 22BL:** Image Source/Getty Images; **p. 22TM:** istockphoto.com/Onur Döngel; **p. 22BR:** Comstock Images/JupiterImages; **p. 23:** Image Source/Punchstock; **p. 24:** PhotoDisc/Getty Images; **p. 25:** Ryan McVay/Getty Images; **p. 26BL:** istockphoto.com/arlindo71; **p. 26BR:** istockphoto.com/arlindo71; **p. 26BM:** W. E. Garrett/National Geographic/Getty Images; **p. 27T:** Frank Lukasseck/Corbis; **p. 27B:** istockphoto.com/noburatti; **p. 28B:** Jae Rew/Getty Images; **p. 28T:** Stockbyte; **p. 29R:** Stockdisc/PunchStock; **p. 29L:** G.K. & Vikki Hart/Getty Images; **p. 30:** ML Harris/Getty Images; **p. 31:** CARL DE SOUZA/AFP/Getty Images.

Chapter 2

pp. 34–35: Punchstock; **p. 36T:** Burke/Triolo Productions/Brand X Pictures/Getty Images; **pp. 36–37:** Hans Neleman/Getty Images; **p. 38:** IT Stock Free/Alamy Images; **p. 39a:** iStockphoto.com/Boris Shapiro; **p. 39b:** iStockphoto.com/Geopaul; **p. 39k:** iStockphoto.com/Lawrence Karn; **p. 39l:** iStockphoto.com/Konstantin Inozemtsev; **p. 39c:** Wayne Calabrese/Getty Images; **p. 39d:** iStockphoto.com; **p. 39i:** Peter Ginte/ Getty Images; **p. 39j:** iStockphoto.com/Julien Grondin; **p. 39h:** iStockphoto.com/Phil Morley; **p. 39e:** iStockphoto.com/Eric Isselée; **p. 39f:** iStockphoto.com/Zeynep Mufti; **p. 39g:** iStockphoto.com/Adam Korzekwa; **p. 40B:** Ahn Young-joon/AP Images; **p. 40T:** iStockphoto.com/Claude Dagenais; **p. 41:** iStockphoto.com/Rafal Zdeb; **p. 42a:** Carl Lyttle/Getty Images; **p. 42b:** iStockphoto.com/Zveiger Alexandre; **p. 42d:** iStockphoto.com/TommL; **p. 42c:** Martin/Fotolia; **p. 42e:** Editorial Image, LLC/Alamy Images; **p. 43:** INTERFOTO Pressebildagentur/Alamy; **p. 44B:** Bettmann/Corbis; **p. 44T:** Photodisc/Getty Images; **p. 46:** StockByte/

Punchstock; p. 47: Nico Hermann/Jupiter Images; p. 48: Michael Nichols/National Geographic Image Collection; p. 49B: Bettmann/Corbis; p. 49T: Photo-Disc/Getty Images; p. 50B: Michael Rosenfeld/Getty Images; p. 50T: Peter Cade/Getty Images; p. 51: Image Source/Corbis; p. 53: Tom Schierlitz/Getty Images; p. 54: Richard Gardette/Jupiter Images; p. 55: Randy Faris/Corbis ; p. 56: Susan Trigg/iStockphoto; p. 57: Corbis; p. 58: Rob Melnychuk/Getty Images, Inc.; p. 59: Steve Cole/Getty Images; p. 60: Spencer Grant/PhotoEdit Inc.; p. 61T: Hill Street Studios/Getty Images; p. 61M: Stockbyte/Getty Images; p. 61B: Louie Psihoyos/Getty Images; p. 62: Stockbyte/Getty Images; p. 63: Ausloeser/zefa/Corbis; p. 64: Brand X Pictures/PunchStock; p. 66: Courtesy of Philip Zimbardo; p. 67: Ingram Publishing/Alamy Images; p. 68: Bob Elsdale/Getty Images; p. 69: Wolfgang Flamisch/zefa/ Corbis; p. 70: Tetra Images/Jupiter Images; p. 71: Wides & Holl/Getty Images.

Chapter 3

p. 74–75: Big Cheese Photo/Punchstock; p. 76T: PhotoAlto/PunchStock; p. 76–77: Dorling Kindersley/Getty Images; p. 77B: Zeynep Mufti/Images and Stories; p. 78T: Gregory Costanzo/Getty Images; p. 78B: Suza Scalora/Getty Images; p. 78ML: iStockphoto.com/Phil Morley; p. 80: Frank Trapper/Corbis; p. 81: Bruce Laurance/Getty Images; p. 82: Andre Cezar/Getty Images; p. 83: Digital Vision/Getty Images; p. 83: James Woodson/Getty Images; p. 84: James Woodson/Getty Images; p. 85: James Woodson/Getty Images; p. 86: Peter Griffith/Getty Images; p. 87: Hybrid Medical/Photo Researchers, Inc.; p. 89: Julia Smith/Getty Images; p. 91: Jim Dowdalls/Photo Researchers, Inc.; p. 92: David Loftus/Getty Images; p. 94: Scott Houston/Sygma/ Corbis; p. 95: Photodisc Collection/Getty Images; p. 96B: PhotoDisc, Inc./Getty Images; p. 96T: G.K. & Vikki Hart/Getty Images; p. 97R: PATRICK BERNARD/AFP/Getty Images; p. 97TL: G.K. & Vikki Hart/Getty Images; p. 98T: Peter Griffith/Getty Images; p. 98BL: Photodisc/Getty Images; p. 98ML: Stockdisc (Stockbyte)/Getty Images; p. 98MR: WEGNER, JORG & PETRA/Animals Animals Enterprises; p. 98BR: The McGraw-Hill Companies, Inc./Photo by JW Ramsey; p. 99: Yasuhide Fumoto/Getty Images; p. 100: Kraig Scarbinsky/Getty Images; p. 101: Rolf Bruderer/Corbis; p. 102: Richard Lord/The Image Works; p.103: ER Productions/Getty Images; p. 108: Hybrid Medical/Photo Researchers, Inc.; p. 109: Chris Pizzello/Corbis; p. 111: Digital Vision/PunchStock; p.113: Peter Kramer/Getty Images; p. 113B: Courtesy of Erika Rosenberg; p. 114T: Philippe Lissac/Corbis; p. 114BL: Photopix/Getty Images; p. 114BM: McGill University, © Collection CNRI/Phototake; p. 114BR: ISM/Phototake; p. 116: PhotoAlto/PunchStock; p.117: Siede Preis/Getty Images; p. 118T: Zeynep Mufti/Images and Stories; p. 118B: Laurence Mouton/Getty Images.

Chapter 4

pp. 122–123: Panoramic Images/Getty Images; pp.124–125: Lyn Holly/Getty Images; p. 125: Dorling Kindersley/Getty Images; p. 126T: Bjorn Wiklander/ Nordic Photos/Getty Images; p. 126BL: altrendo images/Getty Images; p. 126BR: iStockphoto.com/foto-fine-art; p. 127BL: iStockphoto.com/Allen Johnson; p. 127M: iStockphoto.com/Klimenko Aleksandr; p.127T: iStockphoto.com/arlindo71; p. 127TR: PhotoAlto/Alix Minde/Getty Images; p. 127BL: iStockphoto.com/Susan Trigg; p. 128: Thomas Hartwell/ Corbis; p.130: Charlie Edwards/Digital Vision/Getty Images; p.131: Omikron/Photo Researchers, Inc.; p. 135TR: iStockphoto.com/Mark Coffey; p.136–137: ICHIRO/PhotoDisc/Getty Images; p. 137R: Sean Masterson/Getty Images; p. 138: Comstock Images/Alamy; p. 139a: Photodisc/Getty Images; p. 139b: Creatas/PunchStock; p. 139d: Humberto Olarte Cupas/Alamy; p.139c: Ross Barnett/Getty Images; p. 140: Mauro Fermariello/Photo Researchers, Inc.; p. 143T: M.C. Escher's "Sky and Water I" © 2008 The M.C. Escher Company-Holland. All rights reserved; p.143B: Artist: Julian Jusim/Courtesy of Verlagsgruppe Beltz; p. 144: iStockphoto.com/Irina Igumnova; p. 144:

iStockphoto.com/Klaus Sailer; p. 145: Digital Vision/Getty Images; p. 148: HECTOR MATA/AFP/Getty Images; p. 150T: PhotoAlto/Alix Minde/Getty Images; pp. 150–151: TRBfoto/Getty Images; p. 152: Michael A. Keller/Corbis; p. 153: Greg Betz/Getty Images; p. 154: Stockbyte/PunchStock; p. 155: The Tennessean, John Partipilo/AP Images; p. 157: Getty Images; p. 158: PhotoAlto/Alix Minde/Getty Images; p. 159T: Ahn Young-joon/AP Images; p. 159B: iStockphoto.com/Joan Vicent Cantó Roig; p. 160B: Stockbyte/Getty Images; p. 160T: D. Hurst/Alamy; p. 163: TENGKU BAHAR/AFP/Getty Images; p. 164TL: iStockphoto.com/digital skillet.

Chapter 5

pp. 168–169: Karan Kapoor/Getty Images; p. 170B: Image Source/PunchStock; pp. 170–171: Stockbyte/Getty Images; p. 172: David M. Phillips/Photo Researchers, Inc.; p. 174T Ellison; p. 234M: Bloomimage/Co: Anatomical Travelogue/Photo Researchers, Inc.; p. 174B: Artiga Photo/ Masterfile; p. 175L: Penny Gentieu/Babystock/Jupiter Images; p. 175M: Penny Gentieu/Babystock/Jupiter Images; p. 175T: iStockphoto.com/Jani Bryson; p. 176L: Hannah Mentz/zefa/Corbis; p. 176R: Jules Frazier/Getty Images; p.177: Image Source/PunchStock; p. 178: ©Streissguth, A.P., & Little, R.E. (1994). "Unit 5: Alcohol, Pregnancy, and the Fetal Alcohol Syndrome: Second Edition" of the Project Cork Institute Medical School Curriculum (slide lecture series) on Biomedical Education: Alcohol Use and Its Medical Consequences, produced by Dartmouth Medical School. p.179 all: iStockphoto.com/Jaroslaw Wojcik; p. 180: Kevin Peterson/PhotoDisc/Getty Images; p. 181: Enrico Ferorelli; p. 183: Masterfile; p. 184T: Courtesy of Dr. Harry T. Chugani, Children's Hospital of Michigan.; p.184B: Courtesy of Paul Thompson, Laboratory of Neuro Imaging, UCLA; p.186: Alison Barnes Martin/Masterfile; p. 188: Michael Newman/PhotoEdit; p. 190: Corbis Images/Jupiter-Images; p. 191T: iStockphoto.com/Dan Eckert; p. 191B: iStockphoto.com/Catherine Lane; p. 192: David Sacks/Getty Images; p.194: Stockbyte/Getty Images; p. 195: Time & Life Pictures/Getty Images; p.196: Natalie Behring-Chisholm/Getty Images; p. 197: Scott Hancock/Getty Images; p. 198B: Ryan McVay/Getty Images; p.198T: Comstock Images/Alamy; p. 199: Ant Strack/Corbis; p. 200: Radius Images/Masterfile; p.202: Fred Prouser/Reuters/Corbis; p. 203: Steven Vidler/Eurasia Press/Corbis; p. 204: Vicky Kasala/Getty Images; p. 205: Peter Dazeley/Getty Images; p. 206: Michael S. Yamashita/Corbis; p. 207: iStockphoto.com/Anne de Haas; p. 208T: Sarto/Lund/Getty Images; p. 208B: Toni Leon/Getty Images; p.210: Randy Faris/Corbis.

Chapter 6

pp. 214–215: Simon Jarratt/Corbis; p. 216T: Giantstep Inc/Getty Images; pp. 216–217: Karl Weatherly/Getty Images; p. 218: Chev Wilkinson/Getty Images; p. 220: Steve Cole/Getty Images; p. 221: iStockphoto.com/Lori Lee Miller; p. 222: Digital Vision/PUNCHSTOCK; p. 223: Simons, D. J., & Chabris, C. F. (1999). Gorillas in our midst: Sustained inattentional blindness for dynamic events. Perception, 28,1059–1074. Figure provided by Daniel Simons.©1999 Daniel J. Simons. All rights reserved. Image may not be distributed or posted online without written permission; p. 225: Courtesy of David Strayer, Ph.D., Applied Cognition Lab, Department of Psychology, University of Utah; p. 226: CREATAS/PUNCHSTOCK; p. 227: Brand X Pictures/PunchStock; p. 228: Desmond Boylan/Reuters/Corbis; p. 229T: Tonya Jacobs/Courtesy of the author; p. 229B: Image Source/Getty Images; p. 231: Image Source/ Getty Images; p. 232: iStockphoto.com/Duanerbis; p.234T: Purestock/Getty Images; p. 234B: istockphoto.com/Martin McCarthy; p. 235: Anna Peisl/zefa/Corbis; p. 236: C.Dell'iere/Jupiter Images; p. 238: William Thomas Cain/Getty Images; p. 239: istockphoto.com/Chris Bernard; pp. 240–241: PhotoDisc/ Getty Images; p. 243: iStockphoto.com/Kirsty Pargeter; p.244: iStockphoto.com/Yurok; p. 245: OutlineLive Collection/Corbis; p.246BL: iStockphoto.com/Mehmet Salih Guler; p. 246TL: iStockphoto.com/Rafa Irusta;

p. 246TML: iStockphoto.com/P_Wei; p. 246TMR: iStockphoto.com/Manuela Weschke; p. 246TR: iStockphoto.com/Aleaimage; p. 246BR: iStockphoto.com/Studioaraminta; p. 247: iStockphoto.com/Zveiger Alexandre; p. 248: Scott Houston/Corbis; p. 249T: Rod Rolle/Getty Images; p. 249B: iStockphoto.com/Miroslava Holasová; p. 251B: Getty Images; p. 251T: iStockphoto.com/Steve Diddle.

Chapter 7

p.254–255: hasengold/Plain Picture; p. 256B: The McGraw-Hill Companies, Inc./Lars A. Niki; p. 256–257: Digital Vision/Getty Images; p. 259: The McGraw-Hill Companies, Inc./Jacques Cornell photographer; p. 260TL: Heide Benser/zefa/Corbis; p. 260TR: Dylan Ellis/Digital Vision/Getty Images; pp. 260–261: iStockphoto/kycstudio; p. 262: iStockphoto.com/Peter Willems; p. 264: Jason Todd/Getty Images; p. 265: Alex Wong/ Getty Images; p. 266T: Digital Vision; p. 266B: blue jean images/Getty Images; p. 269: Influx Productions/Getty Images; p. 270: BananaStock/PUNCHSTOCK; p. 271: iStockphoto.com/Lisa Thornburg; p. 272: Stockbyte/PunchStock; p. 273: PhotoAlto/Punchstock; p. 275: iStockphoto/Eric Isselée; p. 276: Sean Cayton/The Image Works; p. 277: Tim Laman/National Geographic/Getty Images; p. 279: iStockphoto/Richard Cano; p. 281R: Stephanie Maze/Corbis; p. 281L: Mitch Hrdlicka/Getty Images; p. 282: Stockbyte/PunchStock; p. 283: istockphoto.com/nhuan Nguyen; p. 284: iStockphoto; p. 285: Steve Cole/Getty Images; p. 287: iStockphoto/Nicholas Loran; p. 288: Brand X Pictures/PunchStock; p. 289: Waltraud Grubitzsch/Corbis.

Chapter 8

pp. 292–293: Nicolas Ferrando/Corbis; p. 294: © Brand X Pictures/Punchstock; p. 294–295: Lauren Zeid/eStock Photo; p. 296: Seide Preis/Getty Images; p. 297T: Time & Life Pictures/Getty Images; p. 297B: © Pictorial Press Ltd/Alamy; p. 298TR,BR: iStockphoto.com/Mark Coffey; p. 298MR: iStockphoto.com/Mark Coffey; p. 298ML,BL: iStockphoto.com/Anton Kozlovsky; p.298TL: iStockphoto.com/Leonid Nyshko; p. 298BM: iStockphoto.com/Leonid Nyshko; p. 299R: iStockphoto.com/Mark Coffey; p.300R: iStockphoto.com/Pavel Lebedinsky; p. 300L: iStockphoto.com/jean frooms; p. 301B: Courtesy of Prof. Benjamin Harris, University of New Hampshire; p. 301BL: iStockphoto.com/Dieter Spears; p. 301TM: iStockphoto.com/Juan Monino; p. 301TR: iStockphoto.com/Zsolt Biczó; p. 301TL: iStockphoto.com/Pavel Lebedinsky; p. 303T: Markus Moellenberg/zefa/Corbis; p. 303M: Digital Vision/Getty Images; p. 303B: iStockphoto.com/Nathan Watkins; p.304: Marc Debnam/Digital Vision/Getty Images; p. 305TL: iStockphoto.com/Suzanne Tucker; p. 305TR: iStockphoto.com/Sami Suni; p. 305BL: iStockphoto.com/Jim Pruitt; p. 305BR: iStockphoto.com/Isabel Massé; p. 306: Ryan McVay/Getty Images; p. 307T: Bettmann/Corbis; p. 307B: Photodisc/ Getty Images; p. 308BR: iStockphoto.com/Monika Adamczyk; p. 308M: iStockphoto.com/Juan Monino; p. 308ML: iStockphoto.com/Dieter Spears; p. 308TR: iStockphoto.com/Sami Suni; p. 308L: iStockphoto.com/Pavel Lebedinsky; p. 309a: Sion Touhig/Corbis; p. 309b: WireImageStock/Masterfile; p. 309d: BananaStock/PunchStock; p. 309c: Zucchi Uwe/dpa/Corbis; p. 311: ©Ellen B. Senisi/The Image Works; p. 312T: © JUPITERIMAGES/ Brand X /Alamy; p. 312B: PhotoDisc, Inc./Getty Images; p. 313: C Squared Studios/Getty Images; p. 315TL: iStockphoto.com/April Turner; p. 315BL: iStockphoto.com/eff Clow; p. 315BML,BR: iStockphoto.com/Sharon Dominick; p. 315BMR: iStockphoto.com/Bluestocking; p. 315TML: iStockphoto.com/Mark Coffey; p. 315TMR: iStockphoto.com/Anton Kozlovsky; p. 316: Dorling Kindersley/Getty Images; p. 318: Comstock Images/Alamy; p. 319: Courtesy of Albert Bandura; p. 320: © Virgo Productions/zefa/Corbis; p. 322: Nina Leen/Time & Life Pictures/Getty Images; p. 323: © Gary Salter/zefa/Corbis; p. 324B: Jim Dowdalls/Photo Researchers, Inc.; p. 324T: iStockphoto.com/Paul Merrett; p. 326: inspirestock/www.agefotostock.com; p. 327: Photodisc/Getty Images;

p. 328: PhotoAlto/Alix Minde/Getty Images; p. 329: ©Bob Daemmrich/The Image Works.

Chapter 9

pp. 332–333: PhotoDisc/Punchstock; pp. 334–335: Halfdark/Getty Images; p.335B: C Squared Studios/Getty Images; p. 336: FINBARR O'REILLY/X90055/Reuters/Corbis; p. 338T: PhotoAlto/Punchstock; p. 338B: Bananastock/PictureQuest; p. 339: Datacraft/Getty Images; p.340: Richard T. Nowitz/Corbis; p. 341T: David Rosenberg/Getty Images; p. 341B: BLOOMimage/Getty Images; p. 343: Russell Monk Photography/Getty Images; p. 344: Spike Mafford/Getty Images; p. 346: Frans Lanting/Minden Pictures; p. 347: Burke Triolo Productions/Getty Images; p. 348: Courtesy of Daniel L. Everett; p. 349M: Amos Morgan/PhotoDisc/ Getty Images; p. 349BR: Ross Anania/Getty Images; p. 349TR: Digital Vision/Getty Images; p. 349L: Matthieu Spohn/PhotoAlto; p. 350: Martin Poole/Getty Images; p. 351: Stockbyte/PunchStock; p. 352: Bernhard Lang/Getty Images; p. 353: Ingram Publishing/ SuperStock; p. 354T: BananaStock/Punchstock; p. 354B: Matthieu Spohn/PhotoAlto; p. 355: Digital Zoo/Digital Vision/Getty Images; p. 356: ballyscanlon/PhotoDisc/Getty Images; p. 358: Terry J Alcorn/Getty Images; p. 359: Andrew Gombert/epa/Corbis; p. 360: McGraw-Hill Companies, Inc./Gary He, photographer; p. 363: Eileen Bach/Getty Images; p. 364: Steve Granitz/WireImage/Getty Images; p. 365: PhotosIndia.com/Getty Images; p. 366: Mark Hall/Getty Images; p. 367: Courtesy of Joy Hirsch.

Chapter 10

pp. 370–371: Ellen Rooney/Corbis; p. 372: David Muir/Getty Images; pp. 372–373: Patrik Giardino/Corbis; pp. 374–375: Ryan McVay/Getty Images; p. 376: Andrew Johnson/Getty Images; p. 377: Jessica Rinaldi/Reuters/Corbis; p. 379: C.W. McKeen/Syracuse Newspapers/The Image Works; p. 380: Stockbyte/PunchStock; pp. 382–383: Comstock/PunchStock; p. 384: Commercial Eye/Getty Images; p. 386: Mika/zefa/Corbis; p. 387: Art Akiane LLC; p. 388: Steve McAlister/Getty Images; p. 389: Courtesy of John Duncan; p. 391: Somos Images/Corbis; p. 392: Lawrence Lawry/Getty Images; p. 393: Royalty-free Division/ Masterfile; p.395L: Photodisc/Getty Images; p. 395R: PhotoDisc, Inc./Getty Images; p. 397: Comstock Images/Alamy; p. 398TR: Image Source/Getty Images; p. 398TL: Plush Studios/Getty Images; p. 398B: iStockphoto.com/Diane Diederich; p. 399: Thomas Northcut/PhotoDisc/Getty Images; pp. 400–401: Mark Gabrenya/Alamy; p. 401: Stephanie Diani/Corbis; p. 403: Brand X Pictures; p. 404L: Pixtal/age Fotostock; p. 404ML: Popperfoto/Getty Images; p. 404M: Pixtal/age Fotostock; p. 404MR: Sir Godfrey Kneller/The bridgeman Art Library/Getty Images; p. 404R: Library of Congress Prints and Photographs Division [LC-USZ62-60242]; p.405L: Time Life Pictures/Getty Images; p. 405ML: Imagno/Austrian Archives/Getty Images; p. 405M: Joseph Carl Stieler/The bridgeman Art Library/Getty Images; p. 405MR: FPG Intl./Corbis; p.405R: AFP/Getty Images; pp. 406–407: Michael Wildsmith/Getty Images; p. 407: IMAGEMORE Co.,Ltd./Getty Images; p. 408: Creatas/PunchStock; p. 409: Feature Photo Service.

Chapter 11

p. 412–413: Mike Powell/Getty Images; pp. 414–415: Howie Garber/Getty Images; p. 415: Image Source/Punchstock; p. 416d: TRBfoto/Getty Images; p. 416a: iStockphoto.com/Zoran Ivanovic; p. 416g: iStockphoto.com/Nina Shannon; p. 416b: Ryan McVay/Getty Images; p. 416f: iStockphoto.com/Georgina Palmer; p. 416c: Chris Ware/Getty Images; p. 416e: iStockphoto.com/Grzegorz Lepiarz; p. 418: Kirk Weddle/Getty Images; p. 420: Corbis; p. 421B: Jeffrey Ufberg/Getty Images; p. 421T: Richard Olsenius/Getty Images; p. 422B: Dr. Fred Hossler/Getty Images; p. 422T: iStockphoto.com/christine balderas; p. 424: PhotoAlto/PictureQuest; p. 425T: Steve Cole/Getty Images; p. 425B: The McGraw-Hill Companies, Inc./Jill Braaten, photographer; p.426T: Cathrine Wessel/Corbis; p. 426B: iStockphoto.com/MistikaS; p. 427: Queerstock/Getty Images; p. 428:

blue jean images/Getty Images; p. 429: KEYSTONE/Sigi Tischler, file/AP Images; p. 430: Iconotec/Alamy; p. 431B: Brand X Pictures/Punchstock; p. 431T: Photodisc/Getty Images; p. 432TL: Eric Bean/Getty Images; p. 432R: Elke Van de Velde/Getty Images; p. 432BL: Ian Spanier/Getty Images; p. 433: Jeff Gross/Getty Images; p. 434: Courtesy of Dr. Lenny Kristal and Robert Kong; p. 437: Martin Barraud/Getty Images; p. 438: T-Pool/Getty Images; p. 439: Central Stock/Fotosearch; p. 440T: Réunion des Musées Nationaux /Art Resource, NY; p. 440B: Courtesy of Erika Rosenberg; p. 440B: Courtesy of Erika Rosenberg; p. 442: Ken Graham/Getty Images; p. 443all: The Complete Works of Charles Darwin Online/ University of Cambridge; p. 444T: Courtesy of Paul Ekman; p. 444B: Courtesy of Erika Rosenberg; p. 445: KPPA/Reuters/Corbis; p. 447: Adri Berger/Getty Images; p. 448: Jeremy Woodhouse/Getty Images; p. 449: Sheer Photo, Inc/ Getty Images; p. 450: Ebby May/ Getty Images.

Chapter 12

pp. 454–455: Brand X Pictures/Punchstock; p. 456: Brand X Pictures/Punchstock; pp. 456–457: Spohn Matthieu/Getty Images; p. 458: Masterfile; p. 459a: Peter Dazeley/zefa/Corbis; p. 459b: iStockphoto.com/Anne de Haas; p. 459e: iStockphoto.com/Jaroslaw Wojcik; p. 459d: iStockphoto.com/Franky De Meyer; p.459c: iStockphoto.com/Dr. Heinz Linke; p. 460T: Digital Vision/Getty Images; p. 460B: Brian Gomsak/Getty Images; p. 461: Mike Powell/Getty Images; p. 464: Tom Fox/Dallas Morning News/Corbis; p. 465: Peter Griffith/Getty Images; p. 466L: Christopher Gould/Getty Images; p. 466R: Digital Vision/Punchstock; p. 467B: Peter Hannert/Getty Images; p. 467T: iStockphoto.com/Robert Kneschke; p. 467TM: iStockphoto.com/Damir Cudic; p. 467TB: iStockphoto.com/Andrea Laurita; p. 468: Darius Ramazani/zefa/Corbis; p. 469: Bob Thomas/Corbis; p. 470: Brand X Pictures/PunchStock; pp. 470–471: Kris Timken/Getty Images; p. 473T: Dirk Anschutz/ Getty Images; p. 473B: Steve Prezant/Corbis; p. 474: Nicholas Eveleigh/Getty Images; p. 475: Andrew Olney/ Digital Vision/Punchstock; p. 476: BananaStock; p. 477: Diane Mcdonald/Getty Images; p. 478: Erik Dreyer/Getty Images; p. 479: Somos/Veer/Getty Images; p. 480: Kevin Fleming/Corbis; p. 481: Brand X Pictures/Punch-Stock; p.483: Burke/Triolo/Brand X Pictures; p. 484: BananaStock/Alamy; p. 485B: © The McGraw-Hill Companies/Christopher Kerrigan, photographer; p.485T: Duncan Smith/Getty Images; p. 486 front: iStockphoto.com/Dr. Heinz Linke; p. 486 back: iStockphoto.com/Dr. Heinz Linke; p. 487: Stockdisc/PunchStock; p. 488: NIBSC/Photo Researchers Inc.; p. 489: Brent Stirton/Getty Images.

Chapter 13

pp. 492–493: Titus/Jupiter Images; p. 494: Jody Dole/Getty Images; pp. 494–495: Digital Vision/Getty Images; p. 496: Robert Glenn/Getty Images; p. 497: Ingram Publishing/ AGE Fotostock; p. 498: Phil Walter/Getty Images; p. 500: Miroku/Getty Images; p. 501: Noel Hendrickson/Getty Images; p. 502: Pixland/Corbis; p. 504: Peter Aprahamian/Corbis; p. 507: Alan Bailey/Getty Images; p. 508: Lucasfilm/20th Century Fox/The Kobal Collection; p. 510: Sharon Farmer, Bill & Melinda Gates Foundation/AP Images; p. 511: Michael Rougier/Time & Life Pictures/Getty Images; p. 512: Burke/Triolo/Brand X Pictures/Jupiterimages; p. 516B: Digital Vision/PunchStock; p. 516T: PhotoDisc/ Getty Images; p. 517: Don Farrall/Getty Images; p. 518LT: iStockphoto.com/Eric Isselée; p. 518LM: iStockphoto.com/Eric Isselée; p. 518LB: iStockphoto.com/Sue Mack; p. 518RT: iStockphoto.com/Andrew Johnson; p. 518RMT: Digital Vision/PunchStock; p. 518RMB: iStockphoto.com/Mikhail Soldatenkov; p. 518B: iStockphoto.com/Eduardo Jose Bernardino; p. 519: Don Farrall/Getty Images; p. 520B: Imagesource/Jupiter Images; pp. 520–521: Ed Bock/Corbis; p. 521B: Spencer Grant/ PhotoEdit; p. 523: Mario Tama/Getty Images; p. 525: Hill Street Studios/Getty Images; p. 527T: iStockphoto.com/Scott Griessel; p. 527M: iStockphoto.com/Scott Griessel; p. 527BR: iStockphoto.com/Scott Griesse; p. 527BL: Silverstock/Digital Vision/Getty Images.

Chapter 14

pp. 530–531: altrendo images/Getty Images; pp. 532–533T: altrendo images/Getty Images; pp. 532–533B: Erik Isakson/Getty Images; p. 534: Anthony Plummer/Getty Images; p. 535: Corbis Premium RF/Punchstock; p. 536: Ryan McVay/Getty Images; p. 539: c) 1968 by Stanley Milgram, copyright renewed © 1993 by Alexandra Milgram, and distributed by Penn State Media Sales; p. 540: Rubberball Productions; p. 541: sven hagolani/zefa/Corbis; p. 542: Bruce Laurance/Getty Images; p. 543: Obama Presidential Campaign/AP Images; p. 544B: Peter Dazeley/Getty Images; p. 544M: Digital Vision/Getty Images; p. 544T: Mareen Fischinger/Getty Images; p. 545: Courtesy of Naomi Eisenberger; p. 547: White Packert/Getty Images; p. 548: Jody Dole/Getty Images; p. 549: Jim McIsaac/Getty Images; p. 550T: TIM SLOAN/AFP/Getty Images; p. 550B: bluemagenta/Alamy; p. 551T: iStockphoto.com/Tomasz Borucki; p. 551B: iStockphoto.com/Izabela Habur; p. 552T: Advertising Archive; p. 552B: Steve Cole/Getty Images; p. 553: John Giustina/Getty Images; p. 554: Shannon Fagan/Getty Images; p. 555: Comstock/PunchStock; p. 557: CBS/Courtesy: Everett Collection; p. 558: NY Daily News; p. 559: Ashley Cooper/Corbis; p. 562T: Digital Vision/Getty Images; pp. 562B–563: Courtesy of Connor Principe and the Langlois Social Development Lab, University of Texas, Austin; p. 565: Bettmann/Corbis; p. 566: Bettmann/Corbis.

Chapter 15

pp. 570–571: PhotoAlto/Punchstock; p. 572: Halfdark/Getty Images; pp. 572–573: Peter Miller/Getty Images; p. 573: Erich Lessing/Art Resource, NY; p. 574: Mitchell Funk/ Getty Images; p. 575: iStockphoto.com/Richard Johnson; p. 578L: Nicolas Guerin/ Corbis; pp. 578–579: G.K. & Vikki Hart/Getty Images; p. 579R: Masterfile; p. 580T: Rubberball Productions; p. 580B: Bettmann/Corbis; p. 583: Jae Rew/Getty Images; p. 584L: iStockphoto.com/Don Bayley; p. 584R: iStockphoto.com/Nghe Tran; p. 585: Daniel Grizelj/Getty Images; p. 586: Bob Thomas/Getty Images; p. 588: Jules Frazier/Getty Images; p. 589T: Courtesy of Drs. Lew Baxter & Michael Phelps, UCLA School of Medicine; p. 589B: D. Hurst/Alamy; p. 590: Ingram Publishing/Alamy; p. 594: Chad Baker/Ryan McVay/Getty Images; p. 595: C Squared Studios/Getty Images; p. 596: PhotoDisc/Getty Images; p. 597: Guntmar Fritz/Corbis; p. 598: Courtesy of Dr.Bruce D.Perry; p. 599: Florence Delva/Jupiter Images; p. 601: Photodisc/PunchStock; p. 602T: MDP/New Market/Gene Page/The Kobal Collection; p. 602B: Photodisc Collection/Getty Images; p. 603: VEER Lars Topelmann/Getty Images; p. 604: Nancy Kaszerman/Corbis; p. 605: Digital Vision/PunchStock.

Chapter 16

pp. 610–611: Brand X PicturesPunchstock; pp. 612–613: Gregor Schuster/Getty Images; p. 613B: Tim Hawley/Getty Images; p. 613T: Getty Images; p. 614: Jonathan Nourok/ Getty Images; p. 616: Jeffrey Mayer/Getty Images; p. 617: Comstock/Alamy Images; p. 619T: Hulton Archive/Getty Images; p. 619B: Will & Deni McIntyre/Photo Researchers, Inc.; p. 620: Simon Fraser/University of Durham/Photo Researchers, Inc.; p. 622: Kathy Collins/Getty Images; p. 623T: Courtesy of St. Jude Medical; p. 624: Royalty-Free/Corbis; p. 625: Brian Hagiwara/Brand X/Corbis; p. 626: Michael Rougier/Time-Life Pictures/Getty Images; p. 627TR: istockphoto.com/MorePixels; p. 627TL: iStockphoto.com/arlindo71; p. 627MR: iStockphoto.com/Linda King; p. 627MR: iStockphoto.com/John Bell; p. 627ML: iStockphoto.com/Simone van den Berg; p. 627B: iStockphoto.com/Jake Holmes; p. 628: The Charlotte Observer, Christopher A. Record/ AP Images; p. 629: Gary S Chapman/Getty Images; p. 630: Chad Johnston/Masterfile; p. 631: Ryan McVay/Getty Images; p. 633: Jeff Greenberg/PhotoEdit Inc.; p. 635: Phanie/Photo Researchers, Inc.; p. 636: Brand X Pictures/PunchStock; p. 639BR: Davies and Starr/Getty Images; p. 639BL: Howard J. Radzyner/Phototake; p. 639T: Andrea Morini/Digital Vision/Getty Images; p. 642: Anthony Nagelmann/Getty Images.

name index

McClay, J., 554, 598
McClelland, D. C., 429
McClelland, J. L., 144, 271, 354
McClintock, M. K., 425
McCormack, K. M., 12
McCrae, R. R., 497, 499, 500, 513, 522, 525
McDermott, K. B., 283
McDonald, J., 604
McDowell, M. A., 422
McEachin, J. J., 311
McElree, B., 281
McEvoy, J. P., 618, 637
McEwen, B., 484
McEwen, B. S., 465
McGaugh, J. L., 269
McGee, J. P., 311
McGhee, D. E., 547
McGinnis, S., 622
McGinty, D., 233
McGlone, G., 521
McGowan, B. K., 313
McGrew, K. S., 383
McGuire, E. J., 352
McGuire, M. T., 554
McGuire, P. K., 594
McHugh, P., 596
McKhann, G. M., 485, 486
McKinley, M., 417
McKinney, B. C., 592
McKinney, M. L., 347
McMenamy, J. M., 198
McNeely, H. E., 40, 623
McNulty, J. L., 524
McRae, K., 448
McTiernan, A., 484
Mead, G., 607
Meadows, E. A., 635, 640
Mechelli, A., 366
Mechtcheriakov, S., 244
Medina, A. E., 177
Mednick, M. T., 404
Mednick, S. A., 404
Medvec, V., 437
Meerkerk, G., 580, 581
Meiners, L., 424
Melis, M. R., 424
Mellon, S., 113
Meltzer, H. Y., 637
Meltzoff, A. N., 189, 197, 323, 341, 440
Melzack, R., 156, 157
Mencl, E., 328
Mendl, M., 439
Mendoza-Denton, R., 524
Meng, Z., 198
Mennella, J. A., 175, 425
Menotti, A., 483
Merabet, L. B., 119
Mercado, A. M., 479
Merikangas, K. R., 577, 579, 603, 606, 632
Merrill, J. E., 244
Merskey, H., 154
Merten, J., 448
Merzenich, M. M., 108, 154, 182
Methippara, M., 233
Metter, E. J., 205
Meuret, A. F., 643
Meyer, E., 151
Meyer, J. H., 622
Meyerhoff, D. J., 244
Michael, J., 305

Michel, S., 230
Michela, J. L., 541
Miczek, K. A., 554
Miele, G. M., 468
Mihara, T., 235
Miles, J. N. V., 639
Miles, M., 459
Milgram, S., 66, 67, 496, 537, 538, 539, 540
Mill, J., 554, 598
Miller, A., 352, 406
Miller, A. H., 477
Miller, A. S., 537
Miller, B. L., 103, 202, 273, 447
Miller, G., 417, 498, 562, 563
Miller, G. A., 260, 606
Miller, G. E., 463
Miller, H. L., 615
Miller, L. A., 404
Miller, W. R., 424
Miller-Johnson, S., 393
Millot, J.-L., 163
Milner, B., 257, 258, 277
Milner, P., 448
Mineka, S., 578
Minier, F., 94
Mintun, M., 102, 240
Minturn, A. L., 129
Mirescu, C., 111, 182
Mischel, W., 511, 512, 524
Miselis, R., 417
Mitchell, J. T., 641
Mitchell, K. J., 31
Mitchell, P., 204
Mitchell, P. B., 587
Mitchell, T., 109
Mitchner, L., 617
Miyake, A., 273, 447
Miyaoka, T., 235
Miyashita, T., 271
Mizuno, S., 235
Moffitt, T., 598
Moffitt, T. E., 81, 500, 554, 573, 592, 598
Moghaddam, B., 594
Mohanty, A., 606
Moise-Titus, J., 555
Mojet, J., 205
Mokdad, A. H., 422
Molina, J. C., 318
Moline, J., 152
Moller, J., 482
Montague, D. P. F., 197
Montgomery, G. H., 239
Moody, B. J., 639
Mooney, D., 175
Moore, D. C., 144
Moore, E. S., 177
Moore, M., 637
Moore, M. K., 197, 323, 341, 440
Moore, R. Y., 230
Moradi, A. R., 276
Moray, N., 222
Morelli, G. A., 48
Moreno, S., 183
Morghen, I., 251
Morien, A., 420
Morikawa, H., 341
Morin, C. M., 251
Morinobu, S., 477
Morland, T., 448
Morral, A. R., 307
Morrell, C. H., 205

Morris, J. S., 102, 447
Morris, M. W., 542
Morris, N. M., 424, 425
Morris, P. H., 518
Morris, T. L., 30
Morrison, M., 489
Morrison, R. S., 209
Morrow, J. D., 471, 472
Moruzzi, G., 99
Moscovici, S., 537
Moscovitch, D. A., 643
Moscovitch, M., 263
Moses-Kolko, E. L., 178
Moskowitz, J., 471, 485, 488, 489
Moskowitz, J. T., 470, 471
Mostow, A. J., 437
Motluk, A., 117, 118, 119
Mount, M. K., 522
Mroczek, D., 495, 525
Muchinsky, P. M., 523
Muir, D. W., 174
Mulder, E. J. H., 210
Mulder, I., 483
Muller, D., 227
Müller-Oerlinghausen, B., 588, 589
Munro, M. J., 365
Munsinger, H., 390
Murphy, D. L., 498
Murphy, G., 311
Murphy, M., 632
Murray, A. D., 325
Murray, A. M., 641
Murray, C., 392, 393
Murray, H. A., 429
Murray, R. M., 249, 594, 598
Murvielde, I., 522
Mussell, M., 583
Musselman, L., 563

N

Nacash, N., 635, 640
Nadarajah, B., 94, 173
Nadel, L., 233
Nahin, R. L., 235
Nakazaki, S., 244
Naqvi, N. H., 104
Närvänen, S., 240
Nasar, S., 606
Nash, J. F., Jr., 606
Nash, M. R., 521
National Eye Institute, 360
National Institute of Mental Health (NIMH), 590
National Safety Council, 361
National Science Foundation, 43, 44
National Sleep Foundation, 234
Nauta, W. J. H., 86, 88
Neale, M. C., 422, 582
Neely, M. H., 250
Neisser, U., 373
Nelson, J. D., 325
Nelson-Gray, R. O., 523, 641
Nemeroff, C., 431
Nemeroff, C. B., 637
Nesbit, S. M., 555
Nestler, E. J., 587
Neston, J. D., 481
Nettle, D., 498, 606
Neuberg, S. L., 533, 544, 546, 549

Neugebauer, R., 176
Neville, H., 109
Newall, P., 204
Newcomb, A. F., 203
Newcomb, T. M., 562
Newcombe, N. S., 348
Newman, T. K., 12
Newport, E. L., 339
Neyens, D. M., 225
Nichols, T. N., 102, 240
Nichols, W. C., 604
Nickerson, C., 450
Nicoll, R. A., 249, 250, 277, 420
Nieman, D. C., 450
Nienhuis, R., 234
Nieuwenburg, A., 424
Nisbett, R. E., 60, 163, 542
Nishida, A., 477
Nishikawa, M., 183
Nishino, S., 235, 236
Nissinen, A., 483
Nithianantharajah, J., 207
Niven, H., 587
Nizhnikov, M. E., 318
Noda, H., 485
Noiman, L., 111
Nolan, C. L., 102
Nolen-Hoeksema, S., 14, 484, 591, 601, 620, 626, 640
Nolte, C., 264
Nopoulos, P., 593
Noppeney, U., 366
Norcross, J. C., 10, 634, 635
Nordahl, T. E., 604
Nordborg, C., 111, 326
Norenzayan, A., 163, 542
Nottebohm, F., 110
Novak, M. A., 12
Novick, O., 499
Nowell, A., 393, 394
Nowicki, G. P., 435
Nuechterlein, K., 225
Numminen, J., 240
Nusselder, W., 485

O

Oakley, D. A., 240
Obama, B., 544
Oberman, L. M., 325, 605
O'Brien, C. P., 424
O'Brien, W. H., 482
Ochs, M. T., 108, 154, 182
Ochsner, K. N., 437, 447, 449
O'Cleirigh, C., 468, 489
O'Conner, M. J., 588
O'Connor, C., 482
O'Connor, C. A., 113
Odbert, H. W., 512
Odendaal, H., 177
O'Doherty, J. O., 155, 156, 366, 448, 560, 561
Oeltermann, A., 115
Ogawa, H., 159
Ogden, C. L., 422
O'Hara, L., 403
O'Hara, R., 263
Ohl, F., 485
Öhman, A., 101, 446
Ohnishi, T., 183
Olds, J., 448
O'Leary, D. S., 593
Oliveira, A. J., 251
Oliver, M. B, 425

subject index

brain damage
　distractibility after, 251
　from fetal alcohol spectrum
　　disorder, 177, 178
　Glasgow Coma Scale and, 219
　memory loss after, 274–275,
　　286
　personality change after, 526
　of Phineas Gage, 103–104
　progesterone treatment of,
　　112–113
brain death, 208
brain development
　in adolescence, 201–202
　in adulthood, 205
　in fetuses, 173–176
　in infants, 181–185
　size of, 175
brain maps, 154
brain stem, 99, 118, 151
breathing technique, 226
broaden-and-build model, 435,
　451
broad intelligence, 376
Broca's area, 105, 337–338, 367
Brodmann's Area 25, 621–624
buffering hypothesis, 469
bulimia nervosa, 484
bupropione (Wellbutrin), 616
buspirone, 643
by-products, 27
bystander effect, 46, 557–558

C
caffeine, 242, 246–247
California Psychological
　Inventory, 523
CANOE mnemonic, 513, 515
carbon monoxide, 247
cardiovascular reactivity (CVR)
　model, 481–482
cardiovascular system, 438–439,
　475, 480–483
caregivers, 479, 488
carpentered world, 162
case studies, design of, 47–48
cataplexy, 235–236
catatonic schizophrenia, 592
catecholamines, 116–117,
　461–462
categories, 354–355
catharsis, 626, 643
Catholic Church, witch hunts of,
　13–14
cats, vision development in,
　136–137
Cattell–Horn–Carroll (CHC)
　hierarchical intelligence
　theory, 374, 376, 382–383
caudate nucleus, 582
causal inferences, 356
causation, correlations and, 51
CBT (cognitive–behavioral
　therapy). See cognitive–
　behavioral therapy
CCK (cholecystokinin), 420
cell assemblies, in memory, 277
cell damage, sleep and, 234
cell-phones, 29, 152–153,
　224–225
cells, neuron, 87
cellular immunity, 478
central executive function, 261,
　262, 273

central nervous system (CNS), 83
cerebellum, 99, 182, 274
cerebral cortex, 102–104
cerebral hemispheres, 104–107
　Broca's area, 105, 337–338,
　　367
　communication between,
　　106–107
　creativity and, 403–406
　savant syndrome and, 388
　structure of, 104–105
　vision and, 133
　Wernicke's area, 106, 273, 337,
　　338, 366, 593
cerebral palsy, 196
cerebrum, 102–104
chance mutations, 25
channels, voltage-dependent,
　88–90, 91, 95
CHC (Cattell–Horn–Carroll)
　hierarchical intelligence
　theory, 374, 376, 382–383
"CHC shift," 382–383
chemotherapy, marijuana use
　during, 249
child abuse and neglect, 183–184,
　195, 597–599
child-directed speech, 341
children. See also human
　development; infants
　abuse and neglect of, 183–184,
　　195, 597–599
　attention deficit hyperactivity
　　disorder in, 93, 603, 604,
　　640
　autistic syndrome disorder in,
　　603–604
　brain development in, 181–185
　cognitive development in,
　　185–190
　conduct disorders in, 603
　easy vs. difficult, 210
　emotional competence in,
　　198–199
　language development in,
　　337–340
　moral reasoning development
　　in, 190–192
　myelination in, 184–185
　observational learning of
　　aggression in, 319–321
　peer interaction in, 199
　physical development in, 179–
　　185
　play of, 428, 435
　sexual feelings by, 505, 506
　sleep in, 232–233
　socioemotional development
　　in, 192–194, 197–199
　temperament and personality
　　in, 210
　touch therapy in, 196–197
　well-adjusted vs. inhibited, 210
chimpanzees, sign language
　learned by, 345–347
chlorpromazine (Thorazine), 617
cholecystokinin (CCK), 420
chromosomes, 77–78, 83
chunking, 261
cigarettes. See smoking
cilia, in the nasal cavity, 158
cingulate gyrus, 100, 102
circadian rhythms, 230–231
cirrhosis, 244, 483

civil disobedience, 191–192
classical conditioning, 297–302
　of Little Albert, 301–302
　operant conditioning vs., 308
　Pavlov's dogs, 297–298
　process of, 298–301
　in smoking behavior, 328
　of taste aversion, 293–294, 315
client-centered therapy, 626
clinical psychology, 10, 12–15, 31
clozapine (Clozaril), 617, 637
cocaine, 93, 242, 247–248
cochlea, 150–151
cocktail party effect, 222
codeine, 245
cognition, definition of, 350. See
　also thought
cognitive–behavioral therapy
　(CBT)
　in anxiety disorder treatment,
　　642–643
　dialectical behavior therapy
　　and, 636
　drug therapy combined with,
　　634
　effectiveness of, 639–640
　overview of, 630
cognitive development, 185–190
　in adolescence, 201–202
　in adulthood, 205
　decline with aging, 205–207
　intelligence tests and, 382
　Piaget's stages of, 185–189,
　　201, 382
　theory of mind, 189–190
cognitive dissonance, 550–551,
　567
cognitive maps, 314
cognitive processes, in creative
　thinking, 406–407
cognitive psychology, 8–9, 29,
　350
cognitive symptoms, of
　schizophrenia, 591
cognitive theory, on dreaming,
　237
cognitive therapy, 628–630,
　639–640
cognitivism, 19–21
cold fusion case, 40
collective unconscious, 507–508
collectivism, 501, 537
color blindness, 147
color perception, language and,
　348–349
color vision, 145–147, 161
coma, 219–220, 251
commitment, in love, 564
common sense, science and, 38
communication
　between cerebral hemispheres,
　　106–107
　neural, 88–90, 92
　of scientific results, 42–43
comorbidity, 575
companionate love, 564
compensation, 507
complex cells, 135
compulsion, definition of,
　579–580
compulsive behavior, 242. See
　also obsessive–compulsive
　disorder
computer analogy, 20

concept hierarchy, 353
conception, 172
concepts, 353–355, 366
concrete operational stage,
　188–189
conditioned reinforcers, 304
conditioned response (CR), 298,
　300
conditioned stimulus (CS), 298–
　299, 300
conditioned taste aversion, 293–
　294, 315–318
conditioning, 296–318
　behavior therapies, 626–628
　biological constraints on,
　　312–313
　classical, 297–302, 315, 325,
　　328
　classical vs. operant, 308
　definition of, 296
　of immunosuppression, 476
　language acquisition and, 342
　law of effect in, 302–303
　of Little Albert, 301–302
　operant, 302–312, 328
　Pavlov's dogs, 297–298
　reinforcement and punishment,
　　303–306
　schedules of reinforcement,
　　307–312
　in smoking behavior, 327–329
　in taste aversion, 293–294,
　　315–318
conditioning of reflexes, 298
conduct disorders, 603, 641
cones, 131–132, 145–146
confidentiality, in research,
　67–68
confirmation bias, 356
conformity, 534–547, 566–567
confounding variables, 54
conjunction fallacy, 364
conscientiousness, 517–518, 523
conscious layer, 502
consciousness, 214–253
　AIM model of, 237
　attention, 221–225
　brain injury and, 250–251
　definition of, 217–218
　dreaming, 236–237
　in Freud's theory, 502
　full, 220–221
　in hypnosis, 238–241
　meditation and, 226–228, 229
　minimal, 219–220
　moderate, 220
　psychoactive drugs and, 241–
　　250
　sleeping, 228–236
　wakefulness and awareness in,
　　218–219
conservation, in cognition,
　187–188
consistency, in personality, 496
consistency bias, 283–284
consolidation, in encoding, 269,
　273
construct validity, 384
Continuous Performance Test
　(CPT), 224–225
continuous reinforcement, 308
contralaterality, 103
control groups, 53

conventional level, in moral reasoning, 191
convergence, in vision, 139
convergent thinking problems, 396
cooing, 338
coping, 466–475
　denial as, 489
　dissociative disorders as, 596
　emotion-focused, 467–468
　finding meaning as, 471
　health effects of, 472–475
　meditation as, 485, 487
　positive psychology of, 470–471
　problem-focused, 466–467
　reappraisal as, 488
　social support and, 467, 468–470
cornea, 130–131
coronary artery disease, 482
coronary heart disease, 481–483
corpus callosum
　function of, 105
　location of, 100
　musical training and, 182
　savant syndrome and, 388
　split-brain studies and, 107
correlational designs, 50–51, 52
correlation coefficients, 50–51, 52
cortex, memory storage and, 274
cortical arousal, 514–515
cortical localization, 103
corticotropin releasing factor (CRF), 462
cortisol
　function of, 117
　stress and, 462–463, 465, 475
cost-benefit analysis, 362
counseling psychology, 10
CPT (Continuous Performance Test), 224–225
CR (conditioned response), 298, 300
crack cocaine, 248
creative intelligence, 377
creative thinking, 367, 399
creativity, 400–408
　brain activity and, 403–406
　cognitive processes in, 406–407
　creative personality, 407–408
　definitions of, 401–402
　genius and, 402–403
　mental health and, 605–607
　in self-actualization, 510
　as sexually selected trait, 498
　stages of creative problem solving, 402
CREB protein, 277–278, 280
CRF (corticotropin releasing factor), 462
critical period, in sensory development, 180–181
critical thinking, 356–359
criticism, sensitivity to, 199
cryptomnesia, 283
crystallized intelligence, 375, 382
crystal meth, 248
CS (conditioned stimulus), 298–299, 300
cults, 565–567
cultural differences

in emotional expression, 445–446
in food, 421
intelligence tests and, 375, 385, 392–393
in language and thought, 347–350
in moral reasoning, 192
in personality, 500–501
in sensation and perception, 162–165
in sexual behavior, 425
in smoking behavior, 329
universality of facial expressions of emotion, 442–446
culturally relative, 442
cultural test bias hypothesis, 385
CVR (cardiovascular reactivity) model, 481–482
cyclothymia, 588
cytokines, 477

D

dark adaptation, 132
Darkness Visible (Styron), 585
DBT (dialectical behavior therapy), 636, 640–641
deafness and hearing loss
　age-related, 152, 204–205
　iPods and, 152–153
　noise exposure and, 151
　peripheral vision and, 109
death and dying, 208–209
debriefing, in research, 68
decay, of memories, 281
deception, 68, 542
decibels (dB), 149
decision making, 358–365
　availability heuristic in, 361
　conjunction fallacy in, 364
　heuristics in, 359–361
　nonrational, 362–364
　representativeness heuristic in, 359–361
deductive reasoning, 355
deep brain stimulation, 622–624
defense mechanisms, 504, 506, 508–509, 626, 643
delirium tremens (DTs), 241
delta waves, 232
delusions, 591, 594
dementia, 206. *See also* Alzheimer's disease
dendrites, 87, 90–92, 95, 108, 465
denial, as form of coping, 489
dependence, 241
dependent personality disorder, 601
dependent variables, 52–53
depolarization, in neural communication, 88–90, 92
depressants, 242, 243–246
depression
　brain activity and, 619–620, 621–624
　cognitive therapy for, 628–630, 638
　creativity and, 606
　deep brain stimulation for, 622–624
　drug treatments for, 614–616, 618, 637–638

dysthymia, 585
electroconvulsive therapy for, 619, 639
genetic influences on, 586–587
health effects of, 482–483
mindfulness training with psychotherapy for, 635–636
prefrontal cortex and, 447
prevention of, 632–633
repetitive transcranial magnetic stimulation for, 620
serotonin and, 93–94, 586–587
symptoms of, 585–586
T cell functioning and, 489
treatment effectiveness, 637–640
witch hunts and, 13
depth perception, 138–139, 162
descriptive statistics, 63–64
descriptive studies, 46–50
development. *See* human development
developmental psychology, 9, 30
deviant, definition of, 574
dextroamphetamine (Dexedrine), 248
diabetes, as side effect of clozapine, 637
Diagnostic and Statistical Manual, 4th edition, Text Revision *(DSM-IV-TR)*, 15, 574–575, 599
dialectical behavior therapy (DBT), 636, 640–641
diathesis–stress model, 582, 586
dichotic listening task, 222
DID (dissociative identity disorder), 595–596
diet. *See* eating
difference thresholds, 128–129
diffusion of responsibility, 558
DIGFAST mnemonic, 587
direct effects hypothesis, 469
disabilities, achievement motivation in people with, 429
discrimination, 545
diseases and disorders. *See* illnesses; psychological disorders
disorganized schizophrenia, 592
display rules, 445–446
dispositional attributions, 541
dissociative disorders, 595–596
dissociative identity disorder (DID), 595–596
distancing, 467
distractibility, 251
distressing, definition of, 574
disulfram, 318
divergent thinking problems, 396–397
DNA (deoxyribonucleic acid), 78–79, 82, 498. *See also* genetic influences
domestic violence, 641
dominant genes, 78
dopamine
　antidepressants and, 616
　function of, 92–93
　psychoactive drug use and, 248, 250

release by adrenal glands, 116
schizophrenia and, 594, 617
thrill-seeking behavior and, 498–499
dopamine hypothesis, in schizophrenia, 594
double-blind studies, 55, 57
Down syndrome, 386
dramatic–emotional personality disorders, 600–601
dreaming, 236–237
dream interpretation, 503, 625, 643
drive reduction model, of motivation, 417–418
drives, 416, 417–418. *See also* motivation
drugs and drug therapies. *See also* psychoactive drugs; treatment
　antidepressants, 178, 236, 615, 616, 642
　effectiveness of, 637–639
　for mood and anxiety disorders, 614–617, 642–643
　for pain, 157, 245
　psychotherapy combined with, 634
　for schizophrenia, 617–618
DSM-IV-TR (Diagnostic and Statistical Manual, 4th edition, Text Revision), 15, 574–575, 599
DTs (delirium tremens), 241
Duchenne smile, 440
dysfunctional, definition of, 574
dysthymia, 585

E

ear, 149–151. *See also* hearing
early-onset Alzheimer's, 206
eating
　biology of when we eat, 419–420
　fetal development and, 176–177
　health effects of nutrition, 483–485
　psychology of what we eat, 420–421
　stress and, 483–484
eating disorders, 484–485, 641
echoic memory, 259
ecstasy (MDMA), 94, 242, 248
ECT (electroconvulsive therapy), 619–620, 639
education. *See also* learning
　brain changes from learning, 101, 108, 233, 276–278
　critical thinking beyond the classroom, 358–359
　multiple intelligences theory in, 379
　school shootings, 429
　self-fulfilling prophecies in, 57–58
　social-emotional learning, 438–439
　studying and memory, 287–289
educational psychology, 11
EEG (electroencephalography), 112–114

effect size, 58
effortful processing, 267
ego, 503
egocentrism, 187
egoistic motivation, 560
ejaculation, 200–201
electroconvulsive therapy (ECT), 619–620, 639
electroencephalography (EEG), 112–114
electromagnetic spectrum, 145
embarrassment, 434
embryo, 172
embryonic stage, 172–173
emerging adulthood, 204
emotion(s), 431–451
   affect types, 431–432
   amygdala and, 101–102, 446–447, 449
   appraisal in, 436, 446–448
   arousal and pleasure combinations in, 432–433
   attachment, 192–194, 564–565
   basic, 432
   as behavioral adaptations, 26–27
   brain and, 446–448
   in coping strategies, 467–468
   definition of, 431
   display rules on expression of, 445–446
   education on, 438–439
   emotional response, 437–442
   as evolutionary adaptations, 434–435
   facial expressions, 435–436, 439–440
   gender and, 448–449
   in infants, 192–194, 197–199
   life satisfaction, 449–451
   love, 564–565
   memory and, 275–276
   mood disorders, 583–589
   multiple measurement of, 62
   neuro-cultural theory of, 445
   persistent memories and, 284
   positive, 19, 470–471, 488
   as process, 435–436
   regulation of, 436–437
   self-conscious, 433–434
   from smells, 158
   stress and, 460–461, 474
   subjective experience of, 441–442
   universality in expression of, 442–445
   videotaped data on, 60–61
emotional competence, 198
emotional disclosure, 468, 489
Emotional Intelligence (Goleman), 437
emotional response, 437–442
emotion family, 432
emotion-focused coping, 467–468
emotion regulation, 436–437
empathic motivation, 560
empathy, 560–561
empathy-altruism hypothesis, 560
empirical method, 523
empiricism, 16
enactive learning, 318

encoding, in long-term memory, 266–269
endocannabinoids, 249–250, 420
endocrine system, 115–117, 461
endorphins, 157, 245, 484
environmental influences. *See also* nature–nurture debate
   on aggression, 554
   on brain development, 182–183, 326
   on degenerative brain disorders, 207
   epigenetics and, 82–83
   on fetal development, 176–178
   on intelligence, 389–392
   on language acquisition, 341–342, 344–345
   nature–nurture debate and, 23–24
   on neuron growth, 110–111
   on personality, 499–500
   on schizophrenia, 592
   twin and adoption studies on, 80–81
enzymatic degradation, 92
epigenetics, 82–83, 177
epilepsy, 94, 106–107
epinephrine, 93, 116
episodic buffer, 261–262
episodic memory, 266
ERP (event-related potentials), 112–114
escape-avoidance, 467–468
esteem, need for, 419
estradiol, 200
ethics, in research, 66–69, 302
ethnicity. *See* race and ethnicity
ethology, 322
Eureka insight, 397, 399, 402
European Americans, 329, 547
event-related potentials (ERP), 112–114
evidence-based therapies, 639
evolution
   of altruism, 559–560
   of behavior, 26–28
   definition of, 25
   of emotions, 434–435
   of the human brain, 96–98
   of language, 27–28, 336–337
   mechanisms of, 24–27
   of personality traits, 497
   taste aversion and, 318
"The Evolutionary Foundations of Culture" (Tooby and Cosmides), 21
evolutionary model, of motivation, 417
evolutionary psychology, 21–22, 26
exaptations, 27
excitatory potentials, 92, 95
excitement stage of sexual arousal, 423–424
exercise benefits, 205, 207, 485–486
exhaustion stage, in stress, 463, 464, 472, 474
experiment, definition of, 52
experimental groups, 53
experimental psychology, 9, 17
experimental studies
   characteristics of, 52

design of, 45–46, 52–55
experimenter expectancy effects in, 55–58
explicit memory, 265, 271
explicit prejudice, 546
The Expression of the Emotions in Man and Animals (Darwin), 443
expressive-suppression strategy, 437
extinction, in conditioning, 299, 300, 301, 307
extraversion, 329, 514, 518
eyewitness testimony, 284

F

face recognition, 137
face valid (rational) method, 522
face-vase figure, 142, 143
facial action coding system (FACS), 440, 445
facial attractiveness, 562–563
facial expressions
   anger faces by infants, 198
   culture impacts on, 445–446
   of embarrassment, 434
   in emotion process, 435–436, 439–440
   functional role of, 446
   by peers, 199
   recognition by infants, 197
   universality of, 442–445
FACS (facial action coding system), 440, 445
false-belief task, 189–190
false memories, 255–256, 285
familial-cultural retardation, 386
families
   language acquisition and, 341
   obesity and, 469–470
   puberty and changes in, 203
farsightedness, 133
FASD (fetal alcohol spectrum disorder), 177, 178
fats, evolution of preference for, 25–26
FDA (Food and Drug Administration), 612
fear
   amygdala and, 446–447, 449
   appraisal and, 436, 446–447
   autonomic nervous system and, 437–439
   evolution of, 26, 497
   lack of control and, 436
feature detectors, 135, 138
feedback (homeostasis), 417–418, 464
fertilization, 172
fetal alcohol spectrum disorder (FASD), 177, 178
fetal development. *See* prenatal development
fetal stage, 173
fidelity, 211
figure-ground effects, 142–143, 163–164
fine motor skills, 180
FI (fixed interval) schedule, 310, 311–312
five-factor (Big Five) model of personality, 513, 517

fixation
   in problem solving, 399
   in psychoanalytic theory, 505, 506
fixed interval (FI) schedule, 310, 311–312
fixed ratio (FR) schedule, 309, 311–312
flavor, 160
flexibility of thought, 407
flight-or-fight response, 84
float test for witchcraft, 13
flooding, 628
flow, 220–221, 419
fluid intelligence, 375, 382
fMRI (functional magnetic resonance imaging), 115
folic acid, 176, 177
folk psychology, 6
Food and Drug Administration (FDA), 612
foot-in-the-door technique, 566
forebrain, 98, 99–100
forensic psychology, 11
forgetting, 279–283
forgetting curve, 281–282
formal operational stage, 189–190, 201
forward conditioning, 299
Four Steps training, 636, 641
fovea, 131, 132
frameworks, cognitive, 21
fraternal twins, 80
free association, 625, 643
free radicals damage, sleep and, 234
frequency of sounds, 149, 150–151, 153–154
"friending," 30
frontal lobes
   adolescent development of, 201–202
   aggression and, 554
   alcohol and, 244
   autism and, 605
   meditation training and, 227–228
   pain and, 156
   schizophrenia and, 593
   short-term memory and, 273
   structure of, 102–103
FR (fixed ratio) schedule, 309, 311–312
functional fixedness, 400
functionalism, 18
functional magnetic resonance imaging (fMRI), 115
fundamental attribution errors, 542

G

GABA (gamma-aminobutyric acid)
   anxiety disorders and, 582
   depressants and, 243
   as inhibitory neurotransmitter, 92, 94, 95
   as insomnia treatment, 235
GAD (generalized anxiety disorder), 577–578, 582, 642
ganglion cells, 131, 132

Gardner's multiple intelligences theory, 374, 377–378, 379
GAS (general adaptation syndrome), 463–464, 475
gate control theory of pain, 156–157
gender
  drive for casual sex and, 425–426
  emotion and, 448–449
  intelligence and, 393
  iron deficiency and, 192
  mental rotation tasks and, 353
  moral reasoning and, 192
  peer interaction and, 199
  physical development in puberty, 200–201
  sexual response cycles and, 423–424
  smell perception and, 163, 165
  social networks and, 470
  susceptibility to smoking and, 328–329
gene-by-environment interaction research, 81–82
gene expression, 82–83
general adaptation syndrome (GAS), 463–464, 475
general intelligence, 376
generalized anxiety disorder (GAD), 577–578, 582, 642
generativity, 211
genes. See also genetic influences
  definition of, 78
  dominant and recessive, 78–79
  emotion and, 275
  environment and, 80–83
  in learning and memory, 277–278
  structure of, 77–78
  in twins, 80
genetic influences. See also behavioral genetics; nature–nurture debate
  on aggression, 554
  on anxiety disorders, 582
  on autism, 605
  on behavior, 77–83
  on bipolar disorder, 588
  on body weight, 422
  on color blindness, 147
  on depression, 586–587
  on Down syndrome, 386
  environment and, 80–83
  on intelligence, 389–392, 393–394
  on language learning, 344–345
  on narcolepsy, 236
  nature–nurture debate and, 23–24
  on personality, 498–500, 514–515, 525
  polygenic, 79
  on schizophrenia, 592
  on sexual orientation, 428
genetic markers, 82
genital stage, 505–506
genius, 402–403, 605
genome, 78, 83
germinal stage, 171
Gestalt laws of grouping, 141–144
Gestalt psychology, 19–20

g-factor theory, 375, 376
ghrelin, 420
giftedness, 386–388
ginkgo biloba, 281
Glasgow Coma Scale, 219
glial cells, 85, 156
"global workspace" of consciousness, 218
glucocorticoids, stress and, 461
glucose, 420
glutamate
  in brain development, 64
  depressants and, 243
  as excitatory neurotransmitter, 92, 95
  LSD and, 250
  schizophrenia and, 592, 594, 637
gonads, 200
graded potentials, 92
grammar
  definition of, 336
  as innate, 344–345
  universal, 343, 348
Gross National Happiness (GNH), 414
group living. See social behavior
group therapies, 630–633, 643
groupthink, 536

H

habituation, 296
hair cells, 150–151, 158
hallucinations, in schizophrenia, 590–591, 594
hallucinogenic drugs, 161, 242, 248–250
haloperidol (Haldol), 617
happiness, 414, 440, 449–451
hassles, stress and, 459–460
Hassles and Uplifts Scale, 459
Head Start, 439
health behavior approach, 473, 483–487
health psychology, 11, 31, 473, 488–489
hearing, 148–153
  in adulthood, 204–205
  auditory cortex and, 104, 108–109
  auditory hallucinations, 590–591
  at birth, 180
  brain and, 151
  deafness and hearing loss, 109, 151, 152–153, 204–205
  ear biology and, 149–151
  psychology of, 149
  range of, 149
hearing loss. See deafness and hearing loss
hearing voices, 590–591
heart disease, psychological risk factors for, 480–483
Hebb's law, 276–277
Heinz Dilemma, 190–191
hemispheric specialization. See cerebral hemispheres
heritability, 80–82. See also genetic influences
heroin, 245, 247
hertz (Hz), 149

heuristics, 359–361, 400
hidden observer effect, 239
hierarchies, in memory, 269–270
hierarchy of needs, 419, 450, 509–510
higher needs, 450–451
hindbrain, 98–99
hippocampus
  Alzheimer's disease and, 207
  bipolar disorder and, 588
  effect of learning on, 101, 108, 233
  exercise and, 485–486
  location and function of, 100, 101
  memory and, 257, 273, 275–276
  pain and, 156
  in painting, 118
  schizophrenia and, 593
  stress and, 465
histrionic personality disorder, 600
HIV (human immunodeficiency virus), 488. See also AIDS
homeostasis, 417–418, 464
homophobia, 504
homosexuality, 15, 204
hormones. See also specific hormones
  circadian cycles in, 230
  function of, 115–117
  hunger and, 420
  in puberty, 200
  sex, 116, 200, 427
  stress and, 461, 462–463, 465, 475
hospice, 209
hostile aggression, 553
hostility, 481–482, 508–509. See also aggression; anger
HPA (hypothalamic-pituitary-adrenal) axis, 462, 465, 475, 484
hubristic pride, 433
human development, 168–213
  cognitive, 185–190, 201–202, 205–207
  death and dying, 208–209
  definition of, 171
  environmental influences on, 176–178
  importance of touch in, 194–196
  language in, 337–339
  of moral reasoning, 190–192
  personality across the life span, 209–211
  physical, 179–185, 200–201
  Piaget's stages of, 185–189, 201, 382
  prenatal brain and sensory development, 173–176
  prenatal growth, 171–173
  sensation and perception in adulthood, 204–205
  sleep, over the life span, 232–233
  socioemotional, 48, 192–194, 197–199, 202–204, 207–208
humane treatment, in animal research, 69

human genome, 78, 83
human immunodeficiency virus (HIV), 488. See also AIDS
humanistic approach, 509–511, 515, 626
humanistic–positive psychology theories, 509–511, 515
human research studies, ethical guidelines for, 67–68
hunger, 419–422
Huntington's disease, basal ganglia and, 102
hydrocodone, 245
hyperactivity (attention deficit hyperactivity disorder), 93, 603–604, 640
hypercomplex cells, 135–136
hypersomnia, 236
hypnosis, 238–241
hypothalamic-pituitary-adrenal (HPA) axis
  eating and, 484
  stress and, 462, 465, 475
hypothalamus
  aggression and, 554
  circadian rhythms and, 230–231
  emotions and, 448
  endocrine system and, 116–117
  hunger and, 420
  location and function of, 100
  pain and, 156
  sexual behavior and, 424
  sexual orientation and, 428
  stress and, 461–462
hypotheses, 41, 201

I

IAT (Implicit Associations Test), 547–548
iconic memory, 259
ideal self, 511
ideational fluency, 406, 503
identical twins, 80
identity confusion, 211
identity crisis, 210–211
identity formation, 203–204
idioms, 366
illnesses. See also immune system
  belief in control over, 470–471
  health behavior approach to, 473, 483–487
  stress and, 473–474
imipramine, 614
imitation, 323–325, 341–342
immune system
  conditioned immunosuppression, 476
  cortisol and, 463, 475
  in HIV/AIDS, 488
  inflammation and, 477, 482
  mindfulness meditation and, 487
  overview of, 477–478
  psychological processes and, 475–477
  psychoneuroimmunology, 475, 476–477
  schizophrenia and, 23–24
  stress and, 475–480
Implicit Associations Test (IAT), 547–548

MAO (monoamine oxidase) inhibitors, 614, 637
marijuana, 242, 249–250
massage therapy, 196
mate selection, 563–564
mathematics, musical training and, 183
maze learning, 313–314, 353
MBCT (mindfulness-based cognitive therapy), 635, 640
MBSR (Mindfulness-Based Stress Reduction), 487
MDMA (ecstasy), 94, 242, 248
mean, 63
mechanoreceptors, 153–154
medial geniculate nucleus (MGN), 151
median, 63
meditation
  consciousness and, 226–228, 229
  in coping, 485, 487
  mindfulness, 635–636
  in stress reduction, 485, 487
medulla, 99
melanin, 420
melatonin, 230–231
membrane potentials, 88–90
memory, 254–291
  aging and, 205–207
  brain injury and, 274–275, 286
  brain pathways and, 272–278
  without conscious awareness, 258–259
  definition of, 259
  emotions and, 275–276
  forgetting, 279–283
  learning and, 295
  long-term, 259, 264–271, 274–278, 288–289
  medications to improve, 280–281
  neurotransmitters and, 92, 94
  reconstructions of the past as, 255–256, 283–286
  sensory, 259–260, 272
  short-term, 259, 260–264, 266–267, 273, 383
  in studying, 287–289
  three-stage model of, 259
memory binding, 283
men and boys. *See also* gender
  mate selection by, 563
  puberty in, 200–201
  sexual arousal cycle in, 423
menarche, 200
menstrual cycle, 117, 425
mental age, 380
mental imagery, in creative problem solving, 406
mental representations, 351
mental retardation, 386
mental rotation, 352–353
mental set, 397
mercury poisoning, 391
meta-analysis, 58–59
metabolism, 116
metacognitive thinking, 357–358, 367
methamphetamine (Meth), 248
MGN (medial geniculate nucleus), 151
midbrain, 98–99

middle ear, 149–150
mind–body dualism, 24
mindfulness, 221, 227, 635, 640
mindfulness-based cognitive therapy (MBCT), 635, 640
Mindfulness-Based Stress Reduction (MBSR), 487
Minnesota Multiphasic Personality Inventory (MMPI), 523–524
minority social influence, 537
mirror neurons
  autism and, 605
  experimental discovery of, 324
  in language acquisition, 341–342
  learning and, 88, 324–325
misattribution, 283
"The Misbehavior of Organisms" (Breland and Breland), 313
MMPI (Minnesota Multiphasic Personality Inventory), 523–524
mnemonic devices, 268–269, 289
mode, 63
modeling, 319
monoamine oxidase (MAO) inhibitors, 614, 637
monocular depth cues, 139
monogenic transmission, 79
monosodium glutamate (MSG), 159
mood, definition of, 431–432. *See also* emotion(s)
mood disorders, 583–589, 614–617. *See also* bipolar disorder; depression
moon illusion, 144
moral reasoning development, 190–192
moral treatment movement, 14
morning sickness, 176
morphine, 157, 245
mosquito ringtones, 152–153
motion perception, 138
motion sickness, 293–294
motivation, 415–430
  achievement, 429–430
  to be thin, 421–422
  definition of, 415
  egoistic *vs.* empathic, 560
  happiness and, 450–451
  hunger as, 419–422
  models of, 416–419
  need to belong as, 428–429
  sex as, 423–428
  striving for superiority as, 506–507
motor activity, frontal lobes and, 102–103
motor cortex, 102, 105
motor development, 179–180, 196
motor neurons, 87
MP3 players, hearing loss from, 153
MSG (monosodium glutamate), 159
Müller-Lyer illusion, 143–144, 162
multiple-factor theory of intelligence, 375–378, 379
multiple measurement, 61, 62

multiple personalities, 596
music
  brain changes with training in, 71, 182–183, 205
  hearing loss, 152
  somatosensory cortex and, 154
myelination, 87, 184–185, 202
myelin sheath, 87, 90

N

narcissistic personality disorder, 600
narcolepsy, 235–236
narcotics (opioids), 157, 242, 245–246
narrow intelligence, 376
nativist view of language, 342–344
natural immunity, 477
naturalistic intelligence, 377
naturalistic observation, 48
natural killer cells, 479
natural selection, 25–27
nature–nurture debate
  in aggression, 553–555
  in anxiety disorders, 582–583
  in attitudes, 549
  in depression, 586–587
  factors in, 23–24
  in intelligence, 389–392
  in language learning, 344–345
  in learning, 322, 326, 344–345
  in personality, 497–501
  psychosomatic theory and, 472
  in schizophrenia, 592
  in sexual orientation, 427–428
nature through nurture, 24
Neanderthal brains, 97
nearsightedness, 133
needs, 416, 428–430. *See also* motivation
need to belong, 428–429
need to excel, 429–430
negative punishment, 305
negative reinforcement, 304–305
negative symptoms, of schizophrenia, 591
NEO-Personality Inventory (PI), 500, 522
nervous system, 83–95. *See also* neurons
  autonomic, 83–84, 437–438, 461
  glial cells and neurons, 84–92
  neurotransmission process, 90–92, 95
  neurotransmitters and, 86, 87, 92–95
  organization of, 83–84
  parasympathetic, 84–85, 438–439
  sympathetic, 84–85, 437–438, 462
neural migration, 173–174
neural networks, memory and, 170
neuro-cultural theory of emotion, 445
neuroendocrine system, 461–462
neurogenesis
  Alzheimer's and, 207

  compensation for deficits by, 109
  definition of, 108
  environmental effects on, 110–111
  evidence of, 110
  exercise and, 485–486
  stress and, 465
neuron doctrine, 110
neurons. *See also* neurogenesis
  abuse and, 602
  action potentials, 88–90, 95, 150
  bimodal, 161
  definition of, 86
  emotional events and, 275
  in infants, 181–185
  in learning and memory, 276–278
  mirror, 88, 324–325, 341–342, 605
  motor, 87
  neuroplasticity, 108, 602
  neurotransmission process, 90–92, 95
  in prenatal development, 173
  real movement, 138
  in second-language speakers, 366
  sensory, 87, 158
  structure and types of, 86–88
  in vision, 135–137
neuropeptide Y (NPY), 420
neuroplasticity, 108, 602
neuroscience, 9, 446
neurosis, 508–509, 643
neuroticism, 485, 514, 517–518, 582
neurotic trends, 508–509
neurotransmission, 90–92
neurotransmitters. *See also specific neurotransmitters*
  adrenal glands and, 116–117
  common, 92–95
  function of, 86, 87
  in neurotransmission process, 90–92, 95
  pain control and, 157
  in painting, 118
nicotine, 242, 247, 483. *See also* smoking
night sweats, 455
NMDA, 594
nociceptive pain, 155
nociceptors, 155
nocturnal emissions, 200–201
nodes, in memory, 270–271
nondeclarative (implicit) memory, 264–265, 271
nonhuman behavior, 48
nonrational decision making, 362–364
non-REM sleep, 231, 237
norepinephrine
  antidepressants and, 615, 616
  in bipolar disorder, 588
  function of, 93, 116–117
  stress and, 462
normative social influence, 535
NPY (neuropeptide Y), 420
nutrition, 176–177, 483–485. *See also* eating